ASIA
MAPS 26 – 45

AFRICA
MAPS 46 – 57

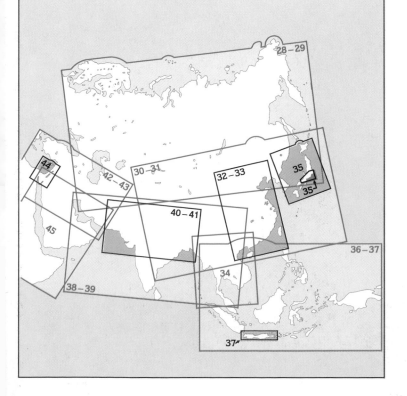

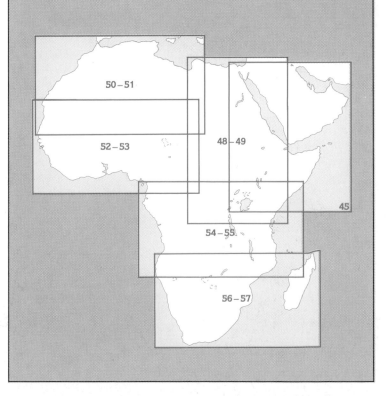

Continued on Back Endpaper

COLLINS
CONCISE ATLAS
OF THE WORLD

COLLINS

CONCISE
Atlas
OF THE
WORLD

HarperCollins*Publishers*

Collins Concise Atlas of the World
First published 1984 by William Collins Sons & Co Ltd
Reprinted 1985, 1986, 1987, 1988, 1989, 1990
2nd Edition 1991
3rd Edition 1993

Maps © HarperCollins*Publishers* and Collins-Longman Atlases
Geographical Encyclopaedia and statistics © HarperCollins*Publishers*
Collins is an imprint of Bartholomew/Times
A Division of HarperCollins*Publishers*
77-85 Fulham Palace Road
Hammersmith
London W6 8JB

Printed in Italy

ISBN 0 00 448022 8

Photograph credits

XII-XIII David Parker/Science Photo Library; Peter Menzell/Science Photo Library; Professor Stewart Lowther/Science
Photo Library

XX-XXI David Campione/Science Photo Library; Dr L. Wright

XXII-XXIII Dr Morley Read/Science Photo Library

XXVI-XXVII D. R. Austen/Telegraph Colour Library; Martin Bond/Science Photo Library

XXVIII-XXIX Marcelo Brodsky/Science Photo Library

XXX-XXXI USGS; The Times Atlas and Encyclopaedia of the Sea

XXXII © Nicholson, produced from the Bartholomew London Digital Database

The Publishers would like to thank the following:

Dr J. Allen, Dr B. Alloway, Professor B. Atkinson, Dr R. Hall and Dr L. Wright
from Queen Mary and Westfield College, University of London

H. A. G. Lewis OBE

Illustrations: Contour Publishing and Swanston Graphics

FOREWORD

MAPS, as essential aids in the understanding of the world around us, would appear to have been made ever since man first moved about the Earth. To begin with they were relatively primitive plans of very limited areas, carved in wood or painted on rock, bark or skins. Later, the highly organized peoples of the ancient civilizations, in conducting their everyday life, made many functional maps on such materials as clay tablets, papyrus and eventually paper.

However, the first attempt to map the whole of the known world, as opposed to producing local plans of small areas, is attributed to the famous Greek cosmographer, Ptolemy (AD 87-150). The many maps of the classical world that accompanied his celebrated manuscript Geographia – itself to be regarded as the standard geographical reference work for many centuries – represent the forerunner of the atlas as we know it today.

ATLASES, in the modern sense of systematic collections of maps of uniform size, were born, much later still, in the Netherlands of the 16th century, during the world's great age of exploration. Indeed, it was the eminent Flemish cartographer Mercator (1512-1594) who first used the word Atlas: taking the name of the ancient Greek mythological titan who symbolically supported the world on his shoulders.

Since the time of these early atlases our knowledge of the world has been greatly increased through continued exploration and scientific discovery. Today, the fast developing space age technology allows man to survey our planet, and beyond, in the most precise detail. The resulting mass of geographical and astronomical data is such that the non-specialist atlas user could easily be overwhelmed. This current information explosion, combined with a new awareness of our world brought about by the views of our planet from space, improved communications, greater opportunity for leisure and travel, and increased media exposure, we believe, calls for a new type of atlas that presents to the general reader, not only an up-to-date collection of well-documented maps, but also an illuminating and readily accessible record of the latest findings and essential facts about our world.

COLLINS CONCISE ATLAS OF THE WORLD, as its title implies, has been specially designed to meet this need. This book is a concise edition of the *Collins Atlas of the World* which, when published in 1983, was widely commended for its modern approach to atlas making, its clarity of presentation, the comprehensiveness of its authoritative content, and its exceptionally good value. Like its parent, this concise atlas makes available in one easily handled volume the latest findings and essential facts about our fast changing world; again presented in three self-contained but interrelated sections first under the heading of geographical encyclopaedia there is an informative and in-depth survey of essential geographical topics. Next, the world atlas section, comprising 96 pages of newly created maps, using the most modern cartographic techniques and up-to-date sources, forms the core of this book. Finally the maps, diagrams and text of these first two sections are complemented by a detailed compendium of world data including a comprehensive index of over 30,000 place names.

The strategy by which the content of the *Collins Atlas of the World* has been reduced to the practical and workmanlike proportions of this concise version has thus carefully avoided wholesale deletion of any one of these essential reference sections. Although there are slightly fewer maps, illustrated encyclopaedia spreads, and indexed place names, a fully balanced coverage of every region in the world and of the major geographical topics is maintained. Again, although the dimensions of the pages of this book are marginally smaller, the scale, area and content of the individual maps has not in any way been reduced. Similarly the presentation of the encyclopaedia texts and data tables contained in this atlas has not suffered any loss of clarity or content.

The resulting COLLINS CONCISE ATLAS OF THE WORLD presents a platform of knowledge from which we can look critically at our fascinating world.

CONTENTS

WORLD ATLAS

GUIDE TO THE ATLAS

COLLINS CONCISE ATLAS OF THE WORLD consists of three self-contained but interrelated sections. First, in the GEOGRAPHICAL ENCYCLOPAEDIA there is a complete and informative guide to contemporary geographical issues. Next, the WORLD ATLAS section, comprising 96 pages of maps, using the most modern cartographic techniques and up-to-date sources, forms the core of this book. Finally, a detailed compendium of WORLD DATA.

GEOGRAPHICAL ENCYCLOPAEDIA

This illustrated section covers essential topics such as the structure of the Earth, earthquakes and volcanoes, atmosphere and climate, vegetation, population, food, minerals and energy. There is a special feature on the use of maps.

WORLD ATLAS

The main section of 96 pages of maps has been carefully planned and designed to meet the contemporary needs of the atlas user. Full recognition has been given to the many different purposes that currently call for map reference.

Map coverage extends to every part of the world in a balanced scheme that avoids any individual country or regional bias. Map areas are chosen to reflect the social, economic, cultural or historical importance of a particular region. Each double spread or single page map has been planned deliberately to cover an entire physical or political unit. Generous map overlaps are included to maintain continuity. Following two world maps, giving separate coverage of the main political and physical features, each of the continents is treated systematically in a subsection of its own. Apart from being listed in the contents, full coverage of all regional maps of each continent is also clearly depicted in the Key to Maps to be found on the front and back endpapers. Also at the beginning of each continental subsection, alongside a special Global View political map, all map coverage, country by country, is identified in an additional handy page index. Finally, as a further aid to the reader in locating the required area, a postage stamp key map is incorporated into the title margin of each map page.

Map projections have been chosen to reflect the different requirements of particular areas. No map can be absolutely true on account of the impossibility of representing a spheroid accurately on a flat surface without some distortion in either area, distance, direction or shape. In a general world atlas it is the equal area property that is most important to retain for comparative map studies and feature size evaluation and this principle has been followed wherever possible in this map section. As a special feature of this atlas, the Global View projections used for each continental political map have been specially devised to allow for a realistic area comparison between the land areas of each continent.

Map scales, as expressions of the relationship which the distance between any two points of the map bears to the corresponding distance on the ground, are in the context of this atlas grouped into three distinct categories.

Large scales, of between 1:1 000 000 (1 centimetre to 10 kilometres or 1 inch to 16 miles) and 1:2 500 000 (1 centimetre to 25 kilometres or 1 inch to 40 miles), are used to cover particularly densely populated areas of Western Europe, United States, Canada and Japan.

Medium scales, of between 1:2 500 000 and 1:7 500 000 are used for maps of important parts of Europe, North America, Australasia, India, China, etc.

Small scales, those of less than 1:7 500 00 (e.g. 1:10 000 000, 1:15 000 000, 1:25 000 000 etc.) are selected for maps of the complete world, continents, oceans, polar regions and many of the larger countries.

The actual scale at which a particular area is mapped therefore reflects its shape, size and density of detail, and as a basic principle the more detail required to be shown of an area, the greater its scale. However, throughout this atlas, map scales have been limited in number, as far as possible, in order to facilitate comparison between maps.

Map measurements give preference to the metric system which is now used in nearly every country throughout the world. All spot heights and ocean depths are shown in metres and the relief and submarine layer delineation is based on metric contour levels. However, all linear scalebar and height reference column figures are given metric and imperial equivalents to facilitate conversion of measurements for the non-metric reader.

Map symbols used are fully explained in the legend to be found on the first page of the World Atlas section. Careful study and frequent reference to this legend will aid in the reader's ability to extract maximum information.

Topography is shown by the combined means of precise spot heights, contouring, layer tinting and three-dimensional hill shading. Similar techniques are also used to depict the sea bed on the World Physical map and those of the oceans and polar regions.

Hydrographic features such as coastlines, rivers, lakes, swamps and canals are clearly differentiated.

Communications are particularly well represented with the contemporary importance of airports and road networks duly emphasized.

International boundaries and national capitals are fully documented and internal administrative divisions are shown with the maximum detail that the scale will allow. Boundary delineation reflects the 'de facto' rather than the 'de jure' political interpretation and where relevant an undefined or disputed boundary is distinguished. However there is no intended implication that the publishers necessarily endorse or accept the status of any political entity recorded on the maps.

Settlements are shown by a series of graded town stamps from major cities to tiny villages.

Other features, such as notable ancient monuments, oases, national parks, oil and gas fields, are selectively included on particular maps that merit their identification.

Lettering styles used in the maps have been chosen with great care to ensure maximum legibility and clear distinction of named feature categories. The size and weight of the various typefaces reflect the relative importance of the features. Town names are graded to correspond with the appropriate town stamp.

Map place names have been selected in accordance with maintaining legibility at a given scale and at the same time striking an appropriate balance between natural and man-made features worthy of note. Name forms have been standardized according to the widely accepted principle, now well established in international reference atlases, of including place names and geographical terms in the local language of the country in question. In the case of non-Roman scripts (e.g. Arabic), transliteration and transcription have either been based on the rules recommended by the Permanent Committee on Geographical Names and the United States Board of Geographical Names, or as in the case of the adopted Pinyin transcription of Chinese names, a system officially proposed by the country concerned. The diacritical signs used in each language or transliteration have been retained on all the maps and throughout the index. However the english language reader's requirements have also been recognised in that the names of all countries, oceans, major seas and land features as well as familiar alternative name versions of important towns are presented in English.

Map sources used in the compilation of this atlas were many and varied, but always of the latest available information. At each stage of their preparation the maps were submitted to a thorough process of research and continual revision to ensure that on publication all data would be as accurate as practicable. A well-documented data bank was created to ensure consistency and validity of all information represented on the maps.

WORLD DATA

This detailed data section forms an appropriate complement to the preceding maps and illustrated texts. There are two parts, each providing a different type of geographical information.

World Facts and Figures Drawn from the latest available official sources, these tables present an easy reference profile of significant world physical, political and demographic as well as national data.

World Index This concluding part of the atlas lists in alphabetical order all individual place names to be found on the maps, which total about 30,000. Each entry in the index is referenced to the appropriate map page number, the country or region in which the name is located and the position of the name on the map, given by its co-ordinates of latitude and longitude. A full explanation of how to use the index is to be found on page 103.

EARTH STRUCTURE

The major three-fold division of the solid Earth into an inner core, a mantle and an outer crust is based largely on the physical properties of these layers as revealed by the passage of seismic waves generated by both earthquakes and man-made explosions.

T HE Earth's crust is a thin shell covering the whole surface of the planet, but only accounts for 0.2% of the total mass of the Earth. There is a fundamental difference between the crust of the continents and that beneath the ocean basins. The oceanic crust is very thin (average 7km), and is composed of relatively dense material. By contrast, the continental crust is thicker and less dense. The crust as a whole is split into a number of distinct plates, which float on the chemically distinct and denser second layer, the mantle. The boundary between the crust and the underlying mantle is known as the Mohorovičić Discontinuity (Moho). At the centre of the Earth lies the core itself, which forms 33% of the planet's mass, and is divided into two zones: the outer layer, thought to be liquid, probably metallic iron with sulphur, silicon, oxygen, potassium or hydrogen; and the inner core, which evidence suggests consists of nickel-iron alloy.

The measurement by a world-wide network of seismographic stations of the vibrational waves generated by earthquakes has provided a relatively accurate picture of where the boundaries between the layers of the Earth lie. The velocity of seismic waves depends on the composition and physical state of the transmitting medium. At the point where the physical or chemical properties of the Earth change, the velocity and path of the waves are changed, too.

The outer layer, the crust in conjuction with that part of the upper mantle immediately below, is in a constant state of movement. Plate tectonics is the name given to the study of the processes which produce faults, joints or folds or cause magma (hot molten rock) to rise to the surface in response to forces deep within the Earth. At the mid-ocean ridges, new crust is created by the rise of magma. This intrusion of new material forces the plates apart. Where two plates meet, pushing from different directions, one plate is forced under the other. Where plates slide past each other, along fault lines, crust is neither created or destroyed.

By studying the way in which new crust has been formed in the ocean beds, a fairly authoritative account can be given of the way the continents have drifted over the past 200 million years. Only a very incomplete picture can be inferred of the preceding 400 million years, and only a sketchy picture before that.

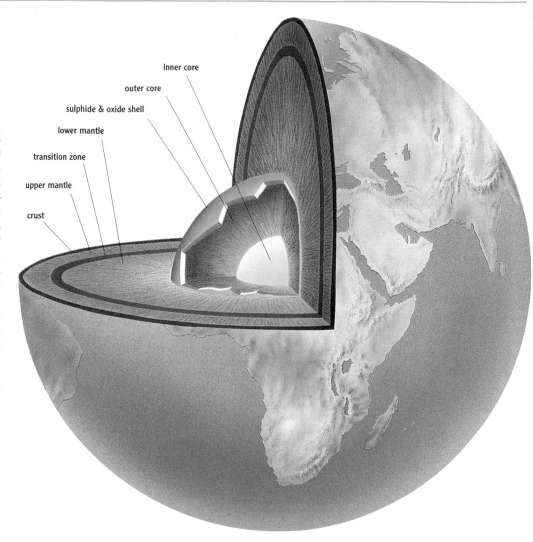

inner core
outer core
sulphide & oxide shell
lower mantle
transition zone
upper mantle
crust

(above) *A section through the Earth's crust. Internally, the Earth is divided into three main areas: crust, mantle and core. The mantle is divided into two parts separated by a transition zone. The core, likewise, is divided into two parts. The solid inner core is surrounded by a liquid outer layer.*

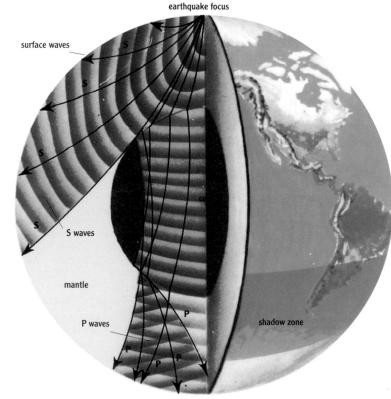

earthquake focus
surface waves
S
S
S
S
S waves
mantle
P waves
P
P
P
co
shadow zone

(right) *In an earthquake, the shock generates vibrations, or seismic waves, which radiate from the focus. Surface waves cause most motion at ground level. The body waves, both primary (P) and secondary (S), reveal by the way they travel, the internal layers of the Earth.*

50 million years ago

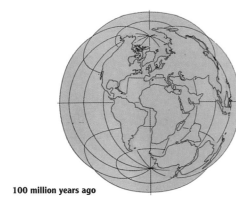

100 million years ago

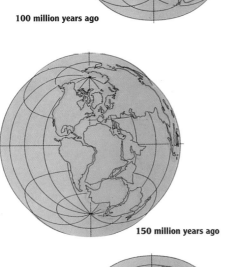

150 million years ago

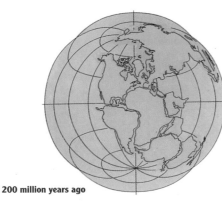

200 million years ago

(left) *From around 200 million years ago, when the Earth's landmasses formed one giant super-continent known as Pangaea, the continents have drifted, divided and collided to produce the present disposition of land and sea.*

(right) *Plate tectonic cycle from continental rifting to continental collision. (1) Rifting following old faults. (2) Continental break-up with the formation of new oceanic crust. Transform faults follow continental fractures. (3) A large Atlantic-type ocean has now formed on the site of the former continent. A mountain belt is formed where the subduction zone dips beneath the continent. (4) Where continental collision occurs a Himalayan-type mountain belt is formed.*

(right) *Faults occur when the Earth's surface breaks. When tension stretches the crust, normal faulting occurs and the rocks on one side of the fault-plane override those on the other. A horst is a block of the crust thrust up between faults; the reverse is a graben or rift valley.*

(below) *Particular features are associated with different types of mineral deposits: continental rifts with tin and fluorine, mid-ocean ridges with marine metallic sulphides, island arcs and cordilleran-type mountains with a variety of metallic deposits.*

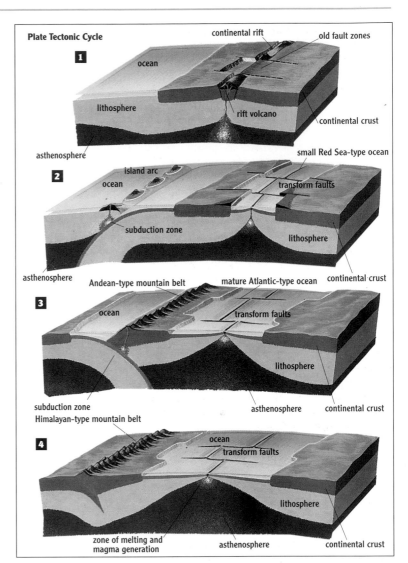

Plate Tectonic Cycle

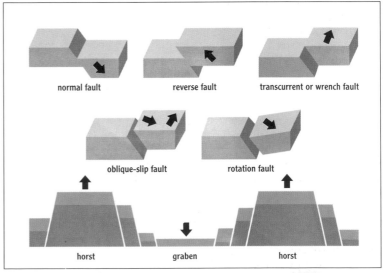

EARTHQUAKES AND VOLCANOES

Violent earthquakes and spectacular volcanic eruptions, the most destructive natural events, are controlled by processes occurring deep below the Earth's surface. Although we understand broadly why and where they happen, we are still some way from being able to predict the exact time and place of the next catastrophic event.

MAJOR zones of seismic and volcanic activity follow the boundaries of the tectonic plates into which the Earth's rigid surface layers are divided (see map right). Where these are moving apart from each other (in the deep oceans), the lithosphere is relatively thin and pliant, earthquakes are shallow and weak, and volcanic lava flows out of long fissures, solidifying to make new ocean floor (see diagram bottom right). If the flow of lava is copious and sustained, a giant shield volcano may build up on the ocean floor and project above the surface as a island. Hawaii is part of a chain of shield volcanoes that have grown over a sustained source of lava, called a hot spot, which is unrelated to plate boundaries and has remained active while the Pacific ocean plate has moved slowly over it.

The most powerful earthquakes and most violent volcanic eruptions occur at boundaries where two plates are in collision. When a thick continental plate meets a thin oceanic plate then the latter is overridden by the former, a process known as subduction. The oceanic plate remains rigid to depths of a few hundred kilometres, causing earthquakes along an inclined surface (referred to as the Wadati-Benioff zone). The frictional heat developed along this zone encourages local partial melting of the rocks; the rather sticky lava ascends slowly to the surface, where highly explosive eruptions send vast clouds of ash and larger fragments into the atmosphere. While the lightest particles may reach the stratosphere and be carried all round the world, most of the material falls back to earth where, in combination with intermittent flows of lava, a massive stratovolcano builds up. Some volcanic eruptions produce searingly hot dense clouds of gas and ash (known as *nuées ardentes*) that descend from the crater at very high speeds, hugging the ground and destroying everything in their path.

Where the colliding plates are both oceanic, subduction of one of the plates results in a similar descending zone of violent earthquakes, and the accompanying volcanic activity builds up an arc of islands on the overriding plate. However, if both plates carry thick continental crust, subduction is no longer possible and volcanic activity ceases, but, as in the Himalayas, the compressive forces continue to generate powerful earthquakes along the collision zone.

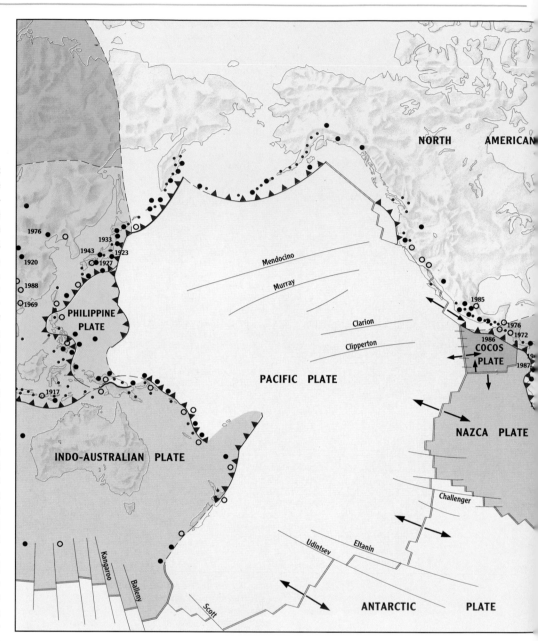

(left) The San Andreas Fault in California marks the boundary between the Pacific plate and the American plate.
(top right) Mauna Loa on the Island of Hawaii, a shield volcano.
(centre right) Mount St. Helens, a stratovolcano, in the Cascade Range. The violent eruption of 18 May 1980 killed 57 people.
(below) The place at which an earthquake originates within the Earth's crust is known as the focus, while the point on the surface directly above is called the epicentre. The strain energy released by the earthquake spreads out in all directions as shock waves from the focus.

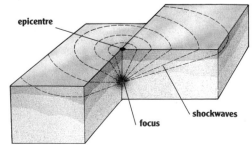

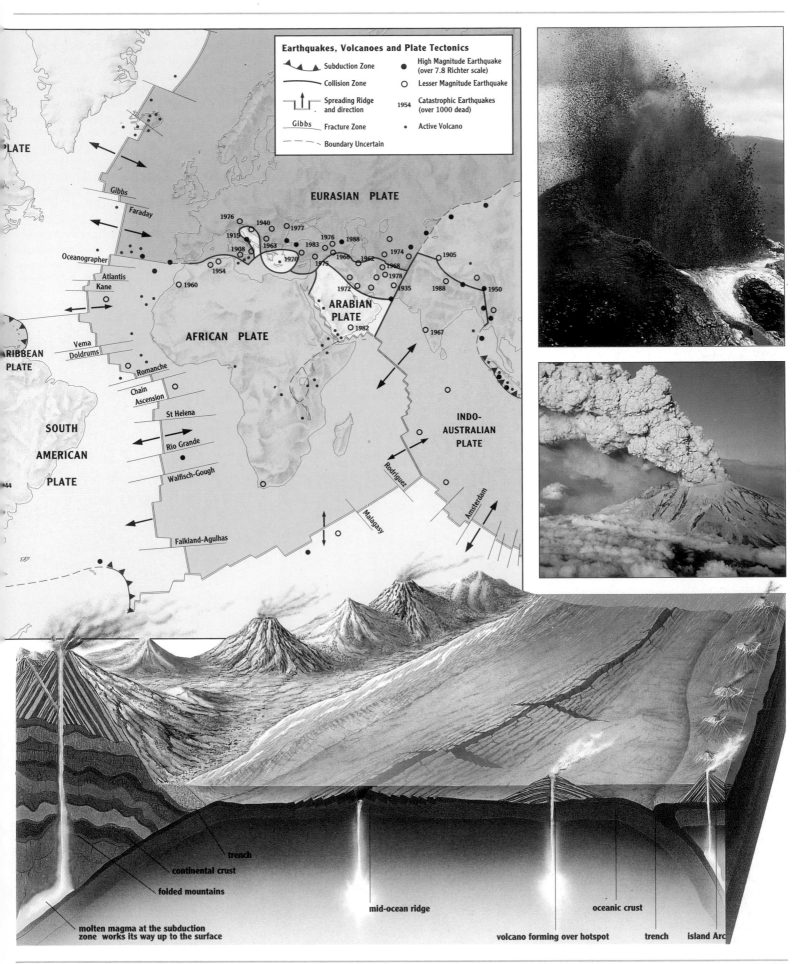

Earthquakes, Volcanoes and Plate Tectonics

⏐⏡⏡	Subduction Zone	●	High Magnitude Earthquake (over 7.8 Richter scale)
—	Collision Zone	○	Lesser Magnitude Earthquake
⊔↑	Spreading Ridge and direction	1954	Catastrophic Earthquakes (over 1000 dead)
Gibbs	Fracture Zone	•	Active Volcano
– – –	Boundary Uncertain		

PLATE

EURASIAN PLATE

Gibbs

Faraday

Oceanographer

Atlantis
Kane

Vema
Doldrums

Romanche

Chain
Ascension

St Helena

Rio Grande

Walfisch-Gough

Falkland-Agulhas

ARIBBEAN
PLATE

SOUTH
AMERICAN
PLATE

44

AFRICAN   PLATE

ARABIAN
PLATE

INDO-
AUSTRALIAN
PLATE

Rodriguez

Malagasy

Amsterdam

1976   1940   1977
1915   1976   1988
1908   1963   1983
1954   1970   1975   1960   1952   1974   1905
1968
1978
1972   1935   1988   1950
1982
1967

1960

trench

continental crust

folded mountains

molten magma at the subduction
zone works its way up to the surface

mid-ocean ridge

volcano forming over hotspot

oceanic crust

trench   island Arc

OCEANS

Covering some 70% of the Earth's surface, oceans have long been vital for navigation, and they are becoming increasingly important for their resources of food, minerals and energy, and also as a final depository for waste. They affect our daily weather and influence long-term changes of climate, but their relative inaccessibility means our knowledge of them is fragmentary.

THE dramatic topography of the ocean floors has been fully revealed only within the last 40 years (see map below right). Its most striking feature, the world's longest mountain chain, is the system of mid-oceanic ridges that extends from the Arctic southwards through the Atlantic, then passes eastwards through the Indian Ocean and northwards into the Pacific. It marks the boundary where adjacent tectonic plates are moving apart from each other as new ocean floor is created from solidifying lava flows. This junction is typically marked by a deep rift valley along the crest of the ridge, and the rugged topography of the ridge flanks is dissected by the cliff-like features of innumerable fracture zones.

Away from the ridges, the level of topography of the deep ocean floors, or abyssal plains, is disturbed by extinct submarine volcanoes.

Some project above sea level as isolated islands, while others, whose tops have been planed off by the erosive power of the waves, may provide a foundation for coral atolls. In the Pacific Ocean, they often occur in long chains where a deep source of lava, or hot spot, has remained active while the Pacific plate has moved slowly over it. The Hawaiian-Emperor chain formed over a period of 75 million years, the sharp bend west of Midway Island signifying a change in the direction of plate movement about 45 million years ago. Elsewhere, sustained volcanic activity combined with plate motion has produced linear features, such as the Walvis Ridge in the eastern South Atlantic. Iceland has formed on the North Atlantic ridge over an unusually active and relatively immobile source of lava.

Deep narrow trenches are a feature of the margins of the Pacific Ocean. The margins of other oceans, especially the North Atlantic, are characterized by wide continental shelves; geologically these are part of the continents, not the oceans, and their width has varied over time in response to changing sea levels. Significant fragments of largely submerged continental lithosphere have been identified in the deep oceans; for example, the Faeroe-Rockall Plateau in the North Atlantic.

The surface waters of the oceans are driven

by the prevailing wind systems in the large-scale circulatory patterns, or gyres, which are broadly symmetrical north and south of the equator (see map below). Along the western boundaries of the major ocean basins, intense warm currents, such as the Gulf Stream, travel polewards; these are counterbalanced by less intense cool currents flowing towards the equator along the eastern margins. Close to the equator an eastwards flowing countercurrent separates the circulations of the two hemispheres. The pattern of currents in the northern Indian Ocean reverses seasonally with the monsoon. In the North Atlantic and Pacific Oceans, weaker anticlockwise circulations complement the main gyres, while in the Southern Ocean the vigorous Antarctic Circumpolar current is unimpeded by the presence of any land masses.

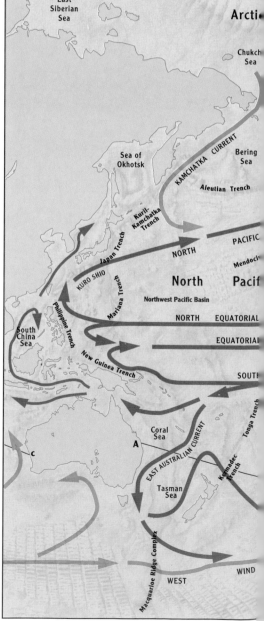

SOUTH PACIFIC OCEAN

A — rise basin ridge trench basin seamount chain ridge fracture zone abyssal plain — A

(above and right) *The relative proportions of the topographic features in the three ocean basins relate to their tectonic geological histories. An extensive mid-oceanic ridge dominates the relatively narrow Atlantic; its margins are tectonically passive with wide continental shelves. The much larger Pacific Ocean, in contrast, has a less extensive ridge system, with active trenches around most of its margins and generally narrow continental shelves. Like the Pacific, the Indian Ocean is dominated by deep ocean floor and has poorly developed continental margins, but it shares with the Atlantic its relative lack of island arcs and trenches.*

SOUTH ATLANTIC OCEAN

B — continental shelf abyssal plain basin rise basin ridge fracture zone — B

INDIAN OCEAN

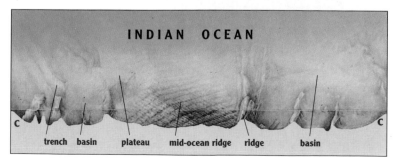

C — trench basin plateau mid-ocean ridge ridge basin — C

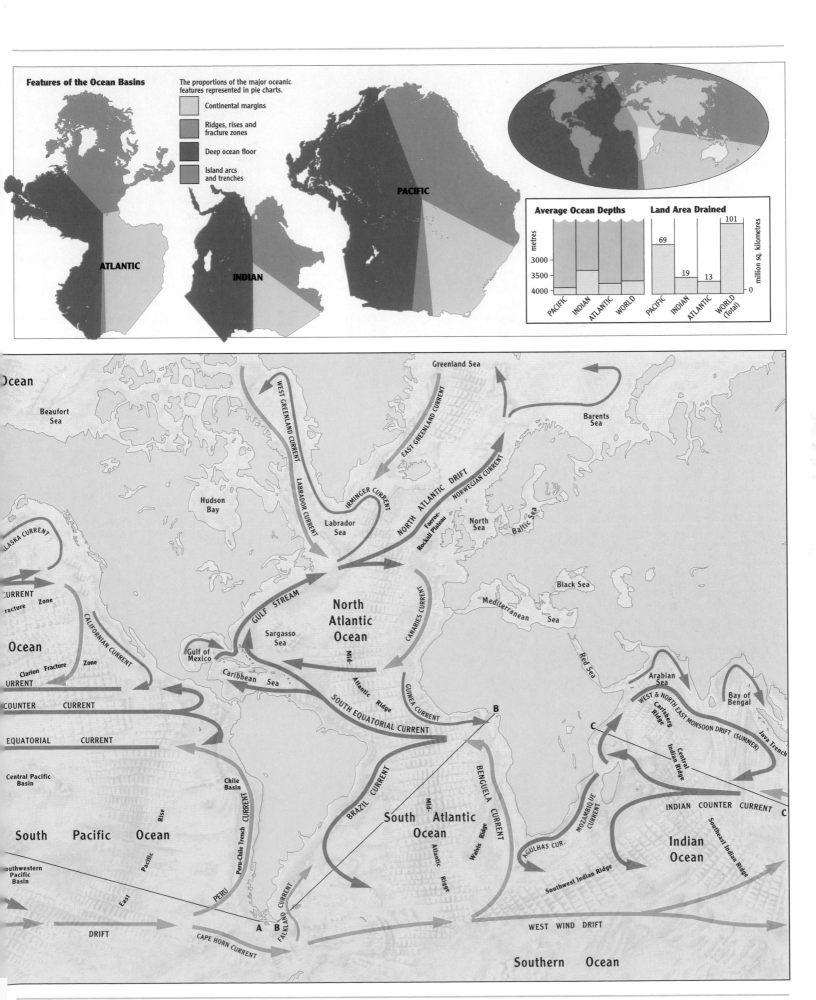

ATMOSPHERE

The atmosphere is a mixture of gases with constant proportions up to a height of 80km. The main constituents are: nitrogen (78%); oxygen (21%); and argon; (less than 1%). Other minor constituents include carbon dioxide, ozone and water vapour. All three have important effects on the energy budget of the atmosphere.

OZONE, lying largely in the stratosphere, absorbs ultraviolet solar radiation which would otherwise damage lifeforms. A reduction in ozone, the ozone hole, is therefore cause for concern. Carbon dioxide, being an effective absorber of terrestrial long-wave radiation, is an important 'greenhouse' gas. If it increases, it may lead to an increase in temperature – global warming. Water vapour is also an important greenhouse gas and varies in quantity from 1-4% by volume.

As air is compressible, its lower layers are much more dense than those above. Half of the total mass of air is found below 5km, with the average surface pressure being 1013.25 millibars.

The atmosphere receives heat from the sun by solar radiation, and loses heat by terrestrial radiation. In general the input and output balance and the Earth's climate changes relatively little. Nevertheless, such changes as do occur create the glacial and inter-glacial periods such as experienced in the past million years. The mean temperature structure of the atmosphere reveals five layers: troposphere; stratosphere; mesosphere; thermosphere and exosphere. About 80% of the atmosphere lies in the troposphere, where all weather occurs.

The input and output of radiation vary in different ways with latitude. There is a net input between latitudes 38º, and a net output in other latitudes. This inequality leads to pressure gradients that drive the winds. In turn, these broadly transfer heat down the thermal gradient produced by the radiation distribution. Such a transfer could be achieved by a single large cell comprising air rising at low latitudes, moving polewards at high levels, sinking over the poles, and returning equatorwards at low levels. The rotation of the earth prevents such an occurrence, leading instead to two regimes: the Hadley cell in the tropics; and the Rossby waves in the extra-tropics. The former is associated with the Trade Winds, the latter with the Westerlies. Within these large wind regimes, frontal cyclones, hurricanes and anticyclones form in preferred locations, and within these systems, smaller circulations (for example, sea breezes) and individual clouds bring our day-to-day weather.

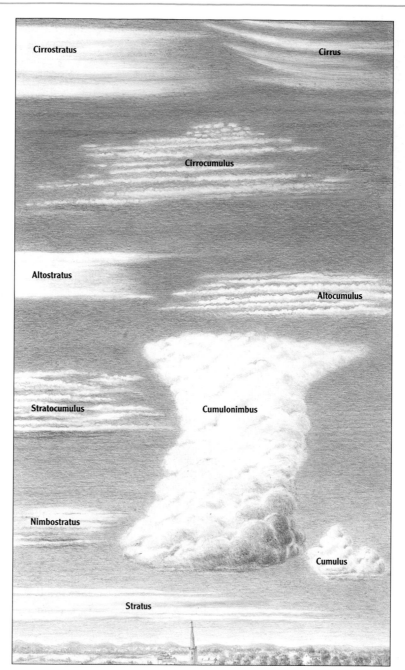

Cirrostratus

Cirrus

Cirrocumulus

Altostratus

Altocumulus

Stratocumulus

Cumulonimbus

Nimbostratus

Cumulus

Stratus

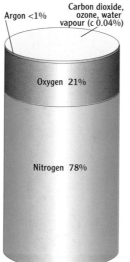

Argon <1%

Carbon dioxide, ozone, water vapour (c 0.04%)

Oxygen 21%

Nitrogen 78%

(left) Ten major cloud types are recognized in the International Cloud Classification.

At high levels: cirrus; cirrocumulus; cirrostratus.

At middle levels: alto-cumulus; altostratus .

At low and middle levels: cumulus

At low levels: nimbostratus; stratus; stratocumulus.

At all levels: cumulonimbus.

The high-level clouds comprise ice; the middle and low-level clouds usually comprise a mixture of ice and water, the latter frequently supercooled with temperatures between 0° C and -15° C. Cumuliform clouds are heaped; stratiform clouds are layered. The cumulonimbus frequently has an anvil-shaped top and may cause thunder and lightning.

(right) The vertical distribution of mean temperature highlights five layers in the atmosphere. The troposphere has a mean lapse rate of 6.5° C/km. Temperature increases in the stratosphere to values a little less than those at the surface. At the top of the mesosphere, temperatures fall to about -90° C and then increase into the thermosphere. The exosphere starts at heights of 500 - 750km where the atmosphere is very tenuous indeed.

(left) Over three-quarters of the atmosphere is nitrogen. Water vapour, carbon dioxide (greenhouse gases) and ozone are very small in quantity but critical in their effects on the planetary energy balance.

(right) The atmospheric circulation is three-dimensional, and comprises two main regimes: vertical over-turning in the Hadley cell, and waves in the Rossby regime. These are manifest as the Trade Winds (which meet in the Inter-Tropical Convergence Zone) and the Westerlies.

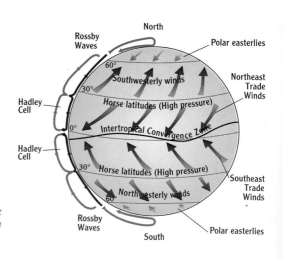

North

Rossby Waves

Polar easterlies

Southwesterly winds

Northeast Trade Winds

Hadley Cell

Horse latitudes (High pressure)

Intertropical Convergence Zone

Hadley Cell

Horse latitudes (High pressure)

Northwesterly winds

Southeast Trade Winds

Rossby Waves

Polar easterlies

South

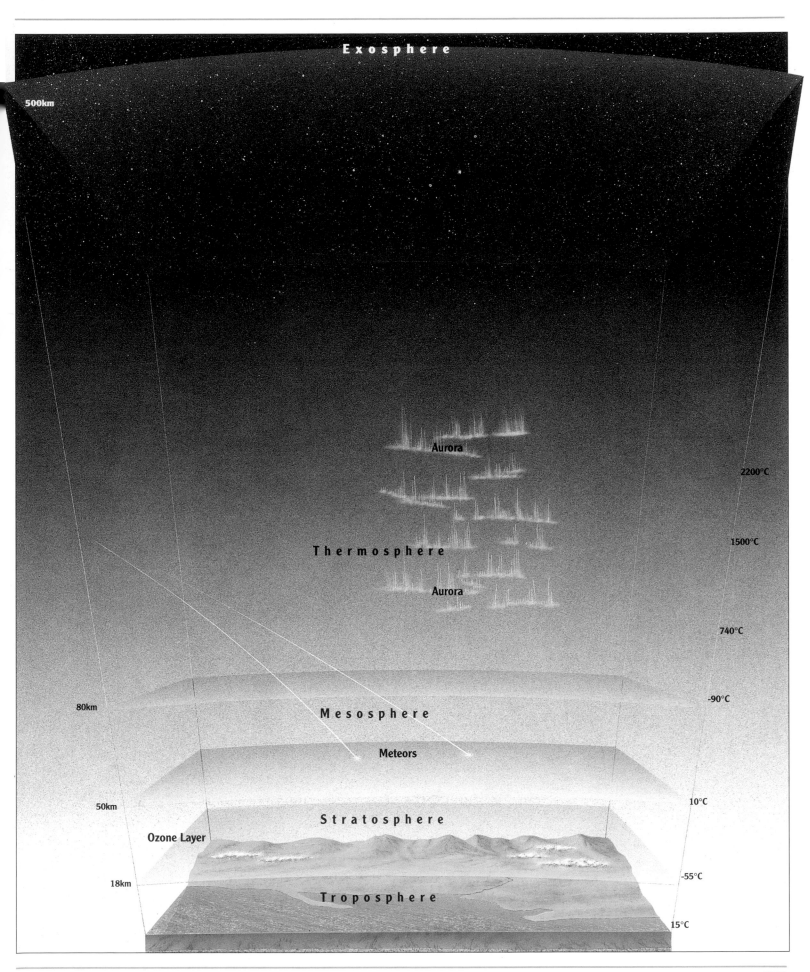

Exosphere

500km

Aurora

2200°C

1500°C

Thermosphere

Aurora

740°C

-90°C

80km

Mesosphere

Meteors

50km

10°C

Stratosphere

Ozone Layer

-55°C

18km

Troposphere

15°C

CLIMATE

The climate of an area is represented by the statistical description of its weather conditions during a specified time. Weather consists of short-term atmospheric variations, most particularly temperature, humidity, precipitation, cloudiness and wind. Earth's climate results from the general circulation of its atmosphere, which produces different regimes of atmospheric variables in different parts of the globe. This allows us to identify different climatic types.

THE mean conditions so frequently used to describe climate result from transfers and transformations of energy, water and momentum between the atmosphere and the Earth. The main source of energy is the Sun, which radiates energy at a virtually constant rate. The Earth's daily rotation and annual precession around the Sun mean that more solar radiation is received near the surface in lower than in higher latitudes. As the Earth's long-wave radiation out to space is distributed more evenly with latitude, the net radiation (input minus output) is positive between latitudes 38 degrees and negative in other latitudes. This energy imbalance leads to pressure gradients that drive the general circulation, which in turn transports heat polewards and upwards. These transports mean that climatic gradients of temperature are smaller than they would be in the absence of the transports.

Nevertheless, it is clear that surface temperatures in January (map top right) range from about -40°C to +40°C, the lowest values being in the continental areas of the northern hemisphere. Land areas gain and lose heat far more rapidly than water areas. As the Sun is in the southern hemisphere in January, the hottest areas are in the Australian desert and parts of South America. In July (map centre right) the desert stretching from the west coast of North Africa to Iran has the highest temperatures. The more maritime southern hemisphere does not reveal very low land temperatures in its winter season, with the notable exception of Antarctica.

The annual precipitation distribution (map below right) also reflects the general circulation. The large amounts in the tropics result from the frequent occurrence of deep cloud systems capable of producing heavy downpours. In the sub-tropics, subsiding air leads to the classic, hot deserts such as the Sahara and Central Australia. Further polewards eastward-moving cyclones produce wet west-coast regimes such as in the UK. In the continental interiors precipitation amounts are less. Further polewards again, precipitation amounts are low, but the water remains on the surface as ice, which gives the impression of a high precipitation area.

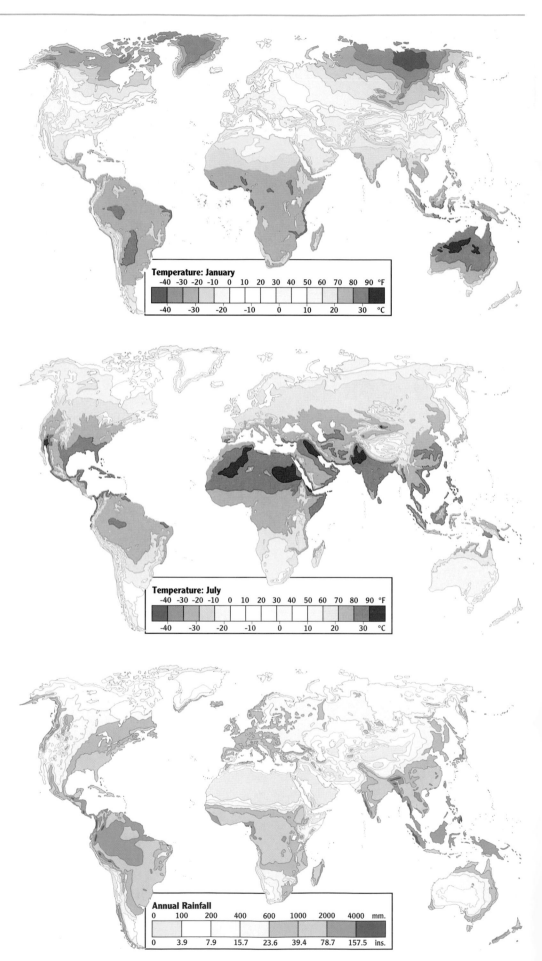

Temperature: January

-40	-30	-20	-10	0	10	20	30	40	50	60	70	80	90	°F
-40		-30		-20		-10		0		10		20		30	°C

Temperature: July

-40	-30	-20	-10	0	10	20	30	40	50	60	70	80	90	°F
-40		-30		-20		-10		0		10		20		30	°C

Annual Rainfall

0	100	200	400	600	1000	2000	4000	mm.
0	3.9	7.9	15.7	23.6	39.4	78.7	157.5	ins.

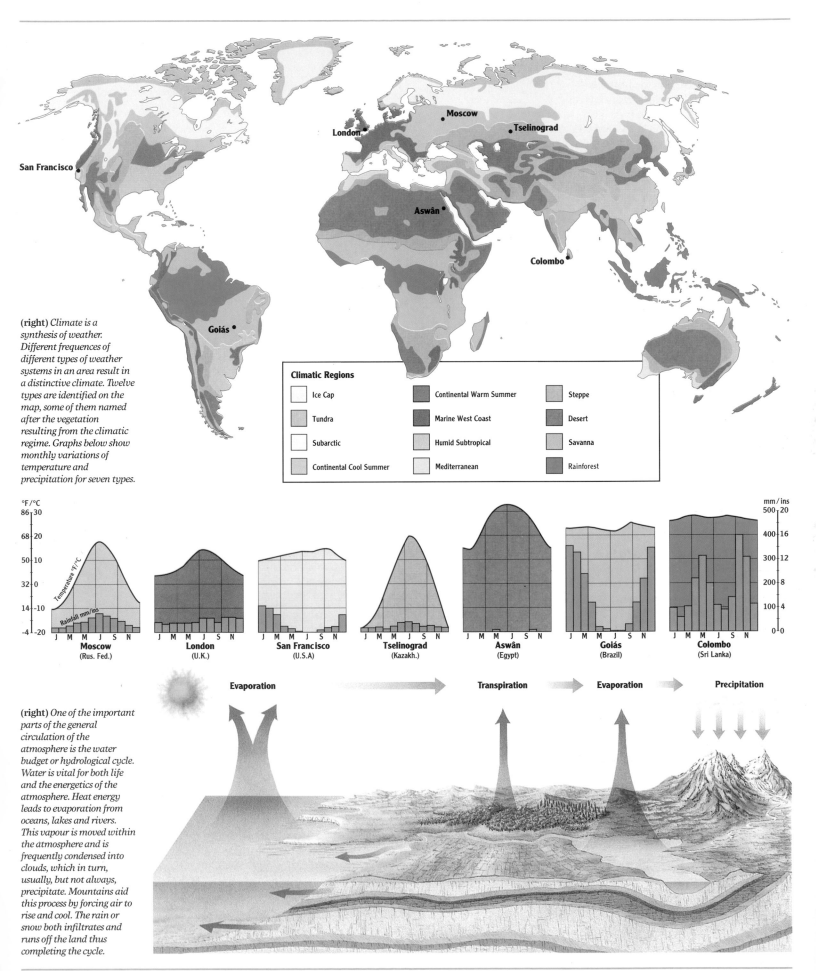

(right) *Climate is a synthesis of weather. Different frequences of different types of weather systems in an area result in a distinctive climate. Twelve types are identified on the map, some of them named after the vegetation resulting from the climatic regime. Graphs below show monthly variations of temperature and precipitation for seven types.*

Climatic Regions

- Ice Cap
- Tundra
- Subarctic
- Continental Cool Summer
- Continental Warm Summer
- Marine West Coast
- Humid Subtropical
- Mediterranean
- Steppe
- Desert
- Savanna
- Rainforest

San Francisco

London · Moscow · Tselinograd

Aswân

Colombo

Goiás

°F/°C
86 · 30
68 · 20
50 · 10
32 · 0
14 · -10
-4 · -20

Temperature °F/°C

Rainfall mm/ins

mm/ins
500 · 20
400 · 16
300 · 12
200 · 8
100 · 4
0 · 0

| Moscow (Rus. Fed.) | London (U.K.) | San Francisco (U.S.A) | Tselinograd (Kazakh.) | Aswân (Egypt) | Goiás (Brazil) | Colombo (Sri Lanka) |

Evaporation   Transpiration   Evaporation   Precipitation

(right) *One of the important parts of the general circulation of the atmosphere is the water budget or hydrological cycle. Water is vital for both life and the energetics of the atmosphere. Heat energy leads to evaporation from oceans, lakes and rivers. This vapour is moved within the atmosphere and is frequently condensed into clouds, which in turn, usually, but not always, precipitate. Mountains aid this process by forcing air to rise and cool. The rain or snow both infiltrates and runs off the land thus completing the cycle.*

LANDSCAPES

The shape of the Earth's surface has been produced through a combination of internal and external forces. The former tend to produce the major landforms of structural origin, notably the great mountain ranges and oceanic rises (underwater mountains) but also volcanic cones, lava fields and faulted (crevassed) landscapes. The externally driven forces of running water, ice, waves and wind produce a greater variety of features, though on a smaller scale. To both of these must be added the landforms produced by weathering processes, notably the erosional and depositional features of limestone (karst) areas.

JUST a few areas of the Earth's surface appear to have been exposed to the external processes continually for tens and even hundreds of millions of years. The area around the Macdonnell Range in Central Australia is one such example. However, most of the landforms we see today are geologically quite young. Most date in large part from the Quaternary Era, which began 2 million years ago, and many have been created in the past 25,000 years as the ice sheets in the northern hemisphere began their final retreat, and the sea level started to rise from its low point.

Our planet's surface today is probably more dynamic and varied than at almost any time in its history. Tertiary (occurring from 65 million years ago) and Quaternary mountain building coupled with the effects of the Ice Age have combined to produce great relief and an intricately varied land surface. This contrasts with the extensive plains and more uniform climate that seem to have been the norm through most of geological time.

The ever-changing nature of the land surface is illustrated by the occurrence of landslip seas and the huge amounts of sediments that are moved annually by the world's rivers and by coastal waves and currents. Sometimes erosion and deposition are so rapid that the surface form can be seen to be changing. More often the full extent of the changes going on can only be determined by careful field measurements. The development of instruments and techniques to record these data has been a major advance over the past few years.

(right) *Stalactites are icicle-like growths of calcium carbonate formed by moisture percolating through calcareous substance, usually the roof of a limestone cave. The mineral is deposited from solution and over time increases in length and width.*

(far right) *Landslips usually require a trigger action. In this case it was a small earthquake but, more often, it is a heavy rainstorm. The basic movement is initially in the form of a fall, slide or flow, but as movement proceeds, clear distinction disappears.*

1 *Solution in limestone areas produces karst landforms: swallow holes, polje and caves. There is often little surface drainage.*

2 *Fluvial (stream) action creates distinctive river patterns, meanders, ox-bow lakes, gorges, flood plains and river terraces. In rivers with shingle beds, braiding occurs.*

3 *Glacial erosion in mountain areas may create cirques (deep semicircular basins) and glacial troughs which may later become lakes.*

4 *Deltas form where large river sediment loads enter the sea (or lake), where wave and current action is weak. The classic delta shape (e.g. the Nile) is just one of the many forms.*

5 Desert landforms include both windblown sand deposits (seif dunes, barchans) and eroded areas littered with stones or bare rock.

6 Glaciers help create pyramidal peaks and sharp ridges (aretes). They also carry rock debris (moraine).

7 Landslides occur on steep slopes and under favourable geological conditions, notably on clays and especially in areas of heavy rainfall.

8 Hard-rock coasts have steep cliffs and often offshore rocks and natural arches. The slope of the cliff is variable and depends on the interaction between geology, climate and the energy of the waves at the base.

9 U-shaped valleys may result from glacial erosion. Beyond the ice limit fluvio-glacial deposition and erosion occurs, often creating terraces.

10 Soft-rock coasts are characterized by deposition. Beaches abound. Spits may dominate river mouths, and salt marsh accumulates in sheltered localities.

NATURAL VEGETATION

Our natural vegetation has evolved in conjunction with the other elements of the environment to produce clear-cut patterns. Climate is an especially important control, but many other factors are influential. Vegetation is a resource for human-kind, and as such has been subject to modification and destruction at an ever-increasing rate.

THE natural vegetation has increased in diversity and complexity over the past 400 million years. Trees are the dominant plant form. Gymnosperms (conifers) evolved first, but have been out-stripped by the angiosperms (flowering plants) and now only dominate in harsher, often cooler, environments. Exceptions include the famous redwood forests on the Pacific coast of North America, and the Podocarp forests of New Zealand.

Most plants require warmth, moisture and sunlight for growth, and a soil to act as an anchor and provide nutrients. Equatorial regions provide the optimum conditions for growth, and support the greatest diversity of tree species. A 10 x 1000m sample area of vegetation through the Amazon forest might contain over 150 species. A similar area in an ancient woodland in Britain might reveal only 15-20 tree types. Species diversity is even lower in northern coniferous forests.

Plants are adapted to the prevailing climate. In equatorial regions there are few limits to growth, and trees are tall, rarely deciduous, and often large leaved. In the absence of strong winds, pollination is mainly by insects, bats and birds. Brightly coloured, highly scented flowers are characteristic. Competition for light is important, and many plants (lianes) scramble and climb up existing trunks or grow directly on the branches (epiphytes).

In drier areas, conservation of moisture is necessary. Leaf loss, small leaves, sunken stomata (similar to skin pores), and aromatic oils within leaves are some of the many survival strategies adopted. Eventually moisture availability is insufficient to support trees, which are replaced by scrub and grass communities.

The impact of human action has been more dramatic and speedy than the gradual evolution of the pattern of natural vegetation over the past 2 million years. The effects have been especially marked in the last 50 years on both forests and rangelands. The speed and scale of tropical forest destruction for timber, settlements, shifting agriculture and large-scale ranching have raised fears about soil erosion and climatic change both locally and globally. Destruction of rangeland vegetation through fire, over-grazing and ploughing has prompted fears of desertification. One resolution is to establish conservation areas but their successful implementation is very difficult.

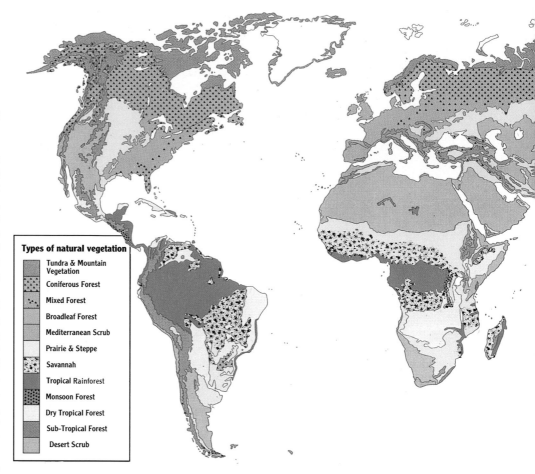

Types of natural vegetation
- Tundra & Mountain Vegetation
- Coniferous Forest
- Mixed Forest
- Broadleaf Forest
- Mediterranean Scrub
- Prairie & Steppe
- Savannah
- Tropical Rainforest
- Monsoon Forest
- Dry Tropical Forest
- Sub-Tropical Forest
- Desert Scrub

The Amazon rainforest is the largest area of natural tropical forest remaining, but it too, is now being exploited by human activities, particularly since a road network has been pushed through the area. Much of the forest is being burnt to provide pasture land or land for peasant farms, or is cleared for the timber industry. Mineral extraction and oil exploration (right) are other causes of deforestation. It is expected that forest destruction will cause climatic changes to Amazonia, and there may also be globally felt effects.

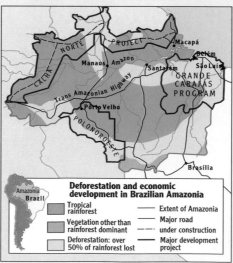

Deforestation and economic development in Brazilian Amazonia
- Tropical rainforest
- Vegetation other than rainforest dominant
- Deforestation: over 50% of rainforest lost
- Extent of Amazonia
- Major road
- under construction
- Major development project

Shrinking Forests

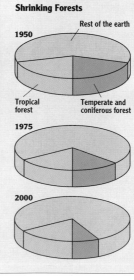

1950 — Rest of the earth / Tropical forest / Temperate and coniferous forest

1975

2000

In 1950 the forests of the temperate and tropical areas covered about 40% of the Earth's land surface. European forests had almost been depleted. Since 1950 there has been a dramatic increase in forest destruction. By 1975 forests occupied 30% of the land surface; by 1985 this had declined towards 20%. Destruction is taking place in both temperate and tropical areas although most publicity has focused on the tropical rain forests.

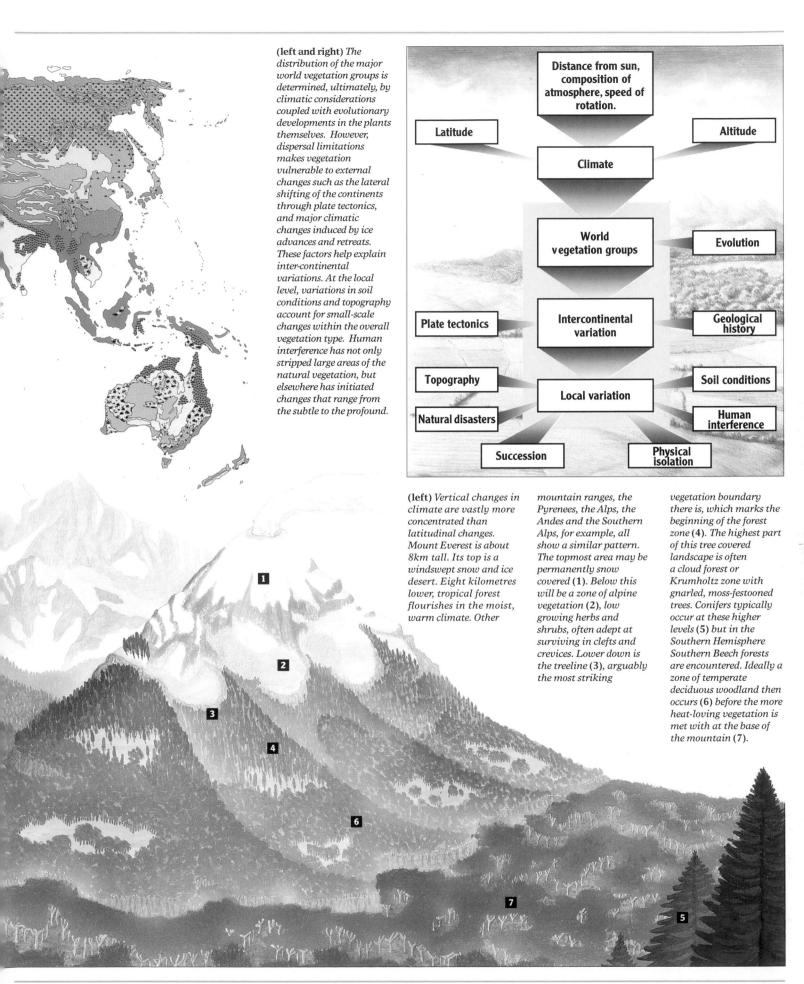

(left and right) *The distribution of the major world vegetation groups is determined, ultimately, by climatic considerations coupled with evolutionary developments in the plants themselves. However, dispersal limitations makes vegetation vulnerable to external changes such as the lateral shifting of the continents through plate tectonics, and major climatic changes induced by ice advances and retreats. These factors help explain inter-continental variations. At the local level, variations in soil conditions and topography account for small-scale changes within the overall vegetation type. Human interference has not only stripped large areas of the natural vegetation, but elsewhere has initiated changes that range from the subtle to the profound.*

Distance from sun, composition of atmosphere, speed of rotation.

Latitude

Altitude

Climate

World vegetation groups

Evolution

Plate tectonics

Intercontinental variation

Geological history

Topography

Soil conditions

Local variation

Natural disasters

Human interference

Succession

Physical isolation

(left) *Vertical changes in climate are vastly more concentrated than latitudinal changes. Mount Everest is about 8km tall. Its top is a windswept snow and ice desert. Eight kilometres lower, tropical forest flourishes in the moist, warm climate. Other mountain ranges, the Pyrenees, the Alps, the Andes and the Southern Alps, for example, all show a similar pattern. The topmost area may be permanently snow covered (1). Below this will be a zone of alpine vegetation (2), low growing herbs and shrubs, often adept at surviving in clefts and crevices. Lower down is the treeline (3), arguably the most striking vegetation boundary there is, which marks the beginning of the forest zone (4). The highest part of this tree covered landscape is often a cloud forest or Krumholtz zone with gnarled, moss-festooned trees. Conifers typically occur at these higher levels (5) but in the Southern Hemisphere Southern Beech forests are encountered. Ideally a zone of temperate deciduous woodland then occurs (6) before the more heat-loving vegetation is met with at the base of the mountain (7).*

POPULATION

The growth of world population is among the most important features of this century, and has sparked debate about its economic, social and environmental implications. Growth may not cease until numbers reach over 12 billion, more than double present figures. The most rapidly growing populations are in poorer regions, and the pressures on resources are enormous.

WORLD population reached 5.5 billion in mid-1992, and is projected to grow to 6.2 billion by the year 2000. Numbers have increased rapidly in the second half of the 20th century, with growth rates reaching 2.1% per annum in the 1960s. The present growth rate is 1.7% per annum (an extra 93 million people each year), and is projected to decline to about 1.0% per annum by 2025 when population is projected to be 8.5 billion.

The exceptional nature of this growth is apparent when placed in the context of world population history. In the past, population growth was exceedingly slow, with birth and death rates generally in balance. Growth rates began to increase around the beginning of the 18th century, and the first thousand million was reached in the early 19th century. In 1900 the world total was less than 1.7 billion.

The major impetus behind growth has been the lowering of mortality and improvements in life expectancy. These have been especially important in the period after the Second World War for the populations of the less developed regions of the world. Meanwhile, declines in birth rates have been much less rapid; parts of Africa have even seen increases in fertility. The result has been explosive rates of growth, particularly in the less developed world, where between 1950 and 1990 the population increased by 143% compared with 45% elsewhere.

Today, growth is most rapid in Africa, parts of Asia and Latin America. Growth is projected to remain high in Africa well into the next century, so that by 2025 Africa will account for 35% of world population growth (20% in 1990) and make up 19% of total world population (12% in 1990). Kenya has one of the highest rates of growth of any country, and population here is expected to increase 13 times from the 1950 total.

How rapidly world population growth decelerates depends on the speed with which birth rates are reduced in those countries where they are still high. Fertility reduction depends on many factors, including the education levels and status of women. For many poor people, children remain their greatest security. The success of government efforts to lower birth rates will depend to a great extent on how successfully they also improve economic and social conditions for their people.

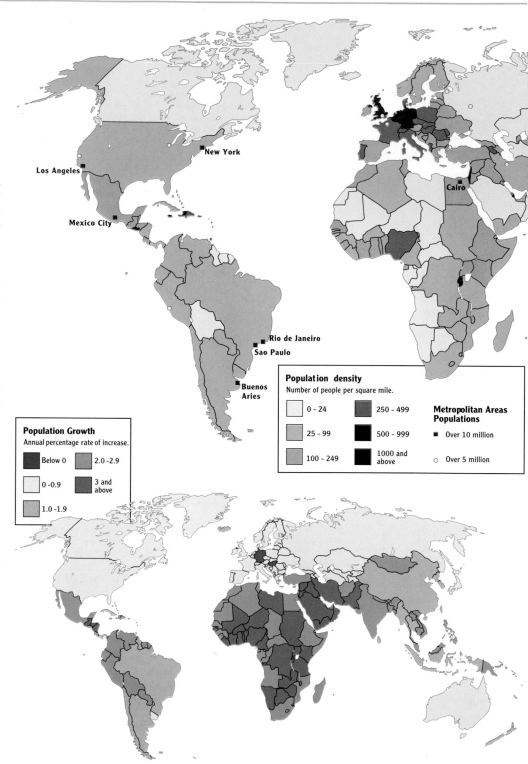

Population Growth
Annual percentage rate of increase.

- Below 0
- 0 -0.9
- 1.0 -1.9
- 2.0 -2.9
- 3 and above

Population density
Number of people per square mile.

- 0 - 24
- 25 - 99
- 100 - 249
- 250 - 499
- 500 - 999
- 1000 and above

Metropolitan Areas Populations
- ■ Over 10 million
- ○ Over 5 million

(above) World population growth rates show a clear north-south division with dramatic growth gradients evident where the less developed world impinges on the more developed world. This is particularly evident in the countries surrounding the Mediterranean Sea where some of the faster growing populations of the world in north Africa are adjacent to the slowest growing in Europe.

(above right) World population grew at a steady rate until the 18th century when the rate of growth accelerated dramatically.

(right) Demographic transition model showing the four broad stages of development as undeveloped societies with high birth and death rates and low rates of growth progress through periods of rapidly growing population before reaching stage 4 where birth and death rates are very low and growth rates stable or even declining.

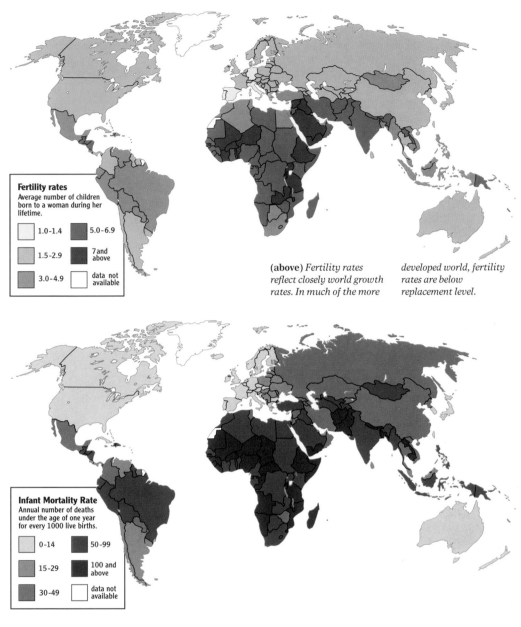

Fertility rates
Average number of children born to a woman during her lifetime.

- 1.0-1.4
- 1.5-2.9
- 3.0-4.9
- 5.0-6.9
- 7 and above
- data not available

(above) *Fertility rates reflect closely world growth rates. In much of the more* *developed world, fertility rates are below replacement level.*

(Map, above left) — labels: Beijing, Seoul, Tokyo/Yokohama, Shanghai, Calcutta

(above left) *Unevenly distributed, about two-thirds of world population is concentrated in south and east Asia and Europe.*

In developing countries, there is increasingly uneven distribution due to migration from rural to urban areas

World population (millions)

Y-axis: 1000, 2000, 3000, 4000, 5000, 6000, 7000, 8000
X-axis: BC 7000-6000, AD 1, 1650, 1750, 1850, 1950, 2050 — **Year**

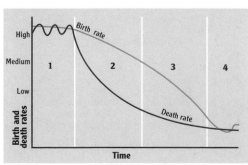

Graph: Birth rate, Death rate, stages 1, 2, 3, 4. Y-axis: High, Medium, Low — **Birth and death rates**. X-axis: **Time**

Infant Mortality Rate
Annual number of deaths under the age of one year for every 1000 live births.

- 0-14
- 15-29
- 30-49
- 50-99
- 100 and above
- data not available

(above) *Until parents can be confident that children will survive they are unlikely to reduce their fertility. The contrasts in infant mortality rates are dramatic: while in Japan fewer than 5 babies for every 1000 born die in their first year, well over 100 will die in much of Africa and some countries of Asia.*

(right) *Contrasts in life expectancy between the more and the less developed world have narrowed since 1950 from 24 years to just over 12 years. How rapidly improvements continue to take place depends on improvements in public health and medicine as well as rising standards of* *living. AIDS may well result in improvements slowing down in Africa and the latest UN projections suggest that the population* *of some African countries will grow more slowly than previously expected because of rising death rates from AIDS.*

Life Expectancy
Average number of years a newborn baby can be expected to live.

- 40-54
- 55-64
- 65-69
- 70-74
- 75 and above
- data not available

XXV

FOOD

Enough food is produced in the world to satisfy the basic needs of all its 5.5 billion inhabitants, yet malnutrition and famine are commonplace. While food production has increased steadily in nearly all countries over the last 50 years, the UN nevertheless estimates that under-nourishment still afflicts one person out of every five.

ABOUT one third of the world's land area is too cold, dry or mountainous for food production. Of the rest, about 10% is under intensive cultivation and 25% used for extensive grazing, with some of the remaining land, mostly semi-arid or forested, potentially available for agricultural use (see map right). The most productive regions of the oceans are nearly all located in relatively shallow waters.

Since 1950, world food production has been increasing at an annual rate of between 2 and 3%. Today the more developed countries produce half the world's food with less than 10% of its agricultural workforce through the intense application of chemicals and widespread use of machinery, giving very high yields per hectare of land. In many developing countries, especially in Africa, farming is labour intensive and yields are low; over much of the Far East and Latin America, on the other hand, the development of high-yielding varieties of cereals, together with increased use of irrigation, fertilizers and pesticides (often referred to as the green revolution), has achieved much greater yields.

The sea is an important source of food for many coastal and island peoples, particularly in the Far East, but opportunities for further expansion of the marine harvest appear limited. Food production in many developing countries has generally kept pace with population growth, and a few, such as Thailand, have become net exporters of food. Most countries in Africa, on the other hand, have experienced a decline in food availability as their population has grown faster than the food supply; technological innovations there have often been in respect of high-value crops intended for export (so-called cash crops), rather than staple foods such as cereals.

Over much of Africa, together with parts of Asia and Latin America, average daily food consumption is below optimum levels both in quantity, or energy content, as well as quality, or nutritional make-up. In contrast, a similar proportion of the population in nearly all developed countries suffers from over-nutrition, with its attendant problems of obesity and dietary-related diseases. This inequality is apparent not only in the average daily intake of food energy (see diagram top right), but more especially in the proportion of the diet derived from animal sources (see map bottom right).

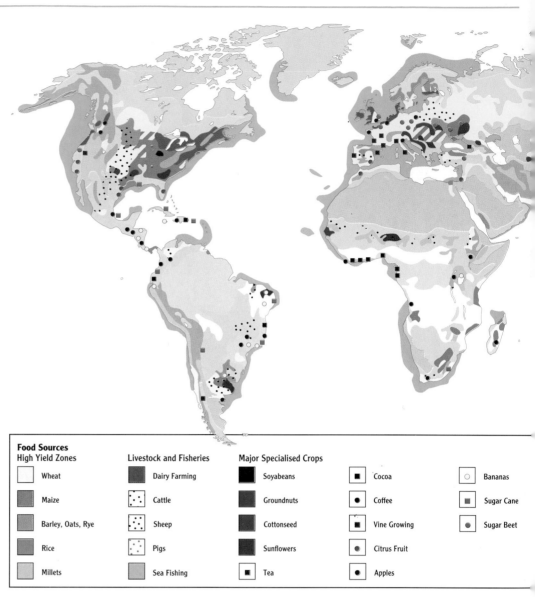

Food Sources

High Yield Zones
- Wheat
- Maize
- Barley, Oats, Rye
- Rice
- Millets

Livestock and Fisheries
- Dairy Farming
- Cattle
- Sheep
- Pigs
- Sea Fishing

Major Specialised Crops
- Soyabeans
- Groundnuts
- Cottonseed
- Sunflowers
- Tea
- Cocoa
- Coffee
- Vine Growing
- Citrus Fruit
- Apples
- Bananas
- Sugar Cane
- Sugar Beet

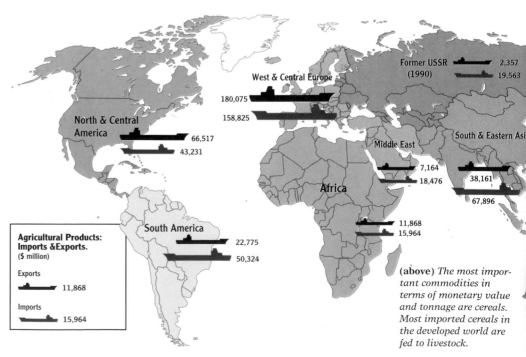

Agricultural Products: Imports & Exports. ($ million)

Exports — 11,868

Imports — 15,964

- Former USSR (1990): 2,357 / 19,563
- West & Central Europe: 180,075 / 158,825
- North & Central America: 66,517 / 43,231
- Middle East: 7,164 / 18,476
- South & Eastern Asia: 38,161 / 67,896
- Africa: 11,868 / 15,964
- South America: 22,775 / 50,324

(above) The most important commodities in terms of monetary value and tonnage are cereals. Most imported cereals in the developed world are fed to livestock.

Low Yield Zones

- Tundra, Ice-cap
- Forest
- Mountain
- Extensive Grassland
- Desert, Semi-desert

Daily Food Consumption
Vegetable/Animal Products

84% = percentage of total calorie intake, per person.

(2171) = total calorie intake per person.

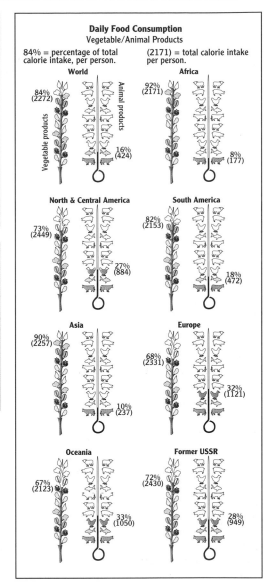

World
Vegetable products
84% (2272)
Animal products
16% (424)

Africa
92% (2171)
8% (177)

North & Central America
73% (2449)
27% (884)

South America
82% (2153)
18% (472)

Asia
90% (2257)
10% (237)

Europe
68% (2331)
32% (1121)

Oceania
67% (2123)
33% (1050)

Former USSR
72% (2430)
28% (949)

The green revolution has brought dramatic increases in food production from high-yielding varieties of cereals requiring the application of chemicals to supply essential nutrients and to protect from pests and diseases.

(top) In SE Asia highly controllable irrigation techniques applied to early maturing varieties of crops allow two or three harvests each year.

(above) In temperate regions productivity has been further increased through extensive mechanization; over much of Europe this has resulted in the amalgamation of small fields, which now resemble the great expanses of North American monoculture.

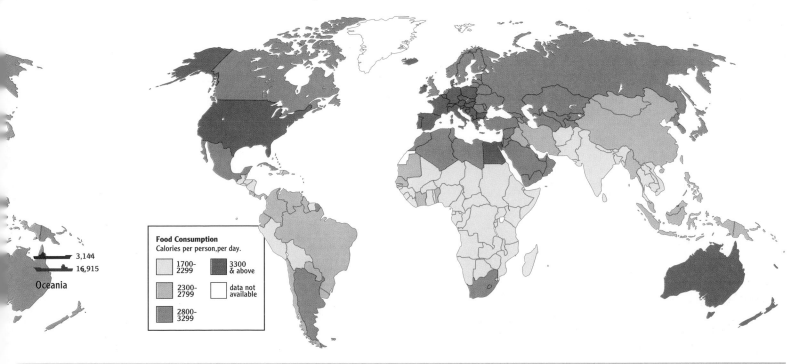

3,144
16,915

Oceania

Food Consumption
Calories per person, per day.

- 1700-2299
- 2300-2799
- 2800-3299
- 3300 & above
- data not available

MINERALS AND ENERGY

Life for most people in the world today is sustained by the consumption of both minerals and energy, often in quite considerable quantities. Knowledge of their location and availability is therefore of great importance, and in many cases the search for new or alternative sources has very high priority.

WHILE metal-yielding minerals are widely distributed in the Earth's crust, it is usually only where they have been concentrated into an ore body that exploitation is possible. The quantity of ore that can be extracted at sufficient profit is known as the reserve of that mineral; its size will change in response to variations in demand and technological advances, as well as to findings of new deposits.

Although no metal is destroyed by use, the proportion that can be recycled seldom exceeds 50%, so there is a continuing need for new sources of supply or the introduction of substitutes. While metals such as aluminium and iron are widely distributed and relatively plentiful, the supply of others, such as copper, has only been maintained with recourse to increasingly less concentrated ore deposits. A few important metals are intrinsically rare and deposits are limited to very few countries; for example, metals of the platinum group occur mainly in South Africa. The economy of many developing countries is largely dependent upon the export of one particular metal (Guinea and Jamaica rely extensively on their reserves of aluminium).

Compared with metals, non-metalliferous minerals (those that do not yield or contain metals) generally have lower intrinsic value but a wider distribution; they are, however, rarely capable of being recycled. The most important sources of energy, fossil hydrocarbon fuels, are totally consumed by use. Whereas coal and lignite are widely distributed and relatively abundant, reserves of gas and oil are more localized. World dependence on oil and gas has increased dramatically since 1945, and supplies are predicted to approach exhaustion during the next century. Nuclear and hydro-power each account for about 20% of world electricity supply, but the uranium fuel on which the former depends has few rich deposits and is non-renewable. Hydro-power, however, constitutes an inexhaustible resource in principle, though most of its potential contribution resides in developing countries.

The amount of energy obtained from fuel-wood is estimated to be comparable with that supplied by nuclear and hydro-power. It is the dominant fuel in much of Africa and parts of Latin America and southeast Asia. Although it is a renewable resource, many developing countries are already experiencing an acute shortage of this source of energy.

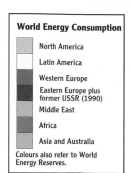

World Energy Consumption

- North America
- Latin America
- Western Europe
- Eastern Europe plus former USSR (1990)
- Middle East
- Africa
- Asia and Australia

Colours also refer to World Energy Reserves.

(above) *The industrialized world's high standard of living requires the consumption of huge quantities of energy.*

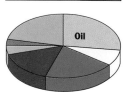

(left) *Because it supplies essential fuels for transport, and despite political uncertainties, oil remains the world's most important source of energy.*

(right) *Widely available, coal is a significant source of energy, and is especially prominent in the (former) communist states and in many developing countries.*

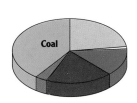

(left) *Consumption of natural gas has doubled over the last 20 years, and is now the principal energy source for many industrialized countries.*

Renewable sources are making an increasing contribution to world energy needs. One of the most promising is wind power (see diagram and photograph below), which already supplies some 2% of electricity demand in both California and Denmark and also has a realistic potential contribution of up to 20% in many countries. The cost of solar cells is still falling, encouraging an expansion of applications mainly within tropical latitudes. In favoured locations electricity from the sea (from both tidal energy and wave power), and geothermal heat can be significant. As valuable replacements for fossil hydrocarbons, similar fuels can be derived from organic material (biomass) of many kinds, including crops such as sugar cane or timber which is grown specifically for the purpose, as well as agricultural or domestic wastes.

European Wind Energy Resources
The potential for wind energy development based upon mean speeds greater than 5m/s.

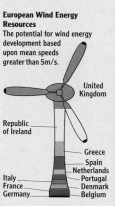

United Kingdom
Republic of Ireland
Greece
Spain
Netherlands
Portugal
Italy
Denmark
France
Germany
Belgium

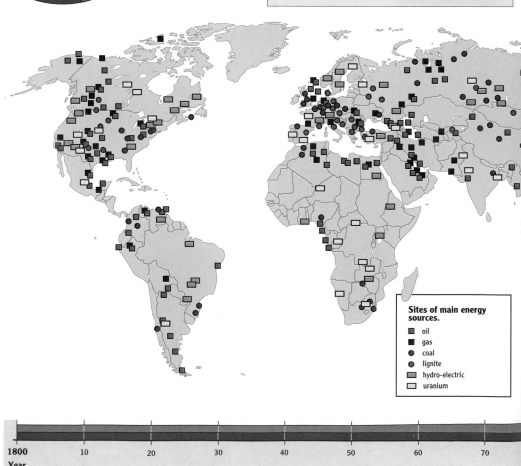

Sites of main energy sources.
- oil
- gas
- coal
- lignite
- hydro-electric
- uranium

1800 Year — 10 — 20 — 30 — 40 — 50 — 60 — 70

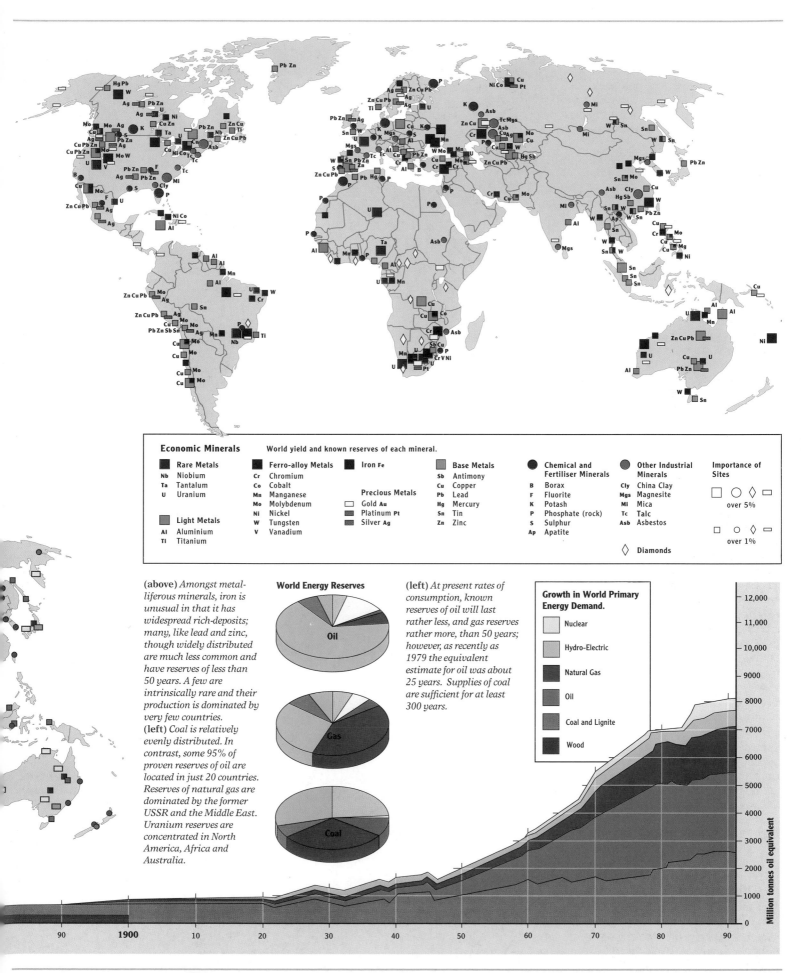

Economic Minerals   World yield and known reserves of each mineral.

| ◼ | **Rare Metals** | | ◼ | **Ferro-alloy Metals** | | ◼ | **Iron** Fe | | ◼ | **Base Metals** | | ● | **Chemical and Fertiliser Minerals** | | ● | **Other Industrial Minerals** | | **Importance of Sites** |

Nb	Niobium
Ta	Tantalum
U	Uranium

Cr	Chromium
Co	Cobalt
Mn	Manganese
Mo	Molybdenum
Ni	Nickel
W	Tungsten
V	Vanadium

Precious Metals
◻	Gold Au
◪	Platinum Pt
◪	Silver Ag

Sb	Antimony
Cu	Copper
Pb	Lead
Hg	Mercury
Sn	Tin
Zn	Zinc

B	Borax
F	Fluorite
K	Potash
P	Phosphate (rock)
S	Sulphur
Ap	Apatite

Cly	China Clay
Mgs	Magnesite
Mi	Mica
Tc	Talc
Asb	Asbestos

◼ **Light Metals**
| Al | Aluminium |
| Ti | Titanium |

◇ **Diamonds**

Importance of Sites: ◻ ○ ◇ ▭ over 5%   ▫ ○ ◇ ▭ over 1%

(above) *Amongst metalliferous minerals, iron is unusual in that it has widespread rich-deposits; many, like lead and zinc, though widely distributed are much less common and have reserves of less than 50 years. A few are intrinsically rare and their production is dominated by very few countries.*

(left) *Coal is relatively evenly distributed. In contrast, some 95% of proven reserves of oil are located in just 20 countries. Reserves of natural gas are dominated by the former USSR and the Middle East. Uranium reserves are concentrated in North America, Africa and Australia.*

World Energy Reserves

Oil

Gas

Coal

(left) *At present rates of consumption, known reserves of oil will last rather less, and gas reserves rather more, than 50 years; however, as recently as 1979 the equivalent estimate for oil was about 25 years. Supplies of coal are sufficient for at least 300 years.*

Growth in World Primary Energy Demand.

| Nuclear |
| Hydro-Electric |
| Natural Gas |
| Oil |
| Coal and Lignite |
| Wood |

Million tonnes oil equivalent

12,000 · 11,000 · 10,000 · 9000 · 8000 · 7000 · 6000 · 5000 · 4000 · 3000 · 2000 · 1000 · 0

90   **1900**   10   20   30   40   50   60   70   80   90

THE USE OF MAPS

The scale and content of a map are determined by the purpose for which it was designed. Thematic maps are a valuable aid in the presentation of complex statistical data. Computers aid their production and increase their scope. Modern databases offer access to map data in digital form to an ever-widening range of users as well as providing new types of maps and related products.

MORE than 1000 years ago the Greeks distinguished geography from chorography. Geography was concerned with the whole world and chorography with only a local area. The word chorography has passed from our vocabulary but the word topography (to do with places) is used in its place. A topographic map contains details of the land surface appropriate for its scale. It is usually part of a map series whose sheets cover all or part of a country. It is typically the standard map of a national map series. Cadastral maps are maps of very large scale which serve the purposes of land ownership, valuation and taxation.

Scale is the dominant factor in determining the contents of maps. A compromise has to be made between what is desired and what can be achieved in the quantity of information included. Choice of scale and type of map is critical in the use of maps. Small scale maps are used for general planning but the need for larger scales becomes evident when more detailed information is needed of a specific area.

The English language, unlike other languages, makes a distinction between a chart and a map. In its original use, the word chart implied a nautical chart but aviators took over the word for their own navigational charts. Nautical charts pay little attention to the land. Aeronautical charts require much less topographical information than maps used on the ground. Elevations are in feet to conform with aircraft instrumentation. Originally aeronautical charts were of the same size as land maps but increases in the speed of aircraft necessitated a change in size. Many charts are four times their previous size to reduce the number handled by the navigator. Both at sea and in the air the nautical mile (1852m) is used for measuring distance.

Maps play an important part in recording and disseminating statistical information. Those maps which are specifically designed for a particular topic are known as thematic maps (maps with a theme). They range from simple diagrams to complex forms of the conventional map. Numerous special symbols have been invented in the presentation of statistics. Among the commonest terms are isopleths (lines of equal area), choropleths

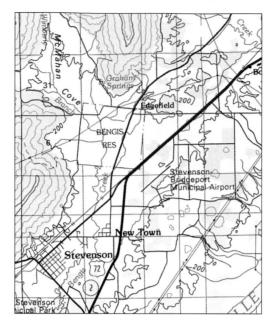

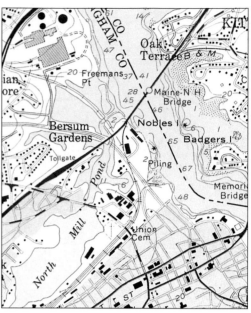

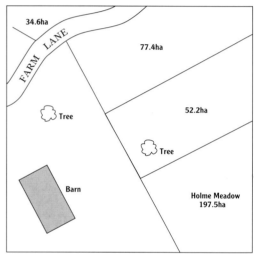

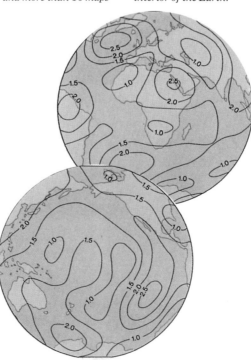

(above) A topographic map at 1:100 000 scale has a wide range of uses, including study of terrain, land use, environmental planning, transportation and hydrological studies. Road widths and individual buildings are exaggerated. Other map detail is displaced.
(above right) A topographic map at a scale of 1:24 000 contains much more detail and has less exaggeration in the size of features than the map at 1:100 000. One mm represents 24m and more than 16 maps

are required to cover the same area of ground as a map at 1:100 000 scale.
(right) In a cadastral map at 1:1000 scale, map detail is drawn to scale without generalization. Maps of this type are used for recording land ownership, taxation and urban planning. Unless such maps are contoured, they are of limited use in engineering works.
(below) Isopleths, or isorithms, are lines which join points of the same numerical value. The maps use isopleths to show heat flow from the interior of the Earth.

(top right) Nautical charts show depths of water by soundings and bathymetric contours. Attention is paid to under-sea features, rocks, wrecks and other hazards and to lights, beacons and aids to navigation, including magnetic variation. The Mercator projection is used for sea charts.
(right) Relief, including man-made vertical obstructions, is of great importance in aeronautical charts. Navigation aids, aerodromes and other air information are shown at the expense of map detail not essential to air use. Elevations are in feet.
(top far right) Maps which show relief, like the one on the right, must, of necessity, be highly coloured and this

makes political information difficult to extract when it is included in the same map. For this reason a separate political map, like the one on the left, is required.
(centre right) Choropleth (measure per area) maps show statistical data by use of line patterns, or colour, applied to areas. Choropleth maps can be used to show density of population by country, state or province using data from a census.
(below right) Dot maps belong to the family of distribution maps. In a population map the dot represents a certain number of people. On the example shown, the density of dots gives an immediate impression of the distribution of world population.

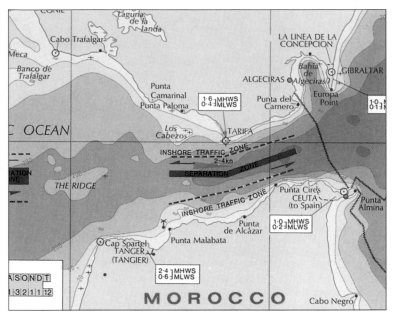

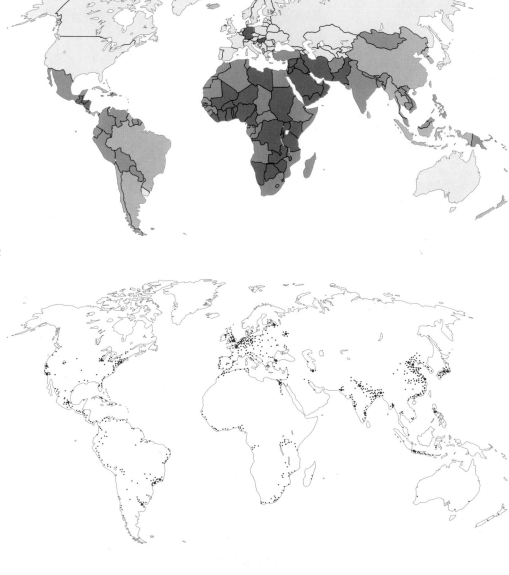

(areas of equal measure) and isorithms (lines of equal number).

Dots, circles, squares, cubes and spheres, as well as an untold number of pictorial symbols, graphs and bar charts are among the items used for thematic maps.

Cartograms are widely used in conveying statistical information. As its name implies, a cartogram is neither a true map nor a diagram. Roman road maps were an early type of cartogram. Road distances were given, but true road alignments were ignored. Determining relative areas of countries by visual comparison on a map is extremely difficult. The areas can be readily compared when they are converted to rectangular form in a cartogram. Some ingenuity is required in arranging the rectangular figures to preserve their geographical position in relation to other countries similarly portrayed.

A popular form of symbol is the pie-chart or pie-graph. It can be used like any other circular symbol, the value of the quantity being in proportion to the area of the circle. Giving the pie-graph thickness can add another set of values.

The computer processing of economic and other types of statistical data led to a requirement for systems capable of handling geographic information by computer. Geographic information systems (GIS) were developed as a tool for handling vast amounts of geographical information and associated data to supply an infinite range of outputs which include graphs, diagrams, cartograms, tabular summaries and maps. Applying the same computer techniques to the production of the ordinary topographic map was not feasible until computers of sufficient power and capacity were available at low cost. A major obstacle was the unavoidable requirement for a very large database whose creation demanded a colossal amount of time and manpower. The benefits which flow from its creation are undeniable. Maps can be designed, produced and stored without going through the conventional processes of manual drafting and printing. Maps held in the computer can be displayed on a screen or can be transmitted from computer to computer. An infinite variety of data can be superimposed. The output can be a map or part of a map or a combination of parts of several maps extracted from the individual source maps which are stored in the database. Perspective views can be generated and construction and engineering problems solved on the computer screen. Such is the ultimate goal in the management of geographic information. That does not mean the end of the paper map. On the contrary, it promises a future in which an endless variety of paper maps can be produced to suit any purpose.

(far left) *A cartogram showing countries by area. In cartograms geographic shape is lost but the rectangular outline which replaces it allows areas to be readily compared. Economic and other statistical data are conveniently presented in this way.*
(below right) *Pie-charts or pie-graphs are used to present statistical data. When used on a map, the diameter of the circle can be made proportion-* *ate to the quantity involved.*
(below left) *Map data stored in a database can be viewed on a graphics screen in whole, or in part, in a range of scales. Any element can be selected for display. Information can be superimposed. Aerial photography or satellite imagery can be combined with the map data. Output can be in plotted form or as digital data.*

WORLD ATLAS

SYMBOLS

Relief

		Feet	Relief	Metres	
⬭	Land contour				
		16404		5000	
▲ 8848	Spot height (metres)	9843		3000	
		6562		2000	
⋈	Pass	3281		1000	
▭	Permanent ice cap	1640		500	
		656		200	
		0		Sea Level	
		Land Dep. 656		200	
		13123		4000	
		22966		7000	

Hydrography

- ⬭ Submarine contour
- ▼11034 Ocean depth (metres)
- (217) Lake level (metres)
- ᷍ Reef
- 〜 River
- ⌁ Intermittent river
- ⌁ Falls
- ⌁ Dam
- ⌁ Gorge
- ⊔⊔⊔ Canal
- ⬭ Lake/Reservoir
- ⬭ Intermittent lake
- ⁖ Marsh/Swamp

Communications

- Tunnel ─── Main railway
- ⊕ Main airport
- - - - - Track

Road representation varies with the scale category.

══════ Principal road	} 1:1M-1:2½M
─────── Other main road	
─────── Principal road	} 1:2½M-1:7½M
─────── Other main road	
─────── Principal road	1:7½M or smaller

Administration

- ───── International boundary
- ─ ─ ─ Undefined/Disputed international boundary
- ─·─·─ Internal division : First order
- ─··─··─ Internal division : Second order
- ▨ ⊚ ⊡ / ⊙ ▯ ▪ National capitals

Settlement

Each settlement is given a town stamp according to its relative importance and scale category.

	1:1M-1:2½M	1:2½M-1:7½M	1:7½M or smaller
▨	Major City	Major City	Major City
⊙	City	City	City
⊚	Large Town	Large Town	Large Town
⊙	Town	Town	Town
○	Small Town	Small Town	—
•	Village	—	—
⬖	Urban area (1:1M-1:2½M only)		

The size of type used for each settlement is graded to correspond with the appropriate town stamp.

Other features

- ∴ Ancient monument
- ‿ Oasis
- ⬭ National Park
- ▲ Oil field
- △ Gas field
- ─·─·─ Oil/Gas pipeline

Lettering

Various styles of lettering are used - each one representing a different type of feature.

ALPS	Physical feature	KENYA	Country name
Red Sea	Hydrographic feature	IOWA	Internal division
Paris	Settlement name	*(Fr.)*	Territorial administration

THE WORLD : Political

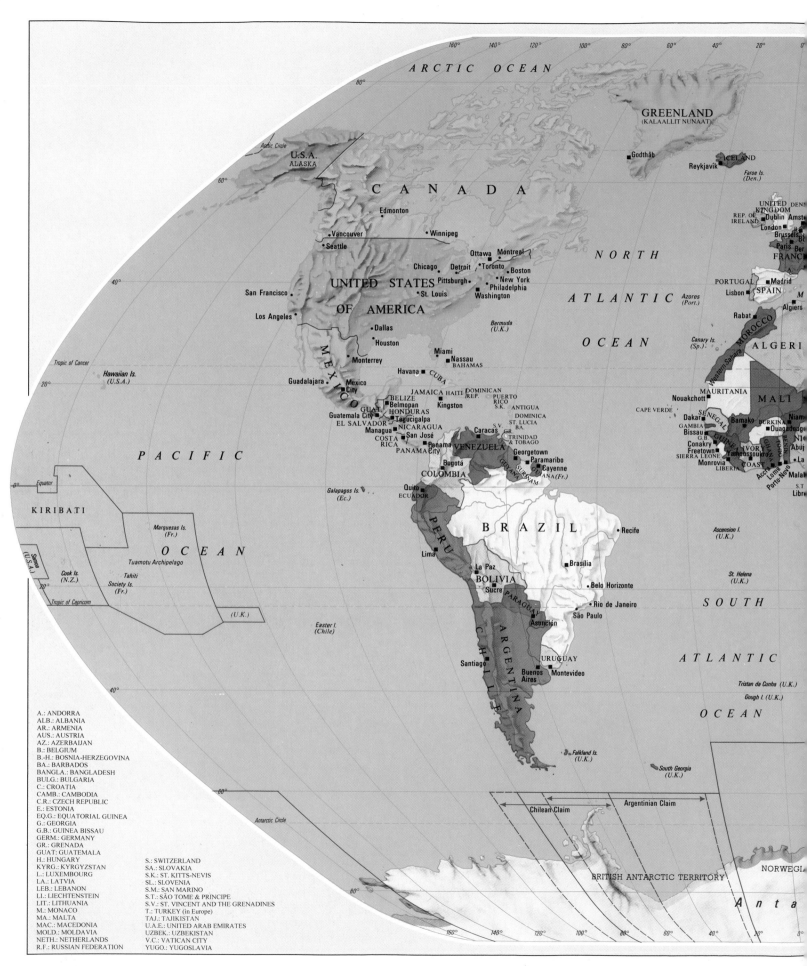

ARCTIC OCEAN

GREENLAND
(KALAALLIT NUNAAT)

Godthåb

ICELAND
Reykjavík
*Faroe Is.
(Den.)*

U.S.A.
ALASKA

C A N A D A

Edmonton

Vancouver
Seattle
Winnipeg

Ottawa Montreal
Chicago Detroit Toronto
Pittsburgh Boston
New York

UNITED
KINGDOM
REP. OF Dublin Amst
IRELAND
London
Brussels
Paris Ber
FRANC

UNITED STATES
OF AMERICA

San Francisco

St. Louis
Washington
Philadelphia

N O R T H

A T L A N T I C

O C E A N

PORTUGAL Madrid
Lisbon SPAIN
Azores
(Port.)

Algiers
Rabat

Los Angeles

Dallas

Houston

Miami
Nassau
BAHAMAS

Monterrey

Havana CUBA

Bermuda
(U.K.)

MOROCCO

ALGERI

Tropic of Cancer

Hawaiian Is.
(U.S.A.)

Guadalajara Mexico
City

JAMAICA HAITI
Belize
Belmopan Kingston

DOMINICAN
REP.
PUERTO
RICO
S.K. ANTIGUA
DOMINICA
ST. LUCIA

Canary Is.
(Sp.)

Western Sahara

MALI

MAURITANIA

Nouakchott

CAPE VERDE

Dakar SENEGAL
GAMBIA Bamako BURKINA
Bissau
G.B. GUINEA

Niam
Ouagadougou
NI

Guatemala City GUAT
EL SALVADOR
Managua
COSTA
RICA San José
PANAMA City

HONDURAS
Tegucigalpa
NICARAGUA

Caracas
S.V.
GR.
TRINIDAD
& TOBAGO

BA.

Conakry
SIERRA LEONE Freetown
Monrovia
LIBERIA IVOR
COAST

Abuj

La

P A C I F I C

VENEZUELA
Bogotá
COLOMBIA

Georgetown
Paramaribo
Cayenne
GUIANA (Fr.)

Accra Lome Mala
Porto-Novo
S.T
Libre

KIRIBATI

O C E A N

Equator

Galapagos Is.
(Ec.)

Quito
ECUADOR

SURINAM

B R A Z I L

Recife

Ascension I.
(U.K.)

Samoa
(U.S.A.)

Marquesas Is.
(Fr.)

PERU

Lima

Cook Is.
(N.Z.) Tahiti
Society Is.
(Fr.)

Tuamotu Archipelago

La Paz
BOLIVIA
Sucre

Brasília

Belo Horizonte

St. Helena
(U.K.)

Tropic of Capricorn

(U.K.)

Easter I.
(Chile)

PARAGUAY
Asunción

Rio de Janeiro
São Paulo

S O U T H

A T L A N T I C

CHILE

ARGENTINA

URUGUAY
Buenos Montevideo
Aires

Tristan da Cunha (U.K.)

Gough I. (U.K.)

Santiago

O C E A N

A.: ANDORRA
ALB.: ALBANIA
AR.: ARMENIA
AUS.: AUSTRIA
AZ.: AZERBAIJAN
B.: BELGIUM
B.-H.: BOSNIA-HERZEGOVINA
BA.: BARBADOS
BANGLA.: BANGLADESH
BULG.: BULGARIA
C.: CROATIA
CAMB.: CAMBODIA
C.R.: CZECH REPUBLIC
E.: ESTONIA
EQ.G.: EQUATORIAL GUINEA
G.: GEORGIA
G.B.: GUINEA BISSAU
GERM.: GERMANY
GR.: GRENADA
GUAT.: GUATEMALA
H.: HUNGARY
KYRG.: KYRGYZSTAN
L.: LUXEMBOURG
LA.: LATVIA
LEB.: LEBANON
LI.: LIECHTENSTEIN
LIT.: LITHUANIA
M.: MONACO
MA.: MALTA
MAC.: MACEDONIA
MOLD.: MOLDAVIA
R.F.: RUSSIAN FEDERATION

Falkland Is.
(U.K.)

South Georgia
(U.K.)

Argentinian Claim
Chilean Claim

Antarctic Circle

NORWEGI

S.: SWITZERLAND
SA.: SLOVAKIA
S.K.: ST. KITTS-NEVIS
SL.: SLOVENIA
S.M.: SAN MARINO
S.T.: SÃO TOME & PRINCIPE
S.V.: ST. VINCENT AND THE GRENADINES
T.: TURKEY (in Europe)
TAJ.: TAJIKISTAN
U.A.E.: UNITED ARAB EMIRATES
UZBEK.: UZBEKISTAN
V.C.: VATICAN CITY
YUGO.: YUGOSLAVIA

BRITISH ANTARCTIC TERRITORY

Anta

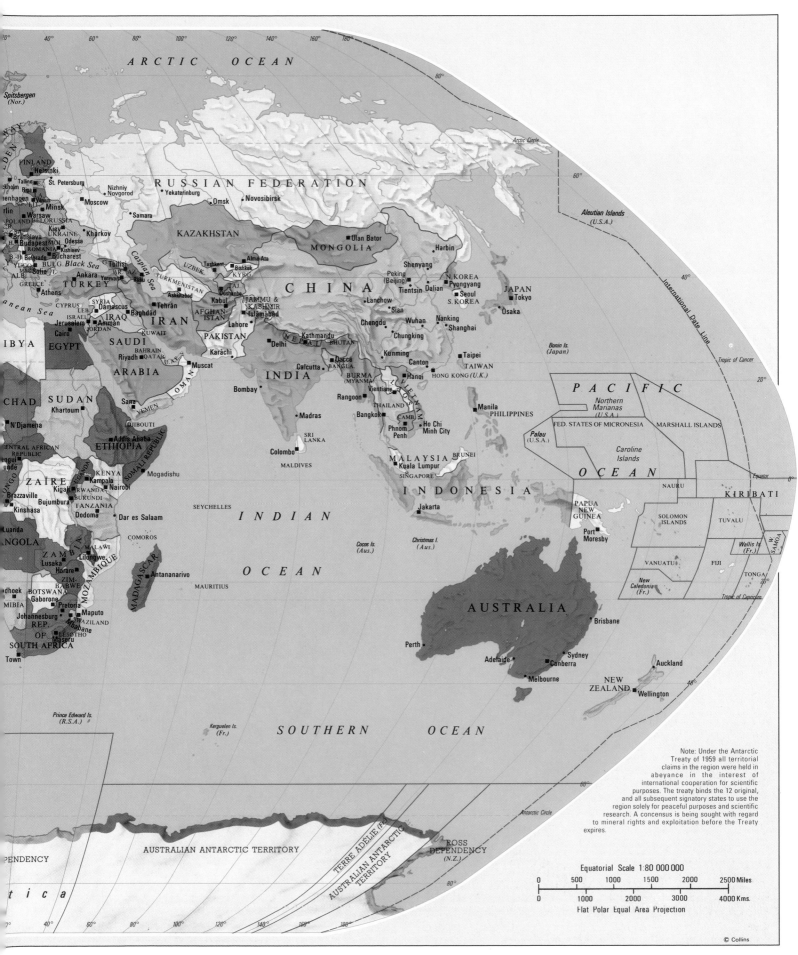

ARCTIC OCEAN

Spitsbergen
(Nor.)

RUSSIAN FEDERATION

Arctic Circle

Aleutian Islands
(U.S.A.)

FINLAND
Helsinki
St. Petersburg
Nizhniy
Novgorod
Yekaterinburg
Omsk
Novosibirsk
Tallinn
Riga
Vilnius
Moscow
Minsk
Samara
Warsaw
KAZAKHSTAN
MONGOLIA
Ulan Bator
Harbin
Shenyang
N.KOREA
Pyongyang
JAPAN
Tokyo
Kiev
UKRAINE
Kharkov
Odessa
Bucharest
Tashkent
Bishkek
UZBEK
Alma-Ata
Peking
(Beijing)
Tientsin
Dalian
Seoul
S.KOREA
Ōsaka
ROMANIA
Kishinev
Tbilisi
Black Sea
KYRG.
Lanchow
Sian
Wuhan
Shanghai
Nanking
BULG.
TURKMENISTAN
Baku
Yerevan
Ashkhabad
TAJ.
Dushanbe
CHINA
GREECE
Athens
TURKEY
Ankara
Caspian Sea
Chengdu
Chungking
Kathmandu
Delhi
BHUTAN
CYPRUS
Damascus
SYRIA
Tehrān
AFGHAN-
ISTAN
JAMMU &
KASHMIR
Islamabad
Kunming
Canton
Taipei
Jerusalem
Amman
IRAQ
Baghdād
IRAN
Kabul
Lahore
NEPAL
Dacca
BANGLA.
Hanoi
TAIWAN
HONG KONG (U.K.)
ISRAEL
JORDAN
KUWAIT
PAKISTAN
Karāchi
Calcutta
BURMA
(MYANMA)
Bonin Is.
(Japan)
Tropic of Cancer
Cairo
SAUDI
Riyadh
BAHRAIN
QATAR
U.A.E.
Muscat
INDIA
Bombay
Rangoon
Vientiane
LAOS
VIETNAM
Manila
PACIFIC
EGYPT
ARABIA
OMAN
Madras
THAILAND
Bangkok
CAMB.
PHILIPPINES
Northern
Marianas
(U.S.A.)
SUDAN
Sana
YEMEN
Phnom
Penh
Ho Chi
Minh City
FED. STATES OF MICRONESIA
MARSHALL ISLANDS
CHAD
Khartoum
DJIBOUTI
SRI
LANKA
Palau
(U.S.A.)
Caroline
Islands
N'Djamena
CENTRAL AFRICAN
REPUBLIC
ETHIOPIA
Addis Ababa
Colombo
MALDIVES
MALAYSIA
Kuala Lumpur
BRUNEI
OCEAN
KENYA
SOMALI REPUBLIC
Mogadishu
SINGAPORE
INDONESIA
NAURU
KIRIBATI
ZAÏRE
Kampala
Nairobi
SEYCHELLES
INDIAN
PAPUA
NEW
GUINEA
Brazzaville
Kinshasa
RWANDA
BURUNDI
Bujumbura
TANZANIA
Dodoma
Dar es Salaam
Jakarta
SOLOMON
ISLANDS
TUVALU
Wallis Is.
(Fr.)
W.
SAMOA
ANGOLA
COMOROS
Cocos Is.
(Aus.)
Christmas I.
(Aus.)
Port
Moresby
VANUATU
FIJI
ZAMBIA
Lusaka
MALAWI
Lilongwe
MADAGASCAR
OCEAN
MAURITIUS
New
Caledonia
(Fr.)
TONGA
Harare
ZIM-
BABWE
MOZAMBIQUE
Antananarivo
Tropic of Capricorn
BOTSWANA
Gaborone
Pretoria
Maputo
SWAZILAND
AUSTRALIA
Brisbane
Johannesburg
REP.
OF
SOUTH AFRICA
LESOTHO
Maseru
Perth
Adelaide
Canberra
Sydney
Auckland
Melbourne
NEW
ZEALAND
Wellington

Prince Edward Is.
(R.S.A.)

Kerguelen Is.
(Fr.)

SOUTHERN   OCEAN

Note: Under the Antarctic
Treaty of 1959 all territorial
claims in the region were held in
abeyance in the interest of
international cooperation for scientific
purposes. The treaty binds the 12 original,
and all subsequent signatory states to use the
region solely for peaceful purposes and scientific
research. A concensus is being sought with regard
to mineral rights and exploitation before the Treaty
expires.

Antarctic Circle

AUSTRALIAN ANTARCTIC TERRITORY
TERRE ADÉLIE (Fr.)
AUSTRALIAN ANTARCTIC TERRITORY
ROSS
DEPENDENCY
(N.Z.)
DEPENDENCY

Equatorial Scale 1:80 000 000

| 0 | 500 | 1000 | 1500 | 2000 | 2500 Miles |

| 0 | 1000 | 2000 | 3000 | 4000 Kms. |

Flat Polar Equal Area Projection

© Collins

3

THE WORLD : Physical

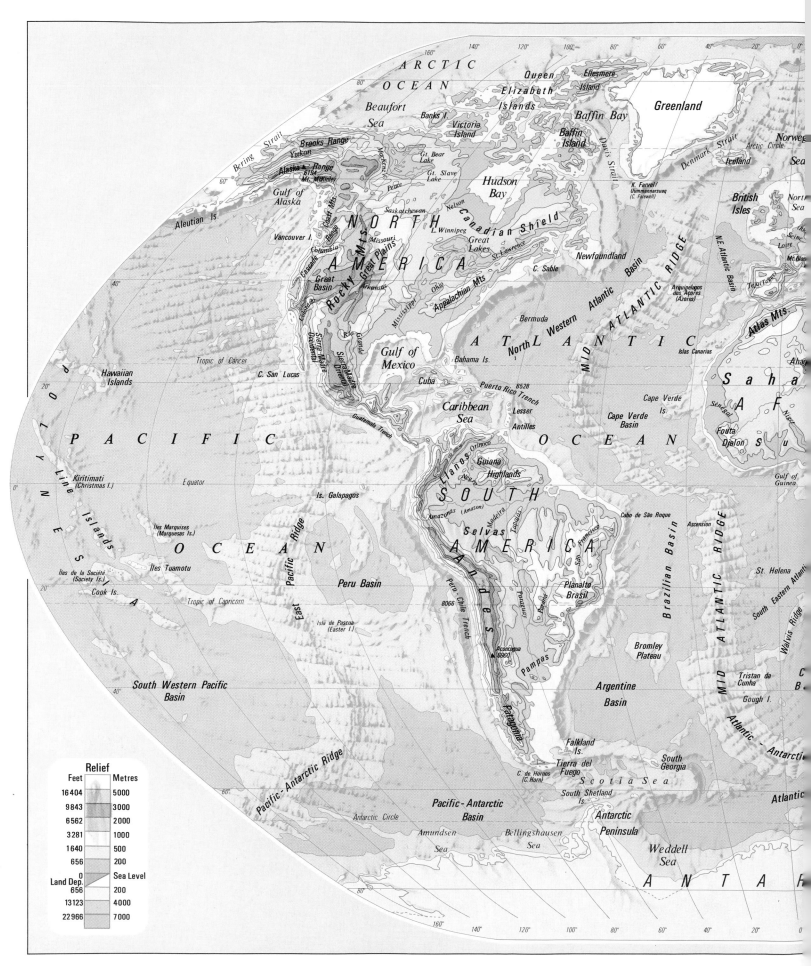

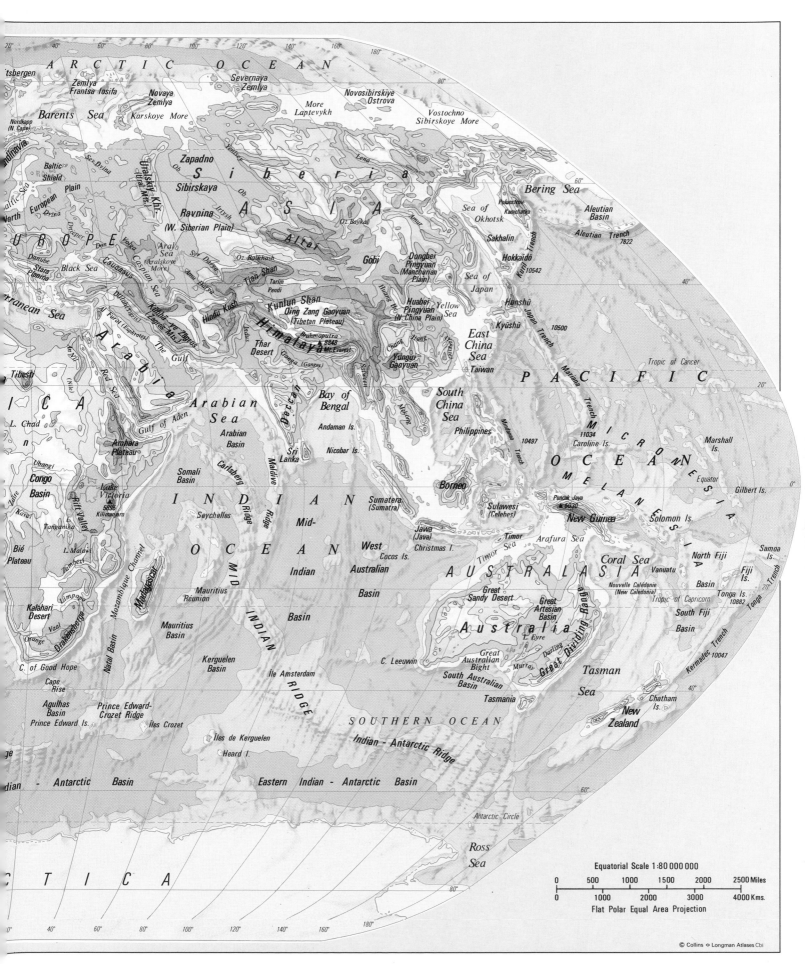

ARCTIC OCEAN

Severnaya
Zemlya

Zemlya
Frantsa Iosifa

Novosibirskiye
Ostrova

Novaya
Zemlya

Barents Sea

Nordkapp
(N. Cape)

Karskoye More

More
Laptevykh

Vostochno
Sibirskoye More

80°

Bering Sea

60°

Zapadno

Siberia

ASIA

Scandinavia

Baltic
Shield

Sev. Dvina

Ob

Yenisey

Lena

Sibirskaya

Poluostrov
Kamchatka

Aleutian
Basin

Aleutian Trench
7822

Baltic Sea

European

North

Drina

Ural'skiy Khr.
(Ural Mts.)

Ravnina

(W. Siberian Plain)

Irtysh

Ob

Oz. Baykal

Amur

Sea of
Okhotsk

EUROPE

Don

Volga

Aral
Sea
(Aral'skoye
More)

Altai

Gobi

Sakhalin

Hokkaidō

Kuril Trench
10542

40°

Dnieper

Dnister

Caspian Sea

Oz. Balkhash

Dongbei
Pingyuan
(Manchurian
Plain)

Sea of
Japan

Danube

Caucasus

Syr Dar'ya

Tian Shan

Tarim
Pendi

Honshū

Japan Trench
10500

Stara
Planina

Black Sea

Amu Dar'ya

Kyūshū

Kizilirmak
(Zagros Mts.)

Hindu Kush

Kunlun Shan

Huang He

Huabei
Pingyuan
(N. China Plain)

Yellow
Sea

Mediterranean Sea

Al Furat (Euphrates)

Qing Zang Gaoyuan
(Tibetan Plateau)

East
China
Sea

PACIFIC

Tropic of Cancer

An Nil
(Nile)

Arabia

Himalaya

Brahmaputra
8848
Mt. Everest

Chang Jiang

Taiwan

20°

Red Sea

The Gulf

Thar
Desert

Ganga (Ganges)

Xi Jiang

Yungui
Gaoyuan

Tibesti

Gulf of Aden

Arabian
Sea

Deccan

Bay of
Bengal

Salween

South
China
Sea

MICRONESIA

L. Chad

Mekong

OCEANIA

Amhara
Plateau

Andaman Is.

Philippines

Mariana Trench
11034

Marshall
Is.

Ubangi

Congo
Basin

Somali
Basin

Carlsberg

Sri
Lanka

Nicobar Is.

Mindanao
Trench
10497

Caroline Is.

Equator

Zaire

Lake
Victoria
5895
Kilimanjaro

Seychelles

Ridge

INDIAN

Maldive

Mid-

Sumatera
(Sumatra)

Borneo

MELANESIA

Gilbert Is.

Kasai

Rift Valley

Ridge

Indian

West
Australian

Puncak Jaya
5030

Solomon Is.

Bié
Plateau

Tanganika

OCEAN

Basin

Jawa
(Java)

Christmas I.

Cocos Is.

Sulawesi
(Celebes)

New Guinea

Zambezi

L. Malawi

MID

Timor

Timor
Sea

Arafura Sea

AUSTRALASIA

Coral Sea

North Fiji
Basin

Samoa
Is.

Kalahari
Desert

Limpopo

Madagascar

Mozambique Channel

Mauritius
Réunion

Basin

Great
Sandy Desert

Great
Artesian
Basin

Vanuatu

Nouvelle Calédonie
(New Caledonia)

Fiji
Is.

20°

Orange

Vaal

Drakensberg

Natal Basin

Mauritius
Basin

INDIAN

Australia

L. Eyre

Great Dividing Range

Tropic of Capricorn

South Fiji
Basin

Tonga Is.
10882

Tonga Trench

C. of Good Hope

Cape Rise

Kerguelen
Basin

Île Amsterdam

RIDGE

C. Leeuwin

Great
Australian
Bight

Murray

Darling

Tasman
Sea

Kermadec Trench
10047

Agulhas
Basin

Prince Edward-
Crozet Ridge

South Australian
Basin

Chatham
Is.

40°

Prince Edward Is.

Îles Crozet

Îles de Kerguelen

Tasmania

New
Zealand

Antarctic Basin

Heard I.

SOUTHERN OCEAN

Indian - Antarctic Ridge

Eastern Indian - Antarctic Basin

60°

Antarctic Circle

ANTARCTICA

Ross
Sea

80°

0°   40°   60°   80°   100°   120°   140°   160°   180°

Equatorial Scale 1:80 000 000

| 0 | 500 | 1000 | 1500 | 2000 | 2500 Miles |

| 0 | 1000 | 2000 | 3000 | 4000 Kms. |

Flat Polar Equal Area Projection

© Collins ◇ Longman Atlases Cbi

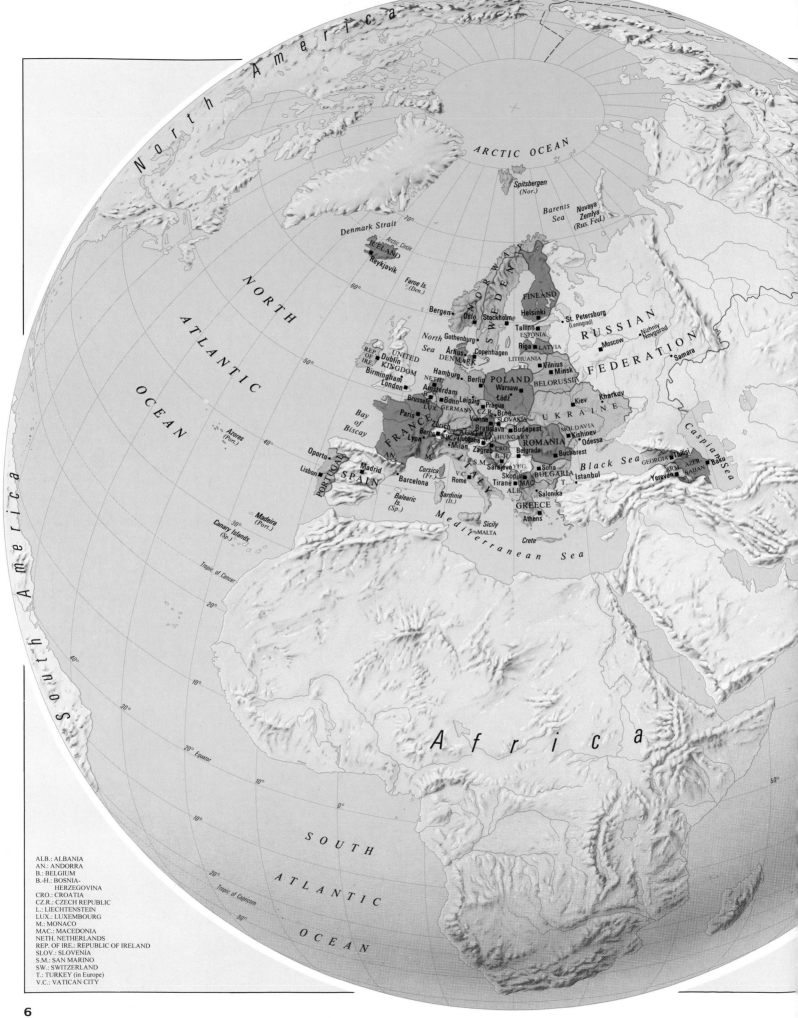

ARCTIC OCEAN

North America

North America

South America

South America

NORTH

ATLANTIC

OCEAN

Spitsbergen
(Nor.)

Barents
Sea

Novaya
Zemlya
(Rus. Fed.)

Denmark Strait

Arctic Circle

ICELAND

Reykjavik

Faroe Is.
(Den.)

Bergen

Oslo   Stockholm

Helsinki

St. Petersburg
(Leningrad)

FINLAND

NORWAY

SWEDEN

Tallinn

ESTONIA

RUSSIAN

Moscow

Nizhniy
Novgorod

North
Sea

Gothenburg

Århus

Copenhagen

Riga   LATVIA

LITHUANIA

FEDERATION

Samara

REP.
OF
IRE.

Dublin

UNITED

KINGDOM

DENMARK

Hamburg

Vilnius   Minsk

Birmingham

NETH.

Berlin

POLAND

BELORUSSIA

London

Amsterdam

Warsaw

Kiev   Kharkov

Brussels

Bonn

Leipzig

Łódź

LUX.

GERMANY

Prague

UKRAINE

Paris

Vienna

CZ.R.   Brno

SLOVAKIA

Zurich

Bratislava   Budapest

MOLDAVIA

Bay
of
Biscay

FRANCE

Berne

A. SLOV.

Lyon

SW.

LIECH.

HUNGARY

Kishinev

Odessa

AUS.

Ljubljana

CRO.

Milan

Zagreb

ROMANIA

V.C.

B.-H.

Belgrade

Bucharest

GEORGIA

Tbilisi

Caspian Sea

Oporto

AN.

M.

I.S.M.

Sarajevo

YUG.

Black Sea

ARM.

AZER-

Baku

Lisbon

Madrid

Corsica
(Fr.)

ITALY

Skopje

Sofia

BAIJAN

PORTUGAL

SPAIN

Barcelona

Rome

Tirane

MAC.

BULGARIA

Istanbul

Yerevan

ALB.

T.

Balearic
Is.
(Sp.)

Sardinia
(It.)

GREECE

Salonika

Azores
(Port.)

Madeira
(Port.)

Athens

Canary Islands
(Sp.)

Sicily

MALTA

Crete

Tropic of Cancer

Mediterranean Sea

Africa

Africa

SOUTH

ATLANTIC

OCEAN

Equator

Tropic of Capricorn

ALB.: ALBANIA
AN.: ANDORRA
B.: BELGIUM
B.-H.: BOSNIA-
          HERZEGOVINA
CRO.: CROATIA
CZ.R.: CZECH REPUBLIC
L.: LIECHTENSTEIN
LUX.: LUXEMBOURG
M.: MONACO
MAC.: MACEDONIA
NETH. NETHERLANDS
REP. OF IRE.: REPUBLIC OF IRELAND
SLOV.: SLOVENIA
S.M.: SAN MARINO
SW.: SWITZERLAND
T.: TURKEY (in Europe)
V.C.: VATICAN CITY

EUROPE

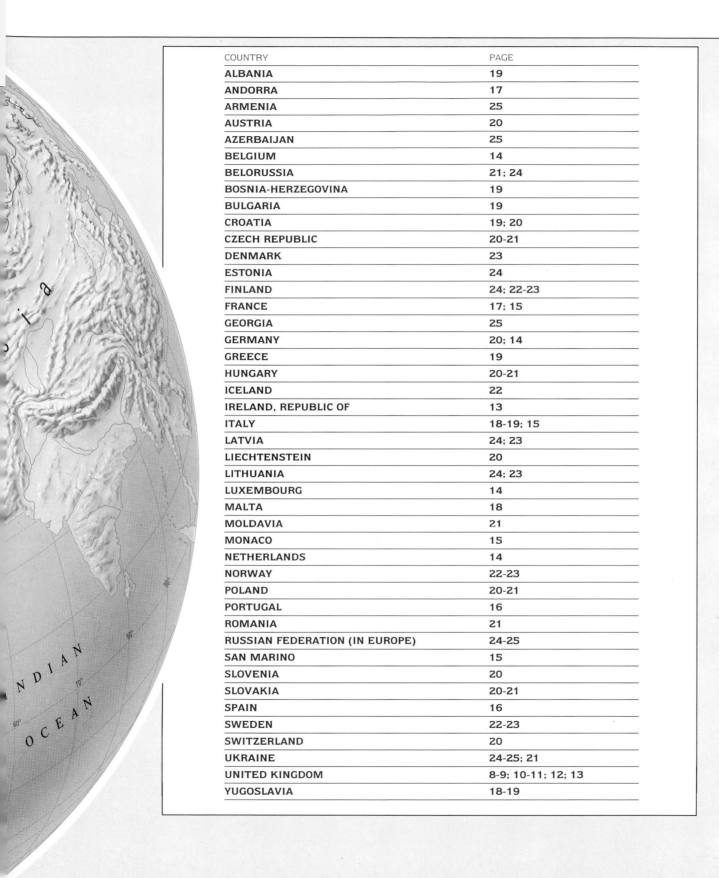

BRITISH ISLES

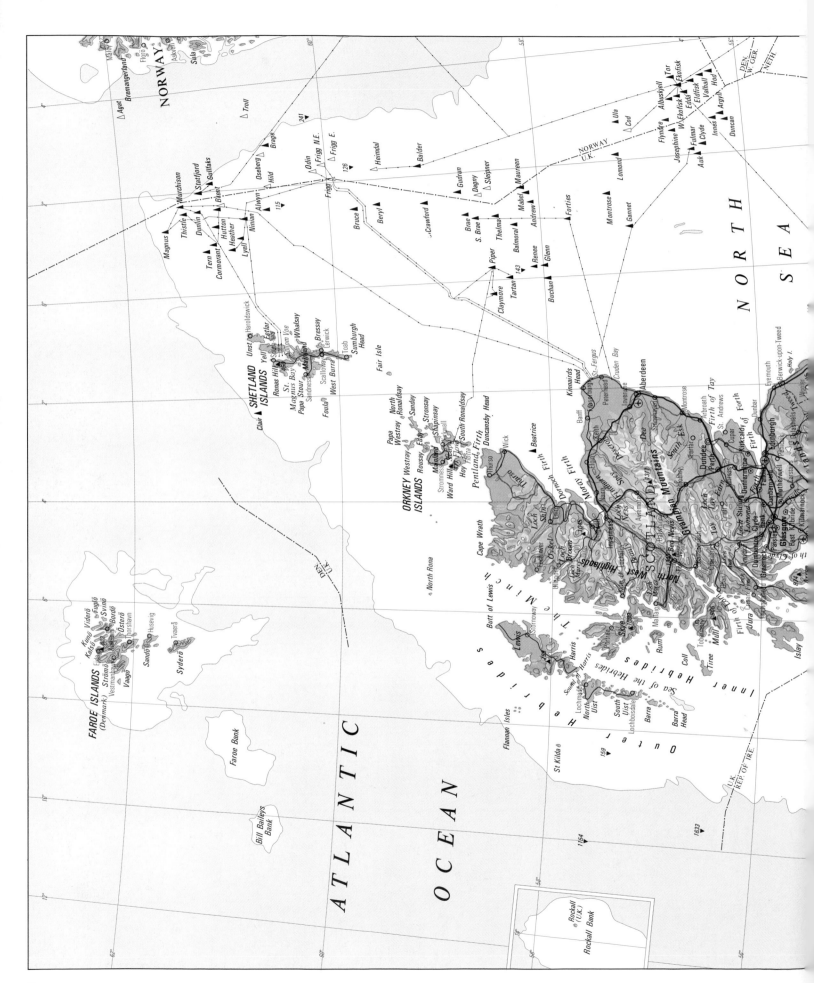

NORWAY

NORTH SEA

ATLANTIC OCEAN

FAROE ISLANDS
(Denmark)

SHETLAND
ISLANDS

ORKNEY
ISLANDS

NORTH SCOTTISH Dee
Grampian Mountains
West Highlands

Inner Hebrides

Outer Hebrides

Sea of the Hebrides

The Minch

Aberdeen

Glasgow
Edinburgh

Rockall
(U.K.)

Rockall Bank

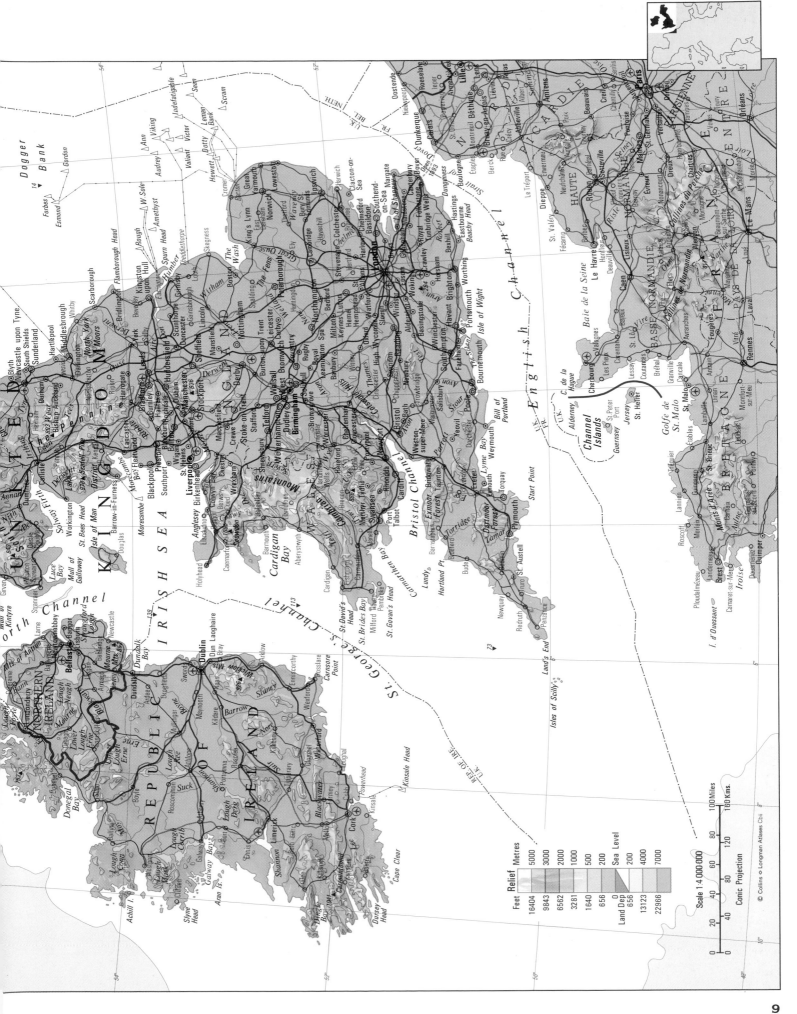

ENGLAND AND WALES

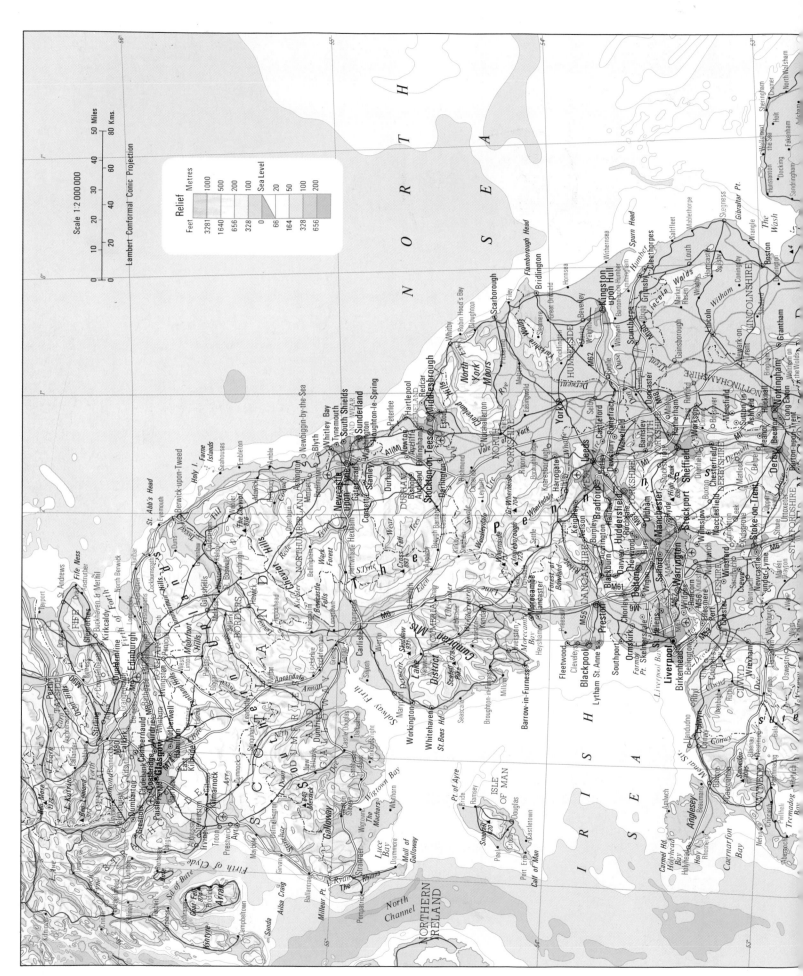

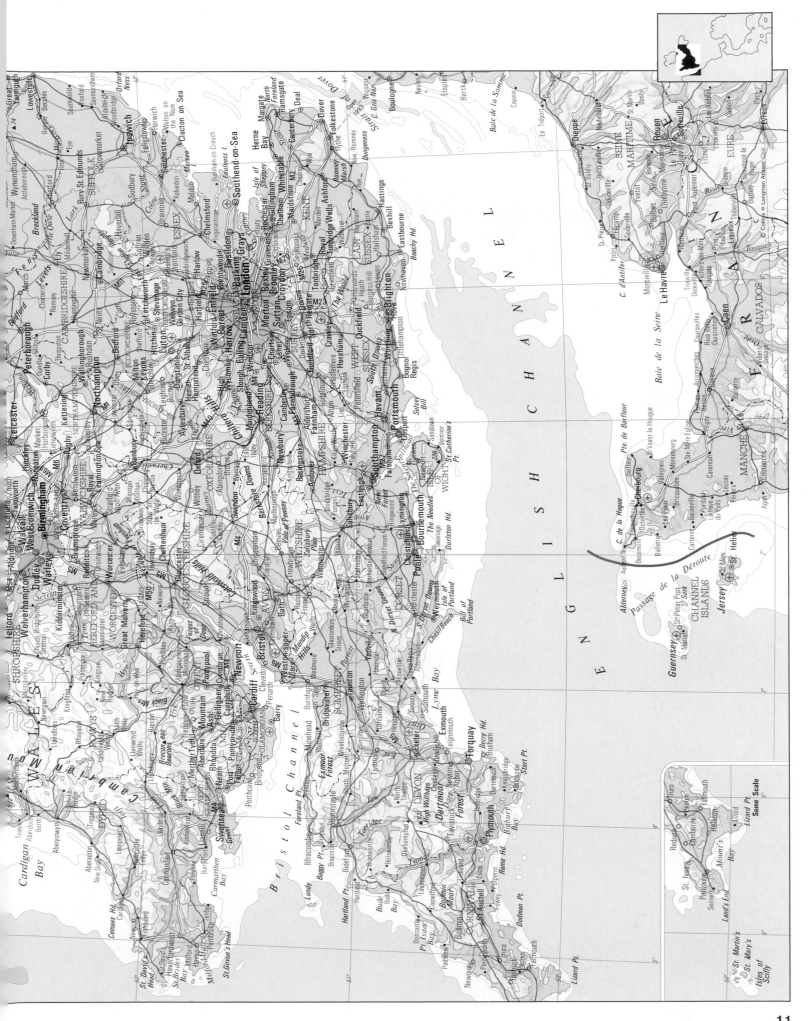

SCOTLAND

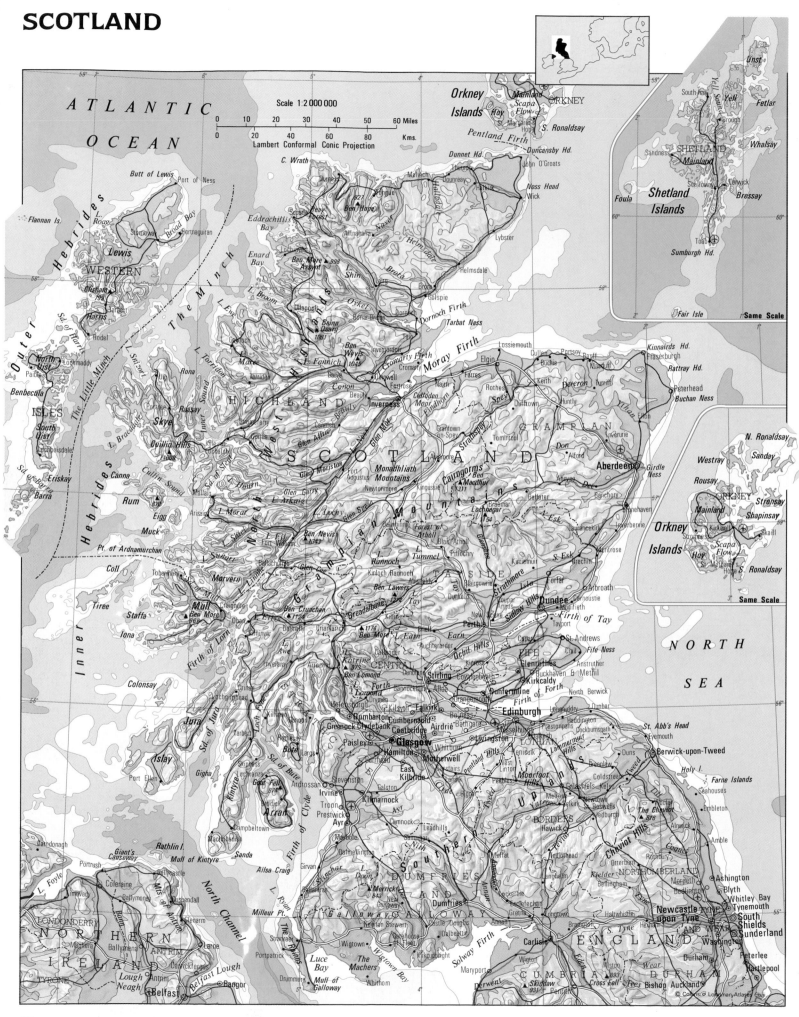

IRELAND

Relief

Feet		Metres
3281		1000
1640		500
656		200
328		100
0	Sea Level	0
66		20
164		50
328		100
656		200

Scale 1 : 2 000 000

Miles
0   10   20   30   40 Miles

Kms.
0   20   40   60 Kms.

Lambert Conformal Conic Projection

© Collins • Longman Atlases Cbiii

THE LOW COUNTRIES

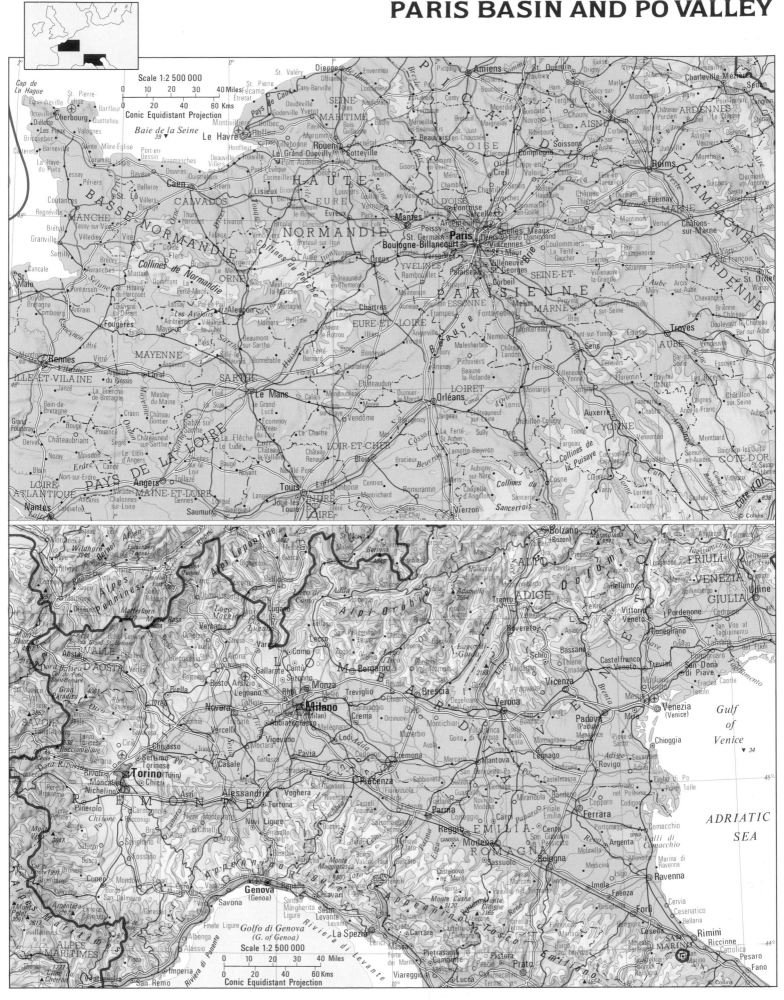

SPAIN AND PORTUGAL

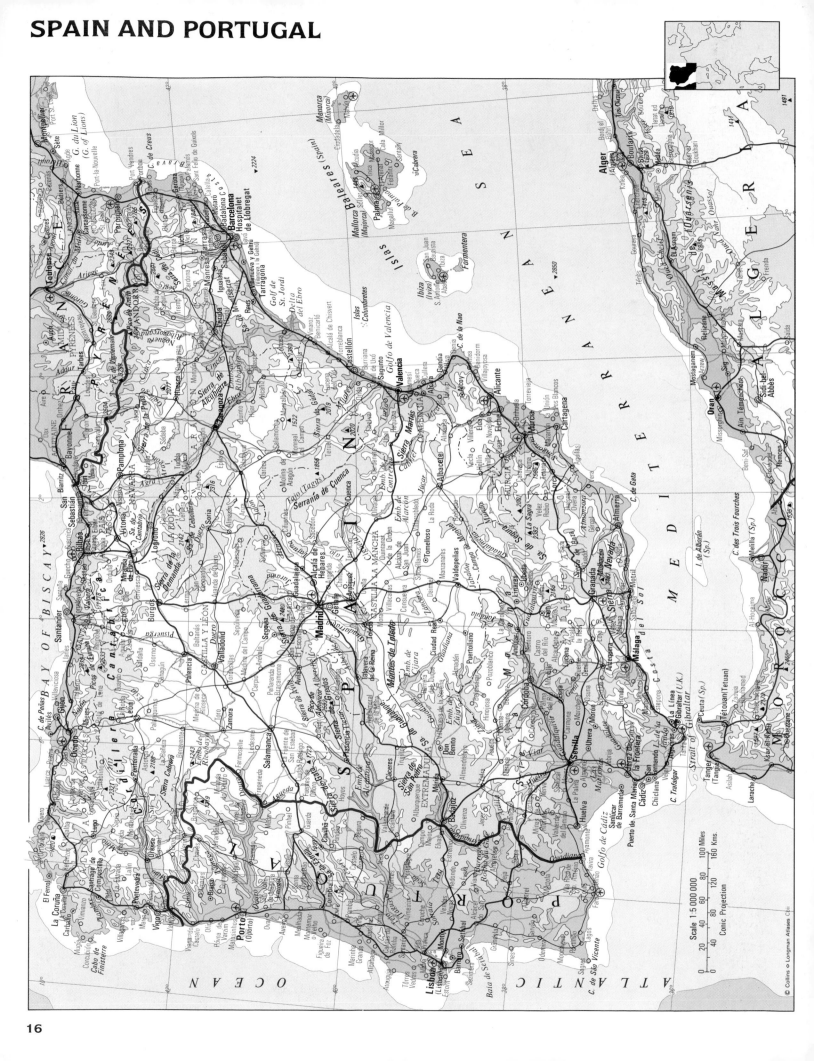

Scale 1:5 000 000
Conic Projection

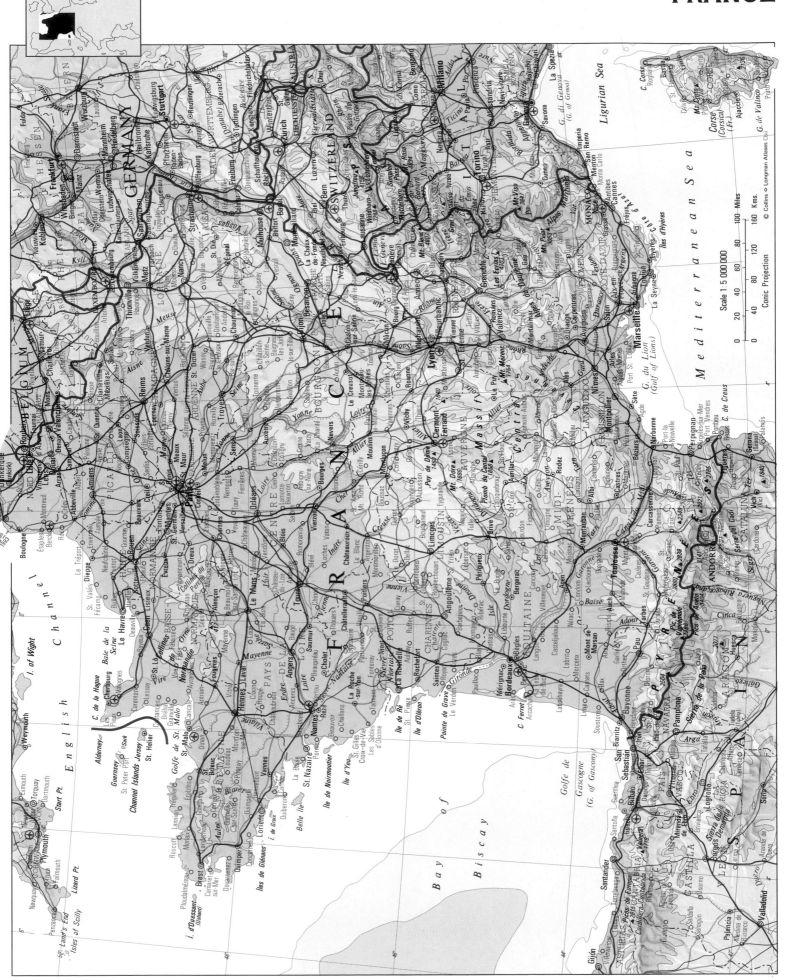

ITALY AND THE BALKANS

CENTRAL EUROPE

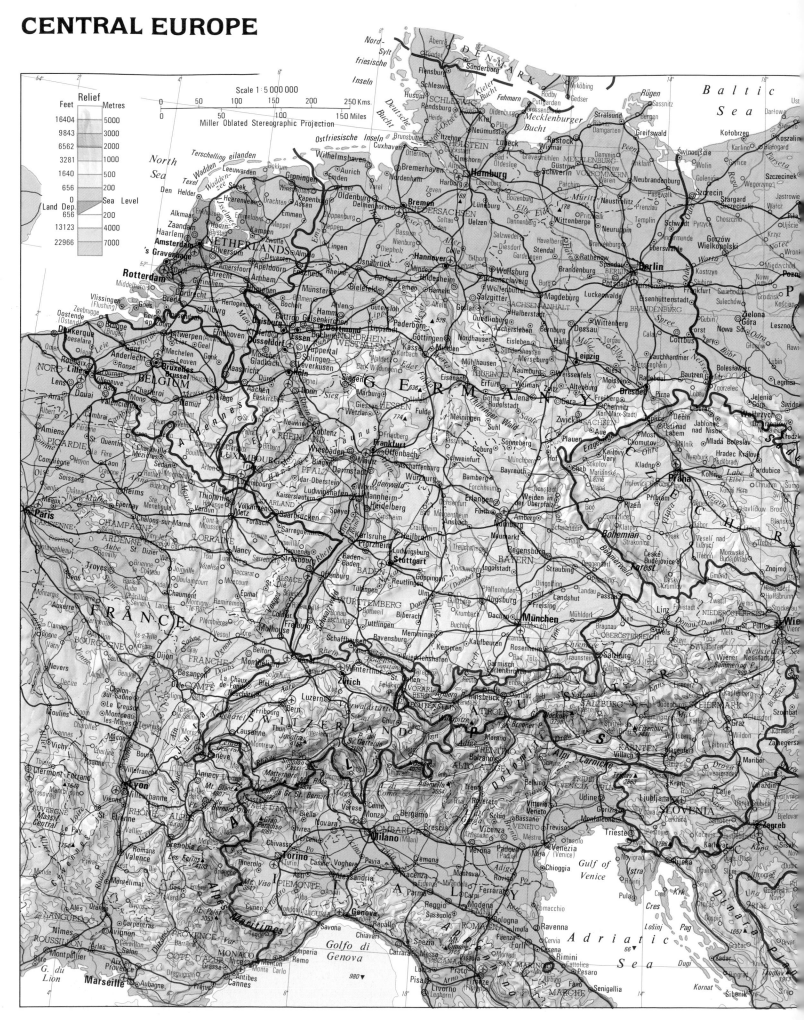

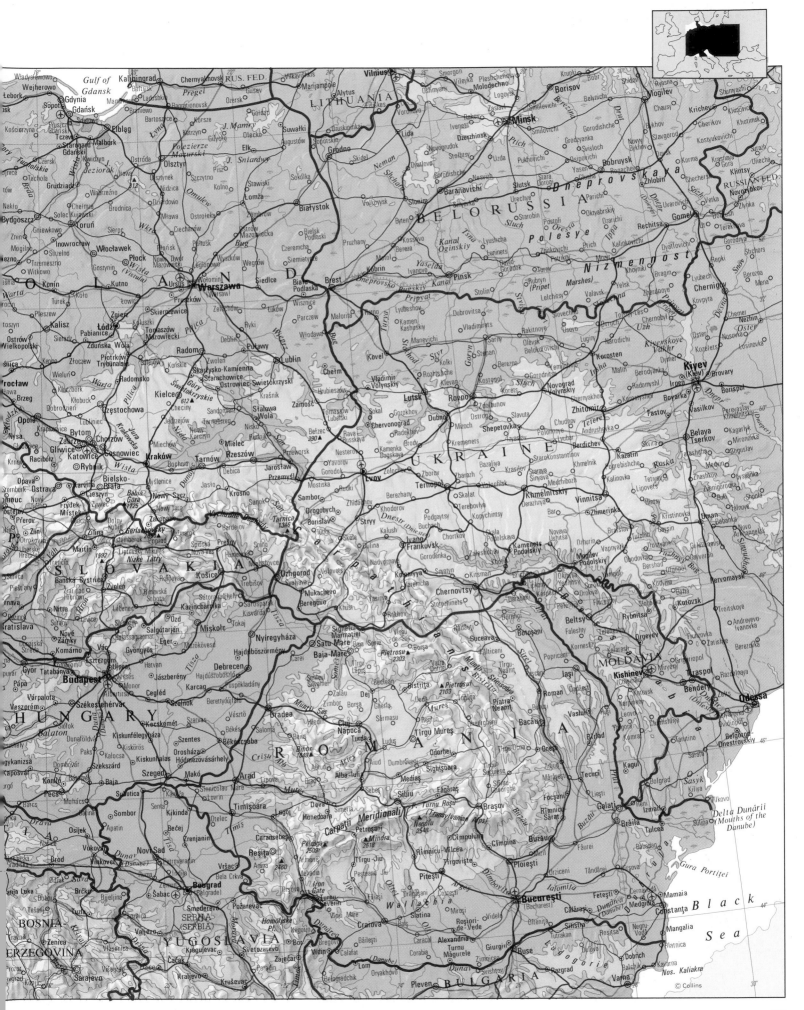

21

SCANDINAVIA AND BALTIC LANDS

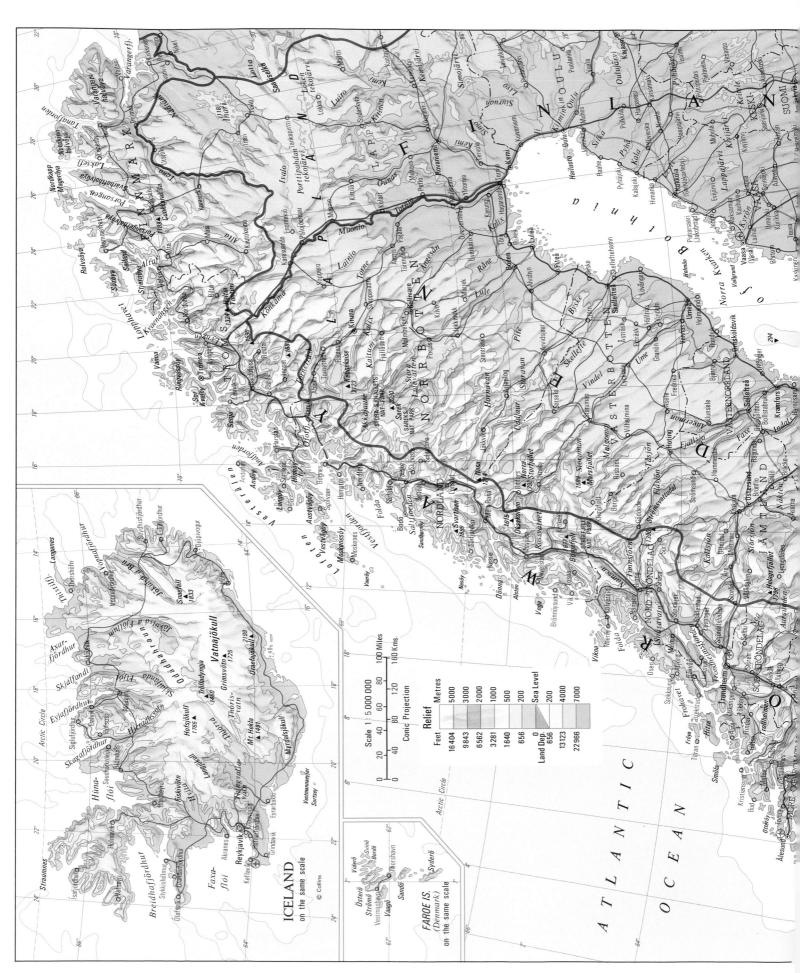

Relief

Metres		Feet
5000		16404
3000		9843
2000		6562
1000		3281
500		1640
200		656
Sea Level	0	
Land Dep.	656	
200		
4000		13123
7000		22966

Scale 1: 5 000 000

Conic Projection

ICELAND
on the same scale

© Collins

FARÖE IS.
(Denmark)
on the same scale

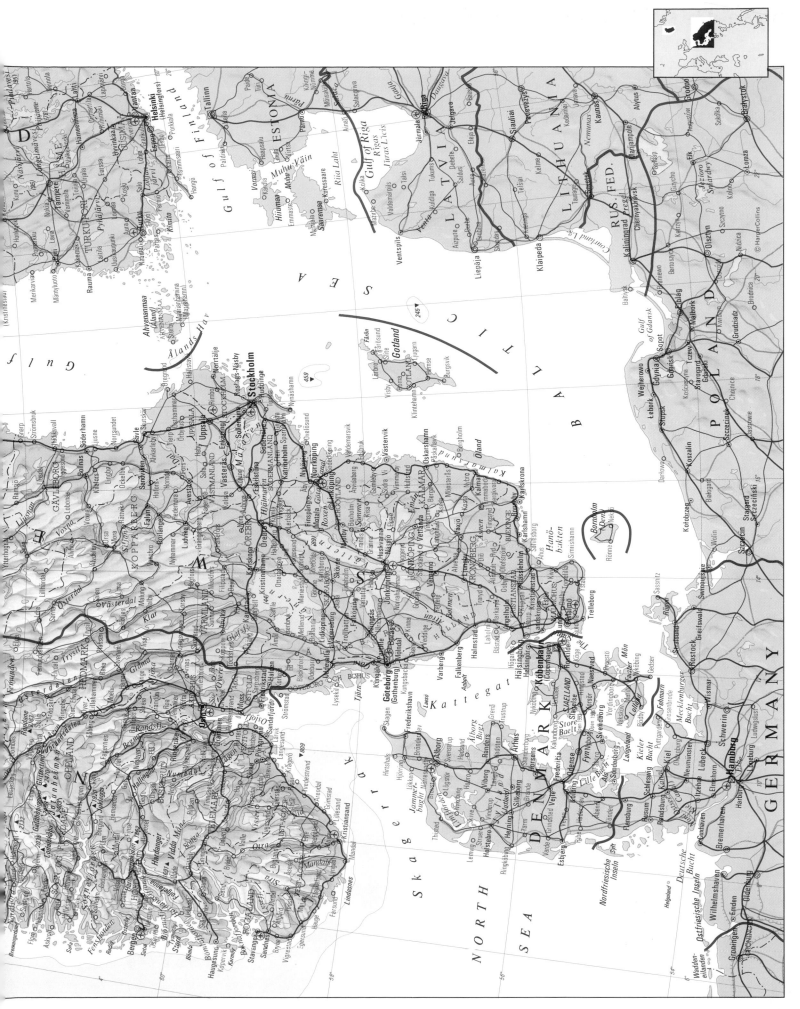

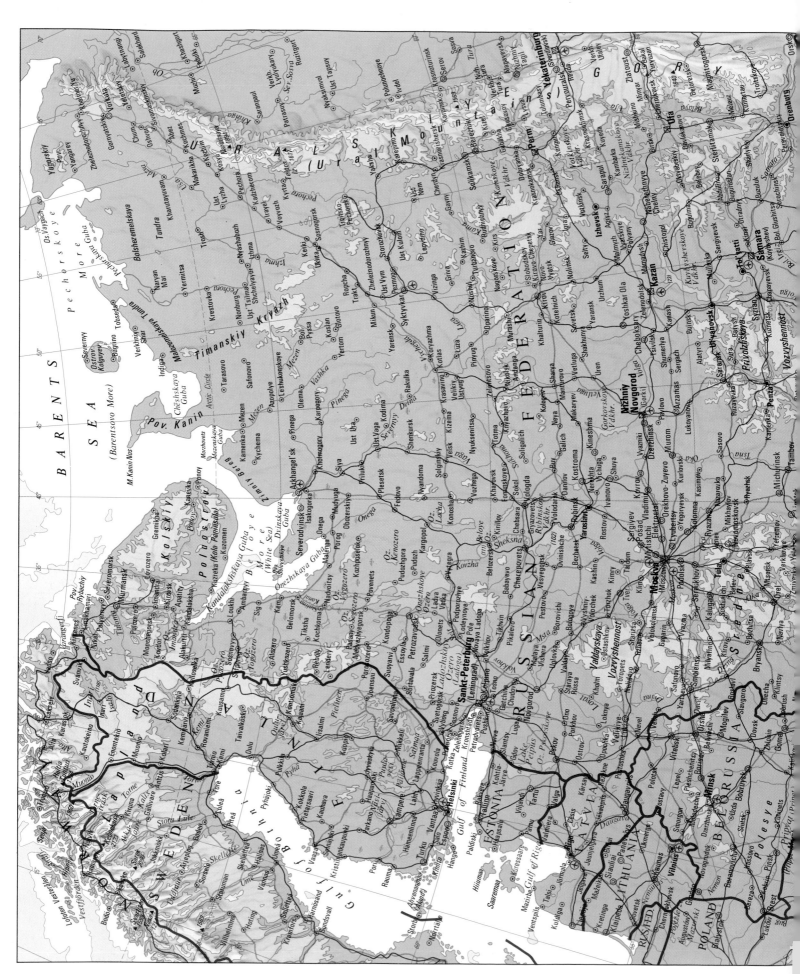

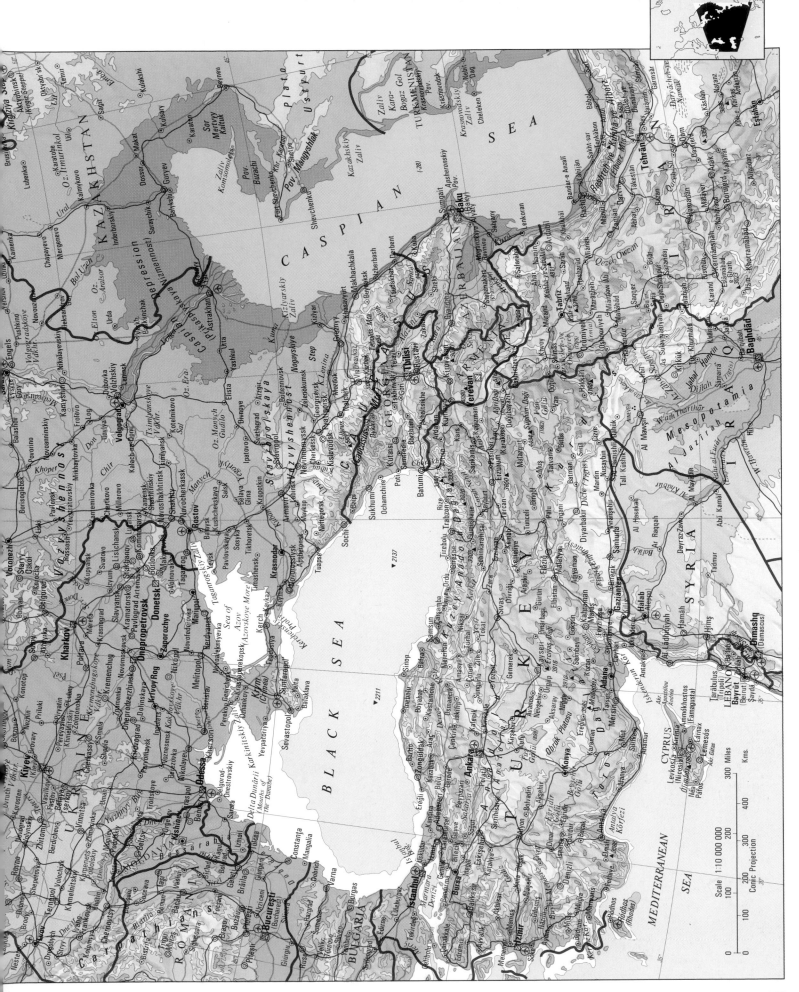

25

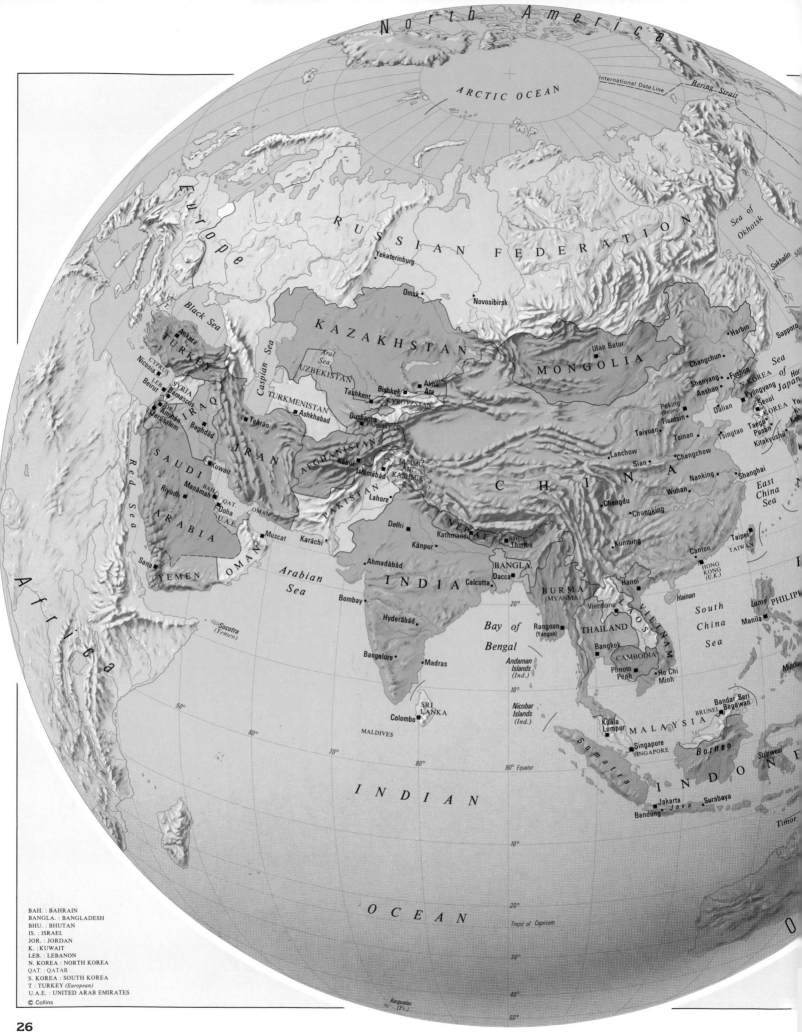

North America

ARCTIC OCEAN
International Date Line
Bering Strait

Europe

RUSSIAN FEDERATION

Sea of Okhotsk

Yekaterinburg
Omsk
Novosibirsk
Sakhalin

KAZAKHSTAN

Aral Sea
Caspian Sea
Black Sea
T.
Ankara
TURKEY
CYPRUS
Nicosia
SYRIA
LEB.
Beirut
Damascus
JOR.
Amman
Jerusalem
IRAQ
Baghdad
IS.

UZBEKISTAN
TURKMENISTAN
Ashkhabad
Tashkent
Bishkek
Alma Ata
KYRGYZSTAN
Dushanbe
TAJIKISTAN
Tehrän

MONGOLIA
Ulan Bator

Harbin
Changchun
Shenyang
Fushun
Anshan
N. KOREA
Pyongyang
Seoul
Peking (Beijing)
Tientsin
Dalian
S. KOREA
Taegu
Pusan
Tsingtao
Kitakyushu

Sapporo

Sea of Japan

IRAN

AFGHANISTAN
Kabul
Islamabad
JAMMU AND KASHMIR

Taiyuan
Tsinan
Lanchow
Sian
Chengchow
Nanking
Shanghai

CHINA

SAUDI
Kuwait
K.
Riyadh
BAH.
Manamah
QAT.
Doha
U.A.E.
OMAN

PAKISTAN
Lahore

Chengdu
Chungking
Wuhan

East China Sea

ARABIA
Muscat
Karächi

Delhi
Känpur
NEPAL
Kathmandu
BHU.
Thimbu

Kunming

Canton
Taipei
TAIWAN

Red Sea

Sana
YEMEN
OMAN

Ahmadäbäd

BANGLA.
Calcutta
Dacca

HONG KONG (U.K.)

Africa

Socotra (Yemen)

Arabian Sea

INDIA
Bombay

Hyderäbäd

BURMA (MYANMAR)

Hanoi
Hainan

South China Sea

Manila
Luzon
PHILIP

Bay of Bengal

Rangoon (Yangon)
THAILAND
Bangkok

Vientiane
LAOS
VIETNAM

Bangalore
Madras

Andaman Islands (Ind.)

CAMBODIA
Phnom Penh
Ho Chi Minh

Mindan

50°

SRI LANKA
Colombo

Nicobar Islands (Ind.)

Bandar Seri Begawan
BRUNEI

60°

MALDIVES

70°

80°

90° Equator

Kuala Lumpur
MALAYSIA
Singapore
SINGAPORE

Borneo

Sulawesi

INDON

10°

INDIAN

Sumatra
Java
Jakarta
Surabaya
Bandung

Timor

10°

OCEAN

20°

Tropic of Capricorn

BAH. : BAHRAIN
BANGLA. : BANGLADESH
BHU. : BHUTAN
IS. : ISRAEL
JOR. : JORDAN
K. : KUWAIT
LEB. : LEBANON
N. KOREA : NORTH KOREA
QAT. : QATAR
S. KOREA : SOUTH KOREA
T : TURKEY (European)
U.A.E. : UNITED ARAB EMIRATES

© Collins

30°

40°

50°

Kerguelen (Fr.)

ASIA

NORTH ASIA

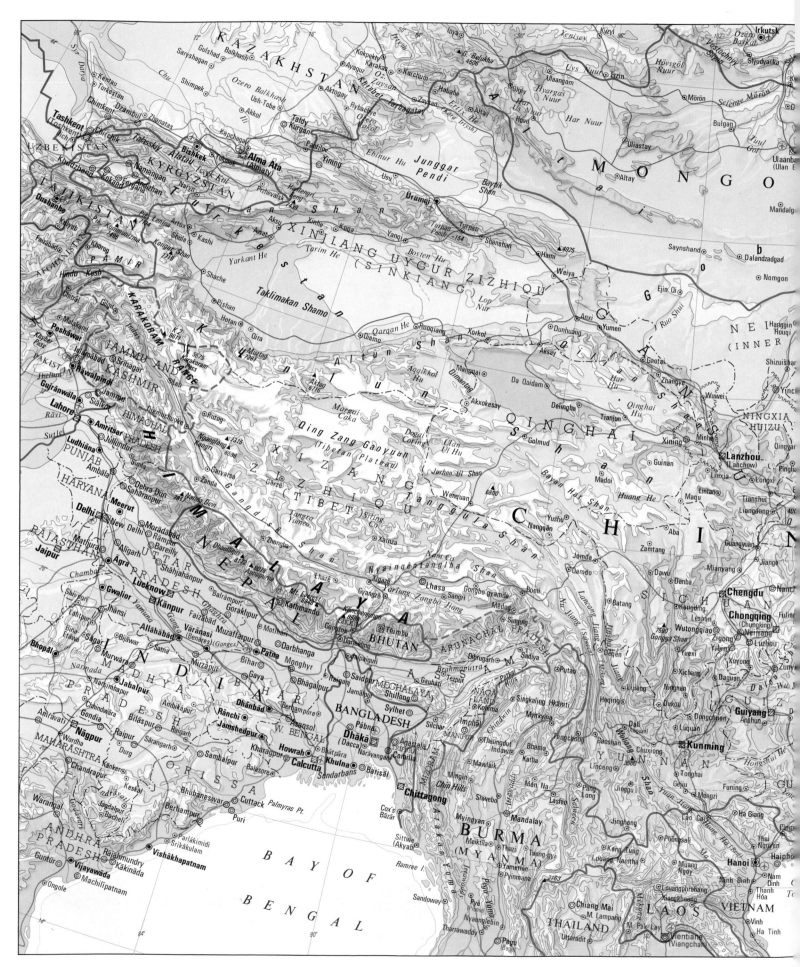

Relief

Feet		Metres
16 404		5000
9843		3000
6562		2000
3281		1000
1640		500
656		200
0	Sea Level	
Land Dep.		
656		200
13123		4000
22966		7000

Scale 1:16 000 000

0   100   200   300   400   500 Miles
0   200   400   600   800 Kms.

Conic Projection

© Collins ○ Longman Atlases Cbi

31

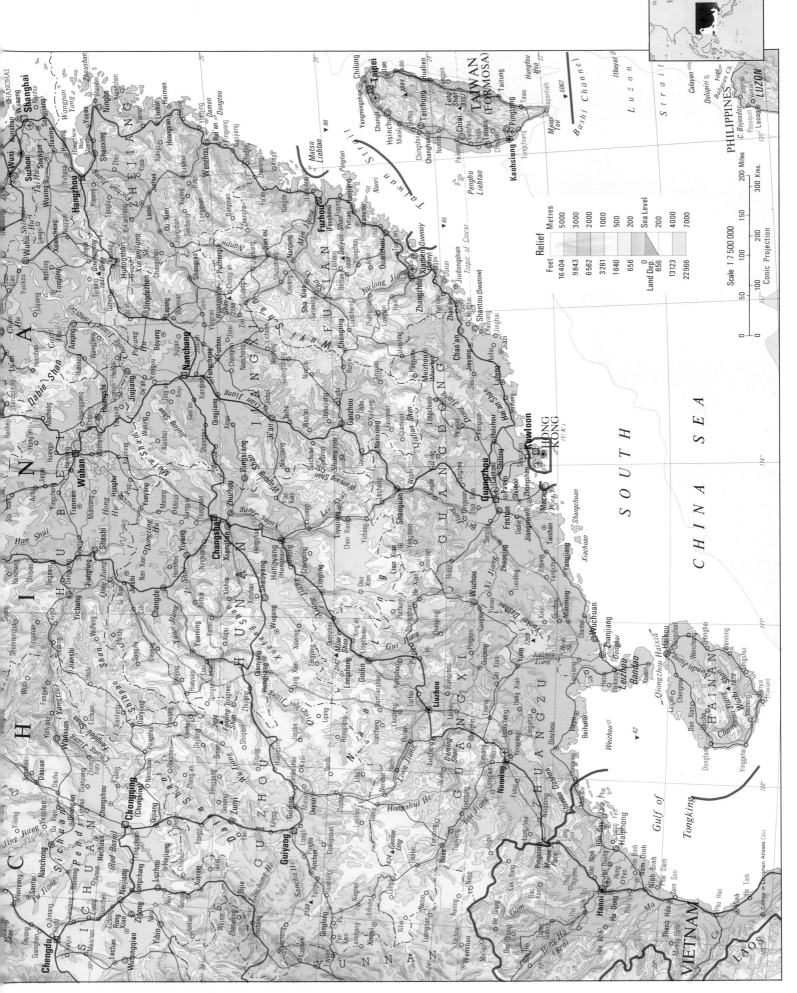

INDO-CHINA

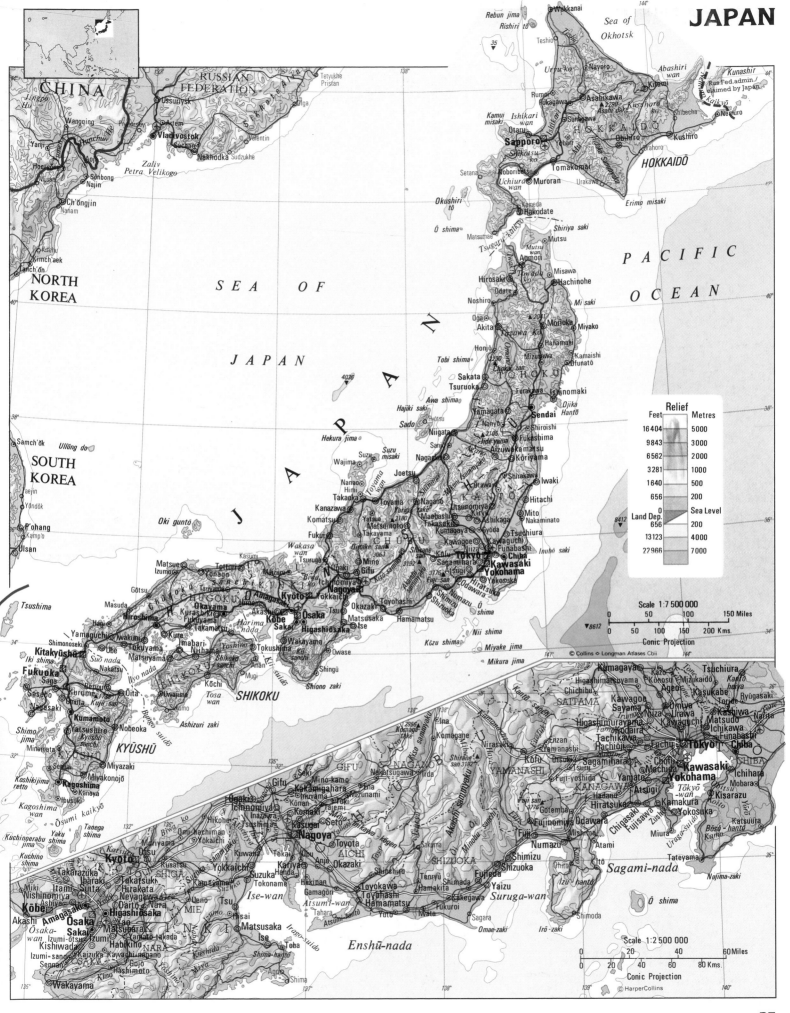

JAPAN

35

SOUTHEAST ASIA

Scale 1:15 000 000

| 0 | 100 | 200 | 300 | 400 | 500 Miles |

| 0 | 200 | 400 | 600 | 800 Kms |

Bonne Projection

© Collins ○ Longman Atlases Cbi

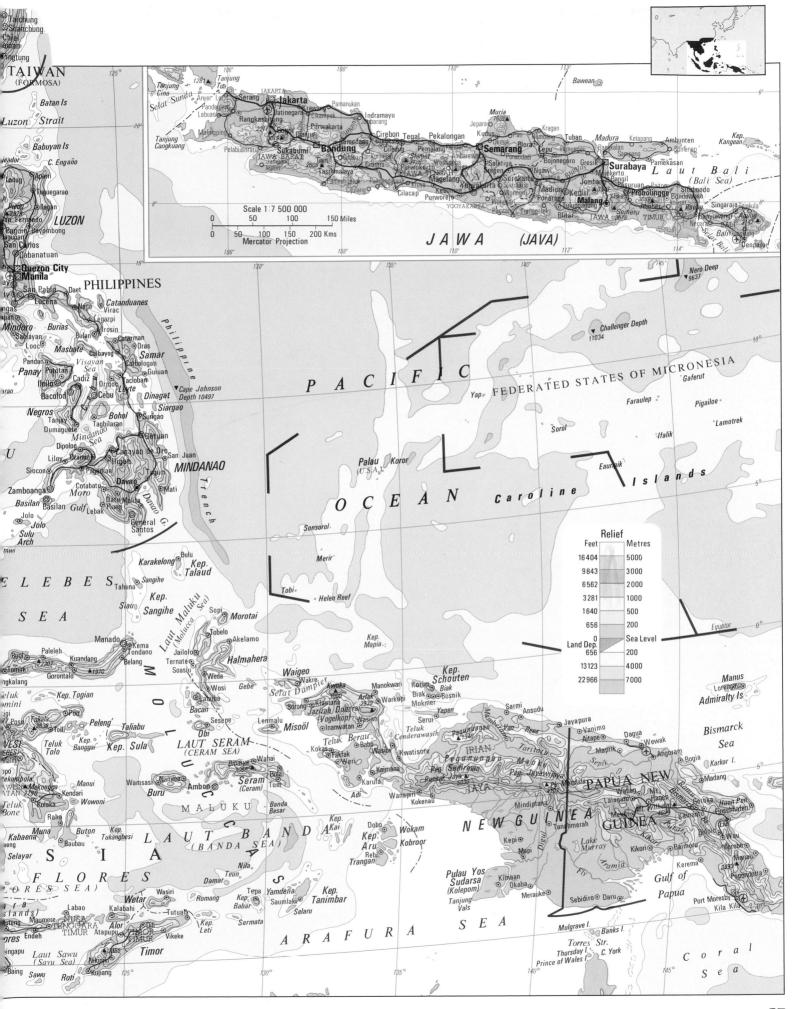

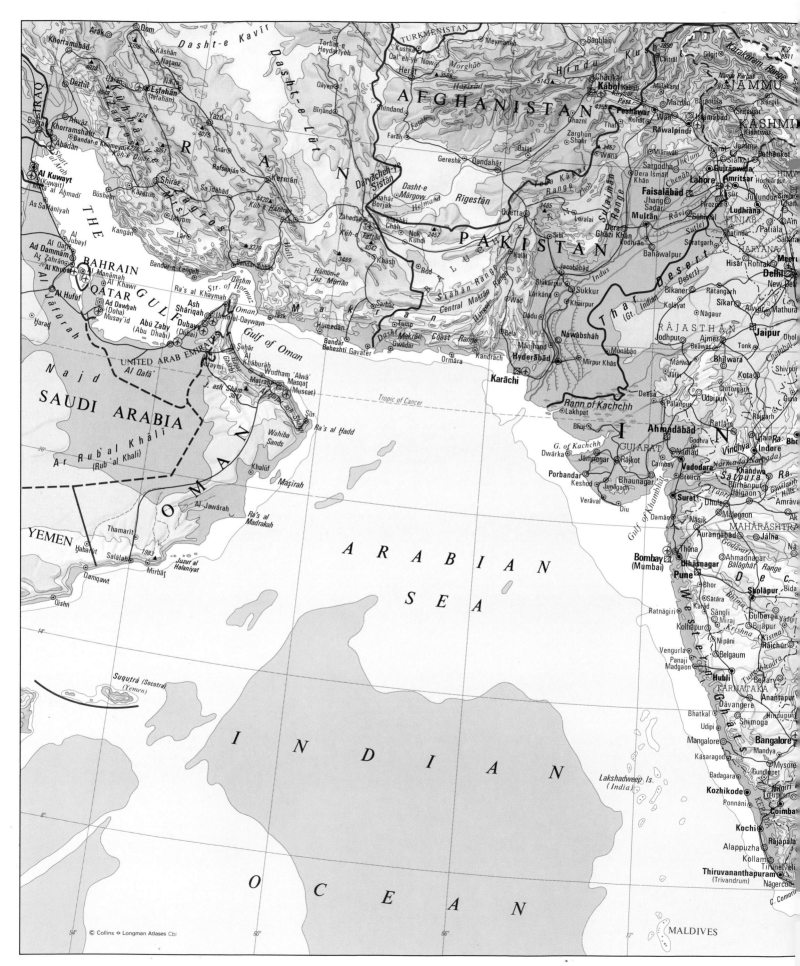

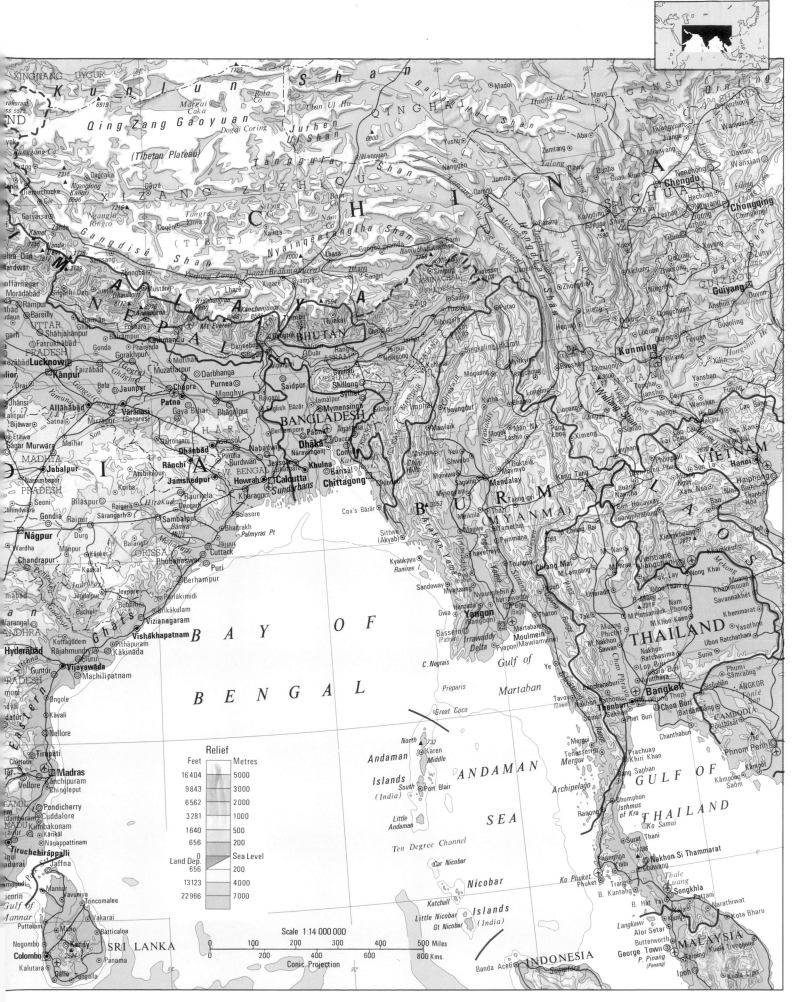

NORTHERN INDIA, PAKISTAN AND BANGLADESH

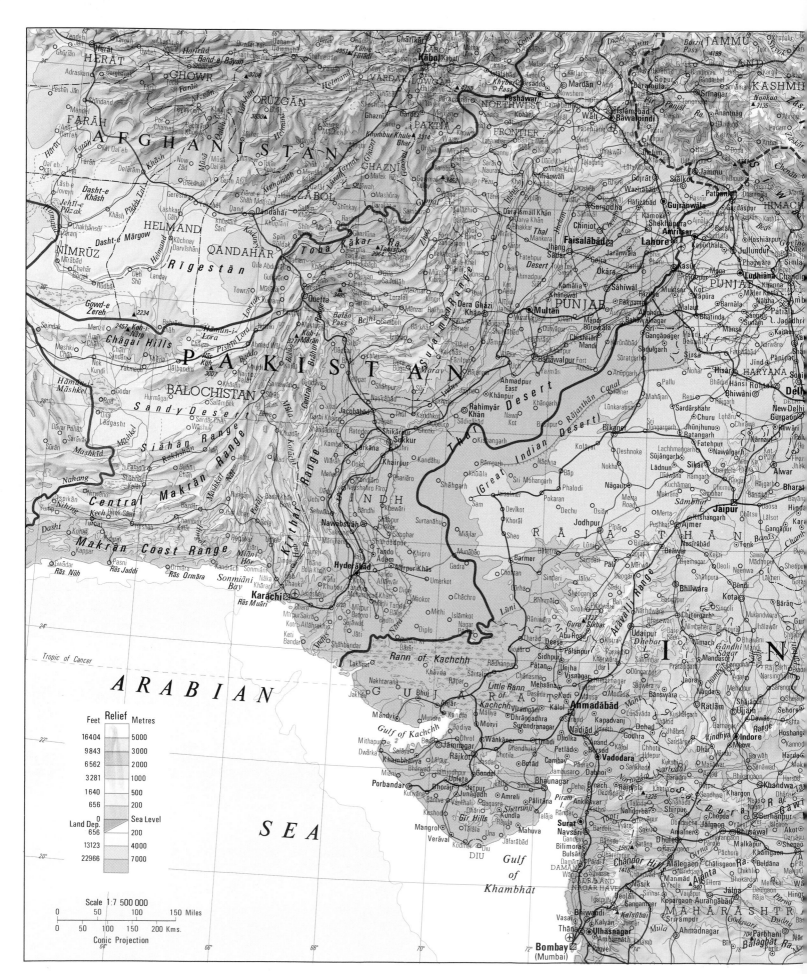

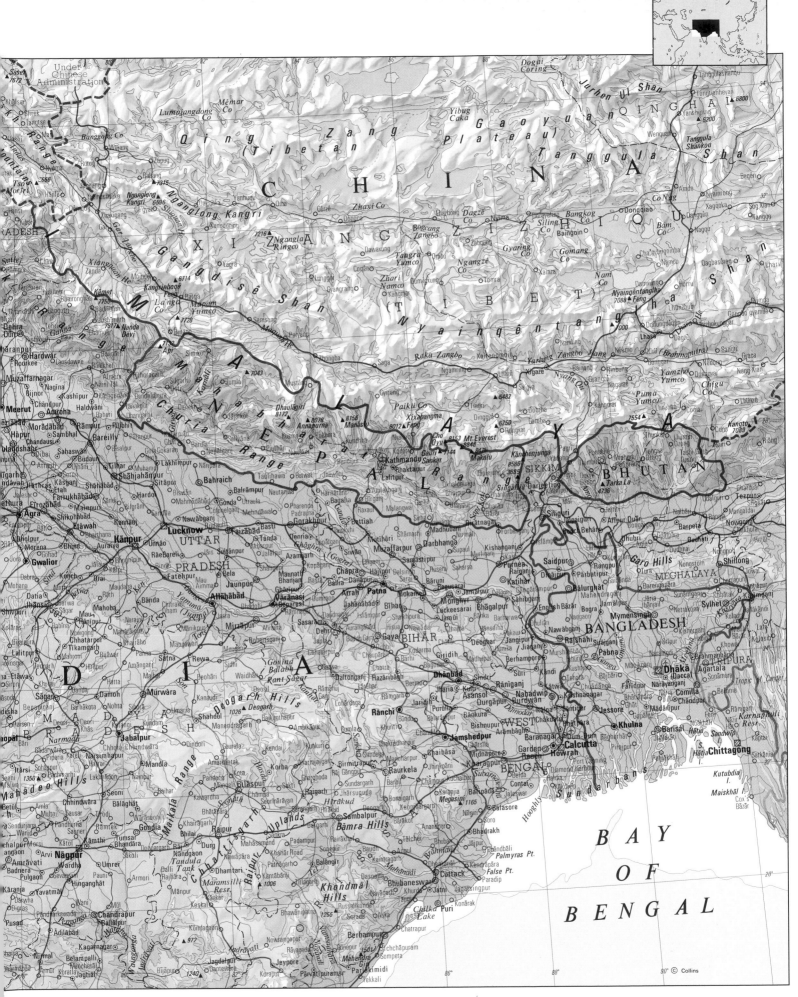

41

SOUTHWEST ASIA

THE LEVANT

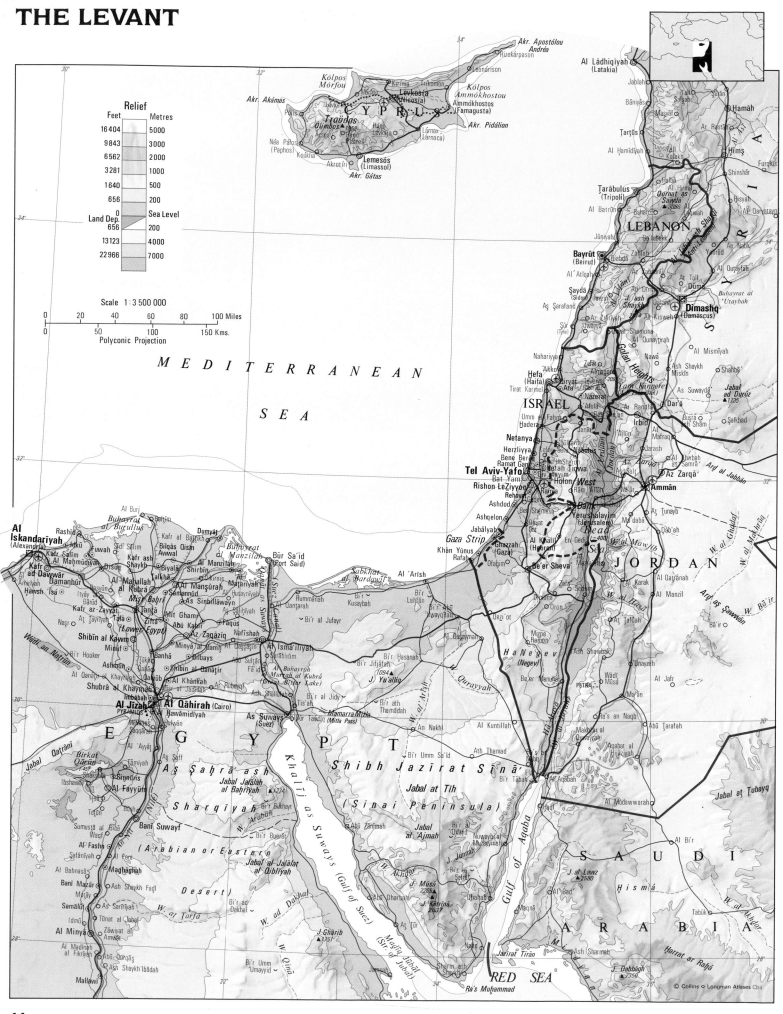

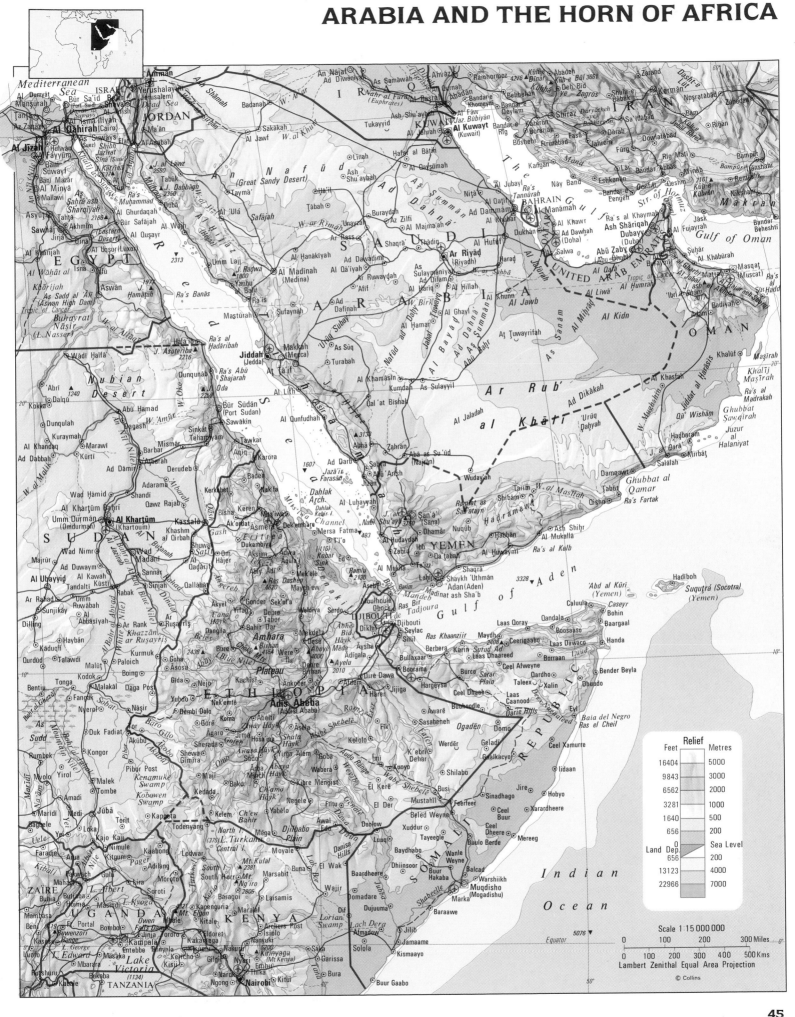

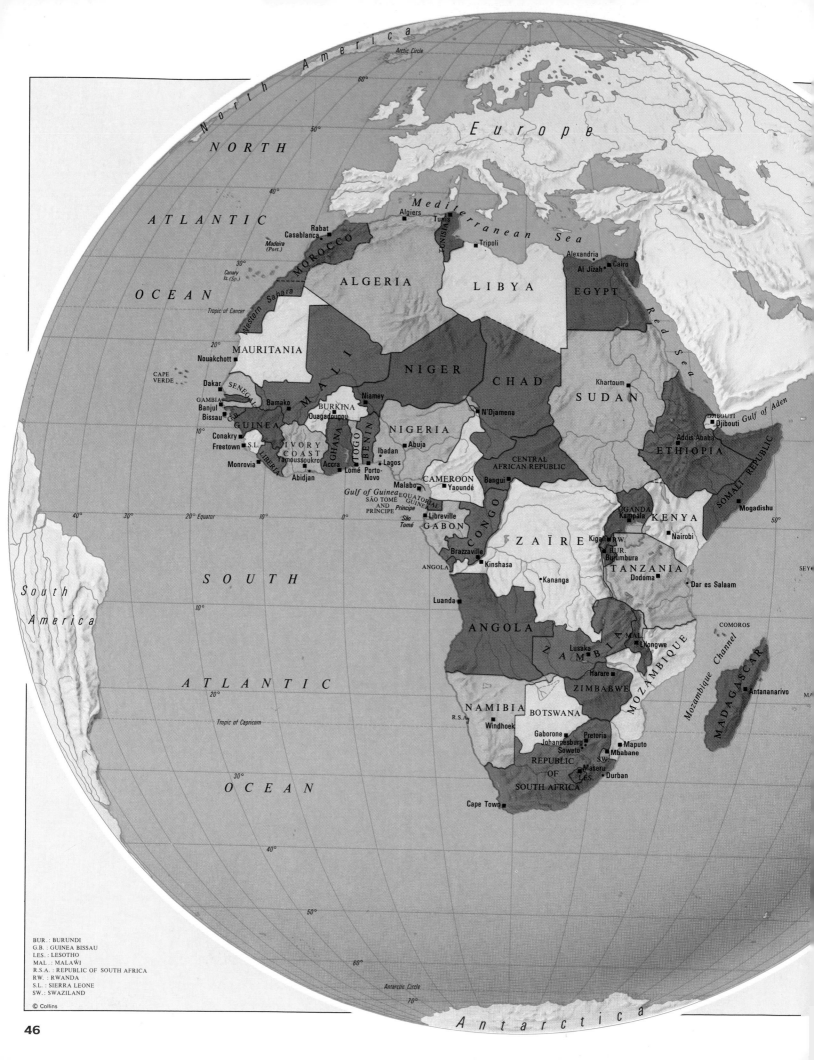

North America

Arctic Circle

NORTH

60°

Europe

50°

ATLANTIC

40°

Mediterranean Sea

Algiers
Tunis
Rabat
Casablanca

MOROCCO

Tripoli

Alexandria
Al Jizah
Cairo

OCEAN

30°
Madeira
(Port.)
Canary
Is. (Sp.)

ALGERIA

LIBYA

EGYPT

Tropic of Cancer

Western Sahara

20°

MAURITANIA

NIGER

CHAD

Red Sea

Nouakchott

Khartoum

CAPE
VERDE

Dakar
SENEGAL

Bamako

MALI

NIGER

SUDAN

DJIBOUTI
Djibouti
Gulf of Aden

GAMBIA
Banjul
Bissau
G.B.

Niamey

BURKINA

Ouagadougou

N'Djamena

10°

GUINEA

Conakry
Freetown
S.L.
Monrovia

LIBERIA

IVORY
COAST
Yamoussoukro
Abidjan

GHANA
TOGO
BENIN

NIGERIA

Ibadan
Abuja
Lagos
Lomé Porto-
Novo
Accra

Addis Ababa

ETHIOPIA

SOMALI REPUBLIC

CENTRAL
AFRICAN REPUBLIC

Bangui

Mogadishu

40°

30°

20° Equator

10°

0°

Gulf of Guinea
SÃO TOMÉ
AND
PRINCIPE
Príncipe
São
Tomé

CAMEROON
Yaoundé
Malabo
EQUATORIAL
GUINEA

Libreville

GABON

CONGO

ZAÏRE

UGANDA
Kampala

Kigali RW.
BUR.
Bujumbura

KENYA

Nairobi

50°

SOUTH

Brazzaville
Kinshasa

Kananga

TANZANIA

Dodoma

Dar es Salaam

ANGOLA

Luanda

10°

ATLANTIC

20°

ANGOLA

Lusaka
ZAMBIA

MAL.
Lilongwe

COMOROS

Mozambique Channel

South
America

Harare

MOZAMBIQUE

ZIMBABWE

MADAGASCAR

Antananarivo

Tropic of Capricorn

NAMIBIA

BOTSWANA

Windhoek
R.S.A.

Gaborone
Johannesburg
Soweto

Pretoria

SW.
Mbabane

Maputo

OCEAN

30°

REPUBLIC
OF
SOUTH AFRICA

Maseru
LES.

Durban

Cape Town

40°

50°

SEY

60°

Antarctic Circle

70°

BUR.: BURUNDI
G.B.: GUINEA BISSAU
LES.: LESOTHO
MAL.: MALAWI
R.S.A.: REPUBLIC OF SOUTH AFRICA
RW.: RWANDA
S.L.: SIERRA LEONE
SW.: SWAZILAND

© Collins

Antarctica

AFRICA

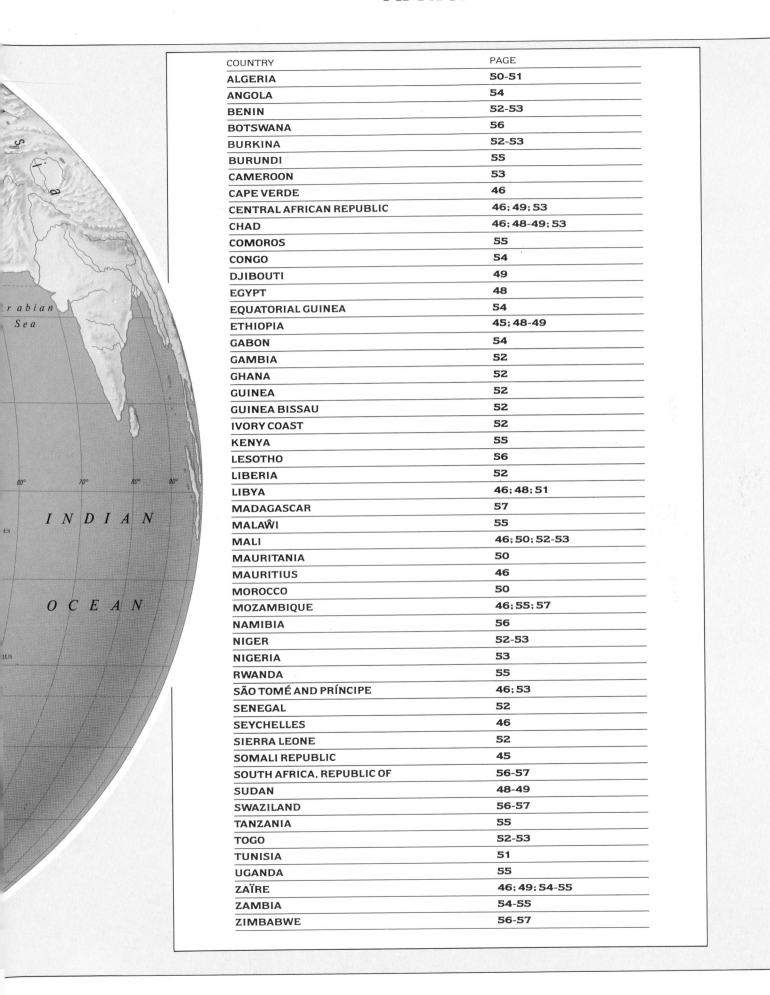

NILE VALLEY

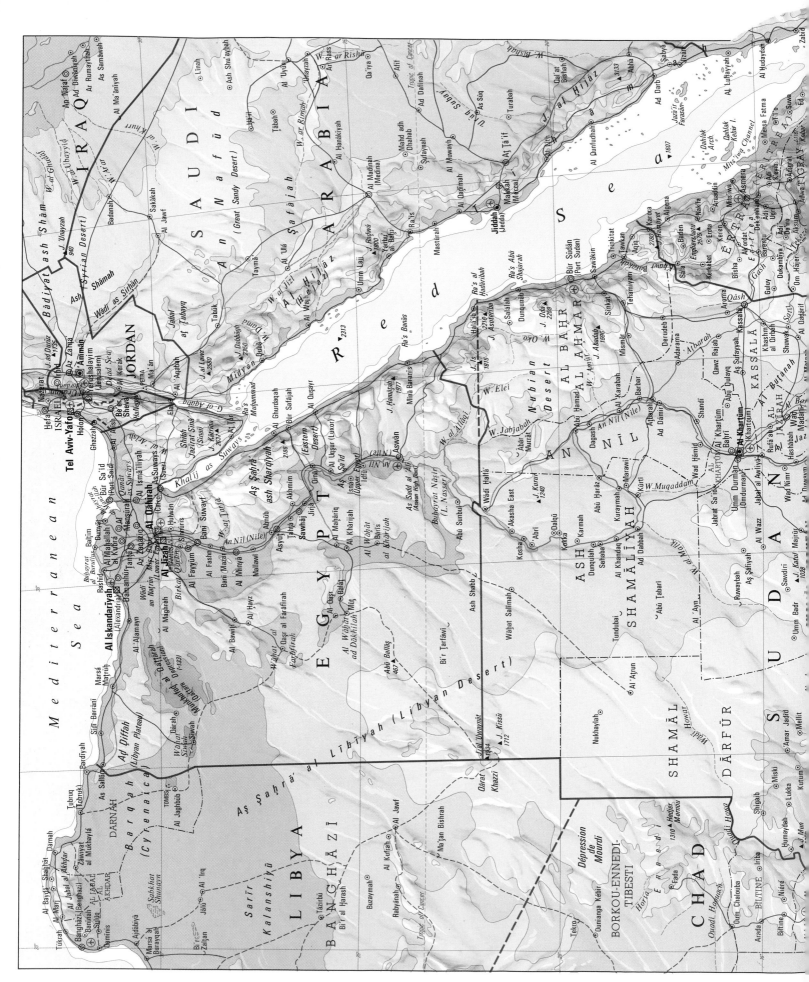

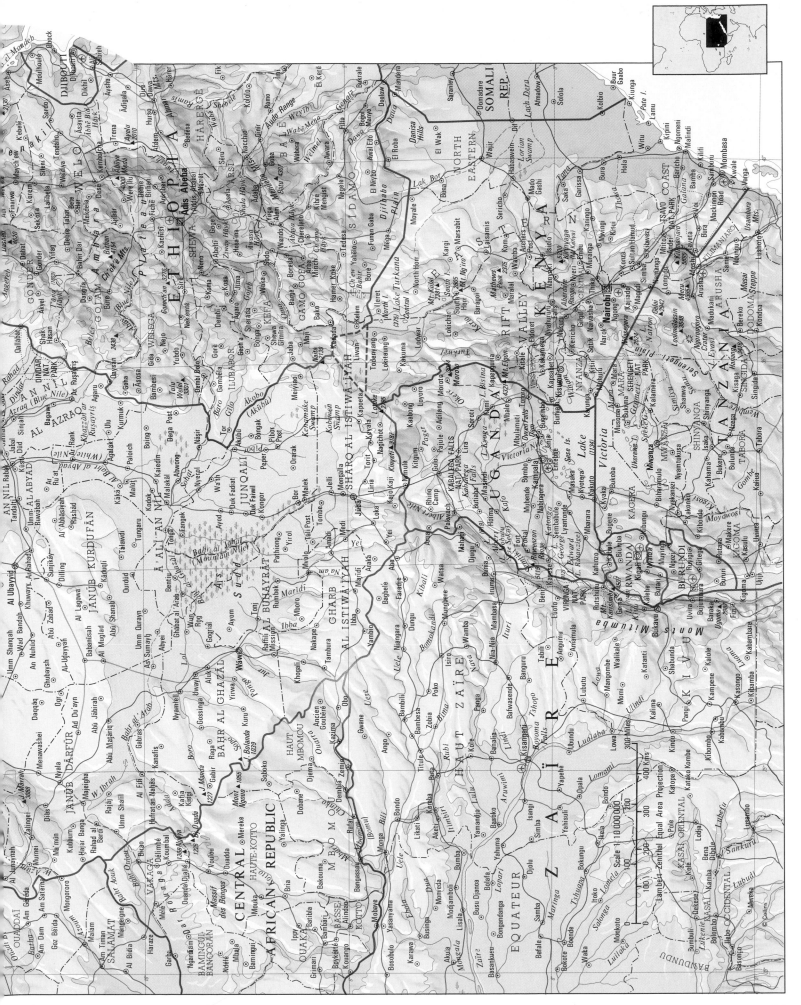

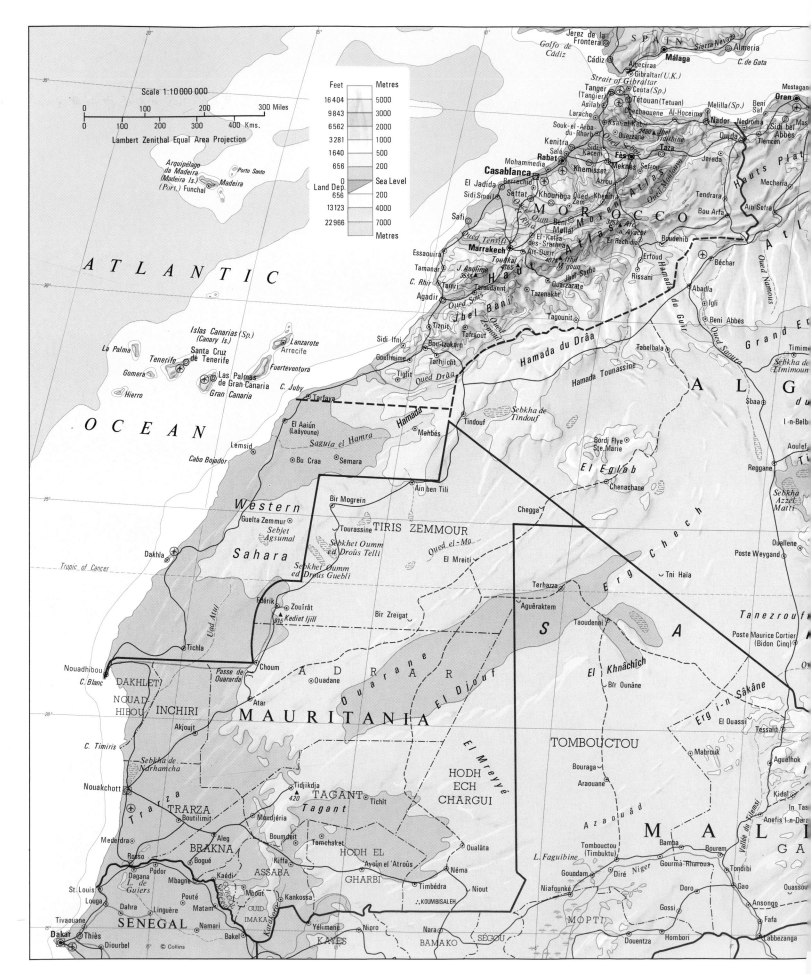

Scale 1:10 000 000

0   100   200   300 Miles

0 100 200 300 400 Kms.

Lambert Zenithal Equal Area Projection

Feet	Metres
16 404	5000
9843	3000
6562	2000
3281	1000
1640	500
656	200
0	Sea Level
Land Dep.	
656	200
13 123	4000
22 966	7000
Metres	Metres

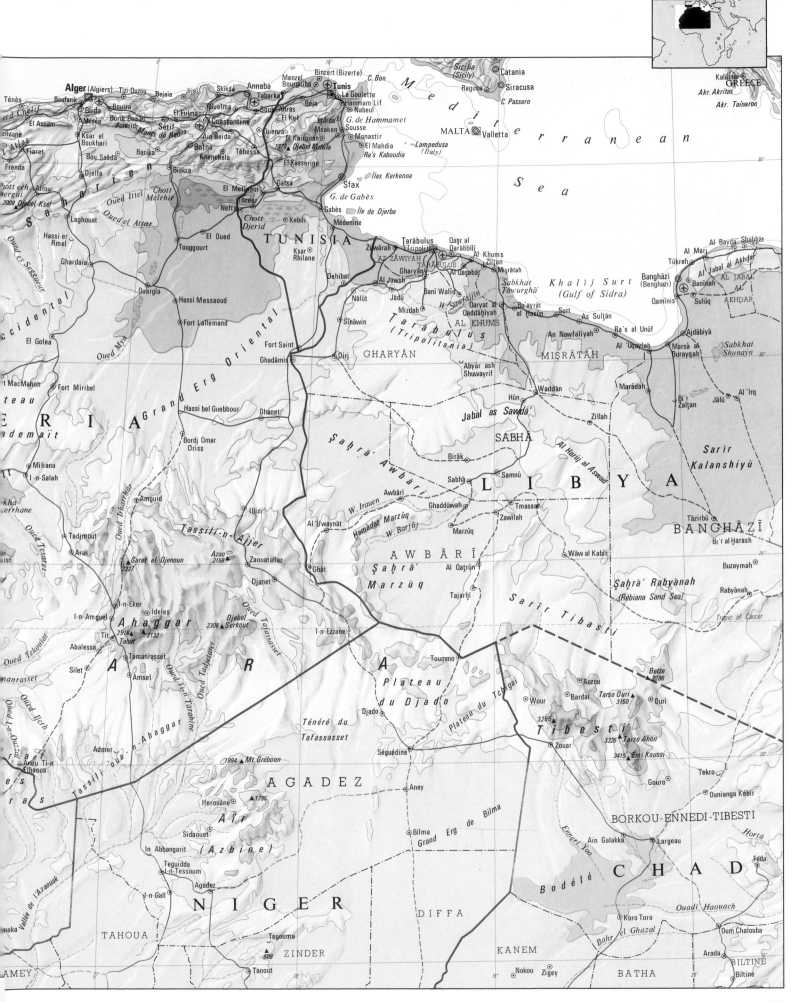

WEST AFRICA

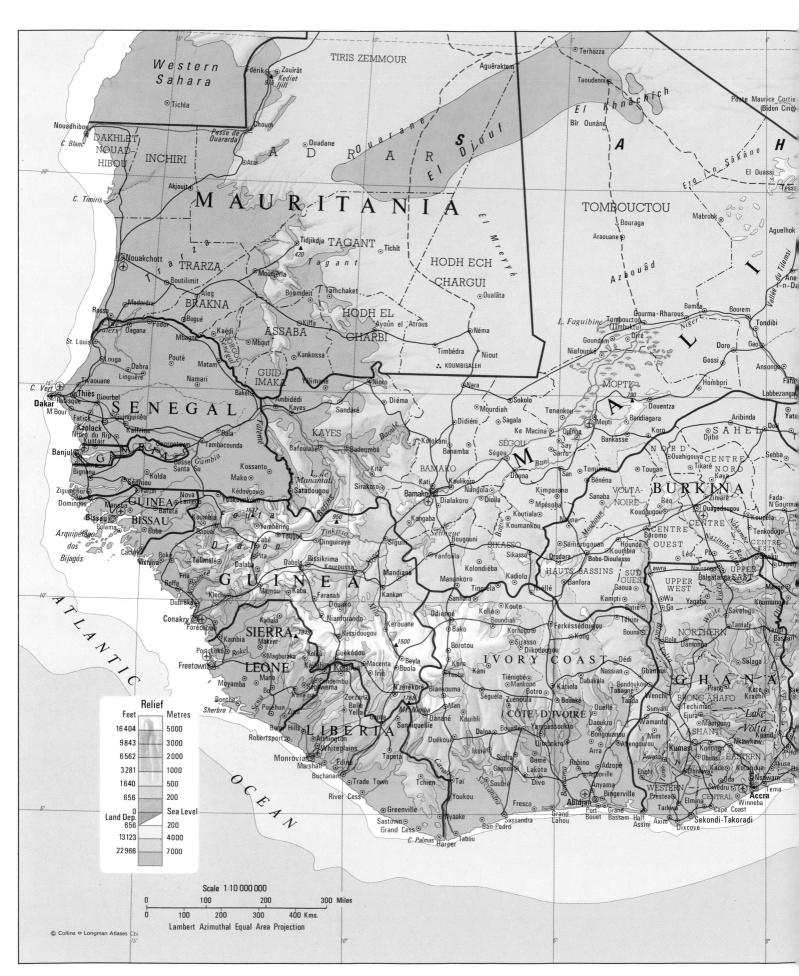

Feet | Relief | Metres
16404 | | 5000
9843 | | 3000
6562 | | 2000
3281 | | 1000
1640 | | 500
656 | | 200
0 | | Sea Level
656 | Land Dep. | 200
13123 | | 4000
22966 | | 7000

Scale 1:10 000 000

0   100   200   300 Miles

0   100   200   300   400 Kms.

Lambert Azimuthal Equal Area Projection

© Collins ◇ Longman Atlases Cbi

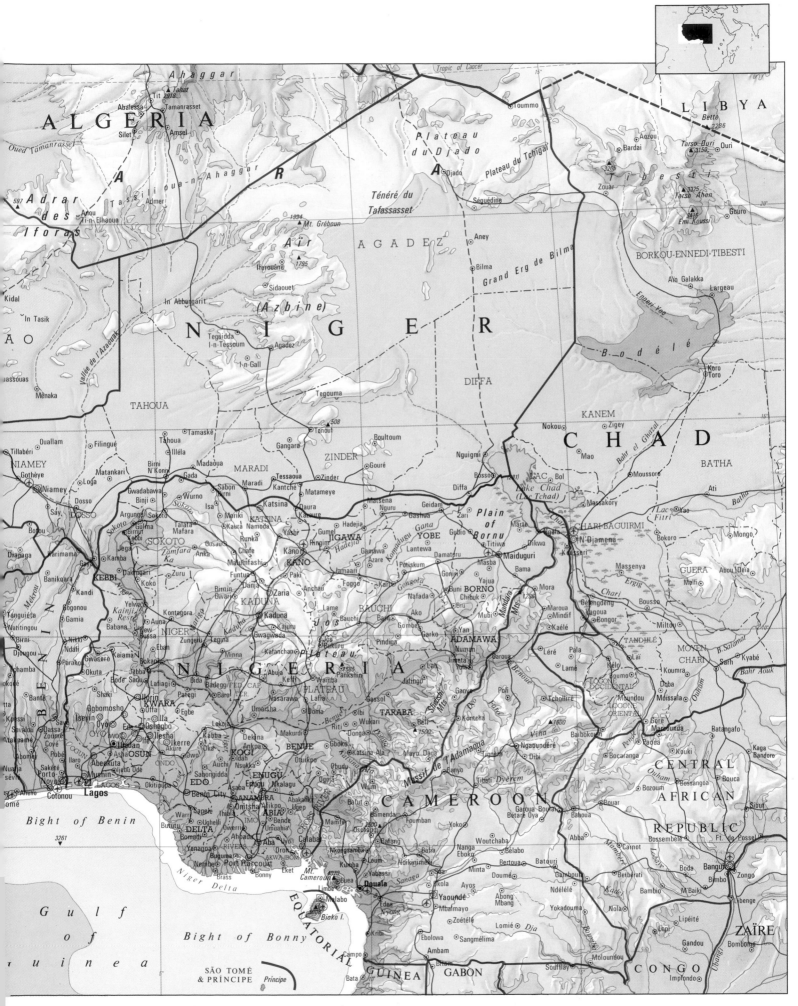

CENTRAL AND EAST AFRICA

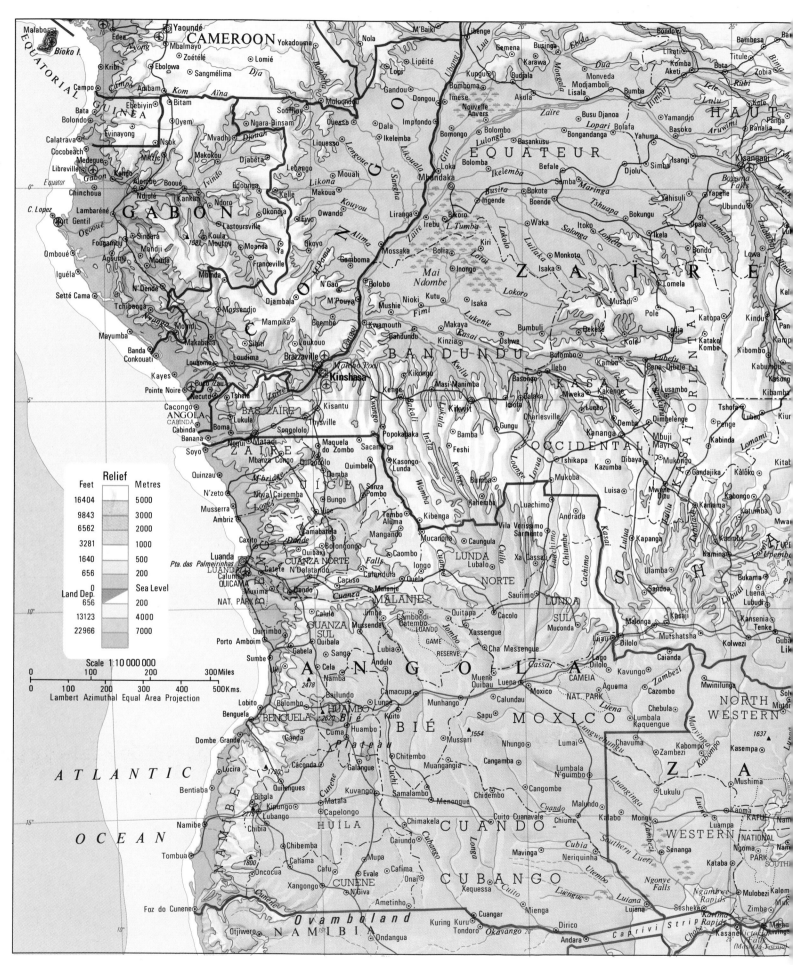

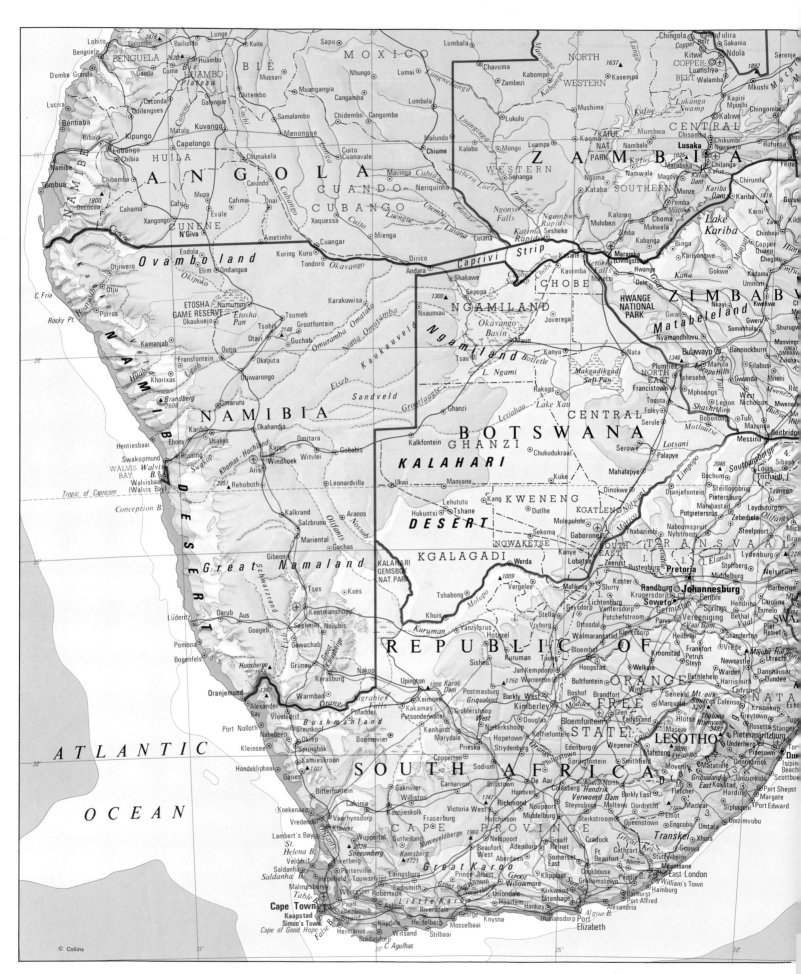

I N D I A N

O C E A N

MOZAMBIQUE CHANNEL

Mozambique Channel

Relief

Feet	Metres
16 404	5000
9843	3000
6562	2000
3281	1000
1640	500
656	200
0	Sea Level
Land Dep.	
656	200
13 123	4000
22 966	7000

Scale 1:10 000 000

0	100	200	300 Miles
0 100	200 300	400	500 Kms.

Lambert Azimuthal Equal Area Projection

Independent homelands
numbered on map

1. BOPHUTHATSWANA
2. CISKEI
3. TRANSKEI
4. VENDA

N O R T H

Tropic of Cancer

P A C I F I C

O C E A N

A S I A

Philippine
Sea

M I C R O N E S I A

Northern
Marianas
(U.S.A.)

Guam (U.S.A.)

Palau
(U.S.A.)

FED. STATES OF MICRONESIA

Caroline Islands

MARSHALL

ISLANDS

Equator

NAURU

Gilbert
Is.

Phoenix
Island   KIRIBATI

Hawaiian
Islands
(U.S.A.)

M E L A N E S I A

New
Ireland

Bougainville

New
Britain

SOLOMON
ISLANDS

Guadalcanal

Santa Cruz
Is.

PAPUA
NEW
GUINEA

Port
Moresby

Arafura Sea

M E L A N E S I A

TUVALU

Tokelau
Is.

WESTERN
SAMOA
Apia

(U.S.A.)

Cook

(N.Z.)

Islands

Tuamotu

Papeete

Tahiti

(Fran

Espíritu
Santo
Malekula

VANUATU

Vila

(France) Wallis
Is.

Vanua
Levu

FIJI   Suva

TONGA

Alofi
Niue

Avarua

Timor
Sea

Coral
Sea

New
Caledonia
(France)
Nouméa

Loyalty Is.

Nuku'alofa

Tropic of Capricorn

P O L Y N E S I A

S O U T

INDIAN

Brisbane

AUSTRALIA

Sydney
Canberra

Adelaide   Melbourne

Perth

Tasmania   Hobart

Tasman
Sea

North
Island

Auckland

NEW
Wellington

ZEALAND

South
Island   Christchurch

Dunedin

Stewart I.

Chatham
Is.

International Date Line

PACIFI

OCEAN

OCEAN

SOUTHERN

OCEAN

Antarctic Circle

Antarctica

© Collins

OCEANIA

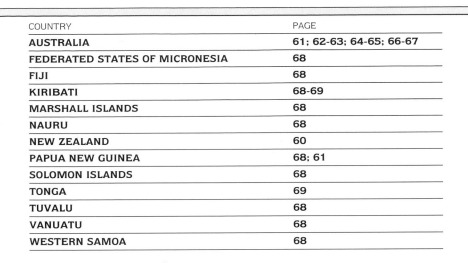

Oceania as a continental name is used for the area extending from Australia in the west, to the most easterly island of Polynesia and from New Zealand in the south, to the Hawaiian Islands in the north. Australasia is that portion of Oceania which lies between the equator and 47°S but in general the term is not often used because of confusion with Australia the country name.

NEW ZEALAND

INDONESIA

Selat Makasar
Mamuju
Majene
Rantekombela 3455
Kendari
Watampone
Takalar
Ujung Pandang
Buton
Buru
Namlea
Ambon
Seram (Ceram)
Bula
Fakfak
Wasian
Serui
Sarmi
Admiralty Is.
New Hanover
New Ireland
Bismarck Sea
New Britain

Kep Sula
Misool
Wasior
Jayapura
Aitape
Wewak
Madang
Hoskins
Finschhafen
Solomon Sea

LAUT BANDA
(BANDA SEA)
7440
Kep. Kai
Kep. Aru
Pegunungan Maoke
Puncak Jaya 5030
Kokenau
NEW GUINEA
PAPUA NEW
GUINEA
Mendi
Mt. Hagen
Mt. Wilhelm 4694
Goroka
Lae
Wau
Mt. Victoria 4073
Owen Stanley Range
Popondetta

LAUT FLORES
(FLORES SEA)
4520
Kep. Tanimbar
Pulau Yos Sudarsa (Kolepom)
Tandjung Vals
Digul
Fly
Kikori

Lombok
Raba
Flores
Ruteng
Maumere
Alor
Wetar
Dili
Kep. Leti
ARAFURA
SEA
Merauke
Daru
Gulf of Papua
Port Moresby

Sumbawa
Ende
Sumba
Waingapu
Baing
Timor
Nikiniki
Kupang
Roti

TIMOR SEA

C. Londonderry
Bonaparte Archipelago
Joseph Bonaparte Gulf
Melville I.
Bathurst I.
Darwin
Batchelor
Arnhem Land
Egbourg Pen.
C. Wessel
Wessel Is.
C. Arnhem
Groote Eylandt
Gulf of Carpentaria
Vanderlin I.
60
Bamaga
C. York
C. Grenville
Weipa
Cape York Peninsula
Coen
C. Melville
4520
CORAL SEA

C. Lévêque
King Leopold Range
Wyndham
Kununurra
Victoria River Downs
Katherine
Roper
Daly Waters
Mataranka
Borroloola
Wellesley Is.
Normanton
Croydon
Georgetown
Forsayth
Coektown
Laura
Cairns 1611
Innisfail
Ingham
Great Barrier Reef

Broome
Derby
Fitzroy Crossing
Kimberley Plateau
Hall's Creek
Gordon Downs
NORTHERN
Tennant Creek
Hatches Creek
Camooweal
Avon Downs
Burketown
Mount Isa
Cloncurry
Duchess
Hughenden
Charters Towers
Townsville
Home Hill
Bowen
Proserpine

Eighty Mile Beach
Lagrange
Great Sandy Desert
South Esk Tablelands
TERRITORY
Kajabbi
Dajarra
Winton
Blair Athol
Mackay
Sarina
C. Townshend

Port Hedland
Goldsworthy
Barrow I.
Dampier
Marble Bar
Nullagine
Percival Lakes
L. Mackay
Mt. Ziel 1511
Macdonnell Ranges
Urandangi
Boulia
Longreach
Barcaldine
QUEENSLAND
Emerald
Springsure
Rockhampton
Gladstone

Onslow
Exmouth
Hamersley Range
Tom Price
Newman
L. Disappointment
Gibson Desert
L. Hopkins
Alice Springs
Simpson Desert
Bedourie
Great Artesian
Windorah
Yaraka
Monto
Bundaberg

I. MacLeod
Carnarvon
Ashburton
Tropic of Capricorn
Barlee Range
Gascoyne
WESTERN
L. Carnegie
Tomkinson Ranges
Petermann Ranges
Musgrave Ranges
L. Amadeus
Warburton
Cooper Creek
Basin
Grey Range
Quilpie
Charleville
Mitchell
Roma
Miles
Wandoan
Maryborough
Gympie

Denham
AUSTRALIA
Meekatharra
Nannine
Cue
Mount Magnet
Leonora
Laverton
Oodnadatta
SOUTH
L. Eyre
Birdsville
Augathella
Cunnamulla
St. George
Dirranbandi
Goondiwindi
Toowoomba
Dalby
Brisbane

Northampton
Geraldton
Mullewa
L. Barlee
Malcolm
Great Victoria Desert
Warrina
Coober Pedy
AUSTRALIA
Tibooburra
Bourke
Warwick
Tenterfield
Lismore
Casino
Grafton

Dongara
Moora
L. Moore
Leonora
Southern Cross
Kalgoorlie
Zanthus
Rawlinna
AUSTRALIA
Leigh Creek
Tarcoola
L. Torrens
Woomera
Pimba
L. Frome
Broken Hill
Wilcannia
Cobar
Nyngan
Narrabri
Armidale 1433
Coff's Harbour

Perth
Meera
Northam
York
Coolgardie
L. Cowan
Norseman
Nullarbor Plain
Penong
Ceduna
L. Gairdner
Port Augusta
Peterborough
Ivanhoe
Roto
NEW SOUTH WALES
Parkes
Orange
Dubbo
Bathurst
Katoomba
Maitland
Newcastle

Fremantle
Pinjarra
Brookton
Newdegate
SOUTHERN OCEAN
Great Australian Bight
Kimba
Whyalla
Port Pirie
Kadina
Radium
Mildura
Hay
Lachlan
Griffith
Wagga Wagga
Goulburn
Sydney
Wollongong

Bunbury
Busselton
Augusta
C. Leeuwin
Pemberton
Denmark
Narrogin
Kojonup
Mount Barker
Albany
Hopetoun
Esperance
Eyre Pen.
Port Lincoln
Spencer Gulf
Adelaide
Murray Bridge
Kangaroo I.
Bordertown
Pinnaroo
Naracoorte
Murray
Murrumbidgee
Albury
Deniliquin
Shepparton
Benalla
Wangaratta
Mt. Kosciusko 2228
Snowy Mts
AUST. CAP. TER.
Canberra
Bega
C. Howe

5670
Mount Gambier
Portland
Warrnambool
Hamilton
Ballarat
Bendigo
VICTORIA
Geelong
Melbourne
Morwell
Sale
Barnsdale
Wilson's Promontory
TASMAN SEA

5635
King I.
Bass Strait
Flinders I.
Smithton
Burnie
Devonport
Launceston

TASMANIA
Queenstown
Mt. Ossa 1617
New Norfolk
Hobart
South East C.

Scale 1:20 000 000
0 100 200 300 400 500 Miles
0 200 400 600 800 Kms.
Lambert Azimuthal Equal Area Projection

WESTERN AUSTRALIA

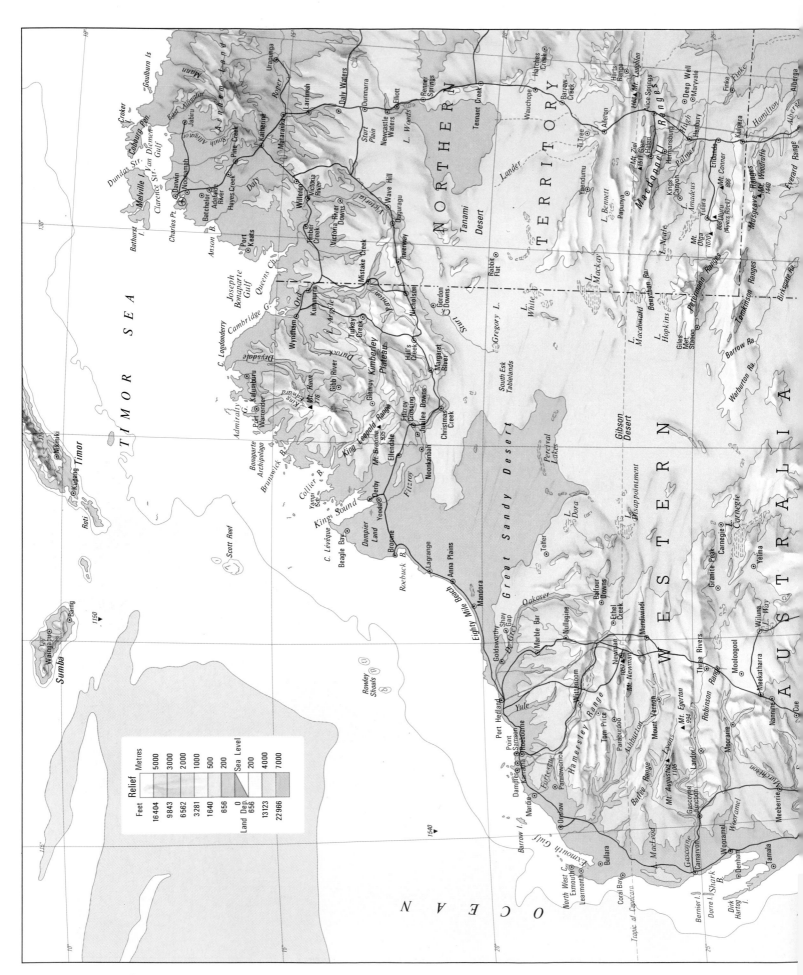

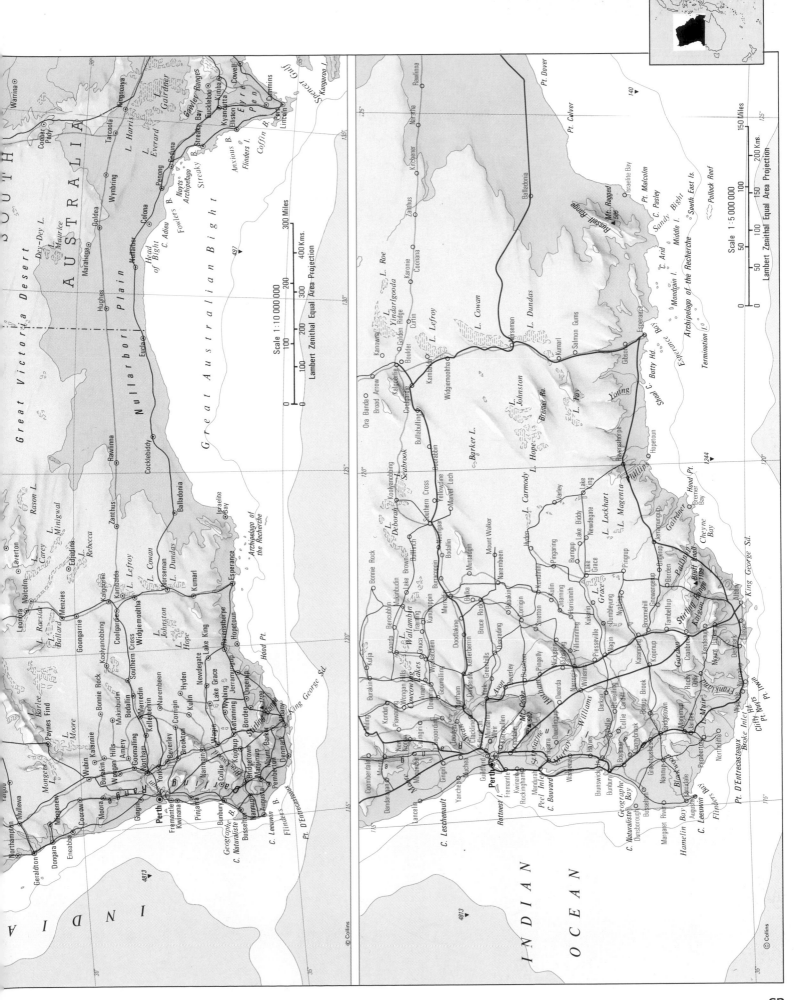

EASTERN AUSTRALIA

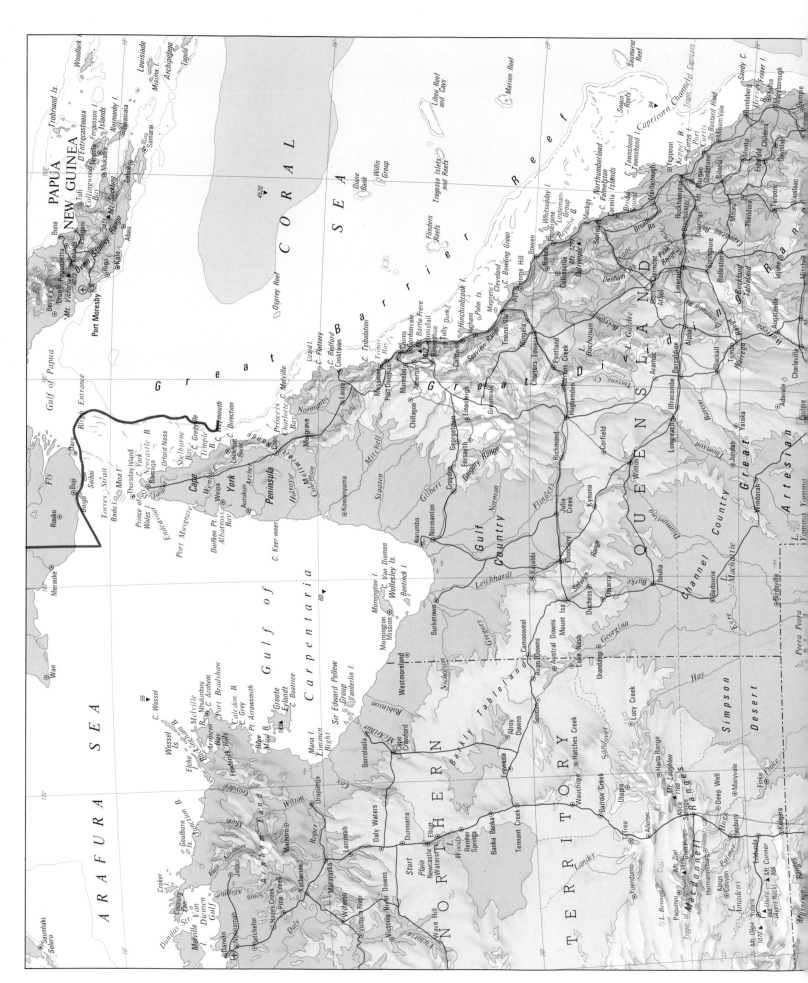

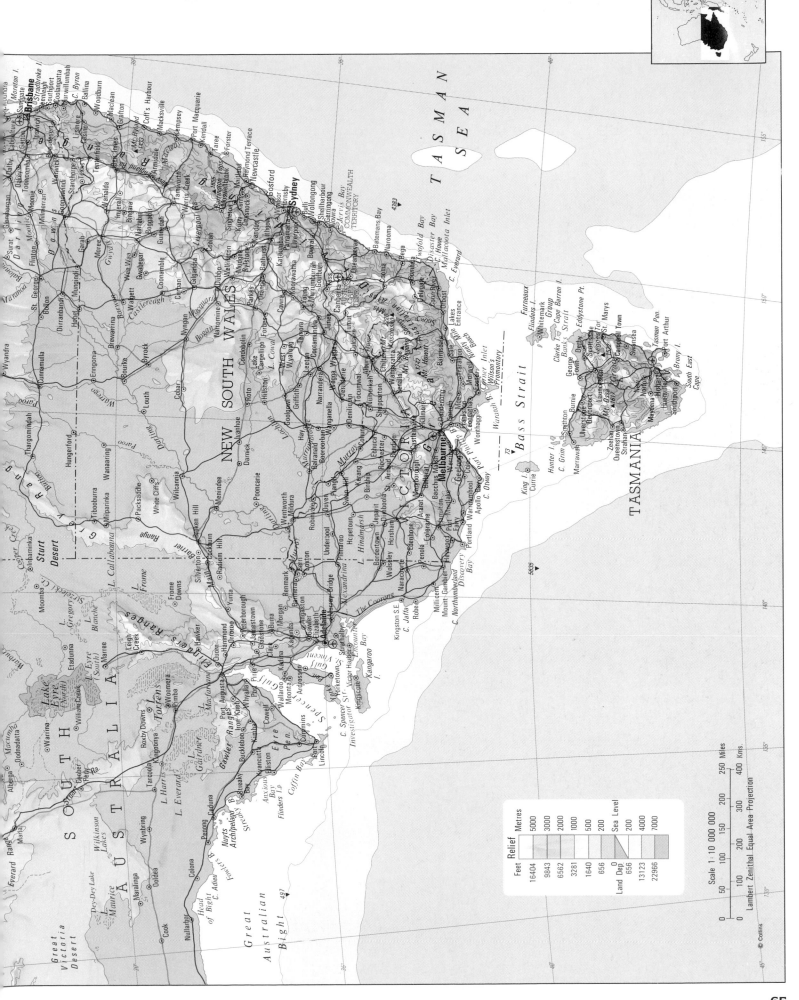

SOUTHEAST AUSTRALIA

67

PACIFIC OCEAN

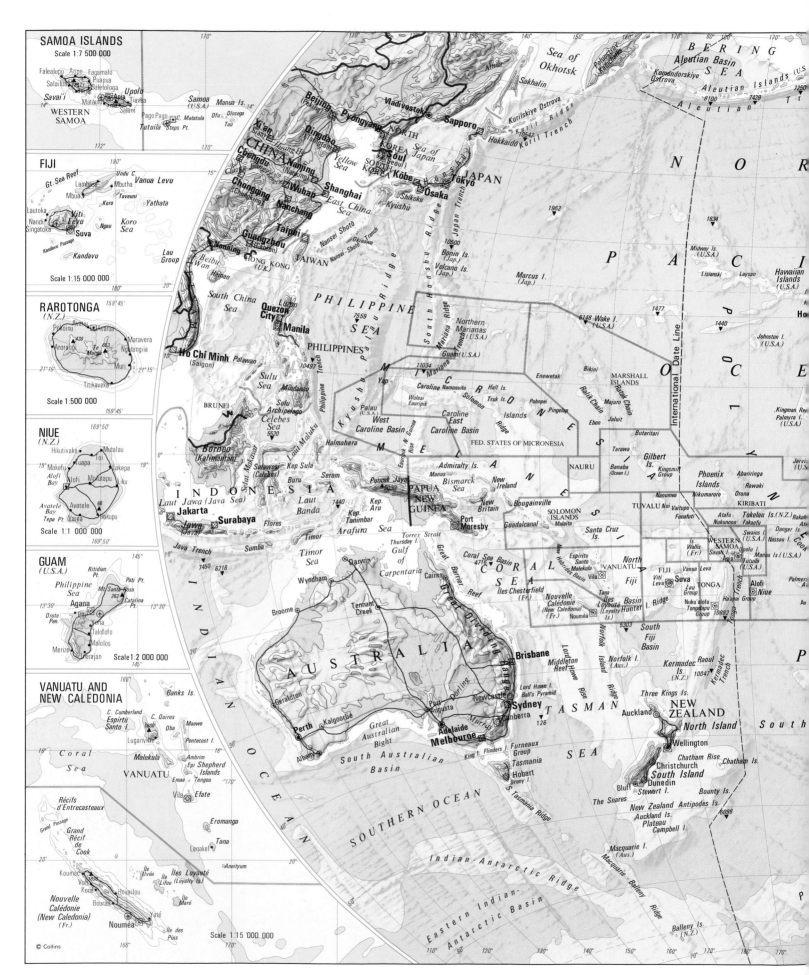

SAMOA ISLANDS
Scale 1:7 500 000

Falealupo Aopo Fagamalo
Salailua Puapua
Salailua Saleologa
Savai'i Upolu
Matautu Apia Tiavea
WESTERN Salani
SAMOA Pago Pago Manua Is.
Tutuila Steps Pt. Ofu Olosega
Tau
Samoa C. Matatula

FIJI
Gt. Sea Reef Undu C.
Lambasa Vanua Levu
Mbua Mbutha Taveuni
Koro Yathata
Lautoka Viti Ngau Koro
Nandi Levu Sea
Singatoka Suva
Kandavu Passage Lau
Kandavu Group
Scale 1:15 000 000

RAROTONGA 159°45'
(N.Z.)
Pokoinu Avatiu Avarua
Te 1438 Matavera
Arorangi Manga Ngatangiia
653
Muri
Titikaveka
Scale 1:500 000 159°45'

NIUE 169°50'
(N.Z.)
Hikutavake Mutalau
Tuapa Toi
Makefu Lakepa
Alofi Mutuapu Liku
Bay Alofi
Avatele 66
Avatele Hakupu
Bay Naiea
Tepa Pt.
Scale 1:1 000 000 169°50'

GUAM 145°
(U.S.A.)
Ritidian Pt.
Philippine Pati Pt.
Sea Mt. Santa Rosa 262
Agana Catalina
Pt.
Orote Yana
Pen. Talofofo
Malolos
Merizo Inarajan
Scale 1:2 000 000 145°

**VANUATU AND
NEW CALEDONIA** 166°
Banks Is.
C. Cumberland C. Quiros
Espiritu Isabel
Santo I. Oba Maewo
Luganville Pentecost I.
Coral Malekula Ambrim
Sea Epi Shepherd
Islands
VANUATU Emae Tongoa
Vila Efate

Récifs
d'Entrecasteaux
Grand Passage
Grand
Récif
de
Cook
Koumac Ile d'Uvéa
Voh 1628 Lifou Iles Loyauté
Kone (Loyalty Is.)
Houailou
Nouvelle Bourail Ile
Calédonie Maré
(New Fr.) Noumea Ile des
Pins
Scale 1:15 000 000 170°

© Collins

68

B E R I N G
Aleutian Basin S E A
Komandorskiye Aleutian Islands (US
Ostrova
8100 7429 7250
Aleutian Tr
Sea of
Okhotsk P-plunsten
Kamchatka
Amur
Sakhalin
Vladivostok Sapporo
Pyongyang Kurilskiye Ostrova
NORTH Hokkaido Kuril Trench
Xi'an Qingdao KOREA 10542
(Sian) Sea of
Beijing SOUTH Japan
(Peking) Seoul Kobe Tokyo
Chengdu KOREA JAPAN
Nanjing Osaka
CHINA (Nanking) Shikoku
Chongqing Shanghai Kyushu 1962
(Chungking) Wuhan
Nanchang East China 1634
Taipei Sea Nansei Shoto
Guangzhou Okinawa Midway Is.
(Canton) TAIWAN Nansei Shoto Trench (U.S.A.)
Nanning HONG KONG Bonin Is. 1477 Laysan
(U.K.) (Jap.) 10500 Lisianski Hawaiian
Hainan Volcano Is. 1440 Islands
Beibu (Jap.) Marcus I. (U.S.A.)
Wan (Jap.)
South China PHILIPPINE 6148 Wake I. Johnston I.
Sea SEA (U.S.A.) (U.S.A.)
Quezon Northern
City Manila 7559 Marianas
(U.S.A.) Bikini MARSHALL
Ho Chi Minh Enewetak ISLANDS
(Saigon) Palawan Guam (U.S.A.) Ralik Chain
10497 11034 Yap Ratak Chain
Sulu Mindanao Mariana Hall Is. Majuro Kingman Re
Sea Trench Caroline Namonuito Truk Is. Pohnpei Jaluit Palmyra I.
BRUNEI Sulu West Palau Woleai Ebon (U.S.A.)
Archipelago Celebes Caroline Basin Caroline Islands
Sea East
Borneo 5520 Caroline Basin Butaritari
(Kalimantan) Halmahera FED. STATES OF MICRONESIA Tarawa Gilbert Jarvis
Laut Maluku Admiralty Is. NAURU Is. (U.S
Sulawesi Kep Sula Manus Banaba Kingsmill Phoenix Abariringa
(Celebes) Seram Bismarck New (Ocean I.) Group Islands Rawaki
INDONESIA Buru Puncak Jaya Sea Ireland Nanumea Nikumaroro Orona
5030 New Nui Vaitupu KIRIBATI
Laut Jawa (Java Sea) Laut 7440 PAPUA Britain TUVALU Takelau Is.(N.Z.) Rakah
Jakarta Banda Kep. NEW Bougainville Funafuti Fakaofu Danger Is.
Jawa Surabaya Tanimbar GUINEA SOLOMON Atafu Nassau I. Cook
(Java) Flores Kep. Aru Port ISLANDS Nukunono WESTERN
Sumba Timor Moresby Guadalcanal Malaita Swains I. SAMOA
Java Trench Arafura Sea Santa Cruz Wallis Savai'i Apia
7450 6218 Torres Strait Is. (Fr.) Upolu I. Tutuila I. (U.S.A.)
Timor Thursday I. Coral Sea Espiritu North FIJI Alofi
Sea Gulf 4719 Basin Santo Viti Vanua Levu
Darwin of Malekula New Hebrides Basin Levu Suva TONGA Niue
Wyndham Carpentaria Iles Chesterfield Vila VANUATU Fiji Lau
Cairns (Fr.) Nouvelle Tana Group Ha'apai
Great Calédonie Iles Nuku'alofa Group
Broome Barrier (New Caledonia) Loyauté Hunter I. Ridge Tongatapu 10882 Av
Tennant Reef (Fr.) Noumea (Loyalty Is.) Group Tonga Trench
Creek 5303 South
Great Dividing Fiji Palme
Geraldton Darling Basin
Range Norfolk Kermadec Raoul
Brisbane Island Norfolk I. Is. I.
Middleton (Aus.) (N.Z.) 10047 Kermadec Trench
Perth Reef Lord
Kalgoorlie Newcastle Lord Howe I. Howe Three Kings Is. NEW
Port Sydney Ball's Pyramid Rise Auckland ZEALAND
Augusta Canberra Ridge North Island
Murray 126 TASMAN Wellington
Adelaide King I. Flinders Chatham Rise Chatham Is.
Alban Melbourne Furneaux SEA Christchurch South Island
South Australian Group Dunedin
Basin Tasmania Bluff Stewart I. Bounty Is.
Hobart The Snares New Zealand Antipodes Is.
Bruny I. Antarctic
AUSTRALIA S. Tasmania Ridge Plateau 6098
Auckland Is.
Campbell I.
SOUTHERN OCEAN
Indian-Antarctic Ridge Macquarie I.
(Aus.)
Eastern Indian- Balleny Is.
Antarctic Basin (N.Z.)

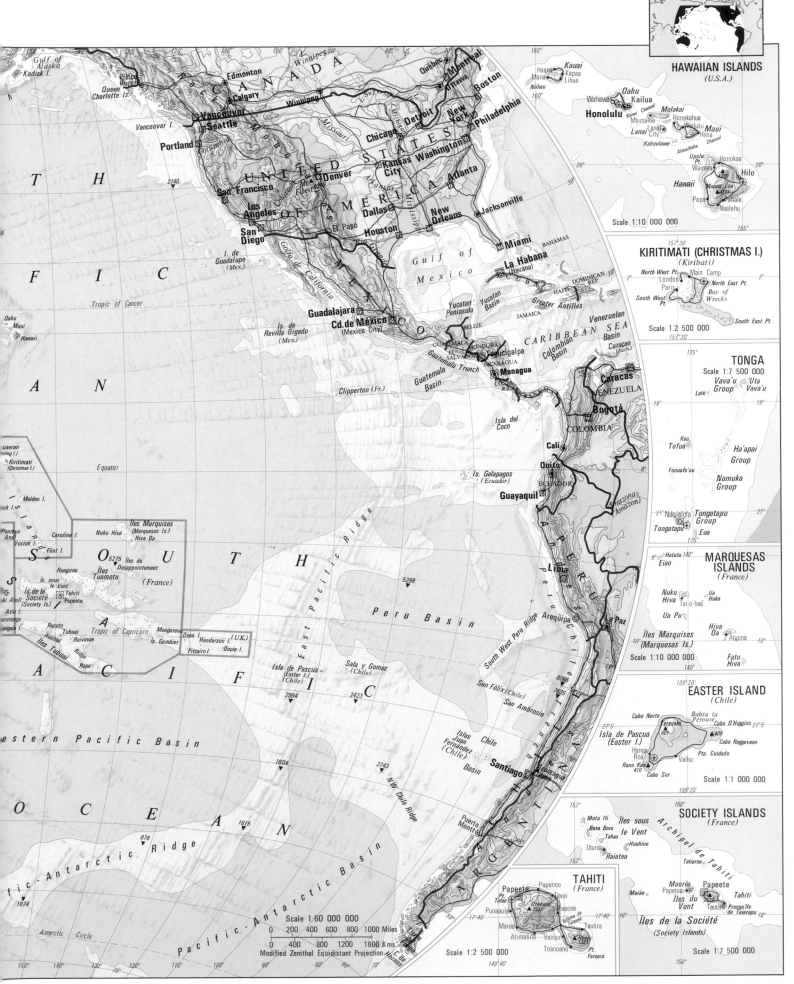

HAWAIIAN ISLANDS
(U.S.A.)

Scale 1:10 000 000

KIRITIMATI (CHRISTMAS I.)
(Kiribati)

Scale 1:2 500 000

TONGA
Scale 1:7 500 000

MARQUESAS ISLANDS
(France)

Scale 1:10 000 000

EASTER ISLAND
(Chile)

Scale 1:1 000 000

SOCIETY ISLANDS
(France)

TAHITI
(France)

Scale 1:2 500 000

Scale 1:7 500 000

Scale 1:60 000 000

0   200 400 600 800 1000 Miles

0   400   800 1200 1600 Kms.

Modified Zenithal Equidistant Projection

69

NORTH AMERICA

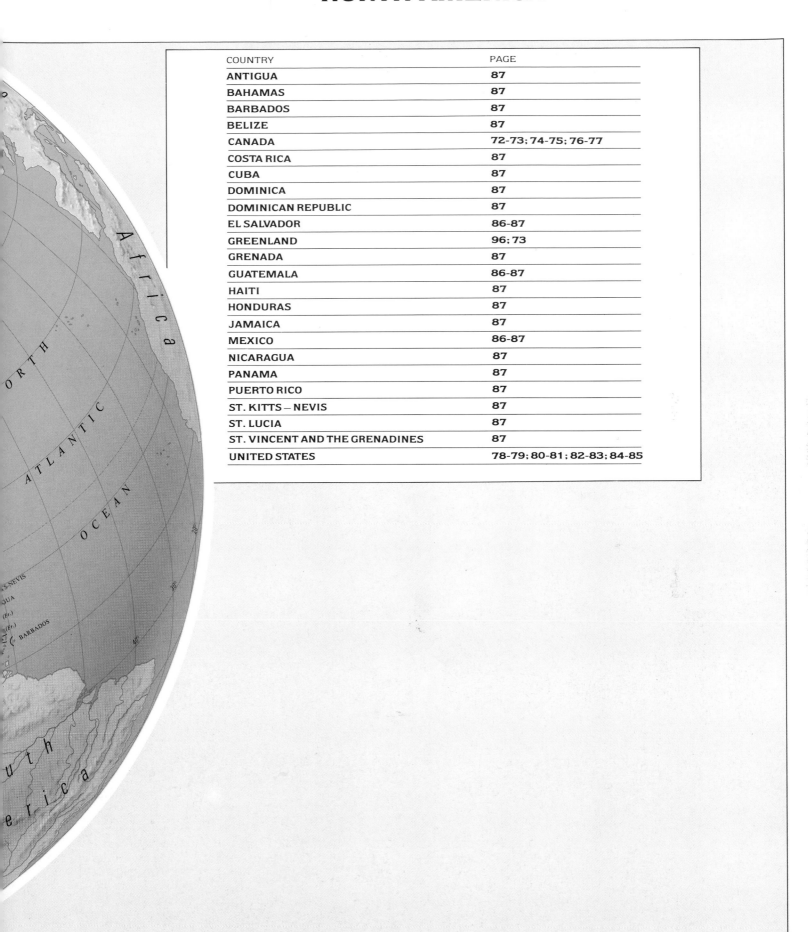

CANADA AND ALASKA

Relief

Feet	Metres
16 404	5000
9843	3000
6562	2000
3281	1000
1640	500
656	200
0	Sea Level
Land Dep.	
656	200
13 123	4000
22 966	7000

Scale 1 : 17 000 000

| 0 | 100 | 200 | 300 | 400 | 500 Miles |
| 0 | 100 | 200 | 300 | 400 | 500 | 600 | 700 | 800 Kms. |

Bonne Projection

WESTERN CANADA

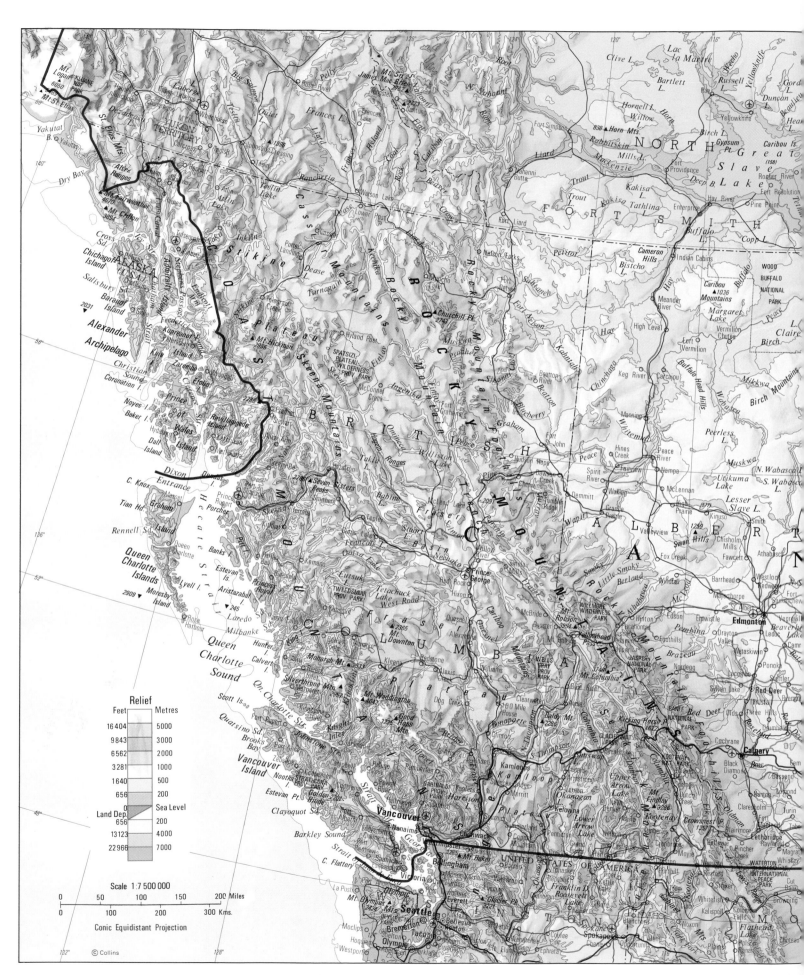

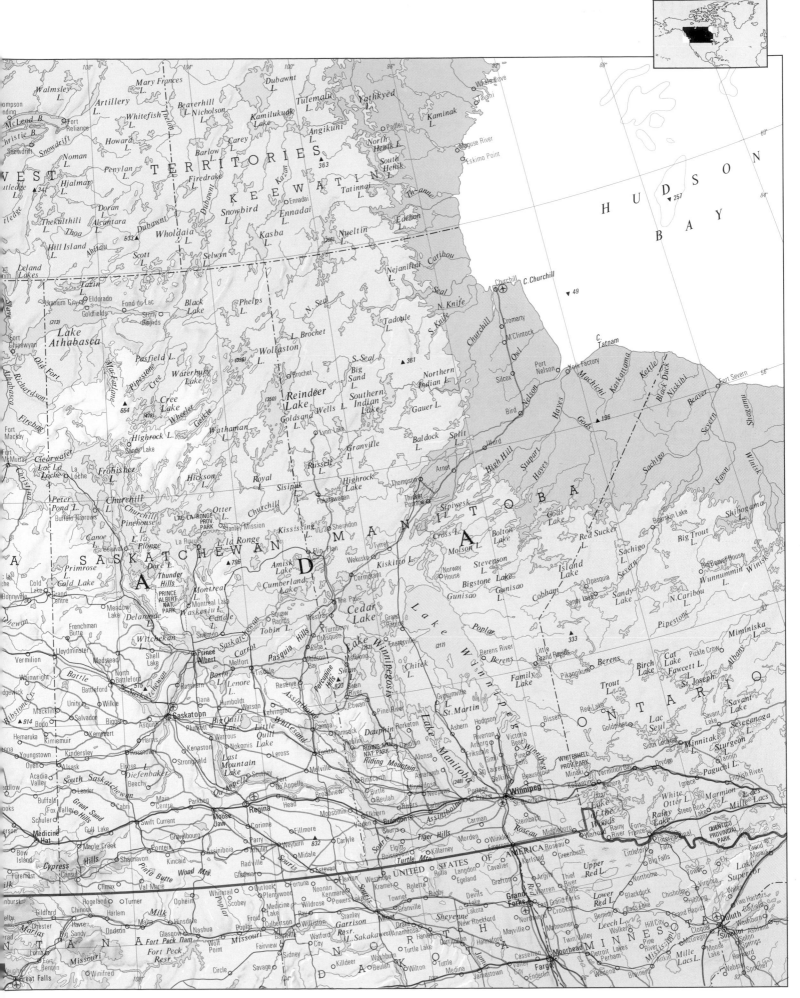

EASTERN CANADA

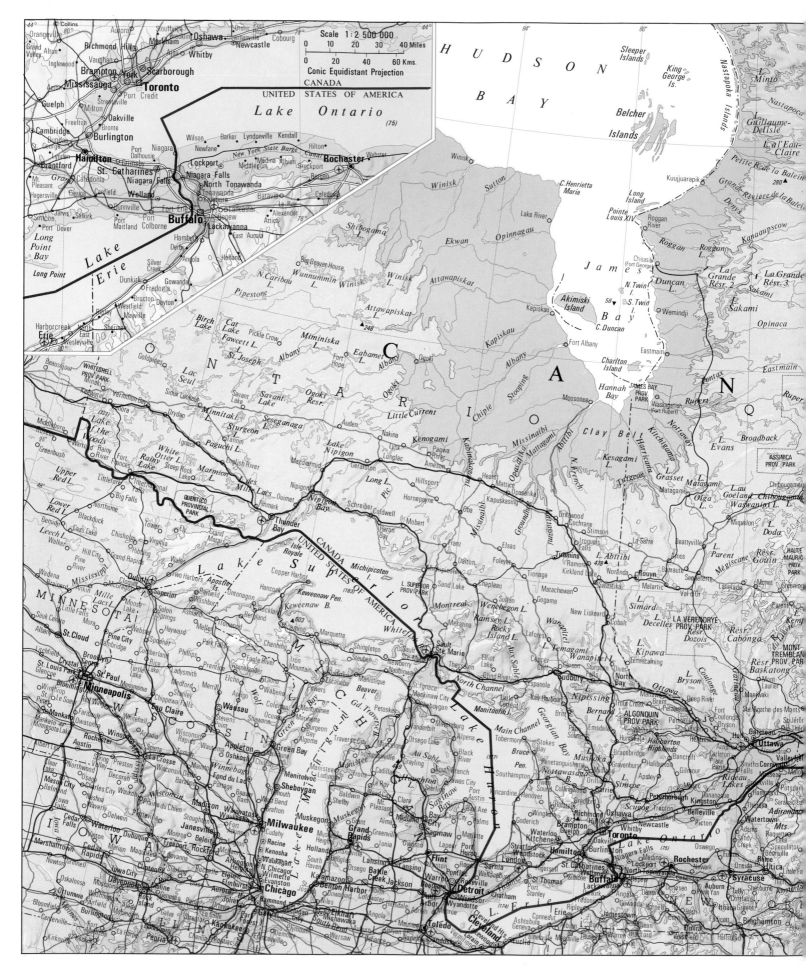

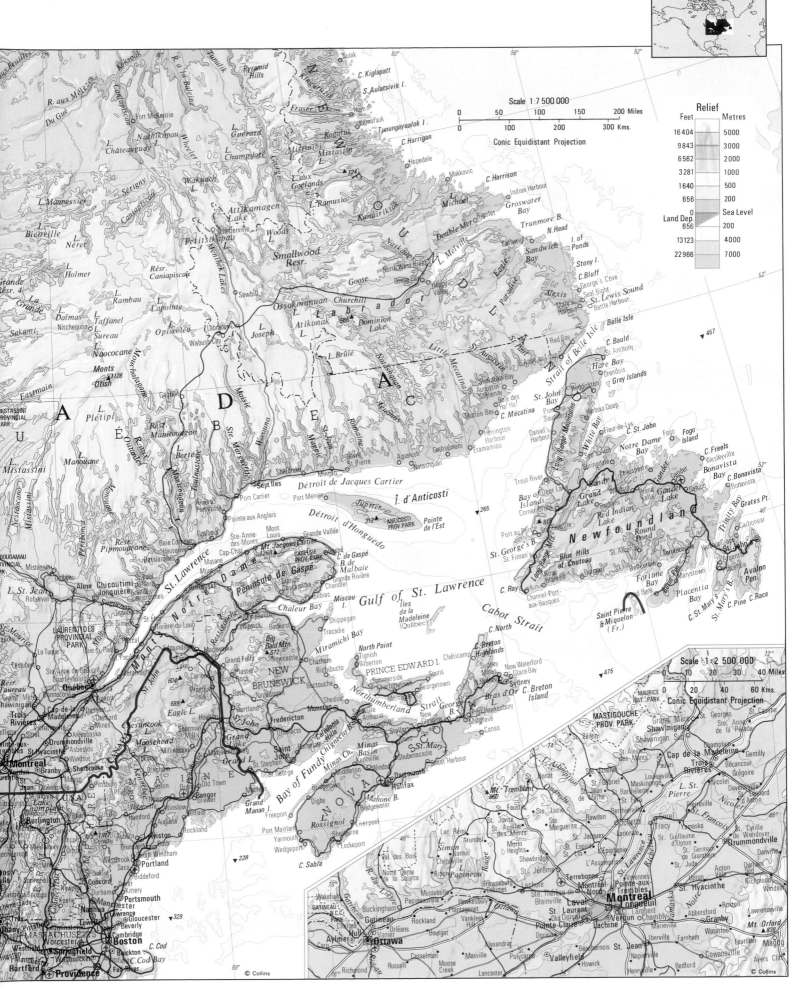

Scale 1:7 500 000

0   50   100   150   200 Miles

0   100   200   300 Kms.

Conic Equidistant Projection

Relief

Feet		Metres
16 404		5000
9843		3000
6562		2000
3281		1000
1640		500
656		200
Land Dep.		Sea Level
656		200
13 123		4000
22 966		7000

Scale 1:2 500 000

0   10   20   30   40 Miles

0   20   40   60 Kms.

Conic Equidistant Projection

© Collins

© Collins

UNITED STATES

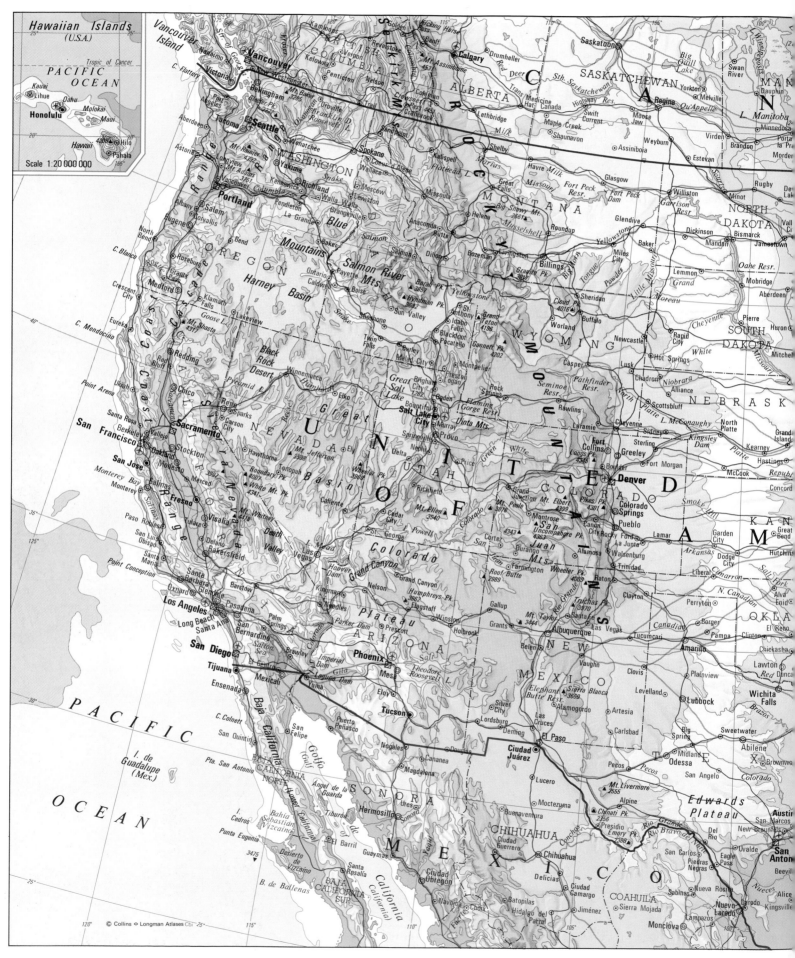

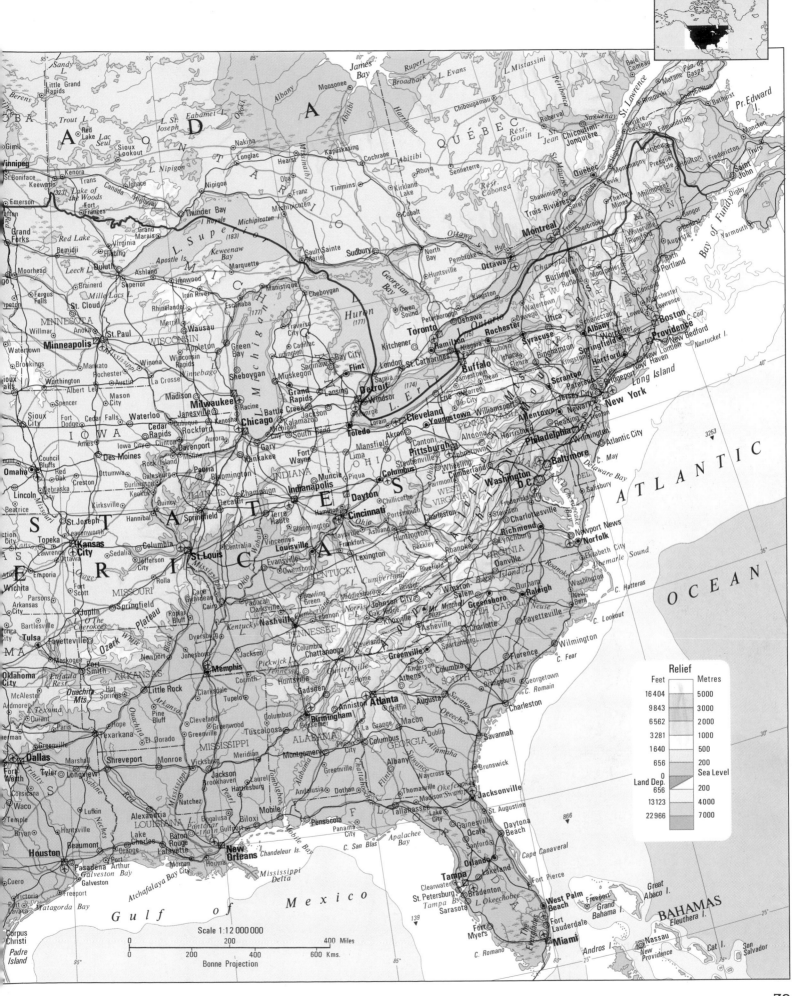

Scale 1:12 000 000

0   200   400 Miles

0   200   400   600 Kms.

Bonne Projection

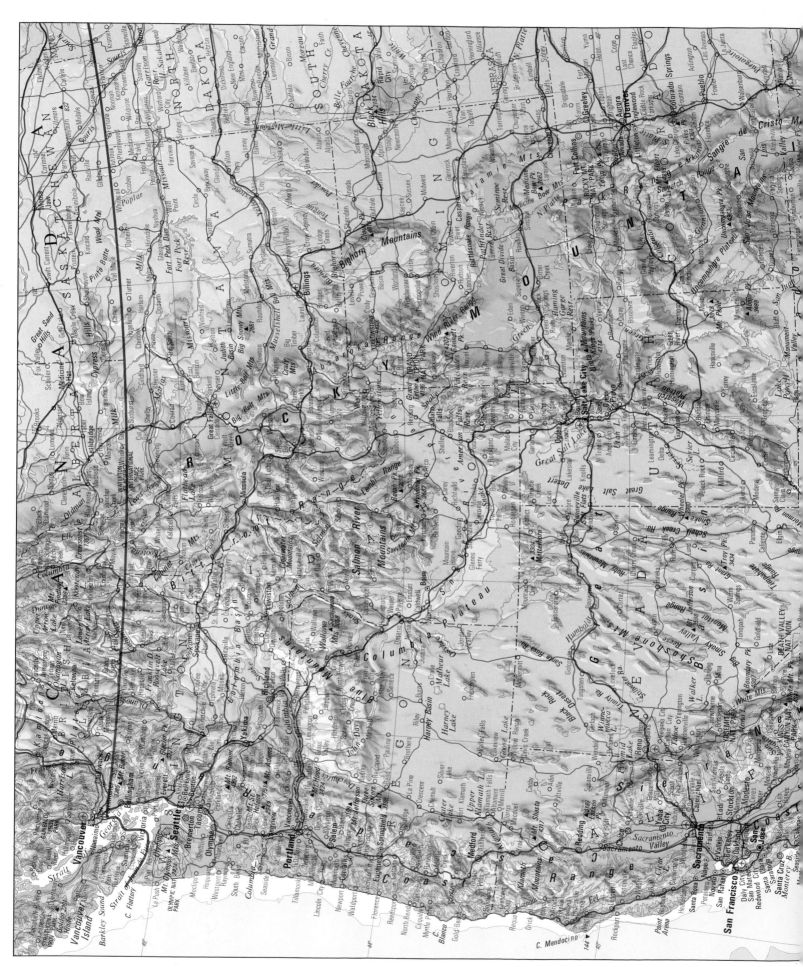

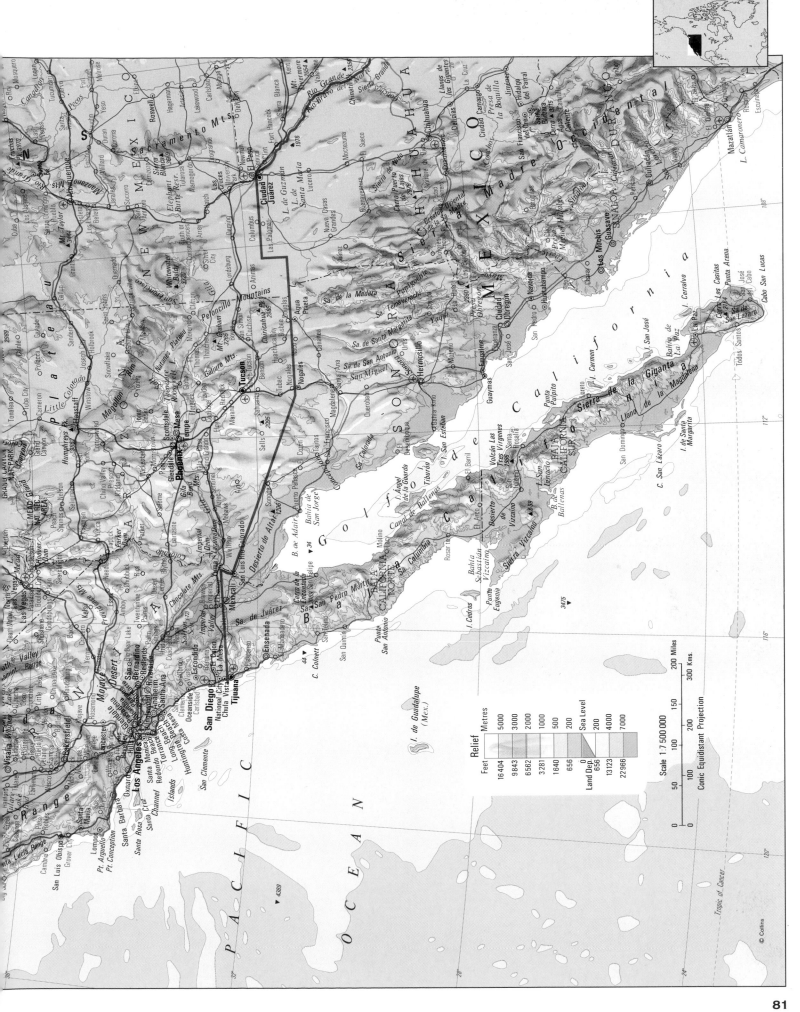

CENTRAL UNITED STATES

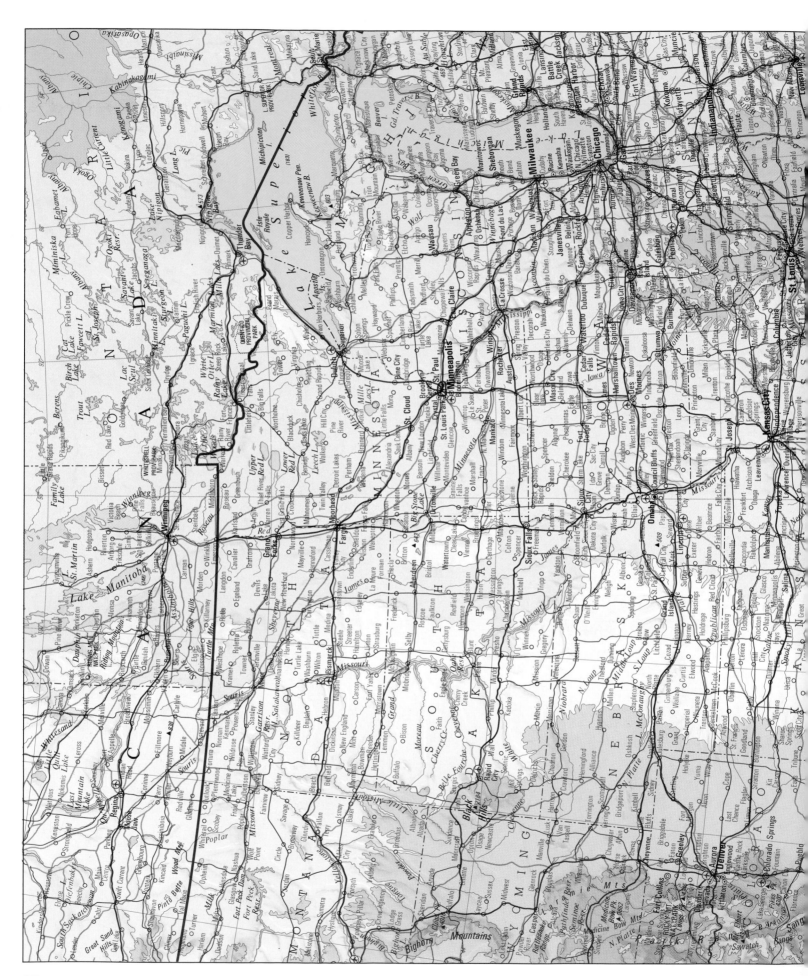

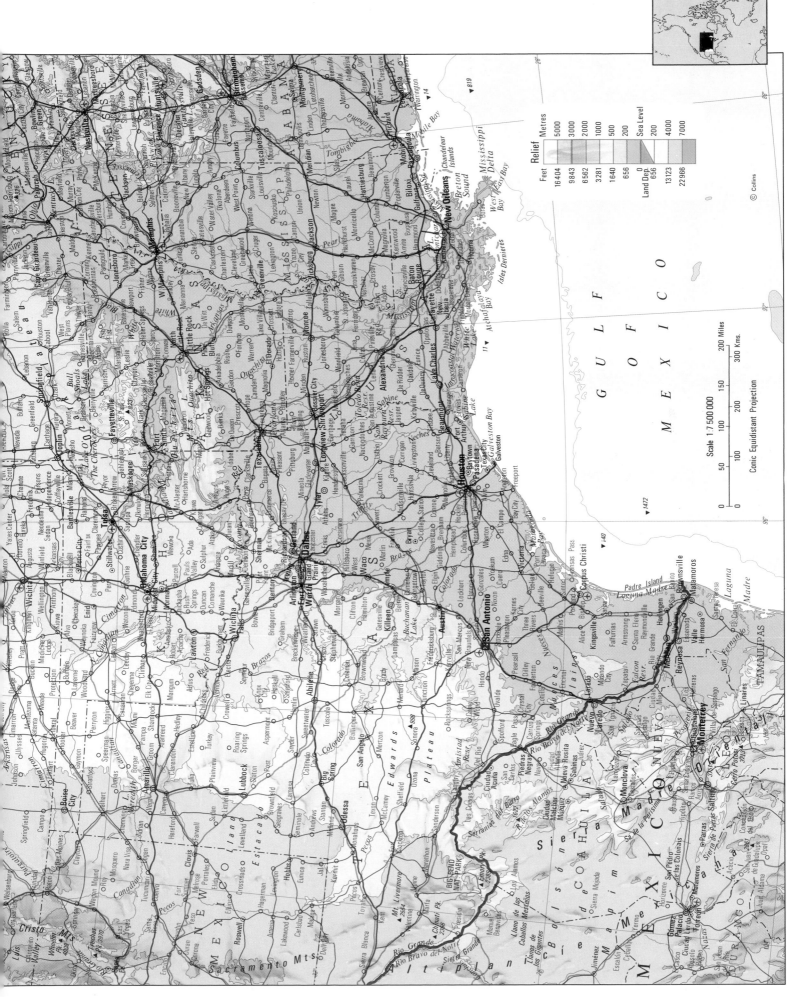

EASTERN UNITED STATES

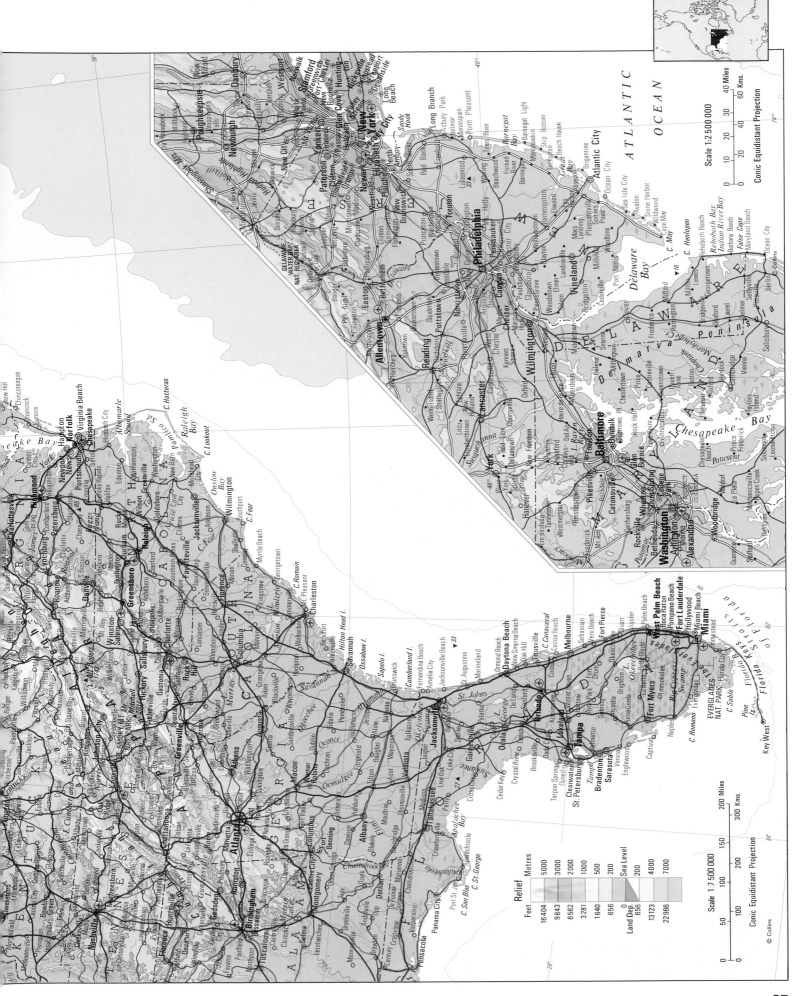

CENTRAL AMERICA AND THE CARIBBEAN

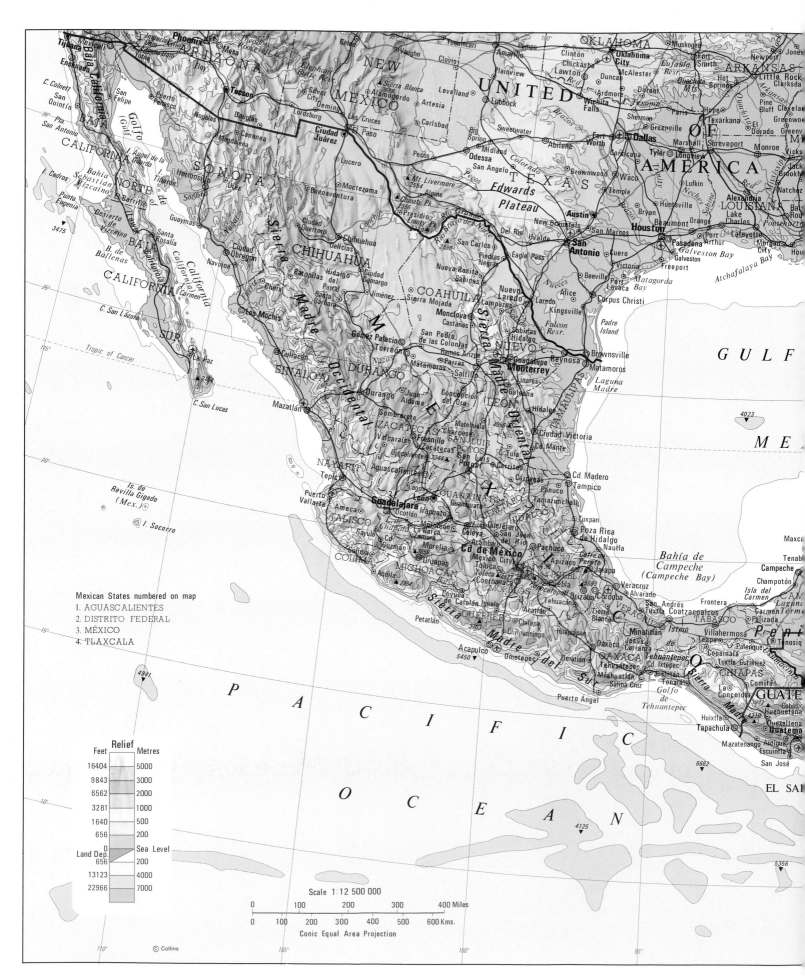

Mexican States numbered on map
1. AGUASCALIENTES
2. DISTRITO FEDERAL
3. MÉXICO
4. TLAXCALA

Relief

Feet		Metres
16404		5000
9843		3000
6562		2000
3281		1000
1640		500
656		200
0		Sea Level
Land Dep.		
656		200
13123		4000
22966		7000

Scale 1:12 500 000

0	100	200	300	400 Miles
0	100 200	300 400	500	600 Kms.

Conic Equal Area Projection

© Collins

North America

NORTH

ATLANTIC

40°

30°

OCEAN

Tropic of Cancer

20°

Caribbean Sea

10°

Barranquilla
Maracaibo · Caracas
TRINIDAD
AND TOBAGO

VENEZUELA
Georgetown
Paramaribo

Medellín
Bogotá
GUYANA
SURINAM
GUIANA
(Fr.)
Cayenne

Cali
COLOMBIA

Quito
ECUADOR
Belém

40°

Equator
30°

Galapagos
Is. (Ec.)
90°
Guayaquil

100°

Fortaleza

B R A Z I L

110°

Lima
P
E
R
U

Recife

120°

La Paz
BOLIVIA
Brasília
10°

Sucre
Belo
Horizonte

130°

PARAGUAY
Rio de
Janeiro
São Paulo
Santo André

140°

SOUTH

Asunción
Curitiba
20°

Tropic of Capricorn

San Félix (Chile)
San Ambrosio
A
R
G
E
N
T
I
N
A
Pôrto
Alegre
A T L

Córdoba
URUGUAY

Islas
Juan
Fernández
(Chile)
Valparaíso
Rosario
30°

Santiago
Buenos
Aires
Montevideo
La
Plata

PACIFIC
C
H
I
L
E

OC

40°

OCEAN

Falkland
Is. (U.K.)

50°

South
Georgia
(U.K.)

Tierra del
Fuego

60°

Antarctic Circle

70°

International Date Line

Antarctica

© Collins

88

SOUTH AMERICA

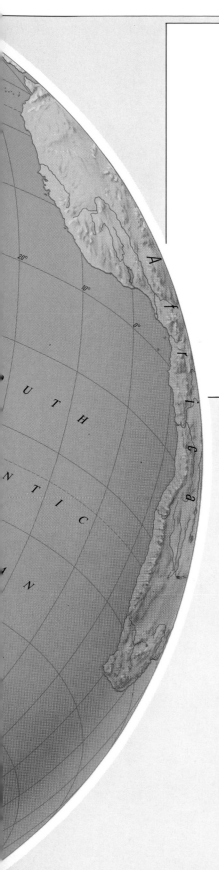

South America as a continental name is used for the land area extending south from the Isthmus of Panama to Cape Horn and lying between 34°W and 82°W. Latin America is a term widely used to cover those parts of the Americas where Spanish, or Portuguese as in Brazil, are the adopted national languages, and thus refers to an area that includes all of South America, Central America, Mexico and the Caribbean, except for the few English, French and Dutch speaking countries and dependencies.

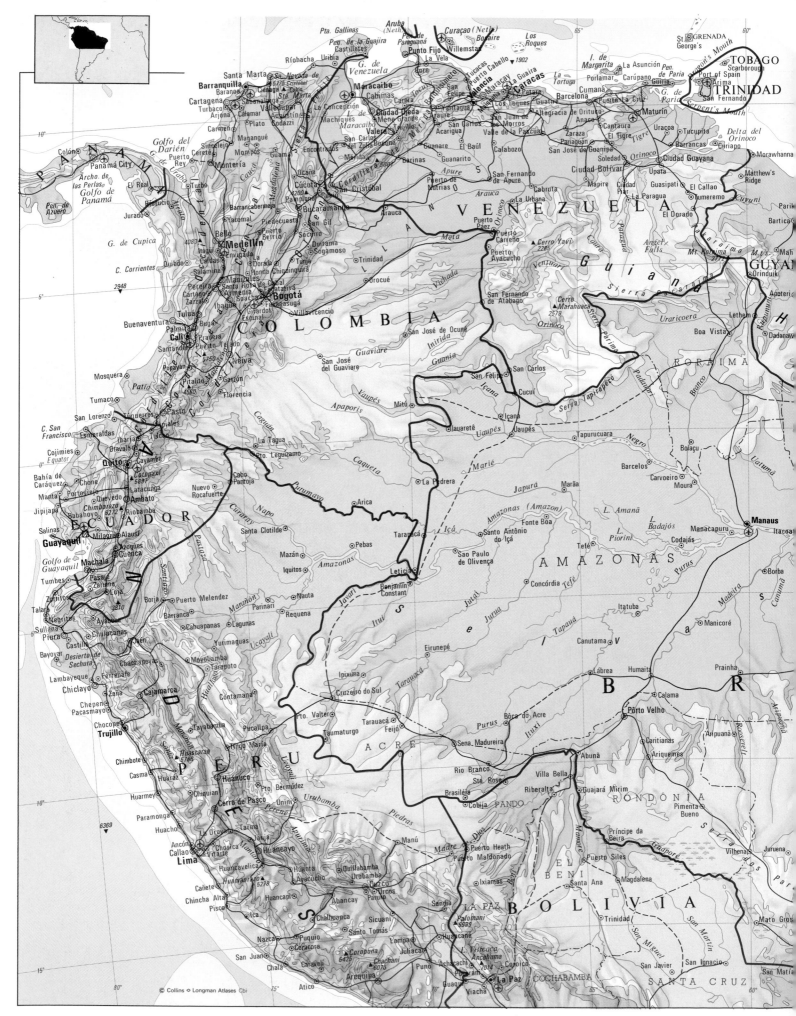

Relief

Feet		Metres
16 404		5000
9843		3000
6562		2000
3281		1000
1640		500
656		200
0		Sea Level
Land Dep.		
656		200
13123		4000

Scale 1:12 500 000

0   100   200   300   400   500 Miles
0 100 200 300 400 500 600 700 800 Kms.

Lambert Azimuthal Equal Area Projection

getown
New Amsterdam
Paramaribo
Nieuw
Nickerie
Afobaka
W.J. Van
Blommestein Meer
SURINAM
Albina
St. Laurent
du Maroni
Kaw
C. Orange
St. Georges
Camopi
GUIANA
(Fr.)
Tumuc Humac Mts.
Amapá
A M A P Á
Serra do Navio
Araguari
C. Norte
Meriruma
Pto. Grande
Estuario do
Rio Amazonas
(Amazon Delta)
Macapá
Ilha
Caviana
Mazagão
Chaves
I. Grande
do Gurupá
Salinópolis
Bragança
Capanema
Viseu
I. de Marajó
Muaná
Icoraci
Belém
Turiaçu
Cururupu
Obidos
Monte
Alegre
Prainha
Gurupá
Pôrto de Moz
Abaetetuba
Acará
Cametá
Baião
Guimarães
São Luís
Viana
Rosário
Tutóia
Parnaíba
Camocim
Granja
Faro
Juruti
Amazonas
(Amazon)
Santarém
Belterra
Altamira
Tucuruí
Itapecuru
Mirim
Caroatá
Piracuruca
Sobral
Antônio Bezerra
Parangaba
Fortaleza
Parintins
Maués
P A R A
Represa de
Tucuruí
Bacabal
Codó
Campo
Maior
Ipu
CEARÁ
Aracati
Itaituba
Bacabal
Caxias
Teresina
Crateús
Areia Branca
Bacabal
Marabá
Itacajuna
Tocantinópolis
M A R A N H Ã O
Barra do
Corda
Colinas
Amarante
Iguatu
Mossoró
Macau
Imperatriz
Pôrto Franco
Represa da Boa
Esperança
Floriano
Oeiras
Senador
Pompeu
RIO GRANDE
DO NORTE
Açu
Natal
Carolina
Loreto
Riachão
Uruçui
Picos
PIAUÍ
Crato
Juazeiro
do Norte
Caicó
Souza
Pombal
Patos
Guarabira
B   R   A   Z   I   L
Piaçá
Conceição
do Araguaia
Sta.
Filomena
São João
do Piauí
Paulistana
Serra Talhada
Cajazeiras
PARAÍBA
Campina Grande
João
Pessoa
Araguacema
Chapada das
Gurgueia
Itaim
Sargueiro
Pesqueira
Caruaru
Itabaiana
Olinda
Recife
Pedro
Afonso
Sta. Isabel
do Morro
T O C A N T I N S
Mangabeiras
Parnaguá
Remanso
Petrolina
Juàzeiro
Paulo Afonso
Ascoverde
Belo
Jardim
Garanhuns
Palmares
PERNAMBUCO
Pto. Nacional
Balsas
Barra
Represa
de Sobradinho
Senhor do Bonfim
Palmeira
dos Índios
Viçosa
Rio
Largo
ALAGOAS
Maceió
Peixe
Paranã
Xique Xique
Jacobina
Quemadas
Propriá
Penedo
Diamantino
B A H I A
Barreiras
Ibotirama
Feira de
Santana
Serrinha
Pedrinhas
SERGIPE
Aracaju
Estância
Niquelândia
Posse
Planalto
Carinhanha
Brumado
Alagoinhas
Cachoeira
Maragogipe
Nazaré
Salvador
Goiás
DIST. FED.
Brasília
Formosa
Luziânia
Brasil
(Brazilian Highlands)
Januária
Monte Azul
Vitória da
Conquista
Valença
Jequié
Ipiaú
Ibicaraí
Ilhéus
Itabuna
Anápolis
Goiânia
M I N A S   G E R A I S
Itapetinga
Salto da
Divisa
Canavieiras
Cuiabá
M a t o   G r o s s o
G O Á S
Alto Araguaia
Rondonópolis
Aragarças
M A T O   G R O S S O
P l a n a l t o   d o
Diamantino
Pouso Alegre
Sta. Formosa

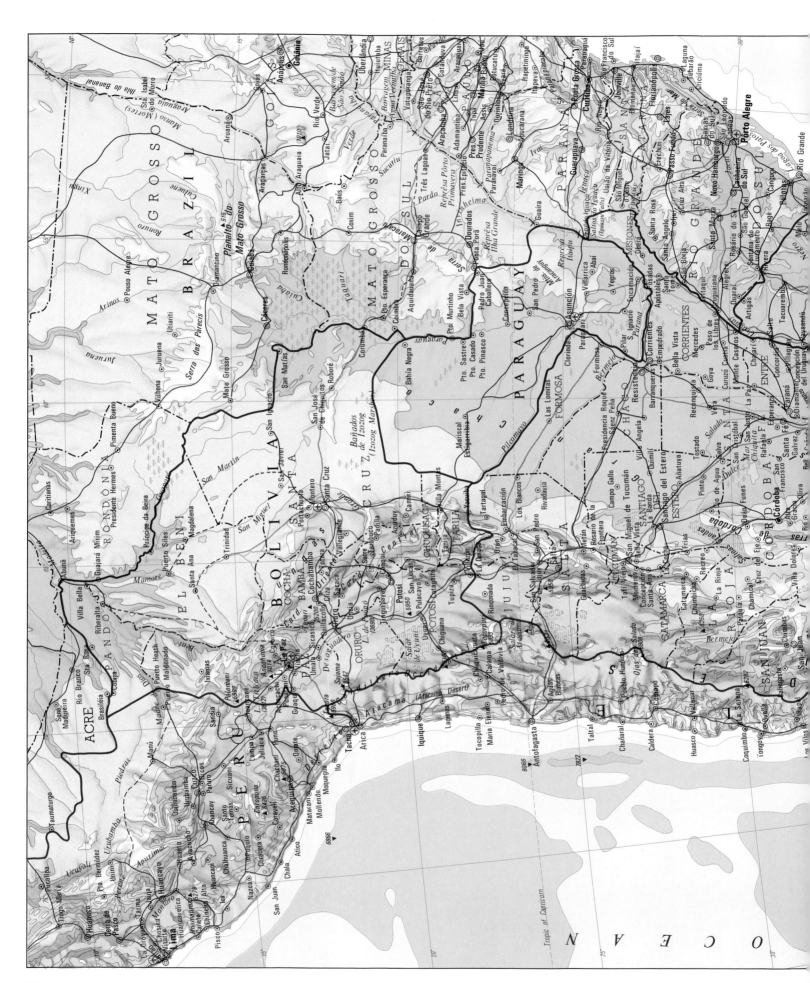

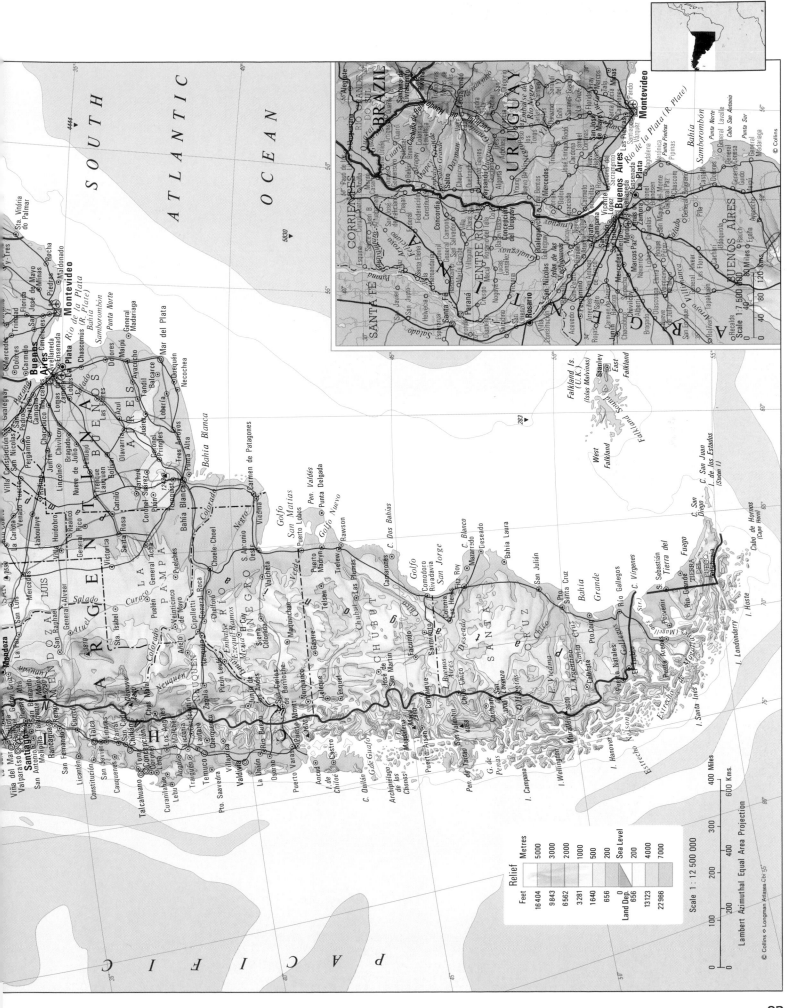

Guaporé Juruena Utiarita Vilhena
Planalto do Mato Grosso
Serra dos Parecis
TOCANTINS
Ibotirama Planalto BAHIA Brasil
Jequié
Diamantino ▲915
MATO GROSSO
Cuiabá
Cáceres
San Javier San Ignacio
San Matías
Goiás Brasília DISTRITO FEDERAL Formosa
GOIÁS
Goiânia ▲1010
Luziânia
Januária
Montes Claros
Vitória da Conquista
Itabuna Ilhéus
SANTA CRUZ
BOLIVIA
Montero Santa Cruz
San José de Chiquitos Roboré
Bañados de Izozog (Izozog Marshes)
Corumbá
MATO GROSSO DO SUL
Campo Grande
MINAS GERAIS
Belo Horizonte
Teófilo Otoni
Governador Valadares
ESPÍRITO SANTO
Vitória Vila Velha
Villa Montes
Mariscal Estigarribia
Pto. Sastre Pto. Casado Pto. Pinasco
PARAGUAY
Pedro Juan Caballero
Concepción
Represa Ilha Grande
SÃO PAULO
Ribeirão Preto
São Paulo
RIO DE JANEIRO
Rio de Janeiro
Niterói
CHACO
FORMOSA
Asunción
Paraguari Villarrica
Represa Itaipu Foz do Iguaçú Saltos do Iguaçú (Iguassu Falls)
PARANÁ
Curitiba
Paranaguá
SANTA CATARINA
Florianópolis
CORRIENTES
ARGENTINA
Corrientes Resistencia
Posadas
MISIONES
Passo Fundo
RIO GRANDE DO SUL
Caxias do Sul
Novo Hamburgo
Pôrto Alegre
SANTA FE
Paraná
ENTRE RIOS
URUGUAY
Rosario
Buenos Aires
La Plata
Montevideo
BUENOS AIRES
Lagoa dos Patos
Rio Grande
PAMPA
Bahía Blanca
Mar del Plata
Tropic of Capricorn

Relief
Feet	Metres
16404	5000
9843	3000
6562	2000
3281	1000
1640	500
656	200
0	Sea Level
Land Dep.	
656	200
13123	4000

Scale 1:12 500 000
0 100 200 300 400 Miles
0 100 200 300 400 500 600 Kms.
Lambert Azimuthal Equal Area Projection

Scale 1:7 500 000
0 40 80 Miles
0 40 80 120 Kms.

© Collins ◇ Longman Atlases Cbi

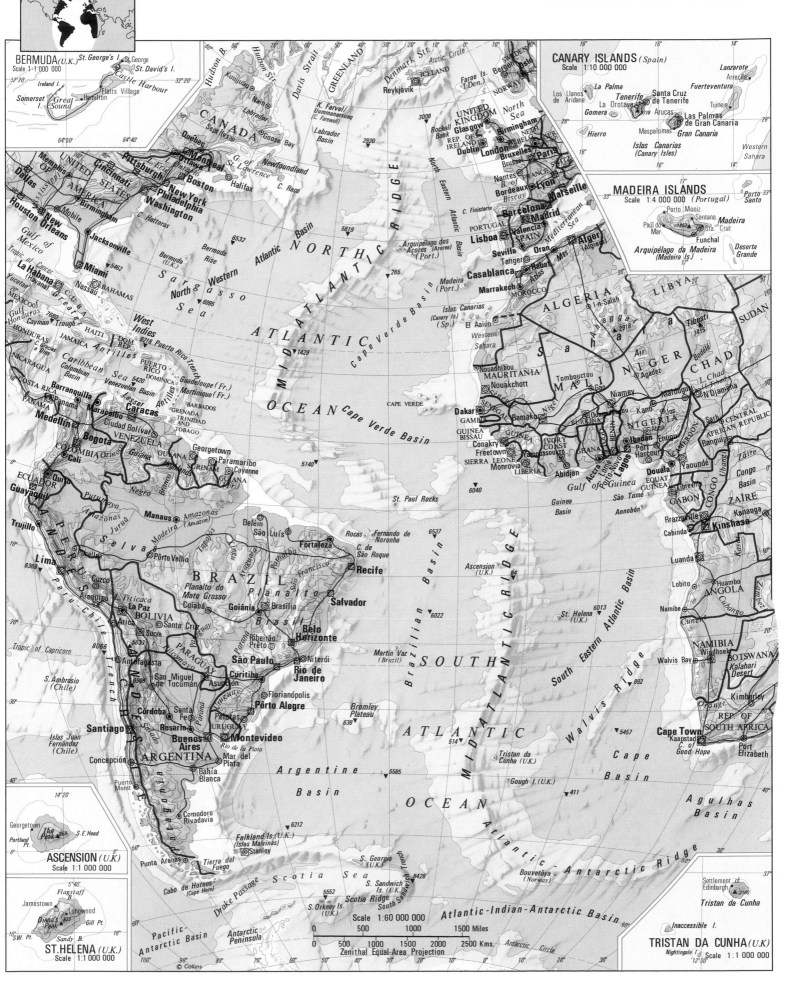

ATLANTIC OCEAN

BERMUDA (U.K.)
Scale 1:1 000 000

CANARY ISLANDS (Spain)
Scale 1:10 000 000

MADEIRA ISLANDS
Scale 1:4 000 000 (Portugal)

ASCENSION (U.K.)
Scale 1:1 000 000

ST. HELENA (U.K.)
Scale 1:1 000 000

TRISTAN DA CUNHA (U.K.)
Scale 1:1 000 000

Scale 1:60 000 000
Zenithal Equal-Area Projection

POLAR REGIONS

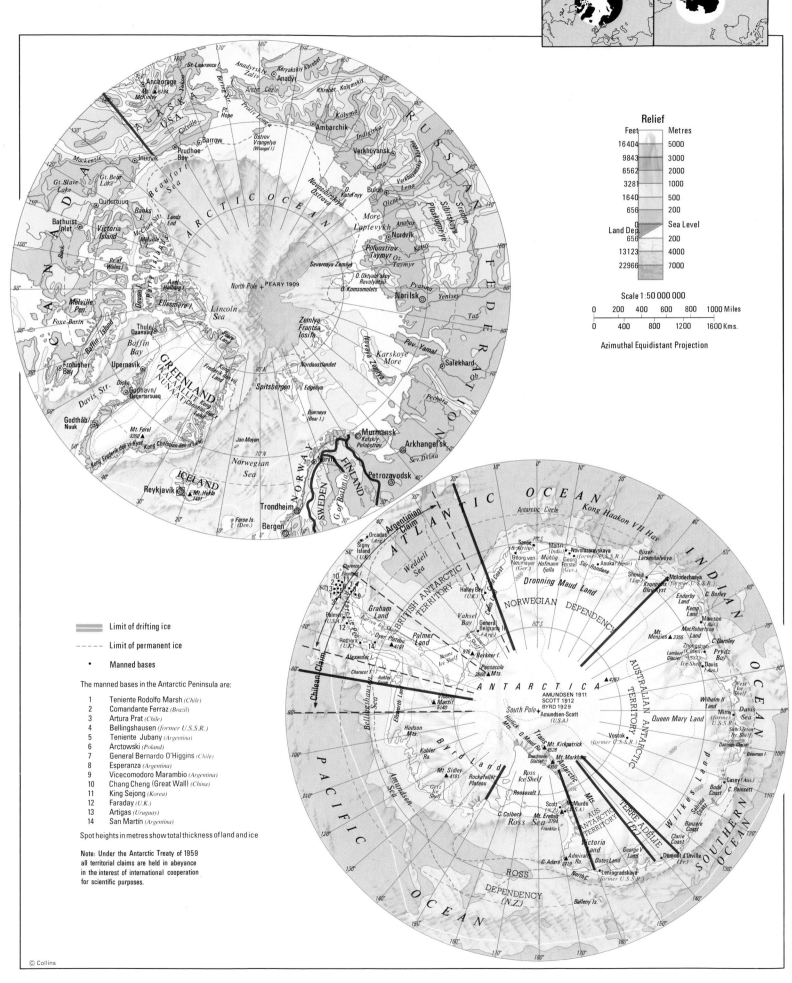

Relief

Feet		Metres
16404		5000
9843		3000
6562		2000
3281		1000
1640		500
656		200
	Sea Level	
Land Dep.		
656		200
13123		4000
22966		7000

Scale 1:50 000 000

0   200   400   600   800   1000 Miles

0   400   800   1200   1600 Kms.

Azimuthal Equidistant Projection

━━━━ Limit of drifting ice

╌╌╌╌ Limit of permanent ice

• Manned bases

The manned bases in the Antarctic Peninsula are:

1   Teniente Rodolfo Marsh *(Chile)*
2   Comandante Ferraz *(Brazil)*
3   Artura Prat *(Chile)*
4   Bellingshausen *(former U.S.S.R.)*
5   Teniente Jubany *(Argentina)*
6   Arctowski *(Poland)*
7   General Bernardo O'Higgins *(Chile)*
8   Esperanza *(Argentina)*
9   Vicecomodoro Marambio *(Argentina)*
10 Chang Cheng (Great Wall) *(China)*
11 King Sejong *(Korea)*
12 Faraday *(U.K.)*
13 Artigas *(Uruguay)*
14 San Martín *(Argentina)*

Spot heights in metres show total thickness of land and ice

Note: Under the Antarctic Treaty of 1959 all territorial claims are held in abeyance in the interest of international cooperation for scientific purposes.

WORLD DATA

Part 1

WORLD FACTS AND FIGURES 98-102

Part 2

WORLD INDEX 103-160

WORLD PHYSICAL DATA

Earth's Dimensions

Superficial area	196 936 679 miles^2	510 066 000 km^2
Land surface	57 268 725 miles^2	148 326 000 km^2
Water surface	139 667 953 miles^2	361 740 000 km^2
Equatorial circumference	24 902 miles	40 075 km
Meridional circumference	24 859 miles	40 007 km
Volume	259 902x10^6 miles^3	1 083 230x10^6 km^3
Mass	5.882x10^{21} tons	5.976x10^{21} tonnes

The Continents

Asia	16 837 065 miles^2	43 608 000 km^2
Africa	11 720 077 miles^2	30 355 000 km^2
North America	9 787 258 miles^2	25 349 000 km^2
South America	6 799 613 miles^2	17 611 000 km^2
Antarctica	5 150 000 miles^2	13 338 500 km^2
Europe	4 053 281 miles^2	10 498 000 km^2
Oceania	3 300 000 miles^2	8 547 000 km^2

Oceans and Sea Areas

Pacific Ocean	63 854 826 miles^2	165 384 000 km^2
Atlantic Ocean	31 744 015 miles^2	82 217 000 km^2
Indian Ocean	28 371 042 miles^2	73 481 000 km^2
Arctic Ocean	5 427 027 miles^2	14 056 000 km^2
Mediterranean Sea	967 181 miles^2	2 505 000 km^2
South China Sea	894 980 miles^2	2 318 000 km^2
Bering Sea	876 061 miles^2	2 269 000 km^2
Caribbean Sea	750 193 miles^2	1 943 000 km^2
Gulf of Mexico	596 138 miles^2	1 544 000 km^2
Okhotskoye More	589 961 miles^2	1 528 000 km^2
East China Sea	481 853 miles^2	1 248 000 km^2
Hudson Bay	476 061 miles^2	1 233 000 km^2
Sea of Japan	389 189 miles^2	1 008 000 km^2
North Sea	222 007 miles^2	575 000 km^2
Black Sea	177 992 miles^2	461 000 km^2

Island Areas

Greenland; Arctic / Atlantic Ocean	839 998 miles^2	2 175 597 km^2
New Guinea; Indonesia / P. N. G.	312 166 miles^2	808 510 km^2
Borneo; Malaysia / Indonesia / Brunei	292 297 miles^2	757 050 km^2
Madagascar; Indian Ocean	229 413 miles^2	594 180 km^2
Sumatera (Sumatra) ; Indonesia	202 355 miles^2	524 100 km^2
Baffin Island; Canada	183 810 miles^2	476 068 km^2
Honshū; Japan	88 978 miles^2	230 455 km^2
Great Britain; United Kingdom	88 751 miles^2	229 867 km^2
Ellesmere Island; Canada	82 118 miles^2	212 688 km^2
Victoria Island; Canada	81 930 miles^2	212 199 km^2
Sulawesi (Celebes) ; Indonesia	72 988 miles^2	189 040 km^2
South Island; New Zealand	58 093 miles^2	150 461 km^2
Jawa (Java) ; Indonesia	51 754 miles^2	134 045 km^2
North Island; New Zealand	44 281 miles^2	114 688 km^2
Cuba; Caribbean Sea	44 218 miles^2	114 525 km^2

River Lengths

An Nīl (Nile) ; Africa	4160 miles	6695 km
Amazonas (Amazon) ; South America	4048 miles	6516 km
Chang Jiang (Yangtze) ; Asia	3964 miles	6380 km
Mississippi - Missouri; North America	3740 miles	6020 km
Ob-Irtysh; Asia	3461 miles	5570 km
Huang He (Hwang Ho) ; Asia	3395 miles	5464 km
Zaïre; Africa	2900 miles	4667 km
Mekong; Asia	2749 miles	4425 km
Amur; Asia	2744 miles	4416 km
Lena; Asia	2734 miles	4400 km
Mackenzie; North America	2640 miles	4250 km
Yenisey; Asia	2541 miles	4090 km
Niger; Africa	2504 miles	4030 km
Murray - Darling; Oceania	2330 miles	3750 km
Volga; Europe	2291 miles	3688 km

Mountain Heights (Selected)

Everest; Nepal / China	29 028 feet	8848 m
K2; Jammu & Kashmir / China	28 251 feet	8611 m
Kānchenjunga; Nepal / India	28 169 feet	8586 m
Dhaulāgiri; Nepal	26 794 feet	8167 m
Annapurna; Nepal	26 545 feet	8091 m
Aconcagua; Argentina	22 834 feet	6960 m
Ojos del Salado; Argentina / Chile	22 664 feet	6908 m
McKinley; Alaska, U.S.A.	20 321 feet	6194 m
Logan; Canada	19 524 feet	5951 m
Kilimanjaro; Tanzania	19 340 feet	5895 m
Elbrus; Russian Federation	18 510 feet	5642 m
Kirinyaga; Kenya	17 060 feet	5200 m
Vinson Massif; Antarctica	16 860 feet	5139 m
Puncak Jaya; Indonesia	16 502 feet	5030 m
Blanc; France / Italy	15 774 feet	4808 m

Lake and Inland Sea Areas

Some areas are subject to seasonal variations.

Caspian Sea; Central Asia	143 550 miles^2	371 795 km^2
Lake Superior; U.S.A. / Canada	32 150 miles^2	83 270 km^2
Lake Victoria; East Africa	26 828 miles^2	69 485 km^2
Lake Huron; U.S.A. / Canada	23 436 miles^2	60 700 km^2
Lake Michigan; U.S.A.	22 400 miles^2	58 016 km^2
Aral Sea; Central Asia	14 092 miles^2	36 500 km^2
Lake Tanganyika; East Africa	12 700 miles^2	32 893 km^2
Great Bear Lake; Canada	12 274 miles^2	31 792 km^2
Ozero Baikal (Lake Baykal) ; Rus. Fed.	11 779 miles^2	30 510 km^2
Great Slave Lake; Canada	11 169 miles^2	28 930 km^2
Lake Erie; U.S.A. / Canada	9910 miles^2	25 667 km^2
Lake Winnipeg; Canada	9464 miles^2	24 514 km^2
Lake Malaŵi; Malaŵi / Mozambique	8683 miles^2	22 490 km^2
Lake Ontario; U.S.A. / Canada	7540 miles^2	19 529 km^2
Ladozhskoye Ozero (Lake Ladoga) ; Rus. Fed.	7100 miles^2	18 390 km^2

Volcanoes (Selected)

	Last Eruption	Height	Height
Cameroun; Cameroon	1922	13 353 feet	4070 m
Cotopaxi; Ecuador	1975	19 347 feet	5897 m
Elbrus; Russian Federation	extinct	18 510 feet	5642 m
Erebus; Antarctica	1979	12 447 feet	3794 m
Etna; Sicilia, Italy	1983	10 958 feet	3340 m
Fuji san (Fujiyama) ; Japan	extinct	12 388 feet	3776 m
Hekla; Iceland	1981	4891 feet	1491 m
Kilimanjaro; Tanzania	extinct	19 340 feet	5895 m
Mauna Loa; Hawaii	1978	13 684 feet	4171 m
Ngauruhoe; New Zealand	1975	7516 feet	2291 m
Popocatépetl; Mexico	1920	17 887 feet	5452 m
St. Helens; U.S.A.	1981	9675 feet	2949 m
Stromboli; Italy	1975	3038 feet	926 m
Tristan da Cunha; Atlantic Ocean	1962	7086 feet	2160 m
Vesuvio (Vesuvius) ; Italy	1944	4189 feet	1277 m

WORLD POLITICAL DATA

National Areas

Russian Federation; Asia / Europe	6 593 822 miles²	17 078 000 km²
Canada; North America	3 831 036 miles²	9 922 385 km²
China; Asia	3 698 455 miles²	9 579 000 km²
United States; North America	3 615 108 miles²	9 363 130 km²
Brazil; South America	3 286 472 miles²	8 511 965 km²
Australia; Oceania	2 966 138 miles²	7 682 300 km²
India; Asia	1 222 714 miles²	3 166 830 km²
Argentina; South America	1 072 515 miles²	2 777 815 km²
Sudan; Africa	967 496 miles²	2 505 815 km²
Saudi Arabia; Asia	926 988 miles²	2 400 900 km²
Algeria; Africa	919 592 miles²	2 381 745 km²
Zaïre; Africa	905 563 miles²	2 345 410 km²
Greenland; North America	840 000 miles²	2 175 600 km²
Mexico; North America	761 600 miles²	1 972 545 km²
Indonesia; Asia	741 098 miles²	1 919 445 km²
Libya; Africa	679 359 miles²	1 759 540 km²
Iran; Asia	636 293 miles²	1 648 000 km²
Mongolia; Asia	604 247 miles²	1 565 000 km²
Peru; South America	496 222 miles²	1 285 215 km²
Chad; Africa	495 752 miles²	1 284 000 km²

National Populations

China; Asia	1 139 060 000
India; Asia	843 931 000
United States; North America	249 975 000
Indonesia; Asia	179 300 000
Brazil; South America	150 368 000
Russian Federation; Asia / Europe	148 263 000
Japan; Asia	123 537 000
Bangladesh; Asia	115 594 000
Pakistan; Asia	112 049 000
Nigeria; Africa	88 500 000
Mexico; North America	86 154 000
Germany; Europe	79 479 000
Vietnam; Asia	66 200 000
Philippines; Asia	61 480 000
Italy; Europe	57 662 000
United Kingdom; Europe	57 411 000
Thailand; Asia	57 196 000
France; Europe	56 440 000
Turkey; Asia / Europe	56 098 000
Iran; Asia	54 608 000

World Cities

Ciudad de México (Mexico City) ; Mexico	20 200 000
Tōkyō; Japan	18 100 000
São Paulo; Brazil	17 400 000
New York; United States	16 200 000
Shanghai; China	13 400 000
Chicago; United States	11 900 000
Calcutta; India	11 800 000
Buenos Aires; Argentina	11 500 000
Bombay; India	11 200 000
Sŏul (Seoul) ; South Korea	11 000 000
Beijing (Peking) ; China	10 800 000
Rio de Janeiro; Brazil	10 700 000
Tianjin; China	9 400 000
Jakarta; Indonesia	9 300 000
Al Qāhirah (Cairo) ; Egypt	9 000 000

Major International Organisations

United Nations - On December 1990 the United Nations had 160 members. Independent States not represented include Liechtenstein, Monaco, Nauru, North Korea, San Marino, South Korea, Switzerland, Taiwan, Tonga.

Commonwealth

Antigua	Australia	Bahamas	Bangladesh
Barbados	Belize	Botswana	Brunei
Canada	Cyprus	Dominica	Fiji
Gambia	Ghana	Grenada	Guyana
Hong Kong	India	Jamaica	Kenya
Kiribati	Lesotho	Malaŵi	Malaysia
Maldives	Malta	Mauritius	Nauru
New Zealand	Nigeria	Pakistan	Papua New Guinea
St. Kitts & Nevis	St. Lucia	St. Vincent	Seychelles
Sierra Leone	Singapore	Solomon Islands	Sri Lanka
Swaziland	Tanzania	Tonga	Trinidad & Tobago
Tuvalu	Uganda	United Kingdom	Vanuatu
Western Samoa	Zambia	Zimbabwe	

OAU - Organisation of African Unity

Algeria	Angola	Benin	Botswana
Burkina	Burundi	Cameroon	Cape Verde
Central African Rep.	Chad	Comoros	Congo
Djibouti	Egypt	Equatorial Guinea	Ethiopia
Gabon	Gambia	Ghana	Guinea
Guinea Bissau	Ivory Coast	Kenya	Lesotho
Liberia	Libya	Madagascar	Malaŵi
Mali	Mauritania	Mauritius	Mozambique
Namibia	Niger	Nigeria	Rwanda
São Tomé & Príncipe	Senegal	Seychelles	Sierra Leone
Somali Rep.	Sudan	Swaziland	Tanzania
Togo	Tunisia	Uganda	Western Sahara
Zaïre	Zambia	Zimbabwe	

OAS - Organisation of American States

Antigua	Argentina	Bahamas	Barbados
Bolivia	Brazil	Chile	Colombia
Costa Rica	Dominica	Dominican Rep.	Ecuador
El Salvador	Grenada	Guatemala	Haiti
Honduras	Jamaica	Mexico	Nicaragua
Panama	Paraguay	Peru	St. Kitts & Nevis
St. Lucia	St. Vincent	Surinam	Trinidad & Tobago
United States	Uruguay	Venezuela	

EEC - European Economic Community

Belgium	Denmark	France	Germany
Greece	Ireland	Italy	Luxembourg
Netherlands	Portugal	Spain	United Kingdom

EFTA - European Free Trade Association

Austria	Finland (assoc.)	Iceland	Norway
Sweden	Switzerland		

ASEAN - Association of Southeast Asian Nations

Brunei	Indonesia	Malaysia	Philippines
Singapore	Thailand		

ECOWAS - Economic Community of West African States

Benin	Burkina	Cape Verde	Gambia
Ghana	Guinea	Guinea Bissau	Ivory Coast
Liberia	Mali	Mauritania	Niger
Nigeria	Senegal	Sierra Leone	Togo

CARICOM - Caribbean Community and Common Market

Antigua	Bahamas	Barbados	Belize
Dominica	Grenada	Guyana	Jamaica
Montserrat	St. Kitts & Nevis	St. Lucia	St. Vincent
Trinidad & Tobago			

NATIONS OF THE WORLD

COUNTRY	AREA		POPULATION			FORM OF GOVERNMENT	CAPITAL CITY	MAIN LANGUAGES	CURRENCY
	miles²	km²	total	density per mile²	km²				
AFGHANISTAN	251,824	652,225	16,120,000	64	25	republic	Kābol	Pushtu,Dari	afghani
ALBANIA	11,100	28,750	3,250,000	293	113	republic	Tiranë	Albanian	lek
ALGERIA	919,593	2,381,745	25,012,000	27	11	republic	Alger (Algiers)	Arabic	dinar
ANDORRA	180	465	52,000	290	112	principality	Andorra	Catalan	French franc,Spanish peseta
ANGOLA	481,351	1,246,700	10,020,000	21	8	republic	Luanda	Portuguese	kwanza
ANTIGUA & BARBUDA	171	442	77,000	451	174	constitutional monarchy	St John's	English	East Caribbean dollar
ARGENTINA	1,072,515	2,777,815	32,322,000	30	12	federal republic	Buenos Aires	Spanish	austral
ARMENIA	11,506	29,800	3,324,000	289	112	republic	Yerevan	Armenian,Russian	rouble
AUSTRALIA	2,966,139	7,682,300	17,086,000	6	2	monarchy (federal)	Canberra	English	dollar
AUSTRIA	32,376	83,855	7,712,000	238	92	federal republic	Wien (Vienna)	German	schilling
AZERBAIJAN	33,436	86,600	7,153,000	214	83	republic	Baku	Azerbaijani,Russian	rouble
BAHAMAS	5353	13,865	253,000	47	18	constitutional monarchy	Nassau	English	dollar
BAHRAIN	255	661	503,000	1971	761	emirate	Al Manāmah	Arabic	dinar
BANGLADESH	55,598	144,000	115,594,000	2079	803	republic	Dhaka	Bengali	taka
BARBADOS	166	430	255,000	1536	593	constitutional monarchy	Bridgetown	English	dollar
BELGIUM	11,784	30,520	9,845,000	835	323	constitutional monarchy	Bruxelles (Brussels) Brussel	French,Dutch, German	franc
BELIZE	8867	22,965	188,000	21	8	constitutional monarchy	Belmopan	English	dollar
BELORUSSIA (BELARUS)	80,309	208,000	10,278,000	128	49	republic	Minsk	Belorussian	rouble
BENIN	43,483	112,620	4,736,000	109	42	republic	Porto-Novo	French	CFA franc
BHUTAN	18,000	46,620	1,517,000	84	33	constitutional monarchy	Thimbu	Dzongkha	Indian rupee,ngultrum
BOLIVIA	424,160	1,098,575	7,400,000	17	7	republic	La Paz / Sucre	Spanish,Aymara	boliviano
BOSNIA-HERZEGOVINA	19,741	51,130	4,200,000	213	82	republic	Sarajevo	Serbo-Croat	dinar
BOTSWANA	231,804	600,372	1,291,000	6	2	republic	Gaborone	English,Tswana	pula
BRAZIL	3,286,473	8,511,965	150,368,000	46	18	federal republic	Brasília	Portuguese	cruzeiro
BRUNEI	2226	5,765	266,000	120	46	sultanate	Bandar Seri Begawan	Malay	dollar
BULGARIA	42,822	110,910	8,980,000	210	81	people's republic	Sofiya (Sofia)	Bulgarian	lev
BURKINA	105,869	274,200	9,001,000	85	33	republic	Ouagadougou	French	CFA franc
BURMA (MYANMA)	261,788	678,030	41,675,000	159	61	military regime	Yangon (Rangoon)	Burmese	kyat
BURUNDI	10,747	27,834	5,458,000	508	196	republic	Bujumbura	French,Kirundi	franc
CAMBODIA	69,884	181,000	8,246,000	118	46	republic	Phnom Penh	Cambodian,Khmer	riel
CAMEROON	183,591	475,500	11,834,000	64	25	republic	Yaoundé	French,English	CFA franc
CANADA	3,831,037	9,922,385	26,603,000	7	3	monarchy (federal)	Ottawa	English,French	dollar
CAPE VERDE	1558	4,035	370,000	237	92	republic	Praia	Portuguese,Creole	escudo
CENTRAL AFRICAN REPUBLIC	241,303	624,975	3,039,000	13	5	republic	Bangui	French,Sango	CFA franc
CHAD	495,753	1,284,000	5,679,000	11	4	republic	N'Djamena	French,Arabic	CFA franc
CHILE	290,203	751,625	13,173,000	45	18	republic	Santiago	Spanish	peso
CHINA	3,698,456	9,579,000	1,139,060,000	308	119	people's republic	Beijing (Peking)	Mandarin	yuan
COLOMBIA	439,736	1,138,915	32,987,000	75	29	republic	Bogotá	Spanish	peso
COMOROS	718	1,860	551,000	767	296	federal republic	Moroni	Comoran,Arabic,French	CFA franc
CONGO	132,046	342,000	2,271,000	17	7	republic	Brazzaville	French	CFA franc
COSTA RICA	19,653	50,900	2,994,000	152	59	republic	San José	Spanish	colon
CROATIA	21,830	56,540	4,600,000	211	81	republic	Zagreb	Serbo-Croat	Dinar
CUBA	44,218	114,525	10,609,000	240	93	people's republic	La Habana (Havana)	Spanish	peso
CYPRUS	3571	9,250	702,000	197	76	republic	Levkosía (Nicosia)	Greek	pound
CZECH REPUBLIC	30,448	78,864	10,300,000	340	131	federal republic	Praha (Prague)	Czech	koruna
DENMARK	16,631	43,075	5,140,000	309	119	constitutional monarchy	Köbenhavn (Copenhagen)	Danish	krone
DJIBOUTI	8880	23,000	409,000	46	18	republic	Djibouti	French,Somali,Afar	franc
DOMINICA	290	751	83,000	286	111	republic	Roseau	English,French	East Caribbean dollar
DOMINICAN REPUBLIC	18,703	48,440	7,170,000	383	148	republic	Santo Domingo	Spanish	peso
ECUADOR	178,176	461,475	10,782,000	61	23	republic	Quito	Spanish	sucre
EGYPT	386,197	1,000,250	53,153,000	138	53	republic	Al Qāhirah (Cairo)	Arabic	pound
EL SALVADOR	8261	21,395	5,252,000	636	245	republic	San Salvador	Spanish	colón
EQUATORIAL GUINEA	10,830	28,050	348,000	32	12	republic	Malabo	Spanish	CFA franc
ESTONIA	17,413	45,100	1,583,000	91	35	republic	Tallinn	Estonian,Russian	kroon
ETHIOPIA	471,776	1,221,900	50,974,000	108	42	people's republic	Ādīs Ābeba (Addis Ababa)	Amharic	birr
FEDERATED STATES OF MICRONESIA	271	702	99,000	365	141	federal republic	Palikir on Pohnpei	English,Kosrean,Yapese, Pohnpeian,Trukese	US dollar
FIJI	7077	18,330	765,000	108	42	republic	Suva	English,Fiji,Hindustani	dollar
FINLAND	130,127	337,030	4,986,000	38	15	republic	Helsinki	Finnish,Swedish	markka
FRANCE	210,025	543,965	56,440,000	269	104	republic	Paris	French	franc
GABON	103,346	267,665	1,172,000	11	4	republic	Libreville	French	CFA franc
GAMBIA	4127	10,690	861,000	209	81	republic	Banjul	English	dalasi
GEORGIA	26,911	69,700	5,464,000	203	78	republic	Tbilisi	Georgian,Russian	rouble
GERMANY	138,173	357,868	79,479,000	575	222	federal republic	Berlin,Bonn	German	mark
GHANA	92,010	238,305	15,028,000	163	63	military regime	Accra	English	cedi

COUNTRY	AREA		POPULATION			FORM OF GOVERNMENT	CAPITAL CITY	MAIN LANGUAGES	CURRENCY
	miles²	km²	total	density per mile²	km²				
GREECE	50,959	131,985	10,123,000	199	77	republic	Athinai (Athens)	Greek	drachma
GRENADA	133	345	85,000	638	246	constitutional monarchy	St George's	English	East Caribbean dollar
GUATEMALA	42,042	108,890	9,197,000	219	84	republic	Guatemala	Spanish	quetzal
GUINEA	98,400	254,855	5,756,000	58	23	military regime	Conakry	French	franc
GUINEA-BISSAU	13,948	36,125	965,000	69	27	republic	Bissau	Portuguese	peso
GUYANA	83,000	214,970	796,000	10	4	republic	Georgetown	English	dollar
HAITI	10,714	27,750	6,486,000	605	234	republic	Port-au-Prince	French,Creole	gourde
HONDURAS	43,276	112,085	5,105,000	118	46	republic	Tegucigalpa	Spanish	lempira
HUNGARY	35,919	93,030	10,553,000	294	113	republic	Budapest	Magyar	forint
ICELAND	39,699	102,820	255,000	6	2	republic	Reykjavík	Icelandic	króna
INDIA	1,222,714	3,166,830	843,931,000	676	266	republic	New Delhi	Hindi,English	rupee
INDONESIA	741,098	1,919,445	179,300,000	242	93	republic	Jakarta	Bahasa Indonesia	rupiah
IRAN	636,293	1,648,000	54,608,000	86	33	Islamic republic	Tehrān	Persian	rial
IRAQ	169,284	438,445	18,920,000	112	43	republic	Baghdād	Arabic,Kurdish	dinar
IRELAND, REPUBLIC OF	26,600	68,895	3,503,000	132	51	republic	Dublin	English,Irish	punt
ISRAEL	8019	20,770	4,659,000	581	224	republic	Yerushalayim (Jerusalem)	Hebrew	shekel
ITALY	116,311	301,245	57,662,000	496	191	republic	Roma (Rome)	Italian	lira
IVORY COAST (CÔTE D'IVOIRE)	124,504	322,465	11,998,000	96	37	republic	Yamoussoukro	French	CFA franc
JAMAICA	4411	11,425	2,420,000	549	212	constitutional monarchy	Kingston	English	dollar
JAPAN	142,741	369,700	123,537,000	865	334	monarchy	Tōkyō	Japanese	yen
JORDAN	37,066	96,000	4,010,000	108	42	monarchy	Ammān	Arabic	dinar
KAZAKHSTAN	1,049,151	2,717,300	16,742,000	16	6	republic	Alma-Ata	Kazakh,Russian	rouble
KENYA	224,959	582,645	24,032,000	107	41	republic	Nairobi	Kiswahili,English	shilling
KIRGHIZIA (KYRGYZSTAN)	76,641	198,500	4,394,000	57	22	republic	Bishkek	Kirghiz,Russian	rouble
KIRIBATI	264	684	66,000	250	96	republic	Bairiki on Tarawa Atoll	English,Gilbertese, I-Kiribati	Australian dollar
KUWAIT	9375	24,280	2,143,000	229	88	emirate	Al Kuwayt (Kuwait)	Arabic	dinar
LAOS	91,400	236,725	4,139,000	45	17	people's republic	Vientiane (Viangchan)	Lao	new kip
LATVIA	24,595	63,700	2,686,000	109	42	republic	Rīga	Latvian,Russian	Latvian rouble
LEBANON	4015	10,400	2,701,000	673	260	republic	Bayrūt (Beirut)	Arabic	pound
LESOTHO	11,716	30,345	1,774,000	151	58	monarchy	Maseru	English,Sesotho	maluti
LIBERIA	43,000	111,370	2,607,000	61	23	republic	Monrovia	English	dollar
LIBYA	679,359	1,759,540	4,545,000	7	3	socialist state	Tarābulus (Tripoli)	Arabic	dinar
LIECHTENSTEIN	62	160	29,000	469	181	constitutional monarchy	Vaduz	German	Swiss franc
LITHUANIA	25,174	65,200	3,731,000	148	57	republic	Vilnius	Lithuanian	rouble,Litas prop.
LUXEMBOURG	998	2,585	381,000	382	147	constitutional monarchy	Luxembourg	Letzeburgish,French, German	franc
MADAGASCAR	229,413	594,180	11,197,000	49	19	republic	Antananarivo	Malagasy,French	Malagasy franc
MALAŴI	36,324	94,080	8,289,000	228	88	republic	Lilongwe	English,Chichewa	Kwacha
MALAYSIA	128,558	332,965	17,861,000	139	54	constitutional monarchy	Kuala Lumpur	Bahasa Malay	ringgit
MALDIVES	115	298	215,000	1869	721	republic	Malé	Divehi	rufiyaa
MALI	478,819	1,240,140	8,156,000	17	7	republic	Bamako	French,Bambara	CFA franc
MALTA	122	316	354,000	2901	1120	republic	Valletta	Maltese,English	pound
MARSHALL ISLANDS	70	181	40,000	572	221	republic	Dalap-Uliga-Darrit	Marshallese,English	US dollar
MAURITANIA	397,954	1,030,700	2,025,000	5	2	republic	Nouakchott	Arabic,French	ouguiya
MAURITIUS	720	1,865	1,075,000	1493	576	constitutional monarchy	Port Louis	English,Creole	rupee
MEXICO	761,600	1,972,545	86,154,000	113	44	federal republic	Ciudad de México (Mexico City)	Spanish	peso
MOLDAVIA (MOLDOVA)	13,012	33,700	4,368,000	336	130	republic	Kishinev	Romanian,Russian	rouble
MONACO	1	2	29,000	29,000	14500	constitutional monarchy	Monaco	French	French franc
MONGOLIA	604,247	1,565,000	2,190,000	4	1	republic	Ulaanbaatar (Ulan Bator)	Khalka Mongol	tugrik
MOROCCO	172,413	446,550	25,061,000	145	56	monarchy	Rabat	Arabic	dirham
MOZAMBIQUE	302,994	784,755	15,656,000	52	20	republic	Maputo	Portuguese	metical
NAMIBIA	318,261	824,295	1,781,000	6	2	republic	Windhoek	Afrikaans,English	Namibian dollar
NAURU	8	21	10,000	1233	476	republic	Yaren	Nauruan,English	Australian dollar
NEPAL	54,600	141,415	18,916,000	346	134	monarchy	Kathmandu	Nepali	rupee
NETHERLANDS	15,892	41,160	14,935,000	940	363	constitutional monarchy	Amsterdam	Dutch	guilder
NEW ZEALAND	102,375	265,150	3,346,000	33	13	constitutional monarchy	Wellington	English,Maori	dollar
NICARAGUA	57,143	148,000	3,871,000	68	26	republic	Managua	Spanish	córdoba
NIGER	458,073	1,186,410	7,732,000	17	7	republic	Niamey	French	CFA Franc
NIGERIA	356,699	923,850	88,500,000	248	96	federal republic	Abuja	English	naira
NORTH KOREA	47,224	122,310	21,773,000	461	178	people's republic	Pyŏngyang	Korean	won
NORWAY	125,056	323,895	4,242,000	34	13	constitutional monarchy	Oslo	Norwegian	krone
OMAN	105,000	271,950	1,502,000	14	6	sultanate	Masqaṭ (Muscat)	Arabic	rial
PAKISTAN	310,402	803,940	112,049,000	361	139	federal Islamic republic	Islāmābād	Urdu,Punjabi,English	rupee
PANAMA	30,315	78,515	2,418,000	80	31	republic	Panamá City	Spanish	balboa

NATIONS OF THE WORLD

COUNTRY	AREA miles²	AREA km²	POPULATION total	density per mile²	density per km²	FORM OF GOVERNMENT	CAPITAL CITY	MAIN LANGUAGES	CURRENCY
PAPUA NEW GUINEA	178,703	462,840	3,699,000	21	8	constitutional monarchy	Port Moresby	English,Pidgin,Motu	kina
PARAGUAY	157,046	406,750	4,277,000	27	11	republic	Asunción	Spanish,Guarani	guaraní
PERU	496,222	1,285,215	21,550,000	43	17	republic	Lima	Spanish,Quechua	sol
PHILIPPINES	115,830	300,000	61,480,000	531	205	republic	Manila	Pilipino,English	peso
POLAND	120,728	312,685	38,180,000	316	122	republic	Warszawa (Warsaw)	Polish	zloty
PORTUGAL	34,340	88,940	10,525,000	306	118	republic	Lisboa (Lisbon)	Portuguese	escudo
QATAR	4415	11,435	486,000	110	43	emirate	Ad Dawhaḩ (Doha)	Arabic	riyal
ROMANIA	91,699	237,500	23,200,000	253	98	republic	Bucureşti (Bucharest)	Romanian	leu
RUSSIAN FEDERATION	6,593,822	17,078,000	148,263,000	22	9	republic	Moskva (Moscow)	Russian	rouble
RWANDA	10,166	26,330	7,181,000	706	273	republic	Kigali	Kinyarwanda,French	franc
ST KITTS-NEVIS	101	261	44,000	437	169	constitutional monarchy	Basseterre	English	East Caribbean dollar
ST LUCIA	238	616	151,000	635	245	constitutional monarchy	Castries	English,French	East Caribbean dollar
ST VINCENT & THE GRENADINES	150	389	116,000	772	298	constitutional monarchy	Kingstown	English	East Caribbean dollar
SAN MARINO	24	61	24,000	1019	393	republic	San Marino	Italian	Italian lira
SÃO TOMÉ & PRÍNCIPE	372	964	121,000	325	126	republic	São Tomé	Portuguese,Creole	dobra
SAUDI ARABIA	926,988	2,400,900	14,870,000	16	6	monarchy	Ar Riyāḍ (Riyadh)	Arabic	riyal
SENEGAL	75,954	196,720	7,327,000	96	37	republic	Dakar	French	CFA franc
SEYCHELLES	156	404	67,000	430	166	republic	Victoria	English,French,Creole	rupee
SIERRA LEONE	27,925	72,325	4,151,000	149	57	republic	Freetown	English	leone
SINGAPORE	238	616	3,003,000	12,626	4875	republic	Singapore	Bahasa Malay,English, Chinese,Tamil	dollar
SLOVAKIA	18,933	49,035	5,300,000	278	108	republic	Bratislava	Slovak	koruna
SLOVENIA	7819	20,250	1,900,000	243	94	republic	Ljubljana	Slovene	dinar
SOLOMON ISLANDS	11,502	29,790	321,000	28	11	constitutional monarchy	Honiara	English	dollar
SOMALI REPUBLIC	243,243	630,000	7,497,000	31	12	republic	Muqdisho (Mogadishu)	Arabic,Somali,Italian, English	shilling
SOUTH AFRICA,REPUBLIC OF	457,461	1,184,825	35,282,000	77	30	republic	Cape Town (Kaapstad) / Pretoria	Afrikaans,English	rand
SOUTH KOREA	38,010	98,445	42,793,000	1126	435	republic	Sŏul (Seoul)	Korean	won
SPAIN	194,934	504,880	38,959,000	200	77	constitutional monarchy	Madrid	Spanish	peseta
SRI LANKA	25,332	65,610	16,993,000	671	259	republic	Colombo	Sinhala,Tamil	Rupee
SUDAN	967,496	2,505,815	25,204,000	26	10	military regime	Al Kharţūm (Khartoum)	Arabic	pound
SURINAM	53,251	163,820	422,000	7	3	republic	Paramaribo	Dutch,English	guilder
SWAZILAND	6705	17,365	768,000	115	44	monarchy	Mbabane	English,Siswati	lilangeni
SWEDEN	173,664	449,790	8,559,000	49	19	constitutional monarchy	Stockholm	Swedish	krona
SWITZERLAND	15,940	41,285	6,712,000	421	163	federal republic	Bern (Berne)	German,French,Italian, Romansh	franc
SYRIA	71,691	185,680	12,116,000	169	65	republic	Dimashq (Damascus)	Arabic	pound
TAIWAN	13,896	35,990	20,300,000	1461	564	republic	Taipei	Mandarin	dollar
TAJIKISTAN	55,251	143,100	5,303,000	96	37	republic	Dushanbe	Tajik,Russian	rouble
TANZANIA	362,842	939,760	25,635,000	71	27	republic	Dodoma	Kiswahili,English	shilling
THAILAND	198,456	514,000	57,196,000	288	111	monarchy	Bangkok (Krung Thep)	Thai	baht
TOGO	21,925	56,785	3,531,000	161	62	republic	Lomé	French	CFA franc
TONGA	270	699	95,000	352	136	constitutional monarchy	Nuku'alofa	English,Tongan	pa'anga
TRINIDAD AND TOBAGO	1981	5,130	1,227,000	619	239	republic	Port of Spain	English	dollar
TUNISIA	63,378	164,150	8,180,000	129	50	republic	Tunis	Arabic	dinar
TURKEY	300,946	779,450	56,098,000	186	72	republic	Ankara	Turkish	lira
TURKMENISTAN	188,456	488,100	3,670,000	19	8	republic	Ashkhabad	Turkmenian	rouble
TUVALU	10	25	10,000	1036	400	constitutional monarchy	Funafuti	English,Tuvaluan	Australian dollar
UGANDA	91,344	236,580	18,795,000	206	79	republic	Kampala	Kiswahili,English	shilling
UKRAINE	233,089	603,700	51,857,000	222	86	republic	Kiev	Ukrainian,Russian	rouble
UNITED ARAB EMIRATES	29,015	75,150	1,589,000	55	21	federation of emirates	Abū Ẓaby (Abu Dhabi)	Arabic	dirham
UNITED KINGDOM	94,500	244,755	57,411,000	608	235	constitutional monarchy	London	English	pound
UNITED STATES OF AMERICA	3,615,108	9,363,130	249,975,000	69	27	federal republic	Washington	English	dollar
URUGUAY	72,172	186,925	3,096,000	43	17	republic	Montevideo	Spanish	peso
UZBEKISTAN	172,741	447,400	20,531,000	119	46	republic	Tashkent	Uzbek,Russian	rouble
VANUATU	5701	14,765	147,000	26	10	republic	Vila	English,French,Bislama	vatu
VATICAN CITY	0.5	1	1000	2000	1000	ecclesiastical state	Vatican City	Italian	lira
VENEZUELA	352,141	912,045	19,735,000	56	22	federal republic	Caracas	Spanish	bolívar
VIETNAM	127,245	329,565	66,200,000	520	201	people's socialist republic	Hanoi	Vietnamese	dong
WESTERN SAMOA	1097	2,840	164,000	150	58	constitutional monarchy	Apia	Samoan,English	tala
YEMEN	203,850	527,969	11,282,000	55	21	republic	San'a	Arabic	rial,dinar
YUGOSLAVIA	49,376	127,885	10,000,000	203	78	federal republic	Beograd (Belgrade)	Serbo-Croat, Macedonian,Albanian	dinar
ZAÏRE	905,564	2,345,410	35,562,000	39	15	republic	Kinshasa	French,Lingala	zaïre
ZAMBIA	290,585	752,615	7,818,000	27	10	republic	Lusaka	English	kwacha
ZIMBABWE	150,699	390,310	9,369,000	62	24	republic	Harare	English	dollar

Introduction to World Index

The index includes an alphabetical list of all names appearing on the maps in the World Atlas section. Each entry indicates the country or region of the world in which the name is located. This is followed by a page reference and finally the name's location on the map, given by latitude and longitude co-ordinates. Most features are indexed to the largest scale map on which they appear, however when the name applies to countries or other extensive features it is generally indexed to the map on which it appears in its entirety. Areal features are generally indexed using co-ordinates which indicate the centre of the feature. The latitude and longitude indicated for a point feature gives the location of the point on the map. In the case of rivers the mouth or confluence is always taken as the point of reference.

Names in the index are generally in the local language and where a conventional English version exists, this is cross referenced to the entry in the local language. Names of features which extend across the boundaries of more than one country are usually named in English if no single official name exists. Names in languages not written in the Roman alphabet have been transliterated using the official system of the country if one exists, e.g. Pinyin system for China, otherwise the systems recognised by the United States Board on Geographical Names have been used.

Names abbreviated on the maps are given in full in the Index. Abbreviations are used for both geographical terms and administrative names in the Index. All abbreviations used in the Index are listed below.

Abbreviations of Geographical Terms

b., **B.**	bay, Bay
c., **C.**	cape, Cape
d.	internal division e.g county, region, state
des.	desert
est.	estuary
f.	physical feature e.g. valley, plain, geographic district or region
g., **G.**	gulf, Gulf
i., **I.**, **is.**, **Is.**	island, Island, islands, Islands
l., **L.**	lake, Lake
mtn., Mtn.	mountain, Mountain
mts., Mts.	mountains, Mountains
pen., Pen.	peninsula, Peninsula
Pt.	Point
r.	river
resr., Resr.	reservoir, Reservoir
Sd.	Sound
str., Str.	strait, Strait

Abbreviations of Country / Administrative Names

Afghan.	Afghanistan	Man.	Manitoba	Raj.	Rājasthān
A.H. Prov.	Alpes de Haut Provence	Mass.	Massachusetts	Rep. of Ire.	Republic of Ireland
Ala.	Alabama	Md.	Maryland	Rhein.-Pfalz	Rheinland-Pfalz
Alas.	Alaska	Mich.	Michigan	R.I.	Rhode Island
Alta.	Alberta	Minn.	Minnesota	R.S.A.	Republic of South Africa
Ariz.	Arizona	Miss.	Mississippi	Russian Fed.	Russian Federation
Ark.	Arkansas	Mo.	Missouri	S.A.	South Australia
Baja Calif.	Baja California	Mont.	Montana	Sask.	Saskatchewan
Baja Calif. Sur	Baja California Sur	M.-Pyr.	Midi-Pyrénées	S.C.	South Carolina
Bangla.	Bangladesh	N.B.	New Brunswick	Sch.-Hol.	Schleswig-Holstein
B.C.	British Columbia	N.C.	North Carolina	S. Dak.	South Dakota
Bos.-Her.	Bosnia-Herzegovina	N. Dak.	North Dakota	S. Korea	South Korea
B.-Würt	Baden-Württemberg	Nebr.	Nebraska	S. Mar.	Seine Maritime
Calif.	California	Neth.	Netherlands	Sogn og Fj.	Sogn og Fjordane
C.A.R.	Central African Republic	Nev.	Nevada	Somali Rep.	Somali Republic
Char. Mar.	Charente Maritime	Nfld.	Newfoundland	Switz.	Switzerland
Colo.	Colorado	N.H.	New Hampshire	Tas.	Tasmania
Conn.	Connecticut	N. Ireland	Northern Ireland	Tenn.	Tennessee
C.P.	Cape Province	N.J.	New Jersey	Tex.	Texas
D.C.	District of Columbia	N. Korea	North Korea	T.G.	Tarn-et-Garonne
Del.	Delaware	N. Mex	New Mexico	Trans.	Transvaal
Dom. Rep.	Dominican Republic	Nschn.	Niedersachsen	U.A.E.	United Arab Emirates
Equat. Guinea	Equatorial Guinea	N.S.W.	New South Wales	U.K.	United Kingdom
Eth.	Ethiopia	N. Trönd.	North Tröndelag	U.S.A.	United States of America
Fla.	Florida	N.T.	Northern Territory	Uttar P.	Uttar Pradesh
Ga.	Georgia	N.-Westfalen	Nordrhein-Westfalen	Va.	Virginia
Guang. Zhuang	Guangxi Zhuangzu	N.W.T.	Northwest Territories	Vic.	Victoria
H.-Gar.	Haute Garonne	N.Y.	New York State	Vt.	Vermont
Himachal P.	Himachal Pradesh	O.F.S.	Orange Free State	W.A.	Western Australia
H. Zaïre	Haut Zaïre	Okla.	Oklahoma	Wash.	Washington
Ill.	Illinois	Ont.	Ontario	W. Bengal	West Bengal
Ind.	Indiana	Oreg.	Oregon	Wisc.	Wisconsin
Kans.	Kansas	P.E.I.	Prince Edward Island	W. Sahara	Western Sahara
K. Occidental	Kasai Occidental	Penn.	Pennsylvania	W. Va.	West Virginia
K. Oriental	Kasai Oriental	Phil.	Philippines	Wyo.	Wyoming
Ky.	Kentucky	P.N.G.	Papua New Guinea	Xin. Uygur	Xinjiang Uygur Zizhiqu
La.	Louisiana	Poit.-Char.	Poitou-Charente	Yugo.	Yugoslavia
Liech.	Liechtenstein	Pyr. Or.	Pyrénées Orientales		
Lux.	Luxembourg	Qld.	Queensland		
Madhya P.	Madhya Pradesh	Que.	Québec		

Aachen to Aldershot

A

Aachen Germany 14 50.46N 6.06E
A 'âlî an Nîl d. Sudan 49 9.35N 31.05E
Aalsmeer Neth. 14 52.17N 4.46E
Aalst Belgium 14 50.57N 4.03E
Äänekoski Finland 22 62.36N 25.44E
Aarau Switz. 20 47.24N 8.04E
Aardenburg Neth. 14 51.16N 3.26E
Aare r. Switz. 20 47.37N 8.13E
Aarschot Belgium 14 50.59N 4.50E
Aba China 39 32.55N 101.42E
Aba Nigeria 53 5.06N 7.21E
Aba Zaïre 49 3.52N 30.14E
Abâ as Su'ûd Saudi Arabia 45 17.28N 44.06E
Abadab, Jabal mtn. Sudan 48 18.53N 35.59E
Âbâdân Iran 43 30.21N 48.15E
Abadan, Jazîreh-ye i. Iran 43 30.10N 48.30E
Âbâdeh Iran 43 31.10N 52.40E
Abadla Algeria 50 31.01N 2.44W
Abaetetuba Brazil 91 1.45S 48.54W
Abagnar Qi China 32 43.58N 116.02E
Abag Qi China 32 43.53N 114.33E
Abaí Paraguay 92 26.01S 55.57W
Abajo Peak mtn. U.S.A. 80 37.51N 109.28W
Abakaliki Nigeria 53 6.17N 8.04E
Abakan Russian Fed. 29 53.43N 91.25E
Abalessa Algeria 51 22.54N 4.50E
Abancay Peru 92 13.35S 72.55W
Abariringa i. Kiribati 68 2.50S 171.40W
Âbâr Murrât wells Sudan 48 21.03N 32.55E
Abasolo Mexico 83 25.18N 104.40W
Abau P.N.G. 64 10.10S 148.40E
Abay Kazakhstan 28 49.40N 72.47E
Âbây r. Ethiopia see Azraq, Al Baḩr al r. r. Sudan 48
Âbaya Hâyk' l. Ethiopia 49 6.20N 37.55E
Abba C.A.R. 53 5.20N 15.11E
Abbeville France 17 50.06N 1.51E
Abbeville La. U.S.A. 83 29.58N 92.08W
Abbeville S.C. U.S.A. 85 34.10N 82.23W
Abbiategrasso Italy 15 45.24N 8.54E
Abbotsbury U.K. 11 50.40N 2.36W
Abbotsford Canada 77 45.27N 72.55W
Abbottâbâd Pakistan 40 34.09N 73.13E
'Abd al Kûrî i. Yemen 45 12.12N 52.13E
Abdulino Russian Fed. 24 53.42N 53.40E
Abéché Chad 48 13.49N 20.49E
Âbeltî Ethiopia 49 8.10N 37.37E
Abengourou Ivory Coast 52 6.42N 3.27W
Âbenrå Denmark 23 55.02N 9.26E
Abeokuta Nigeria 53 7.10N 3.26E
Aberayron U.K. 11 52.15N 4.16W
Abercrombie r. Australia 67 33.50S 149.10E
Aberdare U.K. 11 51.43N 3.27W
Aberdare Range mts. Kenya 55 0.20S 36.40E
Aberdeen Australia 67 32.10S 150.54E
Aberdeen R.S.A. 56 32.28S 24.03E
Aberdeen U.K. 12 57.08N 2.07W
Aberdeen Md. U.S.A. 85 39.30N 76.10W
Aberdeen Miss. U.S.A. 83 33.49N 88.33W
Aberdeen Ohio U.S.A. 84 38.39N 83.46W
Aberdeen S. Dak. U.S.A. 82 45.28N 98.29W
Aberdeen Wash. U.S.A. 80 46.59N 123.50W
Aberdovey U.K. 11 52.33N 4.03W
Aberfeldy U.K. 12 56.37N 3.54W
Abergavenny U.K. 11 51.49N 3.01W
Abersoch U.K. 10 52.50N 4.31W
Aberystwyth U.K. 11 52.25N 4.06W
Abetone Italy 15 44.08N 10.40E
Abez Russian Fed. 24 66.33N 61.51E
Abhâ Saudi Arabia 48 18.13N 42.30E
Abhar Iran 43 36.09N 49.13E
Âbhê Bid Hâyk l. Ethiopia 49 11.06N 41.50E
Abia d. Nigeria 53 5.45N 7.40E
Abidjan Ivory Coast 52 5.19N 4.01W
Abilene Kans. U.S.A. 82 38.55N 97.13W
Abilene Tex. U.S.A. 83 32.27N 99.44W
Abingdon U.K. 11 51.40N 1.17W
Abisko Sweden 22 68.20N 18.51E
Abitau r. Canada 75 59.53N 109.03W
Abitibi r. Canada 76 51.03N 80.55W
Abitibi, L. Canada 76 48.42N 79.45W
Âbiy Âdî Ethiopia 49 13.36N 39.00E
Abnûb Egypt 42 27.16N 31.09E
Âbo see Turku Finland 23
Abohar India 40 30.08N 74.12E
Abomey Benin 53 7.14N 2.00E
Abong Mbang Cameroon 53 3.59N 13.12E
Abou Deïa Chad 53 11.20N 19.20E
Aboyne U.K. 12 57.05N 2.48W
Abrantes Portugal 16 39.28N 8.12W
'Abrî Sudan 48 20.48N 30.20E
Abring Jammu & Kashmir 40 33.42N 76.35E
Abrud Romania 21 46.17N 23.04E
Abruzzi d. Italy 18 42.05N 13.45E
Absaroka Range mts. U.S.A. 80 44.45N 109.50W
Absecon U.S.A. 85 39.26N 74.30W
Abû 'Arîsh Saudi Arabia 45 16.58N 42.50E
Abû Baḩr f. Saudi Arabia 45 21.30N 48.15E
Abû Ballâş hill Egypt 48 24.26N 27.39E
Abu Dhabi see Abû Ẓaby U.A.E. 43
Abû Dharbah Egypt 44 28.29N 33.20E
Abû Dulayq Sudan 48 15.54N 33.49E
Abû Ḩamad Sudan 48 19.32N 33.19E
Abû Ḩarâz Sudan 48 19.04N 32.07E
Abuja Nigeria 53 9.12N 7.11E
Abû Jâbirah Sudan 49 11.04N 26.51E
Abû Kabîr Egypt 44 30.44N 31.40E
Abû Kamâl Syria 42 34.27N 40.55E
Abû Madd, Ra's c. Saudi Arabia 42 24.50N 37.07E
Abû Maţâriq Sudan 49 10.58N 26.17E
Abunã Brazil 90 9.41S 65.20W
Abû Qurqâş Egypt 44 27.56N 30.50E
Abu Road town India 40 24.29N 72.47E
Abû Shajarah, Ra's c. Sudan 48 21.04N 37.14E
Abû Shanab Sudan 49 10.47N 29.32E
Abû Sulţân Egypt 44 30.25N 32.19E
Abû Sunbul Egypt 42 22.18N 31.40E
Abû Ţabarî well Sudan 48 17.35N 28.31E
Abû Ţarafah Jordan 44 30.00N 35.56E
Abû Tîj Egypt 42 27.06N 31.17E
Abuya Mexico 81 24.16N 107.01W
Âbuyê Mêda mtn. Ethiopia 49 10.28N 39.44E
Abû Zabad Sudan 49 12.21N 29.15E
Abû Ẓaby U.A.E. 43 24.27N 54.23E
Abû Zanîmah Egypt 44 29.03N 33.06E
Abwong Sudan 49 9.07N 32.12E
Âby Sweden 23 58.40N 16.11E
Abyaḑ Sudan 48 13.46N 26.28E
Abyaḑ, Al Baḩr al r. Sudan 48 15.38N 32.31E
Abyâr ash Shuwayrif wells Libya 51 29.59N 14.16E
Abyei Sudan 49 9.36N 28.26E
Acacio Mexico 83 24.50N 102.44W
Acadia Valley town Canada 75 51.08N 110.13W
Acámbaro Mexico 86 20.01N 101.42W
Acapulco Mexico 86 16.51N 99.56W
Acará Brazil 91 1.57S 48.11W
Acarigua Venezuela 90 9.35N 69.12W
Acatlán Mexico 86 18.12N 98.02W
Accra Ghana 52 5.33N 0.15W
Accrington U.K. 10 53.46N 2.22W
Aceh d. Indonesia 36 4.00N 97.30E
Acevedo Argentina 93 33.46S 60.27W
Achacachi Bolivia 92 16.03S 68.43W
Achalpur India 41 21.16N 77.31E
Achar Uruguay 93 32.25S 56.10W
Acheng China 31 45.32N 126.59E
Achill I. Rep. of Ire. 13 53.57N 10.00W
Âchîn Afghan. 40 34.08N 70.42E
Achinsk Russian Fed. 28 56.10N 90.10E
Acklin's I. Bahamas 87 22.30N 74.10W
Aconcagua mtn. Argentina 92 32.39S 70.00W
Açores, Arquipélago dos is. Atlantic Oc. 95 38.30N 28.00W
A Coruña see La Coruña Spain 16
Acqui Italy 15 44.41N 8.28E
Acraman, L. Australia 66 32.02S 135.26E
Acre d. Brazil 90 8.50S 71.30W
Acton Canada 76 43.37N 80.02W
Acton Vale Canada 77 45.39N 72.34W
Açu Brazil 91 5.35S 36.57W
Acuña Argentina 93 29.54S 57.57W
Ada U.S.A. 83 34.46N 96.41W
Âdaba Ethiopia 49 7.07N 39.20E
Adair, Bahía de b. Mexico 81 31.30N 113.50W
Adair, C. Canada 73 71.24N 71.13W
Adam Oman 45 22.23N 57.32E
Adamantina Brazil 94 21.42S 51.04W
Adamaoua, Massif de l' mts. Cameroon / Nigeria 53 7.05N 12.00E
Adamawa d. Nigeria 53 9.55N 12.30E
Adamello mtn. Italy 15 46.10N 10.35E
Adaminaby Australia 67 36.04S 148.42E
Adamintina Brazil 92 21.42S 51.04W
Adams U.S.A. 84 43.49N 76.01W
Adams, Mt. U.S.A. 80 46.12N 121.28W
'Adan Yemen 45 12.50N 45.00E
Adana Turkey 42 37.00N 35.19E
Adapazari Turkey 42 40.45N 30.23E
Adarama Sudan 48 17.05N 34.54E
Adare, C. Antarctica 96 71.30S 171.00E
Adavale Australia 64 25.55S 144.36E
Adda r. Italy 15 45.08N 9.55E
Aḑ Ḑab'ah Egypt 42 31.02N 28.26E
Ad Dabbah Sudan 48 18.03N 30.57E
Ad Dafinah Saudi Arabia 42 23.18N 41.58E
Ad Dahnâ' des. Saudi Arabia 43 26.00N 47.00E
Ad Dâmir Sudan 48 17.35N 33.58E
Ad Dammâm Saudi Arabia 43 26.23N 50.08E
Ad Darb Saudi Arabia 48 17.44N 42.15E
Ad Dawâdimî Saudi Arabia 43 24.29N 44.23E
Ad Dawḩah Qatar 43 25.15N 51.34E
Aḑ Ḑiffah f. Africa 42 30.45N 26.00E
Ad Dikâkah f. Saudi Arabia 45 19.25N 51.30E
Ad Dilam Saudi Arabia 43 23.59N 47.10E
Ad Dimâs Syria 44 33.35N 36.05E
Addis Ababa see Âdîs Âbeba Ethiopia 49
Ad Dîwânîyah Iraq 43 31.59N 44.57E
Ad Du'ayn Sudan 49 11.26N 26.09E
Ad Duwaym Sudan 48 14.00N 32.19E
Adel U.S.A. 85 31.07N 83.27W
Adelaide Australia 66 34.56S 138.36E
Adelaide Pen. Canada 73 68.09N 97.45W
Adelaide River town Australia 62 13.14S 131.06E
Adelong Australia 67 35.21S 148.04E
Aden see 'Adan Yemen 45
Aden, G. of Indian Oc. 45 13.00N 50.00E
Adendorp R.S.A. 56 32.18S 24.31E
Adi i. Indonesia 37 4.10S 133.10E
Âdî Da'iro Ethiopia 48 14.27N 38.16E
Adieu, C. Australia 63 31.59S 132.09E
Âdîgala Ethiopia 49 10.25N 42.17E
Adige r. Italy 15 45.10N 12.20E
Âdîgrat Ethiopia 48 14.18N 39.31E
Âdî K'eyih Ethiopia 48 14.49N 39.23E
Âdilâbâd India 41 19.40N 78.32E
Adilang Uganda 55 2.44N 33.28E
Adin U.S.A. 80 41.12N 120.57W
Adirondack Mts. U.S.A. 84 44.00N 74.00W
Âdîs Âbeba Ethiopia 49 9.03N 38.42E
Âdî Ugrî Ethiopia 48 14.55N 38.53E
Adiyaman Turkey 42 37.46N 38.15E
Adjud Romania 21 46.04N 27.11E
Admer well Algeria 51 20.23N 5.27E
Admiralty G. Australia 62 14.20S 125.50E
Admiralty I. U.S.A. 74 57.50N 134.30W
Admiralty Is. P.N.G. 37 2.30S 147.20E
Admiralty Range mts. Antarctica 96 72.00S 164.00E
Adour r. France 17 43.28N 1.35W
Adra Spain 16 36.43N 3.03W
Adrano Italy 18 37.39N 14.49E
Adrar d. Mauritania 50 21.00N 10.00W
Adrar des Iforas mts. Mali / Algeria 51 20.00N 2.30E
Adraskan Afghan. 40 33.39N 62.16E
Adria Italy 15 45.03N 12.03E
Adrian Mich. U.S.A. 84 41.55N 84.01W
Adrian Mo. U.S.A. 82 38.24N 94.21W
Adrian Tex. U.S.A. 83 35.16N 102.40W
Adriatic Sea Med. Sea 18 42.30N 16.00E
Âdwa Ethiopia 48 14.12N 38.56E
Adzopé Ivory Coast 52 6.07N 3.49W
Adzva r. Russian Fed. 24 66.30N 59.30E
Aegean Sea Med. Sea 19 39.00N 25.00E
Âfdem Ethiopia 49 9.26N 41.02E
Afghanistan Asia 40 32.45N 65.00E
'Afif Saudi Arabia 42 23.53N 42.59E
Afikpo Nigeria 53 5.53N 7.55E
Afjord Norway 22 63.57N 10.12E
Aflou Algeria 51 34.07N 2.06E
Afmadow Somali Rep. 55 0.27N 42.05E
Afobaka Surinam 91 5.00N 55.05W
Afognak I. U.S.A. 72 58.15N 152.30W
Afonso Cláudio Brazil 94 20.05S 41.06W
Afsluitdijk f. Neth. 14 53.04N 5.11E
'Afula Israel 44 32.36N 35.17E
Afyon Turkey 42 38.46N 30.32E
Agadez Niger 53 17.00N 7.56E
Agadez d. Niger 53 19.25N 11.00E
Agadir Morocco 50 30.26N 9.36W
Agalak Sudan 49 11.01N 32.42E
Agana Guam 68 13.28N 144.45E
Agapa Russian Fed. 29 71.29N 86.16E
Agar India 40 23.42N 76.01E
Âgaro Ethiopia 49 7.50N 36.40E
Agartala India 41 23.49N 91.16E
Agaru Sudan 49 10.59N 34.44E
Agboville Ivory Coast 52 5.55N 4.15W
Agde France 17 43.19N 3.28E
Agen France 17 44.12N 0.38E
Ageo Japan 35 35.58N 139.36E
Agger r. Germany 14 50.45N 7.06E
Aghada Rep. of Ire. 13 51.50N 8.13W
Agia India 41 26.05N 90.32E
Aginskoye Russian Fed. 29 51.10N 114.32E
Agnew Australia 63 28.01S 120.30E
Ago Japan 35 34.17N 136.48E
Agordo Italy 15 46.17N 12.02E
Agouma Gabon 54 1.33S 10.08E
Âgra India 41 27.11N 78.01E
Agra r. Spain 16 42.12N 1.43W
Agraciada Uruguay 93 33.48S 58.15W
Agreda Spain 16 41.51N 1.55W
Agri r. Italy 19 40.13N 16.45E
Agri Turkey 42 39.44N 43.04E
Agri Dagi mtn. Turkey 43 39.45N 44.15E
Agrigento Italy 18 37.19N 13.36E
Agropoli Italy 18 40.21N 15.00E
Agryz Russian Fed. 24 56.30N 53.00E
Agsumal, Sebjet f. W. Sahara 50 24.21N 12.52W
Agua Caliente, Cerro mtn. Mexico 81 26.27N 106.12W
Aguanish Canada 77 50.16N 62.10W
Aguanus r. Canada 77 50.12N 62.10W
Agua Prieta Mexico 81 31.18N 109.34W
Aguas Blancas Chile 92 24.13S 69.50W
Aguascalientes Mexico 86 21.51N 102.18W
Aguascalientes d. Mexico 86 22.00N 102.00W
Agudos Brazil 94 22.27S 49.03W
Águeda r. Spain 16 41.00N 6.56W
Aguelhok Mali 50 19.28N 0.52E
Aguema Angola 54 12.03S 21.52E
Aguêraktem well Mali 50 23.07N 6.12W
Aguilar de Campóo Spain 16 42.47N 4.15W
Aguilas Spain 16 37.25N 1.35W
Aguit China 32 41.42N 113.20E
Âgula'i Ethiopia 48 13.42N 39.35E
Agulhas, C. R.S.A. 56 34.50S 20.00E
Agulhas Basin f. Indian Oc. 95 43.00S 25.00E
Agulhas Negras mtn. Brazil 94 22.20S 44.43W
Agung, Gunung mtn. Indonesia 37 8.20S 115.28E
Ahaggar f. Algeria 51 23.36N 5.50E
Ahar Iran 43 38.25N 47.07E
Ahaura New Zealand 60 42.21S 171.33E
Ahaus Germany 14 52.04N 7.01E
Ahklun Mts. U.S.A. 72 59.15N 161.00W
Ahlen Germany 14 51.47N 7.52E
Ahmadâbâd India 40 23.02N 72.37E
Aḩmadî Iran 43 27.56N 56.42E
Ahmadnagar India 40 19.05N 74.44E
Ahmadpur East Pakistan 40 29.09N 71.16E
Ahmadpur Siâl Pakistan 40 30.41N 71.46E
Ahmad Wâl Pakistan 40 29.25N 65.56E
Ahmar Mts. Ethiopia 49 9.15N 41.00E
Ahoada Nigeria 53 5.06N 6.39E
Ahr r. Germany 14 50.34N 7.16E
Ahram Iran 43 28.52N 51.16E
Ahraura India 41 25.01N 83.01E
Aḩsâ', Wâḩat al oasis Saudi Arabia 43 25.37N 49.40E
Ähtäri Finland 22 62.34N 24.06E
Âhus Sweden 23 55.55N 14.17E
Ahvâz Iran 43 31.17N 48.44E
Ahvenanmaa d. Finland 23 60.15N 20.00E
Ahvenanmaa is. Finland 23 60.15N 20.00E
Aichi d. Japan 35 35.02N 137.15E
Aigle Switz. 15 46.19N 6.58E
Aigues-Mortes France 17 43.34N 4.11E
Aiken U.S.A. 85 33.34N 81.44W
Aileron Australia 64 22.38S 133.20E
Ailette r. France 14 49.35N 3.09E
Ailsa Craig i. U.K. 12 55.15N 5.07W
Aim Russian Fed. 29 58.50N 134.15E
Aimorés Brazil 94 19.30S 41.04W
Ain r. France 17 45.47N 5.12E
Aïna r. Gabon 54 0.38N 12.47E
Ainaži Estonia 23 57.52N 24.21E
Aïn Beïda Algeria 51 35.50N 7.27E
Aïn ben Tili Mauritania 50 26.00N 9.32W
Aïn Galakka Chad 51 18.04N 18.24E
Aïn Sefra Algeria 50 32.45N 0.35W
Aïr mts. Niger 53 18.30N 8.30E
Airdrie U.K. 12 55.52N 3.59W
Aire France 17 43.39N 0.15W
Aire r. France 15 49.19N 4.49E
Aire r. U.K. 10 53.42N 0.54W
Aisne d. France 15 49.30N 3.30E
Aisne r. France 15 49.27N 2.51E
Aitape P.N.G. 37 3.10S 142.17E
Aitkin U.S.A. 82 46.32N 93.43W
Aït Ourir Morocco 50 31.38N 7.42W
Aitutaki Atoll Cook Is. 69 18.52S 159.46W
Aiud Romania 21 46.19N 23.44E
Aix-en-Provence France 17 43.31N 5.27E
Aix-les-Bains France 17 45.42N 5.55E
Aíyina i. Greece 19 37.43N 23.30E
Aíyion Greece 19 38.15N 22.05E
Aizpute Latvia 23 56.43N 21.38E
Ajaccio France 17 41.55N 8.43E
Ajanta Range mts. India 40 20.15N 75.30E
Ajax Canada 76 43.51N 79.02W
Ajdâbiyâ Libya 48 30.46N 20.14E
Ajibar Ethiopia 49 10.41N 38.37E
'Ajlûn Jordan 44 32.20N 35.45E
'Ajmah, Jabal al f. Egypt 44 29.12N 33.58E
'Ajmân U.A.E. 43 25.23N 55.26E
Ajmer India 40 26.27N 74.38E
Ajnâla India 40 31.51N 74.47E
Ajo U.S.A. 81 32.22N 112.52W
Akaishi sammyaku mts. Japan 35 35.20N 138.10E
Akámas, Akrotírion c. Cyprus 44 35.06N 32.17E
Akaroa New Zealand 60 43.50S 172.59E
'Akasha East Sudan 48 21.05N 30.43E
Akashi Japan 35 34.38N 134.59E
Akbarpur India 41 26.25N 82.33E
Akbulak Russian Fed. 25 51.00N 55.40E
Akelamo Indonesia 37 1.35N 129.40E
Akershus d. Norway 23 60.00N 11.10E
Aketi Zaïre 54 2.46N 23.51E
Akhaltsikhe Georgia 42 41.37N 42.59E
Akhḑar, Al Jabal al mts. Libya 48 32.30N 21.30E
Akhḑar, Al Jabal al mts. Oman 43 23.10N 57.25E
Akhḑar, Wâdî r. Egypt 44 28.42N 33.41E
Akhḑar, Wâdî al r. Saudi Arabia 44 28.30N 36.48E
Akhelóös Greece 19 38.20N 21.04E
Akhisar Turkey 19 38.54N 27.49E
Akhmîm Egypt 42 26.34N 31.44E
Akhtyrka Ukraine 25 50.19N 34.54E
Akimiski I. Canada 76 53.00N 81.20W
Akita Japan 35 39.44N 140.05E
Akjoujt Mauritania 50 19.44N 14.26W
Akkajaure l. Sweden 22 67.40N 17.30E
'Akko Israel 44 32.55N 35.04E
Akkol Kazakhstan 30 45.04N 75.39E
Aklavik Canada 72 68.12N 135.00W
Ako Nigeria 53 10.19N 10.48E
Âkobo r. Ethiopia 49 8.30N 33.15E
Akola India 40 20.44N 77.00E
Âk'ordat Ethiopia 48 15.35N 37.55E
Akot India 40 21.11N 77.04E
Akpatok I. Canada 73 60.30N 68.30W
Akranes Iceland 22 64.19N 22.05W
Akron Colo. U.S.A. 82 40.10N 103.13W
Akron Ohio U.S.A. 84 41.04N 81.31W
Akrotíri Cyprus 44 34.36N 32.57E
Aksaray Turkey 42 38.22N 34.02E
Aksarka Russian Fed. 28 66.31N 67.50E
Aksay China 30 39.28N 94.15E
Aksay Kazakhstan 25 51.24N 52.11E
Akşehir Turkey 42 38.22N 31.24E
Aksu China 30 42.10N 80.00E
Âksum Ethiopia 48 14.08N 38.48E
Aktag mtn. China 30 36.45N 84.40E
Aktogay Kazakhstan 30 46.59N 79.42E
Aktyubinsk Kazakhstan 25 50.16N 57.13E
Akûbû Sudan 49 7.47N 33.01E
Akûbû r. see Âkobo r. Sudan 49
Akula Zaïre 54 2.22N 20.11E
Akure Nigeria 53 7.14N 5.08E
Akureyri Iceland 22 65.41N 18.04W
Akuse Ghana 52 6.04N 0.12E
Akwa-Ibom d. Nigeria 53 4.45N 7.50E
Akxokesay China 30 36.48N 91.06E
Akyab see Sittwe Burma 34
Akyel Ethiopia 49 12.30N 37.04E
Âl Norway 23 60.38N 8.34E
Alabama d. U.S.A. 85 32.50N 87.00W
Alabama r. U.S.A. 83 31.08N 87.57W
Al 'Abbâsîyah Sudan 49 14.27N 33.31E
Alâdâgh, Kûh-e mts. Iran 43 37.15N 57.30E
Alagoas d. Brazil 91 9.30S 37.00W
Alagoinhas Brazil 91 12.09S 38.21W
Alagón Spain 16 41.46N 1.12W
Alakol, Ozero l. Kazakhstan 30 46.00N 81.40E
Alakurtti Russian Fed. 24 67.00N 30.23E
Al 'Alamayn Egypt 42 30.49N 28.57E
Al 'Amârah Iraq 43 31.52N 47.50E
Al Âmirîyah Egypt 44 31.01N 29.48E
Alamogordo U.S.A. 81 32.54N 105.57W
Alamos, Rio de los r. Mexico 83 27.53N 101.12W
Alamosa U.S.A. 80 37.28N 105.52W
Åland is. see Ahvenanmaa is. Finland 23
Ålands Hav sea Finland 23 60.00N 19.30E
Alanreed U.S.A. 83 35.14N 100.45W
Alanya Turkey 42 36.32N 32.02E
Alaotra, Lac l. Madagascar 57 17.30S 48.30E
Alapayevsk Russian Fed. 24 57.55N 61.42E
Alappuzha India 38 9.30N 76.22E
Al 'Aqabah Jordan 44 29.32N 35.00E
Al 'Aramah f. Saudi Arabia 43 25.30N 46.30E
Alarcón, Embalse de resr. Spain 16 39.36N 2.10W
Al 'Arish Egypt 44 31.08N 33.48E
Alaşehir Turkey 19 38.22N 28.29E
Alaska d. U.S.A. 72 65.00N 153.00W
Alaska, G. of U.S.A. 72 58.45N 145.00W
Alaska Pen. U.S.A. 72 56.00N 160.00W
Alaska Range mts. U.S.A. 72 62.10N 152.00W
Alassio Italy 15 44.00N 8.10E
Al 'Atiqah Lebanon 44 33.42N 35.27E
Al 'Aţrun Sudan 48 18.11N 26.36E
Alatyr Russian Fed. 24 54.51N 46.35E
Alausí Ecuador 90 2.00S 78.50W
Alavus Finland 22 62.35N 23.37E
Alawoona Australia 66 34.44S 140.33E
Al 'Ayn wells Sudan 48 16.36N 29.19E
Al 'Ayyâţ Egypt 44 29.37N 31.15E
Alazani r. Georgia 43 41.06N 46.40E
Alba Italy 15 44.42N 8.02E
Albacete Spain 16 39.00N 1.52W
Al Bad' Saudi Arabia 44 28.29N 35.02E
Al Badârî Egypt 42 26.59N 31.25E
Al Bahnasâ Egypt 44 28.32N 30.39E
Al Baḩr al Aḩmar d. Sudan 48 19.30N 35.30E
Alba-Iulia Romania 21 46.04N 23.33E
Albania Europe 19 41.00N 20.00E
Albany Australia 63 34.57S 117.54E
Albany r. Canada 76 52.10N 82.00W
Albany Ga. U.S.A. 85 31.37N 84.10W
Albany Ky. U.S.A. 85 36.42N 85.08W
Albany Minn. U.S.A. 82 45.38N 94.34W
Albany N.Y. U.S.A. 84 42.39N 73.45W
Albany Oreg. U.S.A. 80 44.38N 123.06W
Al Başrah Iraq 43 30.33N 47.50E
Al Bâţinah f. Oman 43 24.25N 56.50E
Albatross B. Australia 64 12.45S 141.43E
Al Batrûn Lebanon 44 34.16N 35.40E
Al Bawîţî Egypt 42 28.21N 25.52E
Al Bayâḑ f. Saudi Arabia 45 22.00N 47.00E
Al Bayḑâ' Libya 51 32.46N 21.43E
Albemarle Sd. U.S.A. 79 36.10N 76.00W
Albenga Italy 15 44.03N 8.13E
Alberche r. Spain 16 40.00N 4.45W
Alberga Australia 65 27.12S 135.28E
Alberga r. Australia 65 27.12S 135.28E
Albermarle U.S.A. 85 35.21N 80.12W
Albermarle Sd. U.S.A. 85 36.03N 76.12W
Albert Australia 67 32.21S 147.33E
Albert France 14 50.02N 2.38E
Albert, L. Australia 66 35.38S 139.17E
Albert, L. Uganda / Zaïre 55 1.45N 31.00E
Alberta d. Canada 74 54.00N 115.00W
Alberti Argentina 93 35.01S 60.16W
Albertirsa Hungary 21 47.15N 19.38E
Albert Kanaal canal Belgium 14 51.00N 5.15E
Albert Lea U.S.A. 82 43.39N 93.22W
Albert Nile r. Uganda 55 3.30N 32.00E
Alberton Canada 77 46.49N 64.04W
Albi France 17 43.56N 2.08E
Al Bidia Chad 49 10.33N 20.13E
Albin U.S.A. 80 41.26N 104.08W
Albina Surinam 91 5.30N 54.03W
Albino Italy 15 45.46N 9.47E
Albion Mich. U.S.A. 84 42.14N 84.45W
Albion Mont. U.S.A. 80 45.11N 104.15W
Albion Nebr. U.S.A. 82 41.42N 98.00W
Albion N.Y. U.S.A. 76 43.15N 78.12W
Albion Penn. U.S.A. 84 41.53N 80.22W
Al Bi'r Saudi Arabia 44 28.52N 36.15E
Alborán, Isla de i. Spain 16 35.55N 3.10W
Ålborg Denmark 23 57.03N 9.56E
Ålborg Bugt b. Denmark 23 56.45N 10.30E
Alborz, Reshteh-ye Kûhhâ-ye mts. Iran 43 36.00N 52.30E
Albuquerque U.S.A. 81 35.05N 106.40W
Al Buraymî U.A.E. 43 24.15N 55.45E
Al Burj Egypt 44 31.35N 30.59E
Alburquerque Spain 16 39.13N 6.59W
Albury Australia 67 36.03S 146.53E
Al Buţanah f. Sudan 48 14.50N 34.30E
Alby Sweden 22 62.30N 15.25E
Alcácer do Sal Portugal 16 38.22N 8.30W
Alcalá de Chisvert Spain 16 40.19N 0.13E
Alcalá de Henares Spain 16 40.28N 3.22W
Alcalá la Real Spain 16 37.28N 3.55W
Alcamo Italy 18 37.59N 12.58E
Alcañiz Spain 16 41.03N 0.09W
Alcántara, Embalse de resr. Spain 16 39.45N 6.25W
Alcantara L. Canada 75 60.57N 108.09W
Alcaudete Spain 16 37.35N 4.05W
Alcázar de San Juan Spain 16 39.24N 3.12W
Alcira Spain 16 39.10N 0.27W
Alcobaça Portugal 16 39.33N 8.59W
Alcova U.S.A. 80 42.35N 106.34W
Alcoy Spain 16 38.42N 0.29W
Alcubierre, Sierra de mts. Spain 16 41.40N 0.20W
Alcudia Spain 16 39.51N 3.09E
Aldan Russian Fed. 29 58.44N 125.22E
Aldan r. Russian Fed. 29 63.30N 130.00E
Aldeburgh U.K. 11 52.09N 1.35E
Alderney i. Channel Is. Europe 11 49.42N 2.11W
Aldershot U.K. 11 51.15N 0.47W

Alderson to Angara

Alderson Canada 75 50.20N111.25W
Aldridge U.K. 11 52.36N 1.55W
Aledo U.S.A. 82 41.12N 90.45W
Aleg Mauritania 50 17.03N 13.55W
Alegre Brazil 94 20.44S 41.30W
Alegrete Brazil 93 29.46S 55.46W
Aleksandrov Gay Russian Fed. 25 50.08N 48.34E
Aleksandrovsk Sakhalinskiy Russian Fed. 29 50.55N142.12E
Alembe Gabon 54 0.03N 10.57E
Além Paraíba Brazil 94 21.49S 42.36W
Alençon France 15 48.25N 0.05E
Alenuihaha Channel Hawaiian Is. 69 20.26N156.00W
Aleppo see Ḥalab Syria 42
Aléria France 17 42.05N 9.30E
Alès France 17 44.08N 4.05E
Alessandria Italy 15 44.54N 8.37E
Ålesund Norway 22 62.28N 6.11E
Aleutian Basin Bering Sea 68 57.00N179.00E
Aleutian Is. U.S.A. 68 52.00N176.00W
Aleutian Range mts. U.S.A. 72 58.00N156.00W
Aleutian Trench Pacific Oc. 68 50.00N176.00W
Alexander U.S.A. 76 42.54N 78.16W
Alexander Archipelago is. U.S.A. 74 56.30N134.30W
Alexander Bay town R.S.A. 56 28.36S 16.26E
Alexander I. Antarctica 96 72.00S 70.00W
Alexandra Australia 67 37.12S145.14E
Alexandra New Zealand 60 45.14S169.26E
Alexandria B.C. Canada 74 52.35N122.27W
Alexandria Ont. Canada 77 45.18N 74.39W
Alexandria see Al Iskandarīyah Egypt 44
Alexandria Romania 21 43.58N 25.20E
Alexandria R.S.A. 56 33.39S 26.24E
Alexandria La. U.S.A. 83 31.18N 92.27W
Alexandria Minn. U.S.A. 82 45.53N 95.22W
Alexandria Va. U.S.A. 85 38.48N 77.03W
Alexandrina, L. Australia 66 35.26S139.10E
Alexandroúpolis Greece 19 40.50N 25.53E
Alexis r. Canada 77 52.32N 56.08W
Alexis Creek town Canada 74 52.05N123.20W
Aleysk Russian Fed. 28 52.32N 82.45E
Al Fant Egypt 44 28.46N 30.53E
Alfaro Spain 16 42.11N 1.45W
Al Fāshir Sudan 49 13.38N 25.21E
Al Fashn Egypt 44 28.49N 30.54E
Al Fāw Iraq 43 29.57N 48.30E
Al Fayyūm Egypt 44 29.19N 30.50E
Alfeld Germany 20 51.59N 9.50E
Alfenas Brazil 94 21.28S 45.48W
Al Fifi Sudan 49 10.03N 25.01E
Alfiós r. Greece 19 37.37N 21.27E
Alfonsine Italy 15 44.30N 12.03E
Alford U.K. 12 57.14N 2.42W
Al Fujayrah U.A.E. 43 25.10N 56.20E
Alga Kazakhstan 28 49.49N 57.16E
Ålgård Norway 23 58.46N 5.51E
Al Gebir Sudan 49 13.43N 29.49E
Algeciras Spain 16 36.08N 5.27W
Algemesí Spain 16 39.11N 0.27W
Algena Ethiopia 48 16.20N 38.34E
Alger Algeria 51 36.50N 3.00E
Algeria Africa 50 28.00N 2.00E
Al Ghayl Saudi Arabia 43 22.36N 46.19E
Alghero Italy 18 40.33N 8.20E
Al Ghurdaqah Egypt 42 27.14N 33.50E
Algiers see Alger Algeria 51
Algoa B. R.S.A. 56 33.50S 26.00E
Algoma U.S.A. 82 44.36N 87.27W
Algona U.S.A. 82 43.04N 94.14W
Algonquin Prov. Park Canada 76 45.27N 78.26W
Algorta Uruguay 93 32.25S 57.23W
Al Ḥajar al Gharbī mts. Oman 43 24.00N 56.30E
Al Ḥajar ash Sharqī mts. Oman 43 22.45N 58.45E
Alhama Spain 16 37.51N 1.25W
Al Ḥamād des. Saudi Arabia 42 31.45N 39.00E
Al Ḥamar Saudi Arabia 43 22.26N 46.12E
Alhambra U.S.A. 81 34.06N118.08W
Al Ḥamīdīyah Syria 44 34.43N 35.56E
Al Ḥanākīyah Saudi Arabia 42 24.53N 40.30E
Al Ḥarīq Saudi Arabia 43 23.37N 46.31E
Al Harūj al Aswad hills Libya 51 27.00N 17.10E
Al Ḥasakah Syria 42 36.29N 40.45E
Al Ḥawāmidīyah Egypt 44 29.54N 31.15E
Al Ḥayz Egypt 42 28.02N 28.39E
Al Ḥijāz f. Saudi Arabia 42 26.00N 37.30E
Al Ḥillah Iraq 43 32.28N 44.29E
Al Ḥillah Saudi Arabia 43 23.30N 46.51E
Al Hirmil Lebanon 44 34.25N 36.23E
Al-Hoceima Morocco 50 35.15N 3.55W
Al Ḥudaydah Yemen 48 14.50N 42.58E
Al Hufūf Saudi Arabia 43 25.20N 49.34E
Al Ḥumrah des. U.A.E. 43 22.45N 55.10E
Al Ḥusayhīyah Egypt 44 30.52N 31.55E
Al Ḥuwaymī Yemen 45 14.05N 47.44E
Alīābād, Kūh-e mtn. Iran 43 34.09N 50.48E
Aliákmon r. Greece 19 40.30N 22.38E
Alicante Spain 16 38.21N 0.29W
Alice R.S.A. 56 32.47S 26.49E
Alice U.S.A. 83 27.45N 98.04W
Alice Arm Canada 74 55.29N129.31W
Alice Springs town Australia 64 23.42S133.52E
Alīgarh India 41 27.53N 78.05E
Alīgūdarz Iran 43 33.25N 49.38E
'Alījūq, Kūh-e mtn. Iran 43 31.27N 51.43E
Alima r. Congo 54 1.36S 16.35E
Alindao C.A.R. 49 5.02N 21.13E
Alingsås Sweden 23 57.56N 12.31E
Alīpur Pakistan 40 29.23N 70.55E
Alīpur Duār India 41 26.29N 89.44E
Alīpur Janūbī Pakistan 40 30.13N 71.18E
Aliquippa U.S.A. 84 40.38N 80.16W
Al 'Irq Libya 51 29.05N 15.48E
Ali Sabieh Djibouti 49 11.09N 42.42E
Al Iskandarīyah Egypt 44 31.13N 29.55E
Al Ismā'īlīyah Egypt 44 30.36N 32.15E
Aliwal North R.S.A. 56 30.41S 26.41E
Al Jabal al Akhḍar d. Libya 51 32.00N 21.30E
Al Jafr Jordan 44 30.16N 36.11E
Al Jāfūrah des. Saudi Arabia 43 24.40N 50.20E
Al Jaghbūb Libya 48 29.45N 24.31E
Al Jahrah Kuwait 43 29.20N 47.41E
Al Jaladah f. Saudi Arabia 45 18.30N 46.25E
Al Jawārah Oman 38 18.55N 57.17E
Al Jawb f. Saudi Arabia 43 23.00N 50.00E
Al Jawf Libya 48 24.12N 23.18E
Al Jawf Saudi Arabia 42 29.49N 39.52E
Al Jawsh Libya 51 32.00N 11.40E
Al Jazīrah f. Iraq 42 35.00N 41.00E
Al Jazīrah d. Sudan 48 14.35N 33.30E
Al Jazīrah f. Sudan 48 14.25N 33.00E
Al Jifārah Saudi Arabia 43 23.59N 45.11E
Al Jīzah Egypt 44 30.01N 31.12E
Al Jubayl Saudi Arabia 43 27.59N 49.40E
Al Junaynah Sudan 49 13.27N 22.27E
Aljustrel Portugal 16 37.55N 8.10W
Al Karabah Sudan 48 18.33N 33.42E
Al Karak Jordan 44 31.11N 35.42E
Al Kawah Sudan 49 13.44N 32.30E
Al Khābūr r. Syria 42 35.07N 40.30E
Al Khābūrah Oman 43 23.58N 57.10E
Al Khalīl Jordan 44 31.32N 35.06E
Al Khamāsīn Saudi Arabia 45 20.29N 44.49E
Al Khandaq Sudan 48 18.36N 30.34E
Al Khānkah Egypt 44 30.12N 31.21E
Al Khārijah Egypt 42 25.26N 30.33E
Al Kharṭūm Sudan 48 15.33N 32.35E
Al Kharṭūm d. Sudan 48 15.45N 32.30E
Al Kharṭūm Baḥrī Sudan 48 15.39N 32.34E
Al Khasfah well Oman 45 19.45N 54.19E
Al Khawr Qatar 43 25.39N 51.32E
Al Khirbah as Samrā' Jordan 44 32.11N 36.10E
Al Khubar Saudi Arabia 43 26.18N 50.06E
Al Khufayfīyah Saudi Arabia 43 24.55N 44.42E
Al Khums Libya 51 32.39N 14.16E
Al Khums d. Libya 51 31.20N 14.10E
Al Khunn Saudi Arabia 43 23.18N 49.15E
Al Kidn des. Saudi Arabia 43 22.20N 54.20E
Al Kiswah Syria 44 33.21N 36.14E
Alkmaar Neth. 14 52.37N 4.44E
Al Kufrah Libya 48 24.14N 23.15E
Al Kuntillah Egypt 44 30.00N 34.41E
Al Kūt Iraq 43 32.30N 45.51E
Al Kuwayt Kuwait 43 29.20N 48.00E
Al Labwah Lebanon 44 34.11N 36.21E
Al Lādhiqīyah Syria 44 35.31N 35.47E
Al Lagowa Sudan 49 11.24N 29.08E
Allahābād India 41 25.27N 81.51E
Allakaket U.S.A. 72 66.30N152.45W
Allanche France 17 45.14N 2.56E
'Allāqī, Wādī al r. Egypt 42 22.55N 33.02E
Allegheny r. U.S.A. 84 40.27N 80.00W
Allegheny Mts. U.S.A. 84 38.30N 80.00W
Allen, Lough Rep. of Ire. 13 54.07N 8.04W
Allentown U.S.A. 85 40.37N 75.30W
Aller r. Germany 20 52.57N 9.11E
Alliance U.S.A. 82 42.06N102.52W
Allier r. France 17 46.58N 3.04E
Al Līṭānī r. Lebanon 44 33.22N 35.14E
Al Līth Saudi Arabia 48 20.09N 40.16E
Al Līwā' f. U.A.E. 45 23.00N 54.00E
Alloa U.K. 12 56.07N 3.49W
Allos France 17 44.14N 6.38E
Al Luḥayyah Yemen 48 15.43N 42.42E
Alluitsup-Paa see Sydpröven Greenland 73
Alma Canada 77 48.32N 71.40W
Alma Ga. U.S.A. 85 31.33N 82.29W
Alma Mich. U.S.A. 84 43.23N 84.40W
Al Ma'ānīyah well Iraq 42 30.44N 43.00E
Alma-Ata Kazakhstan 30 43.19N 76.55E
Almadén Spain 16 38.47N 4.50W
Al Madīnah Saudi Arabia 42 24.30N 39.35E
Al Madīnah al Fikrīyah Egypt 44 27.56N 30.49E
Al Mafraq Jordan 44 32.20N 36.12E
Al Maghrah well Egypt 42 30.14N 28.56E
Almagor Israel 44 32.55N 35.36E
Al Maḥallah al Kubrá Egypt 44 30.59N 31.12E
Al Maḥāriq Egypt 42 25.37N 30.39E
Al Maḥmūdīyah Egypt 44 31.10N 30.30E
Al Majma'ah Saudi Arabia 43 25.52N 45.25E
Al Manāmah Bahrain 43 26.12N 50.36E
Almanor U.S.A. 80 40.15N121.08W
Almansa Spain 16 38.52N 1.06W
Al Manshāh Egypt 42 26.28N 31.48E
Al Manṣūrah Egypt 44 31.03N 31.23E
Al Manzil Jordan 44 31.03N 36.01E
Al Manzilah Egypt 44 31.10N 31.56E
Almanzor, Pico de mtn. Spain 16 40.20N 5.22W
Almanzora r. Spain 16 37.16N 1.49W
Al Marj Libya 48 32.30N 20.50E
Al Maṭarīyah Egypt 44 31.12N 32.02E
Al Matnah Sudan 48 13.47N 35.03E
Almaty see Alma-Ata Kazakhstan 30
Al Mawṣil Iraq 42 36.21N 43.08E
Al Mayādīn Syria 42 35.01N 40.28E
Almazán Spain 16 41.29N 2.31W
Al Mazra'ah Jordan 44 31.16N 35.31E
Almeirim Portugal 16 39.12N 8.37W
Almelo Neth. 14 52.21N 6.40E
Almendralejo Spain 16 38.41N 6.26W
Almería Spain 16 36.50N 2.26W
Älmhult Sweden 23 56.33N 14.08E
Al Midhnab Saudi Arabia 43 25.52N 44.15E
Al Miḥrāḍ des. Saudi Arabia 43 20.00N 52.30E
Al Minyā Egypt 44 28.06N 30.45E
Al Mismīyah Syria 44 33.08N 36.24E
Almonte Spain 16 37.16N 6.31W
Almora India 41 29.37N 79.40E
Al Mudawwarah Jordan 44 29.20N 36.00E
Al Muglad Sudan 49 11.02N 27.44E
Al Muḥarraq Bahrain 43 26.16N 50.38E
Al Mukallā Yemen 45 14.34N 49.09E
Al Mukhā Yemen 49 13.19N 43.15E
Almuñécar Spain 16 36.44N 3.41W
Al Muwayh Saudi Arabia 42 22.41N 41.37E
Alnwick U.K. 10 55.25N 1.41W
Alofi Niue 68 19.03S169.55W
Alofi B. Niue 68 19.02S169.55W
Alónnisos i. Greece 19 39.08N 23.50E
Alonsa Canada 75 50.50N 99.00W
Alor i. Indonesia 37 8.20S124.30E
Alor Setar Malaysia 36 6.06N100.23E
Alozero Russian Fed. 24 65.02N 31.10E
Alpena U.S.A. 84 45.04N 83.27W
Alpes Maritimes mts. France 17 44.07N 7.08E
Alpha Australia 64 23.39S146.38E
Alphen Neth. 14 52.08N 4.40E
Alpine U.S.A. 83 30.22N103.40W
Alps mts. Europe 17 46.00N 7.30E
Al Qaḍārif Sudan 48 14.02N 35.24E
Al Qaḍīmah Saudi Arabia 48 22.21N 39.09E
Al Qafā' des. U.A.E. 43 23.30N 53.30E
Al Qāhirah Egypt 44 30.03N 31.15E
Al Qā'īyah Saudi Arabia 42 24.18N 43.30E
Al Qā'īyah well Saudi Arabia 43 26.27N 45.35E
Al Qalībah Saudi Arabia 42 28.24N 37.42E
Al Qanāṭir al Khayrīyah Egypt 44 30.12N 31.08E
Al Qanṭarah Egypt 44 30.52N 32.20E
Al Qaryatayn Syria 44 34.13N 37.13E
Al Qaṣabāt Libya 51 32.35N 14.03E
Al Qaṣr Egypt 42 25.43N 28.54E
Al Qaṣṣāṣīn Egypt 44 30.34N 31.56E
Al Qaṭīf Saudi Arabia 43 26.31N 50.00E
Al Qaṭrānah Jordan 44 31.15N 36.03E
Al Qaṭrūn Libya 51 24.56N 14.38E
Al Qayṣūmah Saudi Arabia 43 28.20N 46.07E
Al Qunayṭirah Syria 44 33.08N 35.49E
Al Qunfudhah Saudi Arabia 48 19.08N 41.05E
Al Qurnah Iraq 43 31.00N 47.26E
Al Quṣaymah Egypt 44 30.40N 34.22E
Al Quṣayr Egypt 42 26.06N 34.17E
Al Qūṣīyah Egypt 42 27.26N 30.49E
Al Quṭayfah Syria 44 33.44N 36.36E
Alroy Downs town Australia 64 19.18S136.04E
Als i. Denmark 23 54.59N 9.55E
Alsace d. France 17 48.25N 7.40E
Alsask Canada 75 51.23N109.59W
Alsasua Spain 16 42.54N 2.10W
Älsborg d. Sweden 23 58.00N 12.20E
Alsek Ranges mts. Canada 74 59.21N137.05W
Alsfeld Germany 20 50.45N 9.16E
Alsten i. Norway 22 65.55N 12.35E
Alston U.K. 12 54.48N 2.26W
Alta Norway 22 70.00N 23.15E
Alta r. Norway 22 69.50N 23.30E
Altafjorden est. Norway 22 70.10N 23.00E
Alta Gracia Argentina 92 31.40S 64.26W
Altagracia de Orituco Venezuela 90 9.54N 66.24W
Altai mts. Mongolia 30 46.30N 93.30E
Altamaha r. U.S.A. 85 31.19N 81.17W
Altamira Brazil 91 3.12S 52.12W
Altamont U.S.A. 80 42.12N121.44W
Altamura Italy 19 40.50N 16.32E
Altar, Desierto de des. Mexico 81 31.50N114.15W
Altavista U.S.A. 85 37.07N 79.18W
Altay China 30 47.48N 88.07E
Altay Mongolia 30 46.20N 97.00E
Altea Spain 16 38.37N 0.03W
Altenburg Germany 20 50.59N 12.27E
Altenkirchen Germany 14 50.41N 7.40E
Altiplanicie Mexicana mts. Mexico 83 29.00N105.00W
Altnaharra U.K. 12 58.16N 4.26W
Alto Araguaia Brazil 91 17.19S 53.10W
Alto Molocue Mozambique 55 15.38S 37.42E
Alton Canada 76 43.52N 80.04W
Alton U.K. 11 51.08N 0.59W
Alton U.S.A. 82 38.55N 90.10W
Altona Germany 20 53.32N 9.56E
Altoona U.S.A. 84 40.30N 78.24W
Altun Shan mts. China 30 38.10N 87.50E
Altus U.S.A. 83 34.38N 99.20W
Al Ubayyiḍ Sudan 49 13.11N 30.13E
Al Uḍayyah Sudan 49 12.03N 28.17E
Aluk Sudan 49 8.26N 27.32E
Al 'Ulá Saudi Arabia 42 26.39N 37.58E
Al 'Uqaylah Libya 51 30.16N 19.12E
Al Uqṣur Egypt 42 25.41N 32.24E
Al Urduun r. Asia 44 31.47N 35.31E
Al 'Uwaynah well Saudi Arabia 43 26.46N 48.13E
Al 'Uwaynāt Libya 51 25.48N 10.33E
Al 'Uyūn Saudi Arabia 43 26.32N 43.41E
Alva U.S.A. 83 36.48N 98.40W
Alvarado Mexico 86 18.49N 95.46W
Älvdalen Sweden 23 61.14N 14.02E
Alvesta Sweden 23 56.54N 14.33E
Älvho Sweden 23 61.30N 14.46E
Alvin U.S.A. 83 29.25N 95.15W
Älvkarleby Sweden 23 60.34N 17.27E
Älvsbyn Sweden 22 65.39N 20.59E
Al Wajh Saudi Arabia 42 26.16N 36.28E
Al Wakrah Qatar 43 25.09N 51.36E
Alwar India 40 27.34N 76.36E
Al Wazz Sudan 48 15.01N 30.10E
Al Yamāmah Saudi Arabia 43 24.11N 47.21E
Alyaty Azerbaijan 43 39.59N 49.20E
Alytus Lithuania 21 54.24N 24.03E
Alzada U.S.A. 80 45.01N104.26W
Alzette r. Lux. 14 49.52N 6.07E
Amadeus, L. Australia 62 24.50S130.45E
Amadi Sudan 49 5.31N 30.20E
Amadjuak Canada 73 64.00N 72.50W
Amadjuak L. Canada 73 65.00N 71.00W
Amagasaki Japan 35 34.43N135.25E
Åmål Sweden 23 59.03N 12.42E
Amaliás Greece 19 37.48N 21.21E
Amalner India 40 21.03N 75.04E
Amami ō shima i. Japan 31 28.20N129.30E
Amamula Zaïre 55 0.17S 27.49E
Amanã, L. Brazil 90 2.35S 64.40W
Amānganj India 41 24.26N 80.02E
Amangeldy Kazakhstan 28 50.12N 65.11E
Amapá Brazil 91 2.00N 50.50W
Amapá d. Brazil 91 2.00N 52.00W
Amarante Brazil 91 6.14S 42.51W
Amaranth Canada 75 50.36N 98.43W
Amareleja Portugal 16 38.12N 7.13W
Amares Portugal 16 41.38N 8.21W
Amarillo U.S.A. 83 35.13N101.49W
Amar Jadīd Sudan 48 14.28N 25.14E
Amarkantak India 41 22.40N 81.45E
Amaro, Monte mtn. Italy 18 42.06N 14.04E
Amasya Turkey 42 40.37N 35.50E
Amazon r. see Amazonas r. Brazil 91
Amazonas d. Brazil 90 4.50S 64.00W
Amazonas r. Brazil 91 2.00S 52.00W
Amazonas, Estuario do Rio f. Brazil 91 0.00 50.30W
Amazon Delta see Amazonas, Estuario do Rio f. Brazil 91
Amb Pakistan 40 34.19N 72.51E
Ambāla India 40 30.23N 76.46E
Ambalavao Madagascar 57 21.50S 46.56E
Ambam Cameroon 53 2.25N 11.16E
Ambarawa Indonesia 37 7.12S110.30E
Ambarchik Russian Fed. 29 69.39N162.27E
Ambarnāth India 40 19.11N 73.10E
Ambarnyy Russian Fed. 24 65.59N 33.53E
Ambato Ecuador 90 1.18S 78.36W
Ambato-Boeni Madagascar 57 16.28S 46.43E
Ambatofinandrahana Madagascar 57 20.33S 46.48E
Ambatolampy Madagascar 57 19.23S 47.25E
Ambatondrazaka Madagascar 57 17.50S 48.25E
Amberg Germany 20 49.27N 11.52E
Ambergris Cay i. Belize 87 18.00N 87.58W
Ambérieu France 17 45.57N 5.21E
Ambikāpur India 41 23.07N 83.12E
Ambilobe Madagascar 57 13.12S 49.04E
Amble U.K. 10 55.20N 1.34W
Ambleside U.K. 10 54.26N 2.58W
Ambodifototra Madagascar 57 16.59S 49.52E
Ambohidratrimo Madagascar 57 18.50S 47.26E
Ambohimahasoa Madagascar 57 21.07S 47.13E
Ambohimanga du Sud Madagascar 57 20.52S 47.36E
Amboise France 15 47.25N 1.00E
Ambon Indonesia 37 4.50S128.10E
Ambositra Madagascar 57 20.31S 47.15E
Ambovombe Madagascar 57 25.11S 46.05E
Amboy U.S.A. 81 34.33N115.44W
Ambrières France 15 48.24N 0.38W
Ambrim i. Vanuatu 68 16.15S168.10E
Ambriz Angola 54 7.54S 13.12E
Ambunten Indonesia 37 6.55S113.45E
Am Dam Chad 49 12.46N 20.29E
Amderma Russian Fed. 28 69.44N 61.35E
Amdo China 41 32.22N 91.07E
Ameca Mexico 86 20.33N104.02W
Ameland i. Neth. 14 53.28N 5.48E
Amelia City U.S.A. 85 30.37N 81.27W
Americana Brazil 94 22.44S 47.19W
American Falls Resr. U.S.A. 80 43.00N113.00W
American Fork U.S.A. 80 40.23N111.48W
Americus U.S.A. 85 32.04N 84.14W
Amersfoort Neth. 14 52.10N 5.23E
Amery Australia 63 31.09S117.05E
Ames U.S.A. 82 42.02N 93.37W
Ameson Canada 76 49.50N 84.35W
Ametinho Angola 54 17.20S 17.20E
Amga Russian Fed. 29 60.51N131.59E
Amga r. Russian Fed. 29 62.40N135.20E
Am Géréda Chad 49 12.52N 21.10E
Amgu Russian Fed. 31 45.48N137.36E
Amguid Algeria 51 26.26N 5.22E
Amgun r. Russian Fed. 29 53.10N139.47E
Amhara Plateau f. Ethiopia 49 11.00N 38.00E
Amherst Canada 77 45.49N 64.14W
Amiata mtn. Italy 18 42.53N 11.37E
Amiens France 15 49.54N 2.18E
Amīr Chāh well Pakistan 40 29.13N 62.28E
Amisk L. Canada 75 54.35N102.13W
Amistad Resr. U.S.A. 83 29.34N101.15W
Amite U.S.A. 83 30.44N 90.33W
Amla India 41 21.56N 78.07E
Amlekhganj Nepal 41 27.17N 85.00E
Åmli Norway 23 58.47N 8.30E
Amlwch U.K. 10 53.24N 4.21W
'Ammān Jordan 44 31.57N 35.56E
Ammanford U.K. 11 51.48N 4.00W
Ammassalik Greenland 73 65.40N 38.00W
Ammókhostos Cyprus 44 35.07N 33.57E
Ammókhostou, Kólpos b. Cyprus 44 35.12N 34.05E
Amo r. India 41 25.58N 89.36E
Āmol Iran 43 36.26N 52.24E
Amorgós i. Greece 19 36.50N 25.55E
Amory U.S.A. 83 33.59N 88.29W
Amos Canada 76 48.35N 78.05W
Amoy see Xiamen China 33
Ampala Honduras 87 13.16N 87.39W
Ampanihy Madagascar 57 24.42S 44.45E
Amparo Brazil 94 22.44S 46.44W
Ampezzo Italy 15 46.25N 12.48E
Amqui Canada 77 48.28N 67.26W
Amrāvati India 41 20.56N 77.45E
Amreli India 40 21.37N 71.14E
Amritsar India 40 31.38N 74.53E
Amroha India 41 28.55N 78.28E
Am Saterna Chad 49 12.26N 21.25E
Amsel Algeria 51 22.37N 5.26E
Amstelveen Neth. 14 52.18N 4.51E
Amsterdam Neth. 14 52.22N 4.54E
Amsterdam U.S.A. 84 42.57N 74.11W
Am Timan Chad 49 11.02N 20.17E
Amu Darya r. Uzbekistan 28 43.50N 59.00E
Amulet Canada 75 49.40N104.45W
Amundsen G. Canada 72 70.30N122.00W
Amundsen Sea Antarctica 96 72.00S120.00W
Amuntai Indonesia 36 2.24S115.14E
Amur r. Russian Fed. 29 53.17N140.00E
'Amūr, Wādī r. Sudan 48 18.56N 33.34E
Amurzet Russian Fed. 31 47.50N131.05E
Anabar r. Russian Fed. 29 72.40N113.30E
Anabranch r. Australia 66 34.08S141.46E
Anaco Venezuela 90 9.27N 64.28W
Anaconda U.S.A. 80 46.08N112.57W
Anadarko U.S.A. 83 35.04N 98.15W
Anadolu f. Turkey 42 38.00N 35.00E
Anadyr Russian Fed. 29 64.40N177.32E
Anadyr r. Russian Fed. 29 65.00N176.00E
Anadyrskiy Zaliv g. Russian Fed. 29 64.30N177.50W
Anáfi i. Greece 19 36.21N 25.50E
Anaheim U.S.A. 81 33.51N117.57W
Analalava Madagascar 57 14.38S 47.45E
Anambas, Kepulauan is. Indonesia 36 3.00N106.10E
Anambra d. Nigeria 53 6.20N 7.25E
Anamoose U.S.A. 82 47.53N100.15W
Anamur Turkey 42 36.06N 32.49E
Ānand India 40 22.34N 72.56E
Anandpur India 41 21.16N 86.13E
Anantapur India 38 14.41N 77.36E
Anantnāg Jammu & Kashmir 40 33.44N 75.09E
Anápolis Brazil 91 16.19S 48.58W
Anapú r. Brazil 91 1.53S 50.53W
Anār Iran 43 30.54N 55.18E
Anārak Iran 43 33.20N 53.42E
Anār Darreh Afghan. 40 32.46N 61.39E
Anatolia f. see Anadolu f. Turkey 42
Anatone U.S.A. 80 46.08N117.09W
Añatuya Argentina 92 28.26S 62.48W
Ancenis France 15 47.21N 1.10W
Anchau Nigeria 53 11.00N 8.23E
Anchorage U.S.A. 72 61.10N150.00W
Ancien Goubéré C.A.R. 49 5.51N 26.46E
Ancohuma mtn. Bolivia 92 16.05S 68.36W
Ancón Peru 90 11.50S 77.10W
Ancona Italy 18 43.37N 13.33E
Ancuabe Mozambique 55 13.00S 39.50E
Ancud Chile 93 41.05S 73.50W
Ancy-le-Franc France 15 47.46N 4.10E
Anda China 31 46.25N125.20E
Andalsnes Norway 22 62.33N 7.43E
Andalucía d. Spain 16 37.36N 4.30W
Andalusia U.S.A. 85 31.20N 86.30W
Andaman Is. India 34 12.00N 92.45E
Andaman Sea Indian Oc. 34 10.00N 95.00E
Andamooka Australia 66 30.27S137.12E
Andanga Russian Fed. 24 59.11N 45.44E
Andara Namibia 56 18.04S 21.26E
Andelot France 17 48.15N 5.18E
Andenes Norway 22 69.18N 16.10E
Andenne Belgium 14 50.29N 5.04E
Anderlecht Belgium 14 50.51N 4.18E
Andernach Germany 14 50.25N 7.24E
Anderson r. Canada 72 69.45N129.00W
Anderson Ind. U.S.A. 84 40.05N 85.41W
Anderson S.C. U.S.A. 85 34.30N 82.39W
Andes mts. S. America 93 32.40S 70.00W
Andevoranto Madagascar 57 18.57S 49.06E
Andfjorden est. Norway 22 68.55N 16.00E
Andhra Pradesh d. India 39 17.00N 79.00E
Andikíthira i. Greece 19 35.52N 23.18E
Andizhan Uzbekistan 30 40.48N 72.23E
Andoany Madagascar 57 13.25S 48.16E
Andong S. Korea 31 36.37N128.44E
Andorra town Andorra 17 42.30N 1.31E
Andorra Europe 17 42.30N 1.32E
Andover U.K. 11 51.13N 1.29W
Andover U.S.A. 85 40.59N 74.45W
Andöy i. Norway 22 69.05N 15.40E
Andrada Angola 54 7.41S 21.22E
Andrews N.C. U.S.A. 85 35.13N 83.49W
Andrews Tex. U.S.A. 83 32.19N102.33W
Andreyevo-Ivanovka Ukraine 21 47.28N 30.29E
Andria Italy 18 41.13N 16.18E
Andriba Madagascar 57 17.36S 46.55E
Androka Madagascar 57 25.02S 44.05E
Ándros Greece 19 37.50N 24.57E
Ándros i. Greece 19 37.50N 24.50E
Andros I. Bahamas 87 24.25N 78.00W
Andros Town Bahamas 87 24.43N 77.47W
Andrushevka Ukraine 21 50.00N 28.59E
Andújar Spain 16 38.02N 4.03W
Andulo Angola 54 11.28S 16.43E
Anefis I-n-Darane Mali 52 17.57N 0.35E
Anegada i. B.V.Is. 87 18.46N 64.24W
Anécho Togo 53 6.17N 1.40E
Aneityum i. Vanuatu 68 20.12S169.45E
Añelo Argentina 93 38.20S 68.45W
Aneto, Pico de mtn. Spain 16 42.40N 0.19E
Aney Niger 53 19.24N 12.56E
Angara r. Russian Fed. 29 58.00N 93.00E

Angarsk Russian Fed. 29 52.31N103.55E
Angaston Australia 65 34.30S139.03E
Angatuba Brazil 94 23.27S 48.25W
Ange Sweden 22 62.31N 15.40E
Ángel de la Guarda, Isla i. Mexico 81 29.20N113.25W
Angel Falls f. Venezuela 90 5.55N 62.30W
Ängelholm Sweden 23 56.15N 12.50E
Angels Camp U.S.A. 80 38.04N120.32W
Ångereb r. Ethiopia 49 13.45N 36.40E
Ångerman r. Sweden 22 63.00N 17.43E
Angermünde Germany 20 53.01N 14.00E
Angers France 15 47.29N 0.32W
Angerville France 15 48.19N 2.00E
Ängesan r. Sweden 22 66.22N 22.58E
Angikuni L. Canada 75 62.00N100.00W
Angkor ruins Cambodia 34 13.30N103.50E
Anglesey i. U.K. 10 53.16N 4.25W
Angleton U.S.A. 83 29.10N 95.26W
Ango Zaïre 49 4.02N 25.52E
Angoche Mozambique 57 16.10S 39.57E
Angol Chile 93 37.48S 72.43W
Angola Africa 54 11.00S 18.00E
Angola Ind. U.S.A. 84 41.38N 85.01W
Angola N.Y. U.S.A. 84 42.39N 79.02W
Angoram P.N.G. 37 4.04S144.04E
Angoulême France 17 45.40N 0.10E
Angra dos Reis Brazil 94 22.59S 44.17W
Ang Thong Thailand 34 14.35N100.25E
Anguilla i. Leeward Is. 87 18.14N 63.05W
Angul India 41 20.51N 85.06E
Angumu Zaïre 55 0.10S 27.38E
Anholt i. Denmark 23 56.42N 11.34E
Anholt Germany 14 51.51N 6.26E
Anh Son Vietnam 34 18.54N105.18E
Anhua China 33 28.24N111.13E
Anhui d. China 33 32.00N117.00E
Aniak U.S.A. 72 61.32N159.40W
Animas U.S.A. 81 31.57N108.48W
Anin Burma 34 15.40N 97.46E
Anina Romania 21 45.05N 21.51E
Anivorano Madagascar 57 18.44S 48.58E
Anjad India 40 22.02N 75.03E
Anjangaon India 40 21.10N 77.18E
Anjār India 40 23.08N 70.01E
Anjō Japan 35 34.57N137.05E
Anjouan i. Comoros 55 12.25S 44.28E
Anjozorobe Madagascar 57 18.24S 47.52E
Anju N. Korea 31 39.36N125.42E
Anka Nigeria 53 12.06N 5.56E
Ankang China 32 32.38N109.12E
Ankara Turkey 42 39.55N 32.50E
Ankaramena Madagascar 57 21.57S 46.39E
Ankazoabo Madagascar 57 22.18S 44.31E
Ankazobe Madagascar 57 18.21S 47.07E
Anklam Germany 20 53.51N 13.41E
Anklesvar India 40 21.38N 72.59E
Ānkober Ethiopia 49 9.30N 39.44E
Ankpa Nigeria 53 7.26N 7.38E
Anlong China 33 25.06N105.31E
Anlu China 33 31.15N113.40E
Anna U.S.A. 83 37.28N 89.15W
Annaba Algeria 51 36.55N 7.47E
An Nabk Syria 44 34.02N 36.43E
Anna Creek town Australia 66 28.50S136.07E
An Nafūd des. Saudi Arabia 42 28.40N 41.30E
An Najaf Iraq 43 31.59N 44.19E
An Nakhl Egypt 44 29.55N 33.45E
Annam Highlands see Annamitique, Chaîne mts. Laos / Vietnam 34
Annamitique, Chaîne mts. Laos / Vietnam 34 17.00N106.00E
Annan U.K. 12 54.59N 3.16W
Annan r. U.K. 12 54.58N 3.16W
Annandale f. U.K. 12 55.12N 3.25W
Anna Plains Australia 62 19.18S121.34E
Annapolis U.S.A. 85 38.59N 76.30W
Annapurna mtn. Nepal 41 28.34N 83.50E
An Naqirah well Saudi Arabia 43 27.53N 48.15E
Ann Arbor U.S.A. 84 42.18N 83.43W
An Nāşirīyah Iraq 43 31.04N 46.16E
An Nawfalīyah Libya 51 30.47N 17.50E
Annecy France 17 45.54N 6.07E
An Nil d. Sudan 48 18.30N 33.10E
An Nil al Abyad d. Sudan 49 13.10N 32.00E
An Nil al Azraq d. Sudan 49 13.00N 34.00E
Anniston U.S.A. 85 33.38N 85.50W
Annobón i. Equat. Guinea 95 1.25S 5.36E
Annonay France 17 45.15N 4.40E
Annuello Australia 66 34.52S142.54E
An Nuhūd Sudan 49 12.42N 28.26E
Anoka U.S.A. 82 45.11N 93.20W
Anorotsangana Madagascar 57 13.56S 47.55E
Anou Ti-n Elhaoua well Algeria 51 20.02N 2.55E
Anpu China 33 21.27N110.01E
Anqing China 33 30.40N117.03E
Ansbach Germany 20 49.18N 10.36E
Anshan China 32 41.06N122.58E
Anshun China 33 26.11N105.50E
Anson B. Australia 62 13.10S130.00E
Ansongo Mali 52 15.40N 0.30E
Anstruther U.K. 12 56.14N 2.42W
Ansudu Indonesia 37 2.11S139.22E
Antakya Turkey 42 36.12N 36.10E
Antalaha Madagascar 57 14.53S 50.16E
Antalya Turkey 42 36.53N 30.42E
Antalya Körfezi g. Turkey 42 36.38N 31.00E
Antananarivo Madagascar 57 18.55S 47.31E
Antarctica 96
Antarctic Pen. f. Antarctica 95 65.00S 64.00W
Antas Brazil 91 10.20S 38.20W
Antequera Spain 16 37.01N 4.34W
Anthony U.S.A. 83 37.09N 89.02W
Antibes France 17 43.35N 7.07E
Anticosti, Île d' i. Canada 77 49.20N 63.00W
Anticosti Prov. Park Canada 77 49.20N 63.00W
Antifer, Cap d' c. France 15 49.41N 0.10E
Antigo U.S.A. 82 45.09N 89.09W
Antigua Guatemala 86 14.33N 90.42W
Antigua i. Leeward Is. 87 17.09N 61.49W
Anti-Lebanon mts. see Sharqī, Al Jabal ash mts. Lebanon 44
Antipodes Is. Pacific Oc. 68 49.42S178.50E
Antlers U.S.A. 83 34.14N 95.47W
Antofagasta Chile 92 23.39S 70.24W
Antônio Bezerra Brazil 91 3.44S 38.35W
Antônio Carlos Brazil 94 21.18S 43.48W
Antonito U.S.A. 80 37.05N106.00W
Antrain France 15 48.28N 1.30W
Antrim U.K. 13 54.43N 6.14W
Antrim d. U.K. 13 54.58N 6.20W
Antrim, Mts. of U.K. 13 55.00N 6.10W
Antsalova Madagascar 57 18.40S 44.37E
Antsirabé Madagascar 57 19.51S 47.02E
Antsiranana Madagascar 57 12.16S 49.17E
Antsohihy Madagascar 57 14.52S 47.59E
Anttis Sweden 22 67.16N 22.52E
Antwerp see Antwerpen Belgium 14
Antwerpen Belgium 14 51.13N 4.25E
Antwerpen d. Belgium 14 51.16N 4.45E
Anūpgarh India 40 29.11N 73.12E
Anvik U.S.A. 72 62.38N160.20W
Anxi Fujian China 33 25.03N118.13E
Anxi Gansu China 30 40.32N 95.57E
Anxious B. Australia 66 33.25S134.35E
Anyama Ivory Coast 52 5.30N 4.03W
Anyang China 32 36.05N114.20E
Anyer Lor Indonesia 37 6.02S105.57E
Anyi China 33 28.50N115.32E
Anyuan China 33 25.09N115.21E
Anyue China 33 30.09N105.18E
Anzhero-Sudzhensk Russian Fed. 28 56.10N 86.10E
Anzio Italy 18 41.27N 12.37E
Ao Ban Don b. Thailand 34 9.00N 99.20E
Aohan Qi China 32 42.23N119.59E
Aoji N. Korea 35 42.31N130.23E
Aomori Japan 35 40.50N140.43E
Aopo W. Samoa 68 13.29S172.30W
Aosta Italy 15 45.43N 7.19E
Aoulef Algeria 50 26.58N 1.05E
Aoulime, Jbel mtn. Morocco 50 30.48N 8.50W
Aozou Chad 53 21.49N 17.25E
Apache U.S.A. 83 34.54N 98.22W
Apalachee B. U.S.A. 85 30.00N 84.13W
Apalachicola U.S.A. 85 29.43N 85.01W
Apalachicola r. U.S.A. 85 29.44N 84.59W
Apaporis r. Colombia 90 1.40S 69.20W
Aparri Phil. 37 18.22N121.40E
Apatin Yugo. 19 45.40N 18.59E
Apatity Russian Fed. 24 67.32N 33.21E
Apeldoorn Neth. 14 52.13N 5.57E
Api mtn. Nepal 41 30.01N 80.56E
Apia W. Samoa 68 13.48S171.45W
Apizaco Mexico 86 19.25N 98.09W
Apoka Uganda 49 3.42N 33.38E
Apollo Bay town Australia 66 38.45S143.40E
Apostle Is. U.S.A. 82 46.50N 90.30W
Apóstoles Argentina 92 27.55S 55.45W
Apostólou Andréa, Akrotírion c. Cyprus 44 35.40N 34.35E
Apoteri Guyana 90 4.02N 58.32W
Appalachian Mts. U.S.A. 84 41.00N 77.00W
Appennino mts. Italy 18 42.00N 13.30E
Appennino Ligure mts. Italy 15 44.30N 9.00E
Appennino Tosco-Emiliano mts. Italy 15 44.05N 11.00E
Appiano Italy 15 46.28N 11.15E
Appingedam Neth. 14 53.18N 6.52E
Appleby U.K. 10 54.35N 2.29W
Appleton U.S.A. 82 44.16N 88.25W
Apsheronsk Russian Fed. 25 44.26N 39.45E
Apsheronskiy Poluostrov pen. Azerbaijan 43 40.28N 50.00E
Apsley Australia 66 36.58S141.08E
Apsley Canada 76 44.45N 78.06W
Apucarana Brazil 94 23.34S 51.28W
Apure r. Venezuela 90 7.40N 66.30W
Apurimac r. Peru 90 10.43S 73.55W
Aqaba, G. of Asia 44 28.45N 34.45E
Aqabat al Ḩijāzīyah Jordan 44 29.40N 35.55E
'Aqdā Iran 43 32.25N 53.38E
'Aqiq Sudan 48 18.14N 38.12E
Aqqikkol Hu l. China 30 35.44N 81.34E
Aquidauana Brazil 92 20.27S 55.45W
Aquila Mexico 86 18.30N103.50W
Aquitaine d. France 17 44.40N 0.00
'Arab, Baḩr al r. Sudan 49 9.12N 29.28E
Arabādād Iran 43 33.02N 57.41E
'Arabah, Wādī r. Egypt 44 29.07N 32.40E
Arabian Sea Asia 38 16.00N 65.00E
Araç Turkey 42 41.14N 33.20E
Aracaju Brazil 91 10.54S 37.07W
Aracanguy, Montañas de mts. Paraguay 92 24.00S 55.50W
Aracati Brazil 91 4.32S 37.45W
Araçatuba Brazil 94 21.12S 50.24W
Arad Romania 21 46.12N 21.19E
Arada Chad 51 15.01N 20.40E
Arafura Sea Austa. 64 9.00S133.00E
Aragarças Brazil 91 15.55S 52.12W
Aragats mtn. Armenia 43 40.32N 44.11E
Aragón d. Spain 16 41.25N 1.00W
Aragón r. Spain 16 42.20N 1.45W
Araguacema Brazil 91 8.50S 49.34W
Araguaia r. Brazil 91 5.20S 48.30W
Araguari Brazil 94 18.38S 48.13W
Araguari r. Brazil 91 1.15N 50.05W
Arak Algeria 51 25.18N 3.45E
Arāk Iran 43 34.06N 49.44E
Araka Sudan 49 4.16N 30.21E
Arakan d. Burma 34 19.00N 94.15E
Arakan Yoma mts. Burma 34 19.30N 94.30E
Araks r. Azerbaijan 43 40.00N 48.28E
Aral Sea Asia 28 45.00N 60.00E
Aralsk Kazakhstan 28 46.56N 61.43E
Aralskoye More sea see Aral Sea Asia 28
Aralsor, Ozero l. Kazakhstan 25 49.00N 48.40E
Aramac Australia 64 22.59S145.14E
Arāmbāgh India 41 22.53N 87.47E
Aramia r. P.N.G. 37 8.00S143.20E
Aranda de Duero Spain 16 41.40N 3.41W
Aran I. Rep. of Ire. 13 53.07N 9.38W
Aran Is. Rep. of Ire. 13 53.07N 9.38W
Aranjuez Spain 16 40.02N 3.37W
Aranos Namibia 56 24.09S 19.09E
Aransas Pass town U.S.A. 83 27.54N 97.09W
Araouane Mali 52 18.53N 3.31W
Arapahoe U.S.A. 82 40.18N 99.54W
Arapey Uruguay 93 30.58S 57.30W
Arapey Grande r. Uruguay 93 30.55S 57.49W
Arapiraca Brazil 91 9.45S 36.40W
Arapkir Turkey 42 39.03N 38.29E
'Ar'ar, Wādī r. Iraq 42 32.00N 42.30E
Araraquara Brazil 94 21.46S 48.08W
Araras Brazil 94 22.20S 47.23W
Ararat Australia 66 37.20S143.00E
Ararat mtn. see Ağri Daği mtn. Turkey 43
Aras r. Turkey see Araks r. Azerbaijan 42
Arauca Colombia 90 7.04N 70.41W
Arauca r. Venezuela 90 7.05N 70.45W
Araure Venezuela 90 9.36N 69.15W
Arāvalli Range mts. India 40 25.00N 73.45E
Araxá Brazil 94 19.37S 46.50W
Araxes r. Iran see Araks r. Azerbaijan 43
Ārba Minch' Ethiopia 49 6.02N 37.40E
Arbatax Italy 18 39.56N 9.41E
Arboga Sweden 23 59.24N 15.50E
Arborg Canada 75 50.55N 97.15W
Arbroath U.K. 12 56.34N 2.35W
Arcachon France 17 44.40N 1.11W
Arcadia Fla. U.S.A. 85 27.12N 81.52W
Arcadia Wisc. U.S.A. 82 44.15N 91.30W
Arcata U.S.A. 80 40.52N124.05W
Archer r. Australia 64 13.28S141.41E
Archers Post Kenya 55 0.42N 37.40E
Arcis-sur-Aube France 15 48.32N 4.08E
Arckaringa r. Australia 66 27.56S134.45E
Arco Italy 15 45.55N 10.53E
Arco U.S.A. 80 43.38N113.18W
Arcoona Australia 66 31.06S137.19E
Arcos Brazil 94 20.12S 45.30W
Arcos Spain 16 36.45N 5.45W
Arcoverde Brazil 91 8.23S 37.00W
Arctic Bay town Canada 73 73.05N 85.20W
Arctic Ocean 96
Arctic Red r. Canada 72 67.26N133.48W
Arctic Red River town Canada 72 67.27N133.46W
Arda r. Greece 19 41.39N 26.30E
Ardabīl Iran 43 38.15N 48.18E
Ardahan Turkey 42 41.08N 42.41E
Årdalstangen Norway 23 61.14N 7.43E
Ardara Rep. of Ire. 13 54.46N 8.25W
Ard aş Şawwān f. Jordan 44 30.45N 37.15E
Ardèche r. France 17 44.31N 4.40E
Ardee Rep. of Ire. 9 53.51N 6.33W
Ardennes mts. Belgium 14 50.10N 5.30E
Ardennes d. France 15 49.40N 4.40E
Ardennes, Canal des France 15 49.26N 4.02E
Ardestān Iran 43 33.22N 52.25E
Ardfert Rep. of Ire. 13 52.20N 9.48W
Ardila r. Portugal 16 38.10N 7.30W
Ardlethan Australia 67 34.20S146.53E
Ardmore Rep. of Ire. 13 51.58N 7.43W
Ardmore Okla. U.S.A. 83 34.10N 97.08W
Ardmore Penn. U.S.A. 85 40.01N 75.18W
Ardnamurchan, Pt. of U.K. 12 56.44N 6.14W
Ardrossan Australia 66 34.25S137.55E
Ardrossan U.K. 12 55.38N 4.49W
Ards Pen. U.K. 13 54.30N 5.30W
Åre Sweden 22 63.25N 13.05E
Arecibo Puerto Rico 87 18.29N 66.44W
Areia Branca Brazil 91 4.56S 37.07W
Arena, Pt. U.S.A. 78 38.58N123.44W
Arena, Punta c. Mexico 81 23.32N109.30W
Arendal Norway 23 58.27N 8.48E
Arequipa Peru 90 16.25S 71.32W
Arès France 17 44.47N 1.08W
Arévalo Spain 16 41.03N 4.43W
Arezzo Italy 18 43.27N 11.52E
Arfak mtn. Indonesia 37 1.30S133.50E
Arganda Spain 16 40.19N 3.26W
Argelès-sur-Mer France 17 42.33N 3.01E
Argens r. France 17 43.10N 6.45E
Argenta Italy 15 44.37N 11.50E
Argentan France 15 48.45N 0.01W
Argentera Italy 15 44.24N 6.57E
Argentera mtn. Italy 15 44.10N 7.18E
Argenteuil France 15 48.57N 2.15E
Argentia Canada 77 47.18N 53.59W
Argentina S. America 93 36.00S 63.00W
Argentine Basin f. Atlantic Oc. 95 40.00S 40.00W
Argentino, L. Argentina 93 50.15S 72.25W
Argenton France 17 46.36N 1.30E
Argentré France 15 48.05N 0.39W
Argentré du Plessis France 15 48.03N 1.08W
Argeş r. Romania 19 44.13N 26.22E
Arghandāb r. Afghan. 40 31.27N 64.23E
Árgos Greece 19 37.37N 22.45E
Argostólion Greece 19 38.10N 20.30E
Arguello, Pt. U.S.A. 81 34.35N120.39W
Argun r. Russian Fed. 31 53.30N121.48E
Argungu Nigeria 53 12.45N 4.35E
Argyle U.S.A. 82 48.20N 96.49W
Ar Horqin Qi China 32 43.45N120.00E
Århus Denmark 23 56.09N 10.13E
Ariah Park town Australia 67 34.20S147.10E
Ariano Italy 18 41.04N 15.00E
Ariano nel Polesine Italy 15 44.56N 12.07E
Aribinda Burkina 52 14.17N 0.52W
Arica Chile 92 18.29S 70.20W
Arica Colombia 90 2.07S 71.46W
Arid, C. Australia 63 33.58S123.05E
Arieş r. Romania 21 46.26N 23.59E
Ārifwāla Pakistan 40 30.17N 73.04E
Arīḩā Al Quds Jordan 44 31.51N 35.27E
Arima Trinidad 90 10.38N 61.17W
Arinos r. Brazil 91 10.20S 57.35W
Aripuanā Brazil 90 9.10S 60.38W
Aripuanā r. Brazil 90 5.05S 60.30W
Ariquemes Brazil 90 9.56S 63.04W
Aris Namibia 56 22.48S 17.10E
Arisaig U.K. 12 56.55N 5.51W
'Arīsh, Wādī al r. Egypt 44 31.09N 33.49E
Aristazabal I. Canada 74 52.40N129.10W
Arivonimamo Madagascar 57 19.01S 47.15E
Ariza Spain 16 41.19N 2.03W
Arizona d. U.S.A. 78 34.00N112.00W
Årjäng Sweden 23 59.23N 12.08E
Arjeplog Sweden 22 66.00N 17.58E
Arjona Colombia 90 10.14N 75.22W
Arkadelphia U.S.A. 83 34.07N 93.04W
Arkaig, Loch U.K. 12 56.58N 5.08W
Arkansas d. U.S.A. 83 34.20N 92.00W
Arkansas r. U.S.A. 83 33.48N 91.04W
Arkansas City U.S.A. 83 37.04N 97.02W
Arkhangel'sk Russian Fed. 24 64.32N 41.10E
Árki i. Greece 19 37.22N 26.45E
Arklow Rep. of Ire. 13 52.47N 6.10W
Arkville U.S.A. 84 42.09N 74.37W
Arlberg Pass Austria 20 47.00N 10.05E
Arles France 17 43.41N 4.38E
Arlington Colo. U.S.A. 80 38.20N103.19W
Arlington Oreg. U.S.A. 80 45.16N120.13W
Arlington Tex. U.S.A. 83 32.44N 97.07W
Arlington Va. U.S.A. 85 38.52N 77.05W
Arlington Heights town U.S.A. 82 42.06N 88.00W
Arlon Belgium 14 49.41N 5.49E
Armadale Australia 63 32.10S115.57E
Armagh U.K. 13 54.21N 6.41W
Armagh d. U.K. 13 54.16N 6.35W
Armançon r. France 15 47.57N 3.30E
Armavir Russian Fed. 25 44.59N 41.10E
Armenia Colombia 90 4.32N 75.40W
Armenia Europe 43 40.00N 45.00E
Armeniş Romania 21 45.12N 22.19E
Armentières France 14 50.41N 2.53E
Armidale Australia 67 30.32S151.40E
Armori India 41 20.28N 79.59E
Armstrong Canada 74 50.25N119.10W
Armstrong U.S.A. 83 26.55N 97.47W
Ārmūr India 41 18.48N 78.17E
Arnaud r. Canada 73 60.00N 69.45W
Årnes Norway 23 60.09N 11.28E
Arnett U.S.A. 83 36.08N 99.46W
Arnhem Neth. 14 52.00N 5.55E
Arnhem, C. Australia 64 12.10S137.00E
Arnhem B. Australia 64 12.20S136.12E
Arnhem Land f. Australia 64 13.10S134.30E
Arno r. Italy 18 43.43N 10.17E
Arno Bay town Australia 66 33.54S136.34E
Arnot Canada 75 55.46N 96.41W
Arnprior Canada 76 45.26N 76.21W
Arnsberg Germany 14 51.24N 8.03E
Aroma Sudan 48 15.49N 36.08E
Arona Italy 15 45.46N 8.34E
Arorangi Rarotonga Cook Is. 68 21.13S159.49W
Arpajon France 15 48.35N 2.15E
Arra Ivory Coast 52 6.42N 3.57W
Arrah India 41 25.34N 84.40E
Ar Rahad Sudan 49 12.43N 30.39E
Ar Ramādī Iraq 42 33.27N 43.19E
Ar Ramthā Jordan 44 32.34N 36.00E
Arran i. U.K. 12 55.35N 5.14W
Ar Rank Sudan 49 11.45N 32.48E
Ar Raqqah Syria 42 35.57N 39.03E
Arras France 14 50.17N 2.46E
Ar Rass Saudi Arabia 42 25.54N 43.30E
Ar Rastān Syria 44 34.55N 36.44E
Arrecife Canary Is. 50 28.57N 13.32W
Arrecifes Argentina 93 34.05S 60.05W
Arrey U.S.A. 81 32.51N107.19W
Ar Riyāḑ Saudi Arabia 43 24.39N 46.44E
Arrochar U.K. 12 56.12N 4.44W
Arromanches France 15 49.20N 0.38W
Arrow, Lough Rep. of Ire. 13 54.03N 8.20W
Arrowsmith, Pt. Australia 64 13.18S136.24E
Arrowtown New Zealand 60 44.56S168.50E
Arroyo Feliciano r. Argentina 93 31.06S 59.53W
Arroyo Villimanca r. Argentina 93 35.36S 59.05W
Ar Ru'at Sudan 49 12.21N 32.17E
Ar Rub' al Khālī des. Saudi Arabia 38 20.20N 52.30E
Ar Rubayqī Egypt 44 30.10N 31.46E
Ar Rumaythah Iraq 43 31.32N 45.12E
Ar Ruşayriş Sudan 49 11.51N 34.23E
Ar Ruţbah Iraq 42 33.40N 39.59E
Ar Ruwayḑah Saudi Arabia 43 23.46N 44.46E
Ārsī d. Ethiopia 49 7.50N 39.50E
Ársos Cyprus 44 34.50N 32.46E
Árta Greece 19 39.10N 20.57E
Artemovsk Ukraine 25 48.35N 38.00E
Artenay France 15 48.05N 1.53E
Artesia U.S.A. 81 32.51N104.24W
Arthabaska Canada 77 46.02N 71.55W
Arthal Jammu & Kashmir 40 33.16N 76.11E
Arthington Liberia 52 6.35N 10.45W
Arthur's Pass New Zealand 60 42.50S171.45E
Artigas Uruguay 93 30.24S 56.28W
Artillery L. Canada 75 63.09N107.52W
Artois f. France 14 50.16N 2.50E
Artux China 30 39.40N 75.49E
Artvin Turkey 42 41.12N 41.48E
Aru, Kepulauan is. Indonesia 37 6.00S134.30E
Arua Uganda 55 3.02N 30.56E
Aruaddin Ethiopia 48 16.16N 38.46E
Aruanã Brazil 91 14.54S 51.05W
Aruba i. Neth. Ant. 87 12.30N 70.00W
Arucas Canary Is. 95 28.08N 15.32W
Arun r. U.K. 9 50.48N 0.32W
Arunachal Pradesh d. India 39 28.40N 94.60E
Arundel Canada 77 45.58N 74.37W
Arusha Tanzania 55 3.21S 36.40E
Arusha d. Tanzania 55 4.00S 37.00E
Aruwimi r. Zaïre 54 1.20N 23.36E
Arvada Colo. U.S.A. 80 39.50N105.05W
Arvada Wyo. U.S.A. 80 44.39N105.05W
Arvagh Rep. of Ire. 13 53.56N 7.35W
Arvi India 41 20.59N 78.14E
Arvidsjaur Sweden 22 65.35N 19.07E
Arvika Sweden 23 59.39N 12.36E
Arzamas Russian Fed. 24 55.24N 43.48E
Arzgir Russian Fed. 25 45.24N 44.04E
Arzignano Italy 15 45.31N 11.20E
Asaba Nigeria 53 6.12N 6.44E
Asadābād Afghan. 40 34.52N 71.09E
Asahi dake mtn. Japan 35 43.42N142.54E
Asahikawa Japan 35 43.50N142.20E
Asansol India 41 23.41N 86.59E
Åsarna Sweden 22 62.40N 14.20E
Āsayita Ethiopia 49 11.33N 41.30E
Asbestos Canada 77 45.46N 71.57W
Asbury Park U.S.A. 85 40.14N 74.00W
Ascension i. Atlantic Oc. 95 7.57S 14.22W
Aschaffenburg Germany 20 49.58N 9.10E
Aschendorf Germany 14 53.03N 7.20E
Aschersleben Germany 20 51.46N 11.28E
Ascoli Piceno Italy 18 42.52N 13.36E
Ascona Switz. 15 46.09N 8.46E
Āseb Ethiopia 49 13.01N 42.47E
Åseda Sweden 23 57.10N 15.20E
Asedjrad Algeria 51 24.42N 1.40E
Āsela Ethiopia 49 7.59N 39.08E
Åsele Sweden 22 64.10N 17.20E
Åsenbruk Sweden 23 58.54N 12.40E
Asenovgrad Bulgaria 19 42.00N 24.53E
Åseral Norway 23 58.37N 7.25E
Asfeld France 15 49.27N 4.05E
Asha Nigeria 53 7.07N 3.43E
Ashanti d. Ghana 52 6.30N 1.30W
Ashbourne Rep. of Ire. 13 53.31N 6.25W
Ashburn U.S.A. 85 31.42N 83.41W
Ashburton r. Australia 62 21.15S115.00E
Ashburton New Zealand 60 43.54S171.46E
Ashby de la Zouch U.K. 11 52.45N 1.29W
Ashcroft Canada 74 50.40N121.20W
Ashdod Israel 44 31.48N 34.38E
Asheboro U.S.A. 85 35.42N 79.50W
Ashern Canada 75 51.11N 98.21W
Asheville U.S.A. 85 35.35N 82.35W
Ashewat Pakistan 40 31.22N 68.32E
Ash Flat town U.S.A. 83 36.12N 91.38W
Ashford Australia 67 29.19S151.07E
Ashford U.K. 11 51.08N 0.53E
Ash Fork U.S.A. 81 35.13N112.29W
Ashgabat see Ashkhabad Turkmenistan 43
Ashington U.K. 10 55.11N 1.34W
Ashiya Japan 35 34.43N135.17E
Ashkhabad Turkmenistan 43 37.58N 58.24E
Ashland Ky. U.S.A. 84 38.28N 82.40W
Ashland Oreg. U.S.A. 80 42.12N122.42W
Ashland Wisc. U.S.A. 82 46.35N 90.53W
Ashley Australia 67 29.19S149.52E
Ashley U.S.A. 82 38.20N 89.10W
Ashley Snow I. Antarctica 96 72.30S 77.00W
Ashmūn Egypt 44 30.18N 30.59E
Ashoknagar India 41 24.34N 77.43E
Ashqelon Israel 44 31.40N 34.35E
Ash Shabb well Egypt 48 22.19N 29.46E
Ash Shallūfah Egypt 44 30.07N 32.34E
Ash Shāmah des. Saudi Arabia 42 31.20N 38.00E
Ash Shamālīyah d. Sudan 48 19.30N 29.50E
Ash Shāmīyah des. Iraq 43 30.30N 45.30E
Ash Shāriqah U.A.E. 43 25.20N 55.26E
Ash Sharmah Saudi Arabia 44 28.01N 35.14E
Ash Shawbak Jordan 44 30.33N 35.35E
Ash Shaykh Faḑl Egypt 44 28.29N 30.50E
Ash Shaykh 'Ibādah Egypt 44 27.48N 30.52E
Ash Shaykh Miskīn Syria 44 32.49N 36.09E
Ash Shiḩr Yemen 45 14.45N 49.36E
Ash Shu'aybah Iraq 43 30.30N 47.40E
Ash Shu'aybah Saudi Arabia 42 27.53N 42.43E
Ash Shumlūl Saudi Arabia 43 26.29N 47.20E
Ashta India 40 23.01N 76.43E
Ashtabula U.S.A. 84 41.53N 80.47W
Ashton R.S.A. 56 33.49S 20.04E
Ashton U.S.A. 80 44.04N111.27W
'Āsī r. Lebanon 44 34.37N 36.30E
Asiago Italy 15 45.52N 11.30E
Asilah Morocco 50 35.32N 6.00W
Asinara i. Italy 18 41.04N 8.18E
Asinara, Golfo dell' g. Italy 18 41.00N 8.32E
'Asīr f. Saudi Arabia 45 19.00N 42.00E
Aska India 41 19.36N 84.39E
Askeaton Rep. of Ire. 13 52.36N 9.00W
Askersund Sweden 23 58.53N 14.54E
Askim Norway 23 59.35N 11.10E
Askvoll Norway 23 61.21N 5.04E
Āsmera Ethiopia 48 15.20N 38.58E
Åsnen l. Sweden 23 56.38N 14.42E
Asola Italy 15 45.13N 10.24E

Āsosa Ethiopia 49 10.03N 34.32E
Asoteriba, Jabal mtn. Sudan 48 21.51N 36.30E
Aspen U.S.A. 80 39.11N106.49W
Aspermont U.S.A. 83 33.08N100.14W
Aspiring, Mt. New Zealand 60 44.20S168.45E
Asquith Canada 75 52.08N107.13W
Assaba d. Mauritania 50 16.40N 11.40W
As Sadd al 'Ālī dam Egypt 48 23.59N 32.54E
Aş Şaff Egypt 44 29.34N 31.17E
As Saffāniyah Saudi Arabia 43 28.00N 48.48E
Aş Şāfiyah Sudan 48 15.31N 30.07E
Aş Şa'īd f. Egypt 42 25.30N 32.00E
Aş Şāliḥīyah Egypt 44 30.47N 31.59E
As Sallūm Egypt 42 31.31N 25.09E
As Salt Jordan 44 32.03N 35.44E
As Salwa Saudi Arabia 43 24.44N 50.50E
Assam d. India 39 26.30N 93.00E
As Samāwah Iraq 43 31.18N 45.18E
As Sanām f. Saudi Arabia 45 22.00N 51.10E
Aş Şarafand Lebanon 44 33.27N 35.18E
Aş Şarīrīyah Egypt 44 28.20N 30.45E
Assebroek Belgium 14 51.11N 3.16E
Assen Neth. 14 53.00N 6.34E
As Sinbillāwayn Egypt 44 30.53N 31.27E
Assiniboia Canada 75 49.38N105.59W
Assiniboine r. Canada 75 49.53N 97.08W
Assinica Prov. Park Canada 76 50.24N 75.00W
Assis Brazil 94 22.37S 50.25W
As Sudd Sudan 49 7.50N 30.00E
Aş Şufayyah Sudan 48 15.30N 34.42E
As Sulaymānīyah Iraq 43 35.32N 45.27E
As Sulaymānīyah Saudi Arabia 43 24.10N 47.20E
As Sulayyil Saudi Arabia 45 20.27N 45.34E
As Sulṭān Libya 51 31.07N 17.09E
Aş Şumayḥ Sudan 49 9.49N 27.39E
Aş Şummān f. Saudi Arabia 43 27.00N 47.00E
As Sūq Saudi Arabia 48 21.55N 42.00E
As Suwaydā' Syria 44 32.43N 36.33E
As Suways Egypt 44 29.59N 32.33E
Asti Italy 15 44.54N 8.13E
Astipálaia i. Greece 19 36.35N 26.25E
Astorga Spain 16 42.30N 6.02W
Astoria U.S.A. 80 46.11N123.50W
Åstorp Sweden 23 56.08N 12.57E
Astrakhan Russian Fed. 25 46.22N 48.00E
Åsträsk Sweden 22 64.38N 20.00E
Asturias d. Spain 16 43.20N 6.00W
Asunción Paraguay 94 25.15S 57.40W
Aswān Egypt 42 24.05N 32.56E
Aswan High Dam see As Sadd al 'Ālī Egypt 42
Asyūṭ Egypt 42 27.14N 31.07E
Atacama, Desierto des. S. America 92 20.00S 69.00W
Atacama, Salar de f. Chile 92 23.30S 68.46W
Atacama Desert see Atacama, Desierto des. S. America 92
Atafu Pacific Oc. 68 8.40S172.40W
Atakpamé Togo 53 7.34N 1.14E
Atami Japan 35 35.05N139.04E
Atapupu Indonesia 37 9.00S124.51E
Atar Mauritania 50 20.32N 13.08W
Atara Russian Fed. 29 63.10N129.10E
Atasu Kazakhstan 28 48.42N 71.38E
'Aṭbarah Sudan 48 17.42N 33.59E
'Aṭbarah r. Sudan 48 17.40N 33.58E
Atchafalaya B. U.S.A. 83 29.25N 91.20W
Atchison U.S.A. 82 39.34N 95.07W
Ath Belgium 14 50.38N 3.45E
Athabasca Canada 74 54.45N113.20W
Athabasca r. Canada 74 58.30N110.50W
Athabasca, L. Canada 75 59.07N110.00W
Athea Rep. of Ire. 13 52.28N 9.19W
Athenry Rep. of Ire. 13 53.18N 8.45W
Athens see Athínai Greece 19
Athens Ga. U.S.A. 85 33.57N 83.24W
Athens Tenn. U.S.A. 85 35.27N 84.38W
Athens Tex. U.S.A. 83 32.13N 95.51W
Atherton Australia 64 17.15S145.29E
Athínai Greece 19 37.59N 23.42E
Athlone Rep. of Ire. 13 53.26N 7.57W
Atholl, Forest of U.K. 12 56.50N 3.55W
Áthos mtn. Greece 19 40.09N 24.19E
Ath Thamad Egypt 44 29.40N 34.18E
Ati Chad 53 13.11N 18.20E
Atico Peru 90 16.12S 73.37W
Atikonak L. Canada 77 52.40N 64.30W
Atimaono Tahiti 69 17.46S149.28W
Atkarsk Russian Fed. 25 51.55N 45.00E
Atkinson U.S.A. 85 34.33N 78.12W
Atlanta Ga. U.S.A. 85 33.45N 84.23W
Atlanta Tex. U.S.A. 83 33.07N 94.10W
Atlantic U.S.A. 82 41.24N 95.01W
Atlantic-Antarctic Ridge f. Atlantic Oc. 95 53.00S 0.00
Atlantic City U.S.A. 85 39.22N 74.26W
Atlantic-Indian-Antarctic Basin f. Atl.Oc./Ind.Oc. 95 61.00S 0.00
Atlantic Ocean 95
Atlas Sahariën mts. Algeria 51 34.00N 2.00E
Atlin Canada 74 59.31N133.41W
Atlin L. Canada 74 59.26N133.45W
Atmore U.S.A. 85 31.02N 87.29W
Atnarko Canada 74 52.25N126.00W
Atnosen Norway 23 61.44N 10.49E
Atoka U.S.A. 83 34.23N 96.08W
Atouat mtn. Laos 34 16.03N107.17E
Atouguia Portugal 16 39.20N 9.20W
Atrak r. Iran see Atrek r. Asia 43
Ätran r. Sweden 23 56.53N 12.30E
Atrato r. Colombia 90 8.15N 76.58W
Atrauli India 41 28.02N 78.17E
Atrek r. Asia 43 37.23N 54.00E
Atsugi Japan 35 35.27N139.22E
Atsumi-hantō pen. Japan 35 34.40N137.20E
Atsumi-wan b. Japan 35 34.45N137.10E

Aṭ Ṭafīlah Jordan 44 30.52N 35.36E
Aṭ Ṭā'if Saudi Arabia 48 21.15N 40.21E
At Tall Syria 44 33.36N 36.18E
Attapu Laos 34 14.51N106.56E
Attar, Oued el wadi Algeria 51 33.23N 5.12E
Attawapiskat r. Canada 76 53.00N 82.30W
Attawapiskat L. Canada 76 52.20N 88.00W
Aṭ Ṭayrīyah Egypt 44 30.39N 30.46E
Attendorn Germany 14 51.07N 7.54E
Attica U.S.A. 76 42.52N 78.17W
Attigny France 15 49.29N 4.35E
Attikamagen L. Canada 77 55.00N 66.38W
Attleborough U.K. 11 52.31N 1.01E
Attleboro U.S.A. 11 52.31N 1.01E
Aṭ Ṭubayq mts. Saudi Arabia 42 29.30N 37.15E
Aṭ Ṭunayb Jordan 44 31.48N 35.56E
Aṭ Ṭūr Egypt 44 28.14N 33.36E
At Ṭuwayrifah well Saudi Arabia 45 21.30N 49.35E
Atucha Argentina 93 33.58S 59.17W
Atuel r. Argentina 93 36.15S 66.55W
Atui, Uad wadi Mauritania 50 20.03N 15.35W
Atui I. Cook Is. 69 20.00S158.07W
Atuona Is. Marquises 69 9.48S139.02W
Åtvidaberg Sweden 23 58.12N 16.00E
Atwater U.S.A. 80 37.21N120.36W
Atwood U.S.A. 82 39.48N101.03W
Aubagne France 17 43.17N 5.35E
Aube d. France 15 48.15N 4.05E
Aube r. France 15 48.30N 3.37E
Aubenton France 15 49.50N 4.12E
Auberive France 15 47.47N 5.03E
Aubigny-sur-Nère France 15 47.29N 2.26E
Aubin France 17 44.32N 2.14E
Auburn Ala. U.S.A. 85 32.38N 85.38W
Auburn Calif. U.S.A. 80 38.54N121.04W
Auburn Ind. U.S.A. 84 41.22N 85.02W
Auburn Maine U.S.A. 84 44.06N 70.14W
Auburn N.Y. U.S.A. 84 42.57N 76.34W
Auburn Wash. U.S.A. 80 47.18N122.13W
Aubusson France 17 45.57N 2.11E
Auce Latvia 23 56.28N 22.53E
Auch France 17 43.40N 0.36E
Auchi Nigeria 53 7.05N 6.16E
Auchterarder U.K. 12 56.18N 3.43W
Auckland New Zealand 60 36.55S174.45E
Auckland d. New Zealand 60 36.45S174.45E
Auckland Is. Pacific Oc. 68 50.35S166.00E
Aude r. France 17 43.13N 3.15E
Auden Canada 76 50.17N 87.54W
Audo Range mts. Ethiopia 49 6.30N 41.30E
Audubon U.S.A. 82 41.43N 94.55W
Aue Germany 20 50.35N 12.42E
Augathella Australia 64 25.48S146.35E
Augrabies Falls f. R.S.A. 56 28.33S 20.27E
Augsburg Germany 20 48.21N 10.54E
Augusta Australia 63 34.19S115.09E
Augusta Ga. U.S.A. 85 33.29N 82.00W
Augusta Ill. U.S.A. 82 40.14N 90.56W
Augusta Kans. U.S.A. 83 37.41N 96.58W
Augusta Maine U.S.A. 84 44.19N 69.47W
Augustín Codazzi Colombia 90 10.01N 73.10W
Augustów Poland 21 53.51N 22.59E
Augustus, Mt. Australia 62 24.20S116.49E
Aulla Italy 15 44.12N 9.58E
Aulnay France 17 46.02N 0.22W
Aulne r. France 17 48.30N 4.11W
Aulnoye-Aymeries France 15 50.13N 3.50E
Ault U.S.A. 80 40.35N104.44W
Aumale France 15 49.46N 1.45E
Aumont-Aubrac France 17 44.43N 3.17E
Auna Nigeria 53 10.11N 4.46E
Auneau France 15 48.27N 1.46E
Aura Finland 23 60.36N 22.34E
Auraiya India 41 26.28N 79.31E
Aurangābād Bihār India 41 24.45N 84.22E
Aurangābād Mahār India 40 19.53N 75.20E
Aurdal Norway 23 60.56N 9.24E
Aure Norway 22 63.16N 8.34E
Aurich Germany 14 53.28N 7.29E
Aurillac France 17 44.56N 2.26E
Aurora Canada 76 44.00N 79.28W
Aurora Colo. U.S.A. 80 39.44N104.52W
Aurora Ill. U.S.A. 82 41.45N 88.20W
Aurora Mo. U.S.A. 83 36.58N 93.43W
Aursunden l. Norway 22 62.37N 11.40E
Aurukun Australia 64 13.20S141.42E
Aus Namibia 56 26.41S 16.14E
Au Sable r. U.S.A. 84 44.27N 83.21W
Aust-Agder d. Norway 23 58.50N 8.20E
Austin Minn. U.S.A. 82 43.40N 92.59W
Austin Nev. U.S.A. 80 39.30N117.04W
Austin Penn. U.S.A. 84 41.38N 78.05W
Austin Tex. U.S.A. 83 30.16N 97.45W
Austin, L. Australia 62 27.40S118.00E
Austral Downs town Australia 64 20.28S137.55E
Australia Austa. 61
Australian Alps mts. Australia 65 36.30S148.30E
Australian Antarctic Territory Antarctica 96 73.00S 90.00E
Australian Capital Territory d. Australia 67 35.30S149.00E
Austral Ridge Pacific Oc. 69 24.00S148.00W
Austria Europe 20 47.30N 14.00E
Austvågöy i. Norway 22 68.20N 14.40E
Autun France 17 46.58N 4.18E
Auvergne d. France 17 45.20N 3.00E
Auxerre France 17 47.48N 3.35E
Aux Sables r. Canada 76 46.13N 82.04W
Auzances France 17 46.02N 2.29E
Ava Burma 34 21.49N 95.57E
Avallon France 17 47.30N 3.54E
Avaloirs, Les hills France 15 48.28N 0.07W
Avalon U.S.A. 85 39.06N 74.43W

Avalon Pen. Canada 77 47.00N 53.15W
Avanos Turkey 42 38.44N 34.51E
Avaré Brazil 94 23.06S 48.57W
Avarua Rarotonga Cook Is. 68 21.12S159.46W
Avatele Niue 68 19.06S169.55W
Avatele B. Niue 68 19.05S169.56W
Avatiu Rarotonga Cook Is. 68 21.12S159.47W
Aveiro Portugal 16 40.40N 8.35W
Avellaneda Argentina 93 34.40S 58.20W
Avellino Italy 18 40.55N 14.46E
Aversa Italy 18 40.58N 14.12E
Avery U.S.A. 80 47.15N115.49W
Avesnes France 14 50.08N 3.57E
Avesta Sweden 23 60.09N 16.12E
Aveyron r. France 17 44.09N 1.10E
Avezzano Italy 18 42.03N 13.26E
Aviemore U.K. 12 57.12N 3.50W
Avignon France 17 43.56N 4.48E
Ávila Spain 16 40.39N 4.42W
Ávila, Sierra de mts. Spain 16 40.35N 5.08W
Avilés Spain 16 43.35N 5.57W
Avoca Australia 66 37.04S143.29E
Avoca r. Australia 66 35.56S143.44E
Avola Canada 74 51.45N119.19W
Avola Italy 18 36.56N 15.08E
Avon r. Australia 63 31.40S116.07E
Avon d. U.K. 11 51.35N 2.40W
Avon r. Australia 63 31.40S116.07E
Avon r. Avon U.K. 9 51.30N 2.43W
Avon r. Dorset U.K. 11 50.43N 1.45W
Avon r. Glos. U.K. 11 52.00N 2.10W
Avon Downs town Australia 64 20.05S137.30E
Avonmouth U.K. 11 51.30N 2.42W
Avon Park town U.S.A. 85 27.36N 81.30W
Avranches France 15 48.42N 1.21W
Avre r. France 15 49.53N 2.20E
Awal Edo Ethiopia 49 4.14N 40.39E
Awara Ethiopia 45 4.14N 41.22E
Aware Ethiopia 45 8.15N 44.10E
Āwasa Hāyk' l. Ethiopia 49 7.05N 38.25E
Āwash r. Ethiopia 49 11.45N 41.05E
Awaso Ghana 52 6.20N 2.22W
Awat China 30 40.38N 80.22E
Awbārī Libya 51 26.35N 12.46E
Awbārī d. Libya 51 25.10N 12.45E
Awbārī, Şaḥrā' des. Libya 51 27.30N 11.30E
Awdah, Hawr al l. Iraq 43 31.36N 46.53E
Awe, Loch U.K. 12 56.18N 5.24W
Awjilah Libya 51 29.08N 21.07E
Axarfjördhur est. Iceland 22 66.10N 16.30W
Axat France 17 42.48N 2.14E
Axel Heiberg I. Canada 73 79.30N 90.00W
Axim Ghana 52 4.53N 2.14W
Axiós r. Greece 19 40.31N 22.43E
Axminster U.K. 11 50.47N 3.01W
Ayabaca Peru 90 4.40S 79.53W
Ayachi, Ari n' mtn. Morocco 50 32.29N 4.57W
Ayacucho Argentina 93 37.10S 58.30W
Ayacucho Peru 90 13.10S 74.15W
Ayaguz Kazakhstan 30 48.00N 80.27E
Ayamonte Spain 16 37.12N 7.24W
Ayan Russian Fed. 29 56.29N138.00E
Aydin Turkey 42 37.52N 27.50E
Ayelu mtn. Ethiopia 49 10.04N 40.46E
Ayers Cliff town Canada 77 45.10N 72.03W
Ayers Rock see Uluru Australia 64
Áyios Evstrátios i. Greece 19 39.30N 25.00E
Aylesbury U.K. 11 51.48N 0.49W
Aylmer Canada 77 45.23N 75.51W
Aylmer L. Canada 72 64.05N108.30W
Aylsham U.K. 10 52.48N 1.16E
'Ayn, Wādī al r. Oman 43 22.18N 55.35E
'Ayn Dāllah well Egypt 42 27.19N 27.20E
Ayod Sudan 49 8.07N 31.26E
Ayom Sudan 49 7.52N 28.23E
Ayon, Ostrov i. Russian Fed. 29 70.00N169.00E
Ayos Cameroon 53 3.55N 12.30E
'Ayoûn el 'Atroûs Mauritania 50 16.40N 9.37W
Ayr Australia 64 19.35S147.24E
Ayr U.K. 12 55.28N 4.37W
Ayr r. U.K. 12 55.28N 4.38W
Ayre, Pt. of I.o.M. Europe 10 54.25N 4.22W
Āysha Ethiopia 49 10.46N 42.37E
Ayutthaya Thailand 34 14.20N100.40E
Ayvalik Turkey 19 39.19N 26.42E
Azamgarh India 41 26.04N 83.11E
Azangaro Peru 90 14.57S 70.13W
Azaouâd des. Mali 52 18.00N 3.00W
Azaouad mtn. Algeria 51 21.12N 8.08E
Azare Nigeria 53 11.40N 10.08E
Azbine mts. see Aïr mts. Niger 53
Azerbaijan Europe 43 40.10N 47.50E
Azogues Ecuador 90 2.35S 78.00W
Azopolye Russian Fed. 24 65.15N 45.18E
Azores is. see Açores, Arquipélago dos is. Atlantic Oc. 95
Azoum r. Chad 49 10.53N 20.15E
Azov, Sea of Ukraine / Russian Fed. 25 46.00N 36.30E
Azovskoye More sea see Azov, Sea of Ukraine / Russian Fed. 25
Azraq, Al Baḥr al r. Sudan 48 15.38N 32.31E
Azrou Morocco 50 33.27N 5.14W
Aztec U.S.A. 81 32.48N113.26W
Azua Dom. Rep. 87 18.29N 70.44W
Azuaga Spain 16 38.16N 5.40W
Azuero, Península de pen. Panama 87 7.30N 80.30W
Azul Argentina 93 36.46S 59.50W
'Azūm, Wādī r. Sudan see Azoum r. Chad 49
Azurduy Bolivia 92 19.59S 64.29W
Az Zāb al Kabir r. Iraq 43 35.37N 43.20E
Az Zāb aş Şaghir r. Iraq 43 35.16N 43.27E
Az Zabdānī Syria 44 33.43N 36.05E
Az Zaqāziq Egypt 44 30.36N 31.30E
Az Zarqā' Jordan 44 32.04N 36.05E
Az Zarqā' r. Jordan 44 32.08N 35.32E
Az Zāwiyah Libya 51 32.40N 12.10E

Azzel Matti, Sebkha f. Algeria 50 26.00N 0.55E
Az Zilfī Saudi Arabia 43 26.15N 44.50E
Az Zrārīyah Lebanon 44 33.21N 35.20E
A1 Buḥayrāt d. Sudan 49 6.50N 29.40E

B

Baan Baa Australia 67 30.28S149.58E
Baardheere Somali Rep. 55 2.18N 42.18E
Baargaal Somali Rep. 45 11.18N 51.07E
Baarle-Hertog Neth. 14 51.26N 4.56E
Babadag Romania 21 44.54N 28.43E
Babahoyo Ecuador 90 1.53S 79.31W
Babai Gaxun China 32 40.30N104.43E
Babakin Australia 63 32.11S117.58E
Babana Nigeria 53 10.26N 3.51E
Babanka Ukraine 21 48.41N 30.30E
Babanūsah Sudan 49 11.20N 27.48E
Babar, Kepulauan is. Indonesia 37 8.00S129.30E
Babayevo Russian Fed. 24 59.24N 35.50E
B'abdā Lebanon 44 33.50N 35.31E
Babia Gora mtn. Slovakia / Poland 21 49.38N 19.38E
Babina India 41 25.15N 78.28E
Babine L. Canada 74 54.48N126.00W
Babo Indonesia 37 2.33S133.25E
Bābol Iran 43 36.32N 52.42E
Baboua C.A.R. 53 5.49N 14.51E
Babuyan Channel Phil. 33 18.40N121.30E
Babuyan Is. Phil. 37 19.20N121.30E
Babylon ruins Iraq 43 32.33N 44.25E
Bacabal Maranhão Brazil 91 4.15S 44.45W
Bacabal Para Brazil 91 5.20S 56.45W
Bacău Romania 21 46.32N 26.59E
Baccarat France 17 48.27N 6.45E
Bacchus Marsh town Australia 66 37.41S144.27E
Bacharach Germany 14 50.03N 7.48E
Bacheli India 39 18.40N 81.16E
Bachelina Russian Fed. 28 57.45N 67.20E
Back r. Canada 73 66.37N 96.00W
Bac Lieu Vietnam 34 9.16N105.45E
Bac Ninh Vietnam 34 21.10N106.04E
Bacolod Phil. 37 10.38N122.58E
Bac Phan f. Vietnam 34 22.00N105.00E
Bac Quang Vietnam 33 22.30N104.52E
Badagara India 38 11.36N 75.35E
Badajós, Lago l. Brazil 90 3.15S 62.47W
Badajoz Spain 16 38.53N 6.58W
Badal Khān Goth Pakistan 40 26.31N 67.06E
Badalona Spain 16 41.27N 2.15E
Badanah Saudi Arabia 42 30.59N 41.02E
Bad Axe U.S.A. 84 43.49N 82.59W
Baddo r. Pakistan 40 28.15N 65.00E
Badeggi Nigeria 53 9.04N 6.09E
Bad Ems Germany 14 50.21N 7.42E
Baden Austria 20 48.01N 16.14E
Baden Ethiopia 48 17.00N 38.00E
Baden-Baden Germany 20 48.45N 8.15E
Baden-Württemberg d. Germany 20 48.30N 9.00E
Badgastein Austria 20 47.07N 13.09E
Bad Godesberg Germany 14 50.41N 7.09E
Bad Honnef Germany 14 50.39N 7.13E
Badin Pakistan 40 24.39N 68.50E
Bad Ischl Austria 20 47.43N 13.38E
Bādiyat ash Shām des. Asia 42 32.00N 39.00E
Bad Kissingen Germany 20 50.12N 10.04E
Bad Kreuznach Germany 14 49.51N 7.52E
Bad Mergentheim Germany 20 49.30N 9.46E
Bad Münstereifel Germany 14 50.34N 6.47E
Badnera India 41 20.52N 77.44E
Bad Neuenahr-Ahrweiler Germany 14 50.33N 7.07E
Bad Oldesloe Germany 20 53.48N 10.22E
Badong China 33 31.02N110.20E
Badou Togo 52 7.37N 0.37E
Badoumbé Mali 52 13.42N 10.09W
Badrīnāth India 41 30.44N 79.29E
Bad Tölz Germany 20 47.46N 11.34E
Badu Australia 64 10.07S142.08E
Bad Wildungen Germany 20 51.07N 9.07E
Baerami Australia 67 32.23S150.30E
Baeza Spain 16 37.57N 3.25W
Bafang Cameroon 53 5.11N 10.12E
Bafatá Guinea Bissau 52 12.09N 14.38W
Baffin Canada 73 66.00N 72.00W
Baffin B. Canada 73 74.00N 70.00W
Baffin I. Canada 73 68.50N 70.00W
Bafia Cameroon 53 4.39N 11.14E
Bafing r. Mali 52 11.44N 12.10W
Bafoulabé Mali 52 13.49N 10.50W
Bāfq Iran 43 31.35N 55.21E
Bafra Turkey 42 41.34N 35.56E
Bafut Cameroon 53 6.06N 10.02E
Bafwasende Zaïre 55 1.09N 27.12E
Bagaha India 41 27.06N 84.05E
Bagamoyo Tanzania 55 6.26S 38.55E
Bagasra India 40 21.29N 70.57E
Bagawi Sudan 49 12.19N 34.21E
Bagé Brazil 94 31.22S 54.06W
Baggy Pt. U.K. 11 51.08N 4.15W
Baghdād Iraq 43 33.20N 44.26E

Bāgherhāt Bangla. 41 22.40N 89.48E
Bagheria Italy 18 38.05N 13.30E
Baghlān Afghan. 38 36.11N 68.44E
Baghrān Khowleh Afghan. 40 33.01N 64.58E
Bagni di Lucca Italy 15 44.01N 10.35E
Bagnols-sur-Cèze France 17 44.10N 4.37E
Bago see Pegu Burma 34
Bagodar India 41 24.05N 85.52E
Bagoé r. Mali 52 12.34N 6.30W
Bagolino Italy 15 45.49N 10.28E
Bagrationovsk Russian Fed. 21 54.26N 20.38E
Baguio Phil. 37 16.25N120.37E
Bāh India 41 26.53N 78.36E
Bahamas C. America 87 24.15N 76.00W
Bahāwalnagar Pakistan 40 29.59N 73.16E
Bahāwalpur Pakistan 40 29.24N 71.41E
Baheri India 41 28.47N 79.30E
Bahi Tanzania 55 5.59S 35.15E
Bahia d. Brazil 91 12.30S 42.30W
Bahía, Islas de la is. Honduras 87 16.10N 86.30W
Bahía Blanca Argentina 94 38.45S 62.15W
Bahía de Caráquez Ecuador 90 0.40S 80.25W
Bahía Kino Mexico 81 28.50N111.55W
Bahía Laura Argentina 93 48.18S 66.30W
Bahía Negra Paraguay 92 20.15S 58.12W
Bahir Dar Ethiopia 49 11.35N 37.28E
Bahraich India 41 27.35N 81.36E
Bahrain Asia 43 26.00N 50.35E
Baḥr al Ghazāl d. Sudan 49 8.00N 26.30E
Bahrām Chāh Afghan. 40 29.26N 64.03E
Bahr Aouk r. C.A.R. 53 8.50N 18.50E
Bahr el Ghazal r. Chad 53 12.26N 15.25E
Bahr Salamat r. Chad 53 9.30N 18.10E
Bāhū Kalāt Iran 43 25.42N 61.28E
Baia-Mare Romania 21 47.40N 23.35E
Baião Brazil 91 2.41S 49.41W
Baia Sprie Romania 21 47.40N 23.42E
Baïbokoum Chad 53 7.46N 15.43E
Baicheng China 32 45.40N122.52E
Baie Comeau Canada 77 49.13N 68.10W
Baie des Ha! Ha! town Canada 77 50.56N 58.58W
Baie St. Paul town Canada 77 47.27N 70.30W
Baigneux-les-Juifs France 15 47.31N 4.39E
Baihar India 41 22.06N 80.33E
Baijnāth India 41 29.55N 79.37E
Baikunthapur India 41 23.15N 82.33E
Bāilești Romania 21 44.02N 23.21E
Bailleul France 14 50.44N 2.44E
Bailundo Angola 54 12.13S 15.46E
Baimuru P.N.G. 37 7.30S144.49E
Bainang China 41 29.10N 89.15E
Bainbridge U.S.A. 85 30.54N 84.35W
Bain-de-Bretagne France 15 47.50N 1.41W
Baing Indonesia 62 10.15S120.34E
Baingoin China 41 31.45N 89.50E
Bā'ir Jordan 44 30.46N 36.41E
Bā'ir, Wādī r. Jordan 44 31.10N 36.55E
Baird Mts. U.S.A. 72 67.35N161.30W
Bairin Zuoqi China 32 43.59N119.11E
Bairnsdale Australia 67 37.51S147.38E
Bais France 15 48.15N 0.22W
Baise r. France 17 44.15N 0.20E
Baisha China 33 19.13N109.26E
Baiyang Dian l. China 32 38.55N116.00E
Baiyin China 32 36.40N104.15E
Baja Hungary 21 46.12N 18.58E
Baja California pen. Mexico 81 28.40N114.40W
Baja California Norte d. Mexico 81 29.45N115.30W
Baja California Sur d. Mexico 81 26.00N113.00W
Bakal Russian Fed. 24 54.58N 58.45E
Bakali r. Zaïre 54 3.58S 17.10E
Bakel Senegal 52 14.54N 12.26W
Baker Calif. U.S.A. 81 35.16N116.04W
Baker Mont. U.S.A. 80 46.22N104.17W
Baker Oreg. U.S.A. 80 44.47N117.50W
Baker, Mt. U.S.A. 80 48.47N121.49W
Baker I. U.S.A. 74 55.20N133.36W
Baker Lake town Canada 73 64.20N 96.10W
Bakersfield U.S.A. 81 35.23N119.01W
Bâ Kêv Cambodia 34 13.42N107.12E
Bako Ethiopia 49 5.50N 36.40E
Bako Ivory Coast 52 9.08N 7.40W
Bakouma C.A.R. 49 5.42N 22.47E
Baku Azerbaijan 43 40.22N 49.53E
Baky see Baku Azerbaijan 43
Bala Senegal 52 14.01N 13.08W
Bala U.K. 10 52.54N 3.36W
Balabac i. Phil. 36 7.57N117.01E
Balabac Str. Malaysia / Phil. 36 7.30N117.00E
Ba'labakk Lebanon 44 34.00N 36.12E
Bālāghāt India 41 21.48N 80.11E
Bālāghāt Range mts. India 40 19.00N 76.30E
Balaguer Spain 16 41.50N 0.50E
Balaka Malaŵi 55 15.00S 34.56E
Balaklava Australia 66 34.08S138.24E
Balaklava Ukraine 25 44.31N 33.35E
Balakovo Russian Fed. 24 52.04N 47.46E
Balama Mozambique 55 13.19S 38.35E
Bālā Morghāb Afghan. 43 35.34N 63.20E
Balāngīr India 41 20.43N 83.29E
Balarāmpur India 41 23.07N 86.13E
Balashov Russian Fed. 25 51.30N 43.10E
Balasore India 41 21.30N 86.56E
Balassagyarmat Hungary 21 48.05N 19.18E
Balāt Egypt 42 25.33N 29.19E
Balaton l. Hungary 21 46.55N 17.50E
Balboa Panama 87 8.57N 79.33W
Balbriggan Rep. of Ire. 13 53.36N 6.12W
Balcad Somali Rep. 45 2.22N 45.25E
Balcarce Argentina 93 37.52S 58.15W
Balchik Bulgaria 21 43.24N 28.10E

107

Balclutha to Bealanana

Balclutha New Zealand 60 46.16S169.46E
Baldock L. Canada 75 56.33N 97.57W
Baldwin Fla. U.S.A. 85 30.18N 81.59W
Baldwin Mich. U.S.A. 84 43.54N 85.50W
Baldwin Penn. U.S.A. 84 40.23N 79.58W
Baldy Mt. Canada 74 51.28N120.02W
Balē Ethiopia 49 6.30N 40.45E
Baleanoona Australia 66 30.33S139.22E
Baleares, Islas *is.* Spain 16 39.30N 2.30E
Baleine, Grande rivière de la *r.* Canada 76 55.20N 77.40W
Baleine, Petite rivière de la *r.* Canada 76 56.00N 76.45W
Balfate Honduras 87 15.48N 86.25W
Balfour Downs *town* Australia 62 22.57S120.46E
Bali India 40 25.50N 74.05E
Bali *d.* Indonesia 37 8.45S114.56E
Bali *i.* Indonesia 37 8.20S115.07E
Bali, Laut *sea* Indonesia 37 7.30S115.15E
Bali, Selat *str.* Indonesia 37 8.21S114.30E
Balikesir Turkey 19 39.38N 27.51E
Balīkh *r.* Syria 42 35.58N 39.05E
Balikpapan Indonesia 36 1.15S116.50E
Bali Sea *see* Bali, Laut Indonesia 37
Balkan Mts. *see* Stara Planina *mts.* Bulgaria 19
Balkhash Kazakhstan 30 46.51N 75.00E
Balkhash, Ozero *l.* Kazakhstan 30 46.40N 75.00E
Ballachulish U.K. 12 56.40N 5.08W
Balladonia Australia 63 32.27S123.51E
Ballālpur India 41 19.50N 79.22E
Ballandean Australia 67 28.39S151.50E
Ballantrae U.K. 12 55.06N 5.01W
Ballarat Australia 66 37.36S143.58E
Ballard, L. Australia 63 29.27S120.55E
Ballater U.K. 12 57.03N 3.03W
Ballenas, Bahía de *b.* Mexico 81 26.45N113.25W
Ballenas, Canal de *str.* Mexico 81 29.10N113.30W
Balleny Is. Antarctica 96 66.30S163.00E
Balleroy France 15 49.11N 0.50W
Ballia India 41 25.45N 84.10E
Ballina Australia 67 28.50S153.37E
Ballina Rep. of Ire. 13 54.08N 9.10W
Ballinasloe Rep. of Ire. 13 53.20N 8.15W
Ballingeary Rep. of Ire. 13 51.50N 9.15W
Ballinger U.S.A. 83 31.44N 99.57W
Ball's Pyramid *i.* Pacific Oc. 68 31.45S159.15E
Ballybay Rep. of Ire. 13 54.08N 6.56W
Ballycastle U.K. 13 55.12N 6.15W
Ballyclare U.K. 13 54.45N 6.00W
Ballyconnell Rep. of Ire. 13 54.06N 7.37W
Ballydehob Rep. of Ire. 13 51.34N 9.28W
Ballydonegan Rep. of Ire. 13 51.38N 10.04W
Ballygar Rep. of Ire. 13 53.32N 8.20W
Ballygawley U.K. 13 54.28N 7.03W
Ballykelly U.K. 13 55.03N 7.00W
Ballymena U.K. 13 54.52N 6.17W
Ballymoney U.K. 13 55.04N 6.31W
Ballyquintin Pt. U.K. 13 54.40N 5.30W
Ballyragget Rep. of Ire. 13 52.47N 7.21W
Ballyshannon Rep. of Ire. 13 54.30N 8.11W
Ballyvaughan Rep. of Ire. 13 53.06N 9.09W
Ballyvourney Rep. of Ire. 13 51.57N 9.10W
Balmoral Australia 66 37.17S141.50E
Balochistān *d.* Pakistan 40 28.30N 65.00E
Balombo Angola 54 12.20S 14.45E
Balonne *r.* Australia 67 28.30S148.20E
Bālotra India 40 25.50N 72.14E
Balrāmpur India 41 27.26N 82.11E
Balranald Australia 66 34.37S143.37E
Balş Romania 21 44.21N 24.06E
Balsas *r.* Brazil 91 9.00S 48.10W
Balsas *r.* Mexico 86 18.10N102.05W
Balta Ukraine 21 47.58N 29.39E
Baltanás Spain 16 41.56N 4.15W
Baltasar Brum Uruguay 93 30.44S 57.19W
Baltic Sea Europe 23 57.00N 20.00E
Balṭîm Egypt 44 31.34N 31.05E
Baltimore Md. U.S.A. 85 39.17N 76.37W
Baltiysk Russian Fed. 23 54.39N 19.55E
Baluchistan *f.* Pakistan 38 28.00N 66.00E
Balumbah Australia 66 33.16S136.14E
Bālurghāt India 41 25.13N 88.46E
Balygychan Russian Fed. 29 63.55N154.12E
Balykshi Kazakhstan 25 47.04N 51.55E
Bām Iran 43 29.07N 58.20E
Bama Nigeria 53 11.35N 13.40E
Bamaga Australia 64 10.52S142.23E
Bamako Mali 52 12.40N 7.59W
Bamako *d.* Mali 52 12.40N 7.55W
Bamba Kenya 55 3.33S 39.32E
Bamba Mali 52 17.05N 1.23W
Bamba Zaïre 54 5.45S 18.23E
Bambari C.A.R. 49 5.45N 20.40E
Bamberg Germany 20 49.54N 10.53E
Bambesa Zaïre 54 3.27N 25.43E
Bambesi Ethiopia 49 9.45N 34.40E
Bambili Zaïre 54 3.34N 26.07E
Bambio C.A.R. 53 3.55N 16.57E
Bambuí Brazil 94 20.01S 45.59W
Bam Co *l.* China 41 31.30N 91.10E
Bamenda Cameroon 53 5.55N 10.09E
Bāmīān Afghan. 40 34.50N 67.50E
Bamingui C.A.R. 49 7.34N 20.11E
Bamingui Bangoran *d.* C.A.R. 49 8.30N 20.30E
Bampton U.K. 11 51.00N 3.29W
Bampūr Iran 43 27.13N 60.29E
Bampūr *r.* Iran 43 27.18N 59.02E
Bāmra Hills India 41 21.20N 84.30E
Banaba *i.* Kiribati 68 0.52S169.35E
Banagher Rep. of Ire. 13 53.12N 8.00W
Banalia Zaïre 54 1.33N 25.23E
Banamba Mali 52 13.29N 7.22W
Banana Zaïre 54 5.55S 12.27E
Bananal, Ilha do *f.* Brazil 91 11.30S 50.15W
Ban Aranyaprathet Thailand 34 13.43N102.31E
Banās *r.* India 40 25.54N 76.45E
Banâs, Ra's *c.* Egypt 42 23.54N 35.48E
Ban Ban Laos 34 19.38N103.34E
Banbridge U.K. 13 54.21N 6.17W
Ban Bua Chum Thailand 34 15.15N101.15E
Banbury U.K. 11 52.04N 1.21W
Banchory U.K. 12 57.03N 2.30W
Bancroft Canada 76 45.03N 77.51W
Band Afghan. 40 33.17N 68.39E
Banda Gabon 54 3.47S 11.04E
Banda Madhya P. India 41 24.03N 78.57E
Bānda Uttar P. India 41 25.29N 80.20E
Banda, Laut *sea* Indonesia 37 5.00S128.00E
Banda Aceh Indonesia 36 5.35N 95.20E
Banda Besar *i.* Indonesia 37 4.30S129.55E
Bānda Dāūd Shāh Pakistan 40 33.16N 71.11E
Bandama *r.* Ivory Coast 52 5.10N 4.59W
Bandar 'Abbās Iran 43 27.10N 56.15E
Bandar Beheshtī Iran 43 25.17N 60.41E
Bandar-e Anzalī Iran 43 37.26N 49.29E
Bandar-e Deylam Iran 43 30.05N 50.11E
Bandar-e Khomeynī Iran 43 30.25N 49.03E
Bandar-e-Lengeh Iran 43 26.34N 54.53E
Bandar-e Rīg Iran 43 29.30N 50.40E
Bandar-e Torkeman Iran 43 36.55N 54.05E
Bandar Seri Begawan Brunei 36 4.56N114.58E
Banda Sea *see* Banda, Laut *sea* Indonesia 37
Bandawe Malaŵi 55 11.57S 34.11E
Bandeira *mtn.* Brazil 94 20.25S 41.45W
Bāndhi Pakistan 40 26.36N 68.18E
Bandiagara Mali 52 14.12N 3.29W
Bāndikūi India 40 27.03N 76.34E
Bandīpur Nepal 41 27.56N 84.25E
Bandipura Jammu & Kashmir 40 34.25N 74.39E
Bandirma Turkey 19 40.22N 28.00E
Bandon Rep. of Ire. 13 51.45N 8.45W
Bandon *r.* Rep. of Ire. 13 51.43N 8.38W
Bandundu Zaïre 54 3.20S 17.24E
Bandundu *d.* Zaïre 54 4.00S 18.30E
Bandung Indonesia 37 6.57S107.34E
Banes Cuba 87 20.59N 75.24W
Banff Canada 74 51.10N115.34W
Banff U.K. 12 57.40N 2.31W
Banff Nat. Park Canada 74 51.30N116.15W
Banfora Burkina 52 10.36N 4.45W
Bangalore India 38 12.58N 77.35E
Bangassou C.A.R. 49 4.50N 23.07E
Banggai, Kepulauan *is.* Indonesia 37 1.30S123.10E
Banggi *i.* Malaysia 36 7.17N117.12E
Banggong Co *l.* China 41 33.45N 79.15E
Banghāzī Libya 51 32.07N 20.05E
Banghāzī *d.* Libya 51 25.40N 21.00E
Bangil Indonesia 37 7.34S112.47E
Bangka *i.* Indonesia 36 2.20S106.10E
Bangkalan Indonesia 37 7.05S112.44E
Bangkog Co *l.* China 41 31.45N 89.30E
Bangkok Thailand 34 13.44N100.30E
Bangladesh Asia 41 24.30N 90.00E
Bangor Rep. of Ire. 13 54.09N 9.44W
Bangor Down U.K. 13 54.40N 5.41W
Bangor Gywnnedd U.K. 10 53.13N 4.09W
Bangor Maine U.S.A. 84 44.49N 68.47W
Bangor Penn. U.S.A. 85 40.52N 75.13W
Bang Saphan Thailand 34 11.14N 99.31E
Bangui C.A.R. 53 4.23N 18.37E
Bangui Phil. 33 18.33N120.45E
Banguru Zaïre 55 0.30N 27.10E
Bangweulu, L. Zambia 55 11.15S 29.45E
Banhā Egypt 44 30.28N 31.11E
Ban Hat Yai Thailand 34 7.10N100.28E
Ban Houayxay Laos 34 20.21N100.32E
Bani *r.* Mali 52 14.30N 4.15W
Bani, Jbel *mtn.* Morocco 50 30.00N 8.00W
Banikoara Benin 53 11.21N 2.25E
Banī Mazār Egypt 44 28.29N 30.48E
Banīnah Libya 51 32.05N 20.16E
Banī Suwayf Egypt 44 29.05N 31.05E
Banī Walīd Libya 51 31.46N 13.59E
Bāniyās Syria 44 35.09N 35.58E
Banja Luka Bosnia-Herzegovina 19 44.47N 17.10E
Banjarmasin Indonesia 36 3.22S114.36E
Banjul Gambia 52 13.28N 16.39W
Bānka India 41 24.53N 86.55E
Banka Banka Australia 64 18.48S134.01E
Ban Kan Vietnam 34 22.08N105.49E
Ban Kantang Thailand 34 7.25N 99.35E
Bankasse Mali 52 14.01N 3.29W
Banks I. B.C. Canada 74 53.25N130.10W
Banks I. N.W.T. Canada 72 73.00N122.00W
Banks Is. Vanuatu 68 13.50S167.30E
Banks Pen. New Zealand 60 43.45S173.10E
Banks Str. Australia 65 40.37S148.07E
Bānkura India 41 23.15N 87.04E
Ban-m'drack Vietnam 34 12.45N108.50E
Bann *r.* U.K. 13 55.10N 6.46W
Ban Na San Thailand 34 8.53N 99.17E
Bannockburn U.K. 12 56.06N 3.55W
Bannockburn Zimbabwe 56 20.16S 29.51E
Bannu Pakistan 40 32.59N 70.36E
Ban Pak Phraek Thailand 34 8.13N100.13E
Bānsda India 40 20.45N 73.22E
Banská Bystrica Slovakia 21 48.44N 19.07E
Bānswāra India 40 23.33N 74.27E
Bantaeng Indonesia 36 5.32S119.58E
Banté Benin 53 8.26N 1.54E
Bantry Rep. of Ire. 13 51.41N 9.27W
Bantry B. Rep. of Ire. 13 51.40N 9.40W
Bāntva India 40 21.29N 70.05E
Banyak, Kepulauan *is.* Indonesia 36 2.15N 97.10E
Banyo Cameroon 53 6.47N 11.50E
Banyuwangi Indonesia 37 8.12S114.22E
Banzare Coast *f.* Antarctica 96 66.30S125.00E
Baode China 32 39.00N111.05E
Baoding China 32 38.50N115.26E
Bao Ha Vietnam 33 22.10N104.22E
Baoji China 32 34.20N107.17E
Baojing China 33 28.43N109.37E
Bao-Loc Vietnam 34 11.30N107.54E
Baoshan China 39 25.07N 99.08E
Baotou China 32 40.35N109.59E
Baoulé *r.* Mali 52 13.47N 10.45W
Bāp India 40 27.23N 72.21E
Bapaume France 14 50.07N 2.51E
Baqên China 41 31.56N 94.00E
Ba'qūbah Iraq 43 33.45N 44.38E
Bar Albania 19 42.05N 19.06E
Bar Ukraine 21 49.05N 27.40E
Bara Nigeria 53 10.24N 10.43E
Baraawe Somali Rep. 55 1.02N 44.02E
Barabinsk Russian Fed. 28 55.20N 78.18E
Baraboo U.S.A. 82 43.28N 89.50W
Baracoa Cuba 87 20.23N 74.31W
Baradero Argentina 93 33.50S 59.30W
Baradine Australia 67 30.56S149.05E
Baradine *r.* Australia 67 30.17S148.27E
Baragoi Kenya 49 1.47N 36.47E
Bârah Sudan 49 13.42N 30.22E
Barahona Dom. Rep. 87 18.13N 71.07W
Baraka Zaïre 55 4.09S 29.05E
Baraki Barak Afghan. 40 33.56N 68.55E
Barākot India 41 21.33N 85.01E
Bārāmūla Jammu & Kashmir 40 34.12N 74.21E
Bārān India 40 25.06N 76.31E
Baranagar India 41 22.38N 88.22E
Baranoa Colombia 90 10.50N 74.55W
Baranof I. U.S.A. 74 57.00N135.00W
Baranovichi Belorussia 21 53.09N 26.00E
Baratta Australia 66 32.01S139.10E
Barbacena Brazil 94 21.13S 43.47W
Barbados Lesser Antilles 87 13.20N 59.40W
Barbar Sudan 48 18.01N 33.59E
Barbastro Spain 16 42.02N 0.07E
Barberton R.S.A. 56 25.46S 31.02E
Barbezieux France 17 45.28N 0.09W
Barbil India 41 22.06N 85.20E
Barbuda *i.* Leeward Is. 87 17.41N 61.48W
Barcaldine Australia 64 23.31S145.15E
Barcellona Italy 18 38.10N 15.13E
Barcelona Spain 16 41.25N 2.10E
Barcelona Venezuela 90 10.08N 64.43W
Barcelos Brazil 90 0.59S 62.58W
Barcoo *r.* Australia 64 25.30S142.50E
Barcs Hungary 21 45.58N 17.28E
Bardai Chad 53 21.21N 16.56E
Bardejov Slovakia 21 49.18N 21.16E
Bardi Italy 15 44.38N 9.44E
Bardīa Nepal 41 28.18N 81.23E
Bardīyah Libya 48 31.46N 25.06E
Bardoli India 40 21.07N 73.07E
Bardsey *i.* U.K. 10 52.45N 4.48W
Bardu Norway 22 68.54N 18.20E
Bardufoss Norway 22 69.00N 18.30E
Bareilly India 41 28.21N 79.25E
Barellan Australia 67 34.17S146.34E
Barengapāra India 41 25.14N 90.14E
Barentsovo More *see* Barents Sea Arctic Oc. 24
Barents Sea Arctic Oc. 24 73.00N 40.00E
Barentu Ethiopia 48 15.04N 37.37E
Barfleur France 15 49.40N 1.15W
Barga China 41 30.51N 81.20E
Bargarh India 41 21.20N 83.37E
Barge Ethiopia 49 6.15N 37.00E
Barge Italy 15 44.43N 7.20E
Barghanak Afghan. 40 33.56N 62.26E
Barguzin Russian Fed. 29 53.40N109.35E
Barham Australia 66 35.37S144.10E
Barharwa India 41 24.52N 87.47E
Barhi India 41 24.18N 85.25E
Bāri Madhya P. India 41 23.03N 78.05E
Bāri Rāj. India 41 26.39N 77.36E
Bari Italy 19 41.08N 16.52E
Baricho Kenya 55 3.07S 39.47E
Barika Algeria 51 35.25N 5.19E
Barīm *i.* Yemen 45 12.40N 43.24E
Barinas Venezuela 90 8.36N 70.15W
Baripāda India 41 21.56N 86.43E
Bariri Brazil 94 22.04S 48.41W
Bârîs Egypt 42 24.40N 30.36E
Bari Sādri India 40 24.25N 74.28E
Barisāl Bangla. 41 22.42N 90.22E
Barisan, Pegunungan *mts.* Indonesia 36 3.30S102.30E
Barito *r.* Indonesia 36 3.35S114.35E
Barjūj, Wādī Libya 51 26.03N 12.50E
Barker U.S.A. 76 43.20N 78.33W
Barker L. Australia 63 31.45S120.05E
Bārkhān Pakistan 40 29.54N 69.31E
Barking U.K. 11 51.32N 0.05E
Barkley Sd. Canada 74 48.53N125.20W
Barkly East R.S.A. 56 30.58S 27.33E
Barkly Tableland *f.* Australia 64 19.00S136.40E
Barkly West R.S.A. 56 28.32S 24.29E
Bar-le-Duc France 17 48.46N 5.10E
Barlee, L. Australia 63 29.10S119.30E
Barlee Range *mts.* Australia 62 23.40S116.00E
Barletta Italy 18 41.20N 16.15E
Barlow L. Canada 75 62.00N103.00W
Barmedman Australia 67 34.08S147.25E
Barmer India 40 25.45N 71.23E
Barmera Australia 66 34.15S140.31E
Barm Firūz, Kūh-e *mtn.* Iran 43 30.21N 52.00E
Barmouth U.K. 10 52.44N 4.03W
Barnagar India 40 23.03N 75.22E
Barnāla India 40 30.22N 75.33E
Barnard Castle *town* U.K. 10 54.33N 1.55W
Barnato Australia 67 31.38S144.59E
Barnaul Russian Fed. 28 53.21N 83.15E
Barnegat U.S.A. 85 39.45N 74.13W
Barnegat B. U.S.A. 85 39.52N 74.07W
Barnegat Light U.S.A. 85 39.46N 74.06W
Barnet U.K. 11 51.39N 0.11W
Barneveld Neth. 14 52.10N 5.39E
Barneville France 15 49.23N 1.45W
Barneys L. Australia 66 33.16S144.13E
Barnsley U.K. 10 53.33N 1.29W
Barnstaple U.K. 11 51.05N 4.03W
Baro *r.* Ethiopia 49 8.26N 33.13E
Baro Nigeria 53 8.37N 6.19E
Barpeta India 41 26.19N 91.00E
Barqah *f.* Libya 48 31.00N 23.00E
Barquisimeto Venezuela 90 10.03N 69.18W
Barra Brazil 91 11.06S 43.15W
Barra *i.* U.K. 12 56.59N 7.28W
Barra, Sd. of U.K. 12 57.04N 7.20W
Barraba Australia 67 30.24S152.36E
Barra do Corda Brazil 91 5.30S 45.15W
Barra do Piraí Brazil 94 22.28S 43.49W
Barragem Agua Vermelha *resr.* Brazil 94 19.50S 50.00W
Barragem de São Simão *resr.* Brazil 94 18.35S 50.00W
Barra Head U.K. 8 56.47N 7.36W
Barra Mansa Brazil 94 22.35S 44.12W
Barranca Peru 90 4.50S 76.40W
Barrancabermeja Colombia 90 7.06N 73.54W
Barrancas Venezuela 90 8.45N 62.13W
Barrancos Portugal 16 38.10N 7.01W
Barranqueras Argentina 94 27.30S 58.55W
Barranquilla Colombia 90 11.10N 74.50W
Barraute Canada 76 48.26N 77.39W
Barre U.S.A. 84 44.12N 72.30W
Barreiras Brazil 91 12.09S 44.58W
Barreiro Portugal 16 38.40N 9.05W
Barreiros Brazil 91 8.49S 35.12W
Barrême France 20 43.57N 6.22E
Barretos Brazil 94 20.37S 48.38W
Barrhead Canada 74 54.10N114.24W
Barrhead U.K. 12 55.47N 4.24W
Barrie Canada 76 44.22N 79.42W
Barrier Range *mts.* Australia 66 31.25S141.25E
Barrington Tops *mts.* Australia 67 32.30S151.28E
Barringun Australia 67 29.01S145.43E
Barron U.S.A. 80 48.44N120.43W
Barrow *r.* Rep. of Ire. 13 52.17N 7.00W
Barrow U.S.A. 72 71.16N156.50W
Barrow Creek *town* Australia 64 21.32S133.53E
Barrow I. Australia 62 21.40S115.27E
Barrow-in-Furness U.K. 10 54.08N 3.15W
Barrow Range *mts.* Australia 62 26.04S127.28E
Barry U.K. 11 51.23N 3.19W
Barstow U.S.A. 81 34.54N117.01W
Bar-sur-Aube France 15 48.14N 4.43E
Bar-sur-Seine France 15 48.07N 4.22E
Bartica Guyana 90 6.24N 58.38W
Bartin Turkey 42 41.37N 32.20E
Bartle Frere, Mt. Australia 64 17.23S145.49E
Bartlesville U.S.A. 83 36.45N 95.59W
Bartlett L. Canada 74 63.05N118.20W
Bartolomeu Dias Mozambique 57 21.10S 35.09E
Barton-upon-Humber U.K. 10 53.41N 0.27W
Bartoszyce Poland 21 54.16N 20.49E
Bartow U.S.A. 85 27.54N 81.51W
Bāruni India 41 25.29N 85.59E
Barwāh India 40 22.16N 76.03E
Barwāni India 40 22.02N 74.54E
Barwa Sāgar India 41 25.23N 78.44E
Barwon *r.* Australia 67 30.00S148.05E
Barysh Russian Fed. 24 53.40N 47.09E
Basāl Pakistan 40 33.33N 72.15E
Basankusu Zaïre 54 1.12N 19.50E
Basavilbaso Argentina 93 32.20S 58.52W
Basel Switz. 20 47.33N 7.36E
Bashi Channel Taiwan / Phil. 33 21.30N121.00E
Basilan Phil. 37 6.40N121.59E
Basilan *i.* Phil. 37 6.40N122.10E
Basildon U.K. 11 51.34N 0.25E
Basilicata *d.* Italy 18 40.30N 16.20E
Basin U.S.A. 80 44.23N108.02W
Basingstoke U.K. 11 51.15N 1.05W
Basin L. Canada 75 52.38N105.18W
Baskatong, Résr. Canada 76 46.48N 75.50W
Basmat India 40 19.19N 77.10E
Bāsoda India 41 23.51N 77.56E
Basoko Zaïre 49 1.20N 23.36E
Basongo Zaïre 49 4.23S 20.28E
Bassano Canada 74 50.48N112.20W
Bassano Italy 15 45.46N 11.44E
Bassari Togo 52 9.12N 0.18E
Bassein Burma 34 16.46N 94.45E
Basse-Kotto *d.* C.A.R. 49 5.00N 21.30E
Basse Normandie *d.* France 15 49.00N 0.00
Basse Santa Su Gambia 52 13.23N 14.15W
Basse-Terre Guadeloupe 87 16.00N 61.43W
Bassett U.S.A. 82 42.35N 99.32W
Bass Str. Australia 65 39.45S146.00E
Bassum Germany 20 52.51N 8.43E
Båstad Sweden 23 56.26N 12.51E
Bastak Iran 43 27.15N 54.26E
Bastelica France 17 42.00N 9.03E
Basti India 41 26.48N 82.43E
Bastia France 17 42.41N 9.26E
Bastogne Belgium 14 50.00N 5.43E
Bastrop U.S.A. 83 32.47N 91.55W
Basyūn Egypt 44 30.57N 30.49E
Bas Zaïre *d.* Zaïre 54 5.15S 14.00E
Bata Equat. Guinea 54 1.51N 9.49E
Batabanó, Golfo de *g.* Cuba 87 23.15N 82.30W
Batāla India 40 31.48N 75.13E
Batalha Portugal 16 39.39N 8.50W
Batang China 39 30.02N 99.01E
Batangafo C.A.R. 53 7.27N 18.11E
Batangas Phil. 37 13.46N121.01E
Batan Is. Phil. 37 20.50N121.55E
Bátaszék Hungary 21 46.12N 18.44E
Batatais Brazil 94 20.54S 47.37W
Batavia U.S.A. 76 43.00N 78.11W
Bataysk Russian Fed. 25 47.09N 39.46E
Batchelor Australia 64 13.04S131.01E
Bātdâmbâng Cambodia 34 13.06N103.12E
Batemans Bay *town* Australia 67 35.55S150.09E
Batesville Ark. U.S.A. 83 35.46N 91.39W
Batesville Miss. U.S.A. 83 34.18N 90.00W
Bath Canada 77 46.31N 67.37W
Bath U.K. 11 51.22N 2.22W
Bath Maine U.S.A. 84 43.55N 69.49W
Bath N.Y. U.S.A. 84 42.20N 77.19W
Batha *d.* Chad 53 14.30N 18.30E
Batha *r.* Chad 53 12.47N 17.34E
Baṭhā, Wādī al *r.* Oman 43 20.01N 59.39E
Bathgate U.K. 12 55.44N 3.38W
Bathurst Australia 67 33.27S149.35E
Bathurst Canada 77 47.36N 65.39W
Bathurst R.S.A. 56 33.30S 26.48E
Bathurst, C. Canada 72 70.30N128.00W
Bathurst I. Australia 62 11.45S130.15E
Bathurst I. Canada 73 76.00N100.00W
Bathurst Inlet *town* Canada 72 66.48N108.00W
Batibla C.A.R. 49 5.56N 21.09E
Batié Burkina 52 9.42N 2.53W
Batina Croatia 21 45.51N 18.51E
Batley U.K. 10 53.43N 1.38W
Batlow Australia 67 35.32S148.10E
Batman Turkey 42 37.52N 41.07E
Batna Algeria 51 35.35N 6.11E
Baton Rouge U.S.A. 83 30.23N 91.11W
Batopilas Mexico 81 27.00N107.45W
Batouri Cameroon 53 4.26N 14.27E
Batson U.S.A. 83 30.15N 94.37W
Batticaloa Sri Lanka 39 7.43N 81.42E
Battle *r.* Canada 75 52.43N108.15W
Battle U.K. 11 50.55N 0.30E
Battle Creek *town* U.S.A. 84 42.20N 85.11W
Battleford Canada 75 52.45N108.15W
Battle Harbour Canada 77 52.17N 55.35W
Batu *mtn.* Ethiopia 49 6.55N 39.46E
Batu, Kepulauan *is.* Indonesia 36 0.30S 98.20E
Batumi Georgia 42 41.37N 41.36E
Batu Pahat Malaysia 36 1.50N102.48E
Baturaja Indonesia 36 4.10S104.10E
Baturité Brazil 91 4.20S 38.53W
Bat Yam Israel 44 32.01N 34.45E
Baubau Indonesia 37 5.30S122.37E
Bauchi Nigeria 53 10.16N 9.50E
Bauchi *d.* Nigeria 53 10.40N 10.00E
Baudh India 41 20.50N 84.19E
Baugé France 15 47.33N 0.06W
Bauld, C. Canada 77 51.38N 55.25W
Bauru Brazil 94 22.19S 49.07W
Baús Brazil 94 18.19S 53.10W
Bauska Latvia 23 56.24N 24.14E
Bautzen Germany 20 51.11N 14.29E
Bavay France 14 50.18N 3.48E
Bawean *i.* Indonesia 37 5.50S112.39E
Bawku Ghana 52 11.05N 0.13W
Bayamo Cuba 87 20.23N 76.39W
Bayamón Puerto Rico 87 18.24N 66.10W
Bāyan, Band-e *mts.* Afghan. 40 34.20N 65.00E
Bayāna India 40 26.54N 77.17E
Bayan Har Shan *mts.* China 30 34.00N 97.20E
Bayan Nur China 32 38.14N103.56E
Bayburt Turkey 42 40.15N 40.16E
Bay City Mich. U.S.A. 84 43.35N 83.52W
Bay City Tex. U.S.A. 83 28.59N 95.58W
Baydaratskaya Guba *b.* Russian Fed. 28 70.00N 66.00E
Baydhabo Somali Rep. 55 3.08N 43.34E
Bayern *d.* Germany 20 48.30N 11.30E
Bayeux France 15 49.16N 0.42W
Bayfield U.S.A. 82 46.49N 90.49W
Baykal, Ozero *l.* Russian Fed. 30 53.30N100.00E
Baykit Russian Fed. 29 61.45N 96.22E
Baykonyr Kazakhstan 28 47.50N 66.03E
Bay of Plenty *d.* New Zealand 60 38.00S177.10E
Bayombong Phil. 37 16.27N121.10E
Bayonne France 17 43.30N 1.28W
Bayovar Peru 90 5.50S 81.03W
Bayreuth Germany 20 49.56N 11.35E
Bayrūt Lebanon 44 33.52N 35.30E
Baytik Shan *mts.* China 30 45.15N 90.50E
Baytown U.S.A. 83 29.44N 94.58W
Bay View New Zealand 60 39.26S176.52E
Baza Spain 16 37.30N 2.45W
Baza, Sierra de *mts.* Spain 16 37.15N 2.45W
Bazaliya Ukraine 21 49.42N 26.29E
Bazaruto, Ilha do *i.* Mozambique 57 21.40S 35.28E
Bazas France 17 44.26N 0.13W
Bazdār Pakistan 40 26.21N 65.03E
Bazhong China 33 31.51N106.42E
Bazmān Iran 43 27.48N 60.12E
Bazmān, Kūh-e *mtn.* Iran 43 28.06N 60.00E
Beach U.S.A. 82 46.55N103.52W
Beach Haven U.S.A. 85 39.34N 74.14W
Beachport Australia 66 37.29S140.01E
Beachwood U.S.A. 85 39.56N 74.12W
Beachy Head U.K. 11 50.43N 0.15E
Beacon U.S.A. 85 41.30N 73.58W
Beagle Bay *town* Australia 62 16.58S122.40E
Bealanana Madagascar 57 14.33S 48.44E

Beardstown to Bilāspur

Beardstown U.S.A. 82 40.01N 90.26W
Bear I. see Bjørnøya i. Arctic Oc. 96
Bear L. U.S.A. 80 42.00N111.20W
Bearskin Lake town Canada 75 53.58N 91.02W
Beas r. India 40 31.10N 75.00E
Beatrice U.S.A. 82 40.16N 96.44W
Beatrice, C. Australia 64 14.15S136.59E
Beatton r. Canada 74 56.15N120.45W
Beatton River town Canada 74 57.26N121.20W
Beatty U.S.A. 80 36.54N116.46W
Beattyville Canada 76 48.53N 77.10W
Beauce f. France 15 48.22N 1.50E
Beaudesert Australia 67 27.58S153.01E
Beaufort Australia 66 37.28S143.28E
Beaufort U.S.A. 85 32.26N 80.40W
Beaufort Sea N. America 72 72.00N141.00W
Beaufort West R.S.A. 56 32.20S 22.34E
Beaugency France 15 47.47N 1.38E
Beauharnois Canada 77 45.19N 73.52W
Beaulieu r. Canada 74 62.03N113.11W
Beauly U.K. 12 57.29N 4.29W
Beauly r. U.K. 12 57.29N 4.25W
Beaumaris U.K. 10 53.16N 4.07W
Beaumetz-lès-Loges France 14 50.15N 2.36E
Beaumont Belgium 14 50.14N 4.16E
Beaumont Miss. U.S.A. 83 31.11N 88.55W
Beaumont Tex. U.S.A. 83 30.05N 94.06W
Beaumont-le-Roger France 15 49.05N 0.47E
Beaumont-sur-Sarthe France 15 48.13N 0.07E
Beaune France 17 47.02N 4.50E
Beaune-la-Rolande France 15 48.04N 2.26E
Beaupréau France 17 47.12N 0.59W
Beauséjour Canada 75 50.04N 96.33W
Beauvais France 15 49.26N 2.05E
Beauval Canada 75 55.09N107.35W
Beauvoir France 17 46.55N 2.01W
Beaver r. N.W.T. Canada 74 59.43N124.16W
Beaver r. Ont. Canada 75 55.55N 87.50W
Beaver Alas. U.S.A. 72 66.22N147.24W
Beaver Okla. U.S.A. 83 36.49N100.31W
Beaver Dam town U.S.A. 82 43.28N 88.50W
Beaverhill L. Alta. Canada 74 53.27N112.32W
Beaverhill L. N.W.T. Canada 75 63.02N104.22W
Beaver I. U.S.A. 84 45.42N 85.28W
Beāwar India 40 26.06N 74.19E
Bebedouro Brazil 94 20.54S 48.31W
Bebington U.K. 10 53.23N 3.01W
Bécancour Canada 77 46.20N 72.26W
Beccles U.K. 11 52.27N 1.33E
Bečej Yugo. 21 45.37N 20.03E
Béchar Algeria 50 31.37N 2.13W
Beckley U.S.A. 85 37.46N 81.12W
Beckum Germany 14 51.45N 8.02E
Beclean Romania 21 47.11N 24.10E
Bédarieux France 17 43.35N 3.10E
Bedēsa Ethiopia 49 8.50N 40.45E
Bedford Canada 77 45.07N 72.59W
Bedford U.K. 11 52.08N 0.29W
Bedford U.S.A. 84 38.51N 86.30W
Bedford, C. Australia 64 15.14S145.21E
Bedford Levels f. U.K. 11 52.35N 0.08W
Bedfordshire d. U.K. 11 52.04N 0.28W
Bedi India 40 22.30N 70.02E
Bedlington U.K. 10 55.08N 1.34W
Bedourie Australia 64 24.21S139.28E
Beech Grove U.S.A. 84 39.42N 86.06W
Beechworth Australia 67 36.23S146.42E
Beenleigh Australia 67 27.43S153.09E
Be'er Menuha Israel 44 30.19N 35.08E
Be'er Sheva' Israel 44 31.15N 34.47E
Beerta Neth. 14 53.12N 7.07E
Beeston U.K. 10 52.55N 1.11W
Beeville U.S.A. 83 28.24N 97.45W
Befale Zaïre 54 0.27N 21.01E
Befandriana Madagascar 57 22.06S 43.54E
Befandriana Madagascar 57 15.16S 48.32E
Beg, Lough U.K. 13 54.47N 6.29W
Bega Australia 67 36.41S149.50E
Begamganj India 41 23.36N 78.20E
Bègles France 17 44.48N 0.32W
Begna r. Norway 23 60.32N 10.00E
Begusarai India 41 25.25N 86.08E
Behara Madagascar 57 25.00S 46.25E
Behbehān Iran 43 30.35N 50.17E
Bei'an China 31 48.17N126.33E
Beihai China 33 21.29N109.09E
Bei Jiang r. China 33 23.19N112.51E
Beijing China 32 39.55N116.25E
Beijing d. China 32 40.00N116.30E
Beijing Shi d. China 31 40.15N116.30E
Beilen Neth. 14 52.51N 6.31E
Beinn Dearg mtn. U.K. 12 57.47N 4.55W
Beipa'a P.N.G. 64 8.30S146.35E
Beipiao China 32 41.47N120.40E
Beira Mozambique 57 19.49S 34.52E
Beirut see Bayrūt Lebanon 44
Beitang China 32 39.06N117.43E
Beitbridge Zimbabwe 56 22.10S 30.01E
Beiuş Romania 21 46.40N 22.21E
Beja Portugal 16 38.01N 7.52W
Béja Tunisia 51 36.44N 9.11E
Bejaïa Algeria 51 36.45N 5.05E
Béjar Spain 16 40.24N 5.45W
Bejestān Iran 43 34.32N 58.08E
Bejhi r. Pakistan 40 29.47N 67.58E
Bejoording Australia 63 31.22S116.30E
Békés Hungary 21 46.46N 21.08E
Békéscsaba Hungary 21 46.41N 21.06E
Bekily Madagascar 57 24.13S 45.19E
Bela India 41 25.56N 81.59E
Bela Pakistan 40 26.14N 66.19E
Bélabo Cameroon 53 5.00N 13.20E
Bela Crkva Yugo. 21 44.54N 21.26E
Bel Air U.S.A. 85 39.32N 76.21W
Belalcázar Spain 16 38.35N 5.10W
Belampalli India 41 19.02N 79.30E
Belang Indonesia 37 0.58N124.56E
Bela Vista Brazil 92 22.05S 56.22W
Bela Vista Mozambique 57 26.20S 32.41E
Belaya r. Russian Fed. 28 55.40N 52.30E
Belaya Glina Russian Fed. 25 46.04N 40.54E
Belaya Tserkov Ukraine 21 49.49N 30.10E
Belcher Is. Canada 76 56.00N 79.00W
Belcoo U.K. 13 54.18N 7.53W
Belda India 41 22.05N 87.21E
Belebey Russian Fed. 24 54.05N 54.07E
Beled Weyne Somali Rep. 45 4.47N 45.12E
Belém Brazil 91 1.27S 48.29W
Belem Mozambique 57 14.11S 35.59E
Belén Uruguay 93 30.47S 57.47W
Belen U.S.A. 81 34.40N106.46W
Belén, Cuchilla de mts. Uruguay 93 30.49S 56.28W
Beles r. Ethiopia 45 11.10N 35.10E
Belev Russian Fed. 24 53.50N 36.08E
Belfast U.K. 13 54.36N 5.57W
Belfast U.S.A. 84 44.27N 69.01W
Belfast Lough U.K. 13 54.42N 5.45W
Belfield U.S.A. 82 46.53N103.12W
Belfort France 17 47.38N 6.52E
Belfry U.S.A. 80 45.09N109.01W
Belgaum India 38 15.54N 74.36E
Belgium Europe 14 51.00N 4.30E
Belgorod Russian Fed. 25 50.38N 36.36E
Belgorod-Dnestrovskiy Ukraine 21 46.10N 30.19E
Belgrade see Beograd Yugo. 21
Beli Nigeria 53 7.53N 10.59E
Belitung i. Indonesia 36 3.00S108.00E
Belize Belize 87 17.29N 88.20W
Belize C. America 87 17.00N 88.30W
Belka Australia 63 31.45S118.09E
Bellac France 17 46.07N 1.04E
Bella Coola Canada 74 52.25N126.40W
Bellagio Italy 15 45.59N 9.15E
Bellaire U.S.A. 83 29.44N 95.03W
Bellaria Italy 15 44.09N 12.28E
Bellary India 38 15.11N 76.54E
Bellata Australia 67 29.55S149.50E
Bella Unión Uruguay 93 30.15S 57.35W
Bella Vista Corrientes Argentina 92 28.30S 59.00W
Bella Vista Tucuman Argentina 92 27.02S 65.19W
Bellbrook Australia 67 30.48S152.30E
Bellefontaine U.S.A. 84 40.22N 83.45W
Belle Fourche r. U.S.A. 82 44.26N102.19W
Belle Glade U.S.A. 85 26.41N 80.41W
Belle Île France 17 47.20N 3.10W
Belle Isle Canada 77 51.55N 55.20W
Belle Isle, Str. of Canada 77 51.35N 56.30W
Bellême France 15 48.22N 0.34E
Belleoram Canada 77 47.32N 55.28W
Belleville Canada 76 44.10N 77.22W
Belleville U.S.A. 82 39.49N 97.38W
Bellevue Canada 74 49.35N114.22W
Bellevue Idaho U.S.A. 80 43.28N114.16W
Bellevue Penn. U.S.A. 84 40.32N 80.08W
Bellevue Wash. U.S.A. 80 47.37N122.12W
Belle Yella Liberia 52 7.24N 10.09W
Bellingen Australia 67 30.28S152.43E
Bellingham U.K. 10 55.09N 2.15W
Bellingham U.S.A. 80 48.46N122.29W
Bellingshausen Sea Antarctica 96 70.00S 88.00W
Bellinzona Switz. 15 46.11N 9.02E
Bello Colombia 90 6.20N 75.41W
Bellpat Pakistan 40 28.59N 68.00E
Belluno Italy 15 46.09N 12.13E
Bell Ville Argentina 93 32.35S 62.41W
Belmar U.S.A. 85 40.11N 74.01W
Bélmez Spain 16 38.17N 5.17W
Belmond U.S.A. 82 42.51N 93.37W
Belmont Australia 67 33.02S151.40E
Belmopan Belize 87 17.25N 88.46W
Belmullet Rep. of Ire. 13 54.14N 10.00W
Belogradchik Bulgaria 21 43.38N 22.41E
Belo Horizonte Brazil 94 19.45S 43.54W
Beloit Kans. U.S.A. 82 39.28N 98.06W
Beloit Wisc. U.S.A. 82 42.31N 89.02W
Belo Jardim Brazil 91 8.22S 36.22W
Belokorovichi Ukraine 21 51.04N 28.00E
Belomorsk Russian Fed. 24 64.34N 34.45E
Belonia India 41 23.15N 91.27E
Beloretsk Russian Fed. 24 53.59N 58.20E
Belorussia Europe 21 53.30N 28.00E
Beloye More sea Russian Fed. 24 65.30N 38.00E
Beloye Ozero l. Russian Fed. 24 60.12N 37.45E
Belozersk Russian Fed. 24 60.00N 37.49E
Belper U.K. 10 53.02N 1.29W
Beltana Australia 66 30.40S138.27E
Belterra Brazil 91 2.38S 54.57W
Belton Australia 66 32.12S138.45E
Belton U.S.A. 83 31.04N 97.28W
Beltsy Moldavia 21 47.45N 27.59E
Belukha, Gora mtn. Russian Fed. 30 49.48N 86.40E
Belvidere U.S.A. 85 40.49N 75.05W
Belyando r. Australia 64 21.38S146.50E
Belyayevka Ukraine 21 46.30N 30.12E
Belynichi Belorussia 21 54.00N 29.42E
Belyy, Ostrov Russian Fed. 28 73.10N 70.45E
Belyy Yar Russian Fed. 28 58.28N 85.03E
Belzec Poland 21 50.24N 23.26E
Bemaraha, Plateau du mts. Madagascar 57 20.00S 45.15E
Bemarivo r. Madagascar 57 15.27S 47.40E
Bemidji U.S.A. 82 47.29N 94.53W
Bena Dibele Zaïre 54 4.07S 22.50E
Benagerie Australia 66 31.30S140.21E
Benalla Australia 67 36.35S145.58E
Benanee Australia 66 34.32S142.56E
Benares see Vārānasi India 41
Benavente Spain 16 42.00N 5.40W
Benbecula i. U.K. 12 57.26N 7.18W
Bencha China 32 32.31N120.53E
Ben Cruachan mtn. U.K. 12 56.26N 5.18W
Bencubbin Australia 63 30.48S117.52E
Bend U.S.A. 80 44.03N121.19W
Bende Nigeria 53 5.34N 7.37E
Bendemeer Australia 67 30.52S151.10E
Bender Beyla Somali Rep. 45 9.30N 50.30E
Bendery Moldavia 21 46.50N 29.29E
Bendigo Australia 66 36.48S144.21E
Bendoc Australia 67 37.10S148.55E
Bendorf Germany 14 50.26N 7.34E
Bénéna Mali 52 13.09N 4.17W
Benenitra Madagascar 57 23.27S 45.05E
Benešov Czech Republic 20 49.45N 14.22E
Benevento Italy 18 41.07N 14.46E
Bengal, B. of Indian Oc. 41 20.00N 90.00E
Bengbu China 32 32.53N117.26E
Benghazi see Banghāzī Libya 51
Bengkulu Indonesia 36 3.46S102.16E
Bengo d. Angola 54 9.00S 13.40E
Benguela Angola 54 12.34S 13.24E
Benguela d. Angola 54 12.45S 14.00E
Ben Hope mtn. U.K. 12 58.24N 4.36W
Beni r. Bolivia 92 10.23S 65.24W
Beni Zaïre 55 0.29N 29.27E
Beni Abbes Algeria 50 30.08N 2.10W
Benicarló Spain 16 40.25N 0.25E
Benidorm Spain 16 38.33N 0.09W
Beni-Mellal Morocco 50 32.22N 6.29W
Benin Africa 53 9.00N 2.30E
Benin, Bight of Africa 53 5.30N 3.00E
Benin City Nigeria 53 6.19N 5.41E
Beni Saf Algeria 50 35.19N 1.23W
Benjamin Constant Brazil 90 4.22S 70.02W
Benkelman U.S.A. 82 40.03N101.32W
Ben Lawers mtn. U.K. 12 56.33N 4.14W
Ben Lomond mtn. U.K. 12 56.12N 4.38W
Ben Macdhui mtn. U.K. 12 57.04N 3.40W
Ben More mtn. Central U.K. 12 56.23N 4.31W
Ben More mtn. Strath. U.K. 12 56.26N 6.02W
Ben More Assynt mtn. U.K. 12 58.07N 4.52W
Bennett Canada 74 59.49N135.01W
Bennett, L. Australia 64 22.50S131.01E
Bennettsville U.S.A. 85 34.36N 79.40W
Ben Nevis mtn. U.K. 12 56.48N 5.00W
Benneydale New Zealand 60 38.31S175.21E
Benoni R.S.A. 56 26.12S 28.18E
Bénoué r. Cameroon see Benue r. Nigeria 53
Benson Ariz. U.S.A. 81 31.58N110.18W
Benson Minn. U.S.A. 82 45.19N 95.36W
Bentiaba Angola 54 14.19S 12.23E
Bentinck I. Australia 64 17.04S139.30E
Bentiu Sudan 49 9.14N 29.50E
Benton U.S.A. 82 38.01N 88.54W
Benton Harbor U.S.A. 84 42.07N 86.27W
Benue d. Nigeria 53 7.20N 8.00E
Benue r. Nigeria 53 7.52N 6.45E
Ben Wyvis mtn. U.K. 12 57.40N 4.35W
Benxi China 32 41.21N123.47E
Beograd Yugo. 21 44.49N 20.28E
Beohāri India 41 24.03N 81.23E
Beowawe U.S.A. 80 40.35N116.29W
Berat Albania 19 40.42N 19.59E
Berau, Teluk b. Indonesia 37 2.20S133.00E
Berbera Somali Rep. 45 10.28N 45.02E
Berbérati C.A.R. 53 4.19N 15.51E
Berceto Italy 15 44.31N 9.59E
Berchem Belgium 14 50.48N 3.32E
Berck France 17 50.25N 1.36E
Bercu France 14 50.32N 3.15E
Berdichev Ukraine 21 49.54N 28.39E
Berdsk Russian Fed. 28 54.51N 82.51E
Berdyansk Ukraine 25 46.45N 36.47E
Beregovo Ukraine 21 48.13N 22.39E
Bereko Tanzania 55 4.27S 35.43E
Berens r. Canada 75 52.21N 97.02W
Berens River town Canada 75 52.22N 97.02W
Beresford Australia 66 29.14S136.40E
Berettyóújfalu Hungary 21 47.14N 21.32E
Berevo Madagascar 57 19.44S 44.58E
Bereza Belorussia 21 52.32N 25.00E
Berezhany Ukraine 21 49.27N 24.56E
Berezina r. Belorussia 21 54.10N 28.10E
Berezna Ukraine 21 51.34N 31.46E
Berezniki Russian Fed. 24 59.26N 56.49E
Berezno Ukraine 21 51.00N 26.41E
Berezovka Ukraine 21 47.12N 30.56E
Berezovo Russian Fed. 28 63.58N 65.00E
Berga Spain 16 42.06N 1.48E
Berga Sweden 23 57.14N 16.03E
Bergama Turkey 19 39.08N 27.10E
Bergamo Italy 15 45.42N 9.40E
Bergen Germany 20 54.25N 13.26E
Bergen Neth. 14 52.40N 4.41E
Bergen Norway 23 60.23N 5.20E
Bergen U.S.A. 76 43.05N 77.57W
Bergen op Zoom Neth. 14 51.30N 4.17E
Bergerac France 17 44.50N 0.29E
Bergheim Germany 14 50.58N 6.39E
Berghem Neth. 14 51.46N 5.32E
Bergisch Gladbach Germany 14 50.59N 7.10E
Bergkamen Germany 14 51.35N 7.39E
Bergkvara Sweden 23 56.23N 16.05E
Bergland U.S.A. 84 46.36N 89.33W
Bergues France 14 50.58N 2.21E
Bergum Neth. 14 53.14N 5.59E
Berhampore India 41 24.06N 88.15E
Berhampur India 41 19.19N 84.47E
Bering Sea N. America/Asia 72 65.00N170.00W
Bering Str. Russian Fed./U.S.A. 72 65.00N170.00W
Berislav Ukraine 25 46.51N 33.26E
Berja Spain 16 36.50N 2.56W
Berkåk Norway 22 62.48N 10.03E
Berkel r. Neth. 14 52.10N 6.12E
Berkeley U.S.A. 80 37.57N122.18W
Berkner I. Antarctica 96 79.30S 50.00W
Berkshire d. U.K. 11 51.25N 1.03W
Berkshire Downs hills U.K. 11 51.32N 1.36W
Berland r. Canada 74 54.00N116.50W
Berlin Germany 20 52.32N 13.25E
Berlin d. Germany 20 52.30N 13.20E
Berlin Md. U.S.A. 85 38.20N 75.13W
Berlin N.H. U.S.A. 84 44.29N 71.10W
Bermagui Australia 67 36.28S150.03E
Bermejo r. San Juan Argentina 92 31.40S 67.15W
Bermejo r. Tucumán Argentina 92 26.47S 58.30W
Bermo India 41 23.47N 85.57E
Bermuda Atlantic Oc. 95 32.18N 64.45W
Bermuda Rise f. Atlantic Oc. 95 34.00N 60.00W
Bern Switz. 20 46.57N 7.26E
Bernard L. Canada 76 45.44N 79.24W
Bernay France 15 48.06N 0.36E
Bernburg Germany 20 51.48N 11.44E
Berne see Bern Switz. 17
Bernier I. Australia 62 24.51S113.09E
Bernina mtn. Italy/Switz. 15 46.22N 9.57E
Bernkastel Germany 14 49.55N 7.05E
Beroroha Madagascar 57 21.41S 45.10E
Beroun Czech Republic 20 49.58N 14.04E
Berrechid Morocco 50 33.17N 7.35W
Berri Australia 66 34.17S140.36E
Berridale Australia 67 36.21S148.51E
Berrigan Australia 67 35.41S145.48E
Berry Head U.K. 11 50.24N 3.28W
Berryville U.S.A. 83 36.22N 93.34W
Bersenbrück Germany 14 52.36N 7.58E
Bershad Ukraine 21 48.20N 29.30E
Berté, Lac l. Canada 77 50.47N 68.30W
Berthierville Canada 77 46.05N 73.10W
Bertinoro Italy 15 44.09N 12.08E
Bertoua Cameroon 53 4.34N 13.42E
Bertraghboy B. Rep. of Ire. 13 53.23N 9.52W
Berwick-upon-Tweed U.K. 10 55.46N 2.00W
Besalampy Madagascar 57 16.45S 44.30E
Besançon France 17 47.14N 6.02E
Bessarabia f. Moldavia 21 46.30N 28.40E
Bessemer U.S.A. 85 33.22N 87.00W
Betafo Madagascar 57 19.50S 46.51E
Betanzos Spain 16 43.17N 8.13W
Bétaré Oya Cameroon 53 5.34N 14.09E
Bete Hor Ethiopia 49 11.40N 39.00E
Bethal R.S.A. 56 26.26S 29.27E
Bethany Beach town U.S.A. 85 38.31N 75.04W
Bethel U.S.A. 72 60.48N161.46W
Bethesda U.S.A. 85 38.59N 77.06W
Bethlehem R.S.A. 56 28.13S 28.18E
Bethlehem U.S.A. 85 40.36N 75.22W
Béthune France 14 50.32N 2.38E
Béthune r. France 15 49.53N 1.09E
Betim Brazil 94 19.55S 44.07W
Betioky Madagascar 57 23.42S 44.22E
Betroka Madagascar 57 23.16S 46.06E
Bet She'an Israel 44 32.30N 35.30E
Bet Shemesh Israel 44 31.45N 35.00E
Betsiamites Canada 77 48.56N 68.38W
Betsiboka r. Madagascar 57 16.03S 46.36E
Bette mtn. Libya 51 22.00N 19.12E
Bettiah India 41 26.48N 84.30E
Bettles U.S.A. 72 66.53N151.51W
Betūl India 41 21.55N 77.54E
Betwa r. India 41 25.55N 80.12E
Betws-y-Coed U.K. 9 53.05N 3.48W
Betzdorf Germany 14 50.48N 7.54E
Beulah Australia 66 35.59S142.26E
Beulah Canada 75 50.16N101.02W
Beulah U.S.A. 82 47.16N101.47W
Beuvron r. France 15 47.29N 3.31E
Beverley Australia 63 32.06S116.56E
Beverley U.K. 10 53.52N 0.26W
Beverley Hills town U.S.A. 81 34.04N118.26W
Beverly U.S.A. 84 42.33N 70.53W
Beverwijk Neth. 14 52.29N 4.40E
Bewcastle Fells hills U.K. 10 55.05N 2.50W
Bexhill U.K. 11 50.51N 0.29E
Bexley U.K. 11 51.26N 0.10E
Beyla Guinea 52 8.42N 8.39W
Beyneu Kazakhstan 25 45.16N 55.04E
Beypazari Turkey 42 40.10N 31.56E
Beyşehir Gölü l. Turkey 42 37.47N 31.30E
Bezhanovo Bulgaria 19 43.13N 24.26E
Bezhetsk Russian Fed. 24 57.49N 36.40E
Bezhitsa Russian Fed. 24 53.19N 34.17E
Béziers France 17 43.21N 3.13E
Bhadohi India 41 25.25N 82.34E
Bhādra India 40 29.07N 75.10E
Bhadrakh India 41 21.04N 86.30E
Bhāg Pakistan 40 29.02N 67.49E
Bhāgalpur India 41 25.15N 87.00E
Bhāi Pheru Pakistan 40 31.12N 73.57E
Bhaironghāti India 41 31.01N 78.53E
Bhaisa India 41 19.06N 77.58E
Bhakkar Pakistan 40 31.38N 71.04E
Bhaktapur Nepal 41 27.42N 85.27E
Bhalwāl Pakistan 40 32.16N 72.54E
Bhamo Burma 34 24.10N 97.30E
Bhandāra India 41 21.10N 79.39E
Bhānvad India 40 21.56N 69.47E
Bharatpur India 41 27.13N 77.29E
Bharthana India 41 26.45N 79.14E
Bhātāpāra India 41 21.44N 81.56E
Bhatewar India 40 24.40N 74.05E
Bhātiāpāra Ghāt Bangla. 41 23.12N 89.42E
Bhatinda India 40 30.13N 74.56E
Bhatkal India 38 13.58N 74.34E
Bhātpāra India 41 22.52N 88.24E
Bhaunagar India 40 21.46N 72.09E
Bhawāni Mandi India 40 24.25N 75.50E
Bhawānipatna India 41 19.54N 83.10E
Bhera Pakistan 40 32.29N 72.55E
Bhikangaon India 40 21.52N 75.57E
Bhilai India 41 21.13N 81.26E
Bhīlwāra India 40 25.21N 74.38E
Bhima r. India 38 16.30N 77.10E
Bhind India 41 26.34N 78.48E
Bhinmāl India 40 25.00N 72.15E
Bhiwandi India 40 19.18N 73.04E
Bhiwāni India 40 28.47N 76.08E
Bhognīpur India 41 26.12N 79.48E
Bhojpur Nepal 41 27.11N 87.02E
Bhokardan India 40 20.16N 75.46E
Bhopāl India 41 23.16N 77.24E
Bhor India 38 18.12N 73.53E
Bhuban India 41 20.53N 85.50E
Bhubaneswar India 41 20.15N 85.50E
Bhuj India 40 23.16N 69.40E
Bhusāwal India 40 21.03N 75.46E
Bhutan Asia 41 27.15N 91.00E
Bia, Phou mtn. Laos 34 18.59N103.11E
Biābānak Afghan. 40 32.11N 64.11E
Biak Indonesia 37 1.10S136.05E
Biak i. Indonesia 37 0.55S136.00E
Biała Podlaska Poland 21 52.02N 23.06E
Białogard Poland 20 54.00N 16.00E
Białystok Poland 21 53.09N 23.10E
Biankouma Ivory Coast 52 7.51N 7.34W
Biaora India 40 23.55N 76.54E
Biarritz France 17 43.29N 1.33W
Biasca Switz. 15 46.22N 8.58E
Bibā Egypt 44 28.56N 30.59E
Bibala Angola 54 14.46S 13.21E
Biberach Germany 20 48.20N 9.30E
Bic Canada 77 48.22N 68.42W
Bicas Brazil 94 21.44S 43.04W
Bicester U.K. 11 51.53N 1.09W
Bida Nigeria 53 9.06N 5.59E
Bidar India 38 17.54N 77.33E
Biddeford U.S.A. 84 43.30N 70.26W
Bideford U.K. 11 51.01N 4.13W
Bidon Cinq see Poste Maurice Cortier Algeria 50
Bi Doup mtn. Vietnam 34 12.05N108.40E
Bié d. Angola 54 12.30S 17.30E
Biel Switz. 17 47.09N 7.16E
Bielefeld Germany 20 52.02N 8.32E
Biella Italy 15 45.34N 8.03E
Bielsko-Biała Poland 21 49.49N 19.02E
Bielsk Podlaski Poland 21 52.47N 23.12E
Bien Hoa Vietnam 34 10.58N106.50E
Bienville, Lac l. Canada 77 55.05N 72.40W
Bié Plateau f. Angola 54 13.00S 16.00E
Big Bald Mtn. Canada 77 47.12N 66.25W
Big Bear Lake town U.S.A. 81 34.15N116.53W
Big Beaver House town Canada 76 52.59N 89.50W
Big Belt Mts. U.S.A. 80 46.40N111.25W
Big Bend Nat. Park U.S.A. 83 29.12N103.12W
Bigbury B. U.K. 11 50.15N 3.56W
Big Cypress Swamp f. U.S.A. 85 26.10N 81.38W
Big Falls town U.S.A. 82 48.12N 93.48W
Biggar Canada 75 52.04N107.59W
Biggar U.K. 12 55.38N 3.31W
Bighorn r. U.S.A. 80 46.09N107.28W
Bighorn L. U.S.A. 80 45.06N108.08W
Bighorn Mts. U.S.A. 80 44.00N107.30W
Bight, Head of b. Australia 65 31.29S131.16E
Bignasco Switz. 15 46.20N 8.36E
Bignona Senegal 52 12.48N 16.18W
Big Pine U.S.A. 80 37.10N118.17W
Big Piney U.S.A. 80 42.32N110.07W
Big Quill L. Canada 75 51.55N104.22W
Big Salmon Canada 72 61.53N134.55W
Big Salmon r. Canada 74 61.52N134.56W
Big Sand L. Canada 75 57.45N 99.42W
Big Sandy U.S.A. 80 48.11N110.07W
Big Smoky Valley f. U.S.A. 80 38.30N117.15W
Big Snowy Mtn. U.S.A. 80 46.50N109.30W
Big Spring town U.S.A. 83 32.15N101.28W
Big Stone Gap town U.S.A. 85 36.52N 82.46W
Bigstone L. Canada 75 53.42N 95.44W
Big Stone L. U.S.A. 82 45.25N 96.40W
Big Sur U.S.A. 81 36.15N121.48W
Big Timber U.S.A. 80 45.50N109.57W
Big Trout L. Canada 75 53.40N 90.00W
Bihać Bosnia-Herzegovina 18 44.49N 15.53E
Bihar India 41 25.11N 85.31E
Bihar d. India 41 24.30N 86.00E
Biharamulo Tanzania 55 2.34S 31.20E
Bihor mtn. Romania 21 46.26N 22.43E
Bihu China 33 28.21N119.47E
Bijagós, Arquipélago dos is. Guinea Bissau 52 11.30N 16.00W
Bijainagar India 40 25.56N 74.38E
Bijaipura India 41 24.46N 77.48E
Bijāpur India 38 16.52N 75.47E
Bijāpur India 41 18.48N 80.49E
Bijār Iran 43 35.52N 47.39E
Bijāwar India 41 24.38N 79.30E
Bijbān Chāh Pakistan 40 26.54N 64.42E
Bijeljina Bosnia-Herzegovina 19 44.45N 19.13E
Bijeypur India 40 26.03N 77.22E
Bijie China 33 27.28N105.20E
Bijnor India 41 29.22N 78.08E
Bīkaner India 40 28.42N 73.25E
Bikin Russian Fed. 31 46.52N134.15E
Bikini i. Pacific Oc. 68 11.35N165.23E
Bikoro Zaïre 54 0.45S 18.09E
Bilāra India 40 26.10N 73.42E
Bilāspur Himachal P. India 40 31.19N 76.45E

Bilāspur to Borotou

Bilāspur Madhya P. India 41 22.05N 82.09E
Bilauktaung Range *mts.* Thailand 34 13.00N 99.15E
Bilbao Spain 16 43.15N 2.56W
Bilbays Egypt 44 30.25N 31.34E
Bilecik Turkey 42 40.10N 29.59E
Bilgrām India 41 27.11N 80.02E
Bili *r.* Zaïre 49 4.09N 22.29E
Bilibino Russian Fed. 29 68.02N 166.15E
Bilimora India 40 20.45N 72.57E
Billabong Creek *r.* Australia 66 35.04S 144.06E
Bill Baileys Bank *f.* Atlantic Oc. 8 60.45N 10.30W
Billingham U.K. 10 54.36N 1.18W
Billings U.S.A. 80 45.47N 108.27W
Bill of Portland *c.* U.K. 11 50.32N 2.28W
Bilma Niger 51 18.41N 12.56E
Biloela Australia 64 24.24S 150.30E
Biloxi U.S.A. 83 30.24N 88.53W
Bilqās Qism Awwal Egypt 44 31.14N 31.22E
Biltine Chad 51 14.32N 20.55E
Biltine *d.* Chad 51 15.00N 21.00E
Bilto Norway 22 69.26N 21.35E
Bima *r.* Zaïre 54 3.24N 25.10E
Bimberi, Mt. Australia 67 35.40S 148.47E
Bimbo C.A.R. 53 4.15N 18.33E
Bina-Etāwa India 41 24.11N 78.11E
Binaiya *mtn.* Indonesia 37 3.10S 129.30E
Bīnālūd, Kūh-e *mts.* Iran 43 36.15N 59.00E
Binbee Australia 64 20.20S 147.55E
Binche Belgium 14 50.25N 4.10E
Bindki India 41 26.02N 80.36E
Bindura Zimbabwe 57 17.18S 31.20E
Binga Zimbabwe 56 17.38S 27.19E
Binga, Mt. Zimbabwe 57 19.47S 33.03E
Bingara Australia 67 29.51S 150.38E
Bingen Germany 14 49.58N 7.55E
Bingerville Ivory Coast 52 5.20N 3.53W
Bingham U.K. 10 52.57N 0.57W
Bingham U.S.A. 84 45.03N 69.53W
Binghamton U.S.A. 84 42.08N 75.54W
Bingkor Malaysia 36 5.26N 116.15E
Bingöl Turkey 25 38.54N 40.29E
Bingol Dağlari *mtn.* Turkey 42 39.21N 41.22E
Binhai China 32 34.00N 119.55E
Binh Dinh Vietnam 34 13.53N 109.07E
Binjai Indonesia 36 3.37N 98.25E
Binji Nigeria 53 13.12N 4.55E
Binnaway Australia 67 31.32S 149.23E
Binscarth Canada 75 50.37N 101.16W
Bintan *i.* Indonesia 36 1.10N 104.30E
Bintulu Malaysia 36 3.12N 113.01E
Bin Xian China 32 35.02N 108.04E
Binyang China 33 23.12N 108.48E
Binzert Tunisia 51 37.17N 9.51E
Biograd Croatia 18 43.56N 15.27E
Bioko I. Equat. Guinea 53 3.25N 8.45E
Bīr India 40 18.59N 75.46E
Bīr, Ras *c.* Djibouti 45 11.59N 43.25E
Bi'r Abū 'Uwayqīlah *well* Egypt 44 30.50N 34.07E
Bi'r ad Dakhal *well* Egypt 44 28.40N 32.24E
Birāk Libya 51 27.32N 14.17E
Bi'r al Ḩarash *well* Libya 51 25.30N 22.06E
Bi'r al Jidy *well* Egypt 44 30.13N 33.03E
Bi'r al Jufayr *well* Egypt 44 30.49N 32.40E
Bi'r al 'Udayd *well* Egypt 44 28.59N 34.05E
Birao C.A.R. 49 10.17N 22.47E
Bi'r aş Şafrā' *well* Egypt 44 28.46N 34.20E
Bi'r ath Thamadah *well* Egypt 44 30.10N 33.28E
Birātnagar Nepal 41 26.18N 87.17E
Bi'r Buerāt *well* Egypt 44 28.59N 32.10E
Bi'r Bukhayt *well* Egypt 44 29.13N 32.17E
Birch *r.* Canada 74 58.30N 112.15W
Birchip Australia 66 35.59S 142.59E
Birch L. N.W.T. Canada 74 62.04N 116.33W
Birch L. Ont. Canada 76 51.24N 92.20W
Birch Mts. Canada 74 57.30N 112.30W
Bird Canada 75 56.30N 94.13W
Birdsboro U.S.A. 85 40.16N 75.48W
Birdsville Australia 64 25.54S 139.22E
Birecik Turkey 42 37.03N 37.59E
Birganj Nepal 41 27.01N 84.54E
Birhan *mtn.* Ethiopia 49 11.00N 37.50E
Bi'r Ḩasanah *well* Egypt 44 30.29N 33.47E
Bi'r Hooker *well* Egypt 44 30.23N 30.20E
Bīrjand Iran 43 32.54N 59.10E
Bi'r Jifjafah *well* Egypt 44 30.28N 33.11E
Birk, Wādī *r.* Saudi Arabia 43 24.08N 47.35E
Birkenfeld Germany 14 49.39N 7.10E
Birkenhead U.K. 10 53.24N 3.01W
Birksgate Range *mts.* Australia 62 27.10S 129.45E
Bi'r Kusaybah *well* Egypt 44 22.41N 29.55E
Bîrlad Romania 21 46.14N 27.40E
Bi'r Lahfān *well* Egypt 44 31.01N 33.52E
Birmingham U.K. 11 52.30N 1.55W
Birmingham U.S.A. 85 33.30N 86.55W
Birmitrapur India 41 22.24N 84.46E
Bir Mogreïn Mauritania 50 25.14N 11.35W
Birni Benin 53 9.59N 1.34E
Birnin Gwari Nigeria 53 11.02N 6.47E
Birnin Kebbi Nigeria 53 12.30N 4.11E
Birni N'Konni Niger 53 13.49N 5.19E
Birobidzhan Russian Fed. 31 48.49N 132.54E
Bir Ounâne *well* Mali 50 21.02N 3.18W
Birr Rep. of Ire. 13 53.06N 7.56W
Birrie *r.* Australia 67 29.43S 146.37E
Birsilpur India 40 28.11N 72.15E
Birsk Russian Fed. 24 55.28N 55.31E
Bi'r Tābah *well* Egypt 44 29.30N 34.53E
Bi'r Ţarfāwī *well* Egypt 48 22.55N 28.53E
Birtle Canada 75 50.32N 101.02W
Bi'r Umm Sa'īd *well* Egypt 44 29.40N 33.34E
Bi'r Umm 'Umayyid *well* Egypt 44 27.53N 32.30E
Biržai Lithuania 24 56.10N 24.48E
Bi'r Zalţan *well* Libya 51 28.27N 19.46E
Bir Zreigat Mauritania 50 22.27N 8.53W
Bīsalpur India 41 28.18N 79.48E
Bisbee U.S.A. 81 31.27N 109.55W
Biscay, B. of France 17 45.30N 4.00W
Bisceglie Italy 19 41.14N 16.31E
Bisha Ethiopia 48 15.28N 37.34E
Bishkek Kyrgyzstan 30 42.53N 74.46E
Bishnupur India 41 23.05N 87.19E
Bishop Calif. U.S.A. 80 37.22N 118.24W
Bishop Tex. U.S.A. 83 27.35N 97.48W
Bishop Auckland U.K. 10 54.40N 1.40W
Bishop's Stortford U.K. 11 51.53N 0.09E
Bisina, L. Uganda 55 1.35N 34.08E
Biskra Algeria 51 34.48N 5.40E
Bismarck U.S.A. 82 46.48N 100.47W
Bismarck Range *mts.* P.N.G. 37 6.00S 145.00E
Bismarck Sea Pacific Oc. 37 4.00S 146.30E
Bison U.S.A. 82 45.31N 102.28W
Bīsotūn Iran 43 34.22N 47.29E
Bispgården Sweden 22 63.02N 16.40E
Bissau Guinea Bissau 52 11.52N 15.39W
Bissett Canada 75 51.02N 95.40W
Bissikrima Guinea 52 10.50N 10.58W
Bistcho L. Canada 74 59.45N 118.50W
Bistrița Romania 21 47.08N 24.30E
Bistrița *r.* Romania 21 46.30N 26.54E
Biswān India 41 27.30N 81.00E
Bitam Gabon 54 2.05N 11.30E
Bitburg Germany 14 49.58N 6.31E
Bitéa, Ouadi *wadi* Chad 49 13.11N 20.10E
Bitlis Turkey 42 38.23N 42.04E
Bitola Macedonia 19 41.02N 21.21E
Bitter Creek *town* U.S.A. 80 41.31N 109.27W
Bitterfontein R.S.A. 56 31.02S 18.14E
Bitterroot Range *mts.* U.S.A. 80 47.06N 115.10W
Biu Nigeria 53 10.36N 12.11E
Biumba Rwanda 55 1.38S 30.02E
Biwa ko *l.* Japan 35 35.10N 136.00E
Biyalā Egypt 44 31.11N 31.13E
Biysk Russian Fed. 28 52.35N 85.16E
Bizerte *see* Binzert Tunisia 51
Bjelovar Croatia 19 45.54N 16.51E
Bjorli Norway 23 62.16N 8.13E
Björna Sweden 22 63.32N 18.36E
Björnafjorden *est.* Norway 23 60.06N 5.22E
Bjornøya *i.* Arctic Oc. 96 74.30N 19.00E
Black *r.* U.S.A. 83 35.38N 91.19W
Black *r. see* Đà *r.* Vietnam 34
Blackall Australia 64 24.25S 145.28E
Blackburn U.K. 10 53.44N 2.30W
Black Diamond Canada 74 50.45N 114.14W
Black Duck *r.* Canada 75 56.51N 89.02W
Blackduck U.S.A. 82 47.44N 94.33W
Blackfoot U.S.A. 80 43.11N 112.20W
Black Hills U.S.A. 82 44.00N 104.00W
Black L. Canada 75 59.10N 105.20W
Black Mtn. U.K. 11 51.52N 3.50W
Black Mts. U.K. 11 51.52N 3.09W
Blackpool U.K. 10 53.48N 3.03W
Black River *town* Jamaica 87 18.02N 77.52W
Black River *town* U.S.A. 84 44.51N 83.21W
Black Rock *town* U.S.A. 80 38.41N 113.02W
Black Rock Desert U.S.A. 80 41.10N 119.00W
Black Sand Desert *see* Karakumy, Peski Turkmenistan 43
Black Sea Europe 21 44.00N 30.00E
Blacksod B. Rep. of Ire. 13 54.04N 10.00W
Blackstone U.S.A. 85 37.05N 78.02W
Black Sugarloaf Mt. Australia 67 31.24S 151.34E
Blackville Australia 67 31.34S 150.10E
Blackville U.S.A. 85 33.22N 81.17W
Black Volta *r.* Ghana 52 8.14N 2.11W
Blackwater Australia 64 23.34S 148.53E
Blackwater *r.* Rep. of Ire. 13 51.58N 7.52W
Blackwater *r.* U.K. 9 54.31N 6.36W
Blackwell U.S.A. 83 36.48N 97.17W
Blackwood *r.* Australia 63 34.15S 115.10E
Blaenau Ffestiniog U.K. 10 53.00N 3.57W
Blagoevgrad Bulgaria 19 42.02N 23.04E
Blagoveshchensk Russian Fed. 31 50.19N 127.30E
Blain France 15 47.29N 1.46W
Blair U.S.A. 82 41.33N 96.08W
Blair Athol Australia 64 22.42S 147.33E
Blair Atholl U.K. 12 56.46N 3.51W
Blairgowrie U.K. 12 56.36N 3.21W
Blairmore Canada 74 49.40N 114.25W
Blairsville U.S.A. 85 34.52N 83.52W
Blakely U.S.A. 85 31.22N 84.58W
Blanc, Cap *c.* Mauritania 52 20.44N 17.05W
Blanc, Mont *mtn.* Europe 17 45.50N 6.52E
Blanca, Bahía *b.* Argentina 93 39.20S 62.00W
Blanca, Sierra *mtn.* U.S.A. 81 33.23N 105.48W
Blanchard U.S.A. 80 48.01N 116.59W
Blanche, L. Australia 66 29.15S 139.40E
Blanchetown Australia 66 34.21S 139.38E
Blanco, C. Argentina 93 47.12S 65.20W
Blanco, C. Costa Rica 87 9.36N 85.06W
Blanco, C. U.S.A. 80 42.50N 124.34W
Bland *r.* Australia 67 33.42S 147.30E
Blandford Forum U.K. 11 50.52N 2.10W
Blankenberge Belgium 14 51.18N 3.08E
Blansko Czech Republic 20 49.22N 16.39E
Blantyre Malaŵi 55 15.46S 35.00E
Blarney Rep. of Ire. 13 51.56N 8.34W
Blatnica Bulgaria 21 43.42N 28.31E
Blavet *r.* France 17 47.43N 3.18W
Blaye France 17 45.08N 0.40W
Blayney Australia 67 33.32S 149.19E
Blednaya, Gora *mtn.* Russian Fed. 28 76.23N 65.08E
Bleiburg Austria 20 46.35N 14.48E
Blekinge *d.* Sweden 23 56.20N 15.00E
Blenheim New Zealand 60 41.32S 173.58E
Bléré France 15 47.20N 0.59E
Blerick Neth. 14 51.22N 6.08E
Bletchley U.K. 11 51.59N 0.45W
Blida Algeria 51 36.30N 2.50E
Bligh Entrance Australia 64 9.18S 144.10E
Blind River *town* Canada 76 46.15N 83.00W
Blinman Australia 66 31.05S 138.11E
Blitar Indonesia 37 8.06S 112.12E
Blitta Togo 53 8.23N 1.06E
Bloemfontein R.S.A. 56 29.07S 26.14E
Bloemhof R.S.A. 56 27.37S 25.34E
Blois France 15 47.36N 1.20E
Blönduós Iceland 22 65.39N 20.18W
Bloody Foreland *c.* Rep. of Ire. 13 55.09N 8.17W
Bloomfield Iowa U.S.A. 82 40.45N 92.25W
Bloomfield Nebr. U.S.A. 82 42.36N 97.39W
Bloomfield N.J. U.S.A. 85 40.48N 74.12W
Bloomington Ill. U.S.A. 82 40.29N 89.00W
Bloomington Ind. U.S.A. 84 39.10N 86.31W
Bloomington Minn. U.S.A. 82 44.50N 93.17W
Bloomsburg U.S.A. 84 41.00N 76.27W
Blora Indonesia 37 6.55S 111.29E
Blueberry *r.* Canada 74 56.45N 120.49W
Bluefield U.S.A. 85 37.14N 81.17W
Bluefields Nicaragua 87 12.00N 83.49W
Blue Hills of Couteau Canada 77 47.59N 57.43W
Blue Mts. Australia 67 33.16S 150.19E
Blue Mts. U.S.A. 80 45.30N 118.15W
Blue Mud B. Australia 64 13.26S 135.56E
Blue Nile *r. see* Azraq, Al Baḩr al *r.* Sudan 48
Bluenose L. Canada 72 68.30N 119.35W
Blue River *town* Canada 74 52.05N 119.09W
Blue Stack Mts. Rep. of Ire. 13 54.44N 8.09W
Bluff New Zealand 60 46.38S 168.21E
Bluff U.S.A. 80 37.17N 109.33W
Bluff, C. Canada 77 52.48N 55.53W
Bluff Knoll *mtn.* Australia 63 34.25S 118.15E
Blumenau Brazil 94 26.55S 49.07W
Blunt U.S.A. 82 44.31N 99.59W
Blyth U.K. 10 55.07N 1.29W
Blythe U.S.A. 81 33.37N 114.36W
Bö Nordland Norway 22 68.38N 14.35E
Bö Telemark Norway 23 59.25N 9.04E
Bo Sierra Leone 52 7.58N 11.45W
Boa Esperança Brazil 94 21.03S 45.37W
Boa Esperança, Représa da *resr.* Brazil 91 6.45S 44.15W
Bo'ai China 32 35.10N 113.04E
Boane Mozambique 57 26.02S 32.19E
Boa Vista Brazil 90 2.51N 60.43W
Bobadah Australia 67 32.18S 146.42E
Bobadilla Spain 16 37.02N 4.44W
Bobbili India 39 18.34N 83.22E
Bobbio Italy 15 44.46N 9.23E
Bobo-Dioulasso Burkina 52 11.11N 4.18W
Bobonong Botswana 56 21.59S 28.29E
Bobr Belorussia 21 54.19N 29.18E
Bóbr *r.* Poland 20 52.04N 15.04E
Bobruysk Belorussia 21 53.08N 29.10E
Bôca do Acre Brazil 90 8.45S 67.23W
Bocaranga C.A.R. 53 7.01N 15.35E
Boca Raton U.S.A. 85 26.22N 80.05W
Bochnia Poland 21 49.58N 20.26E
Bocholt Germany 14 51.49N 6.37E
Bochum Germany 14 51.28N 7.11E
Bochum R.S.A. 56 23.12S 29.12E
Bockum-Hövel Germany 14 51.42N 7.41E
Boconó Venezuela 90 9.17N 70.17W
Boda C.A.R. 53 4.19N 17.26E
Bodalla Australia 67 36.05S 150.03E
Bodallin Australia 63 31.22S 118.52E
Bodélé *f.* Chad 53 16.50N 17.10E
Boden Sweden 22 65.50N 21.42E
Bodensee *l.* Europe 20 47.40N 9.30E
Bode Sadu Nigeria 53 8.57N 4.49E
Bodfish U.S.A. 81 35.36N 118.30W
Bodmin U.K. 11 50.28N 4.44W
Bodmin Moor U.K. 11 50.53N 4.35W
Bodo Canada 75 52.11N 110.04W
Bodö Norway 22 67.18N 14.26E
Bodrum Turkey 42 37.03N 27.28E
Boembé Congo 54 2.59S 15.34E
Boende Zaïre 54 0.15S 20.49E
Boffa Guinea 52 10.12N 14.02W
Bogale Burma 34 16.17N 95.24E
Bogalusa U.S.A. 83 30.47N 89.52W
Bogan *r.* Australia 67 30.00S 146.20E
Bogan Gate *town* Australia 67 33.08S 147.50E
Bogata U.S.A. 83 33.28N 95.13W
Bogcang Zangbo *r.* China 41 31.50N 87.25E
Bogenfels Namibia 56 27.26S 15.22E
Boggabilla Australia 67 28.36S 150.21E
Boggabri Australia 67 30.42S 150.02E
Boggeragh Mts. Rep. of Ire. 13 52.03N 8.53W
Bogia P.N.G. 37 4.16S 145.00E
Bognes Norway 22 68.15N 16.00E
Bognor Regis U.K. 11 50.47N 0.40W
Bog of Allen *f.* Rep. of Ire. 13 53.17N 7.00W
Bogol Manyo Ethiopia 49 4.32N 41.32E
Bogong, Mt. Australia 67 36.45S 147.21E
Bogor Indonesia 36 6.34S 106.45E
Bogotá Colombia 90 4.38N 74.05W
Bogra Bangla. 41 24.51N 89.22E
Bogué Mauritania 50 16.35N 14.16W
Boguslav Ukraine 21 49.32N 30.52E
Bo Hai *b.* China 32 38.30N 119.30E
Bohain France 14 49.59N 3.28E
Bohai Wan *b.* China 32 38.30N 117.55E
Bohemian Forest *see* Böhmerwald *mts.* Germany 20
Bohin Somali Rep. 45 11.42N 51.17E
Böhmerwald *mts.* Germany 20 49.20N 13.10E
Bohol *i.* Phil. 37 9.45N 124.10E
Boiaçu Brazil 90 0.27S 61.46W
Boigu *i.* Australia 64 9.16S 142.12E
Boing Sudan 49 9.58N 33.44E
Bois, Lac des *l.* Canada 72 66.40N 125.15W
Boise U.S.A. 80 43.37N 116.13W
Boise City U.S.A. 83 36.44N 102.31W
Bois-Guillaume France 15 49.28N 1.08E
Boissevain Canada 75 49.15N 100.00W
Boizenburg Germany 20 53.22N 10.43E
Bojador, Cabo *c.* W. Sahara 50 26.08N 14.30W
Bojeador, C. Phil. 33 18.30N 120.36E
Bojnūrd Iran 43 37.28N 57.20E
Bojonegoro Indonesia 37 7.06S 111.50E
Bokani Nigeria 53 9.27N 5.13E
Boké Guinea 52 10.57N 14.13W
Bokhara *r.* Australia 67 29.55S 146.42E
Boknafjorden *est.* Norway 23 59.10N 5.35E
Bokoro Chad 53 12.17N 17.04E
Bokote Zaïre 54 0.05S 20.08E
Bokpyin Burma 34 11.16N 98.46E
Bokungu Zaïre 54 0.44S 22.28E
Bol Chad 53 13.27N 14.40E
Bolac Lake *town* Australia 66 37.42S 142.50E
Bolafa Zaïre 54 1.23N 22.06E
Bolama Guinea Bissau 52 11.35N 15.30W
Bolān *r.* Pakistan 40 29.05N 67.45E
Bolanda, Jabal *mtn.* Sudan 49 7.44N 25.28E
Bolān Pass Pakistan 40 29.45N 67.35E
Bolbec France 15 49.34N 0.28E
Bole Ghana 52 9.03N 2.23W
Bolesławiec Poland 20 51.16N 15.34E
Bolgatanga Ghana 52 10.42N 0.52W
Bolgrad Ukraine 21 45.42N 28.40E
Bolia Zaïre 54 1.36S 18.23E
Bolívar Argentina 93 36.14S 61.07W
Bolivar U.S.A. 83 35.16N 88.59W
Bolivia S. America 92 17.00S 65.00W
Bollnäs Sweden 23 61.21N 16.25E
Bollon Australia 65 28.02S 147.28E
Bollstabruk Sweden 22 62.59N 17.42E
Bolmen *l.* Sweden 23 56.55N 13.40E
Bolobo Zaïre 54 2.10S 16.17E
Bologna Italy 15 44.30N 11.20E
Bologoye Russian Fed. 24 57.58N 34.00E
Bolomba Zaïre 54 0.30N 19.13E
Bolombo Zaïre 54 3.59S 21.22E
Bolondo Equat. Guinea 54 1.40N 9.38E
Bolongongo Angola 54 8.28S 15.16E
Bolovens, Plateau des *f.* Laos 34 15.10N 106.30E
Bolsena, Lago di *l.* Italy 18 42.36N 11.55E
Bolshaya Glushitsa Russian Fed. 24 52.28N 50.30E
Bolshaya Pyssa Russian Fed. 24 64.11N 48.44E
Bolsherechye Russian Fed. 28 56.07N 74.40E
Bol'shevik, Ostrov *i.* Russian Fed. 29 78.30N 102.00E
Bolshezemelskaya Tundra *f.* Russian Fed. 24 67.00N 56.10E
Bolshoy Atlym Russian Fed. 28 62.17N 66.30E
Bol'shoy Balkhan, Khrebet *mts.* Turkmenistan 43 39.38N 54.30E
Bol'shoy Irgiz *r.* Russian Fed. 24 52.00N 47.20E
Bol'shoy Lyakhovskiy, Ostrov *i.* Russian Fed. 29 73.30N 142.00E
Bol'shoy Onguren Russian Fed. 29 53.40N 107.40E
Bolshoy Uzen *r.* Kazakhstan 25 49.00N 49.40E
Bolsover U.K. 10 53.14N 1.18W
Bolton U.K. 10 53.35N 2.26W
Bolton L. Canada 75 54.16N 95.47W
Bolu Turkey 42 40.45N 31.38E
Bolus Head Rep. of Ire. 13 51.47N 10.20W
Bolvadin Turkey 42 38.43N 31.02E
Bolzano Italy 15 46.30N 11.20E
Boma Zaïre 54 5.50S 13.03E
Bomaderry Australia 67 34.21S 150.34E
Bomadi Nigeria 53 5.13N 6.01E
Bombala Australia 67 36.55S 149.16E
Bombay India 40 18.58N 72.50E
Bombo Uganda 55 0.35N 32.32E
Bomboma Zaïre 54 2.25N 18.54E
Bom Despacho Brazil 94 19.46S 45.15W
Bomi China 30 29.50N 95.45E
Bomi Hills Liberia 52 7.01N 10.38W
Bømlafjorden *est.* Norway 23 59.39N 5.20E
Bömlo *i.* Norway 23 59.46N 5.13E
Bomokandi *r.* Zaïre 55 3.37N 26.09E
Bomongo Equateur Zaïre 54 1.30N 18.21E
Bomu *r.* Zaïre *see* Mbomou *r.* C.A.R. 49
Bon, Cap *c.* Tunisia 51 37.05N 11.03E
Bonaigarh India 41 21.50N 84.57E
Bonaire *i.* Neth. Antilles 90 12.15N 68.27W
Bonanza U.S.A. 80 40.01N 109.11W
Bonaparte *r.* Canada 74 50.46N 121.17W
Bonaparte Archipelago *is.* Australia 62 14.17S 125.18E
Bonar-Bridge *town* U.K. 12 57.53N 4.21W
Bonavista Canada 77 48.39N 53.07W
Bonavista, C. Canada 77 48.42N 53.05W
Bonavista B. Canada 77 48.45N 53.20W
Bon Bon Australia 66 30.26S 135.28E
Bondeno Italy 15 44.53N 11.25E
Bondo Equateur Zaïre 54 3.47N 23.45E
Bondo Haut-Zaïre Zaïre 54 1.22S 23.53E
Bondoukou Ivory Coast 52 8.03N 2.15W
Bondowoso Indonesia 37 7.54S 113.50E
Bone, Teluk *b.* Indonesia 37 4.00S 120.50E
Bo'ness U.K. 12 56.01N 3.36W
Bonga Ethiopia 49 7.17N 36.15E
Bongaigaon India 41 26.28N 90.34E
Bongak Sudan 49 7.27N 33.14E
Bongandanga Zaïre 54 1.28N 21.03E
Bongor Chad 53 10.18N 15.20E
Bongos, Massif des *mts.* C.A.R. 49 8.20N 21.35E
Bongouanou Ivory Coast 52 6.44N 4.10W
Bonham U.S.A. 83 33.35N 96.11W
Bonifacio, Str. of Med. Sea 18 41.18N 9.10E
Bonin Is. Japan 68 27.00N 142.10E
Bonn Germany 14 50.44N 7.06E
Bonners Ferry U.S.A. 80 48.41N 116.18W
Bonnétable France 15 48.11N 0.26E
Bonneval France 15 48.11N 1.24E
Bonneville Salt Flats *f.* U.S.A. 80 40.45N 113.52W
Bonney, L. Australia 66 37.47S 140.23E
Bonnie Rock *town* Australia 63 30.32S 118.21E
Bonny Nigeria 53 4.25N 7.10E
Bonny, Bight of Africa 53 2.58N 7.00E
Bonnyville Canada 75 54.16N 110.44W
Bonshaw Australia 67 29.08S 150.53E
Bontang Indonesia 36 0.05N 117.31E
Bonthe Sierra Leone 52 7.32N 12.30W
Bonython Range *mts.* Australia 62 23.51S 129.00E
Bookaloo Australia 66 31.56S 137.21E
Boola Guinea 52 8.22N 8.41W
Booleroo Centre Australia 66 32.53S 138.21E
Booligal Australia 67 33.54S 144.54E
Boom Belgium 14 51.07N 4.21E
Boomrivier R.S.A. 56 29.34S 20.26E
Boone U.S.A. 82 42.04N 93.53W
Booneville U.S.A. 83 34.39N 88.34W
Boonville Mo. U.S.A. 82 38.58N 92.44W
Boonville N.Y. U.S.A. 84 43.29N 75.20W
Boorabbin Australia 63 31.14S 120.21E
Boorama Somali Rep. 45 9.58N 43.07E
Boorindal Australia 67 30.23S 146.11E
Booroorban Australia 67 34.56S 144.46E
Boorowa Australia 67 34.26S 148.48E
Boort Australia 66 36.08S 143.46E
Boosaaso Somali Rep. 45 11.13N 49.08E
Boothia, G. of Canada 73 70.00N 90.00W
Boothia Pen. Canada 73 70.30N 95.00W
Bootra Australia 66 30.00S 143.00E
Booué Gabon 54 0.00 11.58E
Bopeechee Australia 66 29.36S 137.23E
Bophuthatswana Africa 56 27.00S 23.30E
Boppard Germany 14 50.13N 7.35E
Boquilla, Presa de la *l.* Mexico 81 27.30N 105.30W
Bor Czech Republic 20 49.43N 12.47E
Bor Sudan 49 6.12N 31.33E
Bor Yugo. 19 44.05N 22.07E
Bora Bora *i.* Îs. de la Société 69 16.30S 151.45W
Borah Peak *mtn.* U.S.A. 80 44.08N 113.38W
Borås Sweden 23 57.43N 12.55E
Borāzjān Iran 43 29.14N 51.12E
Borba Brazil 90 4.24S 59.35W
Borda Cape *town* Australia 66 35.44S 136.37E
Bordeaux France 17 44.50N 0.34W
Borden Australia 63 34.05S 118.16E
Borden I. Canada 72 78.30N 111.00W
Borden Pen. Canada 73 73.00N 83.00W
Borders *d.* U.K. 12 55.30N 2.53W
Bordertown Australia 66 36.18S 140.49E
Bordheyri Iceland 22 65.12N 21.06W
Bordighera Italy 15 43.46N 7.39E
Bordj Bou Arreridj Algeria 51 36.04N 4.46E
Bordj Flye Sainte Marie Algeria 50 27.17N 2.59W
Bordj Omar Driss Algeria 51 28.09N 6.49E
Bordö *i.* Faroe Is. 22 62.10N 7.13W
Bore Ethiopia 49 4.40N 37.40E
Boreda Ethiopia 49 6.32N 37.48E
Borgå Finland 23 60.24N 25.40E
Borga Sweden 22 64.49N 15.05E
Börgefjell *mtn.* Norway 22 65.20N 13.45E
Börgefjell Nat. Park Norway 22 65.00N 13.58E
Borger Neth. 14 52.57N 6.46E
Borger U.S.A. 83 35.39N 101.24W
Borgholm Sweden 23 56.53N 16.39E
Borghorst Germany 14 52.08N 7.27E
Borgo Italy 15 46.03N 11.27E
Borgomanero Italy 15 45.42N 8.28E
Borgo San Dalmazzo Italy 15 44.20N 7.30E
Borgo San Lorenzo Italy 15 43.57N 11.23E
Borgosesia Italy 15 45.43N 8.16E
Borgo Val di Taro Italy 15 44.29N 9.46E
Borgund Norway 23 61.03N 7.49E
Borislav Ukraine 21 49.18N 23.28E
Borisoglebsk Russian Fed. 25 51.23N 42.02E
Borisov Belorussia 21 54.09N 28.30E
Borispol Ukraine 21 50.21N 30.59E
Borja Peru 90 4.20S 77.40W
Borken Germany 14 51.50N 6.52E
Borkou-Ennedi-Tibesti *d.* Chad 51 18.15N 20.00E
Borkum Germany 14 53.34N 6.41E
Borkum *i.* Germany 14 53.35N 6.45E
Borlänge Sweden 23 60.29N 15.25E
Borley, C. Antarctica 96 66.15S 55.00E
Bormio Italy 15 46.28N 10.22E
Borndiep *g.* Neth. 14 53.28N 5.35E
Borneo *i.* Asia 36 1.00N 114.00E
Bornheim Germany 14 50.45N 7.00E
Bornholm *i.* Denmark 23 55.10N 15.00E
Borno *d.* Nigeria 53 11.20N 12.40E
Bornu, Plain of *f.* Nigeria 53 12.30N 13.00E
Boro *r.* Sudan 49 8.52N 26.11E
Borodyanka Ukraine 21 50.38N 29.59E
Boromo Burkina 52 11.43N 2.53W
Borotou Ivory Coast 52 8.46N 7.30W

Boroughbridge to **Bunyan**

Boroughbridge U.K. **10** 54.06N 1.23W
Borovichi Russian Fed. **24** 58.22N 34.00E
Borraan Somali Rep. **45** 10.10N 48.48E
Borrika Australia **66** 35.00S140.05E
Borroloola Australia **64** 16.04S136.17E
Borşa Romania **21** 46.56N 23.40E
Borşa Romania **21** 47.39N 24.40E
Borsad India **40** 22.25N 72.54E
Borth U.K. **11** 52.29N 4.03W
Borūjerd Iran **43** 33.54N 48.47E
Bory Tucholskie *f.* Poland **21** 53.45N 17.30E
Borzhomi Georgia **25** 41.49N 43.23E
Borzna Ukraine **25** 51.15N 32.25E
Borzya Russian Fed. **29** 50.24N116.35E
Bosa Italy **18** 40.18N 8.29E
Bosanska Gradiška Croatia **19** 45.09N 17.15E
Bosanski Novi Bosnia-Herzegovina **20** 45.03N 16.23E
Boscastle U.K. **11** 50.42N 4.42W
Bose China **33** 23.58N106.32E
Boshan China **32** 36.29N117.50E
Boshof R.S.A. **56** 28.32S 25.12E
Bosna *r.* Bosnia-Herzegovina **19** 45.04N 18.27E
Bosnia-Herzegovina Europe **19** 44.00N 18.10E
Bosnik Indonesia **37** 1.09S136.14E
Bosobolo Zaïre **49** 4.11N 19.54E
Bōsō-hantō *pen.* Japan **35** 35.08N140.00E
Bosporus *str. see* Istanbul Bogazi *str.* Turkey **19**
Bossangoa C.A.R. **53** 6.27N 17.21E
Bossembélé C.A.R. **53** 5.10N 17.44E
Bossier City U.S.A. **83** 32.31N 93.43W
Bosso Niger **53** 13.43N 13.19E
Bostān Pakistan **40** 30.26N 67.02E
Bosten Hu *l.* China **30** 42.00N 87.00E
Boston U.K. **10** 52.59N 0.02W
Boston U.S.A. **84** 42.21N 71.04W
Botād India **40** 22.10N 71.40E
Botany B. Australia **67** 34.04S151.08E
Botev *mtn.* Bulgaria **19** 42.43N 24.55E
Botevgrad Bulgaria **19** 42.55N 23.57E
Bothnia, G. of Europe **22** 63.30N 20.30E
Botletle *r.* Botswana **56** 21.06S 24.47E
Botoşani Romania **21** 47.44N 26.41E
Botou Burkina **53** 12.47N 2.02E
Botrange *mtn.* Belgium **14** 50.30N 6.04E
Botro Ivory Coast **52** 7.51N 5.19W
Botswana Africa **56** 22.00S 24.15E
Bottrop Germany **14** 51.31N 6.55E
Botucatu Brazil **94** 22.52S 48.30W
Bouaflé Ivory Coast **52** 7.01N 5.47W
Bouaké Ivory Coast **52** 7.42N 5.00W
Bouar C.A.R. **53** 5.58N 15.35E
Bou Arfa Morocco **50** 32.30N 1.59W
Bouca C.A.R. **53** 6.30N 18.21E
Bouchoir France **15** 49.45N 2.41E
Boudenib Morocco **50** 31.57N 4.38W
Boufarik Algeria **51** 36.36N 2.54E
Bougainville *i.* Pacific Oc. **68** 6.00S155.00E
Bougouni Mali **52** 11.25N 7.28W
Bouillon Belgium **14** 49.48N 5.03E
Bouïra Algeria **51** 36.23N 3.54E
Bou-Izakarn Morocco **50** 29.09N 9.44W
Boulder Australia **63** 30.55S121.32E
Boulder U.S.A. **82** 40.01N105.17W
Boulder City U.S.A. **81** 35.59N114.50W
Boulia Australia **64** 22.54S139.54E
Boulogne France **17** 50.43N 1.37E
Boulogne-Billancourt France **15** 48.50N 2.15E
Boultoum Niger **53** 14.45N 10.25E
Boumba *r.* Cameroon **53** 2.00N 15.10E
Boumdeit Mauritania **50** 17.26N 9.50W
Boumo Chad **53** 9.01N 16.24E
Bouna Ivory Coast **52** 9.19N 2.53W
Boundary Peak *mtn.* U.S.A. **80** 37.51N118.21W
Boundiali Ivory Coast **52** 9.30N 6.31W
Bountiful U.S.A. **80** 40.53N111.53W
Bounty Is. Pacific Oc. **68** 48.00S178.30E
Bouraga *well* Mali **52** 19.00N 3.36W
Bourail N. Cal. **68** 21.34S165.30E
Bourem Mali **52** 16.59N 0.20W
Bourg France **17** 46.12N 5.13E
Bourganeuf France **17** 45.57N 1.44E
Bourges France **17** 47.05N 2.23E
Bourget Canada **77** 45.26N 75.09W
Bourg Madame France **17** 42.26N 1.55E
Bourgogne *d.* France **17** 47.10N 4.20E
Bourgogne, Canal de France **15** 47.58N 3.30E
Bourgoin France **17** 45.35N 5.17E
Bourgueil France **15** 47.17N 0.10E
Bourke Australia **67** 30.09S145.59E
Bournemouth U.K. **11** 50.43N 1.53W
Bou Saâda Algeria **51** 35.12N 4.11E
Boussac France **17** 46.22N 2.13E
Bousso Chad **53** 10.32N 16.45E
Boutilimit Mauritania **50** 17.33N 14.42W
Bouvard, C. Australia **63** 32.40S115.34E
Bouvetöya *i.* Atlantic Oc. **95** 54.26S 3.24E
Bovill U.S.A. **80** 46.51N116.24W
Bovril Argentina **93** 31.22S 59.25W
Bow *r.* Canada **74** 51.10N115.00W
Bowelling Australia **63** 33.25S116.27E
Bowen Australia **64** 20.00S148.15E
Bowen, Mt. Australia **67** 37.11S148.34E
Bowie Ariz. U.S.A. **81** 32.19N109.29W
Bowie Tex. U.S.A. **83** 33.34N 97.51W
Bow Island *town* Canada **75** 49.52N111.22W
Bowling Green U.S.A. **85** 37.00N 86.29W
Bowling Green, C. Australia **64** 19.19S146.25E
Bowman U.S.A. **82** 46.11N103.24W
Bowman I. Antarctica **96** 65.00S104.00E
Bowmanville Canada **76** 43.55N 78.41W
Bowral Australia **67** 34.30S150.24E
Bowser Australia **67** 36.19S146.23E
Boxholm Sweden **23** 58.12N 15.03E
Bo Xian China **32** 33.50N115.46E
Boxing China **32** 37.08N118.05E
Box Tank Australia **66** 32.13S142.17E
Boxtel Neth. **14** 51.36N 5.20E
Boyabat Turkey **42** 41.27N 34.45E
Boyang China **33** 28.59N116.42E
Boyanup Australia **63** 33.29S115.40E
Boyarka Ukraine **21** 50.20N 30.26E
Boyd *r.* Australia **67** 29.51S152.25E
Boykétté C.A.R. **49** 5.28N 20.50E
Boyle Rep. of Ire. **13** 53.58N 8.19W
Boyne *r.* Rep. of Ire. **13** 53.43N 6.17W
Boyoma Falls *f.* Zaïre **54** 0.18N 25.32E
Boyup Brook Australia **63** 33.50S116.22E
Bozca Ada *i.* Turkey **19** 39.49N 26.03E
Bozeman U.S.A. **80** 45.41N111.02W
Bozen *see* Bolzano Italy **15**
Bozoum C.A.R. **53** 6.16N 16.22E
Bra Italy **15** 44.42N 7.51E
Brabant *d.* Belgium **14** 50.47N 4.30E
Brač *i.* Croatia **19** 43.20N 16.38E
Bracadale, Loch U.K. **12** 57.22N 6.30W
Bracebridge Canada **76** 45.02N 79.19W
Bracieux France **15** 47.33N 1.33E
Bräcke Sweden **22** 62.44N 15.30E
Brad Romania **19** 46.06N 22.48E
Bradano *r.* Italy **19** 40.23N 16.52E
Bradenton U.S.A. **85** 27.29N 82.33W
Bradford Canada **76** 44.07N 79.34W
Bradford U.K. **10** 53.47N 1.45W
Bradford U.S.A. **84** 41.58N 78.39W
Bradley U.S.A. **83** 33.06N 93.39W
Bradworthy U.K. **11** 50.54N 4.22W
Brady U.S.A. **83** 31.08N 99.20W
Braemar U.K. **12** 57.01N 3.24W
Braga Portugal **16** 41.32N 8.26W
Bragado Argentina **93** 35.10S 60.30W
Bragança Brazil **91** 1.03S 46.46W
Bragança Portugal **16** 41.47N 6.46W
Bragança Paulista Brazil **94** 22.59S 46.32W
Bragin Belorussia **21** 51.49N 30.16E
Brāhmanbāria Bangla. **41** 23.59N 91.07E
Brāhmani *r.* India **41** 20.39N 86.46E
Brahmaputra *r.* Asia **41** 23.50N 89.45E
Braidwood Australia **67** 35.27S149.50E
Brăila Romania **21** 45.18N 27.58E
Brainerd U.S.A. **79** 46.20N 94.10W
Braintree U.K. **11** 51.53N 0.32E
Brakna *d.* Mauritania **50** 17.00N 13.20W
Brålanda Sweden **23** 58.34N 12.22E
Bramfield Australia **66** 33.37S134.59E
Brampton Canada **76** 43.41N 79.46W
Brampton U.K. **10** 54.56N 2.43W
Bramsche Germany **14** 52.26N 7.59E
Branco *r.* Brazil **90** 1.00S 62.00W
Brandberg *mtn.* Namibia **56** 21.08S 14.35E
Brandbu Norway **23** 60.28N 10.30E
Brande Denmark **23** 55.57N 9.07E
Brandenburg Germany **20** 52.25N 12.34E
Brandenburg *d.* Germany **20** 52.15N 13.10E
Brandfort R.S.A. **56** 28.41S 26.27E
Brandon Canada **75** 49.50N 99.57W
Brandon Mtn. Rep. of Ire. **13** 52.14N 10.15W
Brandon Pt. Rep. of Ire. **13** 52.17N 10.11W
Braniewo Poland **21** 54.24N 19.50E
Bransby Australia **66** 28.40S142.00E
Branson U.S.A. **83** 36.39N 93.13W
Brantas *r.* Indonesia **37** 7.13S112.45E
Brantford Canada **76** 43.08N 80.16W
Bras d'Or L. Canada **77** 45.52N 60.50W
Brasil, Planalto *mts.* Brazil **91** 17.02S 50.00W
Brasiléia Brazil **90** 11.00S 68.44W
Brasília Brazil **91** 15.45S 47.57W
Braşov Romania **21** 45.40N 25.35E
Brass Nigeria **53** 4.20N 6.15E
Brasschaat Belgium **14** 51.18N 4.28E
Bratislava Slovakia **21** 48.10N 17.10E
Bratsk Russian Fed. **29** 56.20N101.15E
Bratsk Vodokhranilishche *resr.* Russian Fed. **29** 54.40N103.00E
Bratslav Ukraine **21** 48.49N 28.51E
Braunau Austria **20** 48.15N 13.02E
Braunschweig Germany **20** 52.15N 10.30E
Braunton U.K. **11** 51.06N 4.09W
Bravo del Norte, Rio *r.* Mexico *see* Rio Grande *r.* Mexico / U.S.A. **83**
Brawley U.S.A. **81** 32.59N115.31W
Bray France **15** 48.25N 3.14E
Bray Rep. of Ire. **13** 53.12N 6.07W
Bray Head Rep. of Ire. **13** 51.53N 10.26W
Brazeau *r.* Canada **74** 52.55N115.15W
Brazilian Basin *f.* Atlantic Oc. **95** 15.00S 25.00W
Brazilian Highlands *see* Brasil, Planalto *mts.* Brazil **91**
Brazos *r.* U.S.A. **83** 28.53N 95.23W
Brazzaville Congo **54** 4.14S 15.10E
Brčko Bosnia-Herzegovina **21** 44.53N 18.48E
Brda *r.* Poland **21** 53.07N 18.08E
Breadalbane *f.* U.K. **12** 56.30N 4.20W
Bream B. New Zealand **60** 36.00S174.30E
Brebes Indonesia **37** 6.54S109.00E
Brécey France **15** 48.44N 1.10W
Brechin U.K. **12** 56.44N 2.40W
Breckenridge U.S.A. **83** 32.45N 98.54W
Breckland *f.* U.K. **11** 52.28N 0.40E
Břeclav Czech Republic **20** 48.46N 16.53E
Brecon U.K. **11** 51.57N 3.23W
Brecon Beacons *mts.* U.K. **11** 51.53N 3.27W
Breda Neth. **14** 51.35N 4.46E
Bredasdorp R.S.A. **56** 34.31S 20.03E
Bredbo Australia **67** 35.57S149.10E
Bregenz Austria **20** 47.31N 9.46E
Bregovo Bulgaria **19** 44.08N 22.39E
Bréhal France **15** 48.53N 1.30W
Breidhafjördhur *est.* Iceland **22** 65.15N 23.00W
Breim Norway **23** 61.44N 6.25E
Brekstad Norway **22** 63.42N 9.40E
Bremangerland *i.* Norway **23** 61.51N 5.02E
Bremen Germany **20** 53.05N 8.48E
Bremer Bay *town* Australia **63** 34.21S119.20E
Bremerhaven Germany **20** 53.33N 8.35E
Bremer Range *mts.* Australia **63** 32.40S120.55E
Bremerton U.S.A. **80** 47.34N122.38W
Brenham U.S.A. **83** 30.10N 96.24W
Brenner Pass Italy / Austria **20** 47.00N 11.30E
Breno Italy **15** 45.57N 10.18E
Brent Canada **76** 46.00N 78.24W
Brenta *r.* Italy **15** 45.25N 12.15E
Brentwood U.K. **11** 51.38N 0.18E
Brescia Italy **15** 45.33N 10.12E
Breskens Neth. **14** 51.24N 3.34E
Bressay *i.* U.K. **12** 60.08N 1.05W
Bressuire France **17** 46.50N 0.28W
Brest Belorussia **21** 52.08N 23.40E
Brest France **17** 48.23N 4.30W
Bretagne *d.* France **17** 48.15N 2.30W
Breteuil France **15** 49.38N 2.18E
Breteuil-sur-Iton France **15** 48.50N 0.55E
Breton Sd. U.S.A. **83** 29.30N 89.30W
Brett, C. New Zealand **60** 35.15S174.20E
Breuil-Cervinia Italy **15** 45.56N 7.38E
Brevik Norway **23** 59.04N 9.42E
Brewarrina Australia **67** 29.57S147.54E
Brewer U.S.A. **84** 44.48N 68.46W
Brewster U.S.A. **85** 41.24N 73.37W
Brewton U.S.A. **85** 31.07N 87.04W
Brezovo Bulgaria **19** 42.20N 25.06E
Bria C.A.R. **49** 6.32N 21.59E
Briançon France **17** 44.53N 6.39E
Briare France **15** 47.38N 2.44E
Bribbaree Australia **67** 34.07S147.51E
Brichany Moldavia **21** 48.20N 27.01E
Bricquebec France **15** 49.28N 1.38W
Bride I.o.M. Europe **10** 54.23N 4.24W
Bridge *r.* Canada **74** 50.50N122.40W
Bridgend U.K. **11** 51.30N 3.35W
Bridgeport Calif. U.S.A. **80** 38.10N119.13W
Bridgeport Conn. U.S.A. **84** 41.12N 73.12W
Bridgeport Nebr. U.S.A. **82** 41.40N103.06W
Bridgeport Tex. U.S.A. **83** 33.13N 97.45W
Bridger U.S.A. **80** 45.18N108.55W
Bridgeton U.S.A. **85** 39.26N 75.14W
Bridgetown Australia **63** 33.57S116.08E
Bridgetown Barbados **87** 13.06N 59.37W
Bridgetown Canada **77** 44.51N 65.18W
Bridgetown Rep. of Ire. **13** 52.14N 6.33W
Bridgeville U.S.A. **85** 38.45N 75.36W
Bridgewater Canada **77** 44.23N 64.31W
Bridgewater, C. Australia **66** 38.25S141.28E
Bridgnorth U.K. **11** 52.33N 2.25W
Bridgwater U.K. **11** 51.08N 3.00W
Bridlington U.K. **10** 54.06N 0.11W
Brie *f.* France **15** 48.40N 3.20E
Brienne-le-Château France **15** 48.24N 4.32E
Brig Switz. **15** 46.19N 8.00E
Brigantine U.S.A. **85** 39.24N 74.22W
Brigg U.K. **10** 53.33N 0.30W
Briggsdale U.S.A. **82** 40.38N104.20W
Brigham City U.S.A. **80** 41.31N112.01W
Bright Australia **67** 36.42S146.58E
Brighton U.K. **11** 50.50N 0.09W
Brighton Colo. U.S.A. **80** 39.59N104.49W
Brighton Fla. U.S.A. **85** 27.13N 81.06W
Brikama Gambia **52** 13.15N 16.39W
Brindisi Italy **19** 40.38N 17.57E
Brinkley U.S.A. **83** 34.53N 91.12W
Brinkworth Australia **66** 33.42S138.24E
Brionne France **15** 49.12N 0.43E
Briouze France **15** 48.42N 0.22W
Brisbane Australia **67** 27.30S153.00E
Brisighella Italy **15** 44.13N 11.46E
Bristol U.K. **11** 51.26N 2.35W
Bristol Penn. U.S.A. **85** 40.06N 74.52W
Bristol S.Dak. U.S.A. **82** 45.21N 97.45W
Bristol Tenn. U.S.A. **85** 36.33N 82.11W
Bristol B. U.S.A. **72** 58.00N158.50W
Bristol Channel U.K. **11** 51.17N 3.20W
British Antarctic Territory Antarctica **96** 70.00S 50.00W
British Columbia *d.* Canada **74** 55.00N125.00W
British Mts. Canada **72** 69.00N140.20W
British Virgin Is. C. America **87** 18.30N 64.30W
Britstown R.S.A. **56** 30.34S 23.30E
Britt Canada **76** 45.46N 80.35W
Britton U.S.A. **82** 45.48N 97.45W
Brive France **17** 45.09N 1.32E
Briviesca Spain **16** 42.33N 3.19W
Brixham U.K. **11** 50.24N 3.31W
Brno Czech Republic **20** 49.11N 16.39E
Broach India **40** 21.42N 72.58E
Broad Arrow Australia **63** 30.32S121.20E
Broad B. U.K. **12** 58.15N 6.15W
Broadback *r.* Canada **76** 51.20N 78.50W
Broadford Australia **67** 37.16S145.03E
Broadmere Australia **64** 25.30S149.30E
Broad Sd. Australia **64** 22.20S149.50E
Broadsound Range *mts.* Australia **64** 22.30S149.30E
Broadus U.S.A. **80** 45.27N105.25W
Broadview Canada **75** 50.20N102.30W
Broadway U.K. **11** 52.02N 1.51W
Brochet Canada **75** 57.53N101.40W
Brochet, L. Canada **75** 58.36N101.35W
Brockport U.S.A. **76** 43.13N 77.56W
Brockton U.S.A. **84** 42.05N 71.01W
Brockville Canada **84** 44.35N 75.41W
Brockway U.S.A. **80** 47.15N105.45W
Brocton U.S.A. **76** 42.23N 79.27W
Brod Croatia **21** 45.09N 18.02E
Brodeur Pen. Canada **73** 73.00N 88.00W
Brodick U.K. **12** 55.34N 5.09W
Brodnica Poland **21** 53.16N 19.23E
Brody Ukraine **21** 50.05N 25.08E
Broglie France **15** 49.01N 0.32E
Broke Inlet Australia **63** 34.55S116.25E
Broken Arrow U.S.A. **83** 36.03N 95.48W
Broken B. Australia **67** 33.34S151.18E
Broken Bow U.S.A. **82** 41.24N 99.38W
Broken Hill *town* Australia **66** 31.57S141.30E
Bromley U.K. **11** 51.24N 0.02E
Bromley Plateau *f.* Atlantic Oc. **95** 30.00S 34.00W
Bromsgrove U.K. **9** 52.20N 2.03W
Brönderslev Denmark **23** 57.16N 9.58E
Brong-Ahafo *d.* Ghana **52** 7.45N 1.30W
Brönnöysund Norway **22** 65.30N 12.10E
Bronte Canada **76** 43.23N 79.43W
Brooke's Point *town* Phil. **36** 8.50N117.52E
Brookfield U.S.A. **82** 39.47N 93.04W
Brookhaven U.S.A. **83** 31.35N 90.26W
Brookings Oreg. U.S.A. **80** 42.03N124.17W
Brookings S.Dak. U.S.A. **82** 44.19N 96.48W
Brooklin Canada **76** 43.57N 78.57W
Brooklyn Center U.S.A. **82** 45.05N 93.20W
Brooks Canada **72** 50.35N111.53W
Brooks B. Canada **74** 50.15N127.55W
Brooks Range *mts.* U.S.A. **72** 68.50N152.00W
Brooksville U.S.A. **85** 28.34N 82.24W
Brookton Australia **63** 32.22S117.01E
Broom, Loch U.K. **12** 57.52N 5.07W
Broome Australia **62** 17.58S122.15E
Broome, Mt. Australia **62** 17.21S125.23E
Broomehill *town* Australia **63** 33.50S117.35E
Brora U.K. **12** 58.01N 3.52W
Brora *r.* U.K. **12** 58.00N 3.51W
Brosna *r.* Rep. of Ire. **13** 53.13N 7.58W
Brothers U.S.A. **80** 43.49N120.36W
Brou France **15** 48.13N 1.11E
Brough England U.K. **10** 54.32N 2.19W
Brough Scotland U.K. **12** 60.29N 1.12W
Broughton *r.* Australia **66** 33.21S137.46E
Broughton in Furness U.K. **10** 54.17N 3.12W
Brouwershaven Neth. **14** 51.44N 3.53E
Brovary Ukraine **21** 50.30N 30.45E
Brovst Denmark **23** 57.06N 9.32E
Brown, Mt. Australia **66** 32.33S138.02E
Brownfield U.S.A. **83** 33.11N102.16W
Browning U.S.A. **80** 48.34N113.01W
Brownsburg Canada **77** 45.41N 74.25W
Brownsville Tenn. U.S.A. **83** 35.36N 89.15W
Brownsville Tex. U.S.A. **83** 25.54N 97.30W
Brownwood U.S.A. **83** 31.43N 98.59W
Bruay-en-Artois France **14** 50.29N 2.36E
Bruce Pen. Canada **76** 44.50N 81.20W
Bruce Rock *town* Australia **63** 31.52S118.09E
Bruges *see* Brugge Belgium **14**
Brugge Belgium **14** 51.13N 3.14E
Brühl Germany **14** 50.50N 6.55E
Brûlé, Lac *l.* Canada **77** 52.17N 63.52W
Brumadinho Brazil **94** 20.09S 44.11W
Brumado Brazil **91** 14.13S 41.40W
Brunei Asia **36** 4.56N114.58E
Brünen Germany **14** 51.45N 6.41E
Brunflo Sweden **22** 63.04N 14.50E
Brunner New Zealand **60** 42.28S171.12E
Brunsbüttel Germany **20** 53.44N 9.05E
Brunssum Neth. **14** 50.57N 5.59E
Brunswick Ga. U.S.A. **85** 31.09N 81.30W
Brunswick Maine U.S.A. **84** 43.55N 69.58W
Brunswick B. Australia **62** 15.05S125.00E
Brunswick Junction Australia **63** 33.15S115.45E
Bruny I. Australia **65** 43.15S147.16E
Brusilovka Kazakhstan **25** 50.39N 54.59E
Brussel *see* Bruxelles Belgium **14**
Brussels *see* Bruxelles Belgium **14**
Bruthen Australia **67** 37.44S147.49E
Bruton U.K. **11** 51.06N 2.28W
Bruxelles Belgium **14** 50.50N 4.23E
Bryan Ohio U.S.A. **84** 41.30N 84.34W
Bryan Tex. U.S.A. **83** 30.40N 96.22W
Bryan, Mt. Australia **66** 33.26S138.27E
Bryansk Russian Fed. **24** 53.15N 34.09E
Bryne Norway **23** 58.44N 5.39E
Bryson Canada **76** 45.41N 76.37W
Bryson, Lac *l.* Canada **76** 46.19N 77.27W
Bryson City U.S.A. **85** 35.26N 83.27W
Brzeg Poland **21** 50.52N 17.27E
Bsharrī Lebanon **44** 34.15N 36.00E
Bua *r.* Malaŵi **55** 12.42S 34.15E
Bua Yai Thailand **34** 15.34N102.24E
Bu'ayrāt al Ḥasūn Libya **51** 31.24N 15.44E
Buba Guinea Bissau **52** 11.36N 14.55W
Būbiyān, Jazīrat *i.* Kuwait **43** 29.45N 48.15E
Bubye *r.* Zimbabwe **56** 22.18S 31.00E
Bucak Turkey **42** 37.28N 30.36E
Bucaramanga Colombia **90** 7.08N 73.10W
Buchach Ukraine **21** 49.09N 25.20E
Buchanan Liberia **52** 5.57N 10.02W
Buchanan, L. Australia **64** 21.28S145.52E
Buchanan L. U.S.A. **83** 30.48N 98.25W
Buchan Ness *c.* U.K. **12** 57.28N 1.47W
Buchans Canada **77** 48.49N 56.52W
Bucharest *see* Bucureşti Romania **21**
Buchloe Germany **20** 48.02N 10.44E
Buchy France **15** 49.35N 1.22E
Buckambool Mt. Australia **67** 31.55S145.40E
Buckhaven and Methil U.K. **10** 56.11N 3.03W
Buckie U.K. **12** 57.40N 2.58W
Buckingham Canada **77** 45.35N 75.25W
Buckingham U.K. **11** 52.00N 0.59W
Buckingham B. Australia **64** 12.10S135.46E
Buckinghamshire *d.* U.K. **11** 51.50N 0.48W
Buckland Tableland *f.* Australia **64** 25.00S148.00E
Buckleboo Australia **66** 32.55S136.12E
Buckley U.S.A. **82** 40.35N 88.04W
Bucklin U.S.A. **83** 37.33N 99.38W
Buco Zau Angola **54** 4.46S 12.34E
Bucquoy France **14** 50.09N 2.43E
Bu Craa W. Sahara **50** 26.21N 12.57W
Buctouche Canada **77** 46.28N 64.43W
Bucureşti Romania **21** 44.25N 26.06E
Bucyrus U.S.A. **84** 40.47N 82.57W
Bud Norway **22** 62.54N 6.56E
Budapest Hungary **21** 47.30N 19.03E
Budaun India **41** 28.03N 79.07E
Budda Australia **66** 31.12S144.16E
Budd Coast *f.* Antarctica **96** 67.00S112.00E
Buddh Gaya India **41** 24.42N 84.59E
Bude U.K. **11** 50.49N 4.33W
Bude B. U.K. **11** 50.50N 4.40W
Budennovsk Russian Fed. **25** 44.50N 44.10E
Budjala Zaïre **54** 2.38N 19.48E
Buea Cameroon **53** 4.09N 9.13E
Buenaventura Colombia **90** 3.54N 77.02W
Buenaventura Mexico **81** 29.51N107.29W
Buena Vista U.S.A. **85** 37.44N 79.22W
Buenos Aires Argentina **93** 34.40S 58.25W
Buenos Aires *d.* Argentina **93** 36.30S 59.00W
Buenos Aires, L. Argentina / Chile **93** 46.35S 72.00W
Buffalo Canada **75** 50.49N110.42W
Buffalo *r.* Canada **74** 60.55N115.00W
Buffalo Mo. U.S.A. **83** 37.39N 93.06W
Buffalo N.Y. U.S.A. **84** 42.52N 78.55W
Buffalo Okla. U.S.A. **83** 36.50N 99.38W
Buffalo S.Dak. U.S.A. **82** 45.35N103.33W
Buffalo Wyo. U.S.A. **80** 44.21N106.42W
Buffalo Head Hills Canada **74** 57.25N115.55W
Buffalo L. Canada **74** 60.10N115.30W
Buffalo Narrows *town* Canada **75** 55.51N108.30W
Bug *r.* Poland **21** 52.29N 21.11E
Buga Colombia **90** 3.53N 76.17W
Bugaldie Australia **67** 31.02S149.08E
Bugembe Uganda **55** 0.26N 33.16E
Bugene Tanzania **55** 1.34S 31.07E
Buggs Island L. U.S.A. **85** 36.35N 78.28W
Bugrino Russian Fed. **24** 68.45N 49.15E
Bugt China **31** 48.45N121.58E
Bugulma Russian Fed. **24** 54.32N 52.46E
Buguma Nigeria **53** 4.43N 6.53E
Buguruslan Russian Fed. **24** 53.36N 52.30E
Buhera Zimbabwe **57** 19.21S 31.25E
Buhuşi Romania **21** 46.43N 26.41E
Builth Wells U.K. **11** 52.09N 3.24W
Buinsk Russian Fed. **24** 54.58N 48.15E
Bu'in-Sofiā Iran **43** 35.51N 46.02E
Buitenpost Neth. **14** 53.15N 6.09E
Buji P.N.G. **64** 9.07S142.26E
Bujumbura Burundi **55** 3.22S 29.21E
Bukama Zaïre **54** 9.16S 25.52E
Bukavu Zaïre **55** 2.30S 28.49E
Bukene Tanzania **55** 4.13S 32.52E
Bukhara Uzbekistan **43** 39.47N 64.26E
Buki Ukraine **21** 49.02N 30.29E
Bukima Tanzania **55** 1.48S 33.25E
Bukittinggi Indonesia **36** 0.18S100.20E
Bukoba Tanzania **55** 1.20S 31.49E
Bukrale Ethiopia **49** 4.30N 42.03E
Bukuru Nigeria **53** 9.48N 8.52E
Būl, Kūh-e *mtn.* Iran **43** 30.48N 52.45E
Bula Indonesia **37** 3.07S130.27E
Bulahdelah Australia **67** 32.25S152.13E
Bulan Phil. **37** 12.40N123.53E
Bulandshahr India **41** 28.24N 77.51E
Bulawayo Zimbabwe **56** 20.10S 28.43E
Buldāna India **40** 20.32N 76.11E
Buldern Germany **14** 51.52N 7.21E
Bulgan Mongolia **30** 48.34N103.12E
Bulgaria Europe **19** 42.30N 25.00E
Bullabulling Australia **63** 31.05S120.52E
Bullara Australia **62** 22.40S114.03E
Bullaxaar Somali Rep. **45** 10.23N 44.27E
Buller *r.* New Zealand **60** 41.45S171.35E
Buller, Mt. Australia **67** 37.11S146.26E
Bullfinch Australia **63** 30.59S119.06E
Bulli Australia **67** 34.20S150.55E
Bull Mts. U.S.A. **80** 46.05N109.00W
Bulloo *r.* Australia **66** 28.43S142.27E
Bulloo Downs *town* Australia **66** 28.30S142.45E
Bull Shoals L. U.S.A. **83** 36.30N 92.50W
Bulolo P.N.G. **37** 7.13S146.35E
Bulsār India **40** 20.38N 72.56E
Bultfontein R.S.A. **56** 28.17S 26.09E
Bulu Indonesia **37** 4.34N126.45E
Bulu, Gunung *mtn.* Indonesia **36** 3.00N116.00E
Bulun Russian Fed. **29** 70.50N127.20E
Bulunde Tanzania **55** 4.19S 32.57E
Bumba Bandundu Zaïre **54** 6.55S 19.16E
Bumba Equateur Zaïre **54** 2.15N 22.32E
Bumbuli Zaïre **54** 3.25S 20.30E
Buna Kenya **55** 2.49N 39.27E
Buna P.N.G. **64** 8.40S148.25E
Bunbury Australia **63** 33.20S115.34E
Buncrana Rep. of Ire. **13** 55.08N 7.27W
Bundaberg Australia **64** 24.50S152.21E
Bundaleer Australia **67** 28.39S146.31E
Bundarra Australia **67** 30.11S151.04E
Bunde Germany **14** 53.12N 7.16E
Bundella Australia **67** 31.35S149.59E
Būndi India **40** 25.27N 75.39E
Bundoran Rep. of Ire. **13** 54.28N 8.17W
Būndu India **41** 23.11N 85.35E
Bungay U.K. **11** 52.27N 1.26E
Bungo Angola **54** 7.26S 15.23E
Bungu Tanzania **55** 7.37S 39.07E
Buni Nigeria **53** 11.20N 11.59E
Bunia Zaïre **55** 1.30N 30.10E
Buninyong Australia **66** 37.41S143.58E
Bunkie U.S.A. **83** 30.57N 92.11W
Bunyala Kenya **55** 0.07N 34.00E
Bunyan Australia **67** 36.11S149.09E

Buol to **Carinhanha**

Buol Indonesia 37 1.12N121.28E
Buqayq Saudi Arabia 43 25.55N 49.40E
Bura Coast Kenya 55 1.09S 39.55E
Bura Coast Kenya 55 3.30S 38.19E
Burakin Australia 63 30.30S117.08E
Burang China 41 30.16N 81.11E
Buras U.S.A. 83 29.21N 89.32W
Buraydah Saudi Arabia 43 26.18N 43.58E
Burcher Australia 67 33.32S147.18E
Burco Somali Rep. 45 9.30N 45.30E
Burdur Turkey 25 37.44N 30.17E
Burdwān India 41 23.15N 87.51E
Bure Ethiopia 49 10.40N 37.04E
Burg Germany 20 52.17N 11.51E
Burgas Bulgaria 19 42.30N 27.29E
Burgenland d. Austria 20 47.30N 16.20E
Burgeo Canada 77 47.36N 57.34W
Burgess Hill U.K. 11 50.57N 0.07W
Burgos Spain 16 42.21N 3.41W
Burgsteinfurt Germany 14 52.09N 7.21E
Burgsvik Sweden 23 57.03N 18.16E
Burhānpur India 40 21.18N 76.14E
Buri Brazil 94 23.46S 48.39W
Burias i. Phil. 37 12.50N123.10E
Burica, Punta c. Panama 87 8.05N 82.50W
Burin Pen. Canada 77 47.00N 55.40W
Buriram Thailand 34 14.59N103.08E
Burkburnett U.S.A. 83 34.06N 98.34W
Burke r. Australia 64 23.12S139.33E
Burketown Australia 64 17.44S139.22E
Burkina Africa 52 12.30N 2.00W
Burley U.S.A. 80 42.32N113.48W
Burlington Canada 76 43.19N 79.48W
Burlington Iowa U.S.A. 82 40.49N 91.14W
Burlington Kans. U.S.A. 82 38.12N 95.45W
Burlington N.C. U.S.A. 85 36.05N 79.27W
Burlington N.J. U.S.A. 85 40.04N 74.49W
Burlington Vt. U.S.A. 84 44.29N 73.13W
Burlington Wisc. U.S.A. 82 42.41N 88.17W
Burma Asia 34 21.45N 97.00E
Burngup Australia 63 33.00S118.39E
Burnham-on-Crouch U.K. 11 51.37N 0.50E
Burnham-on-Sea U.K. 11 51.15N 3.00W
Burnie Australia 65 41.03S145.55E
Burnley U.K. 10 53.47N 2.15W
Burns Oreg. U.S.A. 80 43.35N119.03W
Burns Wyo. U.S.A. 80 41.11N104.21W
Burnside r. Canada 72 66.51N108.04W
Burns Lake town Canada 74 54.20N125.45W
Buronga Australia 66 34.08S142.11E
Burra Australia 66 33.40S138.57E
Burracoppin Australia 63 31.22S118.30E
Burragorang, L. Australia 67 33.58S150.27E
Burren Junction Australia 67 30.08S148.59E
Burrewarra Pt. Australia 67 35.56S150.12E
Burriana Spain 16 39.54N 0.05W
Burrinjuck Australia 67 35.01S148.33E
Burrinjuck Resr. Australia 67 35.00S148.40E
Burro, Serranías del mts. Mexico 83 29.20N102.00W
Burry Port U.K. 11 51.41N 4.17W
Bursa Turkey 19 40.11N 29.04E
Būr Safājah Egypt 42 26.44N 33.56E
Būr Sa'īd Egypt 44 31.17N 32.18E
Būr Sūdān Sudan 48 19.39N 37.01E
Burta Australia 66 32.30S141.05E
Būr Tawfīq Egypt 44 29.57N 32.34E
Burton upon Trent U.K. 10 52.58N 1.39W
Burtundy Australia 66 33.45S142.22E
Buru i. Indonesia 37 3.30S126.30E
Burullus, Buḥayrat al l. Egypt 44 31.30N 30.45E
Burundi Africa 55 3.00S 30.00E
Bururi Burundi 55 3.58S 29.35E
Burutu Nigeria 53 5.20N 5.31E
Bury U.K. 10 53.36N 2.19W
Bury St. Edmunds U.K. 11 52.15N 0.42E
Burzil Jammu & Kashmir 40 34.52N 75.07E
Burzil Pass Jammu & Kashmir 40 34.54N 75.06E
Busalla Italy 15 44.34N 8.57E
Busca Italy 15 44.31N 7.29E
Būsh Egypt 44 29.09N 31.07E
Būshehr Iran 43 28.57N 50.52E
Bushkill U.S.A. 85 41.06N 75.00W
Bushmanland f. R.S.A. 56 29.25S 19.40E
Busi Ethiopia 45 5.30N 44.30E
Busigny France 14 50.03N 3.29E
Businga Zaïre 54 3.16N 20.55E
Busira r. Zaïre 54 0.05N 18.18E
Buskerud Norway 23 60.20N 9.00E
Buṣrá ash Shām Syria 44 32.30N 36.29E
Busselton Australia 63 33.43S115.15E
Bussum Neth. 14 52.17N 5.10E
Bustard Head c. Australia 64 24.02S151.48E
Busto Arsizio Italy 15 45.37N 8.51E
Busu Djanoa Zaïre 54 1.42N 21.23E
Buta Zaïre 54 2.50N 24.50E
Butare Rwanda 55 2.38S 29.43E
Butaritari i. Kiribati 68 3.07N172.48E
Bute Australia 66 33.24S138.01E
Bute i. U.K. 12 55.51N 5.07W
Bute, Sd. of U.K. 12 55.44N 5.10W
Butedale Canada 74 53.12N128.45W
Butiaba Uganda 55 1.48N 31.15E
Butler Mo. U.S.A. 83 38.16N 94.20W
Butler N.J. U.S.A. 85 41.00N 74.21W
Buton i. Indonesia 37 5.00S122.50E
Butte Mont. U.S.A. 80 46.00N112.32W
Butte Nebr. U.S.A. 82 42.58N 98.51W
Butterworth Malaysia 36 5.24N100.22E
Buttevant Rep. of Ire. 13 52.14N 8.41W
Butt of Lewis c. U.K. 12 58.31N 6.15W
Butty Head Australia 63 33.52S121.35E
Butuan Phil. 37 8.56N125.31E
Butwal Nepal 41 27.42N 83.28E
Buuhoodle Somali Rep. 45 8.16N 46.24E
Buulo Berdi Somali Rep. 45 3.52N 45.40E
Buur Gaabo Somali Rep. 49 1.10S 41.50E
Buur Hakaba Somali Rep. 55 2.43N 44.10E
Buxton U.K. 10 53.16N 1.54W
Buy Russian Fed. 24 58.23N 41.27E
Buyaga Russian Fed. 29 59.42N126.59E
Buynaksk Russian Fed. 25 42.48N 47.07E
Büyük Menderes r. Turkey 19 37.30N 27.05E
Buzachi, Poluostrov pen. Kazakhstan 25 45.00N 51.55E
Buzancy France 15 49.30N 4.59E
Buzău Romania 21 45.10N 26.49E
Buzău r. Romania 21 45.24N 27.48E
Buzaymah Libya 51 24.55N 22.02E
Buzi r. Mozambique 57 19.52S 34.00E
Buzuluk Russian Fed. 24 52.49N 52.19E
Bwasiaia P.N.G. 64 10.06S150.48E
Byala Bulgaria 19 42.53N 27.55E
Byam Martin I. Canada 72 75.15N104.00W
Bydgoszcz Poland 21 53.16N 17.33E
Byemoor Canada 74 52.00N112.17W
Bygland Norway 23 58.48N 7.50E
Byhalia U.S.A. 83 34.52N 89.41W
Bykhov Belorussia 21 53.30N 30.15E
Bykle Norway 23 59.21N 7.20E
Bylot I. Canada 73 73.00N 78.30W
Byrd Land f. Antarctica 96 79.30S125.00W
Byrock Australia 67 30.40S146.25E
Byron, C. Australia 67 28.37S153.40E
Byron Bay town Australia 67 28.43S153.34E
Byrranga, Gory mts. Russian Fed. 29 74.50N101.00E
Byske Sweden 22 64.57N 21.12E
Byske r. Sweden 22 64.57N 21.13E
Byten Belorussia 21 52.50N 25.28E
Bytom Poland 21 50.22N 18.54E
Bzipi Georgia 25 43.15N 40.24E

C

Ca r. Vietnam 33 18.47N105.40E
Caballos Mesteños, Llano de los f. Mexico 83 28.15N104.00W
Cabanatuan Phil. 37 15.30N120.58E
Cabimas Venezuela 90 10.26N 71.27W
Cabinda Angola 54 5.34S 12.12E
Cabinet Mts. U.S.A. 80 48.08N115.46W
Cabo Delgado d. Mozambique 55 12.30S 39.00E
Cabo Frio town Brazil 94 22.51S 42.03W
Cabonga, Résr. Canada 76 47.35N 76.40W
Cabool U.S.A. 83 37.07N 92.06W
Caboolture Australia 65 27.05S152.57E
Cabo Pantoja Peru 90 1.00S 75.10W
Cabot Str. Canada 77 47.20N 59.30W
Cabras Italy 18 39.56N 8.32E
Cabrera i. Spain 16 39.08N 2.56E
Cabrera, Sierra mts. Spain 16 42.10N 6.30W
Cabri Canada 75 50.37N108.28W
Cabriel r. Spain 16 39.13N 1.07W
Cabruta Venezuela 90 7.40N 66.16W
Čačak Yugo. 21 43.53N 20.21E
Caçapava Brazil 94 23.05S 45.40W
Cáceres Brazil 91 16.05S 57.40W
Cáceres Spain 16 39.29N 6.23W
Cacharí Argentina 93 36.23S 59.29W
Cachimo r. Zaïre 54 7.02S 21.13E
Cachoeira Brazil 91 12.35S 38.59W
Cachoeira do Sul Brazil 94 30.03S 52.52W
Cachoeiro de Itapemirim Brazil 94 20.51S 41.07W
Cacín r. Spain 16 37.10N 4.01W
Cacine Guinea 52 11.08N 14.57W
Cacolo Angola 54 10.09S 19.15E
Caconda Angola 54 13.46S 15.06E
Cacongo Angola 54 5.11S 12.10E
Cacuso Angola 54 9.26S 15.43E
Čadca Slovakia 21 49.26N 18.48E
Cader Idris mtn. U.K. 11 52.40N 3.55W
Cadí, Serra del mts. Spain 16 42.12N 1.35E
Cadibarrawirracanna, L. Australia 66 28.52S135.27E
Cadillac U.S.A. 84 44.15N 85.23W
Cadiz Phil. 37 10.57N123.18E
Cádiz Spain 16 36.32N 6.18W
Cádiz, Golfo de g. Spain 16 37.00N 7.10W
Cadomin Canada 74 53.02N117.20W
Cadoux Australia 63 30.47S117.05E
Caen France 15 49.11N 0.22W
Caernarfon U.K. 10 53.08N 4.17W
Caernarfon B. U.K. 10 53.05N 4.25W
Caerphilly U.K. 11 51.34N 3.13W
Caeté Brazil 94 19.54S 43.37W
Cafima Angola 54 16.34S 16.30E
Cafu Angola 54 16.30S 15.14E
Cagayan de Oro Phil. 37 8.29N124.40E
Cagliari Italy 18 39.14N 9.07E
Cagliari, Golfo di g. Italy 18 39.07N 9.15E
Cagnes France 15 43.40N 7.09E
Caguán r. Colombia 90 0.08S 74.18W
Caguas Puerto Rico 87 18.08N 66.00W
Cahama Angola 54 16.16S 14.23E
Caha Mts. Rep. of Ire. 13 51.44N 9.45W
Caherciveen Rep. of Ire. 13 51.51N 10.14W
Cahir Rep. of Ire. 13 52.23N 7.56W
Cahora Bassa Dam Mozambique 55 15.36S 32.41E
Cahore Pt. Rep. of Ire. 13 52.34N 6.12W
Cahors France 17 44.28N 0.26E
Cahuapanas Peru 90 5.15S 77.00W
Caianda Angola 54 11.02S 23.29E
Caibarién Cuba 87 22.31N 79.28W
Caicó Brazil 91 6.25S 37.04W
Caicos Is. Turks & Caicos Is. 87 21.30N 72.00W
Caird Coast f. Antarctica 96 75.00S 20.00W
Cairngorms mts. U.K. 12 57.04N 3.30W
Cairns Australia 64 16.51S145.43E
Cairo see Al Qāhirah Egypt 44
Cairo U.S.A. 83 37.01N 89.09W
Cairo Montenotte Italy 15 44.24N 8.16E
Caiundo Angola 54 15.43S 17.30E
Caiwarro Australia 67 28.38S144.45E
Caizhai China 32 37.20N118.10E
Caizi Hu l. China 33 30.50N117.06E
Cajamarca Peru 90 7.09S 78.32W
Cajàzeiras Brazil 91 6.52S 38.31W
Cajuru Brazil 94 21.15S 47.18W
Čakovec Croatia 20 46.23N 16.26E
Calabar Nigeria 53 4.56N 8.22E
Calabozo Venezuela 90 8.58N 67.28W
Calabria d. Italy 19 39.00N 16.30E
Calafat Romania 21 43.59N 22.57E
Calafate Argentina 93 50.20S 72.16W
Calahorra Spain 16 42.18N 1.58W
Calais France 17 50.57N 1.52E
Calama Brazil 90 8.03S 62.53W
Calama Chile 92 22.30S 68.55W
Calamar Colombia 90 10.15N 74.55W
Calamian Group is. Phil. 37 12.00N120.05E
Cala Millor Spain 16 39.35N 3.22E
Calamocha Spain 16 40.54N 1.18W
Calapan Phil. 37 13.23N121.10E
Călăraşi Romania 21 44.11N 27.21E
Calatayud Spain 16 41.21N 1.39W
Calatrava Equat. Guinea 54 1.09N 9.24E
Calau Germany 20 51.45N 13.56E
Calayan i. Phil. 33 19.20N121.25E
Calbayog Phil. 37 12.04N124.58E
Calcutta India 41 22.32N 88.22E
Caldaro Italy 15 46.25N 11.14E
Caldas Colombia 90 6.05N 75.36W
Caldas da Rainha Portugal 16 39.24N 9.08W
Caldera Chile 92 27.04S 70.50W
Caldwell Idaho U.S.A. 80 43.40N116.41W
Caldwell Ohio U.S.A. 84 39.44N 81.32W
Caledon r. R.S.A. 56 30.27S 26.12E
Caledon B. Australia 64 12.58S136.52E
Caledonia Canada 76 43.04N 79.56W
Caledonia Hills Canada 77 45.40N 65.00W
Calella Spain 16 41.37N 2.40E
Calexico Mexico 81 32.40N115.30W
Calf of Man i. I.o.M. Europe 10 54.03N 4.49W
Calgary Canada 74 51.00N114.10W
Cali Colombia 90 3.24N 76.30W
Caliente U.S.A. 80 37.37N114.31W
California d. U.S.A. 80 37.29N119.58W
California, G. of see California, Golfo de g. Mexico 86
California, Golfo de g. Mexico 81 28.00N112.00W
Calingasta Argentina 92 31.15S 69.30W
Calingiri Australia 63 31.07S116.27E
Callabonna, L. Australia 66 29.47S140.07E
Callabonna Creek r. Australia 66 29.37S140.08E
Callander U.K. 12 56.15N 4.13W
Callao Peru 92 12.05S 77.08W
Caloocan Phil. 37 14.38N120.58E
Caloundra Australia 65 26.47S153.08E
Caltagirone Italy 18 37.14N 14.30E
Caltanissetta Italy 18 37.30N 14.05E
Calulo Angola 54 10.05S 14.56E
Calumbo Angola 54 9.08S 13.24E
Calumet Canada 77 45.39N 74.41W
Calundau Angola 54 12.05S 19.10E
Caluula Somali Rep. 45 11.58N 50.48E
Calvados d. France 15 49.10N 0.30W
Calvert I. Canada 74 51.30N128.00W
Calvi France 17 42.34N 8.44E
Calvinia R.S.A. 56 31.29S 19.44E
Cam r. U.K. 11 52.34N 0.21E
Camabatela Angola 54 8.20S 15.29E
Camacupa Angola 54 12.01S 17.22E
Camagüey Cuba 87 21.25N 77.55W
Camagüey, Archipiélago de Cuba 87 22.30N 78.00W
Camaiore Italy 15 43.56N 10.18E
Camarès France 17 43.49N 2.53E
Camaret-sur-Mer France 17 48.16N 4.37W
Camarón, C. Honduras 87 15.59N 85.00W
Camaronero, Laguna l. Mexico 81 23.00N106.07W
Camarones Argentina 93 44.45S 65.40W
Camas U.S.A. 80 45.35N122.24W
Cambay India 40 22.18N 72.37E
Camberley U.K. 11 51.21N 0.45W
Cambodia Asia 34 12.45N105.00E
Camborne U.K. 11 50.12N 5.19W
Cambrai Australia 66 34.39S139.17E
Cambrai France 17 50.10N 3.14E
Cambria U.S.A. 81 35.34N121.05W
Cambrian Mts. U.K. 11 52.33N 3.33W
Cambridge Canada 76 43.22N 80.19W
Cambridge New Zealand 60 37.53S175.29E
Cambridge U.K. 11 52.13N 0.08E
Cambridge Idaho U.S.A. 80 44.34N116.41W
Cambridge Mass. U.S.A. 84 42.22N 71.06W
Cambridge Md. U.S.A. 85 38.34N 76.04W
Cambridge Minn. U.S.A. 82 45.31N 93.14W
Cambridge Bay town Canada 72 69.09N105.00W
Cambridge G. Australia 62 15.00S128.05E
Cambridgeshire d. U.K. 11 52.15N 0.05E
Cambundi-Catembo Angola 54 10.09S 17.35E
Camden U.K. 11 51.33N 0.10W
Camden Ark. U.S.A. 83 33.35N 92.50W
Camden N.J. U.S.A. 85 39.57N 75.07W
Camden S.C. U.S.A. 85 34.16N 80.36W
Cameia Nat. Park Angola 54 12.00S 21.30E
Camelford U.K. 11 50.37N 4.41W
Cameron Ariz. U.S.A. 81 35.51N111.25W
Cameron La. U.S.A. 83 29.48N 93.19W
Cameron Mo. U.S.A. 82 39.44N 94.14W
Cameron Tex. U.S.A. 83 30.51N 96.59W
Cameron Hills Canada 74 59.48N118.00W
Cameron Mts. New Zealand 60 45.50S167.00E
Cameroon Africa 53 6.00N 12.30E
Cameroun, Mont mtn. Cameroon 53 4.20N 9.05E
Cametá Brazil 91 2.12S 49.30W
Camiri Bolivia 92 20.03S 63.31W
Camocim Brazil 91 2.55S 40.50W
Camooweal Australia 64 19.55S138.07E
Camopi Guiana 91 3.12N 52.15W
Campana Argentina 93 34.10S 58.57W
Campana, Isla i. Chile 93 48.25S 75.20W
Campania d. Italy 18 41.00N 14.30E
Campbell, C. New Zealand 60 41.45S174.15E
Campbell I. Pacific Oc. 68 52.30S169.02E
Campbellpore Pakistan 40 33.46N 72.22E
Campbell River town Canada 74 50.05N125.20W
Campbellsville U.S.A. 85 37.20N 85.21W
Campbellton Canada 77 48.00N 66.40W
Campbell Town Australia 67 41.55S147.30E
Campbelltown Australia 67 34.04S150.49E
Campbeltown U.K. 12 55.25N 5.36W
Campeche Mexico 86 19.50N 90.30W
Campeche d. Mexico 86 19.00N 90.00W
Campeche, Bahía de b. Mexico 86 19.30N 94.00W
Campeche B. see Campeche, Bahía de b. Mexico 86
Camperdown Australia 66 38.15S143.14E
Cam Pha Vietnam 34 21.07N107.19E
Campina Grande Brazil 91 7.15S 35.50W
Campinas Brazil 94 22.54S 47.06W
Campo Cameroon 53 2.22N 9.50E
Campo r. Cameroon 54 2.21N 9.51E
Campo U.S.A. 83 37.06N102.35W
Campobasso Italy 18 41.34N 14.39E
Campo Belo Brazil 94 20.52S 45.16W
Campo Gallo Argentina 92 26.35S 62.50W
Campo Grande Brazil 92 20.24S 54.35W
Campo Maior Brazil 91 4.50S 42.12W
Campo Maior Portugal 16 39.01N 7.04W
Campos Brazil 94 21.45S 41.18W
Campos Belos Brazil 91 13.09S 47.03W
Campos do Jordão Brazil 94 23.28S 46.10W
Camp Wood U.S.A. 83 29.40N100.01W
Cam Ranh Vietnam 34 11.54N109.14E
Camrose Canada 74 53.00N112.50W
Canada N. America 72 60.00N105.00W
Cañada de Gómez Argentina 92 32.49S 61.25W
Canadian U.S.A. 83 35.55N100.23W
Canadian r. U.S.A. 83 35.27N 95.03W
Çanakkale Turkey 19 40.09N 26.26E
Çanakkale Boğazi str. Turkey 19 40.15N 26.30E
Canal du Midi France 17 43.18N 2.00E
Cananea Mexico 81 30.57N110.18W
Canarias, Islas is. Atlantic Oc. 50 28.00N 15.00W
Canary Is. see Canarias, Islas is. Atlantic Oc. 50
Canastra, Serra da mts. Brazil 94 20.05S 46.30W
Canaveral, C. U.S.A. 85 28.27N 80.32W
Canavieiras Brazil 91 15.44S 38.58W
Canbelego Australia 67 31.33S146.19E
Canberra Australia 67 35.18S149.08E
Canby Calif. U.S.A. 80 41.27N120.52W
Canby Minn. U.S.A. 82 44.43N 96.16W
Cancale France 15 48.40N 1.50W
Cancon France 17 44.32N 0.38E
Candé France 15 47.34N 1.02W
Candeias Brazil 94 20.44S 45.18W
Candeleda Spain 16 40.10N 5.14W
Candle L. Canada 75 53.50N105.18W
Canelli Italy 15 44.43N 8.17E
Canelones Uruguay 93 34.32S 56.17W
Cañete Peru 90 13.00S 76.30W
Canfield Canada 76 42.59N 79.43W
Cangamba Angola 54 13.40S 19.50E
Cangas de Narcea Spain 16 43.11N 6.33W
Cangkuang, Tanjung c. Indonesia 37 6.45S105.15E
Cangombe Angola 54 14.27S 20.00E
Canguçu Brazil 92 31.24S 52.41W
Cangwu China 33 23.27N111.17E
Cangzhou China 32 38.15N116.58E
Caniapiscau r. Canada 77 57.40N 69.30W
Caniapiscau, Résr. l. Canada 77 54.10N 69.55W
Çankiri Turkey 42 40.35N 33.37E
Canna i. U.K. 12 57.03N 6.30W
Cannes France 17 43.33N 7.00E
Cannich U.K. 12 57.20N 4.45W
Cannock U.K. 11 52.42N 2.02W
Cann River town Australia 67 37.35S149.06E
Canõas Brazil 94 29.55S 51.10W
Canoe L. Canada 75 55.11N108.15W
Canonba Australia 67 31.19S147.22E
Canon City U.S.A. 80 38.27N105.14W
Canopus Australia 66 33.30S140.57E
Canora Canada 75 51.37N102.26W
Canossa site Italy 15 44.35N 10.27E
Canowindra Australia 67 33.34S148.30E
Canso Canada 77 45.20N 61.00W
Cantabria d. Spain 16 43.10N 4.15W
Cantabria, Sierra de mts. Spain 16 42.40N 2.30W
Cantábrica, Cordillera mts. Spain 16 42.55N 5.10W
Cantagalo Brazil 94 21.59S 42.22W
Cantaura Venezuela 90 9.22N 64.24W
Canterbury d. New Zealand 60 43.30S172.00E
Canterbury U.K. 11 51.17N 1.05E
Canterbury Bight New Zealand 60 44.15S172.00E
Can Tho Vietnam 34 10.03N105.40E
Canton see Guangzhou China 33
Canton Miss. U.S.A. 83 32.37N 90.02W
Canton N.C. U.S.A. 85 35.33N 82.51W
Canton Ohio U.S.A. 84 40.48N 81.23W
Canton Okla. U.S.A. 83 36.03N 98.35W
Cantù Italy 15 45.44N 9.08E
Cantua Creek town U.S.A. 81 36.30N120.19W
Cantung Canada 74 62.00N128.09W
Cañuelas Argentina 93 35.03S 58.44W
Canumã r. Brazil 90 3.55S 59.10W
Canutama Brazil 90 6.32S 64.20W
Canutillo Mexico 81 26.21N105.25W
Cany-Barville France 15 49.47N 0.38E
Canyon Tex. U.S.A. 83 34.59N101.55W
Canyon Wyo. U.S.A. 80 44.43N110.32W
Cao Bang Vietnam 33 22.37N106.18E
Caombo Angola 54 8.45S 16.50E
Caorle Italy 15 45.36N 12.53E
Capanema Brazil 91 1.08S 47.07W
Cap-Chat Canada 77 48.56N 66.53W
Cap-de-la-Madeleine town Canada 77 46.22N 72.32W
Cape Barren I. Australia 65 40.25S148.15E
Cape Basin f. Atlantic Oc. 95 38.00S 10.00E
Cape Breton Highlands Canada 77 46.45N 60.45W
Cape Breton I. Canada 77 46.00N 60.30W
Cape Coast town Ghana 52 5.10N 1.13W
Cape Cod B. U.S.A. 84 41.50N 70.17W
Cape Crawford town Australia 64 16.38S135.43E
Cape Dyer town Canada 73 66.30N 61.20W
Cape Girardeau town U.S.A. 83 37.19N 89.32W
Cape Johnson Depth Pacific Oc. 37 10.20N127.20E
Capellen Lux. 14 49.39N 5.59E
Capelongo Angola 54 14.55S 15.03E
Cape May town U.S.A. 85 38.56N 74.55W
Cape Province d. R.S.A. 56 31.30S 23.30E
Cape Town R.S.A. 56 33.55S 18.27E
Cape Verde Atlantic Oc. 95 16.00N 24.00W
Cape Verde Basin f. Atlantic Oc. 95 15.00N 35.00W
Cape York Pen. Australia 64 12.40S142.20E
Cap-Haïtien town Haiti 87 19.47N 72.17W
Capim r. Brazil 91 1.40S 47.47W
Capoompeta, Mt. Australia 67 29.22S151.59E
Cappoquin Rep. of Ire. 13 52.09N 7.52W
Capraia i. Italy 18 43.03N 9.50E
Caprera i. Italy 18 41.48N 9.27E
Capri i. Italy 18 40.33N 14.13E
Caprivi Strip f. Namibia 56 17.50S 23.10E
Captains Flat Australia 67 35.34S149.28E
Captiva U.S.A. 85 26.31N 82.12W
Caquetá r. Colombia 90 1.20S 70.50W
Caracal Romania 21 44.08N 24.18E
Caracas Venezuela 90 10.35N 66.56W
Caragabal Australia 67 33.49S147.46E
Caraguatatuba Brazil 94 23.39S 45.26W
Carandaí Brazil 94 20.55S 43.46W
Carangola Brazil 94 20.44S 42.03W
Caransebeş Romania 21 45.25N 22.13E
Caratasca, Laguna de b. Honduras 87 15.10N 84.00W
Caratinga Brazil 94 19.50S 42.06W
Caravaca Spain 16 38.06N 1.51W
Caravaggio Italy 15 45.30N 9.38E
Caravelí Peru 90 15.45S 73.25W
Carballo Spain 16 43.13N 8.41W
Carbenyabba Creek r. Australia 66 29.02S143.28E
Carberry Canada 75 49.52N 99.20W
Carbonara, Capo c. Italy 18 39.06N 9.32E
Carbondale Ill. U.S.A. 83 37.44N 89.13W
Carbondale Penn. U.S.A. 84 41.35N 75.30W
Carbonear Canada 77 47.45N 53.14W
Carbonia Italy 18 39.11N 8.32E
Carcajou Canada 74 57.47N117.06W
Carcassonne France 17 43.13N 2.21E
Carcross Canada 74 60.13N134.45W
Cárdenas Cuba 87 23.02N 81.12W
Cárdenas Mexico 86 22.00N 99.40W
Cardenete Spain 16 39.46N 1.42W
Cardiff U.K. 11 51.28N 3.11W
Cardigan U.K. 11 52.06N 4.41W
Cardigan B. U.K. 11 52.30N 4.30W
Cardona Spain 16 41.56N 1.40E
Cardona Uruguay 93 33.53S 57.23W
Cardwell Australia 64 18.21S146.04E
Carei Romania 21 47.42N 22.28E
Carentan France 15 49.18N 1.14W
Carey U.S.A. 80 43.18N113.56W
Carey, L. Australia 63 29.05S122.15E
Carey L. Canada 75 62.12N102.55W
Carhaix France 17 48.16N 3.35W
Carhué Argentina 93 37.11S 62.45W
Caribbean Sea C. America 87 15.00N 75.00W
Cariboo Mts. Canada 74 53.00N121.00W
Caribou r. Man. Canada 75 59.20N 94.44W
Caribou r. N.W.T. Canada 74 61.27N125.45W
Caribou U.S.A. 84 46.52N 68.01W
Caribou Is. Canada 74 61.55N113.15W
Caribou Mts. Canada 74 59.12N115.40W
Carignan France 15 49.38N 5.10E
Carinda Australia 67 30.29S147.45E
Carinhanha Brazil 91 14.18S 43.47W

Carini to **Cheju do**

Carini Italy **18** 38.08N 13.11E
Caritianas Brazil **90** 9.25S 63.06W
Carleton Place Canada **76** 45.08N 76.09W
Carlingford Rep. of Ire. **13** 54.03N 6.12W
Carlingford Lough Rep. of Ire. **13** 54.03N 6.09W
Carlinville U.S.A. **82** 39.17N 89.52W
Carlisle U.K. **10** 54.54N 2.55W
Carlos Reyles Uruguay **93** 33.03S 56.29W
Carlow Rep. of Ire. **13** 52.50N 6.46W
Carlow *d.* Rep. of Ire. **13** 52.43N 6.50W
Carlsbad Calif. U.S.A. **81** 33.10N117.21W
Carlsbad N.Mex. U.S.A. **81** 32.25N104.14W
Carlyle Canada **75** 49.38N102.16W
Carmacks Canada **72** 62.04N136.21W
Carmagnola Italy **15** 44.51N 7.43E
Carman Canada **75** 49.32N 98.00W
Carmarthen U.K. **11** 51.52N 4.20W
Carmarthen B. U.K. **11** 52.30N 4.30W
Carmaux France **17** 44.03N 2.09E
Carmel U.S.A. **85** 41.26N 73.41W
Carmel Head U.K. **10** 53.24N 4.35W
Carmelo Uruguay **93** 34.00S 58.17W
Carmen Colombia **90** 9.46N 75.06W
Carmen Mexico **86** 18.38N 91.50W
Carmen Uruguay **93** 33.15S 56.01W
Carmen, Isla *i.* Mexico **81** 25.55N111.10W
Carmen, Isla del *i.* Mexico **86** 18.35N 91.40W
Carmen de Areco Argentina **93** 34.20S 59.50W
Carmen de Patagones Argentina **93** 40.48S 63.00W
Carmi U.S.A. **82** 38.05N 88.11W
Carmichael U.S.A. **80** 38.38N121.19W
Carmila Australia **64** 21.55S149.25E
Carmo Brazil **94** 21.56S 42.37W
Carmody, L. Australia **63** 32.27S119.20E
Carmona Spain **16** 37.28N 5.38W
Carnac France **17** 47.35N 3.05W
Carnarvon Australia **62** 24.53S113.40E
Carnarvon R.S.A. **56** 30.58S 22.07E
Carndonagh Rep. of Ire. **13** 55.15N 7.15W
Carnegie Australia **62** 25.43S122.59E
Carnegie, L. Australia **62** 26.15S123.00E
Carnew Rep. of Ire. **13** 52.43N 6.31W
Carniche, Alpi *mts.* Austria / Italy **18** 46.40N 12.48E
Car Nicobar *i.* India **34** 9.11N 92.45E
Carnot C.A.R. **53** 4.59N 15.56E
Carnot, C. Australia **66** 34.57S135.38E
Carnoustie U.K. **12** 56.30N 2.44W
Carnsore Pt. Rep. of Ire. **13** 52.10N 6.21W
Carolina Brazil **91** 7.20S 47.25W
Carolina Puerto Rico **87** 18.23N 65.57W
Carolina R.S.A. **56** 26.04S 30.07E
Caroline I. Kiribati **69** 10.00S150.30W
Caroline Is. Pacific Oc. **37** 7.50N145.00E
Caroline-Solomon Ridge Pacific Oc. **68** 8.00N150.00E
Caroní *r.* Venezuela **90** 8.20N 62.42W
Carora Venezuela **90** 10.12N 70.07W
Carp Canada **77** 45.21N 76.02W
Carpathians *mts.* Europe **21** 48.45N 23.45E
Carpaţii Meridionali *mts.* Romania **21** 45.35N 24.40E
Carpentaria, G. of Australia **64** 14.00S139.00E
Carpentras France **17** 44.03N 5.03E
Carpi Italy **15** 44.47N 10.53E
Carpio Spain **16** 41.13N 5.07W
Carquefou France **15** 47.18N 1.30W
Carra, Lough Rep. of Ire. **13** 53.41N 9.15W
Carrara Italy **15** 44.04N 10.06E
Carrathool Australia **67** 34.25S145.24E
Carrauntoohil *mtn.* Rep. of Ire. **13** 52.00N 9.45W
Carrickfergus U.K. **13** 54.43N 5.49W
Carrickmacross Rep. of Ire. **13** 53.58N 6.43W
Carrick-on-Shannon Rep. of Ire. **13** 53.57N 8.06W
Carrick-on-Suir Rep. of Ire. **13** 52.21N 7.26W
Carrieton Australia **66** 32.28S138.34E
Carrington U.S.A. **82** 47.27N 99.08W
Carrizo Springs *town* U.S.A. **83** 28.31N 99.52W
Carrizozo U.S.A. **81** 33.38N105.53W
Carroll U.S.A. **82** 42.04N 94.52W
Carrollton U.S.A. **82** 39.22N 93.30W
Carrot *r.* Canada **75** 53.50N101.17W
Carrowmore Lough Rep. of Ire. **13** 54.11N 9.47W
Carrum Australia **67** 38.05S145.08E
Çarşamba Turkey **42** 41.13N 36.43E
Çarşamba *r.* Turkey **42** 37.52N 31.48E
Carson U.S.A. **82** 46.25N101.34W
Carson City U.S.A. **80** 39.10N119.46W
Carstairs U.K. **12** 55.42N 3.41W
Cartagena Colombia **90** 10.24N 75.33W
Cartagena Spain **16** 37.36N 0.59W
Cartago Colombia **90** 4.45N 75.55W
Cartago Costa Rica **87** 9.50N 83.52W
Carter U.S.A. **80** 41.27N110.25W
Carteret France **15** 49.22N 1.48W
Cartersville U.S.A. **85** 34.09N 84.49W
Carterton New Zealand **60** 41.01S175.31E
Carthage Mo. U.S.A. **83** 37.11N 94.19W
Carthage S.Dak. U.S.A. **82** 44.10N 97.43W
Carthage Tex. U.S.A. **83** 32.09N 94.20W
Cartwright Canada **77** 53.50N 56.45W
Caruarú Brazil **91** 8.15S 35.55W
Carúpano Venezuela **90** 10.39N 63.14W
Caruthersville U.S.A. **83** 36.11N 89.39W
Carvin France **14** 50.30N 2.58E
Carvoeiro Brazil **90** 1.24S 61.59W
Caryapundy Swamp Australia **66** 29.00S142.36E
Casablanca Morocco **50** 33.39N 7.35W
Casa Branca Brazil **94** 21.45S 47.06W
Casa Grande U.S.A. **81** 32.53N111.45W
Casale Italy **15** 45.08N 8.27E
Casarano Italy **19** 40.00N 18.10E
Cascade Idaho U.S.A. **80** 44.31N116.02W
Cascade Mont. U.S.A. **80** 47.16N111.42W
Cascade Pt. New Zealand **60** 44.01S168.22E
Cascade Range *mts.* U.S.A. **80** 46.15N121.00W
Caserta Italy **18** 41.06N 14.21E
Cashel Rep. of Ire. **13** 52.31N 7.54W
Casilda Argentina **93** 33.03S 61.10W
Casimiro de Abreu Brazil **94** 22.28S 42.12W
Casino Australia **67** 28.50S153.02E
Casma Peru **90** 9.30S 78.20W
Caspe Spain **16** 41.14N 0.03W
Casper U.S.A. **80** 42.51N106.19W
Caspian Depression *f.* Russian Fed. / Kazakhstan **25** 47.00N 48.00E
Caspian Sea Europe / Asia **25** 42.00N 51.00E
Cassai *r.* Angola **54** 10.38S 22.15E
Cassano allo Ionio Italy **19** 39.47N 16.20E
Cass City U.S.A. **84** 43.37N 83.11W
Casselman Canada **77** 45.19N 75.05W
Casselton U.S.A. **82** 46.54N 97.13W
Cassiar Canada **74** 59.16N129.40W
Cassiar Mts. Canada **74** 59.00N129.00W
Cassilis Australia **67** 32.01S149.59E
Cass Lake *town* U.S.A. **82** 47.22N 94.35W
Castaños Mexico **83** 26.48N101.26W
Castelfranco Veneto Italy **15** 45.40N 11.55E
Casteljaloux France **17** 44.19N 0.06W
Castell' Arquato Italy **15** 44.51N 9.52E
Castelli Argentina **93** 36.07S 57.50W
Castellón Spain **16** 39.59N 0.03W
Castelmassa Italy **15** 45.01N 11.18E
Castelnovo ne'Monti Italy **15** 44.26N 10.24E
Castelnuovo di Garfagnana Italy **15** 44.06N 10.24E
Castelo Brazil **94** 20.33S 41.14W
Castelo Branco Portugal **16** 39.50N 7.30W
Castel San Giovanni Italy **15** 45.04N 9.26E
Castelvetrano Italy **18** 37.41N 12.47E
Casterton Australia **66** 37.35S141.25E
Castets France **17** 43.53N 1.09W
Castilla Peru **90** 5.16S 80.36W
Castilla la Mancha *d.* Spain **16** 40.00N 3.45W
Castilla y León *d.* Spain **16** 41.50N 4.15W
Castilletes Colombia **90** 11.55N 71.20W
Castlebar Rep. of Ire. **13** 53.52N 9.19W
Castleblayney Rep. of Ire. **13** 54.08N 6.46W
Castle Douglas U.K. **12** 54.56N 3.56W
Castleford U.K. **10** 53.43N 1.21W
Castlegar Canada **74** 49.20N117.40W
Castlegate U.S.A. **80** 39.44N110.52W
Castle Harbour *b.* Bermuda **95** 32.20N 64.40W
Castleisland Rep. of Ire. **13** 52.13N 9.28W
Castlemaine Australia **66** 37.05S144.19E
Castlerea Rep. of Ire. **13** 53.45N 8.30W
Castlereagh *r.* Australia **67** 30.12S147.32E
Castle Rock *town* Colo. U.S.A. **80** 39.22N104.51W
Castle Rock *town* Wash. U.S.A. **80** 46.17N122.54W
Castletown I.o.M. Europe **10** 54.04N 4.38W
Castletownshend Rep. of Ire. **13** 51.32N 9.12W
Castres France **17** 43.36N 2.14E
Castries St. Lucia **87** 14.01N 60.59W
Castro Chile **93** 42.30S 73.46W
Castro del Río Spain **16** 37.41N 4.29W
Casula Mozambique **55** 15.26S 33.32E
Cataguases Brazil **94** 21.23S 42.39W
Çatalca Turkey **19** 41.09N 28.29E
Catalina Pt. Guam **68** 13.31N144.55E
Cataluña *d.* Spain **16** 42.00N 2.00E
Catamarca Argentina **92** 28.30S 65.45W
Catamarca *d.* Argentina **92** 27.45S 67.00W
Catanduanes *i.* Phil. **37** 13.45N124.20E
Catanduva Brazil **94** 21.03S 49.00W
Catania Italy **18** 37.31N 15.05E
Catanzaro Italy **19** 38.55N 16.35E
Catarman Phil. **37** 12.28N124.50E
Catbalogan Phil. **37** 11.46N124.55E
Catete Angola **54** 9.09S 13.40E
Cathcart Australia **67** 36.49S149.25E
Cathcart R.S.A. **56** 32.17S 27.08E
Cat I. Bahamas **87** 24.33N 75.36W
Cat L. Canada **76** 51.40N 91.50W
Catoche, C. Mexico **87** 21.38N 87.08W
Catonsville U.S.A. **85** 39.16N 76.44W
Catriló Argentina **93** 36.23S 63.24W
Catterick U.K. **10** 54.23N 1.38W
Cattolica Italy **15** 43.58N 12.44E
Catuane Mozambique **57** 26.49S 32.17E
Cauca *r.* Colombia **90** 8.57N 74.30W
Caucasus *mts.* Europe **25** 43.00N 44.00E
Caudry France **17** 50.07N 3.22E
Caungula Angola **54** 8.26S 18.35E
Cauquenes Chile **93** 35.58S 72.21W
Caura *r.* Venezuela **90** 7.38N 64.53W
Cavaillon France **17** 43.50N 5.02E
Cavalese Italy **15** 46.17N 11.26E
Cavalier U.S.A. **82** 48.48N 97.37W
Cavally *r.* Ivory Coast **52** 4.25N 7.39W
Cavan Rep. of Ire. **13** 54.00N 7.22W
Cavan *d.* Rep. of Ire. **13** 53.58N 7.10W
Cavarzere Italy **15** 45.08N 12.05E
Caviana, Ilha *i.* Brazil **91** 0.02N 50.00W
Cawndilla L. Australia **66** 32.30S142.18E
Caxambu Brazil **94** 21.59S 44.54W
Caxias Brazil **91** 4.53S 43.20W
Caxias do Sul Brazil **94** 29.14S 51.10W
Caxito Angola **54** 8.32S 13.38E
Cayambe Ecuador **90** 0.03N 78.08W
Cayenne Guiana **91** 4.55N 52.18W
Cayman Brac *i.* Cayman Is. **87** 19.44N 79.48W
Cayman Is. C. America **87** 19.00N 81.00W
Cayman Trough Carib. Sea **95** 18.00N 8.00W
Cayuga Canada **76** 42.56N 79.51W
Cazères France **17** 43.13N 1.05E
Cazombo Angola **54** 11.54S 22.56E
Ceara *d.* Brazil **91** 4.50S 39.00W
Ceba Canada **75** 53.07N102.14W
Ceballos Mexico **83** 26.32N104.09W
Cebollera, Sierra de *mts.* Spain **16** 41.58N 2.30W
Cebu Phil. **37** 10.17N123.56E
Cebu *i.* Phil. **37** 10.15N123.45E
Cecina Italy **18** 43.18N 10.30E
Cedar City U.S.A. **78** 37.40N113.04W
Cedar Falls *town* U.S.A. **82** 42.32N 92.27W
Cedar Key U.S.A. **85** 29.08N 83.03W
Cedar L. Canada **75** 53.20N100.00W
Cedar Rapids *town* U.S.A. **82** 41.59N 91.40W
Cedarville U.S.A. **85** 39.20N 75.12W
Cedros, Isla *i.* Mexico **81** 28.10N115.15W
Ceduna Australia **66** 32.07S133.42E
Ceel Afweyne Somali Rep. **45** 9.55N 47.14E
Ceel Buur Somali Rep. **45** 4.40N 46.40E
Ceel Dhaab Somali Rep. **45** 8.58N 46.38E
Ceel Dheere Somali Rep. **45** 3.55N 47.10E
Ceel Xamurre Somali Rep. **45** 7.11N 48.55E
Ceepeecee Canada **74** 49.52N126.42W
Ceerigaabo Somali Rep. **45** 10.40N 47.20E
Cefalù Italy **18** 38.01N 14.03E
Cegléd Hungary **21** 47.10N 19.48E
Cela Angola **54** 11.26S 15.05E
Celaya Mexico **86** 20.32N100.48W
Celebes *i. see* Sulawesi *i.* Indonesia **37**
Celebes Sea Indonesia **37** 3.00N122.00E
Celina U.S.A. **84** 40.34N 84.35W
Celje Slovenia **18** 46.15N 15.16E
Celle Germany **20** 52.37N 10.05E
Cemaes Head U.K. **11** 52.08N 4.42W
Cenderawasih, Teluk *b.* Indonesia **37** 2.20S135.50E
Ceno *r.* Italy **15** 44.41N 10.05E
Center Cross U.S.A. **85** 37.48N 76.48W
Centerville Iowa U.S.A. **82** 40.43N 92.52W
Centerville S.Dak. U.S.A. **82** 43.07N 96.58W
Centerville Tenn. U.S.A. **85** 35.45N 87.29W
Cento Italy **15** 44.43N 11.17E
Central *d.* Botswana **56** 21.45S 26.15E
Central *d.* Ghana **52** 5.30N 1.10W
Central *d.* Kenya **55** 0.30S 37.00E
Central *d.* U.K. **12** 56.10N 4.20W
Central *d.* Zambia **56** 14.30S 29.30E
Central, Cordillera *mts.* Bolivia **92** 18.30S 65.00W
Central, Cordillera *mts.* Colombia **90** 5.00N 75.20W
Central Brāhui Range *mts.* Pakistan **40** 29.15N 67.15E
Central City Ky. U.S.A. **85** 37.17N 87.08W
Central City Nebr. U.S.A. **82** 41.07N 98.00W
Central I. Kenya **55** 3.30N 36.02E
Centralia Ill. U.S.A. **82** 38.32N 89.08W
Centralia Wash. U.S.A. **80** 46.43N122.58W
Central Makrān Range *mts.* Pakistan **40** 26.30N 65.00E
Central Siberian Plateau *see* Sredne Sibirskoye Ploskogor'ye *e Ploskogor'ye* Russian Fed. **29**
Centre *d.* Burkina **52** 11.50N 1.10W
Centre *d.* France **17** 47.40N 1.45E
Centre Est *d.* Burkina **52** 11.20N 0.10W
Centre Nord *d.* Burkina **52** 13.30N 1.00W
Centre Ouest *d.* Burkina **52** 12.00N 2.20W
Centreville Ala. U.S.A. **85** 32.57N 87.08W
Centreville Md. U.S.A. **85** 39.03N 76.04W
Century U.S.A. **85** 30.59N 87.18W
Cepu Indonesia **37** 7.07S111.35E
Ceram *i. see* Seram *i.* Indonesia **37**
Ceram Sea *see* Seram, Laut *sea* Pacific Oc. **37**
Ceres U.S.A. **80** 37.35N120.57W
Ceresole Reale Italy **15** 45.26N 7.15E
Cereté Colombia **90** 8.54N 75.51W
Cerignola Italy **18** 41.17N 15.53E
Cérilly France **17** 46.37N 2.50E
Cerisiers France **15** 48.08N 3.29E
Cerknica Slovenia **18** 45.48N 14.22E
Cernavodă Romania **21** 44.20N 28.02E
Cerralvo, Isla *i.* Mexico **81** 24.17N 109.52W
Cerritos Mexico **86** 22.26N100.17W
Cerro de Pasco Peru **90** 10.43S 76.15W
Cervera Spain **16** 41.40N 1.16E
Cervia Italy **15** 44.15N 12.22E
Cervignano del Friuli Italy **15** 45.49N 13.20E
Cervo Spain **16** 43.40N 7.24W
Cesena Italy **15** 44.08N 12.15E
Cesenatico Italy **15** 44.12N 12.24E
Cēsis Latvia **24** 57.18N 25.18E
České Budějovice Czech Republic **20** 49.00N 14.30E
České Zemé *d.* Czech Republic **20** 49.50N 15.50E
Český Krumlov Czech Republic **20** 48.49N 14.19E
Cessnock Australia **67** 32.51S151.21E
Cetinje Yugo. **19** 42.24N 18.55E
Ceuta Spain **16** 35.53N 5.19W
Ceva Italy **15** 44.23N 8.01E
Cévennes *mts.* France **17** 44.25N 4.05E
Ceyhan Turkey **42** 37.02N 35.48E
Ceyhan *r.* Turkey **42** 36.54N 34.58E
Chablis France **15** 47.47N 3.48E
Chacabuco Argentina **93** 34.38S 60.29W
Chachani *mtn.* Peru **90** 16.12S 71.32W
Chachapoyas Peru **90** 6.13S 77.54W
Chāchro Pakistan **40** 25.07N 70.15E
Chaco *d.* Argentina **92** 26.30S 60.00W
Chad, L. Africa **53** 13.30N 14.00E
Chadron U.S.A. **82** 42.50N103.02W
Chafe Nigeria **53** 11.56N 6.55E
Chāgai Pakistan **40** 29.18N 64.42E
Chāgai Hills Pakistan **40** 29.10N 63.35E
Chagda Russian Fed. **29** 58.44N130.38E
'Chaghcharān Afghan. **40** 34.32N 65.15E
Cha'gyüngoinba China **41** 31.10N 90.42E
Chahār Borjak Afghan. **40** 30.17N 62.03E
Chāh Sandan *well* Pakistan **40** 28.59N 63.27E
Chaibāsā India **41** 22.34N 85.49E
Chainat Thailand **34** 15.10N100.10E
Chaiyaphum Thailand **34** 15.46N101.57E
Chajarí Argentina **93** 30.45S 57.59W
Chākāi India **41** 24.34N 86.24E
Chākdaha India **41** 23.05N 88.31E
Chake Chake Tanzania **55** 5.13S 39.46E
Chakhānsūr Afghan. **40** 31.10N 62.04E
Chakradharpur India **41** 22.42N 85.38E
Chakwāl Pakistan **40** 32.56N 72.52E
Chala Peru **90** 15.48S 74.20W
Chaleur B. Canada **77** 48.00N 65.45W
Chalhuanca Peru **90** 14.20S 73.10W
Chālisgaon India **40** 20.28N 75.01E
Challans France **17** 46.51N 1.52W
Challenger Depth Pacific Oc. **37** 11.19N142.15E
Challis U.S.A. **80** 44.30N114.14W
Chalonnes-sur-Loire France **15** 47.21N 0.46W
Châlons-sur-Marne France **15** 48.58N 4.22E
Chalon-sur-Saône France **17** 46.47N 4.51E
Cham Germany **20** 49.13N 12.41E
Chama U.S.A. **80** 36.54N106.35W
Chama Zambia **55** 11.09S 33.10E
Chaman Pakistan **40** 30.55N 66.27E
Chamba India **40** 32.34N 76.08E
Chambal *r.* India **41** 26.29N 79.15E
Chamberlain U.S.A. **82** 43.49N 99.20W
Chambersburg U.S.A. **84** 39.56N 77.39W
Chambéry France **17** 45.34N 5.55E
Chambeshi Zambia **55** 10.57S 31.04E
Chambeshi *r.* Zambia **55** 11.15S 30.37E
Chambly Canada **77** 45.27N 73.17W
Chambly France **15** 49.10N 2.15E
Chamburi Kalāt Pakistan **40** 26.09N 64.43E
Cha Messengue Angola **54** 11.04S 18.56E
Chamical Argentina **92** 30.22S 66.19W
Ch'amo Hāyk' *l.* Ethiopia **49** 5.49N 37.35E
Chamoli India **41** 30.24N 79.21E
Chamonix France **17** 45.55N 6.52E
Chāmpa India **41** 22.03N 82.39E
Champagne Canada **74** 60.47N136.29W
Champagne-Ardenne *d.* France **14** 49.42N 4.30E
Champaign U.S.A. **82** 40.07N 88.14W
Champdoré, Lac *l.* Canada **77** 55.55N 65.50W
Champéry Switz. **15** 46.10N 6.52E
Champlain Canada **77** 46.27N 72.21W
Champlain, L. U.S.A. **84** 44.45N 73.15W
Champotón Mexico **86** 19.21N 90.43W
Chāmpua India **41** 22.05N 85.40E
Chañaral Chile **92** 26.21S 70.37W
Chānasma India **40** 23.43N 72.07E
Chandausi India **41** 28.27N 78.46E
Chāndbāli India **41** 20.46N 86.49E
Chandeleur Is. U.S.A. **83** 29.48N 88.51W
Chandīgarh India **40** 30.44N 76.47E
Chandīgarh *d.* India **40** 30.45N 76.45E
Chāndil India **41** 22.58N 86.03E
Chandler Canada **77** 48.21N 64.41W
Chandler U.S.A. **83** 35.42N 96.53W
Chāndor Hills India **40** 20.30N 74.00E
Chāndpur Bangla. **39** 22.08N 91.55E
Chāndpur Bangla. **41** 23.13N 90.39E
Chāndpur India **41** 29.09N 78.16E
Chandrapur India **41** 19.57N 79.18E
Chāndvad India **40** 20.20N 74.15E
Chānf Iran **43** 26.40N 60.31E
Chang, Ko *i.* Thailand **34** 12.04N102.23E
Changchun China **32** 43.51N125.15E
Changde China **33** 29.00N111.35E
Changfeng China **32** 32.27N117.09E
Changhua Jiang *r.* China **33** 19.20N108.38E
Chang Jiang *r.* China **33** 31.40N121.15E
Changjin N. Korea **31** 40.21N127.20E
Changle China **32** 36.42N118.49E
Changli China **32** 39.43N119.08E
Changling China **32** 44.16N123.58E
Changning China **33** 26.24N112.24E
Changping China **32** 40.12N116.12E
Changsha China **33** 28.09N112.59E
Changshan China **33** 28.57N118.31E
Changshan Qundao *is.* China **32** 39.20N123.00E
Changshou China **33** 29.50N107.02E
Changshu China **33** 31.48N120.52E
Changshun China **33** 25.59N106.25E
Changting China **33** 25.42N116.20E
Changyi China **32** 36.51N119.23E
Changzhi China **32** 36.10N113.00E
Changzhou China **33** 31.46N119.58E
Channel Is. Europe **11** 49.28N 2.13W
Channel Is. U.S.A. **81** 34.00N120.00W
Channel-Port-aux-Basques *town* Canada **77** 47.35N 59.11W
Channing Mich. U.S.A. **84** 46.08N 88.06W
Channing Tex. U.S.A. **83** 35.41N102.20W
Chantada Spain **16** 42.36N 7.46W
Chanthaburi Thailand **34** 12.35N102.05E
Chantilly France **15** 49.12N 2.28E
Chanute U.S.A. **83** 37.41N 95.27W
Chao'an China **33** 23.40N116.32E
Chao Hu *l.* China **33** 31.32N117.30E
Chaonde Mozambique **57** 13.43S 40.31E
Chao Phraya *r.* Thailand **34** 13.34N100.35E
Chao Xian China **33** 31.36N117.52E
Chaoyang Guangdong China **33** 23.25N116.31E
Chaoyang Liaoning China **32** 41.35N120.20E
Chapada das Mangabeiras *mts.* Brazil **91** 10.00S 46.30W
Chapada Diamantina Brazil **94** 13.30S 42.30W
Chapala, Lago de *l.* Mexico **86** 20.00N103.00W
Chapayevo Kazakhstan **25** 50.12N 51.09E
Chapayevsk Russian Fed. **24** 52.58N 49.44E
Chapelle-d'Angillon France **15** 47.22N 2.26E
Chapicuy Uruguay **93** 31.39S 57.54W
Chapleau Canada **76** 47.50N 83.24W
Chāpra India **41** 25.46N 84.45E
Chaqui Bolivia **92** 19.36S 65.32W
Characot I. Antarctica **96** 70.00S 75.00W
Charay Mexico **81** 26.01N108.50W
Charcas Mexico **86** 23.08N101.07W
Chard U.K. **11** 50.52N 2.59W
Charduār India **41** 26.52N 92.46E
Chardzhou Turkmenistan **43** 39.09N 63.34E
Charente *r.* France **17** 45.57N 1.00W
Chari *r.* Chad **53** 13.00N 14.30E
Chari-Baguirmi *d.* Chad **53** 12.20N 15.30E
Chārīkār Afghan. **40** 35.01N 69.11E
Charing U.K. **11** 51.12N 0.49E
Chariton U.S.A. **82** 41.01N 93.19W
Charleroi Belgium **14** 50.25N 4.27E
Charlesbourg Canada **77** 46.52N 71.16W
Charles City U.S.A. **82** 43.04N 92.40W
Charles Pt. Australia **62** 12.23S130.37E
Charleston Miss. U.S.A. **83** 34.00N 90.04W
Charleston S.C. U.S.A. **85** 32.48N 79.58W
Charleston W.Va. U.S.A. **84** 38.23N 81.40W
Charlestown Rep. of Ire. **13** 53.57N 8.48W
Charlestown Ind. U.S.A. **84** 38.28N 85.40W
Charlesville Zaïre **54** 5.27S 20.58E
Charleville Australia **64** 26.25S146.13E
Charleville-Mézières France **15** 49.46N 4.43E
Charlieu France **17** 46.10N 4.10E
Charlotte N.C. U.S.A. **85** 35.03N 80.50W
Charlotte Va. U.S.A. **85** 37.03N 78.44W
Charlottesville U.S.A. **85** 38.02N 78.29W
Charlottetown Canada **77** 46.14N 63.08W
Charlton Australia **66** 36.18S143.27E
Charlton I. Canada **76** 52.00N 79.30W
Charly-sur-Marne France **15** 48.58N 3.17E
Charolles France **17** 46.26N 4.17E
Chārsadda Pakistan **40** 34.09N 71.44E
Charters Towers Australia **64** 20.05S146.16E
Chartres France **15** 48.27N 1.30E
Chascomús Argentina **93** 35.35S 58.00W
Chase City U.S.A. **85** 36.59N 78.30W
Châteaubriant France **15** 47.43N 1.22W
Château-du-Loir France **15** 47.42N 0.25E
Châteaudun France **15** 48.04N 1.20E
Château Gontier France **15** 47.50N 0.42W
Châteauguay, Lac *l.* Canada **77** 56.27N 70.05W
Château Landon France **15** 48.09N 2.42E
Château-la-Vallière France **15** 47.33N 0.19E
Châteauneuf-en-Thymerais France **15** 48.35N 1.15E
Châteauneuf-sur-Loire France **15** 47.52N 2.14E
Chateauneuf-sur-Sarthe France **15** 47.41N 0.30W
Château-Porcien France **15** 49.32N 4.15E
Château Renault France **15** 47.35N 0.55E
Châteauroux France **17** 46.49N 1.41E
Château-Thierry France **15** 49.03N 3.24E
Châtelet Belgium **14** 50.24N 4.32E
Châtellerault France **17** 46.49N 0.33E
Chatham N.B. Canada **77** 47.02N 65.28W
Chatham Ont. Canada **76** 42.24N 82.11W
Chatham U.K. **11** 51.23N 0.32E
Chatham U.S.A. **74** 57.30N135.00W
Chatham Is. Pacific Oc. **68** 44.00S176.35W
Chatham Rise Pacific Oc. **68** 43.30S178.00W
Chatham Str. U.S.A. **74** 57.30N134.45W
Châtillon Italy **15** 45.45N 7.37E
Châtillon-Coligny France **15** 47.50N 2.51E
Châtillon-sur-Seine France **15** 47.52N 4.35E
Chatra India **41** 24.13N 84.52E
Chatrapur India **41** 19.21N 84.59E
Chātsu India **40** 26.36N 75.57E
Chattahoochee U.S.A. **85** 30.42N 84.51W
Chattahoochee *r.* U.S.A. **85** 30.52N 84.57W
Chattanooga U.S.A. **85** 35.02N 85.18W
Chatteris U.K. **11** 52.27N 0.03E
Chauk Burma **34** 20.52N 94.50E
Chaulnes France **15** 49.49N 2.48E
Chaumont France **17** 48.07N 5.08E
Chaumont-en-Vexin France **15** 49.16N 1.53E
Chaungwabyin Burma **34** 13.41N 98.22E
Chauny France **15** 49.37N 3.13E
Chaupāran India **41** 24.23N 85.15E
Chau Phu Vietnam **34** 10.42N105.03E
Chausy Belorussia **21** 53.49N 30.57E
Chavanges France **15** 48.31N 4.34E
Chaves Brazil **91** 0.10S 49.55W
Chaves Portugal **16** 41.44N 7.28W
Chavuma Zambia **54** 13.04S 22.43E
Chawang Thailand **34** 8.25N 99.32E
Cheb Czech Republic **20** 50.04N 12.20E
Cheboksary Russian Fed. **24** 56.08N 47.12E
Cheboygan U.S.A. **84** 45.40N 84.28W
Chebsara Russian Fed. **24** 59.14N 38.59E
Chebula Angola **54** 12.27S 23.49E
Chech, Erg *des.* Mali / Algeria **50** 24.30N 2.30W
Chechaouene Morocco **50** 35.10N 5.16W
Chechersk Belorussia **21** 52.54N 30.54E
Checiny Poland **21** 50.48N 20.28E
Cheduba I. Burma **34** 18.50N 93.35E
Chegdomyn Russian Fed. **29** 51.09N133.01E
Chegga *well* Mauritania **50** 25.30N 5.46W
Chegutu Zimbabwe **56** 18.09S 30.07E
Chehalis U.S.A. **80** 46.40N122.58W
Cheil, Ras el *c.* Somali Rep. **45** 7.45N 49.48E
Cheiron, Cime du *mtn.* France **15** 43.49N 6.58E
Cheju S. Korea **31** 33.31N126.29E
Cheju do *i.* S. Korea **31** 33.20N126.30E

Cheleken to Coast Range

Cheleken Turkmenistan **43** 39.26N 53.11E
Chelforó Argentina **93** 39.04S 66.33W
Chelif, Oued *r.* Algeria **51** 36.15N 2.05E
Chelkar Kazakhstan **28** 47.48N 59.39E
Chelles France **15** 48.53N 2.36E
Chelm Poland **21** 51.10N 23.28E
Chelmer *r.* U.K. **9** 51.43N 0.40E
Chelmsford U.K. **11** 51.44N 0.28E
Chelmza Poland **21** 53.12N 18.37E
Chelsea Canada **77** 45.29N 75.48W
Cheltenham U.K. **11** 51.53N 2.07W
Chelva Spain **16** 39.45N 1.00W
Chelyabinsk Russian Fed. **28** 55.10N 61.25E
Chelyuskin, Mys *c.* Russian Fed. **29** 77.20N106.00E
Chemainus Canada **74** 48.55N123.48W
Chemba Mozambique **55** 17.11S 34.53E
Chemnitz Germany **20** 50.50N 12.55E
Chemult U.S.A. **80** 43.13N121.47W
Chën, Gora *mtn.* Russian Fed. **29** 65.30N141.20E
Chenāb *r.* Pakistan **40** 29.23N 71.02E
Chenachane Algeria **50** 26.00N 4.15W
Chénéville Canada **77** 45.53N 75.03W
Cheney U.S.A. **80** 47.29N117.34W
Chengchow *see* Zhengzhou China **32**
Chengde China **32** 41.00N117.52E
Chengdu China **33** 30.41N104.05E
Chenggu China **32** 33.10N107.22E
Chenghai China **33** 23.31N116.43E
Chengkou China **33** 31.58N108.48E
Chengmai China **33** 19.44N109.59E
Cheng Xian China **32** 33.42N105.36E
Chenoa U.S.A. **82** 40.44N 88.43W
Chen Xian China **33** 25.45N113.00E
Chepen Peru **90** 7.15S 79.20W
Chepstow U.K. **11** 51.38N 2.40W
Cher *r.* France **15** 47.12N 2.04E
Cherbourg France **15** 49.38N 1.37W
Cherdyn Russian Fed. **24** 60.25N 55.22E
Cherelato Ethiopia **49** 6.00N 38.10E
Cheremkhovo Russian Fed. **29** 53.08N103.01E
Cherepovets Russian Fed. **24** 59.05N 37.55E
Chergui, Chott ech *f.* Algeria **51** 34.21N 0.30E
Cherikov Belorussia **21** 53.35N 31.23E
Cherkassy Ukraine **25** 49.27N 32.04E
Cherkessk Russian Fed. **25** 44.14N 42.05E
Cherkovitsa Bulgaria **19** 43.41N 24.49E
Cherlak Russian Fed. **28** 54.10N 74.52E
Chernigov Ukraine **21** 51.30N 31.18E
Chernikovsk Russian Fed. **24** 54.51N 56.06E
Chernobyl Ukraine **21** 51.17N 30.15E
Chernovtsy Ukraine **21** 48.19N 25.52E
Chernyakhov Ukraine **21** 50.30N 28.38E
Chernyakhovsk Russian Fed. **23** 54.38N 21.49E
Cherokee Iowa U.S.A. **82** 42.45N 95.33W
Cherokee Okla. U.S.A. **83** 36.45N 98.21W
Cherquenco Chile **93** 38.41S 72.00W
Cherrapunji India **41** 25.18N 91.42E
Cherry Creek *r.* U.S.A. **82** 44.36N101.30W
Cherry Creek *town* Nev. U.S.A. **80** 39.54N113.53W
Cherry Creek *town* S.Dak. U.S.A. **82** 44.36N101.26W
Cherskogo, Khrebet *mts.* Russian Fed. **29** 65.50N143.00E
Chertkovo Russian Fed. **25** 49.22N 40.12E
Chertsey U.K. **11** 51.23N 0.27W
Chervonograd Ukraine **21** 50.25N 24.10E
Cherwell *r.* U.K. **11** 51.44N 1.15W
Chesapeake U.S.A. **85** 36.43N 76.15W
Chesapeake B. U.S.A. **84** 38.40N 76.25W
Chesapeake Beach *town* U.S.A. **85** 38.41N 76.32W
Chesham U.K. **11** 51.43N 0.38W
Cheshire *d.* U.K. **10** 53.14N 2.30W
Chëshskaya Guba *g.* Russian Fed. **24** 67.20N 46.30E
Chesht-e Sharīf Afghan. **40** 34.21N 63.44E
Chesil Beach *f.* U.K. **11** 50.37N 2.33W
Chester U.K. **10** 53.12N 2.53W
Chester Mont. U.S.A. **80** 48.31N110.58W
Chester Penn. U.S.A. **85** 39.51N 75.21W
Chesterfield U.K. **10** 53.14N 1.26W
Chesterfield, Îles *is.* N. Cal. **68** 20.00S159.00E
Chesterfield Inlet *town* Canada **73** 63.00N 91.00W
Chestertown U.S.A. **85** 39.13N 76.04W
Chesuncook L. U.S.A. **84** 46.00N 69.20W
Chéticamp Canada **77** 46.38N 61.01W
Chetumal Mexico **87** 18.30N 88.17W
Chetumal B. Mexico **87** 18.30N 88.00W
Chetwynd Canada **74** 55.45N121.45W
Cheviot New Zealand **60** 42.49S173.16E
Cheviot U.S.A. **84** 39.10N 84.32W
Ch'ew Bahir *l.* Ethiopia **49** 4.40N 36.50E
Cheyenne Okla. U.S.A. **83** 35.37N 99.40W
Cheyenne *r.* U.S.A. **82** 44.40N101.15W
Cheyenne Wyo. U.S.A. **80** 41.08N104.49W
Cheyne B. Australia **63** 34.35S118.50E
Chhabra India **40** 24.40N 76.50E
Chhātak Bangla. **41** 25.02N 91.40E
Chhatarpur Bihār India **41** 24.23N 84.11E
Chhatarpur Madhya P. India **41** 24.54N 79.36E
Chhattīsgarh *f.* India **41** 21.00N 82.00E
Chhindwāra India **41** 22.04N 78.56E
Chhota-Chhindwāra India **41** 23.03N 79.29E
Chhota Udepur India **40** 22.19N 74.01E
Chiali Taiwan **33** 23.10N120.11E
Chiang Mai Thailand **34** 18.48N 98.59E
Chiapas *d.* Mexico **86** 16.30N 93.00W
Chiari Italy **15** 45.32N 9.56E
Chiavari Italy **15** 44.19N 9.19E
Chiavenna Italy **15** 46.19N 9.24E
Chiba Japan **35** 35.36N140.07E
Chiba *d.* Japan **35** 35.10N140.00E
Chibemba Angola **56** 15.43S 14.07E
Chibia Angola **54** 15.10S 13.32E
Chibougamau Canada **76** 49.56N 74.24W
Chibougamau Lac *l.* Canada **76** 49.50N 74.20W
Chibougamau Prov. Park Canada **77** 49.25N 73.50W
Chibuk Nigeria **53** 10.52N 12.50E
Chibuto Mozambique **57** 24.41S 33.32E
Chicago U.S.A. **82** 41.50N 87.45W
Chichagof I. U.S.A. **72** 57.55N135.45W
Chicheng China **32** 40.52N115.50E
Chichester U.K. **11** 50.50N 0.47W
Chichibu Japan **35** 35.59N139.05E
Chickasha U.S.A. **83** 35.02N 97.58W
Chiclana Spain **16** 36.26N 6.09W
Chiclayo Peru **90** 6.47S 79.47W
Chico *r.* Chubut Argentina **93** 43.45S 66.10W
Chico *r.* Santa Cruz Argentina **93** 50.03S 68.35W
Chico U.S.A. **80** 39.44N121.50W
Chicomo Mozambique **57** 24.33S 34.11E
Chicoutimi-Jonquière Canada **77** 48.26N 71.06W
Chicualacuala Mozambique **57** 22.06S 31.42E
Chidambaram India **39** 11.24N 79.42E
Chidembo Angola **54** 14.34S 19.17E
Chidenguele Mozambique **57** 24.54S 34.13E
Chidley, C. Canada **73** 60.30N 65.00W
Chiemsee *l.* Germany **20** 47.55N 12.30E
Chiengi Zambia **55** 8.42S 29.07E
Chieri Italy **15** 45.01N 7.49E
Chieti Italy **18** 42.22N 14.12E
Chifeng China **32** 42.13N118.56E
Chigasaki Japan **35** 35.19N139.24E
Chignecto B. Canada **77** 45.35N 64.45W
Chiguana Bolivia **92** 21.05S 67.58W
Chigubo Mozambique **57** 22.38S 33.18E
Chigu Co *l.* China **41** 28.40N 91.50E
Chihuahua Mexico **81** 28.38N106.05W
Chihuahua *d.* Mexico **81** 28.40N106.00W
Chiili Kazakhstan **28** 44.10N 66.37E
Chikhli India **40** 20.21N 76.15E
Chikumbi Zambia **55** 15.14S 28.21E
Chikwawa Malaŵi **55** 16.00S 34.54E
Chil *r.* Iran **43** 25.12N 61.30E
Chilanga Zambia **56** 15.33S 28.17E
Chilapa Mexico **86** 17.38N 99.11W
Chilcoot U.S.A. **80** 39.49N120.08W
Childers Australia **64** 25.14S152.17E
Childress U.S.A. **83** 34.25N100.13W
Chile S. America **92** 32.30S 71.00W
Chile Basin Pacific Oc. **69** 34.20S 80.00W
Chile Chico Chile **93** 46.33S 71.44W
Chilka L. India **41** 19.46N 85.20E
Chilko L. Canada **72** 51.20N124.05W
Chillagoe Australia **64** 17.09S144.32E
Chillán Chile **93** 36.36S 72.07W
Chillicothe Mo. U.S.A. **82** 39.48N 93.33W
Chillicothe Ohio U.S.A. **84** 39.20N 82.59W
Chilliwack Canada **74** 49.10N122.00W
Chiloé, Isla de *i.* Chile **93** 43.00S 73.00W
Chilonga Zambia **55** 12.02S 31.17E
Chilpancingo Mexico **86** 17.33N 99.30W
Chiltern Australia **67** 36.11S146.36E
Chiltern Hills U.K. **11** 51.40N 0.53W
Chilton U.S.A. **82** 44.04N 88.10W
Chilumba Malaŵi **55** 10.25S 34.18E
Chilwa, L. Malaŵi **55** 15.15S 35.45E
Chimakela Angola **54** 15.12S 16.58E
Chimanimani Zimbabwe **57** 19.48S 32.52E
Chimay Belgium **14** 50.03N 4.20E
Chimbas Argentina **92** 31.28S 68.30W
Chimbay Uzbekistan **28** 42.56N 59.46E
Chimborazo *mtn.* Ecuador **90** 1.29S 78.52W
Chimbote Peru **90** 9.04S 78.34W
Chimishliya Moldavia **21** 46.30N 28.50E
Chimkent Kazakhstan **30** 42.16N 69.05E
Chimoio Mozambique **57** 19.04S 33.29E
Chin *d.* Burma **34** 22.00N 93.30E
China Asia **30** 33.00N103.00E
China Lake *town* U.S.A. **81** 35.46N117.39W
Chinandega Nicaragua **87** 12.35N 87.10W
Chinati Peak U.S.A. **81** 29.57N104.29W
Chincha Alta Peru **90** 13.25S 76.07W
Chinchaga *r.* Canada **74** 58.50N118.20W
Chinchilla Australia **65** 26.44S150.39E
Chinchón Spain **16** 40.09N 3.26W
Chinchoua Gabon **54** 0.00 9.48E
Chincoteague U.S.A. **85** 37.55N 75.23W
Chinde Mozambique **57** 18.37S 36.24E
Chindio Mozambique **55** 17.46S 35.23E
Chindwin *r.* Burma **34** 21.30N 95.12E
Chinga Mozambique **55** 15.14S 38.40E
Chingleput India **39** 12.42N 79.59E
Chingola Zambia **55** 12.29S 27.53E
Chingombe Zambia **55** 14.25S 29.56E
Chingshui Taiwan **33** 24.15N120.35E
Chin Hills Burma **34** 22.30N 93.30E
Chinhoyi Zimbabwe **56** 17.22S 30.10E
Chīni India **41** 31.32N 78.15E
Chiniot Pakistan **40** 31.43N 72.59E
Chinjan Pakistan **40** 30.34N 67.58E
Chinkapook Australia **66** 35.11S142.57E
Chinko *r.* C.A.R. **49** 4.50N 23.53E
Chinle U.S.A. **81** 36.09N109.33W
Chinon France **17** 47.10N 0.15E
Chinook U.S.A. **80** 48.35N109.14W
Chino Valley *town* U.S.A. **81** 34.45N112.27W
Chinsali Zambia **55** 10.33S 32.05E
Chintheche Malaŵi **55** 11.50S 34.13E
Chiny Belgium **14** 49.45N 5.20E
Chiôco Mozambique **55** 16.27S 32.49E
Chioggia Italy **15** 45.13N 12.17E
Chipata Zambia **55** 13.37S 32.40E
Chipera Mozambique **55** 15.20S 32.35E
Chipie *r.* Canada **76** 51.25N 83.20W
Chipinge Zimbabwe **57** 20.12S 32.38E
Chippenham U.K. **11** 51.27N 2.07W
Chippewa Falls *town* U.S.A. **82** 44.56N 91.24W
Chipping Norton U.K. **11** 51.56N 1.32W
Chiquian Peru **90** 10.10S 77.00W
Chiquinquirá Colombia **90** 5.37N 73.50W
Chir *r.* Russian Fed. **25** 48.34N 42.53E
Chirāwa India **40** 28.15N 75.38E
Chirchik Uzbekistan **30** 41.28N 69.31E
Chiredzi Zimbabwe **57** 21.03S 31.39E
Chiredzi *r.* Zimbabwe **57** 21.10S 31.50E
Chiricahua Peak *mtn.* U.S.A. **81** 31.52N109.20W
Chiriquí *mtn.* Panama **87** 8.49N 82.38W
Chiriquí, Laguna de *b.* Panama **87** 9.00N 82.00W
Chiromo Malaŵi **55** 16.28S 35.10E
Chirripó *mtn.* Costa Rica **87** 9.31N 83.30W
Chirundu Zimbabwe **56** 16.04S 28.51E
Chisamba Zambia **56** 14.58S 28.23E
Chisasibi Canada **76** 53.50N 79.00W
Chishan Taiwan **33** 22.53N120.29E
Chisholm U.S.A. **82** 47.29N 92.53W
Chisholm Mills Canada **74** 54.55N114.09W
Chishtiān Mandi Pakistan **40** 29.48N 72.52E
Chishui China **33** 28.29N105.38E
Chişinau *see* Kishinev Moldavia **21**
Chisone *r.* Italy **15** 44.49N 7.25E
Chistopol Russian Fed. **24** 55.25N 50.38E
Chita Russian Fed. **31** 52.03N113.35E
Chitek L. Canada **75** 52.25N 99.20W
Chitembo Angola **54** 13.33S 16.47E
Chitipa Malaŵi **55** 9.41S 33.19E
Chitorgarh India **40** 24.53N 74.38E
Chitrakūt Dham India **41** 25.11N 80.52E
Chitrāl Pakistan **38** 35.52N 71.58E
Chittagong Bangla. **41** 22.20N 91.50E
Chittoor India **39** 13.13N 79.06E
Chiumbe *r.* Zaïre **54** 6.37S 21.04E
Chiume Angola **54** 15.08S 21.11E
Chiuta, L. Malaŵi / Mozambique **55** 14.45S 35.50E
Chivasso Italy **15** 45.11N 7.53E
Chivhu Zimbabwe **56** 19.01S 30.53E
Chivilcoy Argentina **93** 34.52S 60.02W
Chiwanda Tanzania **55** 11.21S 34.55E
Chobe *d.* Botswana **56** 18.30S 25.15E
Chobe *r.* Namibia / Botswana **56** 17.48S 25.12E
Chobe Swamp *f.* Namibia **56** 18.20S 23.40E
Chocolate Mts. U.S.A. **81** 33.20N115.15W
Chocope Peru **90** 7.47S 79.12W
Choele-Choel Argentina **93** 39.15S 65.30W
Chōfu Japan **35** 35.39N139.33E
Chohtan India **40** 25.29N 71.04E
Choix Mexico **81** 26.43N108.17W
Chojnice Poland **21** 53.42N 17.32E
Ch'ok'ē Mts. Ethiopia **49** 11.00N 37.30E
Cholet France **17** 47.04N 0.53W
Cholon Vietnam **34** 10.40N106.30E
Choluteca Honduras **87** 13.16N 87.11W
Choma Zambia **55** 16.51S 27.04E
Chomu India **40** 27.10N 75.44E
Chomutov Czech Republic **20** 50.28N 13.25E
Chon Buri Thailand **34** 13.20N101.02E
Chone Ecuador **90** 0.44S 80.04W
Chong'an China **33** 27.46N118.01E
Ch'ŏngjin N. Korea **31** 41.55N129.50E
Ch'ŏngju S. Korea **31** 36.39N127.31E
Chŏng Kal Cambodia **34** 13.57N103.35E
Chongming *i.* China **33** 31.36N121.33E
Chongqing China **33** 29.31N106.35E
Chongren China **33** 27.44N116.02E
Chŏnju S. Korea **31** 35.50N127.05E
Chonos, Archipelago de los *is.* Chile **93** 45.00S 74.00W
Cho Oyu *mtn.* China / Nepal **41** 28.06N 86.40E
Chopda India **40** 21.15N 75.18E
Choptank *r.* U.S.A. **85** 38.38N 76.13W
Chorley U.K. **10** 53.39N 2.39W
Chorokh *r.* Georgia **25** 41.36N 41.35E
Chortkov Ukraine **21** 49.01N 25.42E
Chorzów Poland **21** 50.19N 18.56E
Chosica Peru **90** 11.55S 76.38W
Chos Malal Argentina **93** 37.20S 70.15W
Choszczno Poland **20** 53.10N 15.26E
Choteau U.S.A. **80** 47.49N112.11W
Chotila India **40** 22.25N 71.11E
Choum Mauritania **50** 21.10N 13.00W
Chowchilla U.S.A. **80** 37.07N120.16W
Christchurch New Zealand **60** 43.33S172.40E
Christchurch U.K. **11** 50.44N 1.47W
Christian Sd. U.S.A. **74** 55.56N134.40W
Christianshåb Greenland **73** 68.50N 51.00W
Christie B. Canada **75** 62.32N111.10W
Christina *r.* Canada **75** 56.40N111.03W
Christmas Creek *town* Australia **62** 18.55S125.56E
Christmas I. Indian Oc. **36** 10.30S105.40E
Christmas I. *see* Kiritimati *i.* Kiribati **69**
Chrudim Czech Republic **20** 49.57N 15.48E
Chu *r.* Kazakhstan **30** 42.30N 76.10E
Chuādānga Bangla. **41** 23.38N 88.51E
Chubbuck U.S.A. **81** 34.22N115.20W
Chūbu *d.* Japan **35** 35.25N137.40E
Chubut *d.* Argentina **93** 44.00S 68.00W
Chubut *r.* Argentina **93** 43.18S 65.06W
Chu Chua Canada **74** 51.22N120.10W
Chudleigh U.K. **11** 50.35N 3.36W
Chudnov Ukraine **21** 50.05N 28.01E
Chudovo Russian Fed. **24** 59.10N 31.41E
Chugwater U.S.A. **80** 41.46N104.49W
Chuiquimula Guatemala **87** 15.52N 89.50W
Chukai Malaysia **36** 4.16N103.24E
Chukotskiy Poluostrov *pen.* Russian Fed. **29** 66.00N174.30W
Chukudukraal Botswana **56** 22.30S 23.22E
Chula Vista U.S.A. **81** 32.39N117.05W
Chulman Russian Fed. **29** 56.54N124.55E
Chulucanas Peru **90** 5.08S 80.00W
Chulym Russian Fed. **28** 55.09N 80.59E
Chum Russian Fed. **24** 67.05N 63.15E
Chumbicha Argentina **92** 28.50S 66.18W
Chumikan Russian Fed. **29** 54.40N135.15E
Chumphon Thailand **34** 10.34N 99.15E
Chuna *r.* Russian Fed. **29** 58.00N 94.00E
Ch'unch'ŏn S. Korea **31** 37.53N127.45E
Chungking *see* Chongqing China **33**
Chunya Tanzania **55** 8.31S 33.28E
Chuquicamata Chile **92** 22.20S 68.56W
Chuquisaca *d.* Bolivia **92** 21.00S 64.00W
Chur Switz. **17** 46.52N 9.32E
Churchill Canada **75** 58.46N 94.10W
Churchill *r.* Man. Canada **75** 58.47N 94.12W
Churchill *r.* Nfld. Canada **77** 53.20N 60.11W
Churchill, C. Canada **75** 58.46N 93.12W
Churchill L. Canada **75** 55.55N108.20W
Churchill Peak *mtn.* Canada **74** 58.10N125.10W
Church Stretton U.K. **11** 52.32N 2.49W
Churia Range *mts.* Nepal **41** 28.40N 81.30E
Churu India **40** 28.18N 74.57E
Chusovoy Russian Fed. **24** 58.18N 57.50E
Chu Xian China **32** 32.25N118.15E
Chuxiong China **39** 25.03N101.33E
Chu Yang Sin *mtn.* Vietnam **34** 12.25N108.25E
Ciamis Indonesia **37** 7.20S108.21E
Cianjur Indonesia **37** 6.50S107.09E
Cibatu Indonesia **37** 7.10S107.59E
Ciechanów Poland **21** 52.53N 20.38E
Ciego de Avila Cuba **87** 21.51N 78.47W
Ciénaga Colombia **90** 11.11N 74.15W
Cienfuegos Cuba **87** 22.10N 80.27W
Cieszyn Poland **21** 49.45N 18.38E
Cieza Spain **16** 38.14N 1.25W
Cifuentes Spain **16** 40.47N 2.37W
Cigüela *r.* Spain **16** 39.47N 3.00W
Cijara, Embalse de *resr.* Spain **16** 39.20N 4.50W
Cijulang Indonesia **37** 7.44S108.30E
Cikampek Indonesia **37** 6.21S107.25E
Cilacap Indonesia **37** 7.44S109.00E
Ciledug Indonesia **37** 6.56S108.43E
Cili China **33** 29.24N111.04E
Cimanuk *r.* Indonesia **37** 6.20S108.12E
Cimarron U.S.A. **83** 37.48N100.21W
Cimarron *r.* U.S.A. **83** 36.10N 96.17W
Cimone, Monte *mtn.* Italy **15** 44.12N 10.42E
Cîmpina Romania **19** 45.08N 25.44E
Cîmpulung Romania **19** 45.16N 25.03E
Cinca *r.* Spain **16** 41.22N 0.20E
Cincinnati U.S.A. **84** 39.10N 84.30W
Ciney Belgium **14** 50.17N 5.06E
Cinto, Monte *mtn.* France **17** 42.23N 8.57E
Cipolletti Argentina **93** 38.56S 67.59W
Circle U.S.A. **80** 47.25N105.35W
Circleville Ohio U.S.A. **84** 39.36N 82.57W
Circleville Utah U.S.A. **80** 38.10N112.16W
Cirebon Indonesia **37** 6.46S108.33E
Cirencester U.K. **11** 51.43N 1.59W
Ciriè Italy **15** 45.14N 7.36E
Cirò Marina Italy **19** 39.22N 17.08E
Cisco U.S.A. **83** 32.23N 98.59W
Ciskei Africa **56** 32.45S 27.00E
Citra U.S.A. **85** 29.24N 82.06W
Cittadella Italy **15** 45.39N 11.47E
Cittanova Italy **18** 38.21N 16.05E
Ciudad Acuña Mexico **83** 29.18N100.55W
Ciudad Allende Mexico **83** 28.20N100.51W
Ciudad Bolívar Venezuela **90** 8.06N 63.36W
Ciudad Camargo Mexico **81** 27.40N105.10W
Ciudad de México Mexico **86** 19.25N 99.10W
Ciudadela Spain **16** 40.00N 3.50E
Ciudad Guayana Venezuela **90** 8.22N 62.40W
Ciudad Guerrero Mexico **86** 28.33N107.28W
Ciudad Guzmán Mexico **86** 19.41N103.29W
Ciudad Ixtepec Mexico **86** 16.32N 95.10W
Ciudad Jiménez Mexico **81** 27.08N104.55W
Ciudad Juárez Mexico **81** 31.44N106.29W
Ciudad Lerdo Mexico **83** 25.32N103.32W
Ciudad Madero Mexico **86** 22.19N 97.50W
Ciudad Mante Mexico **86** 22.44N 98.57W
Ciudad Melchor Múzquiz Mexico **83** 27.53N101.31W
Ciudad Mier Mexico **83** 26.26N 99.09W
Ciudad Obregón Mexico **81** 27.29N109.56W
Ciudad Ojeda Venezuela **90** 10.05N 71.17W
Ciudad Piar Venezuela **90** 7.27N 63.19W
Ciudad Real Spain **16** 38.59N 3.55W
Ciudad Rodrigo Spain **16** 40.36N 6.33W
Ciudad Victoria Mexico **86** 23.43N 99.10W
Civitanova Italy **18** 43.19N 13.40E
Civitavecchia Italy **18** 42.06N 11.48E
Civray France **17** 46.09N 0.18E
Çivril Turkey **42** 38.18N 29.43E
Ci Xian China **32** 36.22N114.23E
Cizre Turkey **42** 37.21N 42.11E
Clackline Australia **63** 31.43S116.31E
Clacton on Sea U.K. **11** 51.47N 1.10E
Claire, L. Canada **74** 58.30N112.00W
Clamecy France **15** 47.27N 3.31E
Clanton U.S.A. **85** 32.50N 86.38W
Clara Rep. of Ire. **13** 53.21N 7.37W
Clare N.S.W. Australia **66** 33.27S143.55E
Clare S.A. Australia **66** 33.50S138.38E
Clare *d.* Rep. of Ire. **13** 52.52N 8.55W
Clare *r.* Rep. of Ire. **13** 53.17N 9.04W
Clare U.S.A. **84** 43.49N 84.47W
Clare I. Rep. of Ire. **13** 53.48N 10.00W
Claremore U.S.A. **83** 36.19N 95.36W
Claremorris Rep. of Ire. **13** 53.44N 9.00W
Clarence *r.* Australia **67** 29.25S153.02E
Clarence *r.* New Zealand **60** 42.10S173.55E
Clarence I. Antarctica **96** 61.30S 53.50W
Clarence Str. Australia **62** 12.00S131.00E
Clarence Str. U.S.A. **74** 55.40N132.10W
Clarendon U.S.A. **83** 34.56N100.53W
Claresholm Canada **74** 50.00N113.45W
Clarie Coast *f.* Antarctica **96** 67.00S133.00E
Clarinda U.S.A. **82** 40.44N 95.02W
Clark, L. U.S.A. **72** 60.15N154.15W
Clarke I. Australia **65** 40.30S148.10E
Clark Fork *r.* U.S.A. **80** 48.09N116.15W
Clarksburg U.S.A. **84** 39.16N 80.22W
Clarksdale U.S.A. **83** 34.12N 90.34W
Clarkston U.S.A. **80** 46.26N117.02W
Clarksville Ark. U.S.A. **83** 35.28N 93.28W
Clarksville Tenn. U.S.A. **85** 36.31N 87.21W
Clarksville Tex. U.S.A. **83** 33.37N 95.03W
Clary France **14** 50.05N 3.21E
Clayoquot Sd. Canada **74** 49.11N126.08W
Clayton *r.* Australia **66** 29.06S137.59E
Clayton Idaho U.S.A. **80** 44.16N114.25W
Clayton N.J. U.S.A. **85** 39.39N 75.06W
Clayton N.Mex. U.S.A. **83** 36.27N103.11W
Clear, C. Rep. of Ire. **9** 51.25N 9.32W
Clearfield U.S.A. **80** 41.07N112.01W
Clear I. Rep. of Ire. **13** 51.26N 9.30W
Clear L. U.S.A. **80** 39.02N122.50W
Clear Lake *town* Iowa U.S.A. **82** 43.08N 92.23W
Clear Lake *town* S.Dak. U.S.A. **82** 44.45N 96.41W
Clearwater Canada **74** 51.38N120.02W
Clearwater *r.* Canada **75** 56.40N109.30W
Clearwater U.S.A. **85** 27.57N 82.48W
Clearwater Mts. U.S.A. **80** 46.00N115.30W
Cle Elum U.S.A. **80** 47.12N120.56W
Cleethorpes U.K. **10** 53.33N 0.02W
Clermont Australia **64** 22.49S147.39E
Clermont France **15** 49.23N 2.24E
Clermont-en-Argonne France **15** 49.05N 5.05E
Clermont-Ferrand France **17** 45.47N 3.05E
Clervaux Lux. **14** 50.04N 6.01E
Cles Italy **15** 46.22N 11.02E
Cleve Australia **66** 33.37S136.32E
Clevedon U.K. **11** 51.26N 2.52W
Cleveland *d.* U.K. **10** 54.37N 1.08W
Cleveland Miss. U.S.A. **83** 33.45N 90.50W
Cleveland Ohio U.S.A. **84** 41.30N 81.41W
Cleveland Tenn. U.S.A. **85** 35.10N 84.51W
Cleveland Tex. U.S.A. **83** 30.21N 95.05W
Cleveland, C. Australia **64** 19.11S147.01E
Cleveland Heights *town* U.S.A. **84** 41.30N 81.34W
Cleveland Hills U.K. **10** 54.25N 1.10W
Cleveleys U.K. **10** 53.52N 3.01W
Clew B. Rep. of Ire. **13** 53.50N 9.47W
Clifden Rep. of Ire. **13** 53.29N 10.02W
Cliffy Head Australia **63** 34.58S116.24E
Clifton Ariz. U.S.A. **81** 33.03N109.18W
Clifton N.J. U.S.A. **85** 40.53N 74.08W
Clifton Tex. U.S.A. **83** 31.47N 97.35W
Clifton Forge U.S.A. **85** 37.49N 79.49W
Climax Canada **75** 49.13N108.23W
Clint U.S.A. **81** 31.35N106.14W
Clinton Canada **74** 51.05N121.35W
Clinton New Zealand **60** 46.13S169.23E
Clinton Ark. U.S.A. **83** 35.36N 92.38W
Clinton Ill. U.S.A. **82** 40.10N 88.59W
Clinton Iowa U.S.A. **82** 41.51N 90.12W
Clinton Mo. U.S.A. **82** 38.22N 93.46W
Clinton N.C. U.S.A. **85** 35.00N 78.20W
Clinton N.J. U.S.A. **85** 40.38N 74.55W
Clinton Okla. U.S.A. **83** 35.31N 98.59W
Clintwood U.S.A. **85** 37.09N 82.30W
Clipperton *i.* Pacific Oc. **69** 10.17N109.13W
Clisham *mtn.* U.K. **12** 57.58N 6.50W
Clive L. Canada **74** 63.13N118.54W
Cliza Bolivia **92** 17.36S 65.56W
Cloghan Rep. of Ire. **13** 53.13N 7.54W
Clogher Head Rep. of Ire. **13** 52.09N 10.28W
Clonakilty Rep. of Ire. **13** 51.37N 8.54W
Cloncurry Australia **64** 20.42S140.30E
Clones Rep. of Ire. **13** 54.11N 7.16W
Clonmel Rep. of Ire. **13** 52.21N 7.44W
Clonroche Rep. of Ire. **13** 52.27N 6.45W
Cloppenburg Germany **14** 52.52N 8.02E
Cloquet U.S.A. **82** 46.43N 92.28W
Clorinda Argentina **92** 25.20S 57.40W
Cloud Peak *mtn.* U.S.A. **80** 44.25N107.10W
Cloughton U.K. **10** 54.20N 0.27W
Cloverdale U.S.A. **80** 38.48N123.01W
Clovis Calif. U.S.A. **80** 36.49N119.42W
Clovis N.Mex. U.S.A. **83** 34.24N103.12W
Clowne U.K. **10** 53.18N 1.16W
Cluj-Napoca Romania **21** 46.47N 23.37E
Clunes Australia **66** 37.16S143.47E
Cluny France **17** 46.26N 4.39E
Clusone Italy **15** 45.53N 9.57E
Clutha *r.* New Zealand **60** 46.18S169.05E
Clwyd *d.* U.K. **10** 53.07N 3.20W
Clwyd *r.* U.K. **10** 53.19N 3.30W
Clyde Canada **73** 70.30N 68.30W
Clyde New Zealand **60** 45.11S169.19E
Clyde *r.* U.K. **12** 55.58N 4.53W
Clydebank U.K. **12** 55.53N 4.23W
Coachella U.S.A. **81** 33.41N116.10W
Coahuila *d.* Mexico **83** 27.40N102.00W
Coal *r.* Canada **74** 59.39N126.57W
Coalgate U.S.A. **83** 34.32N 96.13W
Coalinga U.S.A. **81** 36.09N120.21W
Coalville U.K. **11** 52.43N 1.21W
Coast *d.* Kenya **55** 3.00S 39.30E
Coast Mts. Canada **74** 55.00N129.00W
Coast Range *mts.* U.S.A. **80** 42.40N123.30W

Coatbridge to Crosby

Coatbridge U.K. 12 55.52N 4.02W
Coatesville U.S.A. 85 39.59N 75.49W
Coats I. Canada 73 62.30N 83.00W
Coats Land f. Antarctica 96 77.00S 25.00W
Coatzacoalcos Mexico 86 18.10N 94.25W
Cobalt Canada 76 47.25N 79.42W
Cobán Guatemala 86 15.28N 90.20W
Cobar Australia 67 31.32S145.51E
Cobargo Australia 67 36.24S149.52E
Cobden Australia 66 38.21S143.07E
Cobden Canada 76 45.38N 76.53W
Cobh Rep. of Ire. 13 51.50N 8.18W
Cobham L. Australia 66 30.09S142.05E
Cobija Bolivia 92 11.02S 68.44W
Cobourg Canada 76 43.58N 78.10W
Cobourg Pen. Australia 64 11.20S132.15E
Cobram Australia 67 35.56S145.40E
Cobre U.S.A. 80 41.07N114.25W
Cobue Mozambique 55 12.10S 34.50E
Coburg Germany 20 50.15N 10.58E
Coburg I. Canada 73 76.00N 79.25W
Cochabamba Bolivia 92 17.24S 66.09W
Cochabamba d. Bolivia 92 17.30S 65.40W
Cochem Germany 14 50.08N 7.10E
Cochise U.S.A. 81 32.06N109.56W
Cochran U.S.A. 85 32.22N 83.21W
Cochrane Alta. Canada 74 51.11N114.30W
Cochrane Ont. Canada 76 49.00N 81.00W
Cochrane Chile 93 47.20S 72.30W
Cockaleechie Australia 66 34.07S135.53E
Cockburn Australia 66 32.05S141.00E
Cockburnspath U.K. 12 55.56N 2.22W
Cockeysville U.S.A. 85 39.29N 76.39W
Cocklebiddy Australia 63 32.02S126.05E
Coco r. Honduras 87 14.58N 83.15W
Coco, Isla del i. Pacific Oc. 69 5.32N 87.04W
Cocoa U.S.A. 85 28.21N 80.46W
Cocoa Beach town U.S.A. 85 28.19N 80.36W
Cocobeach Gabon 54 0.59N 9.36E
Cocoparra Range mts. Australia 67 34.00S146.00E
Cod, C. U.S.A. 84 41.42N 70.15W
Codăeşti Romania 21 46.52N 27.46E
Codajás Brazil 90 3.55S 62.00W
Codigoro Italy 15 44.49N 12.08E
Codó Brazil 91 4.28S 43.51W
Codogno Italy 15 45.09N 9.42E
Codroipo Italy 15 45.58N 12.59E
Cody U.S.A. 80 44.32N109.03W
Coen Australia 64 13.56S143.12E
Coesfeld Germany 14 51.55N 7.13E
Coeur d'Alene U.S.A. 78 47.40N116.46W
Coevorden Neth. 14 52.39N 6.45E
Coffeyville U.S.A. 83 37.02N 93.37W
Coffin B. Australia 66 34.27S135.19E
Coffin Bay Pen. Australia 66 34.30S135.14E
Coff's Harbour Australia 67 30.19S153.05E
Cofre de Perote mtn. Mexico 86 19.30N 97.10W
Coghinas r. Italy 18 40.57N 8.50E
Cognac France 17 45.42N 0.19W
Cohoes U.S.A. 84 42.46N 73.42W
Cohuna Australia 66 35.47S144.15E
Coiba, Isla de i. Panama 87 7.23N 81.45W
Coihaique Chile 93 45.35S 72.08W
Coimbatore India 38 11.00N 76.57E
Coimbra Brazil 94 19.55S 57.47W
Coimbra Portugal 16 40.12N 8.25W
Coín Spain 16 36.40N 4.45W
Cojimies Ecuador 90 0.20N 80.00W
Cokeville U.S.A. 80 42.05N110.57W
Colac Australia 66 38.22S143.38E
Colatina Brazil 94 19.35S 40.37W
Colbeck, C. Antarctica 96 77.20S159.00W
Colby U.S.A. 82 39.24N101.03W
Colchester U.K. 11 51.54N 0.55E
Cold L. Canada 75 54.33N110.05W
Cold Lake town Canada 75 54.27N110.10W
Coldstream U.K. 12 55.39N 2.15W
Coldwater U.S.A. 84 41.57N 85.01W
Coldwell Canada 76 48.45N 86.30W
Coleambally Australia 67 34.48S145.53E
Coleman r. Australia 64 15.06S141.38E
Coleman Tex. U.S.A. 83 31.50N 99.26W
Coleman Wisc. U.S.A. 82 45.04N 88.02W
Colenso R.S.A. 56 28.43S 29.49E
Coleraine Australia 66 37.36S141.42E
Coleraine U.K. 13 55.08N 6.40W
Colesberg R.S.A. 56 30.43S 25.05E
Colfax U.S.A. 83 31.31N 92.42W
Colgong India 41 25.16N 87.13E
Colico Italy 15 46.08N 9.22E
Colima Mexico 86 19.14N103.41W
Colima d. Mexico 86 19.05N104.00W
Colinas Brazil 91 6.02S 44.14W
Coll i. U.K. 12 56.38N 6.34W
Collarenebri Australia 67 29.33S148.36E
College U.S.A. 72 64.54N147.55W
College Park town Ga. U.S.A. 85 33.39N 84.28W
College Park town Md. U.S.A. 85 39.00N 76.55W
College Station town U.S.A. 83 30.37N 96.21W
Collerina Australia 67 29.22S146.32E
Collie N.S.W. Australia 67 31.41S148.22E
Collie W.A. Australia 63 33.21S116.09E
Collie Cardiff Australia 63 33.27S116.09E
Collier B. Australia 62 16.10S124.15E
Collingswood U.S.A. 85 39.55N 75.04W
Collingwood Canada 76 44.29N 80.13W
Collingwood New Zealand 60 40.41S172.41E
Collingwood B. P.N.G. 64 9.20S149.30E
Collinsville Australia 64 20.34S147.51E
Collin Top mtn. U.K. 13 54.58N 6.08W
Collon Rep. of Ire. 13 53.47N 6.30W
Collooney Rep. of Ire. 13 54.11N 8.29W
Colmar France 17 48.05N 7.21E
Colmenar Viejo Spain 16 40.39N 3.46W
Colne r. U.K. 11 51.50N 0.59E
Colnett, C. Mexico 86 31.00N116.20W
Colnett, Cabo c. Mexico 81 31.00N116.20W
Colo r. Australia 67 33.26S150.53E
Cologne see Köln Germany 14
Colombia S. America 90 4.00N 72.30W
Colombian Basin f. Carib. Sea 95 14.00N 76.00W
Colombo Sri Lanka 39 6.55N 79.52E
Colón Argentina 93 32.15S 58.10W
Colón Panama 90 9.21N 79.54W
Colona Australia 65 31.38S132.05E
Colonelganj India 41 27.08N 81.42E
Colonia del Sacramento Uruguay 93 34.28S 57.51W
Colonia Las Heras Argentina 93 46.33S 68.57W
Colonia Lavelleja Uruguay 93 31.06S 57.01W
Colonsay i. U.K. 12 56.04N 6.13W
Colorado r. Argentina 93 39.50S 62.02W
Colorado d. U.S.A. 80 39.07N105.27W
Colorado r. Ariz. U.S.A. 81 31.45N114.40W
Colorado r. Tex. U.S.A. 83 28.36N 95.58W
Colorado City U.S.A. 83 32.24N100.52W
Colorado Plateau f. U.S.A. 81 36.30N108.00W
Colorado Springs town U.S.A. 80 38.50N104.49W
Colton U.S.A. 82 43.47N 96.56W
Columbia La. U.S.A. 83 32.06N 92.05W
Columbia Miss. U.S.A. 83 31.15N 89.56W
Columbia Mo. U.S.A. 82 38.57N 92.20W
Columbia r. U.S.A. 80 46.15N124.05W
Columbia S.C. U.S.A. 85 34.00N 81.00W
Columbia Tenn. U.S.A. 85 35.37N 87.02W
Columbia, Mt. Canada 74 52.08N117.20W
Columbia, Sierra mts. Mexico 81 29.30N114.50W
Columbia Basin f. U.S.A. 80 46.55N117.36W
Columbia Falls town U.S.A. 80 48.23N114.11W
Columbia Plateau f. U.S.A. 80 44.00N117.30W
Columbretes, Islas is. Spain 16 39.50N 0.40E
Columbus Ga. U.S.A. 85 32.28N 84.59W
Columbus Ind. U.S.A. 84 39.12N 85.57W
Columbus Miss. U.S.A. 83 33.30N 88.25W
Columbus Mont. U.S.A. 80 45.38N109.15W
Columbus Nebr. U.S.A. 82 41.25N 97.22W
Columbus N.Mex. U.S.A. 81 31.50N107.38W
Columbus Ohio U.S.A. 84 39.59N 83.03W
Columbus Tex. U.S.A. 83 29.42N 96.33W
Colville r. U.S.A. 72 70.06N151.30W
Colwyn Bay town U.K. 10 53.18N 3.43W
Comacchio Italy 15 44.42N 12.11E
Comacchio, Valli di b. Italy 15 44.38N 12.06E
Comai China 41 28.28N 91.33E
Comanche U.S.A. 83 34.22N 97.58W
Comayagua Honduras 87 14.30N 87.39W
Comblain-au-Pont Belgium 14 50.29N 5.32E
Combles France 14 50.01N 2.52E
Combourg France 15 48.25N 1.45W
Comboyne Australia 67 31.35S152.27E
Comeragh Mts. Rep. of Ire. 13 52.17N 7.34W
Comilla Bangla. 41 23.28N 91.10E
Comitán Mexico 86 16.15N 92.08W
Commentry France 17 46.17N 2.44E
Commerce U.S.A. 83 33.15N 95.54W
Commonwealth Territory d. Australia 67 35.00S151.00E
Como Italy 15 45.48N 9.04E
Como, Lago di l. Italy 15 46.05N 9.17E
Comodoro Rivadavia Argentina 93 45.50S 67.30W
Comorin, C. India 38 8.04N 77.35E
Comoros Africa 55 12.15S 44.00E
Compiègne France 15 49.24N 2.50E
Cona China 41 27.59N 91.59E
Co Nag l. China 41 32.00N 91.15E
Conakry Guinea 52 9.30N 13.43W
Concarneau France 17 47.53N 3.55W
Conceição Mozambique 57 18.45S 36.10E
Conceição do Araguaia Brazil 91 8.15S 49.17W
Concepción Argentina 92 27.20S 65.36W
Concepción Chile 93 36.50S 73.03W
Concepción r. Mexico 81 30.32N112.59W
Concepción Paraguay 92 23.22S 57.26W
Concepción del Oro Mexico 83 24.38N101.25W
Concepción del Uruguay Argentina 93 32.30S 58.14W
Conception, Pt. U.S.A. 81 34.27N120.27W
Conception B. Namibia 56 23.53S 14.28E
Conches France 15 48.58N 0.58E
Conchillas Uruguay 93 34.15S 58.04W
Conchos r. Mexico 81 29.32N104.25W
Concord N.C. U.S.A. 85 35.25N 80.34W
Concord N.H. U.S.A. 84 43.12N 71.32W
Concordia Argentina 93 31.24S 58.02W
Concórdia Brazil 90 4.35S 66.35W
Concordia Mexico 81 23.17N106.04W
Concordia U.S.A. 82 39.34N 97.39W
Condé France 15 48.51N 0.33W
Condé-sur-l'Escaut France 14 50.28N 3.35E
Condobolin Australia 67 33.03S147.11E
Condom France 17 43.58N 0.22E
Conegliano Italy 15 45.53N 12.18E
Confolens France 17 46.01N 0.40E
Conghua China 33 23.33N113.34E
Congleton U.K. 10 53.10N 2.12W
Congo Africa 54 1.00S 16.00E
Congo r. see Zaïre r. Zaïre 54
Congonhas Brazil 94 20.30S 43.53W
Coningsby U.K. 10 53.07N 0.09W
Coniston U.K. 10 54.22N 3.06W
Conkouati Congo 54 4.00S 11.16E
Conn, Lough Rep. of Ire. 13 54.01N 9.15W
Connah's Quay town U.K. 10 53.13N 3.03W
Conneaut U.S.A. 84 41.58N 80.34W
Connecticut d. U.S.A. 84 41.45N 72.45W
Connecticut r. U.S.A. 84 41.17N 72.21W
Connellsville U.S.A. 84 40.01N 79.35W
Connemara f. Rep. of Ire. 13 53.32N 9.56W
Conner, Mt. Australia 64 25.35S131.49E
Conon r. U.K. 12 57.33N 4.33W
Conrad U.S.A. 80 48.10N111.57W
Conroe U.S.A. 83 30.19N 95.27W
Conselheiro Lafaiete Brazil 94 20.40S 43.48W
Consett U.K. 10 54.52N 1.50W
Con Son is. Vietnam 34 8.45N106.38E
Constance, L. see Bodensee Europe 20
Constanţa Romania 19 44.10N 28.31E
Constantina Spain 16 37.54N 5.36W
Constantine Algeria 51 36.22N 6.38E
Constitución Chile 93 35.20S 72.25W
Constitución Uruguay 93 31.05S 57.50W
Consuegra Spain 16 39.28N 3.43W
Consul Canada 75 49.21N109.30W
Contact U.S.A. 80 41.48N114.46W
Contai India 41 21.47N 87.45E
Contamana Peru 90 7.19S 75.00W
Contas r. Brazil 91 14.15S 39.00W
Contreras, Embalse de resr. Spain 16 39.32N 1.30W
Contres France 15 47.25N 1.26E
Contwoyto L. Canada 72 65.42N110.50W
Conty France 15 49.44N 2.09E
Conway Ark. U.S.A. 83 35.05N 92.26W
Conway N.H. U.S.A. 84 43.59N 71.07W
Conway S.C. U.S.A. 85 33.51N 79.04W
Conway, L. Australia 66 28.17S135.35E
Conwy r. U.K. 9 53.17N 3.49W
Coober Pedy Australia 66 29.01S134.43E
Cooch Behār India 41 26.19N 89.26E
Cook, C. Canada 72 50.08N127.55W
Cook, Mt. New Zealand 60 43.45S170.12E
Cooke, Mt. Australia 63 32.26S116.18E
Cookeville U.S.A. 85 36.10N 85.30W
Cookhouse R.S.A. 56 32.44S 25.47E
Cook Inlet U.S.A. 72 60.30N152.00W
Cook Is. Pacific Oc. 68 15.00S160.00W
Cookstown U.K. 13 54.39N 6.46W
Cook Str. New Zealand 60 41.15S174.30E
Cooktown Australia 64 15.29S145.15E
Coolabah Australia 67 31.02S146.45E
Coolah Australia 67 31.48S149.45E
Coolamara Australia 66 31.59S143.42E
Coolamon Australia 67 34.48S147.12E
Coolangatta Australia 67 28.10S153.26E
Coolgardie Australia 63 31.01S121.12E
Coolidge U.S.A. 81 32.59N111.31W
Cooma Australia 67 36.15S149.07E
Coombah Australia 66 32.58S141.39E
Coomberdale Australia 63 30.29S116.03E
Coonabarabran Australia 67 31.16S149.18E
Coonalpyn Australia 66 35.41S139.52E
Coonamble Australia 67 30.55S148.26E
Coonana Australia 63 31.01S123.05E
Coonawarra Australia 66 37.16S140.50E
Coondambo Australia 66 31.07S135.20E
Cooper Creek r. Australia 66 28.33S137.46E
Coorow Australia 63 29.53S116.01E
Coos Bay town U.S.A. 80 43.22N124.13W
Cootamundra Australia 67 34.41S148.03E
Cootehill Rep. of Ire. 13 54.05N 7.05W
Copainalá Mexico 86 17.05N 93.12W
Copán ruins Honduras 87 14.52N 89.10W
Cope U.S.A. 80 39.40N102.51W
Copenhagen see København Denmark 23
Copiapó Chile 92 27.22S 70.20W
Copparo Italy 15 44.54N 11.49E
Copperbelt d. Zambia 56 13.00S 28.00E
Copper Belt f. Zambia 55 12.40S 28.00E
Copper Center U.S.A. 72 61.58N145.19W
Copper Cliff town Canada 76 46.28N 81.04W
Copper Harbor U.S.A. 84 47.28N 87.54W
Coppermine r. Canada 72 67.54N115.10W
Coppermine see Qurlurtuuq town Canada 72
Copper Mountain town Canada 74 49.20N120.30W
Copper Queen Zimbabwe 56 17.31S 29.20E
Copperton R.S.A. 56 30.00S 22.15E
Copp L. Canada 74 60.14N114.40W
Coqên China 41 31.13N 85.12E
Coquet r. U.K. 10 55.21N 1.35W
Coquille U.S.A. 80 43.11N124.11W
Coquimbo Chile 92 29.58S 71.21W
Corabia Romania 19 43.45N 24.29E
Coracora Peru 90 15.02S 73.48W
Coraki Australia 67 23.00S153.17E
Coral Bay town Australia 62 23.02S113.48E
Coral Harbour town Canada 73 64.10N 83.15W
Coral Sea Pacific Oc. 64 14.30S149.30E
Coral Sea Basin Pacific Oc. 68 14.00S152.00E
Corangamite, L. Australia 66 38.10S143.25E
Corbeil France 15 48.37N 2.29E
Corbeny France 15 49.28N 3.49E
Corbigny France 15 47.15N 3.40E
Corbin U.S.A. 85 36.58N 84.06W
Corby U.K. 11 52.29N 0.41W
Corcubión Spain 16 42.56N 9.12W
Córdoba Argentina 92 31.25S 64.10W
Córdoba d. Argentina 92 30.30S 64.30W
Córdoba Mexico 86 18.55N 96.55W
Córdoba Spain 16 37.53N 4.46W
Córdoba, Sierras de mts. Argentina 92 30.30S 64.40W
Cordova U.S.A. 72 60.33N139.44W
Corentyne r. Guyana 91 5.10N 57.20W
Corfield Australia 64 21.43S143.22E
Corfu i. see Kérkira i. Greece 19
Coricudgy, Mt. Australia 67 32.51S150.25E
Corigliano Italy 19 39.36N 16.31E
Corindi Australia 67 30.00S153.21E
Corinne Canada 75 50.04N104.40W
Corinth U.S.A. 83 34.56N 88.31W
Corinto Nicaragua 87 12.29N 87.14W
Cork Rep. of Ire. 13 51.54N 8.28W
Cork d. Rep. of Ire. 13 52.00N 8.40W
Cork Harbour est. Rep. of Ire. 13 51.50N 8.17W
Cormeilles France 15 49.15N 0.23E
Cormorant Canada 75 54.14N100.35W
Corner Brook town Canada 77 48.57N 57.57W
Corner Inlet b. Australia 67 38.43S146.20E
Corning Ark. U.S.A. 83 36.24N 90.35W
Corning N.Y. U.S.A. 84 42.09N 77.04W
Corno, Monte mtn. Italy 18 42.29N 13.33E
Cornwall Canada 76 45.02N 74.45W
Cornwall d. U.K. 11 50.26N 4.40W
Cornwallis I. Canada 73 75.00N 95.00W
Coro Venezuela 90 11.27N 69.41W
Coroatá Brazil 91 4.08S 44.08W
Coroico Bolivia 92 16.10S 67.44W
Coromandel New Zealand 60 36.46S175.30E
Coromandel Pen. New Zealand 60 36.45S175.30E
Corona U.S.A. 81 34.15N105.36W
Coronation G. Canada 72 68.00N112.00W
Coronation I. U.S.A. 74 55.52N134.20W
Coronda Argentina 93 31.55S 60.55W
Coronel Chile 93 37.01S 73.08W
Coronel Brandsen Argentina 93 35.10S 58.15W
Coronel Pringles Argentina 93 37.56S 61.25W
Coronel Suárez Argentina 93 37.30S 61.52W
Coropuna mtn. Peru 90 15.31S 72.45W
Corowa Australia 67 36.00S146.20E
Corozal Belize 87 18.23N 88.23W
Corpus Christi U.S.A. 83 27.48N 97.24W
Correggio Italy 15 44.46N 10.47E
Correntes, Cabo das c. Mozambique 57 24.11S 35.35E
Corrib, Lough Rep. of Ire. 13 53.26N 9.14W
Corrientes Argentina 92 27.30S 58.48W
Corrientes d. Argentina 92 28.00S 57.00W
Corrientes, Cabo c. Colombia 90 5.30N 77.34W
Corrigan U.S.A. 83 31.00N 94.50W
Corrigin Australia 63 32.21S117.52E
Corry U.S.A. 84 41.56N 79.39W
Corryong Australia 67 36.11S147.58E
Corse d. France 17 42.00N 9.10E
Corse i. France 17 42.00N 9.10E
Corse, Cap c. France 17 43.00N 9.21E
Corsham U.K. 11 51.25N 2.11W
Corsica i. see Corse i. France 17
Corsicana U.S.A. 83 32.06N 96.28W
Corte France 17 42.18N 9.08E
Cortegana Spain 16 37.55N 6.49W
Cortez Colo. U.S.A. 80 37.21N108.35W
Cortez Nev. U.S.A. 80 40.09N116.38W
Cortina Italy 18 46.32N 12.08E
Cortland U.S.A. 84 42.36N 76.11W
Cortona Italy 18 43.16N 11.59E
Coruche Portugal 16 38.58N 8.31W
Çoruh Nehri r. Turkey see Chorokh r. Georgia 42
Çorum Turkey 42 40.31N 34.57E
Corumbá Brazil 92 19.00S 57.27W
Corumbá r. Brazil 94 18.15S 48.55W
Corvallis U.S.A. 80 44.34N123.16W
Corwen U.K. 10 52.59N 3.23W
Cosenza Italy 18 39.17N 16.14E
Cosne France 15 47.25N 2.55E
Coso Junction U.S.A. 81 36.03N117.58W
Cosson r. France 15 47.30N 1.15E
Costa Brava f. Spain 16 41.30N 3.00E
Costa del Sol f. Spain 16 36.30N 4.00W
Costa Mesa U.S.A. 81 33.39N117.55W
Costa Rica C. America 87 10.00N 84.00W
Costeşti Romania 19 44.40N 24.53E
Cotabato Phil. 37 7.14N124.15E
Cotagaita Bolivia 92 20.50S 65.41W
Côte d'Azur f. France 17 43.20N 6.45E
Côte d'Ivoire see Ivory Coast Africa 52
Côte-d'Or d. France 15 47.30N 4.50E
Côte d'Or f. France 15 47.10N 4.50E
Cotonou Benin 53 6.24N 2.31E
Cotopaxi mtn. Ecuador 90 0.40S 78.28W
Cotswold Hills U.K. 11 51.50N 2.00W
Cottage Grove U.S.A. 80 43.48N123.03W
Cottbus Germany 20 51.43N 14.21E
Cottonvale Australia 67 28.32S151.57E
Cottonwood U.S.A. 81 34.45N112.01W
Cotulla U.S.A. 83 28.26N 99.14W
Coucy France 15 49.31N 3.19E
Couer d'Alene U.S.A. 80 47.41N117.00W
Couesnon r. France 15 48.37N 1.31W
Coulagh B. Rep. of Ire. 13 51.42N 10.00W
Coulee City U.S.A. 80 47.37N119.17W
Coulommiers France 15 48.49N 3.05E
Coulonge r. Canada 76 45.51N 76.46W
Council U.S.A. 72 64.55N163.44W
Council Bluffs U.S.A. 82 41.16N 95.52W
Coupar Angus U.K. 12 56.33N 3.17W
Courland Lagoon Russian Fed. / Lithuania 23 55.00N 21.00E
Courson-les-Carrières France 15 47.36N 3.30E
Courtalain France 15 48.05N 1.09E
Courtenay Canada 74 49.41N125.00W
Courtrai see Kortrijk Belgium 14
Coutances France 15 49.03N 1.29W
Coutras France 17 45.02N 0.07W
Couvin Belgium 14 50.03N 4.30E
Covὲ Benin 53 7.16N 2.20E
Cove City U.S.A. 85 35.11N 77.20W
Coventry U.K. 11 52.25N 1.31W
Covilhã Portugal 16 40.17N 7.30W
Covington Ga. U.S.A. 85 33.35N 83.52W
Covington Ky. U.S.A. 84 39.04N 84.30W
Covington Okla. U.S.A. 83 36.18N 97.35W
Covington Tenn. U.S.A. 83 35.34N 89.38W
Covington Va. U.S.A. 85 37.48N 80.01W
Cowal, L. Australia 67 33.36S147.22E
Cowan Canada 75 52.05N100.45W
Cowan, L. Australia 63 32.00S122.00E
Cowangie Australia 66 35.14S141.28E
Cowansville Canada 77 45.12N 72.45W
Cowcowing Lakes Australia 63 31.01S117.18E
Cowdenbeath U.K. 12 56.07N 3.21W
Cowell Australia 66 33.41S136.55E
Cowes Australia 67 38.27S145.15E
Cowes U.K. 11 50.45N 1.18W
Cowra Australia 67 33.50S148.45E
Cox r. Australia 64 15.19S135.25E
Coxim Brazil 92 18.28S 54.37W
Cox's Bāzār Bangla. 41 21.26N 91.59E
Coyuca de Catalán Mexico 86 18.20N100.39W
Cozad U.S.A. 82 40.52N 99.59W
Cozes France 17 45.35N 0.50W
Cozumel, Isla de i. Mexico 87 20.30N 87.00W
Cradock Australia 66 31.59S138.34E
Cradock R.S.A. 56 32.10S 25.35E
Craig Alas. U.S.A. 74 55.29N133.09W
Craig Colo. U.S.A. 80 40.31N107.33W
Craigavon U.K. 13 54.28N 6.25W
Craignure U.K. 12 56.28N 5.42W
Craigsville U.S.A. 85 38.04N 79.23W
Crail U.K. 12 56.16N 2.38W
Crailsheim Germany 20 49.09N 10.06E
Craiova Romania 19 44.18N 23.46E
Cranbourne Australia 67 38.07S145.19E
Cranbrook Australia 63 34.15S117.32E
Cranbrook Canada 74 49.30N115.46W
Crane U.S.A. 83 31.24N118.34W
Cranston U.S.A. 84 41.47N 71.26W
Craon France 15 47.50N 0.58W
Craonne France 15 49.27N 3.46E
Crater L. U.S.A. 80 42.56N122.06W
Crateús Brazil 91 5.10S 40.39W
Crati r. Italy 19 39.43N 16.29E
Crato Amazonas Brazil 90 7.25S 63.00W
Crato Ceará Brazil 91 7.10S 39.25W
Craughwell Rep. of Ire. 13 53.14N 8.44W
Crawford U.S.A. 82 42.41N103.25W
Crawfordsville U.S.A. 84 40.03N 86.54W
Crawfordville U.S.A. 85 30.12N 84.21W
Crawley U.K. 11 51.07N 0.10W
Crazy Mts. U.S.A. 80 46.08N110.20W
Crécy France 17 50.15N 1.53E
Crécy-sur-Serre France 15 49.42N 3.37E
Cree r. Canada 75 59.00N105.47W
Creede U.S.A. 80 37.51N106.56W
Cree L. Canada 75 57.30N106.30W
Creil France 15 49.16N 2.29E
Crema Italy 15 45.22N 9.41E
Cremona Italy 15 45.08N 10.03E
Crépy France 15 49.36N 3.31E
Crépy-en-Valois France 15 49.14N 2.54E
Cres i. Croatia 18 44.50N 14.20E
Cres town Croatia 18 44.58N 14.25E
Crescent U.S.A. 80 43.29N121.41W
Crescent City U.S.A. 80 41.45N124.12W
Crescent Head town Australia 67 31.10S152.59E
Crespo Argentina 93 32.02S 60.20W
Cressy Australia 66 38.02S143.38E
Crest France 17 44.44N 5.02E
Creston Canada 74 49.10N116.31W
Creston U.S.A. 82 41.04N 94.22W
Creston Oriental de la Sierra Madre mts. Mexico 81 28.40N107.50W
Crestview U.S.A. 85 30.44N 86.34W
Creswick Australia 66 37.25S143.54E
Crete i. see Kriti i. Greece 19
Crete U.S.A. 82 40.38N 96.58W
Crete, Sea of see Kritikón Pélagos sea Greece 19
Creus, Cabo de c. Spain 16 42.20N 3.19E
Creuse r. France 17 47.00N 0.35E
Crewe U.K. 10 53.06N 2.28W
Crianlarich U.K. 12 56.23N 4.37W
Criccieth U.K. 10 52.55N 4.15W
Criciúma Brazil 94 28.40S 49.23W
Crieff U.K. 12 56.23N 3.52W
Crillon, Mt. U.S.A. 74 58.39N137.14W
Crimea pen. see Krym pen. Ukraine 25
Crinan U.K. 12 56.06N 5.34W
Cristóbal Colón mtn. Colombia 90 10.53N 73.48W
Crişu Alb r. Romania 21 46.42N 21.17E
Crna r. Macedonia 19 41.33N 21.58E
Crna Gora d. Yugo. 19 43.00N 19.30E
Croaghnameal mtn. Rep. of Ire. 13 54.40N 7.57W
Croatia Europe 21 45.10N 15.30E
Crockett U.S.A. 83 31.19N 95.28W
Crocodile r. R.S.A. 56 24.11S 26.48E
Croker I. Australia 64 11.12S132.32E
Cromarty Canada 75 58.03N 94.09W
Cromarty U.K. 12 57.40N 4.02W
Cromarty Firth est. U.K. 12 57.41N 4.10W
Cromer U.K. 10 52.56N 1.18E
Cromwell New Zealand 60 45.03S169.14E
Crooked I. Bahamas 87 22.45N 74.00W
Crookhaven Rep. of Ire. 13 51.29N 9.45W
Crookston U.S.A. 82 47.47N 96.37W
Crookwell Australia 67 34.27S149.28E
Croom Rep. of Ire. 13 52.31N 8.43W
Croppa Creek town Australia 67 29.08S150.20E
Crosby I.o.M. Europe 10 54.11N 4.34W
Crosby U.S.A. 83 31.17N 91.04W

Cross City to **Delphos**

Cross City U.S.A. 85 29.39N 83.09W
Crossett U.S.A. 83 33.08N 91.58W
Cross Fell mtn. U.K. 10 54.43N 2.28W
Cross L. Canada 75 54.45N 97.30W
Cross River d. Nigeria 53 5.45N 8.25E
Crossroads U.S.A. 83 33.30N103.21W
Cross Sd. U.S.A. 74 58.10N136.30W
Crossville U.S.A. 85 35.57N 85.02W
Crotone Italy 19 39.05N 17.06E
Crow r. Canada 74 59.41N124.20W
Crow Agency U.S.A. 80 45.36N107.27W
Crowell U.S.A. 83 33.59N 99.43W
Crowl Creek r. Australia 67 31.58S144.53E
Crowsnest Pass Canada 74 49.40N114.40W
Croyde U.K. 11 51.07N 4.13W
Croyden Australia 61 18.12S142.14E
Croydon Australia 64 18.12S142.14E
Croydon U.K. 11 51.23N 0.06W
Crucero U.S.A. 81 35.03N116.10W
Cruger U.S.A. 83 33.14N 90.14W
Cruz, Cabo c. Cuba 87 19.52N 77.44W
Cruz Alta Brazil 94 28.38S 53.38W
Cruz del Eje Argentina 92 30.44S 64.49W
Cruzeiro Brazil 94 22.33S 44.59W
Cruzeiro do Sul Brazil 90 7.40S 72.39W
Crystal U.S.A. 82 45.00N 93.25W
Crystal Brook town Australia 66 33.21S138.13E
Crystal City U.S.A. 83 28.41N 99.50W
Crystal River town U.S.A. 85 28.54N 82.36W
Csorna Hungary 21 47.37N 17.16E
Csurgó Hungary 21 46.16N 17.06E
Cuamba Mozambique 55 14.48S 36.32E
Cuando r. Angola 56 18.30S 23.32E
Cuando-Cubango d. Angola 56 16.00S 20.00E
Cuangar Angola 54 17.34S 18.39E
Cuango r. see Kwango r. Zaïre 54
Cuanza r. Angola 54 9.20S 13.09E
Cuanza Norte d. Angola 54 8.45S 15.00E
Cuanza Sul d. Angola 54 11.00S 15.00E
Cua Rao Vietnam 34 19.16N104.27E
Cuaró Uruguay 93 30.37S 56.54W
Cuaró r. Uruguay 93 30.15S 57.01W
Cuauhtémoc Mexico 81 28.25N106.52W
Cuba C. America 87 22.00N 79.00W
Cuba U.S.A. 81 36.01N107.04W
Cuballing Australia 63 32.50S117.07E
Cubango r. see Okavango r. Angola 54
Cubia r. Angola 54 16.00S 21.46E
Cubo Mozambique 57 23.48S 33.55E
Cuchi r. Angola 56 15.23S 17.12E
Cuckfield U.K. 11 51.00N 0.08W
Cucuí Brazil 90 1.12N 66.50W
Cúcuta Colombia 90 7.55N 72.31W
Cudahy U.S.A. 82 42.57N 87.52W
Cuddalore India 39 11.43N 79.46E
Cue Australia 62 27.25S117.54E
Cuenca Ecuador 90 2.54S 79.00W
Cuenca Spain 16 40.04N 2.07W
Cuenca, Serranía de mts. Spain 16 40.25N 2.00W
Cuernavaca Mexico 86 18.57N 99.15W
Cuero U.S.A. 83 29.06N 97.18W
Cuervo U.S.A. 81 35.02N104.24W
Cuiabá Brazil 91 15.32S 56.05W
Cuiabá r. Brazil 92 18.00S 57.25W
Cuidado, Punta c. I. de Pascua 69 27.08S109.19W
Cuillin Hills U.K. 12 57.12N 6.13W
Cuilo r. see Kwilu r. Zaïre 54
Cuito r. Angola 54 18.01S 20.50E
Cuito Cuanavale Angola 56 15.11S 19.11E
Culbertson U.S.A. 80 48.09N104.31W
Culcairn Australia 67 35.40S147.03E
Culemborg Neth. 14 51.57N 5.14E
Culgoa r. Australia 67 29.56S146.20E
Culiacán Mexico 81 24.48N107.24W
Culiacán r. Mexico 81 24.30N107.31W
Cullen U.K. 12 57.41N 2.50W
Cullera Spain 16 39.10N 0.15W
Cullin Sd. U.K. 12 57.03N 6.13W
Culloden Moor U.K. 12 57.29N 3.55W
Culpeper U.S.A. 84 38.28N 77.53W
Culuene r. Brazil 91 12.56S 52.51W
Culver, Pt. Australia 63 32.52S124.41E
Cuma Angola 54 12.52S 15.05E
Cumaná Venezuela 90 10.29N 64.12W
Cumberland Ky. U.S.A. 85 36.58N 82.59W
Cumberland Md. U.S.A. 84 39.39N 78.46W
Cumberland r. U.S.A. 85 37.09N 88.25W
Cumberland Va. U.S.A. 85 37.31N 78.16W
Cumberland Wisc. U.S.A. 82 45.32N 92.01W
Cumberland, C. Vanuatu 68 14.39S166.37E
Cumberland, L. U.S.A. 85 36.45N 84.51W
Cumberland I. U.S.A. 85 30.51N 81.27W
Cumberland L. Canada 75 54.02N102.17W
Cumberland Pen. Canada 73 66.50N 64.00W
Cumberland Plateau f. U.S.A. 85 36.00N 85.00W
Cumberland Sd. Canada 73 65.00N 65.30W
Cumbernauld U.K. 12 55.57N 4.00W
Cumbria d. U.K. 10 54.30N 3.00W
Cumbrian Mts. U.K. 10 54.32N 3.05W
Cuminá r. Brazil 91 1.30S 56.00W
Cummins Australia 66 34.16S135.44E
Cumnock Australia 67 32.56S148.46E
Cumnock U.K. 12 55.27N 4.15W
Cunderdin Australia 63 31.39S117.15E
Cunene d. Angola 54 16.00S 16.00E
Cunene r. Angola 54 17.15S 11.50E
Cuneo Italy 15 44.22N 7.32E
Cungena Australia 66 32.33S134.40E
Cunnamulla Australia 67 28.04S145.40E
Cuokkaraš'ša mtn. Norway 22 69.57N 24.32E
Cuorgnè Italy 15 45.23N 7.39E
Cupar U.K. 12 56.19N 3.01W
Cupica, Golfo de g. Colombia 90 6.35N 77.25W
Curaçao i. Neth. Antilles 90 12.15N 69.00W
Curacautín Chile 93 38.26S 71.53W
Curaco r. Argentina 93 38.49S 65.01W
Curanilahue Chile 93 37.28S 73.21W
Curaray r. Peru 90 2.20S 74.05W
Curban Australia 67 31.33S148.36E
Curdlawidny L. Australia 66 30.16S136.20E
Cure r. France 15 47.40N 3.41E
Curiapo Venezuela 90 8.33N 61.05W
Curicó Chile 93 34.59S 71.14W
Curitiba Brazil 94 25.24S 49.16W
Curlewis Australia 67 31.08S150.16E
Curnamona Australia 66 31.40S139.35E
Currane, Lough Rep. of Ire. 13 51.50N 10.07W
Currant U.S.A. 80 38.44N115.30W
Curranyalpa Australia 67 30.57S144.33E
Currie Australia 65 39.56S143.52E
Currie U.S.A. 80 40.17N114.44W
Curtin Australia 63 30.50S122.05E
Curtis U.S.A. 82 40.38N100.31W
Curtis I. Australia 64 23.38S151.09E
Curuá r. Brazil 91 5.23S 54.22W
Cururupu Brazil 91 1.50S 44.52W
Curuzú Cuatiá Argentina 93 29.50S 58.05W
Curvelo Brazil 94 18.45S 44.27W
Cushendall U.K. 13 55.06N 6.05W
Cushing U.S.A. 83 35.59N 96.46W
Cusna, Monte mtn. Italy 15 44.17N 10.23E
Cut Bank U.S.A. 80 48.38N112.20W
Cuttaburra Creek r. Australia 67 29.18S145.00E
Cuttack India 41 20.30N 85.50E
Cuxhaven Germany 20 53.52N 8.42E
Cuyuni r. Guyana 90 6.24N 58.38W
Cuzco Peru 90 13.32S 71.57W
Cwmbran U.K. 11 51.39N 3.01W
Cyclades is. see Kikládhes is. Greece 19
Cynthiana U.S.A. 84 38.22N 84.18W
Cypress Hills Canada 75 49.40N109.30W
Cyprus Asia 44 35.00N 33.00E
Cyrenaica f. see Barqah f. Libya 48
Czech Republic Europe 20 49.30N 15.00E
Czeremcha Poland 21 52.32N 23.15E
Czersk Poland 21 53.48N 18.00E
Częstochowa Poland 21 50.49N 19.07E

D

Dà r. Vietnam 34 21.20N105.24E
Da'an China 32 45.30N124.18E
Ḑab'ah Jordan 44 31.36N 36.04E
Dabakala Ivory Coast 52 8.19N 4.24W
Daba Shan mts. China 33 32.00N109.00E
Dabat Ethiopia 49 12.58N 37.48E
Dabbāgh, Jabal mtn. Saudi Arabia 44 27.51N 35.43E
Dabhoi India 40 22.11N 73.26E
Dabie Shan mts. China 33 31.15N115.20E
Dabola Guinea 52 10.48N 11.02W
Dabra India 41 25.54N 78.20E
Dabu China 33 26.47N116.04E
Dacca see Dhākā Bangla. 41
Dachau Germany 20 48.15N 11.26E
Dadanawa Guyana 90 2.30N 59.30W
Dade City U.S.A. 85 28.23N 82.11W
Dādhar Pakistan 40 29.28N 67.39E
Dādra & Nagar Haveli d. India 40 20.05N 73.00E
Dādu Pakistan 40 26.44N 67.47E
Dadu He r. China 39 28.47N104.40E
Daet Phil. 37 14.07N122.58E
Dagali Norway 23 60.25N 8.27E
Dagana Senegal 52 16.28N 15.35W
Daga Post Sudan 49 9.12N 33.58E
Dagash Sudan 48 19.22N 33.24E
Dagu China 32 38.58N117.40E
Dagua P.N.G. 37 3.25S143.20E
Daguan China 30 27.44N103.53E
Dagupan Phil. 37 16.02N120.21E
Daguragu Australia 62 17.33S130.30E
Dagzê China 41 29.45N105.45E
Dagzê Co l. China 41 31.45N 87.50E
Dahan-e Qowmghī Afghan. 40 34.28N 66.31E
Da Hinggan Ling mts. China 31 50.00N122.10E
Dahlak Archipelago is. Ethiopia 48 15.45N 40.30E
Dahlak Kebir I. Ethiopia 48 15.38N 40.11E
Dahlem Germany 20 50.23N 6.33E
Dahlgren U.S.A. 85 38.20N 77.03W
Dahra Senegal 52 15.21N 15.29W
Dahujiang China 33 26.06N114.58E
Dahūk Iraq 42 36.52N 43.00E
Daḩy, Nafūd ad f. Saudi Arabia 45 22.00N 45.25E
Ḑaḩyah, 'Urūq f. Yemen 45 18.45N 51.15E
Dai Hai l. China 32 40.31N112.43E
Dailekh Nepal 41 28.50N 81.43E
Daimiel Spain 16 39.05N 3.35W
Daitō Japan 35 34.42N135.38E
Daiyun Shan mtn. China 33 25.41N118.11E
Dājal Pakistan 40 29.33N 70.23E
Dajarra Australia 64 21.42S139.31E
Dajing China 33 28.25N121.10E
Dakar Senegal 52 14.38N 17.27W
Dakhal, Wādī ad r. Egypt 44 28.49N 32.45E
Dākhilah, Al Wāḩāt ad oasis Egypt 42 25.30N 28.10E
Dakhla W. Sahara 50 23.43N 15.57W
Dakhlet Nouadhibou d. Mauritania 50 20.30N 16.00W
Dakingari Nigeria 53 11.40N 4.06E
Dakota City U.S.A. 82 42.25N 96.25W
Dakovica Yugo. 19 42.23N 20.25E
Dal r. Sweden 23 60.38N 17.27E
Dala Congo 54 1.40N 16.39E
Dalaba Guinea 52 10.47N 12.12W
Dalai Nur l. China 32 43.27N116.25E
Dalandzadgad Mongolia 32 43.30N104.18E
Da Lat Vietnam 34 11.56N108.25E
Dālbandin Pakistan 40 28.53N 64.25E
Dalbeattie U.K. 12 54.55N 3.49W
Dalby Australia 65 27.11S151.12E
Dalby Sweden 23 55.40N 13.20E
Dale Hordaland Norway 23 60.35N 5.49E
Dale Sogn og Fj. Norway 23 61.22N 5.24E
Dalen Norway 23 59.27N 8.00E
Dalhart U.S.A. 83 36.04N102.31W
Dalhousie Canada 77 48.04N 66.23W
Dalhousie Jammu & Kashmir 40 32.32N 75.59E
Dali China 30 25.33N100.09E
Dali China 30 25.42N100.11E
Dalian China 32 38.49N121.48E
Dalkeith U.K. 12 55.54N 3.04W
Dallas Oreg. U.S.A. 80 44.55N123.19W
Dallas Tex. U.S.A. 83 32.47N 96.48W
Dallastown U.S.A. 85 39.54N 76.39W
Dall I. U.S.A. 74 55.00N133.00W
Dalli Rajhāra India 41 20.35N 81.04E
Dalmally U.K. 12 56.25N 4.58W
Dalmas, Lac l. Canada 77 53.27N 71.50W
Dalmellington U.K. 12 55.19N 4.24W
Dalnerechensk Russian Fed. 31 45.55N133.45E
Daloa Ivory Coast 52 6.56N 6.28W
Dalou Shan mts. China 33 28.25N107.15E
Dalqū Sudan 48 20.07N 30.35E
Dalrymple, Mt. Australia 64 21.02S148.38E
Dalsingh Sarai India 41 25.40N 85.50E
Dalton Canada 76 48.10N 84.00W
Dalton U.S.A. 85 34.46N 84.59W
Daltonganj India 41 24.02N 84.04E
Dalupiri i. Phil. 33 19.05N121.13E
Dalvik Iceland 22 65.58N 18.28W
Dalwhinnie U.K. 12 56.56N 4.15W
Daly r. Australia 62 13.20S130.19E
Daly City U.S.A. 80 37.42N122.29W
Daly Waters town Australia 64 16.15S133.22E
Damā, Wādī r. Saudi Arabia 42 27.04N 35.48E
Damān India 40 20.25N 72.51E
Damān d. India 40 20.10N 73.00E
Damanhūr Egypt 44 31.03N 30.28E
Damar i. Indonesia 37 7.10S128.30E
Damascus see Dimashq Syria 44
Damaturu Nigeria 53 11.49N 11.50E
Damāvand, Qolleh-ye mtn. Iran 43 35.47N 52.04E
Damba Angola 54 6.44S 15.17E
Damen i. China 33 27.58N121.05E
Dāmghān Iran 43 36.09N 54.22E
Damiaoshan China 33 24.43N109.15E
Daming Shan mts. China 33 23.23N108.30E
Dammartin-en-Goële France 15 49.03N 2.41E
Dāmodar r. India 41 22.17N 88.05E
Damoh India 41 23.50N 79.27E
Damongo Ghana 52 9.06N 1.48W
Dampier Australia 62 20.40S116.42E
Dampier, Selat str. Pacific Oc. 37 0.30S130.50E
Dampier Land Australia 62 17.20S123.00E
Damqawt Yemen 45 16.34N 52.50E
Damxung China 41 30.32N 91.06E
Dana Canada 75 52.18N105.42W
Danané Ivory Coast 52 7.21N 8.10W
Da Nang Vietnam 34 16.04N108.13E
Dānāpur India 41 25.38N 85.03E
Danba China 30 30.57N101.55E
Danbury U.S.A. 85 41.24N 73.26W
Dand Afghan. 40 31.37N 65.41E
Dandaragan Australia 63 30.40S115.42E
Dande r. Angola 54 8.30S 13.23E
Dandeldhura Nepal 41 29.17N 80.36E
Dandenong Australia 67 37.59S145.14E
Dandong China 32 40.10N124.25E
Danger Is. Cook Is. 68 10.53S165.49W
Dangila Ethiopia 49 11.18N 36.54E
Dangqên China 41 31.41N 91.51E
Dangriga Belize 87 16.58N 88.13W
Dangshan China 32 34.25N116.24E
Dangyang China 33 30.52N111.40E
Daniel U.S.A. 80 42.52N110.04W
Daniel's Harbour Canada 77 50.14N 57.35W
Danilov Russian Fed. 24 58.10N 40.12E
Daning China 32 36.32N110.47E
Danisa Hills Kenya 55 3.10N 39.37E
Danja Nigeria 53 11.29N 7.30E
Danjiangkou Shuiku resr. China 32 32.42N111.20E
Danlí Honduras 87 14.02N 86.30W
Dannenberg Germany 20 53.06N 11.05E
Dannevirke New Zealand 60 40.12S176.08E
Dannhauser R.S.A. 56 28.00S 30.03E
Dansville U.S.A. 84 42.34N 77.41W
Dantewāra India 41 18.54N 81.21E
Danube r. Europe 21 45.26N 29.38E
Danube, Mouths of the see Dunării, Delta f. Romania 21
Danville Canada 77 45.47N 72.01W
Danville Ill. U.S.A. 82 40.09N 87.37W
Danville Ky. U.S.A. 85 37.40N 84.49W
Danville Va. U.S.A. 85 36.34N 79.25W
Dan Xian China 33 19.30N109.35E
Daordeng China 32 40.47N119.05E
Daosa India 40 26.53N 76.20E
Daoukro Ivory Coast 52 7.10N 3.58W
Dao Xian China 33 25.32N111.35E
Daozhen China 33 28.46N107.45E
Dapango Togo 52 10.51N 0.15E
Dapingfang China 32 41.25N120.07E
Da Qaidam China 30 37.44N 95.08E
Daqinggou China 32 41.22N114.13E
Daqing Shan mts. China 32 41.00N111.00E
Daqqāq Sudan 49 12.56N 26.58E
Daqq-e Patargān f. Iran 43 33.30N 60.40E
Dar'ā Syria 44 32.37N 36.06E
Dārāb Iran 43 28.45N 54.34E
Darāban Pakistan 40 31.44N 70.20E
Darabani Romania 21 48.11N 26.35E
Darakht-e Yahyā Afghan. 40 31.50N 68.08E
Dārān Iran 43 33.00N 50.27E
Darband, Kūh-e mtn. Iran 43 31.33N 57.08E
Darbhanga India 41 26.10N 85.54E
Darby Mont. U.S.A. 80 46.01N114.11W
Darby Penn. U.S.A. 85 39.54N 75.15W
D'Arcy Canada 74 50.33N122.32W
Dardanelles see Çanakkale Boğazi str. Turkey 19
Dar es Salaam Tanzania 55 6.51S 39.18E
Dar es Salaam d. Tanzania 55 6.45S 39.10E
Dareton Australia 66 34.04S142.04E
Darfield New Zealand 60 43.29S172.07E
Dargan Ata Turkmenistan 28 40.30N 62.10E
Dargaville New Zealand 60 35.57S173.53E
Dargo Australia 67 37.30S147.16E
Darhan Mongolia 30 49.34N106.23E
Darie Hills Somali Rep. 45 8.15N 47.25E
Darién, Golfo del g. Colombia 90 9.20N 77.30W
Darjeeling India 41 27.02N 88.16E
Darkan Australia 63 33.19S116.42E
Darke Peak mtn. Australia 66 33.28S136.12E
Darling r. Australia 66 34.05S141.57E
Darling Downs f. Australia 65 28.00S149.45E
Darling Range mts. Australia 63 32.00S116.30E
Darlington U.K. 10 54.33N 1.33W
Darlington Point town Australia 67 34.36S146.01E
Darłowe Poland 20 54.26N 16.23E
Darmstadt Germany 20 49.52N 8.30E
Darnah Libya 48 32.45N 22.39E
Darnah d. Libya 48 31.30N 23.30E
Darnétal France 15 49.27N 1.09E
Darnick Australia 66 32.55S143.39E
Darnley, C. Antarctica 96 68.00S 69.00E
Daroca Spain 16 41.09N 1.25W
Darreh Gaz Iran 43 37.22N 59.08E
Dar Rounga f. C.A.R. 49 9.25N 21.30E
Dartmoor Australia 66 37.58S141.19E
Dartmoor Forest hills U.K. 11 50.33N 3.55W
Dartmouth Canada 77 44.40N 63.34W
Dartmouth U.K. 11 50.21N 3.35W
Dartmouth Resr. Australia 67 36.36S147.38E
Dartry Mts. Rep. of Ire. 13 54.23N 8.25W
Daru P.N.G. 64 9.04S143.12E
Darvaza Turkmenistan 28 40.12N 58.24E
Darvel, Teluk b. Malaysia 36 4.40N118.30E
Darwen U.K. 10 53.42N 2.29W
Dārwha India 41 20.19N 77.46E
Darwin Australia 64 12.23S130.44E
Daryācheh-ye Bakhtegān l. Iran 43 29.20N 54.05E
Daryācheh-ye Namak l. Iran 43 34.45N 51.36E
Daryācheh-ye Orūmīyeh l. Iran 43 37.40N 45.28E
Daryācheh-ye Sīstān f. Iran 43 31.00N 61.15E
Darya Khān Pakistan 40 31.48N 71.06E
Daryāpur India 40 20.56N 77.20E
Dasāda India 40 23.19N 71.50E
Dasht r. Pakistan 40 25.10N 61.40E
Dashte-e Mārgow des. Afghan. 43 30.45N 63.00E
Dasht-e Kavīr des. Iran 43 34.40N 55.00E
Dasht-e Lūt des. Iran 43 31.30N 58.00E
Dashui Nur China 32 42.45N116.47E
Daspalla India 41 20.21N 84.51E
Dassa-Zoumé Benin 53 7.50N 2.13E
Dastgardān Iran 43 34.19N 56.51E
Dastjerd Iran 43 34.33N 50.15E
Datia India 41 25.40N 78.28E
Datong China 32 40.10N113.15E
Datteln Germany 14 51.40N 7.20E
Datu, Tanjung c. Malaysia 36 2.00N109.30E
Datu Piang Phil. 37 7.02N124.30E
Daua r. Kenya see Dawa r. Ethiopia 49
Dāud Khel Pakistan 40 32.53N 71.34E
Daudnagar India 41 25.02N 84.24E
Daugavpils Latvia 24 55.52N 26.31E
Daun Germany 14 50.11N 6.50E
Dauphin Canada 75 51.09N100.03W
Dauphiné, Alpes du mts. France 17 44.35N 5.45E
Dauphin L. Canada 75 51.17N 99.48W
Daura Nigeria 53 13.05N 8.18E
Dāvangere India 38 14.30N 75.52E
Davao Phil. 37 7.05N125.38E
Davao G. Phil. 37 6.30N126.00E
Daveluyville Canada 77 46.12N 72.08W
Davenport U.S.A. 82 41.32N 90.36W
Daventry U.K. 11 52.16N 1.10W
David Panama 87 8.26N 82.26W
David-Gorodok Belorussia 21 52.04N 27.10E
Davis U.S.A. 80 38.33N121.44W
Davis Creek town U.S.A. 80 41.44N120.24W
Davis Sea Antarctica 96 66.00S 90.00E
Davis Str. N. America 73 66.00N 58.00W
Davlekanovo Russian Fed. 24 54.12N 55.00E
Davos Switz. 20 46.47N 9.50E
Dawa China 32 40.58N122.00E
Dawa r. Ethiopia 49 4.11N 42.06E
Dawaxung China 41 31.26N 85.06E
Dawei see Tavoy Burma 34
Dawlish U.K. 11 50.34N 3.28W
Dawna Range mts. Burma 34 17.00N 98.00E
Dawson Canada 72 64.04N139.24W
Dawson U.S.A. 85 31.47N 84.27W
Dawson Creek town Canada 74 55.45N120.15W
Dawson Range f. Canada 72 62.40N139.00W
Dawu China 30 31.00N101.09E
Dax France 17 43.43N 1.03W
Daxian China 33 31.10N107.28E
Daxing China 32 39.44N116.20E
Daylesford Australia 66 37.22S144.12E
Dayman r. Uruguay 93 31.25S 58.00W
Dayong China 33 29.06N110.24E
Dayr az Zawr Syria 42 35.20N 40.08E
Dayton N.Y. U.S.A. 76 42.25N 78.58W
Dayton Ohio U.S.A. 84 39.45N 84.10W
Dayton Tenn. U.S.A. 85 35.30N 85.01W
Dayton Wash. U.S.A. 80 46.19N117.59W
Daytona Beach town U.S.A. 85 29.11N 81.01W
Dayu China 33 25.24N114.22E
Da Yunhe canal China 32 39.10N117.12E
Dazhu China 33 30.50N107.12E
De Aar R.S.A. 56 30.39S 24.01E
Dead Sea Jordan 44 31.25N 35.30E
Deal U.K. 11 51.13N 1.25E
De'an China 33 29.20N115.46E
Deán Funes Argentina 92 30.25S 64.20W
Dearborn U.S.A. 84 42.18N 83.14W
Dease r. Canada 74 59.54N128.30W
Dease Arm b. Canada 72 66.52N119.37W
Dease L. Canada 74 58.05N130.04W
Death Valley f. U.S.A. 81 36.30N117.00W
Death Valley town U.S.A. 81 36.18N116.25W
Death Valley Nat. Monument U.S.A. 80 36.30N117.00W
Deauville France 15 49.21N 0.04E
Debar Macedonia 19 41.31N 20.31E
Debica Poland 21 50.04N 21.24E
Deblin Poland 21 51.35N 21.50E
Deborah, L. Australia 63 30.45S119.07E
Debre Birhan Ethiopia 49 9.40N 39.33E
Debrecen Hungary 21 47.30N 21.37E
Debre Tabor Ethiopia 49 11.50N 38.05E
Decatur Ala. U.S.A. 85 34.36N 87.00W
Decatur Ga. U.S.A. 85 33.45N 84.17W
Decatur Ill. U.S.A. 82 39.51N 89.32W
Decatur Ind. U.S.A. 84 40.50N 84.57W
Deccan f. India 38 18.30N 77.30E
Decelles, Lac l. Canada 76 47.40N 78.10W
Dechu India 40 26.47N 72.20E
Děčín Czech Republic 20 50.48N 14.15E
Decize France 20 46.50N 3.27E
De Cocksdorp Neth. 14 53.12N 4.52E
Decorah U.S.A. 82 43.18N 91.48W
Deda Romania 21 46.57N 24.53E
Dédi Ivory Coast 52 8.34N 3.33W
Dediāpada India 40 21.35N 73.40E
Dedza Malaŵi 55 14.20S 34.24E
Dee r. D. and G. U.K. 12 54.50N 4.05W
Dee r. Grampian U.K. 12 57.07N 2.04W
Dee r. Wales U.K. 10 53.13N 3.05W
Deep B. Canada 74 61.15N116.35W
Deep River town Canada 76 46.04N 77.29W
Deepwater Australia 67 29.26S151.51E
Deep Well Australia 64 24.25S134.05E
Deer Lake town Canada 77 49.07N 57.35W
Deer Lodge U.S.A. 80 46.24N112.44W
Deesa India 40 24.15N 72.10E
Deeth U.S.A. 80 41.04N115.18W
Deex Nugaaleed r. Somali Rep. 45 7.58N 49.52E
Defiance U.S.A. 84 41.17N 84.21W
De Funiak Springs town U.S.A. 85 30.41N 86.08W
Deggendorf Germany 20 48.51N 12.59E
De Grey r. Australia 62 20.12S119.11E
Deh Bīd Iran 43 30.38N 53.12E
Dehej India 40 21.42N 72.35E
Dehibat Tunisia 51 32.01N 10.42E
Dehra Dūn India 41 30.19N 78.02E
Dehri India 41 24.52N 84.11E
Deh Shū Afghan. 40 30.28N 63.25E
Dehua China 33 25.30N118.14E
Deinze Belgium 14 50.59N 3.32E
Dej Romania 21 47.08N 23.55E
Deje Sweden 23 59.36N 13.28E
Dejiang China 33 28.19N108.05E
Dek'emhāre Ethiopia 48 15.05N 39.02E
Dekese Zaïre 54 3.25S 21.24E
Dekina Nigeria 53 7.43N 7.04E
De Land U.S.A. 85 29.02N 81.18W
Delano U.S.A. 81 35.41N119.15W
Delārām Afghan. 40 32.11N 63.25E
Delaronde L. Canada 75 54.05N107.05W
Delaware d. U.S.A. 85 39.10N 75.30W
Delaware r. U.S.A. 85 39.20N 75.25W
Delaware town U.S.A. 84 40.18N 83.06W
Delaware B. U.S.A. 85 39.05N 75.15W
Delaware Water Gap town U.S.A. 85 40.59N 75.09W
Delaware Water Gap Nat. Recreation Area U.S.A. 85 41.07N 75.06W
Delegate Australia 67 37.03S148.58E
Delfinópolis Brazil 94 20.21S 46.51W
Delft Neth. 14 52.01N 4.23E
Delfzijl Neth. 14 53.20N 6.56E
Delgado, C. Mozambique 55 10.45S 40.38E
Delhi India 40 28.40N 77.13E
Delhi d. India 40 28.37N 77.10E
Delicias Mexico 81 28.13N105.28W
Délimbé C.A.R. 49 9.53N 22.37E
Delingha China 30 37.16N 97.12E
Dell City U.S.A. 81 31.56N105.12W
Delmar U.S.A. 85 38.27N 75.34W
Delmarva Pen. U.S.A. 85 38.48N 75.47W
Delmenhorst Germany 20 53.03N 8.37E
De Long Mts. U.S.A. 72 68.20N162.00W
Delphos U.S.A. 84 40.50N 84.21W

Del Rio to **Dráma**

Del Rio U.S.A. 83 29.22N100.54W
Delta *d.* Nigeria 53 5.30N 6.00E
Delta Colo. U.S.A. 80 38.44N108.04W
Delta Utah U.S.A. 80 39.21N112.35W
Delungra Australia 67 29.38S150.50E
Demak Indonesia 37 6.53S110.40E
Demba Zaïre 54 5.28S 22.14E
Dembi Ethiopia 49 8.05N 36.27E
Dembia C.A.R. 49 5.07N 24.25E
Dembi Dolo Ethiopia 49 8.30N 34.48E
Demer *r.* Belgium 14 50.59N 4.42E
Deming U.S.A. 81 32.16N107.45W
Demmin Germany 20 53.54N 13.02E
Demmitt Canada 74 55.20N119.50W
Demonte Italy 15 44.19N 7.17E
Demopolis U.S.A. 83 32.31N 87.50W
Demotte U.S.A. 84 41.07N 87.14W
Dêmqog China 41 32.43N 79.29E
Denain France 14 50.20N 3.24E
Denakil *f.* Ethiopia 49 13.00N 41.00E
Denbigh U.K. 10 53.11N 3.25W
Den Burg Neth. 14 53.03N 4.47E
Dendermonde Belgium 14 51.01N 4.07E
Dendre *r.* Belgium 14 51.01N 4.07E
Dengkou China 32 40.18N106.59E
Deng Xian China 32 32.44N112.00E
Denham Australia 62 25.54S113.35E
Denham Range *mts.* Australia 64 21.55S147.46E
Den Helder Neth. 14 52.58N 4.46E
Denia Spain 16 38.51N 0.07E
Deniliquin Australia 67 35.33S144.58E
Denison Iowa U.S.A. 82 42.01N 95.21W
Denison Tex. U.S.A. 83 33.45N 96.33W
Denizli Turkey 42 37.46N 29.05E
Denman Australia 67 32.23S150.42E
Denmark Australia 63 34.54S117.25E
Denmark Europe 23 55.50N 10.00E
Denmark Str. Greenland/Iceland 95 66.00N 25.00W
Den Oever Neth. 14 52.56N 5.01E
Denpasar Indonesia 37 8.40S115.14E
Denton Mont. U.S.A. 80 47.19N109.57W
Denton Tex. U.S.A. 83 33.13N 97.08W
D'Entrecasteaux, Pt. Australia 63 34.50S116.00E
D'Entrecasteaux, Recifs *reef* N. Cal. 68 18.00S163.10E
D'Entrecasteaux Is. P.N.G. 64 9.30S150.40E
Denver U.S.A. 80 39.43N105.01W
Denys *r.* Canada 76 55.05N 77.22W
Deo *r.* Cameroon 53 8.33N 12.45E
Deogarh Madhya P. India 41 24.33N 78.15E
Deogarh *mtn.* India 41 23.32N 82.16E
Deogarh Orissa India 41 21.32N 84.44E
Deogarh Rāj. India 40 25.32N 73.54E
Deogarh Hills India 41 23.45N 82.30E
Deoghar India 41 24.29N 86.42E
Deolāli India 40 19.57N 73.50E
Deoli India 40 25.45N 75.23E
Deori India 41 23.08N 78.41E
Deoria India 41 26.31N 83.47E
Deori Khās India 41 23.24N 79.01E
Deosil India 41 23.42N 82.15E
De Peel *f.* Belgium 14 51.30N 5.50E
Depew U.S.A. 84 42.54N 78.41W
Dêqên China 30 28.45N 98.58E
De Queen U.S.A. 83 34.02N 94.21W
De Quincy U.S.A. 83 30.27N 93.26W
Dera Bugti Pakistan 40 29.02N 69.09E
Dera Ghāzi Khān Pakistan 40 30.03N 70.38E
Dera Ismāīl Khān Pakistan 40 31.50N 70.54E
Derazhnya Ukraine 21 49.18N 27.28E
Derbent Russian Fed. 43 42.03N 48.18E
Derby Tas. Australia 65 41.08S147.47E
Derby W.A. Australia 62 17.19S123.38E
Derby U.K. 10 52.55N 1.28W
Derby U.S.A. 76 42.41N 78.58W
Derbyshire *d.* U.K. 10 52.55N 1.28W
Derg, Lough Donegal Rep. of Ire. 13 54.37N 7.55W
Derg, Lough Tipperary Rep. of Ire. 13 52.57N 8.18W
De Ridder U.S.A. 83 30.51N 93.17W
Dernieres, Isles *is.* U.S.A. 83 29.02N 90.47W
Déroute, Passage de la *str.* France/U.K. 11 49.10N 1.45W
Derrynasaggart Mts. Rep. of Ire. 13 51.58N 9.15W
Derryveagh Mts. Rep. of Ire. 13 55.00N 8.07W
Derudeb Sudan 48 17.32N 36.06E
Derval France 15 47.40N 1.40W
Derwent *r.* Cumbria U.K. 10 54.38N 3.34W
Derwent *r.* Derbys. U.K. 9 52.52N 1.19W
Derwent *r.* N. Yorks. U.K. 10 53.44N 0.57W
Desaguadero *r.* Bolivia 92 18.24S 67.05W
Desappointement, Îles du *is.* Pacific Oc. 69 14.02S141.24W
Descanso Mexico 81 32.14N116.58W
Deschutes *r.* U.S.A. 80 45.38N120.54W
Desē Ethiopia 49 11.05N 39.41E
Deseado Argentina 93 47.39S 65.20W
Deseado *r.* Argentina 93 47.45S 65.50W
Desenzano del Garda Italy 15 45.28N 10.32E
Deserta Grande *is.* Madeira Is. 95 32.32N 16.30W
Desert Center U.S.A. 81 33.44N115.25W
Deshnoke India 40 27.48N 73.21E
Des Moines Iowa U.S.A. 82 41.35N 93.37W
Des Moines N.Mex. U.S.A. 80 36.46N103.50W
Des Moines *r.* U.S.A. 82 40.22N 91.26W
Desna *r.* Ukraine 21 50.32N 30.37E
De Soto U.S.A. 83 38.08N 90.33W
Dessau Germany 20 51.51N 12.15E
Dete Zimbabwe 56 18.39S 26.49E
Detroit U.S.A. 84 42.23N 83.05W
Detroit Lakes *town* U.S.A. 82 46.49N 95.51W
Deūlgaon Rāja India 40 20.01N 76.02E
Deurne Belgium 14 51.13N 4.26E
Deurne Neth. 14 51.29N 5.44E
Deutsche Bucht *b.* Germany 20 54.00N 8.15E
Deva Romania 21 45.54N 22.55E
Deventer Neth. 14 52.15N 6.10E
Deveron *r.* U.K. 12 57.40N 2.30W
Devikot India 40 26.42N 71.12E
Devil's Bridge U.K. 11 52.23N 3.50W
Devils Lake *town* U.S.A. 82 48.07N 98.59W
Devin Bulgaria 19 41.44N 24.24E
Devizes U.K. 11 51.21N 2.00W
Devon *d.* U.K. 11 50.50N 3.40W
Devon I. Canada 73 75.00N 86.00W
Devonport Australia 65 41.09S146.16E
Devrez *r.* Turkey 42 41.07N 34.25E
Dewās India 40 22.58N 76.04E
De Witt U.S.A. 83 34.18N 91.20W
Dewsbury U.K. 10 53.42N 1.38W
Dexter U.S.A. 83 36.48N 89.57W
Deyang China 33 31.05N104.18E
Dey-Dey L. Australia 65 29.12S131.02E
Dez *r.* Iran 43 31.38N 48.54E
Dezadeash L. Canada 74 60.28N136.58W
Dezfūl Iran 43 32.24N 48.27E
Dezhou China 32 37.23N116.16E
Dezh Shāhpūr Iran 43 35.31N 46.10E
Dhahab Egypt 44 28.30N 34.31E
Dhahran *see* Aẓ Ẓahrān Saudi Arabia 43
Dhākā Bangla. 41 23.43N 90.25E
Dhamār Yemen 45 14.33N 44.24E
Dhamtari India 41 20.41N 81.34E
Dhānbād India 41 23.48N 86.27E
Dhandhuka India 40 22.22N 71.59E
Dhangarhi Nepal 41 28.41N 80.38E
Dhankuta Nepal 41 26.59N 87.21E
Dhār India 40 22.36N 75.18E
Dharampur India 40 20.32N 73.11E
Dharān Bāzār Nepal 41 26.49N 87.17E
Dharangaon India 40 21.01N 75.16E
Dhāri India 40 21.20N 71.01E
Dharmābād India 41 18.54N 77.51E
Dharmjaygarh India 41 22.28N 83.13E
Dharmsāla India 40 32.13N 76.19E
Dhārni India 40 21.33N 76.53E
Dhaulāgiri *mtn.* Nepal 41 28.42N 83.31E
Dhebar L. India 40 24.16N 74.00E
Dhenkānāl India 41 20.40N 85.36E
Dhiinsoor Somali Rep. 45 2.28N 43.00E
Dhodhekánisos *is.* Greece 19 37.00N 27.00E
Dholka India 40 22.43N 72.28E
Dholpur India 41 26.42N 77.54E
Dhorāji India 40 21.44N 70.27E
Dhrāngadhra India 40 22.59N 71.28E
Dhrol India 40 22.34N 70.25E
Dhubri India 41 26.02N 89.58E
Dhule India 40 20.54N 74.47E
Dhuliān India 41 24.41N 87.58E
Dhuudo Somali Rep. 45 9.20N 50.14E
Dialakoro Mali 52 12.18N 7.54W
Diamante Argentina 93 32.05S 60.35W
Diamantina *r.* Australia 64 26.45S139.10E
Diamantina Brazil 94 18.17S 43.37W
Diamantina, Chapada *hills* Brazil 91 13.00S 42.30W
Diamantino Brazil 94 14.25S 56.29W
Diamond Harbour India 41 22.12N 88.12E
Diana's Peak *mtn.* St. Helena 95 15.58S 5.42W
Dianbai China 33 21.30N111.01E
Diane Bank *is.* Australia 64 15.50S149.48E
Dianjiang China 33 30.14N107.27E
Diapaga Burkina 53 12.04N 1.48E
Dibai India 41 28.13N 78.15E
Dibaya Zaïre 54 6.31S 22.57E
Dibi Cameroon 53 7.09N 13.43E
Dibrugarh India 39 27.29N 94.56E
Dibs Sudan 49 14.18N 24.23E
Dickinson U.S.A. 82 46.53N102.47W
Dicle *r.* Turkey *see* Dijlah *r.* Asia 42
Didcot U.K. 11 51.36N 1.14W
Didiéni Mali 52 14.05N 7.50W
Dīdwāna India 40 27.24N 74.34E
Die France 17 44.45N 5.23E
Diefenbaker, L. Canada 75 51.00N106.55W
Diekirch Lux. 14 49.52N 6.10E
Diélette France 15 49.33N 1.52W
Diéma Mali 52 14.32N 9.03W
Diemen Neth. 14 52.22N 4.58E
Diemuchuoke Jammu & Kashmir 41 32.42N 79.29E
Dien Bien Phu Vietnam 34 21.23N103.02E
Diepholz Germany 20 52.35N 8.21E
Dieppe France 15 49.55N 1.05E
Dierdorf Germany 14 50.33N 7.38E
Dieren Neth. 14 52.03N 6.06E
Dierks U.S.A. 83 34.07N 94.01W
Diesdorf Germany 20 52.45N 10.52E
Diest Belgium 14 50.59N 5.03E
Dieuze France 17 48.49N 6.43E
Dif Kenya 55 1.04N 40.57E
Diffa Niger 53 13.19N 12.35E
Diffa *d.* Niger 53 16.00N 13.00E
Dig India 40 27.20N 77.25E
Digby Canada 77 44.30N 65.47W
Dighton U.S.A. 82 38.29N100.28W
Digne France 17 44.05N 6.14E
Digoin France 17 46.29N 3.59E
Digras India 41 20.07N 77.43E
Digri Pakistan 40 25.10N 69.07E
Digul *r.* Indonesia 37 7.10S139.08E
Dijlah *r.* Asia 43 31.00N 47.27E
Dijle *r.* Belgium 14 51.02N 4.25E
Dijon France 17 47.20N 5.02E
Dikhil Djibouti 49 11.06N 42.22E
Dikili Turkey 19 39.05N 26.52E
Dikirnis Egypt 44 31.05N 31.35E
Dikodougou Ivory Coast 52 9.00N 5.45W
Diksmuide Belgium 14 51.01N 2.52E
Dikwa Nigeria 53 12.01N 13.55E
Dili Indonesia 37 8.35S125.35E
Dilley U.S.A. 83 28.40N 99.10W
Dilling Sudan 49 12.03N 29.39E
Dillingham U.S.A. 72 59.02N158.29W
Dillon U.S.A. 80 45.13N112.38W
Dilolo Zaïre 54 10.39S 22.20E
Dimashq Syria 44 33.30N 36.19E
Dimbelenge Zaïre 54 5.32S 23.04E
Dimbokro Ivory Coast 52 6.43N 4.46W
Dimboola Australia 66 36.27S142.02E
Dîmboviţa *r.* Romania 21 44.13N 26.22E
Dimitrovgrad Bulgaria 19 42.01N 25.34E
Dimona Israel 44 31.04N 35.01E
Dinagat *i.* Phil. 37 10.15N125.30E
Dinājpur Bangla. 41 25.38N 88.38E
Dinan France 17 48.27N 2.02W
Dinant Belgium 14 50.16N 4.55E
Dinar Turkey 42 38.05N 30.09E
Dīnār, Kūh-e *mtn.* Iran 43 30.45N 51.39E
Dinara Planina *mts.* Europe 20 44.00N 16.30E
Dindar *r.* Sudan 48 14.06N 33.40E
Dindar Nat. Park Sudan 49 12.00N 35.00E
Dindigul India 38 10.23N 78.00E
Dindori India 41 22.57N 81.05E
Dinga Pakistan 40 25.26N 67.10E
Dingbian China 32 37.36N107.38E
Dinggyê China 41 28.18N 88.06E
Dingle Rep. of Ire. 13 52.09N 10.17W
Dingle B. Rep. of Ire. 13 52.05N 10.12W
Dingolfing Germany 20 48.38N 12.31E
Dinguiraye Guinea 52 11.19N 10.49W
Dingwall U.K. 12 57.35N 4.26W
Dingxi China 32 35.33N104.32E
Ding Xian China 32 38.30N115.00E
Dingxing China 32 39.17N115.46E
Dinokwe Botswana 56 23.24S 26.40E
Dinuba U.S.A. 81 36.32N119.23W
Diö Sweden 23 56.38N 14.13E
Diodār India 40 24.06N 71.47E
Dioïla Mali 52 12.30N 6.49W
Diourbel Senegal 52 14.30N 16.10W
Diplo Pakistan 40 24.28N 69.35E
Dipolog Phil. 37 8.34N123.28E
Dirdal Norway 23 58.47N 6.14E
Diré Mali 52 16.16N 3.24W
Direction, C. Australia 64 12.51S143.32E
Dirē Dawa Ethiopia 49 9.35N 41.50E
Dirico Angola 54 17.58S 20.40E
Dirj Libya 51 30.09N 10.26E
Dirk Hartog I. Australia 62 25.50S113.00E
Dirranbandi Australia 67 28.35S148.10E
Disappointment, L. Australia 62 23.30S122.55E
Disaster B. Australia 67 37.20S149.58E
Discovery Canada 72 63.10N113.58W
Discovery B. Australia 66 38.12S141.07E
Disko *i.* Greenland 73 69.45N 53.00W
Diss U.K. 11 52.23N 1.06E
District of Columbia *d.* U.S.A. 85 38.55N 77.00W
Distrito Federal *d.* Brazil 91 15.45S 47.50W
Distrito Federal *d.* Mexico 86 19.20N 99.10W
Disûq Egypt 44 31.09N 30.39E
Diu India 40 20.42N 70.59E
Diu *d.* India 40 20.45N 70.59E
Diver Canada 76 46.44N 79.30W
Dives *r.* France 15 49.19N 0.05W
Divinópolis Brazil 94 20.08S 44.55W
Divnoye Russian Fed. 25 45.55N 43.21E
Divo Ivory Coast 52 5.48N 5.15W
Divriği Turkey 42 39.23N 38.06E
Diwāl Qol Afghan. 40 34.19N 67.54E
Dixcove Ghana 52 4.49N 1.57W
Dixie U.S.A. 80 45.34N115.28W
Dixon Ill. U.S.A. 82 41.50N 89.29W
Dixon N.Mex. U.S.A. 81 36.12N105.33W
Dixon Entrance *str.* U.S.A./Canada 74 54.25N132.30W
Diyālā *r.* Iraq 43 33.13N 44.33E
Diyarbakir Turkey 42 37.55N 40.14E
Dja *r.* Cameroon 54 1.38N 16.03E
Djabéta Gabon 54 0.45N 14.00E
Djado Niger 53 21.00N 12.20E
Djado, Plateau du *f.* Niger 53 22.00N 12.30E
Djambala Congo 54 2.33S 14.38E
Djanet Algeria 51 24.34N 9.29E
Djelfa Algeria 51 34.40N 3.15E
Djema C.A.R. 49 6.03N 25.19E
Djénné Mali 52 13.55N 4.31W
Djerba, Île de *i.* Tunisia 51 33.48N 10.54E
Djerid, Chott *f.* Tunisia 51 33.42N 8.26E
Djibo Burkina 52 14.09N 1.38W
Djibouti Africa 49 12.00N 42.50E
Djibouti *town* Djibouti 49 11.35N 43.11E
Djilbabo Plain *f.* Ethiopia 49 4.00N 39.10E
Djolu Zaïre 54 0.35N 22.28E
Djouah *r.* Gabon 54 1.16N 13.12E
Djougou Benin 53 9.40N 1.47E
Djugu Zaïre 55 1.55N 30.31E
Djúpivogur Iceland 22 64.41N 14.16W
Dmitriya Lapteva, Proliv *str.* Russian Fed. 29 73.00N142.00E
Dnepr *r.* Ukraine *see* Dneiper *r.* Europe 21
Dneprodzerzhinsk Ukraine 25 48.30N 34.37E
Dnepropetrovsk Ukraine 25 48.29N 35.00E
Dneprovskaya Nizmennost *f.* Belorussia 21 52.30N 29.45E
Dneprovsko-Bugskiy Kanal Belorussia 21 52.03N 25.35E
Dnestr *r.* Ukraine *see* Dniester *r.* Europe 21
Dnieper *r.* Europe 21 50.00N 31.00E
Dniester *r.* Europe 21 46.21N 30.20E
Dno Russian Fed. 24 57.50N 30.00E
Doba Chad 53 8.40N 16.50E
Dobane C.A.R. 49 6.24N 24.42E
Dobele Latvia 23 56.37N 23.16E
Dobo Indonesia 37 5.46S134.13E
Doboj Bosnia-Herzegovina 21 44.44N 18.02E
Dobrich Bulgaria 19 43.34N 27.52E
Dobrodzień Poland 21 50.44N 18.27E
Dobruja *f.* Romania 21 44.30N 28.15E
Dobrush Belorussia 21 52.24N 31.19E
Dobryanka Russian Fed. 24 58.30N 56.26E
Dobzha China 41 28.28N 88.13E
Doce *r.* Brazil 94 19.32S 39.57W
Docking U.K. 10 52.55N 0.39E
Doda Jammu & Kashmir 40 33.08N 75.34E
Doda, Lac *l.* Canada 76 49.24N 75.14W
Dodecanese *is. see* Dhodhekánisos *is.* Greece 19
Dodge City U.S.A. 83 37.45N100.01W
Dodman Pt. U.K. 11 50.13N 4.48W
Dodoma Tanzania 55 6.10S 35.40E
Dodoma *d.* Tanzania 55 6.00S 36.00E
Dodson U.S.A. 80 48.24N108.15W
Doetinchem Neth. 14 51.57N 6.17E
Dogai Coring *l.* China 39 34.30N 89.00E
Dog Creek *town* Canada 74 51.35N122.14W
Dogger Bank *f.* North Sea 9 54.45N 2.00E
Dogubayazit Turkey 43 39.32N 44.08E
Do'gyaling China 41 31.58N 88.24E
Doha *see* Ad Dawḩah Qatar 43
Dohad India 40 22.50N 74.16E
Dohhi India 41 24.32N 84.54E
Doilungdêqên China 41 30.06N 90.32E
Dokkum Neth. 14 53.20N 6.00E
Dokri Pakistan 40 27.23N 68.06E
Dolbeau Canada 77 48.53N 72.14W
Dol-de-Bretagne France 15 48.33N 1.45W
Dole France 17 47.05N 5.30E
Dolgellau U.K. 11 52.44N 3.53W
Dolina Ukraine 21 49.00N 23.59E
Dolinskaya Ukraine 25 48.06N 32.46E
Dollard *b.* Germany 14 53.20N 7.10E
Dolny Kubín Slovakia 21 49.12N 19.17E
Dolomiti *mts.* Italy 15 46.25N 11.50E
Dolores Argentina 93 36.19S 57.40W
Dolores Mexico 81 28.53N108.27W
Dolores Uruguay 93 33.33S 58.13W
Dolores U.S.A. 80 37.28N108.30W
Dolphin and Union Str. Canada 72 69.20N118.00W
Doma Nigeria 53 8.23N 8.21E
Domadare Somali Rep. 49 1.48N 41.13E
Domažlice Czech Republic 20 49.27N 12.56E
Dombås Norway 23 62.05N 9.08E
Dombe Grande Angola 54 13.00S 13.06E
Dombey, C. Australia 66 37.12S139.43E
Dombóvár Hungary 21 46.23N 18.08E
Domburg Neth. 14 51.35N 3.31E
Domfront France 15 48.36N 0.39W
Dominica Windward Is. 87 15.30N 61.30W
Dominican Republic C. America 87 18.00N 70.00W
Dominion L. Canada 77 52.40N 61.42W
Dommel *r.* Neth. 14 51.44N 5.17E
Domo Ethiopia 45 7.54N 46.52E
Domodossola Italy 15 46.07N 8.17E
Domuyo *mtn.* Argentina 93 36.37S 70.28W
Don Mexico 81 26.26N109.02W
Don *r.* Russian Fed. 25 47.06N 39.16E
Don *r.* England U.K. 10 53.41N 0.50W
Don *r.* Scotland U.K. 12 57.10N 2.05W
Donaghadee U.K. 13 54.39N 5.33W
Donald Australia 66 36.25S143.04E
Donaldsonville U.S.A. 83 30.06N 90.59W
Donau *r.* Germany *see* Danube *r.* Europe 20
Donaueschingen Germany 20 47.57N 8.29E
Donauwörth Germany 20 48.44N 10.48E
Don Benito Spain 16 38.57N 5.52W
Doncaster U.K. 10 53.31N 1.09W
Dondaicha India 40 21.20N 74.34E
Dondo Angola 54 9.40S 14.25E
Dondo Mozambique 57 19.39S 34.39E
Donegal Rep. of Ire. 13 54.39N 8.06W
Donegal *d.* Rep. of Ire. 13 54.52N 8.00W
Donegal B. Rep. of Ire. 13 54.32N 8.18W
Donegal Pt. Rep. of Ire. 13 52.43N 9.38W
Donetsk Ukraine 25 48.00N 37.50E
Donga Nigeria 53 7.45N 10.05E
Donga *r.* Nigeria 53 8.20N 10.00E
Dongara Australia 63 29.15S114.56E
Dongargarh India 41 21.12N 80.44E
Dongbei Pingyuan *f.* China 32 42.30N123.00E
Dongchuan China 30 26.10N103.02E
Dongco China 41 32.07N 84.35E
Dongfang China 33 19.05N108.39E
Donggala Indonesia 36 0.48S119.45E
Donggou China 32 39.52N124.08E
Dongguang China 32 37.53N116.32E
Donghai China 32 34.35N118.49E
Donghai *i.* China 33 21.02N110.25E
Dong Hoi Vietnam 34 17.32N106.35E
Dong Jiang *r.* China 33 23.00N113.33E
Dongkalang Indonesia 37 0.12N120.07E
Dongling China 32 41.44N123.32E
Dongou Congo 54 2.05N 18.00E
Dongping Hu *l.* China 32 35.55N116.15E
Dongqiao China 41 31.57N 90.30E
Dongsheng China 32 39.49N109.59E
Dongtai China 32 32.42N120.26E
Dongting Hu *l.* China 33 29.10N113.00E
Dongtou *i.* China 33 27.50N121.08E
Dong Ujimqin Qi China 32 45.33N116.50E
Dongxi China 33 28.42N106.40E
Dongxing China 33 21.33N107.58E
Donington U.K. 10 52.55N 0.12W
Donja Stubica Croatia 20 45.59N 15.58E
Dönna *i.* Norway 22 66.05N 12.30E
Donnacona Canada 77 46.40N 71.47W
Donnybrook Australia 63 33.34S115.47E
Donnybrook R.S.A. 56 29.55S 29.51E
Doodlakine Australia 63 31.41S117.23E
Doolow Somali Rep. 45 4.13N 42.08E
Doon, Loch U.K. 12 55.15N 4.23W
Dora, L. Australia 62 22.05S122.55E
Dora Baltea *r.* Italy 15 45.11N 8.05E
Doran L. Canada 75 61.13N108.06W
Dora Riparia *r.* Italy 15 45.05N 7.44E
Dorchester U.K. 11 50.52N 2.28W
Dorchester, C. Canada 73 65.29N 77.30W
Dordogne *r.* France 17 45.03N 0.34W
Dordrecht Neth. 14 51.48N 4.40E
Dordrecht R.S.A. 56 31.22S 27.02E
Dore, Mont *mtn.* France 17 45.32N 2.49E
Doré L. Canada 75 54.46N107.17W
Dori Burkina 52 14.03N 0.02W
Dorion Canada 77 45.23N 74.03W
Dorking U.K. 11 51.14N 0.20W
Dormagen Germany 14 51.05N 6.50E
Dormans France 15 49.04N 3.38E
Dornie U.K. 12 57.16N 5.31W
Dornoch U.K. 12 57.52N 4.02W
Dornoch Firth *est.* U.K. 12 57.50N 4.04W
Dornogovi *d.* Mongolia 32 44.00N110.00E
Dornum Germany 14 53.39N 7.26E
Doro Mali 52 16.09N 0.51W
Dorohoi Romania 21 47.57N 26.24E
Dörpen Germany 14 52.58N 7.20E
Dorre I. Australia 62 25.08S113.06E
Dorrigo Australia 67 30.20S152.41E
Dorris U.S.A. 80 41.58N121.55W
Dorset *d.* U.K. 11 50.48N 2.25W
Dorset, C. Canada 73 64.10N 76.40W
Dorsten Germany 14 51.38N 6.58E
Dortmund Germany 14 51.32N 7.27E
Dortmund-Ems Kanal Germany 14 52.20N 7.30E
Dorval Canada 77 45.27N 73.44W
Dos Bahías, C. Argentina 93 44.55S 65.32W
Dosquet Canada 77 46.28N 71.32W
Dosso Niger 53 13.03N 3.10E
Dosso *d.* Niger 53 13.00N 3.15E
Dossor Kazakhstan 25 47.31N 53.01E
Dothan U.S.A. 85 31.12N 85.25W
Douai France 14 50.22N 3.05E
Douako Guinea 52 9.45N 10.08W
Douala Cameroon 53 4.05N 9.43E
Douarnenez France 17 48.05N 4.20W
Double Mer *g.* Canada 77 54.05N 59.00W
Doubs *r.* France 17 46.57N 5.03E
Doubtless B. New Zealand 60 35.10S173.30E
Doudeville France 15 49.43N 0.48E
Douentza Mali 52 14.58N 2.48W
Douglas I.o.M. Europe 10 54.09N 4.29W
Douglas R.S.A. 56 29.03S 23.45E
Douglas Ariz. U.S.A. 81 31.21N109.33W
Douglas Ga. U.S.A. 85 31.30N 82.54W
Douglas Mich. U.S.A. 84 42.38N 86.13W
Douglas Wyo. U.S.A. 80 42.45N105.24W
Douglas Creek *r.* Australia 66 28.35S136.50E
Doulaincourt France 17 48.19N 5.12E
Doulevant-le-Château France 15 48.23N 4.55E
Doumé Cameroon 53 4.13N 13.30E
Douna Mali 52 12.40N 6.00W
Dounreay U.K. 12 58.35N 3.42W
Dourados Brazil 92 22.09S 54.52W
Dourdan France 15 48.32N 2.01E
Douro *r.* Portugal 16 41.10N 8.40W
Douvres France 15 49.17N 0.23W
Dove *r.* U.K. 10 52.50N 1.35W
Dover U.K. 11 51.07N 1.19E
Dover Del. U.S.A. 85 39.10N 75.32W
Dover N.H. U.S.A. 84 43.12N 70.56W
Dover N.J. U.S.A. 85 40.53N 74.34W
Dover Ohio U.S.A. 84 40.32N 81.30W
Dover Tenn. U.S.A. 85 36.30N 87.50W
Dover, Pt. Australia 63 32.32S125.30E
Dover, Str. of U.K. 11 51.00N 1.30E
Dovey *r.* U.K. 11 52.33N 3.56W
Dovrefjell *mts.* Norway 23 62.06N 9.25E
Dovsk Belorussia 21 53.07N 30.29E
Dowa Malaŵi 55 13.40S 33.55E
Dowagiac U.S.A. 84 41.58N 86.06W
Dowerin Australia 63 31.15S117.00E
Dowlatābād Iran 43 28.19N 56.40E
Dowlat Yār Afghan. 40 34.33N 65.47E
Down *d.* U.K. 13 54.20N 6.00W
Downey U.S.A. 80 42.26N112.07W
Downham Market U.K. 11 52.36N 0.22E
Downpatrick U.K. 13 54.21N 5.43W
Downpatrick Head Rep. of Ire. 13 54.20N 9.22W
Downton, Mt. Canada 74 52.42N124.51W
Dowra Rep. of Ire. 13 54.11N 8.02W
Doylestown U.S.A. 85 40.19N 75.08W
Dozois, Résr. Canada 76 47.30N 77.00W
Drâa, Hamada du *f.* Algeria 50 29.00N 6.00W
Drâa, Oued *wadi* Morocco 50 28.40N 11.06W
Drachten Neth. 14 53.05N 6.06E
Drăgăşani Romania 21 44.40N 24.16E
Dragoman, Pasul *pass* Bulgaria/Yugo. 19 42.56N 22.52E
Dragon's Mouth *str.* Trinidad 90 11.00N 61.35W
Dragovishtitsa Bulgaria 19 42.22N 22.39E
Draguignan France 17 43.32N 6.28E
Drake Australia 67 28.55S152.24E
Drake U.S.A. 82 47.55N100.23W
Drakensberg *mts.* R.S.A./Lesotho 56 30.00S 29.05E
Drake Passage *str.* Atlantic Oc. 95 59.00S 65.00W
Dráma Greece 19 41.09N 24.11E

Drammen to **Elvas**

Drammen Norway 23 59.44N 10.15E
Drās Jammu & Kashmir 40 34.27N 75.46E
Drau *r.* Austria *see* Drava *r.* Slovenia / Croatia 20
Drava *r.* Slovenia / Croatia 21 45.34N 18.56E
Drayton Valley *town* Canada 74 53.25N114.58W
Drenthe *d.* Neth. 14 52.52N 6.30E
Dresden Germany 20 51.03N 13.45E
Dreux France 15 48.44N 1.23E
Driftwood Canada 76 49.08N 81.23W
Drin *r.* Albania 19 41.45N 19.34E
Drina *r.* Bosnia-Herzegovina 21 44.53N 19.20E
Dröbak Norway 23 59.39N 10.39E
Drogheda Rep. of Ire. 13 53.42N 6.23W
Drogobych Ukraine 21 49.10N 23.30E
Droitwich U.K. 11 52.16N 2.10W
Drokiya Moldavia 21 48.07N 27.49E
Dromedary, C. Australia 67 36.18S150.15E
Dronero Italy 15 44.28N 7.22E
Dronfield U.K. 10 53.18N 1.29W
Dronne *r.* France 17 45.02N 0.09W
Dronning Maud Land *f.* Antarctica 96 74.00S 10.00E
Drumheller Canada 74 51.25N112.40W
Drum Hills Rep. of Ire. 13 52.03N 7.42W
Drummond Range *mts.* Australia 64 23.30S147.15E
Drummondville Canada 77 45.53N 72.30W
Drummore U.K. 12 54.41N 4.54W
Druskininkai Lithuania 21 53.48N 23.58E
Drut *r.* Belorussia 21 53.03N 30.42E
Drvar Bosnia-Herzegovina 20 44.22N 16.24E
Dry B. U.S.A. 74 59.08N138.25W
Dryden Canada 76 49.47N 92.50W
Drymen U.K. 12 56.04N 4.27W
Drysdale *r.* Australia 62 13.59S126.51E
Dschang Cameroon 53 5.28N 10.02E
Dua *r.* Zaïre 54 3.12N 20.55E
Du'an China 33 24.01N108.06E
Duaringa Australia 64 23.42S149.40E
Ḑubā Saudi Arabia 42 27.21N 35.40E
Dubai *see* Dubayy U.A.E. 43
Dubawnt *r.* Canada 73 62.50N102.00W
Dubawnt L. Canada 75 63.04N101.42W
Dubayy U.A.E. 43 25.13N 55.17E
Dubbo Australia 67 32.16S148.41E
Dubica Croatia 20 45.11N 16.48E
Dublin Rep. of Ire. 13 53.21N 6.18W
Dublin *d.* Rep. of Ire. 13 53.20N 6.18W
Dublin U.S.A. 85 32.31N 82.54W
Dublin B. Rep. of Ire. 13 53.20N 6.09W
Dubno Ukraine 21 50.28N 25.40E
Dubois Idaho U.S.A. 80 44.10N112.14W
Du Bois Penn. U.S.A. 84 41.07N 78.46W
Dubovka Russian Fed. 25 49.04N 44.48E
Dubréka Guinea 52 9.50N 13.32W
Dubrovitsa Ukraine 21 51.38N 26.40E
Dubrovnik Croatia 19 42.40N 18.07E
Dubuque U.S.A. 82 42.30N 90.41W
Duchesne U.S.A. 80 40.10N110.24W
Duchess Australia 64 21.22S139.52E
Ducie I. Pacific Oc. 69 24.40S124.48W
Du Coüedic, C. Australia 66 36.00S136.10E
Dudhnai India 41 25.59N 90.44E
Dudinka Russian Fed. 29 69.27N 86.13E
Dudley U.K. 11 52.30N 2.05W
Dudna *r.* India 40 19.07N 76.54E
Duékoué Ivory Coast 52 6.50N 7.22W
Duero *r.* Spain *see* Douro *r.* Portugal 16
Duff Creek *town* Australia 66 28.28S135.51E
Dufftown U.K. 12 57.27N 3.09W
Duga Resa Croatia 20 45.27N 15.30E
Dugi *i.* Croatia 20 44.04N 15.00E
Du Gué *r.* Canada 77 57.20N 70.48W
Duifken Pt. Australia 64 12.33S141.38E
Duisburg Germany 14 51.26N 6.45E
Duitama Colombia 90 5.50N 73.01W
Duiveland *i.* Neth. 14 51.39N 4.00E
Dujuuma Somali Rep. 55 1.14N 42.37E
Dukambīya Ethiopia 48 14.42N 37.30E
Duk Fadiat Sudan 49 7.45N 31.25E
Duk Faiwil Sudan 49 7.30N 31.29E
Dukhān Qatar 43 25.24N 50.47E
Duki Pakistan 40 30.09N 68.34E
Dukou China 30 26.33N101.44E
Dukye Dzong Bhutan 41 27.20N 89.30E
Dulce *r.* Argentina 92 30.40S 62.00W
Duleek Rep. of Ire. 13 53.39N 6.24W
Dülmen Germany 14 51.49N 7.17E
Dulovo Bulgaria 21 43.49N 27.09E
Duluth U.S.A. 82 46.47N 92.06W
Dūmā Syria 44 33.33N 36.24E
Dumaguete Phil. 37 9.20N123.18E
Dumai Indonesia 36 1.41N101.27E
Dumaran *i.* Phil. 36 10.33N119.50E
Dumaresq *r.* Australia 67 28.40S150.28E
Dumaring Indonesia 36 1.36N118.12E
Dumas Ark. U.S.A. 83 33.53N 91.29W
Dumas Tex. U.S.A. 83 35.52N101.58W
Dumbarton U.K. 12 55.57N 4.35W
Dumbleyung Australia 63 33.18S117.42E
Dumbrăveni Romania 21 46.14N 24.35E
Dum-Dum India 41 22.35N 88.24E
Dumfries U.K. 12 55.04N 3.37W
Dumfries and Galloway *d.* U.K. 12 55.05N 3.40W
Dumka India 41 24.16N 87.15E
Dumraon India 41 25.33N 84.09E
Dumyāţ Egypt 44 31.26N 31.48E
Duna *r.* Hungary *see* Danube *r.* Europe 21
Dunaföldvár Hungary 21 46.48N 18.55E
Dunajec *r.* Poland 21 50.15N 20.44E
Dunajská Streda Slovakia 21 48.01N 17.35E
Dunany Pt. Rep. of Ire. 13 53.51N 6.15W
Dunărea *r.* Romania *see* Danube *r.* Europe 21
Dunării, Delta *f.* Romania 21 45.05N 29.45E
Dunav *r.* Bulgaria *see* Danube *r.* Europe 21
Dunav *r.* Yugo. *see* Danube *r.* Europe 21
Dunbar U.K. 12 56.00N 2.31W
Dunblane U.K. 12 56.12N 3.59W
Dunboyne Rep. of Ire. 13 53.26N 6.30W
Duncan Canada 74 48.45N123.40W
Duncan *r.* Canada 74 50.11N116.57W
Duncan U.S.A. 83 34.30N 97.57W
Duncan, C. Canada 76 52.40N 80.48W
Duncan L. N.W.T. Canada 74 62.51N113.58W
Duncan L. Que. Canada 76 53.35N 77.55W
Duncansby Head U.K. 12 58.39N 3.01W
Dundalk Rep. of Ire. 13 54.01N 6.25W
Dundalk U.S.A. 85 39.15N 76.31W
Dundalk B. Rep. of Ire. 13 53.55N 6.17W
Dundas Canada 76 43.16N 79.58W
Dundas, L. Australia 63 32.35S121.50E
Dundas I. Canada 74 54.33N130.50W
Dundas Str. Australia 64 11.20S131.35E
Dundee R.S.A. 56 28.09S 30.14E
Dundee U.K. 12 56.28N 3.00W
Dundgovĭ *d.* Mongolia 32 45.00N106.00E
Dundrum U.K. 13 54.16N 5.51W
Dundrum B. U.K. 13 54.12N 5.46W
Dunedin New Zealand 60 45.52S170.30E
Dunedin U.S.A. 85 28.02N 82.47W
Dunedoo Australia 67 32.00S149.25E
Dunfermline U.K. 12 56.04N 3.29W
Dungannon U.K. 13 54.31N 6.47W
Dūngarpur India 40 23.50N 73.43E
Dungarvan Rep. of Ire. 13 52.06N 7.39W
Dungeness *c.* U.K. 11 50.55N 0.58E
Dungiven U.K. 13 54.56N 6.56W
Dungog Australia 67 32.24S151.46E
Dungu Zaïre 55 3.40N 28.40E
Dunhuang China 30 40.00N 94.40E
Dunkeld Qld. Australia 65 26.55S148.00E
Dunkeld Vic. Australia 66 37.40S142.23E
Dunkeld U.K. 12 56.34N 3.36W
Dunkerque France 14 51.02N 2.23E
Dunk I. Australia 64 17.56S146.10E
Dunkirk *see* Dunkerque France 14
Dunkirk U.S.A. 84 42.29N 79.21W
Dunkwa Ghana 52 5.59N 1.45W
Dun Laoghaire Rep. of Ire. 13 53.17N 6.09W
Dunlap U.S.A. 82 41.51N 95.36W
Dunleer Rep. of Ire. 13 53.49N 6.24W
Dunmahon Rep. of Ire. 13 52.09N 7.23W
Dunmarra Australia 64 16.37S133.22E
Dunmore U.S.A. 84 41.25N 75.38W
Dunnet Head U.K. 12 58.40N 3.23W
Dunning U.S.A. 82 41.50N100.06W
Dunnville Canada 76 42.54N 79.36W
Dunolly Australia 66 36.50S143.45E
Dunoon U.K. 12 55.57N 4.57W
Dunqulah Sudan 48 19.10N 30.29E
Dunqunāb Sudan 48 21.06N 37.05E
Duns U.K. 12 55.47N 2.20W
Dunsborough Australia 63 33.37S115.06E
Dunshaughlin Rep. of Ire. 13 53.30N 6.34W
Dunstable U.K. 11 51.53N 0.32W
Dunstan Mts. New Zealand 60 44.45S169.45E
Dunster Canada 74 53.08N119.50W
Dunyāpur Pakistan 40 29.48N 71.44E
Duolun China 32 42.09N116.21E
Duong Dong Vietnam 34 10.12N103.57E
Dupont U.S.A. 84 38.53N 85.30W
Duque de Caxias Brazil 94 22.47S 43.18W
Du Quoin U.S.A. 83 38.01N 89.14W
Duran U.S.A. 81 34.28N105.24W
Durance *r.* France 17 43.55N 4.48E
Durango Mexico 86 24.01N104.00W
Durango *d.* Mexico 83 24.30N104.00W
Durango Spain 16 43.13N 2.40W
Durango U.S.A. 80 37.16N107.53W
Durant U.S.A. 83 34.00N 96.23W
Durazno Uruguay 93 33.22S 56.31W
Durban R.S.A. 56 29.50S 30.59E
Durbe Latvia 23 56.35N 21.21E
Dureji Pakistan 40 25.53N 67.18E
Düren Germany 14 50.48N 6.30E
Durg India 41 21.11N 81.17E
Durgāpur India 41 23.29N 87.20E
Durham U.K. 10 54.47N 1.34W
Durham *d.* U.K. 10 54.42N 1.45W
Durham N.C. U.S.A. 85 36.00N 78.54W
Durham N.H. U.S.A. 84 43.08N 70.56W
Durham Sud Canada 77 45.39N 72.19W
Durlston Head *c.* U.K. 11 50.35N 1.58W
Durmitor *mtn.* Yugo. 19 43.08N 19.03E
Durness U.K. 12 58.33N 4.45W
Durrës Albania 19 41.19N 19.27E
Durrow Rep. of Ire. 13 52.51N 7.25W
Dursey Head Rep. of Ire. 13 51.35N 10.15W
Durūz, Jabal ad *mtn.* Syria 44 32.42N 36.42E
D'Urville I. New Zealand 60 40.45S173.50E
Dushak Turkmenistan 28 37.13N 60.01E
Dushan China 33 25.50N107.30E
Dushanbe Tajikistan 30 38.38N 68.51E
Duskotna Bulgaria 19 42.52N 27.10E
Düsseldorf Germany 14 51.13N 6.47E
Dutch Creek *town* Canada 74 50.18N115.58W
Dutlhe Botswana 56 23.55S 23.47E
Dutton, L. Australia 66 31.49S137.08E
Duxun China 33 23.57N117.37E
Duyun China 33 26.12N107.29E
Dvina *r.* Europe 28 57.03N 24.02E
Dvinskaya Guba *b.* Russian Fed. 24 64.40N 39.30E
Dwarda Australia 63 32.45S116.23E
Dwārka India 40 22.14N 68.58E
Dwellingup Australia 63 32.42S116.04E
Dyatlovichi Belorussia 21 52.08N 30.49E
Dyatlovo Belorussia 21 53.28N 25.28E
Dyer, C. Canada 73 67.45N 61.45W
Dyérem *r.* Cameroon 53 6.36N 13.10E
Dyer Plateau Antarctica 96 70.00S 65.00W
Dyersburg U.S.A. 83 36.03N 89.23W
Dyfed *d.* U.K. 11 52.00N 4.17W
Dykh Tau *mtn.* Russian Fed. 25 43.04N 43.10E
Dymer Ukraine 21 50.50N 30.20E
Dyulevo Bulgaria 19 42.22N 27.10E
Dyultydag *mtn.* Russian Fed. 43 41.55N 46.52E
Dzamïn Üüd Mongolia 32 43.50N111.53E
Dzerzhinsk Belorussia 21 53.40N 27.01E
Dzerzhinsk Russian Fed. 24 56.15N 43.30E
Dzhambul Kazakhstan 30 42.50N 71.25E
Dzhankoy Ukraine 25 45.42N 34.23E
Dzhardzhan Russian Fed. 29 68.49N124.08E
Dzhelinde Russian Fed. 29 70.09N114.00E
Dzhetygara Kazakhstan 28 52.14N 61.10E
Dzhezkazgan Kazakhstan 28 47.48N 67.24E
Dzhizak Uzbekistan 28 40.06N 67.45E
Dzhugdzhur, Khrebet *mts.* Russian Fed. 29 57.30N138.00E
Dzhurin Ukraine 21 48.40N 28.16E
Działdowo Poland 21 53.15N 20.10E
Dzierzoniów Poland 20 50.44N 16.39E
Dzodze Ghana 52 6.14N 1.00E

E

Eabamet L. Canada 76 51.30N 88.00W
Eads U.S.A. 82 38.29N102.47W
Eagle *r.* Canada 77 53.35N 57.25W
Eagle U.S.A. 82 39.39N106.50W
Eagle Butte *town* U.S.A. 82 45.00N101.14W
Eagle Grove U.S.A. 82 42.40N 93.54W
Eagle L. U.S.A. 84 46.17N 69.20W
Eagle Lake *town* U.S.A. 84 47.02N 68.36W
Eagle Pass *town* U.S.A. 83 28.43N100.30W
Eagle River *town* U.S.A. 82 45.55N 89.15W
Ealing U.K. 11 51.31N 0.20W
Earlimart U.S.A. 81 35.53N119.16W
Earn *r.* U.K. 12 56.21N 3.18W
Earn, Loch U.K. 12 56.23N 4.12W
Easingwold U.K. 10 54.08N 1.11W
Easky Rep. of Ire. 13 54.17N 8.58W
Easley U.S.A. 85 34.50N 82.34W
East Alligator *r.* Australia 64 12.25S132.58E
East Anglian Heights *hills* U.K. 11 52.03N 0.15E
East Aurora U.S.A. 76 42.46N 78.37W
East B. U.S.A. 83 29.30N 94.35W
Eastbourne U.K. 11 50.46N 0.18E
East C. New Zealand 60 37.45S178.30E
East Caroline Basin Pacific Oc. 68 3.00N147.00E
East China Sea Asia 31 29.00N125.00E
East Dereham U.K. 9 52.40N 0.57E
Easter I. *see* Pascua, Isla de *i.* Pacific Oc. 69
Eastern *d.* Ghana 52 6.20N 0.45W
Eastern *d.* Kenya 55 0.00 38.00E
Eastern Desert *see* Sharqīyah, Aş Şaḩrā' ash *des.* Egypt 44
Eastern Ghāts *mts.* India 39 16.30N 80.30E
Easterville Canada 75 53.06N 99.53W
East Falkland *i.* Falkland Is. 93 51.45W 58.50W
East Grand Forks U.S.A. 82 47.56N 96.55W
East Grinstead U.K. 11 51.08N 0.01W
East Ilsley U.K. 11 51.33N 1.15W
East Kilbride U.K. 12 55.46N 4.09W
East Lansing U.S.A. 84 42.45N 84.30W
Eastleigh U.K. 11 50.58N 1.21W
East London R.S.A. 56 33.00S 27.54E
Eastmain Canada 76 52.15N 78.30W
Eastmain *r.* Canada 76 52.15N 78.30W
Eastman Canada 77 45.18N 72.19W
Easton Md. U.S.A. 85 38.46N 76.04W
Easton Penn. U.S.A. 85 40.41N 75.13W
Easton Wash. U.S.A. 80 47.14N121.11W
East Orange U.S.A. 85 40.46N 74.14W
East Pacific Ridge Pacific Oc. 69 15.00S112.00W
East Point *town* U.S.A. 85 33.41N 84.29W
East Retford U.K. 10 53.19N 0.55W
East St. Louis U.S.A. 82 38.34N 90.04W
East Sussex *d.* U.K. 11 50.56N 0.12E
Eaton U.S.A. 82 40.32N104.42W
Eau Claire U.S.A. 82 44.50N 91.30W
Eau-Claire, Lac à l' *l.* Canada 76 56.10N 74.30W
Eauripik *i.* Federated States of Micronesia 37 6.42N143.04E
Eaurpik-N. Guinea Rise Pacific Oc. 68 2.00N141.00E
Eban Nigeria 53 9.41N 4.54E
Ebbw Vale U.K. 11 51.47N 3.12W
Ebebiyin Equat. Guinea 54 2.09N 11.20E
Eberswalde Germany 20 52.50N 13.50E
Ebinur Hu *l.* China 30 45.00N 83.00E
Ebola *r.* Zaïre 49 3.20N 20.57E
Eboli Italy 18 40.37N 15.04E
Ebolowa Cameroon 54 2.56N 11.11E
Ebon *i.* Pacific Oc. 68 4.38N168.43E
Ebony Namibia 56 22.05S 15.15E
Ebro *r.* Spain 16 40.43N 0.54E
Ebro, Delta del *f.* Spain 16 40.43N 0.54E
Ecclefechan U.K. 10 55.03N 3.18W
Echeng China 33 30.26N114.00E
Echternach Lux. 14 49.49N 6.25E
Echuca Australia 67 36.10S144.20E
Écija Spain 16 37.33N 5.04W
Écommoy France 15 47.50N 0.16E
Ecuador S. America 90 1.40S 79.00W
Ēd Ethiopia 48 13.52N 41.40E
Ed Sweden 23 58.55N 11.55E
Edam Neth. 14 52.30N 5.02E
Eday *i.* U.K. 8 59.11N 2.47W
Eddrachillis B. U.K. 12 58.17N 5.15W
Eddystone Pt. Australia 65 40.58S148.12E
Ede Neth. 14 52.03N 5.40E
Ede Nigeria 53 7.45N 4.26E
Edea Cameroon 54 3.47N 10.15E
Edehon L. Canada 75 60.25N 97.15W
Eden Australia 67 37.04S149.54E
Eden *r.* U.K. 10 54.57N 3.02W
Eden U.S.A. 80 42.03N109.26W
Edenburg R.S.A. 56 29.44S 25.55E
Edendale New Zealand 60 46.19S168.47E
Edenderry Rep. of Ire. 13 53.21N 7.05W
Edenhope Australia 66 37.04S141.20E
Edenton U.S.A. 85 36.04N 76.39W
Edeowie Australia 66 31.28S138.29E
Eder *r.* Germany 20 51.13N 9.27E
Ederny U.K. 13 54.32N 7.40W
Edgeley U.S.A. 82 40.07N 98.43W
Edgeöya *i.* Arctic Oc. 96 77.45N 22.30E
Edgeworthstown Rep. of Ire. 13 53.42N 7.38W
Édhessa Greece 19 40.47N 22.03E
Ediacara Australia 66 30.18S137.50E
Edina Liberia 52 6.01N 10.10W
Edinburgh U.K. 12 55.57N 3.13W
Edirne Turkey 19 41.40N 26.35E
Edithburgh Australia 66 35.06S137.44E
Edjudina Australia 63 29.48S122.23E
Edmond U.S.A. 83 35.39N 97.29W
Edmonton Canada 74 53.30N113.30W
Edmundston Canada 77 47.22N 68.20W
Edna U.S.A. 83 28.59N 96.39W
Edo *r.* Japan 35 35.37N139.53E
Edo *d.* Nigeria 53 6.20N 5.55E
Edolo Italy 15 46.11N 10.20E
Edounga Gabon 54 0.03S 13.43E
Edremit Turkey 19 39.35N 27.02E
Edsbruk Sweden 23 58.02N 16.28E
Edson Canada 74 53.35N116.26W
Edward, L. Uganda / Zaïre 55 0.30S 29.30E
Edwards Plateau *f.* U.S.A. 83 31.20N101.00W
Eeklo Belgium 14 51.11N 3.34E
Eel *r.* U.S.A. 80 40.40N124.20W
Efate *i.* Vanuatu 68 17.40S168.25E
Effingham U.S.A. 82 39.07N 88.33W
Egaña Argentina 93 36.57S 59.06W
Egbe Nigeria 53 8.13N 5.31E
Egeland U.S.A. 82 48.38N 99.10W
Eger Hungary 21 47.54N 20.23E
Egersund Norway 23 58.27N 6.00E
Egerton, Mt. Australia 62 24.44S117.40E
Egg Harbor U.S.A. 85 39.32N 74.39W
Egmont, Mt. New Zealand 60 39.20S174.05E
Eğridir Turkey 42 37.52N 30.51E
Eğridir Gölü *l.* Turkey 42 38.04N 30.55E
Egypt Africa 48 26.00N 30.00E
Eiao *i.* Îs. Marquises 69 8.00S140.40W
Éibar Spain 16 43.11N 2.28W
Eidsvåg Norway 22 62.47N 8.03E
Eidsvold Australia 64 25.23S151.08E
Eifel *f.* Germany 14 50.10N 6.45E
Eigg *i.* U.K. 12 56.53N 6.09W
Eighty Mile Beach *f.* Australia 62 19.00S121.00E
Eil, Loch U.K. 12 56.51N 5.12W
Eildon, L. Australia 67 37.10S146.00E
Einasleigh Australia 64 18.31S144.05E
Eindhoven Neth. 14 51.26N 5.30E
Eirunepé Brazil 90 6.40S 69.52W
Eiseb *r.* Namibia 56 20.26S 20.05E
Eisenach Germany 20 50.59N 10.19E
Eisenerz Austria 20 47.33N 14.53E
Eisenhut *mtn.* Austria 20 47.00N 13.45E
Eisenhüttenstadt Germany 20 52.09N 14.41E
Eišiškes Lithuania 21 54.09N 24.55E
Eisleben Germany 20 51.32N 11.33E
Eitort Germany 14 50.46N 7.27E
Ejde Faroe Is. 8 62.03N 7.06W
Ejin Qi China 30 41.50N100.50E
Ejura Ghana 52 7.24N 1.20W
Ekalaka U.S.A. 80 45.53N104.33W
Eket Nigeria 53 4.39N 7.56E
Eketahuna New Zealand 60 40.39S175.44E
Ekibastuz Kazakhstan 28 51.45N 75.22E
Ekimchan Russian Fed. 29 53.09N133.00E
Eksjö Sweden 23 57.40N 14.47E
Ekträsk Sweden 22 64.29N 19.50E
Ekuku Zaïre 54 0.42S 21.38E
Ekwan *r.* Canada 76 53.30N 84.00W
El Aaiún W. Sahara 50 27.09N 13.12W
Elands *r.* R.S.A. 56 24.52S 29.20E
El Arco Mexico 81 28.00N113.25W
El Arenal Spain 16 39.30N 2.45E
El Asnam Algeria 51 36.10N 1.20E
Elat Israel 44 29.33N 34.56E
Elâziğ Turkey 42 38.41N 39.14E
Elba *i.* Italy 18 42.47N 10.17E
El Barril Mexico 81 28.22N113.00W
Elbasan Albania 19 41.07N 20.04E
El Baúl Venezuela 90 8.59N 68.16W
Elbe *r.* Germany 20 53.33N 10.00E
El Beni *d.* Bolivia 92 14.00S 65.30W
Elbert, Mt. U.S.A. 82 39.07N106.27W
Elberton U.S.A. 85 34.05N 82.54W
Elbeuf France 15 49.17N 1.01E
Elbistan Turkey 42 38.14N 37.11E
Elbląg Poland 21 54.10N 19.25E
Elbrus *mtn.* Russian Fed. 25 43.21N 42.29E
Elburg Neth. 14 52.27N 5.50E
Elburz Mts. *see* Alborz, Reshteh-ye Kūhhā-ye *ye* Iran 43
El Cajon U.S.A. 81 32.48N116.58W
El Callao Venezuela 90 7.18N 61.48W
El Campo U.S.A. 83 29.12N 96.16W
El Casco Mexico 83 25.34N104.35W
El Centro U.S.A. 81 32.48N115.34W
Elche Spain 16 38.16N 0.41W
Elcho U.S.A. 82 45.26N 89.11W
Elcho I. Australia 64 11.55S135.45E
El Corral Mexico 83 25.09N 97.58W
El Cozón Mexico 81 31.18N112.29W
El Cuy Argentina 93 39.57S 68.20W
Elda Spain 16 38.29N 0.47W
Elde *r.* Germany 20 53.17N 12.40E
El Der Ethiopia 45 5.08N 43.08E
Elder, L. Australia 66 30.39S140.13E
El Desemboque Mexico 81 29.30N112.27W
El Djouf *des.* Mauritania 50 20.30N 7.30W
Eldon U.S.A. 82 38.21N 93.35W
Eldorado Canada 75 59.35N108.30W
El Dorado Ark. U.S.A. 83 33.13N 92.40W
El Dorado Kans. U.S.A. 83 37.49N 96.52W
El Dorado Venezuela 90 6.45N 61.37W
Eldoret Kenya 55 0.31N 35.17E
Electra U.S.A. 83 34.02N 98.55W
El Eglab *f.* Algeria 50 26.30N 4.15W
Elei, Wādī Sudan 48 22.04N 34.27E
Eleja Latvia 23 56.26N 23.42E
Elektrostal Russian Fed. 24 55.46N 38.30E
Elephant Butte Resr. U.S.A. 81 33.19N107.10W
Elephant I. Antarctica 96 61.00S 55.00W
El Eulma Algeria 51 36.09N 5.41E
Eleuthera I. Bahamas 87 25.15N 76.20W
Elevtheroúpolis Greece 19 40.55N 24.16E
El Ferrol Spain 16 43.29N 8.14W
Elgå Norway 23 62.11N 11.07E
Elgin Canada 75 49.26N100.15W
Elgin U.K. 12 57.39N 3.20W
Elgin Ill. U.S.A. 82 42.03N 88.19W
Elgin Nev. U.S.A. 80 37.21N114.30W
Elgin Oreg. U.S.A. 80 45.34N117.55W
Elgin Tex. U.S.A. 83 30.21N 97.22W
El Golea Algeria 51 30.34N 2.53E
Elgon, Mt. Kenya / Uganda 55 1.07N 34.35E
Elida U.S.A. 83 33.57N103.39W
Elim Namibia 56 17.47S 15.30E
Elista Russian Fed. 25 46.18N 44.14E
Elizabeth Australia 66 34.45S138.39E
Elizabeth N.J. U.S.A. 85 40.40N 74.13W
Elizabeth W.Va. U.S.A. 84 39.04N 81.24W
Elizabeth City U.S.A. 85 36.18N 76.16W
Elizabethtown Ky. U.S.A. 85 37.41N 85.51W
Elizabethtown Penn. U.S.A. 85 40.09N 76.36W
El Jadida Morocco 50 33.16N 8.30W
Elk *r.* Canada 74 49.10N115.14W
Elk Poland 21 53.50N 22.22E
El Kairouan Tunisia 51 35.41N 10.07E
El Kasserine Tunisia 51 35.11N 8.48E
Elk City U.S.A. 83 35.25N 99.25W
El Kef Tunisia 51 36.11N 8.43E
El-Kelâa-des-Srarhna Morocco 50 32.02N 7.23W
Ēl Kerē Ethiopia 49 5.48N 42.10E
Elkhart Ind. U.S.A. 82 41.52N 85.56W
Elkhart Kans. U.S.A. 83 37.00N101.54W
El Khnâchîch *f.* Mali 52 21.50N 3.45W
Elkhorn Canada 75 49.58N101.14W
Elkhovo Bulgaria 19 42.10N 26.35E
Elkins N.Mex. U.S.A. 81 33.41N104.04W
Elkins W.Va. U.S.A. 84 38.55N 79.51W
Elko U.S.A. 80 40.50N115.46W
Elkton U.S.A. 85 39.36N 75.50W
Elleker Australia 63 34.55S117.40E
Ellen, Mt. U.S.A. 78 38.06N110.50W
Ellendale Australia 62 17.56S124.48E
Ellensburg U.S.A. 80 47.00N120.32W
Ellesmere I. Canada 73 78.00N 82.00W
Ellesmere Port U.K. 10 53.17N 2.55W
Elliot R.S.A. 56 31.19S 27.49E
Elliot Lake *town* Canada 76 46.35N 82.35W
Elliott Australia 64 17.33S133.31E
Ellis U.S.A. 82 38.56N 99.34W
Elliston Australia 66 33.39S134.55E
Ellon U.K. 12 57.22N 2.05W
Ellora India 40 20.01N 75.10E
El Mahdía Tunisia 51 35.30N 11.04E
Elmali Turkey 42 36.43N 29.56E
El Maneadero Mexico 81 31.45N116.35W
Elmer U.S.A. 85 39.36N 75.10W
El Metlaoui Tunisia 51 34.20N 8.24E
Elmhurst U.S.A. 82 41.54N 87.56W
Elmina Ghana 52 5.07N 1.21W
Elmira U.S.A. 84 42.06N 76.49W
Elmore Australia 67 36.30S144.40E
El Mreiti *well* Mauritania 50 23.29N 7.52W
El Mreyyé *f.* Mauritania 50 19.30N 7.00W
Elmshorn Germany 20 53.46N 9.40E
El Niybo Ethiopia 49 4.32N 39.59E
El Ouassi *well* Mali 52 20.23N 0.12E
El Oued Algeria 51 33.20N 6.53E
Eloy U.S.A. 81 32.45N111.33W
El Paso U.S.A. 81 31.45N106.29W
El Portal U.S.A. 80 37.41N119.47W
El Quelite Mexico 81 23.32N106.28W
El Real Panama 87 8.06N 77.42W
El Reno U.S.A. 83 35.32N 97.57W
El Roba Kenya 55 3.57N 40.01E
Elrose Canada 75 51.13N108.01W
El Salto Mexico 81 23.47N105.22W
El Salvador C. America 87 13.30N 89.00W
Elsas Canada 76 48.32N 82.55W
Elsdorf Germany 14 50.56N 6.35E
Elsinore U.S.A. 80 38.41N112.09W
El Sueco Mexico 81 29.54N106.24W
El Tabacal Argentina 92 23.15S 64.14W
El Tigre Venezuela 90 8.44N 64.18W
Elton, Ozero *l.* Russian Fed. 25 49.10N 46.34E
El Turbio Argentina 93 51.41S 72.05W
Elūru India 39 16.45N 81.10E
Elvas Portugal 16 38.53N 7.10W

Elvdal to Fernlee

Elvdal Norway 23 61.38N 11.56E
Elverum Norway 23 60.53N 11.34E
Elvira Argentina 93 35.15S 59.30W
El Wak Kenya 55 2.45N 40.52E
Elwood Nebr. U.S.A. 82 40.36N 99.52W
Elwood N.J. U.S.A. 85 39.35N 74.43W
Ely U.K. 9 52.24N 0.16E
Ely Minn. U.S.A. 82 47.53N 91.52W
Ely Nev. U.S.A. 80 39.15N114.53W
Elyria U.S.A. 84 41.22N 82.06W
Emae i. Vanuatu 68 17.04S168.24E
Emāmshahr Iran 43 36.25N 55.00E
Emån r. Sweden 23 57.08N 16.30E
Emba Kazakhstan 28 48.47N 58.05E
Emba r. Kazakhstan 25 46.38N 53.00E
Embarcación Argentina 92 23.15S 64.10W
Embleton U.K. 10 55.30N 1.37W
Embrun France 17 44.34N 6.30E
Embu Kenya 55 0.32S 37.28E
Emden Germany 14 53.23N 7.13E
Emerald Australia 64 23.32S148.10E
Emerson Canada 75 49.00N 97.12W
Emi Koussi mtn. Chad 53 19.58N 18.30E
Emilia-Romagna d. Italy 15 44.35N 11.00E
Emlichheim Germany 14 52.37N 6.50E
Emmaboda Sweden 23 56.38N 15.32E
Emmaste Estonia 23 58.42N 22.36E
Emmaus U.S.A. 85 40.32N 75.30W
Emmaville Australia 67 29.25S151.39E
Emmeloord Neth. 14 52.43N 5.46E
Emmen Neth. 14 52.48N 6.55E
Emmerich Germany 14 51.49N 6.16E
Emmett U.S.A. 80 43.52N116.30W
Emmitsburg U.S.A. 85 39.42N 77.20W
Emory Peak mtn. U.S.A. 83 29.13N103.17W
Empalme Mexico 81 27.58N110.51W
Empangeni R.S.A. 57 28.45S 31.54E
Empedrado Argentina 92 27.59S 58.47W
Emporia Kans. U.S.A. 82 38.24N 96.11W
Emporia Va. U.S.A. 85 36.42N 77.33W
Ems r. Germany 14 53.14N 7.25E
Emsdale Canada 76 45.28N 79.18W
Emsdetten Germany 14 52.14N 7.32E
Ems-Jade Kanal Germany 14 53.28N 7.40E
Emyvale Rep. of Ire. 13 54.20N 6.59W
Enard B. U.K. 12 58.05N 5.20W
Encarnación Paraguay 94 27.20S 55.50W
Enchi Ghana 52 5.53N 2.48W
Encinal U.S.A. 83 28.02N 99.21W
Encino U.S.A. 81 34.39N105.28W
Encontada, Cerro de la mtn. Mexico 81 27.03N112.31W
Encontrados Venezuela 90 9.03N 72.14W
Encounter B. Australia 66 35.35S138.44E
Endeavour Str. Australia 64 10.50S142.15E
Endeh Indonesia 37 8.51S121.40E
Enderbury I. Kiribati 68 3.08S171.05W
Enderby Canada 74 50.35N119.10W
Enderby Land f. Antarctica 96 67.00S 53.00E
Enderlin U.S.A. 82 46.37N 97.36W
Endicott U.S.A. 84 42.06N 76.03W
Endicott Arm f. U.S.A. 74 57.38N133.22W
Endicott Mts. U.S.A. 72 68.00N152.00W
Endola Namibia 56 17.37S 15.50E
Eneabba Australia 63 29.48S115.16E
Enewetak i. Pacific Oc. 68 11.30N162.15E
Enfida Tunisia 51 36.08N 10.22E
Enfield U.K. 11 51.40N 0.05W
Engaño, C. Phil. 37 18.30N122.20E
Engcobo R.S.A. 56 31.39S 28.01E
'En Gedi Israel 44 31.28N 35.23E
Engels Russian Fed. 25 51.30N 46.07E
Enggano i. Indonesia 36 5.20S102.15E
Enghershatu mtn. Ethiopia 48 16.40N 38.20E
Enghien Belgium 14 50.42N 4.02E
England U.K. 10 53.00N 2.00W
Englewood Colo. U.S.A. 80 39.39N104.59W
Englewood Fla. U.S.A. 85 26.58N 82.21W
English Bāzār India 41 25.00N 88.09E
English Channel U.K. 11 50.15N 1.00W
English River town Canada 76 49.20N 91.00W
Enid U.S.A. 83 36.19N 97.48W
Enkhuizen Neth. 14 52.42N 5.17E
Enköping Sweden 23 59.38N 17.04E
Enna Italy 18 37.34N 14.15E
Ennadai Canada 75 61.08N100.53W
Ennadai L. Canada 75 61.00N101.00W
Ennedi f. Chad 48 17.15N 22.00E
Enneri Yoo wadi Chad 53 19.24N 16.38E
Enngonia Australia 67 29.20S145.53E
Ennis Rep. of Ire. 13 52.51N 9.00W
Ennis U.S.A. 83 32.20N 96.38W
Enniscorthy Rep. of Ire. 13 52.30N 6.35W
Enniskillen U.K. 13 54.21N 7.40W
Ennistymon Rep. of Ire. 13 52.56N 9.18W
Enns r. Austria 20 48.14N 14.22E
Enontekiö Finland 22 68.23N 23.38E
Enping China 33 22.11N112.18E
Ensay Australia 67 37.24S147.52E
Enschede Neth. 14 52.13N 6.54E
Ensenada Argentina 93 34.51S 57.55W
Ensenada Baja Calif. Norte Mexico 81 31.52N116.37W
Ensenada Nuevo León Mexico 83 25.56N 97.50W
Enshi China 33 30.18N109.29E
Enshū-nada sea Japan 35 34.30N137.30E
Entebbe Uganda 55 0.08N 32.29E
Enterprise Canada 74 60.47N115.45W
Entre Ríos d. Argentina 93 32.10S 59.00W
Entre Rios de Minas Brazil 94 20.39S 44.06W
Entwistle Canada 74 53.30N115.00W
Enugu Nigeria 53 6.20N 7.29E
Enugu d. Nigeria 53 6.30N 7.30E
Envermeu France 15 49.53N 1.15E
Envigado Colombia 90 6.09N 75.35W
Enza r. Italy 15 44.54N 10.31E
Enzan Japan 35 35.42N138.44E
Eolie, Isole is. Italy 18 38.35N 14.45E
Epe Neth. 14 52.21N 5.59E
Epernay France 15 49.02N 3.58E
Ephraim U.S.A. 80 39.22N111.35W
Ephrata Penn. U.S.A. 85 40.11N 76.10W
Ephrata Wash. U.S.A. 80 47.19N119.33W
Epi i. Vanuatu 68 16.43S168.15E
Épila Spain 16 41.36N 1.17W
Épinal France 17 48.10N 6.28E
Epping U.K. 11 51.42N 0.07E
Epsom U.K. 11 51.20N 0.16W
Epte r. France 15 49.04N 1.37E
Equateur d. Zaïre 54 0.00 21.00E
Equatorial Guinea Africa 54 2.00N 10.00E
Equerdreville France 15 49.40N 1.40W
Era, Ozero l. Russian Fed. 25 47.38N 45.18E
Eraclea Italy 15 45.35N 12.40E
Erciyaş Daği mtn. Turkey 42 38.33N 35.25E
Erdre r. France 15 47.27N 1.34W
Erebus, Mt. Antarctica 96 77.40S167.20E
Erechim Brazil 94 27.35S 52.15W
Eregli Konya Turkey 42 37.30N 34.02E
Eregli Zonguldak Turkey 42 41.17N 31.26E
Erenhot China 32 43.48N112.00E
Ērer r. Ethiopia 45 7.35N 42.05E
Erfoud Morocco 50 31.28N 4.10W
Erft r. Germany 14 51.12N 6.45E
Erfurt Germany 20 50.58N 11.02E
Ergani Turkey 42 38.17N 39.44E
Ergel Mongolia 32 43.08N109.05E
Ergene r. Turkey 19 41.02N 26.22E
Ergig r. Chad 53 11.30N 15.30E
Erica Neth. 14 52.44N 6.56E
Erie U.S.A. 84 42.07N 80.05W
Erie, L. Canada/U.S.A. 76 42.15N 81.00W
Eriksdale Canada 75 50.52N 98.06W
Eriskay i. U.K. 12 57.04N 7.17W
Eritrea see Ērtra d. Ethiopia 48
Eritrea f. Ethiopia 48 15.30N 38.00E
Erkelenz Germany 14 51.05N 6.18E
Erlangen Germany 20 49.36N 11.02E
Erldunda Australia 64 25.14S133.12E
Ermelo Neth. 14 52.19N 5.38E
Ermelo R.S.A. 56 26.30S 29.59E
Erne r. Rep. of Ire. 9 54.30N 8.17W
Ernée France 15 48.18N 0.56W
Erode India 38 11.21N 77.43E
Eromanga i. Vanuatu 68 18.45S169.05E
Erota Ethiopia 48 16.13N 37.57E
Er Rachidia Morocco 50 31.58N 4.25W
Errego Mozambique 55 16.02S 37.11E
Errigal Mtn. Rep. of Ire. 13 55.02N 8.08W
Erris Head Rep. of Ire. 13 54.19N 10.00W
Ertix He r. Kazakhstan 30 48.00N 84.20E
Ērtra d. Ethiopia 48 15.30N 39.00E
Erudina Australia 66 31.30S139.23E
Ervy-le-Châtel France 15 48.02N 3.55E
Erzgebirge mts. Germany 20 50.30N 12.50E
Erzin Russian Fed. 30 50.16N 95.14E
Erzincan Turkey 42 39.44N 39.30E
Erzurum Turkey 42 39.57N 41.17E
Esbjerg Denmark 23 55.28N 8.27E
Esbo see Espoo Finland 23
Escalante U.S.A. 80 37.47N111.36W
Escalón Mexico 83 26.45N104.20W
Escanaba U.S.A. 84 45.47N 87.04W
Esch Lux. 14 49.31N 5.59E
Eschweiler Germany 14 50.49N 6.16E
Escondido r. Nicaragua 87 11.58N 83.45W
Escondido U.S.A. 81 33.07N117.05W
Escuinapa Mexico 81 22.51N105.48W
Escuintla Guatemala 86 14.18N 90.47W
Esens Germany 14 53.40N 7.40E
Eşfahān Iran 43 32.42N 51.40E
Esher U.K. 11 51.23N 0.22W
Eshkanān Iran 43 27.10N 53.38E
Eshowe R.S.A. 56 28.53S 31.29E
Esk r. U.K. 10 54.29N 0.37W
Eskifjördhur town Iceland 22 65.05N 14.00W
Eskilstuna Sweden 23 59.22N 16.30E
Eskimo Point town Canada 75 61.10N 94.03W
Eskişehir Turkey 42 39.46N 30.30E
Esla r. Spain 16 41.29N 6.03W
Eslāmābād-e-Gharb Iran 43 34.08N 46.35E
Eslöv Sweden 23 55.50N 13.20E
Esmeraldas Ecuador 90 0.56N 79.40W
Espanola Canada 76 46.15N 81.46W
Espe Kazakhstan 28 43.50N 74.10E
Esperance Australia 63 33.49S121.52E
Esperance B. Australia 63 33.51S121.53E
Esperanza Argentina 93 31.30S 61.00W
Esperanza Mexico 81 27.35N109.56W
Espinal Colombia 90 4.08N 75.00W
Espinhaço, Serra do mts. Brazil 94 17.15S 43.10W
Espírito Santo d. Brazil 94 20.00S 40.30W
Espíritu Santo i. Vanuatu 68 15.50S166.50E
Espoo Finland 23 60.13N 24.40E
Espungabera Mozambique 57 20.28S 32.48E
Esquel Argentina 93 42.55S 71.20W
Esquimalt Canada 74 48.30N123.23W
Esquina Argentina 93 30.00S 59.30W
Essaouira Morocco 50 31.30N 9.47W
Essen Germany 14 51.27N 6.57E
Essequibo r. Guyana 90 6.30N 58.40W
Essex d. U.K. 11 51.46N 0.30E
Essex U.S.A. 81 34.45N115.15W
Essonne d. France 15 48.36N 2.20E
Essoyes France 15 48.04N 4.32E
Essoyla Russian Fed. 24 61.47N 33.11E
Es Suki Sudan 49 13.24N 33.55E
Est d. Burkina 52 12.45N 0.25E
Est, Pointe de l' c. Canada 77 49.08N 61.41W
Estacado, Llano f. U.S.A. 83 33.30N102.40W
Estados, Isla de los i. Argentina 93 54.45S 64.00W
Eşţahbānāt Iran 43 29.05N 54.03E
Estância Brazil 91 11.15S 37.28W
Estand, Kūh-e mtn. Iran 43 31.18N 60.03E
Este Italy 15 45.14N 11.39E
Estelline U.S.A. 83 34.33N100.26W
Estepona Spain 16 36.26N 5.09W
Esternay France 15 48.44N 3.34E
Estevan Canada 75 49.07N103.05W
Estevan Is. Canada 74 53.03N129.38W
Estevan Pt. Canada 74 49.23N126.33W
Estherville U.S.A. 82 43.24N 94.50W
Estissac France 15 48.16N 3.49E
Estivane Mozambique 57 24.07S 32.38E
Eston U.K. 10 54.34N 1.07W
Estonia Europe 24 59.00N 25.00E
Estoril Portugal 16 38.42N 9.23W
Estrela, Serra da mts. Portugal 16 40.20N 7.40W
Estremoz Portugal 16 38.50N 7.35W
Esztergom Hungary 21 47.48N 18.45E
Étables France 17 48.37N 2.50W
Etadunna Australia 66 28.43S138.38E
Etah India 41 27.38N 78.40E
Etamamiou Canada 77 50.16N 59.58W
Étampes France 15 48.26N 2.10E
Étaples France 17 50.31N 1.39E
Etāwah India 41 26.46N 79.02E
Ethel Creek town Australia 62 23.05S120.14E
Ethiopia Africa 49 9.00N 39.00E
Etive, Loch U.K. 12 56.27N 5.15W
Etna, Monte mtn. Italy 18 37.43N 14.59E
Etolin I. U.S.A. 74 56.10N132.30W
Etosha Game Res. Namibia 56 18.50S 15.40E
Etosha Pan f. Namibia 56 18.50S 16.20E
Etowah U.S.A. 85 35.20N 84.30W
Étretat France 15 49.42N 0.12E
Ettelbrück Lux. 14 49.51N 6.06E
Eua i. Tonga 69 21.23S174.55W
Euabalong Australia 67 33.07S146.28E
Eubank U.S.A. 85 37.16N 84.40W
Euboea see Évvoia i. Greece 19
Eucla Australia 63 31.40S128.51E
Euclid U.S.A. 84 41.34N 81.33W
Eucumbene, L. Australia 67 36.05S148.45E
Eudora U.S.A. 83 33.07N 91.16W
Eudunda Australia 66 34.09S139.04E
Eufaula Resr. U.S.A. 79 35.15N 95.35W
Eugene U.S.A. 80 44.02N123.05W
Eugenia, Punta c. Mexico 81 27.50N115.03W
Eugowra Australia 67 33.24S148.25E
Eunice La. U.S.A. 83 30.30N 92.25W
Eunice N.Mex. U.S.A. 83 32.26N103.09W
Eupen Belgium 14 50.38N 6.04E
Euphrates r. see Nahr al Furāt r. Asia 43
Eurdon U.S.A. 83 33.55N 93.09W
Eure d. France 15 49.10N 1.00E
Eure r. France 15 48.18N 1.12E
Eure et Loire d. France 15 48.30N 1.30E
Eureka Calif. U.S.A. 80 40.47N124.09W
Eureka Kans. U.S.A. 83 37.49N 96.17W
Eureka Nev. U.S.A. 80 39.31N115.58W
Eureka Utah U.S.A. 80 39.57N112.07W
Eurinilla r. Australia 66 30.50S140.01E
Euriowie Australia 66 31.22S141.42E
Euroa Australia 67 36.46S145.35E
Euro Disneyland France 15 48.50N 2.50E
Europa, Picos de mts. Spain 16 43.10N 4.40W
Euskirchen Germany 14 50.40N 6.47E
Euston Australia 66 34.34S142.49E
Eutsuk L. Canada 74 53.20N126.45W
Evale Angola 54 16.24S 15.50E
Evans, Lac l. Canada 76 50.50N 77.00W
Evans Head c. Australia 67 29.06S153.25E
Evanston Ill. U.S.A. 82 42.02N 87.41W
Evanston Wyo. U.S.A. 80 41.16N110.58W
Evansville U.S.A. 84 38.00N 87.33W
Evelyn Creek r. Australia 66 28.20S134.50E
Everard, C. Australia 67 37.50S149.16E
Everard, L. Australia 66 31.25S135.05E
Everard Range mts. Australia 65 27.05S132.28E
Everest, Mt. China/Nepal 41 27.59N 86.56E
Everett U.S.A. 80 47.59N122.13W
Everglades U.S.A. 85 25.52N 81.23W
Everglades Nat. Park U.S.A. 85 25.27N 80.53W
Evesham U.K. 11 52.06N 1.57W
Evijärvi Finland 22 63.22N 23.29E
Evinayong Equat. Guinea 54 1.27N 10.34E
Evje Norway 23 58.36N 7.51E
Évora Portugal 16 38.34N 7.54W
Évreux France 15 49.03N 1.11E
Évry France 15 48.38N 2.27E
Évvoia i. Greece 19 38.30N 23.50E
Ewe, Loch U.K. 12 57.48N 5.38W
Ewing U.S.A. 82 42.16N 98.21W
Ewo Congo 54 0.48S 14.47E
Excelsior Springs town U.S.A. 82 39.20N 94.13W
Exe r. U.K. 11 50.40N 3.28W
Exeter U.K. 11 50.43N 3.31W
Exeter U.S.A. 82 40.39N 97.27W
Exmoor Forest hills U.K. 11 51.08N 3.45W
Exmore U.S.A. 85 37.32N 75.49W
Exmouth Australia 62 21.54S114.10E
Exmouth U.K. 11 50.37N 3.24W
Exmouth G. Australia 62 22.00S114.20E
Expedition Range mts. Australia 64 24.30S149.05E
Extremadura d. Spain 16 39.00N 6.00W
Exuma Is. Bahamas 87 24.00N 76.00W
Eyasi, L. Tanzania 55 3.40S 35.00E
Eye U.K. 11 52.19N 1.09E
Eyemouth U.K. 12 55.52N 2.05W
Eygurande France 17 45.40N 2.26E
Eyjafjördhur est. Iceland 22 65.54N 18.15W
Eyl Somali Rep. 45 8.00N 49.51E
Eyrarbakki Iceland 22 63.52N 21.09W
Eyre r. Australia 64 26.40S139.00E
Eyre, L. Australia 66 28.30S137.25E
Eyre Pen. Australia 66 34.00S135.45E
Ezequil Ramos Mexia, Embalse resr. Argentina 93 39.20S 69.00W

F

Faaone Tahiti 69 17.40S149.18W
Fåberg Norway 23 61.10N 10.22E
Fåborg Denmark 23 55.06N 10.15E
Fabriano Italy 18 43.20N 12.54E
Facatativá Colombia 90 4.48N 74.32W
Facundo Argentina 93 45.19S 69.59W
Fada Chad 48 17.14N 21.33E
Fada-N'Gourma Burkina 52 12.03N 0.22E
Faenza Italy 15 44.17N 11.52E
Fafa Mali 52 15.20N 0.43E
Fafen r. Ethiopia 45 6.07N 44.20E
Fagamalo W. Samoa 68 13.24S172.22W
Făgăraş Romania 21 45.51N 24.58E
Fagernes Norway 23 60.59N 9.17E
Fagersta Sweden 23 60.00N 15.47E
Faguibine, Lac l. Mali 52 16.45N 3.54W
Fagus Egypt 44 30.44N 31.47E
Fā'id Egypt 44 30.19N 32.19E
Fairbanks U.S.A. 72 64.50N147.50W
Fairborn U.S.A. 84 39.48N 84.03W
Fairbury U.S.A. 82 40.08N 97.11W
Fairfax U.S.A. 83 36.34N 96.42W
Fairfield Ala. U.S.A. 85 33.29N 86.59W
Fairfield Calif. U.S.A. 80 38.15N122.03W
Fairfield Ill. U.S.A. 82 38.22N 88.23W
Fairfield Iowa U.S.A. 82 40.56N 91.57W
Fair Head U.K. 13 55.13N 6.09W
Fair Isle U.K. 12 59.32N 1.38W
Fairlie New Zealand 60 44.06S170.50E
Fairmont Minn. U.S.A. 82 43.39N 94.28W
Fairmont W.Va. U.S.A. 84 39.28N 80.08W
Fairview Canada 74 56.05N118.25W
Fairview Mont. U.S.A. 80 47.51N104.03W
Fairview Okla. U.S.A. 83 36.16N 98.29W
Fairview Utah U.S.A. 80 39.38N111.26W
Fairweather, Mt. U.S.A. 74 59.00N137.30W
Faisalābād Pakistan 40 31.25N 73.05E
Faith U.S.A. 82 45.02N102.02W
Faizābād India 41 26.47N 82.08E
Fajr, Wādī r. Saudi Arabia 42 30.00N 38.25E
Fakaofo Pacific Oc. 68 9.30S171.15W
Fakenham U.K. 10 52.50N 0.51E
Fakfak Indonesia 37 2.55S132.17E
Falaise France 15 48.54N 0.11W
Falam Burma 34 22.58N 93.45E
Falcarragh Rep. of Ire. 13 55.08N 8.06W
Falcone, Capo del c. Italy 18 40.57N 8.12E
Falcon Resr. U.S.A. 83 26.37N 99.11W
Falealupo W. Samoa 68 13.29S172.47W
Falémé r. Senegal 52 14.55N 12.00W
Faleshty Moldavia 21 47.30N 27.45E
Falfurrias U.S.A. 83 27.14N 98.09W
Falkenberg Sweden 23 56.54N 12.28E
Falkirk U.K. 12 56.00N 3.48W
Falkland Is. Atlantic Oc. 93 51.45W 59.00W
Falkland Sd. str. Falkland Is. 93 51.45W 59.25W
Falköping Sweden 23 58.10N 13.31E
Fallbrook U.S.A. 81 33.23N117.15W
Fallon U.S.A. 80 46.50N105.07W
Fall River town U.S.A. 84 41.43N 71.08W
Falls City U.S.A. 82 40.03N 95.36W
Falmouth U.K. 11 50.09N 5.05W
False B. R.S.A. 56 34.10S 18.40E
False C. U.S.A. 85 38.29N 74.59W
False Pt. India 41 20.22N 86.52E
Falster i. Denmark 23 54.48N 11.58E
Fălticeni Romania 21 47.28N 26.18E
Falun Sweden 23 60.36N 15.38E
Famagusta see Ammókhostos Cyprus 44
Family L. Canada 75 51.54N 95.30W
Famoso U.S.A. 81 35.36N119.14W
Fandriana Madagascar 57 20.14S 47.23E
Fangak Sudan 49 9.04N 30.53E
Fangcheng China 32 33.16N112.59E
Fangdou Shan mts. China 33 30.36N108.45E
Fang Xian China 33 32.04N110.47E
Fanjing Shan mtn. China 33 27.57N108.50E
Fannich, Loch U.K. 12 57.38N 5.00W
Fanning I. see Tabuaeran i. Kiribati 69
Fano Italy 15 43.50N 13.01E
Fan Xian China 32 35.59N115.31E
Faradje Zaïre 55 3.45N 29.43E
Faradofay Madagascar 57 25.02S 47.00E
Farafangana Madagascar 57 22.49S 47.50E
Farāfirah, Wāḩāt al oasis Egypt 42 27.15N 28.10E
Farāh Afghan. 40 32.22N 62.07E
Farāh d. Afghan. 40 33.00N 62.00E
Farāh r. Afghan. 40 31.29N 61.24E
Faranah Guinea 52 10.01N 10.47W
Farasān, Jazā'ir is. Saudi Arabia 48 16.48N 41.54E
Faratsiho Madagascar 57 19.24S 46.57E
Faraulep is. Federated States of Micronesia 37 8.36N144.33E
Fareara, Pt. Tahiti 69 17.52S149.39W
Fareham U.K. 11 50.52N 1.11W
Farewell, C. see Farvel, Kap c. Greenland 73
Farewell, C. New Zealand 60 40.30S172.35E
Fargo U.S.A. 82 46.52N 96.48W
Faribault U.S.A. 82 44.18N 93.16W
Farīdpur Bangla. 41 23.36N 89.50E
Farim Guinea Bissau 52 12.30N 15.09W
Farina Australia 66 30.05S138.20E
Farkwa Tanzania 55 5.26S 35.15E
Farmerville U.S.A. 83 32.47N 92.24W
Farmington Mo. U.S.A. 83 37.47N 90.25W
Farmington N.Mex. U.S.A. 80 36.44N108.12W
Farnborough U.K. 11 51.17N 0.46W
Farne Is. U.K. 10 55.38N 1.36W
Farnham Canada 77 45.17N 72.59W
Farnham U.K. 11 51.13N 0.49W
Faro Brazil 91 2.11S 56.44W
Faro Portugal 16 37.01N 7.56W
Faroe Bank f. Atlantic Oc. 8 61.00N 9.00W
Faroe Is. Europe 8 62.00N 7.00W
Fårön i. Sweden 23 57.56N 19.08E
Fårösund Sweden 23 57.52N 19.03E
Farrell U.S.A. 84 41.13N 80.31W
Farrukhābād India 41 27.24N 79.34E
Fársala Greece 19 39.17N 22.22E
Fārsī Afghan. 40 33.47N 63.15E
Farsund Norway 23 58.05N 6.48E
Fartak, Ra's c. Yemen 45 15.38N 52.15E
Farvel, Kap c. Greenland 73 60.00N 44.20W
Farwell U.S.A. 83 34.23N103.02W
Fasā Iran 43 28.55N 53.38E
Fastov Ukraine 21 50.08N 29.59E
Fatehābād India 40 29.31N 75.28E
Fatehjang Pakistan 40 33.34N 72.39E
Fatehpur Rāj. India 40 27.59N 74.57E
Fatehpur Uttar P. India 41 25.56N 80.48E
Fatehpur Pakistan 40 31.10N 71.13E
Fatehpur Sīkri India 41 27.06N 77.40E
Fatick Senegal 52 14.19N 16.27W
Fatu Hiva i. Is. Marquises 69 10.27S138.39W
Fatwā India 41 25.31N 85.19E
Faulkton U.S.A. 82 45.02N 99.08W
Făurei Romania 21 45.04N 27.15E
Fauske Norway 22 67.17N 15.25E
Favara Italy 18 37.19N 13.40E
Favignana i. Italy 18 37.57N 12.19E
Fawcett Canada 74 54.34N114.06W
Fawcett L. Canada 76 51.20N 91.46W
Fawn r. Canada 75 55.20N 88.20W
Faxaflói b. Iceland 22 64.30N 22.50W
Faxe r. Sweden 22 63.15N 17.15E
Fayette U.S.A. 85 33.42N 87.50W
Fayetteville Ark. U.S.A. 83 36.04N 94.10W
Fayetteville N.C. U.S.A. 85 35.03N 78.53W
Fayetteville Tenn. U.S.A. 85 35.08N 86.33W
Fāzilka India 40 30.24N 74.02E
Fāzilpur Pakistan 40 29.18N 70.27E
Fdérik Mauritania 50 22.30N 12.30W
Feale r. Rep. of Ire. 13 52.28N 9.37W
Fear, C. U.S.A. 85 33.50N 77.58W
Fécamp France 15 49.45N 0.23E
Federación Argentina 93 31.00S 57.55W
Federal Argentina 93 30.55S 58.45W
Federal Capital Territory d. Nigeria 53 8.50N 7.00E
Federated States of Micronesia Pacific Oc. 68 10.00N155.00E
Fedovo Russian Fed. 24 62.22N 39.21E
Fedulki Russian Fed. 24 65.00N 66.10E
Feeagh, Lough Rep. of Ire. 13 53.56N 9.35W
Feerfeer Somali Rep. 45 5.07N 45.07E
Fehmarn i. Germany 20 54.30N 11.05E
Feia, Lagoa l. Brazil 94 22.00S 41.20W
Feijó Brazil 90 8.09S 70.21W
Feilding New Zealand 60 40.10S175.25E
Feira Zambia 55 15.30S 30.27E
Feira de Santana Brazil 91 12.17S 38.53W
Felanitx Spain 16 39.27N 3.08E
Feldkirch Austria 20 47.15N 9.38E
Felixstowe U.K. 11 51.58N 1.20E
Feltre Italy 15 46.01N 11.54E
Femunden l. Norway 23 62.12N 11.52E
Femundsenden Norway 23 61.55N 11.55E
Fengcheng Jiangxi China 33 28.10N115.45E
Fengcheng Liaoning China 32 40.29N124.00E
Fengfeng China 32 36.35N114.28E
Fenggang China 33 27.58N107.47E
Fengjie China 33 31.02N109.31E
Fengnan China 32 39.30N117.58E
Fengpin Taiwan 33 23.36N121.31E
Fengrun China 32 39.51N118.08E
Fen He r. China 32 35.30N110.38E
Feni Bangla. 41 23.01N 91.20E
Fenoarivo Madagascar 57 18.26S 46.34E
Fenoarivo Atsinanana Madagascar 57 17.22S 49.25E
Fensfjorden est. Norway 23 60.51N 4.50E
Fenton U.S.A. 84 42.48N 83.42W
Fenwick U.S.A. 85 38.14N 80.36W
Fenyang China 32 37.10N111.40E
Feodosiya Ukraine 25 45.03N 35.23E
Ferdows Iran 43 34.00N 58.10E
Fère-Champenoise France 15 48.45N 3.59E
Fère-en-Tardenois France 15 48.12N 3.31E
Fergana Uzbekistan 30 40.23N 71.19E
Fergus Falls town U.S.A. 82 46.17N 96.04W
Ferguson U.S.A. 82 38.46N 90.19W
Fergusson I. P.N.G. 64 9.30S150.40E
Ferkéssédougou Ivory Coast 52 9.30N 5.10W
Fermanagh d. U.K. 13 54.21N 7.40W
Fermo Italy 18 43.09N 13.43E
Fermoselle Spain 16 41.19N 6.24W
Fermoy Rep. of Ire. 13 52.08N 8.17W
Fernandina Beach town U.S.A. 85 30.40N 81.26W
Fernando de Noronha i Atlantic Oc. 95 3.50S 32.25W
Fernlee Australia 67 28.12S147.05E

Ferrara to Gainesville

Ferrara Italy 15 44.49N 11.38E
Ferreñafe Peru 90 6.42S 79.45W
Ferret, Cap c. France 17 44.42N 1.16W
Ferriday U.S.A. 83 31.38N 91.33W
Ferrières France 15 48.05N 2.48E
Fès Morocco 50 34.05N 4.57W
Feshi Zaïre 54 6.08S 18.12E
Festubert Canada 77 47.15N 72.40W
Festus U.S.A. 82 38.13N 90.24W
Feteşti Romania 21 44.23N 27.50E
Fethiye Turkey 42 36.37N 29.06E
Fetlar i. U.K. 12 60.37N 0.52W
Feuilles, Rivière aux r. Canada 73 58.47N 70.06W
Fevzipaşa Turkey 42 37.07N 36.38E
Fianarantsoa Madagascar 57 21.26S 47.05E
Fichê Ethiopia 49 9.52N 38.46E
Fidenza Italy 15 44.52N 10.03E
Fier Albania 19 40.43N 19.34E
Fife d. U.K. 12 56.10N 3.10W
Fife Ness c. U.K. 12 56.17N 2.36W
Figeac France 17 44.32N 2.01E
Figueira da Foz Portugal 16 40.09N 8.51W
Figueras Spain 16 42.16N 2.57E
Figueres see Figueras Spain 16
Fihaonana Madagascar 57 18.36S 47.12E
Fiherenana r. Madagascar 57 23.19S 43.37E
Fiji Pacific Oc. 68 18.00S178.00E
Fik' Ethiopia 49 8.10N 42.18E
Filabusi Zimbabwe 56 20.34S 29.20E
Filey U.K. 10 54.13N 0.18W
Filiaşi Romania 21 44.33N 23.31E
Filiatrá Greece 19 37.09N 21.35E
Filingué Niger 53 14.21N 3.22E
Filipstad Sweden 23 59.43N 14.10E
Fillmore Canada 75 49.50N103.25W
Fillmore U.S.A. 81 34.24N118.55W
Filtu Ethiopia 49 5.05N 40.42E
Fimi r. Zaïre 54 3.00S 17.00E
Finale Emilia Italy 15 44.50N 11.17E
Finale Ligure Italy 15 44.10N 8.20E
Finarwa Ethiopia 49 13.05N 38.58E
Findhorn r. U.K. 12 57.38N 3.37W
Findlay U.S.A. 84 41.02N 83.40W
Findlay, Mt. Canada 74 50.04N116.10W
Finisterre, Cabo de c. Spain 16 42.54N 9.16W
Finke Australia 64 25.35S134.34E
Finke r. Australia 65 27.00S136.10E
Finland Europe 24 64.30N 27.00E
Finland, G. of Finland / Estonia 23 59.30N 24.00E
Finlay r. Canada 74 57.00N125.05W
Finley Australia 67 35.40S145.34E
Finmark Canada 76 48.36N 89.44W
Finn r. Rep. of Ire. 13 54.50N 7.30W
Finnmark d. Norway 22 70.10N 26.00E
Finschhafen P.N.G. 37 6.35S147.51E
Finse Norway 23 60.36N 7.30E
Finspång Sweden 23 58.43N 15.47E
Fiorenzuola d'Arda Italy 15 44.56N 9.55E
Firat r. Turkey see Al Furāt r. Asia 42
Firebag r. Canada 75 57.45N111.20W
Firedrake L. Canada 75 61.25N104.30W
Firenze Italy 18 43.46N 11.15E
Firenzuola Italy 15 44.07N 11.23E
Firozābād India 41 27.09N 78.25E
Firozpur India 40 30.55N 74.38E
Firozpur Jhirka India 40 27.48N 76.57E
Firth of Clyde est. U.K. 12 55.35N 4.53W
Firth of Forth est. U.K. 12 56.05N 3.00W
Firth of Lorn est. U.K. 12 56.20N 5.40W
Firth of Tay est. U.K. 12 56.24N 3.08W
Firūzābād Iran 43 28.50N 52.35E
Firyuza Turkmenistan 28 37.55N 58.03E
Fish r. Namibia 56 28.07S 17.45E
Fisher U.S.A. 83 35.30N 90.58W
Fisher Str. Canada 73 63.00N 84.00W
Fishguard U.K. 11 51.59N 4.59W
Fiskenaesset Greenland 73 63.05N 50.40W
Fiskivötn f. Iceland 22 64.50N 20.45W
Fismes France 15 49.18N 3.41E
Fitzgerald U.S.A. 85 31.43N 83.16W
Fitz Roy Argentina 93 47.00S 67.15W
Fitzroy r. Australia 62 17.31S123.35E
Fitzroy Crossing Australia 62 18.13S125.33E
Fivizzano Italy 15 44.14N 10.08E
Fizi Zaïre 55 4.18S 28.56E
Fjällåsen Sweden 22 67.29N 20.10E
Fjällsjo r. Sweden 22 63.27N 17.06E
Flå Norway 23 60.25N 9.26E
Flagler U.S.A. 80 39.18N103.04W
Flagstaff U.S.A. 81 35.12N111.39W
Flagstaff B. St. Helena 95 15.55S 5.40W
Flåm Norway 23 60.50N 7.07E
Flamborough Head U.K. 10 54.06N 0.05W
Flaming Gorge Resr. U.S.A. 80 41.15N109.30W
Flandre f. Belgium 14 50.52N 3.00E
Flannan Is. U.K. 12 58.16N 7.40W
Flåsjön l. Sweden 22 64.06N 15.51E
Flat r. Canada 74 61.51N126.00W
Flathead L. U.S.A. 80 47.52N114.08W
Flatonia U.S.A. 83 29.47N 97.06W
Flattery, C. Australia 64 14.58S145.21E
Flattery, C. U.S.A. 78 48.23N124.43W
Flatts Village Bermuda 95 32.19N 64.44W
Flaxton U.S.A. 82 48.54N102.24W
Fleetwood U.K. 10 53.55N 3.01W
Flekkefjord town Norway 23 58.17N 6.41E
Flemington U.S.A. 85 40.31N 74.52W
Flen Sweden 23 59.04N 16.35E
Flensburg Germany 20 54.47N 9.27E
Flers France 15 48.45N 0.34W
Fleur-de-Lys Canada 77 50.06N 56.08W
Flevoland d. Neth. 14 52.25N 5.30E
Flinders r. Australia 64 17.30S140.45E
Flinders B. Australia 63 34.23S115.19E
Flinders I. S.A. Australia 66 33.44S134.30E
Flinders I. Tas. Australia 65 40.00S148.00E
Flinders Ranges mts. Australia 66 31.25S138.45E
Flinders Reefs Australia 64 17.37S148.31E
Flin Flon Canada 75 54.46N101.53W
Flint U.K. 10 53.15N 3.07W
Flint U.S.A. 84 43.03N 83.40W
Flint r. U.S.A. 85 30.52N 84.38W
Flint I. Kiribati 69 11.26S151.48W
Flinton Australia 65 27.54S149.34E
Flisa Norway 23 60.34N 12.06E
Flora U.S.A. 82 38.40N 88.30W
Florac France 17 44.19N 3.36E
Florence see Firenze Italy 18
Florence Ala. U.S.A. 85 34.48N 87.40W
Florence Ariz. U.S.A. 81 33.02N111.23W
Florence Colo. U.S.A. 80 38.23N105.08W
Florence Oreg. U.S.A. 80 43.58N124.07W
Florence S.C. U.S.A. 85 34.12N 79.44W
Florence, L. Australia 66 28.52S138.08E
Florencia Colombia 90 1.37N 75.37W
Florennes Belgium 14 50.14N 4.35E
Florenville Belgium 14 49.42N 5.19E
Flores i. Indonesia 37 8.40S121.20E
Flores, Laut sea Indonesia 37 7.00S121.00E
Floreshty Moldavia 21 47.52N 28.12E
Flores Sea see Flores, Laut sea Indonesia 37
Floriano Brazil 91 6.45S 43.00W
Florianópolis Brazil 94 27.35S 48.34W
Florida Uruguay 93 34.06S 56.13W
Florida d. U.S.A. 85 28.00N 82.00W
Florida, Str. of U.S.A. 85 24.00N 81.00W
Florida B. U.S.A. 85 25.00N 80.45W
Florida City U.S.A. 85 25.27N 80.30W
Florida Keys is. U.S.A. 85 24.45N 81.00W
Florina Australia 66 32.23S139.58E
Flórina Greece 19 40.48N 21.25E
Florö Norway 23 61.36N 5.00E
Fluessen l. Neth. 14 52.58N 5.23E
Flushing see Vlissingen Neth. 14
Fly r. P.N.G. 64 8.22S142.23E
Focşani Romania 21 45.40N 27.12E
Foggia Italy 18 41.28N 15.33E
Foggo Nigeria 53 11.21N 9.57E
Fogo Canada 77 49.43N 54.17W
Fogo I. Canada 77 49.40N 54.13W
Foix France 17 42.57N 1.35E
Folda est. N. Trönd. Norway 22 64.45N 11.20E
Folda est. Nordland Norway 22 67.36N 14.50E
Folégandros i. Greece 19 36.35N 24.55E
Foley Botswana 56 21.34S 27.21E
Foleyet Canada 76 48.05N 82.26W
Folgares Angola 56 14.55S 15.03E
Folgefonna glacier Norway 23 60.00N 6.20E
Foligno Italy 18 42.56N 12.43E
Folkestone U.K. 11 51.05N 1.11E
Folkston U.S.A. 85 30.49N 82.02W
Folsom U.S.A. 80 38.41N121.15W
Fominskoye Russian Fed. 24 59.45N 42.03E
Fond du Lac Canada 75 59.17N106.00W
Fond du Lac U.S.A. 82 43.48N 88.27W
Fonsagrada Spain 16 43.08N 7.04W
Fonseca, Golfo de g. Honduras 87 13.10N 87.30W
Fontainebleau France 15 48.24N 2.42E
Fonte Boa Brazil 90 2.33S 65.59W
Fontenay France 17 46.28N 0.48W
Fonuafo'ou i. Tonga 69 18.47S173.58W
Foochow see Fuzhou China 33
Foothills town Canada 74 53.04N116.47W
Forbach France 17 49.11N 6.54E
Forbes Australia 67 33.24S148.03E
Forbesganj India 41 26.18N 87.15E
Forchheim Germany 20 49.43N 11.04E
Förde Norway 23 61.27N 5.52E
Ford's Bridge Australia 67 29.46S145.25E
Fordyce U.S.A. 83 33.49N 92.25W
Forécariah Guinea 52 9.28N 13.06W
Forel, Mt. Greenland 73 67.00N 37.00W
Foreland Pt. U.K. 11 51.15N 3.47W
Foremost Canada 75 49.29N111.25W
Forest of Bowland hills U.K. 10 53.57N 2.30W
Forest of Dean f. U.K. 11 51.48N 2.32W
Forfar U.K. 12 56.38N 2.54W
Forked River town U.S.A. 85 39.51N 74.12W
Forlì Italy 15 44.13N 12.02E
Forman U.S.A. 82 46.07N 97.38W
Formby Pt. U.K. 10 53.34N 3.07W
Formentera i. Spain 16 38.41N 1.30E
Formerie France 15 49.39N 1.44E
Formiga Brazil 94 20.30S 45.27W
Formosa Argentina 92 26.06S 58.14W
Formosa d. Argentina 92 25.00S 60.00W
Formosa see Taiwan Asia 33
Formosa Brazil 91 15.30S 47.22W
Formosa, Serra mts. Brazil 91 12.00S 55.20W
Fornovo di Taro Italy 15 44.42N 10.06E
Forres U.K. 12 57.37N 3.38W
Fors Sweden 23 60.13N 16.18E
Forsayth Australia 64 18.35S143.36E
Forssa Finland 23 60.49N 23.38E
Forst Germany 20 51.46N 14.39E
Forster Australia 67 32.12S152.30E
Forsyth U.S.A. 80 46.16N106.41W
Fort Abbās Pakistan 40 29.12N 72.52E
Fort Adams U.S.A. 83 31.05N 91.33W
Fort Albany Canada 76 52.15N 81.35W
Fortaleza Brazil 91 3.45S 38.35W
Fort Atkinson U.S.A. 82 42.56N 88.50W
Fort Augustus U.K. 12 57.09N 4.41W
Fort Beaufort R.S.A. 56 32.46S 26.36E
Fort Benning U.S.A. 85 32.20N 84.58W
Fort Benton U.S.A. 80 47.49N110.40W
Fort Carnot Madagascar 57 21.53S 47.28E
Fort Chimo see Kuujjuaq Canada 73
Fort Chipewyan Canada 75 58.42N111.08W
Fort Collins U.S.A. 80 40.35N105.05W
Fort Coulonge Canada 76 45.51N 76.44W
Fort-de-France Martinique 87 14.36N 61.05W
Fort de Possel C.A.R. 53 5.03N 19.16E
Fort Dodge U.S.A. 82 42.30N 94.10W
Fort Drum U.S.A. 85 27.31N 80.49W
Forte dei Marmi Italy 15 43.57N 10.10E
Fort Erie Canada 76 42.54N 78.56W
Fortescue r. Australia 62 21.00S116.06E
Fort Frances Canada 76 48.35N 93.25W
Fort Franklin Canada 72 65.11N123.45W
Fort Garland U.S.A. 80 37.26N105.26W
Fort George see Chisasibi Canada 76
Fort Good Hope Canada 72 66.16N128.37W
Fort Grahame Canada 74 56.30N124.35W
Forth r. U.K. 12 56.06N 3.48W
Fort Hancock U.S.A. 81 31.17N105.53W
Fort Hope Canada 76 51.32N 88.00W
Fort Klamath U.S.A. 80 42.42N122.00W
Fort Lallemand Algeria 51 31.18N 6.20E
Fort Lauderdale U.S.A. 85 26.08N 80.08W
Fort Liard Canada 74 60.15N123.28W
Fort Lupton U.S.A. 80 40.05N104.49W
Fort Mackay Canada 75 57.12N111.41W
Fort Macleod Canada 74 49.45N113.30W
Fort MacMahon Algeria 51 29.46N 1.37E
Fort Madison U.S.A. 82 40.38N 91.27W
Fort Maguire Malaŵi 55 13.38S 34.59E
Fort McKenzie Canada 77 56.50N 68.59W
Fort McMurray Canada 75 56.45N111.27W
Fort McPherson Canada 72 67.29N134.50W
Fort Miribel Algeria 51 29.26N 3.00E
Fort Morgan U.S.A. 80 40.15N103.48W
Fort Myers U.S.A. 85 26.39N 81.51W
Fort Nelson Canada 74 58.49N122.39W
Fort Nelson r. Canada 74 59.30N124.00W
Fort Norman Canada 72 64.55N125.29W
Fort Peck Dam U.S.A. 80 47.52N106.38W
Fort Peck Resr. U.S.A. 80 47.45N106.50W
Fort Pierce U.S.A. 85 27.28N 80.20W
Fort Portal Uganda 55 0.40N 30.17E
Fort Providence Canada 74 61.21N117.39W
Fort Qu'Appelle Canada 75 50.45N103.50W
Fort Randall U.S.A. 72 55.10N162.47W
Fort Reliance Canada 75 63.00N109.20W
Fort Resolution Canada 74 61.10N113.40W
Fortrose New Zealand 60 46.34S168.48E
Fortrose U.K. 12 57.34N 4.09W
Fort Rupert Canada 74 50.39N127.27W
Fort Saint Tunisia 51 30.19N 9.30E
Fort Sandeman Pakistan 40 31.20N 69.27E
Fort Saskatchewan Canada 74 53.40N113.15W
Fort Scott U.S.A. 83 37.50N 94.42W
Fort Severn Canada 75 56.00N 87.40W
Fort Shevchenko Kazakhstan 25 44.31N 50.15E
Fort Simpson Canada 74 61.46N121.15E
Fort Smith Canada 75 60.00N111.51W
Fort Smith d. Canada 72 63.30N118.00W
Fort Smith U.S.A. 83 35.23N 94.25W
Fort St. John Canada 74 56.15N120.51W
Fort Stockton U.S.A. 83 30.53N102.53W
Fort Sumner U.S.A. 81 34.28N104.15W
Fort Thomas U.S.A. 81 33.02N109.58W
Fortuna Calif. U.S.A. 80 40.36N124.09W
Fortuna N.Dak. U.S.A. 82 48.55N103.47W
Fortune B. Canada 77 47.25N 55.25W
Fort Valley U.S.A. 85 32.32N 83.56W
Fort Vermilion Canada 74 58.24N116.00W
Fort Wayne U.S.A. 84 41.05N 85.08W
Fort William U.K. 12 56.49N 5.07W
Fort Worth U.S.A. 83 32.45N 97.20W
Fort Yates U.S.A. 82 46.05N100.38W
Forty Mile town Canada 72 64.24N140.31W
Fort Yukon U.S.A. 72 66.35N145.20W
Foshan China 33 23.08N113.08E
Fossano Italy 15 44.33N 7.43E
Foster Australia 67 38.39S146.12E
Fostoria U.S.A. 84 41.10N 83.25W
Fougamou Gabon 54 1.10S 10.31E
Fougères France 15 48.21N 1.12W
Foula i. U.K. 12 60.08N 2.05W
Foulness I. U.K. 11 51.35N 0.55E
Foulwind, C. New Zealand 60 41.45S171.30E
Foumban Cameroon 53 5.43N 10.50E
Fountain U.S.A. 80 38.41N104.42W
Fourmies France 14 50.01N 4.02E
Foúrnoi i. Greece 19 37.34N 26.30E
Fouta Djalon f. Guinea 52 11.30N 12.30W
Foveaux Str. New Zealand 60 46.40S168.00E
Fowey U.K. 11 50.20N 4.39W
Fowler U.S.A. 80 38.08N104.01W
Fowlers B. Australia 65 31.59S132.27E
Fowlerton U.S.A. 83 28.28N 98.48W
Fox Creek town Canada 74 54.26N116.55W
Foxe Basin b. Canada 73 67.30N 79.00W
Foxe Channel Canada 73 65.00N 80.00W
Foxe Pen. Canada 73 65.00N 76.00W
Fox Glacier town New Zealand 60 43.28S170.01E
Foxton New Zealand 60 40.27S175.18E
Fox Valley town Canada 75 50.29N109.28W
Foyle r. U.K. 13 55.00N 7.20W
Foyle, Lough U.K. 13 55.05N 7.10W
Foz do Cunene Angola 54 17.15S 11.48E
Foz do Iguaçu Brazil 94 25.33S 54.31W
Franca Brazil 94 20.33S 47.27W
Francavilla Fontana Italy 19 40.31N 17.35E
France Europe 17 47.00N 2.00E
Frances Australia 66 36.41S140.59E
Frances r. Canada 74 60.16N129.10W
Frances L. Canada 74 61.23N129.30W
Frances Lake town Canada 74 61.15N129.12W
Francesville U.S.A. 84 40.59N 86.54W
Franceville Gabon 54 1.38S 13.31E
Franche-Comté d. France 17 47.10N 6.00E
Francia Uruguay 93 32.33S 56.37W
Francistown Botswana 56 21.12S 27.29E
François L. Canada 74 54.00N125.40W
Franeker Neth. 14 53.13N 5.31E
Frankfort R.S.A. 56 27.15S 28.30E
Frankfort Kans. U.S.A. 82 39.42N 96.25W
Frankfort Ky. U.S.A. 84 38.11N 84.53W
Frankfurt Brandenburg Germany 20 52.20N 14.32E
Frankfurt Hessen Germany 20 50.06N 8.41E
Frankland r. Australia 63 34.58S116.49E
Franklin Ky. U.S.A. 85 36.42N 86.35W
Franklin La. U.S.A. 83 29.48N 91.30W
Franklin N.H. U.S.A. 84 43.27N 71.39W
Franklin Tex. U.S.A. 83 31.02N 96.29W
Franklin W.Va. U.S.A. 84 38.39N 79.20W
Franklin B. Canada 72 70.00N126.30W
Franklin D. Roosevelt L. U.S.A. 80 48.20N118.10W
Franklin Harbour Australia 66 33.42S136.56E
Franklin I. Antarctica 96 76.10S168.30E
Frankston Australia 65 38.08S145.07E
Fransfontein Namibia 56 20.12S 15.01E
Frantsa Iosifa, Zemlya is. Russian Fed. 28 81.00N 54.00E
Franz Canada 76 48.28N 84.25W
Franz Josef Land is. see Frantsa Iosifa, Zemlya ya Russian Fed. 28
Fraser r. B.C. Canada 74 49.07N123.11W
Fraser r. Nfld. Canada 77 56.35N 61.55W
Fraser, I. Australia 64 25.15S153.10E
Fraser Basin f. Canada 74 54.29N124.00W
Fraserburg R.S.A. 56 31.55S 21.29E
Fraserburgh U.K. 12 57.42N 2.00W
Fraser Plateau f. Canada 74 52.52N124.00W
Fraustro Mexico 83 25.51N101.04W
Fray Bentos Uruguay 93 33.08S 58.18W
Fray Marcos Uruguay 93 34.11S 55.44W
Frederica U.S.A. 85 39.01N 75.28W
Fredericia Denmark 23 55.35N 9.46E
Frederick Md. U.S.A. 85 39.23N 77.25W
Frederick Okla. U.S.A. 83 34.23N 99.01W
Frederick S.Dak. U.S.A. 82 45.50N 98.30W
Frederick Hills Australia 64 12.41S136.00E
Fredericksburg Tex. U.S.A. 83 30.17N 98.52W
Fredericksburg Va. U.S.A. 79 38.18N 77.30W
Frederick Sd. U.S.A. 74 57.00N133.00W
Fredericton Canada 77 45.58N 66.39W
Frederikshåb Greenland 73 62.05N 49.30W
Frederikshavn Denmark 23 57.26N 10.32E
Fredonia Kans. U.S.A. 83 37.32N 95.49W
Fredonia N.Y. U.S.A. 84 42.27N 79.22W
Fredrika Sweden 22 64.05N 18.24E
Fredrikstad Norway 23 59.13N 10.57E
Freehold U.S.A. 85 40.16N 74.17W
Freels, C. Canada 77 49.15N 53.28W
Freelton Canada 76 43.22N 80.02W
Freeman U.S.A. 82 43.21N 97.26W
Freeport Bahamas 87 26.30N 78.45W
Freeport Canada 77 44.17N 66.19W
Freeport Ill. U.S.A. 82 42.17N 89.38W
Freeport N.Y. U.S.A. 85 40.40N 73.35W
Freeport Tex. U.S.A. 83 28.58N 95.22W
Freetown Sierra Leone 52 8.30N 13.17W
Freiberg Germany 20 50.54N 13.20E
Freiburg Germany 20 48.00N 7.52E
Freilingen Germany 14 50.33N 7.50E
Freising Germany 20 48.24N 11.45E
Freistadt Austria 20 48.31N 14.31E
Fréjus France 17 43.26N 6.44E
Fremantle Australia 63 32.07S115.44E
Fremont Calif. U.S.A. 80 37.34N122.01W
Fremont Nebr. U.S.A. 82 41.26N 96.30W
Fremont Ohio U.S.A. 84 41.21N 83.08W
Frenchglen U.S.A. 80 42.48N118.56W
French I. Australia 67 38.20S145.20E
Frenchman Butte town Canada 75 53.35N109.38W
Frenda Algeria 51 35.04N 1.03E
Freren Germany 14 52.29N 7.32E
Fresco r. Brazil 91 7.10S 52.30W
Fresco Ivory Coast 52 5.03N 5.31W
Freshford Rep. of Ire. 13 52.44N 7.23W
Fresnillo Mexico 86 23.10N102.53W
Fresno U.S.A. 80 36.45N119.45W
Frewena Australia 64 19.25S135.25E
Fria Guinea 52 10.27N 13.38W
Fria, C. Namibia 56 18.25S 12.01E
Frias Argentina 92 28.40S 65.10W
Fribourg Switz. 20 46.50N 7.10E
Friedberg Germany 20 50.20N 8.45E
Friedrichshafen Germany 20 47.39N 9.29E
Friesland d. Neth. 14 53.05N 5.45E
Friesoythe Germany 14 53.02N 7.52E
Frio, Cabo c. Brazil 94 22.59S 42.00W
Friuli-Venezia Giulia d. Italy 15 46.15N 12.45E
Frobisher B. Canada 73 63.00N 66.45W
Frobisher Bay town Canada 73 63.45N 68.30W
Frobisher L. Canada 75 56.25N108.20W
Frohavet est. Norway 22 63.55N 9.05E
Froid U.S.A. 80 48.20N104.30W
Frolovo Russian Fed. 25 49.45N 43.40E
Frome r. Australia 66 29.49S138.40E
Frome U.K. 11 51.16N 2.17W
Frome, L. Australia 66 30.48S139.48E
Frome Downs town Australia 66 31.13S139.46E
Frontera Mexico 86 18.32N 92.38W
Frosinone Italy 18 41.36N 13.21E
Fröya i. Norway 22 63.45N 8.45E
Frunzovka Ukraine 21 47.19N 29.44E
Frýdek-Místek Czech Republic 21 49.41N 18.22E
Fu'an China 33 27.04N119.37E
Fuchū Japan 35 35.40N139.29E
Fuchuan China 33 24.50N111.16E
Fuchun Jiang r. China 33 30.05N120.00E
Fuding China 33 27.18N120.12E
Fuefuki r. Japan 35 35.33N138.28E
Fuente-obejuna Spain 16 38.15N 5.25W
Fuentes de Oñoro Spain 16 40.33N 6.52W
Fuerte r. Mexico 81 25.50N109.25W
Fuerteventura i. Canary Is. 50 28.20N 14.10W
Fuga i. Phil. 33 18.53N121.22E
Fuglö i. Faroe Is. 8 62.22N 6.15W
Fugou China 32 34.04N114.23E
Fugu China 32 39.02N111.03E
Fuji Japan 35 35.09N138.39E
Fuji r. Japan 35 35.07N138.38E
Fujian d. China 33 26.00N118.00E
Fu Jiang r. China 33 30.02N106.20E
Fujieda Japan 35 34.52N138.16E
Fujin China 31 47.15N131.59E
Fujinomiya Japan 35 35.12N138.38E
Fuji san mtn. Japan 35 35.22N138.44E
Fujisawa Japan 35 35.21N139.29E
Fuji-yoshida Japan 35 35.38N138.42E
Fukui Japan 35 36.04N136.12E
Fukuoka Japan 35 33.39N130.21E
Fukuroi Japan 35 34.45N137.55E
Fūlādī, Kūh-e mtn. Afghan. 40 34.38N 67.32E
Fulda Germany 20 50.35N 9.45E
Fulda r. Germany 20 50.33N 9.41E
Fuling China 33 29.40N107.20E
Fulton Mo. U.S.A. 82 38.52N 91.57W
Fulton N.Y. U.S.A. 84 43.20N 76.26W
Fumay France 14 49.59N 4.42E
Funabashi Japan 35 35.42N139.59E
Funafuti Tuvalu 68 8.31S179.13E
Funan Gaba Ethiopia 49 4.22N 37.58E
Funchal Madeira Is. 95 32.40N 16.55W
Fundão Portugal 16 40.08N 7.30W
Fundy, B. of Canada 77 45.00N 66.00W
Funing China 33 23.37N105.36E
Funiu Shan mts. China 32 33.40N112.20E
Funtua Nigeria 53 11.34N 7.18E
Fuping China 32 38.52N114.12E
Fuqing China 33 25.43N119.22E
Furancungo Mozambique 55 14.51S 33.38E
Fürg Iran 43 28.19N 55.10E
Furnas, Reprêsa de resr. Brazil 94 20.45S 46.00W
Furneaux Group is. Australia 65 40.15S148.15E
Furqlus Syria 44 34.38N 37.08E
Fürstenau Germany 14 52.32N 7.41E
Fürstenwalde Germany 20 52.22N 14.04E
Fürth Germany 20 49.28N 11.00E
Furu-tone r. Japan 35 35.58N139.51E
Fusagasugá Colombia 90 4.22N 74.21W
Fushun China 32 41.50N123.55E
Fusong China 31 42.17N127.19E
Fusui China 33 22.35N107.57E
Fuwah Egypt 44 31.12N 30.33E
Fu Xian Liaoning China 32 39.35N122.07E
Fu Xian Shaanxi China 32 36.00N109.20E
Fuxin China 32 42.08N121.45E
Fuyang Anhui China 32 32.52N115.52E
Fuyang Zhejiang China 33 30.03N119.57E
Fuyang He r. China 32 38.10N116.08E
Fuyu China 31 45.12N124.49E
Fuyuan Heilongjiang China 31 48.20N134.18E
Fuyuan Yunnan China 33 25.40N104.14E
Fuzhou Fujian China 33 26.09N119.21E
Fuzhou Jiangxi China 33 28.01N116.13E
Fyn i. Denmark 23 55.20N 10.30E
Fyne, Loch U.K. 12 55.55N 5.23W

G

Ga Ghana 52 9.48N 2.28W
Gaalkacyo Somali Rep. 45 6.49N 47.23E
Gabela Angola 54 10.52S 14.24E
Gabès Tunisia 51 33.53N 10.07E
Gabès, Golfe de g. Tunisia 51 34.00N 10.25E
Gabir Sudan 49 8.35N 24.40E
Gabon Africa 54 0.00 12.00E
Gabon r. Gabon 54 0.15N 10.00E
Gaborone Botswana 56 24.45S 25.55E
Gabras Sudan 49 10.16N 26.14E
Gabrovo Bulgaria 19 42.52N 25.19E
Gacé France 15 48.48N 0.18E
Gach Sārān Iran 43 30.13N 50.49E
Gada Nigeria 53 13.50N 5.40E
Gādarwāra India 41 22.55N 78.47E
Gäddede Sweden 22 64.30N 14.15E
Gadra Pakistan 40 25.40N 70.37E
Gadsden U.S.A. 85 34.00N 86.00W
Gaeta Italy 18 41.13N 13.35E
Gaeta, Golfo di g. Italy 18 41.05N 13.30E
Gaferut i. Federated States of Micronesia 37 9.14N145.23E
Gaffney U.S.A. 85 35.03N 81.40W
Gafsa Tunisia 51 34.25N 8.48E
Gagarin Russian Fed. 24 55.38N 35.00E
Gagnoa Ivory Coast 52 6.04N 5.55W
Gagnon Canada 77 51.53N 68.10W
Gaibānda Bangla. 41 25.19N 89.33E
Gaillac France 17 43.54N 1.53E
Gaillon France 15 49.10N 1.20E
Gainesville Fla. U.S.A. 85 29.37N 82.21W
Gainesville Ga. U.S.A. 85 34.17N 83.50W
Gainesville Mo. U.S.A. 83 36.36N 92.26W
Gainesville Tex. U.S.A. 83 33.37N 97.08W

Gainsborough to Gochas

Gainsborough U.K. 10 53.23N 0.46W
Gairdner r. Australia 63 34.20S119.30E
Gairdner, L. Australia 66 31.30S136.00E
Gairloch U.K. 12 57.43N 5.40W
Gaithersburg U.S.A. 85 39.09N 77.12W
Gai Xian China 32 40.25N122.15E
Galana r. Kenya 55 3.12S 40.09E
Galangue Angola 54 13.40S 16.00E
Galapagos, Islas is. Pacific Oc. 69 0.30S 90.30W
Galashiels U.K. 12 55.37N 2.49W
Galaţi Romania 21 45.27N 27.59E
Galatina Italy 19 40.10N 18.10E
Galdhöpiggen mtn. Norway 23 61.37N 8.17E
Galeana Mexico 83 24.50N100.04W
Galeh Dār Iran 43 27.36N 52.42E
Galena Alas. U.S.A. 72 64.43N157.00W
Galena Md. U.S.A. 85 39.20N 75.55W
Galesburg U.S.A. 82 40.57N 90.22W
Galich Russian Fed. 24 58.20N 42.12E
Galicia d. Spain 16 43.00N 8.00W
Galilee, L. Australia 64 22.21S145.48E
Galiuro Mts. U.S.A. 81 32.40N110.20W
Gallarate Italy 15 45.40N 8.47E
Gallatin U.S.A. 85 36.22N 86.28W
Galle Sri Lanka 39 6.01N 80.13E
Gállego r. Spain 16 41.40N 0.55W
Gallegos r. Argentina 93 51.35S 69.00W
Galley Head Rep. of Ire. 13 51.32N 8.57W
Galliate Italy 15 45.29N 8.42E
Gallinas, Punta c. Colombia 90 12.20N 71.30W
Gallipoli Italy 19 40.02N 18.01E
Gallipoli see Gelibolu Turkey 19
Gallipolis U.S.A. 84 38.49N 82.14W
Gällivare Sweden 22 67.07N 20.45E
Gällö Sweden 22 62.56N 15.15E
Galloway f. U.K. 12 55.00N 4.28W
Gallup U.S.A. 81 35.32N108.44W
Galong Australia 67 34.37S148.34E
Galston U.K. 12 55.36N 4.23W
Galty Mts. Rep. of Ire. 13 52.20N 8.10W
Galva U.S.A. 82 41.10N 90.03W
Galveston U.S.A. 83 29.18N 94.48W
Galveston B. U.S.A. 83 29.36N 94.57W
Galvez Argentina 92 32.03S 61.14W
Galway Rep. of Ire. 13 53.17N 9.04W
Galway d. Rep. of Ire. 13 53.25N 9.00W
Galway B. Rep. of Ire. 13 53.12N 9.07W
Gam r. Vietnam 33 18.47N105.40E
Gamagōri Japan 35 34.50N137.14E
Gamawa Nigeria 53 12.10N 10.31E
Gamba China 41 28.18N 88.32E
Gambēla Ethiopia 49 8.18N 34.37E
Gambia Africa 52 13.10N 16.00W
Gambia r. Gambia 52 13.28N 15.55W
Gambier, Îles is. Pacific Oc. 69 23.10S135.00W
Gambier I. Australia 66 35.12S136.32E
Gambo Canada 77 48.46N 54.14W
Gamboli Pakistan 40 29.50N 68.26E
Gamboma Congo 54 1.50S 15.58E
Gamboula C.A.R. 53 4.05N 15.10E
Gamia Benin 53 10.24N 2.45E
Gamlakarleby see Kokkola Finland 22
Gamleby Sweden 23 57.54N 16.24E
Gamo Gofa d. Ethiopia 49 6.00N 37.00E
Ganado U.S.A. 81 35.43N109.33W
Gananoque Canada 76 44.20N 76.10W
Ganbashao China 33 26.37N107.41E
Ganda Angola 54 12.58S 14.39E
Gandajika Zaïre 54 6.46S 23.58E
Gandak r. India 41 25.40N 85.13E
Gāndarbal Jammu & Kashmir 40 34.14N 74.47E
Gandāva Pakistan 40 28.37N 67.29E
Gander Canada 77 48.57N 54.34W
Gander r. Canada 77 49.15N 54.30W
Gander L. Canada 77 48.55N 54.40W
Gandevi India 40 20.49N 73.00E
Gāndhi Sāgar resr. India 40 24.18N 75.21E
Gandía Spain 16 38.59N 0.11W
Gandou Congo 54 2.25N 17.25E
Ganga r. India 41 23.22N 90.32E
Gangāpur Rāj. India 40 25.13N 74.16E
Gangāpur Rāj. India 40 26.29N 76.43E
Gangara Niger 53 14.35N 8.40E
Gangārāmpur India 41 25.24N 88.31E
Gangdhār India 40 23.57N 75.37E
Gangdisê Shan mts. China 41 31.15N 82.00E
Ganges r. see Ganga r. India 41
Gangotri India 41 30.56N 79.02E
Gangtok India 41 27.20N 88.37E
Gangu China 32 34.30N105.30E
Gan Jiang r. China 33 29.10N116.00E
Ganmain Australia 67 34.47S147.01E
Gannat France 17 46.06N 3.11E
Gannett Peak mtn. U.S.A. 80 43.11N109.39W
Ganquan China 32 36.19N109.19E
Gansu d. China 30 36.00N103.00E
Ganta Liberia 52 7.15N 8.59W
Gantheaume, C. Australia 66 36.05S137.27E
Ganye Nigeria 53 8.24N 12.02E
Ganyu China 32 34.50N119.07E
Ganzhou China 33 25.49N114.50E
Gao Mali 52 16.19N 0.09W
Gao d. Mali 53 17.20N 1.25E
Gao'an China 33 28.25N115.22E
Gaohe China 33 22.46N112.57E
Gaolan China 32 36.23N103.55E
Gaolou Ling mtn. China 33 24.47N106.48E
Gaomi China 32 36.23N119.44E
Gaoping China 32 35.48N112.55E
Gaotai China 30 39.20N 99.58E
Gaoua Burkina 52 10.20N 3.09W
Gaoual Guinea 52 11.44N 13.14W
Gaoxiong Taiwan 33 22.40N120.18E
Gaoyou China 32 32.40N119.30E
Gaoyou Hu l. China 32 32.50N119.25E
Gaozhou China 33 21.58N110.59E
Gap France 17 44.33N 6.05E
Gar China 41 32.11N 79.59E
Gara, Lough Rep. of Ire. 13 53.57N 8.27W
Garah Australia 67 29.04S149.38E
Garanhuns Brazil 91 8.53S 36.28W
Garba C.A.R. 49 9.12N 20.30E
Gārbosh, Kūh-e mtn. Iran 43 32.36N 50.02E
Gard r. France 17 43.52N 4.40E
Garda Italy 15 45.34N 10.42E
Garda, Lago di l. Italy 15 45.40N 10.40E
Gardelegen Germany 20 52.31N 11.23E
Garden City Ala. U.S.A. 85 34.01N 86.55W
Garden City Kans. U.S.A. 83 37.58N100.53W
Garden Reach India 41 22.33N 88.17E
Gardēz Afghan. 40 33.37N 69.07E
Gardiner U.S.A. 80 45.02N110.42W
Gardnerville U.S.A. 80 38.56N119.45W
Gardone Val Trompia Italy 15 45.41N 10.11E
Garessio Italy 15 44.12N 8.02E
Garet el Djenoun mtn. Algeria 51 25.05N 5.25E
Garhākota India 41 23.46N 79.09E
Garhi Khairo Pakistan 40 28.04N 67.59E
Garibaldi Prov. Park Canada 74 49.50N122.40W
Garies R.S.A. 56 30.34S 18.00E
Garigliano r. Italy 18 41.13N 13.45E
Garissa Kenya 55 0.27S 39.49E
Garko Nigeria 53 11.45N 8.53E
Garland Tex. U.S.A. 83 32.54N 96.39W
Garland Utah U.S.A. 80 41.45N112.10W
Garlasco Italy 15 45.12N 8.55E
Garlin France 17 43.34N 0.15W
Garm Āb Afghan. 40 32.14N 65.01E
Garmisch Partenkirchen Germany 20 47.30N 11.05E
Garmsār Iran 43 35.15N 52.21E
Garnett U.S.A. 82 38.17N 95.14W
Garo Hills India 41 25.45N 90.30E
Garonne r. France 17 45.00N 0.37W
Garoua Cameroon 53 9.17N 13.22E
Garoua Boulaï Cameroon 53 5.54N 14.33E
Garrison U.S.A. 83 31.49N 94.30W
Garrison Resr. U.S.A. 82 48.00N102.30W
Garron Pt. U.K. 13 55.03N 5.57W
Garry L. Canada 73 66.20N100.00W
Garson Canada 76 46.34N 80.52W
Garub Namibia 56 26.33S 16.00E
Garut Indonesia 37 7.15S107.55E
Garvão Portugal 16 37.42N 8.21W
Garve U.K. 12 57.37N 4.41W
Garvie Mts. New Zealand 60 45.15S169.00E
Garwa India 41 24.11N 83.49E
Gary U.S.A. 84 41.34N 87.20W
Garyarsa China 30 31.30N 80.40E
Gar Zangbo r. China 41 32.25N 79.40E
Garzón Colombia 90 2.14N 75.37б
Gas City U.S.A. 84 40.28N 85.37W
Gascogne, Golfe de g. France 17 44.00N 2.40W
Gascony, G. of see Gascogne, Golfe de France 17
Gascoyne r. Australia 62 25.00S113.40E
Gascoyne Junction Australia 62 25.02S115.15E
Gash r. Ethiopia see Qāsh r. Sudan 48
Gashua Nigeria 53 12.53N 11.02E
Gaspé Canada 77 48.50N 64.30W
Gaspé, Cap de c. Canada 77 48.45N 64.09W
Gaspé, Péninsule de pen. Canada 77 48.30N 65.00W
Gaspésie Prov. Park Canada 77 48.50N 65.45W
Gassol Nigeria 53 8.34N 10.25E
Gastonia U.S.A. 85 35.14N 81.12W
Gastre Argentina 93 42.17S 69.15W
Gata, Cabo de c. Spain 16 36.45N 2.11W
Gata, Sierra de mts. Spain 16 40.20N 6.30W
Gátas, Akrotírion c. Cyprus 44 34.33N 33.03E
Gatchina Russian Fed. 24 59.32N 30.05E
Gatehouse of Fleet U.K. 12 54.53N 4.12W
Gateshead U.K. 10 54.57N 1.35W
Gatesville U.S.A. 83 31.26N 97.45W
Gatineau Canada 77 45.29N 75.38W
Gatineau r. Canada 77 45.27N 75.40W
Gatineau N.C.C. Park Canada 77 45.30N 75.52W
Gattinara Italy 15 43.37N 8.22E
Gatton Australia 65 27.32S152.18E
Gatun L. Panama 87 9.20N 80.00W
Gauchy France 15 49.49N 3.13E
Gauer L. Canada 75 57.00N 97.50W
Gauhāti India 41 26.11N 91.44E
Gaurela India 41 22.45N 81.54E
Gauri Sankar mtn. China / Nepal 41 27.57N 86.21E
Gavá Spain 16 41.18N 2.00E
Gavāter Iran 43 25.10N 61.31E
Gāv Koshī Iran 43 28.39N 57.13E
Gävle Sweden 23 60.40N 17.10E
Gävleborg d. Sweden 23 61.30N 16.15E
Gávrion Greece 19 37.52N 24.46E
Gawachab Namibia 56 27.03S 17.50E
Gāwilgarh Hills India 40 21.30N 77.00E
Gawler Australia 66 34.38S138.44E
Gawler Ranges mts. Australia 66 32.30S136.00E
Gaya India 41 24.47N 85.00E
Gaya Niger 53 11.53N 3.31E
Gayndah Australia 64 25.37S151.36E
Gayny Russian Fed. 24 60.17N 54.15E
Gaysin Ukraine 21 48.50N 29.29E
Gayvoron Ukraine 21 48.20N 29.52E
Gaza see Ghazzah Egypt 44
Gaza d. Mozambique 57 23.20S 32.35E
Gaza Strip f. Egypt 44 31.32N 34.23E
Gaziantep Turkey 42 37.04N 37.21E
Gbanhui Ivory Coast 52 8.12N 3.02W
Gboko Nigeria 53 7.22N 8.58E
Gcuwa R.S.A. 56 32.20S 28.09E
Gdańsk Poland 21 54.22N 18.38E
Gdansk, G. of Poland 21 54.45N 19.15E
Gdov Russian Fed. 24 58.48N 27.52E
Gdynia Poland 21 54.31N 18.30E
Gebe i. Indonesia 37 0.05S129.20E
Gebze Turkey 42 40.48N 29.26E
Gech'a Ethiopia 49 7.31N 35.22E
Gedera Israel 44 31.48N 34.46E
Gediz r. Turkey 19 38.37N 26.47E
Gedser Denmark 23 54.35N 11.57E
Geel Belgium 14 51.10N 5.00E
Geelong Australia 66 38.10S144.26E
Gê'gyai China 41 32.25N 84.05E
Gehua P.N.G. 64 10.20S150.25E
Geidam Nigeria 53 12.55N 11.55E
Geikie r. Canada 75 57.45N103.52W
Geilenkirchen Germany 14 50.58N 6.08E
Geilo Norway 23 60.31N 8.12E
Gejiu China 30 23.25N103.05E
Gela Italy 18 37.03N 14.15E
Geladī Ethiopia 45 6.58N 44.30E
Gelai mtn. Tanzania 55 2.37S 36.07E
Gelderland d. Neth. 14 52.05N 6.00E
Geldermalsen Neth. 14 51.53N 5.17E
Geldern Germany 14 51.31N 6.19E
Geldrop Neth. 14 51.26N 5.31E
Geleen Neth. 14 50.58N 5.51E
Gélengdeng Chad 53 10.56N 15.32E
Gelibolu Turkey 19 40.25N 26.31E
Gelligaer U.K. 11 51.40N 3.18W
Gelsenkirchen Germany 14 51.30N 7.05E
Gem Canada 74 50.58N112.11W
Gemas Malaysia 36 2.35N102.35E
Gembloux Belgium 14 50.34N 4.42E
Gemena Zaïre 54 3.14N 19.48E
Gemerek Turkey 42 39.13N 36.05E
Gemlik Turkey 42 40.26N 29.10E
Gemona del Friuli Italy 15 46.16N 13.09E
Genalē r. Ethiopia 49 4.15N 42.10E
Genappe Belgium 14 50.37N 4.25E
Gendringen Neth. 14 51.52N 6.26E
General Acha Argentina 93 37.20S 64.35W
General Alvear Buenos Aires Argentina 93 36.00S 60.00W
General Alvear Mendoza Argentina 93 34.59S 67.42W
General Belgrano Argentina 93 35.45S 58.30W
General Campos Argentina 93 31.30S 58.25W
General Conesa Argentina 93 36.30S 57.19W
General Guido Argentina 93 36.40S 57.45W
General Lavalle Argentina 93 36.22S 56.55W
General Madariaga Argentina 93 37.00S 57.05W
General Paz Argentina 93 35.32S 58.18W
General Pico Argentina 93 35.38S 63.46W
General Roca Argentina 93 39.02S 67.33W
General Santos Phil. 37 6.05N125.15E
Geneseo Ill. U.S.A. 82 41.27N 90.09W
Geneseo N.Y. U.S.A. 84 42.46N 77.49W
Geneva see Genève Switz. 20
Geneva Nebr. U.S.A. 82 40.32N 97.36W
Geneva N.Y. U.S.A. 84 42.53N 76.59W
Geneva Ohio U.S.A. 84 41.48N 80.57W
Geneva, L. see Léman, Lac l. Switz. 20
Genève Switz. 20 46.13N 6.09E
Genichesk Ukraine 25 46.10N 34.49E
Genil r. Spain 16 37.42N 5.20W
Genk Belgium 14 50.58N 5.34E
Gennep Neth. 14 51.43N 5.58E
Gennes France 15 47.20N 0.14W
Genoa Australia 67 37.29S149.35E
Genoa see Genova Italy 15
Genoa U.S.A. 82 41.27N 97.44W
Genoa, G. of see Genova, Golfo di g. Italy 15
Genova Italy 15 44.24N 8.54E
Genova, Golfo di g. Italy 15 44.12N 8.55E
Gent Belgium 14 51.02N 3.42E
Gentilly Canada 77 46.24N 72.17W
Geographe B. Australia 63 33.35S115.15E
George r. Australia 66 28.24S136.39E
George r. Canada 73 58.30N 66.00W
George R.S.A. 56 33.57S 22.27E
George, L. N.S.W. Australia 67 35.07S149.22E
George, L. S.A. Australia 66 37.26S140.00E
George, L. Uganda 55 0.00 30.10E
George, L. U.S.A. 85 29.17N 81.36W
George B. Canada 77 45.50N 61.45W
George's Cove Canada 77 52.40N 55.50W
Georgetown Ascension 95 7.56S 14.25W
Georgetown Qld. Australia 64 18.18S143.33E
George Town Tas. Australia 65 41.04S146.48E
Georgetown Canada 77 46.11N 62.32W
Georgetown Cayman Is. 87 19.20N 81.23W
Georgetown Gambia 52 13.31N 14.50W
Georgetown Guyana 90 6.46N 58.10W
George Town Malaysia 36 5.30N100.16E
Georgetown Del. U.S.A. 85 38.42N 75.23W
Georgetown S.C. U.S.A. 85 33.23N 79.18W
Georgetown Tex. U.S.A. 83 30.38N 97.41W
George V Land f. Antarctica 96 69.00S145.00E
Georgia Europe 25 42.00N 43.30E
Georgia d. U.S.A. 85 32.50N 83.15W
Georgia, Str. of Canada 74 49.25N124.00W
Georgian B. Canada 76 45.15N 80.45W
Georgina r. Australia 64 23.12S139.33E
Georgiyevsk Russian Fed. 25 44.10N 43.30E
Gera Germany 20 50.51N 12.11E
Geraardsbergen Belgium 14 50.47N 3.53E
Geral de Goiás, Serra mts. Brazil 91 13.00S 45.40W
Geraldine New Zealand 60 44.05S171.15E
Geral do Paranã, Serra mts. Brazil 91 14.40S 47.30W
Geraldton Australia 63 28.49S114.36E
Geraldton Canada 76 49.44N 86.59W
Gerede Turkey 42 40.48N 32.13E
Gereshk Afghan. 40 31.48N 64.34E
Gérgal Spain 16 37.07N 2.31W
Gering U.S.A. 82 41.50N103.40W
Gerlach U.S.A. 80 40.40N119.21W
Gerlachovsky mtn. Slovakia 21 49.10N 20.05E
Germany Europe 20 51.00N 10.00E
Germiston R.S.A. 56 26.14S 28.10E
Gerolstein Germany 14 50.14N 6.40E
Gerona Spain 16 41.59N 2.49E
Gerringong Australia 67 34.45S150.50E
Gêrzê China 41 32.16N 84.12E
Gescher Germany 14 51.58N 7.00E
Getafe Spain 16 40.18N 3.44W
Gete r. Belgium 14 50.58N 5.07E
Gethsémani Canada 77 50.13N 60.40W
Gettysburg U.S.A. 82 45.01N 99.57W
Gevān Iran 43 26.03N 57.17E
Gevelsberg Germany 14 51.20N 7.20E
Geysdorp R.S.A. 56 26.31S 25.17E
Geyser U.S.A. 80 47.16N110.30W
Geyve Turkey 42 40.32N 30.18E
Ghābat al 'Arab Sudan 49 9.02N 29.29E
Ghadaf, Wādī al r. Jordan 44 31.46N 36.50E
Ghadāmis Libya 51 30.08N 9.30E
Ghaddūwah Libya 51 26.26N 14.18E
Ghāghra r. India 41 25.47N 84.37E
Ghana Africa 52 8.00N 1.00W
Ghanzi Botswana 56 21.42S 21.39E
Ghanzi d. Botswana 56 21.44S 21.38E
Gharb al Istiwā'īyah d. Sudan 49 5.25N 29.00E
Ghardaïa Algeria 51 32.29N 3.40E
Gharghoda India 41 22.10N 83.21E
Ghārib, Jabal mtn. Egypt 44 28.06N 32.54E
Gharo Pakistan 40 24.44N 67.35E
Gharyān Libya 51 32.10N 13.01E
Gharyān d. Libya 51 30.35N 12.00E
Ghāt Libya 51 24.58N 10.11E
Ghātsīla India 41 22.36N 86.29E
Ghazāl, Baḩr al r. Sudan 49 9.31N 30.25E
Ghāziābād India 41 28.40N 77.26E
Ghāzīpur India 41 25.35N 83.34E
Ghazlūna Pakistan 40 31.24N 67.49E
Ghaznī Afghan. 40 33.33N 68.26E
Ghaznī d. Afghan. 40 32.45N 68.30E
Ghaznī r. Afghan. 40 32.35N 67.58E
Ghazzah Egypt 44 31.30N 34.28E
Ghedi Italy 15 45.24N 10.16E
Gheorghe-Gheorghiu-Dej Romania 21 46.14N 26.44E
Gheorgheni Romania 21 46.43N 25.36E
Gherla Romania 21 47.02N 23.55E
Ghotki Pakistan 40 28.01N 69.19E
Ghowr d. Afghan. 40 34.00N 64.15E
Ghubaysh Sudan 49 12.09N 27.21E
Ghudāf, Wādī al r. Iraq 42 32.54N 43.33E
Ghūrīān Afghan. 40 34.21N 61.30E
Gia Dinh Vietnam 34 10.54N106.43E
Gibb River town Australia 62 16.29S126.20E
Gibeon Namibia 56 25.09S 17.44E
Gibraltar Europe 16 36.07N 5.22W
Gibraltar, Str. of Africa / Europe 16 36.00N 5.25W
Gibraltar Pt. U.K. 10 53.05N 0.20E
Gibson Australia 63 33.39S121.48E
Gibson Desert Australia 62 23.10S125.35E
Gīda Ethiopia 49 9.40N 35.16E
Giddings U.S.A. 83 30.11N 96.56W
Gien France 15 47.41N 2.37E
Giessen Germany 20 50.35N 8.42E
Gieten Neth. 14 53.01N 6.45E
Gifford r. Canada 73 70.21N 83.05W
Gifford U.S.A. 80 48.20N118.08W
Gifhorn Germany 20 52.29N 10.33E
Gifu Japan 35 35.25N136.45E
Gifu d. Japan 35 35.32N137.15E
Giganta, Sierra de la mts. Mexico 81 25.30N111.15W
Gigantes, Llanos de los f. Mexico 81 30.00N105.00W
Gigha i. U.K. 12 55.41N 5.44W
Giglio i. Italy 18 42.21N 10.53E
Gijón Spain 16 43.32N 5.40W
Gila r. U.S.A. 81 32.43N114.33W
Gila Bend U.S.A. 81 32.57N112.43W
Gila Bend Mts. U.S.A. 81 33.10N113.10W
Gilbert r. Australia 64 16.35S141.15E
Gilbert Islands Kiribati 68 2.00S175.00E
Gildford U.S.A. 80 48.34N110.18W
Gilé Mozambique 55 16.10S 38.17E
Gilgandra Australia 67 31.42S148.40E
Gil Gil r. Australia 67 29.10S148.50E
Gilgil Kenya 55 0.29S 36.19E
Gilgit Jammu & Kashmir 38 35.54N 74.20E
Gilgunnia Australia 67 32.25S146.04E
Gill, Lough Rep. of Ire. 13 54.15N 8.14W
Gilles, L. Australia 66 32.50S136.45E
Gillette U.S.A. 80 44.18N105.30W
Gillingham U.K. 11 51.24N 0.33E
Gill Pt. c. St. Helena 95 15.59S 5.38W
Gilmour Canada 76 44.48N 77.37W
Gīlo r. Ethiopia 49 8.10N 33.15E
Gimli Canada 75 50.39N 97.00W
Gingin Australia 63 31.21S115.42E
Gīnīr Ethiopia 49 7.07N 40.46E
Ginzo de Limia Spain 16 42.03N 7.47W
Gióna mtn. Greece 19 38.38N 22.14E
Girardot Colombia 90 4.19N 74.47W
Girdle Ness U.K. 12 57.06N 2.02W
Giresun Turkey 42 40.55N 38.25E
Gīr Hills India 40 21.10N 71.00E
Giri r. Zaïre 54 0.30N 17.58E
Giridih India 41 24.11N 86.18E
Girilambone Australia 67 31.14S146.55E
Girna r. India 40 21.08N 75.19E
Girona see Gerona Spain 16
Gironde r. France 17 45.35N 1.00W
Girvan U.K. 12 55.15N 4.51W
Girwa r. India 41 27.20N 81.25E
Gisborne New Zealand 60 38.41S178.02E
Gisborne d. New Zealand 60 38.20S177.45E
Gisors France 15 49.17N 1.47E
Gitega Burundi 55 3.25S 29.58E
Giulianova Italy 18 42.45N 13.57E
Giurgiu Romania 21 43.52N 25.58E
Giv'atayim Israel 44 32.04N 34.49E
Givet France 17 50.08N 4.49E
Gizāb Afghan. 40 33.23N 65.55E
Gizhiga Russian Fed. 29 62.00N160.34E
Gizhiginskaya Guba g. Russian Fed. 29 61.00N158.00E
Giżycko Poland 21 54.03N 21.47E
Gjerstad Norway 23 58.54N 9.00E
Gjirokastër Albania 19 40.05N 20.10E
Gjoa Haven town Canada 73 68.39N 96.08W
Gjövik Norway 23 60.48N 10.42E
Glace Bay town Canada 77 46.12N 59.57W
Glacier Nat. Park Canada 74 51.15N117.30W
Glacier Peak mtn. U.S.A. 80 48.07N121.06W
Gladewater U.S.A. 83 32.33N 94.56W
Gladmar Canada 75 49.12N104.31W
Gladstone Qld. Australia 64 23.52S151.16E
Gladstone S.A. Australia 66 33.17S138.22E
Gladstone Mich. U.S.A. 84 45.52N 87.02W
Gladstone N.J. U.S.A. 85 40.43N 74.40W
Glafsfjorden l. Sweden 23 59.34N 12.37E
Glåma r. Norway 23 59.15N 10.55E
Glamoč Bosnia-Herzegovina 19 44.03N 16.51E
Glan r. Germany 14 49.46N 7.43E
Glanaman U.K. 11 51.49N 3.54W
Glandorf Germany 14 52.05N 8.00E
Glasco U.S.A. 82 39.22N 97.50W
Glasgow U.K. 12 55.52N 4.15W
Glasgow Ky. U.S.A. 85 36.59N 85.56W
Glasgow Mont. U.S.A. 80 48.12N106.38W
Glassboro U.S.A. 85 39.42N 75.07W
Glastonbury U.K. 11 51.09N 2.42W
Glazov Russian Fed. 24 58.09N 52.42E
Gleisdorf Austria 20 47.06N 15.44E
Glen R.S.A. 56 28.57S 26.19E
Glen Affric f. U.K. 12 57.15N 5.03W
Glénans, Îles de is. France 17 47.43N 3.57W
Glenarm U.K. 13 54.57N 5.58W
Glenburnie Australia 66 37.49S140.56E
Glen Burnie U.S.A. 85 39.10N 76.37W
Glencoe Australia 66 37.41S140.05E
Glen Coe f. U.K. 12 56.40N 5.03W
Glencoe U.S.A. 82 44.45N 94.10W
Glen Cove U.S.A. 85 40.52N 73.37W
Glendale Ariz. U.S.A. 81 33.32N112.11W
Glendale Calif. U.S.A. 81 34.10N118.17W
Glendale Oreg. U.S.A. 80 42.44N123.26W
Glen Davis Australia 67 33.07S150.22E
Glendive U.S.A. 80 47.06N104.43W
Glenelg r. Australia 66 38.03S141.00E
Glengarriff Rep. of Ire. 13 51.45N 9.33W
Glen Garry f. U.K. 12 57.03N 5.04W
Glen Head Rep. of Ire. 13 54.44N 8.46W
Glen Helen town Australia 64 23.15S132.35E
Glen Innes Australia 67 29.42S151.45E
Glen Mòr f. U.K. 12 57.15N 4.30W
Glenmora U.S.A. 83 30.59N 92.35W
Glenmorgan Australia 65 27.19S149.40E
Glen Moriston U.K. 12 57.09N 4.50W
Glenns Ferry U.S.A. 80 42.57N115.18W
Glenrock U.S.A. 80 42.52N105.52W
Glenrothes U.K. 12 56.12N 3.10W
Glenroy Australia 62 17.23S126.01E
Glens Falls town U.S.A. 84 43.19N 73.39W
Glenshee f. U.K. 12 56.45N 3.25W
Glen Spean f. U.K. 12 56.53N 4.40W
Glenwood Ark. U.S.A. 83 34.20N 93.33W
Glenwood Iowa U.S.A. 82 41.03N 95.45W
Glenwood Oreg. U.S.A. 80 45.39N123.16W
Glenwood Springs town U.S.A. 80 39.33N107.19W
Glittertind mtn. Norway 23 61.39N 8.33E
Gliwice Poland 21 50.17N 18.40E
Globe U.S.A. 81 33.24N110.47W
Głogów Poland 20 51.40N 16.06E
Glotovo Russian Fed. 24 63.25N 49.28E
Gloucester Australia 67 31.59S151.58E
Gloucester U.K. 11 51.52N 2.15W
Gloucester U.S.A. 84 42.41N 70.39W
Gloucester City U.S.A. 85 39.54N 75.07W
Gloucestershire d. U.K. 11 51.45N 2.00W
Glubczyce Poland 21 50.13N 17.49E
Glückstadt Germany 20 53.47N 9.25E
Glusha Belorussia 21 53.03N 28.55E
Gmünd Austria 20 48.47N 14.59E
Gnarp Sweden 23 62.03N 17.16E
Gnesta Sweden 23 59.03N 17.18E
Gniewkowo Poland 21 52.24N 18.25E
Gniezno Poland 21 52.32N 17.32E
Gnjilane Yugo. 19 42.28N 21.58E
Gnosjö Sweden 23 57.22N 13.44E
Gnowangerup Australia 63 33.57S117.58E
Gnuca Australia 63 31.08S117.24E
Goa d. India 38 15.30N 74.00E
Goageb Namibia 56 26.45S 17.18E
Goālpāra India 41 26.10N 90.37E
Goat Fell mtn. U.K. 12 55.37N 5.12W
Goba Ethiopia 49 7.02N 40.00E
Goba Mozambique 57 26.11S 32.08E
Gobabis Namibia 56 22.28S 18.58E
Gobi des. Asia 32 45.00N108.00E
Goch Germany 14 51.41N 6.09E
Gochas Namibia 56 24.50S 18.48E

Godalming to **Guanare**

Godalming U.K. 11 51.11N 0.37W
Godar Pakistan 40 28.10N 63.14E
Godāvari r. India 39 16.40N 82.15E
Godbout Canada 77 49.19N 67.37W
Goderich Canada 76 43.45N 81.43W
Goderville France 15 49.39N 0.22E
Godhavn Greenland 73 69.20N 53.30W
Godhra India 40 22.45N 73.38E
Godoy Cruz Argentina 93 32.55S 68.50W
Gods r. Canada 75 56.22N 92.51W
Gods L. Canada 75 54.45N 94.00W
Godthåb Greenland 73 64.10N 51.40W
Goéland, Lac au l. Canada 76 49.47N 76.41W
Goélands, Lac aux l. Canada 77 55.25N 64.20W
Goes Neth. 14 51.30N 3.54E
Gogama Canada 76 47.35N 81.35W
Gogeh Ethiopia 49 8.12N 38.27E
Gogonou Benin 53 10.50N 2.50E
Gogra r. see Ghāghra India 41
Gogrial Sudan 49 8.32N 28.07E
Goha Ethiopia 49 10.25N 34.38E
Gohad India 41 26.26N 78.27E
Goiana Brazil 91 7.30S 35.00W
Goiânia Brazil 91 16.43S 49.18W
Goiás Brazil 91 15.57S 50.07W
Goiás d. Brazil 91 15.00S 48.00W
Goichran India 41 31.04N 78.07E
Goito Italy 15 45.15N 10.40E
Gojam d. Ethiopia 49 11.10N 37.00E
Gojeb r. Ethiopia 49 7.10N 37.27E
Gojō Japan 35 34.21N135.42E
Gojra Pakistan 40 31.09N 72.41E
Gökçeada i. Turkey 19 40.10N 25.51E
Göksun Turkey 42 38.03N 36.30E
Gokteik Burma 39 22.26N 97.00E
Gokwe Zimbabwe 56 18.14S 28.54E
Gol Norway 23 60.42N 8.57E
Gola Gokaran Nath India 41 28.05N 80.28E
Golan Heights mts. Syria 44 32.55N 35.42E
Golconda U.S.A. 80 40.57N117.30W
Goldap Poland 21 54.19N 22.19E
Gold Beach town U.S.A. 80 42.25N124.25W
Golden Canada 74 51.20N117.00W
Golden Rep. of Ire. 13 52.30N 7.59W
Golden U.S.A. 80 39.46N105.13W
Golden B. New Zealand 60 40.45S172.50E
Goldendale U.S.A. 80 45.49N120.50W
Golden Hinde mtn. Canada 74 49.40N125.44W
Golden Ridge town Australia 63 30.51S121.42E
Golden Vale f. Rep. of Ire. 13 52.30N 8.07W
Goldfield U.S.A. 80 37.42N117.14W
Goldfields Canada 75 59.28N108.31W
Goldpines Canada 76 50.45N 93.05W
Goldsand L. Canada 75 56.58N101.02W
Goldsboro U.S.A. 85 35.23N 78.00W
Goldsworthy Australia 62 20.20S119.30E
Goleniów Poland 20 53.36N 14.50E
Golets Skalisty mtn. Russian Fed. 29 56.00N130.40E
Golfito Costa Rica 87 8.42N 83.10W
Golfo degli Aranci town Italy 18 41.00N 9.38E
Goliad U.S.A. 83 28.40N 97.23W
Golling Austria 20 47.36N 13.10E
Golmud China 30 36.22N 94.55E
Golovanevsk Ukraine 21 48.25N 30.30E
Golpāyegān Iran 43 33.23N 50.18E
Golspie U.K. 12 57.58N 3.58W
Goma Zaïre 55 1.37S 29.10E
Gomang Co l. China 41 31.10N 89.10E
Gombe Nigeria 53 10.17N 11.20E
Gombe r. Tanzania 55 4.43S 31.30E
Gomel Belorussia 21 52.25N 31.00E
Gomera i. Canary Is. 50 28.08N 17.14W
Gómez Palacio Mexico 83 25.34N103.30W
Gomīshān Iran 43 37.04N 54.06E
Gompa Jammu & Kashmir 40 35.02N 77.20E
Gonaïves Haiti 87 19.29N 72.42W
Gonâve, Golfe de la g. Haiti 87 19.20N 73.00W
Gonâve, Île de la i. Haiti 87 18.50N 73.00W
Gonbad-e Kāvūs Iran 43 37.15N 55.11E
Gonda India 41 27.08N 81.56E
Gondal India 40 21.58N 70.48E
Gonder Ethiopia 49 12.39N 37.29E
Gonder d. Ethiopia 49 12.30N 37.30E
Gondia India 41 21.27N 80.12E
Gongbo'gyamda China 41 29.56N 93.23E
Gonggar China 41 29.15N 90.50E
Gongga Shan mtn. China 30 29.30N101.30E
Gongola r. Nigeria 53 9.30N 12.06E
Gongolgon Australia 67 30.22S146.56E
Goñi Uruguay 93 33.31S 56.24W
Goniri Nigeria 53 11.30N 12.15E
Gonzaga Italy 15 44.57N 10.49E
Gonzales U.S.A. 83 29.30N 97.27W
Good Hope, C. of R.S.A. 56 34.21S 18.28E
Good Hope Mtn. Canada 74 51.09N124.10W
Gooding U.S.A. 80 42.56N114.43W
Goodland U.S.A. 82 39.21N101.43W
Goodooga Australia 67 29.08S147.30E
Goodsprings U.S.A. 81 35.50N115.26W
Goole U.K. 10 53.42N 0.52W
Goolgowi Australia 67 33.59S145.42E
Goolma Australia 67 32.21S149.20E
Gooloogong Australia 67 33.36S148.27E
Goolwa Australia 66 35.31S138.45E
Goomalling Australia 63 31.19S116.49E
Goombalie Australia 67 29.59S145.24E
Goondiwindi Australia 67 28.30S150.17E
Goongarrie Australia 63 30.03S121.09E
Goor Neth. 14 52.16N 6.33E
Goose r. Canada 77 53.18N 60.23W
Goose Bay town Canada 77 53.19N 60.24W
Goose L. U.S.A. 80 41.57N120.25W
Gopālganj Bangla. 41 23.01N 89.50E
Gopālganj India 41 26.28N 84.26E
Göppingen Germany 20 48.43N 9.39E
Gorakhpur India 41 26.45N 83.22E
Goras India 40 25.32N 76.56E
Gordon r. Australia 63 34.12S117.00E
Gordon U.S.A. 82 42.48N102.12W
Gordon Downs town Australia 62 18.43S128.33E
Gordon L. Canada 74 63.05N113.11W
Gordonvale Australia 64 17.05S145.47E
Goré Chad 53 7.57N 16.31E
Gorē Ethiopia 49 8.08N 35.33E
Gore New Zealand 60 46.06S168.58E
Gorgān Iran 43 36.50N 54.29E
Gorgān r. Iran 43 37.00N 54.00E
Gorgol d. Mauritania 50 15.45N 13.00W
Gori Georgia 43 41.59N 44.05E
Gorinchem Neth. 14 51.50N 4.59E
Gorizia Italy 18 45.58N 13.37E
Gorki see Nizhniy Novgorod Russian Fed. 24
Gorkovskoye Vodokhranilishche resr. Russian Fed. 24 56.49N 43.00E
Görlitz Germany 20 51.09N 15.00E
Gorlovka Ukraine 25 48.17N 38.05E
Gorna Oryakhovitsa Bulgaria 19 43.07N 25.40E
Gorno Altaysk Russian Fed. 28 51.59N 85.56E
Gorno Filinskoye Russian Fed. 28 60.06N 69.58E
Gornyatskiy Russian Fed. 24 67.30N 64.03E
Goroch'an mtn. Ethiopia 49 9.22N 37.04E
Gorodenka Ukraine 21 48.40N 25.30E
Gorodishche Belorussia 21 53.18N 26.00E
Gorodishche Belorussia 21 53.45N 29.45E
Gorodnitsa Ukraine 21 50.50N 27.19E
Gorodnya Ukraine 21 51.54N 31.37E
Gorodok Ukraine 21 49.48N 23.39E
Goroka P.N.G. 37 6.02S145.22E
Goroke Australia 66 36.43S141.30E
Gorokhov Ukraine 21 50.30N 24.46E
Gorongosa r. Mozambique 57 20.29S 34.36E
Gorontalo Indonesia 37 0.33N123.05E
Gort Rep. of Ire. 13 53.04N 8.49W
Goryn r. Ukraine 21 52.08N 27.17E
Gorzów Wielkopolski Poland 20 52.42N 15.12E
Gosford Australia 67 33.25S151.18E
Goslar Germany 20 51.54N 10.25E
Gospić Croatia 20 44.34N 15.23E
Gosport U.K. 11 50.48N 1.08W
Gossi Mali 52 15.49N 1.17W
Gossinga Sudan 49 8.39N 25.59E
Gostivar Macedonia 19 41.47N 20.24E
Gostynin Poland 21 52.26N 19.29E
Göta r. Sweden 23 57.42N 11.52E
Göta Kanal Sweden 23 58.50N 13.58E
Göteborg Sweden 23 57.43N 11.58E
Göteborg och Bohus d. Sweden 23 58.30N 11.30E
Gotemba Japan 35 35.18N138.56E
Götene Sweden 23 58.32N 13.29E
Gotha Germany 20 50.57N 10.43E
Gothenburg see Göteborg Sweden 23
Gothenburg U.S.A. 82 40.56N100.09W
Gothèye Niger 53 13.51N 1.31E
Gotland d. Sweden 23 57.30N 18.30E
Gotland i. Sweden 23 57.30N 18.33E
Göttingen Germany 20 51.32N 9.57E
Gouda Neth. 14 52.01N 4.43E
Gough I. Atlantic Oc. 95 40.20S 10.00W
Gouin, Résr. Canada 76 48.38N 74.54W
Goulburn Australia 67 34.47S149.43E
Goulburn r. Australia 67 36.08S144.30E
Goulburn Is. Australia 64 11.33S133.26E
Goulimime Morocco 50 28.56N 10.04W
Goundam Mali 52 17.27N 3.39W
Gourdon France 17 44.45N 1.22E
Gouré Niger 53 13.59N 10.15E
Gourma-Rharous Mali 52 16.58N 1.50W
Gournay France 15 49.29N 1.44E
Gouro Chad 51 19.33N 19.33E
Governador Valadares Brazil 94 18.51S 42.00W
Govind Balabh Pant Sāgar resr. India 41 24.05N 82.50E
Govind Sāgar resr. India 40 31.20N 76.45E
Gowanda U.S.A. 84 42.28N 78.57W
Gowd-e Zereh des. Afghan. 43 30.00N 62.00E
Gower pen. U.K. 11 51.37N 4.10W
Gowmal r. Afghan. see Gumal r. Pakistan 40
Gowmal Kalay Afghan. 40 32.29N 68.55E
Goya Argentina 92 29.10S 59.20W
Goyder r. Australia 64 12.38S135.11E
Goz Bëida Chad 49 12.13N 21.25E
Gozo i. Malta 18 36.03N 14.16E
Graaff Reinet R.S.A. 56 32.15S 24.31E
Gračac Croatia 20 44.18N 15.51E
Grace, L. Australia 63 33.18S118.15E
Gracias á Dios, Cabo c. Honduras / Nicaragua 87 15.00N 83.10W
Grado Italy 15 45.40N 13.23E
Grado Spain 16 43.23N 6.04W
Grafton Australia 67 29.40S152.56E
Grafton N.Dak. U.S.A. 82 48.25N 97.25W
Grafton Wisc. U.S.A. 82 43.20N 87.58W
Grafton W.Va. U.S.A. 84 39.21N 80.03W
Graham r. Canada 74 56.31N122.17W
Graham U.S.A. 83 33.06N 98.35W
Graham, Mt. U.S.A. 81 32.42N109.52W
Graham I. Canada 74 53.40N132.30W
Graham Land f. Antarctica 96 67.00S 60.00W
Grahamstown R.S.A. 56 33.18S 26.32E
Graiguenamanagh Rep. of Ire. 13 52.33N 6.57W
Grajaú r. Brazil 91 3.41S 44.48W
Grampian d. U.K. 12 57.22N 2.35W
Grampian Mts. U.K. 12 56.55N 4.00W
Grampians mts. Australia 66 37.12S142.34E
Granada Nicaragua 87 11.58N 85.59W
Granada Spain 16 37.10N 3.35W
Granby Canada 77 45.23N 72.44W
Gran Canaria i. Canary Is. 50 28.00N 15.30W
Gran Chaco f. S. America 92 22.00S 60.00W
Grand r. Canada 76 42.51N 79.34W
Grand r. U.S.A. 82 45.40N100.32W
Grand Bahama I. Bahamas 87 26.40N 78.20W
Grand Bank town Canada 77 47.06N 55.47W
Grand Bassam Ivory Coast 52 5.14N 3.45W
Grand Canal see Da Yunhe canal China 32
Grand Canyon f. U.S.A. 81 36.10N112.45W
Grand Canyon town U.S.A. 81 36.03N112.09W
Grand Canyon Nat. Park U.S.A. 81 36.15N112.58W
Grand Cayman i. Cayman Is. 87 19.20N 81.30W
Grand Centre Canada 75 54.25N110.13W
Grand Cess Liberia 52 4.40N 8.12W
Grand Couronne France 15 49.21N 1.00E
Grande r. Bolivia 92 15.10S 64.55W
Grande r. Minas Gerais Brazil 92 20.00S 51.00W
Grande r. Bahia Brazil 91 11.05S 43.09W
Grande, Bahía b. Argentina 93 51.30S 67.30W
Grande, Ilha i. Brazil 94 23.07S 44.16W
Grande, Sierra mts. Mexico 81 29.35N104.55W
Grande Cascapédia Canada 77 48.19N 65.54W
Grande Comore i. Comoros 55 11.35S 43.20E
Grande do Gurupá, Ilha i. Brazil 91 1.00S 51.30W
Grande Prairie Canada 74 55.15N118.50W
Grand Erg de Bilma des. Niger 53 18.30N 14.00E
Grand Erg Occidental des. Algeria 50 30.10N 0.20E
Grand Erg Oriental des. Algeria 51 30.00N 7.00E
Grande Rivière town Canada 77 48.24N 64.30W
Grandes, Salinas f. Argentina 92 29.37S 64.56W
Grandes Bergeronnes Canada 77 48.15N 69.33W
Grande Vallée Canada 77 49.14N 65.08W
Grand Falls town N.B. Canada 77 46.55N 67.45W
Grand Falls town Nfld. Canada 77 48.56N 55.40W
Grand Forks Canada 74 49.00N118.30W
Grand Forks U.S.A. 82 47.55N 97.03W
Grand Fougeray France 15 47.44N 1.44W
Grand Island town U.S.A. 82 40.55N 98.21W
Grand Junction U.S.A. 80 39.05N108.33W
Grand L. N.B. Canada 77 45.38N 67.38W
Grand L. Nfld. Canada 77 49.00N 57.25W
Grand L. U.S.A. 84 45.15N 67.50W
Grand Lahou Ivory Coast 52 5.09N 5.01W
Grand Manan I. Canada 77 44.40N 66.50W
Grand Marais U.S.A. 82 47.45N 90.20W
Grand' Mère Canada 77 46.37N 72.41W
Grandois Canada 77 51.07N 55.46W
Grândola Portugal 16 38.10N 8.34W
Grand Passage N. Cal. 68 18.45S163.10E
Grand Prairie town U.S.A. 83 32.45N 96.59W
Grand Rapids town Canada 75 53.08N 99.20W
Grand Rapids town Mich. U.S.A. 84 42.57N 85.40W
Grand Rapids town Minn. U.S.A. 82 47.14N 93.31W
Grand Récif de Cook reef N. Cal. 68 19.25S163.50E
Grand St. Bernard, Col du pass Italy / Switz. 15 45.52N 7.11E
Grand Teton mtn. U.S.A. 80 43.44N110.48W
Grand Teton Nat. Park U.S.A. 80 43.30N110.37W
Grand Traverse B. U.S.A. 84 45.02N 85.30W
Grand Valley Canada 76 43.54N 80.19W
Grand Valley town U.S.A. 80 39.27N108.03W
Grandville U.S.A. 84 42.54N 85.48W
Grangemouth U.K. 12 56.01N 3.44W
Granger U.S.A. 80 41.35N109.58W
Grängesberg Sweden 23 60.05N 14.59E
Grangeville U.S.A. 80 45.56N116.07W
Granite City U.S.A. 82 38.43N 90.04W
Granite Falls town U.S.A. 82 44.49N 95.31W
Granite Peak town Australia 62 25.38S121.21E
Granite Peak mtn. U.S.A. 78 45.10N109.50W
Granity New Zealand 60 41.38S171.51E
Granja Brazil 91 3.06S 40.50W
Gränna Sweden 23 58.01N 14.28E
Granollers Spain 16 41.37N 2.18E
Granön Sweden 22 64.15N 19.19E
Gran Paradiso mtn. Italy 15 45.31N 7.15E
Grant Mich. U.S.A. 84 43.20N 85.49W
Grant Nebr. U.S.A. 82 40.50N101.56W
Grant City U.S.A. 82 40.29N 94.25W
Grantham U.K. 10 52.55N 0.39W
Grantown-on-Spey U.K. 12 57.20N 3.38W
Grant Range mts. U.S.A. 80 38.25N115.30W
Grants U.S.A. 81 35.09N107.52W
Grants Pass town U.S.A. 80 42.26N123.19W
Grantsville U.S.A. 84 38.55N 81.07W
Granville France 15 48.50N 1.35W
Granville U.S.A. 82 48.16N100.47W
Granville L. Canada 75 56.18N100.30W
Gras, Lac de l. Canada 72 64.30N110.30W
Graskop R.S.A. 56 24.55S 30.50E
Grasse France 17 43.40N 6.56E
Grasset, L. Canada 76 49.55N 78.00W
Grass Valley town Calif. U.S.A. 80 39.13N121.04W
Grass Valley town Oreg. U.S.A. 80 45.22N120.47W
Grates Pt. Canada 77 48.09N 52.57W
Grave Neth. 14 51.45N 5.45E
Grave, Pointe de c. France 17 45.35N 1.04W
Gravelbourg Canada 75 49.53N106.34W
Gravenhurst Canada 76 44.55N 79.22W
Gravesend Australia 67 29.35S150.20E
Gravesend U.K. 11 51.27N 0.24E
Gray France 17 47.27N 5.35E
Grayling U.S.A. 84 44.40N 84.43W
Grays U.K. 11 51.29N 0.20E
Graz Austria 20 47.05N 15.22E
Grdelica Yugo. 19 42.54N 22.04E
Great Abaco I. Bahamas 87 26.25N 77.10W
Great Artesian Basin f. Australia 64 26.30S143.02E
Great Australian Bight Australia 63 33.10S129.30E
Great B. U.S.A. 85 39.30N 74.23W
Great Barrier I. New Zealand 60 36.15S175.30E
Great Barrier Reef f. Australia 64 16.30S146.30E
Great Basin f. U.S.A. 80 40.35N116.00W
Great Bear L. Canada 72 66.00N120.00W
Great Bend town U.S.A. 82 38.22N 98.46W
Great Bitter L. see Murrah al Kubrá, Al Buḩayrah al h5ayrah al Egypt 44
Great Blasket I. Rep. of Ire. 13 52.05N 10.32W
Great Coco i. Burma 34 14.06N 93.21E
Great Divide Basin f. U.S.A. 80 42.00N108.10W
Great Dividing Range mts. Australia 67 29.00S152.00E
Great Driffield U.K. 10 54.01N 0.26W
Greater Antilles is. C. America 87 17.00N 70.00W
Greater London d. U.K. 11 51.31N 0.06W
Greater Manchester d. U.K. 10 53.30N 2.18W
Great Exuma i. Bahamas 87 23.00N 76.00W
Great Falls town U.S.A. 80 47.30N111.17W
Great Inagua I. Bahamas 87 21.00N 73.20W
Great Indian Desert see Thar Desert India / Pakistan 40
Great Karoo f. R.S.A. 56 32.40S 22.20E
Great Kei r. R.S.A. 56 32.39S 28.23E
Great L. Australia 65 41.50S146.43E
Great Malvern U.K. 11 52.07N 2.19W
Great Namaland f. Namibia 56 25.30S 17.20E
Great Nicobar i. India 34 7.00N 93.45E
Great Ouse r. U.K. 10 52.47N 0.23E
Great Ruaha r. Tanzania 55 7.55S 37.52E
Great Salt L. U.S.A. 80 41.10N112.30W
Great Salt Lake Desert U.S.A. 80 40.40N113.30W
Great Sand Hills Canada 75 50.35N109.05W
Great Sandy Desert Australia 62 20.30S123.35E
Great Sandy Desert see An Nafūd des. Saudi Arabia 42
Great Sea Reef Fiji 68 16.25S179.20E
Great Slave L. Canada 74 61.23N115.38W
Great Smoky Mountain Nat. Park U.S.A. 85 35.56N 82.48W
Great Sound b. Bermuda 95 32.18N 64.60W
Great Victoria Desert Australia 63 29.00S127.30E
Great Whernside mtn. U.K. 10 54.09N 1.59W
Great Yarmouth U.K. 11 52.40N 1.45E
Great Zimbabwe ruins Zimbabwe 56 20.30S 30.30E
Gréboun, Mont mtn. Niger 51 20.01N 8.35E
Gredos, Sierra de mts. Spain 16 40.18N 5.20W
Greece Europe 19 39.00N 22.00E
Greeley U.S.A. 80 40.25N104.42W
Green r. U.S.A. 80 38.11N109.53W
Green B. U.S.A. 82 45.00N 87.30W
Green Bay town U.S.A. 82 44.30N 88.01W
Greenbush U.S.A. 82 48.42N 96.11W
Greenbushes Australia 63 33.50S116.00E
Greencastle U.S.A. 84 39.39N 86.51W
Greene U.S.A. 84 42.20N 75.46W
Greeneville U.S.A. 85 36.10N 82.50W
Greenfield Ill. U.S.A. 82 39.21N 90.21W
Greenfield Iowa U.S.A. 82 41.18N 94.28W
Greenfield Mo. U.S.A. 83 37.25N 93.51W
Greenhills Australia 63 31.58S117.01E
Greening Canada 76 48.08N 74.55W
Greenland N. America 73 68.00N 45.00W
Greenlaw U.K. 12 55.43N 2.28W
Greenock U.K. 12 55.57N 4.45W
Greenore Pt. Rep. of Ire. 13 52.14N 6.19W
Greenough r. Australia 63 29.22S114.34E
Green River town Utah U.S.A. 80 38.59N110.10W
Green River town Wyo. U.S.A. 80 41.32N109.28W
Greensboro U.S.A. 85 36.04N 79.47W
Greensburg U.S.A. 84 39.20N 85.29W
Greenvale Australia 64 18.57S144.53E
Greenville Canada 74 55.03N129.33W
Greenville Liberia 52 5.01N 9.03W
Greenville Ala. U.S.A. 85 31.50N 86.40W
Greenville Mich. U.S.A. 84 43.11N 85.13W
Greenville Miss. U.S.A. 83 33.25N 91.05W
Greenville Mo. U.S.A. 83 37.08N 90.27W
Greenville N.C. U.S.A. 85 35.36N 77.23W
Greenville S.C. U.S.A. 85 34.52N 82.25W
Greenville Tex. U.S.A. 83 33.08N 96.07W
Greenwich U.S.A. 85 41.05N 73.37W
Greenwood Miss. U.S.A. 83 33.31N 90.11W
Greenwood S.C. U.S.A. 85 34.11N 82.10W
Gregory r. Australia 64 17.53S139.17E
Gregory U.S.A. 82 43.14N 99.26W
Gregory, L. S.A. Australia 66 28.55S139.00E
Gregory L. W.A. Australia 62 20.10S127.20E
Gregory Range mts. Australia 64 19.00S143.05E
Greifswald Germany 20 54.06N 13.24E
Gremikha Russian Fed. 24 68.03N 39.38E
Grenå Denmark 23 56.25N 10.53E
Grenada C. America 87 12.07N 61.40W
Grenade France 17 43.47N 1.10E
Grenfell Australia 67 33.53S148.11E
Grenoble France 17 45.11N 5.43E
Grenville, C. Australia 64 12.00S143.13E
Gresik Indonesia 37 7.12S112.38E
Gretna U.K. 12 55.00N 3.04W
Gretna U.S.A. 83 29.55N 90.03W
Greven Germany 14 52.07N 7.38E
Grevenbroich Germany 14 51.07N 6.33E
Grevesmühlen Germany 20 53.51N 11.10E
Grey r. New Zealand 60 42.28S171.13E
Grey, C. Australia 64 13.00S136.40E
Greybull U.S.A. 80 44.30N108.03W
Grey Is. Canada 77 50.50N 55.37W
Greymouth New Zealand 60 42.28S171.12E
Grey Range mts. Australia 65 27.30S143.59E
Greystones Rep. of Ire. 13 53.09N 6.04W
Greytown R.S.A. 56 29.04S 30.36E
Griffin U.S.A. 79 33.15N 84.17W
Griffith Australia 67 34.18S146.04E
Griggsville U.S.A. 82 39.42N 90.43W
Grignan France 17 44.25N 4.54E
Grigoriopol Moldavia 21 47.08N 29.18E
Grim, C. Australia 65 40.45S144.45E
Grimari C.A.R. 49 5.44N 20.03E
Grimsby Canada 76 43.12N 79.34W
Grimsby U.K. 10 53.35N 0.05W
Grimstad Norway 23 58.20N 8.36E
Grimsvötn mtn. Iceland 22 64.30N 17.10W
Grindavik Iceland 22 63.50N 22.27W
Grindsted Denmark 23 55.45N 8.56E
Grinnell U.S.A. 82 41.45N 92.43W
Griqualand East f. R.S.A. 56 30.40S 29.10E
Griqualand West f. R.S.A. 56 28.50S 23.30E
Griva Russian Fed. 24 60.35N 50.58E
Grobina Latvia 23 56.33N 21.10E
Groblershoop R.S.A. 56 28.55S 20.59E
Grodno Belorussia 21 53.40N 23.50E
Grodzisk Poland 20 52.14N 16.22E
Grodzyanka Belorussia 21 53.30N 28.41E
Groenlo Neth. 14 52.02N 6.36E
Groix, Île de i. France 17 47.38N 3.26W
Gronau Germany 14 52.14N 7.02E
Grong Norway 22 64.27N 12.19E
Groningen Neth. 14 53.13N 6.35E
Groningen d. Neth. 14 53.15N 6.45E
Groom U.S.A. 83 35.12N101.06W
Groot r. C.P. r. R.S.A. 56 33.58S 25.03E
Groote Eylandt i. Australia 64 14.00S136.40E
Grootfontein Namibia 56 19.32S 18.07E
Groot Karasberge mts. Namibia 56 27.20S 18.50E
Grootlaagte r. Botswana 56 20.58S 21.42E
Groot Swartberge mts. R.S.A. 56 33.20S 22.00E
Grossenbrode Germany 20 54.23N 11.07E
Grossenhain Germany 20 51.17N 13.31E
Grosseto Italy 18 42.46N 11.08E
Gross Glockner mtn. Austria 20 47.05N 12.50E
Groswater B. Canada 77 54.20N 57.30W
Grote Nete r. Belgium 14 51.07N 4.20E
Groundhog r. Canada 76 49.40N 82.06W
Grouse Creek town U.S.A. 80 41.22N113.53W
Grover City U.S.A. 81 35.07N120.37W
Groves U.S.A. 83 29.57N 93.55W
Groveton U.S.A. 83 31.03N 95.08W
Groznyy Russian Fed. 25 43.21N 45.42E
Grudziądz Poland 21 53.29N 18.45E
Grumeti r. Tanzania 55 2.05S 33.45E
Grünau Namibia 56 27.44S 18.18E
Grundarfjördhur town Iceland 22 64.55N 23.20W
Grundy U.S.A. 85 37.13N 82.08W
Grungedal Norway 23 59.44N 7.43E
Gryazovets Russian Fed. 24 58.52N 40.12E
Gryfice Poland 20 53.56N 15.12E
Guachipas Argentina 92 25.31S 65.31W
Guacuí Brazil 94 20.44S 41.40W
Guadalajara Mexico 86 20.30N103.20W
Guadalajara Spain 16 40.37N 3.10W
Guadalcanal i. Solomon Is. 68 9.32S160.12E
Guadalete r. Spain 16 36.37N 6.15W
Guadalmena r. Spain 16 38.00N 3.50W
Guadalquivir r. Spain 16 36.50N 6.20W
Guadalupe Mexico 83 25.41N100.15W
Guadalupe, Isla de i. Mexico 81 29.00N118.16W
Guadalupe, Sierra de mts. Spain 16 39.30N 5.25W
Guadarrama r. Spain 16 39.55N 4.10W
Guadarrama, Sierra de mts. Spain 16 41.00N 3.50W
Guadeloupe i. Leeward Is. 87 16.20N 61.40W
Guadiana r. Portugal 16 37.10N 7.36W
Guadix Spain 16 37.19N 3.08W
Guafo, Golfo de g. Chile 93 43.35S 74.15W
Guainía r. Colombia 90 2.01N 67.07W
Guaíra Brazil 92 24.04S 54.15W
Guajará Mirim Brazil 90 10.48S 65.22W
Guajira, Península de la pen. Colombia 90 12.00N 72.00W
Gualeguay Argentina 93 33.10S 59.20W
Gualeguay r. Argentina 93 33.18S 59.38W
Gualeguaychu Argentina 93 33.00S 58.30W
Guam i. Northern Marianas 68 13.30N144.40E
Guamal Colombia 90 9.10N 74.15W
Guanajuato Mexico 86 21.00N101.16W
Guanajuato d. Mexico 86 21.00N101.00W
Guanare Venezuela 90 9.04N 69.45W

Guanarito to Hassi bel Guebbour

Guanarito Venezuela 90 8.43N 69.12W
Guane Cuba 87 22.13N 84.07W
Guang'an China 33 30.30N106.35E
Guangchang China 33 26.50N116.16E
Guangdong *d.* China 33 23.00N113.00E
Guanghan China 33 30.59N104.15E
Guanghua *see* Laohekou China 32
Guangji China 33 29.42N115.39E
Guangming Ding *mtn.* China 33 30.09N118.11E
Guangnan China 33 24.03N105.03E
Guangrao China 32 37.04N118.22E
Guangxi Zhuangzu *d.* China 33 23.30N109.00E
Guangyuan China 32 32.29N105.55E
Guangze China 33 27.27N117.23E
Guangzhou China 33 23.08N113.20E
Guanling China 33 25.57N105.38E
Guantánamo Cuba 87 20.09N 75.14W
Guan Xian Shandong China 32 36.29N115.25E
Guan Xian Sichuan China 39 30.59N103.40E
Guanyun China 32 34.17N119.15E
Guaporé *r.* Bolivia / Brazil 92 12.00S 65.15W
Guaqui Bolivia 92 16.35S 68.51W
Guarabira Brazil 91 6.46S 35.25W
Guarapuava Brazil 94 25.22S 51.28W
Guaratinguetá Brazil 94 22.49S 45.09W
Guarda Portugal 16 40.32N 7.17W
Guardavalle Italy 19 38.30N 16.30E
Guardo Spain 16 42.47N 4.50W
Guareim *r.* Uruguay *see* Quarí *r.* Brazil 93
Guasave Mexico 81 25.34N108.27W
Guasipati Venezuela 90 7.28N 61.54W
Guastalla Italy 15 44.55N 10.39E
Guatemala C. America 87 15.40N 90.00W
Guatemala *town* Guatemala 86 14.38N 90.22W
Guatemala Basin Pacific Oc. 69 12.00N 95.00W
Guatemala Trench Pacific Oc. 69 15.00N 93.00W
Guatire Venezuela 90 10.28N 66.32W
Guaviare *r.* Colombia 90 4.00N 67.35W
Guaxupé Brazil 94 21.17S 46.44W
Guayaquil Ecuador 90 2.13S 79.54W
Guayaquil, Golfo de *g.* Ecuador 90 3.00S 80.35W
Guaymallén Argentina 93 32.54S 68.47W
Guaymas Mexico 81 27.56N110.54W
Guayquiraró *r.* Argentina 93 30.25S 59.36W
Guba Zaïre 54 10.40S 26.26E
Gubakha Russian Fed. 24 58.55N 57.30E
Gubeikou China 32 40.41N117.09E
Gubin Poland 20 51.59N 14.42E
Gubio Nigeria 53 12.31N 12.44E
Guchab Namibia 56 19.40S 17.47E
Gucheng China 32 37.20N115.57E
Gúdar, Sierra de *mts.* Spain 16 40.27N 0.42W
Gudbrandsdalen *f.* Norway 23 61.30N 10.00E
Gudvangen Norway 23 60.52N 6.50E
Guecho Spain 16 43.21N 3.01W
Guékédou Guinea 52 8.35N 10.11W
Guelma Algeria 51 36.28N 7.26E
Guelph Canada 76 43.34N 80.16W
Guelta Zemmur W. Sahara 50 25.15N 12.20W
Guéméné-sur-Scorff France 17 48.04N 3.13W
Guera *d.* Chad 53 11.22N 18.00E
Guérard, Lac *l.* Canada 77 56.20N 65.35W
Guéret France 17 46.10N 1.52E
Guernica Spain 16 43.19N 2.40W
Guernsey *i.* Channel Is. Europe 11 49.27N 2.35W
Guerra Mozambique 55 13.05S 35.12E
Guerrero *d.* Mexico 86 18.00N100.00W
Guiana S. America 91 3.40N 53.00W
Guiana Highlands S. America 90 4.00N 59.00W
Guichón Uruguay 93 32.21S 57.12W
Guidimaka *d.* Mauritania 50 15.20N 12.00W
Guiding China 33 26.32N107.15E
Guidong China 33 26.12N114.00E
Guiers, Lac de *l.* Senegal 52 16.12N 15.50W
Gui Jiang *r.* China 33 23.25N111.20E
Guildford Australia 63 31.55S115.55E
Guildford U.K. 11 51.14N 0.35W
Guilin China 33 25.20N110.10E
Guillaume-Delisle, Lac *l.* Canada 76 56.20N 75.50W
Guimarães Brazil 91 2.08S 44.36W
Guimarães Portugal 16 41.27N 8.18W
Guimeng Ding *mtn.* China 32 35.34N117.50E
Guinan China 30 35.20N100.50E
Guinea Africa 52 10.30N 11.30W
Guinea, G. of Africa 53 3.00N 3.00E
Guinea Basin *f.* Atlantic Oc. 95 0.00 5.00W
Guinea Bissau Africa 52 11.30N 15.00W
Güines Cuba 87 22.50N 82.02W
Guingamp France 17 48.34N 3.09W
Guinguinéo Senegal 52 14.20N 15.57W
Guiping China 33 23.20N110.02E
Guir, Hammada du *f.* Morocco / Algeria 50 31.00N 3.20W
Güiria Venezuela 90 10.37N 62.21W
Guiscard France 15 49.39N 3.03E
Guise France 15 49.54N 3.38E
Guiuan Phil. 37 11.02N125.44E
Guixi China 33 28.12N117.10E
Gui Xian China 33 23.02N109.40E
Guiyang China 33 26.31N106.39E
Guizhou *d.* China 33 27.00N107.00E
Gujarat *d.* India 40 22.20N 70.30E
Gūjar Khān Pakistan 40 33.16N 73.19E
Gujrānwāla Pakistan 40 32.26N 74.33E
Gujrāt Pakistan 40 32.34N 74.05E
Gulang Gansu China 32 37.30N102.54E
Gulargambone Australia 67 31.21S148.32E
Gulbarga India 38 17.22N 76.47E
Gulfport U.S.A. 83 30.22N 89.06W
Gulgong Australia 67 32.20S149.49E
Gulin China 33 28.07N105.51E
Gulistān Pakistan 40 30.36N 66.35E
Gull Lake *town* Canada 75 50.08N108.27W
Gulma Nigeria 53 12.41N 4.24E
Gulshad Kazakhstan 30 46.37N 74.22E
Gulu Uganda 55 2.46N 32.21E
Guluy Ethiopia 48 14.43N 36.45E
Gulwe Tanzania 55 6.27S 36.27E
Gumal *r.* Pakistan 40 32.08N 69.50E
Gumel Nigeria 53 12.39N 9.23E
Gumla India 41 23.03N 84.33E
Gummersbach Germany 14 51.03N 7.32E
Gum Spring *town* U.S.A. 85 37.47N 77.54W
Gümüşhane Turkey 42 40.26N 39.26E
Guna India 40 24.39N 77.19E
Gunbar Australia 67 34.04S145.25E
Gundagai Australia 67 35.07S148.05E
Gundlupet India 38 11.48N 76.41E
Gungu Zaïre 54 5.43S 19.20E
Gunisao *r.* Canada 75 53.54N 97.58W
Gunisao L. Canada 75 53.33N 96.15W
Gunnedah Australia 67 30.59S150.15E
Gunning Australia 67 34.46S149.17E
Gunnison Colo. U.S.A. 80 38.33N106.56W
Gunnison *r.* U.S.A. 80 39.03N108.35W
Gunnison Utah U.S.A. 80 39.09N111.49W
Guntersville U.S.A. 85 34.20N 86.18W
Guntersville L. U.S.A. 85 34.45N 86.03W
Guntūr India 39 16.20N 80.27E
Gunungsitoli Indonesia 36 1.17N 97.37E
Gunupur India 41 19.05N 83.49E
Günzburg Germany 20 48.27N 10.16E
Guochengyi China 32 36.14N104.52E
Gurais Jammu & Kashmir 40 34.38N 74.50E
Gura Portiţei *f.* Romania 21 44.40N 29.00E
Gurban Obo China 32 43.05N112.27E
Gurdāspur Jammu & Kashmir 40 32.02N 75.31E
Gurgaon India 40 28.28N 77.02E
Gurgueia *r.* Brazil 91 6.45S 43.35W
Gūrha India 40 25.14N 71.45E
Gurskøy *i.* Norway 22 62.16N 5.42E
Guruè Mozambique 57 15.30S 36.58E
Gürün Turkey 42 38.44N 37.15E
Gurupá Brazil 91 1.25S 51.39W
Gurupi *r.* Brazil 91 1.13S 46.06W
Guru Sikhar *mtn.* India 40 24.39N 72.46E
Guruve Zimbabwe 56 16.42S 30.40E
Gurvan Sayhan Uul *mts.* Mongolia 32 43.45N103.30E
Guryev Kazakhstan 25 47.08N 51.59E
Gusau Nigeria 53 12.12N 6.40E
Gusev Russian Fed. 21 54.32N 22.12E
Gusong China 33 28.25N105.12E
Guspini Italy 18 39.32N 8.38E
Gustav Holm, Kap *c.* Greenland 73 67.00N 34.00W
Güstrow Germany 20 53.48N 12.11E
Gütersloh Germany 20 51.54N 8.22E
Guthrie Ky. U.S.A. 85 36.40N 87.10W
Guthrie Okla. U.S.A. 83 35.53N 97.25W
Guyana S. America 90 4.40N 59.00W
Guyang China 32 41.03N110.03E
Guymon U.S.A. 83 36.41N101.29W
Guyra Australia 67 30.14S151.40E
Guyuan Hebei China 32 41.40N115.41E
Guyuan Ningxia Huizu China 32 36.00N106.25E
Guzhen China 32 33.19N117.19E
Guzman, Laguna de *l.* Mexico 81 31.25N107.25W
Gwa Burma 39 17.36N 94.35E
Gwabegar Australia 67 30.34S149.00E
Gwadabawa Nigeria 53 13.23N 5.15E
Gwādar Pakistan 40 25.07N 62.19E
Gwagwada Nigeria 53 10.15N 7.15E
Gwai Zimbabwe 56 19.15S 27.42E
Gwai *r.* Zimbabwe 56 17.59S 26.55E
Gwalior India 41 26.13N 78.10E
Gwanda Zimbabwe 56 20.59S 29.00E
Gwane Zaïre 49 4.43N 25.50E
Gwasero Nigeria 53 9.30N 8.30E
Gweebarra B. Rep. of Ire. 13 54.52N 8.28W
Gwent *d.* U.K. 11 51.44N 3.00W
Gweru Zimbabwe 56 19.25S 29.50E
Gwydir *r.* Australia 67 29.35S148.45E
Gwynedd *d.* U.K. 10 53.00N 4.00W
Gyaca China 41 29.05N 92.55E
Gyandzha Azerbaijan 43 40.39N 46.20E
Gyangtse China 41 30.47N 85.09E
Gyangzê China 41 28.57N 89.38E
Gyaring Co *l.* China 41 31.05N 88.00E
Gydanskiy Poluostrov *pen.* Russian Fed. 28 70.00N 78.30E
Gyimda China 41 31.03N 97.18E
Gyirong China 41 29.00N 85.15E
Gympie Australia 64 26.11S152.40E
Gyöngyös Hungary 21 47.47N 19.56E
Györ Hungary 21 47.41N 17.40E
Gypsum Pt. Canada 74 61.53N114.35W
Gypsumville Canada 75 51.45N 98.35W

H

Haan Germany 14 51.10N 7.02E
Ha'apai Group *is.* Tonga 69 19.50S174.30W
Haapajärvi Finland 22 63.45N 25.20E
Haapamäki Finland 22 62.15N 24.28E
Haapavesi Finland 22 64.08N 25.22E
Haapsalu Estonia 23 58.56N 23.33E
Hā Arava *r.* Israel / Jordan 44 30.30N 35.10E
Haarlem Neth. 14 52.22N 4.38E
Haarlem R.S.A. 56 33.46S 23.28E
Hab *r.* Pakistan 40 24.53N 66.41E
Habahe China 30 47.53N 86.12E
Ḩabarūt Yemen 38 17.18N 52.44E
Habaswein Kenya 55 1.06N 39.26E
Habay-la-Neuve Belgium 14 49.45N 5.38E
Ḩabbān Yemen 45 14.21N 47.05E
Hab Chauki Pakistan 40 25.01N 66.53E
Habiganj Bangla. 41 24.23N 91.25E
Habikino Japan 35 34.33N135.37E
Habo Sweden 23 57.55N 14.04E
Hachinohe Japan 35 40.30N141.30E
Hachiōji Japan 35 35.39N139.20E
Hack, Mt. Australia 66 30.44S138.45E
Hadāli Pakistan 40 32.18N 72.12E
Hadano Japan 35 35.22N139.14E
Ḩadāribah, Ra's al *c.* Sudan 48 22.04N 36.54E
Ḩadbaram Oman 45 17.27N 55.15E
Ḩadd, Ra's al *c.* Oman 43 22.32N 59.49E
Haddington U.K. 12 55.57N 2.47W
Hadejia Nigeria 53 12.30N 10.03E
Hadejia *r.* Nigeria 53 12.47N 10.44E
Hadera Israel 44 32.26N 34.55E
Haderslev Denmark 23 55.15N 9.30E
Hadīboh Yemen 45 12.39N 54.02E
Hadjer Mornou *mtn.* Chad 48 17.12N 23.08E
Ha Dong Vietnam 33 20.40N105.58E
Ḩaḑramawt *f.* Yemen 45 16.30N 49.30E
Hadsten Denmark 23 56.20N 10.03E
Hadsund Denmark 23 56.43N 10.07E
Haedo, Cuchilla de *mts.* Uruguay 93 31.50S 56.10W
Haegeland Norway 23 58.15N 7.50E
Haeju N. Korea 31 38.04N125.40E
Haena Hawaiian Is. 69 22.14N159.34W
Ḩafar al Bāţin Saudi Arabia 43 28.28N 46.00E
Hāfizābād Pakistan 40 32.04N 73.41E
Hafnarfjördhur *town* Iceland 22 64.04N 21.58W
Haft Gel Iran 43 31.28N 49.35E
Hagen Germany 14 51.22N 7.27E
Hagerman U.S.A. 81 33.07N104.20W
Hagerstown U.S.A. 84 39.39N 77.43W
Hagersville Canada 76 42.58N 80.03W
Hagfors Sweden 23 60.02N 13.42E
Ha Giang Vietnam 33 22.50N105.00E
Hags Head Rep. of Ire. 13 52.56N 9.29W
Hague, Cap de la *c.* France 15 49.44N 1.56W
Haguenau France 17 48.49N 7.47E
Hai'an Shan *mts.* China 33 23.00N115.30E
Haicheng China 32 40.52N122.48E
Hai Duong Vietnam 34 20.56N106.21E
Haifa *see* Hefa Israel 44
Haifeng China 33 22.58N115.20E
Haikang China 33 20.55N110.04E
Haikou China 33 20.03N110.27E
Ḩā'il Saudi Arabia 42 27.31N 41.45E
Hailākāndi India 41 24.41N 92.34E
Hailar China 31 49.15N119.41E
Hailong China 32 42.39N125.49E
Hailsham U.K. 11 50.52N 0.17E
Hailun China 31 47.29N126.58E
Hailuoto *i.* Finland 22 65.02N 24.42E
Haimen China 33 28.41N121.30E
Hainan *d.* China 33 19.00N109.30E
Hainaut *d.* Belgium 14 50.30N 3.45E
Haines Alas. U.S.A. 74 59.11N135.23W
Haines Oreg. U.S.A. 80 44.55N117.56W
Haines Junction Canada 74 60.45N137.30W
Haining China 33 30.30N120.35E
Haiphong Vietnam 33 20.48N106.40E
Haiti C. America 87 19.00N 73.00W
Haiyang China 32 36.46N121.09E
Haiyuan China 32 36.35N105.40E
Ḩajar Banga Sudan 49 11.30N 23.00E
Hajdúböszörmény Hungary 21 47.41N 21.30E
Hajdúszoboszló Hungary 21 47.27N 21.24E
Hājīpur India 41 25.41N 85.13E
Hakkâri Turkey 43 37.36N 43.45E
Hakodate Japan 35 41.46N140.44E
Hakupu Niue 68 19.07S169.51W
Hala Pakistan 40 25.49N 68.25E
Ḩalab Syria 42 36.14N 37.10E
Ḩalabjah Iraq 43 35.10N 45.59E
Ḩalā'ib Sudan 48 22.13N 36.38E
Ḩalbā Lebanon 44 34.34N 36.05E
Halberstadt Germany 20 51.54N 11.04E
Halden Norway 23 59.09N 11.23E
Haldia India 41 22.05N 88.03E
Haldwāni India 41 29.13N 79.31E
Haleyville U.S.A. 85 34.12N 87.38W
Half Assini Ghana 52 5.04N 2.53W
Halfmoon Bay *town* Canada 74 49.31N123.54W
Halfmoon Bay *town* New Zealand 60 46.45S168.08E
Haliburton Canada 76 45.03N 78.03W
Haliburton Highlands Canada 76 45.20N 78.00W
Halifax Canada 77 44.39N 63.36W
Halifax U.K. 10 53.43N 1.51W
Halifax U.S.A. 85 36.46N 78.57W
Halīl *r.* Iran 38 27.35N 58.44E
Halkett, C. U.S.A. 72 71.00N152.00W
Halkirk U.K. 12 58.30N 3.30W
Halladale *r.* U.K. 12 58.34N 3.54W
Halland *d.* Sweden 23 56.45N 13.00E
Halle Belgium 14 50.45N 4.14E
Halle Germany 20 51.28N 11.58E
Hällefors Sweden 23 59.47N 14.30E
Hallingdal *f.* Norway 23 60.30N 9.00E
Hall Is. Pacific Oc. 68 8.37N152.00E
Hall Lake *town* Canada 73 68.40N 81.30W
Hällnäs Sweden 22 64.19N 19.38E
Hall Pen. Canada 73 63.30N 66.00W
Hallsberg Sweden 23 59.04N 15.07E
Hall's Creek *town* Australia 62 18.13S127.39E
Hallstavik Sweden 23 60.03N 18.36E
Hallstead U.S.A. 84 41.58N 75.45W
Halmahera *i.* Indonesia 37 0.45N128.00E
Halmstad Sweden 23 56.39N 12.50E
Halsa Norway 22 63.03N 8.14E
Hälsingborg Sweden 23 56.03N 12.42E
Haltern Germany 14 51.45N 7.10E
Haltia Tunturi *mtn.* Finland 22 69.17N 21.21E
Haltwhistle U.K. 10 54.58N 2.27W
Ham France 15 49.45N 3.04E
Ḩamaḑ, Wādī al *r.* Saudi Arabia 42 25.49N 36.37E
Hamada *f. see* Drâa, Hamada du *f.* W. Sahara 50
Hamadān Iran 43 34.47N 48.33E
Ḩamādat Marzūq *f.* Libya 51 26.00N 12.30E
Ḩamāh Syria 44 35.09N 36.44E
Hamakita Japan 35 34.48N137.47E
Hamamatsu Japan 35 34.42N137.44E
Hamar Norway 23 60.48N 11.06E
Hamaröy Norway 22 68.05N 15.40E
Ḩamāţah, Jabal *mtn.* Egypt 42 24.11N 35.01E
Hamborn Germany 14 51.29N 6.46E
Hamburg Germany 20 53.33N 10.00E
Hamburg R.S.A. 56 33.17S 27.27E
Hamburg N.J. U.S.A. 85 41.09N 74.35W
Hamburg N.Y. U.S.A. 76 42.43N 78.50W
Hamburg Penn. U.S.A. 85 40.34N 75.59W
Häme *d.* Finland 23 61.20N 24.30E
Hämeenlinna Finland 23 61.00N 24.27E
Hamelin B. Australia 63 34.10S115.00E
Hameln Germany 20 52.06N 9.21E
Hamer Koke Ethiopia 49 5.12N 36.45E
Hamersley Range *mts.* Australia 62 22.00S118.00E
Hamhŭng N. Korea 31 39.54N127.35E
Hami China 30 42.40N 93.30E
Hamilton Australia 66 37.45S142.04E
Hamilton *r.* Australia 65 27.12S135.28E
Hamilton Bermuda 95 32.18N 64.48W
Hamilton Canada 76 43.15N 79.50W
Hamilton New Zealand 60 37.46S175.18E
Hamilton U.K. 12 55.46N 4.10W
Hamilton Mont. U.S.A. 80 46.15N114.09W
Hamilton Ohio U.S.A. 84 39.23N 84.33W
Hamilton Tex. U.S.A. 83 31.42N 98.07W
Hamley Bridge *town* Australia 66 34.21S138.41E
Hamlin U.S.A. 83 32.53N100.08W
Hamm Germany 14 51.40N 7.49E
Hammamet, Golfe de *g.* Tunisia 51 36.05N 10.40E
Hammam Lif Tunisia 51 36.44N 10.20E
Ḩammār, Hawr al *l.* Iraq 43 30.50N 47.00E
Hammerdal Sweden 22 63.35N 15.20E
Hammerfest Norway 22 70.40N 23.42E
Hammond Australia 66 32.33S138.20E
Hammond La. U.S.A. 83 30.30N 90.28W
Hammond N.Y. U.S.A. 84 44.27N 75.42W
Hammonton U.S.A. 85 39.38N 74.48W
Hamoir Belgium 14 50.25N 5.32E
Hamoyet, Jabal *mtn.* Sudan 48 17.33N 38.00E
Hampshire *d.* U.K. 11 51.03N 1.20W
Hampton S.C. U.S.A. 85 32.52N 81.06W
Hampton Va. U.S.A. 85 37.02N 76.23W
Hamra, Saguia el *wadi* W. Sahara 50 27.15N 13.21W
Ḩamrīn, Jabal *mts.* Iraq 43 34.40N 44.10E
Hāmūn-e Jaz Mūrīān *l.* Iran 38 27.20N 58.55E
Hana Hawaiian Is. 69 20.45N155.59W
Hanang *mtn.* Tanzania 55 4.30S 35.21E
Hancheng China 32 35.29N110.30E
Hancock U.S.A. 84 47.08N 88.34W
Handa Japan 35 34.53N136.56E
Handa Somali Rep. 45 10.39N 51.08E
Handan China 32 36.37N114.26E
Handeni Tanzania 55 5.25S 38.04E
HaNegev *des.* Israel 44 30.42N 34.55E
Hanford U.S.A. 81 36.20N119.39W
Hanga Roa I. de Pascua 69 27.09S109.26W
Hanggin Houqi China 32 40.50N107.06E
Hanggin Qi China 32 39.56N108.54E
Hangö Finland 23 59.50N 22.57E
Hangu China 32 39.11N117.45E
Hangu Pakistan 40 33.32N 71.04E
Hangzhou China 33 30.14N120.08E
Hangzhou Wan *b.* China 33 30.25N121.00E
Hanjiang China 33 25.30N119.14E
Hankey R.S.A. 56 33.50S 24.52E
Hankinson U.S.A. 82 46.04N 96.55W
Hanksville U.S.A. 80 38.21N110.44W
Hānle Jammu & Kashmir 41 32.48N 79.00E
Hanmer Springs *town* New Zealand 60 42.31S172.50E
Hann, Mt. Australia 62 15.55S125.57E
Hanna Canada 75 51.38N111.54W
Hannaford U.S.A. 82 47.19N 98.11W
Hannah B. Canada 76 51.20N 80.00W
Hannibal U.S.A. 79 39.41N 91.25W
Hannover Germany 20 52.23N 9.44E
Hannut Belgium 14 50.40N 5.05E
Hanöbukten *b.* Sweden 23 55.45N 14.30E
Hanoi Vietnam 33 21.01N105.53E
Hanover Canada 76 44.09N 81.02W
Hanover R.S.A. 56 31.04S 24.25E
Hanover U.S.A. 85 39.48N 76.59W
Hanover, Isla *i.* Chile 93 50.57S 74.40W
Han Pijesak Bosnia-Herzegovina 19 44.04N 18.59E
Hānsdiha India 41 24.36N 87.05E
Hanshou China 33 28.55N111.58E
Han Shui *r.* China 33 30.32N114.20E
Hānsi Haryana India 40 29.06N 75.58E
Hansi Himachal P. India 41 32.27N 77.50E
Hanson, L. Australia 66 31.02S136.13E
Hantengri Feng *mtn.* China 30 42.09N 80.12E
Han Ul China 32 45.10N119.48E
Hanyang China 33 30.42N113.50E
Hanyin China 32 32.53N108.37E
Hanzhong China 32 33.08N107.04E
Haouach, Ouadi *wadi* Chad 51 16.45N 19.35E
Haparanda Sweden 22 65.50N 24.10E
Happy Valley *town* Canada 77 53.16N 60.14W
Hapsu N. Korea 31 41.12N128.48E
Hāpur India 41 28.43N 77.47E
Ḩaql Saudi Arabia 44 29.14N 34.56E
Ḩaraḑ Saudi Arabia 43 24.12N 49.08E
Harare Zimbabwe 57 17.49S 31.04E
Har-Ayrag Mongolia 32 45.42N109.14E
Haraze Chad 49 9.55N 20.48E
Harbin China 31 45.45N126.41E
Harborcreek U.S.A. 76 42.10N 79.57W
Harbour Deep *town* Canada 77 50.22N 56.27W
Harbour Grace *town* Canada 77 47.42N 53.13W
Harburg Germany 20 53.27N 9.58E
Harda India 40 22.20N 77.06E
Hardangerfjorden *est.* Norway 23 60.10N 6.00E
Hardangerjökulen *mtn.* Norway 23 60.33N 7.26E
Hardanger Vidda *f.* Norway 23 60.20N 7.30E
Hardeeville U.S.A. 85 32.18N 81.05W
Hardenberg Neth. 14 52.36N 6.40E
Harderwijk Neth. 14 52.21N 5.37E
Harding R.S.A. 56 30.34S 29.52E
Hardman U.S.A. 80 45.10N119.40W
Hardoi India 41 27.25N 80.07E
Hardwār India 41 29.58N 78.10E
Hardwicke B. Australia 66 34.52S137.10E
Hardy U.S.A. 83 36.19N 91.29W
Hare B. Canada 77 51.18N 55.50W
Haren Germany 14 52.48N 7.15E
Hārer Ethiopia 49 9.20N 42.10E
Hārergē *d.* Ethiopia 49 8.00N 41.00E
Harfleur France 15 49.30N 0.12E
Hargeysa Somali Rep. 45 9.31N 44.02E
Har Hu *l.* China 30 38.20N 97.40E
Hari *r.* Indonesia 36 1.00S104.15E
Haripur Pakistan 40 33.59N 72.56E
Harīrūd *r.* Afghan. 38 35.42N 61.12E
Harlan U.S.A. 82 41.39N 95.19W
Harlech U.K. 10 52.52N 4.08W
Harlem U.S.A. 80 48.32N108.47W
Harlingen Neth. 14 53.10N 5.25E
Harlingen U.S.A. 83 26.11N 97.42W
Harlow U.K. 11 51.47N 0.08E
Harlowton U.S.A. 80 46.26N109.50W
Harnai Pakistan 40 30.06N 67.56E
Harnātānr India 41 27.19N 84.01E
Harney Basin *f.* U.S.A. 80 43.15N120.40W
Harney L. U.S.A. 80 43.14N119.07W
Härnösand Sweden 22 62.37N 17.55E
Har Nuur *l.* Mongolia 30 48.00N 93.25E
Haroldswick U.K. 8 60.47N 0.50W
Harper Liberia 52 4.25N 7.43W
Harrai India 41 22.37N 79.13E
Harricana *r.* Canada 76 51.10N 79.45W
Harrigan, C. Canada 77 55.50N 60.21W
Harrington Australia 67 31.50S152.43E
Harrington U.S.A. 85 38.56N 75.35W
Harrington Harbour Canada 77 50.31N 59.30W
Harris Canada 75 51.44N107.35W
Harris *i.* U.K. 12 57.50N 6.55W
Harris, L. Australia 66 31.08S135.14E
Harris, Sd. of U.K. 12 57.43N 7.05W
Harrisburg Ill. U.S.A. 83 37.44N 88.33W
Harrisburg Oreg. U.S.A. 80 44.16N123.10W
Harrisburg Penn. U.S.A. 84 40.16N 76.52W
Harrismith Australia 63 32.55S117.50E
Harrismith R.S.A. 56 28.15S 29.07E
Harrison Ark. U.S.A. 83 36.14N 93.07W
Harrison Nebr. U.S.A. 82 42.41N103.53W
Harrison, C. Canada 77 54.55N 57.55W
Harrison L. Canada 74 49.33N121.50W
Harrisonville U.S.A. 82 38.39N 94.21W
Harrodsburg U.S.A. 85 37.46N 84.51W
Harrogate U.K. 10 53.59N 1.32W
Harrow U.K. 11 51.35N 0.21W
Harstad Norway 22 68.48N 16.30E
Harsūd India 40 22.06N 76.44E
Hart, L. Australia 66 31.08S136.24E
Hartford U.S.A. 84 41.45N 72.42W
Hartland Canada 77 46.18N 67.32W
Hartland U.K. 11 50.59N 4.29W
Hartland Pt. U.K. 11 51.01N 4.32W
Hartlepool U.K. 10 54.42N 1.11W
Hartley Bay *town* Canada 74 53.27N129.18W
Hartola Finland 23 61.35N 26.01E
Hartshorne U.S.A. 83 34.51N 95.33W
Harts Range *town* Australia 64 23.06S134.55E
Hartsville U.S.A. 85 34.23N 80.05W
Harūnābād Pakistan 40 29.37N 73.08E
Har Us Nuur *l.* Mongolia 30 48.10N 92.10E
Hārūt *r.* Afghan. 40 31.35N 61.18E
Harvey Australia 63 33.06S115.50E
Harvey Ill. U.S.A. 82 41.37N 87.39W
Harvey N.Dak. U.S.A. 82 47.47N 99.56W
Harwich U.K. 11 51.56N 1.18E
Haryana *d.* India 40 29.15N 76.30E
Ḩasā, Wādī al *r.* Jordan 44 31.01N 35.29E
Hasa Oasis *see* Aḩsā', Wāḩat al *oasis* Saudi Arabia 43
Hasdo *r.* India 41 21.44N 82.44E
Hase *r.* Germany 14 52.42N 7.17E
Haselünne Germany 14 52.40N 7.30E
Hasenkamp Argentina 93 31.30S 59.50W
Hashābah Sudan 48 14.19N 32.19E
Ḩashtrūd Iran 43 37.29N 47.05E
Hashimoto Japan 35 34.19N135.37E
Haskell U.S.A. 83 33.10N 99.44W
Haslemere U.K. 11 51.05N 0.41W
Hasselt Belgium 14 50.56N 5.20E
Hassi bel Guebbour Algeria 51 28.30N 6.41E

Howth Head to Iron River

Howth Head Rep. of Ire. **13** 53.22N 6.03W
Hoy *i.* U.K. **12** 58.51N 3.17W
Höyanger Norway **23** 61.13N 6.05E
Hoyos Spain **16** 40.09N 6.45W
Hradec Králové Czech Republic **20** 50.13N 15.50E
Hron *r.* Slovakia **21** 47.49N 18.45E
Hrubieszów Poland **21** 50.49N 23.55E
Hsenwi Burma **34** 23.18N 97.58E
Hsipaw Burma **34** 22.42N 97.21E
Hsuphāng Burma **34** 20.18N 98.42E
Huab *r.* Namibia **56** 20.55S 13.28E
Huabei Pingyuan *f.* China **32** 35.00N 115.30E
Huachi China **32** 36.32N 108.14E
Huacho Peru **90** 11.05S 77.36W
Huachuca City U.S.A. **81** 31.34N 110.21W
Huade China **32** 41.57N 114.04E
Hua Hin Thailand **34** 12.34N 99.58E
Huahine *i.* Îs. de la Société **69** 16.45S 151.00W
Huai'an Hebei China **32** 40.40N 114.18E
Huai'an Jiangsu China **32** 33.29N 119.15E
Huaibei China **32** 33.58N 116.50E
Huaide China **32** 43.25N 124.50E
Huai He *r.* China **32** 32.58N 118.18E
Huaiji China **33** 23.58N 112.10E
Huailai China **32** 40.25N 115.27E
Huainan China **32** 32.39N 117.01E
Huaining China **33** 30.21N 116.42E
Huairen China **32** 39.50N 113.07E
Huairou China **32** 40.20N 116.37E
Huaiyang China **32** 33.47N 114.59E
Huaiyuan China **32** 32.57N 117.12E
Huajuápan Mexico **86** 17.50N 97.48W
Hualian Taiwan **33** 24.00N 121.39E
Huallaga *r.* Peru **90** 5.02S 75.30W
Huamanrazo *mtn.* Peru **90** 12.54S 75.04W
Huambo Angola **54** 12.47S 15.44E
Huambo *d.* Angola **54** 12.30S 15.45E
Huanan China **31** 46.13N 130.31E
Huancané Peru **90** 15.10S 69.44W
Huancapi Peru **90** 13.35S 74.05W
Huancavelica Peru **90** 12.45S 75.03W
Huancayo Peru **90** 12.05S 75.12W
Huangchuan China **33** 32.07N 115.02E
Huanggang China **33** 30.33N 114.59E
Huanggang Shan *mtn.* China **33** 27.50N 117.47E
Huang Hai *b.* N. Korea **31** 39.30N 123.40E
Huang He *r.* China **32** 38.00N 118.40E
Huanghe Kou *est.* China **32** 37.54N 118.48E
Huanghua China **32** 38.22N 117.20E
Huangling China **32** 35.36N 109.17E
Huangpi China **33** 30.52N 114.22E
Huangping China **33** 26.54N 107.53E
Huangshan China **33** 29.41N 118.22E
Huangshi China **33** 30.10N 115.04E
Huang Xian China **32** 37.38N 120.30E
Huangyan China **33** 28.42N 121.25E
Huan Jiang *r.* China **32** 35.13N 108.00E
Huanren China **32** 41.16N 125.21E
Huanta Peru **90** 12.54S 74.13W
Huánuco Peru **90** 9.55S 76.11W
Huaráz Peru **90** 9.33S 77.31W
Huarmey Peru **90** 10.05S 78.05W
Huascaran *mtn.* Peru **90** 9.08S 77.36W
Huasco Chile **92** 28.28S 71.14W
Huatabampo Mexico **81** 26.50N 109.38W
Huatong China **32** 40.03N 121.56E
Hua Xian Guangdong China **33** 23.22N 113.12E
Hua Xian Shaanxi China **32** 34.31N 109.46E
Huayuan China **33** 28.37N 109.28E
Hubei *d.* China **33** 31.00N 112.00E
Hubli India **38** 15.20N 75.14E
Hückelhoven Germany **14** 51.04N 6.10E
Hucknall U.K. **10** 53.03N 1.12W
Huddersfield U.K. **10** 53.38N 1.49W
Huddinge Sweden **23** 59.14N 17.59E
Hudiksvall Sweden **23** 61.44N 17.07E
Hudson N.Y. U.S.A. **84** 42.15N 73.47W
Hudson *r.* U.S.A. **84** 40.42N 74.02W
Hudson Wyo. U.S.A. **80** 42.54N 108.35W
Hudson B. Canada **73** 58.00N 86.00W
Hudson Bay *town* Canada **75** 52.52N 102.25W
Hudson Highlands U.S.A. **85** 41.24N 74.15W
Hudson Hope Canada **74** 56.03N 121.59W
Hudson Mts. Antarctica **96** 76.00S 99.00W
Hudson Str. Canada **73** 62.00N 70.00W
Hue Vietnam **34** 16.28N 107.40E
Huedin Romania **21** 46.52N 23.02E
Huehuetenango Guatemala **86** 15.19N 91.26W
Huelva Spain **16** 37.15N 6.56W
Huelva *r.* Spain **16** 37.25N 6.00W
Huércal-Overa Spain **16** 37.23N 1.56W
Huesca Spain **16** 42.02N 0.25W
Ḥufrat an Naḥās Sudan **49** 9.45N 24.19E
Hugh *r.* Australia **64** 25.01S 134.01E
Hughenden Australia **64** 20.51S 144.12E
Hughes Australia **65** 30.40S 129.32E
Hughes U.S.A. **72** 66.03N 154.16W
Hugo U.S.A. **83** 34.01N 95.31W
Hugoton U.S.A. **83** 37.11N 101.21W
Hugou China **32** 33.22N 117.07E
Hui'an China **33** 25.02N 118.48E
Huiarau Range *mts.* New Zealand **60** 38.20S 177.15E
Huikou China **33** 29.49N 116.15E
Huíla *d.* Angola **54** 15.10S 15.30E
Huilai China **33** 23.03N 116.17E
Huimin China **32** 37.30N 117.29E
Huining China **32** 35.42N 105.06E
Huisne *r.* France **15** 47.59N 0.11E
Huixtla Mexico **86** 15.09N 92.30W
Huizen Neth. **14** 52.18N 5.12E
Huizhou China **33** 23.05N 114.29E
Hukuntsi Botswana **56** 24.02S 21.48E
Ḥulayfā' Saudi Arabia **42** 26.00N 40.47E
Hulín Czech Republic **21** 49 19N 17.28E
Hull Canada **77** 45.26N 75.45W
Hüls Germany **14** 51.23N 6.30E
Hulst Neth. **14** 51.18N 4.01E
Hultsfred Sweden **23** 57.29N 15.50E
Hulun Nur *l.* China **31** 49.00N 117.27E
Ḥulwân Egypt **44** 29.51N 31.20E
Humaitá Brazil **90** 7.31S 63.02W
Humansdorp R.S.A. **56** 34.02S 24.45E
Ḥumaydah Sudan **48** 14.22N 22.31E
Humber *r.* U.K. **10** 53.40N 0.12W
Humberside *d.* U.K. **10** 53.48N 0.35W
Humble U.S.A. **83** 30.00N 95.16W
Humboldt Canada **75** 52.12N 105.07W
Humboldt U.S.A. **83** 35.49N 88.55W
Humboldt *r.* U.S.A. **80** 40.02N 118.31W
Hume, L. Australia **67** 36.06S 147.05E
Hūmedān Iran **43** 25.24N 59.39E
Humenné Slovakia **21** 48.56N 21.55E
Humphreys Peak *mtn.* U.S.A. **81** 35.20N 111.40W
Hūn Libya **51** 29.07N 15.56E
Húnaflói *b.* Iceland **22** 65.45N 20.50W
Hunan *d.* China **33** 27.30N 111.30E
Hundred Mile House *town* Canada **74** 51.38N 121.18W
Hunedoara Romania **21** 45.45N 22.54E
Hungary Europe **21** 47.30N 19.00E
Hungerford Australia **66** 29.00S 144.26E
Hungerford U.K. **11** 51.25N 1.30W
Hungfou Hsü *i.* Taiwan **33** 22.03N 121.33E
Hüngnam N. Korea **31** 39.49N 127.40E
Hung Yen Vietnam **33** 20.38N 106.05E
Hunsberge *mts.* Namibia **56** 27.40S 17.12E
Hunse *r.* Neth. **14** 53.20N 6.18E
Hunsrück *mts.* Germany **14** 49.44N 7.05E
Hunstanton U.K. **10** 52.57N 0.30E
Hunte *r.* Germany **20** 52.30N 8.19E
Hunter *r.* Australia **67** 32.50S 151.42E
Hunter I. Australia **65** 40.30S 144.46E
Hunter I. Canada **74** 51.55N 128.00W
Hunter Island Ridge Pacific Oc. **68** 21.30S 175.00E
Huntingdon U.K. **11** 52.20N 0.11W
Huntingdon U.S.A. **84** 40.29N 78.01W
Huntington Ind. U.S.A. **84** 40.54N 85.30W
Huntington N.Y. U.S.A. **85** 40.51N 73.25W
Huntington Oreg. U.S.A. **80** 44.21N 117.16W
Huntington Utah U.S.A. **80** 39.20N 110.58W
Huntington W.Va. U.S.A. **85** 38.24N 82.26W
Huntington Beach *town* U.S.A. **81** 33.39N 118.01W
Huntly New Zealand **60** 37.35S 175.10E
Huntly U.K. **12** 57.27N 2.47W
Huntsville Canada **76** 45.20N 79.13W
Huntsville Ala. U.S.A. **85** 34.44N 86.35W
Huntsville Tex. U.S.A. **83** 30.43N 95.33W
Hunyani *r.* Mozambique **57** 15.41S 30.38E
Hunyuan China **32** 39.45N 113.35E
Huon Pen. P.N.G. **37** 6.00S 147.00E
Huonville Australia **65** 43.01S 147.01E
Huoshan China **33** 31.24N 116.20E
Hure Qi China **32** 42.44N 121.44E
Huretin Sum China **32** 40.19N 103.02E
Hurlock U.S.A. **85** 38.38N 75.52W
Hurmāgai Pakistan **40** 28.18N 64.26E
Huron U.S.A. **82** 44.22N 98.13W
Huron, L. Canada / U.S.A. **84** 44.30N 82.15W
Hurso Ethiopia **49** 9.38N 41.38E
Húsavík Iceland **22** 66.03N 17.21W
Husevig Faroe Is. **8** 61.49N 6.41W
Huşi Romania **21** 46.40N 28.04E
Huskvarna Sweden **23** 57.48N 14.16E
Husum Germany **20** 54.29N 9.04E
Hutchinson R.S.A. **56** 31.30S 23.10E
Hutchinson U.S.A. **83** 38.05N 97.56W
Huttig U.S.A. **83** 33.02N 92.11W
Hutuo He *r.* China **32** 39.10N 117.12E
Hut Yanchi *l.* China **32** 39.24N 105.01E
Huy Belgium **14** 50.31N 5.14E
Hvar *i.* Croatia **19** 43.10N 16.45E
Hvita *r.* Iceland **22** 64.33N 21.45W
Hwange Zimbabwe **56** 18.20S 26.29E
Hwange Nat. Park Zimbabwe **56** 19.00S 26.30E
Hwang Ho *r. see* Huang He *r.* China **32**
Hyannis U.S.A. **82** 41.59N 101.44W
Hyargas Nuur *l.* Mongolia **30** 49.30N 93.35E
Hydaburg U.S.A. **74** 55.15N 132.50W
Hyde U.K. **10** 53.26N 2.06W
Hyden Australia **63** 32.27S 118.53E
Hyderābād India **39** 17.22N 78.26E
Hyderābād Pakistan **40** 25.22N 68.22E
Hydesville U.S.A. **80** 40.31N 124.00W
Hyères France **17** 43.07N 6.08E
Hyères, Îles d' *is.* France **17** 43.01N 6.25E
Hyland *r.* Canada **74** 59.50N 128.10W
Hyland, Mt. Australia **67** 30.09S 152.25E
Hyland Post Canada **74** 57.40N 128.10W
Hyllestad Norway **23** 61.10N 5.18E
Hyndman Peak U.S.A. **80** 43.50N 114.10W
Hysham U.S.A. **80** 46.18N 107.14W
Hythe U.K. **11** 51.04N 1.05E
Hyvinkää Finland **23** 60.38N 24.52E

I

Iakoro Madagascar **57** 23.06S 46.40E
Ialomiţa *r.* Romania **21** 44.41N 27.52E
Iar Connacht *f.* Rep. of Ire. **13** 53.21N 9.22W
Iaşi Romania **21** 47.09N 27.38E
Iauaretê Brazil **90** 0.36N 69.12W
Iaupolo P.N.G. **64** 9.34S 150.30E
Ibadan Nigeria **53** 7.23N 3.56E
Ibagué Colombia **90** 4.25N 75.20W
Ibar *r.* Yugo. **19** 43.44N 20.44E
Ibaraki Japan **35** 34.49N 135.34E
Ibarra Ecuador **90** 0.23N 78.05W
Ibb Yemen **45** 13.58N 44.11E
Ibba Sudan **49** 4.48N 29.06E
Ibba *wadi* Sudan **49** 7.09N 28.41E
Ibbenbüren Germany **14** 52.17N 7.44E
Iberville Canada **77** 45.18N 73.14W
Ibi *r.* Japan **35** 35.03N 136.42E
Ibi Nigeria **53** 8.11N 9.44E
Ibiapaba, Serra da *mts.* Brazil **91** 5.30S 41.00W
Ibicaraí Brazil **91** 14.52S 39.37W
Ibicuy Argentina **93** 33.45S 59.13W
Ibina *r.* Zaïre **55** 1.00N 28.40E
Ibitinga Brazil **94** 21.43S 48.47W
Ibiza *i.* Spain **16** 39.00N 1.23E
Ibiza *town* Spain **16** 38.55N 1.30E
Ibotirama Brazil **91** 12.13S 43.12W
Ibrah, Wadi Sudan **49** 10.36N 25.05E
'Ibrī Oman **45** 23.14N 56.30E
Ibshawây Egypt **44** 29.21N 30.40E
Içá *r.* Brazil **90** 3.07S 67.58W
Ica Peru **90** 14.02S 75.48W
Içana Brazil **90** 0.21N 67.19W
Içana *r.* Brazil **90** 0.00 67.10W
Iceland Europe **22** 64.45N 18.00W
Ichchāpuram India **41** 19.07N 84.42E
Ichihara Japan **35** 35.31N 140.05E
Ichikawa Japan **35** 35.44N 139.55E
Ichinomiya Japan **35** 35.18N 136.48E
Icoraci Brazil **91** 1.16S 48.28W
Icy Str. U.S.A. **74** 58.20N 135.30W
Idabel U.S.A. **83** 33.54N 94.50W
Ida Grove U.S.A. **82** 42.21N 95.28W
Idah Nigeria **53** 7.05N 6.45E
Idaho *d.* U.S.A. **80** 44.58N 115.56W
Idaho Falls *town* U.S.A. **80** 43.30N 112.02W
Idar India **40** 23.50N 73.00E
Idar-Oberstein Germany **14** 49.43N 7.19E
Ideles Algeria **51** 23.49N 5.55E
Idfū Egypt **42** 24.58N 32.50E
Ídhi Óros *mtn.* Greece **19** 35.13N 24.45E
Ídhra *i.* Greece **19** 37.20N 23.32E
Idiofa Zaïre **54** 4.58S 19.38E
Idmū Egypt **44** 28.09N 30.41E
Idre Sweden **23** 61.52N 12.43E
Ieper Belgium **14** 50.51N 2.53E
Ierápetra Greece **19** 35.00N 25.45E
Iesi Italy **18** 43.32N 13.15E
Iesolo Italy **15** 45.32N 12.38E
Ifakara Tanzania **55** 8.09S 36.41E
Ifalik *is.* Federated States of Micronesia **37** 7.15N 144.27E
Ifanadiana Madagascar **57** 21.19S 47.39E
Ife Oyo Nigeria **53** 7.33N 4.34E
Iferouâne Niger **53** 19.04N 8.24E
Iga *r.* Japan **35** 34.45N 136.01E
Igatpuri India **40** 19.42N 73.33E
Iggesund Sweden **23** 61.38N 17.04E
Iglesias Italy **18** 39.18N 8.32E
Igli Algeria **50** 30.27N 2.18W
Igloolik Island *town* Canada **73** 69.05N 81.25W
Ignace Canada **76** 49.30N 91.40W
Iğneada Burnu *c.* Turkey **19** 41.50N 28.05E
Igoumenítsa Greece **19** 39.32N 20.14E
Igra Russian Fed. **24** 57.31N 53.09E
Iguaçu *r.* Brazil **94** 25.33S 54.35W
Iguaçu, Saltos do *f.* Brazil / Argentina **94** 25.35S 54.22W
Iguala Mexico **86** 18.21N 99.31W
Igualada Spain **16** 41.35N 1.37E
Iguassu Falls *see* Iguaçu, Saltos do *f.* Brazil / Argentina Brazil / Argentina **94**
Iguatu Brazil **91** 6.22S 39.20W
Iguéla Gabon **54** 1.57S 9.22E
Ihiala Nigeria **53** 5.51N 6.52E
Ihosy Madagascar **57** 22.24S 46.08E
Ihosy *r.* Madagascar **57** 21.58S 43.38E
Ii *r.* Finland **22** 65.19N 25.20E
Iida Japan **35** 35.31N 137.50E
Iīdaan Somali Rep. **45** 6.03N 49.01E
Iisalmi Finland **22** 63.34N 27.11E
Ijebu Ode Nigeria **53** 6.47N 3.54E
Ijill, Kediet *mtn.* Mauritania **50** 22.38N 12.33W
IJmuiden Neth. **14** 52.28N 4.37E
IJssel *r.* Zuid Holland Neth. **14** 51.54N 4.32E
IJssel *r.* Overijssel Neth. **14** 52.34N 5.50E
IJsselmeer *l.* Neth. **14** 52.45N 5.20E
Ijuí Brazil **94** 28.23S 53.55W
Ijzendijke Neth. **14** 51.19N 3.37E
Ijzer *r.* Belgium **14** 51.09N 2.44E
Ikaría *i.* Greece **19** 37.35N 26.10E
Ikdū Egypt **44** 31.18N 30.18E
Ikela Zaïre **54** 1.06S 23.04E
Ikelemba Congo **54** 1.15N 16.38E
Ikelemba *r.* Zaïre **54** 0.08N 18.19E
Ikerre Nigeria **53** 7.30N 5.14E
Ikopa *r.* Madagascar **57** 16.29S 46.43E
Ila Nigeria **53** 8.01N 4.55E
Ilagan Phil. **37** 17.07N 121.53E
Īlām Iran **43** 33.27N 46.27E
Ilām Nepal **41** 26.55N 87.56E
Ilan Taiwan **33** 24.45N 121.44E
Ilangali Tanzania **55** 6.50S 35.06E
Ilaro Nigeria **53** 6.53N 3.03E
Iława Poland **21** 53.37N 19.33E
Ilebo Zaïre **54** 4.20S 20.35E
Ilek *r.* Russian Fed. **25** 51.30N 54.00E
Ileret Kenya **55** 4.22N 36.13E
Ilerh, Oued *wadi* Algeria **51** 20.59N 2.14E
Ilesha Oyo Nigeria **53** 7.39N 4.45E
Ilford Canada **75** 56.04N 95.35W
Ilfracombe Australia **64** 23.30S 144.30E
Ilfracombe U.K. **11** 51.13N 4.08W
Ilhabela Brazil **94** 23.47S 45.20W
Ilha Grande, Baía da *b.* Brazil **94** 23.09S 44.30W
Ilha Grande, Represa *resr.* Brazil **94** 23.10S 53.40W
Ilhéus Brazil **91** 14.50S 39.06W
Ili *r.* Kazakhstan **30** 45.00N 74.20E
Ilia Romania **21** 45.56N 22.39E
Iliamna L. U.S.A. **72** 59.30N 155.00W
Ilich Russian Fed. **30** 40.50N 68.29E
Iligan Phil. **37** 8.12N 124.13E
Ilintsy Ukraine **21** 49.08N 29.11E
Ilion U.S.A. **84** 43.01N 75.02W
Ilkley U.K. **10** 53.56N 1.49W
Illapel Chile **92** 31.38S 71.10W
Ille-et-Vilaine *d.* France **15** 48.10N 1.30W
Illéla Niger **53** 14.30N 5.09E
Iller *r.* Germany **20** 48.23N 9.58E
Illeret Kenya **49** 4.19N 36.13E
Illiers France **15** 48.18N 1.15E
Illinois *d.* U.S.A. **82** 40.30N 89.30W
Illinois *r.* U.S.A. **82** 38.58N 90.27W
Illizi Algeria **51** 26.29N 8.28E
Ilmajoki Finland **22** 62.44N 22.34E
Ilminster U.K. **11** 50.55N 2.56W
Ilo Peru **92** 17.38S 71.20W
Iloilo Phil. **37** 10.45N 122.33E
Ilorin Nigeria **53** 8.32N 4.34E
Ilovlya Russian Fed. **25** 49.19N 44.01E
Īlubabor *d.* Ethiopia **49** 7.50N 34.55E
Imala Mozambique **55** 14.39S 39.34E
Imandra Russian Fed. **24** 67.53N 33.30E
Imandra, Ozero *l.* Russian Fed. **24** 67.30N 32.45E
Imbābah Egypt **44** 30.05N 31.12E
Imese Zaïre **54** 2.07N 18.06E
Īmī Ethiopia **49** 6.28N 42.18E
Immingham U.K. **10** 53.37N 0.12W
Immokalee U.S.A. **85** 26.25N 81.26W
Imo *d.* Nigeria **53** 5.30N 7.20E
Imola Italy **15** 44.21N 11.42E
Imperatriz Brazil **91** 5.32S 47.28W
Imperia Italy **15** 43.53N 8.01E
Imperial Calif. U.S.A. **81** 32.51N 115.34W
Imperial Nebr. U.S.A. **82** 40.31N 101.39W
Imperial Dam U.S.A. **81** 32.55N 114.30W
Imperial Valley *f.* U.S.A. **81** 32.50N 115.30W
Impfondo Congo **54** 1.36N 17.58E
Imphāl India **39** 24.47N 93.55E
Imroz *i. see* Gökçeada *i.* Turkey **19**
Ina Japan **35** 35.50N 137.57E
Ina *r.* Japan **35** 34.43N 135.28E
In Abbangarit *well* Niger **53** 17.49N 6.15E
Inaccessible I. Tristan da Cunha **95** 37.19S 12.44W
I-n-Amguel Algeria **51** 23.40N 5.08E
Inangahua Junction New Zealand **60** 41.53S 171.58E
Inanwatan Indonesia **37** 2.08S 132.10E
Inarajan Guam **68** 13.16N 144.45E
Inari *l.* Finland **22** 69.00N 28.00E
Inari *town* Finland **22** 68.54N 27.01E
Inazawa Japan **35** 35.15N 136.47E
I-n-Belbel Algeria **50** 27.54N 1.10E
Inca Spain **16** 39.43N 2.54E
Incesu Turkey **42** 38.39N 35.12E
Inchiri *d.* Mauritania **50** 20.10N 15.00W
Inch'on S. Korea **31** 37.30N 126.38E
Indals *r.* Sweden **22** 62.30N 17.20E
Indaw Burma **34** 23.40N 94.46E
Independence Calif. U.S.A. **80** 36.48N 118.12W
Independence Kans. U.S.A. **83** 37.13N 95.42W
Independence Mo. U.S.A. **82** 39.05N 94.24W
Inderborskiy Kazakhstan **25** 48.32N 51.44E
India Asia **39** 23.00N 78.30E
Indiana *d.* U.S.A. **84** 40.00N 86.15W
Indiana *town* U.S.A. **84** 40.37N 79.09W
Indianapolis U.S.A. **84** 39.45N 86.10W
Indian Cabins Canada **74** 59.52N 117.02W
Indian Harbour Canada **77** 54.25N 57.20W
Indian Head Canada **75** 50.32N 103.40W
Indianola U.S.A. **82** 41.22N 93.34W
Indian River B. U.S.A. **85** 38.36N 75.05W
Indiga Russian Fed. **24** 67.40N 49.00E
Indigirka *r.* Russian Fed. **29** 71.00N 148.45E
Indija Yugo. **21** 45.03N 20.05E
Indio U.S.A. **81** 33.43N 116.13W
Indonesia Asia **36** 6.00S 118.00E
Indore India **40** 22.43N 75.50E
Indragiri *r.* Indonesia **36** 0.30S 103.08E
Indramayu Indonesia **37** 6.22S 108.20E
Indrāvati *r.* India **41** 18.44N 80.16E
Indre *r.* France **17** 47.16N 0.19W
Indus *r.* Pakistan **40** 24.20N 67.47E
Inebolu Turkey **42** 41.57N 33.45E
Inegöl Turkey **42** 40.06N 29.31E
I-n-Eker Algeria **51** 24.01N 5.05E
I-n-Ezzane *well* Algeria **51** 23.29N 11.15E
Infiesto Spain **16** 43.21N 5.21W
I-n-Gall Niger **53** 16.47N 6.56E
Ingatestone U.K. **11** 51.41N 0.22E
Ingende Zaïre **54** 0.17S 18.58E
Ingenika *r.* Canada **74** 56.43N 125.07W
Ingersoll Canada **76** 43.02N 80.53W
Inggen China **32** 41.35N 104.47E
Ingham Australia **64** 18.35S 146.12E
Ingleborough *mtn.* U.K. **10** 54.10N 2.23W
Inglewood Qld Australia **67** 28.25S 151.02E
Inglewood Vic. Australia **66** 36.33S 143.53E
Inglewood Canada **76** 43.47N 79.56W
Inglewood New Zealand **60** 39.09S 174.12E
Inglewood U.S.A. **81** 33.58N 118.21W
Ingolstadt Germany **20** 48.46N 11.27E
Ingomar Australia **66** 29.38S 134.48E
Ingulets Ukraine **25** 47.43N 33.16E
Ingwiller France **17** 48.52N 7.29E
Inhambane Mozambique **57** 23.51S 35.29E
Inhambane *d.* Mozambique **57** 22.20S 34.00E
Inhaminga Mozambique **57** 18.24S 35.00E
Inharrime Mozambique **57** 24.29S 35.01E
Inhassoro Mozambique **57** 21.32S 35.10E
Inirida *r.* Colombia **90** 3.59N 67.45W
Inishbofin *i.* Rep. of Ire. **13** 53.38N 10.14W
Inisheer *i.* Rep. of Ire. **13** 53.04N 9.32W
Inishmaan *i.* Rep. of Ire. **13** 53.06N 9.36W
Inishmore *i.* Rep. of Ire. **13** 53.08N 9.43W
Inishowen Pen. Rep. of Ire. **13** 55.08N 7.20W
Inishturk *i.* Rep. of Ire. **13** 53.43N 10.08W
Injune Australia **64** 25.51S 148.34E
Inklin Canada **74** 58.56N 133.05W
Inklin *r.* Canada **74** 58.50N 133.10W
Inn *r.* Europe **20** 48.33N 13.26E
Innaminka Australia **65** 27.43S 140.46E
Inner Hebrides *is.* U.K. **12** 56.50N 6.45W
Inner Mongolia *d. see* Nei Monggol Zizhiqu *d.* China China **32**
Inner Sd. U.K. **12** 57.30N 5.55W
Innisfail Australia **64** 17.32S 146.02E
Innisfail Canada **74** 52.00N 113.57W
Innsbruck Austria **20** 47.17N 11.25E
Innset Norway **22** 68.41N 18.50E
Inongo Zaïre **54** 1.55S 18.20E
Inowrocław Poland **21** 52.49N 18.12E
I-n-Salah Algeria **51** 27.13N 2.28E
Insein Burma **34** 16.54N 96.08E
In Tasik *well* Mali **53** 18.03N 2.00E
Interlaken Switz. **20** 46.42N 7.52E
International Falls *town* U.S.A. **82** 48.38N 93.26W
Intracoastal Waterway *canal* U.S.A. **83** 28.45N 95.40W
Intute Mozambique **55** 14.08S 39.55E
Inukjuak Canada **73** 58.25N 78.18W
Inuvik Canada **72** 68.16N 133.40W
Inuvik *d.* Canada **72** 68.00N 130.00W
Inuyama Japan **35** 35.23N 136.56E
Inveraray U.K. **12** 56.24N 5.05W
Inverbervie U.K. **12** 56.51N 2.17W
Invercargill New Zealand **60** 46.26S 168.21E
Inverell Australia **67** 29.46S 151.10E
Invergordon U.K. **12** 57.42N 4.10W
Inverness U.K. **12** 57.27N 4.15W
Inverurie U.K. **12** 57.17N 2.23W
Inverway Australia **62** 17.49S 129.40E
Investigator Group *is.* Australia **66** 33.45S 134.30E
Investigator Str. Australia **66** 35.25S 137.10E
Invinheima *r.* Brazil **92** 22.52S 53.20W
Inya Russian Fed. **28** 50.24N 86.47E
Inyangani *mtn.* Zimbabwe **57** 18.18S 32.50E
Inyonga Tanzania **55** 6.43S 32.02E
Inzia *r.* Zaïre **54** 3.47S 17.57E
Ioánnina Greece **19** 39.39N 20.49E
Iola U.S.A. **83** 37.55N 95.24W
Iona *i.* U.K. **12** 56.20N 6.25W
Iongo Angola **54** 9.11S 17.45E
Ionia U.S.A. **84** 42.58N 85.06W
Ionian Is. *see* Iónioi Nísoi *is.* Greece **19**
Ionian Sea Med. Sea **19** 38.30N 18.45E
Iónioi Nísoi *is.* Greece **19** 38.45N 20.00E
Íos *i.* Greece **19** 36.42N 25.20E
Iowa *d.* U.S.A. **82** 42.00N 93.30W
Iowa *r.* U.S.A. **82** 41.10N 91.02W
Iowa City U.S.A. **82** 41.40N 91.32W
Iowa Falls *town* U.S.A. **82** 42.31N 93.16W
Ipatovo Russian Fed. **25** 45.44N 42.56E
Ipiales Colombia **90** 0.52N 77.38W
Ipiaú Brazil **91** 14.07S 39.43W
Ipixuna Brazil **90** 7.00S 71.30W
Ipoh Malaysia **36** 4.36N 101.02E
Ippa *r.* Belorussia **21** 52.13N 29.08E
Ippy C.A.R. **49** 6.15N 21.12E
Ipswich Australia **67** 27.38S 152.40E
Ipswich U.K. **11** 52.04N 1.09E
Ipu Brazil **91** 4.23S 40.44W
Ipuh Indonesia **36** 2.58S 101.28E
Iquique Chile **92** 20.13S 70.10W
Iquitos Peru **90** 3.51S 73.13W
Irago-suidō *str.* Japan **35** 34.35N 137.00E
Iráklion Greece **19** 35.20N 25.08E
Iran Asia **43** 32.00N 54.30E
Iran, Pegunungan *mts.* Indonesia / Malaysia **36** 3.20N 115.00E
Īrānshahr Iran **43** 27.14N 60.42E
Irapuato Mexico **86** 20.40N 101.40W
Iraq Asia **42** 33.00N 44.00E
Irauen, Wādī Libya **51** 26.28N 12.00E
Irayel Russian Fed. **24** 64.23N 55.25E
Irazú *mtn.* Costa Rica **87** 9.59N 83.52W
Irbid Jordan **44** 32.33N 35.51E
Irbil Iraq **43** 36.12N 44.01E
Irebu Zaïre **54** 0.37S 17.45E
Ireland I. Bermuda **95** 32.19N 64.51W
Irharhar, Oued *wadi* Algeria **51** 23.45N 5.55E
Irian Jaya *d.* Indonesia **37** 4.00S 138.00E
Iriba Chad **48** 15.07N 22.15E
Irié Guinea **52** 8.15N 9.10W
Iringa Tanzania **55** 7.49S 35.39E
Iringa *d.* Tanzania **55** 8.30S 35.00E
Iriomote jima *i.* Japan **31** 24.30N 124.00E
Iriri *r.* Brazil **91** 3.50S 52.40W
Irish Sea U.K. / Rep. of Ire. **13** 53.30N 5.40W
Irkutsk Russian Fed. **30** 52.18N 104.15E
Iron Baron Australia **66** 32.59S 137.09E
Iron Gate *f.* Romania / Yugo. **21** 44.40N 22.30E
Iron Knob Australia **66** 32.44S 137.08E
Iron Mountain *town* U.S.A. **84** 45.51N 88.03W
Iron Mts. Rep. of Ire. **13** 54.10N 7.56W
Iron River *town* U.S.A. **82** 46.05N 88.38W

Irons to **Jiuzhou Jiang**

Irons U.S.A. 84 44.08N 85.55W
Ironton U.S.A. 84 38.32N 82.40W
Ironwood U.S.A. 84 46.25N 90.08W
Iroquois Falls *town* Canada 76 48.40N 80.40W
Irosin Phil. 37 12.45N124.02E
Irō-zaki *c.* Japan 35 34.36N138.51E
Irpen Ukraine 21 50.31N 30.29E
Irrapatana Australia 66 29.03S136.28E
Irrawaddy *d.* Burma 34 17.00N 95.00E
Irrawaddy *r.* Burma 34 15.50N 95.00E
Irrawaddy Delta Burma 34 16.45N 95.00E
Irsha *r.* Ukraine 21 50.45N 29.30E
Irthing *r.* U.K. 9 54.55N 2.50W
Irtysh *r.* Russian Fed. 28 61.00N 68.40E
Iruma *r.* Japan 35 35.57N139.30E
Irumu Zaïre 55 1.29N 29.48E
Irún Spain 16 43.20N 1.48W
Irvine U.K. 12 55.37N 4.40W
Irvinestown U.K. 13 54.29N 7.40W
Irving U.S.A. 83 32.49N 96.56W
Irwin, Pt. Australia 63 35.03S116.20E
Is, Jabal *mtn.* Sudan 48 22.03N 35.28E
Isa Nigeria 53 13.14N 6.24E
Isaac *r.* Australia 64 22.52S149.20E
Isabelia, Cordillera *mts.* Nicaragua 87 13.30N 85.00W
Ísafjördhur *town* Iceland 22 66.05N 23.06W
Isaka Tanzania 55 3.52S 32.54E
Isaka Bandundu Zaïre 54 2.35S 18.48E
Isaka Equateur Zaïre 54 1.49S 20.50E
Isa Khel Pakistan 40 32.41N 71.17E
Isakogorka Russian Fed. 24 64.23N 40.31E
Isangi Zaïre 54 0.48N 24.03E
Isar *r.* Germany 20 48.48N 12.57E
Isbergues France 14 50.38N 2.24E
Ischia *i.* Italy 18 40.43N 13.54E
Ise Japan 35 34.29N136.42E
Iseo, Lago d' *l.* Italy 15 45.43N 10.04E
Isère *r.* France 17 45.02N 4.54E
Iserlohn Germany 14 51.23N 7.42E
Isernia Italy 18 41.36N 14.14E
Ise-wan *b.* Japan 35 34.45N136.40E
Iseyin Nigeria 53 7.59N 3.36E
Isfahan *see* Eşfahān Iran 38
Ishim Russian Fed. 28 56.10N 69.30E
Ishim *r.* Russian Fed. 28 57.50N 71.00E
Ishinomaki Japan 35 38.25N141.18E
Ishpeming U.S.A. 84 46.29N 87.40W
Ishurdi Bangla. 41 24.09N 89.03E
Isigny France 15 49.18N 1.06W
Isiolo Kenya 55 0.20N 37.36E
Isipingo Beach *town* R.S.A. 56 30.00S 30.57E
Isiro Zaïre 55 2.50N 27.40E
Iskenderun Turkey 42 36.37N 36.08E
Iskenderun Körfezi *g.* Turkey 42 36.40N 35.50E
Iskilip Turkey 42 40.45N 34.28E
Iskūr *r.* Bulgaria 19 43.42N 24.27E
Isla *r.* U.K. 12 56.32N 3.22W
Islāmābād Pakistan 40 33.40N 73.10E
Islāmkot Pakistan 40 24.42N 70.11E
Islāmpur Bihār India 41 25.09N 85.12E
Islāmpur W. Bengal India 41 26.16N 88.12E
Island L. Australia 66 31.30S136.40E
Island L. Canada 75 53.47N 94.25W
Island Magee *pen.* U.K. 13 54.48N 5.44W
Islands, B. of Canada 77 49.10N 58.15W
Islands, B. of New Zealand 60 35.15S174.15E
Islay *i.* U.K. 12 55.45N 6.20W
Isle *r.* France 17 45.02N 0.08W
Isle of Portland *f.* U.K. 11 50.32N 2.25W
Isle of Wight *d.* U.K. 11 50.40N 1.17W
Isleta U.S.A. 81 34.55N106.42W
Ismael Cortinas Uruguay 93 33.58S 57.06W
Ismay U.S.A. 80 46.30N104.48W
Isnā Egypt 42 25.16N 32.30E
Isoka Zambia 55 10.06S 32.39E
Isola della Scala Italy 15 45.16N 11.00E
Isparta Turkey 42 37.46N 30.32E
Ispica Italy 18 36.46N 14.55E
Ispikān Pakistan 40 26.14N 62.12E
Israel Asia 44 32.00N 34.50E
Israelite B. Australia 63 33.40S123.55E
Israelite Bay *town* Australia 63 33.37S123.48E
Issia Ivory Coast 52 6.33N 6.33W
Issoire France 17 45.33N 3.15E
Is-sur-Tille France 17 47.30N 5.10E
Issyk Kul *l.* Kyrgyzstan 30 43.30N 77.20E
Istanbul Turkey 19 41.02N 28.58E
Istanbul Bogazi *str.* Turkey 19 41.07N 29.04E
Isthmus of Kra Thailand 34 10.20N 99.10E
Istiaia Greece 19 38.57N 23.09E
Istok Yugo. 19 42.47N 20.29E
Istra *pen.* Croatia 20 45.12N 13.55E
Itabaiana Brazil 91 7.20S 35.20W
Itabira Brazil 94 19.39S 43.14W
Itabirito Brazil 94 20.21S 43.45W
Itabuna Brazil 91 14.48S 39.18W
Itacajuna *r.* Brazil 91 5.20S 49.08W
Itacoatiara Brazil 90 3.06S 58.22W
Itagüí Colombia 90 6.10N 75.36W
Itaí Brazil 94 23.23S 49.05W
Itaim *r.* Brazil 91 6.43S 42.48W
Itaipu, Represa *resr.* Brazil / Paraguay 94 24.30S 54.20W
Itaituba Brazil 91 4.17S 55.59W
Itajaí Brazil 94 26.50S 48.39W
Itajubá Brazil 94 22.24S 45.25W
Itaka Tanzania 55 8.51S 32.48E
Italy Europe 18 43.00N 12.00E
Itami Japan 35 34.46N135.25E
Itapecerica Brazil 94 20.28S 45.09W
Itapecuru Mirim Brazil 91 3.24S 44.20W
Itaperuna Brazil 94 21.14S 41.51W
Itapetinga Brazil 91 15.17S 40.16W
Itapetininga Brazil 94 23.36S 48.07W
Itapeva Brazil 94 23.59S 48.59W
Itapicuru *r.* Brazil 91 11.50S 37.30W
Itapira Brazil 94 22.24S 46.56W
Itaqui Brazil 94 29.07S 56.33W
Itārsi India 41 22.37N 77.45E
Itatiba Brazil 94 22.59S 46.51W
Itatinga Brazil 94 23.06S 48.36W
Itatuba Brazil 90 5.40S 63.20W
Itaúna Brazil 94 20.04S 44.14W
Itbayat *i.* Phil. 33 20.45N121.50E
Ithaca U.S.A. 84 42.26N 76.30W
Itháki Greece 19 38.23N 20.42E
Itimbiri *r.* Zaïre 54 2.02N 22.47E
Itmurinkol, Ozero *l.* Kazakhstan 25 49.30N 52.17E
Itō Japan 35 34.58N139.05E
Itoko Zaïre 54 1.00S 21.45E
Iton *r.* France 15 49.09N 1.12E
Itsa Egypt 44 29.14N 30.47E
Ittel, Oued *wadi* Algeria 51 34.18N 6.02E
Itu Brazil 94 23.17S 47.18W
Ituí *r.* Brazil 90 4.38S 70.19W
Ituiutaba Brazil 94 19.00S 49.25W
Ituri *r.* Zaïre 55 1.45N 27.06E
Iturup *i.* Russian Fed. 31 44.00N147.30E
Ituverava Brazil 94 20.22S 47.48W
Ituxi *r.* Brazil 90 7.20S 64.50W
Ityāy al Bārūd Egypt 44 30.53N 30.40E
Itzehoe Germany 20 53.56N 9.32E
Ivaí *r.* Brazil 94 23.20S 53.23W
Ivalo Finland 22 68.42N 27.30E
Ivalo *r.* Finland 22 68.43N 27.36E
Ivanhoe Australia 66 32.56S144.22E
Ivanhoe U.S.A. 82 44.28N 96.12W
Ivano-Frankovsk Ukraine 21 48.55N 24.42E
Ivanovo Belorussia 21 52.10N 25.13E
Ivanovo Russian Fed. 24 57.00N 41.00E
Ivdel Russian Fed. 24 60.45N 60.30E
Ivenets Belorussia 21 53.50N 26.40E
Ivigtût Greenland 73 61.10N 48.00W
Ivindo Gabon 54 0.02S 12.13E
Ivittuut *see* Ivigtût Greenland 73
Iviza *i. see* Ibiza *i.* Spain 16
Ivohibe Madagascar 57 22.29S 45.52E
Ivory Coast Africa 52 8.00N 5.30W
Ivrea Italy 15 45.28N 7.52E
Ivujivik Canada 73 62.24N 77.55W
Ivybridge U.K. 11 50.24N 3.56W
Iwata Japan 35 34.42N137.48E
Iwo Nigeria 53 7.38N 4.11E
Ixiamas Bolivia 92 13.45S 68.09W
Izabal, Lago de *l.* Guatemala 87 15.30N 89.00W
Izberbash Russian Fed. 25 42.31N 47.52E
Izhevsk Russian Fed. 24 56.49N 53.11E
Izhma Russian Fed. 24 65.03N 53.48E
Izhma *r.* Russian Fed. 24 65.16N 53.18E
Izmail Ukraine 21 45.20N 28.50E
Izmir Turkey 19 38.24N 27.09E
Izmir Körfezi *g.* Turkey 19 38.30N 26.45E
Izmit Turkey 42 40.48N 29.55E
Izozog, Bañados de *f.* Bolivia 92 18.30S 62.05W
Izozog Marshes *f. see* Izozog, Bañados de *f.* Bolivia 92
Izu-hantō *pen.* Japan 35 34.53N138.55E
Izumi Japan 35 34.29N135.26E
Izumi-ōtsu Japan 35 34.30N135.24E
Izumi-sano Japan 35 34.25N135.19E
Izumo *r.* Japan 35 34.38N136.33E
Izyaslav Ukraine 21 50.10N 26.46E
Izyum Ukraine 25 49.12N 37.19E

J

Jaba Ethiopia 49 6.17N 35.12E
Jabal, Bahr al *r.* Sudan 49 9.30N 30.30E
Jabal al Awliyā' Sudan 48 15.14N 32.30E
Jabal Dūd Sudan 49 13.22N 33.09E
Jabalón *r.* Spain 16 38.55N 4.07W
Jabalpur India 41 23.10N 79.57E
Jabālyah Egypt 44 31.32N 34.29E
Jabbān, Ard al *f.* Jordan 44 32.08N 36.35E
Jabiru Australia 64 12.39S132.55E
Jabjabah, Wādī Egypt 48 22.37N 33.17E
Jablah Syria 44 35.22N 35.56E
Jablonec nad Nisou Czech Republic 20 50.44N 15.10E
Jabori Pakistan 40 34.36N 73.16E
Jaboticabal Brazil 94 21.15S 48.17W
Jabrat Sa'īd *wells* Sudan 48 16.06N 31.50E
Jaca Spain 16 42.34N 0.33W
Jacareí Brazil 94 23.17S 45.57W
Jackman U.S.A. 84 45.38N 70.16W
Jackson Ky. U.S.A. 85 37.32N 83.24W
Jackson Mich. U.S.A. 84 42.15N 84.24W
Jackson Miss. U.S.A. 83 32.18N 90.12W
Jackson Mo. U.S.A. 83 37.23N 89.40W
Jackson Ohio U.S.A. 84 39.03N 82.40W
Jackson Tenn. U.S.A. 83 35.37N 88.49W
Jackson Wyo. U.S.A. 80 43.29N110.38W
Jackson Bay *town* Canada 74 50.32N125.57W
Jacksonville Fla. U.S.A. 85 30.20N 81.40W
Jacksonville Ill. U.S.A. 82 39.44N 90.14W
Jacksonville N.C. U.S.A. 85 34.45N 77.26W
Jacksonville Tex. U.S.A. 83 31.58N 95.17W
Jacksonville Beach *town* U.S.A. 85 30.18N 81.24W
Jacobābād Pakistan 40 28.17N 68.26E
Jacobina Brazil 91 11.13S 40.30W
Jacob Lake *town* U.S.A. 81 36.41N112.14W
Jacques Cartier, Détroit de *str.* Canada 77 50.00N 63.30W
Jacques Cartier, Mt. Canada 77 48.59N 65.57W
Jacuí *r.* Brazil 94 29.56S 51.13W
Jacundá *r.* Brazil 91 1.57S 50.26W
Jaddi, Rās *c.* Pakistan 40 25.14N 63.31E
Jade Germany 14 53.21N 8.11E
Jadebusen *b.* Germany 14 53.30N 8.12E
Jādū Libya 51 31.57N 12.01E
Jaén Peru 90 5.21S 78.28W
Jaén Spain 16 37.46N 3.48W
Jāfarābād India 40 20.52N 71.22E
Jaffa *see* Tel Aviv-Yafo Israel 44
Jaffa, C. Australia 66 36.58S139.39E
Jaffna Sri Lanka 39 9.38N 80.02E
Jagādhri India 40 30.10N 77.18E
Jāgan Pakistan 40 28.05N 68.30E
Jagatsingpur India 41 20.16N 86.10E
Jagdalpur India 41 19.04N 82.02E
Jaggang China 41 32.52N 79.45E
Jagtiāl India 41 18.48N 78.56E
Jaguarão Brazil 94 32.30S 53.25W
Jahānābād India 41 25.13N 84.59E
Jahrom Iran 43 28.30N 53.30E
Jailolo Indonesia 37 1.05N127.29E
Jainti India 41 26.42N 89.36E
Jaintiāpur Bangla. 41 25.08N 92.07E
Jaipur India 40 26.53N 75.50E
Jāis India 41 26.15N 81.32E
Jaisalmer India 40 26.55N 70.54E
Jājarkot Nepal 41 28.42N 82.14E
Jajawijaya Mts. Asia 37 4.20S139.10E
Jajjha Pakistan 40 28.45N 70.34E
Jājpur India 41 20.51N 86.20E
Jakarta Indonesia 37 6.08S106.45E
Jakarta *d.* Indonesia 37 6.10S106.48E
Jakhāu India 40 23.13N 68.43E
Jäkkvik Sweden 22 66.23N 17.00E
Jakobstad *see* Pietarsaari Finland 22
Jal U.S.A. 83 32.07N103.12W
Jalālābād Afghan. 40 34.26N 70.28E
Jalālah al Bahrīyah, Jabal *mts.* Egypt 44 29.20N 32.12E
Jalālat al Qiblīyah, Jabal al *mts.* Egypt 44 28.42N 32.23E
Jalālpur India 41 26.19N 82.44E
Jalapa Mexico 86 19.45N 96.48W
Jalāun India 41 26.09N 79.21E
Jaldak Afghan. 40 31.58N 66.44E
Jalesar India 41 27.29N 78.19E
Jaleswar India 41 21.49N 87.13E
Jālgaon Mahār. India 40 21.03N 76.32E
Jālgaon Mahār. India 40 21.01N 75.34E
Jalingo Nigeria 53 8.54N 11.21E
Jalisco *d.* Mexico 86 21.00N103.00W
Jālna India 40 19.50N 75.53E
Jalón *r.* Spain 16 41.47N 1.02W
Jālor India 40 25.21N 72.37E
Jalpaiguri India 41 26.31N 88.44E
Jālū Libya 51 29.02N 21.33E
Jaluit *i.* Pacific Oc. 68 6.00N169.35E
Jalūlā Iraq 43 34.16N 45.10E
Jamaame Somali Rep. 55 0.04N 42.46E
Jamaari Nigeria 53 11.44N 9.53E
Jamaica C. America 87 18.00N 77.00W
Jamālpur Bangla. 41 24.55N 89.56E
Jamālpur India 41 25.18N 86.30E
Jamanxim *r.* Brazil 91 4.43S 56.18W
Jambes Belgium 14 50.28N 4.52E
Jambi Indonesia 36 1.36S103.39E
Jambi *d.* Indonesia 36 2.00S102.30E
Jambusar India 40 22.03N 72.48E
James *r.* S.Dak. U.S.A. 82 42.55N 97.28W
James *r.* Va. U.S.A. 85 36.57N 76.26W
James B. Canada 76 53.30N 80.00W
James Bay Prov. Park Canada 76 51.30N 79.00W
Jamestown Australia 66 33.12S138.38E
Jamestown St. Helena 95 15.56S 5.44W
Jamestown N.Dak. U.S.A. 82 46.54N 98.42W
Jamestown N.Y. U.S.A. 84 42.06N 79.14W
Jamestown Tenn. U.S.A. 85 36.24N 84.58W
Jamjodhpur India 40 21.54N 70.01E
Jammerbugt *b.* Denmark 23 57.20N 9.30E
Jammu Jammu & Kashmir 40 32.42N 74.52E
Jammu & Kashmir Asia 40 34.45N 76.00E
Jāmnagar India 40 22.28N 70.04E
Jamnotri India 41 31.01N 78.27E
Jampang Kulon Indonesia 37 7.18S106.33E
Jāmpur Pakistan 40 28.45N 70.36E
Jamsah Egypt 44 27.39N 33.35E
Jämsänkoski Finland 23 61.55N 25.11E
Jamshedpur India 41 22.48N 86.11E
Jämtland *d.* Sweden 22 63.00N 14.30E
Jamūi India 41 24.55N 86.13E
Jamuna *r.* Bangla. 41 23.51N 89.45E
Jand Pakistan 40 33.26N 72.01E
Janda, Laguna de la *l.* Spain 16 36.15N 5.50W
Jandiāla India 40 31.33N 75.02E
Jándula *r.* Spain 16 38.08N 4.08W
Janesville U.S.A. 82 42.42N 89.02W
Jangamo Mozambique 57 24.06S 35.21E
Jangipur India 41 24.28N 88.04E
Janīn Jordan 44 32.28N 35.18E
Jan Kempdorp R.S.A. 56 27.55S 24.48E
Jan Mayen *i.* Arctic Oc. 96 71.00N 9.00W
Januária Brazil 94 15.28S 44.23W
Janūb Dārfūr *d.* Sudan 49 11.45N 25.00E
Janūb Kurdufān *d.* Sudan 49 11.10N 30.00E
Janzé France 15 47.58N 1.30W
Jaora India 40 23.38N 75.08E
Japan Asia 35 36.00N136.00E
Japan, Sea of Asia 35 40.00N135.00E
Japan Trench Pacific Oc. 68 33.00N142.00E
Japla India 41 24.33N 84.01E
Japurá *r.* Brazil 90 3.00S 64.50W
Jarales U.S.A. 81 34.37N106.46W
Jarama *r.* Spain 16 40.27N 3.32W
Jarānwāla Pakistan 40 31.20N 73.26E
Jarash Jordan 44 32.17N 35.54E
Jardee Australia 63 34.18S116.04E
Jardine *r.* Australia 64 11.07S142.30E
Jardines de la Reina *is.* Cuba 87 20.30N 79.00W
Jardinópolis Brazil 94 20.59S 47.48W
Jargeau France 15 47.52N 2.07E
Jāria Jhānjail Bangla. 41 25.02N 90.39E
Jaridih India 41 23.38N 86.04E
Jarocin Poland 21 51.59N 17.31E
Jarosław Poland 21 50.02N 22.42E
Jarrāhī *r.* Iran 43 30.40N 48.23E
Jartai China 32 39.45N105.46E
Jartai Yanchi *l.* China 32 39.43N105.41E
Jarud Qi China 32 44.30N120.35E
Järvenpää Finland 23 60.28N 25.06E
Jarvis Canada 76 42.53N 80.06W
Jarvis I. Pacific Oc. 68 0.23S160.02W
Jasdan India 40 22.02N 71.12E
Jāsk Iran 43 25.40N 57.45E
Jasło Poland 21 49.45N 21.29E
Jasper Canada 74 52.55N118.05W
Jasper Ala. U.S.A. 85 33.48N 87.18W
Jasper Fla. U.S.A. 85 30.31N 82.58W
Jasper Tex. U.S.A. 83 30.55N 94.01W
Jasper Nat. Park Canada 74 52.50N118.08W
Jasra India 41 25.17N 81.48E
Jastrebarsko Croatia 20 45.40N 15.39E
Jastrowie Poland 20 53.26N 16.49E
Jászberény Hungary 21 47.30N 19.55E
Jataí Brazil 94 17.58S 51.45W
Jāti Pakistan 40 24.21N 68.16E
Jatibarang Indonesia 37 6.26S108.18E
Jatinegara Indonesia 37 6.12S106.51E
Játiva Spain 16 39.00N 0.32W
Jatni India 41 20.10N 85.42E
Jaú Brazil 94 22.11S 48.35W
Jauja Peru 90 11.50S 75.15W
Jaunjelgava Latvia 24 56.34N 25.02E
Jaunpur India 41 25.44N 82.41E
Java *i. see* Jawa *i.* Indonesia 37
Javari *r.* Peru 90 4.30S 71.20W
Java Sea *see* Jawa, Laut *sea* Indonesia 36
Java Trench *f.* Indonesia 36 10.00S110.00E
Jawa *i.* Indonesia 37 7.25S110.00E
Jawa, Laut *sea* Indonesia 36 5.00S111.00E
Jawa Barat *d.* Indonesia 37 7.10S107.00E
Jawa Tengah *d.* Indonesia 37 7.49S110.35E
Jawa Timur *d.* Indonesia 37 8.42S113.10E
Jayah, Wādī al *see* Hā 'Arava Jordan / Israel 44
Jayapura Indonesia 37 2.28S140.38E
Jaynagar India 41 26.32N 86.07E
Jazirah Doberai *f.* Indonesia 37 1.10S132.30E
Jazzīn Lebanon 44 33.32N 35.34E
Jean U.S.A. 81 35.46N115.20W
Jeanerette U.S.A. 83 29.55N 91.40W
Jean Marie River *town* Canada 72 61.32N120.40W
Jebāl Bārez, Kūh-e *mts.* Iran 43 28.40N 58.10E
Jebba Nigeria 53 9.11N 4.49E
Jebri Pakistan 40 27.18N 65.44E
Jedburgh U.K. 12 55.29N 2.33W
Jedda *see* Jiddah Saudi Arabia 48
Jedrzejów Poland 21 50.39N 20.18E
Jefferson, Mt. Nev. U.S.A. 80 38.46N116.55W
Jefferson, Mt. Oreg. U.S.A. 80 44.40N121.47W
Jefferson City U.S.A. 82 38.34N 92.10W
Jeffersonville U.S.A. 84 38.16N 85.45W
Jega Nigeria 53 12.12N 4.23E
Jēkabpils Latvia 24 56.28N 25.58E
Jelenia Góra Poland 20 50.55N 15.45E
Jelgava Latvia 23 56.39N 23.42E
Jelli Sudan 49 5.22N 31.48E
Jember Indonesia 37 8.07S113.45E
Jena Germany 20 50.56N 11.35E
Jena U.S.A. 83 31.41N 92.08W
Jenbach Austria 20 47.24N 11.47E
Jenolan Caves *town* Australia 67 33.53S150.03E
Jepara Indonesia 37 6.32S110.40E
Jeparit Australia 66 36.09S141.59E
Jeppo Finland 22 63.24N 22.37E
Jequié Brazil 91 13.52S 40.06W
Jequitinhonha *r.* Brazil 94 16.46S 39.45W
Jerada Morocco 50 34.17N 2.13W
Jerantut Malaysia 36 3.56N102.22E
Jérémie Haiti 87 18.40N 74.09W
Jerez Spain 16 38.20N 6.45W
Jerez de la Frontera Spain 16 36.41N 6.08W
Jericho *see* Arīhā Jordan 44
Jerilderie Australia 67 35.23S145.41E
Jerome U.S.A. 80 42.43N114.31W
Jerramungup Australia 63 33.57S118.53E
Jersey *i.* Channel Is. Europe 11 49.13N 2.08W
Jersey City U.S.A. 85 40.44N 74.04W
Jerseyville U.S.A. 82 39.07N 90.20W
Jerusalem *see* Yerushalayim Israel / Jordan 44
Jervis B. Australia 67 35.05S150.44E
Jesenice Slovenia 18 46.27N 14.04E
Jessore Bangla. 41 23.10N 89.13E
Jesup U.S.A. 85 31.36N 81.54W
Jesús Carranza Mexico 86 17.26N 95.02W
Jetmore U.S.A. 83 38.03N 99.54W
Jetpur India 40 21.44N 70.37E
Jever Germany 14 53.34N 7.54E
Jevnaker Norway 23 60.15N 10.28E
Jewett U.S.A. 83 31.22N 96.09W
Jeypore India 41 18.51N 82.35E
Jeziorak, Jezioro *l.* Poland 21 53.40N 19.04E
Jhābua India 40 22.46N 74.36E
Jhajha India 41 24.46N 86.22E
Jhal Pakistan 40 28.17N 67.27E
Jhālakāti Bangla. 41 22.39N 90.12E
Jhālawār India 40 24.36N 76.09E
Jhal Jhao Pakistan 40 26.18N 65.35E
Jhālod India 40 23.06N 74.09E
Jhang Sadar Pakistan 40 31.16N 72.20E
Jhānsi India 41 25.26N 78.35E
Jharia India 41 23.45N 86.24E
Jhārsuguda India 41 21.51N 84.02E
Jhawāni Nepal 41 27.35N 84.38E
Jhelum Pakistan 40 32.56N 73.44E
Jhelum *r.* Pakistan 40 31.12N 72.08E
Jhinkpāni India 41 22.25N 85.47E
Jhok Rind Pakistan 40 31.27N 70.26E
Jhūnjhunu India 40 28.08N 75.24E
Jiaganj India 41 24.14N 88.16E
Jialing Jiang *r.* China 33 29.30N106.35E
Jiamusi China 31 46.50N130.21E
Ji'an China 33 27.03N115.00E
Jianchang China 32 40.50N119.50E
Jiange China 32 32.04N105.26E
Jiangling China 33 30.20N112.14E
Jiangmen China 33 22.31N113.08E
Jiangshan China 33 28.43N118.39E
Jiangsu *d.* China 32 33.00N119.30E
Jiangxi *d.* China 33 27.00N115.30E
Jiangyou China 33 31.47N104.45E
Jianhe China 33 26.39N108.35E
Jian'ou China 33 27.04N118.17E
Jianping China 32 41.23N119.40E
Jianshi China 33 30.42N109.20E
Jianyang Fujian China 33 27.19N118.01E
Jianyang Sichuan China 33 30.25N104.32E
Jiaochangba China 32 32.05N103.43E
Jiaohe China 31 43.42N127.19E
Jiaolai He *r.* China 32 43.48N123.00E
Jiaoling China 33 24.40N116.10E
Jiaonan China 32 35.53N119.58E
Jiao Xian China 32 36.16N120.00E
Jiaozou China 32 35.11N113.27E
Jiashan China 32 32.49N118.01E
Jiawang China 32 34.27N117.27E
Jiaxian China 32 38.02N110.29E
Jiaxing China 33 30.52N120.45E
Jiayi Taiwan 33 23.30N120.24E
Jiazi China 33 22.57N116.01E
Jiddah Saudi Arabia 48 21.30N 39.10E
Jiddat al Harāsīs *f.* Oman 45 19.45N 56.30E
Jiepai China 33 31.11N113.42E
Jiexi China 33 23.26N115.52E
Jiexiu China 32 37.00N111.55E
Jieyang China 33 23.29N116.19E
Jigawa *d.* Nigeria 53 12.30N 9.30E
Jihlava Czech Republic 20 49.24N 15.35E
Jijel Algeria 51 36.48N 5.46E
Jijiga Ethiopia 45 9.22N 42.47E
Jilib Somali Rep. 55 0.28N 42.50E
Jilin China 31 43.53N126.35E
Jilin *d.* China 31 44.50N125.00E
Jilong Taiwan 33 25.09N121.45E
Jima Ethiopia 49 7.36N 36.50E
Jimbe Angola 54 10.20S 16.40E
Jiménez Mexico 86 27.08N104.55W
Jimeta Nigeria 53 9.19N 12.25E
Jimo China 32 36.23N120.27E
Jinan China 32 36.40N117.01E
Jind India 40 29.19N 76.19E
Jindabyne Australia 67 36.24S148.37E
Jing'an China 33 28.52N115.22E
Jingbian China 32 37.33N108.36E
Jingchuan China 32 35.15N107.22E
Jingde China 33 30.19N118.31E
Jingdezhen China 33 29.14N117.14E
Jingellic Australia 67 35.54S147.44E
Jinggu Gansu China 32 35.05N103.41E
Jinggu Yunnan China 39 23.29N100.19E
Jinghai China 33 23.02N116.31E
Jing He *r.* China 32 34.26N109.00E
Jinghong China 30 21.59N100.49E
Jingmen China 33 31.02N112.06E
Jingning China 32 35.30N105.45E
Jingou China 32 41.37N120.33E
Jingtai China 32 37.10N104.08E
Jingxi China 33 23.03N106.36E
Jing Xian China 33 26.35N109.41E
Jingyuan Gansu China 32 36.40N104.40E
Jingyuan Ningxia Huizu China 32 35.29N106.20E
Jinhua China 33 29.05N119.40E
Jining Nei Monggol Zizhiqu China 31 40.56N113.00E
Jining Shantung China 32 35.22N116.45E
Jinja Uganda 55 0.27N 33.10E
Jinotepe Nicaragua 87 11.50N 86.10W
Jinsha Jiang *r.* China 39 26.30N101.40E
Jinshi China 33 29.35N111.56E
Jintang China 33 30.51N104.27E
Jinxi Fujian China 33 26.12N117.34E
Jinxi Liaoning China 32 40.48N120.46E
Jinxian China 33 28.13N116.34E
Jin Xian Liaoning China 32 41.10N121.20E
Jin Xian Liaoning China 32 39.06N121.49E
Jinxiang China 32 35.08N116.20E
Jinzhou China 32 41.06N121.05E
Jipijapa Ecuador 90 1.23S 80.35W
Jire Somali Rep. 45 5.22N 48.05E
Jirjā Egypt 48 26.20N 31.53E
Jishui China 33 27.13N115.07E
Jitarning Australia 63 32.48S117.57E
Jiu *r.* Romania 19 43.44N 23.52E
Jiuding Shan *mtn.* China 33 31.36N103.54E
Jiudongshan China 33 23.44N117.32E
Jiujiang China 33 29.39N116.02E
Jiulian Shan *mts.* China 33 24.40N115.00E
Jiuling Shan *mts.* China 33 28.40N114.45E
Jiulong Jiang *r.* China 33 24.30N117.47E
Jiuzhou Jiang *r.* China 33 21.25N109.58E

Jixi China 31 45.17N131.00E
Ji Xian Henan China 32 35.25N114.05E
Ji Xian Tianjin China 32 40.03N117.24E
Jīzān Saudi Arabia 48 16.54N 42.32E
Jīzl, Wādī al r. Saudi Arabia 42 25.37N 38.20E
João Pessoa Brazil 91 7.06S 34.53W
Jódar Spain 16 37.50N 3.21W
Jodhpur India 40 26.17N 73.02E
Jodiya India 40 22.42N 70.18E
Jodoigne Belgium 14 50.45N 4.52E
Joensuu Finland 24 62.35N 29.46E
Joetsu Japan 35 37.07N138.15E
Jogdor China 32 42.30N115.52E
Johannesburg R.S.A. 56 26.11S 28.04E
Johi Pakistan 40 26.41N 67.37E
John Day U.S.A. 80 44.25N118.57W
John Day r. U.S.A. 80 45.44N120.39W
John O'Groats U.K. 12 58.39N 3.02W
Johnson U.S.A. 83 37.34N101.45W
Johnson City U.S.A. 85 36.20N 82.23W
Johnsons Crossing Canada 74 60.29N133.18W
Johnston, L. Australia 63 32.25S120.30E
Johnstone Str. Canada 74 50.28N126.00W
Johnston I. Pacific Oc. 68 16.45N169.32W
Johnstown U.S.A. 84 40.20N 78.55W
Johor Baharu Malaysia 36 1.29N103.40E
Joigny France 15 48.00N 3.20E
Joinville Brazil 94 26.20S 48.49W
Joinville France 17 48.27N 5.08E
Jokkmokk Sweden 22 66.37N 19.50E
Jökulsá á Brú r. Iceland 22 65.33N 14.23W
Jökulsá á Fjöllum r. Iceland 22 66.05N 16.32W
Jolfa Iran 43 32.40N 51.39E
Joliet U.S.A. 82 41.32N 88.05W
Joliette Canada 77 46.02N 73.27W
Jolo i. Phil. 37 5.55N121.20E
Jolo town Phil. 37 6.03N121.00E
Jombang Indonesia 37 7.30S112.21E
Jombo r. Angola 54 10.20S 16.37E
Jomda China 39 31.30N 98.16E
Jonava Lithuania 23 55.05N 24.17E
Jonê China 32 34.35N103.32E
Jonesboro Ark. U.S.A. 83 35.50N 90.42W
Jonesboro La. U.S.A. 83 32.15N 92.43W
Jones Sd. Canada 73 76.00N 85.00W
Jönköping Sweden 23 57.47N 14.11E
Jönköping d. Sweden 23 57.30N 14.30E
Joplin U.S.A. 83 37.06N 94.31W
Jora India 41 26.20N 77.49E
Jordan Asia 42 31.00N 36.00E
Jordan r. see Al Urdunn r. Asia 44
Jordan U.S.A. 80 47.19N106.55W
Jordan Valley town U.S.A. 80 42.58N117.03W
Jorhāt India 39 26.45N 94.13E
Jörn Sweden 22 65.04N 20.02E
Jos Nigeria 53 9.54N 8.53E
José de San Martin Argentina 93 44.04S 70.26W
José Enrique Rodó Uruguay 93 33.41S 57.34W
Joseph, Lac l. Canada 77 52.45N 65.15W
Joseph Bonaparte G. Australia 62 14.00S128.30E
Joseph City U.S.A. 81 34.57N110.20W
Joshīmath India 41 30.34N 79.34E
Jos Plateau f. Nigeria 53 10.00N 9.00E
Jotunheimen mts. Norway 23 61.38N 8.18E
Joué-lès-Tours France 15 47.21N 0.40E
Joure Neth. 14 52.59N 5.49E
Joverega Botswana 56 19.08S 24.15E
Jowai India 41 25.27N 92.12E
Juan Aldama Mexico 83 24.19N103.21W
Juan B. Arruabarrena Argentina 93 30.25S 58.15W
Juan de Fuca, Str. of Canada / U.S.A. 74 48.15N124.00W
Juan de Nova i. Madagascar 57 17.03S 42.45E
Juan Fernández, Islas is. Pacific Oc. 69 34.20S 80.00W
Juárez Argentina 93 37.40S 59.48W
Juárez Chihuahua Mexico 81 30.20N108.03W
Juárez Coahuila Mexico 83 27.37N100.44W
Juárez, Sierra de mts. Mexico 81 32.00N115.45W
Juàzeiro Brazil 91 9.25S 40.30W
Juàzeiro do Norte Brazil 91 7.10S 39.18W
Jūbā Sudan 49 4.51N 31.37E
Jūbāl, Maḍīq str. Egypt 44 27.40N 33.55E
Jubal, Str. of see Jūbāl, Maḍīq str. Egypt 44
Jubba r. Somali Rep. 55 0.20S 42.40E
Jubilee Downs town Australia 62 18.22S125.17E
Juby, Cap c. Morocco 50 27.58N 12.55W
Júcar r. Spain 16 39.10N 0.15W
Juchitán Mexico 86 16.27N 95.05W
Judenburg Austria 20 47.10N 14.40E
Judith Basin f. U.S.A. 80 47.10N109.58W
Juist Germany 14 53.41N 7.01E
Juist i. Germany 14 53.43N 7.00E
Juiz de Fora Brazil 94 21.47S 43.23W
Jujuy d. Argentina 92 23.00S 66.00W
Juklegga mtn. Norway 23 61.03N 8.13E
Juliaca Peru 90 15.29S 70.09W
Julia Creek town Australia 64 20.39S141.45E
Juliana Kanaal canal Neth. 14 51.00N 5.48E
Julianehåb Greenland 73 60.45N 46.00W
Jülich Germany 14 50.55N 6.21E
Jullundur India 40 31.20N 75.35E
Jumboo Somali Rep. 55 0.12S 42.38E
Jumet Belgium 14 50.27N 4.27E
Jumilla Spain 16 38.28N 1.19W
Jumla Nepal 41 29.17N 82.13E
Jumna r. see Yamuna India 41
Junāgadh India 40 21.31N 70.28E
Junan China 32 35.11N118.50E
Junction U.S.A. 83 30.29N 99.46W
Junction B. Australia 64 11.50S134.15E
Junction City Kans. U.S.A. 82 39.02N 96.50W
Junction City Oreg. U.S.A. 80 44.13N123.12W
Jundah Australia 64 24.50S143.02E
Jundiaí Brazil 94 23.10S 46.54W
Juneau U.S.A. 74 58.26N134.30W
Junee Australia 67 34.51S147.40E
Jungfrau mtn. Switz. 17 46.30N 8.00E
Junggar Pendi f. Asia 30 44.20N 86.30E
Junglinster Lux. 14 49.41N 6.13E
Jungshāhi Pakistan 40 24.51N 67.46E
Junín Argentina 93 34.35S 60.58W
Junín de los Andes Argentina 93 39.57S 71.05W
Juniville France 15 49.24N 4.23E
Jūniyah Lebanon 44 33.59N 35.38E
Junlian China 33 28.08N104.29E
Junnah, Jabal mts. Egypt 44 28.52N 34.15E
Junnar India 40 19.12N 73.53E
Junqali d. Sudan 49 7.30N 32.30E
Junsele Sweden 22 63.40N 16.55E
Juntura U.S.A. 80 43.46N118.05W
Jun Xian China 32 32.40N111.18E
Jupiter r. Canada 77 49.29N 63.32W
Jupiter U.S.A. 85 26.57N 80.08W
Jur r. Sudan 49 7.45N 28.00E
Jura mts. Europe 17 46.55N 6.45E
Jura i. U.K. 12 55.58N 5.55W
Jura, Sd. of U.K. 12 56.00N 5.45W
Jurado Colombia 90 7.07N 77.46W
Jura Krakowska mts. Poland 21 50.30N 19.30E
Jurhen Ul Shan mts. China 41 34.00N 91.00E
Jūrmala Latvia 23 56.58N 23.42E
Juruá r. Brazil 90 2.33S 65.50W
Juruena Brazil 92 12.50S 58.58W
Juruena r. Brazil 91 7.20S 57.30W
Juruti Brazil 91 2.09S 56.04W
Jussey France 17 47.49N 5.54E
Jutaí r. Brazil 90 2.35S 67.00W
Juticalpa Honduras 87 14.45N 86.12W
Jutland pen. see Jylland pen. Denmark 23
Juye China 32 35.23N116.06E
Jūyom Iran 43 28.10N 53.52E
Juzur al Halaniyat is. Oman 38 17.30N 56.00E
Jwayyā Lebanon 44 33.14N 35.20E
Jylland pen. Denmark 23 56.00N 9.15E
Jyväskylä Finland 22 62.14N 25.44E

K

Ka r. Nigeria 53 11.35N 4.10E
Kaabong Uganda 55 3.28N 34.08E
Kaapstad see Cape Town R.S.A. 56
Kaba Guinea 52 10.08N 11.49W
Kabaena i. Indonesia 37 5.25S122.00E
Kabala Sierra Leone 52 9.40N 11.36W
Kabale Uganda 55 1.13S 30.00E
Kabalega Falls f. Uganda 55 2.17N 31.46E
Kabalega Falls Nat. Park Uganda 55 2.15N 31.45E
Kabalo Zaïre 55 6.02S 27.00E
Kabambare Zaïre 55 4.40S 27.41E
Kabanga Zambia 56 17.36S 26.45E
Kabba Nigeria 53 7.50N 6.07E
Kabinakagami r. Canada 84 50.20N 84.20W
Kabinda Zaïre 54 6.10S 24.29E
Kabīr Kūh mts. Iran 43 33.00N 47.00E
Kabkābīyah Sudan 49 13.39N 24.05E
Kābol Afghan. 40 34.31N 69.12E
Kābol d. Afghan. 40 34.45N 69.15E
Kabompo Zambia 54 13.35S 24.10E
Kabompo r. Zambia 54 14.17S 23.15E
Kabongo Zaïre 54 7.22S 25.34E
Kabonzo Zaïre 55 6.41S 27.49E
Kaboudia, Ra's c. Tunisia 51 35.14N 11.10E
Kabūd Gonbad Iran 43 37.02N 59.46E
Kabul see Kābol Afghan. 40
Kabumbu Zaïre 54 4.07S 26.17E
Kabunda Zaïre 55 12.27S 29.15E
Kabundi Zaïre 55 10.07S 27.13E
Kabwe Zambia 55 14.27S 28.25E
Kāchā Kūh mts. Iran 43 29.30N 61.20E
Kachchh, G. of India 40 22.40N 69.30E
Kachin d. Burma 34 26.00N 97.30E
Kachiry Kazakhstan 28 53.07N 76.08E
Kachīsī Ethiopia 49 9.39N 37.50E
Kadaney r. Afghan. 40 31.20N 65.47E
Kade Ghana 52 6.08N 0.51W
Kadei r. C.A.R. 53 3.28N 16.05E
Kadi India 40 23.18N 72.20E
Kadina Australia 66 33.58S137.14E
Kadioli Mali 52 10.38N 5.45W
Kadoka U.S.A. 82 43.50N101.31W
Kadoma Zimbabwe 56 18.23S 29.52E
Kaduna Nigeria 53 10.28N 7.25E
Kaduna d. Nigeria 53 11.00N 7.35E
Kaduna r. Nigeria 53 8.45N 5.45E
Kāduqlī Sudan 49 11.01N 29.43E
Kadusam mtn. China 39 28.30N 96.45E
Kadzherom Russian Fed. 24 64.42N 55.59E
Kaédi Mauritania 50 16.09N 13.30W
Kaélé Cameroon 53 10.05N 14.28E
Kaesŏng N. Korea 31 37.59N126.30E
Kafanchan Nigeria 53 9.38N 8.20E
Kaffrine Senegal 52 14.08N 15.34W
Kafia Kingi Sudan 49 9.16N 24.25E
Kafirévs, Ákra c. Greece 19 38.11N 24.30E
Kafr ad Dawwār Egypt 44 31.08N 30.08E
Kafr al Baṭṭīkh Egypt 44 31.24N 31.44E
Kafr ash Shaykh Egypt 44 31.07N 30.56E
Kafr az Zayyāt Egypt 44 30.50N 30.49E
Kafr Salīm Egypt 44 31.09N 30.07E
Kafu r. Uganda 55 1.40N 32.07E
Kafue Zambia 55 15.40S 28.13E
Kafue r. Zambia 55 15.53S 28.55E
Kafue Dam Zambia 55 15.40S 27.10E
Kafue Nat. Park Zambia 54 15.30S 25.35E
Kafunzo Uganda 55 1.05S 30.26E
Kaga Bandoro C.A.R. 53 7.00N 19.10E
Kāgān Pakistan 40 34.47N 73.32E
Kagan Uzbekistan 28 39.45N 64.32E
Kagarlyk Ukraine 21 49.50N 30.50E
Kagaznagar India 41 19.18N 79.50E
Kagera d. Tanzania 55 2.00S 31.20E
Kagizman Turkey 42 40.08N 43.07E
Kagoshima Japan 35 31.37N130.32E
Kagul Moldavia 21 45.54N 28.11E
Kahama Tanzania 55 3.48S 32.38E
Kahayan r. Indonesia 36 3.20S114.04E
Kahemba Zaïre 54 7.20S 19.00E
Kahntah r. Canada 74 58.15N120.55W
Kahnūj Iran 43 27.55N 57.45E
Kahoolawe i. Hawaiian Is. 69 20.33N156.37W
Kahraman Maraş Turkey 42 37.34N 36.54E
Kai, Kepulauan is. Indonesia 37 5.45S132.55E
Kaiama Nigeria 53 9.37N 4.03E
Kaiapoi New Zealand 60 43.23S172.39E
Kaiedin Sudan 49 9.45N 32.11E
Kaifeng China 32 34.46N114.22E
Kaikohe New Zealand 60 35.25S173.49E
Kaikoura New Zealand 60 42.24S173.41E
Kaikoura Range mts. New Zealand 60 42.00S173.40E
Kailahun Sierra Leone 52 8.21N 10.21W
Kaili China 33 26.35N107.55E
Kailu China 32 43.35N121.12E
Kailua Hawaiian Is. 69 21.24N157.44W
Kaimana Indonesia 37 3.39S133.44E
Kaimanawa Mts. New Zealand 60 39.10S176.15E
Kainantu P.N.G. 37 6.16S145.50E
Kainji Resr. Nigeria 53 10.00N 4.35E
Kaintragarh India 41 20.47N 84.40E
Kaipara Harbour New Zealand 60 36.30S174.00E
Kaiserslautern Germany 14 49.27N 7.47E
Kaitaia New Zealand 60 35.08S173.18E
Kaithal India 40 29.48N 76.23E
Kaitum r. Sweden 22 67.30N 21.05E
Kaiwi Channel Hawaiian Is. 69 21.15N157.30W
Kaiyuan China 32 42.45N123.50E
Kaizuka Japan 35 34.27N135.21E
Kajaani Finland 22 64.14N 27.41E
Kajabbi Australia 64 20.02S140.02E
Kajiado Kenya 55 1.50S 36.48E
Kajo Kaji Sudan 49 3.53N 31.40E
Kajuru Nigeria 53 10.19N 7.40E
Kākā Sudan 49 10.36N 32.11E
Kakamas R.S.A. 56 28.44S 20.35E
Kakamega Kenya 55 0.21N 34.47E
Kakamigahara Japan 35 35.28N136.48E
Kākdwīp India 41 21.53N 88.11E
Kakegawa Japan 35 34.46N138.01E
Kakenge Zaïre 54 4.51S 21.55E
Kakhovskoye Vodokhranilishche resr. Ukraine 25 47.33N 34.40E
Kākī Iran 43 28.19N 51.34E
Kākināda India 39 16.59N 82.20E
Kakisa r. Canada 74 61.03N117.10W
Kakisa L. Canada 74 60.55N117.40W
Kakonko Tanzania 55 3.19S 30.54E
Kakuma Kenya 55 3.38N 34.48E
Kakuto Uganda 55 0.54S 31.26E
Kala r. Finland 22 64.17N 23.55E
Kalaallit Nunaat see Greenland N. America 73
Kālābāgh Pakistan 40 32.58N 71.34E
Kalabahi Indonesia 37 8.13S124.31E
Kalabáka Greece 19 39.42N 21.43E
Kalabity Australia 66 31.53S140.18E
Kalabo Zambia 54 14.58S 22.33E
Kalach-na-Donu Russian Fed. 25 48.43N 43.31E
Kaladan r. Burma 34 20.09N 92.55E
Kalahari Desert Botswana 56 23.30S 22.00E
Kalahari Gemsbok Nat. Park R.S.A. 56 25.45S 20.25E
Kalajoki Finland 22 64.15N 23.57E
Kalakan Russian Fed. 29 55.10N116.45E
Kalámai Greece 19 37.02N 22.05E
Kalamazoo U.S.A. 84 42.17N 85.36W
Kalamb India 40 18.56N 73.55E
Kalamera Tanzania 55 2.07S 33.43E
Kalamurra, L. Australia 66 28.00S138.00E
Kalandula Angola 54 9.06S 16.11E
Kalannie Australia 63 30.21S117.04E
Kalanshiyū, Sarīr des. Libya 51 27.00N 21.30E
Kalarash Moldavia 21 47.18N 28.16E
Kalāt Pakistan 40 29.02N 66.35E
Kalb, Ra's al c. Yemen 45 14.02N 48.41E
Kalbarri Australia 63 27.40S114.12E
Kalchās Pakistan 40 29.21N 69.42E
Kalecik Turkey 42 40.06N 33.22E
Kalehe Zaïre 55 2.05S 28.53E
Kalemie Zaïre 55 5.57S 29.10E
Kalgan r. Australia 63 34.55S117.58E
Kalgoorlie Australia 63 30.49S121.29E
Kaliakra, Nos c. Bulgaria 19 43.23N 28.29E
Kalianda Indonesia 36 5.50S105.45E
Kalima Zaïre 54 2.35S 26.34E
Kalimantan d. Indonesia 36 1.00S113.00E
Kalimantan f. Indonesia 36 0.05N112.30E
Kalimantan Barat d. Indonesia 36 0.30N110.00E
Kalimantan Selatan d. Indonesia 36 2.30S115.30E
Kalimantan Tengah d. Indonesia 36 2.00S113.30E
Kalimantan Timur d. Indonesia 36 2.20N116.30E
Kálimnos i. Greece 19 37.00N 27.00E
Kālimpong India 41 27.04N 88.29E
Kaliningrad Russian Fed. 23 54.43N 20.30E
Kalinkovichi Belorussia 21 52.10N 29.13E
Kalinovka Ukraine 21 49.29N 28.30E
Kalisat Indonesia 37 8.02S113.50E
Kāli Sindh r. India 40 25.32N 76.17E
Kalispell U.S.A. 80 48.12N114.19W
Kalisz Poland 21 51.46N 18.02E
Kaliua Tanzania 55 5.08S 31.50E
Kalix r. Sweden 22 65.50N 23.11E
Kalkar Germany 14 51.45N 6.17E
Kalkfontein Botswana 56 22.08S 20.54E
Kalkrand Namibia 56 24.05S 17.34E
Kallsjön l. Sweden 22 63.35N 13.00E
Kalmar Sweden 23 56.40N 16.22E
Kalmar d. Sweden 23 57.20N 16.00E
Kalmarsund str. Sweden 23 56.40N 16.25E
Kalmthout Belgium 14 51.23N 4.28E
Kalmykovo Kazakhstan 25 49.02N 51.55E
Kālna India 41 23.13N 88.22E
Kalo P.N.G. 64 10.05S147.45E
Kalocsa Hungary 21 46.32N 18.59E
Kaloko Zaïre 54 6.47S 25.47E
Kālol Gujarat India 40 22.36N 73.27E
Kālol Gujarat India 40 23.15N 72.29E
Kalole Zaïre 55 3.40S 27.22E
Kalomo Zambia 54 16.55S 26.29E
Kalonje Zambia 55 12.21S 31.06E
Kālpi India 41 26.07N 79.44E
Kāl Qal 'eh Afghan. 40 32.38N 62.32E
Kalsø i. Faroe Is. 8 62.19N 6.42W
Kalsūbai mtn. India 40 19.36N 73.43E
Kaltag U.S.A. 72 64.20N158.44W
Kaluga Russian Fed. 24 54.31N 36.16E
Kālu Khuhar Pakistan 40 25.08N 67.46E
Kalumburu Australia 62 14.14S126.38E
Kalundborg Denmark 23 55.41N 11.06E
Kalush Ukraine 21 49.02N 24.20E
Kalutara Sri Lanka 39 6.35N 79.58E
Kalyān India 40 19.15N 73.09E
Kama r. Russian Fed. 24 55.30N 52.00E
Kamakura Japan 35 35.19N139.33E
Kamālia Pakistan 40 30.44N 72.39E
Kamanashi r. Japan 35 35.33N138.28E
Kamanjab Namibia 56 19.39S 14.50E
Kamarsuk Canada 77 56.18N 61.38W
Kamba Nigeria 53 11.52N 3.42E
Kamba Zaïre 54 4.00S 22.22E
Kambalda Australia 63 31.12S121.40E
Kambar Pakistan 40 27.36N 68.00E
Kambarka Russian Fed. 24 56.18N 54.13E
Kambia Sierra Leone 52 9.09N 12.53W
Kamchatka, Poluostrov pen. Russian Fed. 29 56.00N160.00E
Kamen mtn. Russian Fed. 29 68.40N 94.20E
Kamenets Podolskiy Ukraine 21 48.40N 26.36E
Kamenka Russian Fed. 24 53.10N 44.05E
Kamenka Russian Fed. 24 65.55N 44.02E
Kamenka Bugskaya Ukraine 21 50.07N 24.30E
Kamen Kashirskiy Ukraine 21 51.32N 24.59E
Kamen-na-Obi Russian Fed. 28 53.46N 81.18E
Kamenskoye Russian Fed. 29 62.31N165.15E
Kamensk-Shakhtinskiy Russian Fed. 25 48.20N 40.16E
Kamensk-Ural'skiy Russian Fed. 28 56.29N 61.49E
Kāmet mtn. India / China 41 30.54N 79.37E
Kameyama Japan 35 34.51N136.27E
Kamiah U.S.A. 80 46.14N116.02W
Kamieskroon R.S.A. 56 30.12S 17.53E
Kamilukuak L. Canada 75 62.22N101.40W
Kamina Zaïre 54 8.46S 24.58E
Kaminak L. Canada 75 62.10N 95.00W
Kamloops Canada 74 50.40N120.20W
Kamloops Plateau f. Canada 74 50.00N120.20W
Kamo r. Japan 35 35.00N139.52E
Kāmoke Pakistan 40 31.58N 74.13E
Kamp Germany 14 50.14N 7.37E
Kampa Indonesia 36 1.46S105.26E
Kampala Uganda 55 0.19N 32.35E
Kampar r. Indonesia 36 0.20N102.55E
Kampen Neth. 14 52.33N 5.55E
Kampene Zaïre 54 3.36S 26.40E
Kamphaeng Phet Thailand 34 16.28N 99.31E
Kamp-Lintfort Germany 14 51.34N 6.38E
Kamp'O S. Korea 35 35.48N129.29E
Kâmpóng Cham Cambodia 34 11.59N105.26E
Kâmpóng Chhnăng Cambodia 34 12.16N104.39E
Kâmpóng Saôm Cambodia 34 10.38N103.30E
Kâmpóng Thum Cambodia 34 12.42N104.52E
Kâmpôt Cambodia 34 10.37N104.11E
Kampti Burkina 52 10.07N 3.22W
Kamsack Canada 75 51.34N101.54W
Kamskoye Vodokhranilishche resr. Russian Fed. 24 58.55N 56.20E
Kāmthi India 41 21.14N 79.12E
Kamyshin Russian Fed. 25 50.05N 45.24E
Kana r. Zimbabwe 56 18.30S 26.50E
Kanaaupscow r. Canada 76 53.40N 77.10W
Kanafis Sudan 49 9.48N 25.40E
Kanagawa d. Japan 35 35.25N139.10E
Kanairiktok r. Canada 77 55.05N 60.20W
Kananga Zaïre 54 5.53S 22.26E
Kanash Russian Fed. 24 55.30N 47.27E
Kanaudi India 41 23.36N 81.23E
Kanawha r. U.S.A. 84 38.50N 82.08W
Kanazawa Japan 35 36.35N136.38E
Kanchanaburi Thailand 34 14.02N 99.28E
Kānchenjunga mtn. Nepal / India 41 27.44N 88.11E
Kānchipuram India 39 12.50N 79.44E
Kandāhu Pakistan 40 27.33N 69.24E
Kandalaksha Russian Fed. 24 67.09N 32.31E
Kandalakshskaya Guba g. Russian Fed. 24 66.30N 34.00E
Kandangan Indonesia 36 2.50S115.15E
Kandavu i. Fiji 68 19.05S178.15E
Kandavu Passage Fiji 68 18.45S178.00E
Kandhkot Pakistan 40 28.14N 69.11E
Kandi Benin 53 11.05N 2.59E
Kāndi India 41 23.57N 88.02E
Kandiāro Pakistan 40 27.04N 68.13E
Kandira Turkey 42 41.05N 30.08E
Kandla India 40 23.00N 70.10E
Kandos Australia 67 32.53S149.59E
Kandrāch Pakistan 40 25.29N 65.29E
Kandreho Madagascar 57 17.29S 46.06E
Kandy Sri Lanka 39 7.18N 80.43E
Kane U.S.A. 84 41.40N 78.49W
Kanem d. Chad 53 15.10N 15.30E
Kanevka Russian Fed. 24 67.08N 39.50E
Kang Botswana 56 23.43S 22.51E
Kangaarsussuaq see Parry, Kap c. Greenland 73
Kangaba Mali 52 11.56N 8.25W
Kangān Iran 43 27.50N 52.07E
Kangar Malaysia 36 6.28N100.10E
Kangaroo I. Australia 66 35.50S137.06E
Kangding China 30 30.05N102.04E
Kangean, Kepulauan is. Indonesia 37 7.00S115.30E
Kangerlussuaq see Söndreströmfjord Greenland 73
Kangiqsualujjuaq Canada 73 58.35N 65.59W
Kangiqsujuaq Canada 73 61.30N 72.00W
Kangirsuk Canada 73 60.01N 70.01W
Kangle China 32 35.16N103.39E
Kangmar Xizang Zizhiqu China 41 30.45N 85.43E
Kangmar Xizang Zizhiqu China 41 28.30N 89.45E
Kango Gabon 54 0.15N 10.14E
Kangping China 32 42.45N123.20E
Kangrinboqê Feng mtn. China 41 31.05N 81.21E
Kangto mtn. China 41 27.54N 92.32E
Kanhar r. India 41 24.28N 83.08E
Kani Ivory Coast 52 8.34N 6.35W
Kaniama Zaïre 54 7.32S 24.11E
Kanin, Poluostrov pen. Russian Fed. 24 68.00N 45.00E
Kaningo Kenya 55 0.52S 38.31E
Kanin Nos, Mys c. Russian Fed. 24 68.38N 43.20E
Kaniva Australia 66 36.33S141.17E
Kanjiža Yugo. 21 46.04N 20.04E
Kankakee U.S.A. 82 41.08N 87.52W
Kankan Gabon 54 0.03S 12.14E
Kankan Guinea 52 10.22N 9.11W
Kānker India 41 20.17N 81.29E
Kankossa Mauritania 50 15.58N 11.31W
Kannack Vietnam 34 14.07N108.36E
Kannapolis U.S.A. 85 35.30N 80.36W
Kannauj India 41 27.04N 79.55E
Kannod India 40 22.40N 76.44E
Kano r. Japan 35 35.05N138.52E
Kano Nigeria 53 12.00N 8.31E
Kano d. Nigeria 53 11.45N 8.30E
Kanona Zambia 55 13.03S 30.37E
Kanowna Australia 63 30.36S121.36E
Kānpur India 41 26.28N 80.21E
Kansas d. U.S.A. 82 38.30N 99.00W
Kansas r. U.S.A. 82 39.07N 94.36W
Kansas City Kans. U.S.A. 82 39.07N 94.39W
Kansas City Mo. U.S.A. 82 39.05N 94.35W
Kansenia Zaïre 54 10.19S 26.02E
Kansk Russian Fed. 29 56.11N 95.20E
Kansŏng S. Korea 31 38.20N128.28E
Kantābānji India 41 20.29N 82.55E
Kantché Niger 53 13.31N 8.30E
Kantemirovka Russian Fed. 25 49.40N 39.52E
Kantō d. Japan 35 35.35N139.30E
Kantōheiya f. Japan 35 36.02N140.10E
Kantō-sanchi mts. Japan 35 36.00N138.35E
Kanye Botswana 56 24.58S 25.17E
Kanyu Botswana 56 20.05S 24.39E
Kao i. Tonga 69 19.40S175.01W
Kaoko Veld f. Namibia 56 18.30S 13.30E
Kaolack Senegal 52 14.09N 16.08W
Kaoma Zambia 54 14.55S 24.58E
Kapaa Hawaiian Is. 69 22.05N159.19W
Kapadvanj India 40 23.01N 73.04E
Kapanga Zaïre 54 8.22S 22.37E
Kapchagay Kazakhstan 30 43.51N 77.14E
Kapenguria Kenya 55 1.13N 35.07E
Kapfenberg Austria 20 47.27N 15.18E
Kapiri Mposhi Zambia 55 13.59S 28.40E
Kapiskau Canada 76 52.20N 82.01W
Kapiskau r. Canada 76 52.20N 83.40W
Kapit Malaysia 36 2.01N112.56E
Kapiti I. New Zealand 60 40.50S174.50E
Kapoeta Sudan 49 4.47N 33.35E
Kapongolo Zaïre 55 7.51S 28.12E
Kaposvár Hungary 19 46.22N 17.47E
Kappar Pakistan 40 25.19N 62.42E
Kapps Namibia 56 22.22S 17.52E
Kapsabet Kenya 55 0.12N 35.05E
Kaptai Bangla. 41 22.21N 92.17E
Kapuas r. Indonesia 36 0.13S109.12E
Kapunda Australia 66 34.21S138.54E
Kapūrthala India 40 31.23N 75.23E
Kapuskasing Canada 76 49.25N 82.30W
Kaputar, Mt. Australia 67 30.20S150.10E
Kapuvár Hungary 21 47.36N 17.02E
Kara Russian Fed. 28 69.12N 65.00E

Kara-Bogaz Gol, Zaliv to Khuzdār

Kara-Bogaz Gol, Zaliv *b.* Turkmenistan 43 41.20N 53.40E
Karabük Turkey 42 41.12N 32.36E
Karabutak Kazakhstan 28 49.55N 60.05E
Karāchi Pakistan 40 24.52N 67.03E
Karād India 38 17.17N 74.12E
Karaganda Kazakhstan 28 49.53N 73.07E
Karaginskiy, Ostrov *i.* Russian Fed. 29 59.00N 165.00E
Karakas Kazakhstan 30 48.20N 83.30E
Karakelong *i.* Indonesia 37 4.20N 126.50E
Karakoram Pass Asia 39 35.33N 77.51E
Karakoram Range *mts.* Jammu & Kashmir 38 35.30N 76.30E
Karakoro *r.* Mauritania 50 14.43N 12.03W
Karaköse *see* Ağri Turkey 25
Karakumskiy Kanal *canal* Turkmenistan 43 37.30N 65.48E
Karakumy, Peski *f.* Turkmenistan 43 37.45N 60.00E
Karakuwisa Namibia 56 18.56S 19.43E
Karaman Turkey 42 37.11N 33.13E
Karamay China 30 45.48N 84.30E
Karamea New Zealand 60 41.15S 172.07E
Karamea Bight *b.* New Zealand 60 41.15S 171.30E
Karamürsel Turkey 42 40.42N 29.37E
Karand Iran 43 34.16N 46.15E
Kāranja India 41 20.29N 77.29E
Karanjia India 41 21.47N 85.58E
Karasburg Namibia 56 28.00S 18.46E
Karasjok Norway 22 69.27N 25.30E
Karasuk Russian Fed. 28 53.45N 78.01E
Karatau, Khrebet *mts.* Kazakhstan 25 44.15N 52.10E
Karatobe Kazakhstan 25 49.44N 53.30E
Karaton Kazakhstan 25 46.26N 53.32E
Karauli India 40 26.30N 77.01E
Karawa Zaïre 54 3.12N 20.20E
Karazhal Kazakhstan 28 48.00N 70.55E
Karbalā' Iraq 43 32.37N 44.03E
Karcag Hungary 21 47.19N 20.56E
Kardhítsa Greece 19 39.22N 21.59E
Kärdla Estonia 23 59.00N 22.42E
Kareli India 41 22.55N 79.04E
Karema Tanzania 55 6.50S 30.25E
Karen India 39 12.50N 92.55E
Karepino Russian Fed. 24 61.05N 58.02E
Karesuando Finland 22 68.25N 22.30E
Kargasok Russian Fed. 28 59.07N 80.58E
Kargi Kenya 55 2.31N 37.34E
Kargil Jammu & Kashmir 40 34.34N 76.06E
Kargopol Russian Fed. 24 61.32N 38.59E
Kari Nigeria 53 11.17N 10.35E
Kariba Zimbabwe 56 16.32S 28.50E
Kariba, L. Zimbabwe / Zambia 56 16.50S 28.00E
Kariba Dam Zimbabwe / Zambia 56 16.15S 28.55E
Karibib Namibia 56 21.56S 15.52E
Kārikāl India 39 10.58N 79.50E
Karimama Benin 53 12.02N 3.15E
Karīmganj India 41 24.52N 92.20E
Karin Somali Rep. 45 10.51N 45.45E
Karis Finland 23 60.05N 23.40E
Karisimbi, Mt. Zaïre / Rwanda 55 1.31S 29.25E
Kariya Japan 35 34.59N 136.59E
Kariyangwe Zimbabwe 56 17.57S 27.30E
Karkaralinsk Kazakhstan 28 49.21N 75.27E
Karkar I. P.N.G. 37 4.40S 146.00E
Karkas, Kūh-e *mtn.* Iran 43 33.25N 51.40E
Karkheh *r.* Iran 43 31.45N 47.52E
Karkinitskiy Zaliv *g.* Ukraine 25 45.50N 32.45E
Karkoo Australia 66 34.02S 135.44E
Karlino Poland 20 54.03N 15.51E
Karl-Marx-Stadt *See* Chemnitz Germany 20
Karlovac Croatia 18 45.30N 15.34E
Karlovy Vary Czech Republic 20 50.14N 12.53E
Karlsborg Sweden 23 58.32N 14.31E
Karlshamn Sweden 23 56.10N 14.51E
Karlskoga Sweden 23 59.20N 14.31E
Karlskrona Sweden 23 56.10N 15.35E
Karlsruhe Germany 20 49.00N 8.24E
Karlstad Sweden 23 59.22N 13.30E
Karlstad U.S.A. 82 48.35N 96.31W
Karmah Sudan 48 19.38N 30.25E
Karmöy *i.* Norway 23 59.15N 5.15E
Karnafuli Resr. Bangla. 39 22.40N 92.05E
Karnāl India 40 29.41N 76.59E
Karnāli *r.* Nepal 41 28.45N 81.16E
Karnaphuli Resr. Bangla. 41 22.30N 92.20E
Karnataka *d.* India 38 14.45N 76.00E
Karnes City U.S.A. 83 28.53N 97.54W
Karnobat Bulgaria 19 42.40N 27.00E
Kärnten *d.* Austria 20 46.50N 13.50E
Karoi Zimbabwe 56 16.51S 29.39E
Karokh Afghan. 40 34.28N 62.35E
Karonga Malaŵi 55 9.54S 33.55E
Karonie Australia 63 30.58S 122.32E
Karoonda Australia 66 35.09S 139.54E
Karor Pakistan 40 31.13N 70.57E
Karora Sudan 48 17.42N 38.22E
Karos Dam R.S.A. 56 28.27S 21.39E
Karpach Moldavia 21 48.00N 27.10E
Kárpathos Greece 19 35.30N 27.14E
Kárpathos *i.* Greece 19 35.35N 27.08E
Karpineny Moldavia 21 46.46N 28.18E
Karpinsk Russian Fed. 24 59.48N 59.59E
Karpogory Russian Fed. 24 64.01N 44.30E
Karragullen Australia 63 32.05S 116.03E
Karratha Australia 62 20.44S 116.50E
Karridale Australia 63 34.12S 115.04E
Kars Turkey 42 40.35N 43.05E
Karsakpay Kazakhstan 28 47.47N 66.43E
Kärsämäki Finland 22 63.58N 25.46E
Kārsava Russian Fed. 24 56.45N 27.40E
Karskoye More *sea* Russian Fed. 28 73.00N 65.00E
Kartaly Russian Fed. 28 53.06N 60.37E
Karufa Indonesia 37 3.50S 133.27E
Karumba Australia 64 17.28S 140.50E
Kārūn *r.* Iran 43 30.25N 48.12E
Karunga Kenya 49 1.09S 36.49E
Karungi Sweden 22 66.03N 23.55E
Karungu Kenya 55 0.50S 34.09E
Karviná Czech Republic 21 49.50N 18.30E
Kasai *r.* Zaïre 54 3.10S 16.13E
Kasaï Occidental *d.* Zaïre 54 5.00S 21.30E
Kasaï Oriental *d.* Zaïre 54 5.00S 24.00E
Kasaji Zaïre 54 10.22S 23.27E
Kasama Zambia 55 10.10S 31.11E
Kasane Botswana 56 17.48S 25.09E
Kasanga Tanzania 55 8.27S 31.10E
Kāsaragod India 38 12.30N 75.00E
Kasba India 41 25.51N 87.33E
Kasba L. Canada 75 60.20N 102.10W
Kasempa Zambia 54 13.28S 25.48E
Kasese Uganda 55 0.07N 30.06E
Kāsganj India 41 27.49N 78.39E
Kāshān Iran 43 33.59N 51.31E
Kashi China 30 39.29N 76.02E
Kashin Russian Fed. 24 57.22N 37.39E
Kashīpur India 41 29.13N 78.57E
Kashiwa Japan 35 35.52N 139.59E
Kāshmar Iran 43 35.12N 58.26E
Kashmor Pakistan 40 28.26N 69.35E
Kasia India 41 26.45N 83.55E
Kasimov Russian Fed. 24 54.55N 41.25E
Kaskaskia *r.* U.S.A. 83 37.59N 89.56W
Kaskattama *r.* Canada 75 57.03N 90.07W
Kaskinen Finland 22 62.23N 21.13E
Kaskö *see* Kaskinen Finland 22
Kaslo Canada 74 49.55N 117.00W
Kasongo Zaïre 54 4.32S 26.33E
Kasongo-Lunda Zaïre 54 6.30S 16.47E
Kásos *i.* Greece 19 35.22N 26.56E
Kassalā Sudan 48 15.28N 36.24E
Kassalā *d.* Sudan 48 15.30N 35.00E
Kassel Germany 20 51.18N 9.30E
Kastamonu Turkey 42 41.22N 33.47E
Kastoría Greece 19 40.32N 21.15E
Kasugai Japan 35 35.14N 136.58E
Kasukabe Japan 35 35.58N 139.45E
Kasulu Tanzania 55 4.34S 30.06E
Kasungu Malaŵi 55 13.04S 33.29E
Kasūr Pakistan 40 31.07N 74.27E
Kataba Zambia 54 16.12S 25.05E
Katako Kombe Zaïre 54 3.27S 24.21E
Katangi India 41 23.27N 79.47E
Katanning Australia 63 33.42S 117.33E
Katanti Zaïre 55 2.19S 27.08E
Katarnian Ghāt India 41 28.20N 81.09E
Katchall *i.* India 39 7.57N 93.22E
Katete Zambia 55 14.08S 31.50E
Katha Burma 34 24.11N 95.20E
Katherine Australia 64 14.29S 132.20E
Kāthgodām India 41 29.16N 79.32E
Kathla India 40 32.00N 76.47E
Kathmandu Nepal 41 27.42N 85.20E
Kathor India 40 21.18N 72.57E
Kathua Jammu & Kashmir 40 32.22N 75.31E
Kati Mali 52 12.41N 8.04W
Katihār India 41 25.32N 87.35E
Katima Rapids *f.* Zambia 54 17.15S 24.20E
Katiola Ivory Coast 52 8.10N 5.10W
Kātlang Pakistan 40 34.22N 72.05E
Kātol India 41 21.16N 78.35E
Katonah U.S.A. 85 41.16N 73.41W
Katonga *r.* Uganda 55 0.03N 30.15E
Katoomba Australia 67 33.42S 150.23E
Katopa Zaïre 54 2.45S 25.06E
Katowice Poland 21 50.15N 18.59E
Kātrīnā, Jabal *mtn.* Egypt 44 28.30N 33.57E
Katrine, Loch U.K. 12 56.15N 4.30W
Katrineholm Sweden 23 59.00N 16.12E
Katsina Nigeria 53 13.00N 7.32E
Katsina *d.* Nigeria 53 12.25N 7.55E
Katsina Ala Nigeria 53 7.10N 9.30E
Katsina Ala *r.* Nigeria 53 7.50N 8.58E
Katsura *r.* Japan 35 34.53N 135.42E
Katsuura Japan 35 35.08N 140.18E
Kattegat *str.* Denmark / Sweden 23 57.00N 11.20E
Katul, Jabal *mtn.* Sudan 48 14.16N 29.23E
Katumba Zaïre 54 7.45S 25.18E
Kātwa India 41 23.39N 88.08E
Katwijk aan Zee Neth. 14 52.13N 4.27E
Kauai *i.* Hawaii U.S.A. 78 22.05N 159.30W
Kaub Germany 14 50.07N 7.50E
Kaufbeuren Germany 20 47.53N 10.37E
Kauhajoki Finland 22 62.26N 22.11E
Kauhava Finland 22 63.06N 23.05E
Kaukauna U.S.A. 82 44.20N 88.16W
Kaukauveld *mts.* Namibia 56 20.00S 20.15E
Kauliranta Finland 22 66.26N 23.40E
Kaunas Lithuania 23 54.54N 23.54E
Kaura Namoda Nigeria 53 12.39N 6.38E
Kautokeino Norway 22 69.00N 23.02E
Kavála Greece 19 40.56N 24.24E
Kāvali India 39 14.55N 80.01E
Kavarna Bulgaria 19 43.26N 28.22E
Kavimba Botswana 56 18.05S 24.34E
Kavkaz Russian Fed. 25 45.20N 36.39E
Kavungo Angola 54 11.28S 23.01E
Kaw Guiana 91 4.29N 52.02W
Kawachi-nagano Japan 35 34.25N 135.32E
Kawagoe Japan 35 35.55N 139.29E
Kawaguchi Japan 35 35.48N 139.43E
Kawambwa Zambia 55 9.47S 29.10E
Kawardha India 41 22.01N 81.15E
Kawasaki Japan 35 35.32N 139.43E
Kawerau New Zealand 60 38.05S 176.42E
Kawhia New Zealand 60 38.04S 174.49E
Kawm Sudan 49 13.31N 22.50E
Kawthaung Burma 34 10.09N 98.33E
Kaya Burkina 52 13.04N 1.04W
Kayah *d.* Burma 34 19.15N 97.30E
Kayambi Zambia 55 9.26S 32.01E
Kayan *r.* Indonesia 36 2.47N 117.46E
Kaycee U.S.A. 80 43.43N 106.38W
Kayenta U.S.A. 80 36.44N 110.17W
Kayes Congo 54 4.25S 11.41E
Kayes Mali 52 14.26N 11.28W
Kayes *d.* Mali 52 14.00N 10.55W
Kayin *d.* Burma 34 17.30N 97.45E
Kayonza Rwanda 49 1.53S 30.31E
Kayseri Turkey 42 38.42N 35.28E
Kaysville U.S.A. 80 41.02N 111.56W
Kazachye Russian Fed. 29 70.46N 136.15E
Kazakhskiy Zaliv *b.* Kazakhstan 25 42.43N 52.30E
Kazakhstan Asia 25 48.00N 52.30E
Kazan Russian Fed. 24 55.45N 49.10E
Kazanlŭk Bulgaria 19 42.38N 25.26E
Kazatin Ukraine 21 49.41N 28.49E
Kazaure Nigeria 53 12.40N 8.25E
Kazbek *mtn.* Russian Fed. 25 42.42N 44.30E
Kāzerūn Iran 43 29.35N 51.39E
Kazhim Russian Fed. 24 60.18N 51.34E
Kazima C.A.R. 49 5.16N 26.11E
Kazincbarcika Hungary 21 48.16N 20.37E
Kazo Japan 35 36.07N 139.36E
Kazumba Zaïre 54 6.30S 22.02E
Kbal Dâmrei Cambodia 34 14.03N 105.20E
Kéa *i.* Greece 19 37.36N 24.20E
Kearney U.S.A. 82 40.42N 99.05W
Keban Turkey 42 38.48N 38.45E
Kebbi *d.* Nigeria 53 11.30N 3.45E
K'ebelē Ethiopia 49 12.52N 40.40E
Kebili Tunisia 51 33.42N 8.58E
Kebnekaise *mtn.* Sweden 22 67.53N 18.33E
K'ebrī Dehar Ethiopia 45 6.47N 44.17E
Kebumen Indonesia 37 7.40S 109.41E
Kech *r.* Pakistan 40 26.00N 62.44E
Kechika *r.* Canada 74 59.36N 127.05W
Kecskemét Hungary 21 46.54N 19.42E
Kedada Ethiopia 49 5.20N 36.00E
Kedainiai Lithuania 23 55.17N 24.00E
Kedgwick Canada 77 47.39N 67.21W
Kediri Indonesia 37 7.45S 112.01E
Kédougou Senegal 52 12.35N 12.09W
Keefers Canada 74 50.00N 121.40W
Keele Peak *mtn.* Canada 72 63.15N 129.50W
Keene U.S.A. 84 42.56N 72.17W
Keepit, L. Australia 67 30.52S 150.30E
Keer-Weer, C. Australia 64 13.58S 141.30E
Keetmanshoop Namibia 56 26.34S 18.07E
Keewatin Canada 76 49.46N 94.34W
Keewatin *d.* Canada 73 65.00N 90.00W
Kefa *d.* Ethiopia 49 7.00N 36.30E
Kefallinía *i.* Greece 19 38.15N 20.33E
Kefar Sava Israel 44 32.11N 34.54E
Keffi Nigeria 53 8.52N 7.53E
Keflavík Iceland 22 64.01N 22.35W
K'eftya Ethiopia 48 13.56N 37.13E
Keg River *town* Canada 74 57.54N 117.07W
Kehsi Mānsām Burma 34 21.56N 97.51E
Keighley U.K. 10 53.52N 1.54W
Keila Estonia 23 59.18N 24.29E
Keimoes R.S.A. 56 28.41S 20.58E
Keitele *l.* Finland 22 62.55N 26.00E
Keith Australia 66 36.06S 140.22E
Keith U.K. 12 57.32N 2.57W
Keith Arm *b.* Canada 72 65.20N 122.15W
Kekri India 40 25.58N 75.09E
Kelang Malaysia 36 2.57N 101.24E
Kelberg Germany 14 50.17N 6.56E
Kelem Ethiopia 49 4.48N 36.06E
Kelkit *r.* Turkey 42 40.46N 36.32E
Kelle Congo 54 0.05S 14.33E
Keller U.S.A. 80 48.03N 118.40W
Kellerberrin Australia 63 31.38S 117.43E
Kellet, C. Canada 72 71.59N 125.34W
Kelloselkä Finland 24 66.55N 28.50E
Kells Rep. of Ire. 13 53.44N 6.53W
Kelme Lithuania 23 55.38N 22.56E
Kélo Chad 53 9.21N 15.50E
Kelowna Canada 74 49.50N 119.25W
Kelso U.K. 12 55.36N 2.26W
Kelso Calif. U.S.A. 81 35.01N 115.39W
Kelso Wash. U.S.A. 80 46.09N 122.54W
Keluang Malaysia 36 2.01N 103.18E
Kelvedon U.K. 11 51.50N 0.43E
Kelvington Canada 75 52.10N 103.30W
Kem Russian Fed. 24 64.58N 34.39E
Kema Indonesia 37 1.22N 125.08E
Ke Macina Mali 52 14.05N 5.20W
Kemah Turkey 42 39.35N 39.02E
Kemaliye Turkey 42 39.16N 38.29E
Kemano Canada 74 53.35N 128.00W
Kembolcha Ethiopia 49 11.02N 39.43E
Kemerovo Russian Fed. 28 55.25N 86.10E
Kemi Finland 22 65.49N 24.32E
Kemi *r.* Finland 22 65.47N 24.30E
Kemijärvi Finland 22 66.36N 27.24E
Kemmerer U.S.A. 80 41.48N 110.32W
Kempen *f.* Belgium 14 51.05N 5.00E
Kemp Land *f.* Antarctica 96 69.00S 57.00E
Kempsey Australia 67 31.05S 152.50E
Kempt, Lac *l.* Canada 76 47.25N 74.30W
Kempten Germany 20 47.44N 10.19E
Ken *r.* India 41 25.46N 80.31E
Kenai U.S.A. 72 60.33N 151.15W
Kenamuke Swamp Sudan 49 5.55N 33.48E
Kenaston Canada 75 51.30N 106.18W
Kendai India 41 22.45N 82.37E
Kendal Indonesia 37 6.56S 110.14E
Kendal U.K. 10 54.19N 2.44W
Kendall Australia 67 31.28S 152.40E
Kendall U.S.A. 76 43.20N 78.02W
Kendari Indonesia 37 3.57S 122.36E
Kendenup Australia 63 34.28S 117.35E
Kendrāpāra India 41 20.30N 86.25E
Kendrick U.S.A. 80 46.37N 116.39W
Kenebri Australia 67 30.45S 149.02E
Kenema Sierra Leone 52 7.57N 11.11W
Kenge Zaïre 54 4.56S 17.04E
Kengeja Tanzania 55 5.24S 39.45E
Keng Tung Burma 34 21.16N 99.39E
Kenhardt R.S.A. 56 29.21S 21.08E
Kenilworth U.K. 11 52.22N 1.35W
Kenitra Morocco 50 34.20N 6.34W
Kenli China 32 37.35N 118.34E
Kenmare Rep. of Ire. 13 51.53N 9.36W
Kenmare U.S.A. 80 48.40N 102.05W
Kenmore U.S.A. 76 42.58N 78.53W
Kennebec *r.* U.S.A. 84 44.00N 69.50W
Kenner U.S.A. 83 29.59N 90.15W
Kennet *r.* U.K. 11 51.28N 0.57W
Kennett Square U.S.A. 85 39.51N 75.43W
Kennewick U.S.A. 80 46.12N 119.07W
Kenogami *r.* Canada 76 50.24N 84.20W
Keno Hill *town* Canada 72 63.58N 135.22W
Kenora Canada 76 49.47N 94.29W
Kenosha U.S.A. 82 42.35N 87.49W
Kenozero, Ozero *l.* Russian Fed. 24 62.20N 37.00E
Kent *d.* U.K. 11 51.12N 0.40E
Kent Ohio U.S.A. 84 41.10N 81.20W
Kent Tex. U.S.A. 81 31.04N 104.13W
Kent Wash. U.S.A. 80 47.23N 122.14W
Kentau Kazakhstan 30 43.28N 68.36E
Kentland U.S.A. 84 40.46N 87.26W
Kenton U.S.A. 84 40.38N 83.38W
Kent Pen. Canada 72 68.30N 107.00W
Kentucky *d.* U.S.A. 85 37.30N 85.15W
Kentucky *r.* U.S.A. 85 38.40N 85.09W
Kentucky L. U.S.A. 83 36.25N 88.05W
Kentville Canada 77 45.05N 64.30W
Kenya Africa 55 1.00N 38.00E
Kenya, Mt. *see* Kirinyaga *mtn.* Kenya 55
Keokuk U.S.A. 82 40.24N 91.24W
Keonjhargarh India 41 21.38N 85.35E
Kepi Indonesia 37 6.32S 139.19E
Kepno Poland 21 51.17N 17.59E
Keppel B. Australia 64 23.21S 150.55E
Kerala *d.* India 38 10.30N 76.30E
Kerang Australia 66 35.42S 143.59E
Kerch Ukraine 25 45.22N 36.27E
Kerchenskiy Proliv *str.* Ukraine / Russian Fed. 25 45.15N 36.35E
Kerema P.N.G. 37 7.59S 145.46E
Keren Ethiopia 48 15.46N 38.28E
Kericho Kenya 55 0.22S 35.19E
Kerinci, Gunung *mtn.* Indonesia 36 1.45S 101.20E
Kerio *r.* Kenya 55 3.00N 36.14E
Kerkebet Ethiopia 48 16.13N 37.30E
Kerkenna, Îles *is.* Tunisia 51 34.44N 11.12E
Kerki Russian Fed. 24 63.40N 54.00E
Kerki Turkmenistan 28 37.53N 65.10E
Kérkira Greece 19 39.37N 19.50E
Kérkira *i.* Greece 19 39.35N 19.50E
Kerkrade Neth. 14 50.52N 6.02E
Kermadec Is. Pacific Oc. 68 30.00S 178.30W
Kermadec Trench Pacific Oc. 68 33.30S 176.00W
Kermān Iran 43 30.18N 57.05E
Kermānshāh Iran 43 34.19N 47.04E
Kerme Körfezi *g.* Turkey 19 36.52N 27.53E
Kermit U.S.A. 83 31.51N 103.06W
Kerouane Guinea 52 9.16N 9.00W
Kerpen Germany 14 50.52N 6.42E
Kerrobert Canada 75 51.55N 109.08W
Kerrville U.S.A. 83 30.03N 99.08W
Kerry *d.* Rep. of Ire. 13 52.07N 9.35W
Kerry Head Rep. of Ire. 13 52.24N 9.56W
Kerulen *r.* Mongolia 31 48.45N 117.00E
Kesagami L. Canada 76 50.23N 80.15W
Keşan Turkey 19 40.50N 26.39E
Keshod India 40 21.18N 70.15E
Keskal India 41 20.03N 81.34E
Keski-Suomi *d.* Finland 22 62.30N 25.30E
Keswick U.K. 10 54.35N 3.09W
Keszthely Hungary 21 46.46N 17.15E
Ketapang Jawa Indonesia 37 6.56S 113.14E
Ketapang Kalimantan Indonesia 36 1.50S 110.02E
Ketchikan U.S.A. 74 55.25N 131.40W
Ketchum U.S.A. 80 43.41N 114.22W
Kete Krachi Ghana 52 7.50N 0.03W
Keti Bandar Pakistan 40 24.08N 67.27E
Ketrzyn Poland 21 54.06N 21.23E
Kettering U.K. 11 52.24N 0.44W
Kettering U.S.A. 84 39.41N 84.10W
Kettle *r.* Canada 75 56.55N 89.25W
Kettle Falls *town* U.S.A. 80 48.36N 118.03W
Keweenaw B. U.S.A. 84 46.46N 88.26W
Keweenaw Pen. U.S.A. 84 47.10N 88.30W
Key, Lough Rep. of Ire. 13 54.00N 8.15W
Keyala Sudan 49 4.27N 32.52E
Key Harbour Canada 76 45.52N 80.42W
Keynsham U.K. 11 51.25N 2.30W
Key West U.S.A. 85 24.33N 81.48W
Kezhma Russian Fed. 29 58.58N 101.08E
Kežmarok Slovakia 21 49.08N 20.25E
Kgalagadi *d.* Botswana 56 25.00S 21.30E
Kgatleng *d.* Botswana 56 24.20S 26.20E
Khaanziir, Ras *c.* Somali Rep. 45 10.55N 45.47E
Khabarovsk Russian Fed. 31 48.32N 135.08E
Khairāgarh India 41 21.25N 80.58E
Khairpur Punjab Pakistan 40 29.35N 72.14E
Khairpur Sind Pakistan 40 27.32N 68.46E
Khajrāho India 41 24.50N 79.58E
Khalatse Jammu & Kashmir 40 34.20N 76.49E
Khalkhāl Iran 43 37.36N 48.36E
Khalkís Greece 19 38.27N 23.36E
Khalmer Yu Russian Fed. 24 67.58N 64.48E
Khālsar Jammu & Kashmir 41 34.31N 77.41E
Khalturin Russian Fed. 24 58.38N 48.50E
Khalūf Oman 38 20.31N 58.04E
Khambhāliya India 40 22.12N 69.39E
Khambhāt, G. of India 40 20.30N 71.45E
Khāmgaon India 40 20.41N 76.34E
Khamkeut Laos 34 18.14N 104.44E
Khānaqīn Iraq 43 34.22N 45.22E
Khandela India 40 27.36N 75.30E
Khandwa India 40 21.50N 76.20E
Khāneh Khvodī Iran 43 36.05N 56.04E
Khānewāl Pakistan 40 30.18N 71.56E
Khāngarh Punjab Pakistan 40 28.22N 71.43E
Khāngarh Punjab Pakistan 40 29.55N 71.10E
Khanh Hung Vietnam 34 9.36N 105.55E
Khaniá Greece 19 35.30N 24.02E
Khanka, Ozero *l.* Russian Fed. 31 45.00N 132.30E
Khankendy *see* Stepanakert Azerbaijan 43
Khanna India 40 30.42N 76.14E
Khānozai Pakistan 40 30.37N 67.19E
Khānpur Pakistan 40 28.39N 70.39E
Khanty-Mansiysk Russian Fed. 28 61.00N 69.00E
Khān Yūnus Egypt 44 31.21N 34.18E
Khapalu Jammu & Kashmir 40 35.10N 76.20E
Khapcheranga Russian Fed. 31 49.46N 112.20E
Kharagpur India 41 22.20N 87.20E
Khārān *r.* Iran 43 27.37N 58.48E
Khārān Pakistan 40 28.35N 65.25E
Khargon India 40 21.49N 75.36E
Khāriān Pakistan 40 32.49N 73.52E
Khariār Road *town* India 41 20.54N 82.31E
Khārijah, Al Wāḥāt al *oasis* Egypt 42 24.55N 30.35E
Kharkov Ukraine 25 50.00N 36.15E
Khār Kūh *mtn.* Iran 43 31.37N 53.47E
Kharovsk Russian Fed. 24 59.67N 40.07E
Khartoum *see* Al Kharṭūm Sudan 48
Kharutayuvam Russian Fed. 24 66.51N 59.31E
Khasavyurt Russian Fed. 25 43.16N 46.36E
Khāsh Afghan. 40 31.31N 62.52E
Khāsh *r.* Afghan. 40 31.11N 61.50E
Khāsh Iran 43 28.14N 61.15E
Khāsh, Dasht-e *des.* Afghan. 40 31.50N 62.30E
Khashgort Russian Fed. 24 65.25N 65.40E
Khashm al Qirbah Sudan 48 14.58N 35.55E
Khaskovo Bulgaria 19 41.57N 25.33E
Khatanga Russian Fed. 29 71.50N 102.31E
Khatangskiy Zaliv *g.* Russian Fed. 29 75.00N 112.10E
Khāvda India 40 23.51N 69.43E
Khawr Barakah *r.* Sudan 48 18.13N 37.35E
Khemisset Morocco 50 33.50N 6.03W
Khemmarat Thailand 34 16.00N 105.10E
Khenchela Algeria 51 35.26N 7.08E
Khenifra Morocco 50 33.00N 5.40W
Khersān *r.* Iran 43 31.29N 48.53E
Kherson Ukraine 25 46.39N 32.38E
Kherwāra India 40 23.59N 73.35E
Khetia India 40 21.40N 74.35E
Khewāri Pakistan 40 26.36N 68.52E
Khíos Greece 19 38.23N 26.07E
Khíos *i.* Greece 19 38.23N 26.04E
Khipro Pakistan 40 25.50N 69.22E
Khiva Uzbekistan 43 41.25N 60.49E
Khmelnik Ukraine 21 49.36N 27.59E
Khmelnitskiy Ukraine 21 49.25N 26.49E
Khodorov Ukraine 21 49.20N 24.19E
Khogali Sudan 49 6.08N 27.47E
Khok Kloi Thailand 34 8.19N 98.18E
Kholm Russian Fed. 24 57.10N 31.11E
Kholmogory Russian Fed. 24 63.51N 41.46E
Khomas-Hochland *mts.* Namibia 56 22.50S 16.25E
Khondmāl Hills India 41 20.15N 84.00E
Khonu Russian Fed. 29 66.29N 143.12E
Khoper *r.* Russian Fed. 25 49.35N 42.17E
Khorāl India 40 26.30N 71.14E
Khorixas Namibia 56 20.24S 14.58E
Khorog Tajikistan 30 37.32N 71.32E
Khorramābād Iran 43 33.29N 48.21E
Khorramshahr Iran 43 30.26N 48.09E
Khotimsk Belorussia 21 53.24N 32.36E
Khotin Ukraine 21 48.30N 26.31E
Khouribga Morocco 50 32.54N 6.57W
Khowai India 41 24.06N 91.38E
Khowrnag, Kūh-e *mtn.* Iran 43 32.10N 54.38E
Khowst Afghan. 40 33.22N 69.57E
Khoyniki Belorussia 21 51.54N 30.00E
Khudzhand Tajikistan 30 40.14N 69.40E
Khugīāni Afghan. 40 31.33N 66.15E
Khūgīānī Sānī Afghan. 40 31.31N 66.12E
Khūiāla India 40 27.15N 70.25E
Khuis Botswana 56 26.37S 21.45E
Khulga *r.* Russian Fed. 24 63.33N 61.53E
Khulna Bangla. 41 22.48N 89.33E
Khumbur Khule Ghar *mtn.* Afghan. 40 33.05N 69.00E
Khunti India 41 23.05N 85.17E
Khurai India 41 24.03N 78.19E
Khurda India 41 20.11N 85.37E
Khurja India 41 28.15N 77.51E
Khurli Pakistan 40 28.59N 65.52E
Khurr, Wādī al *r.* Iraq 45 31.02N 42.00E
Khurra Bārīk *r.* Iraq 42 32.00N 44.15E
Khushāb Pakistan 40 32.18N 72.21E
Khust Ukraine 21 48.11N 23.19E
Khuwayy Sudan 49 13.05N 29.14E
Khuzdār Pakistan 40 27.48N 66.37E

Khvājeh Ra'ūf to Korocha

Khvājeh Ra'ūf Afghan. 40 33.19N 64.43E
Khvor Iran 43 33.47N 55.06E
Khvormuj Iran 43 28.40N 51.20E
Khvoy Iran 43 38.32N 45.02E
Khyber Pass Afghan./Pakistan 40 34.06N 71.05E
Kiama Australia 67 34.41S 150.49E
Kibali r. Zaïre 55 3.37N 28.38E
Kibamba Zaïre 54 4.53S 26.33E
Kibar India 41 32.20N 78.01E
Kibenga Zaïre 54 7.55S 17.35E
Kibombo Zaïre 54 3.58S 25.57E
Kibondo Tanzania 55 3.35S 30.41E
Kibre Mengist Ethiopia 49 5.52N 39.00E
Kibungu Rwanda 55 2.10S 30.31E
Kibwesa Tanzania 55 6.30S 29.57E
Kibwezi Kenya 55 2.28S 37.57E
Kichiga Russian Fed. 29 59.50N 163.27E
Kicking Horse Pass Canada 74 51.27N 116.25W
Kidal Mali 53 18.27N 1.25E
Kidderminster U.K. 11 52.24N 2.13W
Kidete Tanzania 55 6.39S 36.42E
Kidsgrove U.K. 10 53.06N 2.15W
Kiel Germany 20 54.20N 10.08E
Kielce Poland 21 50.52N 20.37E
Kielder resr. U.K. 10 55.12N 2.30W
Kieler Bucht b. Germany 20 54.30N 10.30E
Kiev see Kiyev Ukraine 21
Kiffa Mauritania 50 16.38N 11.28W
Kigali Rwanda 55 1.59S 30.05E
Kiglapatt, C. Canada 77 57.05N 61.05W
Kigoma Tanzania 55 4.52S 29.36E
Kigoma d. Tanzania 55 4.45S 30.00E
Kigosi r. Tanzania 55 4.37S 31.29E
Kiiminkin r. Finland 22 65.12N 25.18E
Kikinda Yugo. 21 45.51N 20.30E
Kikládhes is. Greece 19 37.00N 25.00E
Kikongo Zaïre 54 4.16S 17.11E
Kikori P.N.G. 37 7.25S 144.13E
Kikori r. P.N.G. 37 7.10S 144.05E
Kikwit Zaïre 54 5.02S 18.51E
Kil Sweden 23 59.30N 13.19E
Kilafors Sweden 23 61.14N 16.34E
Kila Kila P.N.G. 37 9.31S 147.10E
Kilchu N. Korea 31 40.55N 129.21E
Kilcoy Australia 65 26.57S 152.33E
Kilcullen Rep. of Ire. 13 53.08N 6.46W
Kildare Rep. of Ire. 13 53.10N 6.55W
Kildare d. Rep. of Ire. 13 53.10N 6.50W
Kildonan Zimbabwe 56 17.22S 30.33E
Kilfinan U.K. 12 55.58N 5.18W
Kilgore U.S.A. 83 32.23N 94.53W
Kilifi Kenya 55 3.30S 39.50E
Kilimanjaro d. Tanzania 55 3.45S 37.40E
Kilimanjaro mtn. Tanzania 55 3.02S 37.20E
Kilindoni Tanzania 55 7.55S 39.39E
Kilingi-Nõmme Estonia 23 58.09N 24.58E
Kilis Turkey 42 36.43N 37.07E
Kiliya Ukraine 21 45.30N 29.16E
Kilkee Rep. of Ire. 13 52.41N 9.40W
Kilkenny Rep. of Ire. 13 52.39N 7.16W
Kilkenny d. Rep. of Ire. 13 52.35N 7.15W
Kilkieran B. Rep. of Ire. 13 53.20N 9.42W
Kilkís Greece 19 40.59N 22.51E
Killala B. Rep. of Ire. 13 54.15N 9.10W
Killard Pt. U.K. 13 54.19N 5.31W
Killarney Australia 67 28.18S 152.15E
Killarney Canada 75 49.12N 99.42W
Killarney Rep. of Ire. 13 52.04N 9.32W
Killary Harbour est. Rep. of Ire. 13 53.38N 9.56W
Killdeer U.S.A. 80 47.22N 102.45W
Killeen U.S.A. 83 31.08N 97.44W
Killin U.K. 12 56.29N 4.19W
Killíni mtn. Greece 19 37.56N 22.22E
Killorglin Rep. of Ire. 13 52.07N 9.45W
Killybegs Rep. of Ire. 13 54.38N 8.27W
Killyleagh U.K. 13 54.24N 5.39W
Kilmarnock U.K. 12 55.37N 4.30W
Kilmichael Pt. Rep. of Ire. 13 52.44N 6.09W
Kilmore Australia 67 37.18S 144.58E
Kilninver U.K. 12 56.21N 5.30W
Kilombero r. Tanzania 55 8.30S 37.28E
Kilosa Tanzania 55 6.49S 37.00E
Kilronan Rep. of Ire. 13 53.08N 9.41W
Kilrush Rep. of Ire. 13 52.39N 9.30W
Kilsyth U.K. 12 55.59N 4.04W
Kilvo Sweden 22 66.50N 21.04E
Kilwa Kivinje Tanzania 55 8.45S 39.21E
Kilwa Masoko Tanzania 55 8.55S 39.31E
Kimaan Indonesia 37 7.54S 138.51E
Kimba Australia 66 33.09S 136.25E
Kimball U.S.A. 82 41.14N 103.40W
Kimberley Canada 74 49.40N 115.59W
Kimberley R.S.A. 56 28.44S 24.44E
Kimberley Plateau Australia 62 17.20S 127.20E
Kimch'aek N. Korea 35 40.41N 129.12E
Kimito i. Finland 23 60.10N 22.30E
Kimparana Mali 52 12.52N 4.59W
Kimry Russian Fed. 24 56.51N 37.20E
Kimsquit Canada 74 52.45N 126.57W
Kinabalu mtn. Malaysia 36 6.10N 116.40E
Kincaid Canada 75 49.39N 107.00W
Kincardine Canada 76 44.11N 81.38W
Kindersley Canada 75 51.27N 109.10W
Kindia Guinea 52 10.03N 12.49W
Kindu Zaïre 54 3.00S 25.56E
Kinel Russian Fed. 24 53.17N 50.42E
Kineshma Russian Fed. 24 57.28N 42.08E
Kingaroy Australia 64 26.33S 151.50E
King City U.S.A. 81 36.13N 121.08W
Kingcome Inlet town Canada 74 50.58N 125.15W
King Edward r. Australia 62 14.12S 126.34E
King George Is. Canada 76 57.20N 78.25W
King George Sd. Australia 63 35.03S 117.57E
King I. Australia 65 39.50S 144.00E
King I. Canada 74 52.10N 127.40W
King Leopold Range mts. Australia 62 17.00S 125.30E
Kingman Ariz. U.S.A. 81 35.12N 114.04W
Kingman Kans. U.S.A. 83 37.39N 98.07W
Kingman Reef Pacific Oc. 68 6.24N 162.22W
Kingoonya Australia 66 30.54S 135.18E
Kingri Pakistan 40 30.27N 69.49E
Kings r. U.S.A. 81 36.03N 119.49W
Kingsbridge U.K. 11 50.17N 3.46W
Kings Canyon Australia 64 24.15S 131.33E
Kings Canyon Nat. Park U.S.A. 80 36.48N 118.30W
Kingsclere U.K. 11 51.20N 1.14W
Kingscote Australia 66 35.40S 137.38E
King Sd. Australia 62 17.00S 123.30E
Kingsdown U.K. 11 51.21N 0.17E
Kingsley Dam U.S.A. 78 41.15N 101.30W
King's Lynn U.K. 10 52.45N 0.25E
Kingsmill Group is. Kiribati 68 1.00S 175.00E
Kings Peaks mts. U.S.A. 80 40.46N 110.23W
Kingsport U.S.A. 85 36.33N 82.34W
Kingston Canada 76 44.14N 76.30W
Kingston Jamaica 87 17.58N 76.48W
Kingston New Zealand 60 45.20S 168.43E
Kingston N.Y. U.S.A. 77 41.56N 74.00W
Kingston W.Va. U.S.A. 85 37.58N 81.19W
Kingston S.E. Australia 66 36.50S 139.50E
Kingston upon Hull U.K. 10 53.45N 0.20W
Kingstown St. Vincent 87 13.12N 61.14W
Kingstree U.S.A. 85 33.40N 79.50W
Kingsville U.S.A. 83 27.31N 97.52W
Kingswood U.K. 11 51.27N 2.29W
Kings Worthy U.K. 11 51.06N 1.18W
Kington U.K. 11 52.12N 3.02W
Kingurutik r. Canada 77 56.49N 62.00W
Kingussie U.K. 12 57.05N 4.04W
King William I. Canada 73 69.00N 97.30W
King William's Town R.S.A. 56 32.52S 27.23E
Kinloch Rannoch U.K. 12 56.42N 4.11W
Kinna Sweden 23 57.30N 12.41E
Kinnairds Head U.K. 12 57.42N 2.00W
Kinnegad Rep. of Ire. 13 53.28N 7.08W
Kino r. Japan 35 34.13N 135.09E
Kinross U.K. 12 56.13N 3.27W
Kinsale Rep. of Ire. 13 51.42N 8.32W
Kinshasa Zaïre 54 4.18S 15.18E
Kinsley U.S.A. 83 37.55N 99.25W
Kintyre pen. U.K. 12 55.35N 5.35W
Kinuso Canada 74 55.25N 115.25W
Kinvara Rep. of Ire. 13 53.08N 8.56W
Kinyeti mtn. Sudan 49 3.57N 32.54E
Kinzia Zaïre 54 3.36S 18.26E
Kiowa Kans. U.S.A. 83 37.01N 98.29W
Kiowa Okla. U.S.A. 83 34.43N 95.54W
Kiparissía Greece 19 37.15N 21.40E
Kipawa, Lac l. Canada 76 47.00N 79.00W
Kipengere Range mts. Tanzania 55 9.15S 34.15E
Kipili Tanzania 55 7.30S 30.39E
Kipini Kenya 55 2.31S 40.32E
Kippure mtn. Rep. of Ire. 13 53.11N 6.20W
Kipungo Angola 54 14.49S 14.34E
Kipushi Zaïre 55 11.46S 27.15E
Kirby U.S.A. 80 43.49N 108.10W
Kirbyville U.S.A. 83 30.40N 93.54W
Kircheimbolanden Germany 14 49.39N 8.00E
Kirensk Russian Fed. 29 57.45N 108.00E
Kirgiziya Step f. Kazakhstan 25 50.00N 57.10E
Kirgiz Steppe see Kirgiziya Step f. Kazakhstan 25
Kiri Zaïre 54 1.23S 19.00E
Kiribati Pacific Oc. 68 6.00S 170.00W
Kirikkale Turkey 42 39.51N 33.32E
Kirillov Russian Fed. 24 59.53N 38.21E
Kirínia Cyprus 44 35.20N 33.20E
Kirinyaga mtn. Kenya 55 0.10S 37.19E
Kiritimati i. Kiribati 69 1.52N 157.20W
Kirkby Lonsdale U.K. 10 54.13N 2.36W
Kirkby Stephen U.K. 10 54.27N 2.23W
Kirkcaldy U.K. 12 56.07N 3.10W
Kirkcudbright U.K. 12 54.50N 4.03W
Kirkenes Norway 22 69.40N 30.03E
Kirkland Ariz. U.S.A. 81 34.26N 112.43W
Kirkland Wash. U.S.A. 80 47.41N 122.12W
Kirkland Lake town Canada 76 48.15N 80.00W
Kirklareli Turkey 19 41.44N 27.12E
Kirkpatrick, Mt. Antarctica 96 85.00S 170.00E
Kirksville U.S.A. 82 40.12N 92.35W
Kirkūk Iraq 43 35.28N 44.26E
Kirkwall U.K. 12 58.59N 2.58W
Kirkwood R.S.A. 56 33.25S 25.24E
Kirkwood U.S.A. 82 38.35N 90.24W
Kirn Germany 14 49.47N 7.28E
Kirov Russian Fed. 24 58.38N 49.38E
Kirov Russian Fed. 24 53.59N 34.20E
Kirovakan Armenia 43 40.49N 44.30E
Kirovo-Chepetsk Russian Fed. 24 58.40N 50.02E
Kirovograd Ukraine 25 48.31N 32.15E
Kirovsk Russian Fed. 24 67.37N 33.39E
Kirovskiy Russian Fed. 29 54.25N 155.37E
Kirriemuir Canada 75 51.56N 110.20W
Kirriemuir U.K. 12 56.41N 3.01W
Kirs Russian Fed. 24 59.21N 52.10E
Kirsanoy Kazakhstan 25 51.29N 52.30E
Kirşehir Turkey 42 39.09N 34.08E
Kirthar Range mts. Pakistan 40 27.15N 67.00E
Kiruna Sweden 22 67.51N 20.16E
Kisa Sweden 23 57.59N 15.37E
Kisaga Tanzania 55 4.26S 34.26E
Kisangani Zaïre 54 0.33N 25.14E
Kisantu Zaïre 54 5.07S 15.05E
Kisaran Indonesia 36 2.47N 99.29E
Kisarazu Japan 35 35.23N 139.55E
Kiselevsk Russian Fed. 28 54.01N 86.41E
Kishanganj India 41 26.07N 87.56E
Kishangarh Rāj. India 40 27.52N 70.34E
Kishangarh Rāj. India 40 26.34N 74.52E
Kishinev Moldavia 21 47.00N 28.50E
Kishiwada Japan 35 34.28N 135.22E
Kishorganj Bangla. 41 24.26N 90.46E
Kishtwār Jammu & Kashmir 40 33.19N 75.46E
Kisii Kenya 55 0.40S 34.44E
Kisiju Tanzania 55 7.23S 39.20E
Kiskitto L. Canada 75 54.16N 98.34W
Kiskörös Hungary 21 46.38N 19.17E
Kiskunfélegyháza Hungary 21 46.43N 19.52E
Kiskunhalas Hungary 21 46.26N 19.30E
Kislovodsk Russian Fed. 25 43.56N 42.44E
Kismaayo Somali Rep. 55 0.25S 42.31E
Kiso Japan 35 35.02N 136.45E
Kiso sammyaku mts. Japan 35 35.42N 137.50E
Kissamos Greece 19 35.30N 23.38E
Kissidougou Guinea 52 9.48N 10.08W
Kissimmee U.S.A. 85 28.20N 81.24W
Kississing L. Canada 75 55.10N 101.20W
Kissū, Jabal mtn. Sudan 48 21.35N 25.09E
Kistna r. see Krishna r. India 38
Kisumu Kenya 55 0.07S 34.47E
Kisvárda Hungary 21 48.13N 22.05E
Kita Mali 52 13.04N 9.29W
Kitab Uzbekistan 28 39.08N 66.51E
Kitabu Zaïre 54 6.31S 26.40E
Kitakyūshū Japan 35 33.52N 130.49E
Kitale Kenya 55 1.01N 35.01E
Kit Carson U.S.A. 82 38.46N 102.48W
Kitchener Australia 63 31.01S 124.20E
Kitchener Canada 76 43.27N 80.30W
Kitchigama r. Canada 76 51.12N 78.55W
Kitgum Uganda 55 3.17N 32.54E
Kíthira Greece 19 36.09N 23.00E
Kíthira i. Greece 19 36.15N 23.00E
Kíthnos i. Greece 19 37.25N 24.25E
Kitikmeot d. Canada 72 80.00N 105.00W
Kitimat Canada 74 54.05N 128.38W
Kitinen r. Finland 22 67.20N 27.27E
Kitsman Ukraine 21 48.30N 25.50E
Kittakittaooloo, L. Australia 66 28.09S 138.09E
Kittanning U.S.A. 84 40.49N 79.32W
Kittery U.S.A. 84 43.05N 70.45W
Kittilä Finland 22 67.40N 24.54E
Kitui Kenya 55 1.22S 38.01E
Kitunda Tanzania 55 6.48S 33.17E
Kitwe Zambia 55 12.50S 28.04E
Kiumbi Zaïre 54 5.31S 26.34E
Kiunga Kenya 55 1.46S 41.30E
Kivijärvi l. Finland 22 63.10N 25.09E
Kivik Sweden 23 55.41N 14.15E
Kivu d. Zaïre 55 3.00S 27.00E
Kivu, L. Rwanda/Zaïre 55 2.00S 29.10E
Kiyev Ukraine 21 50.28N 30.29E
Kiyevskoye Vodokhranilishche resr. Ukraine 21 51.00N 30.25E
Kizel Russian Fed. 24 59.01N 57.42E
Kizema Russian Fed. 24 61.12N 44.52E
Kizil r. Turkey 42 41.45N 35.57E
Kizlyar Russian Fed. 25 43.51N 46.43E
Kizlyarskiy Zaliv b. Russian Fed. 25 44.33N 47.00E
Kizu r. Japan 35 34.53N 135.42E
Kizyl-Arvat Turkmenistan 43 39.00N 56.23E
Kizyl Atrek Turkey 43 37.37N 54.49E
Kladno Czech Republic 20 50.10N 14.05E
Klagenfurt Austria 20 46.38N 14.20E
Klaipeda Lithuania 23 55.43N 21.07E
Klakah Indonesia 37 7.55S 113.12E
Klaksvig Faroe Is. 8 62.13N 6.34W
Klamath r. U.S.A. 80 41.33N 124.04W
Klamath Falls town U.S.A. 80 42.14N 121.47W
Klamath Mts. U.S.A. 80 41.40N 123.20W
Klamono Indonesia 37 1.08S 131.28E
Klar r. Sweden 23 59.23N 13.32E
Klatovy Czech Republic 20 49.24N 13.18E
Klawer R.S.A. 56 31.48S 18.34E
Klawock U.S.A. 74 55.33N 133.06W
Kleena Kleene Canada 74 51.58N 124.50W
Kleinsee R.S.A. 56 29.41S 17.04E
Klerksdorp R.S.A. 56 26.51S 26.38E
Klevan Ukraine 21 50.44N 25.50E
Kleve Germany 14 51.47N 6.11E
Klickitat U.S.A. 80 45.49N 121.09W
Klimovichi Belorussia 21 53.36N 31.58E
Klimpfjäll Sweden 22 65.04N 14.52E
Klin Russian Fed. 24 56.20N 36.45E
Klinaklini r. Canada 74 51.21N 125.40W
Klintehamn Sweden 23 57.24N 18.12E
Klintsy Russian Fed. 21 52.45N 32.15E
Klipdale R.S.A. 56 34.18S 19.58E
Klippan Sweden 23 56.08N 13.06E
Klipplaat R.S.A. 56 33.01S 24.19E
Kłobuck Poland 21 50.55N 18.57E
Kłodzko Poland 20 50.27N 16.39E
Klöfta Norway 23 60.04N 11.09E
Klondike Canada 72 64.02N 139.24W
Kluane Nat. Park Canada 74 60.32N 139.40W
Kluczbork Poland 21 50.59N 18.13E
Klukwan U.S.A. 74 59.25N 135.55W
Klungkung Indonesia 37 8.32S 115.25E
Knaresborough U.K. 10 54.01N 1.29W
Knight Inlet f. Canada 74 50.45N 125.40W
Knighton U.K. 11 52.21N 3.02W
Knin Croatia 20 44.02N 16.10E
Knockadoon Head Rep. of Ire. 13 51.52N 7.52W
Knockalongy mtn. Rep. of Ire. 13 54.12N 8.45W
Knockmealdown Mts. Rep. of Ire. 13 52.15N 7.55W
Knokke Belgium 14 51.21N 3.17E
Knolls U.S.A. 80 40.44N 113.18W
Knossos site Greece 19 35.20N 25.10E
Knox, C. Canada 74 54.11N 133.04W
Knox City U.S.A. 83 33.25N 99.49W
Knoxville U.S.A. 85 36.00N 83.57W
Knutsford U.K. 10 53.18N 2.22W
Knyazhevo Russian Fed. 24 59.40N 43.51E
Knysna R.S.A. 56 34.02S 23.03E
Kobar Sink f. Ethiopia 48 14.00N 40.30E
Kōbe Japan 35 34.41N 135.10E
København Denmark 23 55.43N 12.34E
Koblenz Germany 14 50.21N 7.36E
Kobowen Swamp Sudan 49 5.38N 33.54E
Kobrin Belorussia 21 52.16N 24.22E
Kobroor i. Indonesia 37 6.10S 134.30E
Kočani Macedonia 19 41.55N 22.24E
Kočevje Slovenia 18 45.38N 14.52E
Kochi India 38 9.56N 76.15E
Kochkoma Russian Fed. 24 64.03N 34.14E
Kochmes Russian Fed. 24 66.12N 60.48E
Kodaira Japan 35 35.44N 139.29E
Kodari Nepal 41 27.56N 85.56E
Kodarma India 41 24.28N 85.36E
Kodiak U.S.A. 72 57.49N 152.30W
Kodiak I. U.S.A. 72 57.00N 153.50W
Kodima Russian Fed. 24 62.24N 43.57E
Kodinār India 40 20.47N 70.42E
Kodok Sudan 49 9.53N 32.07E
Kodyma Ukraine 21 48.06N 29.04E
Koekelare Belgium 14 51.08N 2.59E
Koekenaap R.S.A. 56 31.30S 18.18E
Koersel Belgium 14 51.04N 5.19E
Koës Namibia 56 25.58S 19.07E
Koffiefontein R.S.A. 56 29.24S 25.00E
Köflach Austria 20 47.04N 15.05E
Koforidua Ghana 52 6.01N 0.12W
Kōfu Japan 35 35.39N 138.35E
Koga Tanzania 55 6.10S 32.21E
Kogaluk r. Canada 77 56.12N 61.45W
Køge Denmark 23 55.27N 12.11E
Køge Bugt b. Greenland 73 65.00N 40.30W
Kogi d. Nigeria 53 7.15N 7.00E
Kohak Pakistan 40 25.44N 62.33E
Kohāt Pakistan 40 33.35N 71.26E
Kohīma India 39 25.40N 94.08E
Kohler Range mts. Antarctica 96 77.00S 110.00W
Kohtla-Järve Estonia 24 59.28N 27.20E
Koidu Sierra Leone 52 8.41N 10.55W
Koito r. Japan 35 35.21N 139.52E
Kojonup Australia 63 33.50S 117.05E
Kokand Uzbekistan 30 40.33N 70.55E
Kokas Indonesia 37 2.45S 132.26E
Kokchetav Kazakhstan 28 53.18N 69.25E
Kokemäki Finland 23 61.15N 22.21E
Kokenau Indonesia 37 4.42S 136.25E
Kokka Sudan 48 20.00N 30.35E
Kokkola Finland 22 63.50N 23.07E
Koko Sokoto Nigeria 53 11.27N 4.35E
Kokoda P.N.G. 64 8.50S 147.45E
Kokomo U.S.A. 84 40.30N 86.09W
Kokpekty Kazakhstan 30 48.45N 82.25E
Koksoak r. Canada 73 58.30N 68.15W
Kokstad R.S.A. 56 30.32S 29.25E
Kokuora Russian Fed. 29 71.33N 144.50E
Kolāchi r. Pakistan 40 26.25N 67.50E
Kolahun Liberia 52 8.24N 10.02W
Kolaka Indonesia 37 4.04S 121.38E
Kola Pen. see Kolskiy Poluostrov pen. Russian Fed. 24
Kolār India 39 13.10N 78.10E
Kolāras India 41 25.14N 77.36E
Kolari Finland 22 67.20N 23.48E
Kolāyat India 40 27.50N 72.57E
Kolbio Kenya 55 1.11S 41.10E
Kolda Senegal 52 12.56N 14.55W
Kolding Denmark 23 55.31N 9.29E
Kole H.Zaïre Zaïre 54 2.07N 25.26E
Kole K.Oriental Zaïre 54 3.28S 22.29E
Kolepom i. see Yos Sudarsa, Pulau i. Indonesia 37
Kolguyev, Ostrov i. Russian Fed. 24 69.00N 49.00E
Kolhāpur India 38 16.43N 74.15E
Kolia Ivory Coast 52 9.46N 6.28W
Kolín Czech Republic 20 50.02N 15.10E
Kolka Latvia 23 57.45N 22.35E
Kolki Ukraine 21 51.09N 25.40E
Kollam India 38 8.53N 76.38E
Köln Germany 14 50.56N 6.57E
Kolno Poland 21 53.25N 21.56E
Koło Poland 21 52.12N 18.37E
Kołobrzeg Poland 20 54.10N 15.35E
Kologriv Russian Fed. 24 58.49N 44.19E
Kolokani Mali 52 13.35N 7.45W
Kolole Ethiopia 49 7.29N 41.58E
Kolomna Russian Fed. 24 55.05N 38.45E
Kolomyya Ukraine 21 48.31N 25.00E
Kolondiéba Mali 52 11.05N 6.54W
Kolosib India 41 24.14N 92.42E
Kolpashevo Russian Fed. 28 58.21N 82.59E
Kolpino Russian Fed. 24 59.44N 30.39E
Kolskiy Poluostrov pen. Russian Fed. 24 67.00N 38.00E
Kolsva Sweden 23 59.36N 15.50E
Koluszki Poland 21 51.44N 19.49E
Kolvereid Norway 22 64.53N 11.35E
Kolwezi Zaïre 54 10.44S 25.28E
Kolyma r. Russian Fed. 29 68.50N 161.00E
Kolymskiy, Khrebet mts Russian Fed. 29 63.00N 160.00E
Kom r. Cameroon 54 2.20N 10.38E
Kom Kenya 55 1.06N 38.00E
Koma Ethiopia 49 8.25N 36.53E
Komadugu Gana r. Nigeria 53 13.06N 12.23E
Komadugu Yobe r. Niger/Nigeria 53 13.43N 13.19E
Komagane Japan 35 35.43N 137.55E
Komaga-take mtn. Japan 35 35.47N 137.48E
Komaki Japan 35 35.17N 136.55E
Komandorskiye Ostrova is. Russian Fed. 68 55.00N 167.00E
Komárno Slovakia 21 47.45N 18.09E
Komarom Hungary 21 47.44N 18.08E
Komatipoort R.S.A. 57 25.25S 31.55E
Komba Zaïre 54 2.52N 24.03E
Komló Hungary 21 46.12N 18.16E
Kommunarsk Ukraine 25 48.30N 38.47E
Kommunizma, Pik mtn. Tajikistan 30 38.39N 72.01E
Komotiní Greece 19 41.07N 25.26E
Komrat Moldavia 21 46.18N 28.40E
Komsberg mtn. R.S.A. 56 32.40S 20.48E
Komsomolets, Ostrov i. Russian Fed. 29 80.20N 96.00E
Komsomolets, Zaliv g. Kazakhstan 25 45.17N 53.30E
Komsomolsk-na-Amure Russian Fed. 29 50.32N 136.59E
Kōnan Japan 35 35.20N 136.53E
Konar r. Afghan. 40 34.26N 70.32E
Konārak India 41 19.54N 86.07E
Konar-e Khās Afghan. 40 34.39N 70.54E
Konch India 41 25.59N 79.09E
Kondagaon India 41 19.36N 81.40E
Kondakovo Russian Fed. 29 69.38N 152.00E
Kondinin Australia 63 32.33S 118.13E
Kondoa Tanzania 55 4.54S 35.49E
Kondopoga Russian Fed. 24 62.12N 34.17E
Kondratyevo Russian Fed. 29 57.22N 98.15E
Kondut Australia 63 30.44S 117.06E
Koné N. Cal. 68 21.04S 164.52E
Kông r. Cambodia 34 13.32N 105.57E
Kong Ivory Coast 52 8.54N 4.36W
Kong Christian den IX Land f. Greenland 73 68.20N 37.00W
Kong Frederik den VI Kyst f. Greenland 73 63.00N 44.00W
Kong Haakon VII Hav sea Antarctica 96 65.00S 25.00E
Kongolo Zaïre 55 5.20S 27.00E
Kongor Sudan 49 7.10N 31.21E
Kongsberg Norway 23 59.39N 9.39E
Kongsvinger Norway 23 60.12N 12.00E
Kongur Shan mtn. China 30 38.40N 75.30E
Kongwa Tanzania 55 6.13S 36.28E
Konin Poland 21 52.13N 18.16E
Konjic Bosnia-Herzegovina 21 43.39N 17.57E
Könkämä r. Sweden/Finland 22 68.29N 22.30E
Konkouré r. Guinea 52 9.55N 13.45W
Konongo Ghana 52 6.38N 1.12W
Konosha Russian Fed. 24 60.58N 40.08E
Kōnosu Japan 35 36.03N 139.31E
Konotop Ukraine 25 51.15N 33.14E
Końskie Poland 21 51.12N 20.26E
Konstanz Germany 20 47.40N 9.10E
Kontagora Nigeria 53 10.24N 5.22E
Kontcha Cameroon 53 7.59N 12.15E
Kontiomäki Finland 24 64.21N 28.10E
Kontum Vietnam 34 14.23N 108.00E
Kontum, Plateau du f. Vietnam 34 14.00N 108.00E
Konya Turkey 42 37.51N 32.30E
Konz Germany 14 49.42N 6.34E
Konza Kenya 55 1.45S 37.07E
Koolkootinnie L. Australia 66 27.58S 137.47E
Koolyanobbing Australia 63 30.48S 119.29E
Koondrook Australia 66 35.39S 144.11E
Koongawa Australia 66 33.11S 135.52E
Koorawatha Australia 67 34.02S 148.33E
Koorda Australia 63 30.50S 117.51E
Kootenay L. Canada 74 49.45N 117.00W
Kootenay Nat. Park Canada 74 51.00N 116.00W
Kootjieskolk R.S.A. 56 31.14S 20.18E
Kopāganj India 41 26.01N 83.34E
Kopargaon India 40 19.53N 74.29E
Kópavogur Iceland 22 64.06N 21.53W
Koper Slovenia 20 45.33N 13.44E
Kopervik Norway 23 59.17N 5.18E
Kopet Dag, Khrebet mts. Turkmenistan 43 38.00N 58.00E
Köping Sweden 23 59.31N 16.00E
Kopparberg d. Sweden 23 60.50N 15.00E
Koppom Sweden 23 59.43N 12.09E
Koprivnica Croatia 20 46.10N 16.50E
Kopychintsy Ukraine 21 49.10N 25.58E
Kor r. Iran 43 29.40N 53.17E
Koraput India 41 18.49N 82.43E
Koratla India 41 18.49N 78.43E
Korba India 41 22.21N 82.41E
Korbach Germany 20 51.16N 8.53E
Korçë Albania 19 40.37N 20.45E
Korčula i. Croatia 19 42.56N 16.53E
Kord Kūy Iran 43 36.48N 54.07E
Korea Str. S. Korea/Japan 31 35.00N 129.20E
Korem Ethiopia 49 12.30N 39.30E
Korets Ukraine 21 50.39N 27.10E
Korhogo Ivory Coast 52 9.22N 5.31W
Korim Indonesia 37 0.58S 136.10E
Korinthiakós Kólpos g. Greece 19 38.15N 22.30E
Kórinthos Greece 19 37.56N 22.55E
Kōriyama Japan 35 37.23N 140.22E
Korma Belorussia 21 53.08N 30.47E
Körmend Hungary 20 47.01N 16.37E
Kornat i. Croatia 18 43.48N 15.20E
Korneshty Moldavia 21 47.21N 28.00E
Kornsjö Norway 23 58.57N 11.39E
Koro i. Fiji 68 17.22S 179.25E
Koro Ivory Coast 52 8.36N 7.28W
Koro Mali 52 14.01N 2.58W
Korocha Russian Fed. 25 50.50N 37.13E

Korogwe to Lainio

Korogwe Tanzania 55 5.10S 38.35E
Koroit Australia 66 38.17S142.26E
Korong Vale town Australia 66 36.22S143.45E
Koror i. Palau 37 7.30N134.30E
Koro Sea Fiji 68 18.00S179.00E
Korosten Ukraine 21 51.00N 28.30E
Korostyshev Ukraine 21 50.19N 29.03E
Koro Toro Chad 53 16.05N 18.30E
Korsör Denmark 23 55.20N 11.09E
Korsze Poland 21 54.10N 21.09E
Kortrijk Belgium 14 50.49N 3.17E
Koryakskiy Khrebet mts. Russian Fed. 29 62.20N171.00E
Koryazhma Russian Fed. 24 61.19N 47.12E
Kos i. Greece 19 36.48N 27.10E
Kosa Ethiopia 49 7.51N 36.51E
Kościan Poland 20 52.06N 16.38E
Kościerzyna Poland 21 54.08N 18.00E
Kosciusko U.S.A. 83 32.58N 89.35W
Kosciusko, Mt. Australia 67 36.28S148.17E
Kosha Sudan 48 20.49N 30.32E
Koshk-e Kohneh Afghan. 43 34.52N 62.29E
Košice Slovakia 21 48.44N 21.15E
Koski Finland 23 60.39N 23.09E
Koslan Russian Fed. 24 63.29N 48.59E
Kossanto Senegal 52 13.12N 11.56W
Kossovo Belorussia 21 52.40N 25.18E
Kosta Sweden 23 56.51N 15.23E
Koster R.S.A. 56 25.51S 26.52E
Kostopol Ukraine 21 50.51N 26.22E
Kostroma Russian Fed. 24 57.46N 40.59E
Kostrzyn Poland 20 52.24N 17.11E
Kostyukovichi Belorussia 21 53.20N 32.01E
Kosyu Russian Fed. 24 65.36N 59.00E
Koszalin Poland 20 54.12N 16.09E
Kota Madhya P. India 41 22.18N 82.02E
Kota Rāj. India 40 25.11N 75.50E
Kota Baharu Malaysia 36 6.07N102.15E
Kota Belud Malaysia 36 6.00N116.00E
Kotabumi Indonesia 36 4.52S104.59E
Kot Addu Pakistan 40 30.28N 70.58E
Kota Kinabalu Malaysia 36 5.59N116.04E
Kotelnich Russian Fed. 24 58.20N 48.10E
Kotelnikovo Russian Fed. 25 47.39N 43.08E
Kotel'nyy, Ostrov i. Russian Fed. 29 75.30N141.00E
Kotka Finland 24 60.26N 26.55E
Kot Kapūra India 40 30.35N 74.49E
Kotlas Russian Fed. 24 61.15N 46.28E
Kotli Jammu & Kashmir 40 33.31N 73.55E
Kotlik U.S.A. 72 63.02N163.33W
Kotor Yugo. 19 42.28N 18.47E
Kotovsk Moldavia 21 46.50N 28.31E
Kotovsk Ukraine 21 47.42N 29.30E
Kot Pūtli India 40 27.43N 76.12E
Kotra India 40 24.22N 73.10E
Kotri Pakistan 40 25.22N 68.18E
Kotri Allāhrakhio Pakistan 40 24.24N 67.50E
Kottagūdem India 39 17.32N 80.39E
Kotto r. C.A.R. 49 4.14N 22.02E
Kotuy r. Russian Fed. 29 71.40N103.00E
Kotzebue U.S.A. 72 66.51N162.40W
Kotzebue Sd. U.S.A. 72 66.20N163.00W
Kouango C.A.R. 49 4.58N 20.00E
Koudougou Burkina 52 12.15N 2.21W
Kouibli Ivory Coast 52 7.09N 7.16W
Kouki C.A.R. 53 7.09N 17.13E
Koúklia Cyprus 44 34.42N 32.34E
Koula Moutou Gabon 54 1.12S 12.29E
Koulikoro Mali 52 12.55N 7.31W
Koumac N. Cal. 68 20.33S164.17E
Koumankou Mali 52 11.58N 6.06W
Koumbal C.A.R. 49 9.26N 22.39E
Koumbia Burkina 52 11.18N 3.38W
Koumbia Guinea 52 11.54N 13.40W
Koumbisaleh site Mauritania 50 15.55N 8.05W
Koumongou Togo 52 10.10N 0.29E
Koumra Chad 53 8.56N 17.32E
Koupéla Burkina 52 12.09N 0.22W
Kouroussa Guinea 52 10.40N 9.50W
Kousseri Chad 53 12.05N 14.56E
Koutiala Mali 52 12.20N 5.23W
Kouto Ivory Coast 52 9.53N 6.25W
Kouvola Finland 24 60.54N 26.45E
Kouyou r. Congo 54 0.40S 16.37E
Kovdor Russian Fed. 24 67.33N 30.30E
Kovel Ukraine 21 51.12N 24.48E
Kovpyta Ukraine 21 51.22N 30.51E
Kovrov Russian Fed. 24 56.23N 41.21E
Kovzha r. Russian Fed. 24 61.05N 36.27E
Kowanyama Australia 64 15.29S141.44E
Kowloon Hong Kong 33 22.19N114.12E
Kowt-e 'Ashrow Afghan. 40 34.27N 68.48E
Koyukuk r. U.S.A. 72 64.50N157.30W
Kozan Turkey 42 37.27N 35.47E
Kozáni Greece 19 40.18N 21.48E
Kozelets Ukraine 21 50.54N 31.09E
Kozhikode India 38 11.15N 75.45E
Kozhim Russian Fed. 24 65.45N 59.30E
Kozhposelok Russian Fed. 24 63.10N 38.10E
Kpandu Ghana 52 7.02N 0.17E
Kpessi Togo 53 8.07N 1.17E
Krabi Thailand 34 8.08N 98.52E
Krâchéh Cambodia 34 12.30N106.00E
Kragan Indonesia 37 6.40S111.33E
Kragerö Norway 23 58.52N 9.25E
Kragujevac Yugo. 19 44.01N 20.55E
Kraków Poland 21 50.03N 19.55E
Kraljevo Yugo. 19 43.44N 20.41E
Kramatorsk Ukraine 25 48.43N 37.33E
Kramer U.S.A. 82 48.20N100.42W
Kramfors Sweden 22 62.55N 17.50E
Kranj Slovenia 20 46.15N 14.21E
Kranskop R.S.A. 56 28.58S 30.52E
Krapkowice Poland 21 50.29N 17.56E
Krasavino Russian Fed. 24 60.58N 46.25E
Krasilov Ukraine 21 49.39N 26.59E
Kraskino Russian Fed. 31 42.42N130.48E
Krasnaya Gora Russian Fed. 21 53.00N 31.36E
Kraśnik Poland 21 50.56N 22.13E
Krasnodar Russian Fed. 25 45.02N 39.00E
Krasnograd Ukraine 25 49.22N 35.28E
Krasnokamsk Russian Fed. 24 58.05N 55.49E
Krasnoperekopsk Ukraine 25 45.56N 33.47E
Krasnoselkup Russian Fed. 28 65.45N 82.31E
Krasnoturinsk Russian Fed. 24 59.46N 60.10E
Krasnoufimsk Russian Fed. 24 56.40N 57.49E
Krasnouralsk Russian Fed. 28 58.25N 60.00E
Krasnovishersk Russian Fed. 24 60.25N 57.02E
Krasnovodsk Turkmenistan 43 40.01N 53.00E
Krasnovodskiy Poluostrov pen. Turkmenistan 43 40.30N 53.10E
Krasnovodskiy Zaliv g. Turkmenistan 43 39.50N 53.15E
Krasnoyarsk Russian Fed. 29 56.05N 92.46E
Krasnyy Yar Russian Fed. 25 46.32N 48.21E
Kratovo Macedonia 19 42.05N 22.11E
Krawang Indonesia 37 6.15S107.15E
Krefeld Germany 14 51.20N 6.32E
Kremenchug Ukraine 25 49.03N 33.25E
Kremenchugskoye Vodokhranilishche resr. Ukraine 25 49.20N 32.30E
Kremenets Ukraine 21 50.05N 25.48E
Kremmling U.S.A. 80 40.03N106.24W
Krems Austria 20 48.25N 15.36E
Krestovka Russian Fed. 24 66.24N 52.31E
Kretinga Lithuania 23 55.53N 21.13E
Kribi Cameroon 53 2.56N 9.56E
Krichev Belorussia 21 53.40N 31.44E
Krishna r. India 39 16.00N 81.00E
Krishnanagar India 41 23.24N 88.30E
Kristiansand Norway 23 58.10N 8.00E
Kristianstad Sweden 23 56.02N 14.08E
Kristianstad d. Sweden 23 56.15N 13.35E
Kristiansund Norway 22 63.07N 7.45E
Kristiinankaupunki Finland 23 62.17N 21.23E
Kristinehamn Sweden 23 59.20N 14.07E
Kristinestad see Kristiinankaupunki Finland 23
Kristinovka Ukraine 21 48.50N 29.58E
Kríti i. Greece 19 35.15N 25.00E
Kritikón Pélagos sea Greece 19 36.00N 25.00E
Krivaja r. Bosnia-Herzegovina 21 44.27N 18.09E
Krivoy Rog Ukraine 25 47.55N 33.24E
Krk i. Croatia 20 45.04N 14.36E
Krnov Czech Republic 21 50.05N 17.41E
Kroken Norway 22 65.23N 14.15E
Krokom Sweden 22 63.20N 14.30E
Krŏng Kaôh Kŏng Cambodia 34 11.37N102.59E
Kronoberg d. Sweden 23 56.45N 14.15E
Kronprins Olav Kyst f. Antarctica 96 69.00S 42.00E
Kronshtadt Russian Fed. 24 60.00N 29.40E
Kroonstad R.S.A. 56 27.38S 27.12E
Kropotkin Russian Fed. 25 45.25N 40.35E
Krosno Poland 21 49.42N 21.46E
Krotoszyn Poland 21 51.42N 17.26E
Kroya Indonesia 37 7.37S109.13E
Kruger Nat. Park R.S.A. 57 24.10S 31.36E
Krugersdorp R.S.A. 56 26.06S 27.46E
Krujë Albania 19 41.30N 19.48E
Krumbach Germany 20 48.14N 10.22E
Krung Thep see Bangkok Thailand 34
Krupki Belorussia 21 54.19N 29.05E
Kruševac Yugo. 21 43.34N 21.20E
Krym pen. Ukraine 25 45.30N 34.00E
Krymsk Russian Fed. 25 44.56N 38.00E
Krzyz Poland 20 52.54N 16.01E
Ksar el Boukhari Algeria 51 35.53N 2.45E
Ksar-el-Kebir Morocco 50 35.01N 5.54W
Ksar Rhilane Tunisia 51 33.00N 9.38E
Ksel, Djebel mtn. Algeria 51 33.44N 1.10E
Kuala Dungun Malaysia 36 4.47N103.26E
Kualakapuas Indonesia 36 3.01S114.21E
Kuala Lipis Malaysia 36 4.11N102.00E
Kuala Lumpur Malaysia 36 3.08N101.42E
Kuala Trengganu Malaysia 36 5.10N103.10E
Kuancheng China 32 40.36N118.27E
Kuandang Indonesia 37 0.53N122.58E
Kuandian China 32 40.47N124.43E
Kuantan Malaysia 36 3.50N103.19E
Kuba Azerbaijan 43 41.23N 48.33E
Kuban r. Russian Fed. 25 45.20N 37.17E
Kubbum Sudan 49 11.47N 23.47E
Kuchaiburi India 41 22.16N 86.10E
Kuchāman India 40 27.09N 74.52E
Kuching Malaysia 36 1.32N110.20E
Kūchnay Darvīshān Afghan. 40 30.59N 64.11E
Kūd Jammu & Kashmir 40 33.05N 75.17E
Kudat Malaysia 36 6.45N116.47E
Kudus Indonesia 37 6.46S110.48E
Kufstein Austria 20 47.36N 12.11E
Kūhpāyeh Iran 43 32.42N 52.25E
Kūhrān, Kūh-e mtn. Iran 43 26.46N 58.15E
Kuito Angola 54 12.25S 16.58E
Kuiu I. U.S.A. 74 56.40N134.00W
Kuivaniemi Finland 22 65.35N 25.11E
Kuke Botswana 56 23.19S 24.29E
Kukerin Australia 63 33.11S118.03E
Kukës Albania 19 42.05N 20.24E
Kukshi India 40 22.12N 74.45E
Kūl r. Iran 43 28.00N 55.45E
Kula Turkey 42 38.33N 28.38E
Kulāchi Pakistan 40 31.56N 70.27E
Kulakshi Kazakhstan 25 47.09N 55.22E
Kulal, Mt. Kenya 55 2.44N 36.56E
Kulaura Bangla. 41 24.30N 92.03E
Kuldīga Latvia 23 56.58N 21.59E
Kulgera Australia 64 25.50S133.18E
Kulin Australia 63 32.40S118.10E
Kulja Australia 63 30.28S117.17E
Kulkyne r. Australia 67 30.16S144.12E
Kulpara Australia 66 34.07S137.59E
Kulsary Kazakhstan 25 46.59N 54.02E
Kulu India 40 31.58N 77.07E
Kulu Turkey 25 39.06N 33.02E
Kulunda Russian Fed. 28 52.34N 78.58E
Kulwin Australia 66 35.02S142.40E
Kulyab Tajikistan 30 37.55N 69.47E
Kuma r. Russian Fed. 25 44.40N 46.55E
Kumagaya Japan 35 36.08N139.23E
Kumai Indonesia 36 2.45S111.44E
Kumamoto Japan 35 32.50N130.42E
Kumanovo Macedonia 19 42.08N 21.40E
Kumara New Zealand 60 42.38S171.11E
Kumarl Australia 63 32.47S121.33E
Kumasi Ghana 52 6.45N 1.35W
Kumayri Armenia 43 40.47N 43.49E
Kumba Cameroon 53 4.39N 9.26E
Kumbakonam India 39 10.59N 79.24E
Kum Dag Turkmenistan 43 39.14N 54.33E
Kumdah Saudi Arabia 45 20.23N 45.05E
Kumertau Russian Fed. 24 52.48N 55.46E
Kumi Uganda 55 1.26N 33.54E
Kumla Sweden 23 59.08N 15.08E
Kumon Range mts. Burma 34 26.30N 97.15E
Kunashir i. Russian Fed. 31 44.25N146.00E
Kunchha Nepal 41 28.08N 84.22E
Kundam India 41 23.13N 80.21E
Kundelungu Mts. Zaïre 55 9.30S 27.50E
Kundiān Pakistan 40 32.27N 71.28E
Kundip Australia 63 33.44S120.11E
Kundla India 40 21.20N 71.18E
Kungälv Sweden 23 57.52N 11.58E
Kungsbacka Sweden 23 57.29N 12.04E
Kungu Zaïre 54 2.47N 19.12E
Kungur Russian Fed. 24 57.27N 56.50E
Kuningan Indonesia 37 7.02S108.30E
Kunkuri India 41 22.45N 83.57E
Kunlong Burma 34 23.25N 98.39E
Kunlun Shan mts. China 30 36.40N 88.00E
Kunming China 30 25.04N102.41E
Kunö i. Faroe Is. 8 62.20N 6.39W
Kunsan S. Korea 31 35.57N126.42E
Kunshan China 33 31.24N121.08E
Kuntair Gambia 52 13.36N 16.20W
Kununoppin Australia 63 31.09S117.53E
Kununurra Australia 61 15.42S128.50E
Kunyo Ethiopia 45 6.20N 42.32E
Kuolayarvi Russian Fed. 22 66.58N 29.12E
Kuopio Finland 24 62.51N 27.30E
Kupa r. Croatia 20 45.30N 16.20E
Kupang Indonesia 37 10.13S123.38E
Kupreanof I. U.S.A. 74 56.50N133.30W
Kupyansk Ukraine 25 49.41N 37.37E
Kuqa China 30 41.43N 82.58E
Kura r. Azerbaijan 43 39.18N 49.22E
Kuraymah Sudan 48 18.33N 31.51E
Kurchum Kazakhstan 30 48.35N 83.39E
Kurdistan f. Asia 43 37.00N 43.30E
Kŭrdzhali Bulgaria 19 41.38N 25.21E
Kuressaare Estonia 23 58.12N 22.30E
Kurgaldzhino Kazakhstan 28 50.35N 70.03E
Kurgan Russian Fed. 28 55.20N 65.20E
Kurīgrām Bangla. 41 25.49N 89.39E
Kurikka Finland 22 62.37N 22.25E
Kuril Ridge Pacific Oc. 68 46.10N152.30E
Kurilskiye Ostrova is. Russian Fed. 31 46.00N150.30E
Kuril Trench Pacific Oc. 68 46.00N155.00E
Kuring Kuru Namibia 56 17.36S 18.36E
Kurlovski Russian Fed. 24 55.26N 40.40E
Kurmuk Sudan 49 10.33N 34.17E
Kurnool India 39 15.51N 78.01E
Kurow New Zealand 60 44.44S170.28E
Kurram Pakistan 40 30.06N 66.31E
Kurri Kurri Australia 67 32.49S151.29E
Kurseong India 41 26.53N 88.17E
Kursk Russian Fed. 25 51.45N 36.14E
Kuršumlija Yugo. 19 43.09N 21.16E
Kūrtī Sudan 48 18.07N 31.33E
Kuru Finland 23 61.52N 23.44E
Kuru Sudan 49 7.43N 26.31E
Kuruman R.S.A. 56 27.28S 23.25E
Kuruman r. R.S.A. 56 26.53S 20.38E
Kurur, Jabal mtn. Sudan 48 20.31N 31.32E
Kusatsu Japan 35 35.02N135.57E
Kusel Germany 14 49.32N 7.21E
Kushālgarh India 40 23.10N 74.27E
Kushchevskaya Russian Fed. 25 46.34N 39.39E
Kushida r. Japan 35 34.36N136.34E
Kushiro Japan 35 42.58N144.24E
Kushka Turkmenistan 43 35.14N 62.15E
Kushtia Bangla. 41 23.55N 89.07E
Kusiyāra r. Bangla. 41 24.36N 91.44E
Kuskokwim B. U.S.A. 72 59.45N162.25W
Kuskokwim Mts. U.S.A. 72 62.50N156.00W
Kusma Nepal 41 28.13N 83.41E
Kustanay Kazakhstan 28 53.15N 63.40E
Küstenkanal Germany 14 53.05N 7.46E
Kūstī Sudan 49 13.10N 32.40E
Kütahya Turkey 42 39.25N 29.56E
Kutaisi Georgia 25 42.15N 42.44E
Kutiyāna India 40 21.38N 69.59E
Kutná Hora Czech Republic 20 49.57N 15.16E
Kutno Poland 21 52.15N 19.23E
Kutu Zaïre 54 2.42S 18.09E
Kutubdia I. Bangla. 41 21.50N 91.52E
Kutum Sudan 48 14.12N 24.40E
Kutztown U.S.A. 85 40.31N 75.47W
Kuujjuaq Canada 73 58.10N 68.15W
Kuujjuarapik Canada 76 55.25N 77.45W
Kuusamo Finland 24 65.57N 29.15E
Kuvango Angola 54 14.28S 16.25E
Kuwait Asia 43 29.20N 47.40E
Kuwait town see Al Kuwayt Kuwait 43
Kuwana Japan 35 35.04N136.42E
Kuybyshev see Samara Russian Fed. 24
Kuybyshevskoye Vodokhranilishche resr. Russian Fed. 24 55.00N 49.00E
Kuyeda Russian Fed. 24 56.25N 55.33E
Kuzey Anadolu Dağlari mts. Turkey 42 40.32N 38.00E
Kuznetsk Russian Fed. 24 53.08N 46.36E
Kuzomen Russian Fed. 24 66.15N 36.51E
Kuzreka Russian Fed. 24 66.35N 34.48E
Kvaenangen est. Norway 22 69.50N 21.30E
Kwale Kenya 55 4.20S 39.25E
Kwamouth Zaïre 54 3.11S 16.16E
Kwangju S. Korea 31 35.07N126.52E
Kwango r. Zaïre 54 3.20S 17.23E
Kwara d. Nigeria 53 8.20N 5.35E
Kwatisore Indonesia 37 3.18S134.50E
Kwa Zulu f. R.S.A. 56 27.30S 32.00E
Kwekwe Zimbabwe 56 18.59S 29.46E
Kweneng d. Botswana 56 24.30S 25.40E
Kwenge r. Zaïre 54 4.53S 18.47E
Kwethluk U.S.A. 72 60.49N161.27W
Kwidzyn Poland 21 53.45N 18.56E
Kwigillingok U.S.A. 72 59.51N163.08W
Kwiguk U.S.A. 72 62.45N164.28W
Kwilu r. Zaïre 54 3.18S 17.22E
Kwinana Australia 63 32.15S115.48E
Kwoka mtn. Indonesia 37 1.30S132.30E
Kyabé Chad 53 9.28N 18.54E
Kyabram Australia 67 36.18S145.05E
Kyaiklat Burma 34 16.25N 95.42E
Kyaikto Burma 34 17.16N 97.01E
Kyaka Tanzania 55 1.16S 31.27E
Kyakhta Russian Fed. 30 50.22N106.30E
Kyalite Australia 66 34.57S143.31E
Kyancutta Australia 66 33.08S135.34E
Kyaukpadaung Burma 34 20.50N 95.08E
Kyaukpyu Burma 34 19.20N 93.33E
Kybybolite Australia 66 36.54S140.58E
Kychema Russian Fed. 24 65.32N 42.42E
Kyle of Lochalsh town U.K. 12 57.17N 5.43W
Kyll r. Germany 14 49.48N 6.42E
Kyllburg Germany 14 50.03N 6.36E
Kyluchevskaya mtn. Russian Fed. 29 56.00N160.30E
Kyneton Australia 66 37.14S144.28E
Kynuna Australia 64 21.35S141.55E
Kyoga, L. Uganda 55 1.30N 33.00E
Kyogle Australia 67 28.36S152.59E
Kyong Burma 34 20.49N 96.40E
Kyonpyaw Burma 34 17.18N 95.12E
Kyotera Uganda 55 0.40S 31.31E
Kyōto Japan 35 35.00N135.45E
Kyōto d. Japan 35 34.55N135.35E
Kyrgyzstan Asia 30 41.30N 75.00E
Kyrön r. Finland 22 63.14N 21.45E
Kyrta Russian Fed. 24 64.02N 57.40E
Kyūshū i. Japan 35 32.50N130.50E
Kyushu Palau Ridge Pacific Oc. 68 15.00N135.00E
Kyustendil Bulgaria 19 42.18N 22.39E
Kywong Australia 67 35.01S146.45E
Kyyiv see Kiyev Ukraine 21
Kyyjärvi Finland 22 63.02N 24.34E
Kyzyl Russian Fed. 30 51.42N 94.28E
Kyzyl Kum, Peski f. Uzbekistan 28 42.00N 64.30E
Kzyl Orda Kazakhstan 28 44.52N 65.28E
K2 mtn. Asia 30 35.53N 76.32E

L

Laas Caanood Somali Rep. 45 8.26N 47.24E
Laas Dawaco Somali Rep. 45 10.22N 49.03E
Laas Dhaareed Somali Rep. 45 10.10N 46.01E
Laas Qoray Somali Rep. 45 11.10N 48.16E
La Asunción Venezuela 90 11.06N 63.53W
Laâyoune see El Aaiún W. Sahara 50
La Baleine r. Canada 73 58.00N 57.50W
La Banda Argentina 92 27.44S 64.15W
La Bañeza Spain 16 42.17N 5.55W
Labao Indonesia 37 8.12S122.49E
La Barca Mexico 86 20.20N102.33W
La Barge U.S.A. 80 42.16N110.12W
La Bassée France 14 50.32N 2.49E
La Baule France 17 47.18N 2.23W
Labbezanga Mali 52 14.57N 0.42E
Labe r. Czech. see Elbe r. Germany 20
Labé Guinea 52 11.17N 12.11W
La Belle U.S.A. 85 26.43N 81.27W
Laberge, L. Canada 74 61.11N135.12W
Labinsk Russian Fed. 25 44.39N 40.44E
La Blanquilla i. Venezuela 87 11.53N 64.38W
Labouheyre France 17 44.13N 0.55W
Laboulaye Argentina 93 34.05S 63.25W
Labrador f. Canada 77 53.00N 62.00W
Labrador Basin f. Atlantic Oc. 95 55.00N 45.00W
Labrador City Canada 77 52.57N 66.54W
Labrador Sea Canada / Greenland 73 57.00N 53.00W
Lábrea Brazil 90 7.16S 64.47W
Labrit France 17 44.07N 0.33W
Labuan Indonesia 37 6.25S105.49E
Labuan i. Malaysia 36 5.20N115.15E
Labuha Indonesia 37 0.37S127.29E
Labutta Burma 34 16.09N 94.46E
Labyrinth, L. Australia 66 30.43S135.07E
Lac d. Chad 53 13.30N 14.35E
La Calera Chile 93 32.47S 71.12W
La Capelle France 14 49.59N 3.57E
La Carlota Argentina 93 33.25S 63.18W
La Carolina Spain 16 38.16N 3.36W
Lacaune France 17 43.42N 2.41E
La Ceiba Honduras 87 15.45N 86.45W
Lacepede B. Australia 66 36.47S139.45E
Lac Giao Vietnam 34 12.41N108.02E
Lacha, Ozero l. Russian Fed. 24 61.25N 39.00E
La Charité France 17 47.11N 3.01E
La Chartre France 15 47.44N 0.35E
La Chaux-de-Fonds Switz. 20 47.07N 6.51E
Lach Dera r. Somali Rep. 55 0.01S 42.45E
Lachhmangarh India 40 27.49N 75.02E
Lachine Canada 77 45.26N 73.40W
Lachlan r. Australia 66 34.21S143.58E
Lachute Canada 77 45.38N 74.20W
Lackan Resr. Rep. of Ire. 13 53.09N 6.31W
Lackawanna U.S.A. 84 42.49N 78.49W
Lac la Biche town Canada 75 54.46N111.58W
Lac la Ronge Prov. Park Canada 75 55.14N104.45W
La Cocha Argentina 92 27.45S 65.35W
Lacombe Canada 74 52.30N113.44W
La Concepción Venezuela 90 10.25N 71.41W
La Concordia Mexico 86 16.05N 92.38W
La Coruña Spain 16 43.22N 8.24W
Lac Rémi town Canada 77 46.01N 74.47W
La Crosse Kans. U.S.A. 82 38.32N 99.18W
La Crosse Wisc. U.S.A. 82 43.48N 91.15W
La Cruz Mexico 81 27.50N105.11W
La Cruz Uruguay 93 33.56S 56.15W
Ladākh Range mts. Jammu & Kashmir 41 34.15N 78.00E
La Demanda, Sierra de mts. Spain 16 42.10N 3.20W
Ladismith R.S.A. 56 33.29S 21.15E
Ladispoli Italy 18 41.56N 12.05E
Lādīz Iran 43 28.57N 61.18E
Lādnun India 40 27.39N 74.23E
Ladoga l. see Ladozhskoye Ozero l. Russian Fed. 24
La Dorada Colombia 90 5.27N 74.40W
Ladozhskoye Ozero l. Russian Fed. 24 61.00N 32.00E
La Dura Mexico 81 28.22N109.33W
Ladushkin Russian Fed. 21 54.30N 20.05E
Ladva Vetka Russian Fed. 24 61.16N 34.23E
Ladybrand R.S.A. 56 29.11S 27.26E
Ladysmith Canada 74 49.58N123.49W
Ladysmith R.S.A. 56 28.32S 29.47E
Ladysmith U.S.A. 82 45.27N 91.07W
Lae P.N.G. 37 6.45S146.30E
Lae Thailand 34 19.25N101.00E
Laesö i. Denmark 23 57.16N 11.01E
La Estrada Spain 16 42.40N 8.30W
La Fayette Ga. U.S.A. 85 34.42N 85.18W
Lafayette Ind. U.S.A. 84 40.25N 86.54W
Lafayette La. U.S.A. 83 30.14N 92.01W
La Fère France 15 49.40N 3.22E
La Ferté-Bernard France 15 48.11N 0.40E
La Ferté-Gaucher France 15 48.47N 3.18E
La Ferté-Macé France 15 48.36N 0.22W
La Ferté-St. Aubin France 15 47.43N 1.56E
Lafia Nigeria 53 8.35N 8.34E
Lafiagi Nigeria 53 8.50N 5.23E
La Flèche France 15 47.42N 0.05W
Lafollette U.S.A. 85 36.23N 84.09W
Laforest Canada 76 47.04N 81.12W
La Fregeneda Spain 16 40.58N 6.54W
La Fuente de San Esteban Spain 16 40.48N 6.15W
Lagan r. U.K. 13 54.37N 5.44W
Lågen r. Akershus Norway 23 60.10N 11.28E
Lågen r. Vestfold Norway 23 59.03N 10.05E
Laghouat Algeria 51 33.49N 2.55E
Lago Dilolo town Angola 54 11.27S 22.03E
Lagos Mexico 86 21.21N101.55W
Lagos Nigeria 53 6.27N 3.28E
Lagos d. Nigeria 53 6.32N 3.30E
Lagos Portugal 16 37.05N 8.40W
La Goulette Tunisia 51 36.49N 10.18E
La Grande r. Canada 76 53.50N 79.00W
La Grande U.S.A. 80 45.20N118.05W
La Grande Résr. 2 Canada 76 53.35N 77.10W
La Grande Résr. 3 Canada 76 53.35N 74.55W
La Grande Résr. 4 Canada 76 53.50N 73.30W
Lagrange Australia 62 18.46S121.49E
La Grange U.S.A. 85 33.02N 85.02W
La Guaira Venezuela 90 10.38N 66.55W
La Guerche-de-Bretagne France 15 47.56N 1.14W
Laguna Brazil 92 28.29S 48.47W
Laguna Dam U.S.A. 81 32.55N114.25W
Lagunas Chile 92 20.59S 69.37W
Lagunas Peru 90 5.10S 73.35W
La Habana Cuba 87 23.07N 82.25W
Lahad Datu Malaysia 36 5.05N118.20E
La Harpe U.S.A. 82 40.35N 90.57W
Lahat Indonesia 36 3.46S103.32E
La Haye-du-Puits France 15 49.18N 1.33W
Laḩij Yemen 45 13.04N 44.53E
Lāhījān Iran 43 37.12N 50.00E
Lahn r. Germany 14 50.18N 7.36E
Lahnstein Germany 14 50.17N 7.38E
Laholm Sweden 23 56.31N 13.02E
Lahore Pakistan 40 31.35N 74.18E
Lahri Pakistan 40 29.11N 68.13E
Lahti Finland 23 60.58N 25.40E
Laï Chad 53 9.22N 16.14E
Laiagam P.N.G. 37 5.31S143.39E
Laibin China 33 23.42N109.16E
Lai Chau Vietnam 34 22.04N103.12E
L'Aigle France 15 48.45N 0.38E
Laignes France 15 47.50N 4.22E
Laihia Finland 22 62.58N 22.01E
Laingsburg R.S.A. 56 33.11S 20.49E
Lainio r. Sweden 22 67.28N 22.50E

Lairg to Lewisporte

Lairg U.K. 12 58.01N 4.25W
Laisamis Kenya 55 1.38N 37.47E
Laissac France 17 44.23N 2.49E
Laitila Finland 23 60.53N 21.41E
Laiyuan China 32 39.19N114.41E
Laizhou Wan b. China 32 37.30N119.30E
Lajes Brazil 94 27.48S 50.20W
La Junta U.S.A. 80 37.59N103.33W
Lakaband Pakistan 40 31.00N 69.30E
Lak Bor r. Kenya 49 1.18N 40.40E
Lak Bor r. Somali Rep. 55 0.32N 42.05E
Lake Biddy town Australia 63 33.01S118.51E
Lake Boga town Australia 66 35.27S143.39E
Lake Brown town Australia 63 30.57S118.19E
Lake Cargelligo town Australia 67 33.19S146.23E
Lake Charles town U.S.A. 83 30.13N 93.12W
Lake City U.S.A. 85 30.12N 82.39W
Lake District f. U.K. 10 54.30N 3.10W
Lake George town U.S.A. 80 38.58N105.23W
Lake Grace town Australia 63 33.06S118.28E
Lake Harbour town Canada 73 62.50N 69.50W
Lake King town Australia 63 33.05S119.40E
Lakeland town U.S.A. 85 28.02N 81.59W
Lake Mead Nat. Recreation Area U.S.A. 81 36.00N114.30W
Lake Nash town Australia 64 21.00S137.55E
Lakepa Niue 68 19.01S169.49W
Lake Placid town U.S.A. 84 44.17N 73.59W
Lake River town Canada 76 54.30N 82.30W
Lakes Entrance town Australia 67 37.53S147.59E
Lakeshore U.S.A. 80 37.15N119.12W
Lakeside U.S.A. 80 41.13N112.54W
Lake Superior Prov. Park Canada 76 47.30N 84.50W
Lakeview U.S.A. 80 42.11N120.21W
Lake Village U.S.A. 83 33.20N 91.17W
Lakewood N.J. U.S.A. 85 40.06N 74.12W
Lakewood N.Mex. U.S.A. 81 32.39N104.39W
Lakewood Ohio U.S.A. 84 41.29N 81.50W
Lākheri India 40 25.40N 76.10E
Lakhīmpur India 41 27.57N 80.46E
Lakhnādon India 41 22.36N 79.36E
Lakhpat India 40 23.49N 68.47E
Lakonikós Kólpos g. Greece 19 36.35N 22.42E
Lakota Ivory Coast 52 5.50N 5.30W
Lakota U.S.A. 82 48.02N 98.21W
Laksefjorden est. Norway 22 70.58N 27.00E
Lakselv Norway 22 70.03N 24.55E
Lakshadweep Is. Indian Oc. 38 11.00N 72.00E
Lala India 41 24.25N 92.40E
Lāla Mūsa Pakistan 40 32.42N 73.58E
Lalaua Mozambique 55 14.20S 38.30E
Lālehzār, Kūh-e mtn. Iran 43 29.26N 56.48E
Lālganj India 41 25.52N 85.11E
Lalibela Ethiopia 49 12.02N 39.02E
La Libertad El Salvador 87 13.28N 89.20W
Lalín Spain 16 42.40N 8.05W
La Línea Spain 16 36.10N 5.21W
Lalitpur India 41 24.41N 78.25E
Lalitpur Nepal 41 27.41N 85.20E
Lālmanir Hāt Bangla. 41 25.54N 89.27E
La Loche Canada 75 56.29N109.27W
La Loche, Lac l. Canada 75 56.25N109.30W
La Loupe France 15 48.28N 1.01E
La Louvière Belgium 14 50.29N 4.11E
Lālpur India 40 22.12N 69.58E
Lālsot India 40 26.34N 76.20E
Lamar U.S.A. 82 38.05N102.37W
Lambaréné Gabon 54 0.40S 10.15E
Lambasa Fiji 68 16.25S179.24E
Lambayeque Peru 90 6.36S 79.50W
Lambay I. Rep. of Ire. 13 53.29N 6.01W
Lambert's Bay town R.S.A. 56 32.06S 18.16E
Lamé Chad 53 9.14N 14.33E
Lame Nigeria 53 10.27N 9.12E
Lamego Portugal 16 41.05N 7.49W
Lameroo Australia 66 35.20S140.33E
La Mesa Calif. U.S.A. 81 32.46N117.01W
Lamesa Tex. U.S.A. 83 32.44N101.57W
Lamía Greece 19 38.53N 22.25E
Lammermuir Hills U.K. 12 55.51N 2.40W
Lammhult Sweden 23 57.09N 14.35E
Lamongan Indonesia 37 7.05S112.26E
Lamont U.S.A. 80 42.12N107.28W
Lamotrek i. Federated States of Micronesia 37 7.28N146.23E
Lamotte-Beuvron France 15 47.37N 2.01E
La Moure U.S.A. 82 46.21N 98.18W
Lampa Peru 90 15.10S 70.30W
Lampasas U.S.A. 83 31.04N 98.12W
Lampazos Mexico 83 27.00N100.30W
Lampedusa i. Italy 18 35.30N 12.35E
Lampeter U.K. 11 52.06N 4.06W
Lampione i. Italy 18 35.33N 12.18E
Lamu Kenya 55 2.20S 40.54E
La Mure France 17 44.54N 5.47E
Lanai i. Hawaiian Is. 69 20.50N156.55W
Lanai City Hawaiian Is. 69 20.50N156.55W
La Nao, Cabo de Spain 16 38.42N 0.15E
Lanark U.K. 12 55.41N 3.47W
Lancang Jiang r. China see Mekong r. Asia 34
Lancashire d. U.K. 10 53.53N 2.30W
Lancaster Canada 77 45.08N 74.30W
Lancaster U.K. 10 54.03N 2.48W
Lancaster Calif. U.S.A. 81 34.42N118.08W
Lancaster N.Y. U.S.A. 76 42.54N 78.40W
Lancaster Ohio U.S.A. 84 39.43N 82.37W
Lancaster Penn. U.S.A. 85 40.02N 76.19W
Lancaster S.C. U.S.A. 85 34.43N 80.47W
Lancaster Tex. U.S.A. 83 32.36N 96.46W
Lancaster Sd. Canada 73 74.00N 85.00W
Lancelin Australia 63 31.01S115.19E
Lanchow see Lanzhou China 32
Lancun China 32 36.24N120.10E
Landau Germany 20 48.40N 12.43E
Landay Afghan. 40 30.31N 63.47E
Landeck Austria 20 47.09N 10.35E
Landen Belgium 14 50.46N 5.04E
Lander r. Australia 64 20.25S132.00E
Lander U.S.A. 80 42.50N108.44W
Landerneau France 17 48.27N 4.16W
Landisville U.S.A. 85 39.31N 74.55W
Landor Australia 62 25.06S116.50E
Landrecies France 14 50.08N 3.40E
Land's End c. U.K. 11 50.03N 5.45W
Landshut Germany 20 48.31N 12.10E
Landskrona Sweden 23 55.52N 12.50E
Lanett U.S.A. 85 32.52N 85.12W
Langå Denmark 23 56.23N 9.55E
La'nga Co l. China 41 30.45N 81.15E
Langadhás Greece 19 40.45N 23.04E
Langanes c. Iceland 22 66.30N 14.30W
Langao China 32 33.22N109.04E
Langdon U.S.A. 82 48.46N 98.22W
Langeais France 15 47.20N 0.24E
Langeland i. Denmark 23 55.00N 10.50E
Längelmävesi l. Finland 23 61.32N 24.22E
Langeoog i. Germany 14 53.46N 7.30E
Langesund Norway 23 59.00N 9.45E
Langholm U.K. 12 55.09N 3.00W
Langjökull ice cap Iceland 22 63.43N 20.03W
Langkawi i. Malaysia 36 6.20N 99.30E
Langlade Canada 76 48.14N 76.00W
Langon France 17 44.33N 0.14W
Langöy i. Norway 22 68.45N 15.00E
Langres France 17 47.53N 5.20E
Langsa Indonesia 36 4.28N 97.59E
Langshan China 32 41.02N107.27E
Lang Shan mts. China 32 41.30N107.10E
Lang Son Vietnam 33 21.49N106.45E
Langtry U.S.A. 83 29.48N101.34W
Languedoc-Roussillon d. France 17 43.50N 3.30E
Langxi China 33 31.08N119.10E
Lannion France 17 48.44N 3.27W
Lanoraie Canada 77 45.58N 73.13W
Lansdale U.S.A. 85 40.15N 75.17W
Lansdowne India 41 29.50N 78.41E
L'Anse au Loup Canada 77 51.34N 56.48W
Lansing U.S.A. 84 42.44N 84.34W
Lanslebourg France 15 45.17N 6.52E
Lantewa Nigeria 53 12.15N 11.45E
Lanxi China 33 29.17N119.31E
Lanzarote i. Canary Is. 50 29.00N 13.40W
Lanzhou China 32 36.01N103.46E
Lanzo Torinese Italy 15 45.16N 7.28E
Laoag Phil. 37 18.14N120.36E
Lào Cai Vietnam 34 22.30N104.00E
Laochang China 33 25.12N104.35E
Laoha He r. China 32 43.30N120.42E
Laohekou China 32 32.26N111.41E
Laois d. Rep. of Ire. 13 53.00N 7.20W
Laojun Shan mtn. China 32 33.45N111.38E
Laon France 15 49.34N 3.37E
Laona U.S.A. 76 45.35N 88.40W
La Orotava Canary Is. 95 28.26N 16.30W
La Oroya Peru 90 11.36S 75.54W
Laos Asia 34 18.30N104.00E
La Palma i. Canary Is. 50 28.50N 18.00W
La Palma Spain 16 37.23N 6.33W
La Pampa d. Argentina 93 37.00S 66.00W
La Paragua Venezuela 90 6.53N 63.22W
La Paz Entre Ríos Argentina 93 30.45S 59.38W
La Paz Mendoza Argentina 93 33.28S 67.34W
La Paz Bolivia 92 16.30S 68.09W
La Paz d. Bolivia 92 16.00S 68.10W
La Paz Mexico 81 24.10N110.18W
La Paz, Bahía de b. Mexico 81 24.15N110.30W
La Pedrera Colombia 90 1.18S 69.43W
Lapeer U.S.A. 84 43.03N 83.09W
La Peña, Sierra de mts. Spain 16 42.30N 0.50W
La Perouse Str. Russian Fed. 29 45.50N142.30E
La Pine U.S.A. 80 43.40N121.30W
Lapinjärvi Finland 23 60.38N 26.13E
Lapland f. Sweden/Finland 22 68.10N 24.10E
La Plata Argentina 93 34.55S 57.57W
La Plata Md. U.S.A. 85 38.32N 76.59W
La Plata Mo. U.S.A. 82 40.02N 92.29W
La Plata, Río de est. Argentina/Uruguay 93 35.15S 56.45W
Lapointe, Lac l. Canada 77 53.32N 68.56W
Lappajärvi l. Finland 22 63.08N 23.40E
Lappeenranta Finland 24 61.04N 28.05E
Lappi d. Finland 22 67.20N 26.00E
Laptevykh, More sea Russian Fed. 29 74.30N125.00E
Lapua Finland 22 62.57N 23.00E
La Push U.S.A. 80 47.55N124.38W
La Quiaca Argentina 92 22.05S 65.36W
L'Aquila Italy 18 42.22N 13.25E
Lār Iran 43 27.37N 54.16E
Lara Australia 66 38.01S144.26E
Larache Morocco 50 35.12N 6.10W
Laramie U.S.A. 80 41.19N105.35W
Laramie Mts. U.S.A. 80 42.00N105.40W
Lärbro Sweden 23 57.47N 18.47E
Larche, Col de France/Italy 15 44.25N 6.53E
Laredo U.S.A. 83 27.31N 99.30W
Laredo Sd. Canada 74 52.30N128.53W
Largeau Chad 53 17.55N 19.07E
Largs U.K. 12 55.48N 4.52W
Lariang Indonesia 36 1.35S119.25E
La Rioja Argentina 92 29.25S 66.50W
La Rioja d. Argentina 92 29.00S 66.00W
La Rioja d. Spain 16 42.15N 2.25W
Lárisa Greece 19 39.36N 22.24E
Lark r. U.K. 11 52.26N 0.20E
Lārkāna Pakistan 40 27.33N 68.13E
Larkspur U.S.A. 80 39.13N104.54W
Larnaca see Lárnax Cyprus 44
Lárnax Cyprus 44 34.54N 33.39E
Larne U.K. 13 54.51N 5.49W
La Robla Spain 16 42.50N 5.41W
La Roche Belgium 14 50.11N 5.35E
La Rochelle France 17 46.10N 1.10W
La Roche-sur-Yon France 17 46.40N 1.25W
La Roda Spain 16 39.13N 2.10W
La Romana Dom. Rep. 87 18.27N 68.57W
La Ronge Canada 75 55.06N105.17W
La Ronge, Lac l. Canada 72 55.07N105.15W
Laroquebrou France 17 44.58N 2.11E
Larrimah Australia 64 15.35S133.12E
Larvik Norway 23 59.04N 10.00E
La Sagra mtn. Spain 16 37.58N 2.35W
La Salle U.S.A. 82 41.20N 89.06W
Las Animas U.S.A. 80 38.04N103.13W
La Sarre Canada 76 48.45N 79.15W
Las Casitas, Cerro mtn. Mexico 81 23.32N109.59W
Las Cruces U.S.A. 81 32.23N106.29W
Las Cuevas Mexico 83 29.38N101.19W
La Seine, Baie de France 17 49.40N 0.30W
La Serena Chile 92 29.54S 71.16W
La Seyne France 17 43.06N 5.53E
Las Flores Argentina 93 36.02S 59.07W
Lāsh-e Joveyn Afghan. 40 31.43N 61.37E
Las Heras Argentina 93 32.50S 68.50W
Lashio Burma 34 22.58N 96.51E
Lashkar Gāh Afghan. 40 31.30N 64.21E
Las Lomitas Argentina 92 24.43S 60.35W
Las Marismas f. Spain 16 37.00N 6.15W
L'Asomption r. Canada 77 45.43N 73.29W
Las Palmas de Gran Canaria Canary Is. 50 28.08N 15.27W
Las Palomas Mexico 81 31.44N107.37W
Las Perlas, Archipelago de Panama 87 8.45N 79.30W
La Spezia Italy 15 44.07N 9.49E
Las Piedras Uruguay 93 34.44S 56.13W
Las Plumas Argentina 93 43.40S 67.15W
Lassay France 15 48.26N 0.30W
Lassen Peak mtn. U.S.A. 80 40.29N121.31W
L'Assomption Canada 77 45.50N 73.25W
Last Chance U.S.A. 80 39.45N103.36W
Last Mountain L. Canada 75 51.05N105.10W
Lastoursville Gabon 54 0.50S 12.47E
Lastovo i. Croatia 19 42.45N 16.52E
Las Tres Vírgenes, Volcán mtn. Mexico 81 27.27N112.37W
Lastrup Germany 14 52.48N 7.55E
La Suze France 15 47.54N 0.02E
Las Vegas Nev. U.S.A. 81 36.11N115.08W
Las Vegas N.Mex. U.S.A. 81 35.36N105.13W
Latacunga Ecuador 90 0.58S 78.36W
La Tagua Colombia 90 0.03S 74.40W
Latakia see Al Lādhiqīyah Syria 44
Latambar Pakistan 40 33.07N 70.52E
Late i. Tonga 69 18.49S174.40W
Lātehār India 41 23.45N 84.30E
La Teste-de-Buch France 17 44.38N 1.09W
Lathen Germany 14 52.54N 7.20E
Lāthi India 40 21.43N 71.23E
Latina Italy 18 41.28N 12.52E
Latisana Italy 15 45.47N 13.00E
La Tortuga i. Venezuela 90 11.00N 65.20W
La Trobe, Mt. Australia 67 39.03S146.25E
La Tuque Canada 77 47.27N 72.47W
Latvia Europe 24 56.45N 25.00E
Lau Nigeria 53 9.14N 11.15E
Lauchhammer Germany 20 51.30N 13.48E
Lauenburg Germany 20 53.22N 10.33E
Laughlen, Mt. Australia 64 23.23S134.23E
Lau Group is. Fiji 68 19.00S178.30W
Launceston Australia 65 41.25S147.07E
Launceston U.K. 11 50.38N 4.21W
La Unión Chile 93 40.15S 73.02W
La Unión Spain 16 37.38N 0.53W
Laura Australia 66 33.08S138.19E
La Urbana Venezuela 90 7.08N 66.56W
Laurel Del. U.S.A. 85 38.33N 75.34W
Laurel Miss. U.S.A. 83 31.42N 89.08W
Laurel Mont. U.S.A. 80 45.40N108.46W
Laurencekirk U.K. 12 56.50N 2.29W
Laurens U.S.A. 85 34.29N 82.01W
Laurentides mts. Canada 77 46.25N 73.28W
Laurentides Prov. Park Canada 77 47.30N 71.30W
Laurieton Australia 67 31.38S152.46E
Laurinburg U.S.A. 85 34.46N 79.29W
Lausanne Switz. 20 46.32N 6.39E
Laut i. Indonesia 36 3.45S116.20E
Lautaro Chile 93 38.31S 72.27W
Lauterecken Germany 14 49.39N 7.36E
Lautoka Fiji 68 17.37S177.27E
Lavagh More mtn. Rep. of Ire. 13 54.45N 8.07W
Lava Hot Springs town U.S.A. 80 42.37N112.01W
Laval Canada 77 45.35N 73.45W
Laval France 15 48.04N 0.45W
La Vega Dom. Rep. 87 19.15N 70.33W
La Vela Venezuela 90 11.27N 69.34W
La Vérendrye Prov. Park Canada 76 47.32N 77.00W
Laverne U.S.A. 83 36.43N 99.54W
Laverton Australia 63 28.49S122.25E
Lavia Finland 23 61.36N 22.36E
Lavik Norway 23 61.06N 5.30E
Lavras Brazil 94 21.15S 44.59W
Lávrion Greece 19 37.44N 24.04E
Lawra Ghana 52 10.40N 2.49W
Lawrence New Zealand 60 45.55S169.42E
Lawrence Kans. U.S.A. 82 38.58N 95.14W
Lawrence Mass. U.S.A. 84 42.42N 71.09W
Lawrenceburg U.S.A. 85 35.16N 87.20W
Lawrenceville Canada 77 45.25N 72.19W
Lawton U.S.A. 83 34.37N 98.25W
Lawz, Jabal al mtn. Saudi Arabia 44 28.40N 35.20E
Laxå Sweden 23 58.59N 14.37E
Laysan i. Hawaiian Is. 68 25.46N171.44W
Laytonville U.S.A. 80 39.41N123.29W
Lazio d. Italy 18 42.20N 12.00E
Lead U.S.A. 82 44.21N103.46W
Leader Canada 75 50.53N109.31W
Leadhills U.K. 12 55.25N 3.46W
Leamington U.S.A. 80 39.31N112.17W
Learmonth Australia 62 22.13S114.04E
Leavenworth U.S.A. 82 39.19N 94.55W
Lebak Phil. 37 6.32N124.03E
Lebango Congo 54 0.24N 14.44E
Lebanon Asia 44 34.00N 36.00E
Lebanon Ind. U.S.A. 84 40.02N 87.28W
Lebanon Kans. U.S.A. 82 39.49N 98.33W
Lebanon Ky. U.S.A. 85 37.33N 85.15W
Lebanon Mo. U.S.A. 83 37.41N 92.40W
Lebanon Oreg. U.S.A. 80 44.32N122.54W
Lebanon Penn. U.S.A. 84 40.20N 76.25W
Lebanon Tenn. U.S.A. 85 36.11N 86.19W
Lebec U.S.A. 81 34.50N118.52W
Lebesby Norway 22 70.34N 27.00E
Le Blanc France 17 46.37N 1.03E
Lebork Poland 21 54.33N 17.44E
Lebrija Spain 16 36.55N 6.10W
Lebu Chile 93 37.37S 73.39W
Le Bugue France 17 44.55N 0.56E
Le Cateau France 14 50.07N 3.33E
Le Catelet France 14 50.00N 3.12E
Lecce Italy 19 40.21N 18.11E
Lecco Italy 15 45.51N 9.23E
Lech r. Germany 20 48.45N 10.51E
Lechang China 33 25.08N113.20E
Le Chesne France 14 49.31N 4.46E
Lechiguanas, Islas de las is. Argentina 93 33.26S 59.42W
Le Creusot France 17 46.48N 4.27E
Lectoure France 17 43.56N 0.38E
Ledbury U.K. 11 52.03N 2.25W
Ledesma Spain 16 41.05N 6.00W
Le Dorat France 17 46.14N 1.05E
Leduc Canada 74 53.20N113.30W
Lee r. Rep. of Ire. 13 51.53N 8.25W
Leech L. U.S.A. 82 47.09N 94.23W
Leedey U.S.A. 83 35.52N 99.21W
Leeds U.K. 10 53.48N 1.34W
Leeds U.S.A. 85 33.32N 86.31W
Leek U.K. 10 53.07N 2.02W
Leer Germany 14 53.14N 7.27E
Leesburg U.S.A. 85 28.49N 81.54W
Leeston New Zealand 60 43.46S172.18E
Leeton Australia 67 34.33S146.24E
Leeuwarden Neth. 14 53.12N 5.48E
Leeuwin, C. Australia 63 34.22S115.08E
Leeward Is. C. America 87 18.00N 61.00W
Lefroy, L. Australia 63 31.15S121.40E
Legazpi Phil. 37 13.10N123.45E
Leggs Tor mtn. Australia 65 41.32S147.40E
Legget U.S.A. 80 39.52N123.34W
Leghorn see Livorno Italy 18
Legion Mine Zimbabwe 56 21.23S 28.33E
Legionowo Poland 21 52.25N 20.56E
Legnago Italy 15 45.11N 11.18E
Legnano Italy 15 45.36N 8.54E
Legnica Poland 20 51.12N 16.10E
Le Grand-Lucé France 15 47.52N 0.28E
Le Grand-Quevilly France 15 49.25N 1.02E
Leh Jammu & Kashmir 41 34.10N 77.35E
Le Havre France 15 49.30N 0.06E
Lehrte Germany 20 52.22N 9.59E
Lehututu Botswana 56 23.54S 21.52E
Leiah Pakistan 40 30.58N 70.56E
Leibnitz Austria 20 46.48N 15.32E
Leicester U.K. 11 52.39N 1.09W
Leicestershire d. U.K. 11 52.29N 1.10W
Leichhardt r. Australia 64 17.35S139.48E
Leiden Neth. 14 52.10N 4.30E
Leie r. Belgium 14 51.03N 3.44E
Leifeng China 33 25.35N118.17E
Leigh Creek r. Australia 66 29.49S138.10E
Leigh Creek town Australia 66 30.31S138.25E
Leighton Buzzard U.K. 11 51.55N 0.39W
Leikanger Norway 23 61.10N 6.52E
Leinster Australia 63 27.59S120.30E
Leipzig Germany 20 51.20N 12.20E
Leiria Portugal 16 39.45N 8.48W
Lei Shui r. China 33 26.57N112.33E
Leithbridge Canada 74 49.40N112.45W
Leitrim d. Rep. of Ire. 13 54.08N 8.00W
Leiyang China 33 26.30N112.42E
Leizhou Bandao pen. China 33 21.00N110.00E
Lek r. Neth. 14 51.55N 4.29E
Leksvik Norway 22 63.40N 10.40E
Leland U.S.A. 83 33.24N 90.54W
Leland Lakes Canada 75 60.00N110.59W
Lelchitsy Belorussia 21 51.48N 28.20E
Leleque Argentina 93 42.24S 71.04W
Leling China 32 37.45N117.13E
Le Lion-d'Angers France 15 47.38N 0.43W
Le Lude France 15 47.39N 0.09E
Lelystad Neth. 14 52.32N 5.29E
Léman, Lac l. Switz. 20 46.30N 6.30E
Le Mans France 15 48.01N 0.10E
Le Mars U.S.A. 82 42.47N 96.10W
Leme Brazil 94 22.10S 47.23W
Le Merlerault France 15 48.42N 0.18E
Lemesós Cyprus 44 34.40N 33.03E
Lemgo Germany 20 52.02N 8.54E
Lemhi Range mts. U.S.A. 80 44.30N113.25W
Lemmer Neth. 14 52.50N 5.43E
Lemmon U.S.A. 82 45.56N102.10W
Lemsid W. Sahara 50 26.32N 13.49W
Lemvig Denmark 23 56.32N 8.18E
Lena r. Russian Fed. 29 72.00N127.10E
Lena U.S.A. 83 31.47N 92.48W
Lenakel Vanuatu 68 19.32S169.16E
Lendery Russian Fed. 24 63.24N 31.04E
Lendinara Italy 15 45.05N 11.36E
Lengerich Germany 14 52.12N 7.52E
Lengoue r. Congo 54 1.15S 16.42E
Lenina, Kanal canal Russian Fed. 25 43.46N 45.00E
Lenina, Pik mtn. Tajikistan 30 40.14N 69.40E
Leningrad see Sankt-Peterburg Russian Fed. 24
Leninogorsk Kazakhstan 28 50.23N 83.32E
Leninsk Russian Fed. 25 48.42N 45.14E
Leninsk Kuznetskiy Russian Fed. 28 54.44N 86.13E
Lenkoran Azerbaijan 43 38.45N 48.50E
Lenmalu Indonesia 37 1.58S130.00E
Lenne r. Germany 14 51.24N 7.30E
Lenoir U.S.A. 85 35.56N 81.31W
Lenora U.S.A. 82 39.38N100.03W
Lenore L. Canada 75 52.30N105.00W
Lens France 14 50.26N 2.50E
Lentini Italy 18 37.17N 15.00E
Lenvik Norway 22 69.22N 18.10E
Léo Burkina 52 11.05N 2.06W
Leoben Austria 20 47.23N 15.06E
Leominster U.K. 11 52.15N 2.43W
Leominster U.S.A. 84 42.32N 71.45W
León Mexico 86 21.10N101.42W
León d. Mexico 83 25.00N100.20W
León Nicaragua 87 12.24N 86.52W
León Spain 16 42.35N 5.34W
Leon U.S.A. 82 40.44N 93.45W
Leonardtown U.S.A. 85 38.17N 76.38W
Leonardville Namibia 56 23.21S 18.47E
Leonárison Cyprus 44 35.28N 34.08E
Leongatha Australia 67 38.29S145.57E
Leonora Australia 63 28.54S121.20E
Leopoldina Brazil 94 21.30S 42.38W
Leopoldsburg Belgium 14 51.08N 5.13E
Leovo Moldavia 21 46.29N 28.12E
Lepel Russian Fed. 24 54.48N 28.40E
Leping China 33 28.58N117.08E
L'Epiphanie Canada 77 45.51N 73.30W
Le Puy France 17 45.03N 3.54E
Le Quesnoy France 14 50.15N 3.39E
Lerbäck Sweden 23 58.56N 15.02E
Léré Chad 53 9.41N 14.17E
Lerici Italy 15 44.04N 9.55E
Lérida Spain 16 41.37N 0.38E
Lerma Spain 16 42.02N 3.46W
Leross Canada 75 51.17N103.53W
Le Roy Kans. U.S.A. 83 38.05N 95.38W
Le Roy Mich. U.S.A. 84 44.03N 85.29W
Le Roy N.Y. U.S.A. 76 42.59N 77.59W
Lerwick U.K. 12 60.09N 1.09W
Les Andelys France 15 49.15N 1.25E
Les Cayes Haiti 87 18.15N 73.46W
Leschenault, C. Australia 63 31.50S115.23E
Les Ecrins mtn. France 17 44.50N 6.20E
Leshan China 33 29.30N103.45E
Leshukonskoye Russian Fed. 24 64.55N 45.50E
Lesjaskog Norway 23 62.15N 8.22E
Leskovac Yugo. 19 43.00N 21.56E
Leslie U.S.A. 83 35.50N 92.34W
Lesotho Africa 56 29.00S 28.00E
Lesozavodsk Russian Fed. 31 45.30N133.29E
Les Pieux France 15 49.35N 1.50W
Les Riceys France 15 47.59N 4.22E
Les Sables d'Olonne France 17 46.30N 1.47W
Lessay France 15 49.14N 1.30W
Lesser Antilles is. C. America 87 13.00N 65.00W
Lesser Slave L. Canada 74 55.30N115.25W
Lesser Sunda Is. see Nusa Tenggara is. Indonesia 36
Lessines Belgium 14 50.43N 3.50E
Lesti r. Finland 22 64.04N 23.38E
Le Sueur U.S.A. 82 44.27N 93.54W
Lésvos i. Greece 19 39.10N 26.16E
Leszno Poland 20 51.51N 16.35E
Letchworth U.K. 11 51.58N 0.13W
Lethbridge Canada 72 49.43N112.48W
Lethem Guyana 90 3.18N 59.46W
Leti, Kepulauan is. Indonesia 37 8.20S128.00E
Letiahau r. Botswana 56 21.16S 24.00E
Leticia Colombia 90 4.09S 69.57W
Leting China 32 39.26N118.56E
Letohatchee U.S.A. 85 32.08N 86.30W
Le Tréport France 17 50.04N 1.22E
Letterkenny Rep. of Ire. 13 54.56N 7.45W
Leuk Switz. 15 46.19N 7.38E
Leuser mtn. Indonesia 36 3.50N 97.10E
Leuven Belgium 14 50.53N 4.45E
Leuze Hainaut Belgium 14 50.36N 3.37E
Leuze Namur Belgium 14 50.34N 4.53E
Levanger Norway 22 63.45N 11.19E
Levanto Italy 15 44.10N 9.38E
Levelland U.S.A. 83 33.35N102.23W
Lévêque, C. Australia 62 16.25S123.00E
Le Verdon France 17 45.33N 1.04W
Leverkusen Germany 14 51.02N 6.59E
Levice Slovakia 21 48.13N 18.37E
Levin New Zealand 60 40.37S175.18E
Lévis Canada 77 46.49N 71.11W
Lévka Cyprus 44 35.06N 32.51E
Levkás Greece 19 38.50N 20.41E
Levkás i. Greece 19 38.44N 20.37E
Levkosía Cyprus 44 35.11N 33.23E
Lewes U.K. 11 50.53N 0.02E
Lewes U.S.A. 85 38.47N 75.08W
Lewis i. U.K. 12 58.10N 6.40W
Lewis Pass f. New Zealand 60 42.30S172.15E
Lewisporte Canada 77 49.15N 55.04W

Lewis Range to Loudéac

Lewis Range mts. U.S.A. 80 48.30N113.15W
Lewiston Idaho U.S.A. 80 46.25N117.01W
Lewiston Maine U.S.A. 84 44.06N 70.13W
Lewistown Mont. U.S.A. 80 47.04N109.26W
Lewistown Penn. U.S.A. 84 40.36N 77.31W
Lexington Ky. U.S.A. 85 38.03N 84.30W
Lexington Miss. U.S.A. 83 33.07N 90.03W
Lexington Nebr. U.S.A. 82 40.47N 99.45W
Lexington Oreg. U.S.A. 80 45.27N119.41W
Leyburn U.K. 10 54.19N 1.50W
Leydsdorp R.S.A. 56 23.59S 30.32E
Leyte i. Phil. 37 10.40N124.50E
Lezignan France 17 43.12N 2.46E
Lhari China 41 30.47N 93.24E
Lhasa China 41 29.39N 91.06E
Lhasa He r. China 41 29.21N 90.45E
Lhazê China 41 29.10N 87.45E
Lhazhong China 41 32.02N 86.34E
Lhokseumawe Indonesia 36 5.09N 97.09E
Lhozhag China 41 28.23N 90.49E
Lhuntsi Dzong Bhutan 41 27.39N 91.09E
Lhünzê China 41 28.26N 92.27E
Lhünzhub China 41 30.00N 91.12E
Li Thailand 34 17.50N 98.55E
Liancheng China 33 25.47N116.48E
Liangcheng China 32 40.31N112.29E
Liangdang China 32 33.59N106.23E
Lianjiang Fujian China 33 26.10N119.33E
Lianjiang Guangdong China 33 21.33N110.19E
Lianshan China 33 24.37N112.02E
Lianshui China 32 33.46N119.18E
Lian Xian China 33 24.52N112.27E
Lianyungang China 32 34.36N119.10E
Liaocheng China 32 36.25N115.58E
Liaodong Bandao pen. China 32 40.00N122.20E
Liaodong Wan b. China 32 40.00N121.00E
Liao He r. China 32 40.40N122.20E
Liaoning d. China 32 41.40N121.20E
Liaoyang China 32 41.17N123.13E
Liaoyuan China 32 42.50N125.08E
Liard r. Canada 74 61.51N121.18W
Liāri Pakistan 40 25.41N 66.29E
Liart France 15 49.46N 4.20E
Libby U.S.A. 80 48.23N115.33W
Libenge Zaïre 54 3.39N 18.39E
Liberal U.S.A. 83 37.02N100.55W
Liberdade Brazil 94 22.01S 44.22W
Liberec Czech Republic 20 50.48N 15.05E
Liberia Africa 52 6.30N 9.30W
Liberia Costa Rica 87 10.39N 85.28W
Liberty U.S.A. 83 30.03N 94.47W
Lībīyah, Aş Şaḩrā' al des. Africa 42 24.00N 25.30E
Libo China 33 25.25N107.53E
Libourne France 17 44.55N 0.14W
Libramont Belgium 14 49.56N 5.22E
Libreville Gabon 54 0.25N 9.30E
Libya Africa 51 26.30N 17.00E
Libyan Desert see Lībīyah, Aş Şaḩrā' al a-' al Africa Africa 42
Libyan Plateau see Aḑ Ḑiffah f. Africa 42
Licantén Chile 93 34.59S 72.00W
Licata Italy 18 37.07N 13.58E
Lichfield U.K. 11 52.40N 1.50W
Lichinga Mozambique 55 13.09S 35.17E
Lichtenburg R.S.A. 56 26.08S 26.09E
Lichtenvoorde Neth. 14 51.59N 6.32E
Lichuan Hubei China 33 30.18N108.51E
Lichuan Jiangxi China 33 27.22N116.59E
Lida Belorussia 21 53.50N 25.19E
Lida U.S.A. 80 37.29N117.29W
Lidköping Sweden 23 58.30N 13.10E
Liechtenstein Europe 20 47.08N 9.35E
Liège Belgium 14 50.38N 5.35E
Liège d. Belgium 14 50.32N 5.35E
Lien-Huong Vietnam 34 11.13N108.48E
Lienz Austria 20 46.50N 12.47E
Liepāja Latvia 23 56.31N 21.01E
Lier Belgium 14 51.08N 4.35E
Lierneux Belgium 14 50.18N 5.50E
Liești Romania 21 45.38N 27.32E
Liévin France 14 50.27N 2.49E
Lièvre, Rivière du r. Canada 77 45.31N 75.26W
Liffey r. Rep. of Ire. 13 53.21N 6.14W
Liffré France 15 48.13N 1.30W
Lifou, Île i. N. Cal. 68 20.53S167.13E
Lightning Ridge town Australia 67 29.27S148.00E
Liguria d. Italy 15 42.25N 8.40E
Ligurian Sea Med. Sea 18 43.30N 9.00E
Lihou Reef and Cays Australia 64 17.25S151.40E
Lihue Hawaiian Is. 69 21.59N159.23W
Lihula Estonia 23 58.41N 23.50E
Lijiang China 39 26.50N100.15E
Lijin China 32 37.29N118.16E
Likasi Zaïre 54 10.58S 26.50E
Likati Zaïre 54 3.21N 23.53E
Likona r. Congo 54 0.11N 16.25E
Likouala r. Congo 54 0.51S 17.17E
Liku Niue 68 19.03S169.48W
Lille France 14 50.39N 3.05E
Lille Baelt str. Denmark 23 55.20N 9.45E
Lillebonne France 15 49.31N 0.33E
Lillehammer Norway 23 61.08N 10.30E
Lillers France 14 50.34N 2.29E
Lillesand Norway 23 58.15N 8.24E
Lilleström Norway 23 59.57N 11.05E
Lillhärdal Sweden 23 61.51N 14.04E
Lillooet Canada 74 50.42N121.56W
Lillooet r. Canada 74 49.15N121.57W
Lilongwe Malaŵi 55 13.58S 33.49E
Liloy Phil. 37 8.08N122.40E
Lilydale Australia 66 32.58S139.59E
Lim r. Bosnia-Herzegovina 19 43.45N 19.13E
Lima Peru 90 12.06S 77.03W
Lima r. Portugal 16 41.40N 8.50W
Lima Sweden 23 60.56N 13.26E
Lima Mont. U.S.A. 80 44.38N112.36W
Lima Ohio U.S.A. 84 40.43N 84.06W
Limassol see Lemesós Cyprus 44
Limavady U.K. 13 55.03N 6.57W
Limay r. Argentina 93 39.02S 68.07W
Limbang Malaysia 36 4.50N115.00E
Limbdi India 40 22.34N 71.48E
Limbe Cameroon 53 4.01N 9.12E
Limbourg Belgium 14 50.36N 5.57E
Limburg d. Belgium 14 50.36N 5.57E
Limburg d. Neth. 14 51.15N 5.45E
Limeira Brazil 94 22.34S 47.25W
Limerick Rep. of Ire. 13 52.40N 8.37W
Limerick d. Rep. of Ire. 13 52.40N 8.37W
Limfjorden str. Denmark 23 56.55N 9.10E
Liminka Finland 22 64.49N 25.24E
Limmen Bight Australia 64 14.45S135.40E
Límnos i. Greece 19 39.55N 25.14E
Limoges France 17 45.50N 1.15E
Limogne France 17 44.24N 1.46E
Limón Costa Rica 87 10.00N 83.01W
Limon U.S.A. 80 39.16N103.41W
Limone Piemonte Italy 15 44.12N 7.34E
Limousin d. France 17 45.45N 1.30E
Limpopo r. Mozambique 57 25.14S 33.33E
Linah Saudi Arabia 43 28.48N 43.45E
Linakhamari Russian Fed. 24 69.39N 31.21E
Linares Chile 93 35.51S 71.36W
Linares Mexico 83 24.52N 99.34W
Linares Spain 16 38.05N 3.38W
Lincang China 30 24.00N100.10E
Lincheng China 32 37.26N114.34E
Lincoln Argentina 93 34.55S 61.30W
Lincoln New Zealand 60 43.38S172.29E
Lincoln U.K. 10 53.14N 0.32W
Lincoln Ill. U.S.A. 82 40.10N 89.21W
Lincoln Nebr. U.S.A. 82 40.48N 96.42W
Lincoln N.H. U.S.A. 84 44.03N 71.40W
Lincoln City U.S.A. 80 44.59N124.00W
Lincoln Sea Greenland 96 82.00N 55.00W
Lincolnshire d. U.K. 10 53.14N 0.32W
Lincoln Wolds hills U.K. 10 53.22N 0.08W
Lindeman Group is. Australia 64 20.28S149.05E
Linden U.S.A. 83 32.18N 87.47W
Lindesnes c. Norway 23 58.00N 7.02E
Líndhos Greece 19 36.05N 28.02E
Lindi Tanzania 55 10.00S 39.41E
Lindi r. Zaïre 54 0.30N 25.06E
Lindsay Canada 76 44.21N 78.44W
Lindsay U.S.A. 81 36.12N119.05W
Line Is. Pacific Oc. 69 3.00S155.00W
Linfen China 32 36.07N111.34E
Lingao China 33 19.54N109.40E
Lingayen Phil. 37 16.02N120.14E
Lingbo Sweden 23 61.03N 16.41E
Lingchuan China 33 25.25N110.20E
Lingen Germany 14 52.32N 7.19E
Lingga i. Indonesia 36 0.20S104.30E
Lingling China 33 26.12N111.30E
Lingshan China 33 22.17N109.27E
Lingshui China 33 18.31N110.00E
Linguère Senegal 52 15.22N 15.11W
Linhai China 33 28.49N121.08E
Linhe China 32 40.50N107.30E
Linköping Sweden 23 58.25N 15.37E
Linnhe, Loch U.K. 12 56.35N 5.25W
Linosa i. Italy 18 35.52N 12.50E
Linquan China 32 33.03N115.17E
Linru China 32 34.12N112.45E
Lins Brazil 94 21.40S 49.44W
Linshui China 33 30.18N106.55E
Lintan China 32 34.33N103.40E
Lintao China 32 35.20N104.00E
Linton Ind. U.S.A. 84 39.01N 87.10W
Linton N.Dak. U.S.A. 82 46.16N100.14W
Lintong China 32 34.24N109.13E
Lintorf Germany 14 51.19N 6.50E
Linxe France 17 43.56N 1.10W
Linxi China 32 43.31N118.02E
Linxia China 32 35.30N103.10E
Lin Xian China 32 37.57N110.57E
Linyi Shandong China 32 35.08N118.20E
Linyi Shanxi China 32 35.12N110.45E
Linz Austria 20 48.19N 14.18E
Linz Germany 14 50.34N 7.19E
Lion, Golfe du g. France 17 43.12N 4.15E
Lions, G. of see Lion, Golfe du g. France 17
Liouesso Congo 54 1.12N 15.47E
Lipéité Congo 54 3.09N 17.22E
Lipetsk Russian Fed. 24 52.37N 39.36E
Liphook U.K. 11 51.05N 0.49W
Liping China 33 26.16N109.08E
Lipkany Moldavia 21 48.18N 26.48E
Lipova Romania 21 46.05N 21.40E
Lipovets Ukraine 21 49.11N 29.01E
Lippe r. Germany 14 51.38N 6.37E
Lippstadt Germany 20 51.41N 8.20E
Liptovský Mikuláš Slovakia 21 49.06N 19.37E
Liptrap, C. Australia 67 38.53S145.55E
Lipu China 33 24.28N110.12E
Lira Uganda 55 2.15N 32.55E
Liranga Congo 54 0.43S 17.32E
Liri r. Italy 18 41.12N 13.45E
Liria Spain 16 39.37N 0.35W
Liria Sudan 49 4.38N 32.05E
Lisala Zaïre 54 2.13N 21.37E
Lisboa Portugal 16 38.44N 9.08W
Lisbon see Lisboa Portugal 16
Lisbon U.S.A. 82 46.27N 97.41W
Lisburn U.K. 13 54.30N 6.03W
Lisburne, C. U.S.A. 72 69.00N165.50W
Liscannor B. Rep. of Ire. 13 52.55N 9.24W
Lishi China 32 37.30N111.07E
Lishui China 33 28.28N119.59E
Lisianski i. Hawaiian Is. 68 26.04N173.58W
Lisichansk Ukraine 25 48.53N 38.25E
Lisieux France 15 49.09N 0.14E
Liskeard U.K. 11 50.27N 4.29W
Liski Russian Fed. 25 51.00N 39.30E
Lismore N.S.W. Australia 67 28.48S153.17E
Lismore Vic. Australia 66 37.58S143.22E
Lismore Rep. of Ire. 13 52.08N 7.57W
Liss U.K. 11 51.03N 0.53W
Lisse Neth. 14 52.18N 4.33E
Listowel Rep. of Ire. 13 52.27N 9.30W
Litang China 33 23.09N109.09E
Litang Qu r. China 39 28.09N101.30E
Litchfield Ill. U.S.A. 82 39.11N 89.40W
Litchfield Minn. U.S.A. 82 45.08N 94.31W
Litchfield Nebr. U.S.A. 82 41.09N 99.09W
Lithgow Australia 67 33.30S150.09E
Lithuania Europe 24 55.30N 24.00E
Lititz U.S.A. 85 40.09N 76.18W
Little Andaman i. India 34 10.40N 92.24E
Little Belt Mts. U.S.A. 80 46.45N110.35W
Little Cayman i. Cayman Is. 87 19.40N 80.00W
Little Coco i. Burma 34 13.59N 93.12E
Little Colorado r. U.S.A. 81 36.11N111.48W
Little Current r. Canada 76 50.00N 84.35W
Little Current town Canada 84 45.58N 81.56W
Little Falls town Minn. U.S.A. 82 45.59N 94.21W
Little Falls town N.Y. U.S.A. 84 43.03N 74.52W
Littlefield U.S.A. 83 33.55N102.20W
Littlefork U.S.A. 82 48.24N 93.33W
Little Grand Rapids town Canada 75 52.05N 95.29W
Littlehampton U.K. 11 50.48N 0.32W
Little Inagua i. Bahamas 87 21.30N 73.00W
Little Karoo f. R.S.A. 56 33.40S 21.40E
Little Lake town U.S.A. 81 35.58N117.53W
Little Mecatina r. Canada 77 50.28N 59.35W
Little Missouri r. U.S.A. 82 47.30N102.25W
Little Nicobar i. India 39 7.20N 93.40E
Little Ouse r. U.K. 11 52.34N 0.20E
Little Quill L. Canada 75 51.55N104.05W
Little Rann of Kachchh f. India 40 23.25N 71.30E
Little Rock town U.S.A. 83 34.44N 92.15W
Little Smoky r. Canada 74 55.42N117.38W
Littleton U.S.A. 80 39.37N105.01W
Little Topar Australia 66 31.44S142.14E
Liuba China 32 33.37N106.55E
Liucheng China 33 24.39N109.14E
Liuchong He r. China 33 26.50N106.04E
Liuli Tanzania 55 11.07S 34.34E
Liulin China 32 37.26N110.52E
Liuzhou China 33 24.19N109.12E
Livarot France 15 49.01N 0.09E
Live Oak U.S.A. 85 30.19N 82.59W
Livermore, Mt. U.S.A. 81 30.39N104.11W
Liverpool Australia 67 33.57S150.52E
Liverpool Canada 77 44.02N 64.43W
Liverpool U.K. 10 53.25N 3.00W
Liverpool, C. Canada 73 73.38N 78.06W
Liverpool B. U.K. 10 53.30N 3.10W
Liverpool Range mts. Australia 67 31.45S150.45E
Livingston U.K. 12 55.54N 3.31W
Livingston Mont. U.S.A. 80 45.40N110.34W
Livingston Tex. U.S.A. 83 30.43N 94.56W
Livingstone see Maramba Zambia 56
Livingstonia Malaŵi 55 10.35S 34.10E
Livo r. Finland 22 65.24N 26.48E
Livorno Italy 18 43.33N 10.18E
Liwale Tanzania 55 9.47S 38.00E
Liwan Sudan 49 4.55N 35.41E
Li Xian Gansu China 32 34.11N105.02E
Li Xian Hunan China 33 29.38N111.45E
Liyujiang China 33 25.59N113.12E
Lizard U.K. 11 49.58N 5.12W
Lizard I. Australia 64 14.39S145.28E
Lizard Pt. U.K. 11 49.57N 5.15W
Ljubljana Slovenia 18 46.04N 14.28E
Ljugarn Sweden 23 57.19N 18.42E
Ljungan r. Sweden 23 62.19N 17.23E
Ljungby Sweden 23 56.50N 13.56E
Ljungdalen Sweden 22 62.54N 12.45E
Ljusdal Sweden 23 61.50N 16.05E
Ljusnan r. Sweden 23 61.12N 17.08E
Ljusne Sweden 23 61.13N 17.08E
Llandeilo U.K. 11 51.54N 4.00W
Llandovery U.K. 11 51.59N 3.49W
Llandrindod Wells U.K. 11 52.15N 3.23W
Llandudno U.K. 10 53.19N 3.49W
Llanelli U.K. 11 51.41N 4.11W
Llanes Spain 16 43.25N 4.45W
Llangadfan U.K. 11 52.41N 3.28W
Llangollen U.K. 10 52.58N 3.10W
Llanidloes U.K. 11 52.28N 3.31W
Llanos f. S. America 90 7.30N 70.00W
Llanwrtyd Wells U.K. 11 52.06N 3.39W
Lleida see Lérida Spain 16
Llerena Spain 16 38.14N 6.00W
Lloret de Mar Spain 16 41.41N 2.53E
Lloret de Mar Spain 16 41.41N 2.53E
Lloydminster Canada 75 53.17N110.00W
Loange r. Zaïre 54 4.18S 20.05E
Lobatse Botswana 56 25.12S 25.39E
Löbau Germany 20 51.05N 14.40E
Lobaye r. C.A.R. 53 3.40N 18.35E
Lobería Argentina 93 38.08S 58.48W
Lobito Angola 54 12.20S 13.34E
Lobonäs Sweden 23 61.33N 15.20E
Lobos Argentina 93 35.10S 59.05W
Locarno Switz. 20 46.10N 8.48E
Lochboisdale town U.K. 12 57.09N 7.19W
Lochem Neth. 14 52.10N 6.25E
Loches France 17 47.08N 1.00E
Lochgilphead U.K. 12 56.02N 5.26W
Lochinver U.K. 12 58.09N 5.15W
Lochmaddy town U.K. 12 57.36N 7.10W
Lochnagar mtn. U.K. 12 56.57N 3.15W
Lochranza U.K. 12 55.42N 5.18W
Loch Raven Resr. U.S.A. 85 39.27N 76.36W
Lochy, Loch U.K. 12 56.58N 4.55W
Lock Australia 66 33.34S135.46E
Lockeport Canada 77 43.42N 65.07W
Lockerbie U.K. 12 55.07N 3.21W
Lockhart Australia 67 35.16S146.42E
Lockhart U.S.A. 83 29.53N 97.41W
Lockhart, L. Australia 63 33.27S119.00E
Lockhart River town Australia 64 12.58S143.29E
Lock Haven U.S.A. 84 41.08N 77.27W
Lockport U.S.A. 84 43.11N 78.39W
Loc Ninh Vietnam 34 11.51N106.35E
Lodalskåpa mtn. Norway 23 61.47N 7.13E
Loddon r. Australia 66 35.40S143.59E
Lodeynoye Pole Russian Fed. 24 60.43N 33.30E
Lodge Grass U.S.A. 80 45.19N107.22W
Lodhrān Pakistan 40 29.32N 71.38E
Lodi Italy 15 45.19N 9.30E
Lodi U.S.A. 80 38.08N121.16W
Lodja Zaïre 54 3.29S 23.33E
Lodwar Kenya 55 3.06N 35.38E
Łódź Poland 21 51.49N 19.28E
Loei Thailand 34 17.32N101.34E
Lofoten Vesterålen is. Norway 22 68.15N 13.50E
Log Russian Fed. 25 49.28N 43.51E
Loga Niger 53 13.40N 3.15E
Logan N.Mex. U.S.A. 81 35.22N103.25W
Logan Utah U.S.A. 80 41.44N111.50W
Logan, Mt. Canada 74 60.34N140.24W
Logansport U.S.A. 84 40.45N 86.25W
Loge r. Angola 54 7.52S 13.08E
Logone r. Cameroon / Chad 53 12.10N 15.00E
Logone Occidental d. Chad 53 8.40N 15.50E
Logone Oriental d. Chad 53 8.10N 16.00E
Logoysk Belorussia 21 54.08N 27.42E
Logroño Spain 16 42.28N 2.26W
Lögstör Denmark 23 56.58N 9.15E
Lohārdaga India 41 23.26N 84.41E
Lohāru India 40 28.27N 75.49E
Lohja Finland 23 60.15N 24.05E
Lohjanjärvi l. Finland 23 60.15N 23.55E
Loikaw Burma 34 19.40N 97.17E
Loimaa Finland 23 60.51N 23.03E
Loir r. France 15 47.29N 0.32W
Loire r. France 15 47.18N 2.00W
Loiret d. France 15 47.55N 2.20E
Loir-et-Cher d. France 15 47.30N 1.30E
Loja Ecuador 90 3.59S 79.16W
Loja Spain 16 37.10N 4.09W
Loka Sudan 49 4.16N 31.01E
Loka Zaïre 54 0.20N 17.57E
Löken Norway 23 59.48N 11.29E
Loken tekojärvi resr. Finland 22 67.55N 27.40E
Lokeren Belgium 14 51.06N 3.59E
Lokichar Kenya 55 2.23N 35.39E
Lokitaung Kenya 55 4.15N 35.45E
Lokka Finland 22 67.49N 27.44E
Løkken Denmark 23 57.22N 9.43E
Lökken Norway 22 63.06N 9.43E
Loknya Russian Fed. 24 56.49N 30.00E
Lokoja Nigeria 53 7.49N 6.44E
Lokolo r. Zaïre 54 0.45S 19.36E
Lokoro r. Zaïre 54 1.40S 18.29E
Lol r. Sudan 49 9.11N 29.12E
Lolland i. Denmark 23 54.46N 11.30E
Lom Bulgaria 21 43.49N 23.13E
Lom Norway 23 61.50N 8.33E
Loma U.S.A. 80 47.57N110.30W
Lomami r. Zaïre 54 0.45N 24.10E
Lomas de Zamora Argentina 93 34.46S 58.24W
Lombardia d. Italy 15 45.25N 10.00E
Lombok i. Indonesia 36 8.30S116.20E
Lombok, Selat str. Indonesia 37 8.38S115.40E
Lomé Togo 53 6.10N 1.21E
Lomela Zaïre 54 2.15S 23.15E
Lomela r. Zaïre 54 0.14S 20.45E
Lomié Cameroon 53 3.09N 13.35E
Lomme France 14 50.38N 2.59E
Lommel Belgium 14 51.15N 5.18E
Lomond Canada 74 50.21N112.39W
Lomond, Loch U.K. 12 56.07N 4.36W
Lompoc U.S.A. 81 34.38N120.27W
Łomża Poland 21 53.11N 22.04E
Londinières France 15 49.50N 1.24E
London Canada 76 42.58N 81.15W
London Kiribati 69 1.58N157.28W
London U.K. 11 51.32N 0.06W
Londonderry U.K. 13 55.00N 7.21W
Londonderry d. U.K. 13 55.00N 7.00W
Londonderry, C. Australia 62 13.58S126.55E
Londonderry, Isla i. Chile 93 55.03S 70.40W
Londrina Brazil 92 23.30S 51.13W
Lone Pine U.S.A. 81 36.36N118.04W
Longa r. Angola 54 16.15S 19.07E
Longa, Proliv str. Russian Fed. 29 70.00N178.00E
Long'an China 33 23.11N107.41E
Longarone Italy 15 46.16N 12.18E
Long Beach town Calif. U.S.A. 81 33.46N118.11W
Long Beach town N.Y. U.S.A. 85 40.35N 73.41W
Long Branch U.S.A. 85 40.18N 74.00W
Longchamps Belgium 14 50.05N 5.42E
Longchang China 33 29.18N105.20E
Longchuan China 33 24.12N115.25E
Long Creek town U.S.A. 80 44.43N119.06W
Long Eaton U.K. 10 52.54N 1.16W
Longford Rep. of Ire. 13 53.44N 7.48W
Longford d. Rep. of Ire. 13 53.42N 7.45W
Longhua China 32 41.17N117.37E
Long I. Bahamas 87 23.00N 75.00W
Long I. Canada 76 54.55N 79.30W
Long I. U.S.A. 84 40.46N 73.00W
Longido Tanzania 55 2.43S 36.41E
Longiram Indonesia 36 0.05S115.45E
Long Jiang r. China 33 24.12N109.30E
Long L. Canada 76 49.30N 86.50W
Longlac town Canada 76 49.45N 86.25W
Longli China 33 26.29N107.59E
Longlin China 33 24.43N105.26E
Longmont U.S.A. 80 40.10N105.06W
Longnan China 33 24.54N114.47E
Longnawan Indonesia 36 1.54N114.53E
Longniddry U.K. 12 55.58N 2.53W
Long Point B. Canada 76 42.40N 80.14W
Long Pt. Canada 76 42.33N 80.04W
Longquan China 33 28.05N119.07E
Long Range Mts. Nfld. Canada 77 50.00N 57.00W
Long Range Mts. Nfld. Canada 77 48.00N 58.30W
Longreach Australia 64 23.26S144.15E
Longsheng China 33 25.59N110.01E
Longs Peak U.S.A. 80 40.15N105.37W
Longtown U.K. 10 55.01N 2.58W
Longué France 15 47.23N 0.06W
Longueuil Canada 77 45.32N 73.30W
Longuyon France 14 49.27N 5.35E
Longview Tex. U.S.A. 83 32.30N 94.44W
Longview Wash. U.S.A. 80 46.08N122.57W
Longwood St. Helena 95 15.57S 5.42W
Longwy France 14 49.32N 5.46E
Longxi China 32 34.59N104.45E
Long Xian China 32 34.52N106.50E
Long Xuyen Vietnam 34 10.23N105.23E
Longyan China 33 25.10N117.02E
Longzhou China 33 22.24N106.50E
Lonigo Italy 15 45.23N 11.23E
Löningen Germany 14 52.44N 7.46E
Lönsdal Norway 22 66.46N 15.26E
Lonsdale, L. Australia 66 37.05S142.15E
Lons-le-Saunier France 17 46.40N 5.33E
Looc Phil. 37 12.20N122.05E
Looe U.K. 11 50.51N 4.26W
Lookout, C. U.S.A. 85 34.35N 76.32W
Loolmalassin mtn. Tanzania 55 3.00S 35.45E
Loop Head Rep. of Ire. 13 52.33N 9.56W
Lopari Zaïre 49 1.15N 19.59E
Lopari r. Zaïre 54 1.20N 20.22E
Lop Buri Thailand 34 14.49N100.37E
Lopez, C. Gabon 54 0.36S 8.40E
Lopi Congo 54 2.57N 16.47E
Lop Nur l. China 30 40.30N 90.30E
Lopphavet est. Norway 22 70.30N 20.00E
Lopydino Russian Fed. 24 61.10N 52.02E
Lora, Hāmūn-i- l. Pakistan 40 29.20N 64.50E
Lora Creek r. Australia 66 28.10S135.22E
Lorain U.S.A. 84 41.28N 82.11W
Loralai Pakistan 40 30.22N 68.36E
Lorca Spain 16 37.40N 1.41W
Lord Howe I. Pacific Oc. 68 31.28S159.09E
Lord Howe Rise Pacific Oc. 68 29.00S162.30E
Lordsburg U.S.A. 81 32.21N108.43W
Lorena Brazil 94 22.44S 45.07W
Lorengau P.N.G. 37 2.01S147.15E
Lorenzo Geyres Uruguay 93 32.05S 57.55W
Loreto Brazil 91 7.05S 45.09W
Loreto Italy 18 43.26N 13.36E
Loreto Mexico 81 26.01N111.21W
Lorian Swamp Kenya 55 0.35N 39.40E
Lorient France 17 47.45N 3.21W
Lormes France 15 47.17N 3.49E
Lorne Australia 66 38.34S144.01E
Lorraine d. France 17 49.00N 6.20E
Lorris France 15 47.53N 2.31E
Lorup Germany 14 52.58N 7.39E
Los Alamos Mexico 83 28.40N103.30W
Los Alamos U.S.A. 81 35.53N106.19W
Los Andes Chile 93 32.50S 70.37W
Los Angeles Chile 93 37.28S 72.21W
Los Angeles U.S.A. 78 34.00N118.17W
Los Bajios Mexico 81 28.31N108.25W
Los Banos U.S.A. 80 37.04N120.51W
Los Blancos Argentina 92 23.40S 62.35W
Los Blancos Spain 16 37.37N 0.48W
Los Canarreos, Archipiélago de Cuba 87 21.40N 82.30W
Los Herreras Mexico 83 25.55N 99.24W
Lošinj i. Croatia 18 44.36N 14.20E
Losinovka Ukraine 21 50.50N 31.57E
Los Llanos de Aridane Canary Is. 95 28.39N 17.54W
Los Lunas U.S.A. 81 34.48N106.44W
Los Mochis Mexico 86 25.45N108.57W
Los Olivos U.S.A. 81 34.40N120.06W
Los Roques is. Venezuela 90 12.00N 67.00W
Lossiemouth U.K. 12 57.43N 3.18W
Lost Cabin U.S.A. 80 43.19N107.36W
Los Teques Venezuela 90 10.25N 67.01W
Los Vilos Chile 92 31.55S 71.31W
Lot r. France 17 44.17N 0.22E
Lota Chile 93 37.05S 73.10W
Lothian d. U.K. 12 55.50N 3.00W
Lotoi r. Zaïre 54 1.30S 18.30E
Lotsani r. Botswana 56 22.42S 28.11E
Lötschberg Tunnel Switz. 17 46.25N 7.53E
Lotuke mtn. Sudan 49 4.07N 33.48E
Louang Namtha Laos 34 20.57N101.25E
Louangphrabang Laos 34 19.53N102.10E
Loubomo Congo 54 4.09S 12.40E
Loudéac France 17 48.11N 2.45W

Loudima to **Majuba Hill**

Loudima Congo **54** 4.06S 13.05E
Loué France **15** 48.00N 0.09W
Louga Senegal **52** 15.37N 16.13W
Loughborough U.K. **10** 52.47N 1.11W
Loughrea Rep. of Ire. **13** 53.12N 8.35W
Loughros More B. Rep. of Ire. **13** 54.48N 8.32W
Louisburgh Rep. of Ire. **13** 53.46N 9.49W
Louiseville Canada **77** 46.14N 72.56W
Louisiade Archipelago *is.* P.N.G. **64** 11.00S 153.00E
Louisiana *d.* U.S.A. **83** 30.60N 92.30W
Louis Trichardt R.S.A. **56** 23.03S 29.54E
Louisville Ky. U.S.A. **84** 38.13N 85.48W
Louisville Miss. U.S.A. **83** 33.07N 89.03W
Louis XIV, Pointe *c.* Canada **76** 54.35N 79.50W
Loukhi Russian Fed. **24** 66.05N 33.04E
Loukouo Congo **54** 3.38S 14.39E
Loulé Portugal **16** 37.08N 8.02W
Loum Cameroon **53** 4.46N 9.45E
Lourches France **14** 50.19N 3.20E
Lourdes France **17** 43.06N 0.02W
Louth Australia **67** 30.34S 145.09E
Louth *d.* Rep. of Ire. **13** 53.55N 6.30W
Louth U.K. **10** 53.23N 0.00
Louviers France **15** 49.13N 1.10E
Louvigné-du-Désert France **15** 48.29N 1.08W
Lövånger Sweden **22** 64.22N 21.18E
Lovat *r.* Russian Fed. **24** 58.06N 31.37E
Lovech Bulgaria **19** 43.08N 24.44E
Loveland U.S.A. **80** 40.24N 105.05W
Lovell U.S.A. **80** 44.50N 108.24W
Lovelock U.S.A. **80** 40.11N 118.28W
Love Point *town* U.S.A. **85** 39.02N 76.18W
Lovere Italy **15** 45.49N 10.04E
Lovington U.S.A. **83** 32.57N 103.21W
Lovoi *r.* Zaïre **55** 8.14S 26.40E
Lovozero Russian Fed. **24** 68.01N 35.08E
Lovrin Romania **21** 45.58N 20.48E
Lovua *r.* Zaïre **54** 6.08S 20.35E
Lowa Zaïre **54** 1.24S 25.51E
Lowa *r.* Zaïre **54** 1.25S 25.55E
Lowell U.S.A. **84** 42.39N 71.18W
Lower Arrow L. Canada **74** 49.40N 118.05W
Lower California *pen.* see Baja California *pen.* Mexico **86**
Lower Egypt see Mişr Baḩrī *f.* Egypt **44**
Lower Hutt New Zealand **60** 41.13S 174.55E
Lower Lough Erne U.K. **13** 54.28N 7.48W
Lower Post Canada **74** 59.55N 128.30W
Lower Red L. U.S.A. **82** 48.00N 94.50W
Lowestoft U.K. **11** 52.29N 1.44E
Lowgar *d.* Afghan. **40** 34.10N 69.20E
Łowicz Poland **21** 52.06N 19.55E
Lowrah *r.* Afghan. see Pishīn Lora *r.* Pakistan **40**
Loxton Australia **66** 34.38S 140.38E
Loyalty Is. see Loyauté, Îles *is.* N. Cal. **68**
Loyauté, Îles *is.* N. Cal. **68** 21.00S 167.00E
Loyoro Uganda **55** 3.22N 34.16E
Loznica Yugo. **19** 44.32N 19.13E
Lua *r.* Zaïre **54** 2.45N 18.28E
Luabo Mozambique **57** 18.30S 36.10E
Luachimo Angola **54** 7.25S 20.43E
Lualaba *r.* Zaïre **54** 0.18N 25.32E
Luama *r.* Zaïre **55** 4.45S 26.55E
Luampa Zambia **54** 15.04S 24.20E
Lu'an China **33** 31.47N 116.30E
Luancheng Guang. Zhuang. China **33** 22.48N 108.55E
Luancheng Hebei China **32** 37.53N 114.39E
Luanda Angola **54** 8.50S 13.20E
Luanda *d.* Angola **54** 9.00S 13.20E
Luando Game Res. Angola **54** 11.00S 17.45E
Luanginga *r.* Zambia **54** 15.11S 23.05E
Luangwa *r.* Zambia **55** 15.32S 30.28E
Luan He *r.* China **32** 39.25N 119.10E
Luanping China **32** 40.55N 117.17E
Luanshya Zambia **55** 13.09S 28.24E
Luan Xian China **32** 39.45N 118.44E
Luapula *r.* Zambia **55** 9.25S 28.36E
Luarca Spain **16** 43.33N 6.31W
Luau Angola **54** 10.41S 22.09E
Lubalo Angola **54** 9.13S 19.21E
Lubango Angola **54** 14.52S 13.30E
Lubao Zaïre **54** 5.19S 25.43E
Lubbock U.S.A. **83** 33.35N 101.51W
Lubeck Australia **66** 36.47S 142.38E
Lübeck Germany **20** 53.52N 10.40E
Lubefu *r.* Zaïre **54** 4.05S 23.00E
Lubenka Kazakhstan **25** 50.22N 54.13E
Lubersac France **17** 45.27N 1.24E
Lubia Angola **54** 11.01S 17.06E
Lubika Zaïre **55** 7.50S 29.12E
Lubilash *r.* Zaïre **54** 4.59S 23.25E
Lubin Poland **20** 51.24N 16.13E
Lublin Poland **21** 51.18N 22.31E
Lubliniec Poland **21** 50.40N 18.41E
Lubny Ukraine **25** 50.01N 33.00E
Lubudi *r.* K.Occidental Zaïre **54** 4.00S 21.23E
Lubudi Zaïre **54** 9.57S 25.59E
Lubudi *r.* Shaba Zaïre **54** 9.13S 25.40E
Lubumbashi Zaïre **55** 11.44S 27.29E
Lubutu Zaïre **54** 0.48S 26.19E
Lucas González Argentina **93** 32.25S 59.33W
Lucca Italy **15** 43.50N 10.29E
Luce B. U.K. **12** 54.45N 4.47W
Lucena Phil. **37** 13.56N 121.37E
Lucena Spain **16** 37.25N 4.29W
Lucena del Cid Spain **16** 40.09N 0.17W
Lučenec Slovakia **21** 48.20N 19.40E
Lucera Italy **18** 41.30N 15.20E
Lucerne U.S.A. **80** 48.12N 120.36W
Lucero Mexico **81** 30.49N 106.30W
Lucin U.S.A. **80** 41.22N 113.55W
Lucindale Australia **66** 36.59S 140.25E
Lucira Angola **54** 13.51S 12.31E
Luckeesarai India **41** 25.11N 86.05E
Luckenwalde Germany **20** 52.05N 13.11E
Lucknow India **41** 26.51N 80.55E
Lucy Creek *town* Australia **64** 22.25S 136.20E
Lüda see Dalian China **32**
Lüdenscheid Germany **14** 51.13N 7.36E
Lüderitz Namibia **56** 26.37S 15.09E
Ludhiāna India **40** 30.55N 75.51E
Lüdinghausen Germany **14** 51.46N 7.27E
Ludington U.S.A. **84** 43.58N 86.27W
Ludlow U.K. **11** 52.23N 2.42W
Ludogorie *mts.* Bulgaria **21** 43.45N 27.00E
Luduş Romania **21** 46.29N 24.05E
Ludvika Sweden **23** 60.09N 15.11E
Ludwigsburg Germany **20** 48.53N 9.11E
Ludwigshafen Germany **20** 49.29N 8.27E
Luebo Zaïre **54** 5.16S 21.27E
Luena Angola **54** 11.46S 19.55E
Luena *r.* Angola **54** 12.30S 22.37E
Luena Zaïre **54** 9.27S 25.47E
Luena Zambia **55** 10.40S 30.21E
Luena *r.* Zambia **54** 14.47S 23.05E
Luengue *r.* Angola **54** 16.58S 21.15E
Luenha *r.* Mozambique **57** 16.29S 33.40E
Lüeyang China **32** 33.20N 106.03E
Lufeng China **33** 23.01N 115.35E
Lufira *r.* Zaïre **54** 8.15S 26.30E
Lufkin U.S.A. **79** 31.21N 94.47W
Luga Russian Fed. **24** 58.42N 29.49E
Lugano Switz. **15** 46.01N 8.58E
Lugano, Lago di *l.* Switz./Italy **15** 46.00N 9.00E
Lugansk Ukraine **25** 48.35N 39.20E
Luganville Vanuatu **68** 15.32S 167.08E
Lugela Mozambique **57** 16.25S 36.42E
Lugenda *r.* Mozambique **55** 11.23S 38.30E
Luginy Ukraine **21** 51.05N 28.21E
Lugnaquilla Mtn. Rep. of Ire. **13** 52.58N 6.28W
Lugo Italy **15** 44.25N 11.54E
Lugo Spain **16** 43.00N 7.33W
Lugoj Romania **21** 45.42N 21.56E
Luiana Angola **54** 17.08S 22.59E
Luiana *r.* Angola **54** 17.28S 23.02E
Luilaka *r.* Zaïre **54** 0.15S 19.00E
Luilu *r.* Zaïre **54** 6.22S 23.53E
Luino Italy **15** 46.00N 8.44E
Luiro *r.* Finland **22** 67.18N 27.28E
Luisa Zaïre **54** 7.15S 22.27E
Lujiang China **33** 31.14N 117.17E
Lukala Zaïre **54** 5.23S 13.02E
Lukanga Swamp *f.* Zambia **55** 14.15S 27.30E
Lukenie *r.* Zaïre **54** 2.43S 18.12E
Lukka Sudan **48** 14.33N 23.42E
Łuków Poland **21** 51.56N 22.23E
Lukoyanov Russian Fed. **24** 55.03N 44.29E
Lukuga *r.* Zaïre **55** 5.37S 26.58E
Lukula *r.* Zaïre **54** 4.15S 17.59E
Lukulu Zambia **54** 14.35S 23.25E
Lukumbule Tanzania **55** 11.34S 37.24E
Lule *r.* Sweden **22** 65.35N 22.03E
Luleå Sweden **22** 65.34N 22.10E
Lüleburgaz Turkey **19** 41.25N 27.23E
Lüliang Shan *mts.* China **32** 37.00N 111.20E
Lulonga *r.* Zaïre **54** 0.42N 18.26E
Lulu *r.* Zaïre **54** 1.18N 23.42E
Lulua *r.* Zaïre **54** 5.03S 21.07E
Lumai Angola **54** 13.13S 21.13E
Lumajangdong Co *l.* China **41** 34.02N 81.40E
Lumbala Kaquengue Angola **54** 12.37S 22.33E
Lumbala N'guimbo Angola **54** 14.02S 21.35E
Lumberton Miss. U.S.A. **83** 31.00N 89.27W
Lumberton N.Mex. U.S.A. **80** 36.55N 106.56W
Lumsden New Zealand **60** 45.44S 168.26E
Lūnāvāda India **40** 23.08N 73.37E
Lund Sweden **23** 55.42N 13.11E
Lund Nev. U.S.A. **80** 38.52N 115.00W
Lund Utah U.S.A. **80** 38.01N 113.28W
Lunda Norte *d.* Angola **54** 8.30S 19.00E
Lunda Sul *d.* Angola **54** 11.00S 20.00E
Lundazi Zambia **55** 12.19S 33.11E
Lundy *i.* U.K. **11** 51.10N 4.41W
Lune *r.* U.K. **10** 54.03N 2.49W
Lüneburg Germany **20** 53.15N 10.24E
Lünen Germany **14** 51.37N 7.31E
Lunéville France **17** 48.36N 6.30E
Lunga *r.* Zambia **54** 14.28S 26.27E
Lunge Angola **54** 12.13S 16.07E
Lunggar China **41** 31.10N 84.01E
Lungwebungu *r.* Zambia **54** 14.20S 23.15E
Lūni India **40** 26.00N 73.00E
Lūni *r.* India **40** 24.41N 71.15E
Luninets Belorussia **21** 52.18N 26.50E
Luning U.S.A. **80** 38.30N 118.10W
Lūnkaransar India **40** 28.32N 73.50E
Luocheng China **33** 24.47N 108.54E
Luodian China **33** 25.29N 106.39E
Luoding China **33** 22.44N 111.32E
Luofo Zaïre **55** 0.12S 29.15E
Luogosanto Italy **18** 41.02N 9.12E
Luohe China **32** 33.30N 114.04E
Luo He *r.* China **32** 34.40N 110.15E
Luonan China **32** 34.06N 110.10E
Luoyang China **32** 34.48N 112.25E
Lupilichi Mozambique **55** 11.45S 35.15E
Luquan China **39** 25.35N 102.30E
Lūrah *r.* Afghan. **40** 31.20N 65.45E
Lure France **17** 47.42N 6.30E
Lurgan U.K. **13** 54.28N 6.21W
Lurio Mozambique **55** 13.30S 40.30E
Lurio *r.* Mozambique **55** 13.32S 40.31E
Lusaka Zambia **55** 15.20S 28.14E
Lusambo Zaïre **54** 4.59S 23.26E
Luscar Canada **74** 53.05N 117.26W
Lu Shan *mtn.* China **32** 36.18N 118.03E
Lüshi China **32** 34.04N 111.02E
Lushnje Albania **19** 40.56N 19.42E
Lushoto Tanzania **55** 4.48S 38.20E
Lüshun China **32** 38.42N 121.15E
Lusk U.S.A. **80** 42.46N 104.27W
Luton U.K. **11** 51.53N 0.25W
Lutsk Ukraine **21** 50.42N 25.15E
Lutterworth U.K. **11** 52.28N 1.12W
Luud *r.* Somali Rep. **45** 10.25N 51.05E
Luuq Somali Rep. **55** 3.56N 42.32E
Luverne U.S.A. **82** 43.39N 96.13W
Luvua *r.* Zaïre **55** 6.45S 27.00E
Luwegu *r.* Tanzania **55** 8.30S 37.28E
Luwingu Zambia **55** 10.13S 30.05E
Luxembourg *d.* Belgium **14** 49.58N 5.30E
Luxembourg Europe **14** 49.50N 6.15E
Luxembourg *town* Lux. **14** 49.37N 6.08E
Luxi China **33** 28.17N 110.10E
Luxor see Al Uqşur Egypt **42**
Luza Russian Fed. **24** 60.41N 47.12E
Luza *r.* Russian Fed. **24** 60.45N 46.25E
Luzarches France **15** 49.07N 2.25E
Luzern Switz. **20** 47.03N 8.17E
Luzhai China **33** 24.29N 109.29E
Luzhou China **33** 28.48N 105.23E
Luziânia Brazil **91** 16.18S 47.57W
Luzon *i.* Phil. **37** 17.50N 121.00E
Luzon Str. Pacific Oc. **37** 20.20N 122.00E
Lvov Ukraine **21** 49.50N 24.00E
Lyantonde Uganda **55** 0.26S 31.08E
Lybster U.K. **12** 58.18N 3.18W
Lycksele Sweden **22** 64.36N 18.40E
Lydenburg R.S.A. **56** 25.06S 30.27E
Lyell I. Canada **74** 52.40N 131.35W
Lyme B. U.K. **11** 50.40N 2.55W
Lyme Regis U.K. **11** 50.44N 2.57W
Lymington U.K. **11** 50.46N 1.32W
Lyna *r.* Poland **21** 54.37N 21.14E
Lynchburg U.S.A. **85** 37.24N 79.10W
Lynden Canada **76** 43.14N 80.09W
Lyndhurst Australia **66** 30.19S 138.24E
Lyndonville U.S.A. **76** 43.19N 78.23W
Lyngdal Norway **23** 58.08N 7.05E
Lyngen Norway **22** 69.36N 20.10E
Lyngen *est.* Norway **22** 69.35N 20.20E
Lynn U.S.A. **84** 42.28N 70.57W
Lynn Canal U.S.A. **74** 58.38N 135.08W
Lynn Lake *town* Canada **75** 56.51N 101.03W
Lynton U.K. **11** 51.14N 3.50W
Lynx Canada **76** 50.08N 85.55W
Lyon France **17** 45.46N 4.50E
Lyons Australia **66** 30.34S 133.50E
Lyons *r.* Australia **62** 25.02S 115.09E
Lysefjorden *est.* Norway **23** 59.00N 6.14E
Lysekil Sweden **23** 58.16N 11.26E
Lysva Russian Fed. **24** 58.07N 57.49E
Lysyanka Ukraine **21** 49.16N 30.49E
Lysyye Gory Russian Fed. **25** 51.32N 44.48E
Lytham St. Anne's U.K. **10** 53.45N 3.01W
Lyubar Ukraine **21** 49.58N 27.41E
Lyubech Ukraine **21** 51.42N 30.41E
Lyubertsy Russian Fed. **24** 55.38N 37.58E
Lyubeshov Ukraine **21** 51.42N 25.32E
Lyushcha Belorussia **21** 52.28N 26.41E

M

Ma *r.* Vietnam **33** 19.48N 105.55E
Ma, Oued el- *wadi* Mauritania **50** 24.30N 9.10W
Maamakeogh *mtn.* Rep. of Ire. **13** 54.17N 9.29W
Maamturk Mts. Rep. of Ire. **13** 53.32N 9.42W
Ma'ān Jordan **44** 30.11N 35.43E
Ma'anshan China **33** 31.47N 118.33E
Maarianhamina Finland **23** 60.06N 19.57E
Maas *r.* Neth. **14** 51.44N 4.42E
Maaseik Belgium **14** 51.08N 5.48E
Maassluis Neth. **14** 51.58N 4.12E
Maastricht Neth. **14** 50.51N 5.42E
Maave Mozambique **57** 21.06S 34.48E
Maaza Plateau Egypt **44** 27.39N 31.45E
Mabalane Mozambique **57** 23.49S 32.36E
Mablethorpe U.K. **10** 53.21N 0.14E
Mabrouk Mali **52** 19.29N 1.15W
Macá *mtn.* Chile **93** 45.06S 73.12W
Macaé Brazil **94** 22.21S 41.48W
Macalister *r.* Australia **67** 37.55S 146.50E
Macapá Brazil **91** 0.04N 51.04W
Macarthur Australia **66** 38.01S 142.01E
Macau Asia **33** 22.11N 113.33E
Macau Brazil **91** 5.05S 36.37W
Macclesfield U.K. **10** 53.16N 2.09W
Macdiarmid Canada **76** 49.27N 88.08W
Macdoel U.S.A. **80** 41.50N 122.00W
Macdonald, L. Australia **62** 23.30S 129.00E
Macdonnell Ranges *mts.* Australia **64** 23.45S 133.20E
Macduff U.K. **12** 57.40N 2.29W
Macedon, Mt. Australia **67** 37.27S 144.34E
Macedonia Europe **19** 41.35N 21.30E
Maceió Brazil **91** 9.40S 35.44W
Macenta Guinea **52** 8.31N 9.32W
Macerata Italy **18** 43.18N 13.30E
MacFarlane *r.* Canada **75** 59.12N 107.58W
Macfarlane, L. Australia **66** 31.55S 136.42E
Macgillycuddy's Reeks *mts.* Rep. of Ire. **13** 52.00N 9.43W
Machado Brazil **94** 21.39S 45.33W
Machala Ecuador **90** 3.20S 79.57W
Machattie, L. Australia **64** 24.50S 139.48E
Machece Mozambique **57** 19.17S 35.33E
Macheke Zimbabwe **57** 18.08S 31.49E
Macheng China **33** 31.11N 115.02E
Machevna Russian Fed. **29** 60.46N 171.40E
Machias U.S.A. **84** 44.43N 67.28W
Machichi *r.* Canada **75** 57.03N 92.06W
Machida Japan **35** 35.32N 139.27E
Machilipatnam India **39** 16.13N 81.12E
Machiques Venezuela **90** 10.04N 72.37W
Machiya *r.* Japan **35** 35.01N 136.42E
Machrihanish U.K. **12** 55.25N 5.44W
Machynlleth U.K. **11** 52.35N 3.51W
Maciá Argentina **93** 32.11S 59.25W
Macia Mozambique **57** 25.03S 33.10E
Macintyre *r.* Australia **67** 28.50S 150.50E
Mackay Australia **64** 21.09S 149.11E
MacKay U.S.A. **80** 43.55N 113.37W
Mackay, L. Australia **62** 22.30S 149.10E
Mackenzie *r.* Australia **64** 22.48S 149.15E
Mackenzie *r.* Canada **72** 69.20N 134.00W
Mackenzie King I. Canada **72** 77.30N 112.00W
Mackenzie Mts. Canada **72** 64.00N 130.00W
Mackinaw City U.S.A. **84** 45.47N 84.43W
Mackinnon Road *town* Kenya **55** 3.50S 39.03E
Macklin Canada **75** 52.20N 109.56W
Macksville Australia **67** 30.43S 152.55E
Maclean Australia **65** 29.27S 153.14E
Maclear R.S.A. **56** 31.04S 28.21E
Macleay *r.* Australia **67** 30.52S 153.01E
MacLeod, L. Australia **62** 24.10S 113.35E
Maçobere Mozambique **57** 21.14S 32.50E
Macomer Italy **18** 40.16N 8.45E
Mâcon France **17** 46.18N 4.50E
Macon Ga. U.S.A. **85** 32.49N 83.37W
Macon Mo. U.S.A. **82** 39.44N 92.28W
Macquarie *r.* Australia **67** 30.07S 147.24E
Macquarie, L. Australia **67** 33.05S 151.35E
Macquarie-Balleny Ridge Pacific Oc. **68** 58.00S 160.00E
Macquarie I. Pacific Oc. **68** 54.29S 158.58E
Macquarie Marshes Australia **67** 30.50S 147.32E
MacRobertson Land *f.* Antarctica **96** 69.30S 64.00E
Macroom Rep. of Ire. **13** 51.54N 8.58W
Macumba *r.* Australia **65** 27.55S 137.15E
Ma'dabā Jordan **44** 31.44N 35.48E
Madagascar Africa **57** 17.00S 46.00E
Madang P.N.G. **37** 5.14S 145.45E
Madaoua Niger **53** 14.05N 6.27E
Mādārīpur Bangla. **41** 23.10N 90.12E
Madawaska U.S.A. **84** 47.21N 68.20W
Madeira *r.* Brazil **90** 3.20S 59.00W
Madeira *i.* Madeira Is. **95** 32.45N 17.00W
Madeira, Arquipélago da *is.* Atlantic Oc. **95** 32.45N 17.00W
Madeira Is. see Madeira, Arquipélago da *is.* Atlantic Oc. **95**
Madeleine, Îles de la *is.* Canada **77** 47.20N 61.50W
Madera U.S.A. **80** 36.57N 120.03W
Madera, Sierra de la *mts.* Mexico **81** 30.20N 109.00W
Madgaon India **38** 15.26N 73.50E
Madhubani India **41** 26.22N 86.05E
Madhupur India **41** 24.16N 86.39E
Madhya Pradesh *d.* India **41** 23.30N 78.30E
Madibira Tanzania **55** 8.13S 34.47E
Madigan G. Australia **66** 28.55S 137.48E
Madill U.S.A. **83** 34.06N 96.46W
Madīnat ash Sha'b Yemen **45** 12.50N 44.56E
Madison Fla. U.S.A. **79** 30.29N 83.39W
Madison Ind. U.S.A. **84** 38.46N 85.22W
Madison N.J. U.S.A. **85** 40.46N 74.25W
Madison S.Dak. U.S.A. **82** 44.00N 97.07W
Madison Tenn. U.S.A. **85** 36.16N 86.44W
Madison Wisc. U.S.A. **82** 43.05N 89.22W
Madison W.Va. U.S.A. **85** 38.03N 81.50W
Madison Junction U.S.A. **80** 44.39N 110.51W
Madisonville Ky. U.S.A. **85** 37.20N 87.30W
Madisonville Tex. U.S.A. **83** 30.57N 95.55W
Madiun Indonesia **37** 7.37S 111.33E
Madoc Canada **76** 44.30N 77.28W
Mado Gashi Kenya **55** 0.40N 39.11E
Madoi China **30** 34.28N 98.56E
Madonna di Campiglio Italy **15** 46.14N 10.49E
Madrakah, Ra's al *c.* Oman **38** 19.00N 57.50E
Madras India **39** 13.05N 80.18E
Madras U.S.A. **80** 44.38N 121.08W
Madre, Laguna *b.* Mexico **83** 25.00N 97.40W
Madre, Laguna *b.* U.S.A. **83** 27.00N 97.35W
Madre, Sierra *mts.* Mexico/Guatemala **86** 15.20N 92.20W
Madre de Dios *r.* Bolivia **90** 10.24S 65.30W
Madre del Sur, Sierra *mts.* Mexico **86** 17.00N 100.00W
Madre Occidental, Sierra *mts.* Mexico **81** 25.00N 105.00W
Madre Oriental, Sierra *mts.* Mexico **83** 28.10N 102.10W
Madrid Spain **16** 40.25N 3.43W
Madrid *d.* Spain **16** 40.45N 3.40W
Madukani Tanzania **55** 3.57S 35.49E
Madura *i.* Indonesia **37** 7.02S 113.22E
Madurai India **39** 9.55N 78.07E
Mae Klong *r.* Thailand **34** 13.21N 100.00E
Mae Sot Thailand **34** 16.40N 98.35E
Maestra, Sierra *mts.* Cuba **87** 20.10N 76.30W
Maevatanana Madagascar **57** 16.56S 46.49E
Maewo *i.* Vanuatu **68** 15.10S 168.10E
Mafeking Canada **75** 52.43N 100.59W
Mafeteng Lesotho **56** 29.51S 27.13E
Maffra Australia **67** 37.58S 146.59E
Mafia I. Tanzania **55** 7.50S 39.50E
Mafikeng R.S.A. **56** 25.52S 25.36E
Mafra Portugal **16** 38.56N 9.20W
Magadan Russian Fed. **29** 59.38N 150.50E
Magadi Kenya **55** 1.53S 36.18E
Magallanes, Estrecho de *str.* Chile **93** 53.00S 71.00W
Magalluf Spain **16** 39.30N 2.31E
Magangué Colombia **90** 9.14N 74.46W
Magazine U.S.A. **83** 35.10N 93.40W
Magburaka Sierra Leone **52** 8.44N 11.57W
Magdalena Argentina **93** 35.04S 57.32W
Magdalena Bolivia **92** 13.50S 64.08W
Magdalena *r.* Colombia **90** 10.56N 74.58W
Magdalena Mexico **81** 30.38N 110.59W
Magdalena, Isla *i.* Chile **93** 44.42S 73.10W
Magdalena, Llano de la *f.* Mexico **81** 24.55N 111.40W
Magdalene *mtn.* Malaysia **36** 4.25N 117.55E
Magdeburg Germany **20** 52.08N 11.36E
Magé Brazil **94** 22.37S 43.03W
Magee U.S.A. **83** 31.52N 89.44W
Magelang Indonesia **37** 7.28S 110.11E
Magellan's Str. see Magallanes, Estrecho de *str.* Chile **93**
Magenta Italy **15** 45.28N 8.53E
Magenta, L. Australia **63** 33.26S 119.10E
Mageröya *i.* Norway **22** 71.03N 25.45E
Maggiorasca, Monte *mtn.* Italy **15** 44.33N 9.29E
Maggiore, Lago *l.* Italy **15** 46.00N 8.40E
Maghâghah Egypt **44** 28.39N 30.50E
Magherafelt U.K. **13** 54.45N 6.38W
Magna U.S.A. **80** 40.42N 112.06W
Magnetic I. Australia **64** 19.08S 146.50E
Magnitogorsk Russian Fed. **24** 53.28N 59.06E
Magnolia Ark. U.S.A. **83** 33.16N 93.14W
Magnolia Miss. U.S.A. **83** 31.09N 90.28W
Magnolia Tex. U.S.A. **83** 30.13N 95.45W
Magny-en-Vexin France **15** 49.09N 1.47E
Magog Canada **77** 45.16N 72.09W
Magoye Zambia **55** 16.00S 27.38E
Magpie *r.* Canada **77** 50.18N 64.28W
Magrath Canada **74** 49.25N 112.50W
Magude Mozambique **57** 25.01S 32.39E
Magué Mozambique **55** 15.46S 31.42E
Maguse River *town* Canada **75** 61.20N 94.25W
Magwe Burma **34** 20.08N 95.00E
Magwe *d.* Burma **34** 23.00N 95.00E
Mahābād Iran **43** 36.44N 45.44E
Mahābhārat Range *mts.* Nepal **41** 28.00N 84.30E
Mahabo Madagascar **57** 20.23S 44.40E
Mahadday Weyne Somali Rep. **55** 2.58N 45.32E
Mahādeo Hills India **41** 22.15N 78.30E
Mahagi Zaïre **55** 2.16N 30.59E
Mahajamba *r.* Madagascar **57** 15.33S 47.08E
Mahājan India **40** 28.47N 73.50E
Mahajanga Madagascar **57** 15.43S 46.19E
Mahajilo *r.* Madagascar **57** 19.42S 45.22E
Mahalapye Botswana **56** 23.04S 26.47E
Maḩallāt Iran **43** 33.54N 50.28E
Mahānadi India **41** 20.19N 86.45E
Mahānadi *r.* India **39** 20.17N 86.43E
Mahanoro Madagascar **57** 19.54S 48.48E
Mahārājpur India **41** 25.01N 79.44E
Mahārāshtra *d.* India **40** 19.40N 76.00E
Mahāsamund India **41** 21.06N 82.06E
Maha Sarakham Thailand **34** 15.50N 103.47E
Mahavavy *r.* Madagascar **57** 15.57S 45.54E
Mahbés W. Sahara **50** 27.13N 9.44W
Mahd adh Dhahab Saudi Arabia **42** 23.30N 40.52E
Mahdia Guyana **90** 5.10N 59.12W
Mahendraganj India **41** 25.20N 89.45E
Mahenge Tanzania **55** 8.46S 36.38E
Mahi *r.* India **40** 22.30N 72.58E
Mahia Pen. New Zealand **60** 39.10S 177.50E
Mahmūdābād India **41** 27.18N 81.07E
Maḩmūd-e 'Erāqī Afghan. **40** 35.01N 69.20E
Mahnomen U.S.A. **82** 47.19N 96.01W
Maho Sri Lanka **39** 7.49N 80.17E
Mahoba India **41** 25.17N 79.52E
Mahón Spain **16** 39.55N 4.18E
Mahone B. Canada **77** 44.30N 64.15W
Mahroni India **41** 24.35N 78.43E
Mahuva India **40** 21.05N 71.48E
Maiäo *i.* Îs. de la Société **69** 17.23S 150.37W
Maidenhead U.K. **11** 51.32N 0.44W
Maidstone U.K. **11** 51.17N 0.32E
Maiduguri Nigeria **53** 11.53N 13.16E
Maignelay France **15** 49.33N 2.31E
Maihar India **41** 24.16N 80.45E
Maikala Range *mts.* India **41** 21.45N 81.00E
Maiko *r.* Zaïre **54** 0.15N 25.35E
Main *r.* Germany **20** 50.00N 8.19E
Main Camp Kiribati **69** 2.01N 157.25W
Main Centre Canada **75** 50.38N 107.20W
Main Channel *str.* Canada **76** 45.22N 81.50W
Mai Ndombe *l.* Zaïre **54** 2.00S 18.20E
Maine *d.* U.S.A. **84** 45.15N 69.15W
Mainland *i.* Orkney Is. U.K. **12** 59.00N 3.10W
Mainland *i.* Shetland Is. U.K. **12** 60.15N 1.22W
Mainoru Australia **64** 14.02S 134.05E
Mainpuri India **41** 27.14N 79.01E
Maintenon France **15** 48.35N 1.35E
Maintirano Madagascar **57** 18.03S 44.01E
Mainz Germany **20** 50.00N 8.16E
Maipo *mtn.* Argentina **93** 34.10S 69.50W
Maipú Argentina **93** 36.52S 57.54W
Maiquetía Venezuela **90** 10.03N 66.57W
Maiskhāl I. Bangla. **41** 21.36N 91.56E
Maitland N.S.W. Australia **67** 32.33S 151.33E
Maitland S.A. Australia **66** 34.21S 137.42E
Maizhokunggar China **41** 29.50N 91.44E
Majeigha Sudan **49** 11.33N 24.40E
Majene Indonesia **36** 3.33S 118.59E
Maji Ethiopia **49** 6.11N 35.38E
Majiahewan China **32** 37.12N 105.48E
Majiang China **33** 26.30N 107.35E
Majorca *i.* see Mallorca *i.* Spain **16**
Majrūr Sudan **48** 14.01N 30.27E
Majuba Hill R.S.A. **56** 27.26S 29.48E

Majuro to **Marquette**

Majuro *i.* Pacific Oc. **68** 7.09N171.12E
Makabana Congo **54** 3.25S 12.41E
Makale Indonesia **36** 3.06S119.53E
Makalu *mtn.* China / Nepal **41** 27.54N 87.06E
Makarikha Russian Fed. **24** 66.17N 58.28E
Makaryev Russian Fed. **24** 57.52N 43.40E
Makasar, Selat *str.* Indonesia **36** 3.00S118.00E
Makassar Str. *see* Makasar, Selat *str.* Indonesia **36**
Makat Kazakhstan **25** 47.38N 53.16E
Makaw Burma **34** 26.27N 96.42E
Makay, Massif du *mts.* Madagascar **57** 21.15S 45.15E
Makaya Zaïre **54** 3.22S 18.02E
Makedonija *see* Macedonia Europe **19**
Makefu Niue **68** 19.01S169.55W
Makeni Sierra Leone **52** 8.57N 12.02W
Makere Tanzania **55** 4.15S 30.26E
Makeyevka Ukraine **25** 48.01N 38.00E
Makgadikgadi Salt Pan *f.* Botswana **56** 20.50S 25.45E
Makhachkala Russian Fed. **25** 42.59N 47.30E
Makham Thailand **34** 12.40N102.12E
Makhfar al Quwayrah Jordan **44** 29.49N 35.18E
Makhrūq, Wādī al *r.* Jordan **44** 31.30N 37.10E
Makinsk Kazakhstan **28** 52.40N 70.28E
Makkah Saudi Arabia **48** 21.26N 39.49E
Makkovik Canada **77** 55.00N 59.10W
Makó Hungary **21** 46.13N 20.30E
Mako Senegal **52** 13.00N 12.26W
Makokou Gabon **54** 0.38N 12.47E
Makoua Congo **54** 0.01S 15.40E
Makrai India **40** 22.04N 77.06E
Makran *f.* Asia **43** 26.30N 61.20E
Makrāna India **40** 27.03N 74.43E
Makrān Coast Range *mts.* Pakistan **40** 25.30N 64.30E
Maksamaa Finland **22** 63.14N 22.05E
Makuliro Tanzania **55** 9.34S 37.26E
Makurdi Nigeria **53** 7.44N 8.35E
Māl India **41** 26.52N 88.44E
Malabo Equat. Guinea **53** 3.45N 8.48E
Malacca *see* Melaka Malaysia **36**
Malacca, Str. of Indian Oc. **36** 3.00N100.30E
Malad City U.S.A. **80** 42.12N112.15W
Málaga Spain **16** 36.43N 4.25W
Malaga U.S.A. **81** 32.14N104.04W
Malaimbandy Madagascar **57** 20.20S 45.36E
Malaita Solomon Is. **68** 9.00S161.00E
Malakāl Sudan **49** 9.31N 31.39E
Malakand Pakistan **40** 34.34N 71.56E
Malam Chad **49** 11.27N 20.59E
Malang Indonesia **37** 7.59S112.45E
Malangwa Nepal **41** 26.52N 85.34E
Malanje Angola **54** 9.36S 16.21E
Malanje *d.* Angola **54** 8.40S 16.50E
Mälaren *l.* Sweden **23** 59.30N 17.12E
Malartic Canada **76** 48.09N 78.09W
Malatya Turkey **42** 38.22N 38.18E
Malaut India **40** 30.11N 74.30E
Malaŵi Africa **55** 12.00S 34.00E
Malaŵi, L. Africa **55** 12.00S 34.30E
Malaya Vishera Russian Fed. **24** 58.53N 32.08E
Malāyer Iran **43** 34.19N 48.51E
Malaysia Asia **36** 5.00N110.00E
Malazgirt Turkey **42** 39.09N 42.31E
Malbaie *r.* Canada **77** 47.40N 70.05W
Malbaie, Baie de *b.* Canada **77** 48.35N 64.16W
Malbooma Australia **66** 30.41S134.11E
Malbork Poland **21** 54.02N 19.01E
Malcolm Australia **63** 28.56S121.30E
Malcolm, Pt. Australia **63** 33.47S123.44E
Malden U.S.A. **83** 36.34N 89.57W
Malden I. Kiribati **69** 4.03S154.49W
Maldives Indian Oc. **38** 6.20N 73.00E
Maldon U.K. **11** 51.43N 0.41E
Maldonado Uruguay **94** 34.57S 54.59W
Male Italy **15** 46.21N 10.55E
Maléa, Ákra *c.* Greece **19** 36.27N 23.11E
Malebo Pool *f.* Zaïre **54** 4.15S 15.25E
Mālegaon India **40** 20.33N 74.32E
Malek Sudan **49** 6.04N 31.36E
Malek Din Afghan. **40** 32.25N 68.04E
Malekula *i.* Vanuatu **68** 16.15S167.30E
Malema Mozambique **55** 14.55S 37.09E
Malenga Russian Fed. **24** 63.50N 36.50E
Māler Kotla India **40** 30.32N 75.53E
Malesherbes France **15** 48.18N 2.25E
Malgomaj *l.* Sweden **22** 64.47N 16.12E
Malheur L. U.S.A. **80** 43.20N118.45W
Mali Africa **52** 17.30N 2.30E
Mali *r.* Burma **34** 25.43N 97.29E
Malik, Wādī al Sudan **48** 18.02N 30.58E
Malili Indonesia **37** 2.38S121.06E
Malin Ukraine **21** 50.48N 29.08E
Malinau Indonesia **36** 3.35N116.38E
Malindi Kenya **55** 3.14S 40.08E
Malingping Indonesia **37** 6.45S106.01E
Malin Head Rep. of Ire. **13** 55.23N 7.24W
Malin More Rep. of Ire. **13** 54.42N 8.48W
Malipo China **33** 23.11N104.41E
Malita Phil. **37** 6.19N125.39E
Māliya India **40** 23.05N 70.46E
Malkāpur India **40** 20.53N 76.12E
Mallacoota Australia **67** 37.34S149.43E
Mallacoota Inlet *b.* Australia **67** 37.34S149.43E
Mallaig U.K. **12** 57.00N 5.50W
Mallawī Egypt **44** 27.44N 30.50E
Mallorca *i.* Spain **16** 39.35N 3.00E
Mallow Rep. of Ire. **13** 52.08N 8.39W
Malm Norway **22** 64.04N 11.12E
Malmberget Sweden **22** 67.10N 20.40E
Malmédy Belgium **14** 50.25N 6.02E
Malmesbury R.S.A. **56** 33.28S 18.43E
Malmö Sweden **23** 55.36N 13.00E
Malmöhus *d.* Sweden **23** 55.45N 13.30E
Malmyzh Russian Fed. **24** 56.34N 50.41E
Maloja Switz. **15** 46.24N 9.41E
Malolos Guam **68** 13.18N144.46E
Malone U.S.A. **84** 44.51N 74.17W
Malonga Zaïre **54** 10.26S 23.10E
Malorita Belorussia **21** 51.50N 24.08E
Mälöy Norway **23** 61.56N 5.07E
Malozemelskaya Tundra *f.* Russian Fed. **24** 67.40N 50.10E
Malpas Australia **66** 34.44S140.43E
Malta Europe **18** 35.55N 14.25E
Malta U.S.A. **80** 48.21N107.52W
Malta Channel Med. Sea **18** 36.20N 14.45E
Maltby U.K. **10** 53.25N 1.12W
Malton U.K. **10** 54.09N 0.48W
Maluku *d.* Indonesia **37** 4.00S129.00E
Maluku, Laut *sea* Pacific Oc. **37** 2.00N127.00E
Malumfashi Nigeria **53** 11.48N 7.36E
Malundo Angola **54** 14.51S 22.00E
Malung Sweden **23** 60.40N 13.44E
Malūţ Sudan **49** 10.26N 32.12E
Malvinas, Islas *see Falkland Is.* Atlantic Oc. **93**
Mama Russian Fed. **29** 58.20N112.55E
Mamadysh Russian Fed. **24** 55.43N 51.20E
Mamaia Romania **21** 44.15N 28.37E
Mambasa Zaïre **55** 1.20N 29.05E
Mamberamo *r.* Indonesia **37** 1.45S137.25E
Mambéré *r.* C.A.R. **53** 3.30N 16.08E
Mambilima Falls *town* Zambia **55** 10.32S 28.45E
Mamers France **15** 48.21N 0.23E
Mamfe Cameroon **53** 5.46N 9.18E
Mamonovo Russian Fed. **21** 54.30N 19.59E
Mamore *r.* Bolivia **92** 12.00S 65.15W
Mamou Guinea **52** 10.24N 12.05W
Mampika Congo **54** 2.58S 14.38E
Mampikony Madagascar **57** 16.06S 47.38E
Mampong Ghana **52** 7.06N 1.24W
Mamry, Jezioro *l.* Poland **21** 54.08N 21.42E
Mamuju Indonesia **36** 2.41S118.55E
Ma'mūn Sudan **49** 12.15N 22.41E
Man Ivory Coast **52** 7.31N 7.37W
Man Jammu & Kashmir **41** 33.51N 78.32E
Man, Isle of Europe **10** 54.15N 4.30W
Mana *r.* Guiana **91** 5.35N 53.55W
Mana Hawaiian Is. **69** 22.02N156.46W
Manacapuru Brazil **90** 3.16S 60.37W
Manacor Spain **16** 39.32N 3.12E
Manado Indonesia **37** 1.30N124.58E
Managua Nicaragua **87** 12.06N 86.18W
Managua, Lago de *l.* Nicaragua **87** 12.10N 86.30W
Manahawkin U.S.A. **85** 39.42N 74.16W
Manakara Madagascar **57** 22.08S 48.01E
Manāli India **40** 32.16N 77.10E
Manambao *r.* Madagascar **57** 17.43S 43.57E
Mananara Madagascar **57** 16.10S 49.46E
Mananara *r.* Madagascar **57** 23.21S 47.42E
Manangatang Australia **66** 35.02S142.54E
Mananjary Madagascar **57** 21.13S 48.20E
Manankoro Mali **52** 10.25N 7.26W
Manantali, Lac de *l.* Mali **52** 13.00N 10.20W
Manantenina Madagascar **57** 24.17S 47.19E
Manapouri, L. New Zealand **60** 45.30S167.00E
Manār *r.* India **40** 18.39N 77.44E
Manāslu *mtn.* Nepal **41** 28.33N 84.35E
Manasquan U.S.A. **85** 40.07N 74.03W
Manau P.N.G. **37** 8.02S148.00E
Manaus Brazil **90** 3.06S 60.00W
Manāwar India **40** 22.14N 75.05E
Manawatu-Wanganui *d.* New Zealand **60** 39.00S175.25E
Mancelona U.S.A. **84** 44.54N 85.03W
Manche *d.* France **15** 49.00N 1.10W
Mancherāl India **41** 18.52N 79.26E
Manchester U.K. **10** 53.30N 2.15W
Manchester Conn. U.S.A. **84** 41.47N 72.31W
Manchester N.H. U.S.A. **84** 42.59N 71.28W
Manchurian Plain *f. see* Dongbei Pingyuan *f.* China **31**
Mand *r.* Iran **43** 28.09N 51.16E
Manda Iringa Tanzania **55** 10.30S 34.37E
Manda Mbeya Tanzania **55** 7.59S 32.27E
Manda, Jabal *mtn.* Sudan **49** 8.39N 24.27E
Mandabe Madagascar **57** 21.03S 44.55E
Mandal Norway **23** 58.02N 7.27E
Mandala Peak Indonesia **37** 4.45S140.15E
Mandalay Burma **34** 21.58N 96.04E
Mandalay *d.* Burma **34** 22.00N 96.00E
Mandalgovi Mongolia **32** 45.40N106.10E
Mandals *r.* Norway **23** 58.02N 7.28E
Mandan U.S.A. **82** 46.50N100.54W
Mandara Mts. Nigeria / Cameroon **53** 10.30N 13.30E
Mandasor India **40** 24.04N 75.04E
Mandeb, Bāb el *str.* Asia **49** 13.00N 43.10E
Mandel Afghan. **40** 33.17N 61.52E
Mandera Kenya **55** 3.55N 41.50E
Mandi India **40** 31.42N 76.55E
Mandiana Guinea **52** 10.37N 8.39W
Mandi Būrewāla Pakistan **40** 30.09N 72.41E
Mandi Dabwāli India **40** 29.58N 74.42E
Mandji Gabon **54** 1.37S 10.53E
Mandla India **41** 22.36N 80.23E
Mandora Australia **62** 19.45S120.50E
Mandoto Madagascar **57** 19.34S 46.17E
Mandra Pakistan **40** 33.22N 73.14E
Mandritsara Madagascar **57** 15.50S 48.49E
Māndu India **40** 22.22N 75.23E
Mandurah Australia **63** 32.31S115.41E
Manduria Italy **19** 40.24N 17.38E
Māndvi India **40** 22.50N 69.22E
Mandya India **38** 12.33N 76.54E
Måne *r.* Norway **23** 59.55N 8.48E
Manendragarh India **41** 23.13N 82.13E
Manerbio Italy **15** 45.21N 10.08E
Manevichi Ukraine **21** 51.19N 25.35E
Manfredonia Italy **18** 41.38N 15.54E
Manfredonia, Golfo di *g.* Italy **18** 41.35N 16.05E
Mangaia I. Cook Is. **69** 21.56S157.56W
Mangaldai India **41** 26.26N 92.02E
Mangalia Romania **21** 43.50N 28.35E
Mangalore India **38** 12.54N 74.51E
Mangando Angola **54** 8.02S 17.08E
Mangareva *i.* Pacific Oc. **69** 23.07S134.57W
Mangawān India **41** 24.41N 81.33E
Mangaweka New Zealand **60** 38.49S175.48E
Mangeigne Chad **49** 10.31N 21.19E
Mangnai China **30** 37.52N 91.26E
Mango Togo **52** 10.23N 0.30E
Mangochi Malaŵi **55** 14.29S 35.15E
Mangoky *r.* Madagascar **57** 21.29S 43.41E
Mangombe Zaïre **55** 1.23S 26.50E
Mangonui New Zealand **60** 35.00S173.34E
Mangoro *r.* Madagascar **57** 20.00S 48.45E
Māngrol India **40** 21.07N 70.07E
Mangueira, L. Brazil **94** 33.06S 52.48W
Mangum U.S.A. **83** 34.53N 99.30W
Mangyshlak, Poluostrov *pen.* Kazakhstan **25** 44.00N 52.30E
Manhattan U.S.A. **82** 39.11N 96.35W
Manhiça Mozambique **57** 25.24S 32.49E
Manhuaçu Brazil **94** 20.16S 42.01W
Manhumirim Brazil **94** 20.22S 41.57W
Mania *r.* Madagascar **57** 19.42S 45.22E
Maniago Italy **15** 46.10N 12.43E
Maniamba Mozambique **55** 12.30S 35.05E
Manica Mozambique **57** 19.00S 33.00E
Manica *d.* Mozambique **57** 20.00S 34.00E
Manicoré Brazil **90** 5.49S 61.17W
Manicouagan *r.* Canada **77** 49.15N 68.20W
Manicouagan, Résr. Canada **77** 51.20N 68.48W
Maniitsoq *see* Sukkertoppen Greenland **73**
Mānikganj Bangla. **41** 23.19N 87.03E
Mānikpur India **41** 25.04N 81.07E
Manila Phil. **37** 14.36N120.59E
Manila U.S.A. **80** 40.59N109.43W
Manildra Australia **67** 33.12S148.41E
Manilla Australia **67** 30.45S150.45E
Maningory *r.* Madagascar **57** 17.13S 49.28E
Manipur *d.* India **39** 25.00N 93.40E
Manisa Turkey **19** 38.37N 27.28E
Manistee U.S.A. **84** 44.14N 86.20W
Manistee *r.* U.S.A. **84** 44.14N 86.20W
Manistique U.S.A. **84** 45.58N 86.17W
Manitoba *d.* Canada **75** 55.00N 96.00W
Manitoba, L. Canada **75** 51.00N 98.45W
Manitoulin I. Canada **76** 45.45N 82.30W
Manitowoc U.S.A. **82** 44.06N 87.40W
Maniwaki Canada **76** 46.23N 75.58W
Manizales Colombia **90** 5.03N 75.32W
Manja Madagascar **57** 21.26S 44.20E
Manjakandriana Madagascar **57** 18.55S 47.47E
Mānjhand Pakistan **40** 25.55N 68.14E
Manjil Iran **43** 36.44N 49.29E
Manjimup Australia **63** 34.14S116.06E
Mankato U.S.A. **82** 44.10N 94.01W
Mankera Pakistan **40** 31.23N 71.26E
Mankono Ivory Coast **52** 8.01N 6.09W
Manly Australia **67** 33.47S151.17E
Manmād India **40** 20.15N 74.27E
Mann *r.* Australia **64** 12.20S134.07E
Mann *r.* N.S.W. Australia **67** 29.38S152.21E
Mān Na Burma **34** 23.27N 97.14E
Manna Indonesia **36** 4.27S102.55E
Mannahill Australia **66** 32.26S139.59E
Mannar Sri Lanka **39** 8.59N 79.54E
Mannar, G. of India / Sri Lanka **39** 8.20N 79.00E
Mannessier, Lac *l.* Canada **77** 55.28N 70.38W
Mannheim Germany **20** 49.30N 8.28E
Mannin B. Rep. of Ire. **13** 53.28N 10.06W
Manning Canada **74** 56.53N117.39W
Manning U.S.A. **85** 33.42N 80.12W
Mannu *r.* Italy **18** 39.16N 9.00E
Mannum Australia **66** 34.50S139.20E
Mano Sierra Leone **52** 8.04N 12.02W
Manoharpur India **41** 22.23N 85.12E
Manokwari Indonesia **37** 0.53S134.05E
Manombo Madagascar **57** 22.57S 43.28E
Manono Zaïre **55** 7.18S 27.24E
Manorhamilton Rep. of Ire. **13** 54.18N 8.10W
Manosque France **17** 43.50N 5.47E
Manouane *r.* Canada **77** 49.29N 71.13W
Manouane, Lac *l.* Canada **77** 50.40N 70.45W
Mānpur India **41** 20.22N 80.43E
Manresa Spain **16** 41.43N 1.50E
Mānsa Gujarat India **40** 23.26N 72.40E
Mānsa Punjab India **40** 29.59N 75.23E
Mansa Zambia **55** 11.10S 28.52E
Mānsehra Pakistan **40** 34.20N 73.12E
Mansel I. Canada **73** 62.00N 80.00W
Mansfield U.K. **10** 53.08N 1.12W
Mansfield La. U.S.A. **83** 32.02N 93.43W
Mansfield Mass. U.S.A. **84** 42.02N 71.13W
Mansfield Ohio U.S.A. **84** 40.46N 82.31W
Manso *r.* Brazil **92** 11.59S 50.25W
Mansôa Guinea Bissau **52** 12.08N 15.18W
Manta Ecuador **90** 0.59S 80.44W
Mantaro *r.* Peru **90** 12.00S 74.00W
Manteca U.S.A. **80** 37.48N121.13W
Mantes France **15** 49.00N 1.41E
Mantiqueira, Serra da *mts.* Brazil **94** 22.25S 45.00W
Mantova Italy **15** 45.09N 10.47E
Mänttä Finland **23** 62.02N 24.38E
Manturovo Russian Fed. **24** 58.20N 44.42E
Mäntyluoto Finland **23** 61.35N 21.29E
Manú Peru **90** 12.14S 70.51W
Manua Is. Samoa **68** 14.13S169.35W
Manuel Benavides Mexico **83** 29.05N103.55W
Manui *i.* Indonesia **37** 3.35S123.08E
Manukau New Zealand **60** 36.59S174.53E
Manukau Harbour *est.* New Zealand **60** 37.10S174.00E
Manunda Creek *r.* Australia **66** 32.50S138.58E
Manus *i.* P.N.G. **37** 2.00S147.00E
Manville U.S.A. **80** 42.47N104.37W
Manyane Botswana **56** 23.23S 21.44E
Manyara, L. Tanzania **55** 3.40S 35.50E
Manych *r.* Russian Fed. **25** 47.14N 40.20E
Manych Gudilo, Ozero *l.* Russian Fed. **25** 46.20N 42.45E
Manyinga *r.* Zambia **56** 13.28S 24.25E
Manyoni Tanzania **55** 5.46S 34.50E
Mānzai Pakistan **40** 30.07N 68.52E
Manzanares Spain **16** 39.00N 3.23W
Manzanillo Cuba **87** 20.21N 77.21W
Manzano Mts. U.S.A. **81** 34.48N106.12W
Manzhouli China **31** 49.36N117.28E
Manzil Pakistan **40** 29.15N 63.05E
Manzilah, Buḩayrat al *l.* Egypt **44** 31.20N 32.00E
Manzini Swaziland **56** 26.29S 31.24E
Mao Chad **53** 14.06N 15.11E
Maobitou *c.* Taiwan **33** 22.00N120.45E
Maoke, Pegunungan *mts.* Indonesia **37** 4.00S137.30E
Maokui Shan *mtn.* China **32** 33.55N111.33E
Maoming China **33** 21.50N110.58E
Maoniu Shan *mtn.* China **32** 33.00N103.56E
Mapai Mozambique **57** 22.51S 32.00E
Mapam Yumco *l.* China **41** 30.40N 81.20E
Mapi Indonesia **37** 7.06S139.23E
Mapia, Kepulauan *is.* Indonesia **37** 1.00N134.15E
Mapimí, Bolsóne de *des.* Mexico **83** 27.30N103.15W
Mapinhane Mozambique **57** 22.19S 35.03E
Mapire Venezuela **90** 7.46N 64.41W
Maple Creek *town* Canada **75** 49.55N109.27W
Maprik P.N.G. **37** 3.38S143.02E
Mapuera *r.* Brazil **91** 2.00S 55.40W
Maputo Mozambique **57** 25.58S 32.35E
Maputo *d.* Mozambique **57** 26.00S 32.30E
Maqnā Saudi Arabia **44** 28.26N 34.44E
Maqu China **39** 34.05N102.15E
Maquan He *r.* China **41** 29.35N 84.10E
Maquela do Zombo Angola **54** 6.06S 15.12E
Maquinchao Argentina **93** 41.15S 68.44W
Maquoketa U.S.A. **82** 42.04N 90.40W
Mar, Serra do *mts.* Brazil **94** 23.00S 44.40W
Mara Tanzania **55** 1.30S 34.31E
Mara *d.* Tanzania **55** 1.45S 34.30E
Mara *r.* Tanzania **55** 1.30S 33.52E
Maraã Brazil **90** 1.50S 65.22W
Maraa Tahiti **69** 17.46S149.34W
Marabá Brazil **91** 5.23S 49.10W
Marabastad R.S.A. **56** 23.58S 29.21E
Maracaibo Venezuela **90** 10.44N 71.37W
Maracaibo, Lago de *l.* Venezuela **90** 9.50N 71.30W
Maracaju, Serra de *mts.* Brazil **94** 21.38S 55.10W
Maracay Venezuela **90** 10.20N 67.28W
Marādah Libya **51** 29.14N 19.13E
Maradi Niger **53** 13.29N 7.10E
Maradi *d.* Niger **53** 14.00N 8.10E
Marāgheh Iran **43** 37.25N 46.13E
Maragogipe Brazil **91** 12.48S 38.59W
Marahuaca, Cerro *mtn.* Venezuela **90** 3.37N 65.25W
Marajó, Ilha de *i.* Brazil **91** 1.00S 49.40W
Maralal Kenya **55** 1.15N 36.48E
Maralinga Australia **63** 30.13S131.32E
Maramba Zambia **54** 17.40S 25.50E
Maramsilli Resr. India **41** 20.32N 81.41E
Mārān, Koh-i- *mtn.* Pakistan **40** 29.33N 66.53E
Marana U.S.A. **81** 32.27N111.13W
Marand Iran **43** 38.25N 45.50E
Maranhão *d.* Brazil **91** 6.00S 45.30W
Maranoa *r.* Australia **65** 27.55S148.30E
Marañón *r.* Peru **90** 4.40S 73.20W
Marão Mozambique **57** 24.21S 34.07E
Marapi *mtn.* Indonesia **36** 0.20S100.45E
Mărăşeşti Romania **21** 45.52N 27.14E
Marathón Greece **19** 38.10N 23.59E
Marathon U.S.A. **83** 30.12N103.15W
Maratua *i.* Indonesia **36** 2.10N118.35E
Marāveh Tappeh Iran **43** 37.55N 55.57E
Marav L. Pakistan **40** 29.04N 69.18E
Marawī Sudan **48** 18.29N 31.49E
Marbella Spain **16** 36.31N 4.53W
Marble Bar Australia **62** 21.16S119.45E
Marburg Germany **20** 50.49N 8.36E
Marcaria Italy **15** 45.07N 10.32E
March U.K. **11** 52.33N 0.05E
Marche Belgium **14** 50.13N 5.21E
Marche *d.* Italy **18** 43.35N 13.00E
Marchena Spain **16** 37.20N 5.24W
Mar Chiquita *l.* Argentina **92** 30.42S 62.36W
Marcos Paz Argentina **93** 34.49S 58.51W
Marcounda C.A.R. **53** 7.37N 16.59E
Marcq-en-Baroeul France **14** 50.40N 3.01E
Marcus Hook U.S.A. **85** 39.49N 75.25W
Marcus I. Pacific Oc. **68** 24.18N153.58E
Mardān Pakistan **40** 34.12N 72.02E
Mar del Plata Argentina **93** 38.00S 57.32W
Marden U.K. **11** 51.11N 0.30E
Mardie Australia **62** 21.14S115.57E
Mardin Turkey **42** 37.19N 40.43E
Maré, Île *i.* N. Cal. **68** 21.30S168.00E
Maree, Loch U.K. **12** 57.41N 5.28W
Mareeba Australia **64** 17.00S145.26E
Marettimo *i.* Italy **18** 37.58N 12.05E
Marfa U.S.A. **83** 30.18N104.01W
Margai Caka *l.* China **39** 35.11N 86.57E
Margaret *r.* Australia **66** 29.26S137.00E
Margaret Bay *town* Canada **74** 51.20N127.20W
Margaret L. Canada **74** 58.56N115.25W
Margaret River *town* W. Aust. Australia **63** 33.57S115.04E
Margaret River *town* W. Aust. Australia **62** 18.38S126.52E
Margarita, Isla de *i.* Venezuela **90** 11.00N 64.00W
Margate R.S.A. **56** 30.51S 30.22E
Margate U.K. **11** 51.23N 1.24E
Mārgow, Dasht-e *des.* Afghan. **40** 30.45N 63.10E
Maria Elena Chile **92** 22.21S 69.40W
María Grande Argentina **93** 31.40S 59.55W
Maria I. Australia **64** 14.52S135.40E
Mariana Brazil **94** 20.23S 43.23W
Marianao Cuba **87** 23.03N 82.29W
Mariana Ridge Pacific Oc. **68** 17.00N146.00E
Mariana Trench Pacific Oc. **68** 16.00N148.00E
Marianna Ark. U.S.A. **83** 34.46N 90.46W
Marianna Fla. U.S.A. **85** 30.45N 85.15W
Mariánské Lázně Czech Republic **20** 49.59N 12.43E
Marias *r.* U.S.A. **80** 47.56N110.30W
Maribo Denmark **23** 54.46N 11.31E
Maribor Slovenia **20** 46.35N 15.40E
Marico *r.* R.S.A. **56** 24.12S 26.57E
Maricopa U.S.A. **81** 35.03N119.24W
Marīdī Sudan **49** 4.55N 29.28E
Marīdī *r.* Sudan **49** 6.55N 29.00E
Marié *r.* Brazil **90** 0.27S 66.26W
Marieburg Belgium **14** 50.07N 4.30E
Marie-Galante *i.* Guadeloupe **87** 15.54N 61.11W
Mariehamn *see* Maarianhamina Finland **23**
Mariemberg Neth. **14** 52.32N 6.35E
Mariental Namibia **56** 24.38S 17.58E
Mariestad Sweden **23** 58.43N 13.51E
Marietta Ga. U.S.A. **85** 33.57N 84.34W
Marietta Ohio U.S.A. **84** 39.26N 81.27W
Marieville Canada **77** 45.26N 73.10W
Mariga *r.* Nigeria **53** 9.37N 5.55E
Marijampolė Lithuania **23** 54.33N 23.21E
Marília Brazil **94** 22.13S 50.20W
Marín Spain **16** 42.23N 8.42W
Marina di Ravenna Italy **15** 44.29N 12.17E
Marineland U.S.A. **85** 29.39N 81.13W
Marinette U.S.A. **82** 45.06N 87.38W
Maringá Brazil **94** 23.36S 52.02W
Maringa Zaïre **49** 1.14N 20.00E
Maringa *r.* Zaïre **54** 1.13N 19.50E
Maringue Mozambique **57** 17.55S 34.24E
Marinha Grande Portugal **16** 39.45N 8.55W
Marion Ill. U.S.A. **83** 37.44N 88.56W
Marion Ind. U.S.A. **84** 40.33N 85.40W
Marion Iowa U.S.A. **82** 42.02N 91.36W
Marion Ohio U.S.A. **84** 40.35N 83.08W
Marion S.C. U.S.A. **85** 34.11N 79.23W
Marion Va. U.S.A. **85** 36.51N 81.30W
Marion, L. U.S.A. **85** 33.30N 80.25W
Marion Bay *town* Australia **66** 35.13S137.00E
Marion Reef Australia **64** 19.10S152.17E
Mariposa U.S.A. **80** 37.29N119.58W
Mariscal Estigarribia Paraguay **94** 22.03S 60.35W
Maritsa *r.* Turkey **19** 41.00N 26.15E
Mariupol' Ukraine **25** 47.05N 37.34E
Marka Somali Rep. **55** 1.42N 44.47E
Markaryd Sweden **23** 56.26N 13.36E
Marked Tree U.S.A. **83** 35.32N 90.25W
Marken *i.* Neth. **14** 52.28N 5.03E
Markerwaard *f.* Neth. **14** 52.30N 5.15E
Market Drayton U.K. **10** 52.55N 2.30W
Market Harborough U.K. **11** 52.29N 0.55W
Market Rasen U.K. **10** 53.24N 0.20W
Market Weighton U.K. **10** 53.52N 0.04W
Markha *r.* Russian Fed. **29** 63.37N119.00E
Markham Canada **76** 43.52N 79.16W
Markham, Mt. Antarctica **96** 83.00S164.00E
Marks Russian Fed. **25** 51.43N 46.45E
Marla Australia **65** 27.22S133.48E
Marla Australia **64** 27.22S133.48E
Marlborough Australia **64** 22.51S149.50E
Marlborough U.K. **11** 51.26N 1.44W
Marle France **15** 49.44N 3.46E
Marlette U.S.A. **84** 43.20N 83.04W
Marlin U.S.A. **83** 31.18N 96.53W
Marlo Australia **67** 37.50S148.35E
Marmara *i.* Turkey **19** 40.38N 27.37E
Marmara, Sea of *see* Marmara Denizi *sea* Turkey **19**
Marmara Denizi *sea* Turkey **19** 40.45N 28.15E
Marmaris Turkey **19** 36.50N 28.17E
Marmarth U.S.A. **82** 46.18N103.54W
Marmion L. Canada **76** 48.55N 91.25W
Marmolada *mtn.* Italy **15** 46.26N 11.51E
Marne *d.* France **15** 48.55N 4.10E
Marne *r.* France **15** 48.50N 2.25E
Marnoo Australia **66** 36.40S142.55E
Maroantsetra Madagascar **57** 15.26S 49.44E
Marobi Pakistan **40** 32.36N 69.52E
Marolambo Madagascar **57** 20.02S 48.07E
Maromme France **15** 49.28N 1.02E
Marondera Zimbabwe **57** 18.11S 31.31E
Maroni *r.* Guiana **91** 5.30N 54.00W
Maroochydore Australia **65** 26.40S153.07E
Maroua Cameroon **53** 10.35N 14.20E
Marovoay Madagascar **57** 16.06S 46.39E
Marquard R.S.A. **56** 28.39S 27.25E
Marquesas Is. *see* Marquises, Îles *is.* Pacific Oc. **69**
Marquette U.S.A. **84** 46.33N 87.23W

Marquises, Îles to **Meridian**

Marquises, Îles *is.* Pacific Oc. **69** 9.00S139.30W
Marra Australia **66** 31.11S144.03E
Marra *r.* Australia **67** 30.05S147.05E
Marracuene Mozambique **57** 25.44S 32.41E
Marradi Italy **15** 44.04N 11.37E
Marrah, Jabal *mtn.* Sudan **49** 13.10N 24.22E
Marrakech Morocco **50** 31.49N 8.00W
Marrawah Australia **65** 40.55S144.42E
Marree Australia **66** 29.40S138.04E
Marromeu Mozambique **57** 18.20S 35.56E
Marrupa Mozambique **55** 13.10S 37.30E
Marsá al Burayqah Libya **48** 30.25N 19.35E
Marsabit Kenya **55** 2.20N 37.59E
Marsala Italy **18** 37.48N 12.27E
Marsá Maṭrūḥ Egypt **42** 31.21N 27.14E
Marsden Australia **67** 33.46S147.35E
Marseille France **17** 43.18N 5.22E
Marseille-en-Beauvaisis France **15** 49.35N 1.57E
Marsfjället *mtn.* Sweden **22** 65.05N 15.28E
Marshall Liberia **52** 6.10N 10.23W
Marshall Ark. U.S.A. **83** 35.55N 92.38W
Marshall Minn. U.S.A. **82** 44.27N 95.47W
Marshall Mo. U.S.A. **82** 39.07N 93.12W
Marshall Tex. U.S.A. **83** 32.33N 94.23W
Marshall Is. Pacific Oc. **68** 10.00N172.00E
Marshalltown U.S.A. **82** 42.03N 92.55W
Marshyhope Creek *r.* U.S.A. **85** 38.32N 75.45W
Martaban Burma **34** 16.32N 97.35E
Martaban, G. of Burma **34** 15.10N 96.30E
Martapura Indonesia **36** 3.22S114.56E
Marte Nigeria **53** 12.23N 13.46E
Martelange Belgium **14** 49.50N 5.44E
Martés, Sierra *mts.* Spain **16** 39.10N 1.00W
Marthaguy Creek *r.* Australia **67** 30.16S147.35E
Martha's Vineyard *i.* U.S.A. **84** 41.25N 70.40W
Martigny Switz. **20** 46.07N 7.05E
Martin Slovakia **21** 49.05N 18.55E
Martin U.S.A. **82** 43.10N101.44W
Martina Franca Italy **19** 40.42N 17.21E
Martinique *i.* Windward Is. **87** 14.40N 61.00W
Martin L. U.S.A. **85** 32.50N 85.55W
Martin Pt. U.S.A. **72** 70.10N143.50W
Martinsburg U.S.A. **84** 39.27N 77.58W
Martins Ferry *town* U.S.A. **84** 40.07N 80.45W
Martinsville Ind. U.S.A. **84** 39.25N 86.25W
Martinsville Va. U.S.A. **85** 36.43N 79.53W
Martin Vaz *is.* Atlantic Oc. **95** 20.30S 28.51W
Marton New Zealand **60** 40.04S175.25E
Martos Spain **16** 37.44N 3.58W
Martre, Lac la *l.* Canada **74** 63.15N116.55W
Martti Finland **22** 67.28N 28.28E
Marudi Malaysia **36** 4.15N114.19E
Ma'rūf Afghan. **40** 31.34N 67.03E
Marula Zimbabwe **56** 20.26S 28.06E
Marum Neth. **14** 53.06N 6.16E
Marvejols France **17** 44.33N 3.18E
Marvel Loch *town* Australia **63** 31.31S119.30E
Mārwār India **40** 25.44N 73.36E
Mary Turkmenistan **28** 37.42N 61.54E
Maryborough Qld. Australia **64** 25.32S152.36E
Maryborough Vic. Australia **66** 37.05S143.47E
Marydale R.S.A. **56** 29.24S 22.06E
Mary Frances L. Canada **75** 63.19N106.13W
Maryland *d.* U.S.A. **84** 39.00N 76.45W
Maryland Beach *town* U.S.A. **85** 38.26N 74.59W
Maryport U.K. **10** 54.43N 3.30W
Mary's Harbour Canada **77** 52.18N 55.51W
Marystown Canada **77** 47.11N 55.10W
Marysvale U.S.A. **80** 38.27N112.11W
Marysville Kans. U.S.A. **82** 39.51N 96.39W
Maryvale Australia **64** 24.41S134.04E
Maryville Mo. U.S.A. **82** 40.21N 94.52W
Maryville Tenn. U.S.A. **85** 35.45N 83.59W
Marzūq Libya **51** 25.55N 13.55E
Marzūq, Ṣaḥrā' *des.* Libya **51** 24.30N 13.00E
Masāhim, Kūh-e *mtn.* Iran **43** 30.26N 55.08E
Masai Steppe *f.* Tanzania **55** 4.30S 37.00E
Masaka Uganda **55** 0.20S 31.46E
Masan S. Korea **31** 35.10N128.35E
Masasi Tanzania **55** 10.43S 38.48E
Masba Nigeria **53** 10.35N 13.01E
Masbate *i.* Phil. **37** 12.00N123.30E
Mascara Algeria **50** 35.24N 0.08E
Maseru Lesotho **56** 29.18S 27.28E
Mashhad Iran **43** 36.16N 59.34E
Mashkai *r.* Pakistan **40** 26.02N 65.19E
Māshkel *r.* Pakistan **40** 28.02N 63.25E
Māshkel, Hāmūn-i- *l.* Pakistan **40** 28.15N 63.00E
Mashki Chāh Pakistan **40** 29.01N 62.27E
Mashonaland *f.* Zimbabwe **57** 18.20S 32.00E
Mashūray Afghan. **40** 32.12N 68.21E
Masi Norway **22** 69.26N 23.40E
Masīlah, Wādī al *f.* Yemen **45** 15.10N 51.08E
Masi-Manimba Zaïre **54** 4.47S 17.54E
Masindi Uganda **55** 1.41N 31.45E
Maṣīrah *i.* Oman **38** 20.30N 58.50E
Maṣīrah, Khalīj *b.* Oman **45** 20.10N 58.10E
Masjed Soleymān Iran **43** 31.59N 49.18E
Mask, Lough Rep. of Ire. **13** 53.38N 9.22W
Maskinongé Canada **77** 46.35N 73.30W
Mason U.S.A. **83** 30.45N 99.14W
Mason City U.S.A. **82** 43.09N 93.12W
Maspalomas Canary Is. **95** 27.42N 15.34W
Masqaṭ Oman **43** 23.36N 58.37E
Massa Italy **15** 44.02N 10.09E
Massachusetts *d.* U.S.A. **84** 42.15N 71.50W
Massakory Chad **53** 13.02N 15.43E
Massa Marittima Italy **18** 43.03N 10.53E
Massangena Mozambique **57** 21.31S 33.03E
Massangulo Mozambique **57** 13.54S 35.24E
Massarosa Italy **15** 43.52N 10.20E
Massena U.S.A. **84** 44.56N 74.54W
Massenya Chad **53** 11.21N 16.09E
Masset Canada **74** 54.00N132.09W
Massif Central *mts.* France **17** 45.00N 3.30E
Massillon U.S.A. **84** 40.48N 81.32W
Massinga Mozambique **57** 23.20S 35.25E
Massingir Mozambique **57** 23.49S 32.04E
Masterton New Zealand **60** 40.57S175.39E
Mastung Pakistan **40** 29.48N 66.51E
Mastūrah Saudi Arabia **42** 23.06N 38.50E
Masvingo Zimbabwe **56** 20.10S 30.49E
Maṣyāf Syria **44** 35.03N 36.21E
Matabeleland *f.* Zimbabwe **56** 19.50S 28.15E
Matachewan Canada **76** 47.56N 80.39W
Matadi Zaïre **54** 5.50S 13.36E
Matagami Canada **76** 49.45N 77.34W
Matagami, L. Canada **76** 49.50N 77.40W
Matagorda B. U.S.A. **83** 28.35N 96.20W
Matakana Australia **67** 32.59S145.53E
Matakana I. New Zealand **60** 37.35S176.15E
Matala Angola **54** 14.45S 15.02E
Matam Senegal **50** 15.40N 13.15W
Matamata New Zealand **60** 37.49S175.46E
Matameye Niger **53** 13.26N 8.28E
Matamoros Coahuila Mexico **83** 25.32N103.15W
Matamoros Tamaulipas Mexico **83** 25.53N 97.30W
Ma'ṭan Bishrah *well* Libya **48** 22.58N 22.39E
Matandu *r.* Tanzania **55** 8.44S 39.22E
Matane Canada **77** 48.51N 67.32W
Matang China **33** 29.30N113.08E
Matankari Niger **53** 13.47N 4.00E
Matanzas Cuba **87** 23.04N 81.35W
Mataram Indonesia **37** 8.36S116.07E
Matarani Peru **92** 16.58S 72.07W
Mataranka Australia **62** 14.56S133.07E
Mataró Spain **16** 41.32N 2.27E
Matatiele R.S.A. **56** 30.19S 28.48E
Matatula, C. Samoa **68** 14.15S170.35W
Mataura *r.* New Zealand **60** 46.34S168.45E
Matautu W. Samoa **68** 13.57S171.56W
Matavera Rarotonga Cook Is. **68** 21.13S159.44W
Matawai New Zealand **60** 38.21S177.32E
Maṭāy Egypt **44** 28.25N 30.46E
Matehuala Mexico **86** 23.40N100.40W
Mateke Hills Zimbabwe **56** 21.48S 31.00E
Matera Italy **19** 40.41N 16.36E
Matetsi Zimbabwe **56** 18.17S 25.57E
Matfors Sweden **23** 62.21N 17.02E
Mathews Peak *mtn.* Kenya **55** 1.18N 37.20E
Mathis U.S.A. **83** 28.06N 97.50W
Mathoura Australia **67** 35.49S144.54E
Mathura India **41** 27.30N 77.41E
Mati Phil. **37** 6.55N126.15E
Matias Barbosa Brazil **94** 21.52S 43.21W
Matipó Brazil **94** 20.16S 42.17W
Mātli Pakistan **40** 25.02N 68.39E
Matlock U.K. **10** 53.09N 1.32W
Matochkin Shar Russian Fed. **28** 73.15N 56.35E
Mato Grosso *d.* Brazil **92** 13.00S 55.00W
Mato Grosso *town* Brazil **92** 15.05S 59.57W
Mato Grosso, Planalto do *f.* Brazil **92** 16.00S 54.00W
Mato Grosso do Sul *d.* Brazil **92** 20.00S 54.30W
Matope Malaŵi **55** 15.20S 34.57E
Matopo Hills Zimbabwe **56** 20.45S 28.30E
Matosinhos Portugal **16** 41.11N 8.42W
Maṭraḥ Oman **43** 23.37N 58.33E
Matsena Nigeria **53** 13.13N 10.04E
Matsiatra *r.* Madagascar **57** 21.25S 45.33E
Matsubara Japan **35** 34.34N135.33E
Matsudo Japan **35** 35.47N139.54E
Matsue Japan **35** 35.29N133.00E
Matsusaka Japan **35** 34.34N136.32E
Matsuyama Japan **35** 33.50N132.47E
Mattagami *r.* Canada **76** 50.43N 81.29W
Mattawa Canada **76** 46.19N 78.42W
Mattawamkeag U.S.A. **84** 45.31N 68.21W
Matterhorn *mtn.* Italy / Switz. **15** 45.58N 7.38E
Matterhorn *mtn.* U.S.A. **80** 41.49N115.23W
Matthews Ridge *town* Guyana **90** 7.30N 60.10W
Matthew Town Bahamas **87** 20.57N 73.40W
Mattice Canada **76** 49.39N 83.20W
Mattmar Sweden **22** 63.19N 13.45E
Mattoon U.S.A. **82** 39.29N 88.21W
Matua Indonesia **36** 2.58S110.52E
Maturín Venezuela **90** 9.45N 63.10W
Maua Mozambique **57** 13.53S 37.10E
Mau Aimma India **41** 25.42N 81.55E
Maubeuge France **14** 50.17N 3.58E
Maudaha India **41** 25.41N 80.07E
Maude Australia **66** 34.27S144.21E
Maués Brazil **91** 3.24S 57.42W
Mauganj India **41** 24.41N 81.53E
Maui *i.* Hawaii U.S.A. **78** 20.45N156.15W
Maulvi Bāzār Bangla. **41** 24.29N 91.42E
Maumee U.S.A. **84** 41.34N 83.41W
Maumee *r.* U.S.A. **84** 41.40N 83.35W
Maumere Indonesia **37** 8.35S122.13E
Maun Botswana **56** 19.52S 23.40E
Maunaloa Hawaiian Is. **69** 21.08N157.13W
Mauna Loa *mtn.* Hawaiian Is. **69** 19.29N155.36W
Maunath Bhanjan India **41** 25.57N 83.33E
Mau Rānīpur India **41** 25.15N 79.08E
Maurice, L. Australia **65** 29.28S130.58E
Maurice Nat. Park Canada **77** 46.42N 73.00W
Mauritania Africa **50** 20.00N 10.00W
Mauston U.S.A. **82** 43.48N 90.05W
Mavinga Angola **54** 15.47S 20.21E
Mavuradonha Mts. Zimbabwe **57** 16.30S 31.20E
Mawjib, Wādī al *r.* Jordan **44** 31.28N 35.34E
Mawlaik Burma **34** 23.50N 94.30E
Mawlamyine *see* Moulmein Burma **34**
Maxcanú Mexico **86** 20.35N 89.59W
Maxville Canada **77** 45.17N 74.51W
May, C. U.S.A. **85** 38.58N 74.55W
Maya Spain **16** 43.12N 1.29W
Mayaguana I. Bahamas **87** 22.30N 73.00W
Mayagüez Puerto Rico **87** 18.13N 67.09W
Mayāmey Iran **43** 36.27N 55.40E
Maya Mts. Belize **87** 16.30N 89.00W
Maybole U.K. **12** 55.21N 4.41W
Maych'ew Ethiopia **45** 13.02N 39.34E
Maydena Australia **65** 42.45S146.38E
Maydh Somali Rep. **45** 10.57N 47.06E
Mayen Germany **14** 50.19N 7.14E
Mayenne France **15** 48.18N 0.37W
Mayenne *d.* France **15** 48.05N 0.40W
Mayenne *r.* France **15** 47.30N 0.37W
Mayerthorpe Canada **74** 53.57N115.08W
Mayfield U.S.A. **83** 36.44N 88.38W
Maykop Russian Fed. **25** 44.37N 40.48E
Maymyo Burma **34** 22.05N 96.28E
Maynooth Rep. of Ire. **13** 53.23N 6.37W
Mayo *r.* Mexico **81** 26.45N109.47W
Mayo *d.* Rep. of Ire. **13** 53.47N 9.07W
Mayo, Plains of *f.* Rep. of Ire. **13** 53.46N 9.05W
Mayo Daga Nigeria **53** 6.59N 11.25E
Mayo Landing Canada **72** 63.45N135.45W
Mayor I. New Zealand **60** 37.15S176.15E
Mayotte, Île *i.* Comoros **55** 12.50S 45.10E
May Pen Jamaica **87** 17.58N 77.14W
Mays Landing U.S.A. **85** 39.27N 74.44W
Maysville U.S.A. **84** 38.38N 83.46W
Mayumba Gabon **54** 3.23S 10.38E
Mayville N.Dak. U.S.A. **82** 47.30N 97.19W
Mayville N.Y. U.S.A. **76** 42.15N 79.30W
Mazabuka Zambia **55** 15.50S 27.47E
Mazagão Brazil **91** 0.07S 51.17W
Mazamba Mozambique **57** 18.32S 34.50E
Mazamet France **17** 43.30N 2.24E
Mazán Peru **90** 3.15S 73.00W
Mazarredo Argentina **93** 47.00S 66.45W
Mazarrón Spain **16** 37.38N 1.19W
Mazatenango Guatemala **86** 14.31N 91.30W
Mazatlán Mexico **81** 23.13N106.25W
Mažeikiai Lithuania **23** 56.19N 22.20E
Mazirbe Latvia **23** 57.41N 22.21E
Mazowe *r.* Mozambique **57** 16.32S 33.25E
Mazowe Zimbabwe **57** 17.30S 30.58E
Mazu Liedao *is.* China **31** 26.12N120.00E
Mazunga Zimbabwe **56** 21.45S 29.52E
Mazurski, Pojezierze *lakes* Poland **21** 53.50N 21.00E
Mbabane Swaziland **56** 26.19S 31.08E
Mbagne Mauritania **50** 16.06N 14.47W
M'Baiki C.A.R. **53** 3.53N 18.01E
Mbala C.A.R. **49** 7.48N 20.51E
Mbala Zambia **55** 8.50S 31.24E
Mbale Uganda **55** 1.04N 34.12E
Mbalmayo Cameroon **53** 3.35N 11.31E
Mbamba Bay *town* Tanzania **55** 11.18S 34.50E
Mbandaka Zaïre **54** 0.03N 18.21E
Mbanza Congo Angola **54** 6.18S 14.16E
Mbarara Uganda **55** 0.36S 30.40E
Mbari *r.* C.A.R. **49** 4.34N 22.43E
Mbeya Tanzania **55** 8.54S 33.29E
Mbeya *d.* Tanzania **55** 8.30S 32.30E
Mbinda Congo **54** 2.11S 12.55E
Mbogo Tanzania **55** 7.26S 33.26E
Mbomou *d.* C.A.R. **49** 5.10N 23.00E
Mbomou *r.* C.A.R. **49** 4.08N 22.26E
Mboro Sudan **49** 6.18N 28.45E
M'Bour Senegal **52** 14.22N 16.54W
Mbout Mauritania **50** 16.02N 12.35W
M'bridge *r.* Angola **54** 7.12S 12.55E
Mbua Fiji **68** 16.48S178.37E
Mbuji Mayi Zaïre **54** 6.08S 23.39E
Mbulamuti Uganda **55** 0.50N 33.05E
Mbura Tanzania **55** 11.14S 35.25E
Mbutha Fiji **68** 16.39S179.50E
Mbuzi Zambia **55** 12.20S 32.17E
McAlester U.S.A. **83** 34.56N 95.46W
McAllen U.S.A. **83** 26.12N 98.15W
McArthur *r.* Australia **64** 15.54S136.40E
McBride Canada **74** 53.20N120.10W
McCamey U.S.A. **83** 31.08N102.13W
McClintock Canada **75** 57.50N 94.10W
McClintock Channel Canada **73** 71.20N102.00W
McClure Str. Canada **72** 74.30N116.00W
McComb U.S.A. **83** 31.14N 90.27W
McConaughy, L. U.S.A. **82** 41.15N102.00W
McConnel Creek *town* Canada **74** 56.53N126.30W
McCook U.S.A. **82** 40.12N100.38W
McDermitt U.S.A. **80** 41.59N117.36W
McDouall Peak Australia **66** 29.51S134.55E
McGrath U.S.A. **72** 62.58N155.40W
McGregor U.S.A. **82** 46.36N 93.19W
McHenry U.S.A. **82** 42.21N 88.16W
Mchinja Tanzania **55** 9.44S 39.45E
Mchinji Malaŵi **55** 13.48S 32.55E
McIlwraith Range *mts.* Australia **64** 14.00S143.10E
McKeesport U.S.A. **84** 40.21N 79.52W
McKenzie U.S.A. **83** 36.08N 88.31W
McKinley, Mt. U.S.A. **72** 63.00N151.00W
McKinney U.S.A. **83** 33.12N 96.37W
McKittrick U.S.A. **81** 35.18N119.37W
McLaughlin U.S.A. **82** 45.49N100.49W
McLennan Canada **74** 55.42N116.50W
McLeod *r.* Canada **74** 54.08N115.42W
McLeod B. Canada **75** 62.53N110.00W
Mcleod Lake *town* Canada **74** 54.58N123.00W
M'Clintock Canada **74** 60.35N134.25W
McMinnville Oreg. U.S.A. **80** 45.13N123.12W
McMinnville Tenn. U.S.A. **85** 35.40N 85.49W
McNary U.S.A. **81** 34.04N109.51W
McPherson U.S.A. **82** 38.22N 97.40W
McPherson Range *mts.* Australia **67** 28.15S153.00E
Mdantsane R.S.A. **56** 32.54S 27.24E
Mead, L. U.S.A. **81** 36.05N114.25W
Meade U.S.A. **83** 37.17N100.20W
Meadow Lake *town* Canada **75** 54.07N108.20W
Meadville U.S.A. **84** 41.38N 80.09W
Mealhada Portugal **16** 40.22N 8.27W
Meander River *town* Canada **74** 59.02N117.42W
Mearim *r.* Brazil **91** 3.20S 44.20W
Meath *d.* Rep. of Ire. **13** 53.32N 6.40W
Meaux France **15** 48.58N 2.54E
Mécatina, Cap *c.* Canada **77** 50.45N 59.01W
Mecca *see* Makkah Saudi Arabia **48**
Mecca U.S.A. **81** 33.35N116.03W
Mechanicsville U.S.A. **85** 38.26N 76.44W
Mechelen Belgium **14** 51.01N 4.28E
Mecheria Algeria **50** 33.33N 0.17W
Mecklenburger Bucht *b.* Germany **20** 54.05N 11.00E
Mecklenburg-Vorpommern *d.* Germany **20** 53.30N 13.15E
Meconta Mozambique **55** 15.00S 39.50E
Mecufi Mozambique **55** 13.20S 40.32E
Meda Portugal **16** 40.58N 7.16W
Medan Indonesia **36** 3.35N 98.39E
Mede Italy **15** 45.06N 8.44E
Médéa Algeria **51** 36.15N 2.48E
Mededsiz *mtn.* Turkey **42** 37.33N 34.38E
Medegue Gabon **54** 0.37N 10.08E
Medellín Colombia **90** 6.15N 75.36W
Medemblik Neth. **14** 52.48N 5.06E
Médenine Tunisia **51** 33.21N 10.30E
Mederdra Mauritania **52** 17.02N 15.41W
Medford Oreg. U.S.A. **80** 42.19N122.52W
Medford Wisc. U.S.A. **82** 45.09N 90.20W
Medgidia Romania **21** 44.15N 28.16E
Medi Sudan **49** 5.04N 30.44E
Media U.S.A. **85** 39.54N 75.23W
Mediaș Romania **21** 46.10N 24.21E
Medicina Italy **15** 44.28N 11.38E
Medicine Bow Mts. U.S.A. **80** 41.10N106.10W
Medicine Bow Peak *mtn.* U.S.A. **80** 41.21N106.19W
Medicine Hat Canada **75** 50.03N110.40W
Medicine Lake *town* U.S.A. **80** 48.30N104.30W
Medicine Lodge U.S.A. **83** 37.17N 98.35W
Medina *see* Al Madīnah Saudi Arabia **42**
Medina N.Dak. U.S.A. **82** 46.54N 99.18W
Medina N.Y. U.S.A. **84** 43.14N 78.23W
Medina del Campo Spain **16** 41.20N 4.55W
Medina de Ríoseco Spain **16** 41.53N 5.03W
Mêdog China **30** 29.19N 95.19E
Medstead Canada **75** 53.19N108.02W
Medveditsa *r.* Russian Fed. **25** 49.35N 42.45E
Medvezhyegorsk Russian Fed. **24** 62.56N 34.28E
Medvin Ukraine **21** 49.25N 30.48E
Medway *r.* U.K. **11** 51.24N 0.31E
Medzhibozh Ukraine **21** 49.29N 27.28E
Meeberrie Australia **62** 26.58S115.51E
Meekatharra Australia **62** 26.35S118.30E
Meeker U.S.A. **80** 40.02N107.55W
Meer Belgium **14** 51.27N 4.46E
Meerhusener Moor *f.* Germany **14** 53.36N 7.33E
Meerut India **41** 28.59N 77.42E
Mēga Ethiopia **49** 4.07N 38.16E
Mégara Greece **19** 38.00N 23.21E
Megasini *mtn.* India **41** 21.38N 86.21E
Meghalaya *d.* India **41** 25.30N 91.00E
Meghna *r.* Bangla. **41** 22.50N 90.50E
Mégiscane *r.* Canada **76** 48.36N 76.00W
Mehadia Romania **21** 44.55N 22.22E
Mehar Pakistan **40** 27.11N 67.49E
Mehekar India **40** 20.09N 76.34E
Mehidpur India **40** 23.49N 75.40E
Mehndāwal India **41** 26.59N 83.07E
Mehsāna India **40** 23.36N 72.24E
Mehtar Lām Afghan. **40** 34.39N 70.10E
Meiktila Burma **34** 20.53N 95.50E
Meiningen Germany **20** 50.34N 10.25E
Meishan China **33** 30.02N103.50E
Meissen Germany **20** 51.10N 13.28E
Meixian *see* Meizhou China **33**
Meiyino Sudan **49** 6.12N 34.40E
Meizhou China **33** 24.20N116.15E
Mekatina Canada **76** 46.58N 84.05W
Mekdela Ethiopia **49** 11.28N 39.23E
Mek'elē Ethiopia **49** 13.33N 39.30E
Mekerrhane, Sebkha *f.* Algeria **50** 26.22N 1.20E
Mekhtar Pakistan **40** 30.28N 69.22E
Meknès Morocco **50** 33.53N 5.37W
Mekong *r.* Asia **34** 10.00N106.40E
Mekong Delta Vietnam **34** 10.00N105.40E
Mekongga *mtn.* Indonesia **37** 3.39S121.15E
Mékôngk *r.* Kampuchea *see* Mekong *r.* Asia **34**
Mékrou *r.* Benin **53** 12.20N 2.47E
Melaka Malaysia **36** 2.11N102.16E
Melanesia *is.* Pacific Oc. **68** 5.00N165.00E
Melbourne Australia **67** 37.45S144.58E
Melbourne U.S.A. **85** 28.04N 80.38W
Mélé C.A.R. **49** 9.46N 21.33E
Melegnano Italy **15** 45.21N 9.19E
Meleuz Russian Fed. **24** 52.58N 55.56E
Mélèzes, Rivière aux *r.* Canada **77** 57.40N 69.29W
Melfi Chad **53** 11.04N 18.03E
Melfi Italy **18** 40.59N 15.39E
Melilla Morocco **50** 35.17N 2.57W
Melilla Spain **16** 35.17N 2.57W
Melipilla Chile **93** 33.42S 71.13W
Melitopol Ukraine **25** 46.51N 35.22E
Melk Austria **20** 48.14N 15.20E
Mellen U.S.A. **82** 46.20N 90.40W
Mellerud Sweden **23** 58.42N 12.28E
Mellit Sudan **48** 14.08N 25.33E
Melmore Pt. Rep. of Ire. **13** 55.15N 7.49W
Melnik Bulgaria **19** 41.30N 23.22E
Mělník Czech Republic **20** 50.20N 14.29E
Melo Uruguay **94** 32.22S 54.10W
Melrhir, Chott *f.* Algeria **51** 34.20N 6.20E
Melrose U.K. **12** 55.36N 2.43W
Melrose Mont. U.S.A. **80** 45.37N112.41W
Melrose N.Mex U.S.A. **81** 34.26N103.38W
Melstone U.S.A. **80** 46.36N107.52W
Meltaus Finland **22** 66.54N 25.22E
Melton Australia **67** 37.41S144.36E
Melton Mowbray U.K. **10** 52.46N 0.53W
Melun France **15** 48.32N 2.40E
Melvich U.K. **12** 58.33N 3.55W
Melville Canada **75** 50.55N102.48W
Melville, C. Australia **64** 14.11S144.30E
Melville, L. Canada **77** 53.45N 59.30W
Melville B. Australia **64** 12.10S136.32E
Melville Hills Canada **72** 69.20N122.00W
Melville I. Australia **64** 11.30S131.00E
Melville I. Canada **72** 75.30N110.00W
Melville Pen. Canada **73** 68.00N 84.00W
Melvin, Lough Rep. of Ire. / U.K. **13** 54.26N 8.12W
Melzo Italy **15** 45.30N 9.25E
Mêmar Co *l.* China **41** 34.10N 82.15E
Memba Mozambique **57** 14.16S 40.30E
Memboro Indonesia **36** 9.22S119.32E
Memmingen Germany **20** 47.59N 10.11E
Memphis *ruins* Egypt **44** 29.52N 31.12E
Memphis U.S.A. **83** 35.08N 90.03W
Mena Ukraine **21** 51.30N 32.15E
Mena U.S.A. **83** 34.35N 94.15W
Menai Str. U.K. **10** 53.17N 4.20W
Ménaka Mali **51** 15.55N 2.24E
Mènam Khong *r.* Laos *see* Mekong *r.* Asia **34**
Menarandra *r.* Madagascar **57** 25.17S 44.30E
Menard U.S.A. **83** 30.55N 99.47W
Menawashei Sudan **49** 12.40N 24.59E
Mendawai *r.* Indonesia **36** 3.17S113.20E
Mende France **17** 44.32N 3.30E
Mendebo Mts. Ethiopia **49** 7.00N 39.30E
Mendi P.N.G. **37** 6.13S143.39E
Mendip Hills U.K. **11** 51.15N 2.40W
Mendocino, C. U.S.A. **80** 40.25N124.25W
Mendooran Australia **67** 31.48S149.08E
Mendoza Argentina **93** 32.54S 68.50W
Mendoza *d.* Argentina **93** 34.30S 68.00W
Mendung Indonesia **36** 0.31N103.12E
Mene Grande Venezuela **90** 9.51N 70.57W
Menemen Turkey **42** 38.34N 27.03E
Menen Belgium **14** 50.48N 3.07E
Menfi Italy **18** 37.36N 12.59E
Mengcheng China **32** 33.16N116.33E
Mengzi China **39** 23.20N103.21E
Menihek Lakes Canada **77** 54.00N 66.35W
Menindee Australia **66** 32.23S142.30E
Menindee L. Australia **66** 32.21S142.20E
Menominee U.S.A. **82** 45.07N 87.37W
Menomonie U.S.A. **82** 44.53N 91.55W
Menongue Angola **54** 14.40S 17.41E
Menorca *i.* Spain **16** 40.00N 4.00E
Mentawai, Kepulauan *is.* Indonesia **36** 2.50S 99.00E
Mentekab Malaysia **36** 3.29N102.21E
Mentok Indonesia **36** 2.04S105.12E
Menton France **17** 43.47N 7.30E
Menyapa, Gunung *mtn.* Indonesia **36** 1.00N116.20E
Menzel Bourguiba Tunisia **51** 37.10N 9.48E
Menzies Australia **63** 29.41S121.02E
Menzies, Mt. Antarctica **96** 71.50S 61.00E
Meppel Neth. **14** 52.42N 6.12E
Meppen Germany **14** 52.42N 7.17E
Mer France **15** 47.42N 1.30E
Merano Italy **18** 46.41N 11.10E
Merauke Indonesia **64** 8.30S140.22E
Merbein Australia **66** 34.11S142.04E
Mercato Saraceno Italy **15** 43.57N 12.12E
Merced U.S.A. **80** 37.18N120.29W
Mercedes Buenos Aires Argentina **93** 34.40S 59.25W
Mercedes Corrientes Argentina **92** 29.15S 58.05W
Mercedes San Luis Argentina **93** 33.40S 65.30W
Mercedes Uruguay **93** 33.16S 58.01W
Mercy, C. Canada **73** 65.00N 63.30W
Mere U.K. **11** 51.05N 2.16W
Meredith Australia **66** 37.50S144.05E
Meredith, L. U.S.A. **83** 35.36N101.42W
Mereeg Somali Rep. **45** 3.47N 47.18E
Merefa Ukraine **25** 49.49N 36.05E
Mereke C.A.R. **49** 7.34N 23.09E
Mergenevo Kazakhstan **25** 49.59N 51.19E
Mergui Burma **34** 12.26N 98.38E
Mergui Archipelago *is.* Burma **34** 11.15N 98.00E
Meribah Australia **66** 34.42S140.53E
Meriç *r.* Turkey **19** 40.52N 26.12E
Mérida Mexico **87** 20.59N 89.39W
Mérida Spain **16** 38.55N 6.20W
Mérida Venezuela **90** 8.24N 71.08W
Mérida, Cordillera de *mts.* Venezuela **90** 8.30N 71.00W
Meridian U.S.A. **83** 32.22N 88.42W

Mérignac to **Montbéliard**

Mérignac France **17** 44.50N 0.42W
Merigur Australia **66** 34.21S141.23E
Merikarvia Finland **23** 61.51N 21.30E
Merimbula Australia **67** 36.52S149.55E
Merino Australia **66** 37.45S141.35E
Merir *i.* Pacific Oc. **37** 4.19N132.18E
Merirumã Brazil **91** 1.15N 54.50W
Merizo Guam **68** 13.16N144.40E
Merksem Belgium **14** 51.14N 4.25E
Merlo Argentina **93** 34.40S 58.45W
Merredin Australia **63** 31.29S118.16E
Merrick *mtn.* U.K. **12** 55.08N 4.29W
Merrill Oreg. U.S.A. **80** 42.01N121.36W
Merrill Wisc. U.S.A. **82** 45.11N 89.41W
Merriman U.S.A. **82** 42.55N101.42W
Merritt Canada **74** 50.10N120.45W
Merriwa Australia **67** 32.08S150.20E
Mersa Fatma Ethiopia **48** 14.55N 40.20E
Mersch Lux. **14** 49.44N 6.05E
Mersea I. U.K. **11** 51.47N 0.58E
Merseburg Germany **20** 51.22N 12.00E
Mersey *r.* U.K. **10** 53.22N 2.37W
Merseyside *d.* U.K. **10** 53.28N 3.00W
Mersin Turkey **42** 36.47N 34.37E
Mersing Malaysia **36** 2.25N103.50E
Merta India **40** 26.39N 74.02E
Merta Road *town* India **40** 26.43N 73.55E
Merthyr Tydfil U.K. **11** 51.45N 3.23W
Mértola Portugal **16** 37.38N 7.40W
Merton U.K. **11** 51.25N 0.12W
Mertzon U.S.A. **83** 31.16N100.49W
Méru France **15** 49.14N 2.08E
Meru *mtn.* Tanzania **55** 3.15S 36.44E
Méry France **15** 48.30N 3.53E
Merzifon Turkey **42** 40.52N 35.28E
Merzig Germany **14** 49.26N 6.39E
Mesa U.S.A. **81** 33.25N111.50W
Mesagne Italy **19** 40.33N 17.49E
Meslay-du-Maine France **15** 47.57N 0.33W
Mesocco Switz. **15** 46.23N 9.14E
Mesolóngion Greece **19** 38.23N 21.23E
Mesopotamia *f.* Iraq **43** 33.30N 44.30E
Messalo *r.* Mozambique **55** 11.38S 40.27E
Messina Italy **18** 38.13N 15.34E
Messina R.S.A. **56** 22.20S 30.03E
Messina, Stretto di *str.* Italy **18** 38.10N 15.35E
Messíni Greece **19** 37.03N 22.00E
Messiniakós, Kólpos *g.* Greece **19** 36.50N 22.05E
Mesta *r.* Bulgaria *see* Néstos *r.* Greece **19**
Mestre Italy **15** 45.29N 12.15E
Meta *r.* Venezuela **90** 6.10N 67.30W
Metán Argentina **92** 25.30S 65.00W
Metangula Mozambique **55** 12.41S 34.51E
Metković Croatia **19** 43.03N 17.38E
Metlakatla U.S.A. **74** 55.09N131.35W
Métsovon Greece **19** 39.46N 21.11E
Metz France **17** 49.07N 6.11E
Meulaboh Indonesia **36** 4.10N 96.09E
Meulan France **15** 49.01N 1.54E
Meuse *r.* Belgium *see* Maas *r.* Neth. **14**
Mexia U.S.A. **83** 31.41N 96.29W
Mexicali Mexico **81** 32.40N115.29W
Mexico C. America **86** 20.00N100.00W
México *d.* Mexico **86** 19.45N 99.30W
Mexico U.S.A. **82** 39.10N 91.53W
Mexico, G. of N. America **86** 25.00N 90.00W
Mexico City *see* Ciudad de México Mexico **86**
Meydân Kalay Afghan. **40** 32.25N 66.44E
Meydân Khvolah Afghan. **40** 33.36N 69.51E
Meymaneh Afghan. **38** 35.54N 64.43E
Mezen Russian Fed. **24** 65.50N 44.20E
Mezen *r.* Russian Fed. **24** 65.50N 44.18E
Mézenc, Mont *mtn.* France **17** 44.54N 4.11E
Mezenskaya Guba *g.* Russian Fed. **24** 66.30N 44.00E
Mezökövesd Hungary **21** 47.50N 20.34E
Mezzolombardo Italy **15** 46.13N 11.05E
Mhow India **40** 22.33N 75.46E
Miahuatlán Mexico **86** 16.20N 96.36W
Miājlar India **40** 26.15N 70.23E
Miami Fla. U.S.A. **85** 25.45N 80.15W
Miami Okla. U.S.A. **83** 36.53N 94.53W
Miami Tex. U.S.A. **83** 35.42N100.38W
Miami Beach *town* U.S.A. **85** 25.47N 80.07W
Miāndow Āb Iran **43** 36.57N 46.06E
Miandrivazo Madagascar **57** 19.31S 45.28E
Miāneh Iran **43** 37.23N 47.45E
Miang, Phukao *mtn.* Thailand **34** 16.55N101.00E
Miāni India **40** 21.51N 69.23E
Miāni Hōr *b.* Pakistan **40** 25.34N 66.19E
Miānwāli Pakistan **40** 32.35N 71.33E
Mianyang Hubei China **33** 30.25N113.30E
Mianyang Sichuan China **33** 31.26N104.45E
Miao'er Shan *mtn.* China **33** 25.50N110.22E
Miaoli Taiwan **33** 24.34N120.48E
Miarinarivo Madagascar **57** 18.57S 46.55E
Miass Russian Fed. **28** 55.00N 60.00E
Mibu *r.* Japan **35** 35.49N137.57E
Mica R.S.A. **56** 24.09S 30.49E
Micang Shan *mts.* China **32** 32.40N107.28E
Michael, L. Canada **77** 54.32N 58.15W
Michalovce Slovakia **21** 48.45N 21.55E
Michelson, Mt. U.S.A. **72** 69.19N144.17W
Michigan *d.* U.S.A. **84** 44.00N 85.00W
Michigan, L. U.S.A. **84** 44.00N 87.00W
Michigan City U.S.A. **84** 41.43N 86.54W
Michipicoten Canada **76** 47.59N 84.55W
Michipicoten I. Canada **76** 47.40N 85.50W
Michoacán *d.* Mexico **86** 19.20N101.00W
Michurin Bulgaria **19** 42.09N 27.51E
Michurinsk Russian Fed. **24** 52.54N 40.30E
Micronesia *is.* Pacific Oc. **68** 8.00N160.00E
Midale Canada **75** 49.22N103.27W
Mid Atlantic Ridge *f.* Atlantic Oc. **95** 20.00N 45.00W
Middelburg Neth. **14** 51.30N 3.36E
Middelburg C.P. R.S.A. **56** 31.29S 25.00E
Middelburg Trans. R.S.A. **56** 25.45S 29.27E
Middelharnis Neth. **14** 51.46N 4.09E
Middenmeer Neth. **14** 52.51N 4.59E
Middleboro Canada **75** 49.01N 95.21W
Middlebury U.S.A. **84** 44.01N 73.10W
Middle I. Australia **63** 34.07S123.12E
Middle Loup *r.* U.S.A. **82** 41.17N 98.23W
Middleport U.S.A. **76** 43.13N 78.29W
Middlesboro U.S.A. **85** 36.37N 83.43W
Middlesbrough U.K. **10** 54.34N 1.13W
Middleton Canada **77** 44.57N 65.04W
Middleton Reef Pacific Oc. **68** 29.28S159.06E
Middletown Del. U.S.A. **85** 39.25N 75.47W
Middletown Ind. U.S.A. **84** 39.31N 84.13W
Middletown N.Y. U.S.A. **85** 41.27N 74.25W
Mid Glamorgan *d.* U.K. **11** 51.38N 3.25W
Midi-Pyrénées *d.* France **17** 44.10N 2.00E
Midland Canada **76** 44.45N 79.53W
Midland Mich. U.S.A. **84** 43.38N 84.14W
Midland Tex. U.S.A. **83** 32.00N102.05W
Midland Junction Australia **63** 31.54S115.57E
Midleton Rep. of Ire. **13** 51.55N 8.10W
Midnapore India **41** 22.26N 87.20E
Midongy-Sud Madagascar **57** 23.35S 47.01E
Midway Is. Hawaiian Is. **68** 28.15N177.25W
Midwest U.S.A. **80** 43.25N106.16W
Midwest City U.S.A. **83** 35.27N 97.24W
Midyan *f.* Saudi Arabia **44** 27.50N 35.30E
Midye Turkey **19** 41.37N 28.07E
Midžor *mtn.* Bulgaria / Yugo. **19** 43.23N 22.42E
Mie *d.* Japan **35** 34.42N136.08E
Miechów Poland **21** 50.23N 20.01E
Miedzychód Poland **20** 52.36N 15.55E
Mielec Poland **21** 50.18N 21.25E
Mienga Angola **54** 17.16S 19.50E
Mieres Spain **16** 43.15N 5.46W
Migang Shan *mtn.* China **32** 35.32N106.13E
Miguel Hidalgo, Presa *resr.* Mexico **81** 26.41N108.19W
Migyaunglaung Burma **34** 14.40N 98.09E
Mijares *r.* Spain **16** 39.58N 0.01W
Mikhaylov Russian Fed. **24** 54.14N 39.00E
Mikhaylovgrad Bulgaria **19** 43.25N 23.11E
Mikhaylovka Russian Fed. **25** 50.05N 43.15E
Miki Japan **35** 34.48N134.59E
Mikínai Greece **19** 37.44N 22.45E
Mikindani Tanzania **55** 10.16S 40.05E
Mikkeli Finland **24** 61.44N 27.15E
Mikkwa *r.* Canada **74** 58.25N114.46W
Mikonos *i.* Greece **19** 37.29N 25.25E
Mikumi Tanzania **55** 7.22S 37.00E
Mikun Russian Fed. **24** 62.20N 50.01E
Milagro Ecuador **90** 2.11S 79.36W
Milan *see* Milano Italy **15**
Milan U.S.A. **82** 40.12N 93.07W
Milange Mozambique **55** 16.09S 35.44E
Milano Italy **15** 45.28N 9.10E
Milâs Turkey **19** 37.18N 27.48E
Milbank U.S.A. **82** 45.14N 96.38W
Milbanke Sd. Canada **74** 52.18N128.33W
Mildenhall U.K. **11** 52.20N 0.30E
Mildura Australia **66** 34.14S142.13E
Miles Australia **64** 26.40S150.11E
Miles City U.S.A. **80** 46.25N105.51W
Milford Del. U.S.A. **85** 38.55N 75.25W
Milford Utah U.S.A. **80** 38.24N113.01W
Milford Haven *town* U.K. **11** 51.43N 5.02W
Milford Sound *town* New Zealand **60** 44.41S167.56E
Miliana Algeria **51** 27.21N 2.28E
Miling Australia **63** 30.27S116.20E
Milk *r.* U.S.A. **80** 48.05N106.15W
Millau France **17** 44.06N 3.05E
Millbrook U.S.A. **85** 41.47N 73.42W
Mille Lacs, Lac des *l.* Canada **76** 48.45N 90.35W
Mille Lacs L. U.S.A. **82** 46.10N 93.45W
Miller *r.* Australia **66** 30.05S136.07E
Millerovo Russian Fed. **25** 48.55N 40.25E
Millersburg U.S.A. **84** 45.21N 84.02W
Milleur Pt. U.K. **12** 55.01N 5.07W
Millicent Australia **66** 37.36S140.22E
Millington U.S.A. **85** 39.16N 75.50W
Millinocket U.S.A. **84** 45.39N 68.43W
Millmerran Australia **65** 27.51S151.17E
Millom U.K. **10** 54.13N 3.16W
Mills L. Canada **74** 61.30N118.10W
Millville U.S.A. **85** 39.24N 75.02W
Milne Inlet *town* Canada **73** 72.30N 80.59W
Milo *r.* Guinea **52** 11.05N 9.05W
Mílos Greece **19** 36.45N 24.27E
Mílos *i.* Greece **19** 36.40N 24.26E
Milparinka Australia **66** 29.45S141.55E
Milton Australia **67** 35.19S150.24E
Milton Canada **76** 43.31N 79.53W
Milton U.S.A. **85** 38.47N 75.19W
Milton Keynes U.K. **11** 52.03N 0.42W
Miltou Chad **53** 10.10N 17.30E
Miluo China **33** 28.50N113.05E
Milwaukee U.S.A. **82** 43.02N 87.55W
Milwaukie U.S.A. **80** 45.27N122.38W
Milyatino Russian Fed. **24** 54.30N 34.20E
Mim Ghana **52** 6.55N 2.34W
Miminiska L. Canada **76** 51.32N 88.33W
Mina U.S.A. **80** 38.24N118.07W
Mīnā 'al Aḥmadī Kuwait **38** 29.04N 48.08E
Mīnāb Iran **43** 27.07N 57.05E
Mīnā Baranīs Egypt **48** 23.55N 35.28E
Minaki Canada **76** 50.00N 94.48W
Minas Uruguay **93** 34.23S 55.14W
Minas Basin *b.* Canada **77** 45.20N 64.00W
Minas Channel *str.* Canada **77** 45.15N 64.45W
Minas de Corrales Uruguay **93** 31.35S 55.28W
Minas de Riotinto Spain **16** 37.41N 6.37W
Minas Gerais *d.* Brazil **94** 18.00S 45.00W
Minatitlán Mexico **86** 17.59N 94.32W
Minbu Burma **34** 20.09N 94.52E
Mindanao *i.* Phil. **37** 7.30N125.00E
Mindanao Sea Phil. **37** 9.10N124.25E
Minden Germany **20** 52.18N 8.54E
Minden U.S.A. **83** 32.37N 93.17W
Mindif Cameroon **53** 10.25N 14.23E
Mindiptana Indonesia **37** 5.45S140.22E
Mindona L. Australia **66** 33.09S142.09E
Mindoro *i.* Phil. **37** 13.00N121.00E
Mindoro Str. Pacific Oc. **37** 12.30N120.10E
Mindra *mtn.* Romania **21** 45.20N 23.32E
Minehead U.K. **11** 51.12N 3.29W
Mineola U.S.A. **83** 32.40N 95.29W
Minerva Australia **64** 24.00S148.05E
Mingan Canada **77** 50.18N 64.02W
Mingary Australia **66** 32.09S140.46E
Mingela Australia **64** 19.53S146.40E
Mingenew Australia **63** 29.11S115.26E
Mingin Burma **34** 22.52N 94.39E
Mingin Range *mts.* Burma **34** 24.00N 95.45E
Minhe China **32** 36.12N102.59E
Minidoka U.S.A. **80** 42.46N113.30W
Minigwal, L. Australia **63** 29.35S123.12E
Min Jiang *r.* China **33** 26.06N119.15E
Minlaton Australia **66** 34.46S137.37E
Minna Nigeria **53** 9.39N 6.32E
Minneapolis Kans. U.S.A. **82** 39.08N 97.42W
Minneapolis Minn. U.S.A. **82** 44.59N 93.13W
Minnedosa Canada **75** 50.14N 99.51W
Minnesota *d.* U.S.A. **82** 46.00N 94.00W
Minnesota *r.* U.S.A. **82** 44.54N 93.10W
Minnesota Lake *town* U.S.A. **82** 43.51N 93.50W
Minnipa Australia **66** 32.51S135.09E
Minnitaki L. Canada **76** 50.00N 91.50W
Mino Japan **35** 35.34N136.56E
Miño *r.* Spain **16** 41.50N 8.52W
Minobu-sanchi *mts.* Japan **35** 35.05N138.15E
Mino-kamo Japan **35** 35.26N137.01E
Mino-mikawa-kōgen *mts.* Japan **35** 35.16N137.10E
Minorca *i. see* Menorca *i.* Spain **16**
Minot U.S.A. **82** 48.16N101.19W
Minqin China **32** 38.42N103.11E
Minsen Germany **14** 53.44N 7.59E
Min Shan *mts.* China **32** 32.40N104.40E
Minsk Belorussia **21** 53.51N 27.30E
Minto, L. Canada **73** 51.00N 73.37W
Minto, Lac *l.* Canada **76** 57.15N 74.50W
Minturno Italy **18** 41.15N 13.45E
Minûf Egypt **44** 30.28N 30.56E
Min Xian China **32** 34.26N104.02E
Minyā al Qamḥ Egypt **44** 30.31N 31.21E
Minyar Russian Fed. **24** 55.06N 57.29E
Miquelon Canada **76** 49.25N 76.32W
Mira Italy **15** 45.26N 12.08E
Mīrābād Afghan. **40** 30.25N 61.50E
Miracema Brazil **94** 21.22S 42.09W
Mirah, Wādī al *r.* Iraq **42** 32.27N 41.21E
Miraj India **38** 16.51N 74.42E
Miramichi B. Canada **77** 47.08N 65.08W
Mīram Shāh Pakistan **40** 33.01N 70.04E
Mīrān Pakistan **40** 31.24N 70.43E
Miranda de Ebro Spain **16** 42.41N 2.57W
Miranda do Douro Portugal **16** 41.30N 6.16W
Mirande France **17** 43.31N 0.25E
Mirandela Portugal **16** 41.28N 7.10W
Mirando City U.S.A. **83** 27.26N 99.00W
Mirandola Italy **15** 44.53N 11.04E
Mīr Bachcheh Kūt Afghan. **40** 34.45N 69.08E
Mirbāṭ Oman **38** 17.00N 54.45E
Mirecourt France **17** 48.18N 6.08E
Miri Malaysia **36** 4.28N114.00E
Miriam Vale *town* Australia **64** 24.20S151.34E
Mirim, L. Brazil **94** 33.10S 53.30W
Mirintu Creek *r.* Australia **66** 28.58S143.18E
Mironovka Ukraine **21** 49.40N 30.59E
Miroşi Romania **21** 44.25N 24.58E
Mīrpur Jammu & Kashmir **40** 33.15N 73.55E
Mīrpur Batoro Pakistan **40** 24.44N 68.16E
Mīrpur Khās Pakistan **38** 25.33N 69.05E
Mīrpur Sakro Pakistan **40** 24.33N 67.37E
Miryeny Moldavia **21** 47.00N 29.06E
Mīrzāpur India **41** 25.09N 82.35E
Miscou I. Canada **77** 47.57N 64.33W
Mishawaka U.S.A. **84** 41.38N 86.10W
Mishima Japan **35** 35.07N138.55E
Mishkino Russian Fed. **24** 55.34N 56.00E
Misima I. P.N.G. **64** 10.40S152.45E
Misiones *d.* Argentina **92** 27.00S 54.40W
Miskī Sudan **48** 14.51N 24.13E
Miskolc Hungary **21** 48.07N 20.47E
Mismār Sudan **48** 18.13N 35.38E
Misool *i.* Indonesia **37** 1.50S130.10E
Miṣr al Jadīdah Egypt **44** 30.06N 31.20E
Miṣrātah Libya **51** 32.23N 15.06E
Miṣrātah *d.* Libya **51** 30.30N 17.00E
Miṣr Baḥrī *f.* Egypt **44** 30.30N 31.00E
Missinaibi *r.* Canada **76** 50.44N 81.29W
Mission U.S.A. **82** 43.18N100.40W
Mississauga Canada **76** 43.35N 79.37W
Mississippi *d.* U.S.A. **83** 32.40N 90.00W
Mississippi *r.* U.S.A. **83** 29.00N 89.15W
Mississippi Delta U.S.A. **83** 29.10N 89.15W
Mississippi Sd. U.S.A. **83** 30.15N 88.40W
Missoula U.S.A. **80** 46.52N114.01W
Missouri *d.* U.S.A. **82** 38.30N 92.00W
Missouri *r.* U.S.A. **82** 38.50N 90.08W
Missouri Valley *town* U.S.A. **82** 41.33N 95.53W
Mistake Creek *town* Australia **62** 17.06S129.04E
Mistassini Canada **77** 48.54N 72.13W
Mistassini *r.* Canada **77** 48.53N 72.14W
Mistassini, Lac *l.* Canada **77** 51.15N 73.10W
Mistassini Prov. Park Canada **77** 51.30N 73.20W
Mistastin Canada **77** 55.55N 63.30W
Mistinibi, L. Canada **77** 55.55N 64.10W
Mistretta Italy **18** 37.56N 14.22E
Mitchell Australia **64** 26.29S147.58E
Mitchell *r.* Qld. Australia **64** 15.12S141.35E
Mitchell *r.* Vic. Australia **67** 37.53S147.41E
Mitchell Oreg. U.S.A. **80** 44.34N120.09W
Mitchell S.Dak. U.S.A. **82** 43.40N 98.00W
Mitchell, Mt. U.S.A. **85** 35.47N 82.16W
Mitchelstown Rep. of Ire. **13** 52.16N 8.17W
Mīt Ghamr Egypt **44** 30.43N 31.16E
Mithapur India **40** 22.25N 69.00E
Mithi Pakistan **40** 24.44N 69.48E
Mitilíni Greece **19** 39.06N 26.34E
Mitla, Mamarr *pass* Egypt **44** 30.00N 32.53E
Mitla Pass *see* Mitla, Mamarr *pass* Egypt **44**
Mitrovica Yugo. **19** 42.54N 20.51E
Mitsinjo Madagascar **57** 16.01S 45.52E
Mits'iwa Ethiopia **48** 15.36N 39.29E
Mits'iwa Channel Ethiopia **48** 15.30N 40.00E
Mittagong Australia **67** 34.27S150.25E
Mittelandkanal Germany **14** 52.24N 7.52E
Mitú Colombia **90** 1.08N 70.03W
Mitumba, Monts *mts.* Zaïre **55** 3.00S 28.30E
Mitwaba Zaïre **55** 8.32S 27.20E
Mitzic Gabon **54** 0.48N 11.30E
Miura Japan **35** 35.08N139.37E
Miya *r.* Japan **35** 34.32N136.44E
Miyako jima *i.* Japan **31** 24.45N125.25E
Miyakonojō Japan **35** 31.43N131.02E
Miyazaki Japan **35** 31.58N131.50E
Mizdah Libya **51** 31.26N 12.59E
Mizen Head Rep. of Ire. **13** 51.27N 9.50W
Mizil Romania **21** 45.00N 26.26E
Mizoch Ukraine **21** 50.30N 25.50E
Mizoram *d.* India **39** 23.40N 92.40E
Mizpe Ramon Israel **44** 30.36N 34.48E
Mizukaidō Japan **35** 36.01N139.59E
Mizunami Japan **35** 35.22N137.15E
Mjölby Sweden **23** 58.19N 15.08E
Mjösa *l.* Norway **23** 60.40N 11.00E
Mkata Tanzania **55** 5.47S 38.18E
Mkushi Zambia **55** 13.40S 29.26E
Mkuze R.S.A. **57** 27.10S 32.00E
Mkwaja Tanzania **55** 5.46S 38.51E
Mkwiti Tanzania **55** 10.27S 39.18E
Mladá Boleslav Czech Republic **20** 50.26N 14.55E
Mława Poland **21** 53.06N 20.23E
Mljet *i.* Croatia **19** 42.45N 17.30E
Mneni Zimbabwe **56** 20.38S 30.03E
Moab U.S.A. **80** 38.35N109.33W
Moa I. Australia **64** 10.12S142.16E
Moama Australia **67** 36.05S144.50E
Moamba Mozambique **57** 25.35S 32.13E
Moanda Gabon **54** 1.25S 13.18E
Moapa U.S.A. **81** 36.40N114.39W
Moatize Mozambique **57** 16.10S 33.40E
Moba Zaïre **55** 7.03S 29.42E
Mobara Japan **35** 35.25N140.18E
Mobaye C.A.R. **49** 4.19N 21.11E
Moberly U.S.A. **82** 39.25N 92.26W
Mobert Canada **76** 48.41N 85.40W
Mobile U.S.A. **83** 30.42N 88.05W
Mobile B. U.S.A. **83** 30.25N 88.00W
Mobridge U.S.A. **82** 45.32N100.26W
Mobutu Sese Seko, L. *see* Albert, L. Uganda / Zaïre **55**
Moçambique *town* Mozambique **55** 15.00S 40.47E
Mocimboa da Praia Mozambique **55** 11.19S 40.19E
Mocimboa do Ruvuma Mozambique **55** 11.05S 39.15E
Moclips U.S.A. **80** 47.14N124.13W
Mococa Brazil **94** 21.28S 47.00W
Moctezuma Mexico **81** 30.10N106.28W
Mocuba Mozambique **55** 16.52S 37.02E
Modane France **17** 45.12N 6.40E
Modāsa India **40** 23.28N 73.18E
Modder *r.* R.S.A. **56** 29.03S 23.56E
Modena Italy **15** 44.39N 10.55E
Modena U.S.A. **80** 37.48N113.57W
Modesto U.S.A. **80** 37.39N121.00W
Modica Italy **18** 36.51N 14.51E
Modjamboli Zaïre **54** 2.28N 22.06E
Moe Australia **67** 38.10S146.15E
Moebase Mozambique **57** 17.04S 38.41E
Moelv Norway **23** 60.56N 10.42E
Moffat U.K. **12** 55.20N 3.27W
Moga India **40** 30.48N 75.10E
Mogadishu *see* Muqdisho Somali Rep. **55**
Mogaung Burma **34** 25.15N 96.54E
Mogi das Cruzes Brazil **94** 23.33S 46.14W
Mogi-Guaçu Brazil **94** 20.55S 48.06W
Mogilev Belorussia **21** 53.54N 30.20E
Mogilev Podolskiy Ukraine **21** 48.29N 27.49E
Mogilno Poland **21** 52.40N 17.58E
Mogi-Mirim Brazil **94** 22.29S 46.55W
Mogincual Mozambique **55** 15.33S 40.29E
Mogliano Veneto Italy **15** 45.33N 12.14E
Mogok Burma **34** 23.00N 96.30E
Mogollon Rim *f.* U.S.A. **81** 32.30N111.00W
Mogumber Australia **63** 31.01S116.02E
Mohács Hungary **21** 45.59N 18.42E
Mohammedia Morocco **50** 33.44N 7.24W
Mohana India **41** 25.54N 77.45E
Mohawk U.S.A. **81** 32.41N113.47W
Mohéli *i.* Comoros **55** 12.22S 43.45E
Mohon France **15** 49.45N 4.44E
Mohoro Tanzania **55** 8.09S 39.07E
Mohoru Kenya **55** 1.01S 34.07E
Moi Norway **23** 58.28N 6.32E
Moincêr China **41** 31.10N 80.52E
Moindi Gabon **54** 3.24S 11.43E
Mointy Kazakhstan **28** 47.10N 73.18E
Mo-i-Rana Norway **22** 66.19N 14.10E
Mõisaküla Estonia **23** 58.06N 25.11E
Moisdon France **15** 47.37N 1.22W
Moisie *r.* Canada **77** 50.13N 66.02W
Moissac France **17** 44.07N 1.05E
Moïssala Chad **53** 8.20N 17.40E
Mojave U.S.A. **81** 35.03N118.10W
Mojave Desert U.S.A. **81** 35.00N117.00W
Mojokerto Indonesia **37** 7.25S112.31E
Mokameh India **41** 25.24N 85.55E
Mokau New Zealand **60** 38.41S174.37E
Mokmer Indonesia **37** 1.13S136.13E
Mokpo S. Korea **31** 34.50N126.25E
Mol Belgium **14** 51.11N 5.09E
Molchanovo Russian Fed. **28** 57.39N 83.45E
Mold U.K. **10** 53.10N 3.08W
Moldavia Europe **21** 47.30N 28.30E
Molde Norway **22** 62.44N 7.08E
Molepolole Botswana **56** 24.26S 25.34E
Molfetta Italy **19** 41.12N 16.36E
Molihong Shan *mtn.* China **32** 42.11N124.43E
Molina de Aragón Spain **16** 40.50N 1.54W
Moline U.S.A. **82** 41.30N 90.30W
Molinella Italy **15** 44.37N 11.40E
Molino Lacy Mexico **81** 30.05N114.24W
Moliro Zaïre **55** 8.11S 30.29E
Molise *d.* Italy **18** 41.40N 15.00E
Mollendo Peru **92** 17.02S 72.01W
Mölndal Sweden **23** 57.39N 12.01E
Molodechno Belorussia **21** 54.16N 26.50E
Molokai *i.* Hawaii U.S.A. **78** 21.20N157.00W
Molong Australia **67** 33.08S148.53E
Molopo *r.* R.S.A. **56** 28.30S 20.22E
Moloundou Cameroon **54** 2.55N 12.01E
Molson L. Canada **75** 54.12N 96.45W
Molt U.S.A. **82** 46.22N102.20W
Molteno R.S.A. **56** 31.23S 26.21E
Moluccas *is.* Indonesia **37** 4.00S128.00E
Molucca Sea *see* Maluku, Laut *sea* Pacific Oc. **37**
Moma Mozambique **55** 16.40S 39.10E
Mombasa Kenya **55** 4.04S 39.40E
Momi Zaïre **55** 1.42S 27.03E
Mompós Colombia **90** 9.15N 74.29W
Mon *d.* Burma **34** 16.45N 97.25E
Mön *i.* Denmark **23** 55.00N 12.20E
Mona *i.* Puerto Rico **87** 18.06N 67.54W
Monaco Europe **17** 43.40N 7.25E
Monadhliath Mts. U.K. **12** 57.09N 4.08W
Monaghan Rep. of Ire. **13** 54.15N 6.58W
Monaghan *d.* Rep. of Ire. **13** 54.10N 7.00W
Monahans U.S.A. **83** 31.36N102.54W
Monarch Mt. Canada **74** 51.55N125.57W
Monastir Tunisia **51** 35.35N 10.50E
Moncalieri Italy **15** 45.00N 7.40E
Monchegorsk Russian Fed. **24** 67.55N 33.01E
Mönchen-Gladbach Germany **14** 51.12N 6.25E
Monchique Portugal **16** 37.19N 8.33W
Monclova Mexico **83** 26.54N101.25W
Moncton Canada **77** 46.06N 64.47W
Mondo Tanzania **55** 5.00S 35.54E
Mondoubleau France **15** 47.59N 0.54E
Mondovì Italy **15** 44.24N 7.50E
Mondrain I. Australia **63** 34.08S122.15E
Monessen U.S.A. **84** 40.08N 79.54W
Monet Canada **76** 48.10N 75.40W
Monett U.S.A. **83** 36.55N 93.55W
Monfalcone Italy **18** 45.49N 13.32E
Monforte Spain **16** 42.32N 7.30W
Monga Zaïre **49** 4.12N 22.49E
Mongala *r.* Zaïre **54** 1.58N 19.55E
Mongalla Sudan **49** 5.12N 31.46E
Mong Cai Vietnam **33** 21.36N107.55E
Mongers L. Australia **63** 29.15S117.05E
Monghyr India **41** 25.23N 86.28E
Mongo Chad **53** 12.14N 18.45E
Mongolia Asia **30** 46.30N104.00E
Mongororo Chad **49** 12.01N 22.28E
Mongu Zambia **54** 15.10S 23.09E
Monifieth U.K. **12** 56.29N 2.50W
Monitor Range *mts.* U.S.A. **80** 38.45N116.30W
Monkoto Zaïre **49** 1.38S 20.39E
Monmouth U.K. **11** 51.48N 2.43W
Monmouth Ill. U.S.A. **82** 40.54N 90.39W
Monmouth Oreg. U.S.A. **80** 44.51N123.14W
Monocacy *r.* U.S.A. **85** 39.13N 77.27W
Mono L. U.S.A. **80** 38.00N119.00W
Monopoli Italy **19** 40.56N 17.19E
Monor Hungary **21** 47.21N 19.27E
Monreal del Campo Spain **16** 40.47N 1.20W
Monroe La. U.S.A. **83** 32.33N 92.07W
Monroe Mich. U.S.A. **84** 41.56N 83.21W
Monroe N.C. U.S.A. **85** 35.00N 80.35W
Monroe N.Y. U.S.A. **85** 41.20N 74.11W
Monroe Wisc. U.S.A. **82** 42.36N 89.38W
Monroe City U.S.A. **82** 39.39N 91.44W
Monroeville U.S.A. **85** 31.32N 87.21W
Monrovia Liberia **52** 6.20N 10.46W
Mons Belgium **14** 50.27N 3.57E
Monselice Italy **15** 45.14N 11.45E
Mönsterås Sweden **23** 57.02N 16.26E
Montabaur Germany **14** 50.27N 7.51E
Montagnana Italy **15** 45.14N 11.28E
Montague Canada **77** 46.10N 62.39W
Montalbán Spain **16** 40.50N 0.48W
Montalto di Castro Italy **18** 42.21N 11.37E
Montana Switz. **15** 46.18N 7.29E
Montana *d.* U.S.A. **80** 47.14N109.26W
Montargis France **15** 48.00N 2.44E
Montauban France **17** 44.01N 1.20E
Montbard France **15** 47.37N 4.20E
Montbéliard France **17** 47.31N 6.48E

Montbrison to Müritzsee

Montbrison France 17 45.37N 4.04E
Montceau-les-Mines France 17 46.40N 4.22E
Mont Cenis, Col du pass France 17 45.15N 6.55E
Montcornet France 15 49.41N 4.01E
Mont de Marsan town France 17 43.54N 0.30W
Montdidier France 15 49.39N 2.34E
Monte Alegre town Brazil 91 2.01S 54.04W
Monte Azul town Brazil 94 15.53S 42.53W
Montebello Canada 77 45.39N 74.56W
Monte Carlo Monaco 17 43.44N 7.25E
Monte Caseros Argentina 93 30.15S 57.38W
Montecatini Terme Italy 15 43.53N 10.46E
Montecristo i. Italy 18 42.20N 10.19E
Montego Bay town Jamaica 87 18.27N 77.56W
Montélimar France 17 44.33N 4.45E
Montemor-o-Velho Portugal 16 40.10N 8.41W
Montenegro see Crna Gora d. Yugo. 19
Montepuez Mozambique 57 13.09S 39.33E
Montereau France 15 48.22N 2.57E
Monterey U.S.A. 80 36.37N121.55W
Monterey B. U.S.A. 80 36.45N121.55W
Montería Colombia 90 8.45N 75.54W
Montero Bolivia 92 17.20S 63.15W
Monteros Argentina 92 27.10S 65.30W
Monterrey Mexico 83 25.40N100.19W
Monte Santu, Capo di c. Italy 18 40.05N 9.44E
Montes Claros Brazil 94 16.45S 43.52W
Montevideo Uruguay 93 34.53S 56.11W
Montevideo U.S.A. 82 44.57N 95.43W
Montezuma U.S.A. 83 37.36N100.26W
Montfort-sur-Meu France 15 48.08N 1.57W
Montgomery U.K. 11 52.34N 3.09W
Montgomery U.S.A. 85 32.22N 86.20W
Montguyon France 17 45.13N 0.11W
Monthey Switz. 15 46.15N 6.57E
Monthois France 15 49.19N 4.43E
Monticello Ark. U.S.A. 83 33.38N 91.47W
Monticello Miss. U.S.A. 83 31.33N 90.07W
Monticello Utah U.S.A. 80 37.52N109.21W
Montichiari Italy 15 45.25N 10.23E
Montiel, Campo de f. Spain 16 38.46N 2.44W
Montigny-le-Roi France 17 48.00N 5.30E
Montijo Portugal 16 38.42N 8.59W
Montijo Dam Spain 16 38.52N 6.20W
Montilla Spain 16 37.36N 4.40W
Montivilliers France 15 49.33N 0.12E
Mont Joli town Canada 77 48.35N 68.14W
Mont Laurier town Canada 76 46.33N 75.31W
Mont Louis town Canada 77 49.15N 65.46W
Montluçon France 17 46.20N 2.36E
Montmagny Canada 77 46.59N 70.33W
Montmédy France 14 49.31N 5.21E
Montmirail France 15 48.52N 3.32E
Montmorillon France 17 46.26N 0.52E
Montmort France 15 48.55N 3.49E
Monto Australia 64 24.52S151.07E
Montoro Spain 16 38.02N 4.23W
Montpelier Idaho U.S.A. 80 42.20N111.20W
Montpelier Vt. U.S.A. 84 44.16N 72.35W
Montpellier France 17 43.36N 3.53E
Montreal Canada 77 45.30N 73.36W
Montreal r. Canada 76 47.13N 84.40W
Montreal L. Canada 75 54.20N105.40W
Montreal Lake town Canada 75 54.03N105.46W
Montréal-Nord Canada 77 45.36N 73.38W
Montrejeau France 17 43.05N 0.33E
Montreuil France 17 50.28N 1.46E
Montreux Switz. 20 46.27N 6.55E
Montrichard France 15 47.21N 1.11E
Montrose U.K. 12 56.43N 2.29W
Montrose U.S.A. 80 38.29N107.53W
Montserrat i. Leeward Is. 87 16.45N 62.14W
Montserrat, Serra de mts. Spain 16 41.20N 1.00E
Mont Tremblant Prov. Park Canada 76 46.30N 74.30W
Monument Valley f. U.S.A. 80 36.50N110.20W
Monveda Zaïre 54 2.57N 21.27E
Monywa Burma 34 22.05N 95.15E
Monza Italy 15 45.35N 9.16E
Monze Zambia 55 16.16S 27.28E
Monzón Spain 16 41.52N 0.10E
Moolawatana Australia 66 29.55S139.43E
Mooloogool Australia 62 26.06S119.05E
Moomba Australia 65 28.08S140.16E
Moomin Creek r. Australia 67 29.35S148.45E
Moonbi Range mts. Australia 67 31.00S151.10E
Moonie Australia 65 27.40S150.19E
Moonie r. Australia 65 29.30S148.40E
Moonta Australia 66 34.04S137.37E
Moora Australia 63 30.40S116.01E
Mooraberree Australia 64 25.02S140.54E
Moorarie Australia 62 25.56S117.35E
Moorcroft U.S.A. 80 44.16N104.57W
Moore r. Australia 63 31.22S115.29E
Moore, L. Australia 63 29.30S117.30E
Mooréa i. Îs. de la Société 69 17.32S149.50W
Moorfoot Hills U.K. 12 55.43N 3.03W
Moorhead U.S.A. 82 46.53N 96.45W
Moornanyah L. Australia 66 33.02S143.58E
Mooroopna Australia 67 36.24S145.22E
Moose Creek town Canada 77 45.15N 74.58W
Moosehead L. U.S.A. 84 45.40N 69.40W
Moose Jaw Canada 75 50.23N105.32W
Moose Lake town U.S.A. 82 46.26N 92.45W
Moosomin Canada 75 50.07N101.40W
Moosonee Canada 76 51.17N 80.39W
Mootwingee Australia 66 31.52S141.14E
Mopanzhang China 32 33.07N117.22E
Mopêia Velha Mozambique 57 17.58S 35.40E
Mopti Mali 52 14.29N 4.10W
Mopti d. Mali 50 15.30N 3.40W
Moqor Afghan. 40 32.55N 67.40E
Moquegua Peru 92 17.20S 70.55W
Mora Cameroon 53 11.02N 14.07E
Mora Spain 16 39.41N 3.46W
Mora Sweden 23 61.00N 14.33E
Mora U.S.A. 82 45.53N 93.18W
Morādābād India 41 28.50N 78.47E
Morafenobe Madagascar 57 17.49S 44.45E
Moralana Australia 66 31.42S138.12E
Moramanga Madagascar 57 18.56S 48.12E
Morar, Loch U.K. 12 56.56N 4.00W
Morava r. Czech Republic 21 48.10N 16.59E
Morava r. Yugo. 21 44.43N 21.02E
Moravské Budějovice Czech Republic 20 49.03N 15.49E
Morawhanna Guyana 90 8.17N 59.44W
Moray Firth est. U.K. 12 57.35N 5.15W
Morbach Germany 14 49.49N 7.05E
Morbegno Italy 15 46.08N 9.34E
Morcenx France 17 44.02N 0.55W
Morden Australia 66 30.30S142.23E
Morden Canada 75 49.11N 98.05W
Mordovo Russian Fed. 25 52.06N 40.45E
Moreau r. U.S.A. 82 45.18N100.43W
Morecambe U.K. 10 54.03N 2.52W
Morecambe B. U.K. 10 54.05N 3.00W
Moree Australia 67 29.29S149.53E
Morée France 15 47.55N 1.15E
Morehead U.S.A. 85 38.11N 83.27W
Morehead City U.S.A. 85 34.43N 76.44W
Morelia Mexico 86 19.40N101.11W
Morella Spain 16 40.37N 0.06W
Morelos d. Mexico 86 18.40N 99.00W
Morena India 41 26.30N 78.09E
Morena, Sierra mts. Spain 16 38.10N 5.00W
Morenci U.S.A. 81 33.05N109.22W
Moreno Mexico 81 28.29N110.41W
Möre og Romsdal d. Norway 22 63.00N 9.00E
Moresby I. Canada 74 52.30N131.40W
Moreton I. Australia 65 27.10S153.25E
Morez France 17 46.31N 6.02E
Mórfou Cyprus 44 35.12N 33.00E
Mórfou, Kólpos b. Cyprus 44 35.15N 32.50E
Morgan Australia 66 34.02S139.40E
Morgan U.S.A. 83 32.01N 97.37W
Morgan City U.S.A. 83 29.42N 91.12W
Morganfield U.S.A. 85 37.41N 87.55W
Morgantown U.S.A. 84 39.38N 79.57W
Morghāb r. Afghan. 38 36.50N 63.00E
Moriki Nigeria 53 12.55N 6.30E
Morin Heights Canada 77 45.54N 74.21W
Morioka Japan 35 39.43N141.08E
Morisset Australia 67 33.06S151.29E
Moriyama Japan 35 35.04N135.59E
Morlaix France 17 48.35N 3.50W
Mormon Range mts. U.S.A. 80 37.08N114.20W
Mornington I. Australia 64 16.33S139.24E
Mornington Mission Australia 64 16.40S139.10E
Morobe P.N.G. 37 7.45S147.35E
Morocco Africa 50 32.30N 5.00W
Moro G. Phil. 37 6.30N123.20E
Morogoro Tanzania 55 6.47S 37.40E
Morogoro d. Tanzania 55 8.30S 37.00E
Moroleón Mexico 86 20.08N101.12W
Morombe Madagascar 57 21.45S 43.22E
Morón Argentina 93 34.39S 58.37W
Morón Cuba 87 22.08N 78.39W
Mörön Mongolia 30 49.36N100.08E
Morón Spain 16 37.06N 5.28W
Morondava Madagascar 57 20.17S 44.17E
Moroni Comoros 55 11.40S 43.19E
Morotai i. Indonesia 37 2.10N128.30E
Moroto Uganda 55 2.32N 34.41E
Moroto, Mt. Uganda 55 2.30N 34.46E
Morpeth U.K. 10 55.10N 1.40W
Morrilton U.S.A. 83 35.09N 92.45W
Morrinsville New Zealand 60 37.39S175.32E
Morris U.S.A. 82 45.35N 95.55W
Morristown Ariz. U.S.A. 81 33.51N112.37W
Morristown N.J. U.S.A. 85 40.48N 74.29W
Morristown S.Dak. U.S.A. 82 45.56N101.43W
Morristown Tenn. U.S.A. 85 36.13N 83.18W
Morrumbene Mozambique 57 23.41S 35.25E
Morsbach Germany 14 50.52N 7.44E
Morsi India 41 21.21N 78.00E
Mortagne France 15 48.32N 0.33E
Mortain France 15 48.39N 0.56W
Mortara Italy 15 45.15N 8.44E
Mortes r. see Manso r. Brazil 92
Mortes r. Brazil 94 21.09S 45.06W
Mortlake town Australia 66 38.05S142.48E
Morundah Australia 67 34.56S146.18E
Moruya Australia 67 35.56S150.06E
Morven Australia 64 26.25S147.05E
Morvern f. U.K. 12 56.37N 5.45W
Morvi India 40 22.49N 70.50E
Morwell Australia 67 38.14S146.25E
Morzhovets i. Russian Fed. 24 66.45N 42.30E
Mosby Norway 23 58.14N 7.54E
Moscow see Moskva Russian Fed. 24
Moscow U.S.A. 80 46.44N117.00W
Mosel r. Germany 14 50.23N 7.37E
Moselle r. see Mosel r. France / Lux. 14
Moses Lake town U.S.A. 80 47.08N119.17W
Mosgiel New Zealand 60 45.53S170.22E
Moshi Tanzania 55 3.20S 37.21E
Mosjöen Norway 22 65.50N 13.10E
Moskenes Norway 22 67.55N 13.00E
Moskenesöy i. Norway 22 67.55N 13.00E
Moskva Russian Fed. 24 55.45N 37.42E
Moskva r. Russian Fed. 24 55.08N 38.50E
Mosquera Colombia 90 2.30N 78.29W
Mosquero U.S.A. 81 35.47N103.58W
Mosquitia Plain Honduras 87 15.00N 84.00W
Mosquitos, Costa de f. Nicaragua 87 13.00N 84.00W
Mosquitos, Golfo de los g. Panama 87 9.00N 81.00W
Moss Norway 23 59.26N 10.42E
Mossaka Congo 54 1.20S 16.44E
Mossburn New Zealand 60 45.41S168.15E
Mosselbaai R.S.A. 56 34.11S 22.08E
Mossendjo Congo 54 2.52S 12.46E
Mossgiel Australia 67 33.18S144.05E
Mossman Australia 64 16.28S145.22E
Mossoró Brazil 91 5.10S 37.18W
Mossuril Mozambique 57 14.58S 40.42E
Moss Vale town Australia 67 34.33S150.24E
Most Czech Republic 20 50.31N 13.39E
Mostaganem Algeria 50 35.56N 0.05E
Mostar Bosnia-Herzegovina 19 43.20N 17.50E
Mösting, Kap c. Greenland 73 64.00N 41.00W
Mostiska Ukraine 21 49.48N 23.05E
Mosul see Al Mawṣil Iraq 42
Motagua r. Guatemala 87 15.56N 87.45W
Motala Sweden 23 58.33N 15.03E
Moth India 41 25.43N 78.57E
Motherwell U.K. 12 55.48N 4.00W
Motīhāri India 41 26.39N 84.55E
Motloutse r. Botswana 56 22.15S 29.00E
Motol Belorussia 21 52.25N 25.05E
Motou China 32 32.17N120.35E
Motril Spain 16 36.44N 3.37W
Mott U.S.A. 80 46.22N102.20W
Motueka New Zealand 60 41.08S173.01E
Motu Iti i. Îs. de la Société 69 16.15S151.50W
Motutapu Niue 68 19.02S169.52W
Mouali Congo 54 0.10N 15.33E
Mouchalagane r. Canada 77 53.32N 69.00W
Moúdhros Greece 19 39.52N 25.16E
Moudjéria Mauritania 50 17.53N 12.20W
Mouhoun r. Burkina see Black Volta r. Ghana 52
Mouila Gabon 54 1.50S 11.02E
Mouka C.A.R. 49 7.16N 21.52E
Moulamein Australia 66 35.03S144.05E
Moulhoulé Djibouti 49 12.36N 43.12E
Moulins France 17 46.34N 3.20E
Moulins-la-Marche France 15 48.39N 0.29E
Moulmein Burma 34 16.55N 97.49E
Moulouya, Oued r. Morocco 50 35.05N 2.25W
Moultrie U.S.A. 85 31.11N 83.47W
Moultrie, L. U.S.A. 85 33.20N 80.05W
Mound City U.S.A. 82 40.07N 95.14W
Moundou Chad 53 8.36N 16.02E
Moundsville U.S.A. 84 39.54N 80.44W
Moundville U.S.A. 83 32.59N 87.38W
Mountain Ash U.K. 11 51.42N 3.22W
Mountain City U.S.A. 80 41.50N115.58W
Mountain Home Ark. U.S.A. 83 36.20N 92.23W
Mountain Home Idaho U.S.A. 80 43.08N115.41W
Mountain Nile r. see Jabal, Bahr al r. Sudan 49
Mountain Village U.S.A. 72 62.05N163.44W
Mount Airy town Md. U.S.A. 85 39.23N 77.09W
Mount Airy town N.C. U.S.A. 85 36.31N 80.38W
Mount Barker town S.A. Australia 66 35.06S138.52E
Mount Barker town W.A. Australia 63 34.36S117.37E
Mount Beauty town Australia 67 36.43S147.11E
Mount Bellew town Rep. of Ire. 13 53.28N 8.30W
Mount Carmel town Ill. U.S.A. 82 38.25N 87.46W
Mount Darwin town Zimbabwe 57 16.46S 31.36E
Mount Drysdale town Australia 67 31.11S145.51E
Mount Eba town Australia 66 30.12S135.33E
Mount Fletcher town R.S.A. 56 30.41S 28.30E
Mount Gambier town Australia 66 37.51S140.50E
Mount Hagen town P.N.G. 37 5.54S144.13E
Mount Holly town U.S.A. 85 39.59N 74.47W
Mount Hope town N.S.W. Australia 67 32.49S145.48E
Mount Hope town S.A. Australia 66 34.07S135.23E
Mount Hopeless town Australia 66 29.42S139.41E
Mount Isa town Australia 64 20.50S139.29E
Mount Lofty Range mts. Australia 66 34.40S139.03E
Mount Magnet town Australia 63 28.06S117.50E
Mount Manara town Australia 66 32.28S143.59E
Mountmellick Rep. of Ire. 13 53.08N 7.21W
Mount Morgan town Australia 64 23.39S150.23E
Mount Murchison town Australia 66 31.23S143.42E
Mount Pleasant town Canada 76 43.05N 80.19W
Mount Pleasant town Mich. U.S.A. 84 43.36N 84.46W
Mount Pleasant town S.C. U.S.A. 85 32.48N 79.54W
Mount Pleasant town Tex. U.S.A. 83 33.09N 94.58W
Mount Robson town Canada 74 52.56N119.15W
Mount's B. U.K. 11 50.05N 5.25W
Mount Sterling town U.S.A. 85 38.03N 83.56W
Mount Vernon town Australia 62 24.09S118.10E
Mount Vernon town Ill. U.S.A. 82 38.19N 88.52W
Mount Vernon town N.Y. U.S.A. 85 40.54N 73.50W
Mount Vernon town Wash. U.S.A. 80 48.25N122.20W
Mount Walker town Australia 63 27.47S152.32E
Mount Willoughby Australia 66 27.58S134.08E
Moura Australia 64 24.33S149.58E
Moura Brazil 90 1.27S 61.38W
Moura Chad 48 13.47N 21.13E
Mourdi, Dépression de f. Chad 48 18.10N 23.00E
Mourdiah Mali 52 14.35N 7.25W
Mourne r. U.K. 9 54.50N 7.29W
Mourne Mts. U.K. 13 54.10N 6.02W
Mouscron Belgium 14 50.46N 3.10E
Moussoro Chad 53 13.41N 16.31E
Moxico Angola 54 11.50S 20.05E
Moxico d. Angola 54 13.00S 21.00E
Moy r. Rep. of Ire. 13 54.10N 9.09W
Moyale Kenya 55 3.31N 39.04E
Moyamba Sierra Leone 52 8.04N 12.03W
Moyen Atlas mts. Morocco 50 33.30N 5.00W
Moyen-Chari d. Chad 53 9.20N 17.35E
Moyeni Lesotho 56 30.24S 27.41E
Moyie Canada 74 49.17N115.50W
Moyobamba Peru 90 6.04S 76.56W
Moyowosi r. Tanzania 55 4.59S 30.58E
Mozambique Africa 57 17.30S 35.45E
Mozambique Channel Indian Oc. 57 16.00S 42.30E
Mozdok Russian Fed. 25 43.45N 44.43E
Mozyr Belorussia 21 52.02N 29.10E
Mpala Zaïre 55 6.45S 29.31E
M'Pama r. Congo 54 0.59S 15.40E
Mpanda Tanzania 55 6.21S 31.01E
Mpésoba Mali 52 12.31N 5.39W
Mphoengs Zimbabwe 56 21.10S 27.51E
Mpika Zambia 55 11.52S 31.30E
Mponela Malaŵi 55 13.32S 33.43E
Mporokoso Zambia 55 9.22S 30.06E
M'Pouya Congo 54 2.38S 16.08E
Mpunde mtn. Tanzania 55 6.12S 33.48E
Mpwapwa Tanzania 55 6.23S 36.38E
M'qoun, Irhil mtn. Morocco 50 31.31N 6.25W
Mrhila, Djebel mtn. Tunisia 51 35.25N 9.14E
Msaken Tunisia 51 35.42N 10.33E
Mseleni R.S.A. 57 27.21S 32.33E
Msingu Tanzania 55 4.52S 39.08E
Msta r. Russian Fed. 24 58.28N 31.20E
Mtakuja Tanzania 55 7.21S 30.37E
Mtama Tanzania 55 10.20S 39.19E
Mtito Andei Kenya 55 2.32S 38.10E
Mtsensk Russian Fed. 24 53.18N 36.35E
Mtwara Tanzania 55 10.17S 40.11E
Mtwara d. Tanzania 55 10.00S 38.30E
Muaná Brazil 91 1.32S 49.13W
Muangangia Angola 54 13.33S 18.04E
Muang Chiang Rai Thailand 34 19.56N 99.51E
Muang Khammouan Laos 34 17.22N104.50E
Muang Khon Kaen Thailand 34 16.25N102.52E
Muang Lampang Thailand 34 18.16N 99.30E
Muang Lamphun Thailand 34 18.36N 99.02E
Muang Nakhon Phanom Thailand 34 17.22N104.45E
Muang Nakhon Sawan Thailand 34 15.42N100.04E
Muang Nan Thailand 34 18.47N100.50E
Muang Ngoy Laos 34 20.43N102.41E
Muang Pak Lay Laos 34 18.12N101.25E
Muang Phaya Thailand 34 19.10N 99.55E
Muang Phetchabun Thailand 34 16.25N101.08E
Muang Phichit Thailand 34 16.29N100.21E
Muang Phitsanulok Thailand 34 16.45N100.18E
Muang Phrae Thailand 34 18.07N100.09E
Muang Sakon Nakhon Thailand 34 17.10N104.08E
Muang Sing Laos 34 21.11N101.09E
Muang Soum Laos 34 18.46N102.36E
Muang Ubon Thailand 34 15.15N104.50E
Muar Malaysia 36 2.01N102.35E
Muara Brunei 36 5.01N115.01E
Muara Indonesia 36 0.32S101.20E
Muarakaman Indonesia 36 0.02S116.45E
Muaratewe Indonesia 36 0.57S114.53E
Muāri, Rās c. Pakistan 40 24.49N 66.40E
Mubende Uganda 55 0.30N 31.24E
Mubi Nigeria 53 10.16N 13.17E
Mucanona Angola 54 8.13S 16.39E
Muchea Australia 63 31.36S115.57E
Muchinga Mts. Zambia 55 12.15S 31.00E
Muck i. U.K. 12 56.50N 6.14W
Mucojo Mozambique 55 12.05S 40.26E
Muconda Angola 54 10.31S 21.20E
Mudanjiang China 31 44.36N129.42E
Mudgee Australia 67 32.37S149.36E
Mudon Burma 34 16.15N 97.44E
Mudyuga Russian Fed. 24 63.45N 39.29E
Muêda Mozambique 55 11.40S 39.31E
Muene Quibau Angola 54 11.27S 19.14E
Mufulira Zambia 55 12.30S 28.12E
Mufu Shan mts. China 33 29.30N114.45E
Muganskaya Ravnina f. Azerbaijan 43 39.40N 48.30E
Mughshin, Wādī Oman 45 19.44N 55.15E
Mugía Spain 16 43.06N 9.14W
Muğla Turkey 19 37.12N 28.22E
Muhamdi India 41 27.57N 80.13E
Muḥammad, Ra's c. Egypt 44 27.42N 34.13E
Mühldorf Germany 20 48.15N 12.32E
Mühlhausen Germany 20 51.12N 10.27E
Mühlig Hofmann fjella mts. Antarctica 96 72.30S 5.00E
Muhola Finland 22 63.20N 25.05E
Muhos Finland 22 64.48N 25.59E
Muhu i. Estonia 23 58.32N 23.20E
Muhuru Kenya 49 1.01S 34.07E
Muhu Väin str. Estonia 23 58.45N 23.30E
Mui Ca Mau c. Vietnam 34 8.30N104.35E
Muine Bheag town Rep. of Ire. 13 52.42N 6.58W
Muir, L. Australia 63 34.30S116.30E
Mukachevo Ukraine 21 48.26N 22.45E
Mukah Malaysia 36 2.56N112.02E
Mukandwara India 40 24.49N 75.59E
Mukawa P.N.G. 64 9.48S150.00E
Mukeriān India 40 31.57N 75.37E
Mukinbudin Australia 63 30.52S118.08E
Muko r. Japan 35 34.41N135.23E
Mukoba Zaïre 54 6.50S 20.50E
Mukongo Zaïre 54 6.32S 23.30E
Muktsar India 40 30.28N 74.31E
Mukwela Zambia 54 17.00S 26.40E
Mūl India 41 20.04N 79.40E
Mula r. India 40 19.35N 74.50E
Mūla r. Pakistan 40 27.57N 67.37E
Mulanje Mts. Malaŵi 55 15.57S 35.33E
Mulchén Chile 93 37.43S 72.14W
Mulde r. Germany 20 51.10N 12.48E
Mulgathing Australia 66 30.15S134.00E
Mulgrave Canada 77 45.37N 61.23W
Mulhacén mtn. Spain 16 37.04N 3.22W
Mülheim N.-Westfalen Germany 14 51.25N 6.50E
Mülheim N.-Westfalen Germany 14 50.58N 7.00E
Mulhouse France 17 47.45N 7.21E
Mull i. U.K. 12 56.28N 5.56W
Mull, Sd. of str. U.K. 12 56.32N 5.55W
Mullaghanattin mtn. Rep. of Ire. 13 51.56N 9.51W
Mullaghareirk Mts. Rep. of Ire. 13 52.19N 9.06W
Mullaghmore mtn. U.K. 13 54.51N 6.51W
Mullaley Australia 67 31.06S149.55E
Mullen U.S.A. 82 42.03N101.01W
Mullengudgery Australia 67 31.40S147.23E
Mullens U.S.A. 85 37.35N 81.25W
Mullet Pen. Rep. of Ire. 13 54.12N 10.04W
Mullewa Australia 63 28.33S115.31E
Mullingar Rep. of Ire. 13 53.31N 7.21W
Mull of Galloway c. U.K. 12 54.39N 4.52W
Mull of Kintyre c. U.K. 12 55.17N 5.45W
Mullovka Russian Fed. 24 54.12N 49.26E
Mullumbimby Australia 67 28.32S153.30E
Mulobezi Zambia 55 16.49S 25.09E
Muloorina Australia 66 29.10S137.51E
Multai India 41 21.46N 78.15E
Multān Pakistan 40 30.11N 71.29E
Multyfarnham Rep. of Ire. 13 53.37N 7.25W
Mulyungarie Australia 66 31.30S140.45E
Mumbai see Bombay India 40
Mumbwa Zambia 55 14.57S 27.01E
Mun r. Thailand 34 15.15N104.50E
Mun, Jabal mtn. Sudan 48 14.08N 22.42E
Muna i. Indonesia 37 5.00S122.30E
Munābāo India 40 25.45N 70.17E
Munan Pass China / Vietnam 33 22.06N106.46E
Münchberg Germany 20 50.11N 11.47E
München Germany 20 48.08N 11.35E
Muncho Lake town Canada 74 59.00N125.50W
Muncie U.S.A. 84 40.11N 85.23W
Mundaring Weir Australia 63 31.59S116.13E
Münden Germany 20 51.25N 9.39E
Mundiwindi Australia 62 23.50S120.07E
Mundo r. Spain 16 38.20N 1.50W
Mundra India 40 22.51N 69.44E
Mungari Mozambique 57 17.12S 33.31E
Mungbere Zaïre 55 2.40N 28.25E
Mungeli India 41 22.04N 81.41E
Mungerannie Australia 66 28.00S138.36E
Mungindi Australia 67 28.58S148.56E
Munhango Angola 54 12.10S 18.36E
Munich see München Germany 20
Muniz Freire Brazil 94 20.25S 41.23W
Munkfors Sweden 23 59.50N 13.32E
Munning r. Australia 67 31.50S152.30E
Münster Germany 14 51.58N 7.37E
Muntadgin Australia 63 31.41S118.32E
Munyati r. Zimbabwe 56 17.32S 29.23E
Muong Hinh Vietnam 33 19.49N105.03E
Muonio Finland 22 67.57N 23.42E
Muonio r. Finland / Sweden 22 67.10N 23.40E
Mupa Angola 56 16.07S 15.45E
Mupa r. Mozambique 57 19.07S 35.50E
Muping China 32 37.23N121.35E
Muqaddam, Wādī Sudan 48 18.04N 31.30E
Muqdisho Somali Rep. 55 2.02N 45.21E
Mur r. Austria see Mura r. Croatia 20
Mura r. Croatia 20 46.18N 16.53E
Murallón mtn. Argentina / Chile 93 49.48S 73.25W
Muranga Kenya 55 0.43S 37.10E
Murashi Russian Fed. 24 59.20N 48.59E
Murchison Australia 67 36.36S145.14E
Murchison r. Australia 62 27.30S114.10E
Murchison New Zealand 60 41.48S172.20E
Murcia Spain 16 37.59N 1.08W
Murcia d. Spain 16 38.15N 1.50W
Murdo U.S.A. 82 43.53N100.43W
Mureş r. Romania 21 46.16N 20.10E
Muret France 17 43.28N 1.19E
Murewa Zimbabwe 57 17.40S 31.47E
Murfreesboro U.S.A. 85 35.50N 86.25W
Murgha Faqirzai Pakistan 40 31.03N 67.48E
Murgha Kibzai Pakistan 40 30.44N 69.25E
Murgon Australia 64 26.15S151.57E
Murguía Spain 16 42.57N 2.49W
Muri Cook Is. 68 21.14S159.43W
Muria, Gunung mtn. Indonesia 37 6.39S110.51E
Muriaé Brazil 94 21.08S 42.33W
Müritzsee l. Germany 20 52.25N 12.45E

Murjek to Neijiang

Murjek Sweden 22 66.29N 20.50E
Murliganj India 41 25.54N 86.59E
Murmansk Russian Fed. 24 68.59N 33.08E
Murnei Sudan 49 12.57N 22.52E
Murom Russian Fed. 24 55.04N 42.04E
Muroran Japan 35 42.21N 140.59E
Murrah al Kubrá, Al Buḩayrah al *l.* Egypt 44 30.20N 32.20E
Murra Murra Australia 67 28.18S 146.48E
Murray *r.* S.A. Australia 66 35.23S 139.20E
Murray *r.* W.A. Australia 63 32.35S 115.46E
Murray *r.* Canada 74 56.11N 120.45W
Murray Ky. U.S.A. 83 36.37N 88.19W
Murray Utah U.S.A. 80 40.40N 111.53W
Murray, L. P.N.G. 37 7.00S 141.30E
Murray, L. U.S.A. 85 34.04N 81.23W
Murray Bridge *town* Australia 66 35.10S 139.17E
Murrayville Australia 66 35.16S 141.14E
Murree Pakistan 40 33.54N 73.24E
Murringo Australia 67 34.19S 148.36E
Murrumbidgee *r.* Australia 66 34.38S 143.10E
Murrumburrah Australia 67 34.33S 148.21E
Murrurundi Australia 67 31.47S 150.51E
Murshidābād India 41 24.11N 88.16E
Murtoa Australia 66 36.40S 142.31E
Murud *mtn.* Malaysia 36 3.45N 115.30E
Murwāra India 41 23.51N 80.24E
Murwillumbah Australia 67 28.20S 153.24E
Muş Turkey 42 38.45N 41.30E
Mūsá, Jabal *mtn.* Egypt 44 28.31N 33.59E
Musadi Zaïre 54 2.31S 22.50E
Mūsa Khel Pakistan 40 32.38N 71.44E
Mūsa Khel Bāzār Pakistan 40 30.52N 69.49E
Musala *mtn.* Bulgaria 19 42.11N 23.35E
Musan N. Korea 35 42.14N 129.13E
Mūsā Qal 'eh Afghan. 40 32.05N 64.51E
Mūsā Qal 'eh *r.* Afghan. 40 32.22N 64.46E
Musay'īd Qatar 43 24.47N 51.36E
Mūsāzai Pakistan 40 30.23N 66.32E
Muscat *see* Masqaţ Oman 43
Muscatine U.S.A. 82 41.25N 91.03W
Musgrave Australia 64 14.47S 143.30E
Musgrave Ranges *mts.* Australia 62 26.10S 131.50E
Mushie Zaïre 54 2.59S 16.55E
Mushima Zambia 56 14.13S 25.05E
Mushin Nigeria 53 6.33N 3.22E
Musi *r.* Indonesia 36 2.20S 104.57E
Muskegon U.S.A. 84 43.13N 86.15W
Muskegon *r.* U.S.A. 84 43.13N 86.16W
Muskegon Heights *town* U.S.A. 84 43.03N 86.16W
Muskogee U.S.A. 83 35.45N 95.22W
Muskoka, L. Canada 76 45.00N 79.25W
Muskwa *r.* Alta. Canada 74 56.16N 114.06W
Muskwa *r.* B.C. Canada 74 58.47N 122.48W
Musoma Tanzania 55 1.31S 33.48E
Mussari Angola 56 13.07S 17.56E
Musselburgh U.K. 12 55.57N 3.04W
Musselkanaal Neth. 14 52.57N 7.01E
Musselshell *r.* U.S.A. 80 47.21N 107.58W
Mussende Angola 54 10.33S 16.02E
Musserra Angola 54 7.31S 13.02E
Mustahil Ethiopia 45 5.12N 44.17E
Mustāng Nepal 41 29.11N 83.57E
Mustjala Estonia 23 58.28N 22.14E
Muswellbrook Australia 67 32.17S 150.55E
Mūţ Egypt 48 25.29N 28.59E
Mut Turkey 42 36.38N 33.27E
Mutala Mozambique 57 15.54S 37.51E
Mutalau Niue 68 18.58S 169.50W
Mutanda Zambia 54 12.23S 26.16E
Mutare Zimbabwe 57 18.59S 32.40E
Mutoko Zimbabwe 57 17.23S 32.13E
Mutooroo Australia 66 32.30S 140.58E
Mutoray Russian Fed. 29 61.20N 100.32E
Mutshatsha Zaïre 54 10.39S 24.27E
Mutton Bay *town* Canada 77 50.47N 59.02W
Muwale Tanzania 55 6.22S 33.46E
Muxima Angola 54 9.33S 13.58E
Muya Russian Fed. 29 56.28N 115.50E
Muyinga Burundi 55 2.48S 30.21E
Muzaffarābād Jammu & Kashmir 40 34.22N 73.28E
Muzaffargarh Pakistan 40 30.04N 71.12E
Muzaffarnagar India 41 29.28N 77.41E
Muzaffarpur India 41 26.07N 85.24E
Muzhi Russian Fed. 24 65.25N 64.40E
Muzoka Zambia 56 16.43S 27.18E
Muztag *mtn.* China 30 36.25N 87.25E
Mvadhi Gabon 54 1.13N 13.10E
Mvolo Sudan 49 6.03N 29.56E
Mvomero Tanzania 55 6.18S 37.26E
Mvuma Zimbabwe 56 19.16S 30.30E
Mvurwi Range *mts.* Zimbabwe 56 17.10S 30.45E
Mwali *see* Mohéli *i.* Comoros 55
Mwanza Tanzania 55 2.30S 32.54E
Mwanza *d.* Tanzania 55 3.00S 32.30E
Mwanza Zaïre 54 7.51S 26.43E
Mwaya Tanzania 55 9.33S 33.56E
Mweka Zaïre 54 4.51S 21.34E
Mwene Ditu Zaïre 54 7.04S 23.27E
Mwenezi *r.* Mozambique 57 22.42S 31.45E
Mwenezi Zimbabwe 56 21.22S 30.45E
Mweru, L. Zaïre / Zambia 55 9.00S 28.40E
Mwingi Kenya 55 1.00S 38.04E
Mwinilunga Zambia 54 11.44S 24.24E
Mya, Oued *wadi* Algeria 51 31.40N 5.15E
Myanaung Burma 39 18.25N 95.10E
Myanma *see* Burma Asia 34
Myaungmya Burma 34 16.33N 94.55E
Myingyan Burma 34 21.22N 95.28E
Myinkyado Burma 34 20.56N 96.42E
Myinmu Burma 34 21.58N 95.43E
Myitkyinā Burma 34 25.24N 97.25E
Mymensingh Bangla. 41 24.45N 90.24E
Myrdal Norway 23 60.44N 7.08E
Myrdalsjökull *ice cap* Iceland 22 63.40N 19.06W
Myrtle Beach *town* U.S.A. 85 33.42N 78.54W
Myrtle Creek *town* U.S.A. 80 43.01N 123.17W
Myrtleford Australia 67 36.35S 146.44E
Myrtle Point *town* U.S.A. 80 43.04N 124.08W
Myślenice Poland 21 49.51N 19.56E
Mysore India 38 12.18N 76.37E
My Tho Vietnam 34 10.27N 106.20E
Mytishchi Russian Fed. 24 55.54N 37.47E
Mziha Tanzania 55 5.53S 37.48E
Mzimba Malaŵi 55 12.00S 33.39E

N

Naab *r.* Germany 20 49.01N 12.02E
Naalehu Hawaiian Is. 69 19.04N 155.35W
Na'ām *r.* Sudan 49 6.48N 29.57E
Naantali Finland 23 60.27N 22.02E
Naas Rep. of Ire. 13 53.13N 6.41W
Näätämö *r.* Norway 22 69.40N 29.30E
Nababeep R.S.A. 56 29.36S 17.44E
Nabadwip India 41 23.25N 88.22E
Nabari *r.* Japan 35 34.45N 136.01E
Naberezhnyye Chelny Russian Fed. 24 55.42N 52.20E
Nabeul Tunisia 51 36.28N 10.44E
Nābha India 40 30.22N 76.09E
Nabingora Uganda 55 0.31N 31.11E
Nabī Shu'ayb, Jabal an *mtn.* Yemen 45 15.17N 43.59E
Naboomspruit R.S.A. 56 24.31S 28.24E
Nabq Egypt 44 28.04N 34.26E
Nābulus Jordan 44 32.13N 35.16E
Nacala Mozambique 57 14.34S 40.41E
Nacchio Ethiopia 49 7.30N 40.15E
Nachikapau L. Canada 77 56.44N 68.00W
Nachingwea Tanzania 55 10.21S 38.46E
Nāchna India 40 27.30N 71.43E
Naco Mexico 81 31.20N 109.56W
Nacogdoches U.S.A. 83 31.36N 94.39W
Nadiād India 40 22.42N 72.52E
Nador Morocco 50 35.12N 2.55W
Nadūshan Iran 43 32.03N 53.33E
Nadvoitsy Russian Fed. 24 63.56N 34.20E
Nadvornaya Ukraine 21 48.37N 24.30E
Nadym Russian Fed. 28 65.25N 72.40E
Naenwa India 40 25.46N 75.51E
Naeröy Norway 22 64.48N 11.17E
Naestved Denmark 23 55.14N 11.46E
Nafada Nigeria 53 11.08N 11.20E
Nafishah Egypt 44 30.34N 32.15E
Naft-e Safid Iran 43 31.38N 49.20E
Nāg Pakistan 40 27.24N 65.08E
Naga Phil. 37 13.36N 123.12E
Nāgāland *d.* India 39 26.10N 94.30E
Nagambie Australia 67 36.48S 145.12E
Nagano Japan 35 36.39N 138.10E
Nagano *d.* Japan 35 35.33N 137.50E
Nagaoka Japan 35 37.30N 138.50E
Nāgappattinam India 39 10.45N 79.50E
Nagara *r.* Japan 35 35.01N 136.43E
Nagar Pārkar Pakistan 40 24.22N 70.45E
Nagarzê China 41 28.58N 90.24E
Nagasaki Japan 35 32.45N 129.52E
Nāgaur India 40 27.12N 73.44E
Nāgāvali *r.* India 41 18.13N 83.56E
Nāgda India 40 23.27N 75.25E
Nagele Neth. 14 52.39N 5.43E
Nāgercoil India 38 8.11N 77.30E
Nagichot Sudan 49 4.16N 33.34E
Nagīna India 41 29.27N 78.27E
Nagles Mts. Rep. of Ire. 13 52.06N 8.26W
Nagorskoye Russian Fed. 24 58.18N 50.50E
Nagoya Japan 35 35.10N 136.55E
Nāgpur India 41 21.09N 79.06E
Nagqên China 39 32.15N 96.13E
Nagqu China 41 31.30N 92.00E
Nagykanizsa Hungary 21 46.27N 17.01E
Naha Japan 31 26.10N 127.40E
Nāhan India 41 30.33N 77.18E
Nahanni Butte *town* Canada 74 61.02N 123.20W
Nahariyya Israel 44 33.01N 35.05E
Nahāvand Iran 43 34.13N 48.23E
Nahe *r.* Germany 14 49.58N 7.54E
Nahr al Furāt *r.* Asia 43 31.00N 47.27E
Nahunta U.S.A. 85 31.12N 82.00W
Nai Ga Burma 34 27.48N 97.30E
Naiman Qi China 32 42.53N 120.40E
Nain Canada 77 57.00N 61.40W
Nā'īn Iran 43 32.52N 53.05E
Naini Tāl India 41 29.23N 79.27E
Nainpur India 41 22.26N 80.07E
Nairn U.K. 12 57.35N 3.52W
Nairobi Kenya 55 1.17S 36.50E
Naita *mtn.* Ethiopia 49 5.31N 35.18E
Naivasha Kenya 55 0.44S 36.26E
Najd *f.* Saudi Arabia 42 25.00N 45.00E
Naj 'Hammādī Egypt 42 26.04N 32.13E
Najrān *see* Abā as Su'ūd Saudi Arabia 45
Nāka Khārari Pakistan 40 25.15N 66.44E
Nakambe *r.* Burkina *see* White Volta *r.* Ghana 52
Nakape Sudan 49 5.47N 28.38E
Nakatsugawa Japan 35 35.29N 137.30E
Nak'fa Ethiopia 48 16.43N 38.32E
Nakhichevan Azerbaijan 43 39.12N 45.24E
Nakhodka Russian Fed. 31 42.53N 132.54E
Nakhola India 41 26.07N 92.11E
Nakhon Pathom Thailand 34 13.50N 100.01E
Nakhon Ratchasima Thailand 34 14.58N 102.06E
Nakhon Si Thammarat Thailand 34 8.24N 99.58E
Nakhtarana India 40 23.20N 69.15E
Nakina Canada 76 50.10N 86.40W
Nakło Poland 21 53.08N 17.35E
Naknek U.S.A. 72 58.45N 157.00W
Nakop Namibia 56 28.05S 19.57E
Nakskov Denmark 23 54.50N 11.09E
Näkten *l.* Sweden 22 65.50N 14.35E
Nakuru Kenya 55 0.16S 36.04E
Nāl *r.* Pakistan 40 26.02N 65.19E
Nalbāri India 41 26.26N 91.30E
Nalchik Russian Fed. 25 43.31N 43.38E
Nalón *r.* Spain 16 43.35N 6.06W
Nālūt Libya 51 31.52N 10.59E
Namacurra Mozambique 55 17.35S 37.00E
Namakī *r.* Iran 43 31.02N 55.20E
Namanga Kenya 55 2.33S 36.48E
Namangan Uzbekistan 30 40.59N 71.41E
Namanyere Tanzania 55 7.34S 31.00E
Namapa Mozambique 57 13.48S 39.44E
Namaponda Mozambique 57 15.51S 39.52E
Namari Senegal 50 15.05N 13.39W
Namarroi Mozambique 57 15.58S 36.55E
Namatele Tanzania 55 10.01S 38.26E
Namba Angola 54 11.32S 15.33E
Nambala Zambia 56 15.07S 27.02E
Nambour Australia 65 26.36S 152.59E
Nambucca Heads *town* Australia 67 30.38S 152.59E
Namco China 41 30.53N 91.06E
Nam Co *l.* China 41 30.45N 90.30E
Nam Dinh Vietnam 33 20.21N 106.09E
Namecala Mozambique 57 12.50S 39.38E
Nametil Mozambique 57 15.41S 39.30E
Namib Desert Namibia 56 23.00S 15.20E
Namibe Angola 54 15.10S 12.10E
Namibe *d.* Angola 54 15.30S 12.30E
Namibia Africa 56 21.30S 16.45E
Namīn Iran 43 38.25N 48.30E
Namlea Indonesia 37 3.15S 127.07E
Namling China 41 29.40N 89.03E
Namoi *r.* Australia 67 30.14S 148.28E
Namonuito *i.* Pacific Oc. 68 8.46N 150.02E
Namous, Oued *wadi* Algeria 50 30.28N 0.14W
Nampa Canada 74 56.02N 117.07W
Nampa U.S.A. 80 43.44N 116.34W
Nam Phan *f.* Vietnam 34 10.40N 106.00E
Nam Phong Thailand 34 16.45N 102.52E
Namp'o N. Korea 31 38.40N 125.30E
Nampula Mozambique 57 15.09S 39.14E
Nampula *d.* Mozambique 57 15.00S 39.00E
Namsen *r.* Norway 22 64.27N 12.19E
Namsos Norway 22 64.28N 11.30E
Namtu Burma 34 23.04N 97.26E
Namu Canada 74 51.52N 127.41W
Namuchabawashan *mtn.* China 39 29.30N 95.10E
Namungua Mozambique 55 13.11S 40.30E
Namur Belgium 14 50.28N 4.52E
Namur *d.* Belgium 14 50.20N 4.45E
Namur Canada 77 45.54N 74.56W
Namutoni Namibia 56 18.48S 16.58E
Namwala Zambia 54 15.44S 26.25E
Nanaimo Canada 74 49.10N 124.00W
Nanam N. Korea 35 41.43N 129.41E
Nanango Australia 65 26.42S 151.58E
Nanchang China 33 28.37N 115.57E
Nancheng China 33 27.35N 116.33E
Nanchong China 33 30.53N 106.05E
Nanchuan China 33 29.12N 107.30E
Nancy France 17 48.42N 6.12E
Nanda Devi *mtn.* India 41 30.23N 79.59E
Nandan China 33 24.59N 107.32E
Nānded India 40 19.09N 77.20E
Nandewar Range *mts.* Australia 67 30.20S 150.45E
Nāndgaon India 40 20.19N 74.39E
Nandi Fiji 68 17.48S 177.25E
Nandu Jiang *r.* China 33 20.04N 110.20E
Nandurbār India 40 21.22N 74.15E
Nandyāl India 39 15.29N 78.29E
Nanfeng China 33 27.10N 116.24E
Nanga Eboko Cameroon 53 4.41N 12.21E
Nānga Parbat *mtn.* Jammu & Kashmir 38 35.10N 74.35E
Nangapinoh Indonesia 36 0.20S 111.44E
Nangola Mali 52 12.41N 6.35W
Nangqên China 30 32.15N 96.13E
Nangrūl Pīr India 40 20.19N 77.21E
Nang Xian China 41 29.03N 93.12E
Nanhui China 33 31.03N 121.46E
Nanjiang China 32 32.21N 106.50E
Nanjing China 33 32.02N 118.52E
Nanking *see* Nanjing China 33
Nanling China 33 30.56N 118.19E
Nan Ling *mts.* China 33 25.10N 110.00E
Nannine Australia 62 26.53S 118.20E
Nanning China 33 22.48N 108.18E
Nannup Australia 63 33.57S 115.42E
Nanortalik Greenland 73 60.09N 45.15W
Nānpāra India 41 27.52N 81.30E
Nanpi China 32 38.02N 116.42E
Nanping China 33 26.38N 118.10E
Nanpu Xi *r.* China 33 26.38N 118.10E
Nanri *i.* China 33 25.13N 119.30E
Nansei shotō *is.* Japan 31 26.30N 125.00E
Nansei-Shotō Trench Pacific Oc. 68 25.00N 129.00E
Nanshan *is.* S. China Sea 36 10.30N 116.00E
Nantes France 15 47.14N 1.35W
Nanteuil-le-Haudouin France 15 49.08N 2.48E
Nanticoke U.S.A. 84 41.12N 76.00W
Nanton Canada 74 50.21N 113.46W
Nantong China 32 32.02N 120.55E
Nantou Taiwan 33 23.54N 120.41E
Nantua France 20 46.09N 5.37E
Nantucket I. U.S.A. 84 41.16N 70.03W
Nantucket Sd. U.S.A. 84 41.30N 70.15W
Nantwich U.K. 10 53.05N 2.31W
Nanumea *i.* Tuvalu 68 5.40S 176.10E
Nanwan Shuiku *resr.* China 33 32.05N 113.55E
Nanxi China 33 28.52N 104.59E
Nan Xian China 33 29.22N 112.25E
Nanxiong China 33 25.10N 114.16E
Nanyang China 32 33.07N 112.30E
Nanzhang China 33 31.47N 111.42E
Naococane, Lac *l.* Canada 77 52.50N 70.40W
Naogaon Bangla. 41 24.47N 88.56E
Naokot Pakistan 40 24.51N 69.27E
Napa U.S.A. 80 38.18N 122.17W
Napadogan Canada 77 46.24N 67.01W
Napè Laos 34 18.18N 105.07E
Napier New Zealand 60 39.29S 176.58E
Napierville Canada 77 45.11N 73.25W
Naples *see* Napoli Italy 18
Naples U.S.A. 85 26.09N 81.48W
Napo China 33 23.23N 105.48E
Napo *r.* Peru 90 3.30S 73.10W
Napoleon U.S.A. 84 41.24N 84.09W
Napoli Italy 18 40.50N 14.14E
Napoli, Golfo di *g.* Italy 18 40.42N 14.15E
Naqb Ishtar Jordan 44 30.00N 35.30E
Nara Japan 35 34.41N 135.50E
Nara *d.* Japan 35 34.27N 135.55E
Nara Mali 50 15.13N 7.20W
Nāra Pakistan 40 24.07N 69.07E
Naracoorte Australia 66 36.58S 140.46E
Naradhan Australia 67 33.39S 146.20E
Naraini India 41 25.11N 80.29E
Narathiwat Thailand 34 6.25N 101.48E
Nara Visa U.S.A. 83 35.37N 103.06W
Nārāyanganj Bangla. 41 23.37N 90.30E
Narbada *r.* *see* Narmada *r.* India 40
Narbonne France 17 43.11N 3.00E
Nardò Italy 19 40.11N 18.02E
Narembeen Australia 63 32.04S 118.23E
Nares Str. Canada 73 78.30N 75.00W
Naretha Australia 63 31.01S 124.50E
Nāri *r.* Pakistan 40 29.10N 67.50E
Naria Bangla. 41 23.18N 90.25E
Narita Japan 35 35.47N 140.19E
Narmada *r.* India 40 21.40N 73.00E
Nārnaul India 40 28.03N 76.06E
Nāro, Koh-i- *mtn.* Pakistan 40 29.15N 63.30E
Narodichi Ukraine 21 51.11N 29.01E
Narodnaya *mtn.* Russian Fed. 24 65.00N 61.00E
Narok Kenya 55 1.04S 35.54E
Narooma Australia 67 36.15S 150.06E
Narrabri Australia 67 30.20S 149.49E
Narrabri West Australia 67 30.22S 149.47E
Narran *r.* Australia 67 29.45S 147.20E
Narrandera Australia 67 34.36S 146.34E
Narran L. Australia 67 29.40S 147.25E
Narrogin Australia 63 32.58S 117.10E
Narromine Australia 67 32.17S 148.20E
Narsimhapur India 41 22.57N 79.12E
Narsingdi Bangla. 41 23.55N 90.43E
Narsinghgarh India 40 23.42N 77.06E
Narubis Namibia 56 26.56S 18.36E
Narva Russian Fed. 24 59.22N 28.17E
Narvik Norway 22 68.26N 17.25E
Narwāna India 40 29.37N 76.07E
Naryan Mar Russian Fed. 24 67.37N 53.02E
Naryilco Australia 66 28.41S 141.50E
Naryn Kyrgyzstan 28 41.24N 76.00E
Nasa *mtn.* Norway 22 66.29N 15.23E
Nasarawa Nigeria 53 8.35N 7.44E
Naseby New Zealand 60 45.01S 170.09E
Nashua Iowa U.S.A. 82 42.57N 92.32W
Nashua Mont. U.S.A. 80 48.08N 106.22W
Nashua N.H. U.S.A. 84 42.46N 71.27W
Nashville U.S.A. 85 36.10N 86.50W
Našice Croatia 21 45.29N 18.06E
Näsijärvi *l.* Finland 23 61.37N 23.42E
Nāsik India 40 19.59N 73.48E
Nāşir Sudan 49 8.36N 33.04E
Nāşir, Buḩayrat *l.* Egypt 48 22.40N 32.00E
Nasīrābād India 40 26.18N 74.44E
Nasīrābād Pakistan 40 28.23N 68.24E
Naskaupi *r.* Canada 77 53.45N 60.50W
Naşr Egypt 44 30.36N 30.23E
Nass *r.* Canada 74 55.00N 129.50W
Nassau Bahamas 87 25.05N 77.21W
Nassau I. Cook Is. 68 11.33S 165.25W
Nasser, L. *see* Nāşir, Buḩayrat *l.* Egypt 48
Nassian Ivory Coast 52 8.33N 3.18W
Nässjö Sweden 23 57.39N 14.41E
Nastapoca *r.* Canada 76 56.55N 76.33W
Nastapoka Is. Canada 76 57.00N 77.00W
Nata Botswana 56 20.12S 26.12E
Natal Brazil 91 5.46S 35.15W
Natal Indonesia 36 0.35N 99.07E
Natal *d.* R.S.A. 56 28.30S 30.30E
Natanes Plateau *f.* U.S.A. 81 33.35N 110.15W
Naţanz Iran 43 33.30N 51.57E
Natashquan Canada 77 50.11N 61.49W
Natashquan *r.* Canada 77 50.06N 61.49W
Natchez U.S.A. 83 31.34N 91.23W
Natchitoches U.S.A. 83 31.46N 93.05W
Nathalia Australia 67 36.02S 145.14E
Nāthdwāra India 40 24.56N 73.49E
National City U.S.A. 81 32.40N 117.06W
Natitingou Benin 53 10.17N 1.19E
Natoma U.S.A. 82 39.11N 99.01W
Natron, L. Tanzania 55 2.18S 36.05E
Naţrūn, Wādī an *f.* Egypt 44 30.25N 30.18E
Natuna Besar *i.* Indonesia 36 4.00N 108.20E
Naturaliste, C. Australia 63 33.32S 115.01E
Naubinway U.S.A. 84 46.05N 85.27W
Naumburg Germany 20 51.09N 11.48E
Nā'ūr Jordan 44 31.53N 35.50E
Nauroz Kalāt Pakistan 40 28.47N 65.38E
Nauru Pacific Oc. 68 0.32S 166.55E
Naushahro Fīroz Pakistan 40 26.50N 68.07E
Naustdal Norway 23 61.31N 5.43E
Nauta Peru 90 4.30S 73.40W
Nautanwa India 41 27.26N 83.25E
Nautla Mexico 86 20.13N 96.47W
Nava Mexico 83 28.25N 100.46W
Nava *r.* Zaïre 55 1.45N 27.06E
Navalmoral de la Mata Spain 16 39.54N 5.33W
Navan Rep. of Ire. 13 53.39N 6.42W
Navāpur India 40 21.15N 73.55E
Navarra *d.* Spain 16 42.40N 1.45W
Navarre Australia 66 36.54S 143.09E
Navarro Argentina 93 35.00S 59.10W
Navasota U.S.A. 83 30.23N 96.05W
Naver *r.* U.K. 12 58.32N 4.14W
Navlya Russian Fed. 24 52.51N 34.30E
Navoi Uzbekistan 28 40.04N 65.20E
Navojoa Mexico 81 27.06N 109.26W
Návpaktos Greece 19 38.24N 21.49E
Návplion Greece 19 37.33N 22.47E
Navrongo Ghana 52 10.51N 1.03W
Navsāri India 40 20.57N 72.59E
Nawá Syria 44 32.53N 36.03E
Nawābganj Bangla. 41 24.36N 88.17E
Nawābganj India 41 26.56N 81.13E
Nawābshāh Pakistan 40 26.15N 68.25E
Nawāda India 41 24.53N 85.32E
Nāwah Afghan. 40 32.19N 67.53E
Nawākot Nepal 41 27.55N 85.10E
Nawa Kot Pakistan 40 28.20N 71.22E
Nawalgarh India 40 27.51N 75.16E
Nawāpāra India 41 20.58N 81.51E
Naxi China 33 28.44N 105.27E
Náxos Greece 19 37.06N 25.23E
Náxos *i.* Greece 19 37.03N 25.30E
Nayāgarh India 41 20.08N 85.06E
Nayak Afghan. 40 34.44N 66.57E
Nayarit *d.* Mexico 86 21.30N 104.00W
Nāy Band Iran 43 32.20N 57.34E
Nāy Band Iran 43 27.23N 52.38E
Nāy Band, Kūh-e *mtn.* Iran 43 32.25N 57.30E
Nazaré Brazil 91 13.00S 39.00W
Nazarovka Russian Fed. 24 54.19N 41.20E
Nazas *r.* Mexico 86 25.34N 103.25W
Nazca Peru 90 14.53S 74.54W
Nazerat Israel 44 32.41N 35.16E
Nazilli Turkey 42 37.55N 28.20E
Nazinon *r.* Burkina *see* Red Volta *r.* Ghana 52
Nāzir Hāt Bangla. 41 22.38N 91.47E
Nazrēt Ethiopia 49 8.32N 39.22E
Nazuo China 33 24.06N 105.19E
Nchanga Zambia 55 12.30S 27.55E
Ncheu Malaŵi 55 14.50S 34.45E
N'dalatando Angola 54 9.12S 14.54E
Ndali Benin 53 9.53N 2.45E
Ndasegera *mtn.* Tanzania 55 1.58S 35.41E
Ndélé C.A.R. 49 8.24N 20.39E
Ndélélé Cameroon 53 4.03N 14.55E
N'Dendé Gabon 54 2.20S 11.23E
Ndikiniméki Cameroon 53 4.46N 10.49E
N'Djamena Chad 53 12.10N 14.59E
Ndjolé Gabon 54 0.07S 10.45E
Ndola Zambia 56 12.58S 28.39E
Ndoro Gabon 54 0.24S 12.34E
Ndrhamcha, Sebkha de *f.* Mauritania 50 18.45N 15.48W
Ndungu Tanzania 55 4.25S 38.04E
Nea *r.* Norway 22 63.15N 11.00E
Neagh, Lough U.K. 13 54.36N 6.25W
Neale, L. Australia 64 24.21S 130.04E
Néa Páfos Cyprus 44 34.45N 32.25E
Neápolis Greece 19 36.30N 23.04E
Neath U.K. 11 51.39N 3.49W
Nebit-Dag Turkmenistan 43 39.31N 54.24E
Nebraska *d.* U.S.A. 82 41.50N 100.06W
Nebraska City U.S.A. 82 40.41N 95.52W
Nebrodi, Monti *mts.* Italy 18 37.53N 14.32E
Nechako *r.* Canada 74 53.30N 122.44W
Neches *r.* U.S.A. 83 29.55N 93.50W
Neckar *r.* Germany 20 49.32N 8.26E
Necochea Argentina 93 38.31S 58.46W
Necuto Angola 54 4.55S 12.38E
Nêdong China 41 29.14N 91.48E
Nedroma Algeria 50 35.00N 1.44W
Needles U.S.A. 81 34.51N 114.37W
Neepawa Canada 75 50.13N 99.29W
Neerpelt Belgium 14 51.13N 5.28E
Nefta Tunisia 51 33.52N 7.33E
Neftegorsk Russian Fed. 25 44.21N 39.44E
Nefyn U.K. 10 52.55N 4.31W
Negara Indonesia 37 8.21S 114.35E
Negaunee U.S.A. 84 46.31N 87.37W
Negele Ethiopia 49 5.20N 39.36E
Negev *des. see* HaNegev *des.* Israel 44
Negoiu *mtn.* Romania 21 45.36N 24.32E
Negomano Mozambique 55 11.26S 38.30E
Negombo Sri Lanka 39 7.13N 79.50E
Negotin Yugo. 21 44.14N 22.33E
Negrais, C. Burma 34 16.00N 94.12E
Negritos Peru 90 4.42S 81.18W
Negro *r.* Argentina 93 40.50S 63.00W
Negro *r.* Brazil 90 3.00S 59.55W
Negro *r.* Uruguay 93 33.27S 58.20W
Negro, Baia del *b.* Somali Rep. 45 7.52N 49.50E
Negros *i.* Phil. 37 10.00N 123.00E
Negru-Vodă Romania 21 43.50N 28.12E
Neijiang China 33 29.29N 105.03E

Nei Monggol Zizhiqu to Ñorquinco

Nei Monggol Zizhiqu d. China 32 41.50N112.30E
Neisse r. Poland/Germany 20 52.05N 14.42E
Neiva Colombia 90 2.58N 75.15W
Nejanilini L. Canada 75 59.33N 97.48W
Nejo Ethiopia 49 9.30N 35.30E
Nek'emtē Ethiopia 49 9.02N 36.31E
Neksö Denmark 23 55.04N 15.09E
Nelidovo Russian Fed. 24 56.13N 32.46E
Neligh U.S.A. 82 42.08N 98.02W
Nelkan Russian Fed. 29 57.40N136.04E
Nelligen Australia 67 35.39S150.06E
Nellore India 39 14.29N 80.00E
Nelson Australia 66 38.04S141.05E
Nelson Canada 74 49.30N117.20W
Nelson r. Canada 75 57.04N 92.30W
Nelson New Zealand 60 41.18S173.17E
Nelson U.K. 10 53.50N 2.14W
Nelson U.S.A. 81 35.30N113.16W
Nelson, C. Australia 66 38.27S141.35E
Nelson, Estrecho str. Chile 93 51.33S 74.40W
Nelson Bay town Australia 67 32.43S152.08E
Nelson Forks Canada 74 59.30N124.00W
Nelson-Marlborough d. New Zealand 60 41.40S173.40E
Nelspoort R.S.A. 56 32.07S 23.00E
Nelspruit R.S.A. 56 25.27S 30.58E
Néma Mauritania 50 16.40N 7.15W
Nembe Nigeria 53 4.32N 6.25E
Nemours France 15 48.16N 2.41E
Nemunas r. Lithuania 23 55.18N 21.23E
Nenagh Rep. of Ire. 13 52.52N 8.13W
Nenana U.S.A. 72 64.35N149.20W
Nene r. U.K. 10 52.49N 0.12E
Nenjiang China 31 49.10N125.15E
Neodesha U.S.A. 83 37.25N 95.41W
Neosho U.S.A. 83 36.52N 94.22W
Neosho r. U.S.A. 82 35.48N 95.18W
Nepal Asia 41 28.00N 84.00E
Nepālganj Nepal 41 28.03N 81.38E
Nepa Nagar India 40 21.28N 76.23E
Nephi U.S.A. 80 39.43N111.50W
Nephin Beg mtn. Rep. of Ire. 13 54.02N 9.38W
Nephin Beg Range mts. Rep. of Ire. 13 54.00N 9.37W
Nera r. Italy 18 42.33N 12.43E
Nérac France 17 44.08N 0.20E
Nerekhta Russian Fed. 24 57.30N 40.40E
Néret, Lac l. Canada 77 54.45N 70.50W
Neretva r. Bosnia-Herzegovina 19 43.02N 17.28E
Neriquinha Angola 56 15.50S 21.40E
Nero Deep Pacific Oc. 37 12.40N145.50E
Néronde France 17 45.50N 4.14E
Nerva Spain 16 37.42N 6.30W
Nes Neth. 14 53.27N 5.46E
Nesbyen Norway 23 60.34N 9.09E
Nesle France 15 49.46N 2.51E
Nesna Norway 22 66.13N 13.04E
Nesöy i. Norway 22 66.35N 12.40E
Ness, Loch U.K. 12 57.16N 4.30W
Nestaocano r. Canada 77 48.40N 73.25W
Nesterov Ukraine 21 50.04N 24.00E
Néstos r. Greece 19 40.51N 24.48E
Nesttun Norway 23 60.19N 5.20E
Nesvizh Belorussia 21 53.16N 26.40E
Netanya Israel 44 32.20N 34.51E
Netcong U.S.A. 85 40.54N 74.42W
Netherlands Europe 14 52.00N 5.30E
Netherlands Antilles S. America 87 12.30N 69.00W
Neto r. Italy 19 39.12N 17.08E
Netrakona Bangla. 41 24.53N 90.43E
Nettilling L. Canada 73 66.30N 70.40W
Neubrandenburg Germany 20 53.33N 13.16E
Neuchâtel Switz. 20 47.00N 6.56E
Neuchâtel, Lac de l. Switz. 20 46.55N 6.55E
Neuenhaus Germany 14 52.30N 6.58E
Neufchâteau Belgium 14 49.51N 5.26E
Neufchâtel France 15 49.44N 1.26E
Neuillé-Pont-Pierre France 15 47.33N 0.33E
Neumarkt Germany 20 49.16N 11.28E
Neumünster Germany 20 54.06N 9.59E
Neuquén Argentina 93 39.00S 68.05W
Neuquén d. Argentina 93 38.30S 70.00W
Neuquén r. Argentina 93 39.02S 68.07W
Neuruppin Germany 20 52.55N 12.48E
Neuse r. U.S.A. 85 35.06N 76.30W
Neusiedler See l. Austria 20 47.52N 16.45E
Neuss Germany 14 51.12N 6.42E
Neustadt Germany 20 49.44N 12.11E
Neustrelitz Germany 20 53.22N 13.05E
Neuvic France 17 45.23N 2.16E
Neuwied Germany 14 50.26N 7.28E
Nevada U.S.A. 83 37.51N 94.22W
Nevada d. U.S.A. 80 39.50N116.10W
Nevada, Sierra mts. Spain 16 37.04N 3.20W
Nevada, Sierra mts. U.S.A. 78 37.30N119.00W
Nevanka Russian Fed. 29 56.31N 98.57E
Nevel Russian Fed. 24 56.20N 29.59E
Nevers France 17 47.00N 3.09E
Nevertire Australia 67 31.52S147.47E
Nevinnomyssk Russian Fed. 25 44.38N 41.59E
Nevşehir Turkey 42 38.38N 34.43E
Newala Tanzania 55 10.56S 39.15E
New Albany Ind. U.S.A. 84 38.17N 85.50W
New Albany Miss. U.S.A. 83 34.29N 89.00W
New Amsterdam Guyana 91 6.18N 57.30W
New Angledool Australia 67 29.06S147.57E
Newark Del. U.S.A. 85 39.41N 75.45W
Newark N.J. U.S.A. 85 40.44N 74.11W
Newark N.Y. U.S.A. 84 43.03N 77.06W
Newark Ohio U.S.A. 84 40.03N 82.25W
Newark-on-Trent U.K. 10 53.06N 0.48E
New Athens U.S.A. 82 38.19N 89.53W
New Bedford U.S.A. 84 41.38N 70.56W
Newberg U.S.A. 80 45.18N122.58W
New Bern U.S.A. 85 35.05N 77.04W
Newberry Mich. U.S.A. 84 46.22N 85.30W
Newberry S.C. U.S.A. 85 34.17N 81.39W
Newbiggin-by-the-Sea U.K. 10 55.11N 1.30W
New Braunfels U.S.A. 83 29.42N 98.08W
New Britain i. P.N.G. 61 6.00S150.00E
New Brunswick d. Canada 77 46.50N 66.00W
New Brunswick U.S.A. 85 40.29N 74.27W
Newburgh U.S.A. 85 41.30N 74.00W
Newbury U.K. 11 51.24N 1.19W
New Bussa Nigeria 53 9.53N 4.29E
New Caledonia is. see Nouvelle Calédonie is. Pacific Oc. 68
Newcastle Australia 67 32.55S151.46E
Newcastle N.B. Canada 77 47.00N 65.34W
Newcastle Ont. Canada 76 43.55N 78.35W
Newcastle R.S.A. 56 27.44S 29.55E
Newcastle U.K. 13 54.13N 5.53W
New Castle Penn. U.S.A. 84 41.00N 80.22W
Newcastle Wyo. U.S.A. 80 43.50N104.11W
Newcastle B. Australia 64 10.50S142.37E
Newcastle Emlyn U.K. 11 52.02N 4.29W
Newcastle-under-Lyme U.K. 10 53.02N 2.15W
Newcastle upon Tyne U.K. 10 54.58N 1.36W
Newcastle Waters town Australia 64 17.24S133.24E
Newcastle West Rep. of Ire. 13 52.26N 9.04W
New City U.S.A. 85 41.09N 73.59W
Newdegate Australia 63 33.06S119.01E
New Delhi India 40 28.36N 77.12E
New Denver Canada 74 50.00N117.25W
New England U.S.A. 82 46.32N102.52W
New England Range mts. Australia 67 30.30S151.50E
Newenham, C. U.S.A. 72 58.37N162.12W
Newent U.K. 11 51.56N 2.24W
Newfane U.S.A. 76 43.17N 78.43W
New Forest f. U.K. 11 50.50N 1.35W
Newfoundland d. Canada 77 54.00N 60.10W
Newfoundland i. Canada 77 48.30N 56.00W
New Freedom U.S.A. 85 39.44N 76.42W
New Galloway U.K. 12 55.05N 4.09W
Newgate Canada 74 49.01N115.08W
New Glasgow Canada 77 45.35N 62.39W
New Guinea i. Austa. 37 5.00S140.00E
New Hampshire d. U.S.A. 84 43.35N 71.40W
New Hanover i. Pacific Oc. 61 2.00S150.00E
Newhaven U.K. 11 50.47N 0.04E
New Haven U.S.A. 84 41.18N 72.55W
New Hebrides Basin Pacific Oc. 68 16.00S162.00E
New Holland U.S.A. 85 40.06N 76.05W
New Iberia U.S.A. 83 30.00N 91.49W
New Ireland i. P.N.G. 61 2.30S151.30E
New Jersey d. U.S.A. 85 40.15N 74.30W
New Liskeard Canada 76 47.31N 79.41W
New London Conn. U.S.A. 84 41.21N 72.06W
New London Minn. U.S.A. 82 45.18N 94.56W
Newman Australia 62 23.22S119.43E
Newman U.S.A. 81 31.55N106.20W
Newman, Mt. Australia 62 23.15S119.33E
Newmarket Rep. of Ire. 13 52.13N 9.00W
Newmarket U.K. 11 52.15N 0.23E
Newmarket on Fergus Rep. of Ire. 13 52.46N 8.55W
New Martinsville U.S.A. 84 39.39N 80.52W
New Meadows U.S.A. 80 44.58N116.32W
New Mexico d. U.S.A. 80 33.30N106.00W
New Milford U.S.A. 85 41.35N 73.25W
Newnan U.S.A. 85 33.23N 84.48W
New Norcia Australia 63 30.58S116.15E
New Norfolk Australia 65 42.46S147.02E
New Orleans U.S.A. 83 29.58N 90.07W
New Philadelphia U.S.A. 84 40.31N 81.28W
New Plymouth New Zealand 60 39.03S174.04E
Newport Mayo Rep. of Ire. 13 53.53N 9.34W
Newport Tipperary Rep. of Ire. 13 52.42N 8.25W
Newport Dyfed U.K. 11 52.01N 4.51W
Newport Essex U.K. 11 51.58N 0.13E
Newport Gwent U.K. 11 51.34N 2.59W
Newport Hants. U.K. 11 50.43N 1.18W
Newport Ark. U.S.A. 83 35.35N 91.16W
Newport Maine U.S.A. 84 44.50N 69.17W
Newport N.H. U.S.A. 84 43.21N 72.09W
Newport Oreg. U.S.A. 80 44.38N124.03W
Newport R.I. U.S.A. 84 41.13N 71.18W
Newport News U.S.A. 85 36.59N 76.26W
New Providence I. Bahamas 87 25.25N 78.35W
Newquay U.K. 11 50.24N 5.06W
New Quay U.K. 11 52.13N 4.22W
New Radnor U.K. 11 52.15N 3.10W
New Rochelle U.S.A. 85 40.55N 73.47W
New Rockford U.S.A. 82 47.41N 99.15W
New Romney U.K. 11 50.59N 0.58E
New Ross Rep. of Ire. 13 52.24N 6.57W
Newry U.K. 13 54.11N 6.21W
New Scone U.K. 12 56.25N 3.25W
New Smyrna Beach town U.S.A. 85 29.01N 80.56W
New South Wales d. Australia 67 32.40S147.40E
Newton Ill. U.S.A. 82 38.59N 88.10W
Newton Iowa U.S.A. 82 41.42N 93.03W
Newton Kans. U.S.A. 83 38.03N 97.21W
Newton Miss. U.S.A. 83 32.19N 89.10W
Newton N.J. U.S.A. 85 41.03N 74.45W
Newton Abbot U.K. 11 50.32N 3.37W
Newton Aycliffe U.K. 10 54.36N 1.34W
Newtonmore U.K. 12 57.04N 4.08W
Newton Stewart U.K. 12 54.57N 4.29W
Newtown U.K. 11 52.31N 3.19W
Newtownabbey U.K. 13 54.39N 5.57W
Newtownards U.K. 13 54.35N 5.41W
Newtown Butler U.K. 13 54.12N 7.22W
Newtown St. Boswells U.K. 12 55.35N 2.40W
Newtownstewart U.K. 13 54.43N 7.25W
New Waterford Canada 77 46.15N 60.05W
New Westminster Canada 74 49.10N122.52W
New York U.S.A. 85 40.40N 73.50W
New York d. U.S.A. 84 43.00N 75.00W
New York State Barge Canal U.S.A. 76 43.05N 78.43W
New Zealand Austa. 60 41.00S175.00E
New Zealand Plateau Pacific Oc. 68 50.00S170.00E
Neya Russian Fed. 24 58.18N 43.40E
Neyagawa Japan 35 34.46N135.38E
Neyrīz Iran 43 29.12N 54.17E
Neyshābūr Iran 43 36.13N 58.49E
Nezhin Ukraine 21 51.03N 31.54E
Ngala Nigeria 53 12.21N 14.10E
Ngambwe Rapids f. Zambia 54 17.08S 24.10E
Ngami, L. Botswana 56 20.32S 22.38E
Ngamiland d. Botswana 56 19.40S 22.00E
Ngamiland f. Botswana 56 20.00S 22.30E
Ngamring China 41 29.14N 87.10E
Ngangla Ringco l. China 41 31.40N 83.00E
Nganglong Kangri mtn. China 41 32.40N 81.00E
Nganglong Kangri mts. China 41 32.15N 82.00E
Ngangzê Co l. China 41 31.00N 87.00E
Nganjuk Indonesia 37 7.36S111.56E
N'Gao Congo 54 2.28S 15.40E
Ngaoundéré Cameroon 53 7.20N 13.35E
Ngara-Binsam Congo 54 1.36N 13.30E
Ngardiam C.A.R. 49 9.00N 20.58E
Ngaruawahia New Zealand 60 37.40S175.09E
Ngaruroro r. New Zealand 60 39.34S176.54E
Ngatangiia Rarotonga Cook Is. 68 21.14S159.44W
Ngau i. Fiji 68 18.02S179.18E
Ngauruhoe mtn. New Zealand 60 39.10S175.35E
Ngawi Indonesia 37 7.23S111.22E
Ngaya mtn. C.A.R. 49 9.18N 23.28E
Ng'iro, Mt. Kenya 55 2.06N 36.44E
N'Giva Angola 56 17.03S 15.47E
Ngoc Linh mtn. Vietnam 34 15.04N107.59E
Ngoma Zambia 54 16.04S 26.06E
Ngomba Tanzania 55 8.16S 32.51E
Ngomeni Kenya 55 3.00S 40.11E
Ngong Kenya 55 1.22S 36.40E
Ngonye Falls f. Zambia 54 16.35S 23.39E
Ngorongoro Crater f. Tanzania 55 3.13S 35.32E
Ngouo, Mont mtn. C.A.R. 49 7.55N 24.38E
Ngozi Burundi 55 2.52S 29.50E
Nguigmi Niger 53 14.00N 13.11E
Nguru Nigeria 53 12.53N 10.30E
Nguruka Tanzania 55 5.08S 30.58E
Ngwaketse d. Botswana 56 25.10S 25.00E
Ngwerere Zambia 55 15.18S 28.20E
Nhacongo Mozambique 57 24.18S 35.14E
Nhachengue Mozambique 57 22.52S 35.10E
Nhandugue r. Mozambique 57 18.47S 34.30E
Nha Trang Vietnam 34 12.15N109.10E
Nhill Australia 66 36.20S141.40E
Nhulunbuy Australia 64 12.11S136.46E
Nhungo Angola 56 13.17S 20.06E
Niafounké Mali 50 15.56N 4.00W
Niagara Canada 76 43.05N 79.20W
Niagara Falls town Canada 76 43.06N 79.04W
Niagara Falls town U.S.A. 84 43.06N 79.02W
Niah Malaysia 36 3.52N113.44E
Niamey Niger 53 13.32N 2.05E
Niamey d. Niger 53 14.00N 1.40E
Nianforando Guinea 52 9.37N 10.36W
Niangara Zaïre 55 3.47N 27.54E
Nia-Nia Zaïre 55 1.30N 27.41E
Nias i. Indonesia 36 1.05N 97.30E
Niassa d. Mozambique 55 13.00S 36.30E
Nicaragua C. America 87 13.00N 85.00W
Nicaragua, Lago de l. Nicaragua 87 11.30N 85.30W
Nicastro Italy 18 38.58N 16.16E
Nice France 17 43.42N 7.16E
Nichelino Italy 15 44.59N 7.38E
Nicholson Australia 62 18.02S128.54E
Nicholson r. Australia 64 17.31S139.36E
Nicholson L. Canada 75 62.40N102.35W
Nicobar Is. India 34 8.00N 93.30E
Nicolet Canada 77 46.13N 72.37W
Nicolet r. Canada 77 46.14N 72.39W
Nicolls Town Bahamas 87 25.08N 78.00W
Nicosia see Levkosía Cyprus 44
Nicoya, Golfo de g. Costa Rica 87 9.30N 85.00W
Nicoya, Península de pen. Costa Rica 87 10.30N 85.30W
Nid r. Norway 23 58.24N 8.48E
Nida r. Poland 21 50.18N 20.52E
Nido, Sierra de mts. Mexico 81 29.30N107.00W
Nidzica Poland 21 53.22N 20.26E
Niederösterreich d. Austria 20 48.20N 15.50E
Niedersachsen d. Germany 14 52.55N 7.40E
Niekerkshoop R.S.A. 56 29.19S 22.48E
Niéllé Ivory Coast 52 10.05N 5.28W
Nienburg Germany 20 52.38N 9.13E
Niéré Chad 48 14.30N 21.09E
Niers r. Neth. 14 51.43N 5.56E
Nieuw Nickerie Surinam 91 5.57N 56.59W
Nieuwpoort Belgium 14 51.08N 2.45E
Nigde Turkey 42 37.58N 34.42E
Niger d. Nigeria 53 9.50N 6.00E
Niger r. Nigeria 53 4.15N 6.05E
Niger Delta Nigeria 53 4.00N 6.10E
Nigeria Africa 53 9.00N 9.00E
Nightcaps New Zealand 60 45.58S168.02E
Nightingale I. Tristan da Cunha 95 37.28S 12.32W
Nihing r. Pakistan 40 26.00N 62.44E
Nihoa i. Hawaiian Is. 68 23.03N161.55W
Niigata Japan 35 37.58N139.02E
Niihau i. Hawaiian Is. 69 21.55N160.10W
Niiza Japan 35 35.48N139.34E
Nijmegen Neth. 14 51.50N 5.52E
Nikel Russian Fed. 22 69.20N 30.00E
Nikiniki Indonesia 62 9.49S124.29E
Nikki Benin 53 9.55N 3.18E
Nikolayev Ukraine 25 46.57N 32.00E
Nikolayevskiy Russian Fed. 25 50.05N 45.32E
Nikolayevsk-na-Amure Russian Fed. 29 53.20N140.44E
Nikolsk Russian Fed. 24 59.33N 45.30E
Nikopol Ukraine 25 47.34N 34.25E
Niksar Turkey 42 40.35N 36.59E
Nikshahr Iran 43 26.14N 60.15E
Nikšić Yugo. 19 42.48N 18.56E
Nikumaroro i. Kiribati 68 4.40S174.32W
Nīl, An r. Egypt 44 31.30N 30.25E
Nila i. Indonesia 37 6.45S129.30E
Nile r. see Nīl, An r. Egypt 44
Nile Delta Egypt 44 31.00N 31.00E
Niles U.S.A. 84 41.51N 86.15W
Nilgiri India 41 21.28N 86.46E
Nilgiri Hills India 38 11.30N 77.30E
Nimach India 40 24.28N 74.52E
Nimai r. Burma 34 25.44N 97.30E
Nimba, Mt. Guinea 52 7.35N 8.28W
Nimbin Australia 67 28.35S153.12E
Nîmes France 17 43.50N 4.21E
Nim Ka Thāna India 40 27.44N 75.48E
Nimrūz d. Afghan. 40 30.40N 62.15E
Nimule Sudan 49 3.36N 32.03E
Nindigully Australia 67 28.20S148.47E
Ninety Mile Beach f. Australia 67 38.07S147.30E
Ninety Mile Beach f. New Zealand 60 34.45S173.00E
Nineveh ruins Iraq 42 36.24N 43.08E
Ningbo China 33 29.56N121.32E
Ningde China 33 26.41N119.32E
Ningdu China 33 26.29N115.46E
Ninggang China 33 26.45N113.58E
Ningguo China 33 30.38N118.58E
Ningming China 33 22.04N107.02E
Ningnan China 30 27.03N102.46E
Ningqiang China 32 32.49N106.13E
Ningwu China 32 38.59N112.12E
Ningxia Huizu d. China 32 37.00N105.00E
Ning Xian China 32 35.27N107.50E
Ningxiang China 33 28.15N112.33E
Ninh Binh Vietnam 34 20.14N106.00E
Ninove Belgium 14 50.50N 4.02E
Niobrara U.S.A. 82 42.45N 98.02W
Niobrara r. U.S.A. 82 42.45N 98.00W
Nioki Zaïre 54 2.43S 17.41E
Nioro Mali 50 15.12N 9.35W
Nioro du Rip Senegal 52 13.40N 15.50W
Niort France 17 46.19N 0.27W
Niout well Mauritania 50 16.03N 6.52W
Nipāni India 38 16.24N 74.23E
Nipigon Canada 76 49.00N 88.17W
Nipigon, L. Canada 76 49.50N 88.30W
Nipigon B. Canada 76 48.55N 88.00W
Nipissing, L. Canada 76 46.17N 80.00W
Niquelândia Brazil 94 14.27S 48.27W
Nirasaki Japan 35 35.42N138.27E
Nirmal India 41 19.06N 78.21E
Nirmali India 41 26.19N 86.35E
Nirwāno Pakistan 40 26.22N 62.43E
Niš Yugo. 19 43.20N 21.54E
Nisa Portugal 16 39.31N 7.39W
Nishi China 33 29.54N110.38E
Nishinomiya Japan 35 34.43N135.20E
Niskibi r. Canada 75 56.28N 88.10W
Nisko Poland 21 50.35N 22.07E
Nissedal Norway 23 59.10N 8.30E
Nisser l. Norway 23 59.10N 8.30E
Niţā' Saudi Arabia 43 27.13N 48.25E
Nitchequon Canada 77 53.12N 70.47W
Niterói Brazil 94 22.54S 43.06W
Nith r. U.K. 12 55.00N 3.35W
Nitra Slovakia 21 48.20N 18.05E
Niue i. Cook Is. 68 19.02S169.52W
Niut, Gunung mtn. Indonesia 36 1.00N110.00E
Nivala Finland 22 63.55N 24.58E
Nivelles Belgium 14 50.36N 4.20E
Nixon U.S.A. 83 29.16N 97.46W
Nizāmābād India 39 18.40N 78.05E
Nizgān r. Afghan. 40 33.05N 63.20E
Nizhneangarsk Russian Fed. 29 55.48N109.35E
Nizhnekamskoye Vodokhranilishche Russian Fed. 24 55.45N 53.50E
Nizhne Kolymsk Russian Fed. 29 68.34N160.58E
Nizhneudinsk Russian Fed. 29 54.55N 99.00E
Nizhnevartovsk Russian Fed. 28 60.57N 76.40E
Nizhniy Novgorod Russian Fed. 24 56.20N 44.00E
Nizhniy Tagil Russian Fed. 24 58.00N 60.00E
Nizhnyaya Tunguska r. Russian Fed. 29 65.50N 88.00E
Nizhnyaya Tura Russian Fed. 24 58.40N 59.48E
Nizke Tatry mts. Slovakia 21 48.54N 19.40E
Nizza Monferrato Italy 15 44.46N 8.21E
Njazidja see Grande Comore i. Comoros 55
Njombe Tanzania 55 9.20S 34.47E
Njombe r. Tanzania 55 7.02S 35.55E
Njoro Tanzania 55 5.16S 36.30E
Nkalagu Nigeria 53 6.28N 7.46E
Nkawkaw Ghana 52 6.35N 0.47W
Nkayi Zimbabwe 56 19.00S 28.54E
Nkhata Bay town Malaŵi 55 11.37S 34.20E
Nkhotakota Malaŵi 55 12.55S 34.19E
Nkongsamba Cameroon 53 4.59N 9.53E
Nkungwe Mt. Tanzania 55 6.15S 29.54E
Noākhāli Bangla. 41 22.51N 91.06E
Noatak U.S.A. 72 67.34N162.59W
Noce r. Italy 15 46.09N 11.04E
Nogales Mexico 81 31.20N110.56W
Nogara Italy 15 45.11N 11.04E
Nogayskiye Step f. Russian Fed. 25 44.25N 45.30E
Nogent-le-Rotrou France 15 48.19N 0.50E
Nogent-sur-Seine France 15 48.29N 3.30E
Nogoyá Argentina 93 32.22S 59.49W
Noguera Ribagorçana r. Spain 16 41.27N 0.25E
Nohar India 40 29.11N 74.46E
Nohta India 41 23.40N 79.34E
Noire r. Canada 77 45.33N 72.58W
Noirmoutier, Île de i. France 17 47.00N 2.15W
Nojima-zaki c. Japan 35 34.56N139.53E
Nokha India 40 27.35N 73.29E
Nokia Finland 23 61.28N 23.30E
Nok Kundi Pakistan 40 28.46N 62.46E
Nokomis Canada 75 51.30N105.00W
Nokou Chad 53 14.35N 14.47E
Nola C.A.R. 53 3.28N 16.08E
Nolinsk Russian Fed. 24 57.38N 49.52E
Noman L. Canada 75 62.15N108.55W
Noma Omuramba r. Botswana 56 19.14S 22.15E
Nombre de Dios Mexico 81 28.41N106.05W
Nome U.S.A. 72 64.30N165.30W
Nomgon Mongolia 32 42.50N105.13E
Nomuka Group is. Tonga 69 20.15S174.46W
Nonancourt France 15 48.47N 1.11E
Nonburg Russian Fed. 24 65.32N 50.37E
Nong Khai Thailand 34 17.50N102.46E
Nongoma R.S.A. 57 27.58S 31.35E
Nongpoh India 41 25.54N 91.53E
Nongstoin India 41 25.31N 91.16E
Nonning Australia 66 32.30S136.30E
Nono Ethiopia 49 8.31N 37.30E
Nonthaburi Thailand 34 13.48N100.11E
Noojee Australia 67 37.57S146.00E
Noonamah Australia 62 12.35S131.03E
Noonan U.S.A. 82 48.54N103.01W
Noongaar Australia 63 31.21S118.55E
Noonkanbah Australia 62 18.30S124.50E
Noonthorangee Range mts. Australia 66 31.00S142.20E
Noorama Creek r. Australia 67 28.05S145.55E
Noord Beveland f. Neth. 14 51.35N 3.45E
Noord Brabant d. Neth. 14 51.37N 5.00E
Noord Holland d. Neth. 14 52.37N 4.50E
Noordoost-Polder f. Neth. 14 52.45N 5.45E
Noordwijk Neth. 14 52.16N 4.29E
Noorvik U.S.A. 72 66.50N161.14W
Noosa Heads town Australia 64 26.23S153.07E
Nootka I. Canada 74 49.32N126.42W
Noqui Angola 54 5.51S 13.25E
Nora Sweden 23 59.31N 15.02E
Noranda Canada 76 48.20N 79.00W
Nord d. Burkina 52 13.50N 2.20W
Nord d. France 14 50.17N 3.14E
Nordaustlandet i. Arctic Oc. 96 79.55N 23.00E
Norddeich Germany 14 53.35N 7.10E
Nordegg Canada 74 52.29N116.05W
Norden Germany 14 53.34N 7.13E
Nordenham Germany 20 53.30N 8.29E
Norderney Germany 14 53.43N 7.09E
Norderney i. Germany 14 53.45N 7.15E
Nordfjord est. Norway 23 61.54N 5.12E
Nordfjordeid Norway 23 61.54N 6.00E
Nordfold Norway 22 67.48N 15.20E
Nordfriesische Inseln is. Germany 20 54.30N 8.00E
Nordhausen Germany 20 51.31N 10.48E
Nordhorn Germany 14 52.27N 7.05E
Nordkapp c. Norway 22 71.11N 25.48E
Nordkinnhalvöya pen. Norway 22 70.55N 27.45E
Nordland d. Norway 22 66.50N 14.50E
Nord-Ostsee-Kanal Germany 20 53.54N 9.12E
Nordreisa Norway 22 69.46N 21.00E
Nordrhein-Westfalen d. Germany 14 51.18N 6.32E
Nord Tröndelag d. Norway 22 64.20N 12.00E
Nordvik Russian Fed. 29 73.40N110.50E
Nore Norway 23 60.10N 9.01E
Nore r. Rep. of Ire. 13 52.25N 6.58W
Norfolk d. U.K. 11 52.39N 1.00E
Norfolk Nebr. U.S.A. 82 42.02N 97.25W
Norfolk Va. U.S.A. 85 36.54N 76.18W
Norfolk Broads f. U.K. 10 52.43N 1.35E
Norfolk I. Pacific Oc. 68 29.02S167.57E
Norfolk Island Ridge Pacific Oc. 68 29.00S167.00E
Norheimsund Norway 23 60.22N 6.08E
Norilsk Russian Fed. 29 69.21N 88.02E
Normal U.S.A. 82 40.31N 89.00W
Norman r. Australia 64 17.28S140.49E
Norman U.S.A. 83 35.13N 97.26W
Normanby r. Australia 64 14.25S144.08E
Normanby New Zealand 60 39.32S174.16E
Normanby I. P.N.G. 64 10.05S151.05E
Normandie, Collines de hills France 15 48.50N 0.40W
Normanton Australia 64 17.40S141.05E
Norman Wells Canada 72 65.19N126.46W
Ñornalup Australia 63 34.58S116.49E
Ñorquinco Argentina 93 41.50S 70.55W

Norrahammar to Oko, Wādī

Norrahammar Sweden 23 57.42N 14.06E
Norra Kvarken str. Sweden/Finland 22 63.36N 20.43E
Norra Storfjället mtn. Sweden 22 65.52N 15.18E
Norrbotten d. Sweden 22 67.00N 19.50E
Nörresundby Denmark 23 57.04N 9.56E
Norris L. U.S.A. 85 36.18N 83.58W
Norristown U.S.A. 85 40.07N 75.20W
Norrköping Sweden 23 58.36N 16.11E
Norrsundet Sweden 23 60.56N 17.08E
Norrtälje Sweden 23 59.46N 18.42E
Norseman Australia 63 32.15S121.47E
Norsk Russian Fed. 29 52.22N129.57E
Norte d. W. Sahara 50 26.50N 11.15W
Norte, C. Brazil 91 1.40N 49.55W
Norte, Cabo c. I. de Pascua 69 27.03S109.24W
Norte, Punta c. Argentina 93 36.17S 56.46W
North, C. Canada 77 47.01N 60.28W
Northallerton U.K. 10 54.20N 1.26W
Northam Australia 63 31.41S116.40E
Northampton Australia 63 28.21S114.37E
Northampton U.K. 11 52.14N 0.54W
Northampton U.S.A. 85 40.41N 75.30W
Northamptonshire d. U.K. 11 52.18N 0.55W
North Battleford Canada 75 52.47N108.17W
North Bay town Canada 76 46.19N 79.28W
North Bend U.S.A. 80 43.24N124.14W
North Berwick U.K. 12 56.04N 2.43W
North Bourke Australia 67 30.01S145.59E
North C. Antarctica 96 71.00S166.00E
North C. New Zealand 60 34.28S173.00E
North Canadian r. U.S.A. 83 35.17N 95.31W
North Caribou L. Canada 76 52.50N 90.50W
North Carolina d. U.S.A. 85 35.30N 80.00W
North Channel str. Canada 76 46.02N 82.50W
North Channel U.K. 13 55.15N 5.52W
North Chicago U.S.A. 82 42.20N 87.51W
North China Plain f. see Huabei Pingyuan f. China 32
Northcliffe Australia 63 34.36S116.04E
North Dakota d. U.S.A. 82 47.00N100.00W
North Dorset Downs hills U.K. 11 50.46N 2.25W
North Downs hills U.K. 11 51.18N 0.40E
North East d. Botswana 56 20.45S 27.05E
North East U.S.A. 76 42.13N 79.50W
North Eastern d. Kenya 55 1.00N 40.00E
North Eastern Atlantic Basin f. Atlantic Oc. 95 45.00N 17.00W
North East Pt. Kiribati 69 1.57N157.16W
Northern d. Ghana 52 9.00N 1.30W
Northern Indian L. Canada 75 57.20N 97.20W
Northern Ireland d. U.K. 13 54.40N 6.45W
Northern Territory d. Australia 64 20.00S133.00E
North Esk r. U.K. 12 56.45N 2.25W
North Fiji Basin Pacific Oc. 68 17.00S173.00E
North Foreland c. U.K. 11 51.23N 1.26E
North French r. Canada 76 51.04N 80.46W
North Frisian Is. see Nordfriesische Inseln is. Germany 20
North Head c. Canada 77 53.42N 56.24W
North Henik L. Canada 75 61.45N 97.40W
North Horr Kenya 55 3.19N 37.00E
North I. Kenya 49 4.04N 36.03E
North I. New Zealand 60 39.00S175.00E
Northiam U.K. 11 50.59N 0.39E
North Knife r. Canada 75 58.53N 94.45W
North Korea Asia 31 40.00N128.00E
Northland d. New Zealand 60 35.25S174.00E
North Las Vegas U.S.A. 81 36.12N115.07W
North Little Rock U.S.A. 83 34.46N 92.14W
North Loup r. U.S.A. 82 41.17N 98.23W
North Mankato U.S.A. 82 44.15N 94.06W
North Nahanni r. Canada 74 62.15N123.20W
North Ogden U.S.A. 80 41.18N112.00W
Northome U.S.A. 82 47.52N 94.17W
North Platte U.S.A. 82 41.08N100.46W
North Platte r. U.S.A. 82 41.15N100.45W
Northport U.S.A. 85 33.14N 87.33W
North Powder U.S.A. 80 45.13N117.55W
North Pt. Canada 77 47.05N 64.00W
North Rona i. U.K. 8 59.09N 5.43W
North Ronaldsay i. U.K. 12 59.23N 2.26W
North Saskatchewan r. Canada 75 53.15N105.06W
North Sea Europe 20 54.00N 4.00E
North Seal r. Canada 75 58.50N 98.10W
North Sporades see Vorìai Sporádhes is. Greece 19
North Sydney Canada 77 46.13N 60.15W
North Taranaki Bight b. New Zealand 60 38.45S174.15E
North Tawton U.K. 11 50.48N 3.55W
North Thompson r. Canada 74 50.40N120.20W
North Tonawanda U.S.A. 84 43.02N 78.54W
North Twin I. Canada 76 53.20N 80.00W
North Uist i. U.K. 12 57.35N 7.20W
Northumberland d. U.K. 10 55.12N 2.00W
Northumberland, C. Australia 66 38.04S140.40E
Northumberland Is. Australia 64 21.40S150.00E
Northumberland Str. Canada 77 46.00N 63.30W
North Wabasca L. Canada 74 56.00N113.55W
North Walsham U.K. 10 52.49N 1.22E
Northway U.S.A. 72 62.58N142.00W
North West C. Australia 62 21.48S114.10E
North West Chile Ridge Pacific Oc. 69 42.00S 90.00W
North Western d. Zambia 56 13.00S 25.00E
North Western Atlantic Basin f. Atlantic Oc. 95 33.00N 55.00W
Northwest Frontier d. Pakistan 40 33.45N 71.00E
North West Highlands U.K. 12 57.30N 5.15W
North West Pt. Kiribati 69 2.02N157.29W
North West River town Canada 77 53.32N 60.09W
Northwest Territories d. Canada 73 66.00N 95.00W
Northwich U.K. 10 53.16N 2.30W
Northwood Iowa U.S.A. 82 43.27N 93.13W
Northwood N. Dak. U.S.A. 82 47.44N 97.34W
North York Moors hills U.K. 10 54.21N 0.50W
North Yorkshire d. U.K. 10 54.14N 1.14W
Norton U.S.A. 82 39.50N 99.53W
Norton Sound b. U.S.A. 72 63.50N164.00W
Nort-sur-Erdre France 15 47.26N 1.30W
Norwalk Conn. U.S.A. 85 41.07N 73.25W
Norwalk Ohio U.S.A. 84 41.14N 82.37W
Norway Europe 22 65.00N 13.00E
Norway House town Canada 75 53.59N 97.50W
Norwegian Dependency Antarctica 96 77.00S 10.00E
Norwegian Sea Europe 96 65.00N 5.00E
Norwich U.K. 11 52.38N 1.17E
Norwood U.S.A. 84 39.12N 84.21W
Noshul Russian Fed. 24 60.04N 49.30E
Nosovka Ukraine 21 50.55N 31.37E
Noşratābād Iran 43 29.54N 59.58E
Noss Head U.K. 12 58.28N 3.03W
Nosy Be i. Madagascar 57 13.20S 48.15E
Nosy Boraha i. Madagascar 57 16.50S 49.55E
Nosy Varika Madagascar 57 20.35S 48.32E
Noteć r. Poland 20 52.44N 15.26E
Nothern Marianas is. Pacific Oc. 68 15.00N145.00E
Noto Italy 18 36.53N 15.05E
Notodden Norway 23 59.34N 9.17E
Notre Dame, Monts mts. Canada 77 48.00N 69.00W
Notre Dame B. Canada 77 49.45N 55.15W
Notre Dame de la Salette Canada 77 45.46N 75.35W
Nottawasaga B. Canada 76 44.40N 80.30W
Nottaway r. Canada 76 51.25N 78.50W
Nottingham U.K. 10 52.57N 1.10W
Nottinghamshire d. U.K. 10 53.10N 1.00W
Notwani r. Botswana 56 23.46S 26.57E
Nouadhibou Mauritania 50 20.54N 17.01W
Nouakchott Mauritania 50 18.09N 15.58W
Nouméa N. Cal. 68 22.16S166.27E
Nouna Burkina 52 12.44N 3.54W
Noupoort R.S.A. 56 31.11S 24.56E
Nouvelle Anvers Zaïre 54 1.38N 19.10E
Nouvelle Calédonie is. Pacific Oc. 68 21.30S165.30E
Nouzonville France 15 49.49N 4.45E
Nova Caipemba Angola 54 7.25S 14.36E
Novafeltria Bagnodi Romagna Italy 15 43.53N 12.17E
Nova Friburgo Brazil 94 22.16S 42.32W
Nova Iguaçu Brazil 94 22.45S 43.27W
Nova Lamego Guinea Bissau 52 12.19N 14.11W
Nova Lima Brazil 94 19.59S 43.51W
Novara Italy 15 45.27N 8.37E
Nova Scotia d. Canada 77 45.00N 63.30W
Nova Sofala Mozambique 57 20.09S 34.24E
Novato U.S.A. 80 38.06N122.34W
Novaya Ladoga Russian Fed. 24 60.09N 32.15E
Novaya Lyalya Russian Fed. 28 59.02N 60.38E
Novaya Sibir, Ostrov i. Russian Fed. 29 75.20N148.00E
Novaya Ushitsa Ukraine 21 48.50N 27.12E
Novaya Zemlya i. Russian Fed. 28 74.00N 56.00E
Novelda Spain 16 38.24N 0.45W
Nové Zámky Slovakia 21 47.59N 18.11E
Novgorod Russian Fed. 24 58.30N 31.20E
Novgorod Severskiy Russian Fed. 24 52.00N 33.15E
Novi di Modena Italy 15 44.54N 10.54E
Novigrad Croatia 20 45.19N 13.34E
Novi Ligure Italy 15 44.46N 8.47E
Novi Pazar Yugo. 19 43.08N 20.28E
Novi Sad Yugo. 21 45.16N 19.52E
Novoalekseyevka Ukraine 25 46.14N 34.36E
Novoanninskiy Russian Fed. 25 50.32N 42.42E
Novo Arkhangel'sk Ukraine 21 48.34N 30.50E
Novocherkassk Russian Fed. 25 47.25N 40.05E
Novofedorovka Ukraine 25 47.04N 35.18E
Novograd Volynskiy Ukraine 21 50.34N 27.32E
Novogrudok Belorussia 21 53.35N 25.50E
Novo Hamburgo Brazil 94 29.37S 51.07W
Novokazalinsk Kazakhstan 28 45.48N 62.06E
Novokuznetsk Russian Fed. 28 53.45N 87.12E
Novomoskovsk Russian Fed. 24 54.06N 38.15E
Novomoskovsk Ukraine 25 48.38N 35.15E
Novorossiysk Russian Fed. 25 44.44N 37.46E
Novoshakhtinsk Russian Fed. 25 47.46N 39.55E
Novosibirsk Russian Fed. 28 55.04N 82.55E
Novosibirskiye Ostrova is. Russian Fed. 29 76.00N144.00E
Novouzensk Russian Fed. 25 50.29N 48.08E
Novo-Vyatsk Russian Fed. 24 58.30N 49.40E
Novozybkov Russian Fed. 21 52.31N 31.58E
Novska Croatia 20 45.21N 16.59E
Nový Jičín Czech Republic 21 49.36N 18.00E
Novyy Bykhov Belorussia 21 53.20N 30.21E
Novyy Port Russian Fed. 28 67.38N 72.33E
Nowa Ruda Poland 20 50.34N 16.30E
Nowa Sól Poland 20 51.49N 15.41E
Nowendoc Australia 67 31.35S151.45E
Nowgong Assam India 41 26.21N 92.40E
Nowgong Madhya P. India 41 25.04N 79.27E
Nowingi Australia 66 34.36S142.15E
Nowra Australia 67 34.54S150.36E
Nowrangapur India 41 19.14N 82.33E
Nowshera Pakistan 40 34.01N 71.59E
Nowy Dwór Mazowiecki Poland 21 52.26N 20.43E
Nowy Korczyn Poland 21 50.19N 20.48E
Nowy Sacz Poland 21 49.39N 20.40E
Nowy Targ Poland 21 49.29N 20.02E
Nowy Tomśyl Poland 20 52.20N 16.07E
Now Zād Afghan. 40 32.24N 64.28E
Noxon U.S.A. 80 48.01N115.47W
Noyant France 15 47.31N 0.08E
Noyes I. U.S.A. 74 55.30N133.40W
Noyon France 15 49.35N 3.00E
Nozay France 15 47.34N 1.38W
Nsanje Malaŵi 55 16.55S 35.12E
Nsawam Ghana 52 5.49N 0.20W
Nsok Equat. Guinea 54 1.10N 11.19E
Nsombo Zambia 55 10.50S 29.56E
Nsukka Nigeria 53 6.51N 7.29E
Nuatja Togo 53 6.59N 1.11E
Nubian Desert Sudan 48 20.30N 34.00E
Nueces r. U.S.A. 83 27.50N 97.30W
Nueces Plains f. U.S.A. 83 28.30N 99.15W
Nueltin L. Canada 75 60.30N 99.30W
Nueva Casas Grandes Mexico 81 30.25N107.55W
Nueva Gerona Cuba 87 21.53N 82.49W
Nueva Helvecia Uruguay 93 34.19S 57.13W
Nueva Palmira Uruguay 93 33.53S 58.25W
Nueva Rosita Mexico 83 27.57N101.13W
Nueve de Julio Argentina 93 35.30S 60.50W
Nuevitas Cuba 87 21.34N 77.18W
Nuevo d. Mexico 83 26.00N100.00W
Nuevo, Golfo g. Argentina 93 42.42S 64.35W
Nuevo Berlín Uruguay 93 32.59S 58.03W
Nuevo Laredo Mexico 83 27.30N 99.31W
Nuevo León d. Mexico 86 26.00N 99.00W
Nuevo Rocafuerte Ecuador 90 0.56S 75.24W
Nūh, Rās c. Pakistan 40 25.05N 62.24E
Nui i. Tuvalu 68 7.12S177.10E
Nu Jiang r. China see Salween r. Burma 39
Nukha Azerbaijan 43 41.12N 47.10E
Nukhaylah Sudan 48 19.03N 26.19E
Nuku'alofa Tonga 69 21.07S175.12W
Nuku Hiva i. Îs. Marquises 69 8.56S140.00W
Nukunonu Pacific Oc. 68 9.10S171.55W
Nulato U.S.A. 72 64.43N158.06W
Nullagine Australia 62 21.56S120.06E
Nullarbor Australia 63 31.26S130.55E
Nullarbor Plain f. Australia 63 31.30S128.00E
Numalla, L. Australia 66 28.45S144.21E
Numan Nigeria 53 9.30N 12.01E
Numazu Japan 35 35.06N138.52E
Numedal f. Norway 23 60.06N 9.06E
Numurkah Australia 67 36.05S145.26E
Nundle Australia 67 31.28S151.08E
Nuneaton U.K. 11 52.32N 1.29W
Nungo Mozambique 57 13.25S 37.45E
Nunivak I. U.S.A. 72 60.00N166.30W
Nunkun mtn. Jammu & Kashmir 40 33.59N 76.01E
Nuoro Italy 18 40.19N 9.20E
Nuqūb Yemen 45 14.59N 45.48E
Nürburg Germany 14 50.20N 6.59E
Nure r. Italy 15 45.03N 9.49E
Nuriootpa Australia 66 34.27S139.02E
Nürnberg Germany 20 49.27N 11.05E
Nurri, Mt. Australia 67 31.44S146.04E
Nusa Tenggara is. Indonesia 36 8.30S118.00E
Nusa Tenggara Barat d. Indonesia 36 8.50S117.30E
Nusa Tenggara Timur d. Indonesia 37 9.30S122.00E
Nusaybin Turkey 42 37.05N 41.11E
Nushki Pakistan 40 29.33N 66.01E
Nutak Canada 77 57.39N 61.50W
Nuuk see Godthåb Greenland 73
Nuwākot Nepal 41 28.08N 83.53E
Nuwaybi'al Muzayyinah Egypt 44 28.58N 34.38E
Nuweveldberge mts. R.S.A. 56 32.15S 21.50E
Nuyts, Pt. Australia 63 35.02S116.32E
Nuyts Archipelago is. Australia 65 32.35S133.17E
Nxaunxau Botswana 56 18.19S 21.04E
Nyaake Liberia 52 4.52N 7.37W
Nyabing Australia 63 33.32S118.09E
Nyahua Tanzania 55 5.25S 33.16E
Nyahururu Falls town Kenya 55 0.04N 36.22E
Nyah West Australia 66 35.11S143.21E
Nyainqêntanglha Feng mtn. China 41 30.27N 90.33E
Nyainqêntanglha Shan mts. China 41 30.00N 90.00E
Nyainrong China 41 32.02N 92.15E
Nyakanazi Tanzania 55 3.05S 31.16E
Nyaksimvol Russian Fed. 24 62.30N 60.52E
Nyala Sudan 49 12.03N 24.53E
Nyalam China 41 28.12N 85.58E
Nyamandhlovu Zimbabwe 56 19.50S 28.15E
Nyamapanda Zimbabwe 57 16.59S 32.50E
Nyamlell Sudan 49 9.07N 26.58E
Nyamtukusa Tanzania 55 3.03S 32.44E
Nyandoma Russian Fed. 24 61.33N 40.05E
Nyanga r. Gabon 54 3.00S 10.17E
Nyang Qu r. China 41 29.19N 88.52E
Nyanza d. Kenya 55 0.30S 34.30E
Nyanza Rwanda 55 2.20S 29.42E
Nyashabozh Russian Fed. 24 65.28N 53.42E
Nyaunglebin Burma 34 17.57N 96.44E
Nyaungu Burma 34 21.12N 94.55E
Nyborg Denmark 23 55.19N 10.48E
Nybro Sweden 23 56.45N 15.54E
Nyda Russian Fed. 28 66.35N 72.58E
Nyêmo China 41 29.25N 90.15E
Nyeri Kenya 55 0.22S 36.56E
Nyerol Sudan 49 8.41N 32.02E
Nyhammar Sweden 23 60.17N 14.58E
Nyika Plateau f. Malaŵi 55 10.25S 33.50E
Nyima China 41 31.50N 87.48E
Nyimba Zambia 55 14.33S 30.49E
Nyíregyháza Hungary 21 47.59N 21.43E
Nyköbing Falster Denmark 23 54.46N 11.53E
Nyköbing Jylland Denmark 23 56.48N 8.52E
Nyköbing Sjaelland Denmark 23 55.55N 11.41E
Nyköping Sweden 23 58.45N 17.00E
Nylstroom R.S.A. 56 24.42S 28.24E
Nymagee Australia 67 32.05S146.20E
Nymboida Australia 67 29.57S152.32E
Nymboida r. Australia 67 29.39S152.30E
Nymburk Czech Republic 20 50.11N 15.03E
Nynäshamn Sweden 23 58.54N 17.57E
Nyngan Australia 67 31.34S147.14E
Nyngynderry Australia 66 32.16S143.22E
Nyoma Jammu & Kashmir 41 33.11N 78.38E
Nyong r. Cameroon 53 3.15N 9.55E
Nyons France 17 44.22N 5.08E
Nysa Poland 21 50.29N 17.20E
Nysa Kłodzka r. Poland 21 50.49N 17.50E
Nyssa U.S.A. 80 43.53N117.00W
Nyuksenitsa Russian Fed. 24 60.24N 44.08E
Nyunzu Zaïre 55 5.55S 28.00E
Nyurba Russian Fed. 29 63.18N118.28E
Nyuri India 41 27.42N 92.13E
Nzega Tanzania 55 4.13S 33.09E
N'zérékoré Guinea 52 7.49N 8.48W
N'zeto Angola 54 7.13S 12.56E
Nzwani see Anjouan i. Comoros 55

O

Oahe Resr. U.S.A. 82 45.30N100.25W
Oahu i. Hawaiian Is. 69 21.30N158.00W
Oakbank Australia 66 33.07S140.33E
Oakdale U.S.A. 83 30.49N 92.40W
Oakesdale U.S.A. 80 47.08N117.15W
Oakey Australia 65 27.26S151.43E
Oak Harbour U.S.A. 80 48.18N122.39W
Oak Hill town U.S.A. 85 28.52N 80.52W
Oakland Calif. U.S.A. 80 37.47N122.13W
Oakland Oreg. U.S.A. 80 43.25N123.18W
Oaklands Australia 67 35.25S146.15E
Oakley U.S.A. 80 42.15N113.53W
Oakover r. Australia 62 20.49S120.40E
Oakridge U.S.A. 80 43.45N122.28W
Oak Ridge town U.S.A. 85 36.02N 84.12W
Oakvale Australia 66 33.01S140.41E
Oakville Canada 76 43.27N 79.41W
Oamaru New Zealand 60 45.07S170.58E
Oates Land f. Antarctica 96 70.00S155.00E
Oaxaca Mexico 86 17.05N 96.41W
Oaxaca d. Mexico 86 17.30N 97.00W
Ob r. Russian Fed. 24 66.50N 69.00E
Oba Canada 76 49.04N 84.07W
Oba i. Vanuatu 68 15.25S167.50E
Oban U.K. 12 56.26N 5.28W
Oberá Argentina 92 27.30S 55.07W
Oberhausen Germany 14 51.28N 6.51E
Oberlin U.S.A. 82 39.49N100.32W
Oberon Australia 67 33.41S149.52E
Oberösterreich d. Austria 20 48.15N 14.00E
Obi i. Indonesia 37 1.45S127.30E
Obidos Brazil 91 1.55S 55.31W
Obitsu r. Japan 35 35.24N139.54E
Obo C.A.R. 49 5.24N 26.30E
Obock Djibouti 49 11.59N 43.16E
Obodovka Ukraine 21 48.28N 29.10E
Oboyan Russian Fed. 25 51.13N 36.17E
Obozerskiy Russian Fed. 24 63.28N 40.29E
Obregón, Presa resr. Mexico 81 28.00N109.50W
Obruk Platosu f. Turkey 42 38.00N 33.30E
Obskaya Guba g. Russian Fed. 28 68.30N 74.00E
Ōbu Japan 35 35.00N136.58E
Obuasi Ghana 52 6.15N 1.36W
Obudu Nigeria 53 6.42N 9.07E
Ocala U.S.A. 85 29.11N 82.09W
Ocaña Colombia 90 8.16N 73.21W
Ocaña Spain 16 39.57N 3.30W
Occidental, Cordillera mts. Colombia 90 5.00N 76.15W
Occidental, Cordillera mts. S. America 92 17.00S 69.00W
Ocean City Md. U.S.A. 85 38.20N 75.05W
Ocean City N.J. U.S.A. 85 39.16N 74.36W
Ocean Falls town Canada 74 52.25N127.40W
Ocean I. see Banaba i. Kiribati 68
Oceanside Calif. U.S.A. 81 33.12N117.23W
Oceanside N.Y. U.S.A. 85 40.38N 73.38W
Ochamchire Georgia 25 42.44N 41.30E
Ochil Hills U.K. 12 56.16N 3.25W
Ochsenfurt Germany 20 49.40N 10.03E
Ockelbo Sweden 23 60.53N 16.43E
Ocmulgee r. U.S.A. 85 31.58N 82.32W
Oconee r. U.S.A. 85 31.58N 82.32W
Oconto U.S.A. 82 44.55N 87.52W
Ocotal Nicaragua 87 13.37N 86.31W
Ocotlán Mexico 86 20.21N102.42W
Octeville France 15 49.37N 1.39W
Ocua Mozambique 57 13.40S 39.46E
Oda Ghana 52 5.55N 0.56W
Oda, Jabal mtn. Sudan 48 20.21N 36.39E
Odádhahraun mts. Iceland 22 65.00N 17.30W
Odawara Japan 35 35.15N139.10E
Odda Norway 23 60.04N 6.33E
Ödeborg Sweden 23 58.33N 12.00E
Odemira Portugal 16 37.36N 8.38W
Ödemiş Turkey 19 38.12N 28.00E
Odense Denmark 23 55.24N 10.23E
Oder r. E. Germany see Odra r. Poland 20
Oderr. Germanysee Odra mts. Germany 20 49.40N 9.20E
Oderzo Italy 15 45.47N 12.29E
Odessa Ukraine 21 46.30N 30.46E
Odessa U.S.A. 83 31.51N102.22W
Odienné Ivory Coast 52 9.36N 7.32W
Odorhei Romania 21 46.18N 25.18E
Odra r. Poland 20 53.30N 14.36E
Odžak Bosnia-Herzegovina 21 45.03N 18.18E
Odzi r. Zimbabwe 57 19.46S 32.22E
Oegstgeest Neth. 14 52.12N 4.31E
Oeiras Brazil 91 7.00S 42.07W
Oelrichs U.S.A. 82 43.10N103.13W
Oelwein U.S.A. 82 42.41N 91.55W
Oeno I. Pacific Oc. 69 23.55S130.45W
Ofanto r. Italy 18 41.22N 16.12E
Ofaqim Israel 44 31.19N 34.37E
Offa Nigeria 53 8.09N 4.44E
Offaly d. Rep. of Ire. 13 53.15N 7.30W
Offenbach Germany 20 50.06N 8.46E
Offenburg Germany 20 48.29N 7.57E
Offerdal Sweden 22 63.28N 14.03E
Offranville France 15 49.52N 1.03E
Ofir Portugal 16 41.31N 8.47W
Ofotfjorden est. Norway 22 68.25N 17.00E
Ofu i. Samoa 68 14.11S169.40W
Ogadēn f. Ethiopia 45 7.50N 45.40E
Ōgaki Japan 35 35.21N136.37E
Ogallala U.S.A. 82 41.08N101.43W
Ogbomosho Nigeria 53 8.05N 4.11E
Ogden Iowa U.S.A. 82 42.02N 94.02W
Ogden Utah U.S.A. 80 41.14N111.58W
Ogeechee r. U.S.A. 85 31.51N 81.06W
Ogilvie Mts. Canada 72 65.00N139.30W
Oginskiy, Kanal canal Belorussia 21 52.25N 25.55E
Oglio r. Italy 15 45.02N 10.39E
Ognon r. France 17 47.20N 5.37E
Ogoja Nigeria 53 6.40N 8.45E
Ogoki Canada 76 51.35N 86.00W
Ogoki r. Canada 76 51.35N 86.00W
Ogoki Resr. Canada 76 51.00N 88.15W
Ogooué r. Gabon 54 1.00S 9.05E
Ogosta r. Bulgaria 19 43.44N 23.51E
Ogr Sudan 49 12.02N 27.06E
Ogulin Croatia 20 45.17N 15.14E
Ogun d. Nigeria 53 6.50N 3.20E
Ohai New Zealand 60 45.56S167.57E
Ohanet Algeria 51 28.40N 8.50E
Ohey Belgium 14 50.26N 5.06E
O'Higgins, Cabo c. I. de Pascua 69 27.05S109.15W
O'Higgins, L. Chile 93 48.03S 73.10W
Ohio d. U.S.A. 84 40.15N 82.45W
Ohio r. U.S.A. 84 36.59N 89.08W
Ōhito Japan 35 34.59N138.56E
Ohře r. Czech Republic 20 50.32N 14.08E
Ohrid Macedonia 19 41.06N 20.48E
Ohrid, L. Albania/Macedonia 19 41.00N 20.43E
Ōi r. Japan 35 34.45N138.18E
Oil City U.S.A. 84 41.26N 79.42W
Oise d. France 15 49.30N 2.30E
Oise r. France 15 49.00N 2.10E
Oisterwijk Neth. 14 51.34N 5.10E
Ojai U.S.A. 81 34.27N119.15W
Ojocaliente Mexico 86 22.35N102.18W
Ojo de Agua Argentina 92 29.30S 63.44W
Ojos del Salado mtn. Argentina/Chile 92 27.05S 68.05W
Oka Canada 77 45.29N 74.06W
Oka Nigeria 53 7.28N 5.48E
Oka r. Russian Fed. 24 56.09N 43.00E
Okaba Indonesia 37 8.06S139.46E
Okahandja Namibia 56 21.58S 16.44E
Okanagan L. Canada 74 50.00N119.30W
Okanogan U.S.A. 80 48.39N120.41W
Okanogan r. U.S.A. 80 48.22N119.35W
Okaputa Namibia 56 20.08S 16.58E
Okāra Pakistan 40 30.49N 73.27E
Okarito New Zealand 60 43.14S 170.07
Okaukuejo Namibia 56 19.12S 15.56E
Okavango r. Botswana 56 18.30S 22.04E
Okavango Basin f. Botswana 56 19.30S 22.30E
Okayama Japan 35 34.40N133.54E
Okeechobee U.S.A. 85 27.14N 80.50W
Okeechobee, L. U.S.A. 85 26.55N 80.45W
Okefenokee Swamp f. U.S.A. 85 30.42N 82.20W
Okehampton U.K. 11 50.44N 4.01W
Okere r. Uganda 55 1.37N 33.53E
Okha Russian Fed. 29 53.35N142.50E
Okhaldhunga Nepal 41 27.19N 86.31E
Okhansk Russian Fed. 24 57.42N 55.20E
Okhotsk Russian Fed. 29 59.20N143.15E
Okhotsk, Sea of Russian Fed. 29 55.00N150.00E
Okhotskiy Perevoz Russian Fed. 29 61.55N135.40E
Okiep R.S.A. 56 29.36S 17.49E
Oki guntō is. Japan 35 36.30N133.20E
Okinawa jima i. Japan 31 26.30N128.00E
Okipoko r. Namibia 56 18.40S 16.03E
Okitipupa Nigeria 53 6.31N 4.50E
Oklahoma d. U.S.A. 83 35.20N 98.00W
Oklahoma City U.S.A. 83 35.28N 97.32W
Okmulgee U.S.A. 83 35.37N 95.58W
Oknitsa Moldavia 21 48.22N 27.30E
Oko, Wādī Sudan 48 21.15N 35.56E

Okola to Pacy-sur-Eure

Okola Cameroon 53 4.03N 11.23E
Okolona U.S.A. 83 34.00N 88.45W
Okondja Gabon 54 0.03S 13.45E
Okoyo Congo 54 1.28S 15.00E
Oksskolten *mtn.* Norway 22 65.59N 14.15E
Oktyabr'sk Kazakhstan 25 49.30N 57.22E
Oktyabrskiy Belorussia 21 52.35N 28.45E
Oktyabrskiy Russian Fed. 24 54.30N 53.30E
Oktyabr'skoy Revolyutsii, Ostrov *i.* Russian Fed. 29 79.30N 96.00E
Okuru New Zealand 60 43.56S 168.55E
Okuta Nigeria 53 9.13N 3.12E
Ola U.S.A. 83 35.02N 93.13W
Ólafsvík Iceland 22 64.53N 23.44W
Olancha U.S.A. 81 36.17N 118.01W
Öland *i.* Sweden 23 56.45N 16.38E
Olary Australia 66 32.18S 140.19E
Olascoaga Argentina 93 35.14S 60.37W
Olavarría Argentina 93 36.57S 60.20W
Oława Poland 21 50.57N 17.17E
Olbia Italy 18 40.55N 9.29E
Old Bar Australia 67 31.59S 152.35E
Old Crow Canada 72 67.34N 139.43W
Oldenburg Nschn. Germany 14 53.08N 8.13E
Oldenburg Sch.-Hol. Germany 20 54.17N 10.52E
Oldenzaal Neth. 14 52.19N 6.55E
Old Forge U.S.A. 84 41.22N 75.44W
Old Fort *r.* Canada 75 58.30N 110.30W
Old Gumbiro Tanzania 55 10.00S 35.24E
Oldham U.K. 10 53.33N 2.08W
Old Head of Kinsale *c.* Rep. of Ire. 13 51.37N 8.33W
Oldman *r.* Canada 75 49.56N 111.42W
Old Moolawatana Australia 66 30.04S 140.02E
Olds Canada 74 51.50N 114.10W
Old Town U.S.A. 84 44.56N 68.39W
Olean U.S.A. 84 42.05N 78.26W
Olecko Poland 21 54.03N 22.30E
Olekma *r.* Russian Fed. 29 60.20N 120.30E
Olekminsk Russian Fed. 29 60.25N 120.00E
Olema Russian Fed. 24 64.25N 40.15E
Olenëk Russian Fed. 29 68.38N 112.15E
Olenëk *r.* Russian Fed. 29 73.00N 120.00E
Olenëkskiy Zaliv *g.* Russian Fed. 29 74.00N 120.00E
Oléron, Île d' *i.* France 17 45.55N 1.16W
Oleśnica Poland 21 51.13N 17.23E
Olevsk Ukraine 21 51.12N 27.35E
Olga Russian Fed. 31 43.46N 135.14E
Olga, Mt. Australia 64 25.18S 130.44E
Olga L. Canada 76 49.44N 77.18W
Ölgiy Mongolia 30 48.54N 90.00E
Olgopol Ukraine 21 48.10N 29.30E
Olhão Portugal 16 37.01N 7.50W
Olifants *r.* Namibia 56 25.28S 19.23E
Olifants *r.* C.P. R.S.A. 56 31.42S 18.10E
Olifants *r.* Trans. R.S.A. 56 24.08S 32.39E
Ólimbos *mtn.* Cyprus 44 34.55N 32.52E
Ólimbos Greece 19 35.44N 27.11E
Ólimbos *mtn.* Greece 19 40.04N 22.20E
Olinda Brazil 91 8.00S 34.51W
Oliva Argentina 92 32.05S 63.35W
Oliva Spain 16 38.58N 0.15W
Olivares Spain 16 39.45N 2.21W
Oliveira Brazil 94 20.39S 44.47W
Olivenza Spain 16 38.41N 7.09W
Olney U.K. 11 52.09N 0.42W
Olney U.S.A. 82 38.45N 88.05W
Olofström Sweden 23 56.16N 14.30E
Olomouc Czech Republic 21 49.36N 17.16E
Olonets Russian Fed. 24 61.00N 32.59E
Oloron France 17 43.12N 0.35W
Olosega *i.* Samoa 68 14.12S 169.38W
Olot Spain 16 42.11N 2.30E
Olovyannaya Russian Fed. 31 50.58N 115.35E
Olpe Germany 14 51.02N 7.52E
Olsztyn Poland 21 53.48N 20.29E
Olsztynek Poland 21 53.36N 20.17E
Olt *r.* Romania 21 43.43N 24.51E
Olteniţa Romania 21 44.05N 26.31E
Olteţ *r.* Romania 21 44.13N 24.28E
Olympia U.S.A. 80 47.03N 122.53W
Olympic Mts. U.S.A. 80 47.50N 123.45W
Olympic Nat. Park U.S.A. 80 47.48N 123.30W
Olympus *mtn. see* Ólimbos *mtn.* Greece 19
Olympus, Mt. U.S.A. 80 47.48N 123.43W
Oma China 41 32.30N 83.14E
Omae-zaki *c.* Japan 35 34.36N 138.14E
Omagh U.K. 13 54.36N 7.20W
Omaha U.S.A. 82 41.16N 95.57W
Oman Asia 38 22.30N 57.30E
Oman, G. of Asia 43 25.00N 58.00E
Omarama New Zealand 60 44.29S 169.58E
Omaruru Namibia 56 21.25S 15.57E
Omate Peru 92 16.40S 70.58W
Omboué Gabon 54 1.38S 9.20E
Ombrone *r.* Italy 18 42.40N 11.00E
Ombu China 41 31.20N 86.34E
Omdurman *see* Umm Durmān Sudan 48
Omegna Italy 15 45.53N 8.24E
Omeo Australia 67 37.05S 147.37E
Ometepec Mexico 86 16.41N 98.25W
Om Hājer Ethiopia 48 14.24N 36.46E
Ōmi-hachiman Japan 35 35.08N 136.06E
Omineca *r.* Canada 74 56.05N 124.30W
Omitara Namibia 56 22.18S 18.01E
Ōmiya Japan 35 35.54N 139.38E
Ommen Neth. 14 52.32N 6.25E
Ömnögovĭ *d.* Mongolia 32 43.00N 105.00E
Omo *r.* Ethiopia 49 4.51N 36.55E
Omolon *r.* Russian Fed. 29 68.50N 158.30E
Omsk Russian Fed. 28 55.00N 73.22E
Omulew *r.* Poland 21 53.05N 21.32E
Omuramba Omatako *r.* Namibia 56 18.19S 19.52E
Ōmuta Japan 35 33.02N 130.26E
Oña Spain 16 42.44N 3.25W
Onaga U.S.A. 82 39.29N 96.10W
Onai Angola 56 16.43S 17.33E
Onancock U.S.A. 85 37.43N 75.46W
Oncocua Angola 56 16.40S 13.25E
Onda Spain 16 39.58N 0.16W
Ondangua Namibia 56 17.59S 16.02E
Ondo *d.* Nigeria 53 7.10N 5.20E
Onega Russian Fed. 24 63.57N 38.11E
Onega *r.* Russian Fed. 24 63.59N 38.11E
Oneida U.S.A. 84 43.06N 75.39W
O'Neill U.S.A. 82 42.27N 98.39W
Onezhskaya Guba *b.* Russian Fed. 24 63.55N 37.30E
Onezhskoye Ozero *l.* Russian Fed. 24 62.00N 35.30E
Ongerup Australia 63 33.58S 118.29E
Ongiyn Gol *r.* Mongolia 32 43.40N 103.45E
Ongniud Qi China 32 43.00N 118.43E
Ongole India 39 15.31N 80.04E
Onilahy *r.* Madagascar 57 23.34S 43.45E
Onitsha Nigeria 53 6.10N 6.47E
Onslow Australia 62 21.41S 115.12E
Onslow B. U.S.A. 85 34.20N 77.20W
Onstwedde Neth. 14 53.04N 7.02E
Ontario *d.* Canada 76 51.00N 88.00W
Ontario Calif. U.S.A. 81 34.04N 117.39W
Ontario Oreg. U.S.A. 80 44.02N 116.58W
Ontario, L. Canada / U.S.A. 76 43.40N 78.00W
Ontonagon U.S.A. 84 46.52N 89.18W
Oodnadatta Australia 65 27.30S 135.27E
Ooldea Australia 65 30.27S 131.50E
Oostelijk-Flevoland *f.* Neth. 14 52.30N 5.40E
Oostende Belgium 14 51.13N 2.55E
Oosterhout Neth. 14 51.38N 4.50E
Oosterschelde *est.* Neth. 14 51.35N 3.57E
Oosthuizen Neth. 14 52.33N 5.00E
Oostmalle Belgium 14 51.18N 4.45E
Oost Vlaanderen *d.* Belgium 14 51.00N 3.45E
Oost Vlieland Neth. 14 53.18N 5.04E
Ootsa L. Canada 74 53.50N 126.20W
Opaka Bulgaria 19 43.28N 26.10E
Opal Mexico 83 24.18N 102.22W
Opala Russian Fed. 29 51.58N 156.30E
Opala Zaïre 54 0.42S 24.15E
Oparino Russian Fed. 24 59.53N 48.10E
Opasatika Canada 76 49.30N 82.50W
Opasatika *r.* Canada 76 50.24N 82.26W
Opasquia Canada 75 53.16N 93.34W
Opava Czech Republic 21 49.56N 17.54E
Opelousas U.S.A. 83 30.32N 92.05W
Opheim U.S.A. 80 48.51N 106.24W
Opinaca *r.* Canada 76 52.20N 78.00W
Opinnagau *r.* Canada 76 54.12N 82.21W
Opiscotéo, Lac *l.* Canada 77 53.10N 68.10W
Opochka Russian Fed. 24 56.41N 28.42E
Opole Poland 21 50.40N 17.56E
Oporto *see* Porto Portugal 16
Opotiki New Zealand 60 38.00S 177.18E
Opp U.S.A. 85 31.16N 86.18W
Oppdal Norway 22 62.36N 9.41E
Oppland *d.* Norway 23 61.30N 9.00E
Opportunity U.S.A. 80 47.39N 117.15W
Opunake New Zealand 60 39.27S 173.51E
Ora Italy 15 46.21N 11.18E
Ora Banda Australia 63 30.27S 121.04E
Oradea Romania 21 47.03N 21.55E
Öraefajökull *mtn.* Iceland 22 64.02N 16.39W
Orai India 41 25.59N 79.28E
Oran Algeria 50 35.42N 0.38W
Orán Argentina 92 23.07S 64.16W
Orange Australia 67 33.19S 149.10E
Orange France 17 44.08N 4.48E
Orange *r.* R.S.A. 56 28.38S 16.38E
Orange U.S.A. 83 30.01N 93.44W
Orange, C. Brazil 91 4.25N 51.32W
Orangeburg U.S.A. 85 33.28N 80.53W
Orange Free State *d.* R.S.A. 56 28.00S 28.00E
Orangevale U.S.A. 80 38.41N 121.13W
Orangeville Canada 76 43.55N 80.06W
Oranienburg Germany 20 52.45N 13.14E
Oranjefontein R.S.A. 56 23.27S 27.40E
Oranjemund Namibia 56 28.35S 16.26E
Orarak Sudan 49 6.15N 32.23E
Oras Phil. 37 12.09N 125.22E
Orbetello Italy 18 42.27N 11.13E
Orbost Australia 67 37.42S 148.30E
Örbyhus Sweden 23 60.14N 17.42E
Orchies France 14 50.28N 3.15E
Orchila *i.* Venezuela 87 11.52N 66.10W
Orco *r.* Italy 15 45.10N 7.52E
Ord *r.* Australia 62 15.30S 128.30E
Ordu Turkey 42 41.00N 37.52E
Orduña Spain 16 43.00N 3.00W
Örebro Sweden 23 59.17N 15.13E
Örebro *d.* Sweden 23 59.30N 15.00E
Oregon *d.* U.S.A. 80 43.49N 120.36W
Oregon City U.S.A. 80 45.21N 122.36W
Öregrund Sweden 23 60.20N 18.26E
Orekhovo-Zuyevo Russian Fed. 24 55.47N 39.00E
Orel Russian Fed. 24 52.58N 36.04E
Orem U.S.A. 80 40.19N 111.42W
Orenburg Russian Fed. 24 51.50N 55.00E
Orense Spain 16 42.20N 7.52W
Oressa *r.* Belorussia 21 52.33N 28.45E
Orestiás Greece 19 41.30N 26.33E
Orfanoú, Kólpos *g.* Greece 19 40.40N 24.00E
Orford U.S.A. 84 43.54N 72.10W
Orford, Mt. Canada 77 45.18N 72.08W
Orford Ness *c.* Australia 64 11.22S 142.50E
Orford Ness *c.* U.K. 11 52.05N 1.36E
Orgeyev Moldavia 21 47.24N 28.50E
Orgūn Afghan. 40 32.55N 69.10E
Orick U.S.A. 80 41.17N 124.04W
Oriental, Cordillera *mts.* Bolivia 92 17.00S 65.00W
Oriental, Cordillera *mts.* Colombia 90 5.00N 74.30W
Origny France 15 49.54N 3.30E
Orihuela Spain 16 38.05N 0.56W
Orillia Canada 76 44.37N 79.25W
Orimattila Finland 23 60.48N 25.45E
Orinduik Guyana 90 4.42N 60.01W
Orinoco *r.* Venezuela 90 9.00N 61.30W
Orinoco, Delta del *f.* Venezuela 90 9.00N 61.00W
Orissa *d.* India 41 20.20N 84.00E
Oristano Italy 18 39.53N 8.36E
Oristano, Golfo di *g.* Italy 18 39.50N 8.30E
Orizaba Mexico 86 18.51N 97.08W
Orkanger Norway 22 63.17N 9.52E
Orkney Is. *d.* U.K. 12 59.00N 3.00W
Orlândia Brazil 94 20.55S 47.54W
Orlando U.S.A. 85 28.33N 81.21W
Orléans Canada 77 45.28N 75.31W
Orléans France 15 47.54N 1.54E
Orléans, Canal d' France 15 47.54N 1.55E
Ormāra Pakistan 40 25.12N 64.38E
Ormāra, Rās *c.* Pakistan 40 25.09N 64.35E
Ormoc Phil. 37 11.00N 124.37E
Ormond New Zealand 60 38.35S 177.58E
Ormond Beach *town* U.S.A. 85 29.26N 81.03W
Ormskirk U.K. 10 53.35N 2.53W
Orne *d.* France 15 48.40N 0.05E
Orne *r.* France 15 49.17N 0.10W
Örnsköldsvik Sweden 22 63.17N 18.50E
Orobie, Alpi *mts.* Italy 15 46.03N 10.00E
Orocué Colombia 90 4.48N 71.20W
Orodara Burkina 52 11.00N 4.54W
Orogrande U.S.A. 81 32.23N 106.28W
Orohena *mtn.* Tahiti 69 17.37S 149.28W
Oromocto Canada 77 45.51N 66.29W
Oron Israel 44 30.55N 35.01E
Oron Nigeria 53 4.49N 8.15E
Orona *i.* Kiribati 68 4.29S 172.10W
Orono Canada 76 43.59N 78.37W
Orono U.S.A. 84 44.53N 68.40W
Orosei Italy 18 40.23N 9.40E
Orosei, Golfo di *g.* Italy 18 40.15N 9.45E
Orosháza Hungary 21 46.34N 20.40E
Orote Pen. Guam 68 13.26N 144.38E
Orotukan Russian Fed. 29 62.16N 151.43E
Oroville Calif. U.S.A. 80 39.31N 121.33W
Oroville Wash. U.S.A. 80 48.56N 119.26W
Orroroo Australia 66 32.46S 138.39E
Orsa Sweden 23 61.07N 14.37E
Orsha Russian Fed. 24 54.30N 30.23E
Orsières Switz. 15 46.02N 7.09E
Orsk Russian Fed. 24 51.13N 58.35E
Orşova Romania 21 44.42N 22.22E
Orta Nova Italy 18 41.19N 15.42E
Orthez France 17 43.29N 0.46W
Ortigueira Spain 16 43.41N 7.51W
Ortona Italy 18 42.21N 14.24E
Ortonville U.S.A. 82 45.18N 96.28W
Orūmīyeh Iran 43 37.32N 45.02E
Oruro Bolivia 92 17.59S 67.09W
Oruro *d.* Bolivia 92 18.00S 72.30W
Orūzgān Afghan. 40 32.56N 66.38E
Orūzgān *d.* Afghan. 40 33.40N 66.00E
Oryakhovo Bulgaria 19 43.42N 23.58E
Orzinuovi Italy 15 45.24N 9.55E
Os Norway 22 62.31N 11.11E
Osa, Península de *pen.* Costa Rica 87 8.20N 83.30W
Osage Iowa U.S.A. 82 43.17N 92.49W
Osage *r.* U.S.A. 79 38.35N 91.57W
Osage Wyo. U.S.A. 80 43.59N 104.25W
Ōsaka Japan 35 34.40N 135.30E
Ōsaka *d.* Japan 35 34.24N 135.25E
Ōsaka-wan *b.* Japan 35 34.30N 135.18E
Osborne U.S.A. 82 39.26N 98.42W
Osby Sweden 23 56.22N 13.59E
Osceola Iowa U.S.A. 82 41.02N 93.46W
Osceola Mo. U.S.A. 83 38.03N 93.42W
Osen Norway 22 64.18N 10.32E
Osh Kyrgyzstan 28 40.37N 72.49E
Oshawa Canada 76 43.53N 78.51W
Ō shima Japan 35 34.43N 139.24E
Oshkosh U.S.A. 82 41.24N 102.21W
Oshmyany Belorussia 21 54.22N 25.52E
Oshnovīyeh Iran 43 37.03N 45.05E
Oshogbo Nigeria 53 7.50N 4.35E
Oshtorān, Kūh *mtn.* Iran 43 33.18N 49.15E
Oshvor Russian Fed. 24 66.59N 62.59E
Oshwe Zaïre 54 3.27S 19.32E
Osiān India 40 26.43N 72.55E
Osijek Croatia 19 45.35N 18.43E
Osipovichi Belorussia 21 53.19N 28.36E
Oskaloosa U.S.A. 82 41.18N 92.39W
Oskarshamn Sweden 23 57.16N 16.26E
Oskol *r.* Ukraine 25 49.08N 37.10E
Oslo Norway 23 59.56N 10.45E
Oslofjorden *est.* Norway 23 59.20N 10.35E
Osmancik Turkey 42 40.58N 34.50E
Osmaniye Turkey 42 37.04N 36.15E
Osnabrück Germany 14 52.17N 8.03E
Osorno Chile 93 40.35S 73.14W
Osorno Spain 16 42.24N 4.22W
Osöyra Norway 23 60.11N 5.30E
Osprey Reef Australia 64 13.55S 146.38E
Oss Neth. 14 51.46N 5.31E
Ossa *mtn.* Greece 19 39.47N 22.41E
Ossa, Mt. Australia 65 41.52S 146.04E
Ossabaw I. U.S.A. 85 31.47N 81.06W
Osse *r.* Nigeria 53 5.55N 5.15E
Ossining U.S.A. 85 41.10N 73.52W
Ossokmanuan L. Canada 77 53.25N 65.00W
Ostashkov Russian Fed. 24 57.09N 33.10E
Ostend *see* Oostende Belgium 14
Oster Ukraine 21 50.55N 30.53E
Oster *r.* Ukraine 21 53.47N 31.46E
Österdal *r.* Sweden 23 61.03N 14.30E
Østerdalen *f.* Norway 23 61.15N 11.10E
Östergötland *d.* Sweden 23 58.25N 15.35E
Österö *i.* Faroe Is. 8 62.16N 6.54W
Osteröy *i.* Norway 23 60.33N 5.35E
Östersund Sweden 22 63.10N 14.40E
Østfold *d.* Norway 23 59.20N 11.10E
Ostfriesische Inseln *is.* Germany 14 53.45N 7.00E
Östhammar Sweden 23 60.16N 18.22E
Ostrava Czech Republic 21 49.50N 18.15E
Ostróda Poland 21 53.43N 19.59E
Ostrog Ukraine 21 50.20N 26.29E
Ostrołeka Poland 21 53.06N 21.34E
Ostrov Russian Fed. 24 57.22N 28.22E
Ostrowiec-Świetokrzyski Poland 21 50.57N 21.23E
Ostrów Mazowiecka Poland 21 52.50N 21.51E
Ostrów Wielkopolski Poland 21 51.39N 17.49E
Ostuni Italy 19 40.44N 17.35E
Osŭm *r.* Bulgaria 19 43.41N 24.51E
Ōsumi shotō *is.* Japan 31 30.30N 131.00E
Osun *d.* Nigeria 53 7.15N 4.30E
Osuna Spain 16 37.14N 5.06W
Oswego U.S.A. 84 43.27N 76.31W
Oswestry U.K. 10 52.52N 3.03W
Otago *d.* New Zealand 60 45.10S 169.20E
Otago Pen. New Zealand 60 45.48S 170.45E
Otaki New Zealand 60 40.45S 175.08E
Otaru Japan 35 43.14N 140.59E
Otavalo Ecuador 90 0.14N 78.16W
Otavi Namibia 56 19.37S 17.21E
Otelec Romania 21 45.36N 20.50E
Otematata New Zealand 60 44.37S 170.11E
Oti *r.* Ghana 52 8.43N 0.10E
Otira New Zealand 60 42.51S 171.33E
Otish, Monts *mts.* Canada 77 52.22N 70.30W
Otisville U.S.A. 85 41.28N 74.32W
Otiwarongo Namibia 56 20.30S 16.39E
Otjiwero Namibia 56 17.59S 13.22E
Otju Namibia 56 18.15S 13.18E
Otočac Croatia 20 44.52N 15.14E
Otog Qi China 32 39.05N 107.59E
Otosquen Canada 75 53.17N 102.01W
Otra *r.* Norway 23 58.09N 8.00E
Otradnyy Russian Fed. 24 53.26N 51.30E
Otranto Italy 19 40.09N 18.30E
Otranto, Str. of Med. Sea 19 40.10N 19.00E
Otrokovice Czech Republic 21 49.13N 17.31E
Otsego U.S.A. 84 42.26N 85.42W
Otsego Lake *town* U.S.A. 84 44.55N 84.41W
Ōtsu Japan 35 35.02N 135.52E
Ōtsuki Japan 35 35.36N 138.57E
Otta Norway 23 61.46N 9.32E
Ottawa Canada 77 45.25N 75.43W
Ottawa *r.* Canada 76 45.23N 73.55W
Ottawa Ill. U.S.A. 82 41.21N 88.51W
Ottawa Kans. U.S.A. 82 38.37N 95.16W
Ottawa Is. Canada 73 59.50N 80.00W
Otter *r.* U.K. 11 50.38N 3.19W
Otterbäcken Sweden 23 58.57N 14.02E
Otterburn U.K. 10 55.14N 2.10W
Otter L. Canada 75 55.35N 104.39W
Otterndorf Germany 20 53.48N 8.53E
Otteröy *i.* Norway 22 62.45N 6.50E
Ottosdal R.S.A. 56 26.48S 26.00E
Ottumwa U.S.A. 82 41.01N 92.25W
Oturkpo Nigeria 53 7.13N 8.10E
Otway, C. Australia 66 38.51S 143.34E
Ou *r.* Laos 34 20.03N 102.19E
Ouachita *r.* U.S.A. 83 31.38N 91.49W
Ouachita, L. U.S.A. 83 34.40N 93.25W
Ouachita Mts. U.S.A. 83 34.40N 94.25W
Ouada, Djebel *mtn.* C.A.R. 49 8.56N 23.26E
Ouadane Mauritania 50 20.56N 11.37W
Ouadda C.A.R. 49 8.04N 22.24E
Ouaddaï *d.* Chad 49 13.00N 21.00E
Ouagadougou Burkina 52 12.20N 1.40W
Ouahigouya Burkina 52 13.31N 2.21W
Ouaka *d.* C.A.R. 49 6.00N 21.00E
Oualâta Mauritania 50 17.18N 7.02W
Ouallam Niger 53 14.23N 2.09E
Ouallene Algeria 50 24.35N 1.17E
Ouanda Djallé C.A.R. 49 8.54N 22.48E
Ouarane *f.* Mauritania 50 21.00N 9.30W
Ouararda, Passe de *pass* Mauritania 50 21.01N 13.03W
Ouareau *r.* Canada 77 45.56N 73.25W
Ouargla Algeria 51 31.57N 5.20E
Ouarra *r.* C.A.R. 49 5.05N 24.26E
Ouarzazate Morocco 50 30.57N 6.50W
Ouassouas *well* Mali 50 16.01N 1.26E
Ouddorp Neth. 14 51.49N 3.57E
Oudenaarde Belgium 14 50.50N 3.37E
Oudenbosch Neth. 14 51.35N 4.30E
Oude Rijn *r.* Neth. 14 52.14N 4.26E
Oudon *r.* France 15 47.47N 1.02W
Oudtshoorn R.S.A. 56 33.35S 22.11E
Oued-Zem Morocco 50 32.55N 6.30W
Ouellé Ivory Coast 52 7.26N 4.01W
Ouenza Algeria 51 35.57N 8.07E
Ouessant, Île d' *i.* France 17 48.28N 5.05W
Ouesso Congo 54 1.38N 16.03E
Ouezzane Morocco 50 34.52N 5.35W
Oughter, Lough Rep. of Ire. 13 54.01N 7.28W
Ouham *r.* Chad 53 9.15N 18.13E
Ouimet Canada 76 48.43N 88.35W
Ouistreham France 15 49.17N 0.15W
Oujda Morocco 50 34.41N 1.45W
Oulu Finland 22 65.01N 25.28E
Oulu *d.* Finland 22 65.00N 27.00E
Oulu *r.* Finland 22 65.01N 25.25E
Oulujärvi *l.* Finland 22 64.20N 27.15E
Oum Chalouba Chad 51 15.48N 20.46E
Oumé Ivory Coast 52 6.25N 5.23W
Oum er Rbia, Oued *r.* Morocco 50 33.19N 8.21W
Oumm ed Droûs Guebli, Sebkhet *f.* Mauritania 50 24.03N 11.45W
Oumm ed Droûs Telli, Sebkhet *f.* Mauritania 50 24.20N 11.30W
Ounas *r.* Finland 22 66.30N 25.45E
Oundle U.K. 11 52.28N 0.28W
Ounianga Kébir Chad 51 19.04N 20.29E
Our *r.* Lux. 14 49.53N 6.16E
Ouray U.S.A. 80 40.06N 109.40W
Ourcq *r.* France 15 49.01N 3.01E
Ourense *see* Orense Spain 16
Ouri Chad 51 21.34N 19.13E
Ourinhos Brazil 94 23.00S 49.54W
Ouro Fino Brazil 94 22.16S 46.25W
Ouro Prêto Brazil 94 20.54S 43.30W
Ourthe *r.* Belgium 14 50.38N 5.36E
Ouse *r.* U.K. 10 53.41N 0.42W
Outardes, Rivière aux *r.* Canada 77 49.04N 68.25W
Outer Hebrides *is.* U.K. 12 57.40N 7.35W
Outjo Namibia 56 20.07S 16.10E
Outlook U.S.A. 80 48.53N 104.47W
Ouyen Australia 66 35.06S 142.22E
Ouzouer-le-Marché France 15 47.55N 1.32E
Ouzzal, Oued I-n- *wadi* Algeria 51 20.54N 2.28E
Ovalle Chile 92 30.36S 71.12W
Ovamboland *f.* Namibia 56 17.45S 16.00E
Ovar Portugal 16 40.52N 8.38W
Ovens *r.* Australia 67 36.20S 146.18E
Overath Germany 14 50.56N 7.18E
Overflakkee *i.* Neth. 14 51.45N 4.08E
Overijssel *d.* Neth. 14 52.25N 6.30E
Överkalix Sweden 22 66.21N 22.56E
Overland Park *town* U.S.A. 82 38.59N 94.40W
Overton U.S.A. 81 36.33N 114.27W
Övertorneå Sweden 22 66.23N 23.40E
Ovidiopol Ukraine 21 46.18N 30.28E
Oviedo Spain 16 43.21N 5.50W
Ovinishche Russian Fed. 24 58.20N 37.00E
Övörhangay *d.* Mongolia 32 45.00N 103.00E
Ovruch Ukraine 21 51.20N 28.50E
Owaka New Zealand 60 46.27S 169.40E
Owando Congo 54 0.30S 15.48E
Owatonna U.S.A. 82 44.06N 93.10W
Owbeh Afghan. 40 34.22N 63.10E
Owel, Lough Rep. of Ire. 13 53.34N 7.24W
Owen Falls Dam Uganda 55 0.30N 33.07E
Owensboro U.S.A. 85 37.46N 87.07W
Owens L. U.S.A. 81 36.25N 117.56W
Owen Sound *town* Canada 76 44.34N 80.56W
Owen Stanley Range *mts.* P.N.G. 64 9.30S 148.00E
Owerri Nigeria 53 5.29N 7.02E
Owl *r.* Canada 75 57.51N 92.44W
Owo Nigeria 53 7.10N 5.39E
Owosso U.S.A. 84 43.00N 84.11W
Owyhee *r.* U.S.A. 80 43.46N 117.02W
Oxelösund Sweden 23 58.40N 17.06E
Oxford U.K. 11 51.45N 1.15W
Oxford Md. U.S.A. 85 38.42N 76.10W
Oxford Penn. U.S.A. 85 39.47N 75.59W
Oxfordshire *d.* U.K. 11 51.46N 1.10W
Oxley Australia 66 34.11S 144.10E
Oxnard U.S.A. 81 34.12N 119.11W
Oyapock *r.* Guiana 91 4.10N 51.40W
Oyem Gabon 54 1.34N 11.31E
Oyen Canada 75 51.22N 110.28W
Öyer Norway 23 61.12N 10.22E
Öyeren *l.* Norway 23 59.48N 11.14E
Oykel *r.* U.K. 12 57.53N 4.21W
Oymyakon Russian Fed. 29 63.30N 142.44E
Oyo Nigeria 53 7.50N 3.55E
Oyo *d.* Nigeria 53 8.10N 3.40E
Oyonnax France 17 46.15N 5.40E
Ozamiz Phil. 37 8.09N 123.59E
Ozarichi Belorussia 21 52.28N 29.12E
Ozark Ala. U.S.A. 85 31.27N 85.40W
Ozark Ark. U.S.A. 83 35.29N 93.50W
Ozark Mo. U.S.A. 83 37.01N 93.12W
Ozark Plateau U.S.A. 83 37.00N 93.00W
Ózd Hungary 21 48.14N 20.18E
Ozernoye Russian Fed. 24 51.45N 51.29E
Ozersk Russian Fed. 21 54.26N 22.00E
Ozinki Russian Fed. 25 51.11N 49.43E
Ozona U.S.A. 83 30.43N 101.12W

P

Paamiut *see* Frederikshåb Greenland 73
Pa-an Burma 34 16.51N 97.37E
Paarl R.S.A. 56 33.44S 18.58E
Pabianice Poland 21 51.40N 19.22E
Pābna Bangla. 41 24.00N 89.15E
Pacaraima, Sierra *mts.* Venezuela 90 4.00N 62.30W
Pacasmayo Peru 90 7.27S 79.33W
Pachmarhi India 41 22.28N 78.26E
Pāchora India 40 20.40N 75.21E
Pachuca Mexico 86 20.10N 98.44W
Pacific-Antarctic Basin Pacific Oc. 69 58.00S 98.00W
Pacific-Antarctic Ridge Pacific Oc. 69 57.00S 145.00W
Pacific Ocean 69
Pacitan Indonesia 37 8.12S 111.05E
Packsaddle Australia 66 30.28S 141.28E
Packwood U.S.A. 80 46.36N 121.40W
Pacy-sur-Eure France 15 49.01N 1.23E

Padam to **Perabumulih**

Padam Jammu & Kashmir **40** 33.28N 76.53E
Padampur India **41** 20.59N 83.04E
Padang Indonesia **36** 0.55S100.21E
Padangpanjang Indonesia **36** 0.30S100.26E
Padangsidempuan Indonesia **36** 1.20N 99.11E
Padany Russian Fed. **24** 63.12N 33.20E
Padauari *r.* Brazil **90** 0.15S 64.05W
Paderborn Germany **20** 51.43N 8.44E
Padilla Bolivia **92** 19.19S 64.20W
Padlei Canada **75** 62.10N 97.05W
Padloping Island *town* Canada **73** 67.00N 62.50W
Padova Italy **15** 45.27N 11.52E
Pādra India **40** 22.14N 73.05E
Padrauna India **41** 26.55N 83.59E
Padre I. U.S.A. **83** 27.00N 97.15W
Padstow U.K. **11** 50.33N 4.57W
Padthaway Australia **66** 36.37S140.28E
Padua *see* Padova Italy **15**
Paducah U.S.A. **83** 37.05N 88.36W
Paeroa New Zealand **60** 37.23S175.41E
Pafúri Mozambique **57** 22.27S 31.21E
Pag *i.* Croatia **20** 44.28N 15.00E
Pagadian Phil. **37** 7.50N123.30E
Pagai Selatan *i.* Indonesia **36** 3.00S100.18E
Pagai Utara *i.* Indonesia **36** 2.42S100.05E
Pagan Burma **34** 21.07N 94.53E
Page U.S.A. **80** 36.57N111.27W
Pager *r.* Uganda **55** 3.05N 32.28E
Paghmān Afghan. **40** 34.36N 68.57E
Pago Pago Samoa **68** 14.16S170.42W
Pagosa Springs *town* U.S.A. **80** 37.16N107.01W
Pagri China **41** 27.45N 89.10E
Paguchi L. Canada **76** 49.38N 91.40W
Pagwa River *town* Canada **76** 50.02N 85.14W
Pahala Hawaii U.S.A. **78** 19.12N155.28W
Pahiatua New Zealand **60** 40.26S175.49E
Paible U.K. **12** 57.35N 7.27W
Paide Estonia **23** 58.54N 25.33E
Paihia New Zealand **60** 35.16S174.05E
Päijänne *l.* Finland **23** 61.35N 25.30E
Paikü Co *l.* China **41** 28.48N 85.36E
Paimboeuf France **17** 47.14N 2.01W
Painan Indonesia **36** 1.21S100.34E
Painesville U.S.A. **84** 41.43N 81.15W
Pains Brazil **94** 20.23S 45.38W
Paintsville U.S.A. **85** 37.49N 82.48W
Paisley U.K. **12** 55.50N 4.26W
País Vasco *d.* Spain **16** 43.00N 2.30W
Paiton Indonesia **37** 7.42S113.30E
Pajala Sweden **22** 67.11N 23.22E
Pajule Uganda **55** 2.58N 32.53E
Pakaraima Mts. Guyana **90** 5.00N 60.00W
Pakaur India **41** 24.38N 87.51E
Paki Nigeria **53** 11.33N 8.08E
Pakistan Asia **40** 29.00N 67.00E
Pakokku Burma **34** 21.20N 95.10E
Pākpattan Pakistan **40** 30.21N 73.24E
Paks Hungary **21** 46.39N 18.53E
Paktīā *d.* Afghan. **40** 33.25N 69.30E
Pakwach Uganda **55** 2.27N 31.18E
Pakxé Laos **34** 15.07N105.47E
Pala Chad **53** 9.25N 15.05E
Palaiokhóra Greece **19** 35.14N 23.41E
Palaiseau France **15** 48.43N 2.15E
Palamós Spain **16** 41.51N 3.08E
Palana Russian Fed. **29** 59.05N159.59E
Palangkaraya Indonesia **36** 2.16S113.56E
Palanguinos Spain **16** 42.27N 5.31W
Pālanpur India **40** 24.10N 72.26E
Palapye Botswana **56** 22.33S 27.07E
Palatka U.S.A. **85** 29.38N 81.40W
Palau *is.* Pacific Oc. **37** 7.00N134.25E
Palaw Burma **34** 12.58N 98.39E
Palawan *i.* Phil. **36** 9.30N118.30E
Paldiski Estonia **23** 59.20N 24.06E
Paleleh Indonesia **37** 1.04N121.57E
Palembang Indonesia **36** 2.59S104.50E
Palencia Spain **16** 42.01N 4.34W
Palenque Mexico **86** 17.32N 91.59W
Palermo Italy **18** 38.09N 13.22E
Palestine U.S.A. **83** 31.46N 95.38W
Paletwa Burma **34** 21.25N 92.49E
Pāli India **40** 25.46N 73.20E
Palimé Togo **52** 6.55N 0.38E
Palisades Resr. U.S.A. **80** 43.15N111.05W
Pālitāna India **40** 21.31N 71.50E
Palizada Mexico **86** 18.15N 92.05W
Palk Str. India / Sri Lanka **39** 10.00N 79.40E
Pallës, Bishti i *c.* Albania **19** 41.24N 19.23E
Pallinup *r.* Australia **63** 34.29S118.54E
Palliser, C. New Zealand **60** 41.35S175.15E
Pallu India **40** 28.56N 74.13E
Palma Mozambique **55** 10.48S 40.25E
Palma Spain **16** 39.36N 2.39E
Palma, Bahía de *b.* Spain **16** 39.30N 2.40E
Palma del Río Spain **16** 37.43N 5.17W
Palmanova Italy **15** 45.54N 13.19E
Palmares Brazil **91** 8.41S 35.36W
Palmas, C. Liberia **52** 4.30N 7.55W
Palmas, Golfo di *g.* Italy **18** 39.00N 8.30E
Palm Beach *town* U.S.A. **85** 26.41N 80.02W
Palmeira dos Indios Brazil **91** 9.25S 36.38W
Palmeirinhas, Punta das Angola **54** 9.09S 12.58E
Palmer *r.* Australia **62** 24.46S133.25E
Palmer U.S.A. **72** 61.36N149.07W
Palmer Land Antarctica **96** 74.00S 61.00W
Palmerston New Zealand **60** 45.29S170.43E
Palmerston, C. Australia **64** 21.32S149.29E
Palmerston Atoll Cook Is. **68** 18.04S163.10W
Palmerston North New Zealand **60** 40.20S175.39E
Palmerton U.S.A. **85** 40.48N 75.37W
Palmetto U.S.A. **85** 27.31N 82.32W
Palmi Italy **18** 38.22N 15.50E
Palmira Colombia **90** 3.33N 76.17W
Palm Is. Australia **64** 18.48S146.37E
Palms U.S.A. **84** 43.37N 82.46W
Palm Springs *town* U.S.A. **81** 33.50N116.33W
Palmyra I. Pacific Oc. **68** 5.52N162.05W
Palmyras Pt. India **41** 20.46N 87.02E
Paloh Indonesia **36** 1.46N109.17E
Paloich Sudan **49** 10.28N 32.32E
Palojoensuu Finland **22** 68.17N 23.05E
Palomani *mtn.* Bolivia **92** 14.38S 69.14W
Palopo Indonesia **37** 3.01S120.12E
Palu Turkey **42** 38.43N 39.56E
Palwal India **40** 28.09N 77.20E
Pama Burkina **52** 11.15N 0.44E
Pamanukan Indonesia **37** 6.16S107.46E
Pamekasan Indonesia **37** 7.11S113.30E
Pameungpeuk Indonesia **37** 7.39S107.40E
Pamiers France **17** 43.07N 1.36E
Pamir *mts.* Tajikistan **30** 37.50N 73.30E
Pamlico Sd. U.S.A. **85** 35.20N 75.55W
Pampa U.S.A. **83** 35.32N100.58W
Pampas *f.* Argentina **93** 34.00S 64.00W
Pamplona Colombia **90** 7.24N 72.38W
Pamplona Spain **16** 42.49N 1.39W
Pana U.S.A. **82** 39.23N 89.05W
Panaca U.S.A. **80** 37.47N114.23W
Panaji India **38** 15.29N 73.50E
Panama C. America **87** 9.00N 80.00W
Panamá *town* Panama **87** 8.57N 79.30W
Panama Sri Lanka **39** 6.46N 81.47E
Panamá, Golfo de *g.* Panama **87** 8.30N 79.00W
Panama City U.S.A. **85** 30.10N 85.41W
Panamint Range *mts.* U.S.A. **81** 36.30N117.20W
Panaro *r.* Italy **15** 44.55N 11.25E
Panay *i.* Phil. **37** 11.10N122.30E
Pandan Phil. **37** 11.45N122.10E
Pandaria India **41** 22.14N 81.25E
Pandeglang Indonesia **37** 6.19S106.05E
Pāndharkawada India **41** 20.01N 78.32E
Pāndhurna India **41** 21.36N 78.31E
Pando *d.* Bolivia **92** 11.20S 67.40W
Pando Uruguay **93** 34.43S 55.57W
Panevežys Lithuania **23** 55.44N 24.21E
Panfilov Kazakhstan **30** 44.10N 80.01E
Panga Zaïre **54** 1.51N 26.25E
Pangandaran Indonesia **37** 7.41S108.40E
Pangani Tanzania **55** 5.21S 39.00E
Pangi Zaïre **54** 3.10S 26.38E
Pangkalpinang Indonesia **36** 2.05S106.09E
Pang Long Burma **39** 23.11N 98.45E
Pangnirtung Canada **73** 66.05N 65.45W
Panīpāt India **40** 29.23N 76.58E
Panjāb Afghan. **40** 34.22N 67.01E
Panjgūr Pakistan **40** 26.58N 64.06E
Panjpāi Pakistan **40** 29.55N 66.30E
Pankshin Nigeria **53** 9.22N 9.25E
Panna India **41** 24.43N 80.12E
Pannawonica Australia **62** 21.42S116.22E
Páno Lévkara Cyprus **44** 34.55N 33.10E
Páno Plátres Cyprus **44** 34.53N 32.52E
Panshan China **32** 41.10N122.01E
Pantano del Esla *l.* Spain **16** 41.40N 5.50W
Pantelleria *i.* Italy **18** 36.48N 12.00E
Panton *r.* Australia **62** 17.05S128.46E
Pánuco Mexico **86** 22.03N 98.10W
Panvel India **40** 18.59N 73.06E
Pan Xian China **33** 25.46N104.39E
Panyu China **33** 23.00N113.30E
Paola Italy **18** 39.21N 16.03E
Paola U.S.A. **82** 38.35N 94.53W
Paoua C.A.R. **53** 7.09N 16.20E
Paôy Pêt Thailand **34** 13.41N102.34E
Papa Hawaiian Is. **69** 19.12N155.53W
Pápa Hungary **21** 47.19N 17.28E
Papa Stour *i.* U.K. **8** 60.20N 1.42W
Papa Westray *i.* U.K. **8** 59.22N 2.54W
Papeete Tahiti **69** 17.32S149.34W
Papenburg Germany **14** 53.05N 7.25E
Papenoo Tahiti **69** 17.30S149.25W
Papetoai Îs. de la Société **69** 17.29S149.52W
Paphos *see* Néa Páfos Cyprus **44**
Papigochic *r.* Mexico **81** 29.09N109.40W
Papillion U.S.A. **82** 41.09N 96.04W
Papineau, Lac *l.* Canada **77** 45.48N 74.46W
Papineauville Canada **77** 45.37N 75.01W
Papua, G. of P.N.G. **64** 8.30S145.00E
Papua New Guinea Austa. **61** 6.00S144.00E
Papun Burma **34** 18.05N 97.26E
Papunya Australia **64** 23.15S131.53E
Para *d.* Brazil **91** 4.00S 53.00W
Paraburdoo Australia **62** 23.12S117.40E
Paracatu Brazil **94** 17.14S 46.52W
Paracatu *r.* Brazil **94** 16.30S 45.10W
Paracel Is. S. China Sea **36** 16.20N112.00E
Parachilna Australia **66** 31.09S138.24E
Pārachinār Pakistan **40** 33.54N 70.06E
Paraćin Yugo. **21** 43.52N 21.24E
Pará de Minas Brazil **94** 19.53S 44.35W
Paradip India **41** 20.15N 86.35E
Paradise *r.* Canada **77** 53.23N 57.18W
Paradise Calif. U.S.A. **80** 39.46N121.37W
Paradise Nev. U.S.A. **81** 36.09N115.10W
Paragonah U.S.A. **80** 37.53N112.46W
Paragould U.S.A. **83** 36.03N 90.29W
Paragua *r.* Venezuela **90** 6.55N 62.55W
Paraguaçu *r.* Brazil **91** 12.35S 38.59W
Paraguaná, Península de *pen.* Venezuela **90** 11.50N 69.59W
Paraguarí Paraguay **94** 25.36S 57.06W
Paraguay *r.* Argentina **94** 27.30S 58.50W
Paraguay S. America **94** 23.00S 57.00W
Paraiba *d.* Brazil **91** 7.30S 36.30W
Paraíba *r.* Brazil **94** 21.45S 41.10W
Paraibuna Brazil **94** 23.29S 45.32W
Paraisópolis Brazil **94** 22.33S 45.48W
Parakou Benin **53** 9.23N 2.40E
Paramagudi India **39** 9.33N 78.36E
Paramaribo Surinam **91** 5.52N 55.14W
Paramonga Peru **90** 10.42S 77.50W
Paraná Argentina **93** 31.45S 60.30W
Paraná *r.* Argentina **93** 34.00S 58.30W
Paranã Brazil **91** 12.33S 47.48W
Paraná *d.* Brazil **94** 24.30S 52.00W
Paranã *r.* Brazil **91** 12.30S 48.10W
Paranaguá Brazil **94** 25.32S 48.36W
Paranaíba Brazil **94** 19.44S 51.12W
Paranaíba *r.* Brazil **94** 20.00S 51.00W
Paranapanema *r.* Brazil **94** 22.30S 53.03W
Paranapiacaba, Serra *mts.* Brazil **94** 24.30S 49.15W
Paranavaí Brazil **94** 23.02S 52.36W
Parangaba Brazil **91** 3.45S 38.33W
Paraparaumu New Zealand **60** 40.55S175.00E
Paratoo Australia **66** 32.46S139.40E
Paray-le-Monial France **17** 46.27N 4.07E
Pārbati *r.* India **40** 25.51N 76.36E
Pārbatipur Bangla. **41** 25.39N 88.55E
Parbhani India **40** 19.16N 76.47E
Parchim Germany **20** 53.25N 11.51E
Parczew Poland **21** 51.39N 22.54E
Pārdi India **40** 20.31N 72.57E
Pardo *r.* Bahia Brazil **94** 15.40S 39.38W
Pardo *r.* Mato Grosso Brazil **94** 21.56S 52.07W
Pardo *r.* São Paulo Brazil **94** 20.10S 48.36W
Pardubice Czech Republic **20** 50.03N 15.45E
Parecis, Serra dos *mts.* Brazil **90** 13.30S 58.30W
Parent Canada **76** 47.55N 74.35W
Parent, Lac *l.* Canada **76** 48.40N 77.03W
Parepare Indonesia **36** 4.03S119.40E
Párga Greece **19** 39.17N 20.23E
Pargas Finland **23** 60.18N 22.18E
Paria, Golfo de *g.* Venezuela **90** 10.30S 62.00W
Paria, Península de *pen.* Venezuela **90** 10.45N 62.30W
Pariaguán Venezuela **90** 8.51N 64.43W
Pariaman Indonesia **36** 0.36S100.09E
Parichi Belorussia **21** 52.48N 29.25E
Parigi Indonesia **37** 0.49S120.10E
Parika Guyana **90** 6.51N 58.25W
Parima, Sierra *mts.* Venezuela **90** 2.30N 64.00W
Parinari Peru **90** 4.35S 74.25W
Paringa Australia **66** 34.10S140.49E
Parintins Brazil **91** 2.36S 56.44W
Paris France **15** 48.52N 2.20E
Paris Kiribati **69** 1.56N157 29W
Paris Ill. U.S.A. **82** 39.35N 87.41W
Paris Ky. U.S.A. **84** 38.13N 84.15W
Paris Tenn. U.S.A. **83** 36.19N 88.20W
Paris Tex. U.S.A. **83** 33.40N 95.33W
Parisienne *d.* France **15** 48.50N 2.20E
Parkano Finland **23** 62.01N 23.01E
Parkbeg Canada **75** 50.28N106.18W
Parker U.S.A. **81** 34.09N114.17W
Parker, C. Canada **73** 75.04N 79.40W
Parker Dam U.S.A. **81** 34.18N114.10W
Parkersburg U.S.A. **84** 39.17N 81.33W
Parkes Australia **67** 33.10S148.13E
Park Falls *town* U.S.A. **82** 45.56N 90.32W
Park Forest *town* U.S.A. **82** 41.35N 87.41W
Parkland U.S.A. **80** 47.09N122.26W
Park Range *mts.* U.S.A. **80** 40.00N106.30W
Parkton U.S.A. **85** 39.38N 76.40W
Parlākimidi India **41** 18.46N 84.05E
Parma Italy **15** 44.48N 10.18E
Parma *r.* Italy **15** 44.56N 10.26E
Parma U.S.A. **84** 41.24N 81.44W
Parnaguá Brazil **91** 10.17S 44.39W
Parnaíba Brazil **91** 2.58S 41.46W
Parnaíba *r.* Brazil **91** 2.58S 41.47W
Parnassós *mtn.* Greece **19** 38.33N 22.35E
Parndana Australia **66** 35.44S137.14E
Pärnu Estonia **23** 58.24N 24.32E
Pärnu *r.* Estonia **23** 58.23N 24.29E
Pārola India **40** 20.53N 75.07E
Paroo *r.* Australia **66** 31.30S143.34E
Páros *i.* Greece **19** 37.04N 25.11E
Parrakie Australia **66** 35.18S140.12E
Parral Chile **93** 36.09S 71.50W
Parramatta Australia **67** 33.50S150.57E
Parras Mexico **83** 25.30N102.11W
Parras, Sierra de *mts.* Mexico **83** 25.20N102.10W
Parrett *r.* U.K. **11** 51.10N 3.00W
Parry Canada **75** 49.47N104.41W
Parry, Kap *c.* Greenland **73** 76.50N 71.00W
Parry Is. Canada **73** 76.00N102.00W
Parry Sound *town* Canada **84** 45.21N 80.02W
Parsad India **40** 24.11N 73.42E
Parsęta *r.* Poland **20** 54.12N 15.33E
Parsnip *r.* Canada **74** 55.10N123.02W
Parsons U.S.A. **83** 37.20N 95.16W
Parthenay France **17** 46.39N 0.14W
Partille Sweden **23** 57.44N 12.07E
Partinico Italy **18** 38.03N 13.07E
Partry Mts. Rep. of Ire. **13** 53.40N 9.30W
Paru *r.* Brazil **91** 1.33S 52.38W
Pārvatīpuram India **41** 18.47N 83.26E
Paryang China **41** 30.04N 83.28E
Parys R.S.A. **56** 26.54S 27.26E
Pasadena Calif. U.S.A. **81** 34.09N118.09W
Pasadena Tex. U.S.A. **83** 29.42N 95.13W
Pasaje Ecuador **90** 3.23S 79.50W
Pasawng Burma **34** 18.52N 97.18E
Pasay Phil. **37** 14.33N121.00E
Pascagoula U.S.A. **83** 30.23N 88.31W
Paşcani Romania **21** 47.15N 26.44E
Pasco U.S.A. **80** 46.14N119.06W
Pascua, Isla de *i.* Pacific Oc. **69** 27.08S109.23W
Pasewalk Germany **20** 53.30N 14.00E
Pasfield L. Canada **75** 58.25N105.20W
Pasinler Turkey **42** 39.59N 41.41E
Pasir Puteh Malaysia **36** 5.50N102.24E
Påskallavik Sweden **23** 57.10N 16.27E
Pasley, C. Australia **63** 33.55S123.30E
Pasmore *r.* Australia **66** 31.07S139.48E
Pasni Pakistan **40** 25.16N 63.28E
Paso de los Libres *town* Argentina **93** 29.45S 57.05W
Paso de los Toros *town* Uruguay **93** 32.49S 56.31W
Paso Robles U.S.A. **81** 35.38N120.41W
Paspébiac Canada **77** 48.01N 65.20W
Pasquia Hills Canada **75** 53.13N102.37W
Pasrūr Pakistan **40** 32.16N 74.40E
Passaic U.S.A. **85** 40.51N 74.08W
Passau Germany **20** 48.35N 13.28E
Passero, C. Italy **18** 36.40N 15.08E
Passo Fundo Brazil **94** 28.16S 52.20W
Passos Brazil **94** 20.45S 46.38W
Pastaza *r.* Peru **90** 4.50S 76.25W
Pasto Colombia **90** 1.12N 77.17W
Pasuquin Phil. **33** 18.25N120.37E
Pasuruan Indonesia **37** 7.38S112.54E
Patagonia *f.* Argentina **93** 42.20S 67.00W
Pātan India **40** 23.50N 72.07E
Patchewollock Australia **66** 35.25S142.14E
Patea New Zealand **60** 39.46S174.29E
Pategi Nigeria **53** 8.44N 5.47E
Pate I. Kenya **55** 2.08S 41.02E
Paternò Italy **18** 37.34N 14.54E
Paterson U.S.A. **85** 40.55N 74.10W
Pathānkot India **40** 32.17N 75.39E
Pathein *see* Bassein Burma **34**
Pathfinder Resr. U.S.A. **80** 42.30N106.50W
Pathiong Sudan **49** 6.46N 30.54E
Pati Indonesia **37** 6.45S111.00E
Patía *r.* Colombia **90** 1.54N 78.30W
Patiāla India **40** 30.19N 76.23E
Pati Pt. Guam **68** 13.36N144.57E
Patkai Hills Burma **34** 26.30N 95.30E
Pátmos *i.* Greece **19** 37.20N 26.33E
Patna India **41** 25.36N 85.07E
Patnāgarh India **41** 20.43N 83.09E
Patos Brazil **91** 6.55S 37.15W
Patos, Lagoa dos *l.* Brazil **94** 31.00S 51.10W
Patos de Minas Brazil **94** 18.35S 46.32W
Patquía Argentina **92** 30.02S 66.55W
Pátrai Greece **19** 38.15N 21.45E
Patraïkós Kólpos *g.* Greece **19** 38.15N 21.35E
Patrasuy Russian Fed. **24** 63.35N 61.50E
Patrickswell Rep. of Ire. **13** 52.36N 8.43W
Pattani Thailand **34** 6.51N101.16E
Pattaya Thailand **34** 12.57N100.53E
Pattoki Pakistan **40** 31.01N 73.51E
Patuākhāli Bangla. **41** 22.21N 90.21E
Patuca *r.* Honduras **87** 15.50N 84.18W
Pātūr India **40** 20.27N 76.56E
Patuxent *r.* U.S.A. **85** 38.18N 76.25W
Pau France **17** 43.18N 0.22W
Pauillac France **17** 45.12N 0.44W
Paúl do Mar Madeira Is. **95** 32.45N 17.14W
Paulina U.S.A. **80** 44.09N119.58W
Paulistana Brazil **91** 8.09S 41.09W
Paulo Afonso Brazil **91** 9.25S 38.15W
Paulsboro U.S.A. **85** 39.50N 75.15W
Pauls Valley *town* U.S.A. **83** 34.44N 97.13W
Paungde Burma **34** 18.30N 95.30E
Pauni India **41** 20.47N 79.38E
Pauri Madhya P. India **40** 25.32N 77.21E
Pauri Uttar P. India **41** 30.09N 78.47E
Pavia Italy **15** 45.10N 9.10E
Pavilly France **15** 49.34N 0.58E
Pavlodar Kazakhstan **28** 52.21N 76.59E
Pavlograd Ukraine **25** 48.34N 35.50E
Pavlovo Russian Fed. **24** 55.58N 43.05E
Pavlovsk Russian Fed. **25** 50.28N 40.07E
Pavlovskaya Russian Fed. **25** 46.18N 39.48E
Pavullo nel Frignano Italy **15** 44.20N 10.50E
Pawnee U.S.A. **83** 36.20N 96.48W
Paxoí *i.* Greece **19** 39.12N 20.12E
Paxton U.S.A. **82** 41.07N101.21W
Payette U.S.A. **80** 44.05N116.56W
Payne, L. Canada **73** 59.25N 74.00W
Paynes Find Australia **63** 29.15S117.41E
Paysandú Uruguay **93** 32.19S 58.05W
Pays de Caux *f.* France **15** 49.40N 0.40E
Pays de la Loire *d.* France **17** 47.30N 1.00W
Pazardzhik Bulgaria **19** 42.10N 24.22E
Peace *r.* Canada **74** 59.00N111.25W
Peace River *town* Canada **74** 56.15N117.18W
Peach Springs *town* U.S.A. **81** 35.32N113.25W
Peacock Hills Canada **72** 66.05N110.45W
Peak, The *mtn.* Ascension **95** 7.57S 14.21W
Peake Creek *r.* Australia **66** 28.05S136.07E
Peak Hill *town* Australia **67** 32.47S148.13E
Peak Range *mts.* Australia **64** 23.18S148.30E
Peale, Mt. U.S.A. **80** 38.26N109.14W
Pearl *r.* U.S.A. **83** 30.11N 89.32W
Pearland U.S.A. **83** 29.34N 95.17W
Pearsall U.S.A. **83** 28.53N 99.06W
Peary Land *f.* Greenland **96** 82.00N 35.00W
Pebane Mozambique **57** 17.14S 38.10E
Pebas Peru **90** 3.17S 71.55W
Peć Yugo. **19** 42.40N 20.17E
Pechenga Russian Fed. **22** 69.28N 31.04E
Pechora Russian Fed. **24** 65.14N 57.18E
Pechora *r.* Russian Fed. **24** 68.10N 54.00E
Pechorskaya Guba *g.* Russian Fed. **24** 69.00N 56.00E
Pechorskoye More *sea* Russian Fed. **24** 69.00N 55.00E
Pecos U.S.A. **83** 31.25N103.30W
Pecos *r.* U.S.A. **83** 29.42N101.22W
Pécs Hungary **21** 46.05N 18.14E
Peddie R.S.A. **56** 33.12S 27.07E
Pedregulho Brazil **94** 20.15S 47.29W
Pedreiras Brazil **91** 4.32S 44.40W
Pedrinhas Brazil **91** 11.12S 37.41W
Pedro Afonso Brazil **91** 8.59S 48.11W
Pedro de Valdivia Chile **92** 22.36S 69.40W
Pedro Juan Caballero Paraguay **94** 22.30S 55.44W
Peebinga Australia **66** 34.55S140.57E
Peebles U.K. **12** 55.39N 3.12W
Peebles U.S.A. **84** 38.57N 83.14W
Peekskill U.S.A. **85** 41.17N 73.55W
Peel *r.* Canada **72** 68.13N135.00W
Peel I.o.M. Europe **10** 54.14N 4.42W
Peel Inlet Australia **63** 32.35S115.44E
Peel Pt. Canada **72** 73.22N114.35W
Peene *r.* Germany **20** 53.53N 13.49E
Peera Peera Poolanna L. Australia **64** 26.43S137.42E
Peerless L. Canada **74** 56.37N114.35W
Pegasus B. New Zealand **60** 43.15S173.00E
Pegu Burma **34** 17.20N 96.36E
Pegu *d.* Burma **34** 17.30N 96.30E
Pegunungan Van Rees *mts.* Indonesia **37** 2.35S138.15E
Pegu Yoma *mts.* Burma **34** 18.30N 96.00E
Pehuajó Argentina **93** 35.50S 61.50W
Peikang Taiwan **33** 23.35N120.19E
Peipus, L. Estonia / Russian Fed. **24** 58.30N 27.30E
Peixe Brazil **91** 12.03S 48.32W
Pei Xian China **32** 34.44N116.55E
Pekalongan Indonesia **37** 6.54S109.37E
Pekanbaru Indonesia **36** 0.33N101.20E
Pekin U.S.A. **82** 40.34N 89.40W
Peking *see* Beijing China **32**
Pelabuanratu Indonesia **37** 7.00S106.32E
Pelat, Mont *mtn.* France **17** 44.17N 6.41E
Peleaga *mtn.* Romania **21** 45.22N 22.54E
Peleng *i.* Indonesia **37** 1.30S123.10E
Peleniya Moldavia **21** 47.58N 27.48E
Pelican U.S.A. **74** 57.55N136.10W
Pelkum Germany **14** 51.38N 7.44E
Pello Finland **22** 66.47N 24.00E
Pelly *r.* Canada **72** 62.50N137.35W
Pelly Bay *town* Canada **73** 68.38N 89.45W
Pelly L. Canada **73** 65.59N101.12W
Peloncillo Mts. U.S.A. **81** 32.16N109.00W
Pelotas Brazil **94** 31.45S 52.20W
Pemalang Indonesia **37** 6.53S109.21E
Pematangsiantar Indonesia **36** 2.59N 99.01E
Pemba Mozambique **57** 13.02S 40.30E
Pemba Zambia **55** 16.33S 27.20E
Pemba I. Tanzania **55** 5.10S 39.45E
Pemberton Australia **63** 34.28S116.01E
Pemberton Canada **74** 50.20N122.48W
Pembina *r.* Canada **74** 54.45N114.15W
Pembroke Canada **76** 45.49N 77.07W
Pembroke U.K. **11** 51.41N 4.57W
Pembroke U.S.A. **85** 32.09N 81.39W
Penang *see* Pinang, Pulau *i.* Malaysia **36**
Peñaranda de Bracamonte Spain **16** 40.54N 5.13W
Pen Argyl U.S.A. **85** 40.52N 75.16W
Penarth U.K. **11** 51.26N 3.11W
Peñas, Cabo de *c.* Spain **16** 43.42N 5.52W
Penas, Golfo de *g.* Chile **93** 47.20S 75.00W
Pende *r.* Chad **53** 7.30N 16.20E
Pendembu Sierra Leone **52** 8.09N 10.42W
Pendine U.K. **11** 51.44N 4.33W
Pendleton U.S.A. **80** 45.40N118.47W
Penedo Brazil **91** 10.16S 36.33W
Penetanguishene Canada **76** 44.47N 79.55W
Penganga *r.* India **41** 19.53N 79.09E
Penge Zaïre **54** 5.31S 24.37E
Penghu Liedao *is.* Taiwan **33** 23.35N119.32E
Pengshui China **33** 29.17N108.13E
Penicuik U.K. **12** 55.49N 3.13W
Peninsular Malaysia *d.* Malaysia **36** 5.00N102.00E
Penneshaw Australia **66** 35.42S137.55E
Pennines, Alpes *mts.* Switz. **15** 46.08N 7.34E
Pennsauken U.S.A. **85** 39.58N 75.04W
Penns Grove U.S.A. **85** 39.43N 75.28W
Pennsylvania *d.* U.S.A. **84** 40.45N 77.30W
Penn Yan U.S.A. **76** 42.40N 77.03W
Penny Highland *mtn.* Canada **73** 67.10N 66.50W
Penobscot *r.* U.S.A. **84** 44.30N 68.50W
Penola Australia **66** 37.23S140.21E
Penong Australia **63** 31.55S133.01E
Penonomé Panama **87** 8.30N 80.20W
Penrhyn Atoll Cook Is. **69** 9.00S158.00W
Penrith Australia **67** 33.47S150.44E
Penrith U.K. **10** 54.40N 2.45W
Penryn U.K. **11** 50.10N 5.07W
Pensacola U.S.A. **85** 30.26N 87.12W
Pensacola Mts. Antarctica **96** 84.00S 45.00W
Penshurst Australia **66** 37.52S142.20E
Pentecost I. Vanuatu **68** 15.42S168.10E
Penticton Canada **74** 49.30N119.30W
Pentland Australia **64** 20.32S145.24E
Pentland Firth *str.* U.K. **12** 58.40N 3.00W
Pentland Hills U.K. **12** 55.50N 3.20W
Penylan L. Canada **75** 61.50N106.20W
Penza Russian Fed. **24** 53.11N 45.00E
Penzance U.K. **11** 50.07N 5.32W
Penzhinskaya Guba *g.* Russian Fed. **29** 61.00N163.00E
Peoria Ariz. U.S.A. **81** 33.35N112.14W
Peoria Ill. U.S.A. **82** 40.43N 89.38W
Peper Sudan **49** 7.04N 33.00E
Perabumulih Indonesia **36** 3.29S104.14E

Perche, Collines du to **Porsangen**

Perche, Collines du *hills* France **15** 48.30N 0.40E
Percival Lakes Australia **62** 21.25S125.00E
Pereira Colombia **90** 4.47N 75.46W
Perekop Ukraine **25** 46.10N 33.42E
Perené *r.* Peru **92** 11.02S 74.19W
Perevolotskiy Russian Fed. **24** 51.10N 54.15E
Pereyaslav-Khmelnitskiy Ukraine **21** 50.05N 31.28E
Pergamino Argentina **93** 33.53S 60.35W
Pergine Valsugana Italy **15** 46.04N 11.14E
Perham U.S.A. **82** 46.36N 95.34W
Péribonca *r.* Canada **77** 48.45N 72.05W
Pericos Mexico **81** 25.03N107.42W
Périers France **15** 49.11N 1.25W
Périgueux France **17** 45.12N 0.44E
Perija, Sierra de *mts.* Venezuela **90** 10.30N 72.30W
Peri L. Australia **66** 30.44S143.34E
Perm Russian Fed. **24** 58.01N 56.10E
Pernambuco *d.* Brazil **91** 8.00S 39.00W
Pernatty L. Australia **66** 31.31S137.14E
Pernik Bulgaria **19** 42.35N 23.03E
Perniö Finland **23** 60.12N 23.08E
Péronne France **14** 49.56N 2.57E
Perosa Argentina Italy **15** 44.58N 7.10E
Pérouse, Bahía la *b.* I. de Pascua **69** 27.04S109.20W
Perpendicular, Pt. Australia **67** 35.03S150.50E
Perpignan France **17** 42.42N 2.54E
Perranporth U.K. **11** 50.21N 5.09W
Perry Fla. U.S.A. **85** 30.08N 83.36W
Perry Iowa U.S.A. **82** 41.50N 94.06W
Perry Okla. U.S.A. **83** 36.17N 97.17W
Perryton U.S.A. **83** 36.24N100.48W
Perryville U.S.A. **83** 37.43N 89.52W
Persepolis *ruins* Iran **43** 29.55N 53.00E
Perth Australia **63** 31.58S115.49E
Perth Canada **76** 44.54N 76.15W
Perth U.K. **12** 56.24N 3.28W
Perth Amboy U.S.A. **85** 40.32N 74.17W
Peru S. America **90** 10.00S 75.00W
Peru U.S.A. **82** 41.19N 89.11W
Peru Basin Pacific Oc. **69** 19.00S 96.00W
Peru-Chile Trench Pacific Oc. **69** 21.00S 72.00W
Perugia Italy **18** 43.06N 12.24E
Péruwelz Belgium **14** 50.32N 3.36E
Pervomaysk Ukraine **21** 48.03N 30.50E
Pervouralsk Russian Fed. **24** 56.59N 59.58E
Pesaro Italy **15** 43.54N 12.54E
Pescara Italy **18** 42.27N 14.13E
Pescara *r.* Italy **18** 42.28N 14.13E
Pescia Italy **15** 43.54N 10.41E
Peshāwar Pakistan **40** 34.01N 71.33E
Peshin Jān Afghan. **40** 33.25N 61.28E
Pesqueira Brazil **91** 8.24S 36.38W
Pesqueria *r.* Mexico **83** 25.55N 99.28W
Pessac France **17** 44.48N 0.38W
Peşteana Jiu Romania **21** 44.50N 23.15E
Pestovo Russian Fed. **24** 58.32N 35.42E
Petah Tiqwa Israel **44** 32.05N 34.53E
Petaluma U.S.A. **80** 38.14N122.39W
Pétange Lux. **14** 49.32N 5.56E
Petare Venezuela **90** 10.31N 66.50W
Petatlán Mexico **86** 17.31N101.16W
Petauke Zambia **55** 14.16S 31.21E
Petawawa Canada **76** 45.54N 77.17W
Peterborough S.A. Australia **66** 33.00S138.51E
Peterborough Vic. Australia **66** 38.36S142.55E
Peterborough Canada **76** 44.19N 78.20W
Peterborough U.K. **11** 52.35N 0.14W
Peterhead U.K. **12** 57.30N 1.46W
Peterlee U.K. **10** 54.45N 1.18W
Petermann Ranges *mts.* Australia **62** 25.00S129.46E
Peter Pond L. Canada **75** 55.55N108.44W
Petersburg Alas. U.S.A. **74** 56.49N132.58W
Petersburg Va. U.S.A. **85** 37.14N 77.24W
Petersburg W.Va. U.S.A. **84** 39.00N 79.07W
Petersfield U.K. **11** 51.00N 0.56W
Petitot *r.* Canada **74** 60.14N123.29W
Petitsikapau L. Canada **77** 54.45N 66.25W
Petit St. Bernard, Col du *pass* France / Italy **15** 45.40N 6.53E
Petlād India **40** 22.30N 72.45E
Petoskey U.S.A. **84** 45.22N 84.59W
Petra *ruins* Jordan **44** 30.19N 35.26E
Petrich Bulgaria **19** 41.25N 23.13E
Petrikov Belorussia **21** 52.09N 28.30E
Petrodvorets Russian Fed. **24** 59.50N 29.57E
Petrolina Brazil **91** 9.22S 40.30W
Petropavlovsk Kazakhstan **28** 54.53N 69.13E
Petropavlovsk Kamchatskiy Russian Fed. **29** 53.03N158.43E
Petrópolis Brazil **94** 22.30S 43.06W
Petroşani Romania **21** 45.25N 23.22E
Petrovaradin Yugo. **21** 45.16N 19.55E
Petrovsk Russian Fed. **24** 52.20N 45.24E
Petrovsk Zabaykal'skiy Russian Fed. **29** 51.20N108.55E
Petrozavodsk Russian Fed. **24** 61.46N 34.19E
Petrus Steyn R.S.A. **56** 27.38S 28.08E
Peureulak Indonesia **36** 4.48N 97.45E
Pevek Russian Fed. **29** 69.41N170.19E
Pézenas France **17** 43.28N 3.25E
Pezinok Slovakia **21** 48.18N 17.17E
Pezmog Russian Fed. **24** 61.50N 51.45E
Pezu Pakistan **40** 32.19N 70.44E
Pfaffenhofen Germany **20** 48.31N 11.30E
Pfalzel Germany **14** 49.47N 6.41E
Pforzheim Germany **20** 48.53N 8.41E
Phagwāra India **40** 31.13N 75.47E
Phalodi India **40** 27.08N 72.22E
Phangan, Ko *i.* Thailand **36** 9.50N100.00E
Phangnga Thailand **34** 8.29N 98.31E
Phan Rang Vietnam **34** 11.34N109.00E
Phan Thiet Vietnam **34** 11.00N108.06E
Pharenda India **41** 27.06N 83.17E
Phariāro Pakistan **40** 27.12N 68.59E
Phat Diem Vietnam **33** 20.06N106.07E
Phatthalung Thailand **34** 7.38N100.04E
Phelps L. Canada **75** 59.15N103.15W
Phenix City U.S.A. **85** 32.28N 85.01W
Phet Buri Thailand **34** 13.00N 99.58E
Philadelphia Miss. U.S.A. **83** 32.46N 89.07W
Philadelphia Penn. U.S.A. **85** 39.57N 75.07W
Philippeville Belgium **14** 50.12N 4.32E
Philippines Asia **37** 13.00N123.00E
Philippine Sea Pacific Oc. **68** 18.00N135.00E
Philippine Trench Pacific Oc. **68** 9.00N127.00E
Philipstown R.S.A. **56** 30.25S 24.26E
Phillip U.S.A. **82** 44.02N101.40W
Phillip I. Australia **67** 38.29S145.14E
Phillips *r.* Australia **63** 33.55S120.01E
Phillips Maine U.S.A. **84** 44.49N 70.21W
Phillips Wisc. U.S.A. **82** 45.41N 90.24W
Phillipsburg Kans. U.S.A. **82** 39.45N 99.19W
Phillipsburg N.J. U.S.A. **85** 40.42N 75.12W
Phillipson, L. Australia **66** 29.28S134.28E
Phnom Penh Cambodia **34** 11.35N104.55E
Phoenix U.S.A. **81** 33.27N112.05W
Phoenix Is. Kiribati **68** 4.00S172.00W
Phoenixville Penn. U.S.A. **85** 40.08N 75.31W
Phon Thailand **34** 15.50N102.35E
Phôngsali Laos **34** 21.40N102.11E
Phou Loi *mtn.* Laos **34** 20.16N103.18E
Phu Huu Vietnam **33** 19.00N105.35E
Phuket Thailand **34** 7.55N 98.23E
Phuket, Ko *i.* Thailand **34** 8.10N 98.20E
Phu Ly Vietnam **33** 20.30N105.58E
Phumi Chuuk Vietnam **34** 10.50N104.28E
Phumi Sâmraông Cambodia **34** 14.12N103.31E
Phu Quoc *i.* Cambodia **34** 10.20N104.00E
Phu Tho Vietnam **34** 21.23N105.13E
Phu Vinh Vietnam **34** 9.57N106.20E
Piacá Brazil **91** 7.42S 47.18W
Piacenza Italy **15** 45.03N 9.42E
Pialba Australia **64** 25.13S152.55E
Pian *r.* Australia **67** 30.03S148.18E
Piana France **17** 42.14N 8.38E
Piangil Australia **65** 35.04S143.20E
Pianoro Italy **15** 44.22N 11.20E
Pianosa *i.* Italy **18** 42.35N 10.05E
Piatra-Neamţ Romania **21** 46.56N 26.22E
Piauí *d.* Brazil **91** 7.45S 42.30W
Piauí *r.* Brazil **91** 6.14S 42.51W
Piave *r.* Italy **15** 45.33N 12.45E
Piawaning Australia **63** 30.51S116.22E
Pibor *r.* Sudan **49** 8.26N 33.13E
Pibor Post Sudan **49** 6.48N 33.08E
Pic *r.* Canada **76** 48.38N 86.25W
Picardie *d.* France **14** 49.47N 3.12E
Pickering U.K. **10** 54.15N 0.46W
Pickle Crow Canada **76** 51.30N 90.04W
Pickwick L. *resr.* U.S.A. **83** 34.55N 88.10W
Picos Brazil **91** 7.05S 41.28W
Picquigny France **15** 49.57N 2.09E
Picton Australia **67** 34.12S150.35E
Picton Canada **76** 44.00N 77.08W
Picton New Zealand **60** 41.17S174.02E
Picún Leufú Argentina **93** 39.30S 69.15W
Pidálion, Akrotírion *c.* Cyprus **44** 34.56N 34.05E
Pidarak Pakistan **40** 25.51N 63.14E
Piedecuesta Colombia **90** 6.59N 73.03W
Piedmont U.S.A. **85** 33.55N 85.39W
Piedras *r.* Peru **90** 12.30S 69.10W
Piedras, Punta *c.* Argentina **93** 35.25S 57.07W
Piedras Negras Mexico **83** 28.40N100.32W
Piedra Sola Uruguay **93** 32.04S 56.21W
Pielavesi Finland **22** 63.14N 26.45E
Pielinen *l.* Finland **24** 63.20N 29.50E
Piemonte *d.* Italy **15** 44.45N 8.00E
Pierce U.S.A. **80** 46.29N115.48W
Pierre U.S.A. **82** 44.22N100.21W
Pierreville Canada **77** 46.04N 72.49W
Piesseville Australia **63** 33.11S117.12E
Piešt'any Slovakia **21** 48.36N 17.50E
Pietarsaari Finland **22** 63.40N 22.42E
Pietermaritzburg R.S.A. **56** 29.36S 30.23E
Pietersburg R.S.A. **56** 23.54S 29.27E
Pietrasanta Italy **15** 43.57N 10.14E
Piet Retief R.S.A. **56** 27.00S 30.49E
Pietrosu *mtn.* Romania **21** 47.36N 24.38E
Pietrosul *mtn.* Romania **21** 47.08N 25.11E
Pieve di Cadore Italy **15** 46.26N 12.22E
Pigailoe *i.* Federated States of Micronesia **37** 8.08N146.40E
Pigna Italy **15** 43.56N 7.40E
Pihtipudas Finland **22** 63.23N 25.34E
Pikalevo Russian Fed. **24** 59.35N 34.07E
Pikangikum Canada **75** 51.49N 94.00W
Pikes Peak *mtn.* U.S.A. **80** 38.51N105.03W
Pikesville U.S.A. **85** 39.25N 77.25W
Piketberg R.S.A. **56** 32.54S 18.43E
Piketon U.S.A. **84** 39.03N 83.01W
Pikeville U.S.A. **85** 37.29N 82.33W
Pila Argentina **93** 36.00S 58.10W
Piła Poland **20** 53.09N 16.44E
Pilar Paraguay **94** 26.52S 58.23W
Pilar do Sul Brazil **94** 23.48S 47.45W
Pilcomayo *r.* Argentina / Paraguay **92** 25.15S 57.43W
Pīlībhīt India **41** 28.38N 79.48E
Pilica *r.* Poland **21** 51.52N 21.17E
Pilliga Australia **67** 30.23S148.55E
Pílos Greece **19** 36.55N 21.40E
Pilot Point *town* U.S.A. **83** 33.24N 96.58W
Pilsum Germany **14** 53.29N 7.06E
Pimba Australia **66** 31.18S136.47E
Pimenta Bueno Brazil **90** 11.40S 61.14W
Pinang, Pulau *i.* Malaysia **36** 5.30N100.10E
Pinarbaşi Turkey **42** 38.43N 36.23E
Pinar del Río Cuba **87** 22.24N 83.42W
Pincher Creek *town* Canada **74** 49.30N113.57W
Píndhos Óros *mts.* Albania / Greece **19** 39.40N 21.00E
Pindiga Nigeria **53** 9.58N 10.53E
Pindi Gheb Pakistan **40** 33.14N 72.16E
Pindwāra India **40** 24.48N 73.04E
Pine *r.* Canada **74** 56.08N120.41W
Pine, C. Canada **77** 46.37N 53.30W
Pine Bluff *town* U.S.A. **83** 34.13N 92.01W
Pine Bluffs *town* U.S.A. **80** 41.11N104.04W
Pine City U.S.A. **82** 45.50N 92.59W
Pine Creek *town* Australia **62** 13.51S131.50E
Pinega Russian Fed. **24** 64.42N 43.28E
Pinega *r.* Russian Fed. **24** 63.51N 41.48E
Pinehouse L. Canada **75** 55.32N106.35W
Pine Is. U.S.A. **85** 26.35N 82.06W
Pine Point *town* Canada **74** 60.50N114.28W
Pine River *town* Canada **75** 51.45N100.40W
Pine River *town* U.S.A. **82** 46.43N 94.24W
Pinerolo Italy **15** 44.53N 7.21E
Pinetown R.S.A. **56** 29.49S 30.52E
Pineville U.S.A. **83** 31.19N 92.26W
Piney France **15** 48.22N 4.20E
Ping *r.* Thailand **34** 15.47N100.05E
Pingaring Australia **63** 34.45S118.34E
Pingba China **33** 26.25N106.15E
Pingdingshan Henan China **32** 33.38N113.30E
Pingdingshan Liaoning China **32** 41.28N124.45E
Pingdong Taiwan **33** 22.44N120.30E
Pingelap *i.* Pacific Oc. **68** 6.15N160.40E
Pingelly Australia **63** 32.34S117.04E
Pingle China **33** 24.38N110.38E
Pingliang China **32** 35.21N107.12E
Pingluo China **32** 38.56N106.34E
Pingnan China **33** 23.33N110.23E
Pingrup Australia **63** 33.33S118.30E
Pingtan *i.* China **33** 25.36N119.48E
Pingwu China **32** 32.25N104.36E
Pingxiang Guang. Zhuang. China **33** 22.07N106.42E
Pingxiang Jiangxi China **33** 27.36N113.48E
Pingyang China **33** 27.40N120.33E
Pingyao China **32** 37.12N112.08E
Pingyi China **32** 35.30N117.36E
Pingyuan China **33** 24.34N115.54E
Pinhal Brazil **94** 22.10S 46.46W
Pinhel Portugal **16** 40.46N 7.04W
Pini *i.* Indonesia **36** 0.10N 98.30E
Piniós *r.* Greece **19** 39.51N 22.37E
Pinjarra Australia **63** 32.37S115.53E
Pinnaroo Australia **66** 35.18S140.54E
Pinos, Isla de *i.* Cuba **87** 21.40N 82.40W
Pinrang Indonesia **36** 3.48S119.41E
Pins, Île des *i.* N. Cal. **68** 22.37S167.30E
Pinsk Belorussia **21** 52.08N 26.01E
Pinto Argentina **92** 29.09S 62.38W
Pinto Butte *mtn.* Canada **75** 49.22N107.25W
Pinyug Russian Fed. **24** 60.10N 47.43E
Piombino Italy **18** 42.56N 10.30E
Piorini, L. Brazil **90** 3.34S 63.15W
Piotrków Trybunalski Poland **21** 51.25N 19.42E
Piove di Sacco Italy **15** 45.18N 12.02E
Pīpār India **40** 26.23N 73.32E
Piparia India **41** 22.45N 78.21E
Pipestone *r.* Ont. Canada **76** 52.48N 89.35W
Pipestone *r.* Sask. Canada **75** 58.40N105.45W
Pipestone U.S.A. **82** 43.58N 96.10W
Pipinas Argentina **93** 35.30S 57.19W
Piplān Pakistan **40** 32.17N 71.21E
Pipmouacane, Résr. Canada **77** 49.35N 70.30W
Piqua U.S.A. **84** 40.08N 84.14W
Piracicaba Brazil **94** 22.45S 47.40W
Piraçicaba *r.* Brazil **94** 22.35S 48.14W
Piracuruca Brazil **91** 3.56S 41.42W
Piraeus *see* Piraiévs Greece **19**
Piraiévs Greece **19** 37.56N 23.38E
Pīram I. India **40** 21.36N 72.41E
Pirassununga Brazil **94** 21.59S 47.25W
Pírgos Greece **19** 37.42N 21.27E
Pirna Germany **20** 50.58N 13.58E
Pirojpur Bangla. **41** 22.34N 89.59E
Pirot Yugo. **19** 43.10N 22.32E
Pīr Panjāl Range *mts.* Jammu & Kashmir **40** 33.50N 74.30E
Piryatin Ukraine **25** 50.14N 32.31E
Pisa Italy **18** 43.43N 10.24E
Pisciotta Italy **18** 40.08N 15.12E
Pisco Peru **90** 13.46S 76.12W
Písek Czech Republic **20** 49.19N 14.10E
Pishan China **30** 37.30N 78.20E
Pishīn Pakistan **40** 30.35N 67.00E
Pishīn Lora *r.* Pakistan **40** 29.09N 64.55E
Pistoia Italy **15** 43.55N 10.54E
Pisuerga *r.* Spain **16** 41.35N 5.40W
Pisz Poland **21** 53.38N 21.49E
Pita Guinea **52** 11.05N 12.15W
Pitalito Colombia **90** 1.51N 76.01W
Pitarpunga, L. Australia **66** 34.23S143.32E
Pitcairn I. Pacific Oc. **69** 25.04S130.06W
Pite *r.* Sweden **22** 65.14N 21.32E
Piteå Sweden **22** 65.20N 21.30E
Piteşti Romania **21** 44.52N 24.51E
Pithāpuram India **39** 17.07N 82.16E
Pithiviers France **15** 48.10N 2.15E
Pithoragarh India **41** 29.35N 80.13E
Piti Guam **68** 13.28N144.41E
Pitlochry U.K. **12** 56.43N 3.45W
Pitt I. Canada **74** 53.35N129.45W
Pittsburg Kans. U.S.A. **83** 37.25N 94.42W
Pittsburg N.H. U.S.A. **84** 45.03N 71.26W
Pittsburg Tex. U.S.A. **83** 32.60N 94.58W
Pittsburgh U.S.A. **84** 40.26N 80.00W
Pittsfield U.S.A. **84** 42.27N 73.15W
Pittston U.S.A. **84** 41.19N 75.47W
Pittsville U.S.A. **85** 38.24N 75.52W
Pittville U.S.A. **80** 41.03N121.20W
Piüí Brazil **94** 20.28S 45.58W
Piura Peru **90** 5.15S 80.38W
Piuthān Nepal **41** 28.06N 82.54E
Placentia Canada **77** 47.15N 53.58W
Placentia B. Canada **77** 47.15N 54.30W
Plain Dealing U.S.A. **83** 32.54N 93.42W
Plainfield U.S.A. **85** 40.37N 74.26W
Plains U.S.A. **80** 47.27N114.53W
Plainview U.S.A. **83** 34.11N101.43W
Plampang Indonesia **36** 8.48S117.48E
Planá Czech Republic **20** 49.52N 12.44E
Plana Cays *is.* Bahamas **87** 21.31N 72.14W
Plantagenet Canada **77** 45.32N 75.00W
Plasencia Spain **16** 40.02N 6.05W
Plassen Norway **23** 61.08N 12.31E
Plaster Rock *town* Canada **77** 46.54N 67.24W
Platani *r.* Italy **18** 37.24N 13.15E
Plate, R. *est. see* La Plata, Río de Argentina / Uruguay **93**
Plateau *d.* Nigeria **53** 8.50N 9.00E
Platí, Ákra *c.* Greece **19** 40.26N 23.59E
Platinum U.S.A. **72** 59.00N161.50W
Plato Colombia **90** 9.54N 74.46W
Platte *r.* U.S.A. **82** 41.04N 95.53W
Platteville U.S.A. **82** 42.44N 90.29W
Plattling Germany **20** 48.47N 12.53E
Plattsburgh U.S.A. **84** 44.42N 73.28W
Plauen Germany **20** 50.29N 12.08E
Plavsk Russian Fed. **24** 53.40N 37.20E
Pleasantville U.S.A. **85** 39.23N 74.32W
Pleasonton U.S.A. **83** 28.58N 98.29W
Pleiku Vietnam **34** 13.57N108.01E
Plenty, B. of New Zealand **60** 37.40S176.50E
Plentywood U.S.A. **80** 48.47N104.34W
Plesetsk Russian Fed. **24** 62.42N 40.21E
Pleshchenitsy Belorussia **21** 54.24N 27.52E
Pleszew Poland **21** 51.54N 17.48E
Plétipi, Lac *l.* Canada **77** 51.44N 70.06W
Pleven Bulgaria **19** 43.25N 24.39E
Pljevlja Yugo. **19** 43.22N 19.22E
Płock Poland **21** 52.33N 19.43E
Ploieşti Romania **21** 44.57N 26.02E
Plomb du Cantal *mtn.* France **17** 45.04N 2.45E
Plombières France **17** 47.58N 6.28E
Plön Germany **20** 54.09N 10.25E
Plonge, Lac la *l.* Canada **75** 55.05N107.15W
Płońsk Poland **21** 52.38N 20.23E
Ploudalmézeau France **17** 48.33N 4.39W
Plovdiv Bulgaria **19** 42.09N 24.45E
Plumtree Zimbabwe **56** 20.30S 27.50E
Plunkett Canada **75** 51.56N105.29W
Plymouth U.K. **11** 50.23N 4.09W
Plymouth Ind. U.S.A. **84** 41.20N 86.19W
Plymouth Wisc. U.S.A. **82** 43.44N 87.58W
Plzeň Czech Republic **20** 49.45N 13.22E
Pô Burkina **52** 11.11N 1.10W
Po *r.* Italy **15** 44.51N 12.30E
Pobé Benin **53** 7.00N 2.56E
Pobeda, Gora *mtn.* Russian Fed. **29** 65.20N145.50E
Pobla de Segur Spain **16** 42.15N 0.58E
Pocahontas Canada **74** 53.15N118.00W
Pocahontas Ark. U.S.A. **83** 36.16N 90.58W
Pocahontas Iowa U.S.A. **82** 42.44N 94.40W
Pocatello U.S.A. **80** 42.52N112.27W
Pocklington U.K. **10** 53.56N 0.48W
Poços de Caldas Brazil **94** 21.48S 46.33W
Podĕbrady Czech Republic **20** 50.08N 15.07E
Podgaytsy Ukraine **21** 49.19N 25.10E
Podgorica Yugo. **19** 42.30N 19.16E
Podkamennaya Tunguska Russian Fed. **29** 61.45N 90.13E
Podkamennaya Tunguska *r.* Russian Fed. **29** 61.40N 90.00E
Podolsk Russian Fed. **24** 55.23N 37.32E
Podor Senegal **52** 16.35N 15.02W
Podporozhye Russian Fed. **24** 60.55N 34.02E
Pofadder R.S.A. **56** 29.08S 19.22E
Pogrebishche Ukraine **21** 49.30N 29.15E
Poh Indonesia **37** 1.00S122.50E
P'ohang S. Korea **31** 36.00N129.26E
Poinsett, C. Antarctica **96** 65.35S113.00E
Point Arena *f.* U.S.A. **80** 38.55N123.41W
Pointe-à-Pitre Guadeloupe **87** 16.14N 61.32W
Pointe aux Anglais *town* Canada **77** 49.34N 67.10W
Pointe-aux-Trembles *town* Canada **77** 45.39N 73.29W
Pointe-Claire Canada **77** 45.26N 73.50W
Pointe Noire *town* Congo **54** 4.46S 11.53E
Point Hope *town* U.S.A. **72** 68.21N166.41W
Point Lookout *town* Australia **67** 30.33S152.20E
Point Pleasant *town* N.J. U.S.A. **85** 40.05N 74.04W
Point Pleasant *town* W.Va. U.S.A. **84** 38.53N 82.07W
Point Samson *town* Australia **62** 20.46S117.10E
Poissy France **15** 48.56N 2.03E
Poitiers France **17** 46.35N 0.20E
Poitou-Charentes *d.* France **17** 46.00N 0.00
Poix France **15** 49.47N 2.00E
Poix-Terron France **15** 49.39N 4.39E
Pokaran India **40** 26.55N 71.55E
Pokhara Nepal **41** 28.12N 83.59E
Poko Zaïre **54** 3.08N 26.51E
Pokoinu Rarotonga Cook Is. **68** 21.12S159.50W
Polacca U.S.A. **81** 35.50N110.23W
Pola de Lena Spain **16** 43.10N 5.49W
Polān Iran **43** 25.29N 61.15E
Poland Europe **21** 52.30N 19.00E
Polatli Turkey **42** 39.34N 32.08E
Polch Germany **14** 50.18N 7.19E
Polda Australia **66** 33.30S135.10E
Pole Zaïre **54** 2.51S 23.12E
Polesye *f.* Belorussia **21** 52.15N 28.00E
Poli Cameroon **53** 8.30N 13.15E
Policastro, Golfo di *g.* Italy **18** 40.00N 15.35E
Poligny France **17** 46.50N 5.42E
Pólis Cyprus **44** 35.02N 32.26E
Políyiros Greece **19** 40.23N 23.27E
Pollino *mtn.* Italy **18** 39.53N 16.11E
Pollock Reef Australia **63** 34.28S123.40E
Polnovat Russian Fed. **28** 63.47N 65.54E
Polonnoye Ukraine **21** 50.10N 27.30E
Polotsk Russian Fed. **24** 55.30N 28.43E
Polperro U.K. **11** 50.19N 4.31W
Polson U.S.A. **80** 47.41N114.09W
Poltava Ukraine **25** 49.35N 34.35E
Polunochnoye Russian Fed. **24** 60.52N 60.28E
Polyarnyy Russian Fed. **24** 69.14N 33.30E
Polynesia *is.* Pacific Oc. **68** 4.00S165.00W
Pomarkku Finland **23** 61.42N 22.00E
Pombal Brazil **91** 6.45S 37.45W
Pombal Portugal **16** 39.55N 8.38W
Pomene Mozambique **57** 22.53S 35.33E
Pomeroy U.S.A. **80** 46.28N117.36W
Pomona Namibia **56** 27.09S 15.18E
Pomona U.S.A. **81** 34.04N117.45W
Pompano Beach *town* U.S.A. **85** 26.14N 80.07W
Pompey's Pillar *town* U.S.A. **80** 45.59N107.56W
Ponape *i.* Pacific Oc. **68** 6.55N158.15E
Ponca City U.S.A. **83** 36.42N 97.05W
Ponce Puerto Rico **87** 18.00N 66.40W
Pondicherry India **39** 11.59N 79.50E
Pond Inlet *str.* Canada **73** 72.30N 75.00W
Ponds, I. of Canada **77** 53.24N 55.55W
Ponferrada Spain **16** 42.32N 6.31W
Pongani P.N.G. **64** 9.05S148.35E
Pongo *r.* Sudan **49** 8.52N 27.40E
Pongola *r.* Mozambique **57** 26.13S 32.38E
Ponnāni India **38** 10.46N 75.54E
Ponnyadaung Range *mts.* Burma **34** 22.30N 94.20E
Ponoka Canada **74** 52.42N113.40W
Ponorogo Indonesia **37** 7.51S111.30E
Ponoy Russian Fed. **24** 67.02N 41.03E
Ponoy *r.* Russian Fed. **24** 67.00N 41.10E
Ponta Grossa Brazil **94** 25.00S 50.09W
Pont-à-Mousson France **17** 48.55N 6.03E
Ponta Porã Brazil **94** 22.27S 55.39W
Pont-Audemer France **15** 49.21N 0.31E
Pontax *r.* Canada **76** 51.30N 78.48W
Pont Canavese Italy **15** 45.25N 7.36E
Pontchartrain, L. U.S.A. **83** 30.10N 90.10W
Pont-d'Ain France **17** 46.03N 5.20E
Pontedera Italy **18** 43.40N 10.38E
Pontefract U.K. **10** 53.42N 1.19W
Ponteix Canada **75** 49.49N107.30W
Ponte Nova Brazil **94** 20.25S 42.54W
Pontevedra Spain **16** 42.25N 8.39W
Pontiac Ill. U.S.A. **82** 40.54N 88.36W
Pontiac Mich. U.S.A. **84** 42.39N 83.18W
Pontianak Indonesia **36** 0.05S109.16E
Pontivy France **17** 48.05N 3.00W
Pont l'Évêque France **15** 49.18N 0.11E
Pontoise France **15** 49.03N 2.05E
Pontorson France **15** 48.33N 1.31W
Pontremoli Italy **15** 44.22N 9.53E
Pontresina Switz. **15** 46.28N 9.53E
Pontrilas U.K. **11** 51.56N 2.53W
Pont-sur-Yonne France **15** 48.17N 3.12E
Pontypool U.K. **11** 51.42N 3.01W
Pontypridd U.K. **11** 51.36N 3.21W
Ponziane, Isole *is.* Italy **18** 40.56N 12.58E
Poochera Australia **66** 32.42S134.52E
Poole U.K. **11** 50.42N 2.02W
Pooncarie Australia **66** 33.23S142.34E
Poopelloe L. Australia **66** 31.39S144.00E
Poopó, Lago de *l.* Bolivia **92** 19.00S 67.00W
Popayán Colombia **90** 2.27N 76.32W
Poperinge Belgium **14** 50.51N 2.44E
Popes Creek *town* U.S.A. **85** 38.09N 76.58W
Popilta L. Australia **66** 33.09S141.45E
Poplar *r.* Canada **75** 53.00N 97.18W
Poplar U.S.A. **80** 48.07N105.12W
Poplar Bluff *town* U.S.A. **83** 36.45N 90.24W
Poplarville U.S.A. **83** 30.51N 89.32W
Popocatépetl *mtn.* Mexico **86** 19.02N 98.38W
Popokabaka Zaïre **54** 5.41S 16.40E
Popondetta P.N.G. **64** 8.45S148.15E
Poprad Slovakia **21** 49.03N 20.18E
Popricani Romania **21** 47.18N 27.31E
Porāli *r.* Pakistan **40** 25.30N 66.25E
Porbandar India **40** 21.38N 69.36E
Por Chaman Afghan. **40** 33.08N 63.51E
Porcher I. Canada **74** 54.00N130.30W
Porcupine *r.* U.S.A. **74** 66.25N145.20W
Porcupine Hills Canada **75** 52.30N101.45W
Pordenone Italy **15** 45.57N 12.39E
Pori Finland **23** 61.29N 21.47E
Porirua New Zealand **60** 41.08S174.50E
Porjus Sweden **22** 66.57N 19.50E
Porkhov Russian Fed. **24** 57.43N 29.31E
Porkkala Finland **23** 59.59N 24.26E
Porlamar Venezuela **90** 11.01N 63.54W
Pornic France **17** 47.07N 2.05W
Porog Russian Fed. **24** 63.50N 38.32E
Poronaysk Russian Fed. **29** 49.13N142.55E
Porosozero Russian Fed. **24** 62.45N 32.48E
Porretta Terme Italy **15** 44.09N 10.59E
Porsangen *est.* Norway **22** 70.58N 25.30E

Porsangerhalvöya to Qatar

Porsangerhalvöya pen. Norway 22 70.50N 25.00E
Porsgrunn Norway 23 59.09N 9.40E
Porsuk r. Turkey 42 39.41N 31.56E
Portachuela Bolivia 92 17.21S 63.24W
Portadown U.K. 13 54.25N 6.27W
Portaferry U.K. 13 54.23N 5.33W
Portage U.S.A. 82 43.33N 89.28W
Portage la Prairie town Canada 75 49.57N 98.25W
Port Alberni Canada 74 49.14N124.48W
Port Albert Australia 67 38.09S146.40E
Portalegre Portugal 16 39.17N 7.25W
Portales U.S.A. 83 34.11N103.20W
Port Alfred R.S.A. 56 33.36S 26.52E
Port Alice Canada 74 50.25N127.25W
Port Angeles U.S.A. 80 48.07N123.27W
Port Antonio Jamaica 87 18.10N 76.27W
Port Arthur Australia 65 43.08S147.50E
Port Arthur U.S.A. 83 29.55N 93.55W
Port Augusta Australia 66 32.30S137.46E
Port au Port Canada 77 48.33N 58.45W
Port-au-Prince Haiti 87 18.33N 72.20W
Port Austin U.S.A. 84 44.04N 82.59W
Port Bergé Madagascar 57 15.33S 47.40E
Port Blair India 34 11.40N 92.40E
Portbou Spain 16 42.25N 3.09E
Port Bouet Ivory Coast 52 5.14N 3.58W
Port Bradshaw b. Australia 64 12.30S136.42E
Port Broughton Australia 66 33.36S137.56E
Port Campbell Australia 66 38.37S143.04E
Port Canning India 41 22.18N 88.40E
Port Cartier Canada 77 50.01N 66.53W
Port Chalmers New Zealand 60 45.49S170.37E
Port Chester U.S.A. 85 41.00N 73.40W
Port Colborne Canada 76 42.53N 79.14W
Port Coquitlam Canada 74 49.20N122.45W
Port Credit Canada 76 43.33N 79.35W
Port Curtis Australia 64 23.50S151.13E
Port Dalhousie Canada 76 43.12N 79.16W
Port-de-Paix Haiti 87 19.57N 72.50W
Port Dover Canada 76 42.47N 80.12W
Port Edward R.S.A. 56 31.03S 30.13E
Portela Brazil 94 21.38S 41.59W
Port Elizabeth R.S.A. 56 33.57S 25.34E
Port Ellen U.K. 12 55.38N 6.12W
Port-en-Bessin France 15 49.21N 0.45W
Port Erin I.o.M. Europe 10 54.05N 4.45W
Porter Landing Canada 74 58.46N130.05W
Porterville R.S.A. 56 33.01S 19.00E
Porterville U.S.A. 81 36.04N119.01W
Port Fairy Australia 66 38.23S142.17E
Port Gentil Gabon 54 0.40S 8.46E
Port Germein Australia 66 33.01S138.00E
Port Gibson U.S.A. 83 31.58N 90.58W
Portglenone U.K. 13 54.52N 6.30W
Port Harcourt Nigeria 53 4.43N 7.05E
Port Harrison see Inukjuak Canada 73
Port Hawkesbury Canada 77 45.37N 61.21W
Porthcawl U.K. 11 51.28N 3.42W
Port Hedland Australia 62 20.24S118.36E
Port Henry U.S.A. 84 44.03N 73.28W
Porthill U.S.A. 80 49.00N116.30W
Porthmadog U.K. 10 52.55N 4.08W
Port Hope Canada 76 43.57N 78.18W
Port Huron U.S.A. 84 42.59N 82.28W
Portimão Portugal 16 37.08N 8.32W
Port Isaac B. U.K. 11 50.36N 4.50W
Portiţei, Gura f. Romania 19 44.40N 29.00E
Port Jervis U.S.A. 85 41.22N 74.40W
Port Keats Australia 62 14.15S129.35E
Port Kembla Australia 67 34.28S150.54E
Port Kenny Australia 66 33.09S134.42E
Portland N.S.W. Australia 67 33.20S150.00E
Portland Vic. Australia 66 38.21S141.38E
Portland Maine U.S.A. 84 43.39N 70.17W
Portland Oreg. U.S.A. 80 45.33N122.36W
Portland Tex. U.S.A. 83 27.53N 97.20W
Portland Pt. Ascension 95 7.58S 14.26W
Port-la-Nouvelle France 17 43.01N 3.03E
Port Laoise Rep. of Ire. 13 53.03N 7.20W
Port Lavaca U.S.A. 83 28.37N 96.38W
Port Lincoln Australia 66 34.43S135.49E
Port Loko Sierra Leone 52 8.50N 12.50W
Port MacDonnell Australia 66 38.03S140.46E
Port Macquarie Australia 67 31.28S152.25E
Port Maitland N.S. Canada 77 43.59N 66.09W
Port Maitland Ont. Canada 76 42.52N 79.34W
Portmarnock Rep. of Ire. 13 53.25N 6.09W
Port Menier Canada 77 49.49N 64.20W
Port Moresby P.N.G. 64 9.30S147.07E
Port Musgrave b. Australia 64 11.59S142.00E
Portnaguiran U.K. 12 58.15N 6.10W
Port Neill Australia 66 34.07S136.20E
Port Nelson Canada 75 57.03N 92.36W
Port Nolloth R.S.A. 56 29.16S 16.54E
Port Norris U.S.A. 85 39.15N 75.02W
Porto Portugal 16 41.09N 8.37W
Pôrto Alegre Brazil 94 30.03S 51.10W
Porto Amboim Angola 54 10.45S 13.43E
Pôrto de Moz Brazil 91 1.45S 52.13W
Pôrto Esperança Brazil 94 19.36S 57.24W
Pôrto Feliz Brazil 94 23.11S 47.32W
Portoferraio Italy 18 42.49N 10.19E
Port of Ness U.K. 12 58.30N 6.13W
Pôrto Franco Brazil 91 6.21S 47.25W
Port of Spain Trinidad 87 10.38N 61.31W
Porto Grande Brazil 91 0.42N 51.24W
Portogruaro Italy 15 45.47N 12.50E
Pörtom Finland 22 62.42N 21.37E
Portomaggiore Italy 15 44.42N 11.48E
Porto Moniz Madeira Is. 95 32.52N 17.12W
Pôrto Murtinho Brazil 94 21.42S 57.52W
Porton U.K. 11 51.08N 1.44W
Pôrto Nacional Brazil 91 10.42S 48.25W
Porto-Novo Benin 53 6.30N 2.47E
Pôrto Primavera, Represa resr. Brazil 94 21.50S 52.00W
Porto San Giorgio Italy 18 43.11N 13.48E
Porto Santo i. Madeira Is. 50 33.04N 16.20W
Porto Tolle Italy 15 44.56N 12.22E
Porto Torres Italy 18 40.49N 8.24E
Pôrto Valter Brazil 90 8.15S 72.45W
Porto Vecchio France 17 41.35N 9.16E
Pôrto Velho Brazil 90 8.45S 63.54W
Portoviejo Ecuador 90 1.07S 80.28W
Portpatrick U.K. 12 54.51N 5.07W
Port Phillip B. Australia 67 38.05S144.50E
Port Pirie Australia 66 33.11S138.01E
Port Radium Canada 72 66.05N118.02W
Portree U.K. 12 57.24N 6.12W
Port Renfrew Canada 74 48.30N124.20W
Port Rupert see Waskaganish Canada 76
Portrush U.K. 13 55.12N 6.40W
Port Said see Bûr Sa'îd Egypt 44
Port Saunders Canada 77 50.39N 57.18W
Portsea Australia 67 38.19S144.43E
Port Shepstone R.S.A. 56 30.44S 30.27E
Port Simpson Canada 74 54.32N130.25W
Portsmouth U.K. 11 50.48N 1.06W
Portsmouth N.H. U.S.A. 84 43.04N 70.46W
Portsmouth Ohio U.S.A. 84 38.45N 82.59W
Portsmouth Va. U.S.A. 85 36.50N 76.20W
Portsoy U.K. 12 57.41N 2.41W
Port Stanley Canada 84 42.40N 81.13W
Portstewart U.K. 13 55.11N 6.43W
Port St. Joe U.S.A. 85 29.49N 85.19W
Port St. Louis France 17 43.25N 4.40E
Port Sudan see Bûr Sûdân Sudan 48
Port Talbot U.K. 11 51.35N 3.48W
Porttipahdan tekojärvi resr. Finland 22 68.08N 26.40E
Port Townsend U.S.A. 80 48.07N122.46W
Portugal Europe 16 39.30N 8.05W
Portumna Rep. of Ire. 9 53.06N 8.14W
Port Vendres France 17 42.31N 3.06E
Port Victoria Australia 66 34.30S137.30E
Port Wakefield Australia 66 34.12S138.11E
Port Warrender Australia 62 14.30S125.50E
Porvenir Chile 93 53.18S 70.22W
Porz Germany 14 50.53N 7.05E
Posada Italy 18 40.38N 9.43E
Posadas Argentina 92 27.25S 55.48W
Poschiavo Switz. 15 46.18N 10.04E
Posht r. Iran 43 29.09N 58.09E
Poso Indonesia 37 1.23S120.45E
Posse Brazil 94 14.05S 46.22W
Post U.S.A. 83 33.12N101.23W
Postavy Lithuania 24 55.07N 26.50E
Poste Maurice Cortier Algeria 50 22.18N 1.05E
Poste Weygand Algeria 50 24.29N 0.40E
Postmasburg R.S.A. 56 28.19S 23.03E
Postojna Slovenia 20 45.47N 14.13E
Postoli Belorussia 21 52.30N 28.00E
Potchefstroom R.S.A. 56 26.42S 27.05E
Poteau U.S.A. 83 35.03N 94.37W
Potenza Italy 18 40.40N 15.47E
Potgietersrus R.S.A. 56 24.11S 29.00E
Poti r. Brazil 91 5.01S 42.48W
Poti Georgia 25 42.11N 41.41E
Potiskum Nigeria 53 11.40N 11.03E
Potomac r. U.S.A. 85 38.00N 76.18W
Potosí Bolivia 92 19.35S 65.45W
Potosí d. Bolivia 92 21.00S 67.00W
Potosi Cerro mtn. Mexico 83 24.50N100.15W
Pototan Phil. 37 10.54N122.38E
Potsdam Germany 20 52.24N 13.04E
Potsdam U.S.A. 84 44.40N 74.59W
Pottstown U.S.A. 85 40.15N 75.38W
Pouancé France 15 47.47N 1.11W
Poughkeepsie U.S.A. 85 41.43N 73.56W
Pouso Alegre Brazil 94 22.13S 45.49W
Pouté Senegal 50 15.42N 14.10W
Poûthisăt Cambodia 34 12.27N103.50E
Povenets Russian Fed. 24 62.52N 34.05E
Póvoa de Varzim Portugal 16 41.22N 8.46W
Povorino Russian Fed. 25 51.12N 42.15E
Powder r. U.S.A. 80 46.44N105.26W
Powder River town U.S.A. 80 43.03N106.58W
Powell U.S.A. 80 44.45N108.46W
Powell, L. U.S.A. 80 37.25N110.45W
Powell River town Canada 74 49.22N124.31W
Powers U.S.A. 76 45.42N 87.31W
Powers Lake town U.S.A. 82 48.34N102.39W
Powys d. U.K. 11 52.26N 3.26W
Poyang Hu l. China 33 29.10N116.20E
Požarevac Yugo. 21 44.38N 21.12E
Poza Rica de Hidalgo Mexico 86 20.34N 97.26W
Poznań Poland 20 52.25N 16.53E
Pozoblanco Spain 16 38.23N 4.51W
Prachin Buri Thailand 34 14.02N101.23E
Prachuap Khiri Khan Thailand 34 11.50N 99.49E
Pradera Colombia 90 3.23N 76.11W
Prades France 17 42.38N 2.25E
Praestö Denmark 23 55.07N 12.03E
Prague see Praha Czech Republic 20
Praha Czech Republic 20 50.05N 14.25E
Prainha Amazonas Brazil 90 7.16S 60.23W
Prainha Para Brazil 91 1.48S 53.29W
Prairie City U.S.A. 80 44.28N118.43W
Prairie du Chien town U.S.A. 82 43.03N 91.09W
Prairie Village U.S.A. 82 39.01N 94.38W
Prang Ghana 52 8.02N 0.58W
Pratāpgarh India 40 24.02N 74.47E
Prato Italy 15 43.52N 11.06E
Pratt U.S.A. 83 37.39N 98.44W
Pravia Spain 16 43.30N 6.12W
Predazzo Italy 15 46.19N 11.36E
Pré-en-Pail France 15 48.27N 0.12W
Preesall U.K. 10 53.55N 2.58W
Pregel r. Russian Fed. 21 54.41N 20.22E
Premer Australia 67 31.26S149.54E
Premier Canada 74 56.04N129.56W
Prentice U.S.A. 82 45.33N 90.17W
Prenzlau Germany 20 53.19N 13.52E
Preparis i. Burma 34 14.51N 93.38E
Přerov Czech Republic 21 49.27N 17.27E
Prescott Ariz. U.S.A. 81 34.33N112.28W
Prescott Ark. U.S.A. 83 33.48N 93.23W
Presho U.S.A. 82 43.54N100.04W
Presidencia Roque Sáenz Peña Argentina 92 26.50S 60.30W
Presidente Epitácio Brazil 94 21.56S 52.07W
Presidente Hermes Brazil 92 11.17S 61.55W
Presidente Prudente Brazil 94 22.09S 51.24W
Presidio U.S.A. 83 29.33N104.23W
Prešov Slovakia 21 49.00N 21.15E
Prespa, L. Albania / Greece / Macedonia 19 40.53N 21.02E
Presque Isle town U.S.A. 84 46.41N 68.01W
Prestea Ghana 52 5.26N 2.07W
Presteigne U.K. 11 52.17N 3.00W
Preston U.K. 10 53.46N 2.42W
Preston Idaho U.S.A. 80 42.06N111.53W
Preston Minn. U.S.A. 82 43.40N 92.04W
Prestonpans U.K. 12 55.57N 3.00W
Prestwick U.K. 12 55.30N 4.36W
Prêto r. Brazil 94 22.00S 43.21W
Pretoria R.S.A. 56 25.43S 28.11E
Préveza Greece 19 38.58N 20.43E
Prey Vêng Cambodia 34 11.29N105.19E
Priboj Yugo. 19 43.35N 19.31E
Příbram Czech Republic 20 49.42N 14.00E
Price Md. U.S.A. 85 39.06N 75.58W
Price Utah U.S.A. 80 39.36N110.48W
Prichard U.S.A. 83 30.44N 88.07W
Prieska R.S.A. 56 29.40S 22.43E
Prijedor Bosnia-Herzegovina 19 44.59N 16.43E
Prikaspiyskaya Nizmennost see Caspian Depression ion Russian Fed. / Kazakhstan 25
Prilep Macedonia 19 41.20N 21.32E
Priluki Russian Fed. 24 63.05N 42.05E
Priluki Ukraine 25 50.35N 32.24E
Primorsk Russian Fed. 24 60.18N 28.35E
Primorskiy Russian Fed. 35 43.10N131.40E
Primrose L. Canada 75 54.55N109.45W
Primstal Germany 14 49.33N 6.59E
Prince Albert Canada 75 53.12N105.46W
Prince Albert R.S.A. 56 33.14S 22.02E
Prince Albert Nat. Park Canada 75 54.00N106.25W
Prince Albert Sd. Canada 72 70.25N115.00W
Prince Alfred C. Canada 72 74.30N125.00W
Prince Charles I. Canada 73 67.50N 76.00W
Prince Edward Island d. Canada 77 46.45N 63.00W
Prince Frederick U.S.A. 85 38.33N 76.35W
Prince George Canada 74 53.50N122.50W
Prince of Wales, C. U.S.A. 72 66.00N168.30W
Prince of Wales I. Australia 64 10.40S142.10E
Prince of Wales I. Canada 73 73.00N 99.00W
Prince of Wales I. U.S.A. 74 55.00N132.30W
Prince Patrick I. Canada 72 77.00N120.00W
Prince Regent Inlet str. Canada 73 73.00N 90.30W
Prince Rupert Canada 74 54.09N130.20W
Princess Charlotte B. Australia 64 14.25S144.00E
Princess Royal I. Canada 74 53.00N128.40W
Princeton Ind. U.S.A. 84 38.21N 87.33W
Princeton Ky. U.S.A. 85 37.06N 87.55W
Princeton Mo. U.S.A. 82 40.24N 93.35W
Princeton N.J. U.S.A. 85 40.21N 74.40W
Príncipe i. São Tomé & Príncipe 53 1.37N 7.27E
Príncipe da Beira Brazil 90 12.23S 64.28W
Prinzapolca Nicaragua 87 13.19N 83.35W
Priozersk Russian Fed. 24 61.01N 30.08E
Pripet r. Europe 21 51.08N 30.30E
Pripet Marshes see Polesye f. Belorussia 21
Pripyat r. Belorussia see Pripet r. Europe 21
Priština Yugo. 19 42.39N 21.10E
Pritzwalk Germany 20 53.09N 12.10E
Privas France 20 44.44N 4.36E
Privolzhskaya Vozvyshennost f. Russian Fed. 24 53.15N 45.45E
Prizren Yugo. 19 42.13N 20.42E
Probolinggo Indonesia 37 7.45S113.09E
Proddatūr India 39 14.44N 78.33E
Progreso Mexico 87 21.20N 89.40W
Prokopyevsk Russian Fed. 28 53.55N 86.45E
Prome see Pyè Burma 34
Prophet r. Canada 74 58.48N122.40W
Propriá Brazil 91 10.15S 36.51W
Proserpine Australia 64 20.24S148.34E
Prostějov Czech Republic 21 49.29N 17.07E
Protection U.S.A. 83 37.12N 99.29W
Provence-Côte d'Azur d. France 17 43.45N 6.00E
Providence U.S.A. 84 41.50N 71.25W
Providence Mts. U.S.A. 81 34.55N115.35W
Providencia, Isla de i. Colombia 87 13.21N 81.22W
Provins France 15 48.34N 3.18E
Provo U.S.A. 80 40.14N111.39W
Prozor Bosnia-Herzegovina 21 43.49N 17.37E
Prudhoe Bay town U.S.A. 72 70.20N148.25W
Prüm Germany 14 50.12N 6.25E
Prüm r. Germany 14 49.50N 6.29E
Pruszcz Gdański Poland 21 54.17N 18.40E
Pruszków Poland 21 52.11N 20.48E
Prut r. Romania / Ukraine 21 45.29N 28.14E
Pruzhany Belorussia 21 52.23N 24.28E
Prydz B. Antarctica 96 68.30S 74.00E
Pryor U.S.A. 83 36.19N 95.19W
Przemyśl Poland 21 49.48N 22.48E
Przeworsk Poland 21 50.05N 22.29E
Przhevalsk Kyrgyzstan 30 42.31N 78.22E
Psará i. Greece 19 38.34N 25.35E
Psel r. Ukraine 25 49.00N 33.30E
Pskov Russian Fed. 24 57.48N 28.00E
Pskovskoye, Ozero l. Russian Fed. 24 58.00N 27.55E
Ptich Belorussia 21 52.15N 28.49E
Ptich r. Belorussia 21 52.09N 28.52E
Ptolemaís Greece 19 40.31N 21.41E
Puán Argentina 93 37.30S 62.45W
Pu'an China 33 25.47N104.57E
Puapua W. Samoa 68 13.34S172.12W
Pucallpa Peru 90 8.21S 74.33W
Pucarani Bolivia 92 16.23S 68.30W
Pucheng China 33 27.56N118.32E
Pudasjärvi Finland 22 65.25N 26.50E
Pūdeh Tal r. Afghan. 40 31.00N 61.50E
Pudozh Russian Fed. 24 61.50N 36.32E
Pudozhgora Russian Fed. 24 62.18N 35.54E
Puebla Mexico 86 19.03N 98.10W
Puebla d. Mexico 86 18.30N 98.00W
Pueblo U.S.A. 80 38.16N104.37W
Pueblo Hundido Chile 92 26.23S 70.03W
Puelches Argentina 93 38.09S 65.58W
Puelén Argentina 93 37.32S 67.38W
Puente Alta Chile 93 33.37S 70.35W
Puente-Genil Spain 16 37.24N 4.46W
Puerto Aisén Chile 93 45.27S 72.58W
Puerto Ángel Mexico 86 15.40N 96.29W
Puerto Armuelles Panama 87 8.19N 82.15W
Puerto Ayacucho Venezuela 90 5.39N 67.32W
Puerto Barrios Guatemala 87 15.41N 88.32W
Puerto Bermúdez Peru 90 10.20S 75.00W
Puerto Berrío Colombia 90 6.28N 74.28W
Puerto Cabello Venezuela 90 10.29N 68.02W
Puerto Cabezas Nicaragua 87 14.02N 83.24W
Puerto Carreño Colombia 90 6.08N 67.27W
Puerto Casado Paraguay 92 22.20S 57.55W
Puerto Coig Argentina 93 50.54S 69.15W
Puerto Cortés Costa Rica 87 8.58N 83.32W
Puerto Cortés Honduras 87 15.50N 87.55W
Puerto de Nutrias Venezuela 90 8.07N 69.18W
Puerto de Santa Maria Spain 16 36.36N 6.14W
Puerto Heath Bolivia 90 12.30S 68.40W
Puerto Juárez Mexico 87 21.26N 86.51W
Puerto La Cruz Venezuela 90 10.14N 64.40W
Puerto Leguízamo Colombia 90 0.12S 74.46W
Puertollano Spain 16 38.41N 4.07W
Puerto Lobos Argentina 93 42.01S 65.04W
Puerto Madryn Argentina 93 42.46S 65.02W
Puerto Maldonado Peru 90 12.37S 69.11W
Puerto Melendez Peru 90 4.30S 77.30W
Puerto Montt Chile 93 41.28S 73.00W
Puerto Natales Chile 93 51.44S 72.31W
Puerto Páez Venezuela 90 6.13N 67.28W
Puerto Peñasco Mexico 81 31.20N113.33W
Puerto Pinasco Paraguay 94 22.36S 57.53W
Puerto Plata Dom. Rep. 87 19.48N 70.41W
Puerto Princesa Phil. 36 9.46N118.45E
Puerto Quepos Costa Rica 87 9.28N 84.10W
Puerto Rey Colombia 90 8.48N 76.34W
Puerto Rico C. America 87 18.20N 66.30W
Puerto Rico Trench Atlantic Oc. 87 19.50N 66.00W
Puerto Saavedra Chile 93 38.47S 73.24W
Puerto Santa Cruz Argentina 93 50.03S 68.35W
Puerto Sastre Paraguay 94 22.02S 58.00W
Puerto Siles Bolivia 92 12.48S 65.05W
Puerto Tejado Colombia 90 3.16N 76.22W
Puerto Vallarta Mexico 86
Puerto Varas Chile 93 41.20S 73.00W
Pugachev Russian Fed. 24 52.02N 48.49E
Puglia d. Italy 19 41.00N 16.40E
Puisaye, Collines de la hills France 15 47.34N 3.28E
Pujehun Sierra Leone 52 7.23N 11.44W
Pukaki, L. New Zealand 60 44.00S170.10E
Pukatawagan Canada 75 55.45N101.20W
Pukekohe New Zealand 60 37.12S174.56E
Pukeuri New Zealand 60 45.02S171.02E
Pukhovichi Belorussia 21 53.28N 28.18E
Pula Croatia 20 44.52N 13.53E
Pulacayo Bolivia 92 20.25S 66.41W
Pulaski Tenn. U.S.A. 85 35.11N 87.02W
Pulaski Va. U.S.A. 85 37.03N 80.47W
Puławy Poland 21 51.25N 21.57E
Pulgaon India 41 20.44N 78.20E
Pulkkila Finland 22 64.16N 25.52E
Pullman U.S.A. 80 46.44N117.10W
Pulog mtn. Phil. 37 16.50N120.50E
Pulozero Russian Fed. 24 68.22N 33.15E
Pulpito, Punta c. Mexico 81 26.31N111.28W
Pułtusk Poland 21 52.42N 21.02E
Puma Tanzania 55 5.02S 34.46E
Puma Yumco l. China 41 28.35N 90.20E
Punaauia Tahiti 69 17.38S149.36W
Punakha Bhutan 41 27.37N 89.52E
Puncak Jaya mtn. Indonesia 37 4.00S137.15E
Pūnch Jammu & Kashmir 40 33.46N 74.06E
Pune India 38 18.34N 73.58E
Punjab d. India 40 30.45N 75.30E
Punjab d. Pakistan 40 30.25N 72.30E
Puno Peru 90 15.53S 70.03W
Punta Alta town Argentina 93 38.50S 62.00W
Punta Arenas town Chile 93 53.10S 70.56W
Puntabie Australia 66 32.15S134.13E
Punta Delgada town Argentina 93 42.43S 63.38W
Punta Gorda town Belize 87 16.10N 88.45W
Punta Gorda town U.S.A. 85 26.56N 82.01W
Puntarenas Costa Rica 87 10.00N 84.50W
Punto Fijo Venezuela 90 11.50N 70.16W
Puolanka Finland 22 64.52N 27.40E
Puqi China 33 29.40N113.52E
Puquio Peru 90 14.44S 74.07W
Pur r. Russian Fed. 28 67.30N 75.30E
Pūranpur India 41 28.31N 80.09E
Purari r. P.N.G. 37 7.49S145.10E
Purcell U.S.A. 83 35.01N 97.22W
Purgatoire r. U.S.A. 80 38.04N103.10W
Puri India 41 19.48N 85.51E
Purisima, Sierra de la mts. Mexico 83 26.28N101.45W
Purli India 40 18.51N 76.32E
Pūrna r. India 40 19.07N 77.02E
Purnea India 41 25.47N 87.31E
Purros Namibia 56 18.38S 12.59E
Purūlia India 41 23.20N 86.22E
Purus r. Brazil 90 3.58S 61.25W
Purwakarta Indonesia 37 6.30S107.25E
Purwodadi Indonesia 37 7.05S110.53E
Purwokerto Indonesia 37 7.28S109.09E
Purworejo Indonesia 37 7.45S110.04E
Pusad India 41 19.54N 77.35E
Pusan S. Korea 31 35.05N129.02E
Pushkar India 40 26.30N 74.33E
Pushkin Russian Fed. 24 59.43N 30.22E
Pushkino Russian Fed. 25 51.16N 47.09E
Püspökladány Hungary 21 47.19N 21.07E
Pustoshka Russian Fed. 24 56.20N 29.20E
Putao Burma 34 27.22N 97.27E
Putaruru New Zealand 60 38.03S175.47E
Putian China 33 25.29N119.04E
Puting, Tanjung c. Indonesia 36 3.35S111.52E
Putorana, Gory mts. Russian Fed. 29 68.30N 96.00E
Putsonderwater R.S.A. 56 29.14S 21.50E
Puttalam Sri Lanka 39 8.02N 79.50E
Puttgarden Germany 20 54.30N 11.13E
Putumayo r. Brazil 90 3.05S 68.10W
Puulavesi l. Finland 23 61.50N 26.42E
Puyallup U.S.A. 80 47.11N122.18W
Puyang China 32 35.40N115.02E
Puy de Dôme mtn. France 17 45.46N 2.56E
Puysegur Pt. New Zealand 60 46.10S166.35E
Pūzak, Jehīl-e l. Afghan. 40 31.30N 61.45E
Pwani d. Tanzania 55 7.00S 39.00E
Pweto Zaïre 55 8.27S 28.52E
Pwllheli U.K. 10 52.53N 4.25W
Pyaozero, Ozero l. Russian Fed. 24 66.00N 31.00E
Pyapon Burma 34 16.15N 95.40E
Pyasina r. Russian Fed. 29 73.10N 84.55E
Pyatigorsk Russian Fed. 25 44.04N 43.06E
Pyè Burma 34 18.50N 95.14E
Pyhä r. Finland 22 64.28N 24.13E
Pyhäjärvi l. Oulu Finland 22 63.35N 25.57E
Pyhäjärvi l. Turku-Pori Finland 23 61.00N 22.20E
Pyhäjoki Finland 22 64.28N 24.14E
Pyinmana Burma 34 19.45N 96.12E
Pyongyang N. Korea 31 39.00N125.47E
Pyramid U.S.A. 80 40.05N119.43W
Pyramid Hill town Australia 66 36.03S144.24E
Pyramid Hills Canada 77 57.35N 65.00W
Pyramid L. U.S.A. 80 40.00N119.35W
Pyramids Egypt 48 29.52N 31.00E
Pyrénées mts. France / Spain 17 42.40N 0.30E
Pyrzyce Poland 20 53.10N 14.55E
Pytteggja mtn. Norway 23 62.13N 7.42E
Pyu Burma 34 18.29N 96.26E

Q

Qaanaaq see Thule Greenland 73
Qā'emshahr Iran 43 36.28N 52.53E
Qagan Nur l. China 32 43.30N114.35E
Qagbasêrag China 41 30.51N 92.42E
Qagcaka China 41 32.32N 81.52E
Qahā Egypt 44 30.17N 31.12E
Qalāt Afghan. 40 32.07N 66.54E
Qal'at Bīshah Saudi Arabia 48 19.50N 42.36E
Qal 'eh Kāh Afghan. 40 32.18N 61.31E
Qal'eh-ye Now Afghan. 43 34.58N 63.04E
Qal'eh-ye Sāber Afghan. 40 34.02N 69.01E
Qallābāt Sudan 49 12.58N 36.09E
Qalyūb Egypt 44 30.11N 31.12E
Qamar, Ghubbat al b. Yemen 45 16.00N 52.30E
Qamdo China 30 31.11N 97.18E
Qamīnis Libya 48 31.40N 20.01E
Qamr-ud-dīn Kārez Pakistan 40 31.39N 68.25E
Qanâtir Muhammad 'Alî Egypt 44 30.12N 31.08E
Qandahār Afghan. 40 31.32N 65.30E
Qandahār d. Afghan. 40 31.00N 65.45E
Qandala Somali Rep. 45 11.23N 49.53E
Qaqortoq see Julianehåb Greenland 73
Qarā, Jabal al mts. Oman 45 17.15N 54.15E
Qārah Egypt 42 27.37N 26.30E
Qārat Khazzī hill Libya 48 21.26N 24.30E
Qardho Somali Rep. 45 9.30N 49.03E
Qareh Sū Iran 43 34.52N 51.25E
Qareh Sū r. Iran 43 35.58N 56.25E
Qarqan He r. China 30 40.56N 86.27E
Qārūn, Birkat l. Egypt 44 29.30N 30.40E
Qaryat al Qaddāḥīyah Libya 51 31.22N 15.14E
Qash r. Sudan 48 16.48N 35.51E
Qasigianguit see Christianshåb Greenland 73
Qaşr al Farāfirah Egypt 42 27.15N 28.10E
Qaşr al Qarābūllī Libya 51 32.45N 13.43E
Qaşr-e Qand Iran 43 26.13N 60.37E
Qa'ṭabah Yemen 45 13.51N 44.42E
Qaṭanā Syria 44 33.27N 36.04E
Qatar Asia 43 25.20N 51.10E

Qaţrānī, Jabal to **Renner Springs**

Qaţrānī, Jabal *mts.* Egypt **44** 29.40N 30.36E
Qattara Depression *see* Qaţţa-rah, Munkhafaḑ al *f.* Egypt **42**
Qaţţārah, Munkhafaḑ al *f.* Egypt **42** 29.40N 27.30E
Qawz Rajab Sudan **48** 16.04N 35.34E
Qāyen Iran **43** 33.44N 59.07E
Qaysān Sudan **49** 10.45N 34.48E
Qāzigund Jammu & Kashmir **40** 33.38N 75.09E
Qazvin Iran **43** 36.16N 50.00E
Qeqertarsuaq *see* Godhavn Greenland **73**
Qeqertarsuatsiaat *see* Fiskenaesset Greenland **73**
Qeshm Iran **43** 26.58N 57.17E
Qeshm *i.* Iran **43** 26.48N 55.48E
Qezel Owzan *r.* Iran **43** 36.44N 49.27E
Qezi'ot Israel **44** 30.52N 34.28E
Qian'an China **32** 45.00N124.00E
Qianjiang China **33** 29.28N108.43E
Qianxi China **32** 40.10N118.19E
Qianyang China **33** 27.22N110.14E
Qiaotou China **32** 42.56N118.54E
Qidong Hunan China **33** 26.47N112.07E
Qidong Jiangsu China **33** 31.49N121.40E
Qiemo China **30** 38.08N 85.33E
Qijiang China **33** 29.00N106.40E
Qila Abdullāh Pakistan **40** 30.43N 66.38E
Qila Lādgasht Pakistan **40** 27.54N 62.57E
Qila Saifullāh Pakistan **40** 30.43N 68.21E
Qilian Shan *mts.* China **30** 38.30N 99.20E
Qimantag *mts.* China **30** 37.45N 89.40E
Qimen China **33** 29.50N117.38E
Qinā Egypt **42** 26.10N 32.43E
Qinā, Wādī *r.* Egypt **42** 26.07N 32.42E
Qingdao China **32** 36.02N120.25E
Qinghai *d.* China **41** 34.20N 91.00E
Qinghai Hu *l.* China **30** 36.40N100.00E
Qingjian China **32** 37.02N110.06E
Qingjiang China **33** 28.01N115.30E
Qing Jiang Shuiku *resr.* China **33** 30.00N112.12E
Qinglong Guizhou China **33** 25.47N105.12E
Qinglong Hebei China **32** 40.24N118.53E
Qingshui Jiang *r.* China **33** 28.08N110.06E
Qing Xian China **32** 38.35N116.48E
Qingxu China **32** 37.36N112.21E
Qingyang China **32** 36.03N107.52E
Qingyuan Guangdong China **33** 23.42N113.00E
Qingyuan Jilin China **32** 42.05N125.01E
Qingyuan Zhejiang China **33** 27.37N119.03E
Qing Zang Gaoyuan *f.* China **30** 33.40N 86.00E
Qinhuangdao China **32** 39.52N119.42E
Qin Ling *mts.* China **32** 33.30N109.00E
Qin Xian China **32** 36.45N112.41E
Qinyang China **32** 35.06N112.57E
Qinzhou China **33** 21.58N108.34E
Qionghai China **33** 19.12N110.31E
Qiongshan China **33** 19.59N110.30E
Qiongzhou Haixia *str.* China **33** 20.09N110.20E
Qipanshan China **32** 42.05N117.37E
Qiqihar China **31** 47.23N124.00E
Qira China **30** 37.02N 80.53E
Qiryat Ata Israel **44** 32.48N 35.06E
Qiryat Gat Israel **44** 31.37N 34.47E
Qiryat Shemona Israel **44** 33.13N 35.35E
Qishn Yemen **38** 15.25N 51.40E
Qiuxizhen China **33** 29.54N104.40E
Qi Xian Henan China **32** 34.30N114.50E
Qi Xian Henan China **32** 35.35N114.08E
Qom Iran **43** 34.40N 50.57E
Qonggyai China **41** 29.03N 91.41E
Qornet'es Sauda *mtn.* Lebanon **44** 34.17N 36.04E
Qoţūr Iran **43** 38.28N 44.25E
Quairading Australia **63** 32.00S117.22E
Quakenbrück Germany **14** 52.41N 7.59E
Quakertown U.S.A. **85** 40.26N 75.21W
Qu'ali China **33** 29.46N117.15E
Quambatook Australia **66** 35.52S143.36E
Quambone Australia **67** 30.54S147.55E
Quang Ngai Vietnam **34** 15.09N108.50E
Quang Tri Vietnam **34** 16.44N107.10E
Quang Yen Vietnam **34** 20.56N106.49E
Quan Long Vietnam **34** 9.11N105.09E
Quannan China **33** 24.45N114.32E
Quantico U.S.A. **85** 38.31N 77.17W
Quanzhou Fujian China **33** 24.57N118.36E
Quanzhou Guang. Zhuang. China **33** 26.00N111.00E
Qu'Appelle *r.* Canada **75** 50.33N101.20W
Quaqtaq Canada **73** 61.05N 69.36W
Quaraí Brazil **93** 30.23S 56.27W
Quaraí *r.* Brazil **93** 30.12S 57.36W
Quarryville U.S.A. **85** 39.54N 76.10W
Quartu Sant'Elena Italy **18** 39.14N 9.11E
Quartzsite U.S.A. **81** 33.40N114.13W
Quatsino Sd. Canada **74** 50.42N127.58W
Qūchān Iran **43** 37.04N 58.29E
Queanbeyan Australia **67** 35.24S149.17E
Québec Canada **77** 46.50N 71.15W
Québec *d.* Canada **77** 51.20N 68.45W
Quebracho Uruguay **93** 31.57S 57.53W
Quedlinburg Germany **20** 51.48N 11.09E
Queen Anne U.S.A. **85** 38.55N 75.57W
Queen Charlotte Canada **74** 53.18N132.04W
Queen Charlotte Is. Canada **74** 53.00N132.00W
Queen Charlotte Sd. Canada **74** 51.30N129.30W
Queen Charlotte Str. Canada **74** 51.00N128.00W
Queen Elizabeth Is. Canada **73** 78.30N 99.00W
Queen Maud G. Canada **73** 68.30N 99.00W
Queen Maud Range *mts.* Antarctica **96** 86.20S165.00W
Queens Channel Australia **62** 14.46S129.24E
Queenscliff Australia **67** 38.17S144.42E
Queensland *d.* Australia **64** 23.30S144.00E
Queenstown Australia **65** 42.07S145.33E
Queenstown New Zealand **60** 45.03S168.41E
Queenstown R.S.A. **56** 31.52S 26.51E
Queenstown U.S.A. **85** 38.59N 76.09W
Queguay Grande *r.* Uruguay **93** 32.09S 58.09W
Queimadas Brazil **91** 10.58S 39.38W
Quela Angola **54** 9.18S 17.05E
Quelimane Mozambique **55** 17.53S 36.57E
Quemado U.S.A. **81** 34.20N108.30W
Quemoy *i.* China **33** 24.30N118.20E
Quentico Prov. Park Canada **76** 48.20N 91.30W
Quequén Argentina **93** 38.34S 58.42W
Querétaro Mexico **86** 20.38N100.23W
Querétaro *d.* Mexico **86** 21.03N100.00W
Querobabi Mexico **81** 30.03N111.01W
Queshan China **32** 32.48N114.01E
Quesnel Canada **74** 53.05N122.30W
Quesnel *r.* Canada **74** 52.58N122.29W
Quetta Pakistan **40** 30.12N 67.00E
Quettehou France **15** 49.36N 1.18W
Quevedo Ecuador **90** 0.59S 79.27W
Quezaltenango Guatemala **86** 14.50N 91.30W
Quezon City Phil. **37** 14.39N121.01E
Quibala Angola **54** 10.48S 14.56E
Quibaxi Angola **54** 8.34S 14.37E
Quibdo Colombia **90** 5.40N 76.38W
Quiberon France **17** 47.29N 3.07W
Quibocolo Angola **54** 6.20S 15.05E
Quicama Nat. Park Angola **54** 9.40S 13.30E
Quiet L. Canada **74** 61.05N133.05W
Quilán, C. Chile **93** 43.16S 74.27W
Quilengues Angola **54** 14.09S 14.04E
Quillabamba Peru **90** 12.50S 72.50W
Quillacollo Bolivia **92** 17.26S 66.17W
Quillota Chile **93** 32.53S 71.16W
Quilpie Australia **64** 26.37S144.15E
Quilpué Chile **93** 33.03S 71.27W
Quimbele Angola **54** 6.29S 16.25E
Quimilí Argentina **92** 27.35S 62.25W
Quimper France **17** 48.00N 4.06W
Quimperlé France **17** 47.52N 3.33W
Quincy Ill. U.S.A. **82** 39.56N 91.23W
Quincy Wash. U.S.A. **80** 47.14N119.51W
Qui Nhon Vietnam **34** 13.47N109.11E
Quintanar de la Orden Spain **16** 39.36N 3.05W
Quintana Roo *d.* Mexico **87** 19.00N 88.00W
Quinter U.S.A. **82** 39.04N100.14W
Quinto Spain **16** 41.25N 0.30W
Quinzau Angola **54** 6.51S 12.46E
Quionga Mozambique **55** 10.37S 40.31E
Quirigua *ruins* Guatemala **87** 15.20N 89.25W
Quirimbo Angola **54** 10.41S 14.16E
Quirindi Australia **67** 31.30S150.42E
Quiros, C. Vanuatu **68** 14.55S167.01E
Quissanga Mozambique **55** 12.24S 40.33E
Quissico Mozambique **57** 24.42S 34.44E
Quitapa Angola **54** 10.10S 18.16E
Quiterajo Mozambique **55** 11.46S 40.25E
Quito Ecuador **90** 0.14S 78.30W
Qu Jiang *r.* China **33** 30.02N106.20E
Qumigxung China **41** 30.53N 86.38E
Quorn Australia **66** 32.20S138.02E
Qurayyah, Wādī *r.* Egypt **44** 30.26N 34.01E
Qurdūd Sudan **49** 10.17N 29.56E
Qurlurtuuq Canada **72** 67.49N115.12W
Qū' Wishām *f.* Oman **45** 18.55N 55.55E
Qu Xian China **33** 28.59N118.56E
Quxian China **33** 30.50N106.54E
Qüzü China **41** 29.21N 90.39E

R

Raahe Finland **22** 64.41N 24.29E
Raalte Neth. **14** 52.22N 6.17E
Raasay *i.* U.K. **12** 57.25N 6.05W
Raas Caseyr *c.* Somali Rep. **45** 11.48N 51.22E
Rába *r.* Hungary **21** 47.42N 17.38E
Raba Indonesia **36** 8.27S118.45E
Rabak Sudan **49** 13.09N 32.44E
Rabang China **41** 33.03N 80.29E
Rabat Morocco **50** 34.02N 6.51W
Rabbit Flat *town* Australia **62** 20.10S129.53E
Rabbitskin *r.* Canada **74** 61.47N120.42W
Rābor Iran **43** 29.18N 56.56E
Rabyānah Libya **48** 24.14N 21.59E
Rabyānah, Şaḩrā' *f.* Libya **51** 24.30N 21.00E
Racconigi Italy **15** 44.46N 9.46E
Race, C. Canada **77** 46.40N 53.10W
Rach Gia Vietnam **34** 10.02N105.05E
Racibórz Poland **21** 50.06N 18.13E
Racine U.S.A. **82** 42.42N 87.50W
Rădăuţi Romania **21** 47.51N 25.55E
Radebeul Germany **20** 51.06N 13.41E
Radekhov Ukraine **21** 50.18N 24.35E
Radford U.S.A. **85** 37.07N 80.34W
Rādhanpur India **40** 23.50N 71.36E
Radium Hill *town* Australia **66** 32.30S140.32E
Radium Hot Springs *town* Canada **74** 50.48N116.12W
Radom Poland **21** 51.26N 21.10E
Radomir Bulgaria **19** 42.32N 22.56E
Radomsko Poland **21** 51.05N 19.25E
Radomyshl Ukraine **21** 50.30N 29.14E
Radöy *i.* Norway **23** 60.38N 5.05E
Radstock U.K. **11** 51.17N 2.25W
Radstock, C. Australia **66** 33.11S134.21E
Radville Canada **75** 49.27N104.17W
Raḑwá, Jabal *mtn.* Saudi Arabia **42** 24.36N 38.18E
Rae Canada **74** 62.50N116.03W
Rāe Bareli India **41** 26.13N 81.14E
Raeren Germany **14** 50.41N 6.07E
Raeside, L. Australia **63** 29.30S122.00E
Rafaela Argentina **92** 31.16S 61.44W
Rafaḩ Egypt **44** 31.18N 34.15E
Rafaï C.A.R. **49** 4.58N 23.56E
Raffili Mission Sudan **49** 6.53N 27.58E
Rafsanjān Iran **43** 30.24N 56.00E
Rafsanjān Iran **38** 30.24N 56.00E
Raga Sudan **49** 8.28N 25.41E
Ragged, Mt. Australia **63** 33.27S123.27E
Ragunda Sweden **22** 63.06N 16.23E
Ragusa Italy **18** 36.56N 14.44E
Raha Indonesia **37** 4.50S122.43E
Raḩā, Ḩarrat ar *f.* Saudi Arabia **44** 28.00N 36.35E
Rahad *r.* Sudan **48** 14.28N 33.31E
Rahad al Bardī Sudan **49** 11.18N 23.53E
Rahim Ki Bāzār Pakistan **40** 24.19N 69.09E
Rahīmyār Khān Pakistan **40** 28.25N 70.18E
Raiatea *i.* Îs. de la Société **69** 16.50S151.25W
Rāichūr India **38** 16.15N 77.20E
Raiganj India **41** 25.37N 88.07E
Raigarh India **41** 21.54N 83.24E
Rainbow Australia **66** 35.56S142.01E
Rainelle U.S.A. **85** 37.58N 80.47W
Rainier, Mt. U.S.A. **80** 46.52N121.46W
Rainy L. Canada / U.S.A. **76** 48.42N 93.10W
Rainy River *town* Canada **76** 48.43N 94.29W
Raipur India **41** 21.14N 81.38E
Raipur Uplands *mts.* India **41** 20.45N 82.30E
Rairākhol India **41** 21.03N 84.23E
Ra's Saudi Arabia **42** 23.35N 38.36E
Raisen India **41** 23.20N 77.48E
Raivavae *i.* Pacific Oc. **69** 23.52S147.40W
Rājahmundry India **39** 17.01N 81.52E
Rajāj Sudan **49** 10.55N 24.43E
Rajang *r.* Malaysia **36** 2.10N112.45E
Rājanpur Pakistan **40** 29.06N 70.19E
Rājapālaiyam India **38** 9.26N 77.36E
Rājasthān *d.* India **40** 26.15N 74.00E
Rājasthān Canal India **40** 31.10N 75.00E
Rājbāri Bangla. **41** 23.46N 89.39E
Rāj Gāngpur India **41** 22.11N 84.36E
Rājgarh Madhya P. India **40** 23.56N 76.58E
Rājgarh Rāj. India **40** 28.38N 75.23E
Rājgarh Rāj. India **40** 27.14N 76.38E
Rājkot India **40** 22.18N 70.47E
Rāj-Nāndgaon India **41** 21.06N 81.02E
Rājpīpla India **40** 21.47N 73.34E
Rājpur India **40** 21.56N 75.08E
Rājshāhi Bangla. **41** 24.22N 88.36E
Rājula India **40** 21.01N 71.34E
Rakahanga Atoll Cook Is. **68** 10.03S161.06W
Rakaia New Zealand **60** 43.45S172.01E
Rakaia *r.* New Zealand **60** 43.52S172.13E
Raka Zangbo *r.* China **41** 29.24N 87.58E
Rakhni Pakistan **40** 30.03N 69.55E
Rakhov Ukraine **21** 48.02N 24.10E
Rakhshān *r.* Pakistan **40** 27.10N 63.25E
Rakitnoye Ukraine **21** 51.18N 27.10E
Rakops Botswana **56** 21.00S 24.32E
Rakov Belorussia **21** 53.58N 26.59E
Rakulka Russian Fed. **24** 62.19N 46.52E
Rakvåg Norway **22** 63.47N 10.10E
Rakvere Estonia **24** 59.22N 26.28E
Raleigh U.S.A. **85** 35.46N 78.39W
Raleigh B. U.S.A. **85** 35.47N 76.09W
Ralik Chain *is.* Pacific Oc. **68** 8.00N168.00E
Ram *r.* Canada **74** 62.01N123.41W
Rama Nicaragua **87** 12.09N 84.15W
Rāmah Saudi Arabia **43** 25.33N 47.08E
Rām Allāh Jordan **44** 31.55N 35.12E
Ramallo Argentina **93** 33.28S 60.02W
Rāmānuj Ganj India **41** 23.48N 83.42E
Ramat Gan Israel **44** 32.05N 34.48E
Rambau, Lac *l.* Canada **77** 53.40N 70.10W
Rambouillet France **15** 48.39N 1.50E
Rām Dās India **40** 31.58N 74.55E
Rame Head Australia **67** 37.50S149.25E
Rame Head U.K. **11** 50.18N 4.13W
Ramelton Rep. of Ire. **13** 55.02N 7.40W
Rāmgarh Bangla. **41** 22.59N 91.43E
Rāmgarh Bihār India **41** 23.38N 85.31E
Rāmgarh Rāj. India **40** 27.15N 75.11E
Rāmgarh Rāj. India **40** 27.22N 70.30E
Rāmhormoz Iran **43** 31.14N 49.37E
Ramillies Belgium **14** 50.39N 4.56E
Ramingstein Austria **20** 47.04N 13.50E
Ramis *r.* Ethiopia **49** 7.59N 41.34E
Ramla Israel **44** 31.56N 34.52E
Ramlu *mtn.* Ethiopia **49** 13.20N 41.45E
Rāmnagar India **41** 25.17N 83.02E
Ramo Ethiopia **49** 6.50N 41.15E
Ramona Calif. U.S.A. **81** 33.08N116.52W
Ramona Okla. U.S.A. **83** 36.32N 95.55W
Ramore Canada **76** 48.30N 80.25W
Ramos Arizpe Mexico **83** 25.33N100.58W
Rāmpur Himachal P. India **41** 31.27N 77.38E
Rāmpur Uttar P. India **41** 28.49N 79.02E
Rampura India **40** 24.28N 75.26E
Ramree I. Burma **34** 19.06N 93.48E
Ramsey I.o.M. Europe **10** 54.19N 4.23W
Ramsey England U.K. **11** 52.27N 0.06W
Ramsey L. Canada **76** 47.10N 82.18W
Ramsgate U.K. **11** 51.20N 1.25E
Rāmshīr Iran **43** 30.54N 49.24E
Ramsjö Sweden **23** 62.11N 15.39E
Rāmtek India **41** 21.24N 79.20E
Ramu *r.* P.N.G. **37** 4.00S144.40E
Ramusio, Lac *l.* Canada **77** 55.04N 63.40W
Ranau Malaysia **36** 5.58N116.41E
Rancagua Chile **93** 34.10S 70.45W
Rancheria *r.* Canada **74** 60.13N129.07W
Rānchī India **41** 23.21N 85.20E
Rand Australia **67** 35.34S146.35E
Randalstown U.K. **13** 54.45N 6.20W
Randburg R.S.A. **56** 26.07S 28.02E
Rānder India **40** 21.14N 72.47E
Randers Denmark **23** 56.28N 10.03E
Randolph U.S.A. **82** 39.27N 96.44W
Randsburg U.S.A. **81** 35.22N117.39W
Randsfjorden *l.* Norway **23** 60.25N 10.24E
Råne *r.* Sweden **22** 65.52N 22.19E
Råneå Sweden **22** 65.52N 22.18E
Rāner India **40** 28.53N 73.17E
Ranfurly New Zealand **60** 45.08S170.08E
Rangdong China **32** 32.51N112.18E
Rangely U.S.A. **80** 40.05N108.48W
Ranger U.S.A. **85** 38.07N 82.10W
Rangia India **41** 26.28N 91.38E
Rangiora New Zealand **60** 43.18S172.38E
Rangiroa *i.* Pacific Oc. **69** 15.00S147.40W
Rangitaiki *r.* New Zealand **60** 37.55S176.50E
Rangkasbitung Indonesia **37** 6.21S106.12E
Rangoon *see* Yangon Burma **34**
Rangpur Bangla. **41** 25.45N 89.15E
Rānīganj India **41** 23.37N 87.08E
Rānīkhet India **41** 29.39N 79.25E
Rāniwāra India **40** 24.45N 72.13E
Rankin Inlet *town* Canada **73** 62.52N 92.00W
Rankins Springs *town* Australia **67** 33.52S146.18E
Rannoch, Loch U.K. **12** 56.41N 4.20W
Rann of Kachchh *f.* India **40** 23.50N 69.50E
Ranohira Madagascar **57** 22.29S 45.24E
Rano Kao *mtn.* I. de Pascua **69** 27.11S109.27W
Ranong Thailand **34** 9.59N 98.40E
Rantauprapat Indonesia **36** 2.05N 99.46E
Rantekombola *mtn.* Indonesia **36** 3.30S119.58E
Rao Co *mtn.* Laos **34** 18.10N105.25E
Raoping China **33** 23.45N117.05E
Raoul *i.* Pacific Oc. **68** 29.15S177.55W
Rapa *i.* Pacific Oc. **69** 27.35S144.20W
Rapallo Italy **15** 44.20N 9.14E
Rāpar India **40** 23.34N 70.38E
Rapid Bay *town* Australia **66** 35.33S138.09E
Rapid City U.S.A. **82** 44.05N103.14W
Raquette Lake *town* U.S.A. **84** 43.49N 74.41W
Rarotonga *i.* Cook Is. **68** 21.14S159.46W
Ra's al Ḩadd *c.* Oman **38** 22.32N 59.49E
Ra's al Khaymah U.A.E. **43** 25.48N 55.56E
Ra's al Unūf Libya **51** 30.31N 18.34E
Ra's an Naqb *town* Egypt **44** 29.36N 34.51E
Ra's an Naqb *town* Jordan **44** 30.30N 35.29E
Ras Dashen *mtn.* Ethiopia **49** 13.20N 38.10E
Râs Ghârib Egypt **44** 28.22N 33.04E
Rashād Sudan **49** 11.51N 31.04E
Rashîd Egypt **44** 31.25N 30.25E
Rashīd Qal 'eh Afghan. **40** 31.31N 67.31E
Rasht Iran **43** 37.18N 49.38E
Raška Yugo. **19** 43.17N 20.37E
Rās Koh *mtn.* Pakistan **40** 28.50N 65.12E
Rason L. Australia **63** 28.46S124.20E
Rasra India **41** 25.51N 83.51E
Ratak Chain *is.* Pacific Oc. **68** 8.00N172.00E
Ratangarh India **40** 28.05N 74.36E
Rat Buri Thailand **34** 13.30N 99.50E
Ratcatchers L. Australia **66** 32.40S143.13E
Rāth India **41** 25.35N 79.34E
Rathcormack Rep. of Ire. **13** 52.05N 8.18W
Rathdrum Rep. of Ire. **13** 52.56N 6.15W
Rathenow Germany **20** 52.37N 12.21E
Rathlin I. U.K. **13** 55.17N 6.15W
Rath Luirc Rep. of Ire. **13** 52.21N 8.41W
Rathmullen Rep. of Ire. **13** 55.06N 7.32W
Ratlām India **40** 23.19N 75.04E
Ratnāgiri India **38** 16.59N 73.18E
Ratno Ukraine **21** 51.40N 24.32E
Ratodero Pakistan **40** 27.48N 68.18E
Raton U.S.A. **80** 36.54N104.24W
Rattlesnake Range *mts.* U.S.A. **80** 42.45N107.10W
Rattray Head U.K. **12** 57.37N 1.50W
Rättvik Sweden **23** 60.53N 15.06E
Rauch Argentina **93** 36.47S 59.05W
Raufoss Norway **23** 60.43N 10.37E
Raul Soares Brazil **94** 20.04S 42.27W
Rauma Finland **23** 61.08N 21.30E
Rauma *r.* Norway **22** 62.32N 7.43E
Raung, Gunung *mtn.* Indonesia **37** 8.07S114.03E
Raurkela India **41** 22.13N 84.53E
Rautas Sweden **22** 68.00N 19.55E
Ravalgaon India **40** 20.38N 74.25E
Rāvar Iran **43** 31.14N 56.51E
Rava-Russkaya Ukraine **21** 50.15N 23.36E
Ravena U.S.A. **84** 42.29N 73.49W
Ravenna Italy **15** 44.25N 12.12E
Ravensburg Germany **20** 47.47N 9.37E
Ravenshoe Australia **64** 17.37S145.29E
Ravensthorpe Australia **63** 33.35S120.02E
Rāver India **40** 21.15N 76.05E
Ravi *r.* Pakistan **38** 30.30N 72.13E
Rawaki *i.* Kiribati **68** 3.43S170.43W
Rāwalpindi Pakistan **40** 33.36N 73.04E
Rawāndūz Iraq **43** 36.38N 44.32E
Rawdon Canada **77** 46.03N 73.44W
Rawene New Zealand **60** 35.24S173.30E
Rawicz Poland **20** 51.37N 16.52E
Rawlinna Australia **63** 31.00S125.21E
Rawlins U.S.A. **80** 41.47N107.14W
Rawson Argentina **93** 34.40S 60.02W
Raxaul India **41** 26.59N 84.51E
Ray U.S.A. **82** 48.21N103.10W
Ray, C. Canada **77** 47.40N 59.18W
Raya *mtn.* Indonesia **36** 0.45S112.45E
Rāyagada India **41** 19.10N 83.25E
Rāyen Iran **43** 29.34N 57.26E
Raymond Canada **74** 49.30N112.35W
Raymond U.S.A. **80** 46.41N123.44W
Raymond Terrace Australia **67** 32.47S151.45E
Raymondville U.S.A. **83** 26.29N 97.47W
Rayong Thailand **34** 12.43N101.20E
Razan Iran **43** 35.22N 49.02E
Razdelnaya Ukraine **21** 46.50N 30.02E
Razgrad Bulgaria **21** 43.32N 26.30E
Ré, Île de *i.* France **17** 46.10N 1.26W
Reading U.K. **11** 51.27N 0.57W
Reading U.S.A. **85** 40.20N 75.56W
Realicó Argentina **93** 35.02S 64.14W
Reay Forest *f.* U.K. **12** 58.17N 4.48W
Rebecca, L. Australia **63** 30.07S122.32E
Rebi Indonesia **37** 6.24S134.07E
Rebiana Sand Sea *see* Rabyānah, Şaḩrā' *f.* Libya **51**
Reboly Russian Fed. **24** 63.50N 30.49E
Recalde Argentina **93** 36.39S 61.05W
Rechāh Lām Afghan. **40** 34.58N 70.51E
Recherche, Archipelago of the *is.* Australia **63** 34.05S122.45E
Rechitsa Belorussia **21** 52.21N 30.24E
Recife Brazil **91** 8.06S 34.53W
Recklinghausen Germany **14** 51.36N 7.11E
Reconquista Argentina **92** 29.08S 59.38W
Recreo Argentina **92** 29.20S 65.04W
Red *r.* Canada **75** 50.20N 96.50W
Red *r.* U.S.A. **83** 31.00N 91.40W
Red *r. see* Hong Hà *r.* Vietnam **34**
Red Bank U.S.A. **85** 40.21N 74.03W
Red Basin *f. see* Sichuan Pendi *f.* China **33**
Red Bay *town* Canada **77** 51.44N 56.45W
Red Bluff U.S.A. **80** 40.11N122.15W
Redcar U.K. **10** 54.37N 1.04W
Red Cliffs *town* Australia **66** 34.22S142.13E
Red Cloud U.S.A. **82** 40.04N 98.31W
Red Deer Canada **74** 52.20N113.50W
Red Deer *r.* Canada **75** 50.56N109.54W
Redding U.S.A. **80** 40.35N122.24W
Redditch U.K. **11** 52.18N 1.57W
Rede *r.* U.K. **10** 55.08N 2.13W
Redfield U.S.A. **82** 44.53N 98.31W
Redhill *town* Australia **66** 33.34S138.12E
Red Indian L. Canada **77** 48.40N 56.50W
Red L. U.S.A. **79** 48.00N 95.00W
Red Lake *town* Canada **75** 51.03N 93.49W
Redlands U.S.A. **81** 34.03N117.11W
Red Lion U.S.A. **85** 39.54N 76.36W
Red Lodge U.S.A. **80** 45.11N109.15W
Redmond U.S.A. **80** 44.17N121.11W
Red Oak U.S.A. **82** 41.01N 95.14W
Redondela Spain **16** 42.15N 8.38W
Redondo Portugal **16** 38.39N 7.33W
Redondo Beach *town* U.S.A. **81** 33.51N118.23W
Red Rock Canada **74** 53.39N122.41W
Redrock U.S.A. **81** 32.35N111.19W
Redruth U.K. **11** 50.14N 5.14W
Red Sea Africa / Asia **45** 20.00N 39.00E
Redstone Canada **74** 52.13N123.50W
Red Sucker L. Canada **75** 54.09N 93.40W
Red Volta *r.* Ghana **52** 10.32N 0.31W
Redwater Canada **74** 53.55N113.06W
Red Wing U.S.A. **82** 44.33N 92.31W
Redwood City U.S.A. **80** 37.29N122.13W
Ree, Lough Rep. of Ire. **13** 53.31N 7.58W
Reed City U.S.A. **84** 43.54N 85.31W
Reeder U.S.A. **82** 46.06N102.57W
Reedsport U.S.A. **80** 43.42N124.06W
Reefton New Zealand **60** 42.07S171.52E
Reese *r.* U.S.A. **80** 40.39N116.54W
Reftele Sweden **23** 57.11N 13.35E
Refuge Cove *town* Canada **74** 50.07N124.50W
Refugio U.S.A. **83** 28.18N 97.17W
Rega *r.* Poland **20** 54.10N 15.18E
Regensburg Germany **20** 49.01N 12.07E
Reggane Algeria **50** 26.42N 0.10E
Reggio Calabria Italy **18** 38.07N 15.38E
Reggio Emilia-Romagna Italy **15** 44.40N 10.37E
Reghin Romania **21** 46.47N 24.42E
Regina Canada **75** 50.25N104.39W
Regiwar Pakistan **40** 25.57N 65.44E
Regnéville France **15** 49.01N 1.33W
Rehoboth Namibia **56** 23.19S 17.10E
Rehoboth B. U.S.A. **85** 38.40N 75.06W
Rehoboth Beach *town* U.S.A. **85** 38.43N 75.05W
Rehovot Israel **44** 31.54N 34.46E
Reidsville U.S.A. **85** 36.21N 79.40W
Reigate U.K. **11** 51.14N 0.13W
Reims France **15** 49.15N 4.02E
Reindeer L. Canada **75** 57.15N102.40W
Reinosa Spain **16** 43.01N 4.09W
Reisterstown U.S.A. **85** 39.38N 76.50W
Relizane Algeria **51** 35.45N 0.33E
Remanso Brazil **91** 9.41S 42.04W
Remarkable, Mt. Australia **66** 32.48S138.10E
Rembang Indonesia **37** 6.45S111.22E
Remeshk Iran **43** 26.52N 58.46E
Remich Lux. **14** 49.34N 6.23E
Remiremont France **17** 48.01N 6.35E
Remscheid Germany **14** 51.10N 7.11E
Rena Norway **23** 61.08N 11.22E
Rendsburg Germany **20** 54.19N 9.39E
Renfrew Canada **76** 45.28N 76.41W
Rengat Indonesia **36** 0.26S102.35E
Rengo Chile **93** 34.25S 70.52W
Renheji China **33** 31.56N115.07E
Reni India **40** 28.41N 75.02E
Reni Ukraine **21** 45.28N 28.17E
Renkum Neth. **14** 51.59N 5.46E
Renmark Australia **66** 34.10S140.45E
Rennell Sd. Canada **74** 53.23N132.35W
Renner Springs *town* Australia **64** 18.20S133.48E

Rennes to Rurutu

Rennes France 15 48.06N 1.40W
Reno r. Italy 15 44.36N 12.17E
Reno U.S.A. 80 39.31N119.48W
Renton U.S.A. 80 47.30N122.11W
Ren Xian China 32 37.07N114.41E
Réo Burkina 52 12.20N 2.27W
Repki Ukraine 21 51.47N 31.06E
Republic U.S.A. 80 48.39N118.44W
Republican r. U.S.A. 82 39.03N 96.48W
Republic of Ireland Europe 13 53.00N 8.00W
Republic of South Africa Africa 56 28.30S 24.50E
Repulse B. Australia 64 20.36S148.43E
Repulse Bay town Canada 73 66.35N 86.20W
Requa U.S.A. 80 41.34N124.05W
Requena Peru 90 5.05S 73.52W
Requena Spain 16 39.29N 1.08W
Reserve Canada 75 52.28N102.39W
Resistencia Argentina 92 27.28S 59.00W
Reşiţa Romania 21 45.17N 21.53E
Resolute Canada 73 74.40N 95.00W
Resolution I. Canada 73 61.30N 65.00W
Resolution I. New Zealand 60 45.40S166.30E
Restigouche r. Canada 77 48.04N 66.20W
Rethel France 15 49.31N 4.22E
Réthimnon Greece 19 35.22N 24.29E
Reus Spain 16 41.10N 1.06E
Reusel Neth. 14 51.21N 5.09E
Reutlingen Germany 20 48.30N 9.13E
Reutte Austria 20 47.29N 10.43E
Revda Russian Fed. 24 56.49N 59.58E
Revelstoke Canada 74 51.00N118.00W
Revilla Gigedo, Islas de is. Mexico 86 19.00N111.00W
Revillagigedo I. U.S.A. 74 55.50N131.20W
Revin France 14 49.58N 4.40E
Revue r. Mozambique 57 19.58S 34.40E
Rewa India 41 24.32N 81.18E
Rewāri India 40 28.11N 76.37E
Rexburg U.S.A. 80 43.49N111.47W
Rexford U.S.A. 80 48.53N115.13W
Rey Iran 43 35.35N 51.27E
Reykjavík Iceland 22 64.09N 21.58W
Reynosa Mexico 83 26.07N 98.18W
Rezé France 17 47.12N 1.34W
Rēzekne Latvia 24 56.30N 27.22E
Rhayader U.K. 11 52.19N 3.30W
Rheden Neth. 14 52.01N 6.02E
Rhein r. Europe 14 51.53N 6.03E
Rheinbach Germany 14 50.39N 6.59E
Rheine Germany 14 52.17N 7.26E
Rheinland-Pfalz d. Germany 14 50.05N 7.09E
Rhenen Neth. 14 51.58N 5.34E
Rheydt Germany 14 51.10N 6.25E
Rhine see Rhein r. Europe 14
Rhinebeck U.S.A. 85 41.56N 73.55W
Rhinelander U.S.A. 82 45.39N 89.23W
Rhino Camp town Uganda 55 2.58N 31.20E
Rhir, Cap c. Morocco 50 30.38N 9.55W
Rho Italy 15 45.32N 9.02E
Rhode Island d. U.S.A. 84 41.40N 71.30W
Rhodes i. see Ródhos i. Greece 19
Rhodopi Planina mts. Bulgaria 19 41.35N 24.35E
Rhondda U.K. 11 51.39N 3.30W
Rhône r. France 17 43.25N 4.45E
Rhône-Alpes d. France 17 45.20N 5.45E
Rhosneigr U.K. 10 53.14N 4.31W
Rhyl U.K. 10 53.19N 3.29W
Riachão Brazil 91 7.22S 46.37W
Riāng India 41 27.32N 92.56E
Riāsi Jammu & Kashmir 40 33.05N 74.50E
Riau d. Indonesia 36 0.00 102.35E
Riau, Kepulauan is. Indonesia 36 0.50N104.00E
Ribadeo Spain 16 43.32N 7.04W
Ribarroja, Embalse de resr. Spain 16 41.12N 0.20E
Ribauè Mozambique 55 14.57S 38.27E
Ribble r. U.K. 10 53.45N 2.44W
Ribe Denmark 23 55.21N 8.46E
Ribeauvillé France 17 48.12N 7.19E
Ribécourt France 15 49.31N 2.55E
Ribeirão Prêto Brazil 94 21.09S 47.48W
Ribérac France 17 45.14N 0.22E
Riberalta Bolivia 92 10.59S 66.06W
Ribnitz-Damgarten Germany 20 54.15N 12.28E
Ribstone Creek r. Canada 75 52.51N110.05W
Riccione Italy 15 43.59N 12.39E
Rice U.S.A. 81 34.06N114.50W
Rice Lake town U.S.A. 82 45.30N 91.43W
Richard's Bay town R.S.A. 57 28.47S 32.06E
Richardson r. Canada 75 58.30N111.30W
Richardson U.S.A. 83 32.57N 96.44W
Richelieu r. Canada 77 46.03N 73.07W
Richfield Idaho U.S.A. 80 43.03N114.09W
Richfield Utah U.S.A. 80 38.46N112.05W
Rich Hill town U.S.A. 83 38.06N 94.22W
Richibucto Canada 77 46.41N 64.52W
Richland U.S.A. 80 46.17N119.18W
Richmond Australia 64 20.44S143.08E
Richmond Ont. Canada 77 45.11N 75.50W
Richmond Que. Canada 77 45.40N 72.09W
Richmond New Zealand 60 41.20S173.10E
Richmond R.S.A. 56 31.24S 23.56E
Richmond U.K. 10 54.24N 1.43W
Richmond Ind. U.S.A. 84 39.50N 84.51W
Richmond Utah U.S.A. 80 41.55N111.48W
Richmond Va. U.S.A. 85 37.34N 77.27W
Richmond Hill town Canada 76 43.52N 79.27W
Richmond Range mts. Australia 67 29.00S152.48E
Ricobayo, Embalse de resr. Spain 16 41.40N 5.50W
Ridderkerk Neth. 14 51.53N 4.39E
Rideau r. Canada 77 45.27N 75.42W
Rideau Lakes Canada 76 44.40N 76.10W
Ridgway U.S.A. 84 41.26N 78.44W
Riding Mtn. Canada 75 50.37N 99.50W
Riding Mtn. Nat. Park Canada 75 50.55N100.25W
Ried Austria 20 48.13N 13.30E
Riemst Belgium 14 50.49N 5.38E
Riesa Germany 20 51.18N 13.18E
Rieti Italy 18 42.24N 12.53E
Rifle U.S.A. 80 39.32N107.47W
Rift Valley d. Kenya 55 1.00N 36.00E
Riga Latvia 23 56.53N 24.08E
Riga, G. of Latvia/Estonia 23 57.30N 23.35E
Rīgān Iran 43 28.40N 58.58E
Rīgas Jūras Līcis g. see Riga, G. of Latvia 23
Rīgestān f. Afghan. 40 30.35N 65.00E
Riggins U.S.A. 80 45.25N116.19W
Rig Matī Iran 43 27.40N 58.11E
Rigo P.N.G. 64 9.50S147.35E
Rigolet Canada 77 54.20N 58.35W
Riia Laht g. see Riga, G. of Estonia 23
Riihimäki Finland 23 60.45N 24.46E
Riiser-Larsenhalvöya pen. Antarctica 96 68.00S 35.00E
Rijeka Croatia 18 45.20N 14.25E
Rijssen Neth. 14 52.19N 6.31E
Rijswijk Neth. 14 52.03N 4.22E
Riley U.S.A. 80 43.31N119.28W
Rimah, Wādī ar r. Saudi Arabia 42 26.10N 44.00E
Rimavská Sobota Slovakia 21 48.23N 20.02E
Rimbo Sweden 23 59.45N 18.22E
Rimini Italy 15 44.01N 12.34E
Rîmnicu-Sărat Romania 21 45.24N 27.06E
Rîmnicu-Vîlcea Romania 21 45.06N 24.22E
Rimouski Canada 77 48.27N 68.32W
Rinbung China 41 29.16N 89.54E
Rinconada Argentina 92 22.26S 66.10W
Rindal Norway 22 63.04N 9.13E
Ringebu Norway 23 61.31N 10.10E
Ringerike Norway 23 60.10N 10.12E
Ringim Nigeria 53 12.09N 9.08E
Ringköbing Denmark 23 56.05N 8.15E
Ringling U.S.A. 80 46.16N110.49W
Ringsted Denmark 23 55.27N 11.49E
Ringus India 40 27.21N 75.34E
Ringvassöy i. Norway 22 69.55N 19.10E
Ringwood U.K. 11 50.50N 1.48W
Riobamba Ecuador 90 1.44S 78.40W
Rio Branco Brazil 90 9.59S 67.49W
Rio Bueno Chile 93 40.20S 72.55W
Rio Casca Brazil 94 20.13S 42.38W
Rio Claro Brazil 94 22.19S 47.35W
Río Cuarto Argentina 93 33.08S 64.20W
Rio de Janeiro Brazil 94 22.53S 43.17W
Rio de Janeiro d. Brazil 94 22.00S 42.30W
Río Gallegos Argentina 93 51.37S 69.10W
Río Grande town Argentina 93 53.50S 67.40W
Rio Grande town Brazil 94 32.03S 52.08W
Rio Grande r. Mexico/U.S.A. 83 25.57N 97.09W
Río Grande r. Nicaragua 87 12.48N 83.30W
Rio Grande City U.S.A. 83 26.23N 98.49W
Rio Grande do Norte d. Brazil 91 6.00S 36.30W
Rio Grande do Sul d. Brazil 94 30.15S 53.30W
Ríohacha Colombia 90 11.34N 72.58W
Rio Largo Brazil 91 9.28S 35.50W
Río Negro d. Argentina 93 40.00S 67.00W
Rio Negro Brazil 94 26.06S 49.48W
Río Negro, Embalse del resr. Uruguay 93 32.45S 56.00W
Rio Novo Brazil 94 21.15S 43.09W
Rio Piracicaba Brazil 94 19.54S 43.10W
Rio Pomba Brazil 94 21.15S 43.12W
Rio Prêto Brazil 94 22.06S 43.52W
Ríosucio Colombia 90 7.27N 77.07W
Río Tercero Argentina 92 32.10S 64.05W
Rio Verde town Brazil 92 17.50S 50.55W
Ripley U.S.A. 84 42.16N 79.43W
Ripon Canada 77 45.47N 75.06W
Ripon U.K. 10 54.08N 1.31W
Rirapora Brazil 94 17.20S 45.02W
Risbäck Sweden 22 64.42N 15.32E
Riscle France 17 43.40N 0.05W
Rishā, Wādī ar r. Saudi Arabia 43 25.40N 44.08E
Rishīkesh India 41 30.07N 78.42E
Rishon LeZiyyon Israel 44 31.57N 34.48E
Risle r. France 15 49.26N 0.23E
Rison U.S.A. 83 33.58N 92.11W
Risör Norway 23 58.43N 9.14E
Rissani Morocco 50 31.23N 4.09W
Riti Nigeria 53 7.57N 9.41E
Ritidian Pt. Guam 68 13.39N144.51E
Ritzville U.S.A. 80 47.08N118.23W
Riva Italy 15 45.53N 10.50E
Rivadavia Argentina 92 24.11S 62.53W
Rivarolo Canavese Italy 15 45.25N 7.36E
Rivas Nicaragua 87 11.26N 85.50W
Rivera Uruguay 93 30.54S 55.31W
River Cess town Liberia 52 5.28N 9.32W
Rivergaro Italy 15 44.55N 9.36E
Riverhead U.S.A. 84 40.55N 72.40W
Riverina f. Australia 67 34.30S145.20E
Rivers Canada 75 50.02N100.12W
Rivers d. Nigeria 53 4.45N 6.35E
Riversdale R.S.A. 56 34.05S 21.15E
Riverside U.S.A. 81 33.59N117.22W
Rivers Inlet town Canada 74 51.40N127.20W
Riverton Australia 66 34.08S138.24E
Riverton Canada 75 50.59N 96.59W
Riverton New Zealand 60 46.21S168.01E
Riverton U.S.A. 80 43.02N108.23W
Riviera di Levante f. Italy 15 44.00N 9.40E
Riviera di Ponente f. Italy 15 43.40N 8.00E
Rivière-du-Loup town Canada 77 47.50N 69.32W
Rivière Pentecôte town Canada 77 49.47N 67.10W
Rivoli Italy 15 45.04N 7.31E
Riyadh see Ar Riyāḑ Saudi Arabia 43
Rize Turkey 42 41.03N 40.31E
Rizhao China 32 35.26N119.27E
Rizokárpason Cyprus 44 35.35N 34.24E
Rizzuto, Capo c. Italy 19 38.54N 17.06E
Rjukan Norway 23 59.52N 8.34E
Roa Norway 23 60.17N 10.37E
Roag, Loch U.K. 12 58.14N 6.50W
Roanne France 17 46.02N 4.05E
Roanoke Ala. U.S.A. 85 33.09N 85.24W
Roanoke r. U.S.A. 85 35.56N 76.43W
Roanoke Va. U.S.A. 85 37.15N 79.58W
Roanoke Rapids town U.S.A. 85 36.28N 77.40W
Roaring Springs U.S.A. 83 33.54N100.52W
Robāţ Iran 43 30.04N 54.49E
Robe Australia 66 37.11S139.45E
Robe, Mt. Australia 66 31.39S141.16E
Robertsganj India 41 24.42N 83.04E
Robertson R.S.A. 56 33.48S 19.52E
Robertsport Liberia 52 6.45N 11.22W
Robertstown Australia 66 33.59S139.03E
Roberval Canada 77 48.31N 72.13W
Robin Hood's Bay town U.K. 10 54.26N 0.31W
Robinson r. Australia 64 16.03S137.16E
Robinson Range mts. Australia 62 25.45S119.00E
Robinvale Australia 66 34.37S142.50E
Robledo Spain 16 38.46N 2.26W
Roblin Canada 75 51.17N101.28W
Roboré Bolivia 92 18.20S 59.45W
Robson, Mt. Canada 74 53.10N119.10W
Rocas i. Atlantic Oc. 95 3.50S 33.50W
Roccella Italy 19 38.19N 16.24E
Rocciamelone mtn. Italy 15 45.12N 7.05E
Rocha Uruguay 94 34.30S 54.22W
Rocha da Gale, Barragem resr. Portugal 16 38.20N 7.35W
Rochdale U.K. 10 53.36N 2.10W
Rochechouart France 17 45.49N 0.50E
Rochefort Belgium 14 50.10N 5.13E
Rochefort France 17 45.57N 0.58W
Rochelle U.S.A. 82 41.55N 89.05W
Rocher River town Canada 74 61.23N112.44W
Rochester Australia 67 36.22S144.42E
Rochester U.K. 11 51.22N 0.30E
Rochester Minn. U.S.A. 82 44.01N 92.27W
Rochester N.Y. U.S.A. 84 43.12N 77.37W
Rochfort Bridge Rep. of Ire. 13 53.25N 7.19W
Rock r. Canada 74 60.07N127.07W
Rock U.S.A. 84 46.03N 87.10W
Rockall i. U.K. 8 57.39N 13.44W
Rockall Bank f. Atlantic Oc. 8 57.30N 14.00W
Rockdale U.S.A. 85 39.21N 76.46W
Rockefeller Plateau Antarctica 96 80.00S140.00W
Rockford U.S.A. 82 42.17N 89.06W
Rock Hall U.S.A. 85 39.08N 76.14W
Rockhampton Australia 64 23.22S150.32E
Rock Hill town U.S.A. 85 34.55N 81.01W
Rockingham Australia 63 32.16S115.21E
Rockingham U.S.A. 85 34.56N 79.47W
Rock Island town U.S.A. 82 41.30N 90.34W
Rockland Canada 77 45.32N 75.19W
Rockland Idaho U.S.A. 80 42.34N112.53W
Rockland Maine U.S.A. 84 44.06N 69.06W
Rockland Mich. U.S.A. 84 46.44N 89.12W
Rocklands Resr. Australia 66 37.13S141.52E
Rockport U.S.A. 80 39.45N123.47W
Rock Rapids town U.S.A. 82 43.26N 96.10W
Rock Sound town Bahamas 87 24.54N 76.11W
Rocksprings Tex. U.S.A. 83 30.01N100.13W
Rock Springs Wyo. U.S.A. 80 41.35N109.13W
Rockville U.S.A. 85 39.05N 77.09W
Rockwood U.S.A. 85 35.52N 84.40W
Rocky Ford U.S.A. 78 38.03N103.44W
Rocky Gully town Australia 63 34.31S117.01E
Rocky Island L. Canada 76 46.55N 82.55W
Rocky Mount town U.S.A. 85 35.56N 77.48W
Rocky Mountain Foothills f. Canada 74 57.17N123.21W
Rocky Mountain Nat. Park U.S.A. 80 40.19N105.42W
Rocky Mountain Trench f. Canada 74 56.45N124.47W
Rocky Mts. N. America 80 43.21N109.50W
Rocky Pt. Namibia 56 19.00S 12.29E
Rocroi France 14 49.56N 4.31E
Rod Pakistan 40 28.06N 63.12E
Rödby Denmark 23 54.42N 11.24E
Roddickton Canada 77 50.52N 56.08W
Rodel U.K. 12 57.44N 6.58W
Rodeo Mexico 83 25.11N104.34W
Rodez France 17 44.21N 2.34E
Ródhos i. Greece 19 36.12N 28.00E
Ródhos town Greece 19 36.24N 28.15E
Rodonit, Kep-i- c. Albania 19 41.34N 19.25E
Roe, L. Australia 63 30.40S122.10E
Roebourne Australia 62 20.45S117.08E
Roebuck B. Australia 62 19.04S122.17E
Roermond Neth. 14 51.12N 6.00E
Roeselare Belgium 14 50.57N 3.06E
Rogachev Belorussia 21 53.05N 30.02E
Rogaland d. Norway 23 59.00N 6.15E
Rogers, Mt. U.S.A. 85 36.35N 81.32W
Rogerson U.S.A. 80 42.14N114.47W
Roggan r. Canada 76 54.24N 78.05W
Roggan L. Canada 76 54.10N 77.58W
Roggan River town Canada 76 54.24N 78.05W
Roggeveen, Cabo c. I. de Pascua 69 27.06S109.16W
Rogliano France 17 42.57N 9.25E
Rogue r. U.S.A. 80 42.26N124.25W
Rohri Pakistan 40 27.41N 68.54E
Rohtak India 40 28.54N 76.34E
Rojas Argentina 93 34.15S 60.44W
Rokan r. Indonesia 36 2.00N101.00E
Rokel r. Sierra Leone 52 8.36N 12.55W
Rola Co l. China 39 35.26N 88.24E
Röldal Norway 23 59.49N 6.48E
Rolette U.S.A. 82 48.40N 99.51W
Rolla Mo. U.S.A. 83 37.57N 91.46W
Rolla N.Dak. U.S.A. 82 48.52N 99.37W
Rolleston Australia 64 24.25S148.35E
Rolleville Bahamas 87 23.41N 76.00W
Rolvsöya i. Norway 22 70.58N 24.00E
Roma Australia 64 26.35S148.47E
Roma Italy 18 41.54N 12.29E
Roma Sweden 23 57.32N 18.28E
Romain, C. U.S.A. 85 33.00N 79.22W
Romaine r. Canada 77 50.18N 63.47W
Roman Romania 21 46.55N 26.56E
Romang i. Indonesia 37 7.45S127.20E
Romania Europe 21 46.30N 24.00E
Romano, C. U.S.A. 85 25.50N 81.41W
Romans France 17 45.03N 5.03E
Rome see Roma Italy 18
Rome Ga. U.S.A. 85 34.01N 85.02W
Rome N.Y. U.S.A. 84 43.13N 75.27W
Romeo U.S.A. 84 42.47N 83.01W
Romilly France 15 48.31N 3.44E
Romney Marsh f. U.K. 11 51.03N 0.55E
Romorantin France 15 47.22N 1.44E
Rona i. U.K. 12 57.33N 5.58W
Ronan U.S.A. 80 47.32N114.06W
Ronas Hill U.K. 8 60.32N 1.26W
Roncesvalles Spain 16 43.01N 1.19W
Ronda Spain 16 36.45N 5.10W
Rondane mtn. Norway 23 61.55N 9.45E
Rondônia d. Brazil 90 12.10S 62.30W
Rondonópolis Brazil 91 16.29S 54.37W
Rongcheng China 32 37.09N122.23E
Ronge, Lac la l. Canada 75 55.07N104.45W
Rongjiang China 33 25.56N108.31E
Rongxar China 41 28.14N 87.44E
Rong Xian China 33 29.28N104.32E
Roniu mtn. Tahiti 69 17.49S149.12W
Rönne Denmark 23 55.06N 14.42E
Ronneby Sweden 23 56.12N 15.18E
Ronse Belgium 14 50.45N 3.36E
Ronuro r. Brazil 91 11.56S 53.33W
Roof Butte mtn. U.S.A. 81 36.28N109.05W
Roorkee India 41 29.52N 77.53E
Roosendaal Neth. 14 51.32N 4.28E
Roosevelt r. Brazil 90 7.35S 60.20W
Roosevelt U.S.A. 80 40.18N109.59W
Roosevelt I. Antarctica 96 79.00S161.00W
Root r. Canada 74 62.50N123.40W
Ropcha Russian Fed. 24 62.50N 51.55E
Roper r. Australia 64 14.40S135.30E
Roque Pérez Argentina 93 35.23S 59.22W
Roraima d. Brazil 90 2.00N 62.00W
Roraima, Mt. Guyana 90 5.14N 60.44W
Rorketon Canada 75 51.26N 99.32W
Röros Norway 22 62.35N 11.23E
Rosa, Monte mtn. Italy/Switz. 15 45.56N 7.51E
Rosamond U.S.A. 81 34.52N118.10W
Rosario Argentina 93 32.57S 60.40W
Rosário Brazil 91 3.00S 44.15W
Rosario Mexico 81 23.00N105.52W
Rosario Uruguay 93 34.19S 57.21W
Rosario de la Frontera Argentina 92 25.50S 64.55W
Rosario del Tala Argentina 93 32.20S 59.10W
Rosário do Sul Brazil 94 30.15S 54.55W
Rosarito Mexico 81 28.38N114.04W
Roscoe U.S.A. 82 45.27N 99.20W
Roscoff France 17 48.44N 4.00W
Roscommon Rep. of Ire. 13 53.38N 8.13W
Roscommon d. Rep. of Ire. 13 53.38N 8.11W
Roscrea Rep. of Ire. 13 52.57N 7.49W
Roseau r. Canada 75 49.10N 97.20W
Roseau Dominica 87 15.18N 61.23W
Roseau U.S.A. 82 48.51N 95.46W
Rose Blanche Canada 77 47.37N 58.43W
Rosebud Australia 67 38.21S144.54E
Rosebud r. Canada 74 51.25N112.37W
Roseburg U.S.A. 80 43.13N123.20W
Rose Harbour Canada 74 52.15N131.10W
Rosenberg U.S.A. 83 29.33N 95.48W
Rosenheim Germany 20 47.51N 12.09E
Roses Spain 16 42.19N 3.10E
Rosetown Canada 75 51.33N108.00W
Rosetta R.S.A. 56 29.18S 29.58E
Roseville Calif. U.S.A. 80 38.45N121.17W
Roseville Mich. U.S.A. 76 42.30N 82.56W
Rosières France 15 49.49N 2.43E
Rosignano Marittimo Italy 18 43.24N 10.28E
Roşiori-de-Vede Romania 21 44.07N 25.00E
Rositsa Bulgaria 21 43.57N 27.57E
Roska r. Ukraine 21 49.27N 29.45E
Roskilde Denmark 23 55.39N 12.05E
Roslags-Näsby Sweden 23 59.26N 18.04E
Roslavl Russian Fed. 24 53.55N 32.53E
Ross New Zealand 60 42.54S170.49E
Rossano Italy 19 39.35N 16.39E
Ross Dependency Antarctica 96 75.00S170.00W
Rossignol, L. Canada 77 44.10N 65.10W
Rossing Namibia 56 22.31S 14.52E
Rosslare Rep. of Ire. 13 52.17N 6.23W
Rosso Mauritania 50 16.30N 15.49W
Ross-on-Wye U.K. 11 51.55N 2.36W
Rossosh Russian Fed. 25 50.12N 39.35E
Ross River town Canada 74 62.30N131.30W
Rössvatnet l. Norway 22 65.45N 14.00E
Rosta Norway 22 68.59N 19.40E
Rosthern Canada 75 52.40N106.17W
Rostock Germany 20 54.06N 12.09E
Rostov Russian Fed. 24 57.11N 39.23E
Rostov Russian Fed. 25 47.15N 39.45E
Roswell Ga. U.S.A. 85 34.02N 84.21W
Roswell N.Mex. U.S.A. 81 33.24N104.32W
Rotem Belgium 14 51.04N 5.44E
Rothbury U.K. 10 55.19N 1.54W
Rother r. U.K. 9 50.56N 0.46E
Rotherham U.K. 10 53.26N 1.21W
Rothes U.K. 12 57.31N 3.13W
Rothesay Canada 77 45.23N 66.00W
Rothesay U.K. 12 55.50N 5.03W
Roti i. Indonesia 62 10.30S123.10E
Roto Australia 67 33.04S145.27E
Rotondella Italy 19 40.10N 16.32E
Rotorua New Zealand 60 38.07S176.17E
Rotorua, L. New Zealand 60 38.00S176.00E
Rotterdam Neth. 14 51.55N 4.29E
Rottnest I. Australia 63 32.01S115.28E
Rottweil Germany 20 48.10N 8.37E
Roubaix France 14 50.42N 3.10E
Rouen France 15 49.26N 1.05E
Rouge r. Canada 77 45.39N 74.41W
Rougé France 15 47.47N 1.26W
Rouku P.N.G. 64 8.40S141.35E
Round Mt. Australia 67 30.26S152.15E
Round Pond l. Canada 77 48.10N 56.00W
Roundup U.S.A. 80 46.27N108.33W
Rousay i. U.K. 12 59.10N 3.02W
Rouyn Canada 76 48.20N 79.00W
Rovaniemi Finland 22 66.30N 25.40E
Rovato Italy 15 45.34N 10.00E
Rovereto Italy 15 45.53N 11.02E
Rovigo Italy 15 45.04N 11.47E
Rovinj Croatia 20 45.06N 13.39E
Rovno Ukraine 21 50.39N 26.10E
Rowena Australia 67 29.49S148.54E
Rowley Shoals f. Australia 62 17.30S119.00E
Roxboro U.S.A. 85 36.24N 79.00W
Roxburgh New Zealand 60 45.33S169.19E
Roxby Downs town Australia 66 30.42S136.46E
Roxen l. Sweden 23 58.30N 15.41E
Roxton Canada 77 45.29N 72.36W
Roy U.S.A. 81 35.57N104.12W
Royale, Isle i. U.S.A. 84 48.00N 89.00W
Royal L. Canada 75 56.00N103.15W
Royal Leamington Spa U.K. 11 52.18N 1.32W
Royal Tunbridge Wells U.K. 11 51.07N 0.16E
Royan France 17 45.37N 1.02W
Roye France 15 49.42N 2.48E
Royston U.K. 11 52.03N 0.01W
Rozhishche Ukraine 21 50.58N 25.15E
Rožňava Slovakia 21 48.40N 20.32E
Rtishchevo Russian Fed. 24 52.16N 43.45E
Ruahine Range mts. New Zealand 60 40.00S176.00E
Ruapehu mtn. New Zealand 60 39.20S175.30E
Ruapuke I. New Zealand 60 46.45S168.30E
Rub 'al Khali des. see Ar Rub 'al Khālī des. Saudi Arabia 38
Rubi r. Zaïre 54 2.50N 24.06E
Rubino Ivory Coast 52 6.04N 4.18W
Rubio Colombia 90 7.42N 72.23W
Rubryn Belorussia 21 51.52N 27.30E
Rubtsovsk Russian Fed. 28 51.29N 81.10E
Ruby Mts. U.S.A. 80 40.25N115.35W
Rūdān r. Iran 43 27.02N 56.53E
Rudauli India 41 26.45N 81.45E
Rūdbār Afghan. 40 30.09N 62.36E
Rudewa Tanzania 55 6.40S 37.08E
Rudki Ukraine 21 49.40N 23.28E
Rudnaya Pristan Russian Fed. 31 44.18N135.51E
Rudnichnyy Russian Fed. 24 59.10N 52.28E
Rudnik Poland 21 50.28N 22.15E
Rudnyy Kazakhstan 28 53.00N 63.05E
Rudolstadt Germany 20 50.44N 11.20E
Rue France 17 50.15N 1.40E
Rufā'ah Sudan 48 14.46N 33.22E
Ruffec France 17 46.02N 0.12E
Rufiji r. Tanzania 55 8.02S 39.19E
Rufino Argentina 93 34.16S 62.45W
Rufisque Senegal 52 14.43N 17.16W
Rufunsa Zambia 55 15.02S 29.35E
Rugao China 32 32.25N120.40E
Rugby U.K. 11 52.23N 1.16W
Rugby U.S.A. 82 48.22N100.00W
Rügen i. Germany 20 54.30N 13.30E
Ruhr f. Germany 14 51.22N 7.26E
Ruhr r. Germany 14 51.27N 6.41E
Rui'an China 33 26.50N120.40E
Ruijin China 33 25.49N116.00E
Ruinen Neth. 14 52.47N 6.21E
Rukwa d. Tanzania 55 7.05S 31.25E
Rukwa, L. Tanzania 55 8.00S 32.20E
Rum i. U.K. 12 57.00N 6.20W
Ruma Yugo. 21 44.59N 19.51E
Rumbek Sudan 49 6.48N 29.41E
Rum Cay i. Bahamas 87 23.41N 74.53W
Rumford U.S.A. 84 44.33N 70.33W
Rummānah Egypt 44 31.01N 32.40E
Runcorn U.K. 10 53.20N 2.44W
Runde r. Zimbabwe 57 21.20S 32.23E
Rundvik Sweden 22 63.30N 19.24E
Rungāni Pakistan 40 26.38N 65.43E
Rungwa Tanzania 55 6.57S 33.35E
Rungwa r. Tanzania 55 7.38S 31.55E
Rungwe Mt. Tanzania 55 9.10S 33.40E
Runka Nigeria 53 12.28N 7.20E
Ruoqiang China 30 39.00N 88.00E
Ruo Shui r. China 30 42.15N101.03E
Rūpar India 40 30.58N 76.32E
Rupert r. Canada 76 51.30N 78.45W
Rupununi r. Guyana 90 4.00N 58.30W
Rur r. Neth. 14 51.12N 5.58E
Rurutu i. Pacific Oc. 69 22.25S151.20W

Rusape to Sambava

Rusape Zimbabwe 57 18.30S 32.08E
Ruşayriş, Khazzān ar resr. Sudan 49 11.40N 34.20E
Ruse Bulgaria 19 43.50N 25.59E
Rusera India 41 25.45N 86.02E
Rushan China 32 36.54N121.30E
Rushden U.K. 11 52.17N 0.37W
Rush Springs town U.S.A. 83 34.47N 97.58W
Rushworth Australia 67 36.38S145.02E
Russell Canada 77 45.17N 75.17W
Russellkonda India 41 19.56N 84.35E
Russell L. Man. Canada 75 56.15N101.30W
Russell L. N.W.T. Canada 74 63.05N115.44W
Russell Pt. Canada 72 73.30N115.00W
Russell Range mts. Australia 63 33.15S123.30E
Russellville U.S.A. 83 35.17N 93.08W
Russian Federation Europe / Asia 28 62.00N 80.00E
Russkaya Polyana Russian Fed. 28 53.48N 73.54E
Rustavi Georgia 25 41.34N 45.03E
Rustenburg R.S.A. 56 25.39S 27.13E
Ruston U.S.A. 83 32.32N 92.38W
Rutana Burundi 55 3.58S 30.00E
Rutanzige, L. see Edward, L. Uganda / Zaïre 55
Rütenbrock Germany 14 52.51N 7.06E
Ruteng Indonesia 37 8.35S120.28E
Rutenga Zimbabwe 56 21.15S 30.46E
Ruth U.S.A. 80 39.17N114.59W
Ruthin U.K. 10 53.07N 3.18W
Rutland U.S.A. 84 43.36N 72.59W
Rutledge r. Canada 75 61.04N112.00W
Rutledge L. Canada 75 61.33N110.47W
Rutog China 41 33.27N 79.43E
Rutshuru Zaïre 55 1.10S 29.26E
Ruvu Tanzania 55 6.50S 38.42E
Ruvuma r. Mozambique / Tanzania 55 10.30S 40.30E
Ruvuma d. Tanzania 55 10.45S 36.15E
Ruwaybah wells Sudan 48 15.39N 28.45E
Ruwenzori Range mts. Uganda / Zaïre 55 0.30N 30.00E
Ruyigi Burundi 55 3.26S 30.14E
Ruzayevka Russian Fed. 24 54.04N 44.55E
Ruzitgort Russian Fed. 24 62.51N 64.52E
Ružomberok Slovakia 21 49.06N 19.18E
Rwanda Africa 55 2.00S 30.00E
Ryan, Loch U.K. 12 54.56N 5.02W
Ryasna Belorussia 21 54.00N 31.14E
Ryazan Russian Fed. 24 54.37N 39.43E
Ryazhsk Russian Fed. 24 53.40N 40.07E
Rybachiy, Poluostrov pen. Russian Fed. 24 69.45N 32.30E
Rybachye Kazakhstan 30 46.27N 81.30E
Rybinsk Russian Fed. 24 58.01N 38.52E
Rybinskoye Vodokhranilishche resr. Russian Fed. 24 58.30N 38.25E
Rybnik Poland 21 50.06N 18.32E
Rybnitsa Moldavia 21 47.42N 29.00E
Ryd Sweden 23 56.28N 14.41E
Rye U.K. 11 50.57N 0.46E
Rye r. U.K. 10 54.10N 0.44W
Ryki Poland 21 51.39N 21.56E
Rylstone Australia 67 32.48S149.58E
Ryūgasaki Japan 35 35.54N140.11E
Ryukyu Is. see Nansei shotō is. Japan 31
Rzeszów Poland 21 50.04N 22.00E
Rzhev Russian Fed. 24 56.15N 34.18E

S

Saa Cameroon 53 4.24N 11.25E
Saale r. Germany 20 51.58N 11.53E
Saanich Canada 74 48.28N123.22W
Saar r. Germany 14 49.43N 6.34E
Saarbrücken Germany 20 49.15N 6.58E
Saarburg Germany 14 49.36N 6.33E
Saaremaa i. Estonia 23 58.25N 22.30E
Saarijärvi Finland 22 62.43N 25.16E
Saariselkä mts. Finland 22 68.15N 28.30E
Saarland d. Germany 14 49.30N 6.50E
Saba i. Leeward Is. 87 17.42N 63.26W
Šabac Yugo. 21 44.45N 19.41E
Sabadell Spain 16 41.33N 2.07E
Sabah d. Malaysia 36 5.30N117.00E
Sabalān, Kūhhā-ye mts. Iran 43 38.15N 47.50E
Sabana, Archipiélago de Cuba 87 23.30N 80.00W
Sabanalarga Colombia 90 10.38N 75.00W
Sabaudia Italy 18 41.18N 13.01E
Sabbioneta Italy 15 45.00N 10.39E
Sabhā Libya 51 27.02N 14.26E
Sabhā d. Libya 51 27.02N 15.30E
Sabinas Mexico 83 27.51N101.07W
Sabinas Hidalgo Mexico 83 26.30N100.10W
Sabine r. U.S.A. 83 30.00N 93.45W
Sabine L. U.S.A. 83 29.50N 93.50W
Sabkhat al Bardawīl l. Egypt 44 31.10N 33.15E
Sablayan Phil. 37 12.50N120.50E
Sable, C. Canada 77 43.25N 65.35W
Sable, C. U.S.A. 85 25.05N 65.50W
Sable I. Canada 73 43.55N 59.50W
Sablé-sur-Sarthe France 15 47.50N 0.20W
Sabon Birni Nigeria 53 13.37N 6.15E
Sabongidda Nigeria 53 6.54N 5.56E
Sabrina Coast f. Antarctica 96 67.00S120.00E
Şabyā Saudi Arabia 48 17.09N 42.37E
Sabzevār Iran 43 36.13N 57.38E
Sacaca Bolivia 92 18.05S 66.25W
Sacajawea mtn. U.S.A. 80 45.15N117.17W
Sacandica Angola 54 5.58S 15.56E
Sac City U.S.A. 82 42.25N 95.00W
Sacedón Spain 16 40.29N 2.44W
Sachigo r. Canada 75 55.00N 89.00W
Sachigo L. Canada 75 53.50N 92.00W
Sachsen d. Germany 20 51.10N 13.15E
Sachsen-Anhalt d. Germany 20 52.05N 11.30E
Sackville Canada 77 45.54N 64.22W
Saco U.S.A. 84 43.29N 70.28W
Sacramento Brazil 94 19.51S 26.47W
Sacramento U.S.A. 80 38.35N121.30W
Sacramento r. U.S.A. 80 38.03N121.56W
Sacramento Mts. U.S.A. 81 33.10N105.50W
Sacramento Valley f. U.S.A. 80 39.15N122.00W
Sádaba Spain 16 42.19N 1.10W
Sadani Tanzania 55 6.00S 38.40E
Sadda Pakistan 40 33.42N 70.20E
Sa Dec Vietnam 34 10.19N105.45E
Sādiqābād Pakistan 40 28.18N 70.08E
Sadiya India 39 27.49N 95.38E
Sādri India 40 25.11N 73.26E
Sadulgarh India 40 29.35N 74.19E
Şafājah des. Saudi Arabia 42 26.30N 39.30E
Şafāniyah Egypt 44 28.49N 30.48E
Şafarābād Iran 43 38.59N 47.25E
Säffle Sweden 23 59.08N 12.56E
Saffron Walden U.K. 11 52.02N 0.15E
Safi Morocco 50 32.20N 9.17W
Safid r. Iran 43 37.23N 50.11E
Safonovo Russian Fed. 24 65.40N 48.10E
Safonovo Russian Fed. 24 55.08N 33.16E
Saga China 41 29.30N 85.09E
Sagaing Burma 34 22.00N 96.00E
Sagaing d. Burma 34 24.00N 95.00E
Sagala Mali 52 14.09N 6.38W
Sagami r. Japan 35 35.14N139.23E
Sagamihara Japan 35 35.32N139.23E
Sagami-nada b. Japan 35 34.55N139.30E
Sāgar India 41 23.50N 78.43E
Sagara Japan 35 34.41N138.12E
Sage U.S.A. 80 41.49N110.59W
Saginaw U.S.A. 84 43.25N 83.54W
Saginaw B. U.S.A. 84 43.56N 83.40W
Sagiz Kazakhstan 25 47.31N 54.55E
Sagres Portugal 16 37.00N 8.56W
Saguache U.S.A. 80 38.05N106.08W
Sagua la Grande Cuba 87 22.55N 80.05W
Saguenay r. Canada 77 48.10N 69.43W
Sagunto Spain 16 39.40N 0.17W
Sāgwāra India 40 23.41N 74.01E
Sa'gya China 41 28.55N 88.03E
Sahaba Sudan 48 18.55N 30.28E
Sahagún Spain 16 42.23N 5.02W
Sahand, Kūh-e mtn. Iran 43 37.37N 46.27E
Sahara des. Africa 51 22.30N 3.00E
Sahāranpur India 41 29.58N 77.33E
Saharsa India 41 25.53N 86.36E
Sahaswān India 41 28.05N 78.45E
Sahbā, Wādī as r. Saudi Arabia 43 23.48N 49.50E
Sahel d. Burkina 52 14.00N 0.50W
Sāhibganj India 41 25.15N 87.39E
Sāhīwāl Punjab Pakistan 40 30.40N 73.06E
Sāhīwāl Punjab Pakistan 40 31.58N 72.20E
Sahtaneh r. Canada 74 59.02N122.28W
Sahuarita U.S.A. 81 31.57N110.58W
Saibai i. Australia 64 9.24S142.40E
Sa'īdābād Iran 43 29.28N 55.43E
Saidpur Bangla. 41 25.47N 88.54E
Saidu Pakistan 40 34.45N 72.21E
Saigon see Ho Chi Minh Vietnam 34
Saimaa l. Finland 24 61.20N 28.00E
Saimbeyli Turkey 42 38.07N 36.08E
Saindak Pakistan 40 29.17N 61.34E
St. Abb's Head U.K. 12 55.54N 2.07W
St. Agapit Canada 77 46.34N 71.26W
St. Alban's Canada 77 47.52N 55.51W
St. Albans U.K. 11 51.46N 0.21W
St. Albans U.S.A. 84 44.49N 73.05W
St. Albert Canada 74 53.37N113.40W
St. Alexis des Monts Canada 77 46.28N 73.08W
St. Amand France 14 50.27N 3.26E
St. Amand-Mont-Rond town France 17 46.43N 2.29E
St. Andrews U.K. 12 56.20N 2.48W
St. Andries Belgium 14 51.12N 3.10E
St. Ann's Bay town Jamaica 87 18.26N 77.12W
St. Anthony Canada 77 51.22N 55.35W
St. Anthony U.S.A. 78 43.59N111.40W
St. Arnaud Australia 66 36.40S143.20E
St. Augustin r. Canada 77 51.14N 58.41W
St. Augustine U.S.A. 85 29.54N 81.19W
St. Augustin Saguenay Canada 77 51.14N 58.39W
St. Austell U.K. 11 50.20N 4.48W
St. Barthélemy Canada 77 46.12N 73.08W
St. Barthélemy i. Leeward Is. 87 17.55N 62.50W
St. Bees Head U.K. 10 54.31N 3.39W
St. Boniface Canada 75 49.55N 97.06W
St. Brides B. U.K. 11 51.48N 5.03W
St. Brieuc France 17 48.31N 2.45W
St. Calais France 15 47.55N 0.45E
St. Casimir Canada 77 46.40N 72.08W
St. Catharines Canada 76 43.10N 79.15W
St. Catherine's Pt. U.K. 11 50.34N 1.18W
St. Céré France 17 44.52N 1.53E
St. Charles U.S.A. 82 38.47N 90.29W
St. Cloud U.S.A. 82 45.33N 94.10W
St. Croix i. U.S.V.Is. 87 17.45N 64.35W
St. Cyrille de Wendover Canada 77 45.56N 72.26W
St. David's U.K. 11 51.54N 5.16W
St. David's I. Bermuda 95 32.23N 64.42W
St. Denis France 15 48.56N 2.21E
St. Dié France 17 48.17N 6.57E
St. Dizier France 15 48.38N 4.58E
St. Donat Canada 77 46.19N 74.13W
Sainte-Agathe-des-Monts Canada 77 46.03N 74.17W
Sainte Anne de Beaupré Canada 77 47.02N 70.56W
Sainte Anne de la Pérade Canada 77 46.35N 72.12W
Sainte-Anne-des-Monts Canada 77 49.07N 66.29W
Sainte Emelie Canada 77 46.19N 73.39W
St. Elias, Mt. U.S.A. 74 60.18N140.55W
St. Elias Mts. Canada 74 60.30N139.30W
St. Éloi Canada 77 48.02N 69.13W
Sainte Lucie Canada 77 46.07N 74.13W
Sainte Marguerite Canada 77 46.03N 74.05W
Sainte Marguerite r. Canada 77 50.10N 66.40W
Sainte Menehould France 15 49.05N 4.54E
Sainte Mère-Église France 15 49.24N 1.19W
Saintes France 17 45.44N 0.38W
St. Espirit Canada 77 45.56N 73.40W
Sainte-Thérèse-de-Blainville Canada 77 45.39N 73.49W
St. Étienne France 17 45.26N 4.26E
St. Fargeau France 15 47.38N 3.04E
St. Faustin Canada 77 46.07N 74.30W
St. Félix Canada 77 46.10N 73.26W
Saintfield U.K. 13 54.28N 5.50W
St. Fintan's Canada 77 48.10N 58.50W
St. Florent France 17 42.41N 9.18E
St. Florentin France 15 48.00N 3.44E
St. Flour France 17 45.02N 3.05E
St. Francis U.S.A. 82 39.47N101.47W
St. Francisville U.S.A. 83 30.47N 91.23W
St. Francois r. Canada 77 46.07N 72.55W
St. Gabriel Canada 77 46.17N 73.23W
St. Gallen Switz. 20 47.25N 9.23E
St. Gaudens France 17 43.07N 0.44E
St. George Australia 65 28.03S148.30E
St. George Bermuda 95 32.24N 64.42W
St. George N.B. Canada 77 45.11N 66.57W
St. George Ont. Canada 76 43.15N 80.15W
St. George U.S.A. 80 37.06N113.35W
St. George, C. U.S.A. 85 29.35N 85.04W
St. Georges Belgium 14 50.37N 5.20E
St. Georges Canada 77 46.37N 72.40W
St. George's Grenada 87 12.04N 61.44W
St. Georges Guiana 91 3.54N 51.48W
St. George's B. Canada 77 48.20N 59.00W
St. George's Channel Rep. of Ire. / U.K. 13 51.30N 6.20W
St. George's I. Bermuda 95 32.24N 64.42W
St. Germain France 15 48.53N 2.04E
St. Germain de Grantham Canada 77 45.50N 72.34W
St. Gheorghe's Mouth est. Romania 19 44.51N 29.37E
St. Gilles-Croix-de-Vie France 17 46.42N 1.56W
St. Girons France 17 42.59N 1.08E
St. Gotthard Pass Switz. 17 46.30N 8.55E
St. Govan's Head U.K. 11 51.36N 4.55W
St. Grégoire Canada 77 46.16N 72.30W
St. Guillaume d'Upton Canada 77 45.53N 72.46W
St. Helena i. Atlantic Oc. 95 15.58S 5.43W
St. Helena B. R.S.A. 56 32.35S 18.05E
St. Helens U.K. 10 53.28N 2.43W
St. Helens U.S.A. 80 45.52N122.48W
St. Helier Channel Is. Europe 11 49.12N 2.07W
St. Hilaire-du-Harcouët France 15 48.35N 1.06W
St. Hubert Belgium 14 50.02N 5.22E
St. Hyacinthe Canada 77 45.38N 72.57W
St. Ignace U.S.A. 84 45.53N 84.44W
St. Ives U.K. 11 50.13N 5.29W
St. Jacques Canada 77 45.57N 73.34W
St. Jean Canada 77 45.18N 73.20W
St. Jean r. Canada 77 50.17N 64.20W
St. Jean France 17 45.17N 6.21E
St. Jean, Lac l. Canada 77 48.35N 72.00W
St. Jean de Matha Canada 77 46.10N 73.30W
St. Jean Pied-de-Port France 17 43.10N 1.14W
St. Jérôme Canada 77 45.47N 74.00W
St. John Canada 77 45.16N 66.03W
St. John r. Canada 77 45.16N 66.04W
St. John U.S.A. 83 38.00N 98.46W
St. John, C. Canada 77 50.00N 55.32W
St. John B. Canada 77 50.40N 57.08W
St. John's Antigua 87 17.07N 61.51W
St. John's Canada 77 47.34N 52.43W
St. Johns U.S.A. 81 34.30N109.22W
St. Johns r. U.S.A. 85 30.24N 81.24W
St. Johnsbury U.S.A. 84 44.25N 72.01W
St. John's Pt. U.K. 13 54.14N 5.39W
St. Jordi, Golf de g. Spain 16 40.50N 1.10E
St. Joseph La. U.S.A. 83 31.55N 91.14W
St. Joseph Mich. U.S.A. 84 42.05N 86.30W
St. Joseph Mo. U.S.A. 82 39.46N 94.51W
St. Joseph, L. Canada 76 51.05N 90.35W
St. Jovite Canada 77 46.07N 74.36W
St. Jude Canada 77 45.46N 72.59W
St. Junien France 17 45.53N 0.55E
St. Just-en-Chaussée France 15 49.30N 2.26E
St. Kilda i. U.K. 8 57.55N 8.20W
St. Kitts-Nevis Leeward Is. 87 17.20N 62.45W
St. Lambert Canada 77 45.30N 73.30W
St. Laurent Man. Canada 75 50.24N 97.56W
St. Laurent Que. Canada 77 45.31N 73.41W
St. Laurent du Maroni Guiana 91 5.30N 54.02W
St. Lawrence r. Canada 77 48.45N 68.30W
St. Lawrence, G. of Canada 77 48.00N 62.00W
St. Lawrence I. U.S.A. 72 63.00N170.00W
St. Léonard d'Aston Canada 77 46.06N 72.22W
St. Lewis Sd. Canada 77 52.20N 55.40W
St. Lin Canada 77 45.51N 73.45W
St. Lô France 15 49.07N 1.05W
St. Louis Senegal 52 16.01N 16.30W
St. Louis U.S.A. 82 38.38N 90.11W
St. Louis Park town U.S.A. 82 44.56N 93.22W
St. Lucia Windward Is. 87 14.05N 61.00W
St. Lucia, L. R.S.A. 57 28.05S 32.26E
St. Magnus B. U.K. 8 60.25N 1.35W
St. Maixent France 17 46.25N 0.12W
St. Malo France 15 48.39N 2.00W
St. Malo, Golfe de g. France 17 49.20N 2.00W
St.-Marc Haiti 87 19.08N 72.41W
St. Margaret's Hope U.K. 12 58.49N 2.57W
St. Maries U.S.A. 80 47.19N116.35W
St. Martin Channel Is. Europe 11 49.27N 2.34W
St. Martin i. Leeward Is. 87 18.05N 63.05W
St. Martin, L. Canada 75 51.37N 98.29W
St. Martin's i. U.K. 11 49.57N 6.16W
St. Mary Channel Is. Europe 11 49.14N 2.10W
St. Mary Peak Australia 66 31.30S138.35E
St. Marys Australia 65 41.33S148.12E
St. Mary's r. Canada 77 45.02N 61.54W
St. Mary's i. U.K. 11 49.55N 6.16W
St. Mary's, C. Canada 77 46.49N 54.12W
St. Mary's B. Canada 77 46.50N 53.47W
St. Matthew I. U.S.A. 72 60.30N172.45W
St. Maur France 15 48.48N 2.30E
St. Maurice r. Canada 77 46.22N 72.32W
St. Moritz Switz. 20 46.30N 9.51E
St. Nazaire France 17 47.17N 2.12W
St. Neots U.K. 11 52.14N 0.16W
St. Niklaas Belgium 14 51.10N 4.09E
St. Omer France 17 50.45N 2.15E
St. Pacôme Canada 77 47.24N 69.57W
St. Pascal Canada 77 47.32N 69.48W
St. Paul r. Canada 77 51.26N 57.40W
St. Paul France 17 42.49N 2.29E
St. Paul Ark. U.S.A. 83 35.50N 93.48W
St. Paul Minn. U.S.A. 82 45.00N 93.10W
St. Paul Nebr. U.S.A. 82 41.13N 98.27W
St. Paul du Nord Canada 77 48.27N 69.15W
St. Paulin Canada 77 46.25N 73.01W
St. Paul Rocks is. Atlantic Oc. 95 1.00N 29.23W
St. Peter U.S.A. 82 44.17N 93.57W
St. Peter Port Channel Is. Europe 11 49.27N 2.32W
St. Petersburg U.S.A. 85 27.45N 82.40W
St. Pierre Char. Mar. France 17 45.57N 1.19W
St. Pierre S. Mar. France 15 49.48N 0.29E
St. Pierre, Lac l. Canada 77 46.12N 72.52W
St. Pierre and Miquelon is. N. America 77 46.55N 56.10W
St. Pierre-Église France 15 49.40N 1.24W
St. Pölten Austria 20 48.13N 15.37E
St. Polycarpe Canada 77 45.18N 74.18W
St. Quentin France 15 49.51N 3.17E
St. Seine-l'Abbaye France 15 47.26N 4.47E
St. Siméon Canada 77 47.55N 69.58W
St. Stephen Canada 77 45.12N 67.17W
St. Thomas Canada 76 42.47N 81.12W
St. Thomas i. U.S.V.Is. 87 18.22N 64.57W
St. Tropez France 17 43.16N 6.39E
St. Truiden Belgium 14 50.49N 5.11E
St. Valéry France 15 49.52N 0.43E
St. Vallier France 17 45.11N 4.49E
St. Vincent, G. Australia 66 35.00S138.05E
St. Vincent and the Grenadines Windward Is. 87 13.00N 61.15W
St. Vith Belgium 14 50.15N 6.08E
St. Wendel Germany 14 49.27N 7.10E
St. Yrieix France 17 45.31N 1.12E
St. Zénon Canada 77 46.33N 73.49W
Saitama d. Japan 35 35.55N139.00E
Sajama mtn. Bolivia 92 18.06S 69.00W
Saka Kenya 55 0.09S 39.18E
Sakai Japan 35 34.35N135.28E
Sakākah Saudi Arabia 42 29.59N 40.12E
Sakakawea, L. see Garrison Resr. U.S.A. 82
Sakami r. Canada 76 53.40N 76.40W
Sakami, Lac l. Canada 76 53.10N 77.00W
Sâkâne, Erg i-n f. Mali 50 21.00N 1.00W
Sakania Zaïre 55 12.44S 28.34E
Sakarya r. Turkey 42 41.08N 30.36E
Sakété Benin 53 6.45N 2.45E
Sakhalin i. Russian Fed. 31 50.00N143.00E
Sākhar Afghan. 40 32.57N 65.32E
Sakhi Sarwar Pakistan 40 29.59N 70.18E
Sakht-Sar Iran 43 36.54N 50.41E
Sākoli India 41 21.05N 79.59E
Sakrand Pakistan 40 26.08N 68.16E
Sakri India 40 21.02N 74.40E
Sakrivier R.S.A. 56 30.53S 20.24E
Sakti India 41 22.02N 82.58E
Sakuma Japan 35 35.05N137.48E
Sal r. Russian Fed. 25 47.33N 40.40E
Sala Ethiopia 48 16.58N 37.27E
Sala Sweden 23 59.55N 16.36E
Salaca r. Latvia 23 57.45N 24.21E
Salacgriva Latvia 23 57.45N 24.21E
Salado r. Buenos Aires Argentina 93 35.44S 57.22W
Salado r. Santa Fé Argentina 93 31.40S 60.41W
Salado r. La Pampa Argentina 93 36.15S 66.55W
Salado r. Mexico 83 26.50N 99.17W
Salaga Ghana 52 8.36N 0.32W
Salailua W. Samoa 68 13.42S172.35W
Şalālah Oman 38 17.00N 54.04E
Salālah Sudan 48 21.19N 36.13E
Salamanca Spain 16 40.58N 5.40W
Salamat d. Chad 49 11.00N 20.40E
Salāmbek Pakistan 40 28.18N 65.09E
Salamina Colombia 90 5.24N 75.31W
Salām Khān Afghan. 40 31.47N 66.45E
Salani W. Samoa 68 14.02S171.35W
Salatiga Indonesia 37 7.15S110.34E
Salāya India 40 22.19N 69.35E
Sala y Gomez i. Pacific Oc. 69 26.28S105.28W
Salbris France 15 47.26N 2.03E
Salcombe U.K. 11 50.14N 3.47W
Saldaña Spain 16 42.32N 4.48W
Saldanha R.S.A. 56 33.00S 17.56E
Saldanha B. R.S.A. 56 33.05S 17.50E
Saldus Latvia 23 56.40N 22.30E
Sale Australia 67 38.06S147.06E
Salé Morocco 50 34.04N 6.50W
Salekhard Russian Fed. 24 66.33N 66.35E
Salelologa W. Samoa 68 13.43S172.13W
Salem India 39 11.38N 78.08E
Salem Ind. U.S.A. 84 38.38N 86.06W
Salem Mo. U.S.A. 83 37.39N 91.32W
Salem N.J. U.S.A. 85 39.34N 75.28W
Salem Oreg. U.S.A. 80 44.57N123.01W
Salem Va. U.S.A. 85 37.17N 80.04W
Sälen Sweden 23 61.10N 13.16E
Salerno Italy 18 40.41N 14.45E
Salerno, Golfo di g. Italy 18 40.30N 14.45E
Salford U.K. 10 53.30N 2.17W
Salgótarján Hungary 21 48.07N 19.48E
Salgueiro Brazil 91 8.04S 39.05W
Salima Malaŵi 55 13.45S 34.29E
Salim's Tanzania 55 10.37S 36.33E
Salina U.S.A. 82 38.50N 97.37W
Salina Cruz Mexico 86 16.11N 95.12W
Salinas Ecuador 90 2.13S 80.58W
Salinas U.S.A. 80 36.40N121.38W
Salinas r. U.S.A. 78 36.45N121.48W
Saline r. U.S.A. 82 38.51N 97.30W
Salinópolis Brazil 91 0.37S 47.20W
Salins France 17 46.56N 5.53E
Salisbury U.K. 11 51.04N 1.48W
Salisbury Md. U.S.A. 85 38.22N 75.36W
Salisbury N.C. U.S.A. 85 35.20N 80.30W
Salisbury Plain f. U.K. 11 51.15N 1.55W
Salisbury Sd. U.S.A. 74 57.30N135.56W
Şalkhad Syria 44 32.29N 36.42E
Sallisaw U.S.A. 83 35.28N 94.47W
Salluit Canada 73 62.10N 75.40W
Sallyāna Nepal 41 28.22N 82.12E
Salmās Iran 43 38.13N 44.50E
Salmi Russian Fed. 24 61.19N 31.46E
Salmon r. Canada 74 54.03N122.40W
Salmon U.S.A. 80 45.11N113.55W
Salmon r. U.S.A. 80 45.51N116.46W
Salmon Gums Australia 63 32.59S121.39E
Salmon River Mts. U.S.A. 80 44.45N115.30W
Salo Finland 23 60.23N 23.08E
Salò Italy 15 45.36N 10.31E
Salobreña Spain 16 36.45N 3.35W
Salome U.S.A. 81 33.47N113.37W
Salon France 17 43.38N 5.06E
Salonga r. Zaïre 54 0.09S 19.52E
Salonta Romania 21 46.48N 21.40E
Salsk Russian Fed. 25 46.30N 41.33E
Salso r. Italy 18 37.07N 13.57E
Salsomaggiore Terme Italy 15 44.49N 9.59E
Salt r. U.S.A. 81 33.23N112.18W
Salta Argentina 92 24.47S 65.24W
Salta d. Argentina 92 25.00S 65.00W
Saltdal Norway 22 67.06N 15.25E
Saltee Is. Rep. of Ire. 13 52.08N 6.36W
Saltfjorden est. Norway 22 67.15N 14.10E
Saltfleet U.K. 10 53.25N 0.11E
Salt Fork r. U.S.A. 79 36.41N 97.05W
Saltillo Mexico 83 25.25N101.00W
Salt Lake City U.S.A. 80 40.46N111.53W
Salto Argentina 93 34.17S 60.15W
Salto Brazil 94 23.10S 47.16W
Salto r. Italy 18 42.23N 12.54E
Salto Uruguay 93 31.23S 57.58W
Salto da Divisa Brazil 91 16.04S 40.00W
Salto Grande, Embalse de resr. Argentina / Uruguay 93 31.00S 57.50W
Salton Sea l. U.S.A. 81 33.19N115.50W
Salūmbar India 40 24.08N 74.03E
Saluzzo Italy 15 44.39N 7.29E
Salvador Brazil 91 12.58S 38.29W
Salvador Canada 75 52.12N109.32W
Salversville U.S.A. 85 37.43N 83.06W
Salween r. Burma 34 16.32N 97.35E
Salyany Azerbaijan 43 39.36N 48.59E
Salzbrunn Namibia 56 24.23S 18.00E
Salzburg Austria 20 47.54N 13.03E
Salzburg d. Austria 20 47.25N 13.15E
Salzgitter Germany 20 52.02N 10.22E
Salzwedel Germany 20 52.51N 11.09E
Sam India 40 26.50N 70.31E
Samalambo Angola 54 14.16S 17.53E
Samālūt Egypt 44 28.18N 30.43E
Samaná Dom. Rep. 87 19.14N 69.20W
Samana Cay i. Bahamas 87 23.05N 73.45W
Samanga Tanzania 55 8.24S 39.18E
Samannūd Egypt 44 30.58N 31.14E
Samar i. Phil. 37 11.45N125.15E
Samara Russian Fed. 24 53.10N 50.15E
Samara r. Russian Fed. 24 53.17N 50.42E
Samarai P.N.G. 64 10.37S150.40E
Samarinda Indonesia 36 0.30S117.09E
Samarkand Uzbekistan 28 39.40N 66.57E
Sāmarrā Iraq 43 34.13N 43.52E
Samāstipur India 41 25.51N 85.47E
Samawāri Pakistan 40 28.34N 66.46E
Samba Zaïre 54 0.14N 21.19E
Sambalpur India 41 21.27N 83.58E
Sambao r. Madagascar 57 16.40S 44.26E
Sambava Madagascar 57 14.16S 50.10E

Sambāza to Sarpsborg

Sambāza Pakistan 40 31.46N 69.20E
Sambhal India 41 28.35N 78.33E
Sāmbhar India 40 26.55N 75.12E
Sāmbhar L. India 40 26.58N 75.05E
Sambor Ukraine 21 49.31N 23.10E
Samborombón, Bahía b. Argentina 93 36.00S 57.00W
Sambre r. Belgium 14 50.29N 4.52E
Samburu Kenya 55 3.46S 39.17E
Samch'ŏk S. Korea 31 37.30N129.10E
Samdari India 40 25.49N 72.35E
Same Tanzania 55 4.10S 37.43E
Samnū Libya 51 27.16N 14.54E
Samoa is. Pacific Oc. 68 14.20S170.00W
Samoa Is. Pacific Oc. 68 14.00S171.00W
Samobor Slovenia 20 45.48N 15.43E
Samorogouan Burkina 52 11.21N 4.57W
Sámos i. Greece 19 37.44N 26.45E
Samothráki i. Greece 19 40.26N 25.35E
Sampang Indonesia 37 7.13S113.15E
Sampit Indonesia 36 2.34S112.59E
Sam Rayburn Resr. U.S.A. 83 31.27N 94.37W
Samsang China 41 30.22N 82.57E
Sam Son Vietnam 33 19.44N105.53E
Samsun Turkey 42 41.17N 36.22E
Samtredia Georgia 25 42.10N 42.22E
Samui, Ko i. Thailand 34 9.30N100.00E
Samur r. Russian Fed. 25 42.00N 48.20E
Samut Prakan Thailand 34 13.32N100.35E
Samut Sakhon Thailand 34 13.31N100.13E
San r. Cambodia 34 13.32N105.57E
San Mali 52 13.21N 4.57W
San r. Poland 21 50.25N 22.20E
Sana r. Bosnia-Herzegovina 20 45.03N 16.23E
Şan'ā' Yemen 45 15.23N 44.14E
Sana see Şan'ā' Yemen 45
Sanaba Burkina 52 12.25N 3.47W
Sanaga r. Cameroon 53 3.35N 9.40E
San Ambrosio i. Pacific Oc. 69 26.28S 79.53W
Sānand India 40 22.59N 72.23E
Sanandaj Iran 43 35.18N 47.01E
San Andreas U.S.A. 80 38.12N120.41W
San Andrés, Isla de i. Colombia 87 12.33N 81.42W
San Andrés Tuxtla Mexico 86 18.27N 95.13W
San Angelo U.S.A. 83 31.28N100.26W
San Antonio Chile 93 33.35S 71.38W
San Antonio N.Mex. U.S.A. 81 33.55N106.52W
San Antonio Tex. U.S.A. 83 29.28N 98.31W
San Antonio, C. Cuba 87 21.50N 84.57W
San Antonio, Cabo c. Argentina 93 36.40S 56.42W
San Antonio, Punta c. Mexico 81 29.45N115.41W
San Antonio, Sierra de mts. Mexico 81 30.00N110.10W
San Antonio Abad Spain 16 38.58N 1.18E
San Antonio de Areco Argentina 93 34.16S 59.30W
San Antonio Oeste Argentina 93 40.44S 64.57W
San Augustine U.S.A. 83 31.32N 94.07W
Sanāwad India 40 22.11N 76.04E
San Benedetto Italy 18 42.57N 13.53E
San Benedetto Po Italy 15 45.02N 10.55E
San Benito Guatemala 87 16.55N 89.54W
San Benito U.S.A. 83 26.08N 97.38W
San Bernardino U.S.A. 81 34.06N117.17W
San Bernardo Chile 93 33.36S 70.43W
San Blas, C. U.S.A. 85 29.40N 85.22W
San Bonifacio Italy 15 45.24N 11.16E
San Carlos Chile 93 36.25S 71.58W
San Carlos Mexico 83 29.01N100.51W
San Carlos Nicaragua 87 11.07N 84.47W
San Carlos Phil. 37 15.59N120.22E
San Carlos Venezuela 90 1.55N 67.04W
San Carlos Venezuela 90 9.39N 68.35W
San Carlos de Bariloche Argentina 93 41.08S 71.15W
San Carlos del Zulia Venezuela 90 9.01N 71.55W
Sancerre France 15 47.20N 2.51E
Sancerrois, Collines du hills France 15 47.25N 2.45E
Sancha He r. China 33 26.50N106.04E
San Clemente U.S.A. 81 33.26N117.37W
San Clemente i. U.S.A. 81 32.54N118.29W
San Cristóbal Argentina 92 30.20S 61.41W
San Cristóbal Dom. Rep. 87 18.27N 70.07W
San Cristóbal Venezuela 90 7.46N 72.15W
Sancti Spíritus Cuba 87 21.55N 79.28W
Sand Norway 23 59.29N 6.15E
Sanda i. U.K. 12 55.17N 5.34W
Sandakan Malaysia 36 5.52N118.04E
Sandaré Mali 52 14.40N 10.15W
Sanday i. U.K. 12 59.15N 2.33W
Sandbach U.K. 10 53.09N 2.23W
Sandefjord Norway 23 59.08N 10.14E
Sanders U.S.A. 81 35.13N109.20W
Sanderson U.S.A. 83 30.09N102.24W
Sandersville U.S.A. 85 32.59N 82.49W
Sandgate Australia 67 27.18S153.00E
Sandhornöy i. Norway 22 67.05N 14.10E
Sāndi India 41 27.18N 79.57E
Sandia Peru 90 14.14S 69.25W
San Diego U.S.A. 81 32.43N117.09W
San Diego, C. Argentina 93 54.38S 65.05W
Sandīla India 41 27.05N 80.31E
Sand Lake town Canada 76 47.45N 84.30W
Sandnes Norway 23 58.51N 5.44E
Sandness U.K. 12 60.18N 1.38W
Sandoá i. Faroe Is. 8 61.50N 6.45W
Sandoa Zaïre 54 9.41S 22.56E
Sandomierz Poland 21 50.41N 21.45E
San Donà di Piave Italy 15 45.38N 12.34E
Sandover r. Australia 64 21.43S136.32E
Sandoway Burma 34 18.28N 94.20E
Sandown U.K. 11 50.39N 1.09W
Sandpoint town U.S.A. 80 48.17N116.34W
Sandringham U.K. 10 52.50N 0.30E
Sandstone Australia 63 27.59S119.17E
Sandu Shuizu Zizhixian China 33 25.59N107.52E
Sandusky U.S.A. 84 41.27N 82.42W
Sandveld f. Namibia 56 21.25S 20.00E
Sandviken Sweden 23 60.37N 16.46E
Sandwich B. Canada 77 53.35N 57.15W
Sandwip I. Bangla. 41 22.29N 91.26E
Sandy U.S.A. 80 40.35N111.53W
Sandy B. St. Helena 95 16.02S 5.42W
Sandy Bight b. Australia 63 33.53S123.25E
Sandy C. Australia 64 24.42S153.17E
Sandy Creek town U.S.A. 84 43.39N 76.05W
Sandy Desert Pakistan 40 28.00N 65.00E
Sandy Hook f. U.S.A. 85 40.27N 74.00W
Sandy L. Nfld. Canada 77 49.16N 57.00W
Sandy L. Ont. Canada 75 53.00N 93.00W
Sandy Lake town Ont. Canada 75 53.00N 93.00W
Sandy Lake town Sask. Canada 75 57.00N107.15W
San Enrique Argentina 93 35.47S 60.22W
San Esteban, Isla i. Mexico 81 28.41N112.35W
San Felipe Chile 93 32.45S 70.44W
San Felipe Colombia 90 1.55N 67.06W
San Felipe Mexico 81 31.00N114.52W
San Felipe Venezuela 90 10.25N 68.40W
San Félix i. Pacific Oc. 69 26.23S 80.05W
San Fernando Argentina 93 34.26S 58.34W
San Fernando Chile 93 34.35S 71.00W
San Fernando r. Mexico 83 24.55N 97.40W
San Fernando Phil. 37 16.39N120.19E
San Fernando Spain 16 36.28N 6.12W
San Fernando Trinidad 90 10.16N 61.28W
San Fernando de Apure Venezuela 90 7.35N 67.15W
San Fernando de Atabapo Venezuela 90 4.03N 67.45W
Sanford r. Australia 62 27.22S115.53E
Sanford Fla. U.S.A. 85 28.49N 81.17W
Sanford N.C. U.S.A. 85 35.29N 79.10W
San Francisco Argentina 92 31.29S 62.06W
San Francisco Mexico 81 30.50N112.40W
San Francisco U.S.A. 80 37.48N122.24W
San Francisco r. U.S.A. 81 32.59N109.22W
San Francisco, C. Ecuador 90 0.50N 80.05W
San Francisco del Oro Mexico 81 26.52N105.51W
San Francisco de Macorís Dom. Rep. 87 19.19N 70.15W
Sanga Angola 54 11.09S 15.21E
Sanga-Tolon Russian Fed. 29 61.44N149.30E
Sang-e Māsheh Afghan. 40 33.08N 67.27E
Sanggan He r. China 32 40.23N115.18E
Sangha r. Congo 54 1.10S 16.47E
Sanghar Pakistan 40 26.02N 68.57E
Sangihe i. Indonesia 37 3.30N125.30E
Sangihe, Kepulauan is. Indonesia 37 2.45N125.20E
San Gil Colombia 90 6.35N 73.08W
San Giovanni in Persiceto Italy 15 44.38N 11.11E
Sangkulirang Indonesia 36 1.00N117.58E
Sāngli India 38 16.55N 74.37E
Sangmélima Cameroon 53 2.55N 12.01E
Sangonera r. Spain 16 37.58N 1.04W
San Gottardo, Passo del pass Switz. 20 46.30N 8.55E
Sangre de Cristo Mts. U.S.A. 80 37.30N105.15W
San Gregorio Uruguay 93 32.37S 55.40W
Sangri China 41 29.18N 92.05E
Sangrūr India 40 30.14N 75.51E
Sangzhi China 33 29.24N110.09E
Sanhala Ivory Coast 52 10.01N 6.48W
San Ignacio Bolivia 92 16.23S 60.59W
San Ignacio Mexico 81 27.27N112.51W
San Ignacio Paraguay 92 26.52S 57.03W
San Ignacio, Laguna l. Mexico 81 26.50N113.11W
San Isidro Argentina 93 34.29S 58.31W
Sanīyah, Hawr as l. Iraq 43 31.52N 46.50E
San Javier Argentina 93 30.40S 59.55W
San Javier Bolivia 92 16.22S 62.38W
San Javier Chile 93 35.35S 71.45W
Sanjāwi Pakistan 40 30.17N 68.21E
San Joaquin r. U.S.A. 80 38.03N121.50W
San Jorge, Bahía de b. Mexico 81 31.08N113.15W
San Jorge, Golfo g. Argentina 93 46.00S 66.00W
San José Costa Rica 87 9.59N 84.04W
San José Guatemala 86 13.58N 90.50W
San José Mexico 81 27.32N110.09W
San Jose U.S.A. 80 37.20N121.53W
San José, Isla i. Mexico 81 25.00N110.38W
San José de Chiquitos Bolivia 92 17.53S 60.45W
San José de Feliciano Argentina 93 30.25S 58.45W
San José de Guanipa Venezuela 90 8.54N 64.09W
San José del Cabo town Mexico 81 23.03N109.41W
San José del Guaviare Colombia 90 2.35N 72.38W
San José de Mayo Uruguay 93 34.20S 56.42W
San José de Ocuné Colombia 90 4.15N 70.20W
San Juan Argentina 92 31.30S 68.30W
San Juan d. Argentina 92 31.00S 68.30W
San Juan r. Costa Rica 87 10.50N 83.40W
San Juan Dom. Rep. 87 18.40N 71.05W
San Juan Peru 92 15.20S 75.09W
San Juan Phil. 37 8.25N126.22E
San Juan Puerto Rico 87 18.29N 66.08W
San Juan r. U.S.A. 80 37.18N110.28W
San Juan, C. Argentina 93 54.45S 63.50W
San Juan Bautista Spain 16 39.05N 1.30E
San Juan de Guadalupe Mexico 83 24.38N102.44W
San Juan del Norte Nicaragua 87 10.58N 83.40W
San Juan de los Morros Venezuela 90 9.53N 67.23W
San Juan del Río Durango Mexico 83 24.47N104.27W
San Juan del Río Querétaro Mexico 86 20.23N100.00W
San Juan Mts. U.S.A. 80 37.35N107.10W
San Julián Argentina 93 49.19S 67.40W
San Justo Argentina 93 30.47S 60.35W
Sankh r. India 41 22.15N 84.48E
Sankheda India 40 22.10N 73.35E
Sānkra India 41 20.18N 82.03E
Sankt Niklaus Switz. 15 46.11N 7.48E
Sankt-Peterburg Russian Fed. 24 59.55N 30.25E
Sankuru r. Zaïre 54 4.20S 20.27E
San Lázaro, Cabo c. Mexico 81 24.50N112.18W
San Lázaro, Sierra de mts. Mexico 81 23.20N110.00W
San Leonardo Spain 16 41.49N 3.04W
Sanliurfa Turkey 42 37.08N 38.45E
San Lorenzo Argentina 93 32.45S 60.44W
San Lorenzo mtn. Chile 93 47.37S 72.19W
San Lorenzo Ecuador 90 1.17N 78.50W
San Lorenzo r. Mexico 81 24.15N107.25W
San Lorenzo de El Escorial Spain 16 40.34N 4.08W
Sanlúcar de Barrameda Spain 16 36.46N 6.21W
Sanlúcar la Mayor Spain 16 37.26N 6.18W
San Lucas Bolivia 92 20.06S 65.07W
San Lucas, Cabo c. Mexico 81 22.50N109.55W
San Luis Argentina 93 33.20S 66.20W
San Luis d. Argentina 93 34.00S 66.00W
San Luis Cuba 87 20.13N 75.50W
San Luis Obispo U.S.A. 81 35.17N120.40W
San Luis Potosí Mexico 86 22.10N101.00W
San Luis Potosí d. Mexico 86 23.00N100.00W
San Luis Río Colorado Mexico 81 32.29N114.48W
San Luis Valley f. U.S.A. 80 37.25N106.00W
San Marcos U.S.A. 83 29.53N 97.57W
San Marino Europe 15 43.55N 12.27E
San Marino town San Marino 15 43.55N 12.27E
San Martín r. Bolivia 92 12.25S 64.25W
San Mateo U.S.A. 80 37.35N122.19W
San Matías Bolivia 90 16.22S 58.24W
San Matías, Golfo g. Argentina 93 41.30S 64.00W
Sanmenxia China 32 35.45N111.22E
San Miguel r. Bolivia 92 12.25S 64.25W
San Miguel r. Bolivia 90 13.52S 63.56W
San Miguel El Salvador 87 13.28N 88.10W
San Miguel del Monte Argentina 93 35.25S 58.49W
San Miguel de Tucumán Argentina 92 26.49S 65.13W
San Miguelito Panama 87 9.02N 79.30W
Sanming China 33 26.25N117.35E
Sannār Sudan 49 13.33N 33.38E
Sannicandro Italy 18 41.50N 15.34E
San Nicolas Argentina 93 33.20S 60.13W
Sanniquellie Liberia 52 7.24N 8.45W
Sanok Poland 21 49.35N 22.10E
San Pablo Phil. 37 13.58N121.10E
San Pedro Buenos Aires Argentina 93 33.40S 59.41W
San Pedro Jujuy Argentina 92 24.14S 64.50W
San Pedro Dom. Rep. 87 18.30N 69.18W
San Pedro Ivory Coast 52 4.45N 6.37W
San Pedro Mexico 81 27.00N109.53W
San Pedro Paraguay 94 24.08S 57.08W
San Pedro, Punta c. Costa Rica 87 8.38N 83.45W
San Pedro, Sierra de mts. Spain 16 39.20N 6.20W
San Pedro de las Colonais Mexico 83 25.45N102.59W
San Pedro Mártir, Sierra mts. Mexico 81 30.45N115.30W
San Pedro Sula Honduras 87 15.26N 88.01W
San Pellegrino Terme Italy 15 45.50N 9.40E
San Pietro i. Italy 18 39.09N 8.16E
Sanquhar U.K. 12 55.22N 3.56W
San Quintín Mexico 81 30.28N115.58W
San Rafael U.S.A. 80 37.59N122.31W
San Raphael Argentina 93 34.40S 68.21W
San Remo Italy 15 43.48N 7.46E
San Salvador Argentina 93 31.37S 58.30W
San Salvador i. Bahamas 87 24.00N 74.32W
San Salvador El Salvador 87 13.40N 89.10W
San Salvador de Jujuy Argentina 92 24.10S 65.20W
San Sebastián Argentina 93 53.15S 68.30W
San Sebastián Spain 16 43.19N 1.59W
San Severo Italy 18 41.40N 15.24E
Sanshui China 33 23.09N112.52E
San Simon U.S.A. 81 32.16N109.14W
Santa r. Peru 90 9.00S 78.35W
Santa Ana Argentina 92 27.20S 65.35W
Santa Ana Bolivia 92 13.45S 65.35W
Santa Ana El Salvador 87 14.00N 89.31W
Santa Ana Mexico 81 30.33N111.07W
Santa Ana U.S.A. 81 33.44N117.54W
Santa Bárbara Mexico 81 26.48N105.49W
Santa Barbara U.S.A. 81 34.25N119.42W
Santa Catarina d. Brazil 94 27.00S 52.00W
Santa Catarina Mexico 83 25.41N100.28W
Santa Clara Cuba 87 22.25N 79.58W
Santa Clara Calif. U.S.A. 80 37.21N121.57W
Santa Clara Utah U.S.A. 80 37.08N113.39W
Santa Clotilde Peru 90 2.25S 73.35W
Santa Comba Dão Portugal 16 40.24N 8.08W
Santa Cruz d. Argentina 93 48.00S 69.30W
Santa Cruz r. Argentina 93 50.03S 68.35W
Santa Cruz Bolivia 92 17.45S 63.14W
Santa Cruz d. Bolivia 92 17.45S 62.00W
Santa Cruz Madeira Is. 95 32.41N 16.48W
Santa Cruz U.S.A. 80 36.58N122.08W
Santa Cruz i. U.S.A. 81 34.01N119.45W
Santa Cruz de Tenerife Canary Is. 50 28.28N 16.15W
Santa Cruz Is. Solomon Is. 68 10.30S166.00E
Santa Domingo Mexico 81 25.32N112.02W
Santa Elena Argentina 93 31.00S 59.50W
Santa Elena U.S.A. 83 26.46N 98.30W
Santa Elena, C. Costa Rica 87 10.54N 85.56W
Santa Fé Argentina 93 31.40S 60.40W
Santa Fé d. Argentina 92 30.00S 61.00W
Santa Fe U.S.A. 81 35.42N106.57W
Santa Filomena Brazil 91 9.07S 45.56W
Santai China 33 31.10N105.02E
Santa Inés, Isla i. Chile 93 53.40S 73.00W
Santa Isabel Argentina 93 36.15S 66.55W
Santa Isabel do Morro Brazil 91 11.36S 50.37W
Sāntalpur India 40 23.45N 71.10E
Santa Lucía Uruguay 93 34.27S 56.24W
Santa Lucía r. Uruguay 93 34.48S 56.22W
Santa Lucia Range mts. U.S.A. 81 36.00N121.20W
Santa Margarita, Isla de i. Mexico 81 24.25N111.50W
Santa Margarita, Sierra de mts. Mexico 81 30.00N110.00W
Santa Margherita Ligure Italy 15 44.20N 9.12E
Santa María Brazil 94 29.40S 53.47W
Santa Maria U.S.A. 81 34.57N120.26W
Santa María, Laguna de l. Mexico 81 31.07N107.17W
Santa Maria di Leuca, Capo c. Italy 19 39.47N 18.24E
Santa Maria Madalena Brazil 94 21.58S 42.02W
Santa Marta Colombia 90 11.18N 74.10W
Santa Marta, Sierra Nevada de mts. Colombia 90 11.20N 73.00W
Santa Monica U.S.A. 81 34.01N118.30W
Santana Madeira Is. 95 32.48N 16.54W
Santana do Livramento Brazil 93 30.53S 55.31W
Santander Colombia 90 3.00N 76.25W
Santander Spain 16 43.28N 3.48W
Santañy Spain 16 39.20N 3.07E
Santarém Brazil 91 2.26S 54.41W
Santarém Portugal 16 39.14N 8.40W
Santa Rosa Argentina 93 36.00S 64.40W
Santa Rosa Bolivia 90 10.36S 67.25W
Santa Rosa Brazil 94 27.52S 54.29W
Santa Rosa Honduras 87 14.47N 88.46W
Santa Rosa Calif. U.S.A. 80 38.26N122.34W
Santa Rosa i. U.S.A. 81 33.58N120.06W
Santa Rosa N.Mex. U.S.A. 81 34.57N104.41W
Santa Rosa, Mt. Guam 68 13.32N144.55E
Santa Rosa de Cabal Colombia 90 4.52N 75.37W
Santa Rosalía Mexico 81 27.19N112.17W
Santa Rosa Range mts. U.S.A. 80 41.00N117.40W
Santa Teresa Mexico 83 25.19N 97.50W
Santa Vitória do Palmar Brazil 94 33.31S 53.21W
San Telmo Mexico 81 31.00N116.06W
Sant Feliu de Guixols Spain 16 41.47N 3.02E
Santhià Italy 15 45.22N 8.10E
Santiago Chile 93 33.27S 70.40W
Santiago Dom. Rep. 87 19.30N 70.42W
Santiago Panama 87 8.08N 80.59W
Santiago r. Peru 90 4.30S 77.48W
Santiago de Compostela Spain 16 42.52N 8.33W
Santiago de Cuba Cuba 87 20.00N 75.49W
Santiago del Estero Argentina 92 27.50S 64.15W
Santiago del Estero d. Argentina 92 27.40S 63.30W
Santiago Vázquez Uruguay 93 34.48S 56.21W
Sāntipur India 41 23.15N 88.26E
Santo Amaro Brazil 91 12.35S 38.41W
Santo André Brazil 94 23.39S 46.29W
Santo Angelo Brazil 94 28.18S 54.16W
Santo Antônio do Içá Brazil 90 3.05S 67.57W
Santo Domingo Dom. Rep. 87 18.30N 69.57W
Santo Domingo Pueblo U.S.A. 81 35.31N106.22W
Santoña Spain 16 43.27N 3.26W
Santos Brazil 94 23.56S 46.22W
Santos Dumont Brazil 94 21.30S 43.34W
Santo Tomás Peru 90 14.34S 72.30W
Santo Tomé Argentina 92 28.31S 56.03W
Santpoort Neth. 14 52.27N 4.38E
San Valentín, Cerro mtn. Chile 93 46.40S 73.25W
San Vicente El Salvador 87 13.38N 88.42W
San Vito al Tagliamento Italy 15 45.54N 12.52E
Sanya China 33 18.19N109.32E
Sanyuan China 32 34.30N108.52E
Sanza Pombo Angola 54 7.20S 16.12E
São Borja Brazil 94 28.35S 56.01W
São Caetano do Sul Brazil 94 23.36S 46.34W
São Carlos Brazil 94 22.01S 47.54W
São Domingos Guinea Bissau 52 12.22N 16.08W
São Francisco r. Brazil 91 10.20S 36.20W
São Francisco do Sul Brazil 94 26.17S 48.39W
São Gabriel Brazil 94 30.20S 54.19W
São Gonçalo do Sapucaí Brazil 94 21.54S 45.35W
Sao Hill town Tanzania 55 8.21S 35.10E
São João da Boa Vista Brazil 94 21.59S 46.45W
São João da Madeira Portugal 16 40.54N 8.30W
São João del Rei Brazil 94 21.08S 44.15W
São João do Piauí Brazil 91 8.21S 42.15W
São Joaquim da Barra Brazil 94 20.36S 47.51W
São José do Calçado Brazil 94 21.01S 41.37W
São José do Rio Prêto Brazil 94 20.50S 49.20W
São José dos Campos Brazil 94 23.07S 45.52W
São Leopoldo Brazil 94 29.46S 51.09W
São Lourenço Brazil 94 22.08S 45.05W
São Luís Brazil 91 2.34S 44.16W
São Manuel Brazil 94 22.40S 48.35W
São Manuel r. see Teles Pires r. Brazil 91
São Miguel d'Oeste Brazil 94 26.45S 53.34W
Saona i. Dom. Rep. 87 18.09N 68.42W
Saône r. France 20 45.46N 4.52E
Saoner India 41 21.23N 78.54E
São Paulo Brazil 94 23.33S 46.39W
São Paulo d. Brazil 94 22.05S 48.00W
São Paulo de Olivença Brazil 90 3.34S 68.55W
São Roque Brazil 94 23.31S 47.09W
São Roque, Cabo de c. Brazil 95 5.00S 35.00W
São Sebastião Brazil 94 23.48S 45.26W
São Sebastião, Ilha de i. Brazil 94 23.53S 45.17W
São Sebastião do Paraíso Brazil 94 20.54S 46.59W
São Tiago Brazil 94 20.54S 44.30W
São Tomé & Príncipe Africa 53 2.00N 6.40E
Saoura, Oued wadi Algeria 50 28.48N 0.50W
São Vicente Brazil 94 23.57S 46.23W
São Vicente, Cabo de c. Portugal 16 37.01N 8.59W
São Vicente de Minas Brazil 94 21.40S 44.26W
Sapé Brazil 91 7.06S 35.13W
Sapele Nigeria 53 5.53N 5.41E
Sapelo I. U.S.A. 85 31.28N 81.15W
Sapporo Japan 35 43.05N141.21E
Sapri Italy 18 40.04N 15.38E
Sapt Kosi r. Nepal 41 26.30N 86.55E
Sapu Angola 54 12.28S 19.26E
Sapulpa U.S.A. 83 36.00N 96.06W
Saqin Sum China 32 42.06N111.03E
Saqqārah Egypt 44 29.51N 31.13E
Saqqez Iran 43 36.14N 46.15E
Sarāb Iran 43 37.56N 47.35E
Sarābiyūm Egypt 44 30.23N 32.17E
Sara Buri Thailand 34 14.30N100.59E
Saragossa see Zaragoza Spain 16
Sarāi Naurang Pakistan 40 32.50N 70.47E
Sarajevo Bosnia-Herzegovina 21 43.52N 18.26E
Saranac Lake town U.S.A. 76 44.20N 74.10W
Sarandí del Yí Uruguay 93 33.21S 55.38W
Sarandí Grande Uruguay 93 33.44S 56.20W
Sārangarh India 41 21.36N 83.05E
Sārangpur India 40 23.34N 76.28E
Saranley Somali Rep. 49 2.28N 42.08E
Saranpaul Russian Fed. 24 64.15N 60.58E
Saransk Russian Fed. 24 54.12N 45.10E
Sarapul Russian Fed. 24 56.30N 53.49E
Sarar Plain Somali Rep. 45 9.35N 46.15E
Sarasota U.S.A. 85 27.20N 82.32W
Sarata Ukraine 21 46.00N 29.40E
Saratoga U.S.A. 80 37.16N122.02W
Saratoga Springs U.S.A. 84 43.05N 73.47W
Saratov Russian Fed. 25 51.30N 45.55E
Saravan Laos 34 15.43N106.24E
Sarawak d. Malaysia 36 2.00N113.00E
Saraychik Kazakhstan 25 47.29N 51.42E
Sarbāz Iran 43 26.39N 61.20E
Sarcelles France 15 49.00N 2.23E
Sardār Chāh Pakistan 40 27.58N 64.50E
Sardārpur India 40 22.39N 74.59E
Sardārshahr India 40 28.26N 74.29E
Sardegna d. Italy 18 40.05N 9.00E
Sardegna i. Italy 18 40.00N 9.00E
Sardinia i. see Sardegna i. Italy 18
Sarek mtn. Sweden 22 67.25N 17.46E
Sareks Nat. Park Sweden 22 67.15N 17.30E
Sargasso Sea Atlantic Oc. 95 28.00N 60.00W
Sargodha Pakistan 38 32.01N 72.40E
Sarh Chad 53 9.08N 18.22E
Sarhro, Jbel mts. Morocco 50 31.00N 5.55W
Sari Iran 43 36.33N 53.06E
Sarikamiş Turkey 42 40.19N 42.35E
Sarikei Malaysia 36 2.07N111.31E
Sarina Australia 64 21.26S149.13E
Sarita U.S.A. 83 27.13N 97.47W
Sark i. Channel Is. Europe 11 49.26N 2.22W
Sarlat France 17 44.53N 1.13E
Sărmasu Romania 21 46.46N 24.11E
Sarmi Indonesia 37 1.51S138.45E
Sarmiento Argentina 93 45.35S 69.05W
Särna Sweden 23 61.41N 13.08E
Sarnia Canada 76 42.58N 82.23W
Sarny Ukraine 21 51.21N 26.31E
Saronno Italy 15 45.38N 9.02E
Saros Körfezi g. Turkey 19 40.32N 26.25E
Sárospatak Hungary 21 48.19N 21.34E
Sarpsborg Norway 23 59.17N 11.07E

Sarrebourg to Shefford

Sarrebourg France 17 48.43N 7.03E
Sarreguemines France 17 49.06N 7.03E
Sarria Spain 16 42.47N 7.25W
Sarro Mali 52 13.40N 5.05W
Sartène France 17 41.36N 8.59E
Sarthe d. France 15 48.00N 0.05E
Sarthe r. France 15 47.29N 0.30W
Sartilly France 15 48.45N 1.27W
Sartynya Russian Fed. 28 63.22N 63.11E
Şarūr Oman 43 23.25N 58.10E
Sárvár Hungary 20 47.15N 16.57E
Saryshagan Kazakhstan 30 46.08N 73.32E
Sarzana Italy 15 44.07N 9.58E
Sasabeneh Ethiopia 45 7.55N 43.39E
Sasarām India 41 24.57N 84.02E
Sasebo Japan 35 33.10N129.42E
Saser mtn. Jammu & Kashmir 41 34.50N 77.50E
Saskatchewan d. Canada 75 55.00N106.00W
Saskatchewan r. Canada 75 53.12N 99.16W
Saskatoon Canada 75 52.07N106.38W
Sasovo Russian Fed. 24 54.21N 41.58E
Sassandra Ivory Coast 52 4.58N 6.08W
Sassandra r. Ivory Coast 52 5.00N 6.04W
Sassari Italy 18 40.43N 8.33E
Sassnitz Germany 20 54.32N 13.40E
Sasso Marconi Italy 15 44.24N 11.15E
Sassuolo Italy 15 44.33N 10.47E
Sastown Liberia 52 4.44N 8.01W
Sasyk, Ozero l. Ukraine 21 45.38N 29.38E
Satadougou Mali 52 12.30N 11.30W
Satāna India 40 20.35N 74.12E
Satanta U.S.A. 83 37.26N100.59W
Sātāra India 38 17.43N 74.05E
Satit r. Sudan 48 14.20N 35.50E
Satkānia Bangla. 41 22.04N 92.03E
Satna India 41 24.35N 80.50E
Sátoraljaújhely Hungary 21 48.24N 21.39E
Sātpura Range mts. India 40 21.30N 76.00E
Satu Mare Romania 21 47.48N 22.52E
Satun Thailand 34 6.38N100.05E
Sauce Argentina 93 30.05S 58.45W
Sauda Norway 23 59.39N 6.20E
Saudi Arabia Asia 42 26.00N 44.00E
Sauk Centre U.S.A. 82 45.44N 94.57W
Saulieu France 15 47.17N 4.14E
Sault Sainte Marie Canada 76 46.32N 84.20W
Sault Sainte Marie U.S.A. 84 46.29N 84.22W
Saumarez Reef Australia 64 21.50S153.40E
Saumlaki Indonesia 64 7.59S131.22E
Saumur France 15 47.16N 0.05W
Saurimo Angola 54 9.38S 20.20E
Sausar India 41 21.42N 78.52E
Sava r. Europe 21 44.50N 20.26E
Savage U.S.A. 80 47.27N104.21W
Savai'i i. W. Samoa 68 13.36S172.27W
Savalou Benin 53 7.55N 1.59E
Savanna U.S.A. 82 42.06N 90.07W
Savannah Ga. U.S.A. 85 32.04N 81.05W
Savannah r. U.S.A. 85 32.02N 80.53W
Savannah Tenn. U.S.A. 83 35.14N 88.14W
Savannakhét Laos 34 16.34N104.48E
Savant L. Canada 76 50.48N 90.20W
Savant Lake town Canada 76 50.20N 90.40W
Savé Benin 53 8.04N 2.37E
Save r. Mozambique 57 20.59S 35.02E
Save r. Zimbabwe 57 21.16S 32.20E
Sāveh Iran 43 35.00N 50.25E
Savelugu Ghana 52 9.39N 0.48W
Saverdun France 17 43.14N 1.35E
Savigliano Italy 15 44.38N 7.40E
Savigny-sur-Braye France 15 47.53N 0.49E
Savona Italy 15 44.18N 8.28E
Savonlinna Finland 24 61.52N 28.51E
Savoonga U.S.A. 72 63.42N170.27W
Savu Sea see Sawu, Laut sea Pacific Oc. 37
Sawai Mādhopur India 40 25.59N 76.22E
Sawākin Sudan 48 19.07N 37.20E
Sawatch Range mts. U.S.A. 82 39.10N106.25W
Sawbridgeworth U.K. 11 51.50N 0.09W
Sawdā', Jabal as hills Libya 51 28.40N 15.00E
Sawdā', Qurnat as mtn. Lebanon 44 34.17N 36.04E
Sawdirī Sudan 48 14.25N 29.05E
Sawfajjin, Wādī Libya 51 31.54N 15.07E
Sawhāj Egypt 42 26.33N 31.42E
Şawqirah, Ghubbat b. Oman 45 18.35N 57.00E
Sawston U.K. 11 52.07N 0.11E
Sawtell Australia 67 30.21S153.05E
Sawtooth Mts. U.S.A. 80 44.03N114.35W
Sawu i. Indonesia 37 10.30S121.50E
Sawu, Laut sea Pacific Oc. 37 9.30S122.30E
Saxmundham U.K. 11 52.13N 1.29E
Saxon Switz. 15 46.09N 7.11E
Say Mali 52 13.50N 4.57W
Say Niger 53 13.08N 2.22E
Sayama Japan 35 35.51N139.24E
Şaydā Lebanon 44 33.32N 35.22E
Sayers Lake town Australia 66 32.46S143.20E
Saynshand Mongolia 32 44.58N110.12E
Saynshand Mongolia 32 43.33N102.13E
Sayula Mexico 86 19.52N103.36W
Sázava r. Czech Republic 20 49.53N 14.21E
Sbaa Algeria 50 28.13N 0.10W
Scafell Pike mtn. U.K. 10 54.27N 3.12W
Scalea Italy 18 39.49N 15.48E
Scalloway U.K. 12 60.08N 1.17W
Scammon Bay town U.S.A. 72 61.50N165.35W
Scapa Flow str. U.K. 12 58.53N 3.05W
Scarborough Canada 76 43.44N 79.16W
Scarborough Tobago 90 11.11N 60.45W
Scarborough U.K. 10 54.17N 0.24W
Scenic U.S.A. 80 43.46N102.32W
Schaerbeek Belgium 14 50.54N 4.20E
Schaffhausen Switz. 20 47.42N 8.38E
Schagen Neth. 14 52.47N 4.47E
Schefferville Canada 73 54.50N 67.00W
Schelde r. Belgium 14 51.13N 4.25E
Schell Creek Range mts. U.S.A. 80 39.10N114.40W
Schenectady U.S.A. 84 42.47N 73.53W
Scheveningen Neth. 14 52.07N 4.16E
Schiedam Neth. 14 51.55N 4.25E
Schiermonnikoog i. Neth. 14 53.28N 6.15E
Schio Italy 15 45.43N 11.21E
Schleiden Germany 14 50.32N 6.29E
Schleswig Germany 20 54.32N 9.34E
Schleswig-Holstein d. Germany 20 54.00N 10.30E
Schouten, Kepulauan is. Indonesia 37 0.45S135.50E
Schouwen i. Neth. 14 51.42N 3.45E
Schreiber Canada 76 48.45N 87.20W
Schuler Canada 75 50.22N110.05W
Schuylkill r. U.S.A. 85 39.53N 75.12W
Schwandorf Germany 20 49.20N 12.08E
Schwaner, Pegunungan mts. Indonesia 36 0.45S113.20E
Schwarzrand mts. Namibia 56 25.40S 16.53E
Schwarzwald f. Germany 20 48.00N 7.45E
Schwedt Germany 20 53.04N 14.17E
Schweich Germany 14 49.50N 6.47E
Schweinfurt Germany 20 50.03N 10.16E
Schwelm Germany 14 51.17N 7.18E
Schwerin Germany 20 53.38N 11.25E
Schwyz Switz. 20 47.02N 8.40E
Sciacca Italy 18 37.31N 13.05E
Scilla Italy 18 38.15N 15.44E
Scilly, Isles of U.K. 11 49.55N 6.20W
Scobey U.S.A. 80 48.47N105.25W
Scone Australia 67 32.01S150.53E
Scotia U.S.A. 80 40.26N123.31W
Scotia Ridge f. Atlantic Oc. 95 60.00S 35.00W
Scotia Sea Atlantic Oc. 95 57.00S 45.00W
Scotland U.K. 12 55.30N 4.00W
Scotsbluff U.S.A. 82 41.52N103.40W
Scottburgh R.S.A. 56 30.17S 30.45E
Scott City U.S.A. 82 38.29N100.54W
Scott Is. Canada 74 50.48N128.40W
Scott L. Canada 75 59.55N106.18W
Scott Reef Australia 62 14.00S121.50E
Scottsbluff U.S.A. 80 41.52N103.40W
Scottsboro U.S.A. 83 34.40N 86.02W
Scottsdale Australia 65 41.09S147.31E
Scottsdale U.S.A. 81 33.30N111.56W
Scottsville U.S.A. 83 36.45N 86.11W
Scranton U.S.A. 84 41.24N 75.40W
Scugog, L. Canada 76 44.10N 78.51W
Scunthorpe U.K. 10 53.35N 0.38W
Scutari, L. Yugo./Albania 19 42.10N 19.18E
Seabrook, L. Australia 63 30.56S119.40E
Seaford U.S.A. 85 38.39N 75.37W
Seagroves U.S.A. 83 32.57N102.34W
Seahouses U.K. 10 55.35N 1.38W
Sea Isle City U.S.A. 85 39.09N 74.42W
Seal r. Canada 75 59.04N 94.48W
Sea Lake town Australia 66 35.31S142.54E
Seal Bight Canada 77 52.27N 55.40W
Searchlight U.S.A. 81 35.28N114.55W
Seascale U.K. 10 54.24N 3.29W
Seaside Calif. U.S.A. 80 36.37N121.50W
Seaside Oreg. U.S.A. 80 46.02N123.55W
Seaton U.K. 11 50.43N 3.05W
Seattle U.S.A. 80 47.36N122.20W
Seaview Range mts. Australia 64 18.56S146.00E
Sebastian U.S.A. 85 27.50N 80.29W
Sebastián Vizcaíno, Bahía b. Mexico 81 28.00N114.30W
Sebba Burkina 52 13.27N 0.33E
Sebeş Romania 21 45.58N 23.34E
Sebidiro P.N.G. 37 9.00S142.15E
Sebinkarahisar Turkey 42 40.19N 38.25E
Sebou, Oued r. Morocco 50 34.15N 6.40W
Sebring U.S.A. 85 27.30N 81.28W
Sechura, Desierto de des. Peru 90 6.00S 80.30W
Seclin France 14 50.34N 3.01E
Sêda r. Portugal 16 38.55N 7.30W
Sedalia U.S.A. 82 38.42N 93.14W
Sedan France 15 49.42N 4.57E
Sedan U.S.A. 83 37.08N 96.11W
Seddon New Zealand 60 41.40S174.04E
Sedgewick Canada 75 52.46N111.41W
Sédhiou Senegal 52 12.44N 15.30W
Sedom Israel 44 31.04N 35.23E
Seeheim Namibia 56 26.50S 17.45E
Sées France 15 48.38N 0.10E
Sefrou Morocco 50 33.50N 4.50W
Segbwema Sierra Leone 52 8.00N 11.00W
Segueur, Oued es wadi Algeria 51 31.44N 2.18E
Ségou Mali 52 13.28N 6.18W
Ségou d. Mali 52 13.55N 6.20W
Segovia Spain 16 40.57N 4.07W
Segozero, Ozero l. Russian Fed. 24 63.15N 33.40E
Segré France 15 47.41N 0.53W
Segre r. Spain 16 41.25N 0.21E
Séguédine Niger 53 20.12N 12.59E
Séguéla Ivory Coast 52 7.58N 6.44W
Seguin U.S.A. 83 29.34N 97.58W
Segura Portugal 16 39.50N 6.59W
Segura r. Spain 16 38.07N 0.14W
Segura, Sierra de mts. Spain 16 38.00N 2.50W
Sehore India 40 23.12N 77.05E
Sehwān Pakistan 40 26.26N 67.52E
Seiches-sur-le-Loir France 15 47.35N 0.22W
Seiland i. Norway 22 70.25N 23.10E
Seinäjoki Finland 22 62.47N 22.50E
Seine r. France 15 49.28N 0.25E
Seine, Baie de la b. France 15 49.25N 0.15E
Seine-et-Marne d. France 15 48.30N 3.00E
Seine-Maritime d. France 15 49.45N 1.00E
Sekayu Indonesia 36 2.58S103.58E
Seki Japan 35 35.29N136.55E
Sekoma Botswana 56 24.41S 23.50E
Sekondi-Takoradi Ghana 52 4.57N 1.44W
Sek'ot'a Ethiopia 49 12.38N 39.03E
Sekūheh Iran 43 30.45N 61.29E
Selaru i. Indonesia 64 8.09S131.00E
Selatan, Tanjung c. Indonesia 36 4.20S114.45E
Selatan Natuna, Kepulauan is. Indonesia 36 3.00N108.50E
Selayar i. Indonesia 37 6.07S120.28E
Selbu Norway 22 63.14N 11.03E
Selby U.K. 10 53.47N 1.05W
Selby U.S.A. 82 45.31N100.02W
Selbyville U.S.A. 85 38.28N 75.13W
Seldovia U.S.A. 72 59.27N151.43W
Sele r. Italy 18 40.30N 14.50E
Selenga r. Russian Fed. 30 52.20N106.20E
Selenge Mörön r. see Selenga Mongolia 30
Sélestat France 20 48.16N 7.28E
Seligman U.S.A. 81 35.20N112.53W
Sélingue, Lac de l. Mali 52 11.25N 8.15W
Seljord Norway 23 59.29N 8.37E
Selkirk Man. Canada 75 50.09N 96.52W
Selkirk Ont. Canada 76 42.49N 79.56W
Selkirk U.K. 12 55.33N 2.51W
Selkirk Mts. Canada 74 50.02N116.20W
Selles-sur-Cher France 15 47.16N 1.33E
Sells U.S.A. 81 31.55N111.53W
Selma Ala. U.S.A. 83 32.25N 87.01W
Selma Calif. U.S.A. 81 36.34N119.37W
Selmer U.S.A. 83 35.11N 88.36W
Selseleh ye Safid Kūh mts. Afghan. 43 34.30N 63.30E
Selsey Bill c. U.K. 11 50.44N 0.47W
Selty Russian Fed. 24 57.19N 52.12E
Sélune r. France 15 48.35N 1.15W
Selva Argentina 94 29.50S 62.02W
Selvas f. Brazil 90 6.00S 65.00W
Selwyn L. Canada 75 60.00N104.30W
Selwyn Mts. Canada 72 63.00N130.00W
Selwyn Range mts. Australia 64 21.35S140.35E
Seman r. Albania 19 40.53N 19.25E
Semara W. Sahara 50 26.44N 14.41W
Semarang Indonesia 37 6.58S110.29E
Sembabule Uganda 55 0.08S 31.27E
Semeru, Gunung mtn. Indonesia 37 8.04S112.53E
Seminoe Resr. U.S.A. 80 42.00N106.50W
Seminole U.S.A. 83 32.43N102.39W
Semiozernoye Kazakhstan 28 52.22N 64.06E
Semipalatinsk Kazakhstan 28 50.26N 80.16E
Semīrom Iran 43 31.31N 52.10E
Semiyarka Kazakhstan 28 50.52N 78.23E
Semliki r. Zaïre 55 1.12N 30.27E
Semmering Pass Austria 20 47.40N 16.00E
Semnān Iran 43 35.31N 53.24E
Semois r. France 14 49.53N 4.45E
Semporna Malaysia 36 4.27N118.36E
Semu r. Tanzania 55 3.57S 34.20E
Semur-en-Auxois France 15 47.29N 4.20E
Sena Mozambique 55 17.36S 35.00E
Senador Pompeu Brazil 91 5.30S 39.25W
Senaja Malaysia 36 6.49N117.02E
Sena Madureira Brazil 90 9.04S 68.40W
Senanga Zambia 54 15.52S 23.19E
Senatobia U.S.A. 83 34.39N 89.58W
Sendai Japan 35 38.16N140.52E
Sendenhorst Germany 14 51.52N 7.50E
Sendhwa India 40 21.41N 75.06E
Sendurjana India 41 21.32N 78.17E
Seneca Oreg. U.S.A. 80 44.08N118.58W
Seneca S.C. U.S.A. 85 34.41N 82.59W
Senegal Africa 52 14.30N 14.30W
Sénégal r. Senegal/Mauritania 52 16.00N 16.28W
Senekal R.S.A. 56 28.18S 27.37E
Senhor do Bonfim Brazil 91 10.28S 40.11W
Senica Slovakia 21 48.41N 17.22E
Senigallia Italy 20 43.42N 13.14E
Senise Italy 18 40.09N 16.18E
Senj Croatia 20 45.00N 14.58E
Senja i. Norway 22 69.15N 17.20E
Senlis France 15 49.12N 2.35E
Senmonoron Vietnam 34 12.27N107.12E
Sennan Japan 35 34.22N135.17E
Sennen U.K. 11 50.04N 5.42W
Senneterre Canada 76 48.25N 77.15W
Sens France 15 48.12N 3.18E
Senta Yugo. 21 45.56N 20.04E
Sentinel U.S.A. 81 32.53N113.12W
Seonāth r. India 41 21.44N 82.28E
Seoni India 41 22.05N 79.32E
Seoni Mālwa India 41 22.27N 77.28E
Seorīnārāyan India 41 21.44N 82.35E
Seoul see Sŏul S. Korea 31
Sepik r. P.N.G. 37 3.54S144.30E
Sepopa Botswana 56 18.45S 22.11E
Sept Îles town Canada 77 50.12N 66.23W
Sepúlveda Spain 16 41.18N 3.45W
Seraing Belgium 14 50.37N 5.33E
Seram i. Indonesia 37 3.10S129.30E
Seram, Laut sea Pacific Oc. 37 2.50S128.00E
Serang Indonesia 37 6.07S106.09E
Serbia d. see Srbija d. Yugo. 21
Serdo Ethiopia 49 11.59N 41.30E
Seremban Malaysia 36 2.42N101.54E
Serengeti Nat. Park Tanzania 55 2.30S 35.00E
Serengeti Plain f. Tanzania 55 3.00S 35.00E
Serenje Zambia 55 13.12S 30.50E
Sergach Russian Fed. 24 55.32N 45.27E
Sergipe d. Brazil 91 11.00S 37.00W
Sergiyev Posad Russian Fed. 24 56.20N 38.10E
Sergiyevsk Russian Fed. 24 53.56N 50.01E
Seria Brunei 36 4.39N114.23E
Serian Malaysia 36 1.10N110.35E
Sericho Kenya 49 1.05N 39.05E
Sérifos i. Greece 19 37.11N 24.31E
Sérigny r. Canada 77 55.59N 68.43W
Serkout, Djebel mtn. Algeria 51 23.40N 6.48E
Serle, Mt Australia 66 30.34S138.55E
Sermata i. Indonesia 37 8.30S129.00E
Serodino Argentina 93 32.37S 60.57W
Serov Russian Fed. 24 59.42N 60.32E
Serowe Botswana 56 22.22S 26.42E
Serpa Portugal 16 37.56N 7.36W
Serpentine r. Australia 63 32.33S115.46E
Serpent's Mouth str. Venezuela 90 9.50N 61.00W
Serpukhov Russian Fed. 24 54.53N 37.25E
Serra do Navio Brazil 91 0.59N 52.03W
Sérrai Greece 19 41.04N 23.32E
Serra Talhada Brazil 91 8.01S 38.17W
Serravalle Scrivia Italy 15 44.43N 8.51E
Serre r. France 14 49.40N 3.22E
Serrinha Brazil 91 11.38S 38.56W
Sēru Ethiopia 49 7.50N 40.28E
Serui Indonesia 37 1.53S136.15E
Serule Botswana 56 21.54S 27.17E
Serviceton Australia 66 36.22S141.02E
Şes, Munţii mts. Romania 21 47.05N 22.30E
Seseganaga L. Canada 76 50.00N 90.10W
Sese Is. Uganda 55 0.20S 32.30E
Sesepe Indonesia 37 1.30S127.59E
Sesheke Zambia 54 17.14S 24.22E
Sesia r. Italy 15 45.05N 8.37E
Sesimbra Portugal 16 38.26N 9.06W
Sestao Spain 16 43.18N 3.00W
Sestri Levante Italy 15 44.16N 9.24E
Sète France 17 43.25N 3.43E
Sete Lagoas Brazil 94 19.29S 44.15W
Sétif Algeria 51 36.10N 5.26E
Seto Japan 35 35.14N137.06E
Settat Morocco 50 33.04N 7.37W
Setté Cama Gabon 54 2.32S 9.46E
Settimo Torinese Italy 15 45.09N 7.46E
Settle U.K. 10 54.05N 2.18W
Settlement of Edinburgh Tristan da Cunha 95 37.03S 12.18W
Setúbal Portugal 16 38.31N 8.54W
Setúbal, Baía de b. Portugal 16 38.20N 9.00W
Seul, Lac l. Canada 76 50.20N 92.30W
Sevagram India 41 20.45N 78.30E
Sevan, Ozero l. Armenia 43 40.22N 45.20E
Sevastopol' Ukraine 25 44.36N 33.31E
Sevenoaks U.K. 11 51.16N 0.12E
Seven Sisters Peaks mts. Canada 74 54.56N128.10W
Sévérac France 17 44.20N 3.05E
Severn r. Australia 67 29.08S150.50E
Severn r. Canada 75 56.00N 87.38W
Severn r. U.K. 11 51.50N 2.21W
Severnaya Zemlya is. Russian Fed. 29 80.00N 96.00E
Severnyy Russian Fed. 24 69.55N 49.01E
Severnyy Donets r. Russian Fed./Ukraine 25 49.08N 37.28E
Severnyy Dvina r. Russian Fed. 24 57.03N 24.00E
Severodvinsk Russian Fed. 24 64.35N 39.50E
Severomorsk Russian Fed. 24 69.05N 33.30E
Sevier r. U.S.A. 80 39.04N113.06W
Sevier L. U.S.A. 80 38.55N113.09W
Sevilla Spain 16 37.24N 5.59W
Sèvre-Nantaise r. France 17 47.12N 1.35W
Sèvre Niortaise r. France 17 46.35N 1.05W
Sewa Sierra Leone 52 7.15N 12.08W
Seward Alas. U.S.A. 72 60.05N149.34W
Seward Nebr. U.S.A. 82 40.55N 97.06W
Seward Pen. U.S.A. 72 65.00N164.10W
Seydhisfjördhur town Iceland 22 65.16N 14.02W
Seylac Somali Rep. 45 11.21N 43.30E
Seym r. Ukraine 25 51.30N 32.30E
Seymour Australia 67 37.01S145.10E
Seymour U.S.A. 83 33.35N 99.16W
Sézanne France 15 48.44N 3.44E
Sfax Tunisia 51 34.45N 10.43E
Sfîntu-Gheorghe Romania 21 45.52N 25.50E
'sGravenhage Neth. 14 52.05N 4.16E
Shaanxi d. China 32 35.00N108.30E
Shaba d. Zaïre 55 8.00S 27.00E
Shabeelle r. Somali Rep. 55 0.30N 43.10E
Shabunda Zaïre 55 2.42S 27.20E
Shache China 30 38.27N 77.16E
Shafter U.S.A. 81 35.30N119.16W
Shaftesbury U.K. 11 51.00N 2.12W
Shagamu r. Canada 75 55.50N 86.48W
Shāhābād India 41 27.39N 79.57E
Shāhāda India 40 21.28N 74.18E
Shahbā' Syria 44 32.51N 36.37E
Shāhbandar Pakistan 40 24.10N 67.54E
Shāhbāz Kalāt Pakistan 40 26.42N 63.58E
Shahdād Iran 43 30.27N 57.44E
Shāhdādkot Pakistan 40 27.51N 67.54E
Shāhdādpur Pakistan 40 25.56N 68.37E
Shahdol India 41 23.17N 81.21E
Shāhganj India 41 26.03N 82.41E
Shāhgarh India 40 27.07N 69.54E
Shaḥḥāt Libya 48 32.50N 21.52E
Shāh Jahān, Kūh-e mts. Iran 43 37.00N 58.00E
Shāhjahānpur India 41 27.53N 79.55E
Shāh Jūy Afghan. 40 32.31N 67.25E
Shāh Kot Pakistan 40 31.34N 73.29E
Shāh Kūh mtn. Iran 43 31.38N 59.16E
Shāhpur Pakistan 40 28.43N 68.25E
Shāhpura India 40 25.35N 75.00E
Shāhpur Chākar Pakistan 40 26.09N 68.39E
Shahrak Afghan. 40 34.06N 64.18E
Shahr-e Bābak Iran 43 30.08N 55.04E
Shahrestān Afghan. 40 34.22N 66.47E
Shahrezā Iran 43 32.00N 51.52E
Shahr Kord Iran 43 32.40N 50.52E
Shahsavār Iran 43 36.49N 50.54E
Sha'ib Abā al Qūr wadi Saudi Arabia 42 31.02N 42.00E
Shaikhpura India 41 25.09N 85.51E
Shājāpur India 40 23.26N 76.16E
Shakawe Botswana 56 18.22S 21.50E
Shaker Heights town U.S.A. 84 41.29N 81.36W
Shakhty Russian Fed. 25 47.43N 40.16E
Shakhunya Russian Fed. 24 57.41N 46.46E
Shaki Nigeria 53 8.41N 3.24E
Shakshūk Egypt 44 29.28N 30.42E
Shala Hāyk' l. Ethiopia 49 7.25N 38.30E
Shalingzi China 32 40.42N114.55E
Shallotte U.S.A. 85 33.58N 78.25W
Shām, Jabal ash mtn. Oman 43 23.14N 57.17E
Shamāl Dārfūr d. Sudan 48 17.15N 25.30E
Shamāl Kurdūfān d. Sudan 48 14.00N 29.00E
Shāmat al Akbād des. Saudi Arabia 42 28.15N 43.05E
Shāmli India 40 29.27N 77.19E
Shamokin U.S.A. 84 40.47N 76.34W
Shamrock U.S.A. 83 35.13N100.15W
Shamva Zimbabwe 57 17.20S 31.38E
Shan d. Burma 34 22.00N 98.00E
Shandī Sudan 48 16.42N 33.26E
Shandong d. China 32 36.00N119.00E
Shandong Bandao pen. China 32 37.00N121.30E
Shangcheng China 33 31.48N115.24E
Shangdu China 32 41.33N113.31E
Shanggao China 33 28.15N114.55E
Shanghai China 33 31.18N121.50E
Shanghai d. China 33 31.00N121.30E
Shanglin China 33 23.26N108.36E
Shangqiu China 32 34.21N115.40E
Shangrao China 33 28.24N117.56E
Shangshui China 32 33.31N114.39E
Shangxian see Shangzhou China 32
Shangyi China 32 41.06N114.00E
Shangyou Shuiku resr. China 33 25.52N114.21E
Shangyu China 33 30.01N120.52E
Shangzhou China 32 33.49N109.56E
Shanhaiguan China 32 39.58N119.45E
Shannon r. Rep. of Ire. 13 52.39N 8.43W
Shannon, Mouth of the est. Rep. of Ire. 13 52.29N 9.57W
Shan Plateau Burma 34 18.50N 98.00E
Shanshan China 30 42.52N 90.10E
Shantarskiy Ostrova is. Russian Fed. 29 55.00N138.00E
Shantou China 33 23.22N116.39E
Shanwa Tanzania 55 3.09S 33.48E
Shanxi d. China 32 37.00N112.00E
Shanyin China 32 39.30N112.50E
Shaoguan China 33 24.53N113.31E
Shaoxing China 33 30.01N120.40E
Shaoyang China 33 27.10N111.14E
Shap U.K. 10 54.32N 2.40W
Shapinsay i. U.K. 12 59.03N 2.51W
Shapur ruins Iran 43 29.42N 51.30E
Shaqrā' Saudi Arabia 43 25.17N 45.14E
Shaqrā' Yemen 45 13.21N 45.42E
Sharan Jogizai Pakistan 40 31.02N 68.33E
Shark B. Australia 62 25.30S113.30E
Sharlyk Russian Fed. 24 52.58N 54.46E
Sharm ash Shaykh Egypt 44 27.51N 34.16E
Sharon U.S.A. 84 41.16N 80.30W
Sharon Springs town U.S.A. 82 38.54N101.45W
Sharq al Istiwā'iyah d. Sudan 49 5.00N 33.00E
Sharqī, Al Jabal ash mts. Lebanon 44 34.00N 36.25E
Sharqiyah, Aş Şaḥrā' ash des. Egypt 44 27.40N 32.00E
Sharya Russian Fed. 24 58.22N 45.50E
Shashi r. Botswana/Zimbabwe 56 22.10S 29.15E
Shashi China 33 30.18N112.20E
Shasta, Mt. U.S.A. 80 41.20N122.20W
Shatt al Arab r. Iraq 43 30.00N 48.30E
Shaunavon Canada 75 49.40N108.25W
Shawangunk Mts. U.S.A. 85 41.35N 74.30W
Shawano U.S.A. 76 44.46N 88.38W
Shawbridge Canada 77 45.52N 74.05W
Shaw I. Australia 64 20.29S149.05E
Shawinigan Canada 77 46.33N 72.45W
Shawinigan Sud Canada 77 46.30N 72.45W
Shawnee U.S.A. 83 35.20N 96.55W
Sha Xi r. China 33 26.38N118.10E
Sha Xian China 33 26.27N117.42E
Shayang China 33 30.42N112.29E
Shay Gap town Australia 62 20.28S120.05E
Shaykh, Jabal ash mtn. Lebanon 44 33.24N 35.52E
Shaykh 'Uthmān Yemen 45 12.52N 44.59E
Shchara r. Belorussia 21 53.27N 24.45E
Shchelyayur Russian Fed. 24 65.16N 53.17E
Shchors Ukraine 21 51.50N 31.59E
Sheboygan U.S.A. 82 43.46N 87.36W
Shebshi Mts. Nigeria 53 8.30N 11.45E
Shediac Canada 77 46.13N 64.32W
Sheeffry Hills Rep. of Ire. 13 53.41N 9.42W
Sheelin, Lough Rep. of Ire. 13 53.48N 7.20W
Sheep Range mts. U.S.A. 81 36.45N115.05W
Sheet Harbour Canada 77 44.55N 62.32W
Sheffield U.K. 10 53.23N 1.28W
Sheffield Ala. U.S.A. 85 34.46N 87.40W
Sheffield Tex. U.S.A. 83 30.41N101.49W
Shefford U.K. 11 52.02N 0.20W

Sneem to Stokes Bay

Sneem Rep. of Ire. 13 51.50N 9.54W
Sneeuwberg mtn. R.S.A. 56 32.30S 19.09E
Śniardwy, Jezioro l. Poland 21 53.46N 21.44E
Snina Slovakia 21 48.59N 22.07E
Snizort, Loch U.K. 12 57.35N 6.30W
Snöhetta mtn. Norway 23 62.20N 9.17E
Snov r. Ukraine 21 51.45N 31.45E
Snowbird L. Canada 75 60.45N103.00W
Snowdon mtn. U.K. 10 53.05N 4.05W
Snowdrift Canada 75 62.24N110.44W
Snowdrift r. Canada 75 62.24N110.44W
Snowflake U.S.A. 81 34.30N110.05W
Snow Hill town U.S.A. 85 38.11N 75.23W
Snowy r. Australia 67 37.48S148.30E
Snowy r. Australia 67 37.49S148.30E
Snowy Mts. Australia 67 36.30S148.20E
Snyatyn Ukraine 21 48.30N 25.50E
Snyder U.S.A. 83 32.44N100.05W
Soacha Colombia 90 4.35N 74.13W
Soalala Madagascar 57 16.06S 45.20E
Soanierana-Ivongo Madagascar 57 16.55S 49.35E
Soasiu Indonesia 37 0.40N127.25E
Soavinandriana Madagascar 57 19.09S 46.45E
Sob r. Ukraine 21 48.42N 29.17E
Sobat r. Sudan 49 9.30N 31.30E
Sobernheim Germany 14 49.47N 7.40E
Soboko C.A.R. 49 6.49N 24.50E
Sobradinho, Represa de resr. Brazil 91 10.00S 42.30W
Sobral Brazil 91 3.45S 40.20W
Sochi Russian Fed. 25 43.35N 39.46E
Société, Îles de la is. Pacific Oc. 69 17.00S150.00W
Society Is. see Société, Îles de la is. Pacific Oc. 69
Socorro Colombia 90 6.30N 73.16W
Socorro U.S.A. 81 34.04N106.54W
Socorro, Isla i. Mexico 86 18.45N110.58W
Socotra i. see Suquţrá i. Yemen 45
Socuéllamos Spain 16 39.16N 2.47W
Sodankylä Finland 22 67.29N 26.32E
Söderhamn Sweden 23 61.18N 17.03E
Söderköping Sweden 23 58.29N 16.18E
Södermanland d. Sweden 23 59.10N 16.35E
Södertälje Sweden 23 59.12N 17.37E
Sodium R.S.A. 56 30.10S 23.08E
Sodo Ethiopia 49 6.52N 37.47E
Södra Vi Sweden 23 57.45N 15.48E
Soest Germany 14 51.34N 8.06E
Sofala Australia 67 33.05S149.42E
Sofala d. Mozambique 57 19.00S 34.39E
Sofia see Sofiya Bulgaria 19
Sofia r. Madagascar 57 15.27S 47.23E
Sofiya Bulgaria 19 42.41N 23.19E
Sofiysk Russian Fed. 29 52.19N133.55E
Sofporog Russian Fed. 24 65.47N 31.30E
Sogamoso Colombia 90 5.43N 72.56W
Sögel Germany 14 52.51N 7.31E
Sognefjorden est. Norway 23 61.06N 5.10E
Sogn og Fjordane d. Norway 23 61.30N 6.50E
Söğüt Turkey 42 40.02N 30.10E
Sog Xian China 41 31.51N 93.40E
Sohâgpur India 41 22.42N 78.12E
Soignies Belgium 14 50.35N 4.04E
Soissons France 15 49.23N 3.20E
Sojat India 40 25.55N 73.40E
Sokal Ukraine 21 50.30N 24.10E
Söke Turkey 19 37.46N 27.26E
Sokodé Togo 53 8.59N 1.11E
Sokol Russian Fed. 24 59.28N 40.04E
Sokółka Poland 21 53.25N 23.31E
Sokolo Mali 52 14.53N 6.11W
Sokolov Czech Republic 20 50.09N 12.40E
Sokoto Nigeria 53 13.02N 5.15E
Sokoto d. Nigeria 53 11.50N 5.05E
Sokoto r. Nigeria 53 13.05N 5.13E
Solbad Hall Austria 20 47.17N 11.31E
Solec Kujawski Poland 21 53.06N 18.14E
Soledad Venezuela 90 8.10N 63.34W
Solesmes France 14 50.12N 3.32E
Solginskiy Russian Fed. 24 61.07N 41.30E
Solheim Norway 23 60.53N 5.27E
Soligalich Russian Fed. 24 59.02N 42.15E
Solihull U.K. 9 52.26N 1.47W
Solikamsk Russian Fed. 24 59.40N 56.45E
Sol-Iletsk Russian Fed. 24 51.09N 55.00E
Solingen Germany 14 51.10N 7.05E
Sollefteå Sweden 22 63.12N 17.20E
Sollentuna Sweden 23 59.28N 17.54E
Sóller Spain 16 39.47N 2.41E
Sollia Norway 23 61.47N 10.24E
Solola Somali Rep. 49 0.08N 41.30E
Solomon Is. Pacific Oc. 68 8.00S160.00E
Solomons U.S.A. 85 38.21N 76.29W
Solomon Sea Pacific Oc. 61 7.00S150.00E
Solon U.S.A. 84 44.57N 69.52W
Solon Springs U.S.A. 82 46.22N 91.48W
Solothurn Switz. 20 47.13N 7.32E
Solovetskiye, Ostrova is. Russian Fed. 24 65.05N 35.30E
Šolta i. Croatia 18 43.23N 16.17E
Soltānābād Iran 43 36.25N 58.02E
Soltau Germany 20 52.59N 9.49E
Sölvesborg Sweden 23 56.03N 14.33E
Solway Firth est. U.K. 10 54.50N 3.30W
Solwezi Zambia 54 12.11S 26.23E
Solzach r. Austria 20 48.35N 13.30E
Soma Turkey 19 39.11N 27.36E
Somabhula Zimbabwe 56 19.40S 29.38E
Somali Republic Africa 45 5.30N 47.00E
Sombor Yugo. 19 45.48N 19.08E
Sombrerete Mexico 86 23.38N103.39W
Somerset d. U.K. 11 51.09N 3.00W
Somerset U.S.A. 85 37.05N 84.38W
Somerset East R.S.A. 56 32.43S 25.33E
Somerset I. Bermuda 95 32.18N 64.53W
Somerset I. Canada 73 73.00N 93.30W
Somers Point town U.S.A. 85 39.20N 74.36W
Somerville U.S.A. 85 40.34N 74.37W
Somes r. Hungary 21 48.40N 22.30E
Somme r. France 17 50.01N 1.40E
Sommen l. Sweden 23 58.01N 15.15E
Sompeta India 41 18.56N 84.36E
Sompuis France 15 48.41N 4.23E
Son r. India 41 25.42N 84.52E
Sonāmarg Jammu & Kashmir 40 34.18N 75.18E
Sonāmura India 41 23.29N 91.17E
Sonbong N. Korea 31 42.19N130.24E
Sönderborg Denmark 23 54.55N 9.47E
Sondershausen Germany 20 51.22N 10.52E
Söndreströmfjord Greenland 73 66.30N 50.52W
Sondrio Italy 15 46.10N 9.52E
Sonepur India 41 20.50N 83.55E
Songa r. Norway 23 59.45N 7.59E
Song-Cau Vietnam 34 13.27N109.13E
Songea Tanzania 55 10.42S 35.39E
Songhua Jiang r. China 31 47.46N132.30E
Songjiang China 33 31.01N121.20E
Songkhla Thailand 34 7.12N100.35E
Songololo Zaïre 54 5.40S 14.05E
Songpan China 32 32.36N103.36E
Songtao Miaozu Zizhixian China 33 28.12N109.12E
Song Xian China 32 34.02N111.48E
Sonid Youqi China 32 42.44N112.40E
Sonid Zuoqi China 32 43.58N113.59E
Sonipat India 40 28.59N 77.01E
Son La Vietnam 34 21.20N103.55E
Sonmiāni Pakistan 40 25.26N 66.36E
Sonmiāni B. Pakistan 40 25.15N 66.30E
Sonneberg Germany 20 50.22N 11.10E
Sonoita Mexico 81 31.51N112.50W
Sonora d. Mexico 81 29.30N110.40W
Sonora r. Mexico 81 28.50N111.33W
Sonora U.S.A. 83 30.34N100.39W
Sonsorol i. Pacific Oc. 37 5.20N132.13E
Son Tay Vietnam 33 21.15N105.17E
Sopi Indonesia 37 2.40N128.28E
Sopo r. Sudan 49 8.51N 26.11E
Sopot Poland 21 54.28N 18.34E
Sopotskin Belorussia 21 53.49N 23.42E
Soppero Sweden 22 68.07N 21.40E
Sopron Hungary 20 47.41N 16.36E
Sop's Arm town Canada 77 49.46N 56.56W
Sopur Jammu & Kashmir 40 34.18N 74.28E
Sorada India 41 19.45N 84.26E
Sorel Canada 77 46.03N 73.06W
Sörfjorden Norway 22 66.29N 13.20E
Sörfold Norway 22 67.30N 15.30E
Sorgono Italy 18 40.01N 9.06E
Soria Spain 16 41.46N 2.28W
Soriano Uruguay 93 33.24S 58.19W
Sor Kvalöy i. Norway 22 69.40N 18.30E
Sörli Norway 22 64.15N 13.50E
Sor Mertvyy Kultuk f. Kazakhstan 25 45.30N 54.00E
Soro India 41 21.17N 86.40E
Sorocaba Brazil 94 23.29S 47.27W
Sorochinsk Russian Fed. 24 52.29N 53.15E
Soroki Moldavia 21 48.08N 28.12E
Sorol i. Federated States of Micronesia 37 8.09N140.25E
Soron India 41 27.53N 78.45E
Sorong Indonesia 37 0.50S131.17E
Soroti Uganda 55 1.40N 33.37E
Söröya i. Norway 22 70.35N 22.30E
Sorraia r. Portugal 16 39.00N 8.51W
Sorrento Italy 18 40.37N 14.22E
Sör-Rondane mts. Antarctica 96 72.30S 22.00E
Sorsele Sweden 22 65.30N 17.30E
Sortavala Russian Fed. 24 61.40N 30.40E
Sortland Norway 22 68.44N 15.25E
Sör Tröndelag d. Norway 22 63.00N 10.20E
Sorūbī Afghan. 40 34.36N 69.43E
Sosnogorsk Russian Fed. 24 63.32N 53.55E
Sosnovo Russian Fed. 24 60.33N 30.11E
Sosnovyy Russian Fed. 24 66.01N 32.40E
Sosnowiec Poland 21 50.18N 19.08E
Sosva Russian Fed. 24 59.10N 61.50E
Sosyka Russian Fed. 25 46.11N 38.49E
Sotik Kenya 55 0.40S 35.08E
Sotra i. Norway 23 60.15N 5.10E
Sotteville France 15 49.25N 1.06E
Soubré Ivory Coast 52 5.50N 6.35W
Souderton U.S.A. 85 40.19N 75.19W
Souflay Congo 54 2.00N 14.54E
Souflíon Greece 19 41.12N 26.18E
Souk Ahras Algeria 51 36.17N 7.57E
Souk-el-Arba-du-Rharb Morocco 50 34.43N 6.01W
Sŏul S. Korea 31 37.30N127.00E
Sources, Mont-aux- mtn. Lesotho 56 28.44S 28.52E
Soure Portugal 16 40.04N 8.38W
Souris Man. Canada 75 49.38N100.15W
Souris P.E.I. Canada 77 46.21N 62.15W
Souris r. Canada 75 49.39N 99.34W
Sous, Oued wadi Morocco 50 30.27N 9.31W
Sousa Brazil 91 6.41S 38.14W
Sous le Vent, Îles is. Îs. de la Société 69 16.30S151.30W
Sousse Tunisia 51 35.48N 10.38E
Soustons France 17 43.45N 1.19W
South Alligator r. Australia 64 12.53S132.29E
Southampton Canada 76 44.29N 81.23W
Southampton U.K. 11 50.54N 1.23W
Southampton I. Canada 73 64.30N 84.00W
South Aulatsivik I. Canada 77 56.45N 61.30W
South Australia d. Australia 66 30.00S137.00E
South Bend Ind. U.S.A. 84 41.40N 86.15W
South Bend Wash. U.S.A. 80 46.40N123.48W
South Boston U.S.A. 85 36.42N 78.58W
South Branch U.S.A. 84 44.29N 83.36W
South Carolina d. U.S.A. 85 34.00N 81.00W
South Cerney U.K. 11 51.40N 1.55W
South China Sea Asia 36 12.30N115.00E
South Dakota d. U.S.A. 82 45.00N100.00W
South Dorset Downs hills U.K. 11 50.40N 2.25W
South Downs hills U.K. 11 50.04N 0.34W
South East d. Botswana 56 25.00S 25.45E
South East C. Australia 65 43.38S146.48E
South Eastern Atlantic Basin f. Atlantic Oc. 95 20.00S 0.00
South East Head c. Ascension 95 7.58S 14.18W
South East Is. Australia 63 34.23S123.30E
South East Pt. Kiribati 69 1.40N157.10W
Southend-on-Sea U.K. 11 51.32N 0.43E
Southern d. Zambia 56 16.30S 26.40E
Southern Alps mts. New Zealand 60 43.20S170.45E
Southern Cross Australia 63 31.14S119.16E
Southern Indian L. Canada 75 57.10N 98.40W
Southern Lueti r. Zambia 56 16.15S 23.12E
Southern Ocean Pacific Oc. 68 44.00S130.00E
Southern Pines U.S.A. 85 35.12N 79.23W
Southern Uplands hills U.K. 12 55.30N 3.30W
South Esk r. U.K. 12 56.43N 2.32W
South Esk Tablelands f. Australia 62 20.50S126.40E
Southey Canada 75 50.56N104.30W
South Fiji Basin Pacific Oc. 68 27.00S176.00E
South Georgia i. Atlantic Oc. 95 54.50S 36.00W
South Glamorgan d. U.K. 11 51.27N 3.22W
South-haa U.K. 12 60.34N 1.17W
South Hātia I. Bangla. 41 22.19N 91.07E
South Haven U.S.A. 84 42.25N 86.16W
South Henik L. Canada 75 61.30N 97.30W
South Honshu Ridge Pacific Oc. 68 22.00N141.00E
South Horr Kenya 55 2.10N 36.45E
South I. Kenya 55 2.36N 36.38E
South I. New Zealand 60 43.00S171.00E
South Knife r. Canada 75 58.55N 94.37W
South Korea Asia 31 36.00N128.00E
South Lake Tahoe town U.S.A. 80 38.57N119.57W
Southland d. New Zealand 60 45.40S168.00E
South Loup r. U.S.A. 82 41.04N 98.40W
South Molton U.K. 11 51.01N 3.50W
South Nahanni r. Canada 74 61.03N123.21W
South Orkney Is. Atlantic Oc. 95 60.50S 45.00W
South Platte r. U.S.A. 82 41.07N100.42W
Southport Qld. Australia 67 27.58S153.20E
Southport Tas. Australia 65 43.25S146.59E
Southport U.K. 10 53.38N 3.01W
Southport U.S.A. 85 33.55N 78.00W
South River town U.S.A. 85 40.27N 74.23W
South Ronaldsay i. U.K. 12 58.47N 2.56W
South Sandwich Is. Atlantic Oc. 95 57.00S 27.00W
South Sandwich Trench f. Atlantic Oc. 95 57.00S 25.00W
South Saskatchewan r. Canada 75 53.15N105.05W
South Seal r. Canada 75 58.48N 98.08W
South Shields U.K. 10 55.00N 1.24W
South Sioux City U.S.A. 82 42.28N 96.24W
South Tasmania Ridge f. Pac. Oc./Ind. Oc. 68 46.00S147.00E
South Thompson r. Canada 74 50.40N120.20W
South Tucson U.S.A. 81 32.12N110.58W
South Twin I. Canada 76 53.00N 79.50W
South Tyne r. U.K. 12 54.59N 2.08W
South Uist i. U.K. 12 57.15N 7.20W
South Wabasca L. Canada 74 55.54N113.45W
Southwest C. New Zealand 60 47.15S167.30E
South Western Pacific Basin Pacific Oc. 69 39.00S148.00W
South West Peru Ridge Pacific Oc. 69 20.00S 82.00W
South West Pt. c. Kiribati 69 1.52N157.33W
South West Pt. c. St. Helena 95 16.00S 5.48W
South Windham U.S.A. 84 43.44N 70.26W
Southwold U.K. 11 52.19N 1.41E
South Yorkshire d. U.K. 10 53.28N 1.25W
Soutpansberg mts. R.S.A. 56 22.58S 29.50E
Sovetsk Lithuania 23 55.05N 21.53E
Sovetsk Russian Fed. 24 57.39N 48.59E
Sovetskaya Gavan Russian Fed. 29 48.57N140.16E
Soweto R.S.A. 56 26.16S 27.51E
Soyo Angola 54 6.12S 12.25E
Soyopa Mexico 81 28.47N109.39W
Sozh r. Belorussia 21 51.57N 30.48E
Spa Belgium 14 50.29N 5.52E
Spain Europe 16 40.00N 4.00W
Spalding Australia 66 33.29S138.40E
Spalding U.K. 10 52.47N 0.09W
Spalding U.S.A. 82 41.41N 98.22W
Spandau Germany 20 52.32N 13.13E
Spanish Fork U.S.A. 80 40.07N111.39W
Sparks U.S.A. 80 39.32N119.45W
Sparrows Point town U.S.A. 85 39.13N 76.26W
Sparta Ga. U.S.A. 85 33.17N 82.58W
Sparta N.J. U.S.A. 85 41.02N 74.38W
Sparta Wisc. U.S.A. 82 43.57N 90.47W
Spartanburg U.S.A. 85 34.56N 81.57W
Spárti Greece 19 37.04N 22.28E
Spartivento, Capo c. Calabria Italy 18 37.55N 16.04E
Spartivento, Capo c. Sardegna Italy 18 38.53N 8.50E
Spátha, Ákra c. Greece 19 35.42N 23.43E
Spatsizi Plateau Wilderness Prov. Park Canada 74 57.13N127.53W
Spearman U.S.A. 83 36.12N101.12W
Speculator U.S.A. 84 43.30N 74.17W
Speke G. Tanzania 55 2.20S 33.30E
Spence Bay town Canada 73 69.30N 93.20W
Spencer Idaho U.S.A. 80 44.21N112.11W
Spencer Iowa U.S.A. 82 43.09N 95.09W
Spencer S.Dak. U.S.A. 82 43.44N 97.36W
Spencer, C. Australia 66 35.18S136.53E
Spencer G. Australia 66 34.00S137.00E
Spences Bridge town Canada 74 50.25N121.20W
Sperrin Mts. U.K. 13 54.49N 7.06W
Spétsai i. Greece 19 37.15N 23.10E
Spey r. U.K. 12 57.40N 3.06W
Speyer Germany 20 49.18N 8.26E
Spiekeroog i. Germany 14 53.48N 7.45E
Spilimbergo Italy 15 46.07N 12.54E
Spilsby U.K. 10 53.10N 0.06E
Spina ruins Italy 15 44.42N 12.08E
Spinazzola Italy 18 40.58N 16.06E
Spin Būldak Afghan. 40 31.01N 66.24E
Spirit River town Canada 74 55.45N118.50W
Spišská Nová Ves Slovakia 21 48.57N 20.34E
Spithead str. U.K. 11 50.45N 1.05W
Spitsbergen is. Arctic Oc. 96 78.00N 17.00E
Spittal an der Drau Austria 20 46.48N 13.30E
Split Croatia 19 43.32N 16.27E
Split L. Canada 75 56.08N 96.15W
Spofford U.S.A. 83 29.11N100.25W
Spokane U.S.A. 80 47.40N117.23W
Spokane r. U.S.A. 80 47.44N118.20W
Spooner U.S.A. 82 45.50N 91.53W
Spratly i. S. China Sea 36 8.45N111.54E
Spray U.S.A. 80 44.50N119.48W
Spree r. Germany 20 52.32N 13.15E
Springbok R.S.A. 56 29.40S 17.50E
Springdale Canada 77 49.30N 56.04W
Springer U.S.A. 80 36.22N104.36W
Springerville U.S.A. 81 34.08N109.17W
Springfield New Zealand 60 43.20S171.56E
Springfield Colo. U.S.A. 83 37.24N102.37W
Springfield Ill. U.S.A. 82 39.49N 89.39W
Springfield Mass. U.S.A. 84 42.07N 72.35W
Springfield Miss. U.S.A. 79 37.11N 93.19W
Springfield Mo. U.S.A. 83 37.14N 93.17W
Springfield Ohio U.S.A. 84 39.55N 83.48W
Springfield Oreg. U.S.A. 80 44.03N123.01W
Springfield Tenn. U.S.A. 85 36.30N 86.54W
Springfield Vt. U.S.A. 84 43.18N 72.29W
Springfontein R.S.A. 56 30.15S 25.41E
Spring Grove U.S.A. 85 39.52N 76.52W
Springhill Canada 77 45.39N 64.03W
Springs town R.S.A. 56 26.16S 28.27E
Springsure Australia 64 24.07S148.05E
Spring Valley town U.S.A. 82 43.41N 92.23W
Springville U.S.A. 80 40.10N111.37W
Spry U.S.A. 80 37.55N112.28W
Spurn Head U.K. 10 53.35N 0.08E
Spuzzum Canada 74 49.37N121.23W
Squamish Canada 74 49.45N123.10W
Squaw Rapids town Canada 75 53.41N103.20W
Squillace Italy 19 38.46N 16.31E
Sragen Indonesia 37 7.24S111.00E
Srbija d. Yugo. 19 44.30N 20.30E
Srednekolymsk Russian Fed. 29 67.27N153.35E
Sredne Russkaya Vozvyshennost f. Russian Fed. 24 53.00N 37.00E
Sredne Sibirskoye Ploskogor'ye f. Russian Fed. 29 66.00N108.00E
Srê Moat Cambodia 34 13.15N107.10E
Srêpôk r. Cambodia 34 13.33N106.16E
Sretensk Russian Fed. 31 52.15N117.52E
Sri Dūngargarh India 40 28.05N 74.00E
Sri Gangānagar India 40 29.55N 73.52E
Srīkākulam India 39 18.18N 83.54E
Sri Lanka Asia 39 7.30N 80.50E
Sri Mohangarh India 40 27.17N 71.14E
Srīnagar Jammu & Kashmir 40 34.05N 74.49E
Sripur Bangla. 41 24.12N 90.29E
Srirampur India 40 19.30N 74.30E
Srnetica Bosnia-Herzegovina 19 44.26N 16.40E
Staaten r. Australia 64 16.24S141.17E
Stadskanaal Neth. 14 53.02N 6.55E
Stadtkyll Germany 14 50.21N 6.32E
Stadtlohn Germany 14 52.00N 6.58E
Staffa i. U.K. 12 56.26N 6.21W
Stafford U.K. 10 52.49N 2.09W
Stafford U.S.A. 85 38.09N 76.51W
Staffordshire d. U.K. 10 52.40N 1.57W
Staines U.K. 11 51.26N 0.31W
Stainforth U.K. 10 53.37N 1.01W
Stakhanov Ukraine 25 48.34N 38.40E
Stalina Kanal canal Russian Fed. 24 64.33N 34.48E
Stamford U.K. 11 52.39N 0.28W
Stamford Conn. U.S.A. 85 41.03N 73.32W
Stamford N.Y. U.S.A. 84 42.25N 74.37W
Stamford Tex. U.S.A. 83 32.57N 99.48W
Stanberry U.S.A. 82 40.13N 94.35W
Standerton R.S.A. 56 26.57S 29.14E
Stanger R.S.A. 56 29.20S 31.17E
Stanley Canada 72 55.45N104.55W
Stanley Falkland Is. 93 51.42S 57.51W
Stanley U.K. 10 54.53N 1.42W
Stanley Idaho U.S.A. 80 44.13N114.35W
Stanley Wisc. U.S.A. 82 44.58N 90.56W
Stanley Mission Canada 75 55.27N104.33W
Stanovoy Khrebet mts. Russian Fed. 29 56.00N125.40E
Stanthorpe Australia 67 28.37S151.52E
Stanton U.S.A. 83 32.08N101.48W
Stapleton U.S.A. 82 41.29N100.31W
Starachowice Poland 21 51.03N 21.04E
Stara Dorogi Belorussia 21 53.02N 28.18E
Stara Planina mts. Bulgaria 19 42.50N 24.30E
Staraya Russa Russian Fed. 24 58.00N 31.22E
Staraya Sinyava Ukraine 21 49.38N 27.39E
Stara Zagora Bulgaria 19 42.26N 25.37E
Starbuck I. Kiribati 69 5.37S155.55W
Stargard Szczeciński Poland 20 53.21N 15.01E
Staritsa Russian Fed. 24 56.29N 34.59E
Starke U.S.A. 85 29.55N 82.06W
Starkville U.S.A. 83 33.28N 88.48W
Starnberg Germany 20 48.00N 11.20E
Starobin Belorussia 21 52.40N 27.29E
Starogard Gdański Poland 21 53.59N 18.33E
Starokonstantinov Ukraine 21 49.48N 27.10E
Start Pt. U.K. 11 50.13N 3.38W
Staryy Oskol Russian Fed. 25 51.20N 37.50E
State College U.S.A. 84 40.48N 77.52W
Staten I. see Estados, Isla de los i. Argentina 93
Statesville U.S.A. 85 35.46N 80.54W
Staunton U.S.A. 85 38.09N 79.04W
Stavanger Norway 23 58.58N 5.45E
Stavelot Belgium 14 50.23N 5.54E
Staveren Neth. 14 52.53N 5.21E
Stavropol' Russian Fed. 25 45.03N 41.59E
Stavropolskaya Vozvyshennost mts. Russian Fed. 25 45.00N 42.30E
Stawell Australia 66 37.06S142.52E
Stawiski Poland 21 53.23N 22.09E
Stayton U.S.A. 80 44.48N122.48W
Steamboat Springs town U.S.A. 80 40.29N106.50W
Steele U.S.A. 82 46.51N 99.55W
Steelpoort R.S.A. 56 24.44S 30.13E
Steelton U.S.A. 84 40.14N 76.49W
Steenbergen Neth. 14 51.36N 4.19E
Steenvoorde France 14 50.49N 2.35E
Steenwijk Neth. 14 52.47N 6.07E
Steep Rock Lake town Canada 76 48.50N 91.38W
Steiermark d. Austria 20 47.10N 15.10E
Steilloopbrug R.S.A. 56 23.26S 28.37E
Steinbach Canada 75 49.32N 96.41W
Steinkjer Norway 22 64.00N 11.30E
Steinkopf R.S.A. 56 29.16S 17.41E
Stella R.S.A. 56 26.32S 24.51E
Stellarton Canada 77 45.34N 62.40W
Stellenbosch R.S.A. 56 33.56S 18.51E
Stenay France 15 49.29N 5.11E
Stendal Germany 20 52.36N 11.52E
Stenträsk Sweden 22 66.20N 19.50E
Stepan Ukraine 21 51.09N 26.18E
Stepanakert Azerbaijan 43 39.48N 46.45E
Stephens Passage str. U.S.A. 74 57.50N133.50W
Stephenville Canada 77 48.33N 58.35W
Stephenville U.S.A. 83 32.13N 98.12W
Stepnyak Kazakhstan 28 52.52N 70.49E
Steps Pt. c. Samoa 68 14.22S170.45W
Sterkstroom R.S.A. 56 31.32S 26.31E
Sterling Colo. U.S.A. 80 40.37N103.13W
Sterling Ill. U.S.A. 82 41.48N 89.43W
Sterling Mich. U.S.A. 84 44.02N 84.02W
Sterlitamak Russian Fed. 24 53.40N 55.59E
Šternberk Czech Republic 21 49.44N 17.18E
Stettler Canada 74 52.19N112.40W
Steuben U.S.A. 84 46.12N 86.27W
Steubenville U.S.A. 84 40.22N 80.39W
Stevenage U.K. 11 51.54N 0.11W
Stevenson L. Canada 75 53.56N 96.09W
Stevens Point town U.S.A. 82 44.32N 89.33W
Stevenston U.K. 12 55.39N 4.45W
Stewart Canada 74 55.56N130.01W
Stewart I. New Zealand 60 47.00S168.00E
Stewart River town Canada 72 63.19N139.26W
Steynsburg R.S.A. 56 31.17S 25.48E
Steyr Austria 20 48.04N 14.25E
Stikine r. Canada/U.S.A. 74 56.40N132.30W
Stikine Mts. Canada 72 59.00N129.00W
Stikine Plateau f. Canada 74 58.45N130.00W
Stiklestad Norway 22 63.48N 11.22E
Stilbaai R.S.A. 56 34.22S 21.22E
Stillwater U.S.A. 83 36.07N 97.04W
Stillwater Range mts. U.S.A. 80 39.50N118.15W
Stilton U.K. 11 52.29N 0.17W
Stimson Canada 76 48.58N 80.36W
Stinchar r. U.K. 12 55.06N 5.00W
Stînisoara, Munţii mts. Romania 21 47.10N 26.00E
Štip Macedonia 19 41.44N 22.12E
Stirling U.K. 12 56.07N 3.57W
Stirling Range mts. Australia 63 34.23S117.50E
Stjernöya i. Norway 22 70.17N 22.40E
Stjördalshalsen Norway 22 63.29N 10.51E
Stockaryd Sweden 23 57.18N 14.35E
Stockbridge U.K. 11 51.07N 1.30W
Stockdale U.S.A. 83 29.14N 97.58W
Stockerau Austria 20 48.23N 16.13E
Stockett U.S.A. 80 47.21N111.10W
Stockholm Sweden 23 59.20N 18.03E
Stockholm d. Sweden 23 59.40N 18.10E
Stockinbingal Australia 67 34.03S147.53E
Stockport U.K. 10 53.25N 2.11W
Stocksbridge U.K. 10 53.30N 1.36W
Stockton Calif. U.S.A. 80 37.57N121.17W
Stockton Kans. U.S.A. 82 39.26N 99.16W
Stockton-on-Tees U.K. 10 54.34N 1.20W
Stoeng Trêng Cambodia 34 13.31N105.59E
Stoffberg R.S.A. 56 25.25S 29.49E
Stoke-on-Trent U.K. 10 53.01N 2.11W
Stokes Bay town Canada 76 44.58N 81.18W

Stokhod to Taleex

Stokhod r. Ukraine 21 51.52N 25.38E
Stokksund Norway 22 64.03N 10.05E
Stolac Bosnia-Herzegovina 19 43.05N 17.58E
Stolberg Germany 14 50.47N 6.12E
Stolbtsy Belorussia 21 53.30N 26.44E
Stolin Belorussia 21 51.52N 26.51E
Stone U.K. 10 52.55N 2.10W
Stone Harbor U.S.A. 85 39.03N 74.45W
Stonehaven U.K. 12 56.58N 2.13W
Stony I. Canada 77 53.00N 55.48W
Stony Rapids town Canada 75 59.16N105.50W
Stooping r. Canada 76 52.08N 82.00W
Stora Lulevatten l. Sweden 22 67.10N 19.16E
Stora Sjöfallets Nat. Park Sweden 22 67.44N 18.16E
Storavan l. Sweden 22 65.40N 18.15E
Storby Finland 23 60.13N 19.34E
Stord i. Norway 23 59.53N 5.25E
Store Baelt str. Denmark 23 55.30N 11.00E
Stor Elvdal Norway 23 61.32N 11.02E
Stören Norway 22 63.03N 10.18E
Storlien Sweden 22 63.20N 12.05E
Storm Lake town U.S.A. 82 42.39N 95.10W
Stornoway U.K. 12 58.12N 6.23W
Storozhevsk Russian Fed. 24 62.00N 52.20E
Storozhinets Ukraine 21 48.11N 25.40E
Storsjön l. Sweden 22 63.10N 14.20E
Storuman Sweden 22 65.06N 17.06E
Storuman l. Sweden 22 65.10N 16.40E
Stouffville Canada 76 43.59N 79.15W
Stoughton U.S.A. 82 42.55N 89.13W
Stour r. Dorset U.K. 11 50.43N 1.47W
Stour r. Kent U.K. 11 51.19N 1.22E
Stour r. Suffolk U.K. 11 51.56N 1.03E
Stourport-on-Severn U.K. 11 52.21N 2.16W
Stowmarket U.K. 11 52.11N 1.00E
Stow on the Wold U.K. 11 51.55N 1.42W
Strabane U.K. 13 54.50N 7.30W
Stradbally Rep. of Ire. 13 53.01N 7.09W
Stradbroke I. Australia 65 27.38S153.45E
Stradella Italy 15 45.05N 9.18E
Straelen Germany 14 51.27N 6.14E
Strahan Australia 65 42.08S145.21E
Strakonice Czech Republic 20 49.16N 13.55E
Stralsund Germany 20 54.18N 13.06E
Strand R.S.A. 56 34.07S 18.50E
Stranda Norway 22 62.19N 6.58E
Strangford Lough U.K. 13 54.28N 5.35W
Strangways Australia 66 29.08S136.35E
Stranraer U.K. 12 54.54N 5.02W
Strasbourg France 17 48.35N 7.45E
Strasburg U.S.A. 82 46.08N100.10W
Stratford Australia 67 37.57S147.05E
Stratford Canada 76 43.22N 80.57W
Stratford New Zealand 60 39.20S174.18E
Stratford U.S.A. 83 36.20N102.04W
Stratford-upon-Avon U.K. 11 52.12N 1.42W
Strathalbyn Australia 66 35.16S138.54E
Strathclyde d. U.K. 12 55.45N 4.45W
Strathcona Prov. Park Canada 74 49.38N125.40W
Strathmore f. U.K. 12 56.44N 2.45W
Strathspey f. U.K. 12 57.25N 3.25W
Stratton U.S.A. 82 39.18N102.36W
Straubing Germany 20 48.53N 12.35E
Straumnes c. Iceland 22 66.30N 23.05W
Strawn U.S.A. 83 32.33N 98.30W
Streaky B. Australia 66 32.36S134.08E
Streaky Bay town Australia 66 32.48S134.13E
Streator U.S.A. 82 41.07N 88.53W
Street U.K. 11 51.07N 2.43W
Streeter U.S.A. 82 46.39N 99.21W
Streetsville Canada 76 43.35N 79.42W
Stresa Italy 15 45.53N 8.32E
Stretton Australia 63 32.30S117.42E
Strimon r. Greece 19 40.47N 23.51E
Stromboli i. Italy 18 38.48N 15.14E
Stromeferry U.K. 12 57.21N 5.34W
Stromness U.K. 12 58.57N 3.18W
Strömö i. Faroe Is. 8 62.08N 7.00W
Strömsbruk Sweden 23 61.53N 17.19E
Strömstad Sweden 23 58.56N 11.10E
Strömsund Sweden 22 63.51N 15.35E
Strömsvattudal f. Sweden 22 64.15N 15.00E
Strongfield Canada 75 51.20N106.36W
Stronsay i. U.K. 12 59.07N 2.36W
Stroud Australia 67 32.25S151.58E
Stroud U.K. 11 51.44N 2.12W
Struan Australia 66 37.08S140.49E
Struer Denmark 23 56.29N 8.37E
Struga Macedonia 19 41.10N 20.41E
Struma r. Bulgaria see Strimon r. Greece 19
Strumica Macedonia 19 41.26N 22.39E
Strydenburg R.S.A. 56 29.56S 23.39E
Stryker U.S.A. 80 48.40N114.44W
Stryy Ukraine 21 49.16N 23.51E
Strzelecki Creek r. Australia 66 29.37S139.59E
Strzelno Poland 21 52.38N 18.11E
Stuart Fla. U.S.A. 85 27.12N 80.16W
Stuart Nebr. U.S.A. 82 42.36N 99.08W
Stuart Creek town Australia 66 29.43S137.01E
Stuart L. Canada 74 54.30N124.30W
Stuart Range mts. Australia 66 29.10S134.56E
Stuart Town Australia 67 32.51S149.08E
Stupart r. Canada 75 56.00N 93.22W
Sturgeon Bay town U.S.A. 82 44.50N 87.23W
Sturgeon Falls town Canada 76 46.22N 79.55W
Sturgeon L. Canada 76 50.00N 90.40W
Sturgis U.S.A. 82 44.25N103.31W
Sturminster Newton U.K. 11 50.56N 2.18W
Sturt B. Australia 66 35.24S137.32E
Sturt Creek r. Australia 62 20.08S127.24E
Sturt Desert Australia 66 28.30S141.12E
Sturt Plain f. Australia 64 17.00S132.48E
Stutterheim R.S.A. 56 32.32S 27.25E
Stuttgart Germany 20 48.47N 9.12E
Stviga r. Belorussia 21 52.04N 27.54E
Stykkishólmur Iceland 22 65.06N 22.48W
Styr r. Belorussia 21 52.07N 26.35E
Suao Taiwan 33 24.36N121.51E
Subarnarekha r. India 41 21.34N 87.24E
Subay', 'Urūq f. Saudi Arabia 48 22.15N 43.05E
Subei Guangai Zongqu canal China 32 34.06N120.19E
Subotica Yugo. 19 46.04N 19.41E
Suceava Romania 21 47.39N 26.19E
Suchan Russian Fed. 35 43.03N133.05E
Suck r. Rep. of Ire. 13 53.16N 8.04W
Suckling, Mt. P.N.G. 64 9.45S148.55E
Sucre Bolivia 92 19.02S 65.17W
Sucuriu r. Brazil 94 20.44S 51.40W
Sudan Africa 48 14.30N 29.00E
Sudan U.S.A. 83 34.04N102.32W
Sudbury Canada 76 46.30N 81.00W
Sudbury U.K. 11 52.03N 0.45E
Sudety mts. Czech Republic/Poland 20 50.30N 16.30E
Sudirman, Pegunungan mts. Indonesia 37 3.50S136.30E
Sud Ouest d. Burkina 52 10.45N 3.10W
Sudzukhe Russian Fed. 35 42.50N133.43E
Sueca Spain 16 39.12N 0.21W
Suez see As Suways Egypt 44
Suez, G. of see Suways, Khalīj as g. Egypt 44
Suez Canal see Suways, Qanāt as canal Egypt 44
Şufaynah Saudi Arabia 42 23.09N 40.32E
Suffolk d. U.K. 11 52.16N 1.00E
Suffolk U.S.A. 85 36.44N 76.37W
Şuḩār Oman 43 24.23N 56.43E
Sühbaatar d. Mongolia 32 45.30N114.00E
Suhl Germany 20 50.37N 10.43E
Sūi Pakistan 40 28.37N 69.19E
Suibin China 31 47.19N131.49E
Suichang China 33 28.36N119.16E
Suichuan China 33 26.24N114.31E
Suide China 32 37.35N110.08E
Suihua China 31 46.39N126.59E
Suileng China 31 47.15N127.05E
Suining Jiangsu China 32 33.54N117.56E
Suining Sichuan China 33 30.31N105.32E
Suipacha Argentina 93 34.47S 59.40W
Suippes France 15 49.08N 4.32E
Suir r. Rep. of Ire. 13 52.17N 7.00W
Suita Japan 35 34.45N135.32E
Sui Xian Henan China 32 34.25N115.04E
Sui Xian Hubei China 33 31.45N113.30E
Suiyang China 33 27.57N107.11E
Suizhong China 32 40.25N120.25E
Suj China 32 42.02N107.58E
Sūjāngarh India 40 27.42N 74.28E
Sujāwal Pakistan 40 24.36N 68.05E
Sukabumi Indonesia 37 6.55S106.50E
Sukadana Indonesia 36 1.15S110.00E
Sukaraja Indonesia 36 2.23S110.35E
Sukhinichi Russian Fed. 24 54.07N 35.21E
Sukhona r. Russian Fed. 24 61.30N 46.28E
Sukhumi Georgia 25 43.01N 41.01E
Sukkertoppen Greenland 73 65.40N 53.00W
Sukkur Pakistan 40 27.42N 68.52E
Sukoharjo Indonesia 37 7.40S110.50E
Sula i. Norway 23 61.08N 4.55E
Sula, Kepulauan is. Indonesia 37 1.50S125.10E
Sulaimān Range mts. Pakistan 40 30.00N 69.50E
Sulak r. Russian Fed. 25 43.18N 47.35E
Sulawesi i. Indonesia 37 2.00S120.30E
Sulawesi Selatan d. Indonesia 37 3.45S120.30E
Sulawesi Utara d. Indonesia 37 1.45S120.30E
Sulechów Poland 20 52.06N 15.37E
Sulejów Poland 21 51.22N 19.53E
Sulina Romania 19 45.08N 29.40E
Sulitjelma Norway 22 67.10N 16.05E
Sullana Peru 90 4.52S 80.39W
Sullivan U.S.A. 82 38.13N 91.10W
Sully France 15 47.46N 2.22E
Sulmona Italy 18 42.04N 13.57E
Sulphur U.S.A. 83 34.31N 96.58W
Sultan Canada 76 47.36N 82.47W
Sultan Hamud Kenya 55 2.02S 37.20E
Sultānpur India 41 26.16N 82.04E
Sulu Archipelago Phil. 37 5.30N121.00E
Sulūq Libya 51 31.40N 20.15E
Sulu Sea Pacific Oc. 37 8.00N120.00E
Sumatera i. Indonesia 36 2.00S102.00E
Sumatera Barat d. Indonesia 36 1.00S100.00E
Sumatera Selatan d. Indonesia 36 3.00S104.00E
Sumatera Utara d. Indonesia 36 2.00N 99.00E
Sumatra see Sumatera i. Indonesia 36
Sumatra U.S.A. 80 46.38N107.31W
Sumba i. Indonesia 36 9.30S119.55E
Sumbar r. Turkmenistan 43 38.00N 55.20E
Sumbawa i. Indonesia 36 8.45S117.50E
Sumbawanga Tanzania 55 7.58S 31.36E
Sumbe Angola 54 11.11S 13.52E
Sumburgh Head U.K. 12 59.51N 1.16W
Sumedang Indonesia 37 6.54S107.55E
Šumen Bulgaria 19 43.15N 26.55E
Sumenep Indonesia 37 7.01S113.51E
Sumgait Azerbaijan 43 40.35N 49.38E
Summerland Canada 74 49.32N119.41W
Summerside Canada 77 46.24N 63.47W
Summerville Ga. U.S.A. 85 34.29N 85.21W
Summerville S.C. U.S.A. 85 33.02N 80.11W
Šumperk Czech Republic 20 49.58N 16.58E
Sumprabum Burma 34 26.33N 97.34E
Sumusţā al Waqf Egypt 44 28.55N 30.51E
Sumy Ukraine 25 50.55N 34.49E
Sunām India 40 30.08N 75.48E
Sunāmganj Bangla. 41 25.04N 91.24E
Sunart, Loch U.K. 12 56.43N 5.45W
Sunburst U.S.A. 80 48.53N111.55W
Sunbury Australia 67 37.36S144.45E
Sunda, Selat str. Indonesia 36 6.00S105.50E
Sundance U.S.A. 80 44.24N104.23W
Sundarbans f. India/Bangla. 41 21.45N 89.00E
Sundargarh India 41 22.07N 84.02E
Sundays r. R.S.A. 56 33.43S 25.50E
Sunderland U.K. 10 54.55N 1.22W
Sundsvall Sweden 23 62.23N 17.18E
Sungai Kolok Thailand 34 6.02N101.58E
Sungaipakning Indonesia 36 1.19N102.00E
Sungaipenuh Indonesia 36 2.00S101.28E
Sungguminasa Indonesia 36 5.14S119.27E
Sungurlu Turkey 42 40.10N 34.23E
Sunjikāy Sudan 49 12.20N 29.46E
Sunne Sweden 23 59.50N 13.09E
Sunnyside U.S.A. 80 46.20N120.00W
Suntar Russian Fed. 29 62.10N117.35E
Suntsar Pakistan 40 25.31N 62.00E
Sun Valley town U.S.A. 78 43.42N114.21W
Sunwu China 31 49.40N127.10E
Sunyani Ghana 52 7.22N 2.18W
Suoyarvi Russian Fed. 24 62.02N 32.20E
Supaul India 41 26.07N 86.36E
Superior Mont. U.S.A. 80 47.12N114.53W
Superior Wisc. U.S.A. 82 46.42N 92.05W
Superior Wyo. U.S.A. 80 41.46N108.58W
Superior, L. Canada/U.S.A. 84 48.00N 88.00W
Suphan Buri Thailand 34 14.14N100.07E
Suphan Buri r. Thailand 34 13.34N100.15E
Süphan Dagi mtn. Turkey 25 38.55N 42.55E
Süphan Daglari mtn. Turkey 42 38.55N 42.55E
Suqian China 32 33.59N118.25E
Suquţrā i. Yemen 45 12.30N 54.00E
Şūr Lebanon 44 33.16N 35.12E
Şūr Oman 43 22.23N 59.32E
Sur d. W. Sahara 50 23.40N 14.15W
Sur, Cabo c. I. de Pascua 69 27.12S109.26W
Sur, Punta c. Argentina 93 36.53S 56.41W
Sura Russian Fed. 24 53.52N 45.45E
Sūrāb Pakistan 40 28.29N 66.16E
Surabaya Indonesia 37 7.14S112.45E
Surakarta Indonesia 37 7.32S110.50E
Şūrān Syria 44 35.18N 36.44E
Šurany Slovakia 21 48.06N 18.14E
Surat Australia 65 27.09S149.05E
Surat India 40 21.12N 72.50E
Sūratgarh India 40 29.18N 73.54E
Surat Thani Thailand 34 9.09N 99.23E
Surazh Russian Fed. 21 53.00N 32.22E
Sûre r. Lux. 14 49.43N 6.31E
Sureau, Lac l. Canada 77 53.10N 70.50W
Surendranagar India 40 22.42N 71.41E
Surfer's Paradise Australia 67 27.58S153.26E
Surgut Russian Fed. 28 61.13N 73.20E
Sūri India 41 23.55N 87.32E
Surigao Phil. 37 9.47N125.29E
Surin Thailand 34 14.58N103.33E
Surinam S. America 91 4.00N 56.00W
Suriname r. Surinam 91 5.52N 55.14W
Surrey d. U.K. 11 51.16N 0.30W
Surt Libya 51 31.13N 16.35E
Surt, Khalīj g. Libya 51 31.45N 17.50E
Surtanāhu Pakistan 40 26.22N 70.00E
Surtsey i. Iceland 22 63.18N 20.30W
Surud Ad mtn. Somali Rep. 45 10.41N 47.18E
Suruga-wan b. Japan 35 34.45N138.30E
Susa Italy 15 45.08N 7.03E
Susanino Russian Fed. 29 52.46N140.09E
Susanville U.S.A. 80 40.25N120.39W
Susquehanna r. U.S.A. 85 39.33N 76.05W
Sussex N.J. U.S.A. 85 41.13N 74.36W
Sussex Wyo. U.S.A. 80 43.42N106.19W
Sutak Jammu & Kashmir 41 33.12N 77.28E
Sutherland Australia 67 34.02S151.04E
Sutherland R.S.A. 56 32.23S 20.38E
Sutherlin U.S.A. 80 43.25N123.19W
Sutlej r. Pakistan 40 29.23N 71.02E
Sutton r. Canada 76 55.22N 83.48W
Sutton U.K. 11 51.22N 0.12W
Sutton Nebr. U.S.A. 82 40.36N 97.52W
Sutton W. Va. U.S.A. 84 38.41N 80.43W
Sutton in Ashfield U.K. 10 53.08N 1.16W
Suva Fiji 68 18.08S178.25E
Suwa Ethiopia 48 14.16N 41.10E
Suwałki Poland 21 54.07N 22.56E
Suwanee r. U.S.A. 85 29.18N 83.09W
Suways, Khalīj as g. Egypt 44 28.48N 33.00E
Suways, Qanāt as canal Egypt 44 30.40N 32.20E
Suwon S. Korea 31 37.16N126.59E
Suzhou China 33 31.22N120.45E
Suzuka Japan 35 34.51N136.35E
Suzuka r. Japan 35 34.54N136.39E
Suzuka-sammyaku mts. Japan 35 35.00N136.20E
Suzzara Italy 15 45.00N 10.45E
Svalyava Ukraine 21 48.33N 23.00E
Svanvik Norway 22 69.25N 30.00E
Svappavaara Sweden 22 67.39N 21.04E
Svarhofthalvöya Norway 22 70.35N 26.00E
Svartenhuk Halvo c. Greenland 73 71.55N 55.00W
Svartisen mtn. Norway 22 66.40N 13.56E
Svatovo Ukraine 25 49.24N 38.11E
Svay Riēng Cambodia 34 11.05N105.48E
Svedala Sweden 23 55.30N 13.14E
Sveg Sweden 23 62.02N 14.21E
Svelgen Norway 23 61.47N 5.15E
Svendborg Denmark 23 55.03N 10.37E
Svenstrup Denmark 23 56.59N 9.52E
Sverdlovsk see Yekaterinburg Russian Fed. 24
Svetlograd Russian Fed. 25 45.25N 42.58E
Svetogorsk Russian Fed. 24 61.07N 28.50E
Svetozarevo Yugo. 19 43.58N 21.16E
Svinö i. Faroe Is. 8 62.17N 6.18W
Svir r. Russian Fed. 24 60.09N 32.15E
Svishtov Bulgaria 19 43.36N 25.23E
Svisloch Belorussia 21 53.28N 29.00E
Svitavy Czech Republic 20 49.45N 16.27E
Svobodnyy Russian Fed. 31 51.24N128.05E
Svolvaer Norway 22 68.15N 14.40E
Swaffham U.K. 11 52.38N 0.42E
Swain Reefs Australia 64 21.40S152.15E
Swains I. Samoa 68 11.03S171.06W
Swakop r. Namibia 56 22.38S 14.32E
Swakopmund Namibia 56 22.40S 14.34E
Swale r. U.K. 10 54.05N 1.20W
Swan r. Australia 63 32.03S115.45E
Swanage U.K. 11 50.36N 1.59W
Swan Hill town Australia 66 35.23S143.37E
Swan Hills Canada 74 54.42N115.24W
Swan L. Canada 75 52.30N100.45W
Swan River town Canada 75 52.10N101.17W
Swansea Australia 65 42.08S148.00E
Swansea U.K. 11 51.37N 3.57W
Swastika Canada 76 48.07N 80.06W
Swatow see Shantou China 33
Swaziland Africa 56 26.30S 32.00E
Sweden Europe 22 63.00N 16.00E
Swedru Ghana 52 5.31N 0.42W
Sweetwater U.S.A. 83 32.28N100.25W
Swidnica Poland 20 50.51N 16.29E
Swiebodzin Poland 20 52.15N 15.32E
Świetokrzyskie, Góry mts. Poland 21 51.00N 20.30E
Swift Current town Canada 75 50.17N107.50W
Swilly, Lough Rep. of Ire. 13 55.10N 7.32W
Swindon U.K. 11 51.33N 1.47W
Świnoujście Poland 20 53.55N 14.18E
Switzerland Europe 17 47.00N 8.00E
Swords Rep. of Ire. 9 53.27N 6.15W
Syderö i. Faroe Is. 8 61.30N 6.50W
Sydney Australia 67 33.55S151.10E
Sydney Canada 77 46.09N 60.11W
Sydney Mines town Canada 77 46.14N 60.14W
Sydpröven Greenland 73 60.30N 45.35W
Syktyvkar Russian Fed. 24 61.42N 50.45E
Sylacauga U.S.A. 85 33.10N 86.15W
Sylhet Bangla. 41 24.54N 91.52E
Sylt i. Germany 20 54.50N 8.20E
Sylte Norway 22 62.31N 7.07E
Sylvan Lake town Canada 74 52.20N114.10W
Syracuse Kans. U.S.A. 83 37.59N101.45W
Syracuse N.Y. U.S.A. 84 43.03N 76.09W
Syr Darya r. Kazakhstan 28 46.00N 61.12E
Syria Asia 42 35.00N 38.00E
Syriam Burma 36 16.45N 96.17E
Syrian Desert see Bādiyat ash Shām des. Asia 42
Syzran Russian Fed. 24 53.10N 48.29E
Szarvas Hungary 21 46.52N 20.34E
Szczecin Poland 20 53.25N 14.32E
Szczecinek Poland 20 53.42N 16.41E
Szczytno Poland 21 53.34N 21.00E
Szécsény Hungary 21 48.06N 19.31E
Szeged Hungary 19 46.16N 20.08E
Székesfehérvár Hungary 21 47.12N 18.25E
Szekszárd Hungary 19 46.22N 18.44E
Szentes Hungary 21 46.39N 20.16E
Szolnok Hungary 21 47.10N 20.12E
Szombathely Hungary 20 47.12N 16.38E
Sztutowo Poland 21 54.20N 19.15E

T

Tabagne Ivory Coast 52 7.59N 3.04W
Ţābah Saudi Arabia 42 27.02N 42.10E
Tabarka Tunisia 51 36.56N 8.43E
Ţabas Khorāsān Iran 43 32.48N 60.14E
Ţabas Khorāsān Iran 43 33.36N 56.55E
Tabasco d. Mexico 86 18.30N 93.00W
Tābask, Kūh-e mtn. Iran 43 29.51N 51.52E
Tabelbala Algeria 50 29.24N 3.15W
Taber Canada 74 49.47N112.08W
Tabili Zaïre 55 0.04N 28.01E
Table B. R.S.A. 56 33.52S 18.26E
Tábor Czech Republic 20 49.25N 14.41E
Tabora Tanzania 55 5.02S 32.50E
Tabora d. Tanzania 55 5.30S 32.50E
Tabou Ivory Coast 52 4.28N 7.20W
Tabrīz Iran 43 38.05N 46.18E
Tabuaeran i. Kiribati 69 3.52N159.20W
Tabūk Saudi Arabia 44 28.23N 36.36E
Tabulam Australia 67 28.50S152.35E
Ţabūt Yemen 45 15.57N 52.09E
Tachia Taiwan 33 24.21N120.37E
Tachikawa Japan 35 35.42N139.25E
Tacloban Phil. 37 11.15N124.59E
Tacna Peru 92 18.01S 70.15W
Tacoma U.S.A. 80 47.15N122.27W
Tacora mtn. Chile 92 17.40S 69.45W
Tacuarembó Uruguay 93 31.44S 55.59W
Tademaït, Plateau du f. Algeria 51 28.30N 2.15E
Tadjetaret, Oued Algeria 51 21.00N 7.30E
Tadjmout Algeria 51 25.30N 3.42E
Tadjoura, Golfe de g. Djibouti 45 11.42N 43.00E
Tadmor New Zealand 60 41.26S172.47E
Tadmur Syria 42 34.36N 38.15E
Tadoule L. Canada 75 58.36N 98.20W
Tadoussac Canada 77 48.09N 69.43W
Taegu S. Korea 31 35.52N128.36E
Taejin S. Korea 35 36.34N129.24E
Taejŏn S. Korea 31 36.20N127.26E
Tafalla Spain 16 42.31N 1.40W
Tafassasset, Oued wadi Niger 51 22.00N 9.55E
Tafassasset, Ténéré du des. Niger 53 21.00N 11.00E
Taffanel, Lac l. Canada 77 53.22N 70.56W
Tafí Viejo Argentina 92 26.45S 65.15W
Tafraout Morocco 50 29.40N 8.58W
Taftān, Kūh-e mtn. Iran 43 28.38N 61.08E
Taga W. Samoa 68 13.47S172.30W
Taganrog Russian Fed. 25 47.14N 38.55E
Taganrogskiy Zaliv g. Ukraine/Russian Fed. 25 47.00N 38.30E
Tagant d. Mauritania 50 18.30N 10.30W
Tagant f. Mauritania 50 18.20N 11.00W
Tagaytay City Phil. 37 14.07N120.58E
Tagbilaran Phil. 37 9.38N123.53E
Tagish Canada 74 60.19N134.16W
Tagliamento r. Italy 15 45.38N 13.06E
Taglio di Po Italy 15 45.00N 12.12E
Tagounit Morocco 50 29.58N 5.36W
Tagula I. P.N.G. 64 11.30S153.30E
Tagum Phil. 37 7.33N125.53E
Tagus r. Portugal/Spain see Tejo r. Portugal 16
Tahaa i. Îs. de la Société 69 16.38S151.30W
Tahara Japan 35 34.40N137.16E
Tahat mtn. Algeria 51 23.18N 5.32E
Tahe China 31 52.35N124.48E
Tahiti i. Îs. de la Société 69 17.37S149.27W
Tahiti, Archipel de is. Îs. de la Société 69 17.00S149.35W
Tahlequah U.S.A. 83 35.55N 94.58W
Tahoe, L. U.S.A. 80 39.07N120.03W
Tahoua Niger 53 14.57N 5.16E
Tahoua d. Niger 53 15.38N 4.50E
Ţahţā Egypt 42 26.46N 31.30E
Tahuna Indonesia 37 3.37N125.29E
Taï Ivory Coast 52 5.52N 7.28W
Tai'an China 32 36.16N117.13E
Taiarapu, Presqu'île de pen. Tahiti 69 17.47S149.14W
Taibai China 32 36.08N108.41E
Taibai Shan mtn. China 32 33.55N107.45E
Taibus Qi China 32 41.55N115.23E
Taidong Taiwan 33 22.49N121.10E
Taigu China 32 37.23N112.34E
Taihang Shan mts. China 32 36.00N113.35E
Taihape New Zealand 60 39.40S175.48E
Taihe Anhui China 32 33.10N115.36E
Taihe Jiangxi China 33 26.48 114.56E
Tai Hu l. China 33 31.15N120.10E
Tailai China 31 46.23N123.24E
Tailem Bend town Australia 66 35.14S139.29E
Tain U.K. 12 57.48N 4.04W
Tainan Taiwan 33 23.01N120.12E
Taínaron, Ákra c. Greece 19 36.22N 22.28E
Tai-o-haé Îs. Marquises 69 8.55S140.04W
Taipei Taiwan 33 25.05N121.30E
Taiping China 33 30.18N118.06E
Taiping Malaysia 36 4.54N100.42E
Taishan China 33 22.10N112.57E
Taito, Península de pen. Chile 93 46.30S 74.25W
Taitze He r. China 32 41.07N122.43E
Taivalkoski Finland 22 65.34N 28.15E
Taiwan Asia 33 24.00N121.00E
Taiwan Str. China/Taiwan 33 24.30N119.30E
Taiyuan China 32 37.48N112.33E
Taiyue Shan mts. China 32 36.40N112.00E
Taizhong Taiwan 33 24.11N120.40E
Taizhou China 32 32.22N119.58E
Ta'izz Yemen 45 13.35N 44.02E
Tajarḩī Libya 51 24.21N 14.28E
Tajikistan Asia 30 39.00N 70.30E
Tajimi Japan 35 35.19N137.08E
Tajitos Mexico 81 30.58N112.18W
Tajo r. Spain see Tejo r. Portugal 16
Tajrīsh Iran 43 35.48N 51.20E
Tajuna r. Spain 16 40.10N 3.35W
Tak Thailand 34 16.51N 99.08E
Takaka New Zealand 60 40.51S172.48E
Takalar Indonesia 36 5.29S119.26E
Takamatsu Japan 35 34.20N134.01E
Takapuna New Zealand 60 36.48S174.47E
Takarazuka Japan 35 34.49N135.21E
Takatsuki Japan 35 34.51N135.37E
Tākestān Iran 43 36.02N 49.40E
Takēv Cambodia 34 11.00N104.46E
Takhādīd well Iraq 43 29.59N 44.30E
Takla L. Canada 74 55.15N125.45W
Taklimakan Shamo des. China 30 38.10N 82.00E
Taku r. Canada/U.S.A. 74 58.30N133.50W
Talā Egypt 44 30.41N 30.56E
Tala Uruguay 93 34.21S 55.46W
Talagang Pakistan 40 32.55N 72.25E
Talagante Chile 93 33.40S 70.56W
Talāja India 40 21.21N 72.03E
Tālāla India 40 21.02N 70.32E
Talangbetutu Indonesia 36 2.48S104.42E
Talara Peru 90 4.38S 81.18W
Talasskiy Alatau mts. Kyrgyzstan 30 42.20N 73.20E
Talata Mafara Nigeria 53 12.37N 6.05E
Talaud, Kepulauan is. Indonesia 37 4.20N126.50E
Talavera de la Reina Spain 16 39.58N 4.50W
Talawdī Sudan 49 10.38N 30.23E
Talbragar r. Australia 67 32.12S148.37E
Talca Chile 93 35.26S 71.40W
Talcahuano Chile 93 36.43S 73.07W
Tālcher India 41 20.57N 85.13E
Taldom Russian Fed. 24 56.49N 37.30E
Taldy Kurgan Kazakhstan 30 45.02N 78.23E
Taleex well Somali Rep. 45 9.12N 48.23E

Talia to Thásos

Talia Australia **66** 33.16S134.53E
Taliabu *i.* Indonesia **37** 1.50S124.55E
Tali Post Sudan **49** 5.54N 30.47E
Talkeetna U.S.A. **72** 62.20N150.09W
Ţalkhā Egypt **44** 31.04N 31.22E
Tallahassee U.S.A. **85** 30.26N 84.19W
Tallangatta Australia **67** 36.14S147.19E
Tallard France **17** 44.28N 6.03E
Tallinn Estonia **23** 59.22N 24.48E
Tall Kalakh Syria **44** 34.40N 36.18E
Tall Kūshik Syria **42** 36.48N 42.04E
Tall Salḩab Syria **44** 35.15N 36.22E
Tallulah U.S.A. **83** 32.25N 91.11W
Talmont France **17** 46.28N 1.36W
Talnoye Ukraine **21** 48.55N 30.40E
Taloda India **40** 21.34N 74.13E
Talofofo Guam **68** 13.21N144.45E
Talsi Latvia **23** 57.15N 22.36E
Taltal Chile **92** 25.24S 70.29W
Talvik Norway **22** 70.05N 22.52E
Talwood Australia **67** 28.29S149.25E
Talyawalka *r.* Australia **66** 31.49S143.25E
Tama *r.* Japan **35** 35.32N139.47E
Tamala Australia **62** 26.42S113.47E
Tamale Ghana **52** 9.26N 0.49W
Tamanar Morocco **50** 31.00N 9.35W
Tamanrasset Algeria **51** 22.47N 5.31E
Tamanrasset, Oued *wadi* Algeria **50** 21.24N 1.00E
Tamanthi Burma **34** 25.19N 95.18E
Tamar *r.* U.K. **11** 50.28N 4.13W
Tamaské Niger **53** 14.55N 5.55E
Tamaulipas *d.* Mexico **83** 24.30N 98.50W
Tamazunchale Mexico **86** 21.16N 98.47W
Tambacounda Senegal **52** 13.45N 13.40W
Tambara Mozambique **55** 16.42S 34.17E
Tambar Springs *town* Australia **67** 31.20S149.50E
Tambellup Australia **63** 34.03S117.36E
Tambo Australia **64** 24.53S146.15E
Tambo *r.* Australia **67** 37.51S147.48E
Tambohorano Madagascar **57** 17.30S 43.58E
Tambor Mexico **81** 25.08N105.27W
Tambov Russian Fed. **24** 52.44N 41.28E
Tambre *r.* Spain **16** 42.50N 8.55W
Tambura Sudan **49** 5.36N 27.28E
Tamchaket Mauritania **50** 17.25N 10.40W
Tâmega *r.* Portugal **16** 41.04N 8.17W
Tamil Nadu *d.* India **39** 11.15N 79.00E
Ţāmiyah Egypt **44** 29.29N 30.58E
Tamkuhi India **41** 26.41N 84.11E
Tam Ky Vietnam **34** 15.34N108.29E
Tammisaari Finland **23** 59.58N 23.26E
Tampa U.S.A. **85** 27.58N 82.38W
Tampa B. U.S.A. **85** 27.45N 82.35W
Tampere Finland **23** 61.30N 23.45E
Tampico Mexico **86** 22.18N 97.52W
Tamri Morocco **50** 30.43N 9.43W
Tamsagbulag Mongolia **31** 47.10N117.21E
Tamworth Australia **67** 31.07S150.57E
Tamworth U.K. **11** 52.38N 1.42W
Tana *r.* Kenya **55** 2.32S 40.32E
Tana Norway **22** 70.26N 28.14E
Tana *r.* Norway **22** 69.45N 28.15E
Tana *i.* Vanuatu **68** 19.30S169.20E
Tanacross U.S.A. **72** 63.12N143.30W
Tanafjorden Norway **22** 70.54N 28.40E
T'ana Hāyk' *l.* Ethiopia **49** 12.00N 37.20E
Tanahgrogot Indonesia **36** 1.55S116.12E
Tanahmerah Indonesia **37** 6.08S140.18E
Tanakpur India **41** 29.05N 80.07E
Tanami Desert Australia **62** 19.50S130.50E
Tanana U.S.A. **72** 65.11N152.10W
Tanana *r.* U.S.A. **72** 65.09N151.55W
Tananarive *see* Antananarivo Madagascar **57**
Tanaro *r.* Italy **15** 45.01N 8.46E
Tanch'on N. Korea **35** 40.27N128.54E
Tānda India **41** 26.33N 82.39E
Tanda Ivory Coast **52** 7.48N 3.10W
Tandaltī Sudan **49** 13.01N 31.50E
Tăndărei Romania **21** 44.38N 27.40E
Tandil Argentina **93** 37.18S 59.10W
Tandjilé *d.* Chad **53** 9.45N 16.28E
Tando Ādam Pakistan **40** 25.46N 68.40E
Tando Allāhyār Pakistan **40** 25.28N 68.43E
Tando Bāgo Pakistan **40** 24.47N 68.58E
Tando Muhammad Khan Pakistan **40** 25.08N 68.32E
Tandou L. Australia **66** 32.38S142.05E
Tandula Tank *resr.* India **41** 20.40N 81.12E
Taneytown U.S.A. **85** 39.40N 77.10W
Tanezrouft *des.* Algeria **50** 22.25N 0.30E
Tanga Tanzania **55** 5.07S 39.05E
Tanga *d.* Tanzania **55** 5.20S 38.30E
Tangalla Sri Lanka **39** 6.02N 80.47E
Tanganyika, L. Africa **55** 6.00S 29.30E
Tanger Morocco **50** 35.48N 5.45W
Tanggo China **41** 31.37N 93.18E
Tanggu China **32** 39.01N117.43E
Tanggula Shan *mts.* China **41** 33.00N 90.00E
Tanggula Shankou *pass* China **41** 32.45N 92.24E
Tanggulashanqu China **41** 34.10N 92.23E
Tanghe China **32** 32.41N112.49E
Tāngi India **41** 19.57N 85.30E
Tangi Pakistan **40** 34.18N 71.40E
Tangier *see* Tanger Morocco **50**
Tangmarg Jammu & Kashmir **40** 34.02N 74.26E
Tangra Yumco *l.* China **41** 31.00N 86.15E
Tangshan China **32** 39.32N118.08E
Tangtse Jammu & Kashmir **41** 34.02N 78.11E
Tanguiéta Benin **53** 10.37N 1.18E
Tanimbar, Kepulauan *is.* Indonesia **37** 7.50S131.30E
Tanintharyi *see* Tenasserim Burma **34**
Tanishpa *mtn.* Pakistan **40** 31.10N 68.24E
Tanjay Phil. **37** 9.31N123.10E
Tanjona Ankaboa *c.* Madagascar **57** 21.57S 43.16E
Tanjona Bobaomby *c.* Madagascar **57** 11.57S 49.17E
Tanjona Masoala *c.* Madagascar **57** 15.59S 50.13E
Tanjona Vilanandro *c.* Madagascar **57** 16.11S 44.27E
Tanjona Vohimena *c.* Madagascar **57** 25.36S 45.08E
Tanjung Indonesia **36** 2.10S115.25E
Tanjungbalai Indonesia **36** 2.59N 99.46E
Tanjungkarang Indonesia **36** 5.28S105.16E
Tanjungpandan Indonesia **36** 2.44S107.36E
Tanjungredeb Indonesia **36** 2.09N117.29E
Tānk Pakistan **40** 32.13N 70.23E
Tankapirtti Finland **22** 68.16N 27.20E
Tännäs Sweden **23** 62.27N 12.40E
Tannin Canada **76** 49.40N 91.00W
Tannu Ola *mts.* Russian Fed. **29** 51.00N 93.30E
Tannūrah, Ra's *c.* Saudi Arabia **45** 26.39N 50.10E
Tano *r.* Ghana **52** 5.07N 2.54W
Tanout Niger **53** 14.55N 8.49E
Ţanţā Egypt **44** 30.48N 31.00E
Tanzania Africa **55** 5.00S 35.00E
Tao'an China **32** 45.20N122.48E
Taole China **32** 38.50N106.40E
Taoudenni Mali **52** 22.45N 4.00W
Tapachula Mexico **86** 14.54N 92.15W
Tapajós *r.* Brazil **91** 2.25S 54.40W
Tapaktuan Indonesia **36** 3.30N 97.10E
Tapalquén Argentina **93** 36.20S 60.02W
Tapanahoni *r.* Surinam **91** 4.20N 54.25W
Tapanlieh Taiwan **33** 21.58N120.47E
Tapanui New Zealand **60** 45.57S169.16E
Tapauá *r.* Brazil **90** 5.40S 64.20W
Tapeta Liberia **52** 6.25N 8.47W
Tapirapecó, Serra *mts.* Venezuela / Brazil **90** 1.00N 64.30W
Tāplejung Nepal **41** 27.21N 87.40E
Tapolca Hungary **21** 46.53N 17.27E
Tāpti *r.* India **40** 21.05N 72.40E
Tapurucuara Brazil **90** 0.24S 65.02W
Taquari *r.* Brazil **94** 19.00S 57.27W
Taquaritinga Brazil **94** 21.23S 48.33W
Tar *r.* U.S.A. **85** 35.33N 77.05W
Tara Russian Fed. **28** 56.55N 74.24E
Tara *r.* Russian Fed. **28** 56.30N 74.40E
Tara *r.* Yugo. **19** 43.23N 18.47E
Taraba *d.* Nigeria **53** 8.15N 11.00E
Tarabine, Oued Ti-n- *wadi* Algeria **51** 21.16N 7.24E
Tarabuco Bolivia **92** 19.10S 64.57W
Ţarābulus Lebanon **44** 34.27N 35.50E
Ţarābulus *d.* Libya **51** 32.40N 13.15E
Ţarābulus *f.* Libya **51** 31.00N 13.30E
Ţarābulus *town* Libya **51** 32.58N 13.12E
Tarago Australia **67** 35.05S149.10E
Tarakan Indonesia **36** 3.20N117.38E
Taranaki *d.* New Zealand **60** 39.00S174.30E
Tarancón Spain **16** 40.01N 3.01W
Taranto Italy **19** 40.28N 17.14E
Taranto, Golfo di *g.* Italy **19** 40.00N 17.20E
Tarapacá Colombia **90** 2.52S 69.44W
Tarapoto Peru **90** 6.31S 76.23W
Tarashcha Ukraine **21** 49.35N 30.20E
Tarasovo Russian Fed. **24** 66.14N 46.43E
Tarauacá Brazil **90** 8.10S 70.46W
Tarauacá *r.* Brazil **90** 6.42S 69.48W
Taravao, Isthme de Tahiti **69** 17.43S149.19W
Tarawa *i.* Kiribati **68** 1.25N173.00E
Tarawera New Zealand **60** 39.02S176.36E
Tarbagatay, Khrebet *mts.* Kazakhstan **30** 47.00N 83.00E
Tarbat Ness *c.* U.K. **12** 57.52N 3.46W
Tarbert Rep. of Ire. **13** 52.34N 9.24W
Tarbert Strath. U.K. **12** 55.51N 5.25W
Tarbert W. Isles U.K. **12** 57.54N 6.49W
Tarbes France **17** 43.14N 0.05E
Tarcento Italy **15** 46.13N 13.13E
Tarcoola Australia **66** 30.41S134.33E
Tarcoon Australia **67** 30.19S146.43E
Tarcutta Australia **67** 35.17S147.45E
Taree Australia **67** 31.54S152.26E
Tarella Australia **66** 30.55S143.06E
Tärendö Sweden **22** 67.10N 22.38E
Ţarfā, Wādī aţ *r.* Egypt **44** 28.36N 30.50E
Tarfaya Morocco **50** 27.58N 12.55W
Tarhjicht Morocco **50** 29.05N 9.24W
Tarifa Spain **16** 36.01N 5.36W
Tarija Bolivia **92** 21.31S 64.45W
Tarija *d.* Bolivia **92** 21.40S 64.20W
Tarim Yemen **45** 16.03N 49.00E
Tarim He *r.* China **30** 41.00N 83.30E
Tarin Kowt Afghan. **40** 32.52N 65.38E
Taritatu *r.* Indonesia **37** 2.54S138.27E
Tarka La *mtn.* Bhutan **41** 27.05N 89.40E
Tarkwa Ghana **52** 5.16N 1.59W
Tarlac Phil. **37** 15.29N120.35E
Tarm Denmark **23** 55.55N 8.32E
Tarma Peru **90** 11.28S 75.41W
Tarn *r.* France **17** 44.15N 1.15E
Tärnaby Sweden **22** 65.43N 15.16E
Tarnak *r.* Afghan. **40** 31.26N 65.31E
Tarnica *mtn.* Poland **21** 49.05N 22.44E
Tarnobrzeg Poland **21** 50.35N 21.41E
Tarnów Poland **21** 50.01N 20.59E
Taro *r.* Italy **15** 45.00N 10.15E
Taroom Australia **64** 25.39S149.49E
Taroudannt Morocco **50** 30.31N 8.55W
Tarpon Springs *town* U.S.A. **85** 28.08N 82.45W
Tarragona Spain **16** 41.07N 1.15E
Tarran Hills Australia **67** 32.27S146.27E
Tarrasa Spain **16** 41.34N 2.00E
Tarrytown U.S.A. **85** 41.05N 73.52W
Tarso Ahon *mtn.* Chad **53** 20.23N 18.18E
Tarso Ouri *mtn.* Chad **53** 21.25N 18.56E
Tarsus Turkey **42** 36.52N 34.52E
Tartagal Argentina **92** 22.32S 63.50W
Tartu Estonia **24** 58.20N 26.44E
Ţarţūs Syria **44** 34.55N 35.52E
Tarutino Ukraine **21** 46.09N 29.04E
Tarutung Indonesia **36** 2.01N 98.54E
Tashan China **32** 40.51N120.56E
Tashauz Uzbekistan **28** 41.49N 59.58E
Tashi Gang Dzong Bhutan **41** 27.19N 91.34E
Tashkent Kyrgyzstan **30** 41.16N 69.13E
Tasiilaq *see* Ammassalik Greenland **73**
Tasikmalaya Indonesia **37** 7.20S108.16E
Täsjön Sweden **22** 64.15N 15.47E
Tasman B. New Zealand **60** 41.00S173.15E
Tasmania *d.* Australia **65** 42.00S147.00E
Tasman Mts. New Zealand **60** 41.00S172.40E
Tasman Pen. Australia **65** 43.08S147.51E
Tasman Sea Pacific Oc. **68** 38.00S162.00E
Tassili-n-Ajjer *f.* Algeria **51** 26.05N 7.00E
Tassili oua-n-Ahaggar *f.* Algeria **51** 20.30N 5.00E
Tataa, Pt. Tahiti **69** 17.33S149.36W
Tatabánya Hungary **21** 47.34N 18.26E
Tatarsk Russian Fed. **28** 55.14N 76.00E
Tatarskiy Proliv *g.* Russian Fed. **29** 47.40N141.00E
Tateyama Japan **35** 34.59N139.52E
Tathlina L. Canada **74** 60.32N117.32W
Tathra Australia **67** 36.44S149.58E
Tatinnai L. Canada **75** 60.55N 97.40W
Tatnam, C. Canada **75** 57.16N 91.00W
Tatong Australia **67** 36.46S146.03E
Tatta Pakistan **40** 24.45N 67.55E
Tatvan Turkey **42** 38.31N 42.15E
Tau *i.* Samoa **68** 14.15S169.30W
Taubaté Brazil **94** 23.00S 45.36W
Taulihawa Nepal **41** 27.32N 83.05E
Taumarunui New Zealand **60** 38.53S175.16E
Taumaturgo Brazil **90** 8.57S 72.48W
Taung R.S.A. **56** 27.32S 24.46E
Taungdwingyi Burma **34** 20.00N 95.30E
Taung-gyi Burma **34** 20.49N 97.01E
Taungup Burma **34** 18.51N 94.14E
Taunoa Tahiti **69** 17.45S149.21W
Taunsa Pakistan **40** 30.42N 70.39E
Taunton U.K. **11** 51.01N 3.07W
Taunus *mts.* Germany **20** 50.07N 7.48E
Taupo New Zealand **60** 38.42S176.06E
Taupo, L. New Zealand **60** 38.45S175.30E
Taurage Lithuania **23** 55.15N 22.17E
Tauranga New Zealand **60** 37.42S176.11E
Taureau, Résr. Canada **77** 46.45N 73.50W
Taurianova Italy **18** 38.21N 16.01E
Taurus Mts. *see* Toros Dağlari *mts.* Turkey **42**
Tautira Tahiti **69** 17.45S149.10W
Tavani Canada **75** 62.10N 93.30W
Tavda Russian Fed. **28** 58.04N 65.12E
Tavda *r.* Russian Fed. **28** 57.40N 67.00E
Taveta Kenya **55** 3.23S 37.42E
Taveuni *i.* Fiji **68** 16.56S179.58W
Tavira Portugal **16** 37.07N 7.39W
Tavistock U.K. **11** 50.33N 4.09W
Tavoy Burma **34** 14.02N 98.12E
Taw *r.* U.K. **11** 51.05N 4.05W
Tawas City U.S.A. **84** 44.16N 83.33W
Tawau Malaysia **36** 4.16N117.54E
Tawitawi *i.* Phil. **37** 5.10N120.05E
Ţawkar Sudan **48** 18.26N 37.44E
Tawu Taiwan **33** 22.22N120.54E
Tāwurghā', Sabkhat *f.* Libya **51** 31.10N 15.15E
Tay *r.* U.K. **12** 56.21N 3.18W
Tay, L. Australia **63** 33.00S120.52E
Tay, Loch U.K. **12** 56.32N 4.08W
Tayabamba Peru **90** 8.15S 77.15W
Tayan Indonesia **36** 0.02S110.05E
Tayeegle Somali Rep. **45** 4.02N 44.36E
Taylor U.S.A. **83** 30.34N 97.25W
Taylor, Mt. U.S.A. **81** 35.14N107.37W
Taylors Island *town* U.S.A. **85** 38.28N 76.18W
Taymā' Saudi Arabia **42** 27.37N 38.30E
Taymyr, Ozero *l.* Russian Fed. **29** 74.20N101.00E
Taymyr, Poluostrov *pen.* Russian Fed. **29** 75.30N 99.00E
Tay Ninh Vietnam **34** 11.21N106.02E
Tayport U.K. **12** 56.27N 2.53W
Tayshet Russian Fed. **29** 55.56N 98.01E
Tayside *d.* U.K. **12** 56.35N 3.28W
Taytay Phil. **36** 10.47N119.32E
Taz *r.* Russian Fed. **28** 67.30N 78.50E
Taza Morocco **50** 34.16N 4.01W
Tazenakht Morocco **50** 30.35N 7.12W
Tazin L. Canada **75** 59.40N109.00W
Tāzirbū Libya **48** 25.45N 21.00E
Tazovskiy Russian Fed. **28** 67.28N 78.43E
Tbilisi Georgia **43** 41.43N 44.48E
Tchad, Lac *see* Chad, L. Africa **53**
Tchamba Togo **53** 9.05N 1.27E
Tchibanga Gabon **54** 2.52S 11.07E
Tchien Liberia **52** 6.00N 8.10W
Tchigaï, Plateau du *f.* Niger / Chad **53** 21.30N 14.50E
Tcholliré Cameroon **53** 8.25N 14.10E
Tczew Poland **21** 54.06N 18.47E
Te Anau New Zealand **60** 45.25S167.43E
Te Anau, L. New Zealand **60** 45.10S167.15E
Teaneck U.S.A. **85** 40.53N 74.01W
Teapa Mexico **86** 17.33N 92.57W
Te Araroa New Zealand **60** 37.38S178.25E
Tébessa Algeria **51** 35.22N 8.08E
Tebingtinggi Sumatera Selatan Indonesia **36** 3.37S103.09E
Tebingtinggi Sumatera Utara Indonesia **36** 3.20N 99.08E
Tebulos Mta *mtn.* Georgia **25** 42.34N 45.17E
Techiman Ghana **52** 7.36N 1.55W
Tecuci Romania **21** 45.49N 27.27E
Tedesa Ethiopia **49** 5.07N 37.45E
Tees *r.* U.K. **10** 54.35N 1.11W
Tefé Brazil **90** 3.24S 64.45W
Tefé *r.* Brazil **90** 3.35S 64.47W
Tegal Indonesia **37** 6.52S109.07E
Tegelen Neth. **14** 51.20N 6.08E
Tegina Nigeria **53** 10.06N 6.11E
Tego Australia **67** 28.48S146.47E
Tegouma *well* Niger **53** 15.33N 9.19E
Tegucigalpa Honduras **87** 14.05N 87.14W
Teguidda I-n-Tessoum Niger **53** 17.21N 6.32E
Tehamiyam Sudan **48** 18.20N 36.32E
Tehata Bangla. **41** 23.43N 88.32E
Téhini Ivory Coast **52** 9.39N 3.32W
Tehrān Iran **43** 35.40N 51.26E
Tehri India **41** 30.23N 78.29E
Tehuacán Mexico **86** 18.30N 97.26W
Tehuantepec Mexico **86** 16.21N 95.13W
Tehuantepec, Golfo de *g.* Mexico **86** 16.00N 95.00W
Tehuantepec, Istmo de *f.* Mexico **86** 17.00N 94.30W
Teifi *r.* U.K. **11** 52.05N 4.41W
Teignmouth U.K. **11** 50.33N 3.30W
Teixeiras Brazil **94** 20.37S 42.52W
Tejakula Indonesia **37** 8.09S115.19E
Tejo *r.* Portugal **16** 39.00N 8.57W
Te Kaha New Zealand **60** 37.44S177.52E
Tekamah U.S.A. **82** 41.47N 96.13W
Tekapo, L. New Zealand **60** 43.35S170.30E
Tekax Mexico **87** 20.12N 89.17W
Tekezē *r.* Ethiopia *see* Safīt *r.* Sudan **48**
Tekirdag Turkey **19** 40.59N 27.30E
Tekkali India **41** 18.37N 84.14E
Tekouiat, Oued *wadi* Algeria **51** 22.20N 2.30E
Tekro *well* Chad **48** 19.30N 20.58E
Te Kuiti New Zealand **60** 38.20S175.10E
Tel *r.* India **41** 20.50N 83.54E
Tela Honduras **87** 15.56N 87.25W
Telavi Georgia **43** 41.56N 45.30E
Tel Aviv-Yafo Israel **44** 32.05N 34.46E
Tele *r.* Zaïre **54** 2.48N 24.00E
Telegraph Creek *town* Canada **74** 57.55N131.10W
Telemark *d.* Norway **23** 59.40N 8.30E
Teleneshty Moldavia **21** 47.35N 28.17E
Teles Pires *r.* Brazil **91** 7.20S 57.30W
Telfer Australia **62** 21.42S122.13E
Telford U.K. **11** 52.42N 2.30W
Telfs Austria **20** 47.19N 11.04E
Telgte Germany **14** 51.59N 7.46E
Télimélé Guinea **52** 10.54N 13.02W
Tell Atlas *mts.* Algeria **51** 36.00N 1.00E
Tell City U.S.A. **85** 37.56N 86.46W
Teller U.S.A. **72** 65.16N166.22N
Telpos-Iz *mtn.* Russian Fed. **24** 63.56N 59.02E
Telsen Argentina **93** 42.25S 67.00W
Telšiai Lithuania **23** 55.59N 22.15E
Telukbetung Indonesia **36** 5.28S105.16E
Teluk Intan Malaysia **36** 4.00N101.00E
Tema Ghana **52** 5.41N 0.01W
Temagami, L. Canada **76** 47.00N 80.05W
Te Manga *mtn.* Rarotonga Cook Is. **68** 21.13S159.45W
Temaverachi, Sierra *mts.* Mexico **81** 29.30N109.30W
Tembo Aluma Angola **54** 7.42S 17.15E
Teme *r.* U.K. **11** 52.10N 2.13W
Temir Kazakhstan **25** 49.09N 57.06E
Temirtau Kazakhstan **28** 50.05N 72.55E
Témiscaming Canada **76** 46.44N 79.05W
Temora Australia **67** 34.27S147.35E
Tempe U.S.A. **81** 33.25N111.56W
Tempino Indonesia **36** 1.55S103.23E
Tempio Italy **18** 40.54N 9.06E
Temple U.S.A. **83** 31.06N 97.21W
Temple B. Australia **64** 12.10S143.04E
Templemore Rep. of Ire. **13** 52.48N 7.51W
Templin Germany **20** 53.07N 13.30E
Temuco Chile **93** 38.44S 72.36W
Tenabo Mexico **86** 20.03N 90.14W
Tenaha U.S.A. **83** 31.57N 94.15W
Tenasserim Burma **34** 12.05N 99.00E
Tenasserim *d.* Burma **34** 13.00N 99.00E
Tenby U.K. **11** 51.40N 4.42W
Tendaho Ethiopia **49** 11.48N 40.52E
Tende France **17** 44.05N 7.36E
Tende, Col de *pass* France / Italy **15** 44.09N 7.34E
Ten Degree Channel Indian Oc. **34** 10.00N 93.00E
Tendrara Morocco **50** 33.04N 1.59W
Tenenkou Mali **52** 14.25N 4.58W
Tenerife *i.* Canary Is. **50** 28.10N 16.30W
Ténès Algeria **51** 36.31N 1.18E
Teng *r.* Burma **34** 19.50N 97.40E
Tengchong China **39** 25.02N 98.28E
Tengger Shamo *des.* China **32** 39.00N104.10E
Tengiz, Ozero *l.* Kazakhstan **28** 50.30N 69.00E
Teng Xian China **32** 35.08N117.20E
Tenke Zaïre **54** 10.34S 26.07E
Tenkodogo Burkina **52** 11.47N 0.19W
Tennant Creek *town* Australia **64** 19.31S134.15E
Tennessee *d.* U.S.A. **85** 35.50N 85.30W
Tennessee *r.* U.S.A. **85** 37.04N 88.33W
Tenosique Mexico **86** 17.29N 91.26W
Tenryū Japan **35** 34.52N137.49E
Tenryū *r.* Japan **35** 34.39N137.47E
Tensift, Oued *r.* Morocco **50** 32.02N 9.22W
Tenterfield Australia **67** 29.01S152.04E
Teófilo Otoni Brazil **94** 17.52S 41.31W
Tepa Indonesia **37** 7.52S129.31E
Tepa Pt. Niue **68** 19.07S169.56W
Tepelenë Albania **19** 40.18N 20.01E
Tepic Mexico **86** 21.30N104.51W
Teplice Czech Republic **20** 50.40N 13.50E
Ter *r.* Spain **16** 42.02N 3.10E
Téra Niger **52** 14.01N 0.45E
Tera *r.* Portugal **16** 38.55N 8.01W
Teramo Italy **18** 42.40N 13.43E
Terang Australia **66** 38.13S142.56E
Tercan Turkey **42** 39.47N 40.23E
Terebovlya Ukraine **21** 49.18N 25.44E
Terekhova Belorussia **21** 52.13N 31.28E
Teresina Brazil **91** 5.09S 42.46W
Teresópolis Brazil **94** 22.26S 42.59W
Terevaka *mtn.* I. de Pascua **69** 27.05S109.23W
Tergnier France **15** 49.39N 3.18E
Terhazza Mali **52** 23.45N 4.59W
Termez Uzbekistan **28** 37.15N 67.15E
Termination I. Australia **63** 34.25S121.53E
Termini Italy **18** 37.59N 13.42E
Términos, Laguna de *b.* Mexico **86** 18.30N 91.30W
Termoli Italy **18** 41.58N 14.59E
Ternate Indonesia **37** 0.48N127.23E
Terneuzen Neth. **14** 51.20N 3.50E
Terni Italy **18** 42.34N 12.44E
Ternopol Ukraine **21** 49.35N 25.39E
Terra Bella U.S.A. **81** 35.58N119.03W
Terrace Canada **74** 54.31N128.35W
Terracina Italy **18** 41.17N 13.15E
Terralba Italy **18** 39.43N 8.38E
Terrassa *see* Tarrasa Spain **16**
Terre Adélie *f.* Antarctica **96** 80.00S140.00E
Terrebonne Canada **77** 45.42N 73.38W
Terre Haute U.S.A. **84** 39.27N 87.24W
Terrenceville Canada **77** 47.42N 54.43W
Terry U.S.A. **80** 46.47N105.19W
Terschelling *i.* Neth. **14** 53.25N 5.25E
Teruel Spain **16** 40.21N 1.06W
Tervola Finland **22** 66.05N 24.48E
Tešanj Bosnia-Herzegovina **21** 44.37N 18.00E
Tesaret, Oued *wadi* Algeria **51** 25.32N 2.52E
Teslin Canada **74** 60.10N132.43W
Teslin *r.* Canada **74** 61.34N134.54W
Teslin L. Canada **74** 60.15N132.57W
Tessalit Mali **52** 20.12N 1.00E
Tessaoua Niger **53** 13.46N 7.55E
Tessy-sur-Vire France **15** 48.58N 1.04W
Test *r.* U.K. **11** 50.55N 1.29W
Têt *r.* France **17** 42.43N 3.00E
Tetachuck L. Canada **74** 53.18N125.55W
Tete Mozambique **57** 16.10S 33.30E
Tete *d.* Mozambique **57** 15.30S 33.00E
Teterev *r.* Ukraine **21** 51.03N 30.30E
Teterow Germany **20** 53.46N 12.34E
Teteven Bulgaria **19** 42.55N 24.16E
Tethul *r.* Canada **74** 60.35N112.12W
Tetiaroa *i.* Is. de la Société **69** 17.05S149.32W
Tetiyev Ukraine **21** 49.22N 29.40E
Tétouan Morocco **50** 35.34N 5.23W
Tetovo Macedonia **19** 42.01N 20.58E
Tetuan *see* Tétouan Morocco **50**
Tetyukhe Pristan Russian Fed. **35** 44.31N135.31E
Teulada Italy **18** 38.58N 8.46E
Teun *i.* Indonesia **37** 6.59S129.08E
Teuva Finland **22** 62.29N 21.44E
Tevere *r.* Italy **18** 41.45N 12.16E
Teverya Israel **44** 32.48N 35.32E
Teviot *r.* U.K. **12** 55.36N 2.27W
Teviotdale *f.* U.K. **10** 55.26N 2.46W
Teviothead U.K. **12** 55.20N 2.56W
Tewkesbury U.K. **11** 51.59N 2.09W
Texarkana Ark. U.S.A. **83** 33.26N 94.02W
Texarkana Tex. U.S.A. **83** 33.26N 94.03W
Texarkana, L. U.S.A. **83** 33.16N 94.14W
Texas Australia **67** 28.50S151.09E
Texas *d.* U.S.A. **83** 31.30N100.00W
Texas City U.S.A. **83** 29.23N 94.54W
Texel *i.* Neth. **14** 53.05N 4.47E
Texoma, L. U.S.A. **83** 33.55N 96.37W
Texon U.S.A. **83** 31.13N101.43W
Teyvareh Afghan. **40** 33.21N 64.25E
Tezpur India **41** 26.38N 92.48E
Tha-anne *r.* Canada **75** 60.31N 94.37W
Thabana Ntlenyana *mtn.* Lesotho **56** 29.28S 29.17E
Thabazimbi R.S.A. **56** 24.36S 27.23E
Thādiq Saudi Arabia **43** 25.18N 45.52E
Thai Binh Vietnam **33** 20.30N106.26E
Thailand Asia **34** 17.00N101.30E
Thailand, G. of Asia **34** 11.00N101.00E
Thai Nguyen Vietnam **33** 21.46N105.52E
Thak Pakistan **40** 30.32N 70.13E
Thal Pakistan **40** 33.22N 70.33E
Thal Desert Pakistan **40** 31.30N 71.40E
Thale Luang *l.* Thailand **34** 7.40N100.20E
Thallon Australia **67** 28.39S148.49E
Thamarīt Oman **38** 17.39N 54.02E
Thames *r.* Canada **76** 42.19N 82.28W
Thames New Zealand **60** 37.08S175.35E
Thames *r.* U.K. **11** 51.30N 0.05E
Thāna India **40** 19.12N 72.58E
Thāna Pakistan **40** 28.55N 63.45E
Thanh Hóa Vietnam **33** 19.47N105.49E
Thanjāvūr India **39** 10.46N 79.09E
Thāno Bula Khān Pakistan **40** 25.22N 67.50E
Tharād India **40** 24.24N 71.38E
Thar Desert Pakistan / India **40** 28.00N 72.00E
Thargomindah Australia **65** 27.59S143.45E
Tharrawaddy Burma **34** 17.37N 95.48E
Tharthār, Wādī ath *r.* Iraq **42** 34.18N 43.07E
Thásos Greece **19** 40.47N 24.42E
Thásos *i.* Greece **19** 40.40N 24.39E

Thatcher to Tralee B.

Thatcher U.S.A. 81 32.51N109.56W
Thaton Burma 34 16.50N 97.21E
Thaungdut Burma 34 24.26N 94.45E
Thayer U.S.A. 83 36.31N 91.33W
Thayetmyo Burma 34 19.20N 95.10E
Thazi Burma 34 20.51N 96.05E
Thebes *ruins* Egypt 42 25.41N 32.40E
The Bight *town* Bahamas 87 24.19N 75.24W
The Cherokees, L. O' U.S.A. 83 36.45N 94.50W
The Cheviot *mtn.* U.K. 10 55.29N 2.10W
The Cheviot Hills U.K. 10 55.22N 2.24W
The Coorong *g.* Australia 66 36.00S139.30E
The Dalles *town* U.S.A. 80 45.36N121.10W
Thedford U.S.A. 82 41.59N100.35W
The Everglades *f.* U.S.A. 85 26.00N 80.40W
The Fens *f.* U.K. 11 55.10N 4.13W
The Gulf Asia 43 27.00N 50.00E
The Hague *see* 'sGravenhage Neth. 14
Thekulthili L. Canada 75 61.03N110.00W
The Little Minch *str.* U.K. 12 57.40N 6.45W
Thelon *r.* Canada 73 64.23N 96.15W
The Machers *f.* U.K. 12 54.45N 4.28W
The Minch *str.* U.K. 12 58.10N 5.50W
The Needles *c.* U.K. 11 50.39N 1.35W
Theodore Australia 64 24.57S150.05E
Theodore Roosevelt L. U.S.A. 81 33.30N110.57W
Theog India 40 31.07N 77.21E
The Pas Canada 75 53.50N101.15W
The Pennines *hills* U.K. 10 55.40N 2.20W
Thérain *r.* France 15 49.15N 2.27E
Theresa U.S.A. 84 44.13N 75.48W
The Rhinns *f.* U.K. 12 54.50N 5.02W
Thermaïkós Kólpos *g.* Greece 19 40.10N 23.00E
Thermopolis U.S.A. 80 43.39N108.13W
Thermopylae, Pass of Greece 19 38.47N 22.34E
The Rock *town* Australia 67 35.16S147.07E
The Salt L. Australia 66 30.05S142.10E
The Snares *is.* New Zealand 68 48.00S166.30E
The Solent *str.* U.K. 11 50.45N 1.20W
The Sound *str.* Denmark/Sweden 23 55.35N 12.40E
Thessalon Canada 76 46.20N 83.30W
Thessaloníki Greece 19 40.38N 22.56E
Thetford U.K. 11 52.25N 0.44E
Thetford Mines *town* Canada 77 46.06N 71.18W
The Twins *town* Australia 66 30.00S135.16E
The Wash *b.* U.K. 10 52.55N 0.15E
The Weald *f.* U.K. 11 51.05N 0.20E
Thibodaux U.S.A. 83 29.48N 90.49W
Thicket Portage Canada 75 55.19N 97.42W
Thief River Falls *town* U.S.A. 82 48.07N 96.10W
Thiene Italy 15 45.42N 11.29E
Thiers France 17 45.51N 3.33E
Thiès Senegal 52 14.50N 16.55W
Thika Kenya 55 1.04S 37.04E
Thimbu Bhutan 41 27.28N 89.39E
Thingvallavatn *l.* Iceland 22 64.10N 21.10W
Thionville France 17 49.22N 6.11E
Thira *i.* Greece 19 36.24N 25.27E
Thirsk U.K. 10 54.15N 1.20W
Thiruvananthapuram India 38 8.41N 76.57E
Thisted Denmark 23 56.57N 8.42E
Thistilfjördhur *b.* Iceland 22 66.11N 15.20W
Thistle I. Australia 66 35.00S136.09E
Thívai Greece 19 38.21N 23.19E
Thjórsá *r.* Iceland 22 63.53N 20.38W
Thoa *r.* Canada 75 60.31N109.47W
Thoen Thailand 34 17.41N 99.14E
Tholen *i.* Neth. 14 51.34N 4.07E
Thomas U.S.A. 84 39.09N 79.30W
Thomaston U.S.A. 85 32.55N 84.20W
Thomasville Ala. U.S.A. 83 31.55N 87.51W
Thomasville Fla. U.S.A. 85 30.50N 83.59W
Thompson Canada 75 55.45N 97.52W
Thompson U.S.A. 80 38.58N109.43W
Thompson Landing Canada 75 62.56N110.40W
Thompsonville U.S.A. 84 44.32N 85.57W
Thomson *r.* Australia 64 25.11S142.53E
Thonburi Thailand 34 13.43N100.27E
Thórisvatn *l.* Iceland 22 64.15N 18.50W
Thorshavn Faroe Is. 8 62.02N 6.47W
Thorshöfn Iceland 22 66.12N 15.17W
Thouars France 17 46.59N 0.13W
Thowa *r.* Kenya 49 1.33S 40.03E
Thrapston U.K. 11 52.24N 0.32W
Three Forks U.S.A. 80 45.54N111.33W
Three Hills *town* Canada 74 51.43N113.15W
Three Kings Is. New Zealand 68 34.09S172.09E
Three Rivers *town* Australia 62 25.07S119.09E
Three Rivers *town* U.S.A. 83 28.28N 98.11W
Three Sisters Mt. U.S.A. 80 44.10N121.46W
Thuin Belgium 14 50.21N 4.20E
Thul Pakistan 40 28.14N 68.46E
Thule Greenland 73 77.30N 69.29W
Thun Switz. 20 46.46N 7.38E
Thunder Bay *town* Canada 76 48.25N 89.14W
Thunder Hills Canada 75 54.30N106.00W
Thung Song Thailand 34 8.10N 99.41E
Thunkar Bhutan 41 27.55N 91.00E
Thuringen *d.* Germany 20 50.50N 11.35E
Thüringer Wald *mts.* Germany 20 50.40N 10.50E
Thurles Rep. of Ire. 13 52.41N 7.50W
Thurloo Downs *town* Australia 66 29.18S143.30E
Thursday I. Australia 68 10.35S142.13E
Thursday Island *town* Australia 64 10.34S142.14E
Thurso U.K. 12 58.35N 3.32W
Thurso *r.* U.K. 8 58.35N 3.32W
Thury-Harcourt France 15 48.59N 0.29W
Thysville Zaïre 54 5.15S 14.52E
Tiandong China 33 23.36N107.08E
Tian'e China 33 25.00N107.10E
Tian Head Canada 74 53.47N133.06W
Tianjin China 32 39.07N117.08E
Tianjin *d.* China 32 39.30N117.20E
Tianjun China 30 37.16N 98.52E
Tianlin China 33 24.18N106.13E
Tianmen China 33 30.40N113.25E
Tian Shan *mts.* Asia 30 42.00N 80.30E
Tianshui China 32 34.25N105.58E
Tiantai China 33 29.09N121.02E
Tianyang China 33 23.45N106.54E
Tiarei Tahiti 69 17.32S149.20W
Tiaret Algeria 51 35.28N 1.21E
Tiavea W. Samoa 68 13.57S171.28W
Tibasti, Sarir *des.* Libya 51 24.00N 17.00E
Tibati Cameroon 53 6.25N 12.33E
Tiber *r.* *see* Tevere *r.* Italy 18
Tiberias *see* Teverya Israel 44
Tiberias, L. *see* Yam Kinneret *l.* Israel 44
Tibesti *mts.* Chad 53 21.00N 17.30E
Tibet *d.* *see* Xizang *d.* China 41
Tibetan Plateau *see* Qing Zang Gaoyuan *f.* China 30
Tibooburra Australia 66 29.28S142.04E
Tiburón, Isla Mexico 81 29.00N112.20W
Tîchît Mauritania 50 18.28N 9.30W
Tichla W. Sahara 50 21.35N 14.58W
Ticino *r.* Italy 15 45.09N 9.12E
Ticonderoga U.S.A. 84 43.51N 73.26W
Tidaholm Sweden 23 58.11N 13.57E
Tidikelt *f.* Algeria 51 27.00N 1.30E
Tidirhine, Jbel *mtn.* Morocco 50 34.50N 4.30W
Tidjikdja Mauritania 50 18.29N 11.31W
Tiel Neth. 14 51.53N 5.26E
Tieling China 32 42.13N123.48E
Tielt Belgium 14 51.00N 3.20E
Tienen Belgium 14 50.49N 4.56E
Tiénigbé Ivory Coast 52 8.11N 5.43W
Tientsin *see* Tianjin China 32
Tierp Sweden 23 60.20N 17.30E
Tierra Amarilla U.S.A. 80 36.42N106.33W
Tierra Blanca Mexico 86 18.28N 96.12W
Tierra del Fuego *d.* Argentina 93 54.30S 67.00W
Tierra del Fuego *i.* Argentina/Chile 93 54.00S 69.00W
Tietar *r.* Spain 16 39.50N 6.00W
Tietê Brazil 94 23.04S 47.41W
Tifton U.S.A. 85 31.27N 83.31W
Tiger U.S.A. 80 48.42N117.24W
Tiger Hills Canada 75 49.25N 99.30W
Tigil Russian Fed. 29 57.49N158.40E
Tiglit Morocco 50 28.31N 10.15W
Tignère Cameroon 53 7.23N 12.37E
Tignish Canada 77 46.57N 64.02W
Tigray *d.* Ethiopia 48 14.10N 39.35E
Tigre *r.* Venezuela 90 9.20N 62.30W
Tigris *r.* *see* Dijlah *r.* Asia 43
Tîh, Jabal at *f.* Egypt 44 28.50N 34.00E
Tihâmah *f.* Saudi Arabia 48 19.00N 41.00E
Tijuana Mexico 81 32.32N117.01W
Tikamgarh India 41 24.44N 78.50E
Tikaré Burkina 52 13.16N 1.44W
Tikhoretsk Russian Fed. 25 45.52N 40.07E
Tikhvin Russian Fed. 24 59.35N 33.29E
Tikitiki New Zealand 60 37.47S178.25E
Tiksha Russian Fed. 24 64.04N 32.35E
Tiksi Russian Fed. 29 71.40N128.45E
Tilburg Neth. 14 51.34N 5.05E
Tilbury U.K. 11 51.28N 0.23E
Tilemsi, Vallée du *f.* Mali 52 16.15N 0.02E
Tilghman U.S.A. 85 38.42N 76.20W
Tilhar India 41 27.59N 79.44E
Till *r.* U.K. 10 55.41N 2.12W
Tillabéri Niger 53 14.28N 1.27E
Tillamook U.S.A. 80 45.27N123.51W
Tilos *i.* Greece 19 36.25N 27.25E
Tilpa Australia 66 30.57S144.24E
Timanskiy Kryazh *mts.* Russian Fed. 24 66.00N 49.00E
Timaru New Zealand 60 44.23S171.41E
Timashevsk Russian Fed. 25 45.38N 38.56E
Timbákion Greece 19 35.04N 24.46E
Timbédra Mauritania 50 16.17N 8.16W
Timber Creek *town* Australia 62 15.38S130.28E
Timboon Australia 66 38.32S143.02E
Timbuktu *see* Tombouctou Mali 52
Timimoun Algeria 50 29.15N 0.15E
Timimoun, Sebkha de *f.* Algeria 50 29.10N 0.05E
Timiris, Cap *c.* Mauritania 52 19.23N 16.32W
Timiş *r.* Yugo./Romania 21 44.49N 20.28E
Timişoara Romania 21 45.47N 21.15E
Timmins Canada 76 48.28N 81.25W
Timok *r.* Yugo. 19 44.13N 22.40E
Timor *i.* Indonesia 62 9.30S125.00E
Timor Sea Austa. 62 11.00S127.00E
Timor Timur *d.* Indonesia 37 9.00S125.00E
Timpahute Range *mts.* U.S.A. 80 37.38N115.34W
Tinahely Rep. of Ire. 13 52.48N 6.19W
Tindouf Algeria 50 27.42N 8.09W
Tindouf, Sebkha de *f.* Algeria 50 27.45N 7.30W
Tingha Australia 67 29.58S151.16E
Tingo María Peru 90 9.09S 75.56W
Tingping China 33 26.10N110.17E
Tingréla Ivory Coast 52 10.26N 6.20W
Tingri China 41 28.30N 86.34E
Tingsryd Sweden 23 56.32N 14.59E
Tinguipaya Bolivia 92 19.11S 65.51W
Tinkisso *r.* Guinea 52 11.25N 9.05W
Tinnenburra Australia 67 28.40S145.30E
Tinnoset Norway 23 59.43N 9.02E
Tinos *i.* Greece 19 37.36N 25.08E
Tinsukia India 39 27.30N 95.22E
Tintinara Australia 66 35.52S140.04E
T'ī'o Ethiopia 48 14.40N 40.15E
Tioman, Pulau *i.* Malaysia 36 2.45N104.10E
Tionaga Canada 76 48.05N 82.00W
Tione di Trento Italy 15 46.02N 10.43E
Tipperary Rep. of Ire. 13 52.29N 8.10W
Tipperary *d.* Rep. of Ire. 13 52.37N 7.55W
Tirân, Jazîrat Saudi Arabia 44 27.56N 34.34E
Tiranë Albania 19 41.20N 19.48E
Tirano Italy 15 46.12N 10.10E
Tiraspol Moldavia 21 46.50N 29.38E
Tirat Karmel Israel 44 32.46N 34.58E
Tirebolu Turkey 42 41.02N 38.49E
Tiree *i.* U.K. 12 56.30N 6.50W
Tîrgovişte Romania 21 44.56N 25.27E
Tîrgu-Jiu Romania 21 45.03N 23.17E
Tîrgu-Lăpuş Romania 21 47.27N 23.52E
Tîrgu Mureş Romania 21 46.33N 24.34E
Tîrgu-Neamţ Romania 21 47.12N 26.22E
Tîrgu-Ocna Romania 21 46.15N 26.37E
Tîrgu-Secuiesc Romania 21 46.00N 26.08E
Tiris Zemmour *d.* Mauritania 50 24.00N 9.00W
Tîrnavos Greece 19 39.45N 22.17E
Tirodi India 41 21.41N 79.42E
Tirol *d.* Austria 20 47.15N 11.20E
Tir Pol Afghan. 43 34.38N 61.19E
Tirso *r.* Italy 18 39.52N 8.33E
Tiruchchirāppalli India 39 10.50N 78.43E
Tirunelveli India 38 8.45N 77.43E
Tirupati India 39 13.39N 79.25E
Tiruppur India 38 11.05N 77.20E
Tisa *r.* Yugo. 21 45.09N 20.16E
Tis'ah Egypt 44 30.02N 32.35E
Tisdale Canada 75 52.51N104.04W
Tisza *r.* Hungary *see* Tisa *r.* Yugo. 21
Tit Algeria 51 22.58N 5.11E
Titicaca, L. Bolivia/Peru 92 16.00S 69.00W
Titikaveka Rarotonga Cook Is. 68 21.16S159.45W
Titiwa Nigeria 53 12.14N 12.53E
Titlagarh India 41 20.18N 83.09E
Titov Veles Macedonia 19 41.43N 21.49E
Titran Norway 22 63.42N 8.22E
Ti Tree Australia 64 22.06S133.17E
Titule Zaïre 54 3.17N 25.32E
Titusville Fla. U.S.A. 85 28.37N 80.50W
Titusville Penn. U.S.A. 84 41.38N 79.41W
Tiuni India 41 30.57N 77.51E
Tivaouane Senegal 52 14.57N 16.49W
Tiverton U.K. 11 50.54N 3.30W
Tivoli Italy 18 41.58N 12.48E
Tizimín Mexico 87 21.10N 88.09W
Tizi Ouzou Algeria 51 36.44N 4.05E
Tiznit Morocco 50 29.43N 9.44W
Tjeuke Meer *l.* Neth. 14 52.55N 5.51E
Tjörn *i.* Sweden 23 58.00N 11.38E
Tlaxcala *d.* Mexico 86 19.45N 98.20W
Tlemcen Algeria 50 34.52N 1.19W
Tmassah Libya 51 26.22N 15.48E
Tni Haïa *well* Algeria 50 24.15N 2.45W
Toab U.K. 12 59.53N 1.16W
Toamasina Madagascar 57 18.10S 49.23E
Toano Italy 15 44.23N 10.34E
Toanoano Tahiti 69 17.52S149.12W
Toba Japan 35 34.29N136.51E
Toba, Danau *l.* Indonesia 36 2.45N 98.50E
Toba Kākar Range *mts.* Pakistan 40 31.15N 68.00E
Tobar U.S.A. 80 40.53N114.54W
Toba Tek Singh Pakistan 40 30.58N 72.29E
Tobelo Indonesia 37 1.45N127.59E
Tobermory Canada 76 45.14N 81.36W
Tobermory U.K. 12 56.37N 6.04W
Tobi *i.* Pacific Oc. 37 3.01N131.10E
Tobin L. Canada 75 53.40N103.35W
Toboali Indonesia 36 3.00S106.30E
Tobol *r.* Russian Fed. 28 58.15N 68.12E
Tobolsk Russian Fed. 28 58.15N 68.12E
Tobruk *see* Ţubruq Libya 48
Tobseda Russian Fed. 24 68.34N 52.16E
Tocantinópolis Brazil 91 6.20S 47.25W
Tocantins *d.* Brazil 91 10.15S 48.30W
Tocantins *r.* Brazil 91 1.50S 49.15W
Toccoa U.S.A. 85 34.34N 83.21W
Töcksfors Sweden 23 59.30N 11.50E
Tocopilla Chile 92 22.05S 70.12W
Tocorpuri *mtn.* Bolivia/Chile 92 22.26S 67.53W
Tocumwal Australia 67 35.51S145.34E
Tocuyo *r.* Venezuela 90 11.03N 68.23W
Todenyang Kenya 55 4.34N 35.52E
Todos Santos Mexico 81 23.27N110.13W
Tofua *i.* Tonga 69 19.45S175.05W
Togian, Kepulauan *is.* Indonesia 37 0.20S122.00E
Togo Africa 52 8.00N 1.00E
Toi Niue 68 18.58S169.52W
Toijala Finland 23 61.10N 23.52E
Toili Indonesia 37 1.25S122.23E
Tojg Afghan. 40 32.04N 61.48E
Tokaj Hungary 21 48.08N 21.27E
Tokala *mtn.* Indonesia 37 1.36S121.41E
Tokat Turkey 42 40.20N 36.35E
Tokelau Is. Pacific Oc. 68 9.00S171.45W
Toki Japan 35 35.21N137.11E
Toki *r.* Japan 35 35.12N136.52E
Tokmak Kyrgyzstan 30 42.49N 75.15E
Tokoname Japan 35 34.53N136.51E
Tokoroa New Zealand 60 38.13S175.53E
Tokuno shima *i.* Japan 31 27.40N129.00E
Tōkyō Japan 35 35.42N139.46E
Tōkyō-wan *b.* Japan 35 35.25N139.45E
Tolaga Bay *town* New Zealand 60 38.22S178.18E
Toledo Spain 16 39.52N 4.02W
Toledo U.S.A. 84 41.40N 83.35W
Toledo, Montes de *mts.* Spain 16 39.35N 4.30W
Toledo Bend Resr. U.S.A. 83 31.46N 93.25W
Toliara Madagascar 57 23.21S 43.40E
Tolmezzo Italy 15 46.24N 13.01E
Tolo, Teluk *g.* Indonesia 37 2.00S122.30E
Tolosa Spain 16 43.09N 2.04W
Tolstyy-Les Ukraine 21 51.24N 29.48E
Tolti Jammu & Kashmir 40 35.02N 76.06E
Toluca Mexico 86 19.20N 99.40W
Toluca *mtn.* Mexico 86 19.10N 99.40W
Tol'yatti Russian Fed. 24 53.32N 49.24E
Tomah U.S.A. 82 43.59N 90.30W
Tomar Portugal 16 39.36N 8.25W
Tomás Gomensoro Uruguay 93 30.26S 57.26W
Tomaszów Lubelski Poland 21 50.28N 23.25E
Tomaszów Mazowiecki Poland 21 51.32N 20.01E
Tombe Sudan 49 5.49N 31.41E
Tombigbee *r.* U.S.A. 83 31.04N 87.58W
Tombos Brazil 94 20.53S 42.03W
Tombouctou Mali 52 16.49N 2.59W
Tombouctou *d.* Mali 52 19.35N 3.20W
Tombua Angola 54 15.55S 11.51E
Tomé Chile 93 36.37S 72.57W
Tomelilla Sweden 23 55.33N 13.57E
Tomelloso Spain 16 39.09N 3.01W
Tomingley Australia 67 32.06S148.15E
Tomini Indonesia 37 0.31N120.30E
Tomini, Teluk *g.* Indonesia 37 0.30S120.45E
Tominian Mali 52 13.17N 4.35W
Tomintoul U.K. 12 57.15N 3.24W
Tomislavgrad Bosnia-Herzegovina 21 43.43N 17.14E
Tomkinson Ranges *mts.* Australia 62 26.11S129.05E
Tom Price Australia 62 22.49S117.51E
Tomra China 41 30.52N 87.30E
Tomra Norway 22 62.34N 6.55E
Tomsk Russian Fed. 28 56.30N 85.05E
Toms River *town* U.S.A. 85 39.57N 74.12W
Tonalá Mexico 86 16.08N 93.41W
Tonalea U.S.A. 81 36.20N110.58W
Tonasket U.S.A. 80 48.42N119.26W
Tonawanda U.S.A. 76 43.01N 78.53W
Tonbridge U.K. 11 51.12N 0.16E
Tondano Indonesia 37 1.19N124.56E
Tönder Denmark 23 54.56N 8.54E
Tondibi Mali 52 16.39N 0.14W
Tondoro Namibia 56 17.45S 18.50E
Tone *r.* Japan 35 35.44N140.51E
Tonga Pacific Oc. 69 20.00S175.00W
Tonga Sudan 49 9.28N 31.03E
Tongaat R.S.A. 56 29.34S 31.07E
Tong'an China 33 24.44N118.09E
Tongatapu *i.* Tonga 69 21.10S175.10W
Tongatapu Group *is.* Tonga 69 21.10S175.10W
Tonga Trench *f.* Pacific Oc. 68 20.00S173.00W
Tongchuan China 32 35.05N109.10E
Tongeren Belgium 14 50.47N 5.28E
Tongguan Hunan China 33 28.27N112.48E
Tongguan Shaanxi China 32 34.32N110.26E
Tonghai China 39 24.07N102.45E
Tonghua China 31 41.40N126.52E
Tongking, G. of China/Vietnam 34 20.00N108.00E
Tongliao China 32 43.40N122.20E
Tongling China 33 30.55N117.42E
Tonglu China 33 29.49N119.40E
Tongo Australia 66 30.30S143.47E
Tongoa *i.* Vanuatu 68 16.54S168.34E
Tongobory Madagascar 57 23.32S 44.20E
Tongoy Chile 92 30.15S 71.30W
Tongren China 33 27.41N109.08E
Tongsa Dzong Bhutan 41 27.31N 90.30E
Tongue U.K. 12 58.28N 4.25W
Tongue *r.* U.S.A. 80 46.24N105.25W
Tongwei China 32 35.18N105.10E
Tong Xian China 32 39.52N116.45E
Tongxin China 32 36.59N105.50E
Tongyu China 32 44.48N123.06E
Tongzi China 33 28.08N106.49E
Tonj Sudan 49 7.17N 28.45E
Tonk India 40 26.10N 75.47E
Tonkābon Iran 43 36.49N 50.54E
Tônlé Sap *l.* Cambodia 34 12.50N104.15E
Tonnerre France 15 47.51N 3.59E
Tonopah U.S.A. 80 38.04N117.14W
Tonota Botswana 56 21.28S 27.24E
Tons *r.* India 41 25.17N 82.04E
Tönsberg Norway 23 59.17N 10.25E
Tonstad Norway 23 58.40N 6.43E
Tonto Basin *town* U.S.A. 81 33.55N111.18W
Toobeah Australia 67 28.22S149.50E
Toodyay Australia 63 31.35S116.26E
Tooele U.S.A. 80 40.32N112.18W
Toolondo Australia 66 36.55S142.00E
Toowoomba Australia 65 27.35S151.54E
Topeka U.S.A. 82 39.03N 95.41W
Topko *mtn.* Russian Fed. 29 57.20N138.10E
Topley Canada 74 54.32N126.05W
Topliţa Romania 21 46.55N 25.21E
Topock U.S.A. 81 34.44N114.27W
Topolovgrad Bulgaria 19 42.05N 26.20E
Topozero, Ozero *l.* Russian Fed. 24 65.45N 32.00E
Toppenish U.S.A. 80 46.23N120.19W
Tor Ethiopia 49 7.53N 33.40E
Tora-Khem Russian Fed. 29 52.31N 96.13E
Torbat-e Ḩeydarīyeh Iran 43 35.16N 59.13E
Torbat-e Jām Iran 43 35.15N 60.37E
Tördal Norway 23 59.10N 8.45E
Tordesillas Spain 16 41.30N 5.00W
Töre Sweden 22 65.54N 22.39E
Töreboda Sweden 23 58.43N 14.08E
Torgau Germany 20 51.34N 13.00E
Torhout Belgium 14 51.04N 3.06E
Toride Japan 35 35.53N140.04E
Torino Italy 15 45.04N 7.40E
Torit Sudan 49 4.24N 32.34E
Tormes *r.* Spain 16 41.18N 6.29W
Torne *r.* Sweden *see* Tornio *r.* Finland 22
Torneträsk Sweden 22 68.15N 19.30E
Torneträsk *l.* Sweden 22 68.20N 19.10E
Tornio Finland 22 65.52N 24.10E
Tornio *r.* Finland 22 65.53N 24.07E
Tornquist Argentina 93 38.06S 62.14W
Toro Spain 16 41.31N 5.24W
Toronaíos Kólpos *g.* Greece 19 40.05N 23.38E
Toronto Canada 76 43.42N 79.25W
Toropets Russian Fed. 24 56.30N 31.40E
Tororo Uganda 55 0.42N 34.13E
Toros Dağlari *mts.* Turkey 42 37.15N 34.15E
Torquay Australia 66 38.20S144.20E
Torquay U.K. 11 50.27N 3.31W
Torrance U.S.A. 81 33.50N118.19W
Torreblanca Spain 16 40.14N 0.12E
Torre de Moncorvo Portugal 16 41.10N 7.03W
Torrelavega Spain 16 43.21N 4.00W
Torremolinos Spain 16 36.38N 4.30W
Torrens, L. Australia 66 31.00S137.50E
Torrens Creek *r.* Australia 64 22.22S145.09E
Torrens Creek *town* Australia 64 20.50S145.00E
Torreón Mexico 83 25.33N103.26W
Torre Pellice Italy 15 44.49N 9.13E
Torres Str. Australia 64 10.00S142.20E
Torres Vedras Portugal 16 39.05N 9.15W
Torrevieja Spain 16 37.59N 0.40W
Torrey U.S.A. 80 38.18N111.25W
Torridge *r.* U.K. 11 51.01N 4.12W
Torridon U.K. 12 57.23N 5.31W
Torridon, Loch U.K. 12 57.35N 5.45W
Torriglia Italy 15 44.31N 9.10E
Torrington U.S.A. 80 42.04N104.11W
Torsby Sweden 23 60.08N 13.00E
Tortola *i.* B.V.Is. 87 18.28N 64.40W
Tortona Italy 15 44.54N 8.52E
Tortosa Spain 16 40.49N 0.31E
Tortue, Île de la *i.* Cuba 87 20.05N 72.57W
Toruń Poland 21 53.01N 18.35E
Tory I. Rep. of Ire. 13 55.16N 8.13W
Tory Sd. Rep. of Ire. 13 55.14N 8.15W
Torzhok Russian Fed. 24 57.02N 34.51E
Toscana *d.* Italy 18 43.35N 11.10E
Tosen Norway 22 65.16N 12.50E
Toshkent *see* Tashkent Kyrgyzstan 30
Tosno Russian Fed. 24 59.38N 30.46E
Tostado Argentina 92 29.15S 61.45W
Totana Spain 16 37.46N 1.30W
Tôtes France 15 49.41N 1.03E
Totma Russian Fed. 24 59.59N 42.44E
Totora Bolivia 92 17.42S 65.09W
Tottenham Australia 67 32.14S147.24E
Tottori Japan 35 35.32N134.12E
Touba Ivory Coast 52 8.22N 7.42W
Toubkal *mtn.* Morocco 50 31.03N 7.57W
Toucy France 15 47.44N 3.18E
Tougan Burkina 52 13.05N 3.04W
Touggourt Algeria 51 33.06N 6.04E
Tougué Guinea 52 11.25N 11.50W
Toul France 17 48.41N 5.54E
Toulnustouc *r.* Canada 77 49.35N 68.25W
Toulon France 17 43.07N 5.53E
Toulouse France 17 43.33N 1.24E
Toummo Niger 51 22.45N 14.08E
Tounassine, Hamada *des.* Algeria 50 28.36N 5.00W
Toungoo Burma 34 18.57N 96.26E
Touques *r.* France 15 49.22N 0.06E
Tourassine *well* Mauritania 50 24.40N 11.20W
Tourcoing France 14 50.44N 3.09E
Tournai Belgium 14 50.36N 3.23E
Tournon France 17 45.04N 4.50E
Tournus France 17 46.33N 4.55E
Tours France 15 47.23N 0.42E
Toury France 15 48.11N 1.56E
Touwsrivier *town* R.S.A. 56 33.20S 20.02E
Towcester U.K. 11 52.07N 0.56W
Tower U.S.A. 82 47.47N 92.19W
Towner U.S.A. 82 48.21N100.25W
Townsend, Mt. Australia 67 36.24S148.15E
Townshend I. Australia 64 22.15S150.30E
Townsville Australia 64 19.13S146.48E
Towrzī Afghan. 40 30.11N 65.59E
Towson U.S.A. 85 39.24N 76.36W
Towyn U.K. 11 52.37N 4.08W
Toyah U.S.A. 83 31.19N103.47W
Toyama Japan 35 36.42N137.14E
Toyo *r.* Japan 35 34.47N137.20E
Toyohashi Japan 35 34.46N137.23E
Toyokawa Japan 35 34.49N137.24E
Toyota Japan 35 35.05N137.09E
Tozeur Tunisia 51 33.55N 8.08E
Traben-Trarbach Germany 14 49.57N 7.07E
Trabzon Turkey 42 41.00N 39.43E
Tracadie Canada 77 47.31N 64.54W
Tracy Canada 77 46.01N 73.09W
Tracy U.S.A. 82 44.14N 95.37W
Trade Town Liberia 52 5.43N 9.56W
Trafalgar, Cabo *c.* Spain 16 36.11N 6.02W
Traiguén Chile 93 38.15S 72.41W
Trail Canada 74 49.05N117.40W
Trajanova Vrata *pass* Bulgaria 19 42.13N 23.58E
Trakt Russian Fed. 24 62.40N 51.26E
Tralee Rep. of Ire. 13 52.16N 9.42W
Tralee B. Rep. of Ire. 13 52.18N 9.55W

Tranås to **Una**

Tranas Sweden **23** 58.03N 14.59E
Trang Thailand **34** 7.35N 99.35E
Trangan *i.* Indonesia **37** 6.30S134.15E
Trangie Australia **67** 32.03S148.01E
Trani Italy **18** 41.17N 16.26E
Tranoroa Madagascar **57** 24.42S 45.04E
Tranqueras Uruguay **93** 31.12S 55.45W
Transkei Africa **56** 31.30S 29.00E
Transkei *f.* R.S.A. **56** 32.12S 28.20E
Transvaal *d.* R.S.A. **56** 24.30S 29.30E
Transylvanian Alps *see* Carpaţii Meridionalimts. *mts.* Romania **19**
Trapani Italy **18** 38.02N 12.30E
Traralgon Australia **67** 38.12S146.32E
Traryd Sweden **23** 56.35N 13.45E
Trarza *d.* Mauritania **50** 18.00N 14.50W
Trarza *f.* Mauritania **50** 18.00N 15.00W
Trasimeno, Lago *l.* Italy **18** 43.09N 12.07E
Trat Thailand **34** 12.14N102.33E
Traunstein Germany **20** 47.52N 12.38E
Travellers L. Australia **66** 33.18S142.00E
Travers, Mt. New Zealand **60** 42.05S172.45E
Traverse City U.S.A. **84** 44.46N 85.38W
Travnik Bosnia-Herzegovina **19** 44.14N 17.40E
Trayning Australia **63** 31.09S117.46E
Trbovlje Slovenia **20** 46.10N 15.03E
Trebbia *r.* Italy **15** 45.04N 9.41E
Třebíč Czech Republic **20** 49.13N 15.55E
Trebinje Bosnia-Herzegovina **19** 42.43N 18.20E
Trebišov Slovakia **21** 48.40N 21.47E
Třeboň Czech Republic **20** 49.01N 14.50E
Trecate Italy **15** 45.26N 8.44E
Tredegar U.K. **11** 51.47N 3.16W
Tregaron U.K. **11** 52.14N 3.56W
Tregosse Islets and Reefs Australia **64** 17.41S150.43E
Tréguier France **17** 48.47N 3.16W
Treinta-y-Tres Uruguay **94** 33.16S 54.17W
Treis Germany **14** 50.10N 7.20E
Trélazé France **15** 47.27N 0.28W
Trelew Argentina **93** 43.15S 65.20W
Trelleborg Sweden **23** 55.22N 13.10E
Trélon France **14** 50.04N 4.05E
Tremadog B. U.K. **10** 52.52N 4.14W
Tremblant, Mont *mtn.* Canada **77** 46.16N 74.35W
Tremp Spain **16** 42.10N 0.52E
Trena Ethiopia **49** 10.45N 40.38E
Trenčín Slovakia **21** 48.54N 18.04E
Trenggalek Indonesia **37** 8.01S111.38E
Trenque Lauquen Argentina **93** 35.56S 62.43W
Trent *r.* U.K. **10** 53.41N 0.41W
Trentino-Alto Adige *d.* Italy **15** 46.30N 11.20E
Trento Italy **15** 46.04N 11.08E
Trenton Canada **76** 44.06N 77.35W
Trenton Mo. U.S.A. **82** 40.05N 93.37W
Trenton Nebr. U.S.A. **82** 40.11N101.01W
Trenton N.J. U.S.A. **85** 40.15N 74.43W
Trepassey Canada **73** 46.44N 53.22W
Tres Árboles Uruguay **93** 32.24S 56.43W
Tres Arroyos Argentina **93** 38.26S 60.17W
Três Corações Brazil **94** 21.44S 45.15W
Três Lagoas Brazil **94** 20.46S 51.43W
Três Marias, Represa *resr.* Brazil **94** 18.15S 45.15W
Três Pontas Brazil **94** 21.23S 45.29W
Três Rios Brazil **94** 22.07S 43.12W
Treuchtlingen Germany **20** 48.57N 10.55E
Treviglio Italy **15** 45.31N 9.35E
Treviso Italy **15** 45.40N 12.14E
Tribulation, C. Australia **64** 16.03S145.30E
Tribune U.S.A. **82** 38.28N101.45W
Trida Australia **67** 33.00S145.01E
Trier Germany **14** 49.45N 6.39E
Trieste Italy **18** 45.40N 13.47E
Triglav *mtn.* Slovenia **18** 46.21N 13.50E
Trikala Greece **19** 39.34N 21.46E
Trikomon Cyprus **44** 35.17N 33.53E
Triman Pakistan **40** 29.38N 69.05E
Trincomalee Sri Lanka **39** 8.34N 81.13E
Trinidad Bolivia **92** 14.47S 64.47W
Trinidad Colombia **90** 5.25N 71.40W
Trinidad Cuba **87** 21.48N 80.00W
Trinidad Uruguay **93** 33.32S 56.54W
Trinidad U.S.A. **80** 37.10N104.31W
Trinidad & Tobago S. America **87** 10.30N 61.20W
Trinity *r.* U.S.A. **83** 29.55N 94.45W
Trinity B. Australia **64** 16.26S145.26E
Trinity B. Canada **77** 48.00N 53.40W
Trinity Range *mts.* U.S.A. **80** 40.13N119.12W
Trinkitat Sudan **48** 18.41N 37.43E
Trino Italy **15** 45.12N 8.18E
Tripoli *see* Ţarābulus Lebanon **44**
Tripoli *see* Ţarābulus Libya **51**
Tripolis Greece **19** 37.31N 22.21E
Tripolitania *f. see* Ţarābulus *f.* Libya **51**
Tripp U.S.A. **82** 43.13N 97.58W
Tripura *d.* India **41** 23.50N 92.00E
Tristan da Cunha *i.* Atlantic Oc. **95** 37.50S 12.30W
Trivandrum *see* Thiruvananthapuram India **38**
Trnava Slovakia **21** 48.23N 17.35E
Troarn France **15** 49.11N 0.11W
Trobriand Is. P.N.G. **64** 8.35S151.05E
Troglav *mtn.* Croatia **19** 43.57N 16.36E
Troisdorf Germany **14** 50.50N 7.07E
Trois-Rivières *town* Canada **77** 46.21N 72.34W
Troitsk Russian Fed. **28** 54.08N 61.33E
Troitsko-Pechorsk Russian Fed. **24** 62.40N 56.08E
Troitskoye Russian Fed. **24** 52.18N 56.26E
Troitskoye Ukraine **21** 47.38N 30.19E
Trölladyngja *mtn.* Iceland **22** 64.54N 17.16W
Trollhättan Sweden **23** 58.16N 12.18E
Trollheimen *mts.* Norway **22** 62.50N 9.15E
Troms *d.* Norway **22** 69.20N 19.30E
Tromsö Norway **22** 69.42N 19.00E
Trondheim Norway **22** 63.36N 10.23E
Trondheimsfjorden *est.* Norway **22** 63.40N 10.30E
Troödos *mts.* Cyprus **44** 34.57N 32.50E
Troon U.K. **12** 55.33N 4.40W
Tropic U.S.A. **80** 37.37N112.05W
Trosh Russian Fed. **24** 66.24N 56.08E
Trostan *mtn.* U.K. **13** 55.03N 6.10W
Trostyanets Ukraine **21** 48.35N 29.10E
Trout *r.* Canada **74** 61.19N119.51W
Trout Creek *town* Canada **76** 45.56N 79.24W
Trout L. N.W.T. Canada **74** 60.35N121.10W
Trout L. Ont. Canada **76** 51.13N 93.20W
Trout River *town* Canada **77** 49.29N 58.08W
Trouville France **15** 49.22N 0.55E
Trowbridge U.K. **11** 51.18N 2.12W
Troy Ala. U.S.A. **85** 31.49N 86.00W
Troy Mo. U.S.A. **82** 38.59N 90.59W
Troy Mont. U.S.A. **80** 48.28N115.53W
Troy N.Y. U.S.A. **84** 42.43N 73.40W
Troy Ohio U.S.A. **84** 40.02N 84.12W
Troyes France **15** 48.18N 4.05E
Troy Peak *mtn.* U.S.A. **80** 38.19N115.30W
Trpanj Croatia **19** 43.00N 17.17E
Truchas Peak *mtn.* U.S.A. **81** 35.58N105.39W
Truckee U.S.A. **80** 39.20N120.11W
Trujillo Honduras **87** 15.55N 86.00W
Trujillo Peru **90** 8.06S 79.00W
Trujillo Spain **16** 39.28N 5.53W
Trujillo Venezuela **90** 9.20N 70.37W
Truk Is. Pacific Oc. **68** 7.23N151.46E
Trundle Australia **67** 32.54S147.35E
Trung-Luong Vietnam **34** 13.55N109.15E
Trunmore B. Canada **77** 53.48N 57.10W
Truro Australia **66** 34.23S139.09E
Truro Canada **77** 45.22N 63.16W
Truro U.K. **11** 50.17N 5.02W
Trustrup Denmark **23** 56.21N 10.47E
Truth or Consequences U.S.A. **81** 33.08N107.15W
Trysil Norway **23** 61.19N 12.16E
Trysil *r.* Norway **23** 61.03N 12.30E
Trzemeszno Poland **21** 52.35N 17.50E
Tsaratanana Madagascar **57** 16.47S 47.39E
Tsaratanana, Massif de *mts.* Madagascar **57** 14.00S 49.00E
Tsau Botswana **56** 20.10S 22.29E
Tsavo Nat. Park Kenya **55** 2.45S 38.45E
Tselinograd Kazakhstan **28** 51.10N 71.28E
Tses Namibia **56** 25.58S 18.08E
Tsévié Togo **53** 6.28N 1.15E
Tshabong Botswana **56** 26.03S 22.25E
Tshane Botswana **56** 24.02S 21.54E
Tshela Zaïre **54** 4.57S 12.57E
Tshesebe Botswana **56** 20.45S 27.31E
Tshikapa Zaïre **54** 6.28S 20.48E
Tshofa Zaïre **54** 5.13S 25.20E
Tshopo *r.* Zaïre **54** 0.30N 25.07E
Tshuapa *r.* Zaïre **54** 0.14S 20.45E
Tsihombé Madagascar **57** 25.18S 45.29E
Tsimlyansk Russian Fed. **25** 47.40N 42.06E
Tsimlyanskoye Vodokhranilishche *resr.* Russian Fed. **25** 48.00N 43.00E
Tsinan *see* Jinan China **32**
Tsingtao *see* Qingdao China **32**
Tsiribihina Madagascar **57** 19.42S 44.31E
Tsiroanomandidy Madagascar **57** 18.46S 46.02E
Tsivilsk Russian Fed. **24** 55.50N 47.28E
Tsivory Madagascar **57** 24.04S 46.05E
Tskhinvali Georgia **25** 42.14N 43.58E
Tsna *r.* Belorussia **21** 52.10N 27.03E
Tsna *r.* Russian Fed. **24** 54.45N 41.54E
Tsobis Namibia **56** 19.27S 17.30E
Tso Moriri *l.* Jammu & Kashmir **41** 32.54N 78.20E
Tsu Japan **35** 34.43N136.31E
Tsuchiura Japan **35** 36.05N140.12E
Tsudakhar Russian Fed. **25** 42.20N 47.11E
Tsumeb Namibia **56** 19.12S 17.43E
Tsuru Japan **35** 35.30N138.56E
Tsushima Japan **35** 35.10N136.43E
Tsushima *i.* Japan **35** 34.30N129.20E
Tuam Rep. of Ire. **13** 53.32N 8.52W
Tuamotu, Îles *is.* Pacific Oc. **69** 17.00S142.00W
Tuapa Niue **68** 18.59S169.54W
Tuapse Russian Fed. **25** 44.06N 39.05E
Tuatapere New Zealand **60** 46.08S167.41E
Tubac U.S.A. **81** 31.37N111.03W
Tuba City U.S.A. **81** 36.08N111.14W
Tuban Indonesia **37** 6.55S112.01E
Tubarão Brazil **94** 28.30S 49.01W
Ţubayq, Jabal aţ *mts.* Saudi Arabia **44** 29.30N 37.15E
Tubbercurry Rep. of Ire. **13** 54.03N 8.45W
Tübingen Germany **20** 48.32N 9.04E
Ţubjah, Wādī *r.* Saudi Arabia **42** 25.35N 38.22E
Ţubruq Libya **48** 32.06N 23.58E
Tubuai *i.* Pacific Oc. **69** 23.23S149.27W
Tubuai Is. Pacific Oc. **69** 23.00S150.00W
Tucacas Venezuela **90** 10.48N 68.19W
Tuchola Poland **21** 53.35N 17.50E
Tuckerton U.S.A. **85** 39.36N 74.20W
Tucson U.S.A. **81** 32.13N110.58W
Tucumán *d.* Argentina **92** 26.30S 65.20W
Tucumcari U.S.A. **81** 35.10N103.44W
Tucupita Venezuela **90** 9.02N 62.04W
Tucuruí Brazil **91** 3.42S 49.44W
Tucuruí, Represa de *resr.* Brazil **91** 4.35S 49.33W
Tudela Spain **16** 42.04N 1.37W
Tufi P.N.G. **64** 9.05S149.20E
Tugela R.S.A. **56** 29.10S 31.25E
Tuguegarao Phil. **37** 17.36N121.44E
Tugur Russian Fed. **29** 53.44N136.45E
Tuineje Canary Is. **95** 28.18N 14.03W
Tukangbesi, Kepulauan *is.* Indonesia **37** 5.30S124.00E
Tukayyid *well* Iraq **43** 29.47N 45.36E
Ţūkh Egypt **44** 30.21N 31.12E
Tūkrah Libya **51** 32.32N 20.34E
Tuktoyaktuk Canada **72** 69.27N133.00W
Tukums Latvia **23** 57.00N 23.10E
Tukuyu Tanzania **55** 9.20S 33.37E
Tula Mexico **86** 23.00N 99.43W
Tula Russian Fed. **24** 54.11N 37.38E
Tūlāk Afghan. **40** 33.58N 63.44E
Tulare U.S.A. **81** 36.13N119.21W
Tulare L. *resr.* U.S.A. **81** 36.03N119.49W
Tularosa U.S.A. **81** 33.04N106.01W
Tulcan Ecuador **90** 0.50N 77.48W
Tulcea Romania **19** 45.10N 28.50E
Tulchin Ukraine **21** 48.40N 28.49E
Tulemalu L. Canada **75** 62.58N 99.25W
Tuli Zimbabwe **56** 21.50S 29.15E
Tuli *r.* Zimbabwe **56** 21.49S 29.00E
Tulia U.S.A. **83** 34.32N101.46W
Ţūlkarm Jordan **44** 32.19N 35.02E
Tullahoma U.S.A. **85** 35.21N 86.12W
Tullamore Australia **67** 32.39S147.39E
Tullamore Rep. of Ire. **13** 53.17N 7.31W
Tulle France **17** 45.16N 1.46E
Tullins France **17** 45.18N 5.29E
Tullow Rep. of Ire. **13** 52.49N 6.45W
Tully Australia **64** 17.55S145.59E
Tully U.S.A. **84** 42.47N 76.06W
Tuloma *r.* Russian Fed. **24** 68.56N 33.00E
Tulsa U.S.A. **83** 36.09N 95.58W
Tulsequah Canada **74** 58.39N133.35W
Tuluá Colombia **90** 4.05N 76.12W
Tulumbasy Russian Fed. **24** 57.27N 57.40E
Tulun Russian Fed. **29** 54.32N100.35E
Tulungagung Indonesia **37** 8.03S111.54E
Tulu Welel *mtn.* Ethiopia **49** 8.53N 34.47E
Tum Indonesia **37** 3.28S130.21E
Tumaco Colombia **90** 1.51N 78.46W
Tumba Sweden **23** 59.12N 17.49E
Tumba, L. Zaïre **54** 0.45S 18.00E
Tumbarumba Australia **67** 35.49S148.01E
Tumbes Peru **90** 3.37S 80.27W
Tumbler Ridge Canada **74** 55.20N120.49W
Tumby Bay *town* Australia **66** 34.20S136.05E
Tumd Youqi China **32** 40.33N110.30E
Tumd Zuoqi China **32** 40.42N111.08E
Tumeremo Venezuela **90** 7.18N 61.30W
Tummel, Loch U.K. **12** 56.43N 3.55W
Tump Pakistan **40** 26.07N 62.22E
Tumsar India **41** 21.23N 79.44E
Tumuc Humac Mts. S. America **91** 2.20N 54.50W
Tumut Australia **67** 35.20S148.14E
Tunari *mtn.* Bolivia **92** 17.18S 66.22W
Tūnat al Jabal Egypt **44** 27.46N 30.44E
Tunceli Turkey **42** 39.07N 39.34E
Tuncurry Australia **67** 32.17S152.29E
Tundubai *well* Sudan **48** 18.31N 28.33E
Tunduma Tanzania **55** 9.19S 32.47E
Tunduru Tanzania **55** 11.08S 37.21E
Tundzha *r.* Bulgaria **19** 41.40N 26.34E
Tungabhadra *r.* India **38** 16.00N 78.15E
Tungaru Sudan **49** 10.14N 30.42E
Tungchiang Taiwan **33** 22.28N120.26E
Tungsten Canada **74** 62.00N128.15W
Tungsten U.S.A. **80** 40.48N118.08W
Tunica U.S.A. **83** 34.41N 90.23W
Tunis Tunisia **51** 36.47N 10.10E
Tunisia Africa **51** 34.00N 9.00E
Tunja Colombia **90** 5.33N 73.23W
Tunnsjöen *l.* Norway **22** 64.45N 13.25E
Tunungayualok I. Canada **77** 56.05N 61.05W
Tunuyán *r.* Argentina **93** 33.33S 67.30W
Tunxi *see* Huangshan China **33**
Tuoy-Khaya Russian Fed. **29** 62.33N111.25E
Tupã Brazil **94** 21.57S 50.28W
Tupelo U.S.A. **83** 34.16N 88.43W
Tupinambaranas, Ilha *f.* Brazil **91** 3.00S 58.00W
Tupiza Bolivia **92** 21.27S 65.43W
Tuquan China **32** 45.22N121.41E
Túquerres Colombia **90** 1.06N 77.37W
Tura India **41** 25.31N 90.13E
Tura Russian Fed. **29** 64.05N100.00E
Tura Tanzania **55** 5.30S 33.50E
Turabah Saudi Arabia **48** 21.13N 41.39E
Turangi New Zealand **60** 38.59S175.48E
Turbaco Colombia **90** 10.20N 75.25W
Turbanovo Russian Fed. **24** 60.05N 50.46E
Turbat Pakistan **40** 25.59N 63.04E
Turbo Colombia **90** 8.06N 76.44W
Turda Romania **21** 46.34N 23.47E
Turek Poland **21** 52.02N 18.30E
Turgeon *r.* Canada **76** 50.00N 78.54W
Tŭrgovishte Bulgaria **19** 43.14N 26.37E
Turgutlu Turkey **19** 38.30N 27.43E
Turhal Turkey **42** 40.23N 36.05E
Türi Estonia **23** 58.48N 25.26E
Turia *r.* Spain **16** 39.27N 0.19W
Turiaçu Brazil **91** 1.41S 45.21W
Turiaçu *r.* Brazil **91** 1.36S 45.19W
Turin Canada **74** 49.59N112.35W
Turin *see* Torino Italy **15**
Turka Ukraine **21** 49.10N 23.02E
Turkana, L. Kenya **55** 4.00N 36.00E
Turkestan *f.* Kazakhstan **30** 43.17N 68.16E
Turkey Asia **42** 39.00N 35.00E
Turkey U.S.A. **83** 34.23N100.54W
Turkey Creek *town* Australia **62** 17.04S128.15E
Turkmenistan Asia **28** 40.00N 60.00E
Turks Is. Turks & Caicos Is. **87** 21.30N 71.10W
Turku Finland **23** 60.27N 22.17E
Turku-Pori *d.* Finland **23** 61.00N 22.35E
Turkwel *r.* Kenya **55** 3.08N 35.39E
Turnagain *r.* Canada **74** 59.06N127.35W
Turnberry Canada **75** 53.25N101.45W
Turneffe Is. Belize **87** 17.30N 87.45W
Turner U.S.A. **80** 48.51N108.24W
Turnhout Belgium **14** 51.19N 4.57E
Turnu Măgurele Romania **19** 43.43N 24.53E
Turnu Roşu, Pasul *pass* Romania **19** 45.37N 24.17E
Turnu-Severin Romania **19** 44.37N 22.39E
Turon *r.* Australia **67** 33.03S149.33E
Turon U.S.A. **83** 37.48N 98.26W
Turov Belorussia **21** 52.04N 27.40E
Turpan China **30** 42.55N 89.06E
Turpan Pendi *f.* China **30** 43.40N 89.00E
Turquino *mtn.* Cuba **87** 20.05N 76.50W
Turriff U.K. **12** 57.32N 2.28W
Turtkul Uzbekistan **43** 41.30N 61.00E
Turtle Lake *town* N.Dak. U.S.A. **82** 47.31N100.53W
Turtle Lake *town* Wisc. U.S.A. **82** 45.23N 92.09W
Turtle Mtn. Canada / U.S.A. **75** 49.05N 99.45W
Turukhansk Russian Fed. **29** 65.21N 88.05E
Turya *r.* Ukraine **21** 51.48N 24.52E
Tuscaloosa U.S.A. **85** 33.12N 87.33W
Tuscarora U.S.A. **80** 41.19N116.14W
Tuscola Ill. U.S.A. **82** 39.48N 88.17W
Tuscola Tex. U.S.A. **83** 32.12N 99.48W
Tuticorin India **39** 8.48N 78.10E
Tutóia Brazil **91** 2.45S 42.16W
Tutrakan Bulgaria **19** 44.02N 26.40E
Tuttle U.S.A. **82** 47.09N100.00W
Tuttlingen Germany **20** 47.59N 8.49E
Tutuala Indonesia **37** 8.24S127.15E
Tutubu Tanzania **55** 5.28S 32.43E
Tutuila *i.* Samoa **68** 14.18S170.42W
Ţuţūn Egypt **44** 29.09N 30.46E
Tuul Gol *r.* Mongolia **30** 48.53N104.35E
Tuvalu Pacific Oc. **68** 8.00S178.00E
Tuwayq, Jabal *mts.* Saudi Arabia **45** 23.30N 46.20E
Tuxpan Mexico **86** 21.00N 97.23W
Tuxtla Gutiérrez Mexico **86** 16.45N 93.09W
Túy Spain **16** 42.03N 8.39W
Tuyen Quang Vietnam **33** 21.48N105.21E
Tuz Gölü *l.* Turkey **42** 38.45N 33.24E
Ţūz Khurmātū Iraq **43** 34.53N 44.38E
Tuzla Bosnia-Herzegovina **19** 44.33N 18.41E
Tvaerå Faroe Is. **8** 61.34N 6.48W
Tvedestrand Norway **23** 58.37N 8.55E
Tveitsund Norway **23** 59.01N 8.32E
Tver' Russian Fed. **24** 56.47N 35.57E
Tweed *r.* U.K. **12** 55.46N 2.00W
Tweed Heads *town* Australia **67** 28.13S153.33E
Tweedsmuir Prov. Park Canada **74** 52.55N126.20W
Twentynine Palms U.S.A. **81** 34.08N116.03W
Twin Bridges *town* U.S.A. **80** 45.33N112.20W
Twin Falls *town* U.S.A. **80** 42.34N114.28W
Twins Creek *r.* Australia **66** 29.10S139.27E
Twin Valley *town* U.S.A. **82** 47.16N 96.16W
Twizel New Zealand **60** 44.15S170.06E
Twofold B. Australia **67** 37.06S149.55E
Two Harbors *town* U.S.A. **82** 47.02N 91.40W
Twyford U.K. **11** 51.01N 1.19W
Tyler Minn. U.S.A. **82** 44.17N 96.08W
Tyler Tex. U.S.A. **83** 32.21N 95.18W
Tyndinskiy Russian Fed. **29** 55.11N124.34E
Tyne *r.* U.K. **10** 55.00N 1.25W
Tyne and Wear *d.* U.K. **10** 54.57N 1.35W
Tynemouth U.K. **10** 55.01N 1.24W
Tynset Norway **23** 62.17N 10.47E
Tyre *see* Şūr Lebanon **44**
Tyrifjorden *l.* Norway **23** 60.02N 10.08E
Tyron U.S.A. **85** 35.13N 82.14W
Tyrone *d.* U.K. **13** 54.35N 7.15W
Tyrone U.S.A. **84** 40.40N 78.14W
Tyrrel Canada **75** 54.35N 99.10W
Tyrrell *r.* Australia **66** 35.28S142.55E
Tyrrell, L. Australia **66** 35.22S142.50E
Tyrrhenian Sea Med. Sea **18** 40.00N 12.00E
Tysnesöy *i.* Norway **23** 60.00N 5.35E
Tyumen Russian Fed. **28** 57.11N 65.29E
Tywi *r.* U.K. **11** 51.46N 4.22W
Tzaneen R.S.A. **56** 23.49S 30.10E

U

Ua Huka *i.* Is. Marquises **69** 8.55S139.32W
Ua Pu *i.* Is. Marquises **69** 9.25S140.00W
Uatumã *r.* Brazil **91** 2.30S 57.40W
Uaupés Brazil **90** 0.07S 67.05W
Uaupés *r.* Brazil **90** 0.00S 67.10W
Ubá Brazil **94** 21.08S 42.59W
Ubangi *r.* Congo / Zaïre **54** 0.25S 17.40E
Ubatuba Brazil **94** 23.26S 45.05W
Ubauro Pakistan **40** 28.10N 69.44E
Ubayyiḑ, Wādī al *r.* Iraq **42** 32.04N 42.17E
Ubeda Spain **16** 38.01N 3.22W
Uberaba Brazil **94** 19.47S 47.57W
Uberlândia Brazil **94** 18.57S 48.17W
Ubombo R.S.A. **57** 27.35S 32.05E
Ubort *r.* Belorussia **21** 52.06N 28.28E
Ubundu Zaïre **54** 0.24S 25.28E
Ucayali *r.* Peru **90** 4.40S 73.20W
Uch Pakistan **40** 29.14N 71.03E
Udaipur India **40** 24.35N 73.41E
Udalguri India **41** 26.46N 92.08E
Udaquiola Argentina **93** 36.35S 58.30W
Udaypur Nepal **41** 26.54N 86.32E
Uddevalla Sweden **23** 58.21N 11.55E
Uddjaur *l.* Sweden **22** 65.55N 17.49E
Udhampur Jammu & Kashmir **40** 32.56N 75.08E
Udine Italy **15** 46.03N 13.15E
Udipi India **38** 13.21N 74.45E
Udon Thani Thailand **34** 17.25N102.45E
Uele *r.* Zaïre **49** 4.09N 22.26E
Uelzen Germany **20** 52.58N 10.34E
Ueno Japan **35** 34.45N136.08E
Uere *r.* Zaïre **49** 3.42N 25.24E
Ufa Russian Fed. **24** 54.45N 55.58E
Ufa *r.* Russian Fed. **24** 54.45N 56.00E
Uffculme U.K. **11** 50.45N 3.19W
Ugab *r.* Namibia **56** 21.12S 13.37E
Ugalla *r.* Tanzania **55** 5.43S 31.10E
Uganda Africa **55** 2.00N 33.00E
Ugep Nigeria **53** 5.48N 8.05E
Ughelli Nigeria **53** 5.33N 6.00E
Uglegorsk Russian Fed. **29** 49.01N142.04E
Uglovka Russian Fed. **24** 58.13N 33.30E
Ugoma *mtn.* Zaïre **55** 4.00S 28.45E
Ugra *r.* Russian Fed. **24** 54.30N 36.10E
Uherske Hradiště Czech Republic **21** 49.05N 17.28E
Uig U.K. **12** 57.35N 6.22W
Uíge Angola **54** 7.40S 15.09E
Uíge *d.* Angola **54** 7.00S 15.30E
Uil Kazakhstan **25** 49.08N 54.43E
Uil *r.* Kazakhstan **25** 48.33N 52.25E
Uinta Mts. U.S.A. **80** 40.45N110.05W
Uitenhage R.S.A. **56** 33.46S 25.23E
Uithuizen Neth. **14** 53.24N 6.41E
Uivlleq *see* Nanortalik Greenland **73**
Ujhāni India **41** 28.01N 79.01E
Uji *r.* Japan **35** 34.53N135.48E
Ujiji Tanzania **55** 4.55S 29.39E
Ujjain India **40** 23.11N 75.46E
Ujpest Hungary **21** 47.33N 19.05E
Ujście Poland **20** 53.04N 16.43E
Ujung Pandang Indonesia **36** 5.09S119.28E
Uka Russian Fed. **29** 57.50N162.02E
Ukerewe I. Tanzania **55** 2.00S 33.00E
Ukhta Russian Fed. **24** 63.33N 53.44E
Ukiah U.S.A. **80** 39.09N123.13W
Ukmerge Lithuania **24** 55.14N 24.49E
Ukraine Europe **21** 49.45N 27.00E
Uku Angola **54** 11.24S 14.15E
Ukwi Botswana **56** 23.22S 20.30E
Ulaanbaatar Mongolia **30** 47.54N106.52E
Ulaangom Mongolia **30** 49.59N 92.00E
Ulamba Zaïre **54** 9.07S 23.40E
Ulan Bator *see* Ulaanbaatar Mongolia **30**
Ulansuhai Nur *l.* China **32** 40.56N108.49E
Ulan-Ude Russian Fed. **30** 51.55N107.40E
Ulan Ul Hu *l.* China **39** 34.45N 90.25E
Ulcinj Yugo. **19** 41.55N 19.11E
Ulenia, L. Australia **66** 29.57S142.24E
Ulhāsnagar India **40** 19.13N 73.07E
Uliastay Mongolia **30** 47.42N 96.52E
Ulindi *r.* Zaïre **54** 1.38S 25.55E
Ulla *r.* Spain **16** 42.38N 8.45W
Ulladulla Australia **67** 35.21S150.25E
Ullånger Sweden **22** 62.58N 18.16E
Ullapool U.K. **12** 57.54N 5.10W
Ullswater *l.* U.K. **10** 54.34N 2.52W
Ulm Germany **20** 48.24N 10.00E
Ulongwé Mozambique **55** 14.34S 34.21E
Ulricehamn Sweden **23** 57.47N 13.25E
Ulsan S. Korea **31** 35.32N129.21E
Ulsan S. Korea **35** 35.34N129.19E
Ulsberg Norway **22** 62.45N 9.59E
Ultima Australia **66** 35.30S143.20E
Ulu Sudan **49** 10.43N 33.29E
Ulúa *r.* Honduras **87** 15.50N 87.38W
Uluguru Mts. Tanzania **55** 7.05S 37.40E
Uluru *mtn.* Australia **64** 25.20S131.01E
Ulverston U.K. **10** 54.13N 3.07W
Ulverstone Australia **65** 41.09S146.10E
Ul'yanovsk Russian Fed. **24** 54.19N 48.22E
Ulysses U.S.A. **83** 37.35N101.22W
Umaisha Nigeria **53** 8.01N 7.12E
Umala Bolivia **92** 17.21S 68.00W
Uman Ukraine **21** 48.45N 30.10E
Umaria India **41** 23.32N 80.50E
Umarkot Pakistan **40** 25.22N 69.44E
Umbria *d.* Italy **18** 42.55N 12.10E
Ume *r.* Sweden **22** 63.47N 20.16E
Ume *r.* Zimbabwe **56** 17.00S 28.22E
Umeå Sweden **22** 63.45N 20.20E
Umfors Sweden **22** 65.56N 15.00E
Umfuli *r.* Zimbabwe **56** 17.32S 29.23E
Umiat U.S.A. **72** 69.25N152.20W
Umm-al-Qaywayn U.A.E. **43** 25.32N 55.34E
Umm Badr Sudan **48** 14.14N 27.57E
Umm Bel Sudan **49** 13.32N 28.04E
Umm Durmān Sudan **48** 15.37N 32.59E
Umm el Fahm Israel **44** 32.31N 35.09E
Umm Kuwaykah Sudan **49** 12.49N 31.52E
Umm Lajj Saudi Arabia **42** 25.03N 37.17E
Umm Qurayn Sudan **49** 9.58N 28.55E
Umm Ruwābah Sudan **49** 12.54N 31.13E
Umm Shalīl Sudan **49** 10.51N 23.42E
Umm Shanqah Sudan **49** 13.14N 27.14E
Umniati Zimbabwe **56** 18.41S 29.45E
Umrer India **41** 20.51N 79.20E
Umreth India **40** 22.42N 73.07E
Umtata R.S.A. **56** 31.35S 28.47E
Umuahia Nigeria **53** 5.31N 7.26E
Umzimkulu R.S.A. **56** 30.15S 29.56E
Umzimvubu R.S.A. **56** 31.37S 29.32E
Una *r.* Bosnia-Herzegovina **19** 45.16N 16.55E
Una India **40** 20.49N 71.02E

Victoria to **Warrumbungle Range**

Victoria *d.* Australia **67** 37.20S145.00E
Victoria *r.* Australia **62** 15.12S129.43E
Victoria Canada **74** 48.30N123.25W
Victoria Chile **93** 38.13S 72.20W
Victoria Guinea **52** 10.50N 14.32W
Victoria U.S.A. **83** 28.48N 97.00W
Victoria, L. Africa **55** 1.00S 33.00E
Victoria, L. Australia **66** 34.00S141.15E
Victoria, Mt. Burma **34** 21.12N 93.55E
Victoria, Mt. P.N.G. **64** 8.55S147.35E
Victoria Beach *town* Canada **75** 50.43N 96.33W
Victoria de las Tunas Cuba **87** 20.58N 76.59W
Victoria Falls *f.* Zimbabwe / Zambia **56** 17.58S 25.45E
Victoria I. Canada **72** 71.00N110.00W
Victoria L. Australia **66** 32.29S143.22E
Victoria Nile *r.* Uganda **55** 2.14N 31.20E
Victoria River *town* Australia **62** 15.36S131.06E
Victoria River Downs *town* Australia **64** 16.24S131.00E
Victoriaville Canada **77** 46.03N 71.58W
Victoria West R.S.A. **56** 31.24S 23.07E
Victorica Argentina **93** 36.15S 65.25W
Vidalia U.S.A. **85** 32.14N 82.24W
Videle Romania **21** 44.16N 25.31E
Viderö *i.* Faroe Is. **8** 62.21N 6.30W
Vidin Bulgaria **21** 43.58N 22.51E
Vidisha India **41** 23.32N 77.49E
Viedma Argentina **93** 40.50S 63.00W
Viedma, L. Argentina **93** 49.40S 72.30W
Vienna *see* Wien Austria **20**
Vienna Md. U.S.A. **85** 38.29N 75.49W
Vienna S.Dak. U.S.A. **82** 44.42N 97.30W
Vienna Va. U.S.A. **85** 38.54N 77.16W
Vienne France **17** 45.32N 4.54E
Vienne *r.* France **17** 47.13N 0.05W
Vientiane Laos **34** 17.59N102.38E
Vieques *i.* Puerto Rico **87** 18.08N 65.30W
Viersen Germany **14** 51.16N 6.22E
Vierwaldstätter See *l.* Switz. **20** 47.10N 8.50E
Vierzon France **15** 47.14N 2.03E
Vietnam Asia **34** 15.00N108.30E
Viet Tri Vietnam **33** 21.20N105.26E
Vieux-Condé France **14** 50.29N 3.31E
Vigan Phil. **37** 17.35N120.23E
Vigevano Italy **15** 45.19N 8.51E
Vignemale, Pic de *mtn.* France **17** 42.46N 0.08W
Vigo Spain **16** 42.15N 8.44W
Vigrestad Norway **23** 58.34N 5.42E
Vihāri Pakistan **40** 30.02N 72.21E
Vihowa Pakistan **40** 31.08N 70.30E
Vijāpur India **40** 23.35N 72.45E
Vijayawāda India **39** 16.34N 80.40E
Vik Norway **22** 65.19N 12.10E
Vikajärvi Finland **22** 66.37N 26.12E
Vikeke Indonesia **37** 8.42S126.30E
Vikersund Norway **23** 59.59N 10.02E
Vikna *i.* Norway **22** 64.52N 10.57E
Vikulovo Russian Fed. **20** 56.51N 70.30E
Vila Vanuatu **68** 17.44S168.19E
Vila da Maganja Mozambique **55** 17.25S 37.32E
Vila Franca Portugal **16** 38.57N 8.59W
Vilaine *r.* France **17** 47.30N 2.25W
Vilanculos Mozambique **57** 21.59S 35.16E
Vilanova i la Geltrú *see* Villanueva y Geltrú Spain Spain **16**
Vila Real Portugal **16** 41.17N 7.45W
Vila Real de Santo António Portugal **16** 37.12N 7.25W
Vila Velha Brazil **94** 20.20S 40.17W
Vila Verissimo Sarmento Angola **54** 8.08S 20.38E
Vileyka Belorussia **21** 54.30N 26.50E
Vilhelmina Sweden **22** 64.37N 16.39E
Vilhena Brazil **90** 12.40S 60.08W
Viliga Kushka Russian Fed. **29** 61.35N156.55E
Viljandi Estonia **24** 58.22N 25.30E
Vilkaviškis Lithuania **21** 54.39N 23.02E
Vil'kitskogo, Proliv *str.* Russian Fed. **29** 77.57N102.30E
Vilkovo Ukraine **21** 45.28N 29.32E
Villa Angela Argentina **92** 27.34S 60.45W
Villa Bella Bolivia **92** 10.23S 65.24W
Villablino Spain **16** 42.57N 6.19W
Villacañas Spain **16** 39.38N 3.20W
Villach Austria **20** 46.37N 13.51E
Villa Clara Argentina **93** 31.46S 58.50W
Villa Constitución Argentina **93** 33.14S 60.21W
Villa de Santiago Mexico **83** 25.26N100.09W
Villa Dolores Argentina **92** 31.58S 65.12W
Villafranca di Verona Italy **15** 45.21N 10.50E
Villagarcía Spain **16** 42.35N 8.45W
Villaguay Argentina **93** 31.55S 59.00W
Villahermosa Mexico **86** 18.00N 92.53W
Villa Hernandarias Argentina **93** 31.15S 59.58W
Villa Huidobro Argentina **93** 34.50S 64.34W
Villaines-la-Juhel France **15** 48.21N 0.17W
Villajoyosa Spain **16** 38.31N 0.14W
Villalba Spain **16** 43.18N 7.41W
Villa María Argentina **92** 32.25S 63.15W
Villa Montes Bolivia **92** 21.15S 63.30W
Villanueva y Geltrú Spain **16** 41.13N 1.43E
Villanueva de la Serena Spain **16** 38.58N 5.48W
Villaputzu Italy **18** 39.28N 9.35E
Villarrica Chile **93** 39.15S 72.15W
Villarrica Paraguay **94** 25.45S 56.28W
Villarrobledo Spain **16** 39.16N 2.36W
Villa San José Argentina **93** 32.12S 58.15W
Villasayas Spain **16** 41.24N 2.39W
Villavicencio Colombia **90** 4.09N 73.38W
Villaviciosa Spain **16** 43.29N 5.26W
Villazón Bolivia **92** 22.06S 65.36W
Villedieu France **15** 48.50N 1.13W
Villefranche France **17** 46.00N 4.43E
Villena Spain **16** 38.39N 0.52W
Villenauxe-la-Grande France **15** 48.35N 3.33E
Villeneuve France **17** 44.25N 0.43E
Villeneuve d'Ascq France **14** 50.37N 3.10E
Villeneuve-St. Georges France **15** 48.44N 2.27E
Villeneuve-sur-Yonne France **15** 48.05N 3.18E
Villers-Bocage France **15** 49.05N 0.39W
Villers-Cotterêts France **15** 49.15N 3.04E
Villers-sur-Mer France **15** 49.21N 0.02W
Villeurbanne France **20** 45.46N 4.54E
Vilnius Lithuania **21** 54.40N 25.19E
Vilvoorde Belgium **14** 50.56N 4.25E
Vilyuy *r.* Russian Fed. **29** 64.20N126.55E
Vilyuysk Russian Fed. **29** 63.46N121.35E
Vimianzo Spain **16** 43.07N 9.02W
Vimmerby Sweden **23** 57.40N 15.51E
Vimoutiers France **15** 48.55N 0.12E
Vina *r.* Chad **53** 7.43N 15.30E
Viña del Mar Chile **93** 33.02S 71.34W
Vinaroz Spain **16** 40.30N 0.27E
Vincennes France **15** 48.51N 2.26E
Vincennes U.S.A. **82** 38.41N 87.32W
Vindel *r.* Sweden **22** 63.54N 19.52E
Vindeln Sweden **22** 64.12N 19.44E
Vinderup Denmark **23** 56.29N 8.47E
Vindhya Range *mts.* India **40** 22.45N 75.30E
Vineland U.S.A. **85** 39.29N 75.02W
Vingåker Sweden **23** 59.02N 15.52E
Vinh Vietnam **34** 18.42N105.41E
Vinh Long Vietnam **34** 10.15N105.59E
Vinita U.S.A. **83** 36.39N 95.09W
Vînju Mare Romania **21** 44.26N 22.52E
Vinkovci Croatia **19** 45.17N 18.38E
Vinnitsa Ukraine **21** 49.11N 28.30E
Vinson Massif Antarctica **96** 78.00S 85.00W
Vintar Phil. **33** 18.16N120.40E
Vinton U.S.A. **82** 42.10N 92.01W
Vioolsdrif R.S.A. **56** 28.45S 17.33E
Vipava Slovenia **20** 45.51N 13.58E
Virac Phil. **37** 13.35N124.15E
Viramgām India **40** 23.07N 72.02E
Viranşehir Turkey **42** 37.13N 39.45E
Virden Canada **75** 49.51N100.55W
Vire France **17** 48.50N 0.53W
Vire *r.* France **15** 49.20N 0.53W
Vírgenes, C. Argentina **93** 52.00S 68.50W
Virgin Gorda *i.* B.V.Is. **87** 18.30N 64.26W
Virginia U.S.A. **82** 47.31N 92.32W
Virginia *d.* U.S.A. **85** 37.30N 78.45W
Virginia Beach *town* U.S.A. **85** 36.51N 75.59W
Virginia City Mont. U.S.A. **80** 45.18N111.56W
Virginia City Nev. U.S.A. **80** 39.19N119.39W
Virovitica Croatia **21** 45.51N 17.23E
Virrat Finland **22** 62.14N 23.47E
Virserum Sweden **23** 57.19N 15.35E
Virton Belgium **14** 49.35N 5.32E
Virtsu Estonia **23** 58.34N 23.31E
Virunga Nat. Park Zaïre **55** 0.30S 29.15E
Vis Croatia **18** 43.03N 16.21E
Vis *i.* Croatia **18** 43.03N 16.10E
Visalia U.S.A. **81** 36.20N119.18W
Visayan Sea Phil. **37** 11.35N123.51E
Visby Sweden **23** 57.38N 18.18E
Visconde do Rio Branco Brazil **94** 21.00S 42.51W
Viscount Melville Sd. Canada **72** 74.30N104.00W
Visé Belgium **14** 50.44N 5.42E
Višegrad Bosnia-Herzegovina **19** 43.47N 19.20E
Viseu Brazil **91** 1.12S 46.07W
Viseu Portugal **16** 40.40N 7.55W
Viseu de Sus Romania **21** 47.44N 24.22E
Vishākhapatnam India **39** 17.42N 83.24E
Visnagar India **40** 23.42N 72.33E
Viso, Monte *mtn.* Italy **15** 44.38N 7.05E
Visp Switz. **15** 46.18N 7.53E
Vista U.S.A. **81** 33.12N117.15W
Vistula *r.* *see* Wisła *r.* Poland **21**
Vitarte Peru **90** 12.03S 76.51W
Vitebsk Belorussia **24** 55.10N 30.14E
Viterbo Italy **18** 42.26N 12.07E
Viti Levu *i.* Fiji **68** 18.00S178.00E
Vitim Russian Fed. **29** 59.28N112.35E
Vitim *r.* Russian Fed. **29** 59.30N112.36E
Vitoria Spain **16** 42.51N 2.40W
Vitória da Conquista Brazil **91** 14.53S 40.52W
Vitória Espírito Santo Brazil **94** 20.19S 40.21W
Vitré France **15** 48.07N 1.12W
Vitry-le-François France **15** 48.44N 4.35E
Vitteaux France **15** 47.24N 4.30E
Vittoria Italy **18** 36.57N 14.21E
Vittorio Veneto Italy **15** 45.59N 12.18E
Viveiro *see* Vivero Spain **16**
Vivero Spain **16** 43.38N 7.35W
Vivonne Bay *town* Australia **66** 35.58S137.10E
Vizcaíno, Desierto de *des.* Mexico **81** 27.40N114.40W
Vizcaíno, Sierra *mts.* Mexico **81** 27.20N114.30W
Vizianagaram India **39** 18.07N 83.30E
Vizinga Russian Fed. **24** 61.06N 50.05E
Vjosë *r.* Albania **19** 40.39N 19.20E
Vlaardingen Neth. **14** 51.55N 4.20E
Vladikavkaz Russian Fed. **25** 43.02N 44.43E
Vladimir Russian Fed. **24** 56.08N 40.25E
Vladimirets Ukraine **21** 51.28N 26.03E
Vladimir Volynskiy Ukraine **21** 50.51N 24.19E
Vladivostok Russian Fed. **31** 43.09N131.53E
Vlasenica Bosnia-Herzegovina **21** 44.11N 18.56E
Vlieland *i.* Neth. **14** 53.15N 5.00E
Vlissingen Neth. **14** 51.27N 3.35E
Vlorë Albania **19** 40.28N 19.27E
Vltava *r.* Czech Republic **20** 50.22N 14.28E
Voerde Germany **14** 51.37N 6.39E
Vogelkop *f.* *see* Jazirah Doberai *f.* Indonesia **37**
Voghera Italy **15** 44.59N 9.01E
Voh N. Cal. **68** 20.58S164.42E
Vohibinany Madagascar **57** 18.49S 49.04E
Vohimarina Madagascar **57** 13.21S 50.02E
Vohipeno Madagascar **57** 22.22S 47.51E
Voi Kenya **55** 3.23S 38.35E
Voiron France **17** 45.22N 5.35E
Volborg U.S.A. **80** 45.50N105.40W
Volcano Is. Japan **68** 25.00N141.00E
Volda Norway **23** 62.09N 6.06E
Volga *r.* Russian Fed. **25** 45.45N 47.50E
Volgograd Russian Fed. **25** 48.45N 44.30E
Volgogradskoye Vodokhranilishche *resr.* Russian Fed. **25** 51.00N 46.05E
Volkhov Russian Fed. **24** 59.54N 32.47E
Volkhov *r.* Russian Fed. **24** 60.15N 32.15E
Völklingen Germany **20** 49.15N 6.50E
Volkovysk Belorussia **21** 53.10N 24.28E
Vollenhove Neth. **14** 52.41N 5.59E
Volnovakha Ukraine **25** 47.36N 37.32E
Volochanka Russian Fed. **29** 70.59N 94.18E
Volochisk Ukraine **21** 49.34N 26.10E
Volodarsk Russian Fed. **24** 56.14N 43.10E
Vologda Russian Fed. **24** 59.10N 39.55E
Volokolamsk Russian Fed. **24** 56.02N 35.56E
Vólos Greece **19** 39.22N 22.57E
Volovets Ukraine **21** 48.44N 23.14E
Volsk Russian Fed. **24** 52.04N 47.22E
Volta *d.* Ghana **52** 7.30N 0.25E
Volta *r.* Ghana **52** 5.50N 0.41E
Volta-Noire *d.* Burkina **52** 12.30N 3.25W
Volta Noire *d.* Ghana **52** 12.30N 3.25W
Volta Redonda Brazil **94** 22.31S 44.05W
Volterra Italy **18** 43.24N 10.51E
Voltri Italy **15** 44.26N 8.45E
Volturno *r.* Italy **18** 41.02N 13.56E
Volzhskiy Russian Fed. **25** 48.48N 44.45E
Vondrozo Madagascar **57** 22.49S 47.20E
Voorburg Neth. **14** 52.05N 4.22E
Vopnafjördhur *est.* Iceland **22** 65.50N 14.30W
Vopnafjördhur *town* Iceland **22** 65.46N 14.50W
Vorarlberg *d.* Austria **20** 47.15N 9.55E
Vordingborg Denmark **23** 55.01N 11.55E
Voríai Sporádhes *is.* Greece **19** 39.00N 24.00E
Vorkuta Russian Fed. **24** 67.27N 64.00E
Vormsi *i.* Estonia **23** 59.00N 23.20E
Voronezh Russian Fed. **25** 51.40N 39.13E
Voronovo Belorussia **21** 54.09N 25.19E
Vosges *mts.* France **20** 48.10N 7.00E
Voss Norway **23** 60.39N 6.26E
Vostochno Sibirskoye More *sea* Russian Fed. **29** 73.00N160.00E
Vostochnyy Sayan *mts.* Russian Fed. **30** 51.30N102.00E
Vostok I. Kiribati **69** 10.05S152.23W
Votkinsk Russian Fed. **24** 57.02N 53.59E
Votkinskoye Vodokhranilishche *resr.* Russian Fed. **24** 57.00N 55.00E
Votuporanga Brazil **92** 20.26S 49.53W
Vouga *r.* Portugal **16** 40.41N 8.38W
Vouillé France **17** 46.38N 0.10E
Voulou C.A.R. **49** 8.33N 22.36E
Vouziers France **15** 49.24N 4.42E
Voves France **15** 48.16N 1.37E
Voxna Sweden **23** 61.20N 15.30E
Voxna *r.* Sweden **23** 61.17N 16.26E
Voyvozh Russian Fed. **24** 64.19N 55.12E
Vozhega Russian Fed. **24** 60.25N 40.11E
Voznesensk Ukraine **25** 47.34N 31.21E
Vrangelya, Ostrov *i.* Russian Fed. **29** 71.00N180.00
Vranje Yugo. **19** 42.34N 21.52E
Vratsa Bulgaria **19** 43.12N 23.33E
Vrbas *r.* Bosnia-Herzegovina **19** 45.06N 17.29E
Vrede R.S.A. **56** 27.24S 29.09E
Vredendal R.S.A. **56** 31.40S 18.28E
Vresse Belgium **14** 49.53N 4.57E
Vries Neth. **14** 53.06N 6.35E
Vrindāvan India **41** 27.35N 77.42E
Vrnograč Bosnia-Herzegovina **18** 45.10N 15.56E
Vršac Yugo. **21** 45.08N 21.18E
Vryburg R.S.A. **56** 26.57S 24.42E
Vught Neth. **14** 51.39N 5.18E
Vukovar Croatia **21** 45.21N 19.00E
Vung Tau Vietnam **34** 10.21N107.04E
Vyāra India **40** 21.07N 73.24E
Vyatka *r.* Russian Fed. **28** 55.40N 51.40E
Vyatskiye Polyany Russian Fed. **24** 56.14N 51.08E
Vyazma Russian Fed. **24** 55.12N 34.17E
Vyazniki Russian Fed. **24** 56.14N 42.08E
Vyborg Russian Fed. **24** 60.45N 28.41E
Vychegda *r.* Russian Fed. **24** 61.15N 46.28E
Vychodné Beskydy *mts.* Europe **21** 49.30N 22.00E
Vygozero, Ozero *l.* Russian Fed. **24** 63.30N 34.30E
Vyrnwy, L. U.K. **10** 52.46N 3.30W
Vyshka Turkmenistan **43** 39.19N 54.10E
Vyshniy-Volochek Russian Fed. **24** 57.34N 34.23E
Vytegra Russian Fed. **24** 61.04N 36.27E

W

Wa Ghana **52** 10.07N 2.28W
Waal *r.* Neth. **14** 51.45N 4.40E
Waalwijk Neth. **14** 51.42N 5.04E
Wabag P.N.G. **37** 5.28S143.40E
Wabasca *r.* Canada **74** 58.22N115.20W
Wabash U.S.A. **82** 40.47N 85.48W
Wabash *r.* U.S.A. **82** 37.46N 88.02W
Wabē Mena *r.* Ethiopia **49** 6.20N 40.41E
Wabeno U.S.A. **82** 45.27N 88.38W
Wabera Ethiopia **49** 6.25N 40.45E
Wabē Shebelē *r.* Ethiopia *see* Shabeelle *r.* Somali Rep. **45**
Wąbrzeźno Poland **21** 53.17N 18.57E
Wabush City Canada **77** 52.53N 66.50W
Waco U.S.A. **83** 31.55N 97.08W
Wacouno *r.* Canada **77** 50.50N 65.58W
Wad Pakistan **40** 27.21N 66.22E
Wad Bandah Sudan **49** 13.06N 27.57E
Waddān Libya **51** 29.10N 16.08E
Waddeneilanden *is.* Neth. **14** 53.20N 5.00E
Waddenzee *b.* Neth. **14** 53.15N 5.05E
Waddikee Australia **66** 33.18S136.12E
Waddington, Mt. Canada **74** 51.23N125.15W
Wadena U.S.A. **82** 46.26N 95.08W
Wad Ḥāmid Sudan **48** 16.30N 32.48E
Wadhurst U.K. **11** 51.03N 0.21E
Wādī Ḥalfā' Sudan **48** 21.56N 31.20E
Wādī Mūsá *town* Jordan **44** 30.19N 35.29E
Wad Madanī Sudan **48** 14.24N 33.32E
Wad Nimr Sudan **48** 14.32N 32.08E
Wafrah Kuwait **43** 28.39N 47.56E
Wageningen Neth. **14** 51.58N 5.39E
Wager B. Canada **73** 65.26N 88.40W
Wager Bay *town* Canada **73** 65.55N 90.40W
Wagga Wagga Australia **67** 35.07S147.24E
Wagin Australia **63** 33.18S117.21E
Wagon Mound *town* U.S.A. **81** 36.01N104.42W
Wāh Pakistan **40** 33.48N 72.42E
Wahai Indonesia **37** 2.48S129.30E
Wāḥāt Salīmah Sudan **48** 21.22N 29.19E
Wahiawa Hawaiian Is. **69** 21.30N158.01W
Wahiba Sands *des.* Oman **38** 21.56N 58.55E
Wahpeton U.S.A. **82** 46.16N 96.36W
Waiau New Zealand **60** 42.39S173.03E
Waidhān India **41** 24.04N 82.20E
Waidhofen Austria **20** 47.58N 14.47E
Waigeo *i.* Indonesia **37** 0.05S130.30E
Waihi New Zealand **60** 37.24S175.50E
Waikato *d.* New Zealand **60** 38.15S175.10E
Waikato *r.* New Zealand **60** 37.19S174.50E
Waikerie Australia **66** 34.11S139.59E
Waikokopu New Zealand **60** 39.05S177.50E
Waikouaiti New Zealand **60** 45.36S170.41E
Wailuku Hawaiian Is. **69** 20.53N156.30W
Waimakariri *r.* New Zealand **60** 43.23S172.40E
Waimate New Zealand **60** 44.45S171.03E
Waimea Hawaiian Is. **69** 20.01N155.41W
Wainganga *r.* India **41** 18.50N 79.55E
Waingapu Indonesia **37** 9.30S120.10E
Wainwright Canada **75** 52.49N110.52W
Wainwright U.S.A. **72** 70.39N160.00W
Waiouru New Zealand **60** 39.39S175.40E
Waipara New Zealand **60** 43.03S172.45E
Waipawa New Zealand **60** 39.56S176.35E
Waipiro New Zealand **60** 38.02S178.21E
Waipu New Zealand **60** 35.59S174.26E
Waipukurau New Zealand **60** 40.00S176.33E
Wairau *r.* New Zealand **60** 41.32S174.08E
Wairoa New Zealand **60** 39.03S177.25E
Waitaki *r.* New Zealand **60** 44.56S171.10E
Waitara New Zealand **60** 38.59S174.13E
Waiuku New Zealand **60** 37.15S174.44E
Wajir Kenya **55** 1.46N 40.05E
Waka Ethiopia **49** 7.07N 37.26E
Waka Zaïre **54** 0.48S 20.10E
Wakatipu, L. New Zealand **60** 45.10S168.30E
Wakayama Japan **35** 34.13N135.11E
Wakefield Canada **77** 45.38N 75.56W
Wakefield U.K. **10** 53.41N 1.31W
Wake I. Pacific Oc. **68** 19.17N166.36E
Wakema Burma **34** 16.36N 95.11E
Wakkanai Japan **35** 45.26N141.43E
Wakre Indonesia **37** 0.30S131.05E
Wakuach, L. Canada **77** 55.37N 67.40W
Walamba Zambia **55** 13.27S 28.44E
Wałbrzych Poland **20** 50.48N 16.19E
Walcha Australia **67** 31.00S151.36E
Walcheren *f.* Neth. **14** 51.32N 3.35E
Wałcz Poland **20** 53.17N 16.28E
Waldbröl Germany **14** 50.52N 7.34E
Waldeck Germany **20** 51.12N 9.04E
Walden U.S.A. **80** 40.34N106.11W
Waldorf U.S.A. **85** 38.37N 76.54W
Waldport U.S.A. **80** 44.26N124.04W
Waldron U.S.A. **83** 34.54N 94.05W
Wales *d.* U.K. **11** 52.30N 3.45W
Wales U.S.A. **82** 47.13N 91.41W
Walgett Australia **67** 30.03S148.10E
Walikale Zaïre **55** 1.29S 28.05E
Walker U.S.A. **82** 47.06N 94.35W
Walker L. U.S.A. **80** 38.44N118.43W
Wall U.S.A. **80** 43.59N102.14W
Wallace Idaho U.S.A. **80** 47.28N115.55W
Wallace Nebr. U.S.A. **82** 40.50N101.10W
Wallaceburg Canada **76** 42.36N 82.23W
Wallachia *f.* Romania **21** 44.35N 25.00E
Wallambin, L. Australia **63** 30.58S117.30E
Wallangarra Australia **67** 28.51S151.52E
Wallaroo Australia **66** 33.57S137.36E
Walla Walla Australia **67** 35.48S146.52E
Walla Walla U.S.A. **80** 46.08N118.20W
Wallis, Îles *is.* Pacific Oc. **68** 13.16S176.15W
Wallkill *r.* U.S.A. **85** 41.51N 74.03W
Wallowa U.S.A. **80** 45.34N117.32W
Wallowa Mts. U.S.A. **80** 45.10N117.30W
Wallsend Australia **67** 32.55S151.40E
Walmsley L. Canada **75** 63.25N108.36W
Walpole Australia **63** 34.57S116.44E
Walsall U.K. **11** 52.36N 1.59W
Walsenburg U.S.A. **80** 37.37N104.47W
Walterboro U.S.A. **85** 32.54N 80.21W
Walton on the Naze U.K. **11** 51.52N 1.17E
Walton on the Wolds U.K. **10** 52.49N 0.49W
Walvis B. R.S.A. **56** 22.55S 14.30E
Walvisbaai R.S.A. **56** 22.57S 14.30E
Walvis Bay *town see* Walvisbaai R.S.A. **56**
Walvis Bay *d.* R.S.A. **56** 22.56S 14.35E
Walvis Ridge *f.* Atlantic Oc. **95** 28.00S 4.00E
Wamanfo Ghana **52** 7.16N 2.44W
Wamba Kenya **55** 0.58N 37.19E
Wamba Nigeria **53** 8.57N 8.42E
Wamba Zaïre **55** 2.10N 27.59E
Wamba *r.* Zaïre **54** 4.35S 17.15E
Wami *r.* Tanzania **55** 6.10S 38.50E
Wamsasi Indonesia **37** 3.27S126.07E
Wan Indonesia **64** 8.23S137.55E
Wāna Pakistan **40** 32.17N 69.35E
Wanaaring Australia **66** 29.42S144.14E
Wanaka New Zealand **60** 44.42S169.08E
Wanaka, L. New Zealand **60** 44.30S169.10E
Wan'an China **33** 26.27N114.46E
Wanapiri Indonesia **37** 4.30S135.50E
Wanapitei *r.* Canada **76** 46.02N 80.51W
Wanapitei L. Canada **76** 46.45N 80.45W
Wanbi Australia **66** 34.46S140.19E
Wandana Australia **66** 32.04S133.45E
Wandoan Australia **64** 26.09S149.51E
Wanganella Australia **67** 35.13S144.53E
Wanganui New Zealand **60** 39.56S175.00E
Wangaratta Australia **67** 36.22S146.20E
Wangary Australia **66** 34.30S135.26E
Wangdu China **32** 38.43N115.09E
Wangdu Phodrang Bhutan **41** 27.29N 89.54E
Wangerooge *i.* Germany **14** 53.50N 7.50E
Wanghai Shan *mtn.* China **32** 41.40N121.43E
Wangianna Australia **66** 29.42S137.32E
Wangjiang China **33** 30.07N116.41E
Wangpan Yang *b.* China **33** 30.30N121.30E
Wangquing China **35** 43.20N129.48E
Wangyuanqiao China **32** 38.24N106.16E
Wani India **41** 20.04N 78.57E
Wānkāner India **40** 22.37N 70.56E
Wanle Weyne Somali Rep. **45** 2.38N 44.55E
Wannian China **33** 28.42N117.03E
Wanning China **33** 18.48N110.22E
Wānow Afghan. **40** 32.38N 65.54E
Wantage U.K. **11** 51.35N 1.25W
Wanxian China **33** 30.52N108.20E
Wanyang Shan *mts.* China **33** 26.01N113.48E
Wanyuan China **32** 32.04N108.02E
Wanzai China **33** 28.06N114.27E
Wāpi India **40** 20.22N 72.54E
Wapiti *r.* Canada **74** 55.05N118.18W
Wappingers Falls U.S.A. **85** 41.36N 73.55W
Wārāh Pakistan **40** 27.27N 67.48E
Warangal India **39** 18.00N 79.35E
Waranga Resr. Australia **67** 36.32S145.04E
Wārāseoni India **41** 21.45N 80.02E
Waratah B. Australia **65** 38.55S146.04E
Warburton *r.* Australia **65** 27.55S137.15E
Warburton Range *mts.* S.A. Australia **66** 30.30S134.32E
Warburton Range *mts.* W.A. Australia **62** 26.09S126.38E
Ward Rep. of Ire. **13** 53.26N 6.20W
Warden R.S.A. **56** 27.49S 28.57E
Wardenburg Germany **14** 53.04N 8.11E
Wardha India **41** 20.45N 78.37E
Wardha *r.* India **41** 19.38N 79.48E
Ward Hill U.K. **8** 58.54N 3.20W
Wardlow Canada **75** 50.54N111.33W
Waren Germany **20** 53.31N 12.40E
Warendorf Germany **14** 51.57N 8.00E
Warialda Australia **67** 29.33S150.36E
Wark Forest *hills* U.K. **10** 55.06N 2.24W
Warkopi Indonesia **37** 1.12S134.09E
Warkworth New Zealand **60** 36.24S174.40E
Warley U.K. **11** 52.29N 2.02W
Warmbad Namibia **56** 28.26S 18.41E
Warminster U.K. **11** 51.12N 2.11W
Warm Springs *town* U.S.A. **80** 39.39N114.49W
Warner Robins U.S.A. **85** 32.35N 83.37W
Waroona Australia **63** 32.51S115.50E
Warracknabeal Australia **66** 36.15S142.28E
Warragul Australia **67** 38.11S145.55E
Warrakalanna, L. Australia **66** 28.13S139.23E
Warrambool *r.* Australia **67** 30.04S147.38E
Warrego *r.* Australia **67** 30.25S145.18E
Warrego Range *mts.* Australia **64** 24.55S146.20E
Warren Australia **67** 31.44S147.53E
Warren Ark. U.S.A. **83** 33.37N 92.04W
Warren Mich. U.S.A. **84** 42.28N 83.01W
Warren Minn. U.S.A. **82** 48.12N 96.46W
Warren Ohio U.S.A. **84** 41.15N 80.49W
Warren Penn. U.S.A. **84** 41.51N 79.08W
Warrenpoint U.K. **13** 54.06N 6.15W
Warrensburg U.S.A. **82** 38.46N 93.44W
Warrenton R.S.A. **56** 28.07S 24.49E
Warri Nigeria **53** 5.36N 5.46E
Warrina Australia **66** 28.10S135.49E
Warriner Creek *r.* Australia **66** 29.15S137.03E
Warrington U.K. **10** 53.25N 2.38W
Warrington U.S.A. **83** 30.23N 87.16W
Warrnambool Australia **66** 38.23S142.03E
Warroad U.S.A. **82** 48.54N 95.19W
Warrumbungle Range *mts.* Australia **67** 31.20S149.00E

Wolmaransstad to Yom

Wolmaransstad R.S.A. 56 27.11S 25.58E
Wolomin Poland 21 52.21N 21.14E
Wolseley Australia 66 36.21S140.55E
Wolvega Neth. 14 52.53N 6.00E
Wolverhampton U.K. 11 52.35N 2.06W
Womelsdorf U.S.A. 85 40.22N 76.11W
Wondai Australia 64 26.19S151.52E
Wongan Hills town Australia 63 30.55S116.41E
Wonogiri Indonesia 37 7.48S110.52E
Wonosari Indonesia 37 7.55S110.39E
Wonosobo Indonesia 37 7.21S109.56E
Wŏnsan N. Korea 31 39.07N127.26E
Wonthaggi Australia 67 38.38S145.37E
Woocalla Australia 66 31.44S137.10E
Woodbine U.S.A. 85 39.14N 74.49W
Woodbridge U.K. 11 52.06N 1.19E
Woodbridge U.S.A. 85 38.39N 77.15W
Wood Buffalo Nat. Park Canada 74 59.00N113.41W
Woodburn Australia 67 29.04S153.21E
Woodbury U.S.A. 85 39.50N 75.10W
Wooded Bluff f. Australia 67 29.22S153.22E
Woodenbong Australia 67 28.28S152.35E
Woodland U.S.A. 80 38.41N121.46W
Woodlark I. P.N.G. 64 9.05S152.50E
Wood Mts. Canada 75 49.14N106.20W
Woodroffe, Mt. Australia 64 26.20S131.45E
Woods, L. Australia 64 17.50S133.30E
Woods, L. of the Canada / U.S.A. 76 49.15N 94.45W
Woodside Australia 67 38.31S146.52E
Woods L. Canada 77 54.40N 64.21W
Woodstock Canada 76 43.08N 80.45W
Woodstock U.K. 11 51.51N 1.20W
Woodstown U.S.A. 85 39.39N 75.20W
Woodville New Zealand 60 40.20S175.52E
Woodward U.S.A. 83 36.26N 99.24W
Wooler U.K. 10 55.33N 2.01W
Woolgoolga Australia 67 30.07S153.12E
Wooltana Australia 66 30.28S139.26E
Woomera Australia 66 31.11S136.54E
Woonsocket U.S.A. 84 42.00N 71.31W
Wooramel Australia 62 25.42S114.20E
Wooramel r. Australia 62 25.47S114.10E
Woorong, L. Australia 66 29.24S134.06E
Worcester R.S.A. 56 33.39S 19.25E
Worcester U.K. 11 52.12N 2.12W
Worcester U.S.A. 84 42.16N 71.48W
Workington U.K. 10 54.39N 3.34W
Worksop U.K. 10 53.19N 1.09W
Workum Neth. 14 53.00N 5.26E
Worland U.S.A. 80 44.01N107.57W
Worms Germany 20 49.38N 8.23E
Worthing U.K. 11 50.49N 0.21W
Worthington Minn. U.S.A. 82 43.37N 95.36W
Worthington Ohio U.S.A. 84 40.03N 83.03W
Worthville U.S.A. 84 38.38N 85.05W
Wosi Indonesia 37 0.15S128.00E
Wour Chad 53 21.21N 15.57E
Woutchaba Cameroon 53 5.13N 13.05E
Wowoni i. Indonesia 37 4.10S123.10E
Wragby U.K. 10 53.17N 0.18E
Wrangel I. see Vrangelya, Ostrov i. Russian Fed. 29
Wrangell U.S.A. 74 56.28N132.23W
Wrangell Mts. U.S.A. 72 62.00N143.00W
Wrangle U.K. 10 53.03N 0.09E
Wrath, C. U.K. 12 58.37N 5.01W
Wray U.S.A. 82 40.05N102.13W
Wrecks, B. of Kiribati 69 1.52N157.17W
Wrexham U.K. 10 53.05N 3.00W
Wrigley Canada 72 63.16N123.39W
Wrocław Poland 21 51.05N 17.00E
Wronki Poland 20 52.43N 16.23E
Września Poland 21 52.20N 17.34E
Wubin Australia 63 30.06S116.38E
Wuchang China 33 30.21N114.19E
Wucheng China 32 37.12N116.04E
Wuchuan Guangdong China 33 21.21N110.40E
Wuchuan Nei Monggol Zizhiqu China 32 41.08N111.24E
Wuda China 32 39.40N106.40E
Wuday 'ah Saudi Arabia 45 16.05N 47.05E
Wudham 'Alwā' Oman 43 23.48N 57.33E
Wudinna Australia 66 33.03S135.28E
Wudu China 32 33.24N104.50E
Wufeng China 33 30.12N110.36E
Wugang China 33 26.42N110.31E
Wugong Shan mts. China 33 27.15N114.00E
Wuhai China 32 39.50N106.40E
Wuhan China 33 30.37N114.19E
Wuhu China 33 31.25N118.25E
Wūjang China 41 33.38N 79.55E
Wu Jiang r. China 33 29.41N107.24E
Wukari Nigeria 53 7.57N 9.42E
Wulian China 32 35.45N119.12E
Wuliang Shan mts. China 30 24.27N100.43E
Wum Cameroon 53 6.25N 10.03E
Wumbulgal Australia 67 34.25S146.16E
Wuming China 33 23.10N108.16E
Wuning China 33 29.17N115.05E
Wunnummin L. Canada 76 52.50N 89.20W
Wun Rog Sudan 49 9.00N 28.21E
Wuppertal Germany 14 51.15N 7.10E
Wuppertal R.S.A. 56 32.16S 19.12E
Wuqi China 32 37.03N108.14E
Wuqiao China 32 37.38N116.22E
Wuqing China 32 39.19N117.05E
Wurno Nigeria 53 13.20N 5.28E
Würzburg Germany 20 49.48N 9.57E
Wusong China 33 31.20N121.30E
Wutongqiao China 33 29.20N103.48E
Wuwei China 32 38.00N102.59E
Wuxi Jiangsu China 33 31.34N120.20E
Wuxi Sichuan China 33 31.28N109.36E
Wuxing China 33 30.59N120.04E
Wuyi Shan mts. China 33 27.00N117.00E
Wuyuan China 32 41.06N108.16E
Wuzhan China 31 50.14N125.18E
Wuzhi Shan mts. China 33 18.50N109.30E
Wuzhou China 33 23.28N111.21E
Wyalkatchem Australia 63 31.21S117.22E
Wyalong Australia 67 33.55S147.17E
Wyandotte U.S.A. 84 42.11N 83.10W
Wyandra Australia 65 27.15S146.00E
Wyangala Resr. Australia 67 33.58S148.55E
Wyara, L. Australia 66 28.42S144.16E
Wycheproof Australia 66 36.04S143.14E
Wye U.K. 11 51.11N 0.56E
Wye r. U.K. 11 51.37N 2.40W
Wymondham U.K. 11 52.34N 1.07E
Wynbring Australia 65 30.33S133.32E
Wyndham Australia 62 15.29S128.05E
Wynne U.S.A. 83 35.14N 90.47W
Wyoming d. U.S.A. 80 43.10N107.36W
Wyong Australia 67 33.17S151.25E
Wyszków Poland 21 52.36N 21.28E
Wytheville U.S.A. 85 36.57N 81.07W

X

Xa Cassau Angola 54 9.02S 20.17E
Xagquka China 41 31.50N 92.46E
Xainza China 41 30.56N 88.40E
Xaitongmoin China 41 29.22N 88.15E
Xai-Xai Mozambique 57 25.05S 33.38E
Xalin well Somali Rep. 45 9.08N 48.47E
Xam Nua Laos 34 20.25N104.10E
Xangdoring China 41 32.06N 82.02E
Xangongo Angola 54 16.31S 15.00E
Xanten Germany 14 51.40N 6.29E
Xánthi Greece 19 41.07N 24.55E
Xarardheere Somali Rep. 45 4.32N 47.53E
Xar Hudag China 32 45.07N114.28E
Xar Moron He r. China 32 43.30N120.42E
Xassengue Angola 54 10.26S 18.32E
Xau, L. Botswana 56 21.15S 24.50E
Xebert China 32 44.02N122.00E
Xenia U.S.A. 84 39.41N 83.56W
Xequessa Angola 54 16.47S 19.05E
Xhora R.S.A. 56 31.58S 28.40E
Xiachuan i. China 33 21.40N112.37E
Xiaguan see Dali China 30
Xiamen China 33 24.30N118.08E
Xi'an China 32 34.11N108.55E
Xianfeng China 33 29.41N109.02E
Xiangcheng China 32 33.50N113.29E
Xiangfan China 33 32.04N112.05E
Xiangfen China 32 35.52N111.24E
Xiang Jiang r. China 33 28.49N112.30E
Xiangkhoang Laos 34 19.21N103.23E
Xiangquan He r. China 41 31.45N 78.40E
Xiangshan China 33 29.29N121.51E
Xiangtan China 33 27.50N112.49E
Xiangtang China 33 28.26N115.58E
Xiangyin China 33 28.41N112.53E
Xiangyuan China 32 36.32N113.02E
Xiangzhou China 33 23.58N109.41E
Xianju China 33 28.51N120.44E
Xianning China 33 29.53N114.13E
Xian Xian China 32 38.12N116.07E
Xianyang China 32 34.20N108.40E
Xianyou China 33 25.28N118.50E
Xiao Hinggan Ling mts. China 31 48.40N128.30E
Xiaojiang China 33 27.34N120.27E
Xiaojiao China 32 38.24N113.42E
Xiaowutai Shan mtn. China 32 39.57N114.59E
Xiapu China 33 26.58N119.57E
Xiayang China 33 26.45N117.58E
Xichang China 30 27.53N102.18E
Xichou China 33 23.27N104.40E
Xichuan China 32 33.15N111.27E
Xifeng China 33 27.06N106.44E
Xigazê China 30 29.18N 88.50E
Xiheying China 32 39.53N114.42E
Xiji China 32 35.52N105.35E
Xi Jiang r. China 33 22.23N113.20E
Xiliao He r. China 32 43.48N123.00E
Xilin China 33 24.30N105.03E
Ximeng China 39 22.45N 99.29E
Xin'anjiang China 33 29.27N119.14E
Xin'anjiang Shuiku resr. China 33 29.32N119.00E
Xincheng Guang. Zhuang. China 33 24.04N108.40E
Xincheng Ningxia Huizu China 32 38.33N106.10E
Xincheng Shanxi China 32 37.57N112.35E
Xindu China 33 30.50N104.12E
Xinfeng Guangdong China 33 24.04N114.12E
Xinfeng Jiangxi China 33 25.27N114.58E
Xing'an China 33 25.35N110.32E
Xingcheng China 32 40.37N120.43E
Xinghua China 32 32.51N119.50E
Xingkai Hu l. see Khanka, Ozero China / Russian Fed. 31
Xingren China 33 25.26N105.14E
Xingshan China 33 31.10N110.51E
Xingtai China 32 37.04N114.26E
Xingu r. Brazil 91 1.40S 52.15W
Xing Xian China 32 38.31N111.04E
Xingyi China 33 25.00N104.59E
Xinhe Hebei China 32 37.22N115.14E
Xinhe Xin. Uygur Zizhiqu China 30 41.34N 82.38E
Xinhua China 33 27.45N111.18E
Xining China 30 36.35N101.55E
Xinji China 32 35.17N115.35E
Xinjiang Uygur Zizhiqu d. China 30 41.15N 87.00E
Xinjie China 32 39.15N109.36E
Xinjin Liaoning China 32 39.27N121.48E
Xinjin Sichuan China 33 30.30N103.47E
Xinle China 32 38.15N114.40E
Xinlitun China 32 42.00N122.09E
Xinmin China 32 42.01N122.48E
Xinning China 33 26.31N110.48E
Xinshao China 33 27.20N111.26E
Xin Xian China 32 38.24N112.47E
Xinxiang China 32 35.12N113.57E
Xinyang China 32 32.08N114.04E
Xinyi Guangdong China 33 22.21N110.57E
Xinyi Jiangsu China 32 34.20N118.30E
Xinyu China 33 27.50N114.55E
Xinzheng China 32 34.25N113.46E
Xinzhu Taiwan 33 24.50N120.58E
Xiping Henan China 32 33.23N114.02E
Xiping Zhejiang China 33 28.27N119.29E
Xique Xique Brazil 91 10.47S 42.44W
Xi Ujimqin Qi China 32 44.32N117.40E
Xiuning China 33 29.48N118.20E
Xiushan China 33 28.27N108.59E
Xiushui China 33 29.01N114.37E
Xixabangma Feng mtn. China 41 28.21N 85.47E
Xixia China 32 33.30N111.30E
Xizang Zizhiqu d. China 41 31.45N 87.00E
Xorkol China 30 39.04N 91.05E
Xuancheng China 33 30.59N118.40E
Xuang r. Laos 34 19.59N102.20E
Xuanhan China 33 31.25N107.38E
Xuanhua China 32 40.30N115.00E
Xuanwei China 33 26.16N104.01E
Xuchang China 32 34.02N113.50E
Xuddur Somali Rep. 45 4.10N 43.53E
Xuefeng Shan mts. China 33 27.30N111.00E
Xueshuiwen China 31 49.15N129.39E
Xugou China 32 34.40N119.26E
Xunyang China 32 32.48N109.27E
Xupu China 33 27.54N110.35E
Xushui China 32 39.01N115.39E
Xuwen China 33 20.25N110.20E
Xuyong China 33 28.17N105.21E
Xuzhou China 32 34.14N117.20E

Y

Ya Gabon 54 1.17S 14.14E
Ya'an China 39 30.00N102.59E
Yaapeet Australia 66 35.48S142.07E
Yabassi Cameroon 53 4.30N 9.55E
Yabēlo Ethiopia 49 4.54N 38.05E
Yablonovyy Khrebet mts. Russian Fed. 29 53.20N115.00E
Yabrai Shan mts. China 32 39.50N103.30E
Yabrai Yanchang China 32 39.24N102.43E
Yabrūd Syria 44 33.58N 36.40E
Yacheng China 33 18.35N109.13E
Yacuiba Bolivia 92 22.00S 63.25W
Yādgīr India 38 16.46N 77.08E
Yadong China 41 27.29N 88.54E
Yagaba Ghana 52 10.13N 1.14W
Yagoua Cameroon 53 10.23N 15.13E
Yagra China 41 31.32N 82.27E
Yahagi r. Japan 35 34.50N136.59E
Yahisuli Zaïre 54 0.08S 24.04E
Yahuma Zaïre 54 1.06N 23.10E
Yaizu Japan 35 34.52N138.20E
Yajua Nigeria 53 11.27N 12.49E
Yakchāl Afghan. 40 31.47N 64.41E
Yakima U.S.A. 80 46.36N120.31W
Yakmach Pakistan 40 28.45N 63.51E
Yaksha Russian Fed. 24 61.51N 56.59E
Yakutat U.S.A. 72 59.33N139.44W
Yakutat U.S.A. 74 59.29N139.49W
Yakutat B. U.S.A. 74 59.29N139.49W
Yakutsk Russian Fed. 29 62.10N129.20E
Yala Thailand 34 6.32N101.19E
Yalgoo Australia 63 28.20S116.41E
Yalinga C.A.R. 49 6.31N 23.15E
Yallourn Australia 67 38.09S146.22E
Yalong Jiang r. China 30 26.35N101.44E
Yalta Ukraine 25 44.30N 34.09E
Yalu Jiang r. China 32 40.10N124.25E
Yalutorovsk Russian Fed. 28 56.41N 66.12E
Yamal, Poluostrov pen. Russian Fed. 28 70.20N 70.00E
Yamanashi Japan 35 35.40N138.40E
Yamanashi d. Japan 35 35.30N138.35E
Yamandjo Zaïre 54 1.38N 23.27E
Yamaska Canada 77 46.01N 72.55W
Yamaska r. Canada 77 46.06N 72.56W
Yamato Japan 35 35.29N139.29E
Yamato-takada Japan 35 34.31N135.45E
Yamba N.S.W. Australia 67 29.26S153.22E
Yamba S.A. Australia 66 34.15S140.54E
Yambéring Guinea 52 11.49N 12.18W
Yambio Sudan 49 4.34N 28.23E
Yambol Bulgaria 19 42.28N 26.30E
Yamdena i. Indonesia 37 7.30S131.00E
Yamenyingzi China 32 42.23N121.03E
Yamethin Burma 34 20.24N 96.08E
Yam Kinneret l. Israel 44 32.49N 35.36E
Yamma Yamma, L. Australia 64 26.20S141.25E
Yamoussoukro Ivory Coast 52 6.51N 5.18W
Yampi Sound Australia 62 16.11S123.30E
Yampol Ukraine 21 48.13N 28.12E
Yamuna r. India 41 25.25N 81.50E
Yamzho Yumco l. China 41 29.00N 90.40E
Yan Nigeria 53 10.05N 12.11E
Yana r. Russian Fed. 29 71.30N135.00E
Yanac Australia 66 36.09S141.29E
Yan'an China 32 36.45N109.22E
Yanbu'al Baḩr Saudi Arabia 42 24.07N 38.04E
Yancannia Australia 66 30.16S142.50E
Yancheng China 32 33.22N120.05E
Yanchep Australia 63 31.32S115.33E
Yanchi China 32 37.47N107.24E
Yanchuan China 32 36.51N110.05E
Yanco Australia 67 34.36S146.25E
Yanco Glen town Australia 66 31.43S141.39E
Yanda r. Australia 67 30.22S145.38E
Yandong China 33 24.02N107.09E
Yandoon Burma 34 17.02N 95.39E
Yanfolila Mali 52 11.11N 8.09W
Yangarey Russian Fed. 24 68.46N 61.29E
Yangchun China 33 22.03N111.46E
Yangcun China 33 23.26N114.30E
Yangjiang China 33 21.50N111.54E
Yangmingshan Taiwan 33 25.18N121.35E
Yangon see Rangoon Burma 34
Yangon Burma 34 16.47N 96.10E
Yangqu China 32 38.03N112.36E
Yangquan China 32 37.49N113.28E
Yangshan Guangdong China 33 24.29N112.38E
Yangshan Liaoning China 32 41.15N120.18E
Yangshuo China 33 24.47N110.30E
Yangtze r. see Chang Jiang r. China 33
Yang Xian China 32 33.10N107.35E
Yangxin China 33 29.50N115.10E
Yangze China 33 26.59N118.19E
Yangzhou China 32 32.22N119.26E
Yanhuqu China 41 32.32N 82.44E
Yanji China 31 42.45N129.25E
Yanko Creek r. Australia 67 35.25S145.27E
Yankton U.S.A. 82 42.53N 97.23W
Yanqi China 30 42.00N 86.30E
Yanshan China 39 23.36N104.20E
Yanshiping China 41 33.35N 92.04E
Yanskiy Zaliv g. Russian Fed. 29 72.00N136.10E
Yantabulla Australia 67 29.13S145.01E
Yantai China 32 37.27N121.26E
Yanxi China 33 28.11N110.58E
Yanzhou China 32 35.35N116.52E
Yao Chad 53 12.52N 17.34E
Yao Japan 35 34.37N135.36E
Yaopu China 33 26.05N105.42E
Yaoundé Cameroon 53 3.51N 11.31E
Yao Xian China 32 34.52N109.01E
Yap i. Federated States of Micronesia 37 9.30N138.09E
Yapehe Zaïre 54 0.10S 24.20E
Yapen i. Indonesia 37 1.45S136.10E
Yaqui r. Mexico 81 27.37N110.39W
Yar Russian Fed. 24 58.13N 52.08E
Yaraka Australia 64 24.53S144.04E
Yaransk Russian Fed. 24 57.22N 47.49E
Yardea Australia 66 32.23S135.32E
Yare r. U.K. 11 52.34N 1.45E
Yaremcha Ukraine 21 48.26N 24.29E
Yarensk Russian Fed. 24 62.10N 49.07E
Yargora Moldavia 21 46.25N 28.20E
Yaritagua Venezuela 90 10.05N 69.07W
Yarkant He r. China 30 40.30N 80.55E
Yarlung Zangbo Jiang r. China see Brahmaputra r. Asia 41
Yarmouth Canada 77 43.50N 66.07W
Yaroslavl Russian Fed. 24 57.34N 39.52E
Yarra r. Australia 67 37.51S144.54E
Yarram Australia 67 38.30S146.41E
Yarrawonga Australia 67 36.02S145.59E
Yarrow r. U.K. 12 55.32N 2.51W
Yar Sale Russian Fed. 28 66.50N 70.48E
Yartsevo Russian Fed. 29 60.17N 90.02E
Yartsevo Russian Fed. 24 55.06N 32.43E
Yarumal Colombia 90 6.59N 75.25W
Yasanyama Zaïre 49 4.18N 21.11E
Yaselda r. Belorussia 21 52.07N 26.28E
Yasen Belorussia 21 53.10N 28.55E
Yashi Nigeria 53 12.23N 7.54E
Yashkul Russian Fed. 25 46.10N 45.20E
Yasinya Ukraine 21 48.12N 24.20E
Yasothon Thailand 34 15.46N104.12E
Yass Australia 67 34.51S148.55E
Yatakala Niger 52 14.52N 0.22E
Yaté N. Cal. 68 22.09S166.57E
Yates Center U.S.A. 83 37.53N 95.44W
Yathkyed L. Canada 75 62.40N 98.00W
Yāval India 40 21.10N 75.42E
Yavatmāl India 41 20.24N 78.08E
Yaví, Cerro mtn. Venezuela 90 5.32N 65.59W
Yavorov Ukraine 21 49.59N 23.20E
Yawng-hwe Burma 34 20.35N 96.58E
Yaxi China 33 27.35N106.40E
Ya Xian see Sanya China 33
Yazd Iran 43 31.54N 54.22E
Yazmān Pakistan 40 29.08N 71.45E
Yazoo r. U.S.A. 83 32.22N 91.00W
Yazoo City U.S.A. 83 32.51N 90.28W
Ybbs Austria 20 48.11N 15.05E
Ye Burma 34 15.15N 97.50E
Yea Australia 67 37.12S145.25E
Yecla Spain 16 38.35N 1.05W
Yedintsy Moldavia 25 48.09N 27.18E
Yeeda Australia 62 17.36S123.39E
Yefremov Russian Fed. 24 53.08N 38.08E
Yegorlyk r. Russian Fed. 25 46.30N 41.52E
Yegoryevsk Russian Fed. 24 55.21N 39.01E
Yegros Paraguay 94 26.24S 56.25W
Yei Sudan 49 4.05N 30.40E
Yei r. Sudan 49 7.20N 30.39E
Yeji China 33 31.51N115.01E
Yekaterinburg Russian Fed. 24 56.52N 60.35E
Yelets Russian Fed. 24 52.36N 38.30E
Yeletskiy Russian Fed. 24 67.04N 64.00E
Yélimané Mali 52 15.08N 10.34W
Yell i. U.K. 12 60.35N 1.05W
Yellowdine Australia 63 31.19S119.36E
Yellowhead Pass Canada 74 52.53N118.25W
Yellowknife Canada 74 62.27N114.21W
Yellowknife r. Canada 74 62.27N114.19W
Yellow Mt. Australia 67 32.19S146.50E
Yellowstone r. U.S.A. 82 47.58N103.59W
Yellowstone r. U.S.A. 78 47.55N103.45W
Yellowstone L. U.S.A. 80 44.25N110.38W
Yellowstone Nat. Park U.S.A. 80 44.30N110.35W
Yell Sd. U.K. 12 60.30N 1.11W
Yelma Australia 62 26.30S121.40E
Yelsk Belorussia 21 51.50N 29.10E
Yelwa Nigeria 53 10.48N 4.42E
Yemen Asia 45 14.00N 47.00E
Yemen f. Yemen 45 15.30N 46.10E
Yemilchino Ukraine 21 50.58N 27.40E
Yenagoa Nigeria 53 4.59N 6.15E
Yenangyaung Burma 34 20.28N 94.54E
Yen Bai Vietnam 34 21.43N104.44E
Yenda Australia 67 34.15S146.13E
Yendi Ghana 52 9.29N 0.01W
Yengan Burma 34 21.06N 96.30E
Yenisey r. Russian Fed. 29 69.00N 86.00E
Yeniseysk Russian Fed. 29 58.27N 92.13E
Yeniseyskiy Zaliv g. Russian Fed. 28 73.00N 79.00E
Yenshui Taiwan 33 23.20N120.16E
Yenyuka Russian Fed. 29 57.57N121.15E
Yeo L. Australia 63 28.04S124.23E
Yeola India 40 20.02N 74.29E
Yeoval Australia 67 32.44S148.39E
Yeovil U.K. 11 50.57N 2.38W
Yepáchic U.S.A. 81 28.27N108.25W
Yeppoon Australia 64 23.08S150.45E
Yerbent Turkmenistan 43 39.23N 58.35E
Yercha Russian Fed. 29 69.34N147.30E
Yerda Australia 66 31.05S135.04E
Yerepol Russian Fed. 29 65.15N168.43E
Yerevan Armenia 43 40.10N 44.31E
Yerington U.S.A. 80 38.59N119.10W
Yermak Kazakhstan 28 52.03N 76.55E
Yermitsa Russian Fed. 24 66.56N 52.20E
Yermo Mexico 83 26.23N104.01W
Yermo U.S.A. 81 34.54N116.50W
Yershov Russian Fed. 25 51.22N 48.16E
Yertom Russian Fed. 24 63.31N 47.51E
Yerushalayim Israel / Jordan 44 31.47N 35.13E
Yeşil r. Turkey 42 41.22N 36.37E
Yeso U.S.A. 81 34.26N104.37W
Yessey Russian Fed. 29 68.29N102.15E
Yetman Australia 67 28.55S150.49E
Yeu Burma 34 22.49N 95.26E
Yeu, Île d' i. France 17 46.43N 2.20W
Yevpatoriya Ukraine 25 45.12N 33.20E
Yevstratovskiy Russian Fed. 25 50.07N 39.45E
Ye Xian China 32 37.10N119.56E
Yeysk Russian Fed. 25 46.43N 38.17E
Yi r. Uruguay 93 33.17S 58.08W
Yiannitsá Greece 19 40.48N 22.25E
Yibin China 33 28.42N104.34E
Yibug Caka l. China 41 33.50N 87.00E
Yichang China 33 30.21N111.21E
Yichuan China 32 34.25N112.26E
Yidu China 32 36.45N118.24E
Yifag Ethiopia 49 12.02N 37.44E
Yijun China 32 35.23N109.07E
Yilan China 31 46.22N129.31E
Yilehuli Shan mts. China 31 51.20N124.20E
Yilliminning Australia 63 32.54S117.22E
Yilong China 33 31.34N106.24E
Yimen China 32 34.21N107.07E
Yinan China 32 35.33N118.27E
Yinchuan China 32 38.27N106.18E
Yindarlgooda, L. Australia 63 30.45S121.55E
Yingcheng China 33 30.57N113.33E
Yingde China 33 24.07N113.20E
Yinggehai China 33 18.31N108.40E
Yingkou China 32 40.39N122.18E
Yingshan China 33 31.06N116.35E
Yingshang China 32 32.42N116.20E
Yingtan China 33 28.11N116.55E
Yinkanie Australia 66 34.21S140.20E
Yinning China 30 43.57N 81.23E
Yin Shan mts. China 32 41.30N109.00E
Yirga' Alem Ethiopia 49 6.52N 38.22E
Yirol Sudan 49 6.33N 30.30E
Yirwa Sudan 49 7.47N 27.15E
Yishan China 33 24.37N108.32E
Yíthion Greece 19 36.46N 22.34E
Yiwu China 33 29.18N120.04E
Yi Xian China 32 41.30N121.14E
Yiyang Henan China 32 34.30N112.10E
Yiyang Hunan China 33 28.20N112.30E
Yiyuan China 32 36.12N118.08E
Yizhang China 33 25.24N112.57E
Ylitornio Finland 22 66.19N 23.40E
Ylivieska Finland 22 64.05N 24.33E
Yoakum U.S.A. 83 29.17N 97.09W
Yobe d. Nigeria 53 12.30N 11.45E
Yodo r. Japan 35 34.41N135.25E
Yogyakarta Indonesia 37 7.48S110.24E
Yogyakarta d. Indonesia 37 7.48S110.22E
Yokadouma Cameroon 53 3.26N 15.06E
Yokkaichi Japan 35 34.58N136.37E
Yoko Cameroon 53 5.29N 12.19E
Yokohama Japan 35 35.27N139.39E
Yokosuka Japan 35 35.18N139.40E
Yola Nigeria 53 9.14N 12.32E
Yom r. Thailand 34 15.47N100.05E

OCEANIA
MAPS 58 – 69

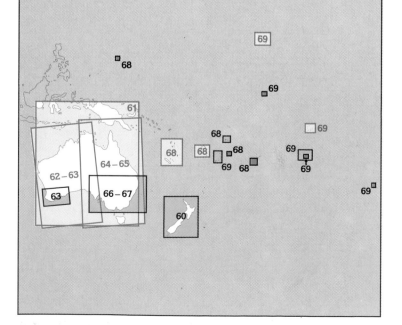

NORTH AMERICA
MAPS 70 – 87

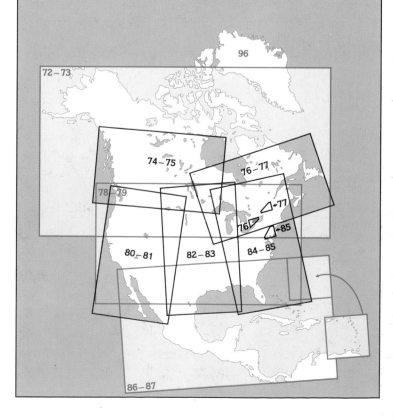

Continuation from Front Endpaper